[redacted]

3839
MAJ

D1345106

THE MISSION AND MESSAGE OF JESUS

The Mission and Message of Jesus

AN EXPOSITION OF THE GOSPELS IN THE LIGHT OF MODERN RESEARCH

by

H. D. A. Major, D.D., F.S.A.
Principal of Ripon Hall, Oxford

T. W. Manson, D.Litt.
Rylands Professor of Biblical Criticism and Exegesis in the University of Manchester

C. J. Wright, B.D., Ph.D.
Professor of Systematic Theology and Philosophy of Religion, Didsbury College, Manchester

MANSFIELD COLLEGE OXFORD LIBRARY
WITHDRAWN

1937
IVOR NICHOLSON AND WATSON
LIMITED · · · LONDON

All Rights Reserved

FIRST PUBLISHED IN MCMXXXVII
BY IVOR NICHOLSON AND WATSON
LIMITED LONDON

PRINTED AND MADE IN GREAT BRITAIN
BY HAZELL WATSON & VINEY LIMITED
LONDON AND AYLESBURY

General Guide to the Volume

GENERAL INTRODUCTION

By H. D. A. MAJOR, D.D., F.S.A.

BOOK I. INCIDENTS IN THE LIFE OF JESUS

By H. D. A. MAJOR, D.D., F.S.A.

BOOK II. THE SAYINGS OF JESUS

By T. W. MANSON, D.Litt.

BOOK III. JESUS: THE REVELATION OF GOD

By C. J. WRIGHT, B.D., Ph.D.

Detailed Contents of the Volume will be found on pages vii–xi, immediately following this General Guide

ACKNOWLEDGEMENTS

The acknowledgements and thanks of the Editor, Authors, and Publishers of this work are due to the Delegates of the Oxford University Press for their kind permission to reprint the Text of the Gospels from the Revised Version

Contents

GENERAL INTRODUCTION

BOOK I

INCIDENTS IN THE LIFE OF JESUS

The Gospel According to St. Mark

BOOK II

THE SAYINGS OF JESUS

Introduction

I.—The Document Q

II.—The Teaching Peculiar to Matthew

III.—The Teaching Peculiar to Luke

BOOK III

JESUS: THE REVELATION OF GOD

A General Introduction

THE FOUR GOSPELS IN THE LIGHT OF MODERN RESEARCH

TO-DAY there is urgent need for an untechnical volume dealing with our four Gospels—Matthew, Mark, Luke, and John—in the light of modern research. A vast mass of information of various degrees of trustworthiness about the Gospels has been accumulated in modern times. This information is in the possession of scholars: not a little of it is of technical character: it is concerned with the origin, purpose, sources, credibility, authorship, date, locality, and literary style of each of the four Gospels.

All these themes are interwoven and hardly a single one of them can be treated satisfactorily without reference to the others. Many of the conclusions, speculative or assured, at which our modern students of the Gospels have arrived have a very serious bearing upon the meaning of the message and also upon the moral and spiritual authority of our Lord Jesus Christ.

Ordinary men and women are conscious that such a state of things exists, but they feel that they have neither the time nor the educational qualifications, nor perhaps even the inclination, to understand these things. For them the Gospels are true, literally true, and are to be read and understood in that way, or else they are false, and in that case no sensible person need trouble about them. But this 'either-or' way of looking at the Gospels is most unsatisfactory: it is detrimental and dangerous. The scholars responsible for the modern research dealing with the origin and character of the Gospels, who are spoken of, unfortunately, as the 'Critics' or the 'Higher Critics,' have thrown much light upon the Gospels. It is most important that those of their results about which there seems to be a general agreement should be known and appreciated, at least by those who believe the Gospels to be of great value, and who reverence our Lord as the supreme authority in things moral and spiritual. The old-fashioned, downright way of insisting that the Gospels must be entirely true or else fallacious fabrications is one which modern study of the Gospels has altogether discredited. The traditional view that every word and phrase of the Gospels is the product of the direct inspiration of the Holy Spirit can no more be accepted to-day than can the view that the writers of the Gospels were impostors who deliberately set out to deceive mankind.

A great English educationist has said: 'Read the Bible like any other book and you will come to find that it is not like any other book.' And so it may be said with equal truth: 'Study the Gospels in the way in which you would study, under a first-rate teacher of English, a play by Shakespeare, or a poem by Browning, and you will find at the conclusion of your course of study, that you have not only learnt a good deal about the mind and method of the author, but that you have also learnt a very great deal about the subject of the play or poem. You will have learnt, indeed, much that you could not possibly have learnt without such a course of study. And you will find that what you have learnt does not come simply in the class of general information but that it is of that deeper kind which purges the soul, inspires the higher nature, deepens the thought, fills the mind with a sense of the majesty and mystery of life: its moral responsibilities and its spiritual potentialities.

It is this kind of study of the Gospels which is needed to-day, which is, on the one hand, entirely open-minded to the results of what is called literary and historical criticism, and is, on the other hand, sensitive and reverent in the spheres of moral and spiritual truth.

This is not a kind of study which is easy either for teacher or for taught. Euclid told his princely pupil that 'there was no royal road to learning,' and this kind of study of the Gospels, as needful for professor as for peasant, demands the service of the whole personality at its highest, as does the worship of God.

'Thou shalt love the Lord thy God with all thy heart, with all thy soul, with all thy mind, and with all thy strength.'

It is with the purpose of promoting this kind of study of the Gospels by ordinary men and women that this book has been undertaken. Its authors have no intention of acquainting their readers with the vast mass of critical speculation, linguistic and antiquarian detail, which the modern study of the Gospels of necessity involves for scholars. The authors conceive it to be their business to make a selection of what they consider is best worth knowing about the Gospels, and to present as lucidly as they can what they hold to be the truest and most significant elements in the teaching of Jesus.

The oldest codices of the Gospels are written in Greek. A number of scholars have maintained that the language in which the Gospels were originally written was Aramaic, the language in which our Lord Himself taught, and of which there are a few fragments preserved in the Greek Gospels. In this book, however, it is the English Revised Version which will be used as the basis for exposition, and as little reference as possible will be made to the original Greek or underlying Aramaic. Roger Ascham, the beloved tutor of Lady Jane Grey, writes in the dedication to his *Toxophilus*:

'Though to have written this book in Latin or Greek had been easier, yet I have written this English matter in the English tongue for English men.'

It was the boast of Wm. Tyndale in Tudor times that he would cause the boy who drives the plough to know more of the Scriptures than did the Bishop of London. The great task for Tyndale was the popularisation of the study of Scripture by translating it from the Hebrew, Greek, and Latin tongues into English, so that once again Christian men might hear in their own tongue wherein they were born the wonderful works of God.

The task to-day before scholars who value the Bible, and especially the Gospels, as the treasury of those moral and spiritual principles upon which personal, social, national, and international life can alone be securely based, is to impart such a knowledge of the Gospels as will revive an interest in their study and develop a growing devotion to that supreme and life-giving Personality who brought the Gospels into existence.

The author of the Fourth Gospel relates that at a feast of the Jews, certain Greeks came to Philip the Apostle and said to him: 'Sir, we would see Jesus.'

There are many to-day, faced as they believe they are by the breakdown of our civilisation, who desire to see Jesus as He really is, in order to learn, if possible, from Him the essential principles and ideals of His Gospel as the only sound basis for human life and for a permanent and progressive civilisation. Their attitude towards Jesus, although they could give no well-informed and reasoned support for their conviction, is that expressed in the words of St. Peter:

'Lord, to whom shall we go? Thou hast the words of Eternal Life.'

Yet they feel that they cannot understand the Gospels as they are: they seem such a strange medley of fact and fiction, of harmony and contradiction, of eternal truth and contemporary Jewish mythology and superstition.

The old popular commentaries on the Gospels appear to them to be in many cases so obscurantist and lacking in discernment that they irritate the modern reader by assuming as true a background of theological presuppositions and underlying beliefs which are impossible for ordinary men and women to-day. On the other hand, our most up-to-date commentaries seem so full of technicalities and are often so hyper-critical and ingeniously speculative as to confuse utterly the serious and common-sense reader. Although there be much good grain in the Gospels to be gathered and garnered, yet these modern commentators seem to be only concerned, like the man with the muckrake in *The Pilgrim's Progress*, 'to gather the dust and the small straws of the floor.' These critics seem to combine ingenuity with scepticism and to show little appreciation of moral and spiritual values. They aptly illustrate, for their disappointed readers, the *dictum* of Thomas Fuller:

'If any man will not feed on the good meat of the Word, let him not marvel if he be choked with its dry bones.'

Their treatment of the Gospels seems to reflect that atheistic spirit which Francis Bacon described when he wrote:

'The true Atheist is he who handles holy things without feeling.' (*Essay on Atheism.*)

Disgruntled readers of our modern critical commentaries do not understand that these commentaries are purely critical and that their authors would regard it as alien to the scope of their work to be either practical or devotional. Yet it is this practical and devotional element, combined with a shrewd, searching, but not meticulous or sceptical, criticism, which modern readers require. To provide such an exposition of the Gospels is no easy task, and it is only the deep sense that such an exposition is required by a vast multitude of modern men and women which has impelled the writers of this book to enter on their undertaking.

Christ's charge against the scribes of His day was that 'they had taken away the key of knowledge,' or, as a variant reading has it, 'had hidden the key of knowledge': that they went not into the Kingdom of God themselves and prevented others who desired to enter from doing so. Here Christ sees the scribe as the adversary of the Kingdom, but in another saying of His He sees the scribe as the friend of the Kingdom:

'Every scribe instructed unto the Kingdom of God bringeth forth out of his treasures things new and old.'

This is the task which we would attempt, mindful of Thomas Carlyle's conviction that:

'The Old never dies till this happen, till all the soul of good that was in it have got itself transfused into the practical New.'

As the following exposition of the Gospels cannot be technically described as 'critical,' so neither can it be described as 'catholic' or 'evangelical.' The authors are not concerned to make the Gospels affirm the declarations of the traditional creeds nor to teach the traditional scheme of salvation.

Archbishop Frederick Temple wrote on one occasion: 'If the conclusions be prescribed, the research is precluded.' So we hold.

These traditional beliefs may or may not be rightly deduced from the teaching and life of Jesus, but the authors of this exposition are not concerned primarily to find them there nor to prove them to be essential elements in the Gospel of Jesus. The authors are only concerned to try to recover, if they be lost, and to present to their readers, the essential and significant truths which Jesus proclaimed in His Mission, preaching, and personality. We may add that such conclusions as the authors have come to they have arrived at independently, and therefore they will not be found to be in complete agreement on every point.

The writers themselves belong to three different Christian denominations and are directly concerned with training ordinands for the Christian ministry in an age when the problems of that ministry were never more difficult of solution nor the need for that ministry greater.

Modern research has brought to light certain important facts about the Gospels of which the Church since the formation of the Gospel Canon in the second century has been unaware.

(1) The Gospel of St. Mark was written before the Gospels of St. Matthew and St. Luke, and both those Gospels make use of St. Mark's Gospel as one of their literary sources.

(2) St. Matthew's and St. Luke's Gospels make use of another literary source consisting mainly, if not entirely, of collections of the Sayings ascribed to Jesus. This document, common to Mt. and Lk., which used to be spoken of as Matthew's Logia or the Logian document, is now called Q, from the German word *Quelle*, which means a source or spring.

(3) St. Matthew's Gospel, besides making use of Mk. and Q, also made use of a source or collection of sources peculiar to it, and which critics represent by the symbol M, i.e. Matthew's special source. Some critics use M to represent all that is peculiar to the First Gospel, other critics seem to restrict M to collections of sayings peculiar to that Gospel.

(4) St. Luke, besides making use of Mk. and Q, also makes use of a source or

sources not used by any of the other Gospel writers and which critics represent by the symbol L, i.e. Luke's special source.

It is now acknowledged generally, if it was ever doubted, that the Fourth Gospel, commonly called St. John's Gospel, was written later than the other three and that the writer of the Fourth Gospel was probably acquainted with all three Synoptic Gospels.

It is these facts which have largely determined the particular arrangement of the contents of this exposition of the Gospels. Mark's Gospel, with its parallels in the other Gospels, will be treated first; incidents (not discourses) recorded in Mt. which have no parallels in Mk. will be treated second; incidents (not discourses) recorded in Lk. which have no parallels in Mk. or Mt. will be treated third; the discourses and sayings of Jesus in Q, in M, and in L, will be treated fourth; the Gospel of St. John will be treated fifth, although some of the passages in that Gospel which have parallels in the Synoptics will have been referred to in the exposition of the first three Gospels.

It will always be possible by reference to the complete index of Gospel passages to discover at once where the exposition of any particular passage may be found. Most Greek and Hebrew words which occur in this Commentary will be transliterated in accordance with the principles made use of in Strong's *Exhaustive Concordance of the Bible.*

A map of Palestine has been inserted. We have thought it a good thing to provide bibliographies, not of books used by the authors, but of books which may be consulted with profit by our readers.

ARE THE GOSPELS TRUE HISTORY?

When a child has been told a story the first question he asks is: Is it true? This is the question which plain men and women ask to-day about the account of Jesus contained in the Gospels. In days which have passed away, when every word of the Bible was believed to have been inspired by the Holy Spirit and so guarded against all form of error and untruth, this question could be answered, if one accepted the doctrine of Biblical infallibility, with a plain 'Yes,' or if one rejected it, with a plain 'No.' For modern students of the Gospels such answers are no longer possible. That the writers of the Gospels were honest and truth-loving men we may well believe, but they were not scientific historians, nor when they wrote their Gospels were they setting out to write scientific history. It is doubtful whether any of them were eye-witnesses of what they describe and relate. They had therefore to depend upon information derived from others, some if not all of whom were eye-witnesses. These 'sources,' as we call them, came to our Evangelists either in the form of oral traditions (i.e. stories told by word of mouth) or as written documents. These sources would not all be of equal historical value. Some would be more precise and accurate than others; some would come direct from those who had actually seen and heard what happened: other accounts would be second-hand or third-hand. A careful modern study of the Gospels enables the student to detect a number of the sources which the Evangelists have used and to assess their comparative value as reliable evidence. Generally speaking, the earlier the source, the more reliable it will be, but this is not always the case, for many other things have to be taken into consideration.

Was the original observer and narrator intelligent and free from prejudices? Was he only concerned to tell historic truth whether it was acceptable or unacceptable, or was he intent upon doing something else, e.g. securing belief in Jesus Christ as the Son of God, or composing a narrative which would be acceptable and edifying to a Christian congregation? If this were so, would it influence the truthfulness of his narrative? These and a number of similar questions have to be answered before we can answer the main question as to the historical value of the Gospels.

Because there are so many of these questions and the difficulty of answering them accurately is so great, we have a great number of contradictory conclusions put forward by those who are known as the 'Higher Critics,' or modern scientific students of the Gospels. These critics can be roughly classified into groups or schools. Each of these groups stands for some particular theory of the way in which the Gospels were composed and how and why they came into existence. As, in our modern studies of the Gospels, references are necessarily made to these schools, it seems to be important to say something about some of them here and the theories and tendencies for which they stand.

Some of these will seem perhaps very far-fetched, absurdly ingenious, and even highly improbable, but inasmuch as they are accepted by some people and as they represent serious, even though mistaken, attempts to explain the origin and character of the Gospels and to answer the great question as to whether the Gospels are true, it is desirable to be acquainted with them.

Four Schools of Thought

(i) *The 'Christ-Myth School'*

First there is the Christ-myth school of criticism. It became popular in the twentieth century pre-War period. It was expounded in Germany by Drews, Kalthoff, and Jensen; in England by the Rt. Hon. J. M. Robertson and George Mead; in America by W. B. Smith.

In Germany it was disposed of by a galaxy of great German Biblical critics headed by von Soden. In England it was hopelessly discredited by F. C. Conybeare in his volume *The Historical Christ.* In America, Professor Shirley Jackson Case and Professor Thorburn dismissed it with costs. Its latest exponent in France appears to be P. L. Couchoud.

Nevertheless, having been almost entirely eliminated from academic lecture halls, the Christ-myth theory survives, and even thrives, in secularist labour circles. It exhibits a variety of forms, but all its exponents are agreed in one conclusion: that there is no Jesus of history. Not because there was no Jesus, but because He had no history, or rather because we have no history of Him. Our Canonical Gospels are not histories of Jesus in any proper historical sense. The sayings and actions assigned to Him in them are fictitious. A man named

Jesus may have existed and have been executed by Pontius Pilate, the Roman Procurator of Judæa, but the Lord Jesus Christ, the Head of the Christian Church and the object of its cultus, is a religious myth and an ecclesiastical legend. These are the conclusions, generally speaking, of the Christ-myth school of critics.

According to this body of critics, Jesus did not create the Christian Church. The Christian Church created Him. This entirely reverses the teaching of our popular hymn, ' The Church's one foundation is Jesus Christ her Lord,' and perhaps what will seem more serious it also reverses the conviction of the primitive Christian apostle, St. Paul, that ' other foundation can no man lay than that which is laid, even Jesus Christ.'

Inspired possibly by the Greek Mystery Religions, with their ' Saviour Gods ' who lived and died and rose again for mankind, the Christian religion thus becomes the product of social conditions, ethical demands, mystical intuitions, and aspirations as they operated in Græco-Roman civilisation in the first century of our era. It is not Galilee or Jerusalem, but Antioch, Ephesus, Corinth, Rome, which are the creative centres of the Christian cultus. These Christ-myth theories must astonish plain readers of the New Testament who believe they find in that volume a wealth of historic evidence for the life and ministry of Jesus. But these people will be told that they are crassly ignorant of the creative power of religious mythical tendencies. Let it be admitted at once that there are mythical elements in our Four Gospels and clear evidences of this myth-creating tendency at work in early Christianity: but this is quite a different thing from believing that the whole Christian religion could have originated in this way.

The French *savant* who desired to found a new religion, and was told by Talleyrand that if he would succeed he must first be crucified and rise again the third day, was seriously misinformed. According to the Christ-myth school, all the founder of a new religion requires is to secure a small group of adherents with no sense of factual veracity but possessed of powerful imaginations, dialectical abilities, and an intuitive perception of the social and religious needs of their environment and how to satisfy them by the creation of a religious myth—and the feat is accomplished.

We are all aware how much great movements and great men have owed to their environment. Men and movements born before their time perish unknown, not because they lack a sacred bard, but because they have an uncongenial environment. Certainly the time and place of the Christian religion constituted important factors in its success. Harnack's great book *The Mission and Expansion of Christianity* demonstrates this. But that will not mean that the Christian religion did not need a personal founder. A supreme personality, and this is pre-eminently the case with a moral and spiritual personality, seems in some mysterious way to inherit, not only all that is most vital in his individual, social, and religious ancestry, but also to draw into himself all that is most vital in his contemporary environment. But this is not all. In him all these forces are united in vital union, not in the form of addition but of multiplication. As a consequence a new moral and spiritual creation ensues. All the higher religions have had personal founders. The highest form of religion is of this ' founded religion ' type. All that is most vital, original, and characteristic in this type of religion is the reflection of the personality of its founder, and so the new religion becomes in varying degree the apotheosis of the personality of its founder. He has created it. It did not create him. This is true of Buddhism, founded by the Buddha, Gautama; of Islam, founded by Mohammed; of Zoroastrianism, founded by Zoroaster; and it is equally true of Christianity, founded by Jesus Christ. It is impossible for any serious student of the origin and evolution of Religion to exclude Christianity from the class of 'founded religions.' The origin of the Christian religion is most adequately accounted for by finding both the sower and the seed in the historic personality of Jesus of Nazareth.

(ii) *The 'Form-Criticism School'*

Akin in some of its conclusions to the Christ-myth school, although entirely different in its working hypothesis and methods, is the Form-criticism school. It is so named to distinguish it from the Source-criticism school, which has achieved such remarkable results. The methods and results of Source-criticism are most adequately presented for English readers in Canon Streeter's monumental work, *The Four Gospels*.

The Form-criticism school makes use of the main results achieved by the Source-criticism school, but it claims to carry back its researches successfully into a much earlier stage in the rise of the Gospel tradition. It is generally accepted that Mark's Gospel was not written until at least a quarter of a century after the Crucifixion of Jesus; the Gospels of Matthew and Luke (in their final form) not until at least half a century after the Crucifixion; and the Fourth Gospel not until nearly three-quarters of a century after the Crucifixion.

Mark's Gospel was thus preceded by a period of oral tradition, in the later part of which period probably Q and possibly proto-Luke were composed. This period of oral teaching gave scope for accounts of the activities and teaching of Jesus being shaped and arranged in accordance with the propagandist needs of the primitive Christian missionaries. How these needs or apologetic tendencies operated in the shaping or formation of the Christian tradition can be learnt by a comparative study of the written sources as we have them in the four Canonical Gospels. The general tendency is to conform Jesus and His acts and teaching, and even His apostles, more and more to the ideals and needs of the primitive Christian community. Hence historical fact becomes blurred and even lost as the idealising apologetic tendency prevails both in oral and written tradition.

These conclusions are not peculiar to the Form-criticism school. The researches of the Source-criticism school brought them to light. The particular contribution of the Form-criticism school consists in what may be described as the unstringing, rearranging, and rethreading of the beads which constitute our Canonical Gospels, particularly the Synoptics, and pre-eminently Mk. All students of Mark's Gospel recognise that a considerable portion of it consists of little paragraphs (later incorporated into Mt. and Lk.) relating actions and words of Jesus. These are the beads. The string upon which they are strung consists of the chronological succession of these incidents which is interwoven with their localisation, which consists not merely of the geographical localities associated with incidents and sayings but is supplemented by such further information as 'on the road,' 'in the boat' (no doubt Peter's), 'in the house' (also Peter's), 'in the mountain,' 'on the beach,' 'in the synagogue.'

The Source-critics regarded Mark's string as of supreme value for the historical understanding of the order of events and the development of the methods of the ministry of Jesus. The Form-critics, for reasons which I cannot give here, regard Mark's string as of no value at all. On this point I find myself in acute disagreement with the Form-critics.

Having unstrung Mark's beads, the Form-critics examine and classify them according to a theory of literary forms: as legends, paradigms, wonder stories, apophthegms, exhortations, etc. This is a task of some difficulty, as the beads in some cases are not easily assigned to a particular class. The Form-critics then arrange these various literary forms in a hypothetical chronological succession which they assume will be the order of the evolution of a religious tradition. Having done this they restring the beads in groups in this order, which they claim to be the true order of the beads, in contrast to the order which they have in Mark's Gospel. Moreover, they do not regard the beads as themselves being actual reminiscences of the actions and words of Jesus (as, for instance, are the sections in the *Memorabilia* of Socrates compiled by his pupil, Xenophon). The beads are for the Form-critics the creation of the primitive Christian teachers and missionaries. The primitive Christian leaders skilfully fashioned some of these beads to satisfy the curiosity and devotional and practical needs of the members of the primitive Christian communities. Other beads they fashioned to meet their own apologetic needs in their work of propaganda, which brought them into conflict with Jewish and pagan opponents.

These beads are thus the creation, very largely, of the oral period of Christian propaganda which preceded the period of literary composition which brought our Synoptic Gospels into existence. Our Synoptic Gospels and their literary sources consist almost entirely of collections of these beads. According to the Form-critics the order of events in the ministry of Jesus has been lost. All we have in its place, and it is supplied to us by the Form-critics, is the order of the growth of the tradition about Jesus, which tradition is not based upon history but is the product of the needs of the Christian community.

Hence, according to the Form-critics, our Gospels present us with an interesting picture of the cultus, practice, expectations, beliefs, problems, prejudices of the Christian Church in the second half of the first century, but not with any reliable historical account of Jesus Himself.

We may rightly concede to the Form-critics that Mark's Gospel does exhibit apologetic tendencies which are more fully developed in later Gospels. This, of course, is not new: the Source-critics were teaching it forty years ago, as may be seen by reference to Menzies' *The Earliest Gospel* (pub. 1896). Nevertheless, although influenced by various apologetic tendencies, especially in the selection of its material and in certain cases in the interpretation of it, Mark's Gospel will be found on examination to provide both in its contents and in the order of events which it relates a generally reliable guide to the understanding of the

Messianic mission of Jesus. The Form-critics have made us aware of the part played by the Church (the particular Christian community for which the Gospel was written). In the composition of the Gospel, the Church did not wield the pen: that was done by the Evangelist; but the Church acted as inheritor of the Christian tradition and cultus, and no Gospel which was not in general harmony with these could hope to survive as authoritative in the Christian Church. Hence, our Gospels are not pure histories: they are primitive Christian apologies or, as some would say, primitive Church catechisms which enshrine primitive Christian traditions, beliefs, and practices. But this must be emphasised: these traditions, beliefs, and practices had *a solid basis in historic fact*. It is this which the more extreme Form-critics deny.

(iii) *The Jewish Prophet School*

Another school of critics is convinced that Jesus was a historical personage —a Jew of Palestine, although possibly not of pure Jewish descent, if we accept what are called ‘ the slanders of the Talmud ’ and the theories of Mr. Houston Chamberlain and his Teutonic allies.

Nevertheless, Jesus was an absolute Jew in His religion and felt Himself called upon, in the spirit of one of the eighth-century prophets (an Amos or a Hosea), to reform that religion. As a consequence He made fierce attacks upon contemporary Judaism and its leaders, and, like other of the goodly fellowship of the Prophets of Israel who had preceded Him, He suffered their fate, but at the hands of the Roman Procurator of Judæa.

Some of His most enthusiastic followers, after His death, became convinced that Jesus, the prophet of Galilee, was more than a prophet, and proclaimed their conviction that He was the Messiah, God's Anointed One, the Son of God. This conviction was stimulated, if not originated, by the report of some of His disciples that they had actually seen Him alive after His crucifixion. As Professor Shirley Jackson Case of Chicago, the ablest and latest exponent of this view, expresses it:

> ‘ The process of idealisation rapidly gathered momentum. Time dimmed historical memories as death removed those who had known Jesus in the flesh.’

And so Jesus, who had never claimed to be the Messiah, is exalted to God's right hand, and His adoring and expectant Church awaits His apocalyptic return from heaven with power and great glory to be the Judge, as God's vice-gerent, of all mankind.

The underlying and basic conviction which all the Gospels preserve is that Jesus undertook His mission simply and solely because He believed Himself to be the Messiah; although according to the earliest Gospel (Mk.) Jesus kept that conviction in His own breast, and until others had surmised it He Himself would not confess it.

The view that the historic Jesus never claimed to be the Messiah seems to us to be open to the fatal objection that it renders His historic ministry inexplicable. If He had claimed to be a prophet, and no more than a prophet, why should His death disillusion His followers as to the validity of His claim? His fate was only too common in the history of the prophets, but no loyal Jew supposed for an instant that martyrdom discredited either their message or their mission. It was because Jesus claimed to be Messiah that His crucifixion discredited His claim in the eyes of His disciples and of Judaism generally, which claim was only revived as the result of His disciples' experiences both of His resurrection and of the outpouring of His Spirit into their hearts.

The Messianic secret with the stages of its unveiling and recognition in Mk. is so unexpected and so original as to make it very difficult to believe that it is not historically true, but is merely a *post-mortem* fiction invented by the primitive disciples of Jesus. This impression is deepened when we observe the tendency in Mt. to confuse or ignore the stages in the unveiling of the Messianic secret as given by Mk. This impression is strengthened by John's deliberate correction of Mk. on this point. Jesus, in the Fourth Gospel, proclaims His Messiahship from the very beginning of His ministry.

We may add that the Messianic conviction of Jesus is enshrined as strongly and clearly in Q (the earliest of our literary sources) as it is in John (the latest of our Canonical Gospels).

It seems to us that unless we are going to regard, not only our Gospels, but the literary sources they use as unhistorical, we must accept the Messianic consciousness of Jesus as one of the best-attested facts we possess in regard to Him. This conclusion in no way contradicts the view that the contemporary Galileans regarded Jesus as a prophet and described Him as such. Nor does it contradict the conviction of His very early disciples that He was a Rabbi possessed of extraordinary wisdom, originality, and insight.

(iv) *The Eschatological School*

Yet a fourth school of critics concludes that the historical Jesus did claim to be the Messiah, and a Messiah of the strictly apocalyptic kind. There seem to have been at least two current and popular conceptions of the Messiahship in existence at this time :

(*a*) The Zealots, a party of fanatical Jewish patriots, expected the Messiah to be a Jew who would claim the Messianic office and as a great political and military leader would deliver Judaism from pagan domination and establish a great Jewish empire on earth. In short, the Messiah was to be the patriotic successor of the Maccabean princes, but on a vaster scale.

(*b*) The second contemporary view of the Messiah was that He was a pre-existent spiritual Being dwelling in the celestial sphere with the most Ancient of Days, and that at the moment determined by Divine decree He would descend from heaven with legions of angels and archangels and by means of their flaming swords utterly destroy the pagan world and establish as Jehovah's vice-gerent a Messianic empire on earth which would last a thousand years or more.

This, with variations, is the conception of the Messiahship contained in the Jewish apocalypses, of which the most significant (with the exception of the Book of Daniel) was the Book of Enoch, written several generations before the birth of Jesus. These Jewish apocalypses seem to have gained a wide popularity among devout Jews. They were bright tracts for dark times, and they gave hope and good cheer to many who through them were led to wait, not to fight with material swords, for the redemption of Israel. Jesus is presumed to have been an ardent student of this kind of literature, and so was led to believe Himself to be the Messiah, and a Messiah of the apocalyptic type. There are many phrases and passages in the Gospels which indicate this. Of course we all recognise in this year of grace that these apocalyptic dreams failed to be realised, both for the Jews and for the Christians. There was no celestial irruption of spiritual champions to rescue Judaism from the Roman yoke, or to deliver the Christian Church from her pagan persecutors. Both Jew and Gentile, as they looked at the sky, asked: Where is the promise of His coming? But no triumphant Messiah descending with His angels from heaven gladdened their sight.

Not a few eminent New Testament scholars who believe in the existence of the historic Jesus and that He claimed to be the Messiah, believe that He claimed to be a Messiah of this strictly apocalyptic type. The scholarly adherents of this view, since Johannes Weiss and Albert Schweitzer first presented it, comprise so formidable an array that it must seem presumptuous in the highest degree to question the correctness of their conclusion.

Is there really no place for a *tertium quid*? Are we absolutely tied to the view that either Jesus did not claim to be the Messiah at all or else that He claimed to be the Messiah in the strictly apocalyptic sense?

I am myself compelled to hold that there is such a *tertium quid*, and that Jesus did claim to be the Messiah but not in the strictly apocalyptic sense. The conclusion that He claimed to be the Messiah in a strictly apocalyptic sense seems to me unconvincing, and for the following reasons:

If Jesus claimed to be a Messiah of the apocalyptic kind, the most fundamental element in His Gospel is lacking in originality. If the mystical narrative of the triple temptation derived from Q is meant to teach that Jesus accepted as His own the apocalyptic model of Messiahship, then He ought to have confuted the Tempter with three quotations from the *Book of Daniel* or the *Similitudes of Enoch*, and not from *Deuteronomy*.

Another objection to the conclusion that Jesus regarded Himself as an apocalyptic Messiah is that there are profound sayings attributed to Him which are not in agreement with apocalyptic conceptions. The Divine Father of Jesus whom Jesus adored is not the avenging Deity of the apocalyptists. The sons of the Kingdom which Jesus proclaimed are not of the seed of Abraham in accordance with the evangel of the apocalyptists, but are all those who possess the moral and spiritual qualities commended in the Beatitudes.

If there be, on these essential issues, such divergence from current apocalypticism, why must we assume that the conception which Jesus held of the Messiahship was strictly apocalyptic? It will no doubt be replied: Because there are many sayings attributed to Jesus in the Gospels which make this identification certain. There are no doubt many such sayings, but can we be sure that they are His? We are quite sure that some of them are not His. Matthew's Gospel, the most Jewish of the Gospels, alters passages taken from Mk. so as to give them an apocalyptic significance. That Gospel omits non-apocalyptic passages which are found in Mk. It also inserts a number of apocalyptic passages. This indicates a strong tendency in primitive Jewish Christianity not only to interpret the teaching of Jesus apocalyptically, but also to ignore teaching attributed to Jesus which conflicted with current apocalyptic beliefs, and even to put into His mouth apocalyptic sayings which are not His.

Moreover, are there not a number of profound and original sayings of Jesus which are in conflict with these crude apocalyptic conceptions? And ought we not to regard this non-apocalyptic element in the recorded teaching of Jesus as that which is essentially His; and the apocalyptic element as having come in from contemporary Judaism through John the Baptist and the early disciples of Jesus, who were all Jews and of the apocalyptic kind?

Further, had not the apocalyptic conception of the Messiahship, as of the Kingdom and as of the Deity, an apologetic value for the early Christian Church which the more profound spiritual and moral elements of the teaching attributed to Jesus had not? Is there no critical justification for the pre-Schweitzerian Liberal view that as Jesus filled the current Jewish concepts of the Kingdom with a new and original content, so He did also those of the Messiahship?

I would not maintain that no apocalyptic elements are to be found in our Lord's original teaching about the Kingdom. Judaism owed much spiritually to certain elements in Apocalypticism, and these, there is good reason to believe, Jesus retained and included: but those aspects of apocalyptic teaching which experience has shown to be false and futile, I am unable, in view of the conflicting character of the evidence, to regard as part of the original Gospel of Jesus. Genius is more prone to create than to borrow, to strike out new paths for itself rather than to follow pedestrians on the highway; and Jesus has claims, although there are many who would deprive Him of every element of originality, to be regarded as a supreme moral and spiritual genius. Jesus, in Matthew Arnold's phrase, is not only above the heads of His reporters, but He is also above the heads of His modern critics.

There is one contributor, however, to the pages of the New Testament who did not take the apocalyptic view either of the Kingdom or of the Messiahship of Jesus. I refer, of course, to the author of the Fourth Gospel. He identified the Kingdom with eternal life to be entered into here and now, and the Messiahship of the Kingdom he identified with the mission of the Life-giver:

'I am come that they may have life, and have it abundantly.'

How far he was historically justified in this view is no easy question to answer, but I am drawn to think that he had a more profound understanding of the essential teaching of Jesus than had those primitive Jewish disciples who are reported to have asked Jesus on the occasion of His ascension:

'Lord, dost thou at this time restore the Kingdom to Israel?'

The Death of Jesus

In connexion with the Messiahship of Jesus it is of importance to indicate here the precise connexion between His Messiahship and His Crucifixion.

Dr. Eisler's widely-circulating volume, *The Messiah Jesus and John the Baptist* (New York, Eng. tr., 1931), propounds the view that an early Russian translation of the original draft of the work of Josephus' *History of the Jewish War* throws important light, by the additional matter it contains, on the origins of the Christian movement. Jesus, it would seem according to this view, was not guiltless of harbouring dreams of a political revolutionary kind akin to those of the Zealots. His crucifixion between two of the revolutionaries was therefore not so inappropriate as it has hitherto seemed to us. It is possible that some of the disciples of Jesus, as the incident of the two swords in Lk. suggests, believed in Zealot methods; but there is no convincing evidence that Jesus did. His entry into Jerusalem on Palm Sunday symbolised His coming as the Prince of Peace. His dictum, 'they that take the sword shall perish by the sword,' is directed against the Zealot propaganda, as are also His pacific exhortations to submit to the oppressive exactions and even injustices of Roman government officials.

Professor Creed [1] has given Professor Eisler's ingenious and erudite theories the *coup de grâce*. Dr. Creed shows, with a high degree of probability, that where the Slavonic Josephus deviates from the received text of Josephus the variants are worthless and have no sound claim to be regarded as genuine.

Sceptics have asserted that the only Article in the Christian Creed which it is possible to accept is that which states that Jesus was crucified under Pontius Pilate. Nevertheless there is still much debate as to why He was crucified. Was He crucified voluntarily, and if so what significance and value did He attach to His death for the purpose of His Messianic mission? To me it seems clear that the death of Jesus was voluntary; that He went up to Jerusalem expecting to die. The fate of many of the great prophets of Israel, the death of John the Baptist, the lot of the Suffering Servant in the Second Isaiah, the growing hostility of the religious and political authorities of His nation all pointed to the inevitability and the appropriateness of His own death. But why in Jerusalem?

It is said that the late Marshal Foch, when a professor at a military academy, used to propound to his pupils this problem: When the enemy are in overwhelming force in front, and both your flanks are in the air and you are without reserves, what must you do—surrender or retreat? Neither. You must advance with all your forces and strike at the enemy's centre.

This was the situation of Jesus. Defeated in Galilee, attacked on both flanks by the religious and political authorities of His nation, He must either take to flight or surrender, or advance on Jerusalem. It was a forlorn hope, but the alternatives were not death or victory, but failure or victory through death. For one brief period in Gethsemane, Jesus was almost overwhelmed by the darkness and horror of the situation, but recognising His Father's hand in it He was able to say 'Thy will be done.' And so, after confessing His Messiahship to the Sanhedrin, He died deliberately and as Messiah, rejected by Judaism.

He might so easily have been got out of the way or been suppressed on some minor charge. That is the real danger which threatens the martyrs and heroes of every great cause. Jesus had the supreme satisfaction of dying for that for which He had lived—His Messianic claim. It was on that claim that His Church

[1] *Harvard Theological Review* for Oct. 1932.

was founded after His death in Jerusalem, and it was the thin red line of the Messiah's blood which separated that Church from Judaism. Only by His death could His Gospel triumph. The view that He died as a propitiatory sacrifice for the sins of His nation or for the sins of mankind, which was the view of St. Paul and of many others in the primitive Christian Church, cannot be convincingly attributed to Jesus Himself, and neither Q, proto-Lk. nor Mk. contain any teaching which identifies the death of Jesus with a propitiatory sacrifice for the forgiveness of sins. He died as Messiah; He did not die as a propitiatory sacrifice; He died on behalf of the many who were to come unto God through Him.

Miracles in the Gospels

In the past, critical study of the Gospels has been much concerned with the historicity of the miracles in the Gospels.

The term ' miracle ' is an ambiguous one and is generally taken to refer to occurrences which are contrary to the known laws of Nature. Inasmuch as in the pre-scientific period in which our Gospels were composed, men did not think of occurrences as being either in harmony with Nature's laws or out of harmony with them it would be misleading to think of the ' Gospel miracles ' in this way. In the Gospels they are spoken of as ' powers ' (*dunameis*), ' wonders ' (*terata*), ' mighty works ' (*dunata erga*), and ' signs ' (*sēmeia*).

They caused wonder to those who witnessed them: they appeared to be special manifestations of the Divine action and presence: they were cited by primitive Christians as testimonies to the Messiahship of Jesus: men came to believe in Jesus on account of them.

The attitude of Jesus towards them differed from that of His contemporaries and followers. In our earliest Gospel sources, Jesus condemns the faith in Him which rests on miracles. He declares that it is an evil and adulterous generation which seeks after a sign; in other words, a generation unfaithful to God which demands signs and wonders as the basis for its religious faith. He pointed to the Ninevites, who were won to repentance, not by the miracles of Jonah, for the prophet wrought none, but by his prophetic preaching. He pointed to the Queen of Sheba, who was converted, not by the miracles of Solomon, but by his wisdom; and declared that in Him His generation possessed one who was greater than either Jonah or Solomon. He asserted that if men would not hear Moses and the prophets, neither would they be persuaded though one rose from the dead.

Again it is abundantly clear that though Jesus was regarded as a healer, possessed of Divine power, yet He Himself sought to escape from this reputation. Again and again, He told those who were healed that their faith had healed them. He told them also to be silent on the subject of their cure. In certain cases they were to offer the prescribed sacrifices in the Temple and they might tell their relations what great things God had done for them, but Jesus did not wish Himself to be proclaimed publicly as their healer.

In this attitude towards miracles Jesus stood far above His contemporaries and indeed above His disciples in every succeeding age of the Church down to the present time. He had no desire to work miracles: He had no desire to be regarded as a worker of miracles: He did not regard faith in miracles as constituting a sound basis for the moral and spiritual life.

In the Fourth Gospel, and in the Longer Ending of Mk. (Mk. 16^9 to end), Jesus is made to claim that miracles are signs of His Messianic authority; but this reflects the beliefs of the primitive Christian Church, not of Jesus Himself.

It may naturally be asked: Even though Jesus took this view of miracles, yet did He not work them? Are the accounts of miracles in our Gospels fabrications? The critic's answer to these questions is both Yes and No.

Undoubtedly many of the acts of healing related in the Gospels are historical. Although the Messianic mission of Jesus consisted primarily in the proclamation of His Gospel of the Kingdom, yet the ministry of healing did secure a subordinate place in the Messianic mission—subordinate in the mind and will of Jesus, but very often dominant in the estimation of the multitudes of sick and diseased who flocked to Him. These miracles were achieved by faith. To-day we are able to regard this as a credible explanation of them.

But all the miracles in the Gospels are not miracles of healing. There are what have been called 'Nature-miracles,' such as the stilling of the storm, the feeding of the five thousand, the withering of the barren fig tree. Here the modern critic applies two tests:

(1) Is the evidence for the alleged miracle sufficient to establish it as a historic fact? If it be accepted that it is a fact, it will not necessarily follow that it is a miracle because those who experienced it interpreted it as a miracle. In the light of our modern knowledge it may be entirely natural, although contemporary interpretations conceived of it as miraculous.

(2) Hence the modern critic strives to discriminate between *fact* and *interpretation* in the miracle-narratives in the Gospels. The interpretation of the fact will of necessity reflect contemporary views of God, the Universe, and the Divine method of action; all of which differ very widely from modern views in these spheres. It may be a fact that a storm ceased with extraordinary suddenness just after Jesus had uttered the words, 'Peace, be still,' but it may be that contemporary interpretation, which made the one the cause of the other, is wrong. It may be fact that after Jesus had exorcised a demoniac, a neighbouring herd of swine rushed over a cliff and were drowned, but the interpretation, that demons passed from the demoniac into the swine and so caused their destruction, may be mistaken.

Yet the Gospel account of the mistaken interpretation, just as its account of the fact which it seeks to interpret, will both be true records of contemporary events.

The older view, that if a single miracle in the Gospels was discredited as unhistorical, then the whole of the Gospels must be regarded as unhistorical, is a product of a belief in the plenary verbal inspiration of Scripture as a whole, which is no longer held by modern-minded students of the Bible.

Literary criticism has shown that the Gospels consist of a great number of different oral and literary sources which vary greatly in their historical value.

Hence all the miraculous narratives belonging to one source might be regarded as absolutely unhistorical without affecting the historical value of narratives derived from other sources. Each miracle narrative, therefore, must be judged on its merits. The fact that, among discerning Christian teachers to-day, miracles are no longer regarded as proofs of the truth of the Christian religion, has relieved the tension with regard to them. No modern-minded student will deny the possibility that miracles might happen; but this becomes to him, from the religious point of view, a profitless speculation since he regards miracles as possessing no validity for proving the truth of the Christian religion. Matthew Arnold put this in a nutshell when he wrote satirically: ' In order to prove to you that what I have written is true, I will turn my pen into a pen-wiper.'

Two Conflicting Tendencies in Gospel Criticism

We observe in modern criticism of the Gospels two conflicting tendencies. The first tendency inclines to strengthen our impression of the historical character of the Synoptic Gospels. The second tendency inclines to weaken our impression of their historical value.

The first tendency is to stress more and more strongly the full humanity of Jesus—not simply the richness and tenderness and insight of His human sympathy, but also His various human limitations, physical and mental. Gore's doctrine of the *Kenosis* sought to explain and justify these human limitations theologically.

The second tendency is to stress the strangeness of Jesus. He is the ' enigma of the centuries.'

' He comes to us as One unknown, without a name, as of old by the lake-side He came to those men who knew Him not. He speaks to us the same word, " Follow thou me! " and sets us to the tasks which He has to fulfil for our time. He commands. And to those who obey Him, whether they be wise or simple, He will reveal Himself in the toils, and conflicts, the sufferings which they shall pass through in His fellowship, and, as an ineffable mystery, they shall learn in their own experience Who He is.'

This famous passage with which Schweitzer concludes *The Quest of the Historical Jesus* has had many imitators among those less gifted as critics and writers.

This most modern tendency to regard Jesus as the Great Unknown is partly the product of reaction, possibly even of scepticism and disillusionment. The elder generation of Gospel critics were perhaps too much at ease in Zion. Weinel asked: Do we know Jesus? And had no hesitation in replying: Yes, we know Him very well indeed.

Loisy's attack on the Jesus of Liberal Protestantism was not without some justification, although the replacement of the Liberal Protestant Jesus, first by the apocalyptic Jesus and then by the Christ who is identified with the Catholic Church, led Loisy in the end to renounce both his Christianity and his Catholicism.

This stress upon the unknown Jesus which gives freedom to critics to assess His personality at every valuation ranging from zero to infinity is to-day appropriately united to the Barthian theology, which proclaims as the supreme article of its faith the unknown God whose only undoubted attribute is His 'otherness.' The doctrine of an unknown God and an unknown Messiah reflects not only the modern flight from a reasonable faith but also from sound New Testament criticism. Yet there is a lesson to be learnt from this. It is contained in the warning of a modern critic: We must seek to become the contemporaries of Jesus, we must not seek to make Him our contemporary.

It is the task of Gospel Criticism to make ourselves the contemporaries of Jesus: to see Him as He really was in the fullness and circumstances of His humanity. Our Lord was not a modern man, although the spirit and principles which proceed from Him are ever new in their creative and transforming power. The ethic of Jesus in its underlying principles (not necessarily in every occasional utterance attributed to Him) is universal and eternal.

The Originality of Jesus

The question of historicity is bound up with that of originality. The Gospel *dicta:* 'What is this? A new teaching! Never man spake as this man'—have been taken to refer, not to the content, but to the manner of His teaching. Many things which used to be supposed to be original in the teaching of Jesus are now shown to be derived from contemporary Judaism. Were there, then, no original elements in His teaching? Yes, there were some: notably His view about miracles; also about forgiveness; also about little children. Harnack has said: What is most remarkable about the religion of Jesus is not what He includes in it but what He excludes from it. The originality of Jesus is seen in two things pre-eminently: (1) in the originality of His selection, (2) in the way in which He filled old terms with new meanings. And yet that is not all. Jesus speaks of the new wine. This was not so much new teaching as a new spirit.

It is this new spirit which is enshrined in the Gospels, and it is no small proof of their essentially historical character. The Gospels preserve for us the impression made on that ancient world by the impact of the personality of Jesus Christ: an impact which awakened in it a spirit of faith, hope, and love.

The Snare of Critical Study

The modern critical study of the Gospels, because it is often so rightly concerned with the study of minute details, is in danger of failing to see the wood for the trees.

Certainly it is the duty of the literary and historic critic to find truth in minute details. But if he only finds truth there, just as much as if he fails to find it there, he has come short in the fulfilment of his task. There is also the truth to be found in the general impression created by the narrative as a whole—its cumulative effect—an effect which is not dissipated by innumerable petty contradictions and discrepancies. The literary critic of the Gospels may very easily develop a temper which begins by being critical and ends by being sceptical—the outcome of excessive concentration upon minute details and failure to harmonise them into a consistent unity. Such a temper unfits him to be a really understanding critic of the literature with which he is dealing. To be an understanding critic many gifts are required. He must have the knowledge which enables him to find the truth in petty details: he must also have the acute intelligence which enables him to find the truth in what Renan called *les nuances*, fine distinctions of phrase and thought; but he must also find the truth in the narrative as a whole. To do this he must be able to take what Plato called a synoptic view—to see the whole, although that whole consists of many minute and superficially conflicting elements.

A great judge, in contrast to a pettifogging attorney, is able to get at the truth behind the contradictions in the evidence because he possesses not only a much wider range of general culture, but also a much deeper and more sympathetic understanding of human nature. Yet it is the spirit of the attorney rather than that of the judge which seems to dominate the conclusions of some New Testament critics. Their basis of judgement is too narrow. They seem to have so little understanding of human nature, comparative religion, and the forces which mould human history.

We do well to remember that while knowledge of the assured results of criticism is an important factor in our knowledge of Jesus, it is only *one* of the factors in the knowledge of Him. It is most important that this should be realised. Besides the critical knowledge of Jesus there is the influence of the spirit and ideals of Jesus upon our Western civilisation. This does not come within the purview of New Testament criticism, yet it provides a very important element in assisting us to estimate the essential significance of Jesus, both for His time and for ours. It is to Him we owe the axiom: 'A tree is known by its fruit.'

After reading these remarks on the theme: Are the Gospels true history? the reader may not unreasonably complain that he does not know what answer he ought to give to that question.

That answer he can only give with some degree of conviction after he has made a first-hand study of the Gospels for himself. When St. Polycarp of Smyrna, in the year A.D. 156, was asked by the Roman pro-consul who was about to condemn him to death: 'Who is this god of the Christians?' Polycarp replied: 'If thou art worthy, thou shalt know.'

BOOK I. INCIDENTS IN THE LIFE OF JESUS

Introduction to St. Mark's Gospel

EVIDENCE concerning the origin, authorship, date, purpose, historicity, etc., of the Gospels is classified as either external or internal. The external evidence is derived from sources outside the Gospel itself, such as the statements of early writers about the Gospel ; the earliest quotations from the Gospel to be found in primitive Church literature ; the date and locality of the earliest codices or manuscripts of the Gospel ; and the earliest versions or translations of it.

The internal evidence is derived from the Gospel itself : what the Gospel tells us, and in most cases inadvertently, about itself. The external evidence may be inaccurate or even entirely fictitious, but the internal evidence, if correctly interpreted, cannot deceive. This does not mean that the external evidence is of little or of no importance. It may be, and often is, of the very highest value especially in helping the reader of the Gospel to interpret the internal evidence correctly. The point, however, to be borne in mind is this: That where there is a conflict between the external evidence and the internal evidence rightly interpreted—and that's the rub—the internal evidence must prevail as against the external.

For instance, if a writer of the second century should tell us that St. Matthew's Gospel was written in Hebrew or Aramaic, and the study of our present Gospel according to St. Matthew should show that the compiler of that work makes use of many passages taken from the Greek Gospel of St. Mark and quoted almost word for word: it is clear that this internal evidence for the original Greek character of our Gospel according to St. Matthew must prevail against the external statement which led some to think that the writer of that Gospel wrote it in Hebrew or Aramaic.

In studying the origin of the Gospels it is usual to begin with the external evidence. We shall, therefore, begin with the external evidence for the origin and authorship of the Second Gospel. From this external evidence only the most significant items will be selected and sufficient to prove the point at issue, but no more.

1. Papias, Bishop of Hierapolis (Asia Minor), writing some years before the middle of the second century in his book, *Expositions of the Oracles of the Lord* (of which only fragments are preserved, mainly in the great *Ecclesiastical History* of Eusebius, written in the days of Constantine the Great), gives the following account of the origin of the Second Gospel:

'And the Elder [i.e. the Presbyter John whom he is citing here] used to say this: Mark having become Peter's interpreter wrote down accurately so far as he remembered what Christ either said or did: not, however, in order (orderly fashion), for he neither heard the Lord, nor followed Him, but subsequently, as I have said, followed Peter, who used to suit his instructions to the needs of his hearers, but with no intention of giving a connected account of the Lord's discourses (*Logia*), so that Mark made no error while he thus wrote some things as he remembered them. For he was careful of one thing—not to omit any of the things which he had heard, and not to state any of them falsely.' (Cited from the *Ecclesiastical History* of Eusebius, Bk. iii. 39.)

We postpone comment on this evidence until later.

2. Our second piece of external testimony is found in the *Dialogue with one Trypho, a Jew*, written by St. Justin Martyr probably before the year A.D. 150. In chapter 106 of this work Justin refers to Mark's Gospel as the *Memoirs of Peter*. The word he uses for Memoirs is the same as that which the great Greek writer Xenophon uses as the title of his *Memoirs of Socrates*, his beloved teacher. Justin Martyr was a well-known figure in the Christian Church in the middle of the second century. Born in Palestine, in Samaritan territory, he became an ardent student of philosophy and journeyed from place to place in order to sit at the feet of the most eminent philosophical teachers. He was converted mysteriously to the Christian religion by one whose name he never knew, and thereafter became an ardent teacher of his new faith and addressed two Apologies or Defences on its behalf to the reigning Roman Emperors. He was finally martyred in Rome, where he had established a Christian congregation.

3. Our third witness to the Gospel of St. Mark is St. Irenæus, a contemporary of St. Justin Martyr, and even more widely and honourably known than he. As a young man he had been a pupil of St. Polycarp, Bishop of Smyrna, the friend of St. Ignatius, the second Bishop of Antioch, who addressed him in an Epistle, which is still extant. St. Irenæus, who had been a presbyter of the Church of Lyons and Vienne in Gaul, became Bishop of that See in the year 178, in succession to the martyred Pothinus. St. Irenæus, in his great work directed against the heretical teaching of the Gnostics, writes:

(*a*) 'Matthew published his Gospel among the Hebrews in their own dialect [i.e. Aramaic] while Peter and Paul were preaching at Rome and founding the Church. After their departure [*exodos*, by which he means their death], Mark, the disciple and interpreter of Peter, also transmitted to us in writing those things that Peter used to preach (*Hær*. iii. i. 1).' Irenæus is thus in agreement with the recently published *Anti-Marcionite Prologue to Mark* (written A.D. 150–180):

'This man was the translator of Peter *after the death of Peter himself*. He also wrote this Gospel in the regions of Italy.'

(*b*) 'Mark, the interpreter and follower of Peter, thus began to write his Gospel—

"The Beginning of the Gospel of Jesus Christ the Son of God, etc."' (*Hær*. iii. 10, 6).

4. Our fourth piece of external evidence is from the North African writer, Tertullian, a barrister and presbyter of Carthage, born about A.D. 155. A man of great learning, he became a brilliant Christian apologist. He writes in his treatise against the heretic Marcion (iv. 5):

'And what Mark published may be said to be Peter's, whose interpreter Mark was.'

5. We have next the evidence of a contemporary of Tertullian, Clement of Alexandria, head of the famous catechetical school in Alexandria about 190–203. He is cited by Eusebius as follows:

'Clement gives the tradition of the earliest presbyters as to the order of the Gospels, in the following manner: "the Gospel according to Mark had this occasion. As Peter had preached the Word publicly at Rome, and declared the Gospel by the Spirit, many who were present requested that Mark, who had followed him for a long time and remembered his sayings, should write them out, and having composed the Gospel he gave it to those who had requested it: when Peter learned of this, he neither directly forbade nor encouraged it!"' (*H.E.* vi. 14, quoting Clement's *Hypotyposes.*)

6. The next piece of evidence is that of Clement's successor in the catechetical school, the famous Origen, surnamed Adamantius, the greatest scholar of the ancient Church and one of its most indomitable teachers and martyrs. He writes, as cited by Eusebius:

'The Second [Gospel] is by Mark, who composed it according to the instructions of Peter, who in his Catholic epistle acknowledges him as a son.' (*H.E.* vi. 25.)

These six pieces of external evidence are agreed in one main affirmation that in Mark's Gospel we have recorded the Gospel preaching of St. Peter, the chief of the Apostles.

This, as the late Professor McGiffert asserts, is 'the universal tradition of antiquity,' and 'is repeated over and over again by the Fathers.'

But this direct external evidence for the origin of the Second Gospel is supplemented by a piece of even more striking indirect internal evidence. Modern research, in the form of the parallel study of the Greek texts of the Gospels of St. Matthew, St. Mark, and St. Luke, proves overwhelmingly that the writers of the First and Third Gospels were not only well acquainted with St. Mark's Gospel but that they regarded it as so valuable an authority for the ministry of Jesus that they incorporated a large part of Mark into the text of their own Gospels.

The more important part of the evidence for this is thus summarised by Professor Stanton in *The Gospels as Historical Documents* (pt. ii., pp. 34 f.):

'With very few exceptions, our first and third evangelists, so far as they omit incidents or sayings given in St. Mark, do not omit the same ones: the result being that almost all the sections in St. Mark are found also in one or other of the two remaining synoptics: . . .

'When the sequence of narratives in St. Matthew or in St. Luke differs from that in St. Mark, the other one agrees with St. Mark. In other words, St. Matthew and St. Luke do not, save in one or two instances, unite against St. Mark as to order. When all three do not agree in respect to it, we have the same sequence in St. Matthew and St. Mark, or in St. Luke and St. Mark. There is, further, an agreement which is generally considerable and sometimes very full between St. Mark and each of the two other Synoptics in the manner in which incidents are related, and in phraseology. All three frequently agree in these respects. But there are also commonly particulars of this kind in which St. Matthew and St. Luke each separately agrees with St. Mark. On the whole the correspondence is closest between St. Matthew and St. Mark; but there are some cases in which the correspondence is closer between St. Luke and the parallel passage in St. Mark than between the latter and a parallel in St. Matthew. Finally, it is to be observed that the amount of agreement in statements or words between St. Matthew and St. Luke alone, in all those portions of their Gospels which are in substance contained in St. Mark, is trifling in comparison with the agreement of each separately and even of both together, with St. Mark. Now, if . . . we suppose that the authors of these Gospels used St. Mark, or a document resembling St. Mark, and each in his own way revised and supplemented it, we have a simple and natural explanation of these phenomena.'

As these two Gospels were almost certainly written not later than A.D. 80, it is clear that St. Mark's Gospel was not only composed at least some years before that date but it was regarded as a most important source, if not the most important source, for the ministry of Jesus. Internal evidence indicates clearly that Mk. was *the* most important source of the First Gospel. In the case of the Third Gospel, although an important source, Mk. was not, so Dr. Streeter has indicated, the most important of the sources used by St. Luke for his Gospel. It would seem to be probable that Luke had already composed a first draft of his Gospel (Proto-Luke) before he came across Mark's Gospel. He then used Mk. in the second draft of his own Gospel. Thus while Mk. is a primary source for Mt., he is a secondary source for Lk. There can be little doubt that it was not simply the early date of Mark's Gospel, but the conviction that it enshrined the actual reminiscences and experiences of St. Peter, the chief apostle of Jesus, which gave it its supreme value in the eyes of the writers of the First and Third Gospels.

There is yet another piece of evidence which must not be overlooked. St. Irenæus makes it clear that our present Gospel canon of four Gospels was in existence when he wrote against the Gnostics. He asserts as there cannot be more, so there cannot be less than four Gospels even as there are four quarters of the Heaven and according to the Scriptures four rivers which watered Paradise. As Irenæus is writing in the last quarter of the second century it is clear that at that time St. Mark's Gospel was one of the sacred four. Yet how was it that it came to be included in the evangelical canon? That great Cambridge scholar, Professor H. B. Swete, pointed out:

'While no doubts are expressed by any early writer as to the genuineness of St. Mark, it cannot be denied that the Gospel received comparatively little attention from the theologians of the ancient Church. This relative neglect is noticeable from the very first.' (Swete's *St. Mark*, p. xxxiv.)

This neglect will seem to some to contradict the conclusion that Mark's Gospel is really St. Peter's. And yet not so. It was this that almost proved its undoing. It was the fact that it was St. Peter's Gospel which led to its incorporation with Matthew and Luke. By incorporating it into their Gospels, which contained a great deal especially of the teaching of Jesus which was not in Mark, they became in primitive Christian circles much more precious and desirable than Mark. And so Mark fell apparently into such extreme neglect that Professor Burkitt believes that the compiler of the First Gospel had only access to a single mutilated copy of Mark from which to make his citations. How was it, in that case, that Mark's Gospel got included among the Four?

It is here that Dr. B. H. Streeter in his great work on *The Four Gospels* suggests a convincing reason for Mark's inclusion in the Gospel canon. It was not simply the great name attached to a Gospel: it was not simply the quality and interest of its contents: it was the fact that it was the familiar and treasured Gospel of a great Christian Church which caused it to be included in the Four. Mark's Gospel, archaic, crude, mutilated, though it might be, was the treasured possession of the great Church of Rome since it contained the preaching to his Roman audiences of St. Peter, the apostolic co-founder of that Church. It was because the Roman Church cherished Mark's Gospel that the Catholic or Universal Church included Mark's Gospel in its evangelical canon.

When we look again at our external evidence we observe a number of points of interest if not of supreme importance.

The first concerns Mark's relationship to St. Peter. Now in the New Testament, except for the passage referred to by Origen in the *First Epistle of St. Peter*, 'Marcus, my son' (5^{13}), we should not think of there being any close relationship between St. Mark and St. Peter. In the *Acts of the Apostles* it is St. Mark's relationship with St. Barnabas, his cousin, and with St. Paul which is emphasised. Nothing is there said of his relationship to St. Peter. He set out with St. Paul and St. Barnabas from Antioch on their first great missionary journey (Acts 12^{25}, 13^{13}) but left them before the completion of it. When St. Barnabas wished him to accompany St. Paul on the second great missionary journey, St. Paul refused to have him on account of his former desertion. This led to a serious difference with St. Barnabas, who accordingly declined to accompany St. Paul on his second missionary journey, and taking St. Mark went with him to do evangelising work in Cyprus about A.D. 47 (Acts 15^{39}).

Many years later, when St. Paul was a prisoner in Rome, we learn that he had become reconciled to St. Mark, as we see from his directions given in his Epistle to the Colossians:

'Aristarchus my fellow prisoner saluteth you and Marcus, sister's son to Barnabas, (touching whom ye received commandments: if he come unto you, receive him)." (Col. 4^{10}; cf. Philem. *vv.* 23, 24.)

In the Second Epistle to Timothy (4^{11}), probably the very latest of St. Paul's letters, he writes:

'Take Mark, and bring him with thee: for he is profitable to me for the ministry.'

St. Mark would appear to have been associated with St. Peter very early in the history of the Christian Church, for Mary, Mark's mother, a widow, owned a large house in Jerusalem where the Christian Church assembled for worship and to which St. Peter went after his release from prison before A.D. 44 (Acts 12^{12}).

St. Peter knew many young men in Jerusalem in those days, and John Mark, the son of this important member of the Christian Church, was no doubt one of them. Nevertheless we have no statement in the New Testament that there was any relationship between St. Peter and St. Mark at this time. It is only many years later and in a single brief reference that we have the relationship between St. Peter and St. Mark revealed. It occurs, as has been noted, in 1 Pet. 5^{13}.

'She in Babylon who is elect with you,' whom St. Peter refers to as sending greetings to the churches in Asia Minor, is no doubt to be understood as the Church in Rome, and her name is coupled with that of 'Marcus, my son.' This would certainly seem to indicate that this First Epistle of St. Peter was written from Rome when St. Mark was an important younger colleague of St. Peter there. This fits in with the other external evidence which we have about St. Mark's Gospel. It need not surprise us that St. Peter should speak of Rome as Babylon, for we see in the Apocalypse that St. John the Divine, that primitive Christian, spoke of Rome by that name. But it was a name apparently only given to Rome by the Christians after Rome had become the cruel persecutor of the Christians in the days of Nero (A.D. 64).

Another point of interest in the external evidence cited is that Mark is spoken of as the Interpreter (*hermeneutes*) of St. Peter. This term, like the modern word dragoman, is given in the Near East to one who translates for another. It will seem strange to those who think of the Pentecostal outpouring of the Holy Spirit as conferring the power upon the Apostles to speak all foreign languages that St. Peter, the chief of the Apostles, should, for the purposes of his Christian ministry in Rome, stand in need of a dragoman whose business it would be to translate St. Peter's native Aramaic into Greek, which was at this time the vernacular of Rome. But it is generally recognised by scholars to-day that the *glossalalia*, or 'speaking with tongues,' was a form of ecstatic emotional utterance and not the power to speak in foreign languages. What those who possessed the gift were sent to do was to speak with 'new' tongues, that is to say, tongues which had never been used before by any human being. St. Paul, who wrote to his Corinthian converts that he spoke with tongues more than they all (1 Cor. 14^{18}), yet was evidently ignorant of the language of the Lycaonians (Acts 14^{11}).

Hence it fits in entirely with our best modern knowledge that St. Peter, the simple Galilean fisherman turned Christian Apostle, should require an interpreter in Rome, and that Mark, a wealthy young Jew belonging to the upper classes in Jerusalem, should be bilingual and act as Peter's interpreter. There is, however, some will feel, a grave difficulty presented by the fact that the First Epistle of St. Peter is written in Greek, and Greek of a quality and style much superior to the Greek of St. Mark's Gospel. This, however, presents no difficulty for those who interpret the passage 1 Pet. 5^{12}—

'By Silvanus, a faithful brother, as I count him, I have written briefly to you,' etc.,

as a statement by St. Peter that he is not using his usual translator Mark but another translator, Silvanus, not known to them as was St. Mark, yet one whom St. Peter counted to be a loyal Christian brother. Under the circumstances there could be nothing more natural than that the Roman Christians who had so often listened to St. Mark interpreting for St. Peter when the Apostle was recounting his reminiscences of Jesus should request St. Mark, when St. Peter had either died or was drawing to the end of his ministry, to give them those reminiscences in written form as an abiding possession.

It will be observed that the external evidence is in apparent conflict on the point as to whether Mark wrote down the Petrine preaching while the Apostle was yet alive or whether he wrote it after his death.

Irenæus appears to say that Mark's Gospel was written after Peter's death. Clement of Alexandria says distinctly that the Gospel was written during St. Peter's lifetime. It is possible to interpret the words of Irenæus that Mark undertook his work, presumably in the Apostle's lifetime, in order that after the Apostle's death his hearers might have a permanent record of his teaching. But this interpretation seems strained.

The point is of little importance for the purpose of dating Mark's Gospel. All are agreed that if it was not written before Peter's death it was written soon after it. There is general agreement that Peter died as a martyr, as did St. Paul, in the days of Nero but later than St. Paul. That is to say that Peter died somewhere between A.D. 64 and 68.

This would seem to agree with the internal evidence of St. Mark's Gospel, which, as we shall see, points to its having been written before the destruction of Jerusalem by Vespasian and Titus in A.D. 70.

Another point of interest in the external evidence is that stressed by Papias when he refers to the somewhat disconnected character of St. Mark's Gospel; the absence of any connected account of Christ's teaching in it, and the lack of order in the record of the actions and sayings of Christ. In the statement, in which he refers to the lack of order in Mk., Papias would seem to be making a subtle contrast between Mark and the other Gospels. Luke's Gospel shows a fine sense of chronological sequence: Matthew's Gospel contains a great body of systematically arranged discourse: John's Gospel conflicts acutely in its order with Mark's.

Papias, who was, as we have said, a bishop in Asia Minor, lived in the sphere in which the great Gospel of the Ephesian Church, St. John's, circulated, and whose authority for the order of events and discourses in our Lord's ministry he no doubt regarded as unable to be challenged.

Since, therefore, the *order* in St. Mark's Gospel is in conflict with the order in St. John's Gospel, Papias would naturally conclude that Mark did not write 'in order.' We shall see, however, that the internal evidence of the Gospel of St. Mark does not support Papias.

On the other hand, Papias is at pains to stress Mark's accuracy and conscientiousness. We shall see that there is much in the internal evidence to support this.

St. Luke tells his readers in his most interesting preface to his Gospel that many had—

'taken in hand to draw up in orderly fashion a narrative concerning those things which are most surely believed among us, even as they delivered them unto us, which from the beginning [of Christ's Ministry] were eyewitnesses, and ministers of the Word.'

St. Luke states in this preface, what is an obvious fact, that the record of the written word was preceded by the ministry of the spoken word. And he also would have his hearers to realise that the record of the written word is in no sense an original invention but is a reproduction in written form of that oral preaching and tradition which preceded it.

The fact that our canonical Gospels are the product of a secondary stage in the history of the Christian tradition (the primary stage being the period of oral preaching during more than a quarter of a century) has seemed to some utterly to deprive of historical value the written Gospels. This is the view of some very extreme Form-critics who in consequence reduce our canonical Gospels to the level of myth and legend. Those who read the researches and conclusions of Bultmann, and other extremists of this school, and compare them with the expositions furnished by this volume, will have abundance of material provided to enable them to form their own conclusions on this point. The fact is that a period of oral teaching and tradition, extending over perhaps thirty years, does not necessarily deprive of historic value and accuracy our written records of the ministry of Jesus. It is quite true that a strong apologetic, or, if we will, propagandist motive, lay behind the Apostolic testimony and preaching and so manifests itself in our written Gospels. But those who would convert others to a new religion have first themselves to be converted to it, and for the purpose of that conversion experiences of no ordinary character are required. St. Peter, in the Acts of the Apostles, is reported as defending his public preaching in Jerusalem by saying:

'We cannot but report the things which we saw and heard' (4^{20}).

The early chapters of the Acts present the Apostles, not as originators, but as witnesses:

'Ye shall be my witnesses both in Jerusalem and in all Judæa and Samaria, and unto the uttermost part of the earth' (Acts 1^{8}).

Of course it is always possible to assume that witnesses are liars if it be to their interest to be liars, but the originality of much of the teaching ascribed to Jesus—the description of His personality and actions in the Gospels, particularly in the

Synoptic Gospels—demand so high a quality of creative and dramatic power as to render it more probable that the authors are relating in many cases actual experiences rather than indulging in the fabrication of forged testimony.

It must not be understood from this statement that we argue here that every portion of the Gospels is historical: that there are no mythical accretions; that there are no misrepresentations or misunderstandings or even exaggerations and inventions on the part of the Evangelists. What we desire to suggest is, that although in large measure dependent upon oral tradition, and although directed to an apologetic end, yet the Gospels will be seen, as the result of critical study, to contain large historical elements. There is no more effective way of disposing of the allegations of the Christ-myth school of critics and the exaggerations of the 'Form-criticism' school than to spend some time in the study of the Apocryphal Gospels, of which a great number exist and which are genuine examples of the working of the spirit of devout and apologetic fiction in the early Church uncontrolled by actual historical experience and by that sense of moral responsibility which seems to have dominated the leading members of the Church.

'We can do nothing against the Truth but for the Truth,' wrote St. Paul, and it is well to remember that it is to the period of the oral tradition that the great Pauline epistles belong. They were written, and they are seen, when carefully studied, to presuppose, or perhaps we ought to say require, the existence of such a personality and such historic experiences as constitute the essential element in the canonical Gospels.[1] We desire to stress this at the outset, because a critical and comparative study of the Gospels, as given in this volume, will provide examples of the growth of myth and legend. But to admit the presence of myth and legend, of error and exaggeration, in a body of ancient narratives does not mean that those narratives may not be, on the whole, historical and reliable. The tendency of ignorant people, as of impatient people, and of very clever but ill-balanced people, is to rush to extremes. If there is anything which modern research, in connexion with the Gospels, has utterly discredited, it is the 'either-or' method of treating these critical problems. The Gospels studied in the light of modern criticism 'turn to scorn with lips divine the falsehood of extremes.'

What gives peculiar value to the Gospel of Mark is that, according to a very strong body of external testimony, supported, as we shall see, by internal testimony, we have contained in Mark's Gospel the reports of the actual reminiscences of St. Peter as delivered by him publicly to audiences of Roman Christians who would be in a position to test the written Gospel by their memory of the oral tradition. The whole notion that it would be possible to have in a living society written Gospels which were not based in the main upon oral teaching, and oral teaching which was not based in the main upon actual historical experience, is something which is more likely to commend itself as probable to the literary theorist than to the experienced historian.

Archbishop Whateley's famous pamphlet *Historic Doubts as to the Existence of Napoleon Buonaparte* constitutes an admirable satire on those schools of critical theorists who not only believe that fiction is stranger than fact but that it has greater vitality.

[1] See Knowling's *The Witness of the Epistles.*

This does not mean that Mark's Gospel, although it contains, according to universal primitive Christian tradition, the memoirs of St. Peter, is absolutely accurate. In some cases St. Peter's memory, after so many years, may have been at fault: in some cases St. Mark may have misunderstood St. Peter, or in other cases have recorded his teaching inaccurately: in some cases he may have omitted things that Peter taught: in other cases he may have made additions which, although non-Petrine, were very highly valued by the Roman Church.

What we do contend, however, is that Mark's Gospel does contain, whatever they may be worth as history, a body of Petrine reminiscences. And in this connexion it is important to note that Mk. (with possibly two exceptions) is a literary unity distinguished by characteristic features. Its style is simple, energetic, varied, picturesque—the style natural to the recounting of his memories by a plain man who visualised what he relates. The constant recurrence of such phrases as 'again,' 'and immediately,' the use of the present tense to describe past events, as well as the use of the imperfect tense to express repeated and continuous action, give dramatic effect and movement to the narrative.

And here we would stress another point: Mark's Gospel is not a biography of Jesus. It seems probable that what is recorded in its pages covers only a single year in that marvellous life. Its contents may be summarised thus: Mark having described briefly the Mission of the Baptist, the Baptism and Temptation of Jesus, tells of the opening of the Mission of Jesus in Galilee in the vicinity of the Lake, beginning after the arrest of the Baptist. Mark stresses the immense impression made by the preaching and healing powers of Jesus, the conflicts which ensued, first with the ecclesiastical authorities, then with the civil authorities; next the flight of Jesus with His disciples to the regions of Tyre and Sidon; then His unexpected return to Western Galilee for a brief visit; then His ascent to Jerusalem, not through the territory of the Samaritans, but by way of Peræa and Jericho; His triumphal entry into Jerusalem; His impressive, almost revolutionary mission in that city; and within a week, His arrest, crucifixion and burial; the visit of the women to His sepulchre, its emptiness; the announcement of His resurrection; the flight of the fearful women; and so the Gospel abruptly closes. If we were, in modern fashion, to describe the book on its title-page, it would be:

MY YEAR WITH THE LORD JESUS

THE REMINISCENCES OF PETER, HIS CHIEF APOSTLE

REPORTED AND TRANSLATED

BY

HIS DRAGOMAN, JOHN MARK

FOR

THE CHRISTIANS IN ROME

TEXT AND COMMENTARY

According to Mark

THIS title is not part of the original Gospel. It is a later addition and takes various forms. *According to Mark* is the shortest of these titles and the earliest. *The Holy Gospel according to Mark* is a later expansion of it. The title does not definitely ascribe authorship and might mean *delivered by* or *derived from* Mark.

STRUCTURE

Of course in the earliest Greek codices of the Gospel there is no division into chapters and verses. Our division into verses we owe, for the Old Testament, to the Jewish Rabbi Nathan in the fifteenth century, and for the New Testament to the famous printer Stephanus or Estienne in the sixteenth century. In its original structure Mark's Gospel consists for the most part of a great number of short detachable sections: a collection of brief anecdotes or discourses. This structure of the Gospel fits in entirely with the universal tradition of the Christian Church that Mark's Gospel consisted of Peter's reminiscences. In this respect it might be compared with Xenophon's memoirs of Socrates. However, in the Eschatological Discourse (Mk. 13) and the Passion narrative (Mk. 14, 15) we have something more consecutive and closely connected.

PREFACE

MK. 1^{1}

1 1 The beginning of the gospel of Jesus
Christ, the Son of God.

MT. 1^{1}

1 1 The book of the generation of Jesus
Christ, the son of David, the son of
Abraham.

LK. 1^{1-4}

1 1 Forasmuch as many have taken in hand
to draw up a narrative concerning those
matters which have been fulfilled among us,
2 even as they delivered them unto us, which
from the beginning were eyewitnesses and
3 ministers of the word, it seemed good to me
also, having traced the course of all things
accurately from the first, to write unto thee
4 in order, most excellent Theophilus; that
thou mightest know the certainty concerning
the things wherein thou wast instructed.

JN. 1^{1-6}

1 1 In the beginning was the Word, and the
Word was with God, and the Word was
2 God. The same was in the beginning
3 with God. All things were made by him;
and without him was not anything made
4 that hath been made. In him was life;
5 and the life was the light of men. And
the light shineth in the darkness; and the
6 darkness apprehended it not.

The first line (The beginning of the gospel of Jesus Christ, the Son of God) is Mark's descriptive Preface to his book.

Each of the Four Gospels has a Preface. Mark's is the briefest. It lacks the literary dignity and extraordinary historical interest of the Preface to Luke's Gospel (Lk. 1^{1-4}) It also lacks the dramatic majesty and theological profundity of the Prologue of the Fourth Gospel (John 1^{1-18}).

GOSPEL

The word Gospel (Gk. *euaggelion*; Lat. *evangelium*) is the key-note of the New Testament and appears appropriately in the first line of the earliest extant account of the Ministry of Jesus. The Greek word meant originally (in the plural) the reward given to one who brought good news. It next came to mean the good news itself. It then came to mean the good news proclaimed by Jesus, and somewhat later the good news proclaimed about Jesus. At a still later stage, the middle of the second century, it was applied (by Justin Martyr, etc.) to the canonical memoirs of Jesus. At a still later stage it came to signify select passages from those memoirs read at the Eucharist.

In modern Protestantism it acquired yet another sense—the plan of salvation by the acceptance of which men were delivered from everlasting death. This is its meaning in the famous *dictum* of the Bishop of Cork on a notable sermon by the Dean of Cork:

'That it did not contain enough Gospel to save the soul of a tomtit.'

It is in the third sense—the good news or glad tidings proclaimed by Jesus Christ—that Mk. uses the word here. The nature of this good news will appear later. The idea of the Messiah as one who should proclaim good news goes back to the great prophecies of the unknown writer who is usually spoken of as the Second Isaiah. The Second Isaiah begins with the words:

'Comfort ye, comfort ye, my people, saith your God.' (Is. 40^{1}.)

It is significant that Jesus takes as His text for the sermon delivered by Him in the Synagogue of Nazareth in the early days of His Ministry another great proclamation of consolation from the same author:

'The Spirit of the Lord is upon me, because he hath anointed me to preach the gospel to the poor: he hath sent me to heal the broken-hearted, to preach deliverance to the captives, and recovering of sight to the blind, to set at liberty them that are bruised, to preach the acceptable year of the Lord.' (Lk. 4^{18}; Is. $61^{1, 2}$, 58^{6}.)

CHRIST

The word Christ attached to the personal name Jesus (which means 'Saviour' or 'God saves' or 'will save') is a title and is the translation of the Hebrew word Messiah which means 'the Anointed One.'

Although high-priests, prophets, in certain cases, and kings in Israel were divinely consecrated for their office by anointing with oil, yet the title the Anointed or the Lord's Anointed was reserved for the King: the King himself being regarded as God's son and vice-gerent. The words in Mk. 1^{1}, 'the Son of God,' are not in the oldest and most reliable Greek texts of the Gospel. These words were undoubtedly added later to explain especially for non-Jewish readers the meaning of the word Christ.

This word Christ was, we know, a great puzzle to pagans who were inclined to connect it, not with the Greek word which means 'anointed,' but with another Greek word which means 'kind.'

THE BAPTIST'S MISSION

MK. 1^{2-8}

1 2 Even as it is written in Isaiah the
prophet,
Behold, I send my messenger before thy
face,
Who shall prepare thy way;
3 The voice of one crying in the wilderness,
Make ye ready the way of the Lord,
Make his paths straight.
4 John came, who baptized in the wilderness and preached the baptism of repent-
5 ance unto remission of sins. And there
went out unto him all the country of
Judæa, and all they of Jerusalem; and they
were baptized of him in the river Jordan,
6 confessing their sins. And John was
clothed with camel's hair, and *had* a leathern
girdle about his loins, and did eat locusts
7 and wild honey. And he preached, saying,
There cometh after me he that is mightier
than I, the latchet of whose shoes I am not
8 worthy to stoop down and unloose. I baptized you with water; but he shall baptize
you with the Holy Ghost.

MT. 3^{1-12}

3 1 And in those days cometh John the
Baptist, preaching in the wilderness of
2 Judæa, saying, Repent ye; for the kingdom
3 of heaven is at hand. For this is he that
was spoken of by Isaiah the prophet,
saying,
The voice of one crying in the wilderness,
Make ye ready the way of the Lord,
Make his paths straight.
4 Now John himself had his raiment of
camel's hair, and a leathern girdle about
his loins; and his food was locusts and wild
5 honey. Then went out unto him Jerusalem, and all Judæa, and all the region
6 round about Jordan; and they were
baptized of him in the river Jordan, con-
7 fessing their sins. But when he saw many
of the Pharisees and Sadducees coming to
his baptism, he said unto them, Ye offspring of vipers, who warned you to flee
8 from the wrath to come? Bring forth
therefore fruit worthy of repentance:
9 and think not to say within yourselves,
We have Abraham to our father: for I
say unto you, that God is able of these
stones to raise up children unto Abraham.
10 And even now is the axe laid unto the
root of the trees: every tree therefore that
bringeth not forth good fruit is hewn down,
11 and cast into the fire. I indeed baptize
you with water unto repentance: but he
that cometh after me is mightier than I,
whose shoes I am not worthy to bear: he
shall baptize you with the Holy Ghost and
12 *with* fire: whose fan is in his hand, and
he will throughly cleanse his threshing-
floor; and he will gather his wheat into
the garner, but the chaff he will burn up
with unquenchable fire.

LK. 3^{1-18}

3 1 Now in the fifteenth year of the reign of
Tiberius Cæsar, Pontius Pilate being
governor of Judæa, and Herod being
tetrarch of Galilee, and his brother Philip
tetrarch of the region of Ituræa and
Trachonitis, and Lysanias tetrarch of
2 Abilene, in the high-priesthood of Annas
and Caiaphas, the word of God came unto
John the son of Zacharias in the wilder-
3 ness. And he came into all the region
round about Jordan, preaching the bap-

JN. $1^{6-8, 19-31}$

1 6 There came a man, sent from God,
7 whose name was John. The same came
for witness, that he might bear witness of
the light, that all might believe through
8 him. He was not the light, but *came* that
he might bear witness of the light.
19 And this is the witness of John, when the
Jews sent unto him from Jerusalem priests
and Levites to ask him, Who art thou?
20 And he confessed, and denied not; and he
21 confessed, I am not the Christ. And they

tism of repentance unto remission of sins;
4 as it is written in the book of the words of
Isaiah the prophet,
The voice of one crying in the wilderness,
Make ye ready the way of the Lord,
Make his paths straight.
5 Every valley shall be filled,
And every mountain and hill shall be
brought low;
And the crooked shall become straight,
And the rough ways smooth;
6 And all flesh shall see the salvation of
God.
7 He said therefore to the multitudes that
went out to be baptized of him, Ye offspring of vipers, who warned you to flee
8 from the wrath to come? Bring forth
therefore fruits worthy of repentance, and
begin not to say within yourselves, We
have Abraham to our father: for I say
unto you, that God is able of these stones
9 to raise up children unto Abraham. And
even now is the axe also laid unto the root
of the trees: every tree therefore that
bringeth not forth good fruit is hewn
10 down, and cast into the fire. And the
multitudes asked him, saying, What then
11 must we do? And he answered and said
unto them, He that hath two coats, let him
impart to him that hath none; and he that
12 hath food, let him do likewise. And there
came also publicans to be baptized, and
they said unto him, Master, what must we
13 do? And he said unto them, Extort no
more than that which is appointed you.
14 And soldiers also asked him, saying, And
we, what must we do? And he said unto
them, Do violence to no man, neither
exact *anything* wrongfully; and be content
with your wages.
15 And as the people were in expectation,
and all men reasoned in their hearts concerning John, whether haply he were the
16 Christ; John answered, saying unto them
all, I indeed baptize you with water; but
there cometh he that is mightier than I,
the latchet of whose shoes I am not
worthy to unloose: he shall baptize you
17 with the Holy Ghost and *with* fire: whose
fan is in his hand, throughly to cleanse his
threshing-floor, and to gather the wheat
into his garner; but the chaff he will burn
up with unquenchable fire.
18 With many other exhortations therefore
preached he good tidings unto the people.

asked him, What then? Art thou Elijah?
And he saith, I am not. Art thou the
22 prophet? And he answered, No. They
said therefore unto him, Who art thou?
that we may give an answer to them that
sent us. What sayest thou of thyself?
23 He said, I am the voice of one crying in
the wilderness, Make straight the way of
24 the Lord, as said Isaiah the prophet. And
they had been sent from the Pharisees.
25 And they asked him, and said unto him,
Why then baptizest thou, if thou art not
the Christ, neither Elijah, neither the
26 prophet? John answered them, saying, I
baptize with water: in the midst of you
27 standeth one whom ye know not, *even* he
that cometh after me, the latchet of whose
28 shoes I am not worthy to unloose. These
things were done in Bethany beyond
Jordan, where John was baptizing.
29 On the morrow he seeth Jesus coming
unto him, and saith, Behold, the Lamb of
God, which taketh away the sin of the
30 world! This is he of whom I said, After
me cometh a man which is become before
31 me: for he was before me. And I knew
him not; but that he should be made
manifest to Israel, for this cause came I
baptizing with water.

The Gospel opens with an account of John the Baptist's ministry which the early Christian Church on looking back regarded as both a fulfilment of Old Testament oracles or predictions and also as a divinely ordained preparation for the Ministry of Jesus, the Christ. Whether Jesus Himself viewed the Baptist,

'our Old Testament quotations in the New Testament are drawn from
gint.
titude of the early Christians towards the Old Testament is very
nd it is of great importance to realise it. They value the Old Testament
as containing an account of God's revelation to mankind, and especially
's, but as a volume full of predictions dealing with the coming of the
They believed that the Old Testament described the nature of His
d experiences and the foundation, privileges, and mission of the Christian

' the great arguments used by early Christian teachers to convince the
: Messiahship of Jesus was to prove to them out of their own Scriptures
was their Messiah because He had fulfilled in His birth, ministry, death,
n, and in His ascension and the gift of the Holy Spirit to His Church a
s of Old Testament predictions on these points. This kind of Christian
has little value to-day for reasons which will appear as this exposition
but we shall fail to understand the early Christian mind and the signifi-
ch it attached to many of the Old Testament passages cited in the New
t unless we bear in mind that primarily it regarded the Old Testament
tion of divine predictions uttered and recorded in order that men might
eir fulfilment in Jesus.

ling to the primitive Christian view, John the Baptist was the Elijah
by Malachi in the closing words of the Old Testament. Indeed, Jesus
recorded as making or affirming this identification, although the Baptist
Jn. 1^{21} is asserted to have explicitly denied it.
'our Gospels and in the Acts of the Apostles John appears as a preacher of
e for the remission of sins. He is also presented as a preacher of right-
especially in Lk. (cf. Lk. 3^{10-14}). His message is marked by sternness
sense of impending judgement. His mission, which was conducted
the southern end of the Jordan valley, appears to have taken place in
an, for his metaphors are derived from the operations of the harvest.
bable that these harvesting operations which he uses to illustrate his
were actually taking place within sight of the audiences he was address-
: offspring of vipers, who warned you to flee from the wrath to come?'
to the religious teachers from Jerusalem, becomes vivid as we picture the
d other vermin being overtaken by the flames of the burning stubble
tumn fields. (Mt. 3^{7}.)
ords:

an is in his hand, and he will throughly cleanse his threshing-floor;
ll gather his wheat into the garner, but the chaff he will burn up with
able fire' (Mt. 3^{12}; cf. Lk. 3^{17})

ie farmer accomplishing the concluding stage of his harvest work. The
een cut and has been carried up to some flat-topped hill where a thresh-
ias been made by removing the soil from the solid limestone. On this
:s have been laid and a sledge composed of sharp spikes drawn by an ox

although He had the highest reverence for him, as strict
is open to question. Jesus seems to have regarded Jo
figure of the old order and Himself as inaugurating a n

That Mark's Gospel should begin with John the Ba
for the Petrine authorship of the Second Gospel, if we
in Acts 1^{21} as historical. Peter there requires as an
apostleship in the case of the successor of Judas, that he

'which have companied with us all the time that the Lo
out among us, beginning from the baptism of John.'

It is no curious coincidence, therefore, that St. Peter'
the Baptist's ministry.

None of the other Gospels begins at this point. Ma
the genealogy of Jesus and with his nativity: Luke's
prediction of the birth of John the Baptist. The Fou
time in that eternal sphere in which the Word dwelt wit

Mk. begins his account of the Baptist's ministry wi
Old Testament. The first from Mal. 3^{1}:

'Behold I send my messenger before thy face who sh

Mk. here makes a mistake by assigning this passag
Mk.'s second citation is derived. This mistake, small a
disposing of the ancient belief in the inerrancy of the
All of them are as liable to error as careful and conscien
copyists of Mk.'s Gospel have tried to gloss over the mista
Isaiah the prophet' the phrase 'in the prophets.'

Mt., who follows Mk. closely here, gets out of Mk.'s
gether the quotation from Malachi.

The quotation from Malachi is part of the prophecy
prediction of the sending of:

'Elijah the prophet before the great and terrible day of
shall turn the heart of the fathers to the children, and th
their fathers; lest I come and smite the earth with a curse

Mk.'s second quotation is from Is. 40^{3}, which predic
the return of the exiles from Babylon across the Arabi
especially prepared for them.[1] Both of these oracles are c
(LXX). The Septuagint was the Greek version or translat
tures and was the Bible of the Greek-speaking Jews and
Dispersion (*diaspora*). This Dispersion existed in its myri
great cities of the Roman Empire.

As many of the early Christian converts outside Palesti
body, the Septuagint and not the Hebrew Scriptures was

[1] Note the misquotation of Is. 40^{3}, 'in the wilderness,' to suit
mission.

the bulk
the Sept

The
singular,
not simp
to the Je
Messiah.
Mission a
Church.

One
Jews of t
that Jesu
resurrec
great ser
apologet
proceeds
cance w
Testame
as a coll
behold t

Acco
predicte
Himself
himself

In a
repenta
eousnes
and th
mainly
the aut
It is p
teachin
ing. '
address
snakes
of the

Th

'Whos
and he
unque

describ
corn h
ing-flo
the sh

has been driven again and again over the sheaves until they are reduced to a mass of chaff and grain. The farmer with his fan, or wooden winnowing-shovel, having waited for the wind, goes up to his floor and tosses the mixture of chaff and grain into the air. The wind separates the chaff from the grain and at the end of the process there is the clean grain lying in a heap on the threshing-floor and the chaff piled up in a great mass outside it. The farmer then gathers up his grain and stores it in the garner or barn and sets light to the chaff, which burns until it is all consumed.

It is in the light of this harvest-home preaching that the meaning of the Baptist's message is best understood. It is a message of judgement—apocalyptic or eschatological judgement—that final judgement which shall terminate once and for all the iniquities and hypocrisies of what Cicero called ' this horrid and polluted scene of human society.' Then there will be complete annihilation of evil men and eternal reward for righteous God-fearers.

Judgement at the door is represented by another autumn metaphor—the woodman's axe lying at the foot of the tree, preliminary to his felling it.

It is true that the Evangelists add other elements to the Baptist's preaching. There is his demand for repentance (*metanoia*), which means primarily not sorrow for past sins but a changed mind, a new outlook, a reformed life. Those who sought and possessed this, the Baptist baptised in Jordan for ' the remission of sins.' (Mk. 1^{4}; cf. Lk. 3^{3}.)

The Evangelists stress the ministry of John as a ministry of preparation for the mission of the Messiah. John is represented as expecting the advent of one mightier than himself, the latchet of whose shoes he is not worthy to unloose, and who, instead of baptising men with water, shall baptise them with the Holy Spirit. (Mk. 1^{7}; cf. Mt. 3^{11}, Lk. 3^{16}, Jn. 1^{26-27}, Acts 1^{5}, 13^{25}.)

There is reason to believe that this prediction by the Baptist of baptism by the Holy Spirit by Him who should come after is a primitive Christian addition to the Baptist's message and forms part of that tendency to make a very important part of the Baptist's ministry his testimony to Jesus. When St. Paul visited Ephesus (Acts $19^{1\,ff.}$) on his second missionary journey he found there certain disciples of John the Baptist whom St. Paul asked whether, on the occasion of their Baptism, they had received the Holy Ghost, and they replied, ' We heard not so much as whether there be any Holy Ghost.'

It is difficult to imagine that if these men had received the Baptist's teaching about the coming baptism by the Holy Ghost they should have made such a reply. Mt. (3^{2}) adds yet another element to the Baptist's preaching. He gives as his message:

' Repent ye; for the kingdom of heaven is at hand,'

thus making John anticipate that which we shall see was the great message of Jesus. (Cf. Mt. 4^{17}.) This assertion by Mt. seems to receive no support elsewhere in the New Testament and cannot be regarded as historical.

These points, however, are significant because they indicate that there was a tendency to confuse the teaching of John the Baptist with that of Jesus. There is good reason to believe that a number of sayings attributed in the Gospels to Jesus are really the sayings of John the Baptist, even as some of the teaching assigned to John the Baptist was not his but the teaching of Jesus.

It is the writer of the Fourth Gospel who brings out the interesting fact that certain of the disciples of Jesus had formerly been the disciples of John the Baptist (Jn. 1^{35-37}): one of them being Andrew, Simon Peter's brother. This fact may well account for this confusion of teaching sources. Such attributing of the sayings of one great teacher to another in the same succession is not infrequent, as the late Sir Herbert Warren pointed out, in the *Colleges of the University of Oxford.*

What is perfectly clear, is that the dominant note of John's preaching was imminent judgement.

Dies irae, dies illa
solvet saeclum in favilla.

John the Baptist was the prophet Amos of the new era; unless we hold him to be the second Elijah with whom the old era closed.

It may seem curious, where John's message was of so much importance, that the Evangelists should concern themselves about his diet and costume. The stress upon his diet, locust (the voracious insect, not the pods of the carob tree) and wild honey, are intended to indicate that he was an ascetic. Lk. regards him as a Nazirite:

'He shall drink no wine nor strong drink' (Lk. 1^{15}; cf. Num. 6^3; Judges 13^4)

but it is possible that he belonged to a numerous body of Jewish ascetics, the Essenes, who at this time inhabited the deserts of Southern Palestine. As for his clothing:

'John was clothed with camel's hair, and had a leathern girdle about his loins.' (Mk. 1^6; cf. Mt. 3^4.)

This is intended to indicate that John was a member of the prophetic order. This order had been extinct for several centuries in Palestine. 'There is no longer any prophet,' sings the Psalmist in Ps. 74, and the Maccabean heroes after driving the Antiochene garrison from the Temple in 165 B.C. laid aside the defiled stones of the great altar of sacrifice until some prophet should arise (1 *Macc.* 4^{45}). The camel's hair was undoubtedly the *'addereth*, the hairy garment (cf. Zech. 13^4) which constituted the famous mantle of Elijah and which became the official garb of Elisha and the sons of the prophets. Probably no one living had ever seen this garment worn until John assumed it.

Lk. adds two interesting details about John, (1) that he was the son of a priest (Lk. i. 5), and (2) that he was the kinsman of Jesus on his mother's side (Lk. i. 36).

JESUS COMES TO BE BAPTISED BY JOHN

MK. 1^{9-11}

1 9 And it came to pass in those days, that
Jesus came from Nazareth of Galilee, and
10 was baptized of John in the Jordan. And
straightway coming up out of the water,
he saw the heavens rent asunder, and the
11 Spirit as a dove descending upon him: and
a voice came out of the heavens, Thou art
my beloved Son, in thee I am well pleased.

MT. 3^{13-17}

3 13 Then cometh Jesus from Galilee to the
Jordan unto John, to be baptized of him.
14 But John would have hindered him, saying,
I have need to be baptized of thee,
15 and comest thou to me? But Jesus
answering said unto him, Suffer *it* now:
for thus it becometh us to fulfil all
righteousness. Then he suffereth him.
16 And Jesus, when he was baptized, went up
straightway from the water: and lo, the
heavens were opened unto him, and he
saw the Spirit of God descending as a
17 dove, and coming upon him; and lo, a
voice out of the heavens, saying, This is
my beloved Son, in whom I am well
pleased.

LK. $3^{21, 22}$

3 21 Now it came to pass, when all the people
were baptized, that, Jesus also having
been baptized, and praying, the heaven
22 was opened, and the Holy Ghost descended
in a bodily form, as a dove, upon
him, and a voice came out of heaven,
Thou art my beloved Son; in thee I am
well pleased.

JN. 1^{32}

1 32 And John bare witness, saying, I have
beheld the Spirit descending as a dove out
of heaven; and it abode upon him.

All four Evangelists seem to be agreed that John baptised Jesus. For Mk., this fact raised no apologetic difficulty as it did for the later Evangelists Matthew and John.

Jewish critics of the Messianic claim made by primitive Christians on behalf of Jesus were swift to ask: Why did Jesus come to John for baptism? And replied to their own question: He did it in order to confess His sins, and have them washed away like those others of whom Mk. relates:

'And there went out unto him [John] all the country of Judæa, and all they of Jerusalem; and they were baptised of him in the river Jordan, confessing their sins.' (Mk. 1^5; cf. Mt. $3^{5, 6}$, Lk. 3^3: 'the baptism of repentance unto remission of sins.')

The inference therefore was that Jesus was a sinful man and so unfit to be the Messiah. Mk., and it is an indication of the archaic character of his Gospel, seems quite unaware of this objection, but Mt. meets it by a dialogue he alone records between Jesus and John:

'Then cometh Jesus from Galilee to the Jordan unto John, to be baptized of him. But John would have hindered him, saying, I have need to be baptized of thee, and comest thou to me? But Jesus answering said unto him, Suffer it now: for thus it becometh us to fulfil all righteousness. Then he suffereth him.' (Mt. 3^{13-15}.)

Although the Baptist recognises that Jesus does not need baptism for the remission of sins, yet he consents to baptise Him in deference to His plea: 'Thus it becometh us to fulfil all righteousness.' In other words, Jesus is baptised as an example to Judaism, not because He personally needs baptism, but because others do.

In the Fourth Gospel, it would seem that the purpose of the Baptism of Jesus is to provide personal testimony for the Baptist that He, Jesus, is the Messiah.

'And John bare witness, saying, I have beheld the Spirit descending as a dove out of heaven; and it abode upon him. And I knew him not: but he that sent me to baptize with water, he said unto me, Upon whomsoever thou shalt see the Spirit descending, and abiding upon him, the same is he that baptizeth with the Holy Spirit. And I have seen, and have borne witness that this is the Son of God.' (Jn. 1^{32-34}.)

The historian will question the historical character of the defences put forward by the First and Fourth Evangelists. There were persistent attempts by Jewish opponents to discredit the moral character of Jesus at every stage both during His Ministry and after His Crucifixion. In consequence, primitive Christian apologists became very sensitive on this point and took care to provide definite confutations of the charge.

Which of you convicteth me of sin? is the indignant question of the Jesus of the Fourth Gospel (Jn. 8^{46}), and in one of the apocryphal Gospels, the Gospel according to the Hebrews (cited by Jerome in his Dialogue against Pelagius, iii. 2), Jesus is represented as asking, Wherein have I sinned that I should go and be baptised of him? Unless peradventure this very thing that I have said is *a sin* of ignorance.

And St. Peter was equally assured of the sinlessness of Jesus, if we may accept as testimony on this point the passage in his First Epistle:

'Who did no sin, neither was guile found in His mouth.' (1 Pet. 2^{22}.)

(See also the sermons attributed to St. Peter in the Acts in which he accuses the Jews of having slain the holy and righteous one, etc.) (Acts 3^{14}, etc.)

This sinlessness of Jesus is also asserted in Heb. 4^{15}: 'one that hath been in all points tempted like as we are, yet without sin.'

If Jesus had no need of repentance, why then was He baptised? Was He never conscious of sin? The whole primitive Christian Church, as we can see from the testimony of the New Testament, was convinced that although fully human Jesus was without sin. On the other hand, many modern writers will have it that to be fully and truly human is to be conscious of sin but also to be capable of contending with sin and overcoming it, and that this qualification, rather than sinlessness, is needful for one who would be the Saviour of sinners.

The early Christian Church stressed the sinlessness of Jesus because it held that the validity of His Messianic claim depended upon His sinlessness, and that to be effectively the sacrifice for the sins of mankind He must be without spot and blemish.

St. Paul in his presentation of Jesus as God's great expiatory sacrifice for the sins of the world writes:

'Him who knew no sin he made to be sin on our behalf.' (2 Cor. 5^{21}.)

What may be called the dogma of the sinlessness of Jesus in contrast to the faith in the goodness of Jesus, the love of Jesus, the courage of Jesus, the truthfulness of Jesus, the loyalty, obedience, and purity of Jesus, is the product of a particular view of the death of Jesus, of its significance and sacrificial efficacy, rather than the outcome of the impression made by our Lord's moral majesty.

Jesus, so the Gospel relates, advanced in wisdom and stature, and in favour with God and men. As a human being there was of necessity growth, and not merely physical, but mental, moral, and spiritual. And by this growth Jesus advanced to perfection.

We can well believe that in the supreme moral and spiritual temptations which beset Him in His Messianic Ministry He proved victorious on every occasion: but to believe this is not the same as to believe in the dogma of the sinlessness of Jesus from His infancy until the time when He felt Himself called to the Messianic Office. Apart from statements made in the latest of the Gospels, there is nothing in the teaching of Jesus which affirms this dogma. The resentment aroused in Jesus by the address 'Good Master' and His sharp retort, 'Why callest thou me good? none is good save one, even God' (Mk. 10^{18})—a dialogue, it is to be noted, which is toned down and radically altered by the later Evangelist (Mt. 19^{17})—does not give convincing support to those who stress the dogma of the sinlessness of Jesus. It is certainly open to doubt whether He would have approved of it. This being so, it seems to us improbable that He went to John's baptism as the Sinless Sin-bearer who by submitting to baptism identified Himself with His sinful and repentant people as later orthodoxy teaches. This is based upon the conception of His death as an expiatory offering for sin and cannot well be conceived of as the intention of One who was not yet conscious of His Messianic Office.

It seems more probable that, attracted by John's personality and preaching, He wished to unite Himself with this call to His nation to make a fresh start, and was baptised, not as one obsessed by a sense of sin, nor as the sin-bearer of His people, but as one inspired by a great hope.

The Baptismal Experience of Jesus

There is a very important difference in the accounts of the Baptism given by the Four Evangelists.

Mk. makes the experience of Jesus at His Baptism purely subjective. It was shared by no one else, not even by John. That experience was the awakening of the Messianic consciousness of Jesus. His divine call to the Messianic Office took a threefold form.

(1) First the cleaving of the heavens asunder—*splitting*, a curious phrase peculiar to Mk.

(2) Secondly, the descent of the Spirit 'as a dove' *into* Him.

(3) Thirdly, a voice from the cloven heavens speaking to Him: 'Thou art my Son, the Beloved One, in Whom I am well pleased.'

Had we been standing on that occasion on the banks of the Jordan we should, according to Mk., have seen John baptise Jesus, but we should not have seen the cloven heavens, the descending Spirit, nor have heard the Divine voice—the *Bath-Qōl* of Hebrew tradition. These were the experiences of Jesus alone.

But in the other evangelical narratives, what is subjective in Mk. becomes objective. Thus spiritual or mystical experience becomes miraculous, and indeed materialistic.

Mt. says that the heavens were opened and He saw the Spirit of God descending as a dove and coming upon Him and Behold a voice out of the heavens saying, '*This* is my Son, the Beloved One in Whom I am well pleased.'

Here the opening of the heavens is objective and the voice from them is objective also. It is not addressed to Jesus but to John or to the spectators.

Lk. says the heavens were opened and the Holy Spirit descended upon Him in the bodily form of a dove. This statement is not only objective, it is materialistic.

Nevertheless, Lk. makes the Divine declaration of Messiahship subjective as does Mk., but with a difference:

'Thou art my Son, the Beloved One. To-day have I begotten thee.'

It is quite true that a number of the manuscripts of Lk. have, like Mk., 'in Thee I am well pleased,' but in the judgement of Canon Streeter, those manuscripts which have 'to-day have I begotten Thee' give us Lk.'s original statement which later scribes harmonised with Mk.

The Fourth Gospel gives no full account of the Baptism, but mentions the descent of the Spirit from heaven beheld with wonder (*tetheamai*) by the Baptist and accepted by him, in accordance with a Divine prediction which he had already received, as a proof of the Messiahship of Jesus. (Jn. $1^{32 f.}$)

This example of the way in which, no doubt in perfect good faith, but in accordance with their particular preconceptions and the tendencies of their religious community, these later Evangelists transmute a subjective, mystical, spiritual experience into an objective, miraculous fact is most significant, and should be carefully noted by the reader, because although we are able to detect it here, there are probably a number of other narratives in the Gospels where the same kind of change has been effected, but proof of it has disappeared.

Some might argue that this view is wrong and that what has taken place is just the reverse. That what was originally an objective, miraculous, materialist experience has under the influence of spiritualising tendencies been transmuted into that which is subjective and mystical. That this is not really the case is proved by an incident concerning John the Baptist which is related by both Mt. and Lk. (Mt. 11^{2-11}; Lk. 7^{18-28}), but derived originally, not from Mk. but from that very early literary source known as Q. There it is related that John heard in the prison the works of Jesus, and he sent his disciples to Jesus with this message: 'Art Thou the Coming One [a familiar Jewish title for the Messiah] or do we look for another?' It seems difficult to believe that John could have asked such a question of Jesus if he (John) had actually received the testimony recorded in the Fourth Gospel to have been given to him, or had seen the miraculous vision of the Third Gospel, or had heard the miraculous voice (*Bath-Qōl*) of the First Gospel. If, however, he had experienced nothing of the kind, as the account in the Second Gospel indicates, his sending messengers to Jesus to ask whether He is the Messiah becomes immediately explicable.

This confirmation of Mk. by Q compels us to accept the Marcan account as historic in preference to the accounts by the other Evangelists, and at the same time provides an example of a contemporary tendency to transmute the account of subjective and mystical experiences into objective and miraculous events.

The Holy Spirit as a Dove

The phrase concerning the Holy Spirit descending as a dove into, or upon, Jesus at His Baptism has been very variously interpreted.

The term 'as a dove' may mean, flying direct to the mark like a dove to its dove-cot, or, to use the Old Testament phrase, as the doves to their windows (Is. 60^{8}), as in the Nazarene Gospel (an early Jewish Christian document of which only fragments remain).

'O my son, in all the prophets I was awaiting thee in order that thou mightest come and I might rest in thee, for thou art My rest.'

With this we may compare the words from some very primitive and spiritual Christian compositions known as *The Odes of Solomon:*

'The dove fluttered over the Messiah because He was her head' (24).

'As the wings of doves over their nestlings . . . so also are the wings of the Spirit over my heart' (28).

The priestly account of creation (Gen. 1^{3}) describes the Spirit of God as hovering like a bird over the chaos, producing life and order. In other words, the metaphor represents the life-giving creative activity of the Divine Spirit. No more suggestive metaphor could be used of that Spirit's activity which at the Baptism of Jesus created in Him the Messianic Consciousness: the sense of unique Divine Sonship and unique Divine Mission. Others have interpreted the phrase 'as a dove' to mean here gently, as in that saying of Jesus addressed to His disciples: 'Be ye harmless as doves.'

It is maintained that the Evangelists are contrasting by this phrase the gentleness of the Spirit in Jesus with the Spirit's violence as often displayed in the Old Testament—that contrast of the Spirit of Elijah with the Spirit of Christ, which appears in Christ's rebuke of John and James when they desired to call down fire from heaven upon the Samaritans, as did Elijah: ' Ye know not what Spirit ye are of.'

Others have interpreted the dove as the spirit of wisdom. What the owl of Minerva was for the Greeks, the dove was for the Rabbis. There is one thing that is quite clear, ' as a dove ' here does not mean what Lk. took it to mean ' *in the bodily form of a dove.*'

THE TEMPTATION

MK. $1^{12, 13}$

1 12 And straightway the Spirit driveth him
13 forth into the wilderness. And he was in
the wilderness forty days tempted of
Satan; and he was with the wild beasts;
and the angels ministered unto him.

HEB. 4^{15}

4 15 For we have not a high priest that cannot
be touched with the feeling of our infirmities; but one that hath been in all points
tempted like as *we are, yet* without sin.

MT. 4^{1-11}

4 1 Then was Jesus led up of the Spirit into
the wilderness to be tempted of the devil.
2 And when he had fasted forty days and
3 forty nights, he afterward hungered. And
the tempter came and said unto him, If
thou art the Son of God, command that
4 these stones become bread. But he
answered and said, It is written, Man shall
not live by bread alone, but by every
word that proceedeth out of the mouth of
5 God. Then the devil taketh him into the
holy city; and he set him on the pinnacle
6 of the temple, and saith unto him, If thou
art the Son of God, cast thyself down: for
it is written,
He shall give his angels charge concerning thee:
And on their hands they shall bear
thee up,
Lest haply thou dash thy foot against
a stone.
7 Jesus said unto him, Again it is written,
Thou shalt not tempt the Lord thy God.
8 Again, the devil taketh him unto an exceeding high mountain, and sheweth him
all the kingdoms of the world, and the
9 glory of them; and he said unto him, All
these things will I give thee, if thou wilt
10 fall down and worship me. Then saith
Jesus unto him, Get thee hence, Satan:
for it is written, Thou shalt worship the
Lord thy God, and him only shalt thou
11 serve. Then the devil leaveth him; and
behold, angels came and ministered unto
him.

LK. 4^{1-13}

4 1 And Jesus, full of the Holy Spirit, returned from the Jordan, and was led by
the Spirit in the wilderness during forty
2 days, being tempted of the devil. And he
did eat nothing in those days: and when
3 they were completed, he hungered. And
the devil said unto him, If thou art the
Son of God, command this stone that it
4 become bread. And Jesus answered unto
him, It is written, Man shall not live by
5 bread alone. And he led him up, and
shewed him all the kingdoms of the world
6 in a moment of time. And the devil said
unto him, To thee will I give all this
authority, and the glory of them: for it hath
been delivered unto me; and to whomso-
7 ever I will I give it. If thou therefore wilt
worship before me, it shall all be thine.
8 And Jesus answered and said unto him,
It is written, Thou shalt worship the Lord
thy God, and him only shalt thou serve.
9 And he led him to Jerusalem, and set him
on the pinnacle of the temple, and said
unto him, If thou art the Son of God, cast
10 thyself down from hence: for it is written,
He shall give his angels charge concerning thee, to guard thee :
11 and,
On their hands they shall bear thee
up,
Lest haply thou dash thy foot against
a stone.
12 And Jesus answering said unto him, It is
said, Thou shalt not tempt the Lord thy
God.
13 And when the devil had completed
every temptation, he departed from him
for a season.

Cf. MT. 16^{23}

16 23 But he turned, and said unto Peter, Get
thee behind me, Satan: thou art a
stumblingblock unto me: for thou
mindest not the things of God, but the
things of men.

Mk.'s account of what is called the Temptation of Jesus is so compressed that we should have little understanding of its significance if we were dependent on his account alone. Fortunately the Temptation (as recounted by Q) is given much more fully in the First and Third Gospels. From these accounts we see that the Temptation arose out of the newly-awakened Messianic Consciousness of Jesus and the difficulties which beset Him in the decision how rightly to fulfil the Messianic Office to which he felt Himself to have been divinely called by the Anointing of the Holy Spirit at His Baptism.

In its way perhaps one of the best interpretations of the nature of that temptation is to be found in John Milton's *Paradise Regained.*

We see in Q (Mt. adheres to its original form and order) that the temptation assumed a threefold form. At first Jesus is tempted, moved by His own physical needs and the poverty-stricken condition of the lower classes in Palestine, to use the Messianic Office as a means of securing economic relief. This seems to be the significance of the temptation to turn stones into bread. The Divine Word as voiced in Dt. 8^3 pointed Him to the inadequacy of this ideal for His Messianic Mission.

'Man doth not live by bread only, but by every thing that proceedeth out of the mouth of the Lord doth man live.'

Bread is a necessity for physical existence, but the basis of a human society collapses where it is solely economic.

Materialism fails because it lacks those moral and spiritual principles upon which a sound and progressive civilisation can alone be securely founded. The higher life is not only the true life of man but it is even a necessity for his economic life.

'Seek first His Kingdom and His righteousness and all these things [needful for the physical life] shall be added unto you.' (Mt. 6^{33}.)

Then next, Jesus (if we follow Mt.'s order) is tempted to make the Messianic Office a miracle-working agency. Not upon materialism, but upon miracles, will He found His Kingdom.

There was a Jewish tradition that Jesus learnt magic in Egypt. We have no knowledge of the evidence upon which this Jewish tradition is based. It is possible that at some earlier stage in His life Jesus was attracted by magic and thought that by practising on men's sense of wonder and mystery they could be won to higher things.

This seems to be the significance of the temptation to cast Himself from the pinnacle of the Temple, secure in the Divine intervention which shall miraculously protect Him. But again the Divine Voice reflected in the words of Dt. 6^{16},

'Ye shall not tempt the Lord your God,'

forbids this use of the miraculous to advance the moral and spiritual progress of mankind. Later in His Ministry, when the religious leaders of the nation came to

Him tempting Him, saying unto Him: 'Shew unto us a sign from Heaven', He replied:

'An evil and an adulterous generation seeketh after a sign; and there shall no sign be given unto it.' (Mt. 16^4.)

A religious movement seeking to base itself on man's innate sense of terror and wonder in the presence of the *mysterium tremendum fascinans*, manifesting itself by the practice of miracle and magic, is no more securely based than a religious movement which seeks its justification in the satisfaction of man's economic needs. They both sin against man's divine nature which is as essentially rational as it is moral and spiritual.

Magic and miracle-mongering achieve their successes, but these successes are short-lived. They are Pyrrhic victories secured by the intimidation and humiliation of man's rational and moral nature.

Last of all Jesus is tempted to resort to political means for the fulfilment of His Messianic office: to make the Maccabean heroes and the Zealot fanatics His model, and to seek by military force to establish God's Kingdom.

No Messianic programme could have been more popular with his countrymen, but again the Divine Spirit forbad this method.

'Thou shalt worship the Lord thy God, and Him only shalt thou serve,'

was the reply of Jesus to the tempter who showed Him all the kingdoms of the world and the glory of them and said unto Him:

'All these things will I give thee, if thou wilt fall down and worship me.'

That temptation came again with terrific force when Jesus, after the confession of His Messiahship at Cæsarea Philippi by Peter, tells his Apostles that Messiahship for Him involves the shame and suffering of the Cross.

When Peter tells Him He is mad, He replies:

'Get thee behind me, Satan: for thou mindest not the things of God but the things of men.' (Mk. 8^{33}; Mt. 16^{23}.)

The Fourth Gospel relates (Jn. $6^{15\,ff.}$) that the people wished to take Jesus and make Him a King; and it is quite possible that an important factor in the popularity which marked the early days of His Ministry was due to the widespread expectation in Galilee that He was preparing to lead a revolt against the political authorities, Herodian and Roman.

Though these temptations to misinterpret and misuse the Messianic Office beset Jesus at the outset of His Mission there can be little doubt that they reappeared during the whole period of it.

The conception of the Messianic Office as one which might only appeal directly to man's spiritual, moral, and rational consciousness to secure support and victory demanded intense moral rectitude, unflinching courage, and an insight as profound as it was self-sacrificing. This conception of the Messianic Office did not on the one hand offer economic benefits, nor on the other hand did it depend upon miraculous agencies or political intrigue and military force.

We cannot feel assured that Jesus at this time foresaw the Cross as the inevitable result of His interpretation of the Messianic Office. The Cross only definitely loomed into sight at a much later stage in His Ministry. In other words, at this point He apprehended, not only His call to the Messianic Office, but also the essential character of that office. But He did not foresee in detail its inevitable outcome.

These points often seem to be confused in the minds of students of the life of Jesus. There are not a few who seem to doubt whether He ever possessed the Messianic Consciousness at all, and whether it was only attributed to Him by His disciples after His death, as the outcome of their interpretation of His personality and mission. Such a view seems to us grotesque. It is quite impossible to explain the Mission of Jesus except on the supposition that He possessed the Messianic Consciousness from the beginning of His Ministry. This alone explains, so it seems to us, the character of this Ministry.

Nevertheless, although Jesus possessed this Messianic Consciousness, a sound interpretation of our historical sources seems to indicate clearly that He did not proclaim it. The Messianic Consciousness was His secret possession, the inspiration of His Mission, but, as we shall see, it was only very gradually unveiled by Him.

Nature of the Temptation Narrative

There are a number of less important points connected with these narratives of the Temptation. Of course it will be recognised by the modern reader that these narratives are mystical, allegorical, symbolic, rather than historical. No modern reader can think, as ancient readers did, and not least John Milton, of Satan appearing in visible form and engaging Jesus in vocal conversation; placing Him on a pinnacle of the Temple; showing Him all the kingdoms of the world and the glory of them from an impossible terrestrial mountain; above all, citing Scripture in order to convince Him. (Ps. 91[11].) It was this last Satanic device which touched the poetic imagination of Shakespeare. He makes Antonio say in the *Merchant of Venice*:

> ‘*The Devil can cite Scripture for his purpose.*
> *An evil soul, producing holy witness,*
> *Is like a villain with a smiling cheek,*
> *A goodly apple rotten at the heart.*’

It has been asserted that Satan deliberately misquoted Scripture by omitting the phrase ‘in all thy ways,’ which, it is maintained, promised the Divine protection to the Messiah in treading the way which God had appointed for Him.

Possibly this dialogue owes its literary form to the Prologue of that great Old Testament drama the Book of Job.

But we can hardly be wrong in assuming that this temptation narrative originated with Jesus Himself. Our Lord's use of the Old Testament here, as always, goes to the very heart of the passage cited: it is significant that all three quotations are from the Book of Deuteronomy—the great practical summary of the prophetic teaching of Israel's Golden Age. Those who think of Jesus as apocalyptic in His conception of the Kingdom and His Mission would have expected Him to cite here not Deuteronomy but Daniel, the chief Old Testament apocalypse. But this is only the first of many occasions on which the reflective reader will find himself asking: Was Jesus, as it is the fashion to-day to affirm, really dominated by current apocalyptic expectations and modes of thought or was it only His Jewish predecessors, contemporaries, disciples, primitive Christian apostles and evangelists who, being dominated by apocalypticism, recorded, interpolated, and interpreted the words of Jesus in accordance with their preconceptions?

This is an extremely difficult question to answer, and it is only a very thorough and comprehensive study, not simply of the words and actions of Jesus but of His personality in relation to His environment, which will help towards the right answer, which again will almost certainly not be of the 'either-or' class.

Satan

It will naturally be asked: Did Jesus believe in the existence of Satan, and does such a being exist?

The old answer was: Yes, Jesus believed in the existence of Satan, and of course such a being exists.

The common modern answer is that Jesus did believe in the existence of Satan and that Satan does not exist.

This does not exhaust the possibilities of the enquiry. Satan became an article of religious belief among the Jews in the Persian period (538 to 333 B.C.), which dates from the ascendancy of Cyrus.

His earliest appearance in the Old Testament Scriptures, not as the principle of evil, but as a personal spiritual being, possessed of a proper title, is in the Prologue to the Book of Job, written possibly in the fifth century before Christ. There, Satan appears as one of the Sons of God (*Elohim*)—a disconcerting son, it is true, but nevertheless loyal.

Satan's next appearance is in Chronicles (written in the post-Exilic period probably in the fourth century B.C.). The Chronicler writes:

'And Satan stood up against Israel, and moved David to number Israel.' (1 Chron. 21[1].)

For this incident of the numbering of Israel by David the Chronicler is dependent upon the Book of Samuel, written several centuries earlier. The parallel passage in 2 Sam. 24[1] runs as follows:

'And again the anger of the Lord was kindled against Israel, and he moved David against them, saying, Go, number Israel and Judah.'

It will be observed that in this older narrative Jehovah is Himself the tempter of David, just as He was of Abraham. And this was the primitive belief in Israel; but in the interval between the writing of Samuel and the writing of Chronicles, a new belief sprang up: that Satan, not God, has the function of tempter, at first, as in Job, in subordination to the Divine permission, but later as an independent agent.

It seems probable that the Jews derived this belief from the dualism of Persian religion. Zoroaster had taught the existence of two principles, good and evil, or light and darkness, embodied in two personal beings, Ormuzd and Ahriman.

Ahriman, the God of Evil and Darkness in eternal conflict with the God of Light and Goodness, becomes the figure of Satan in later Judaism.

Is there any convincing reason, in the light of our modern experience, for believing in the existence of such a Being? We cannot feel that there is. The activities assigned by Jewish and Christian writers to Satan are accounted for in other ways by our scientists. Various forms of physical evil and moral and mental obliquity, which used to be attributed to the instigation and activity of Satan, are now attributed to other causes which account for them in a more adequate manner. As a consequence, there being nothing left for Satan to do, he ceases to exist, as a working hypothesis which is no longer needed.

We do not regard this as necessarily a final answer. Modern science, although it has disposed of Satan and his demons, and has thereby relieved humanity of a terrible incubus of horror and deception, cannot be said to have absolutely disproved the existence of invisible spiritual beings who may be the cause of certain evil temptations and types of insanity. Such things cannot be absolutely disproved. The scientists, however, have provided other working hypotheses which are not only more satisfactory intellectually, but are also more satisfactory morally and socially.

There is no doubt that the contemporaries of Jesus in Palestine believed in the existence of Satan and of countless myriads of demons, hostile both to God and to man. They believed that they caused the more unaccountable forms of disease such as violent insanity, epilepsy, and paralysis: they believed that by exorcism, where the name of God or some other good and powerful personality was invoked, the demons could be put to flight. Did Jesus hold these views?

There is little doubt that these were the views of His disciples and of the Evangelists who recorded His Ministry.

Did Jesus share their limitations or have they misrepresented Him in this matter?

It is usual to-day to assume that they have not; that the views of Jesus in this matter were the views of His contemporaries. And yet it is seldom safe to assume this is the case with men of genius. No doubt they do share: they must needs share in some measure the limitations of their contemporaries: they cannot entirely transcend their environment; but they wear their rue with a difference.

It is difficult to account for many of the words and actions attributed to Jesus in the Gospels without holding that He did believe in the existence of Satan and his Kingdom of Darkness—' the Strong Man ' who had to be bound before his house could be spoiled.

Our Lord's extreme anger at His power to cast out demons being attributed to His league with Beelzebub (Baalzebul, the Prince of the demons) would seem to indicate that He did believe in the reality of these demonic beings. His story of the exorcised demon who returned with seven other demons more evil than himself to dwell in the man who had not taken the precaution to replace his evil guest by a good one, does seem to presuppose our Lord's belief in demonic possession. His remark about the woman with the issue of blood whom Satan had bound eighteen years does seem to show, as for instance does His exorcism of the epileptic boy at the foot of the mountain of Transfiguration, that He did believe in demons being the cause of disease.

On the other hand, He did not use incantations to cast them out. He simply addressed them directly and claimed that the Divine power acted through Him in expelling them. He said:

'If I by the finger of God cast out demons, surely the Kingdom of God has come to you before you have anticipated its arrival.'

Yet He seems undoubtedly to have held—and here His great originality, as we shall see, manifests itself—that the effective action of the Divine power over demons required, as a preliminary, faith on the part of the possessed and afflicted individual and of others near him. Hence we find that Jesus is far less concerned to exorcise the evil spirit than to awaken or strengthen a spirit of faith in the possessed individual, which will enable the demon to be expelled. As a consequence, the really effective element in the cure is faith in God, not demonic exorcism.

Thus Jesus is no ordinary Jewish exorcist who trusts to the magical quality of his incantation and the devices of his art to effect the cure.

With Jesus, as we shall see, it is faith in God on the part of the afflicted, and the reciprocal Divine action, which expelled the demon. It may be argued that if this be so, demons were merely a figure of speech for Him: that He spoke of them and to them because only thus would those who desired His help be able to be cured by Him. To have denied the existence of their demons would at the outset have led them to believe that He did not understand the nature of their case and therefore must be unable to help them.

It may be that this hypothesis of deliberate concession to contemporary human ignorance is sound, but the weight of the evidence seems to us to be against it.

Ascetic Tendency in the Gospels

Mk.'s account of the Satanic Temptation, which extended over forty days, says nothing at all about the fasting of Jesus, but that He was during this period with wild beasts and that angels were ministering unto Him.

Mt. asserts that He fasted for forty days and forty nights; and Lk. stresses the severe character of the fast: that during all this period 'he did eat nothing.'

We observe here in the later Gospels, what is absent from Mk., a tendency to stress the religious value of asceticism.

A. THE BEGINNING OF THE MINISTRY OF JESUS IN GALILEE

MK. 1^{14}

1 14 Now after that John was delivered up, Jesus came into Galilee, preaching the gospel of God.

MT. 4^{12-16}

12 Now when he heard that John was delivered up, he withdrew into Galilee;
13 and leaving Nazareth, he came and dwelt in Capernaum, which is by the sea, in the
14 borders of Zebulun and Naphtali: that it might be fulfilled which was spoken by Isaiah the prophet, saying,

15 The land of Zebulun and the land of Naphtali,
Toward the sea, beyond Jordan,
Galilee of the Gentiles,
16 The people which sat in darkness
Saw a great light,
And to them which sat in the region and shadow of death,
To them did light spring up.

LK. 4^{14}

4 14 And Jesus returned in the power of the Spirit into Galilee: and a fame went out concerning him through all the region round about.

JN. 1^{43}

1 43 On the morrow he was minded to go forth into Galilee, and he findeth Philip: and Jesus saith unto him, Follow me.

Mk., who tells us that Jesus came from Nazareth (in Galilee), opens his account of the Ministry of Jesus in Galilee by saying that it began after the delivering up of John the Baptist. Whether Mark means by this phrase that John was betrayed by one of His disciples to the authorities as was Jesus later is not clear. We have no account in the Gospels or in Josephus of such a betrayal: the phrase, however, is curious.

What is of much importance is the question whether the Ministry of Jesus began after the conclusion of John's ministry, or while John's ministry was in progress.

According to Mk., the Ministry of Jesus began only after the arrest of the Baptist, and it began in Galilee. In this Mk. is followed by Mt. and Lk., but in Jn. it is stated (3^{24}), after a long account of the ministerial activities of Jesus both in Judæa and Galilee, that John was not yet cast into prison. In this period Jesus cleanses the Temple, collects a band of disciples, visits Cana in Galilee, etc.; in short, carries on a ministry which transcends both in power and popularity the ministry of the Baptist, whilst the Baptist still continues his work.

It has been held possible to reconcile this apparent contradiction by assuming that all Mk. is concerned to relate is not the beginning of the Ministry of Jesus but merely the beginning of His Galilean ministry and that Galilean ministry only when Peter himself has actual experience of it at Capernaum on the shores of the Galilean lake.

On the other hand, Jn. begins with the account of an early Judæan ministry of Jesus and a Galilean ministry earlier than Mk.'s Galilean ministry.

Commentators have urged that there is much to be said for the Johannine account as historical. Jesus would seem to have had, according to the Synoptists, a number of adherents or disciples in Judæa, and would seem to have been publicly known to the inhabitants of Jerusalem before his last visit there—the only visit during His Ministry, according to Mk. Mk.'s account of the Ministry would seem to make it only a one-year ministry.

Is it possible that Jesus could have accomplished all He did in a ministry of one brief year? Is not the Johannine account of the Ministry, which seems to include in it at least three Passovers and frequent visits to Jerusalem, much more probable?

St. Irenæus (see Westcott, *St. John, ad. loc.*) suggests that the Ministry of Jesus extended over ten years, and the remark of the Jews in the Fourth Gospel, 'Thou are not yet fifty years old' supports the theory of a longer ministry than Mk. records.

Is it not entirely natural that Peter's public teaching about the Ministry of Jesus should begin with his own personal experience of that ministry, even although he knew by hearsay of earlier ministries of Jesus? His brother Andrew (according to the Fourth Gospel) had been a disciple of the Baptist before he became a disciple of Jesus.

The only earlier incident in the life of Jesus recorded in Mk.'s Gospel before Peter's actual contact with Him at Capernaum is the Baptism and Temptation. As the Baptism and Temptation are both crucially concerned with the call of Jesus to the Messiahship, which Messiahship Peter was the first of the Apostles to recognise, it is only natural that Peter should preface his narrative of the Ministry of Jesus by an account of these two crucial experiences. We can only suppose that these experiences of Jesus in the earliest stage of His Ministry were confided by Him to His disciples after their recognition of His Messiahship.

THE MESSAGE OF JESUS

The Kingdom of God

MK. 1[15]

1 15 The time is fulfilled, and the kingdom of God is at hand: repent ye, and believe in the gospel.

MT. 4[17]

4 17 From that time began Jesus to preach, and to say, Repent ye; for the kingdom of heaven is at hand.

LK. 4[15]

4 15 And he taught in their synagogues, being glorified of all.

Mk.'s account of the theme with which Jesus began His public preaching is very brief. But how it is to be interpreted is a matter of profound difficulty. The theme is thus stated:

'The time is fulfilled, and the Kingdom of God is at hand: repent ye, and believe in the Gospel.'

It is clear enough what is meant by 'the time is fulfilled': Jesus is proclaiming the dawn of a new age. Israel's prophets had taught the people to look forward to a new age because they had taught them to believe in the Divine government of God, which government was marked by a progressive purpose. The Apocalyptists, who succeeded the prophets, had stressed even more emphatically this conception of a Divine plan destined inevitably to be accomplished with precision in each successive stage of human history.

For these thinkers, time was no mere ceaseless round, as it was for the writer of Ecclesiastes, but a progress subdivided into ages, seasons, days, hours: each to be marked by a particular predetermined form of Divine action. For those who accepted this teaching the world was indeed subject to government by God, 'and the soul of time His slave,' as the Battle Hymn of the Great Republic finely phrases it.

There can be little doubt that Jesus viewed human history in this way. He was not a Determinist of the modern materialist scientific type who regards the stages in the creative process as the product of the interaction of blind forces operating mechanistically. Jesus was a Determinist of the personal, moral, and spiritual type who believes that the whole course of things is determined by the Will of a Personal Divine Being 'of infinite power, wisdom, and goodness.' In 'the whole course of things' was not included the opposition of evil men and demons, for these futile and subordinate activities, though divinely permitted, were doomed finally to defeat and dissolution. They possessed neither real power nor permanence.

The new age whose advent Jesus heralded was the Messianic age. It was the consummation of the ages (Heb. 9^{26}), the last of what some of the Apocalyptists regarded as the Seven Ages of the world, each lasting a thousand years. Contemporary speculation on this point of the number and length of the ages was very varied, as the research of Dr. R. H. Charles has shown; but in all cases the Messianic Age was regarded as the last of the time series, the culmination of the world process when time passed into eternity, or perhaps more truly when eternity broke into and shattered time.

Life, like a dome of many-coloured glass,
Stains the white radiance of eternity,
Until Death tramples it to fragments.

It was not, however, death, but the Archangel's trumpet, 'the trump of God,' heralding the Advent (*Parousia*) of the Messiah which concluded the time series.

For Jesus, then, the Messianic Age had dawned because He, the Messiah, had arrived. That age was to inaugurate the Kingdom of God (Mk. and Lk.) or the Kingdom of the heavens (Mt.), a phrase derived from the Jewish apocalypses. Of course this does not mean that God was not ruling all the time in the Kingdom of men. He was, but His rule, according to current views, was being thwarted by evil men: by demons, by rebellious or incompetent angels, who were His vicegerents, and it was believed that in the Messianic Age, under the leadership of the Messiah, humanity would witness the complete triumph of Divine government, when all opposing forces would be utterly and for ever subject to God.

The difficult problem for those who would rightly interpret the Gospel of Jesus is to decide whether He took the precise view of the Kingdom portrayed by the Apocalyptists. In other words, whether He held that His Kingdom would be inaugurated and consummated in the apocalyptic manner—that is to say, by a divine Irruption preceded by the advent of angels and archangels; appalling cataclysms in the heavens and on the earth; and then the visible unveiling of the Divine presence in power and great glory, consuming all the evil and rewarding with eternal felicity the loyal servants of God.

There are, however, great objections to thinking that Jesus' conception, either of the Kingdom or of the mode of its coming, was that pictured by the Apocalyptists.

The apocalyptic conception of the Kingdom was strongly nationalist: it was essentially Jewish. When the Kingdom came the loyal Jew would come into his own: the oppressors of the Jews would be crushed and annihilated. In the coming Kingdom, the Jews, 'the saints of the Most High,' would be supreme.

Jesus teaches that entrance into the Kingdom is dependent, not upon race, but upon character and conduct. 'The good Samaritan' who succoured the half-dead Jew whom priest and Levite had avoided, would undoubtedly find himself within the Kingdom. 'Many,' said Jesus, 'shall come from the East and the West, and shall recline with Abraham, Isaac, and Jacob in the Kingdom of heaven, but the sons of the Kingdom [i.e. the Jews] shall be cast forth.' (Mt. 8^{11-12}; Lk. 13^{26-29}.)

The Beatitudes with which Mt.'s Sermon on the Mount opens present the ideals of character and conduct of the sons of the Kingdom as Jesus conceived them.

The Kingdom of God as the Apocalyptists conceived it was terrestrial. It was on this earth that the Divine triumph would be achieved. There are sayings of Jesus which suggest that He did not think of earth, but of heaven, the spiritual invisible sphere, as not only the sphere in which God reigns supremely now and ever but also as the abiding home of the sons of God.

'Lay not up for yourselves treasures upon the earth, for where thy treasure is there will thy heart be also.' (Mt. 6^{21}; Lk. 12^{34}.)

This point of view is much more fully developed in the discourses of Jesus in the later chapters of the Fourth Gospel (Jn., especially chap. 14, 'In my Father's house are many mansions'), but it is present also in the Synoptists. It is true that Jesus teaches His disciples to pray:

Thy Kingdom come,
Thy Will be done,
On earth as in heaven.

but this is a prayer not for the establishment of a terrestrial empire of God but for His reign in the hearts of men. For Jesus the Kingdom was not objective, but subjective. Its sphere was in the minds and hearts and souls of men. Where God reigns in a human personality, there the Kingdom of God has come on earth, and it is for this kind of advance of the Kingdom that Jesus taught His disciples to pray. 'The Kingdom of God,' said Jesus, 'is within [1] you.' The external localisation of the Kingdom suggested by the words, 'Lo here, Lo there,' He condemned.

The Kingdom was thus the *summum bonum* of the individual, 'the pearl of great price,' 'the purest treasure mortal times afford.' Wise was the man who sought and secured this before every other good.

There was a social side to the Gospel of the Kingdom as taught by Jesus, but it did not find its expression of necessity in an organised human society any more than it realised itself essentially in improved economic conditions and social progress in the terrestrial sphere.

'The gospel is not one of social improvement, but one of spiritual redemption.'[2]

Undoubtedly these social results and many others equally beneficial would follow, but as by-products. 'In many of the processes of applied science, there are certain results known as by-products, which are thrown off or precipitated on the way to the special result desired. It may happen that these by-products are of the utmost value: but none the less they are obtained by the way. Such a by-product is the social teaching of Jesus. It was not the end toward which His mission was directed: it came about as He fulfilled that mission. To reconstruct the gospels so as to make them primarily a programme of social reform is to mistake the by-product for the end specifically sought, and, in the desire to find a place for Jesus within the modern age, to forfeit that which gives him his place in all ages.' [3] Professor Peabody, the author of the above quotation, in his *Jesus Christ and the Social Question* seems to us to point to the right conclusion when he stresses the 'inwardness' of Christ's teaching.

'His way of approach to the life of his age was not by external organisation or mass-movements or force of numbers, or in any way from without: but by interior inspiration, by the quickening of individuals, by the force of personality, or, so to speak, from within. . .

'In short, Jesus approaches the social question from within: he deals with individuals: he makes men. It is for others to serve the world by organisation: he serves it through inspiration' (p. 111).

How was the Kingdom to come?

There were two opposing conceptions in contemporary Judaism as to how the Kingdom of God would come:

(1) Undoubtedly the more popular of the two in Galilee was that of the Zealots—a body of ardent Jewish patriots. The Zealots, true to the Maccabean tradition and example, believed that the Kingdom must come by heroic endeavour and the exertion of military force. Jesus curtly dismissed their programme for bringing in the Messianic Kingdom with the words:

'All they that take the sword shall perish by the sword.' (Mt. 26^{52}.)

[1] Some would translate the Greek word *entos* as *among*, but 'within' is more probably correct.
[2] A. von Harnack.
[3] *Jesus Christ and the Social Question*, p. 79.

(2) On the other hand, the Apocalyptists taught that the Kingdom came not by man's strivings but by God's intervention. The Kingdom was God's, and at the time appointed He would bring it in, not by the scimitars of heroic Zealots, but by the flaming swords of myriads of angels and archangels. This was the view of the Pharisees, who were opposed to the political militarism of the Zealots.

(3) Jesus taught, however, that the Kingdom comes not by military force nor by angelic agency, but by the individual human being accepting and doing the Will of God. When the individual does that he enters into the Kingdom: the Kingdom has come in his heart

Hence for Jesus the Kingdom comes invisibly like the seed growing secretly—like the leaven working in the meal. Nevertheless, the results of the coming of the Kingdom are manifest and may be seen by men as in the case of the growing plant or the leavened dough.

The ultimate and universal triumph of the Kingdom was not less assured for Jesus because it came in this way. The gentle trickle of Shiloah's brook effects more in the long run than does the turgid tide of the Euphrates. The grain of mustard seed would produce a larger plant than all its rivals. The action of the leaven in the three measures of meal does not cease until the *whole* is leavened.

Hence for Jesus the Kingdom has come and is coming: it is present and it is future: it is invisible and it is visible: it is from heaven and it operates on earth. Prayer and preaching, faith and obedience, loyalty and perseverance, are all means by which the Kingdom comes. Thus the complete coming of the Kingdom on earth is dependent upon the co-operation of man with God.

This conception of the Kingdom was profoundly original, not only in its essence and its combination of opposites but also by what it excluded in contemporary popular ideas. It was in consequence extremely difficult for the contemporaries of Jesus and even for His apostles and disciples to apprehend His conception of the Kingdom. They were mystified by much that He taught about it. They believed in Him, but they did not understand Him. He rebuked them for dullness and lack of insight. They deserved it: they could not rid themselves of current Jewish ways of thinking and feeling. The last question which Luke records they put to Him just before His Ascension was:

'Lord, dost thou at this time restore the Kingdom to Israel?'

This indicates their lack of discernment. On this occasion He uttered neither rebuke nor criticism.

There was one, however, 'the beloved disciple,' the author of the Fourth Gospel, who recognised later, if not then, the true significance of the teaching of his Master, and he, in his record of his Master's teaching, substitutes for the term 'Kingdom of God,' the phrase 'Eternal Life.'

And this perhaps is the very best synonym we could have for it, but had Jesus at the outset of His Ministry preached the Gospel of Eternal Life and not the Gospel of the Kingdom of God, few would have been attracted by His message and possibly even fewer would have understood it.

To fill an old term with a new meaning, though a difficult task to accomplish successfully, is often a better method than to introduce a new terminology. At any rate, the former was undoubtedly the method of Jesus; not only the old term Kingdom but also the old term Messiah were each given a new content by Him.

There is one point to be noted. Mt. makes John the Baptist anticipate Jesus by proclaiming that the Kingdom of the Heavens is at hand. In this we believe that Mt. was entirely wrong. John's message for the near future was not the coming of the Kingdom but the coming of apocalyptic Divine Judgement:

'Ye offspring of vipers, who warned you to flee from the wrath to come?' (Mt. 3^{7}.)

That Divine Judgement could only be escaped, so the Baptist taught, by bringing forth the fruits of moral reformation. The practical application of this teaching of the Baptist appears in a more fully developed form in Lk. 3^{10-14}.

THE CALL OF THE FIRST DISCIPLES

MK. 1^{16-20}

1 16 And passing along by the sea of Galilee,
he saw Simon and Andrew the brother of
Simon casting a net in the sea: for they
17 were fishers. And Jesus said unto them,
Come ye after me, and I will make you to
18 become fishers of men. And straightway
they left the nets, and followed him.
19 And going on a little further, he saw James
the *son* of Zebedee, and John his brother,
who also were in the boat mending the
20 nets. And straightway he called them:
and they left their father Zebedee in the
boat with the hired servants, and went
after him.

MT. 4^{18-22}

4 18 And walking by the sea of Galilee, he
saw two brethren, Simon who is called
Peter, and Andrew his brother, casting a
net into the sea; for they were fishers.
19 And he saith unto them, Come ye after
me, and I will make you fishers of men.
20 And they straightway left the nets, and
21 followed him. And going on from thence
he saw other two brethren, James the *son*
of Zebedee, and John his brother, in the
boat with Zebedee their father, mending
22 their nets; and he called them. And they
straightway left the boat and their father,
and followed him.

LK. 5^{1-11}

5 1 Now it came to pass, while the multitude
pressed upon him and heard the word of
God, that he was standing by the lake of
2 Gennesaret; and he saw two boats standing by the lake: but the fishermen had
gone out of them, and were washing their
3 nets. And he entered into one of the
boats, which was Simon's, and asked him
to put out a little from the land. And he
sat down and taught the multitudes out of
4 the boat. And when he had left speaking,
he said unto Simon, Put out into the deep,
5 and let down your nets for a draught. And
Simon answered and said, Master, we
toiled all night, and took nothing: but at
6 thy word I will let down the nets. And
when they had this done, they inclosed a
great multitude of fishes; and their nets

JN. 1^{35-51}

1 35 Again on the morrow John was stand-
36 ing, and two of his disciples; and he looked
upon Jesus as he walked, and saith, Be-
37 hold, the Lamb of God! And the two
disciples heard him speak, and they
38 followed Jesus. And Jesus turned, and
beheld them following, and saith unto
them, What seek ye? And they said unto
him, Rabbi (which is to say, being inter-
39 preted, Master), where abidest thou? He
saith unto them, Come, and ye shall see.
They came therefore and saw where he
abode; and they abode with him that
40 day: it was about the tenth hour. One of
the two that heard John *speak*, and followed him, was Andrew, Simon Peter's
brother. He findeth first his own brother
Simon, and saith unto him, We have

7 were breaking; and they beckoned unto
their partners in the other boat, that they
should come and help them. And they
came, and filled both the boats, so that
8 they began to sink. But Simon Peter,
when he saw it, fell down at Jesus' knees,
saying, Depart from me; for I am a sinful
9 man, O Lord. For he was amazed, and
all that were with him, at the draught of
10 the fishes which they had taken; and so
were also James and John, sons of Zebedee,
which were partners with Simon. And
Jesus said unto Simon, Fear not; from
11 henceforth thou shalt catch men. And
when they had brought their boats to
land, they left all, and followed him.

found the Messiah (which is, being inter-
42 preted, Christ). He brought him unto
Jesus. Jesus looked upon him, and said,
Thou art Simon the son of John: thou
shalt be called Cephas (which is by
interpretation, Peter).
43 On the morrow he was minded to go
forth into Galilee, and he findeth Philip:
and Jesus saith unto him, Follow me.
44 Now Philip was from Bethsaida, of the
45 city of Andrew and Peter. Philip findeth
Nathanael, and saith unto him, We have
found him, of whom Moses in the law, and
the prophets, did write, Jesus of Nazareth,
46 the son of Joseph. And Nathanael said
unto him, Can any good thing come out of
Nazareth? Philip saith unto him, Come
47 and see. Jesus saw Nathanael coming to
him, and saith of him, Behold, an Israelite
48 indeed, in whom is no guile! Nathanael
saith unto him, Whence knowest thou me?
Jesus answered and said unto him, Before
Philip called thee, when thou wast under
49 the fig tree, I saw thee. Nathanael
answered him, Rabbi, thou art the Son of
50 God; thou art King of Israel. Jesus
answered and said unto him, Because I
said unto thee, I saw thee underneath the
fig tree, believest thou? thou shalt see
51 greater things than these. And he saith
unto him, Verily, verily, I say unto you,
Ye shall see the heaven opened, and the
angels of God ascending and descending
upon the Son of man.

The Galilean ministry opens with the call of Simon and his elder brother Andrew, and his partners John and James, the sons of Zebedee, all fishermen on the Lake of Galilee, to become disciples of Jesus.

If Mk. be the Gospel of Peter, then the account of the call of Peter must be a reminiscence, and there are points in the Marcan narrative which support this view. The opening of the account is dramatic. Andrew and Simon are casting their net into the sea. The net used, as we see from the account of Mk. (slightly expanded by Mt.), was an *amphiblestron*—a circular casting net weighted round the edges. The fisherman using it wades on the beach and casts it ahead of him.

Mk. relates that Jesus *spoke* to Andrew and Peter. For He was quite close to them. In the case of James and John He hailed them, for they were out on the lake in their boat repairing their nets and so not within speaking distance.

This fine distinction between speaking and hailing and the difference in the fishing operations of the two pairs of brothers suggest actual recollection.

Again there is another Petrine touch, if we may so call it, in the narrative. It is related by Mk. alone. That when John and James in obedience to the call of Jesus left their father Zebedee, who was in the boat with them, they did not leave the old man unaided to carry on his fishing occupation, for he had with him hired servants. This statement about Zebedee's hired servants occurs nowhere else but in Mk. It probably seemed too trifling a point for anyone else to relate.

This account of the call of Peter and his fellow-disciples has a certain dramatic quality:

'Come ye after me and I will make you fishers of men, and they straightway left the nets and followed Him.'

Yet it is difficult not to suppose that Peter and his fellows must have had some experience of Jesus and His ability as a fisher of men before they obeyed His call.

Lk. gives another account (5^{1-11}) of the call of Peter and his fellow-fishermen to discipleship. It is even more dramatic than that of Mk. It is connected with an incident calculated to touch the heart and fire the imagination of fishermen. It is the story of an enormous catch of fish made in response to the command of Jesus to let down the nets after a night spent in fruitless toil.

At the sight of the catch, Peter fell down at the knees of Jesus saying:

'Depart from me, for I am a sinful man, O Lord.'

And Jesus said unto him:

'Fear not; from henceforth thou shalt catch men.'

Some have thought that Lk.'s story is a doublet of the story told of St. Peter and his fellow-disciples on the Galilean lake in the Epilogue of St. John's Gospel (21^{1-14}) which also relates a great catch of fish. There was evidently some tradition in the early Church which connected Peter with some wonderful catch of fish due to the Lord. Perhaps we have another echo of the tradition in Mt.'s story of Peter catching a fish with a coin in its mouth, in obedience to Christ's command.

Possibly this remarkable fishing experience may have preceded the actual call of Peter to discipleship and have been an important influence in attaching him to Jesus. There is, however, a difficulty about this view, for if Mk.'s Gospel be Peter's memoirs, why is this not related in Mk.'s account of Peter's Call? It may be that while the great catch of fish preceded the Call of Peter it was not actually united to that Call, although Luke, with his love for dramatic and picturesque combinations, has brought the Catch and the Call together.

There was no doubt another incident which influenced Peter's attachment to Jesus, although it is related as following, not preceding, Peter's Call. It was the healing of Peter's mother-in-law by Jesus.

No doubt the magnetic power of Jesus which drew vast multitudes to hear Him, and also to be healed by Him, related as preceding the Call of Peter in Mt. and Lk., but not in Mk., may have proved a powerful influence in inducing Peter to throw in his lot with Jesus. But Mk. does not relate these earlier activities of Jesus by the Lake because they preceded Peter's Call and Peter, we may assume, was accustomed in his Roman preaching to begin his account of the Galilean ministry with his own Call by Jesus.

TEACHING IN THE SYNAGOGUE IN CAPERNAUM

MK. $1^{21, 22}$

1 21 And they go into Capernaum; and
straightway on the sabbath day he entered
22 into the synagogue and taught. And they
were astonished at his teaching: for he
taught them as having authority, and not
as the scribes.

MT. 4^{13}; cf. $7^{28b\ 29}$

4 13 and leaving Nazareth, he came and dwelt
in Capernaum, which is by the sea, in the
borders of Zebulun and Naphtali.
7 28 the multitudes were astonished at his
29 teaching: for he taught them as *one*
having authority, and not as their scribes.

LK. 4^{31-32}

4 31 And he came down to Capernaum, a
city of Galilee. And he was teaching
32 them on the sabbath day: and they were
astonished at his teaching; for his word
was with authority.

Jesus, with his four newly-attached disciples, now takes up His quarters in Capernaum (literally Nahum's village, the modern Tel-Ḥum), pleasantly situated on the western shores of the Lake of Galilee, some miles north of Tiberias which was then in course of being built. His place of residence there was Peter's house, evidently a spacious one, as will appear later. Into this house Peter received, not only Jesus as his guest, but also James and John, who had forsaken the paternal roof (Mk. 1^{29}). Mark's Gospel alone relates this homely recollection.

In Capernaum, Jesus makes use of the synagogue for the purpose of preaching the Glad Tidings. To-day the visitor to Capernaum may see the considerable remains of a very handsome synagogue of the Græco-Roman period: in all probability, the synagogue in which Jesus preached. This was also, no doubt, the synagogue referred to as having been generously built and presented to Capernaum by the devout centurion of Gentile origin who loved the Jews and whose servant (not son) Jesus healed. (Mt. 8^{5ff}.; Lk. 7^{2ff}.)

Synagogues began to be built by the Jews after their return from the Babylonian exile. They served a triple purpose:

(1) Places of worship on the Sabbath.

(2) Schools during the weekdays where the young were taught to read and understand the Scriptures.

(3) Local law courts where lesser offences were tried and the condemned were beaten.

The synagogue was essentially a lay institution. Not less than ten adult male Jews were necessary to found a synagogue in any locality, and they, 'the rulers of the synagogue,' managed it. A lay chazzan or verger was employed by them. The services of a priest were not required, as synagogue religion was entirely non-sacrificial. In the Sabbath services prayers were recited, psalms sung, the Law and the Prophets read in the Hebrew and afterwards paraphrased in Aramaic, the local vernacular in Palestine in our Lord's day. These paraphrases, some of which are still extant, are known as Targums. Sermons were preached when a preacher was procurable. These preachers were for the most part laymen. Distinguished strangers present at the synagogue service who might be expected to have something to say were often invited to address the congregation—as was the case with Paul, Barnabas, Silas, etc.

It would seem more probable from Mk.'s account that Jesus began His evangelical Mission by preaching in the synagogues (as did John Wesley in the English parish churches), and only when His audience became much too great for any synagogue did He resort (as did John Wesley) to open-air preaching. It may be that at the close of His Galilean ministry, Jesus preached in the open air because He had been excommunicated from the local synagogues, but there is no proof that this was the case, although later His disciples were excluded from the Jewish synagogues.

The preaching of Jesus in the synagogue of Capernaum quickly created a sensation. His manner was novel. Unlike the scribes, the contemporary students, copyists, and expounders of the Scripture, who were satisfied in their preaching to confine themselves to the exposition of the Scriptural text and the citation of authoritative comments on it, Jesus cited no authorities to support His message. He preached prophetically, and yet not precisely prophetically, for the prophet prefaced his oracle with the words: 'Thus saith the Lord.' There is no record that Jesus did this. His preaching was rather Messianic: 'Ye have heard that it was said to them of old time . . . but I say unto you' (Mt. 5^{21}). His astonished and gratified audience exclaim:

> 'He teacheth as one having authority and not as do the scribes.'

When to this original and authoritative preaching was added the power of effective exorcism and healing, they were still more impressed by this new teaching, exclaiming:

> 'What is this? A new Teaching! With authority he commands even the unclean spirits and they obey him' (Mk. 1^{27}).

A BUSY SABBATH

(*a*) Exorcising a Demoniac in the Synagogue

MK. 1^{23-28}

1 23 And straightway there was in their
synagogue a man with an unclean spirit;
24 and he cried out, saying, What have we
to do with thee, thou Jesus of Nazareth?
art thou come to destroy us? I know
thee who thou art, the Holy One of God.
25 And Jesus rebuked him, saying, Hold thy
26 peace, and come out of him. And the
unclean spirit, tearing him and crying
with a loud voice, came out of him.
27 And they were all amazed, insomuch that
they questioned among themselves, saying,
What is this? a new teaching! with
authority he commandeth even the un-
28 clean spirits, and they obey him. And
the report of him went out straightway
everywhere into all the region of Galilee
round about.

LK. 4^{33-37}

4 33 And in the synagogue there was a man,
which had a spirit of an unclean devil; and
34 he cried out with a loud voice, Ah! what
have we to do with thee, thou Jesus of
Nazareth? art thou come to destroy us?
I know thee who thou art, the Holy One
35 of God. And Jesus rebuked him, saying,
Hold thy peace, and come out of him.
And when the devil had thrown him down
in the midst, he came out of him, having
36 done him no hurt. And amazement
came upon all, and they spake together,
one with another, saying, What is this
word? for with authority and power he
commandeth the unclean spirits, and they
37 come out. And there went forth a
rumour concerning him into every place
of the region round about.

OMITTED BY MATTHEW

'And immediately,' writes Mk., 'he was in the synagogue.' This curious phrase 'and immediately' is characteristic of Mk. He begins again and again his narrative with it. It lends liveliness to his style and in all probability reproduces a mannerism of St. Peter, as does also Mk.'s use of the historic present, i.e. using the present tense to describe past events.

On this occasion, Jesus has an abnormal member in His synagogue congregation—a man possessed by an unclean spirit, i.e. one mentally deranged. He shouts out: 'What to us and to thee, O Nazarene Jesus?'

This Semitic way of speaking no doubt means: What have we in common? I, a man possessed of demons (notice the plural) and thou the Messiah, the Holy One of God? Jesus silenced the man by bidding the demon: 'Be muzzled, and come forth.'

The man experienced a convulsion and cried with a loud voice and ceased to be possessed. (Luke, the physician, in his account adds 'he took no harm,' 4^{35}.) In consequence a report went abroad through the whole Galilean region of this amazing occurrence.

The Messianic Secret

The most interesting point in this narrative is not the exorcising of a possessed man by Jesus. There were many possessed men in Galilee at this time, and there were many who exorcised them with varying degrees of success. The interesting thing is that this possessed man hailed Jesus as the Messiah.

Orientals would differ from modern Western people in their estimate of the value of such an assertion. The East (this is well brought out in Saladin's conversation with Richard, Cœur de Lion, in Scott's *Talisman*) regarded madmen as inspired. Mk., however, regards the inspiration as demoniacal and not divine. In terror, these Palestinian lunatics, or rather the demons in them, hail Jesus as the Messiah, but it will be noted, not beseeching Him to deliver them, but crying out, Avaunt!

St. James, the Head of the Church in Jerusalem, writes in his Epistle, 'the demons also believe [there is one God] and tremble' (literally their hair stands on end), but such faith, he notes, makes no difference to their character or conduct. Nevertheless, this fact would not affect the value of their testimony to Jesus as the Messiah.

Perhaps the modern man will see in these incidents of demonic testimony evidence of the strength of the personality of Jesus and the force of His Messianic conviction, to which it has been suggested that the mentally unbalanced would be more sensitive than the sane.

Jesus knew Himself to be the Messiah, and His Messianic Consciousness may have telepathically affected them. Jesus, and this will seem most unexpected, bade them be silent, not because they were demons or because what they said was not true, but because He did not wish to have His Messiahship proclaimed in this way and at this time.

In order to achieve an effective and permanent impression it was necessary that His contemporaries should recognise Him as Messiah. His Messiahship is His own secret, and until others find it out it cannot be told.

We can see in Mk.'s Gospel definite stages in the unveiling of the Messiahship of Jesus. These stages are in certain instances blurred, or ignored, or contradicted in the other Canonical Gospels, and yet there can be no reasonable doubt that Mk. records their true order. Mk.'s order is much too unexpected and original to have been invented by him, and it certainly serves no apologetic purpose, and in some ways counteracts prevalent tendencies in the Christian community. The Fourth Gospel provides strong evidence for this. It begins the Messianic Mission of Jesus by making Him proclaim His Messiahship on every occasion.

The stages in Mk.'s Gospel are as follows:

(1) First there is the unveiling of the Messiahship to Jesus Himself alone at His baptism (1^{11}).

(2) Secondly, there is the unveiling of the Messiahship to the insane (the demonised), and their proclamation of it (1^{24}, 3^{11}).

(3) The third stage is the unveiling of the Messiahship to Peter at Cæsarea Philippi. ('Who say ye that I am?' 'Thou art the Christ.') ($8^{27ff.}$)

(4) The fourth stage is the unveiling of the Messiahship to the disciples as a body, when He strives to teach them explicitly the significance of His Messiahship both for Himself and for them. Contrary to all their prepossessions and expectations, He is to be rejected and crucified and they in their turn are to be cross-bearers in His train (8^{31}).

(5) The fifth stage is the unveiling of the Messiahship by His triumphal entry into Jerusalem. He now changes His former policy of concealment and reticence and publicly proclaims His Messiahship by symbolical acts and utterances. He deliberately fulfils certain striking Old Testament Messianic prophecies. The triumphal entry into Jerusalem upon an ass on Palm Sunday was such an act (cf. Zech. 9^{9}), and also the cleansing of the Temple (cf. Mal. 3^{1-3}). In His public teaching in His last days in Jerusalem, in His parable of the vinedressers who slew the heir, and in His reference to the stone which the builders rejected, He unveils His Messiahship and His impending fate (11^{1}).

(6) The sixth stage of the unveiling of the Messiahship is reached when in the presence of the Sanhedrin, being adjured by the High Priest to answer the question: 'Art Thou the Christ, the Son of the Blessed One?' He replies: 'I am.' This is followed by His reply to Pilate's question: 'Art Thou the King of the Jews?' to which Jesus answered: 'Thou sayest it' (Mk. 15^{2}).

(*b*) Healing Peter's Mother-in-law

MK. 1^{29-31}

1 29 And straightway, when they were come
out of the synagogue, they came into the
house of Simon and Andrew, with James
30 and John. Now Simon's wife's mother
lay sick of a fever; and straightway they
31 tell him of her: and he came and took her
by the hand, and raised her up; and the
fever left her, and she ministered unto
them.

MT. 8^{14-15}

8 14 And when Jesus was come into Peter's
house, he saw his wife's mother lying sick
15 of a fever. And he touched her hand,
and the fever left her; and she arose, and
ministered unto him.

LK. 4^{38-39}

4 38 And he rose up from the synagogue,
and entered into the house of Simon.
And Simon's wife's mother was holden
with a great fever; and they besought him
39 for her. And he stood over her, and
rebuked the fever; and it left her: and
immediately she rose up and ministered
unto them.

On leaving the Synagogue with His little group of disciples, Jesus goes into the house of Peter and is told that Peter's mother-in-law is laid up with a fever. (Luke the physician adds 'a great fever.') St. Peter, as we know also from references by St. Paul (1 Cor. 9^{5}), was, like the rest of the Twelve, a married man. When Jesus learns of the sickness of Peter's mother-in-law He at once goes into her room, takes her by the hand, and raises her from her couch. As He does this the fever leaves her and she begins to attend to the needs of her guests.

The immediacy and completeness of the cure on this occasion made a deep impression on her son-in- law, and so we have it recorded in the Gospels.

(c) Healing Many after Sunset

MK. 1^{32-34}

1 32 And at even, when the sun did set, they
brought unto him all that were sick, and
them that were possessed with devils.
33 And all the city was gathered together at
34 the door. And he healed many that were
sick with divers diseases, and cast out
many devils; and he suffered not the
devils to speak, because they knew him.

MT. 8^{16}

8 16 And when even was come, they brought
unto him many possessed with devils:
and he cast out the spirits with a word,
and healed all that were sick.

LK. 4^{40-41}

4 40 And when the sun was setting, all they
that had any sick with divers diseases
brought them unto him; and he laid his
hands on every one of them, and healed
41 them. And devils also came out from
many, crying out, and saying, Thou art
the Son of God. And rebuking them, he
suffered them not to speak, because they
knew that he was the Christ.

'At even when the sun was set' the work of Jesus begins again. At first sight 'when the sun was set' seems tautology, but it is not so, although the writers of the First and Third Gospels show they so regard it. The Jewish Sabbath began at sunset on Friday and extended to sunset on Saturday. Many Roman Christians, for whom Mark's Gospel was written, might not realise this. Moreover, the reference to sunset reflects a personal reminiscence. Watches were not carried in the East in those days. It is said that even to-day at the fast of Ramadhan hungry and thirsty Mohammedans watch eagerly until the sun's disk sinks below the horizon and then a wild rush takes place for coffee, cheroots, and comestibles.

Moved by less selfish reasons, the people of Capernaum and its neighbourhood who had sick relations waited with eagerness until the Jewish law (which forbad men to bear burdens upon the Sabbath) permitted them to bring their sick folk to Jesus to be healed. In the text, the word *brought* should be translated either 'began to bring' or 'brought one after another.' Dr. Swete translates it in this latter way: 'Case after case arrived,' so that the whole town was gathered at the door of Peter's house. *Many*, says Mk., were healed. Mt., following a tendency of his, states that *all* were healed. Mk. relates that the demonised bore testimony to Jesus as the Messiah, but Jesus would not permit them to speak. (Mk. 3^{11}.)

With this incident the busy day concludes.

Mt. consistently omits this testimony of the demonised to the Messiahship of Jesus, just as he also omits the healing of the demonised man in the Synagogue of Capernaum.

SOLITARY PRAYER AND AN EXTENSION OF THE MISSION

MK. I$^{35-39}$

1 35 And in the morning, a great while
before day, he rose up and went out, and
departed into a desert place, and there
36 prayed. And Simon and they that were
37 with him followed after him; and they
found him, and say unto him, All are
38 seeking thee. And he saith unto them,
Let us go elsewhere into the next towns,
that I may preach there also; for to this
39 end came I forth. And he went into their
synagogues throughout all Galilee, preaching
and casting out devils.

LK. 4^{42-44}

4 42 And when it was day, he came out and
went into a desert place: and the multitudes
sought after him, and came unto
him, and would have stayed him, that he
43 should not go from them. But he said
unto them, I must preach the good tidings
of the kingdom of God to the other cities
also: for therefore was I sent.
44 And he was preaching in the synagogues
of Galilee.

Very early next day, it being quite dark, Jesus went forth from Peter's house into a solitary place and began to pray there. Having somehow discovered His absence, Peter, followed by the other disciples, tracks Him down.

Mk.'s explicitness of detail here suggests the reminiscence of an eye-witness. Peter remembered with pardonable pride his scouting achievement.

Mt. omits it altogether and Lk. omits Peter's achievement and says the multitude sought Him and found Him and they laid hold on Him so that He should not leave them.

Mk. relates that on finding Him the disciples say: 'Everyone is seeking Thee' and Jesus replies:

'Let us go elsewhere into the neighbouring country towns that I may proclaim the Gospel there. For this reason I came forth.'

Some ancient commentators have taken this to mean 'it was for the purpose of proclaiming the Gospel, I, the Eternal Word, came forth from God': others, 'for this reason I undertook the Messianic Mission': but as the word used is exactly the same as that used in *v.* 35 it probably means: 'for this very reason that I might prepare for an extension of my Mission I went out to seek a place for solitary prayer.'

Jesus then preaches His Gospel in the synagogues of the whole of Galilee. Lk. says 'in the whole of Judæa.' Lk., as we see from the Acts of the Apostles, uses Judæa in a double sense as either (1) the whole of Palestine or else (2) the southern part of Palestine in contrast to Samaria and Galilee. Cf. Mt. 4^{23-25}.

THE CLEANSING OF A LEPER

MK. 1$^{40-45}$

1 40 And there cometh to him a leper, beseeching him, and kneeling down to him,
and saying unto him, If thou wilt, thou
41 canst make me clean. And being moved
with compassion, he stretched forth his
hand, and touched him, and saith unto
42 him, I will; be thou made clean. And
straightway the leprosy departed from
43 him, and he was made clean. And he
strictly charged him, and straightway sent
44 him out, and saith unto him, See thou say
nothing to any man: but go thy way,
shew thyself to the priest, and offer for
thy cleansing the things which Moses
commanded, for a testimony unto them.
45 But he went out, and began to publish it
much, and to spread abroad the matter,
insomuch that Jesus could no more openly
enter into a city, but was without in
desert places: and they came to him from
every quarter.

MT. 8$^{2-4}$

8 2 And behold, there came to him a leper
and worshipped him, saying, Lord, if thou
3 wilt, thou canst make me clean. And he
stretched forth his hand, and touched him,
saying, I will; be thou made clean. And
4 straightway his leprosy was cleansed. And
Jesus saith unto him, See thou tell no man;
but go thy way, shew thyself to the priest,
and offer the gift that Moses commanded,
for a testimony unto them.

LK. 5$^{12-16}$

5 12 And it came to pass, while he was in
one of the cities, behold, a man full of
leprosy: and when he saw Jesus, he fell on
his face, and besought him, saying, Lord,
if thou wilt, thou canst make me clean.
13 And he stretched forth his hand, and
touched him, saying, I will; be thou made
clean. And straightway the leprosy de-
14 parted from him. And he charged him
to tell no man: but go thy way, and shew
thyself to the priest, and offer for thy
cleansing, according as Moses commanded,
15 for a testimony unto them. But so much
the more went abroad the report concerning him: and great multitudes came
together to hear, and to be healed of their
16 infirmities. But he withdrew himself in
the deserts, and prayed.

A very notable case of healing, presumably the first of its kind, takes place in this extended Galilean Mission. A leper knelt down before Jesus beseeching Him to heal him, saying: ‘ If you wish, you are able to cleanse me,’ and Jesus, filled with pity, touched the leper, saying to him: ‘ I do wish it: be cleansed ’; and he was cleansed immediately. Then Jesus sternly sent him away and said to him, ‘ Take care not to say anything to anyone, but be off, show thyself to the priest, and offer for thy cleansing what Moses commanded for a testimony to them.’ The man went forth and disregarding the command of Jesus told the story of his cleansing everywhere. As a result Jesus was unable to show Himself in inhabited localities.

Mk.’s account of this incident is extraordinarily vivid. Pity, courage, decision, mark the action of Jesus. It was unlawful to touch a leper. If one did one incurred uncleanness with all its disabilities. Jesus shows that His faith is as great as the leper’s when He touches him. On the other hand, it is clear by His stern charge to the leper that Jesus regarded healing as merely subsidiary and did not wish His Mission to be regarded as a healing and not as a preaching mission. The phrase, ‘ for a testimony unto them,’ does not mean, as some have taken it to mean, that Jesus is sending the cleansed leper up to the authorities of the Temple as a testimony to them that the Messiah has come, but that He is merely telling the leper to do what the law of Moses commanded in such cases; for until the leper had done that, he could not return to his home and to his friends.

The priest in Judaism, among his many functions, was the officer of public health, and his acceptance of the leper's sacrifice constituted the public testimony that the leper was cleansed. Had the leper left Galilee silently and immediately, Jesus would not have been thwarted in His preaching mission by the multitudes who came to Him, not to hear, but to be healed.

Mt., who omits anything in Mk. which suggests a limitation of the power of Jesus, omits the whole of *v.* 45 which speaks of the inability of Jesus to show Himself publicly in the Galilean towns at this time.

Lk., in accordance with his custom, supplements Mk.'s narrative by adding that Jesus spent the period of consequent seclusion in prayer.

M. Coué, of Nancy, asserted that he had known a case of a rodent ulcer being cured by faith.

THE RETURN TO CAPERNAUM AND THE HEALING OF A PARALYTIC

MK. 2^{1-12}

2 1 And when he entered again into
Capernaum after some days, it was noised
2 that he was in the house. And many
were gathered together, so that there was
no longer room *for them*, no, not even
about the door: and he spake the word
3 unto them. And they come, bringing
unto him a man sick of the palsy, borne
4 of four. And when they could not come
nigh unto him for the crowd, they uncovered the roof where he was: and when
they had broken it up, they let down the
5 bed whereon the sick of the palsy lay. And
Jesus seeing their faith saith unto the sick
of the palsy, Son, thy sins are forgiven.
6 But there were certain of the scribes sitting
there, and reasoning in their hearts,
7 Why doth this man thus speak? he
blasphemeth: who can forgive sins but
8 one, *even* God? And straightway Jesus,
perceiving in his spirit that they so reasoned within themselves, saith unto them,
Why reason ye these things in your hearts?
9 Whether is easier, to say to the sick of the
palsy, Thy sins are forgiven; or to say,
Arise, and take up thy bed, and walk?
10 But that ye may know that the Son of
man hath power on earth to forgive sins
11 (he saith to the sick of the palsy), I say
unto thee, Arise, take up thy bed, and go
12 unto thy house. And he arose, and
straightway took up the bed, and went
forth before them all; insomuch that they
were all amazed, and glorified God,
saying, We never saw it on this fashion.

MT. 9^{1-8}

9 1 And he entered into a boat, and crossed
2 over, and came into his own city. And
behold, they brought to him a man sick of
the palsy, lying on a bed: and Jesus seeing
their faith said unto the sick of the palsy,
Son, be of good cheer; thy sins are forgiven.
3 And behold, certain of the scribes said
within themselves, This man blasphemeth.
4 And Jesus knowing their thoughts said,
Wherefore think ye evil in your hearts?
5 For whether is easier, to say, Thy sins are
6 forgiven; or to say, Arise, and walk? But
that ye may know that the Son of man hath
power on earth to forgive sins (then saith
he to the sick of the palsy), Arise, and take
7 up thy bed, and go unto thy house. And
8 he arose, and departed to his house. But
when the multitudes saw it, they were
afraid, and glorified God, which had given
such power unto men.

LK. 5^{17-26}

5 17 And it came to pass on one of those
days, that he was teaching; and there were
Pharisees and doctors of the law sitting
by, which were come out of very village of
Galilee and Judæa and Jerusalem: and
the power of the Lord was with him to
18 heal. And behold, men bring on a bed
a man that was palsied: and they sought
to bring him in, and to lay him
19 before him. And not finding by what
way they might bring him in because
of the multitude, they went up to the
housetop, and let him down through the
tiles with his couch into the midst before
20 Jesus. And seeing their faith, he said,
21 Man, thy sins are forgiven thee. And the
scribes and the Pharisees began to reason,
saying, Who is this that speaketh blasphemies? Who can forgive sins, but God
22 alone? But Jesus perceiving their reasonings, answered and said unto them, What
23 reason ye in your hearts? Whether is
easier, to say, Thy sins are forgiven thee;
24 or to say, Arise and walk? But that ye
may know that the Son of man hath
power on earth to forgive sins (he said
unto him that was palsied), I say unto
thee, Arise, and take up thy couch, and
25 go unto thy house. And immediately he
rose up before them, and took up that
whereon he lay, and departed to his
26 house, glorifying God. And amazement
took hold on all, and they glorified God;
and they were filled with fear, saying, We
have seen strange things to-day.

Having completed His preaching Mission in the Galilean synagogues, Jesus returns to Capernaum some days later. It is at once reported that He is ' at home ' (Mk. only). Crowds assemble at the house so that it is impossible even to get to the door. Jesus begins again to preach the ' Word ' to them. While He is doing so, four men bring a paralysed young man on a stretcher or sleeping-rug. They cannot reach Jesus because of the crowd, so they go upstairs and, removing some part of the roof, lower the paralytic down into the presence of Jesus.

What the bearers did to the roof is not easily understood and so Mt. omits it altogether. Lk. says they went up on to the flat roof of the house and actually removed the tiles and lowered the man on a little couch (Mt. says a bed) down to the presence of Jesus. It seems impossible to think that the tiles of the roof could have been removed without great inconvenience and danger to those below. Mk. says: ' they uncovered the roof and when they had broken through lowered the invalid.'

This incident is related, not simply to stress the faith of the bearers, but possibly because the house was Peter's, who was naturally interested in what was done to it on this occasion.

The paralytic believed that his paralysis was due to his sins. Disease was generally recognised among the Jews at this time as being God's punishment for sin. In the Fourth Gospel, the Jews ask of a blind man, ' Did this man sin or his parents that he was born blind? ' Jesus replies: ' Neither did this man sin, nor his parents [that he was born blind].' Jesus, it would seem, in contrast to the prevailing opinion, did not regard disease as necessarily the result of sin. So also in the case of the paralytic at Capernaum. He says to the young man in a tone of kindness and conviction: ' Child, thy sins are forgiven thee.'

This declaration is intended to awaken the spirit of hope and faith in the invalid, which the sense of unforgiven sin inhibited. If God has forgiven him his sins, then there is no reason why his paralysis, which he regarded as the Divine punishment of his sins, should not also be removed. Some scribes who were present (probably with the purpose of making an official investigation of this new religious movement), as Mk. alone relates, ' were seated ' as became persons of their importance, although all the rest (with the exception of the paralytic) were standing. The scribes resented Jesus speaking in this way, but they kept silent. Jesus, however, as psychically sensitive to criticism and opposition as He was to trust and loyalty, challenges their hostile attitude with the words: 'Is it easier to say, thy sins are forgiven thee or to say, arise and walk?' Then turning to the paralytic He says: 'Arise, take up thy bed and be off to thy home.' And the paralytic rose immediately, took up his bed and went out in the presence of them all. General astonishment ensued.

Many critics have regarded the words in Mk. 2^{10} ('In order that ye may know that the Son of Man has authority to forgive sins upon earth, He says to the paralytic, I say to thee') as an interpolation (by way of explanation) into the original narrative.

It is said at this time, in Judaism, only a priest could officially pronounce the Divine forgiveness of sin. Of course a prophet could have done so, as did the prophet Nathan in the case of David, but no prophets were believed to be in existence at this time. For Jesus to do so seemed to the scribes to be arrogant presumption. The views of Jesus both about sin and the condition of its forgiveness were not those of His orthodox contemporaries, as we shall show later. It should be noted here, however, that Jesus Himself did not profess to forgive sins. He did not use to the paralytic the mediæval form of absolution, 'I absolve thee.' What He did was to declare the Divine forgiveness in this case, Thy sins are forgiven thee. If the doubtful words in *v.* 10 are really His, then He uses here for the first time in Mk.'s narrative the term 'Son of Man,' and declares that His action, in pronouncing the Divine forgiveness, proves that the 'Son of Man' has authority on earth to forgive sins.

Son of Man

But much depends upon what, if He used it of Himself on this occasion, Jesus meant by the phrase 'Son of Man.' The term is most ambiguous and is used in various senses in Jewish literature.

(1) In the Psalms it is used of man generally; especially man as he reflects the Divine glory of his Creator and exercises a Divine authority over terrestrial creatures.

> What is man, that thou art mindful of him?
>   And the son of man, that thou visitest him?
> For thou hast made him but little lower than God (Elohim),
>   And crownest him with glory and honour.
> Thou madest him to have dominion over the works of thy hands;
>   Thou hast put all things under his feet:
> All sheep and oxen,
>   Yea, and the beasts of the field; (Ps. 8^{4-7}).

(2) In the Book of Ezekiel it is also used of man generally; but man in his frailty and impermanency, in contrast to the power and eternity of God.

'Stand on thy feet, O son of man, and hear what I shall say unto thee' (Ezek. 2^{1}).

(3) It is used in the Book of Daniel (probably the earliest, and certainly the most important, of the Jewish canonical apocalypses) as the name for the kingdom of the saints of the Most High. In Daniel the great world empires of Assyria, Babylonia, Persia, Greece, are represented by beasts which come up out of the sea; but the Divine Kingdom which is to succeed them all on earth is represented by a Son of Man coming down from God out of Heaven. In other words, the brute empires are to be succeeded by one as far superior to them as man is to the brutes. In this sense, the term Son of Man in Daniel becomes the equivalent of the Kingdom of the Heavens, or the Kingdom of God in the Gospels.

(4) 'Son of Man' is used in the greatest of the extra-canonical apocalypses, the Book of *Enoch* (in that portion known as the *Similitudes of Enoch* probably composed in the century before Christ was born) to describe a pre-existent spiritual being who dwells in heaven with the Ancient of Days, and is about to be revealed upon earth. In other words, in the Book of *Enoch* the Son of Man is the title of the pre-existent, personal, Divine Messiah.

Many critics to-day assume that when Jesus used the phrase Son of Man of Himself in the Gospels He used it in the fourth or Enochic sense.

It is not, however, certain that this is the case. The term Son of Man occurs in all four Gospels, altogether some eighty times. In some cases the term is not used of Jesus Himself, but simply of mankind, as, for instance, in the passage peculiar to Mark:

'The Sabbath was made for man, not man for the Sabbath, therefore the Son of Man is Lord of the Sabbath day.'

But in other cases it is definitely used of Himself by the Lord. This is certainly so in the second half of Mark's Gospel beginning with Peter's confession of Him as the Christ at Cæsarea Philippi (Mk. 8^{27ff}). Where it occurs earlier in Mk.'s Gospel it is not clearly applied by Jesus to Himself.

There are many Messianic titles used of Jesus in the Synoptic Gospels, e.g. The Messiah or Christ (i.e. the Anointed One), the Son of God, the Coming One, the Beloved, the Elect One, the Holy One of God, the Son of David: not one of these Synoptic Messianic titles is applied by Jesus to Himself. The title 'Son of Man' alone has His authority.

For the Synoptists and the primitive Jewish Christians, it certainly had the significance which it possesses in the *Similitudes of Enoch*, where the Son of Man is pre-eminently the Judge of mankind, coming on the clouds of Heaven to bring in the end of the age. But had it this significance for Jesus Himself?

If we answer Yes, as many critics do, then not only is the view which Jesus takes of His Messianic office apocalyptic, but His conception of the Kingdom is also apocalyptic. But there is much to indicate in the Gospels, notwithstanding the prevailing tendency to interpret the teaching of Jesus apocalyptically, that His conception of the Kingdom was not primarily apocalyptic. So there is good reason to believe that His conception of His Messiahship was not identical with that of the Son of Man of the *Similitudes of Enoch*.

Jesus filled the phrase 'Kingdom of God' with a new content which had likenesses to, but also differences from, current beliefs. So also it seems probable that He gave an original meaning to the title 'Son of Man.' The term might mean anything in current usage, ranging from an ordinary human being to the pre-existent, celestial Messiah. The account of the Temptation indicates how widely the ideal of the Messianic office, which Jesus accepted for Himself, differed from contemporary ideals. Hence it is probable, nay certain, that in describing Himself as 'Son of Man,' if He did so, He is using this title to reflect His own original and unique conception of Himself as Messiah. (But see Dr. Manson's profound and original interpretation of the term 'Son of Man' in his exposition of the teaching of Jesus in this work.)

THE CALL OF LEVI (OR MATTHEW) THE TAX-COLLECTOR

MK. 2^{13-17}

2 13 And he went forth again by the sea
side; and all the multitude resorted unto
14 him, and he taught them. And as he
passed by, he saw Levi the *son* of Alphæus
sitting at the place of toll, and he saith
unto him, Follow me. And he arose and
15 followed him. And it came to pass, that
he was sitting at meat in his house, and
many publicans and sinners sat down with
Jesus and his disciples: for there were
16 many, and they followed him. And the
scribes of the Pharisees, when they saw
that he was eating with the sinners and
publicans, said unto his disciples, He
eateth and drinketh with publicans and
17 sinners. And when Jesus heard it, he
saith unto them, They that are whole have
no need of a physician, but they that are
sick: I came not to call the righteous, but
sinners.

MT. 9^{9-13}

9 9 And as Jesus passed by from thence, he
saw a man, called Matthew, sitting at the
place of toll: and he saith unto him,
Follow me. And he arose, and followed
him.
10 And it came to pass, as he sat at meat
in the house, behold, many publicans and
sinners came and sat down with Jesus and
11 his disciples. And when the Pharisees
saw it, they said unto his disciples, Why
eateth your Master with the publicans and
12 sinners? But when he heard it, he said,
They that are whole have no need of a
13 physician, but they that are sick. But go
ye and learn what *this* meaneth, I desire
mercy, and not sacrifice: for I came not
to call the righteous, but sinners.

LK. 5^{27-32}

5 27 And after these things he went forth,
and beheld a publican, named Levi,
sitting at the place of toll, and said unto
28 him, Follow me. And he forsook all, and
29 rose up and followed him. And Levi
made him a great feast in his house: and
there was a great multitude of publicans
and of others that were sitting at meat
30 with them. And the Pharisees and their
scribes murmured against his disciples
saying, Why do ye eat and drink with the
31 publicans and sinners? And Jesus answering said unto them, They that are whole
have no need of a physician; but they
32 that are sick. I am not come to call the
righteous but sinners to repentance.

Jesus next calls Levi, the tax-collector, to be His disciple (Mt. calls him Matthew). As Levi's receipt of custom was by the sea, possibly he collected dues from the fishermen, and so was well known to them. After Levi's call, when Jesus with His disciples was reclining at a meal, it would seem to have been in his house. From the accounts of Mk. and Mt. the meal would seem to be in Peter's house, but in the account in Lk. it is plainly Matthew's own house in which he gives a great reception not only to Jesus and His disciples but to many tax-gatherers and others who were generally regarded as being outside the pale of religious respectability. The word 'sinner' may mean a prostitute, but it is more likely to mean here disreputable in the sense of not observing all those religious practices which strict Jews regarded as essential.

Judaism at this time was, as a whole, fanatically religious, and its standards of judgement were strictly legalist. It was split up into a number of religious organisations, but outside all these organisations was a substratum of careless, ignorant, non-practising Jews: often contemptuously called by the religious leaders—' the people of the earth.' In the Gospels it is these probably who are meant by the term ' sinners.' Respectable Jews avoided them as ' unclean,' just as no Brahmin in India to-day would risk his caste by associating with ' untouchables.' Jesus caused scandal by associating with them freely.

When the scribes of the Pharisees (cf. Acts 23^{9}), that is to say, the trained disputants of the Pharisaic party who were always ready to defend or advance its cause by attacking its opponents, noted this free conduct of Jesus, they complained to His disciples. Jesus replied to their criticism:

' They that are in good [strong] health have no need of a physician, but they that are sick: I came not to call [invite] righteous men but sinners.'

(Luke, the physician, alters the word ' strong ' in Mk.: and Mt. into ' healthy.' Strong men might need a physician, but not healthy men. Lk. also by adding the words ' unto repentance ' makes it clear that Jesus came to invite sinners, not to social enjoyment, but to a new life.)

Mt. makes Jesus cite, in condemning the exclusiveness of the Pharisees, the words of the prophet Hosea in which the prophet declares:

' That what God desires from Israel is not religious offerings or sacrifices but kindness.' (Mt. 9^{13}, cited from Hos. 6^{6}; cf. Mt. 23^{23}.)

DISPUTE ABOUT FASTING

MK. 2^{18-22}

2 18 And John's disciples and the Pharisees
were fasting: and they come and say unto
him, Why do John's disciples and the
disciples of the Pharisees fast, but thy dis-
19 ciples fast not? And Jesus said unto
them, Can the sons of the bride-chamber
fast, while the bridegroom is with them?
as long as they have the bridegroom with
20 them, they cannot fast. But the days will
come, when the bridegroom shall be taken
away from them, and then will they fast in
21 that day. No man seweth a piece of
undressed cloth on an old garment: else
that which should fill it up taketh from it,
the new from the old, and a worse rent is
22 made. And no man putteth new wine
into old wine-skins: else the wine will
burst the skins, and the wine perisheth,
and the skins: but *they put* new wine into
fresh wine-skins.

MT. 9^{14-17}

9 14 Then come to him the disciples of John,
saying, Why do we and the Pharisees fast
15 oft, but thy disciples fast not? And Jesus
said unto them, Can the sons of the bride-
chamber mourn, as long as the bridegroom
is with them? but the days will come,
when the bridegroom shall be taken away
16 from them, and then will they fast. And
no man putteth a piece of undressed cloth
upon an old garment; for that which
should fill it up taketh from the garment,
17 and a worse rent is made. Neither do
men put new wine into old wine-skins: else
the skins burst, and the wine is spilled,
and the skins perish: but they put new
wine into fresh wine-skins, and both are
preserved.

LK. 5^{33-39}

5 33 And they said unto him, The disciples
of John fast often, and make supplications;
likewise also the *disciples* of the Pharisees;
34 but thine eat and drink. And Jesus said
unto them, Can ye make the sons of the
bride-chamber fast, while the bridegroom
35 is with them? But the days will come;
and when the bridegroom shall be taken
away from them, then will they fast in
36 those days. And he spake also a parable
unto them: No man rendeth a piece from
a new garment and putteth it upon an old
garment; else he will rend the new, and
also the piece from the new will not agree
37 with the old. And no man putteth new
wine into old wine-skins; else the new
wine will burst the skins, and itself will be
38 spilled, and the skins will perish. But
new wine must be put into fresh wine-
39 skins. And no man having drunk old
wine desireth new: for he saith The old
is good.

So far the various incidents related by Mk. beginning with the appearance of Jesus on the shore of the Lake of Galilee are closely connected and are given in their correct chronological order. It is important to stress this because from the days of Papias (in the early second century) Mark has not been given credit for observing in his narrative the right order of events, although a high valuation has been put upon the accuracy with which he describes the events themselves.

We believe it is possible to show in almost every case that where the order of Mt., Lk., and Jn. differs from that of Mk., the implicit probabilities are in favour of Mk.'s order being right.

Mk. now seeks to present to his readers a series of incidents, beginning with the association of Jesus with the disreputable classes, which bring Jesus into conflict with the religious leaders in Galilee.

The second of these incidents is connected with fasting. Mk. relates that while the disciples of John and the Pharisees were actually engaged in observing a fast, probably one of the prescribed public fasts of Judaism, they noticed that the disciples of Jesus were neglecting it.

Their subsequent complaint to Him indicates that this failure to fast is not due to negligence, but is deliberate.

The Messianic Mission of Jesus, with its Gospel of freedom and joyousness, finds no place for institutional fasting. No one can fast at a wedding. Jesus Himself is the Bridegroom: His disciples, the Bridegroom's attendants, while the wedding festivities are in progress, should enjoy themselves. He adds with prophetic foresight that when He is no longer with them they shall fast. This is not a command but a prediction. Possibly this is a ' prediction after the event ' and originated with the early Church and reflects its practice.

Two metaphors follow which definitely declare that Jesus cannot make the practice of fasting a part of His Gospel. Fasting, as He sees it, is not going to meet human moral and spiritual needs. Fasting as a religious institution, if insisted on, will not improve the situation but make it worse. It would be like patching an old cloak with a piece of new cloth—the cloth so new that it had not even been shrunken. As a result, the first time the cloak gets wet the patch shrinks and tears away from the cloak and the rent is made worse.

Or it is like putting new wine in a state of violent fermentation into hard and dry old wine skins which are unable to expand and in consequence are burst.

Jesus indicates here His conviction that His Gospel cannot be contained within the limits of Jewish legalism. St. Paul saw this clearly; but Jesus saw it first; and St. Paul recognised that He had done so when he writes to the Galatians: 'With freedom did Christ set us free' (5^1).

Jesus does not forbid fasting, but He definitely refuses to authorise it. He did object to fasting when it was practised ostentatiously, but men, if they would, might fast in secret. His religious contemporaries attached the highest importance to fasting and seem to have placed it on the same level as prayer and almsgiving. Jesus did not. In the saying attributed to Him: 'This kind goeth not forth but by prayer and fasting': the words 'and fasting' are not His, as textual criticism shows, but a later Christian gloss.

We have no account of Jesus observing a statutory fast, although no doubt He often went hungry, e.g. in the wilderness. He said of Himself on one occasion: 'The Son of Man came eating and drinking.' Perhaps with Zoroaster He was convinced that:

'He must eat who would do the heavy work of holiness.'

What is perfectly clear is, that Jesus found no place for fasting as an institution, in His Gospel.

Luke, the artist, adds an additional objection to patching an old cloak with a piece of new cloth. It is grotesque: it creates a disharmony. He also adds a delightful explanation of why Jewish legalists cannot be expected to like the Gospel of Jesus all at once. He makes Jesus say:

'That no man having drunk old wine immediately calls for new, for he says the old is mellow [better].' (Lk. 5^{39}.)

TWO DISPUTES ABOUT SABBATH KEEPING

MK. 2^{23}–3^6

2 23 And it came to pass, that he was going
on the sabbath day through the cornfields;
and his disciples began, as they went, to
24 pluck the ears of corn. And the Pharisees
said unto him, Behold, why do they on
the sabbath day that which is not lawful?
25 And he said unto them, Did ye never read
what David did, when he had need, and
was an hungred, he, and they that were
26 with him? How he entered into the house
of God when Abiathar was high priest,
and did eat the shewbread, which it is not
lawful to eat save for the priests, and gave
27 also to them that were with him? And he
said unto them, The sabbath was made for
28 man, and not man for the sabbath: so that
the Son of man is lord even of the sabbath.

3 1 And he entered again into the synagogue; and there was a man there which
2 had his hand withered. And they watched
him, whether he would heal him on the
sabbath day; that they might accuse him.

MT. 12^{1-14}

12 1 At that season Jesus went on the
sabbath day through the cornfields; and
his disciples were an hungred, and began
2 to pluck ears of corn, and to eat. But
the Pharisees, when they saw it, said unto
him, Behold, thy disciples do that which
it is not lawful to do upon the sabbath.
3 But he said unto them, Have ye not read
what David did, when he was an
hungred, and they that were with him;
4 how he entered into the house of God,
and did eat the shewbread, which it was
not lawful for him to eat, neither for them
that were with him, but only for the
5 priests? Or have ye not read in the law,
how that on the sabbath day the priests
in the temple profane the sabbath, and
6 are guiltless? But I say unto you, that
7 one greater than the temple is here. But
if ye had known what this meaneth, I
desire mercy, and not sacrifice, ye would
8 not have condemned the guiltless. For
the Son of man is lord of the sabbath.

3 And he saith unto the man that had his
4 hand withered, Stand forth. And he
saith unto them, Is it lawful on the
sabbath day to do good, or to do harm?
to save a life, or to kill? But they held
5 their peace. And when he had looked
round about on them with anger, being
grieved at the hardening of their heart, he
saith unto the man, Stretch forth thy
hand. And he stretched it forth: and his
6 hand was restored. And the Pharisees
went out, and straightway with the
Herodians took counsel against him, how
they might destroy him.

9 And he departed thence, and went into
10 their synagogue: and behold, a man having
a withered hand. And they asked him,
saying, Is it lawful to heal on the sabbath
11 day? that they might accuse him. And
he said unto them, What man shall there
be of you, that shall have one sheep, and
if this fall into a pit on the sabbath day,
will he not lay hold on it, and lift it out?
12 How much then is a man of more value
than a sheep! Wherefore it is lawful to
13 do good on the sabbath day. Then saith
he to the man, Stretch forth thy hand.
And he stretched it forth; and it was
14 restored whole, as the other. But the
Pharisees went out, and took counsel
against him, how they might destroy him.

LK. 6^{1-11}

6 1 Now it came to pass on a sabbath, that
he was going through the cornfields; and
his disciples plucked the ears of corn, and
2 did eat, rubbing them in their hands. But
certain of the Pharisees said, Why do ye
that which it is not lawful to do on the
3 sabbath day? And Jesus answering them
said, Have ye not read even this, what
David did, when he was an hungred, he,
4 and they that were with him; how he
entered into the house of God, and did
take and eat the shewbread, and gave also
to them that were with him; which it is
not lawful to eat save for the priests alone?
5 And he said unto them, The Son of man
is lord of the sabbath.
6 And it came to pass on another sabbath,
that he entered into the synagogue and
taught: and there was a man there, and
7 his right hand was withered. And the
scribes and the Pharisees watched him,
whether he would heal on the sabbath;
that they might find how to accuse him.
8 But he knew their thoughts; and he said to
the man that had his hand withered, Rise
up, and stand forth in the midst. And he
9 arose and stood forth. And Jesus said
unto them, I ask you, Is it lawful on the
sabbath to do good, or to do harm? to save
10 a life, or to destroy it? And he looked
round about on them all, and said unto
him, Stretch forth thy hand. And he did
11 *so*: and his hand was restored. But they
were filled with madness; and communed
one with another what they might do to
Jesus.

(Cf. Jn. 9—the man born blind, healed on Sabbath; and subsequent dispute.)

The great religious institution of Judaism was the Sabbath. The Old Testament legislation, particularly that of the priestly code, was strict in demanding its observance, but this strictness had been enormously increased by a great number of sub-regulations formulated by Jewish scribes. These regulations were not only meticulous and irksome, but also, in many cases, casuistical. They were concerned for the most part with what constituted ' lawful ' activity and what ' unlawful ' activity on the Sabbath.

For instance, one might walk 2,000 cubits without being guilty of Sabbath breaking, but to walk farther was to break the Sabbath.

The disciples of Jesus being hungry pluck ears of corn on the Sabbath day. The scribes decided this was unlawful as a form of harvest labour, and according to Lk. the disciples still further transgressed by rubbing the ears in their hands in order to separate the grain from the husk! This was to perform the actions of a mill, and a mill might not be used on the Sabbath day!

The Pharisees express surprise to Jesus at His permitting such law-breaking by His disciples. Jesus replies, ' Their hunger renders their action lawful,' and

He appeals to the case of the High Priest, Abimelech or Ahimelech (wrongly given in the text of Mk. as Abiathar), as having permitted David and his attendant warriors in their need to eat the shewbread which only the priests were normally permitted to eat after it had been removed from the table of shewbread in the tabernacle. The claims of human need have greater authority than ritual regulations.

The Sabbath, Jesus asserts, was instituted to serve man's welfare: not man created to be the Sabbath slave. All therefore that is needful for man's welfare may be lawfully done on the Sabbath day. There seems to have been in existence at this time a Jewish aphorism:

'The Sabbath is delivered unto you, ye are not delivered unto the Sabbath,'

but whether this Jewish saying is as early as the ministry of Jesus is a matter of doubt.

However, to judge from what we know of contemporary Jewish practice and scribal regulations, it had no effect in delivering men from sabbatical tyranny. The golden sentence, 'the Sabbath was made for man, not man for the Sabbath,' is not in Mt. nor Lk.

In Mk. the words 'therefore the Son of Man is Lord even of the Sabbath' indicate that Jesus is asserting, not the Messiah's, but man's authority over the Sabbath.

Mt. and Lk. apparently here take the term 'Son of Man' as a Messianic title, and so express the claim of Jesus as Messiah to regulate Sabbath observance. This is a later development.

Mt. makes Jesus use another argument in justification of His disciples' Sabbath-breaking, namely, that the priests in the Temple on the Sabbath day are compelled by the necessities of their office to break their Sabbath rest and are yet accounted blameless.

The second Sabbath dispute results from Jesus healing a man with a paralysed hand in the synagogue on the Sabbath day. Mk. asserts that Jesus was being 'narrowly watched' on this occasion in order that He might be reported to the ecclesiastical authorities. He is aware of this and takes up the challenge in a spirit of righteous indignation, 'being grieved at their moral imperceptiveness' (the heart in these narratives is regarded not as the seat of emotion but of conscience).

The question which Jesus puts to his would-be accusers:

'Is it lawful on the Sabbath to act kindly or to act maliciously, to save a man's life or to kill him?'

is directed against the plotters who design if possible to secure the death of Jesus as a Sabbath breaker.

Under the Jewish law Sabbath-breaking was a capital offence. Mk. adds very significantly that the Pharisees obtained the support of the Herodians in their machinations against Jesus. Of the Herodians we know nothing. Mk. mentions them again in 12^{13}, where Mt. follows Mk. The Herodians are probably not a political party but simply the officials or *entourage* of Herod Antipas who at that time was Tetrarch of Galilee. He had already suppressed and executed John the Baptist—he might therefore be inclined to do the same by Jesus.

Lk., who seems to have had a unique source of information connected with Herod's Court, relates that at a later stage in the ministry of Jesus certain Pharisees announced to Jesus that Herod desired to kill Him and urged Him to fly the country: and that Jesus sent an insulting message to Herod by them:

'Go and tell that fox, Behold I cast out demons and perform cures to-day and to-morrow, and the third day I shall have finished.' (Lk. 13^{32}.)

Mk. 7^{24} narrates that Jesus had finally to seek refuge outside Herod's dominions.

It was this combination between the ecclesiastical and political authorities, originating in the Sabbath disputes, which wrecked the Messianic Mission in Galilee, and it is to Mark alone, voicing the contemporary knowledge of local conditions by Peter, that we owe this important information.

(Luke describes the opponents of Jesus on this occasion as 'filled with madness.' Lk. 6^{11}.)

THE POPULARITY OF JESUS

MK. 3^{7-12}

3 7 And Jesus with his disciples withdrew to
the sea: and a great multitude from Galilee
8 followed: and from Judæa, and from
Jerusalem, and from Idumæa, and beyond
Jordan, and about Tyre and Sidon, a great
multitude, hearing what great things he
9 did, came unto him. And he spake to his
disciples, that a little boat should wait on
him because of the crowd, lest they should
10 throng him: for he had healed many;
insomuch that as many as had plagues
pressed upon him that they might touch
11 him. And the unclean spirits, whensoever they beheld him, fell down before him,
and cried, saying, Thou art the Son of
12 God. And he charged them much that
they should not make him known.

MT. 12^{15-16}

12 15 And Jesus perceiving *it* withdrew from
thence: and many followed him; and
16 he healed them all, and charged them
that they should not make him known.

LK. 6^{17-19}

6 17 And he came down with them, and stood
on a level place, and a great multitude of
his disciples, and a great number of the
people from all Judæa and Jerusalem, and
the sea coast of Tyre and Sidon, which
came to hear him, and to be healed of
18 their diseases; and they that were troubled
19 with unclean spirits were healed. And all
the multitude sought to touch him: for
power came forth from him, and healed
them all.

The adversaries of Jesus who desired His suppression or destruction were faced with no easy task because of His immense popularity. Mk. asserts that a great multitude from Galilee, from Judæa, and from Jerusalem, and from Idumæa and beyond Jordan, and about Tyre and Sidon came to Him. (Idumæa is Edom, to the south-east of the Dead Sea: beyond Jordan is the district known as Peræa: Tyre and Sidon were on the Mediterranean coast, north of Palestine.)

The source of attraction was the reputation of Jesus as a healer. The pressure of the multitude was so great that Jesus hit upon a device by which He could secure some relief. He ordered His disciples to have a little boat in readiness on the beach, by which He was enabled to get away from the pressure of the crowd and possibly in some cases to teach them from it. Mk. alone records the use of this little boat on this occasion. We may assume that Peter was its owner and rowed it.

It was no doubt the same little boat which Jesus used later as a pulpit in His preaching on the shore of the lake, and there Lk. tells us that it was Peter's (Lk. 5^{3}).

THE APPOINTMENT OF THE TWELVE APOSTLES

MK. 3^{13-19}

3 13 And he goeth up into the mountain,
and calleth unto him whom he himself
14 would: and they went unto him. And he
appointed twelve, that they might be
with him, and that he might send them
15 forth to preach, and to have authority to
16 cast out devils: and Simon he surnamed
17 Peter; and James the *son* of Zebedee, and
John the brother of James; and them he
surnamed Boanerges, which is, Sons of
18 thunder: and Andrew, and Philip, and
Bartholomew, and Matthew, and Thomas,
and James the *son* of Alphæus, and
19 Thaddæus, and Simon the Cananæan, and
Judas Iscariot, which also betrayed him.

MT. 10^{1-4}

10 1 And he called unto him his twelve disciples, and gave them authority over unclean spirits, to cast them out, and to heal all manner of disease and all manner of sickness.
2 Now the names of the twelve apostles
are these: The first, Simon, who is called
Peter, and Andrew his brother; James
the *son* of Zebedee, and John his brother;
3 Philip, and Bartholomew; Thomas, and
Matthew the publican; James the *son* of
4 Alphæus, and Thaddæus; Simon the
Cananæan, and Judas Iscariot, who also
betrayed him.

LK. 6^{12-16}

6 12 And it came to pass in these days, that
he went out into the mountain to pray;
and he continued all night in prayer to
13 God. And when it was day, he called his
disciples: and he chose from them twelve,
14 whom also he named apostles; Simon,
whom he also named Peter, and Andrew
his brother, and James and John, and
15 Philip and Bartholomew, and Matthew
and Thomas, and James *the son* of Alphæus,
and Simon which was called the Zealot,
16 and Judas *the son* of James, and Judas
Iscariot, which was the traitor.

ACTS $1^{13b-26b}$

1 13 both Peter and John and James and
Andrew, Philip and Thomas, Bartholomew and Matthew, James *the son* of
Alphæus, and Simon the Zealot, and
14 Judas *the son* of James. These all with one
accord continued stedfastly in prayer,
with the women, and Mary the mother of
Jesus, and with his brethren.
15 And in these days Peter stood up in the
midst of the brethren, and said (and there
was a multitude of persons *gathered* together, about a hundred and twenty),
16 Brethren, it was needful that the scripture
should be fulfilled, which the Holy Ghost
spake before by the mouth of David concerning Judas, who was guide to them
17 that took Jesus. For he was numbered
among us, and received his portion in this
18 ministry. (Now this man obtained a field
with the reward of his iniquity; and falling
headlong, he burst asunder in the midst,
19 and all his bowels gushed out. And it
became known to all the dwellers at
Jerusalem; insomuch that in their language
that field was called Akeldama, that is,
20 The field of blood.) For it is written in
the book of Psalms,

> Let his habitation be made desolate,
> And let no man dwell therein;

and,

> His office let another take.

21 Of the men therefore which have companied with us all the time that the Lord
Jesus went in and went out among us,
22 beginning from the baptism of John, unto
the day that he was received up from us,
of these must one become a witness with
23 us of his resurrection. And they put
forward two, Joseph called Barsabbas,
who was surnamed Justus, and Matthias.
24 And they prayed, and said, Thou, Lord,
which knowest the hearts of all men, shew
of these two the one whom thou hast
25 chosen, to take the place in this ministry
and apostleship, from which Judas fell
away, that he might go to his own place.
26 And they gave lots for them; and the lot
fell upon Matthias; and he was numbered
with the eleven apostles.

Jesus called His first disciples (Peter, Andrew, James, John, and Levi) on the shores of the lake.

He now takes a further step in the organisation of His Messianic Mission.

He selects twelve whom He names Apostles (i.e. missionaries, those *sent*), in order, says Mark, ' that they might be with him,' and also in order that ' He might send them forth to proclaim the glad tidings.' Their being with Him is obviously in order that He, the *Pastor pastorum*, may instruct them in the Gospel of the Kingdom.

If the Gospel of the Kingdom consisted of the apocalyptic conception of the Kingdom and its mode of advent, there was little need for any instruction at all: for such knowledge appears to have been a commonplace in Judaism at this period. What, under the circumstances, could the proclamation of the Kingdom mean? The Kingdom, according to apocalyptic views, was to be inaugurated by the descent from Heaven of the pre-existent Son of Man. But inasmuch as Jesus believed that the Messiah was already in the midst of them, what form could the proclamation of the Kingdom take? The answer would appear to be that it certainly could not take the form of the proclamation of the Kingdom as an apocalyptic cataclysm.

Mk. narrates that Jesus chose the Twelve in the mountain, and in the presence of others from whom He selected them. He summoned to Him whomsoever He wished. There is something in the phrase which suggests the magnetic power of Jesus. He had but to speak the word at this time and none could resist His invitation. Whether ' the mountain ' here is simply used of the high land around the Lake, in contrast to the plain of Gennesaret in which Capernaum was situated, or whether it be some particular eminence, is not clear. Matthew's first great collection of the ' Sayings of Jesus ' is prefaced by the statement that ' He went up into the mountain ' (Mt. 5^1). It is the very same phrase as is used by St. Mark in 3^{13}.

There is, a few miles from the shores of the Lake, a notable mountain (the scene of the famous battle of Tiberias) called to-day Karnhattin (the Horns of Hattin) because of its two peaks. I found when I climbed it many years ago that it was an extinct volcano and the green bowl of its crater forms a natural amphitheatre. It seems quite possible that Jesus went up into this mountain for the purpose described. This eminence is sometimes spoken of as the Mount of the Beatitudes, but I am unable to find any references to it in modern commentaries.

The number 12 indicates that Jesus intended them to be the apostles for a national mission to his twelve-tribe nation. In that case, when Lk. relates that on another occasion Jesus sent out seventy disciples, it would symbolise a universal mission to all mankind; for according to current Jewish views there were seventy (or seventy-two) nations of the world.

The twelve Apostles fall into three groups of four.

(1) Peter, James, John, and Andrew. Simon, Jesus surnamed Peter, the rock-man. Mt. relates that this surnaming took place when Simon confessed Jesus to be the Christ at Cæsarea Philippi. (Thou art the rock-man and on this rock I will found my Church: Mt. 16^{18}.) James and John He surnamed Boanerges (scholars regard this term as corrupt). Mk. interprets it as ' sons of thunder.' Although Simon and the sons of Zebedee play a prominent part in the Gospel narrative, Andrew (except in the Fourth Gospel) is unnoticed.

(2) Philip, Bartholomew, Matthew, and Thomas form the second group. The Fourth Gospel relates that Philip came from Bethsaida (House of Fish), probably Bethsaida Julias, a little town about a mile from the northern shores of the Lake, said by Jn. to have been the original home of Peter and Andrew. Bartholomew, which means son (*bar*) of Tolmai, is an incomplete designation; cf. Bartimæus, whose full name was Timæus Bar Timæus, or Barabbas, whose full name was probably Jesus Bar Abbas. In consequence it has been assumed that the Bartholomew of the Synoptists is the same as Nathanael (Gift of God) of the Fourth Gospel whom Philip brings to Jesus. His full name in that case would be Nathanael Bar Tolmai, an 'Israelite indeed in whom is no guile.' (Jn. 1^{44-51}.)

Matthew is no doubt the same as Levi, the tax-gatherer, whose call has been related. Thomas means the twin. Hence he is called Thomas Didymus in the Fourth Gospel, Didymus being the Greek for twin. There has been much speculation as to who was his twin brother. In the Mesopotamian Church a legend grew up that he was the twin brother of Jesus. (See Burkitt, *Early Eastern Christianity*, p. 198.) As Peter became the patron saint of Latin Christianity, so Thomas became the patron saint of Oriental Christianity, which extended into India and China. The Fourth Gospel shows him to be a man of strong character, but the Synoptists are silent.

(3) The third group consists of James the son of Alphæus, also called James the Little, i.e. of small stature ; Thaddæus or Lebbæus (the man of heart or feeling), probably to be identified with Judas the (*son? brother?*) of James in Lk.'s apostolic lists (in the Third Gospel and Acts ; Lk. 6^{16}, Acts 1^{13}, but cf. Jude 1) ; Simon, the Zealot, not the Canaanite: the word *Kananaios*, a Zealot, got confused with *Kananites*, a Canaanite. The word *zelotes* (Greek) and *qan'an* (Aramaic) both mean hot and indicate the fervour of the apostle's political and religious fanaticism. Judas Iscariot 'who betrayed Him' comes last on the list. The meaning of Iscariot is doubtful. (*a*) Some have taken it to mean, man of Kerioth. In that case, Judas was probably the only Judæan or Southerner among the Twelve. (*b*) Others have taken Iscariot to mean a member of the Sicarii: the dagger men, the extreme left wing of the Zealots who actively promoted the policy of political assassination (particularly of their compatriots suspected of disloyalty) as the best way of overthrowing the Roman authority and bringing in the Messianic Kingdom. They stood for no half-measures. If Judas were one of them, it throws a strong light on his character. (*c*) Others regard it as a personal designation of hatred and contempt—'the assassin'—given by the primitive Christians to Judas because he betrayed Jesus.

THE MADNESS OF JESUS

MK. 3^{19b-21}

3 19^b-20 And he cometh into a house. And the multitude cometh together again, so that
21 they could not so much as eat bread. And when his friends heard it, they went out to lay hold on him: for they said, He is beside himself.

Mk. alone relates that at this time the relations of Jesus think Him mad and try to lay hold on Him. Early Christian scribes seem to have been much perturbed by this charge and so have attempted to re-write the statement: some making it say, not that Jesus Himself is mad, but that He is turning the multitude mad.

There is, however, no doubt that the charge of madness was made against Jesus by his ecclesiastical opponents : ' He hath a devil and is mad,' just as it was made against John the Baptist. It was a not uncommon charge against the prophets of the Old Testament—' Wherefore came this mad fellow to thee? ' is the question put to Jehu by his fellow-captains.

' *HE HATH BEELEZEBUB* '

MK. 3^{22-30}

3 22 And the scribes which came down from
Jerusalem said, He hath Beelzebub, and,
By the prince of the devils casteth he out
23 the devils. And he called them unto him,
and said unto them in parables, How can
24 Satan cast out Satan? And if a kingdom
be divided against itself, that kingdom
25 cannot stand. And if a house be divided
against itself, that house will not be able to
26 stand. And if Satan hath risen up against
himself, and is divided, he cannot stand,
27 but hath an end. But no one can enter
into the house of the strong *man*, and spoil
his goods, except he first bind the strong
man; and then he will spoil his house.
28 Verily I say unto you, All their sins shall
be forgiven unto the sons of men, and their
blasphemies wherewith soever they shall
29 blaspheme: but whosoever shall blaspheme
against the Holy Spirit hath never
forgiveness, but is guilty of an eternal
30 sin: because they said, He hath an
unclean spirit.

MT. 9^{32-34}, 12^{22-32}

9 32 And as they went forth, behold, there
was brought to him a dumb man pos-
33 sessed with a devil. And when the devil
was cast out, the dumb man spake: and
the multitudes marvelled, saying, It was
34 never so seen in Israel. But the Pharisees
said, By the prince of the devils
casteth he out devils.

12 22 Then was brought unto him one possessed with a devil, blind and dumb: and
he healed him, insomuch that the dumb
23 man spake and saw. And all the multitudes were amazed, and said, Is this the
24 son of David? But when the Pharisees
heard it, they said, This man doth not
cast out devils, but by Beelzebub the
25 prince of the devils. And knowing their
thoughts he said unto them, Every kingdom divided against itself is brought to
desolation; and every city or house
26 divided against itself shall not stand: and
if Satan casteth out Satan, he is divided
against himself; how then shall his king-
27 dom stand? And if I by Beelzebub cast
out devils, by whom do your sons cast
them out? therefore shall they be your
28 judges. But if I by the Spirit of God
cast out devils, then is the kingdom of
29 God come upon you. Or how can one
enter into the house of the strong *man*,
and spoil his goods, except he first bind
the strong *man*? and then he will spoil his
30 house. He that is not with me is against
me; and he that gathereth not with me
31 scattereth. Therefore I say unto you,
Every sin and blasphemy shall be forgiven unto men; but the blasphemy
against the Spirit shall not be forgiven.
32 And whosoever shall speak a word
against the Son of man, it shall be forgiven him; but whosoever shall speak
against the Holy Spirit, it shall not be
forgiven him, neither in this world, nor
in that which is to come.

LK. 11^{14-23}, 12^{10}

11 14 And he was casting out a devil *which*
was dumb. And it came to pass, when
the devil was gone out, the dumb man
spake; and the multitudes marvelled.
15 But some of them said, By Beelzebub the
prince of the devils casteth he out devils.
16 And others, tempting *him*, sought of him
17 a sign from heaven. But he, knowing
their thoughts, said unto them, Every
kingdom divided against itself is brought
to desolation; and a house *divided* against
18 a house falleth. And if Satan also is
divided against himself, how shall his
kingdom stand? because ye say that I
19 cast out devils by Beelzebub. And if I
by Beelzebub cast out devils, by whom
do your sons cast them out? therefore
20 shall they be your judges. But if I by
the finger of God cast out devils, then is
the kingdom of God come upon you.
21 When the strong *man* fully armed
guardeth his own court, his goods are in
22 peace: but when a stronger than he shall
come upon him, and overcome him, he
taketh from him his whole armour
wherein he trusted, and divideth his
23 spoils. He that is not with me is
against me; and he that gathereth not
with me scattereth.

12 10 And every one who shall speak a word
against the Son of man, it shall be forgiven him: but unto him that blasphemeth against the Holy Spirit it shall
not be forgiven.

The charge, however, grows more precise. Mt. 12^{22-32} connects it with Jesus' healing a blind and dumb man. The ecclesiastical inquisitors sent from Jerusalem assert that Jesus exorcises demons by means of Beelzebub or Beelzebul—the Prince of Demons.

Beelzebub was the Philistine God of Ekron. The name probably meant 'Lord of the Heavenly Dwelling.' But by a slight alteration the Jews gave it the offensive sense of 'God of Dung' or 'God of Flies.' When the Jews became Monotheists, they degraded the gods of the surrounding nations to the level of demons. The God of Ekron whom even Ahaziah, King of Israel, consulted (2 Kings 1^2) must have been regarded as a very potent person to be given the rank of the Prince of Demons by the Jews.

In exorcising demons it was necessary to adjure them by one greater than themselves, particularly by the great name of God, to come forth from their victim. It is of interest to observe that Jesus appears never to have exorcised in the name of another, but speaks directly, 'I charge thee.' In this He would appear to have differed from contemporary exorcists. This difference is explained as being due to the fact that He Himself is the Prince of Demons and so He has but to speak to them and they obey—'Satan casts out Satan.'

Jesus deeply resented this charge, for He believed that He cast out demons by the Holy Spirit. Such a charge indicates the absolute moral perversion of those who make it: 'they put evil for good and good for evil, darkness for light and light for darkness.' (Cf. Milton's Satan in *Paradise Lost*: 'Evil, be thou my good.')

In so doing they sin against the Holy Spirit and are guilty of an action which can never receive the Divine forgiveness.

Jesus satirically remarks that if Satan is casting out Satan he is hastening his own destruction and so preparing for the advance of the Kingdom of God. Jesus, however, suggests another solution. No one can rob a strong man's house except he first bind the strong man. Hence Jesus, by robbing Satan of his wretched human victims, is providing proof, if his adversaries could but see it, of the presence of the Kingdom of God in their midst.

These words of Jesus about sin against the Holy Spirit have deeply troubled many sensitive consciences needlessly. These words are not directed against sins of unbelief or sins of sensuality but against that malignant moral blindness which deliberately affirms that that which is good is evil. Only those can be forgiven who are forgivable. The moral state of the man who cannot distinguish good from evil, or deliberately reverses them, is hopeless. In the original text of Mk., Jesus says that such an one is guilty of an eternal sin or is liable to an eternal judgement. The former reading is the better attested. A spiritual sin is not a sin of the lower nature but a sin of the higher nature; the perversion or misuse of the rational, moral, and spiritual nature. This, for Jesus, is the most deadly form of sin. In this valuation Jesus differs as much from His contemporaries as from His successors, who have ever been prone to treat the sins of the lower nature with great severity and the sins of the higher nature far too lightly or even to ignore them altogether.

The Beelzebub charge besides occurring in Mk. is also present in Q. (Mt. 12^{25-28}; Lk. 11^{17-20}.)

'WHO IS MY MOTHER AND WHO ARE MY BROTHERS?'

MK. 3^{31-35}

3 31 And there come his mother and his
brethren; and, standing without, they sent
32 unto him, calling him. And a multitude
was sitting about him; and they say unto
him, Behold, thy mother and thy brethren
33 without seek for thee. And he answereth
them, and saith, Who is my mother and
34 my brethren? And looking round on
them which sat round about him, he saith,
35 Behold, my mother and my brethren! For
whosoever shall do the will of God, the
same is my brother, and sister, and
mother.

MT. 12^{46-50}

12 46 While he was yet speaking to the
multitudes, behold, his mother and his
brethren stood without, seeking to speak
47 to him. And one said unto him, Behold,
thy mother and thy brethren stand
48 without, seeking to speak to thee. But
he answered and said unto him that told
him, Who is my mother? and who are
49 my brethren? And he stretched forth
his hand towards his disciples, and said,
Behold, my mother and my brethren!
50 For whosoever shall do the will of my
Father which is in heaven, he is my
brother, and sister, and mother.

LK. 8^{19-21}

8 19 And there came to him his mother and
brethren, and they could not come at him
20 for the crowd. And it was told him, Thy
mother and thy brethren stand without,
21 desiring to see thee. But he answered and
said unto them, My mother and my
brethren are these which hear the word of
God, and do it.

Jesus, seated in Oriental fashion on the ground, is engaged in teaching His disciples seated in a circle round Him. His mother and His brothers arrive outside the house, possibly with the intention of laying hold on Him as a lunatic, and call on Him to come out to them. He takes no notice until it is announced to Him that His mother and His brothers outside are seeking Him. He asks, Who is my mother and who are my brothers? and answers: Whosoever shall do God's will, the same is my brother and sister and mother.

By this speech Jesus refuses to recognise that His relations have any right to interfere with His Messianic Mission. He also declares that the supreme relationships are not physical but moral and spiritual: and loyalty to these relationships must come first in life.

JESUS BEGINS TO TEACH IN PARABLES

MK. 4^{1-25}

4 1 And again he began to teach by the sea
side. And there is gathered unto him a
very great multitude, so that he entered
into a boat, and sat in the sea; and all the
multitude were by the sea on the land.
2 And he taught them many things in
parables, and said unto them in his teach-
3 ing, Hearken: Behold, the sower went
4 forth to sow: and it came to pass, as he
sowed, some *seed* fell by the way side, and
5 the birds came and devoured it. And
other fell on the rocky *ground*, where it had
not much earth; and straightway it sprang
up, because it had no deepness of earth:
6 and when the sun was risen, it was
scorched; and because it had no root, it
7 withered away. And other fell among
the thorns, and the thorns grew up, and
8 choked it, and it yielded no fruit. And
others fell into the good ground, and
yielded fruit, growing up and increasing;
and brought forth, thirtyfold, and sixty-
9 fold, and a hundredfold. And he said,
Who hath ears to hear, let him hear.
10 And when he was alone, they that were
about him with the twelve asked of him
11 the parables. And he said unto them,
Unto you is given the mystery of the
kingdom of God: but unto them that are
without, all things are done in parables:
12 that seeing they may see, and not perceive; and hearing they may hear, and
not understand; lest haply they should
turn again, and it should be forgiven
13 them. And he saith unto them, Know ye
not this parable? and how shall ye know
14 all the parables? The sower soweth the
15 word. And these are they by the way
side, where the word is sown; and when
they have heard, straightway cometh
Satan, and taketh away the word which
16 hath been sown in them. And these in
like manner are they that are sown upon
the rocky *places*, who, when they have
heard the word, straightway receive it
17 with joy; and they have no root in themselves, but endure for a while; then, when
tribulation or persecution ariseth because
of the word, straightway they stumble.
18 And others are they that are sown among
the thorns; these are they that have heard
19 the word, and the cares of the world, and
the deceitfulness of riches, and the lusts of
other things entering in, choke the word,
20 and it becometh unfruitful. And those
are they that were sown upon the good

MT. 13^{1-23}

13 1 On that day went Jesus out of the
2 house, and sat by the sea side. And
there were gathered unto him great
multitudes, so that he entered into a
boat, and sat; and all the multitude stood
3 on the beach. And he spake to them
many things in parables, saying, Behold,
4 the sower went forth to sow; and as he
sowed, some *seeds* fell by the way side, and
5 the birds came and devoured them: and
others fell upon the rocky places, where
they had not much earth: and straightway they sprang up, because they had no
6 deepness of earth: and when the sun was
risen, they were scorched; and because
they had no root, they withered away.
7 And others fell upon the thorns; and the
8 thorns grew up, and choked them: and
others fell upon the good ground, and
yielded fruit, some a hundredfold, some
9 sixty, some thirty. He that hath ears,
let him hear.
10 And the disciples came, and said unto
him, Why speakest thou unto them in
11 parables? And he answered and said
unto them, Unto you it is given to know
the mysteries of the kingdom of heaven,
12 but to them it is not given. For whosoever hath, to him shall be given, and he
shall have abundance: but whosoever
hath not, from him shall be taken away
13 even that which he hath. Therefore
speak I to them in parables; because
seeing they see not, and hearing they hear
14 not, neither do they understand. And
unto them is fulfilled the prophecy of
Isaiah, which saith,
By hearing ye shall hear, and shall in
no wise understand;
And seeing ye shall see, and shall in
no wise perceive:
15 For this people's heart is waxed gross,
And their ears are dull of hearing,
And their eyes they have closed;
Lest haply they should perceive with
their eyes,
And hear with their ears,
And understand with their heart,
And should turn again,
And I should heal them.
16 But blessed are your eyes, for they see;
17 and your ears, for they hear. For verily
I say unto you, that many prophets and
righteous men desired to see the things
which ye see, and saw them not; and to
hear the things which ye hear, and heard

ground; such as hear the word, and accept
it, and bear fruit, thirtyfold, and sixtyfold,
and a hundredfold.
21 And he said unto them, Is the lamp
brought to be put under the bushel, or
under the bed, *and* not to be put on the
22 stand? For there is nothing hid, save
that it should be manifested; neither was
anything made secret, but that it should
23 come to light. If any man hath ears to
24 hear, let him hear. And he said unto
them, Take heed what ye hear: with what
measure ye mete it shall be measured unto
you: and more shall be given unto you.
25 For he that hath, to him shall be given:
and he that hath not, from him shall be
taken away even that which he hath.

18 them not. Hear then ye the parable of
19 the sower. When any one heareth the
word of the kingdom, and understandeth
it not, *then* cometh the evil *one*, and
snatcheth away that which hath been
sown in his heart. This is he that was
20 sown by the way side. And he that was
sown upon the rocky places, that is he
that heareth the word, and straightway
21 with joy receiveth it; yet hath he not root
in himself, but endureth for a while; and
when tribulation or persecution ariseth
because of the word, straightway he
22 stumbleth. And he that was sown
among the thorns, that is he that heareth
the word; and the care of the world, and
the deceitfulness of riches, choke the
23 word, and he becometh unfruitful. And
he that was sown upon the good ground,
that is he that heareth the word, and
understandeth it; who verily beareth
fruit, and bringeth forth, some a hundredfold, some sixty, some thirty.

LK. 8^{4-17}

8 4 And when a great multitude came together, and they of every city resorted
5 unto him, he spake by a parable: The
sower went forth to sow his seed: and as he
sowed, some fell by the way side; and it
was trodden under foot, and the birds of
6 the heaven devoured it. And other fell on
the rock; and as soon as it grew, it withered away, because it had no moisture.
7 And other fell amidst the thorns; and the
8 thorns grew with it, and choked it. And
other fell into the good ground, and grew,
and brought forth fruit a hundredfold.
As he said these things, he cried, He that
hath ears to hear, let him hear.
9 And his disciples asked him what this
10 parable might be. And he said, Unto you
it is given to know the mysteries of the
kingdom of God: but to the rest in
parables; that seeing they may not see,
and hearing they may not understand.
11 Now the parable is this: The seed is the
12 word of God. And those by the way side
are they that have heard; then cometh the
devil, and taketh away the word from
their heart, that they may not believe and
13 be saved. And those on the rock *are* they
which, when they have heard, receive the
word with joy; and these have no root,
which for a while believe, and in time of
14 temptation fall away. And that which
fell among the thorns, these are they that
have heard, and as they go on their way
they are choked with cares and riches and
pleasures of *this* life, and bring no fruit to
15 perfection. And that in the good ground,
these are such as in an honest and good
heart, having heard the word, hold it fast,
and bring forth fruit with patience.
16 And no man, when he hath lighted a
lamp, covereth it with a vessel or putteth
it under a bed; but putteth it on a stand,
that they which enter in may see the light.
17 For nothing is hid, that shall not be made
manifest; nor *anything* secret, that shall
not be known and come to light.

In Mk.'s Gospel the teaching of Jesus falls into four stages—(1) popular, (2) parabolic, (3) pastoral, and (4) Passion teaching. There is a fifth kind of teaching—polemical, directed by Jesus against His opponents, but this does not constitute a stage. It is absent in the earliest stage of His teaching and appears to grow in intensity as His Ministry approaches its conclusion. At this point Mk. ($4^{33, 34}$) notes that Jesus changes His style of teaching from popular to parabolic. The occasion on which He does so is a striking one. A great crowd has assembled to hear Him on the shore of the Lake. Jesus embarks in a boat, which He uses as a pulpit. He opens His discourse with the oft-repeated exhortation—'He that hath ears to hear, let him hear.'

The parable which He delivers is usually called 'The Sower,' but more accurately to be described as 'The Four Kinds of Soil.' It forms an appropriate introduction to His parabolic teaching, for it stresses the truth that the result of teaching must depend on the quality of the hearing. The criticism of the pulpit by the pew is a commonplace. Here we have criticism of the pew by the pulpit. The skill of the sower and the quality of the seed are unquestionable, yet the results of the sowing are strangely varied. This is accounted for by the quality of the soil—in other words, the moral and spiritual qualities of the different members in the audience. It is these which will determine the attention given to the teaching and the reception accorded to it and the practical and patient endeavour to carry it out.

Jesus, like the Rabbis, divides His hearers into four classes. (Compare Charles Taylor: *Sayings of the Jewish Fathers*, V, 18, 20, 21. There are four characters in scholars. Quick to hear and quick to forget, his gain is cancelled by his loss: slow to hear and slow to forget, his loss is cancelled by his gain: quick to hear and slow to forget, is wise: slow to hear and quick to forget, this is an evil lot. There are four characters in college-goers. He that goes and does not practise, the reward of going is in his hand: he that practises and does not go, the reward of practice is in his hand: he that goes and practises is pious: he that goes not and does not practise is wicked. There are four characters in those who sit under the wise: a sponge; a funnel; a strainer; and a bolt sieve. A sponge, which sucks up all; a funnel, which lets in here and lets out there; a strainer, which lets out the wine and keeps back the dregs; a bolt sieve, which lets out the pollard and keeps back the flour.) The first three classes produce no abiding moral and spiritual results in response to His teaching. The fourth class, which Jesus divides into three sub-classes, produces results in various degrees—some thirty, some sixty, some a hundred fold.

In the first of the three unproductive classes the seed falls upon a hard trodden road which runs through the field and it is immediately gobbled up by the birds. The hearers hear with the outward ear but no impression whatsoever is made by the teaching upon their rational, moral, and spiritual nature.

In the second of the three unproductive classes the seed falls upon a thin coating of soil spread over the underlying rock. Stimulated by the warmth and light of the sun's rays, the seed germinates more rapidly than if buried deeper, but since the soil in which it is sown is incapable of retaining moisture, the seed which sprouted so quickly soon withers up in the dry weather.

The hearers in this case respond eagerly to the new teaching but their emotion quickly disappears. They lack depth. The appeal affects their emotions but does not grip their conscience and reason. When persecution arises as a result of their new loyalty, they possess no staying power.

In the third of the three unproductive classes the seed falls on the rough ground at the edge of the field which has not been properly cleaned and prepared for it. When it springs up, the thorny weeds spring up with it. For a time it survives, a thin and sickly growth, but it produces no grain before it is choked by the thorns.

The hearers in this case respond to the new teaching. But it is only one of many interests in their busy lives and it soon proves not to be the most engrossing interest. Material needs and material cares, worldly pleasures and worldly occupations absorb in time all their attention and all their energy. The new life and its ideals and duties are neglected; moral and spiritual growth is checked; and as a consequence, nothing results.

In the fourth, and productive class, the seed falls on good soil, properly prepared for its reception.

The hearers in this case are deep and strong natures, possessed of good will. (Lk. describes them as possessed of a fair and good heart—a phrase reminiscent of ' the good man ' of the Greek philosophical schools.) Their response to the new teaching is permanent and productive. Each, according to his capacity, shows the influence of the Word in his character and conduct. As Lk. adds: ' He holds it fast and brings forth fruit with perseverance (Lk. 8^{15}). Mt. (13^{23}) stresses that it is a man's understanding of the Word, as well as his hearing of it, which makes it productive.

All three Gospels relate that this interpretation of the parable was delivered by Jesus to the disciples. Mk. adds, ' alone.' There are a number of cases in which the Gospels relate that Jesus gave certain teaching *only* to the disciples. It has been thought that this teaching, esoteric some would call it, does not possess the same authority as the public teaching of Jesus: that it is not really His, but is the creation of early Christian disciples which the primitive Christian Church believed to go back to Jesus Himself. It is of importance to note this because, although in the case of the interpretation of the parable of the four kinds of soil the interpretation would appear to reflect the mind of Jesus, there are other cases where this private or esoteric teaching would seem to contradict the true meaning of the parable it undertakes to interpret, e.g. the parable of the tares sown secretly; and in other cases it would seem to add to the teaching of Jesus what was not part of His original gospel and is possibly in conflict with it, e.g. the eschatological discourse in Mk. 13.

It is probable that from this time onward all systematic public teaching of Jesus, where not directly polemical, is parabolic. Mk. writes: ' With many such like parables He was speaking frequently the Word to them as they were able to hear it, and He made it a practice not to speak to them without a parable; but He interpreted all things to His disciples in secret. ($4^{33, 34}$.)

But why did Jesus change to Parabolic Teaching? (Mk. 4^{2}.)

Jesus had come to realise, possibly as the result of His immense popularity as a healer in comparison with His popularity as a prophetic preacher, which He regarded as His real mission, that His teaching was failing, in the case of the vast majority of His hearers, to have any abiding and effective influence. The direct and immediate salvation of His nation, as the result of His own single-handed efforts, He perceived to be outside the range of His accomplishment. He must have intermediaries. Hence His selection of apostles. He Himself can only henceforth draw into the body of His disciples elect souls who shall in their turn be the means of winning others. These will be won by His parabolic teaching. Their earnestness and sincerity will enable them to understand it, and its more profound aspects will become increasingly manifest to them in proportion to their loyalty and understanding.

The purpose, therefore, of His parabolic teaching is not secretive, as some might allege. Men do not bring a lamp to place it under a bed or a bushel measure, but where it can give light to those in the house. What He says to His disciples into their ear they shall in their turn proclaim to all men from the housetop.

In this connexion it is important to note that Jesus is recorded in the Synoptists to have cited a passage from Is. 6 which relates, not only the call of that prophet, but also the nature and effect of his mission. This passage proclaims for the first time what is known to Old Testament scholars as the ' Doctrine of the Remnant,' namely, that the salvation of the whole people is impossible. Even though they all hear the prophetic message, yet will they not be converted by it: only a remnant can be saved.

In ancient Israel no distinction was made between the effect of the Divine action and its intention. Every result in the sphere of human experience was the expression of the Divine Will. Hence if men were not saved it was argued that it was the express Will of God that they should not be saved. It is this conviction which is expressed in the citation from Is. 6^{9} (Septuagint). ' That seeing they may see, and not perceive: and hearing they may hear, and not understand: lest haply they should turn again, and it should be forgiven them.' (Mk. 4^{12}.) We may not assume that this was the view of Jesus. He plainly recognised the freedom of individuals to determine their fate by their own choice.

The passage cited from Isaiah here is only intended to indicate that Jesus perceived, not the failure of His mission, because there are indications elsewhere that He was convinced of its ultimate success, but that at this stage He recognised its limitation. Only a remnant could be saved. And there is reason to believe, as Dr. Manson has ably pointed out elsewhere, that the view of Jesus transcends that of the First Isaiah, who thinks only of the remnant as being saved for itself alone. Jesus in His vision of salvation passes over into the thought of the Second Isaiah, who thinks of the elect remnant as existing to save not itself but ultimately all the rest (' the many,' cf. Is. $53^{11, 12}$).

There was also an essentially moral purpose in the use of parabolic teaching by Jesus. It differentiated between the careless and the earnest hearer. He who listened as a seeker of the truth received the truth embodied in a tale. He who brought with him neither earnestness nor intelligence received nothing at all. Mk. cites in this connexion words of Jesus which Mt. and Lk. cite in another connexion and with another significance: ' With whatsoever measure ye measure it shall be measured to you . . . for to him that hath it shall be given, but from him that hath not shall be taken away even that which he hath."

It is difficult to express the full force of this epigram. It asserts that not only shall a man be repaid for the trouble he takes, but that his payment shall be in excess of what he gives—' and it shall be *added* unto you ' (Mk. 4^{24b}).

It is the quality of the hearing, therefore, which must determine the benefit of the teaching: Take heed *how* ye hear (Lk. 8^{18}). Mk.'s parallel is: Take heed *what* ye hear. This is due to a mistranslation by Mk. The same word in Aramaic may mean either how or what. Plainly in this saying of our Lord it means ' how.'

Jesus claims (Mk. 4^{11}) that the mystery of the Kingdom is being imparted in these parables to His disciples. Mt. and Lk. in their parallels have 'mysteries.' This is the only passage of our Lord's recorded teaching in which the word 'mystery' occurs. It no doubt means here the very essence of Divine truth: perhaps what the Psalmist means when he says: 'the Lord imparts his secret to the pious.'

THREE PARABLES OF THE KINGDOM'S GROWTH

(*a*) The Parable of the Seed Growing Automatically

MK. 4^{26-29}

4 26 And he said, So is the kingdom of God,
as if a man should cast seed upon the
27 earth; and should sleep and rise night and
day, and the seed should spring up and
28 grow, he knoweth not how. The earth
beareth fruit of herself; first the blade,
then the ear, then the full corn in the ear.
29 But when the fruit is ripe, straightway he
putteth forth the sickle, because the harvest
is come.

Mt. and Lk. have many parables which Mk. has not. Mk. has one parable which they have not. It is the parable of the seed which grew of itself *automatically* and no one knew the secret of its growth. 'That,' said Jesus, 'is the way the Kingdom advances.'

(*b*) The Parable of the Mustard Seed

MK. 4^{30-34}

4 30 And he said, How shall we liken the
kingdom of God? or in what parable shall
31 we set it forth? It is like a grain of
mustard seed, which, when it is sown upon
the earth, though it be less than all the
32 seeds that are upon the earth, yet when it
is sown, groweth up, and becometh greater
than all the herbs, and putteth out great
branches; so that the birds of the heaven
can lodge under the shadow thereof.
33 And with many such parables spake he
the word unto them, as they were able to
34 hear it: and without a parable spake he
not unto them: but privately to his own
disciples he expounded all things.

MT. $13^{31, 32, 34}$

13 31 Another parable set he before them,
saying, The kingdom of heaven is like
unto a grain of mustard seed, which a
32 man took, and sowed in his field: which
indeed is less than all seeds; but when it is
grown, it is greater than the herbs, and
becometh a tree, so that the birds of the
heaven come and lodge in the branches
thereof.
34 All these things spake Jesus in parables
unto the multitudes; and without a
parable spake he nothing unto them.

LK. $13^{18, 19}$

13 18 He said therefore, Unto what is the
kingdom of God like? and whereunto
19 shall I liken it? It is like unto a grain
of mustard seed, which a man took, and
cast into his own garden; and it grew,
and became a tree; and the birds of the
heaven lodged in the branches thereof.

Jesus compares the Kingdom to a grain of mustard seed. The mustard seed, said He, is the smallest of all the seeds which the farmer sows on his land—smaller than wheat and barley and rye—yet when it is full grown it exceeds in size all the cereals and vegetables; it becomes a veritable tree in which the birds build their nests. So it is with the Kingdom. To-day you see it the least of all religious movements but in the end it shall surpass them all. It is only Mk. who brings out the point; not that the mustard seed is the smallest of all seeds, which it is not, but that it is the smallest of all seeds which the Palestinian farmer sows. And no doubt farmers often speculated as to how it was that the smallest seed could produce the largest growth. Those who marked the small beginnings of the Kingdom might well wonder, in the future, by what power it had become so great.

(*c*) The Parable of the Leaven Hid in Three Measures of Meal

These seed parables which present the coming of the Kingdom as a growth, mysterious and inexplicable, are supplemented in Q (Mt. 13^{33}; Lk. 13^{21}) by the parable of the leaven hid in three measures of meal which permeated and leavened the whole ' sponge.'

This presentation of the coming of the Kingdom is not apocalyptic. It seems to present the coming of the Kingdom as a Divine influence, mysteriously and progressively extending itself in human society until mankind is finally conformed to the Divine ideal—first the blade, then the ear, then the full grain in the ear.

There is a quality of originality in this teaching of Jesus about the Kingdom which marks it as His. It is above the level of His contemporaries and His reporters.

THE STILLING OF THE STORM

MK. 4^{35-41}

4 35 And on that day, when even was come,
he saith unto them, Let us go over unto
36 the other side. And leaving the multitude, they take him with them, even as he
was, in the boat. And other boats were
37 with him. And there ariseth a great
storm of wind, and the waves beat into
the boat, insomuch that the boat was now
38 filling. And he himself was in the stern,
asleep on the cushion: and they awake
him, and say unto him, Master, carest
39 thou not that we perish? And he awoke,
and rebuked the wind, and said unto the
sea, Peace, be still. And the wind ceased,
40 and there was a great calm. And he said
unto them, Why are ye fearful? have ye
41 not yet faith? And they feared exceedingly, and said one to another, Who then
is this, that even the wind and the sea
obey him?

MT. $8^{18,\ 23-27}$

8 18 Now when Jesus saw great multitudes
about him, he gave commandment to
depart unto the other side.
23 And when he was entered into a boat,
24 his disciples followed him. And behold,
there arose a great tempest in the sea, insomuch that the boat was covered with the
25 waves: but he was asleep. And they came
to him, and awoke him, saying, Save,
26 Lord; we perish. And he saith unto
them, Why are ye fearful, O ye of little
faith? Then he arose, and rebuked the
winds and the sea; and there was a great
27 calm. And the men marvelled, saying,
What manner of man is this, that even the
winds and the sea obey him?

LK. 8^{22-25}

8 22 Now it came to pass on one of those
days, that he entered into a boat, himself
and his disciples; and he said unto them,
Let us go over unto the other side of the
23 lake: and they launched forth. But as
they sailed he fell asleep: and there came
down a storm of wind on the lake; and
they were filling *with water*, and were in
24 jeopardy. And they came to him, and
awoke him, saying, Master, master, we
perish. And he awoke, and rebuked the
wind and the raging of the water: and
they ceased, and there was a calm.
25 And he said unto them, Where is your
faith? And being afraid they marvelled,
saying one to another, Who then is this,
that he commandeth even the winds and
the water, and they obey him?

Mk. relates that on the evening of the day when Jesus delivered His parables from his boat-pulpit to the congregation standing on the shore, He concluded by saying to His disciples: ‘ Let us go across to the other side.’ Having dismissed the crowd without landing, they put off across the lake; other boats being with them. Mk. alone, giving us no doubt the reminiscences of St. Peter, preserves these details. Jesus, exhausted with His teaching, falls asleep in the stern of the boat on a ‘ pillow ’ (A.V.) or ‘ cushion ’ (R.V.). The word is peculiar to Mk.—another little Petrine reminiscence. Suddenly a storm arises. Storms on the Lake of Galilee can be as sudden and as violent as storms upon the lakes of Northern Italy, and they subside, in many cases, as suddenly as they arise.

The waves wash into the boat. The frightened disciples rudely awake Jesus with a stupid question: ‘ Carest Thou not that we perish? ’ He replies: ‘ Be quiet. Be muzzled.’ The storm ceased at that moment and He, addressing His amazed disciples, says: ‘ Why are ye cowards? Have ye not yet got faith? ’ (Lk. writes: Where is your faith? Mt.: Why are ye of little faith?) More frightened still by the calm than by the storm, they say to one another: ‘ What manner of man is this that even the wind and the sea submit to Him? ’

This incident is usually interpreted as a Nature miracle. That was the way in which Peter and his fellow-disciples interpreted it. Yet is it necessary to interpret it in this way?

The words which Jesus is recorded to have uttered on being awakened might well be addressed to the excited individual who awakened Him, for they are in the singular. (They are omitted by Mt. and Lk.) The curious phrase: ‘ Be muzzled,’ is recorded by Mk. as having been used by Jesus to the demoniac in the synagogue of Capernaum (Mk. 1^{25}). It can be properly addressed to a frantic and voluble individual, but less appropriately to waves and tempests, which in any case would seem to require the plural. The suggestion that Jesus is here addressing ‘ the demon of the storm ’ would be appropriate enough if commenting on an incident in the *Arabian Nights*, but it presupposes that Jesus held a view of the operations of Nature which is without support in His teaching recorded in the Gospels. May we not assume that this wonder-story grew out of a remarkable coincidence. The rebuke administered by Jesus to a voluble and cowardly disciple, coinciding as it did with the subsidence of the storm, was interpreted by His wonder-loving disciples as a rebuke administered to the storm itself.

The story reminds us of Julius Cæsar, in a small boat, encountering a storm which terrified his boatmen. Unperturbed, he calmed their fears by bidding them remember that they carried Cæsar and his Fortune.

Jesus points His disciples to faith, not in Luck but in God, as the source of courage.

THE GERASENE DEMONIAC

MK. 5^{1-20}

5 1 And they came to the other side of the
sea, into the country of the Gerasenes.
2 And when he was come out of the boat,
straightway there met him out of the
3 tombs a man with an unclean spirit, who
had his dwelling in the tombs: and no
man could any more bind him, no, not

MT. 8^{28-34}

8 28 And when he was come to the other side
into the country of the Gadarenes, there
met him two possessed with devils, coming
forth out of the tombs, exceeding fierce,
so that no man could pass by that way.
29 And behold, they cried out, saying, What
have we to do with thee, thou Son of

4 with a chain; because he had been
often bound with fetters and chains, and
the chains had been rent asunder by him,
and the fetters broken in pieces: and no
5 man had strength to tame him. And
always, night and day, in the tombs and
in the mountains, he was crying out, and
6 cutting himself with stones. And when
he saw Jesus from afar, he ran and wor-
7 shipped him; and crying out with a loud
voice, he saith, What have I to do with
thee, Jesus, thou Son of the Most High
God? I adjure thee by God, torment me
8 not. For he said unto him, Come forth,
9 thou unclean spirit, out of the man. And
he asked him, What is thy name? And
he saith unto him, My name is Legion;
10 for we are many. And he besought him
much that he would not send them away
11 out of the country. Now there was there
on the mountain side a great herd of swine
12 feeding. And they besought him, saying,
Send us into the swine, that we may enter
13 into them. And he gave them leave.
And the unclean spirits came out, and
entered into the swine: and the herd
rushed down the steep into the sea, *in
number* about two thousand; and they were
14 choked in the sea. And they that fed
them fled, and told it in the city, and in
the country. And they came to see what
15 it was that had come to pass. And they
come to Jesus, and behold him that was
possessed with devils sitting, clothed and
in his right mind, *even* him that had the
16 legion: and they were afraid. And they
that saw it declared unto them how it
befell him that was possessed with devils,
17 and concerning the swine. And they
began to beseech him to depart from their
18 borders. And as he was entering into the
boat, he that had been possessed with
devils besought him that he might be with
19 him. And he suffered him not, but saith
unto him, Go to thy house unto thy
friends, and tell them how great things the
Lord hath done for thee, and *how* he had
20 mercy on thee. And he went his way,
and began to publish in Decapolis how
great things Jesus had done for him: and
all men did marvel.

God? art thou come hither to torment us
30 before the time? Now there was afar off
from them a herd of many swine feeding.
31 And the devils besought him, saying, If
thou cast us out, send us away into the
32 herd of swine. And he said unto them,
Go. And they came out, and went into
the swine: and behold, the whole herd
rushed down the steep into the sea, and
33 perished in the waters. And they that
fed them fled, and went away into the
city, and told everything, and what was
befallen to them that were possessed with
34 devils. And behold, all the city came out
to meet Jesus: and when they saw him,
they besought *him* that he would depart
from their borders.

LK. 8^{26-39}

8 26 And they arrived at the country of the
Gerasenes, which is over against Galilee.
27 And when he was come forth upon the
land, there met him a certain man out of
the city, who had devils; and for a long
time he had worn no clothes, and abode
28 not in *any* house, but in the tombs. And
when he saw Jesus, he cried out, and fell
down before him, and with a loud voice
said, What have I to do with thee, Jesus,
thou Son of the Most High God? I
29 beseech thee, torment me not. For he
commanded the unclean spirit to come
out from the man. For oftentimes it had
seized him: and he was kept under guard,
and bound with chains and fetters; and
breaking the bands asunder, he was driven
30 of the devil into the deserts. And Jesus

asked him, What is thy name? And he
said, Legion; for many devils were entered
31 into him. And they intreated him that he
would not command them to depart into
32 the abyss. Now there was there a herd of
many swine feeding on the mountain: and
they intreated him that he would give
them leave to enter into them. And he
33 gave them leave. And the devils came
out from the man, and entered into the
swine: and the herd rushed down the steep
34 into the lake, and were choked. And
when they that fed them saw what had
come to pass, they fled, and told it in the
35 city and in the country. And they went
out to see what had come to pass; and
they came to Jesus, and found the man,
from whom the devils were gone out,
sitting, clothed and in his right mind, at
the feet of Jesus: and they were afraid.
36 And they that saw it told them how he
that was possessed with devils was made
37 whole. And all the people of the country
of the Gerasenes round about asked him
to depart from them; for they were holden
with great fear: and he entered into a boat,
38 and returned. But the man from whom
the devils were gone out prayed him that
he might be with him: but he sent him
39 away, saying. Return to thy house, and
declare how great things God hath done
for thee. And he went his way, publishing
throughout the whole city how great
things Jesus had done for him.

After the storm, Jesus and His disciples continued their voyage across the Lake, and came to the region of the Gergesenes. The place where they landed appears in the different texts of the Synoptic Gospels as Gadara, Gerasa, and Gergesa. The first two are important cities of Decapolis. (The region of the ten pagan Greek-speaking cities lying to the east of the Jordan.)

Gadara and Gerasa are, however, much too far from the beach of the Lake to be the scene of the incident recorded. There is, however, a little town on the eastern shore of the Lake, called to-day Khersa, which is rightly identified with the Gergesa of our Gospel texts. It is natural enough that later New Testament scribes, who knew nothing of the local geography, should have altered it to the well-known Gadara or Gerasa.

On leaving the boat they were met by a violent lunatic who dwelt permanently in the sepulchres (burial-caves) of the locality. Attempts had been made to tame him by keeping him in confinement, but he had broken his fetters and plucked his chains asunder. Day and night his cries could be heard as he dashed about the hills cutting himself on the sharp stones.

He espied Jesus afar off and ran to Him crying with a loud voice: ‘ What hast thou to do with me, O Jesus, Son of the most High God ? I adjure Thee by God, not to torment me ’: for Jesus began to command the evil spirit to come out of him.

Then said Jesus to him: ‘ What is thy name ? ’ And the man replied in the name of the demon which he believed possessed him: ‘ Legion, for we are many.’ (The Roman legion consisted of 6,000 soldiers.)

Mt., who shows himself generally uninterested in the details of miracles of healing, omits this question. Jesus would appear to have put it, in order to establish personal contact with the lunatic by inviting him to speak of himself. The lunatic, however, is terrified at the thought of being deprived of his familiar spirits and beseeches Jesus much, not to send them altogether away from that region. Close at hand there was a vast herd of swine browsing and the demons in the man begged Jesus (as it now appears certain that He will expel them from their human victim) that He will send them into the swine. So Jesus gave them permission, as Mk. and Lk. write; but Mt. states that Jesus actually commanded them to depart into the swine. This development of the incident by Mt. is natural enough, but it makes a considerable difference to the precise understanding of what happened.

Jesus did not command the demons to depart into the swine. He simply assented, possibly only by a gesture, to the supplications of the lunatic. But in view of what happened subsequently it was said that He had actually commanded the demons to possess the swine.

Seized with a panic, possibly as the result of the shouts and gesticulations of the lunatic, the swine rush down the slope and tumble over the cliff into the lake. Their keepers fly to the neighbouring town where the owners of the swine dwell and report the occurrence. The townspeople, presumably pagans, for no Jew might keep swine, hasten to the spot and behold the notorious lunatic, clothed and calm, seated at the feet of Jesus. The bystanders confirm the story of the exorcism and the fate of the swine. The townsfolk, perplexed and powerless, beg Jesus to leave their locality. This He does. When Jesus is about to embark, the recent demoniac begs to be allowed to accompany Him, but Jesus refuses permission and says to him: 'Go away unto thy home and to thy relations and tell them what great things the Lord has done for thee.'

Some have supposed that Jesus here, contrary to His general custom, which disclaimed any power for Himself in the healing of the sick, is telling the demoniac to announce to his friends what great things He, Jesus, has done for him. But a reference to the parallel passage in Lk. indicates the mistake of this interpretation. Lk. has: 'Tell what great things God has done for thee.' The word 'Lord' (*Kurios*) is the ordinary way of speaking of Jehovah in the Greek Old Testament.

The recent demoniac, however—and how prophetic this is of the primitive Christian Church—proclaims throughout Decapolis 'what great things Jesus had done for him.'

In Victorian times the Gergesene narrative became the battle-ground between Professor Huxley and Mr. Gladstone—the Professor contending that the whole narrative was fictitious; the Prime Minister contending that it was literally true.

Much water has flowed under the arches since then. There is probably no New Testament scholar of any standing to-day who would maintain that the Gergesene demoniac was actually possessed of a legion of demons and that these were transferred from him to the herd of swine. On the other hand, there are few historical critics who, in view of the vivid and original quality of Mk.'s narrative, would not regard it as substantial fact: but fact interpreted in the light, or rather the darkness, of current and popular demonology.

Whether Jesus actually believed in demons we cannot be certain. Probably He did. That He successfully exorcised demoniacs, there can be no doubt. Some readers of the Gospel have not only felt compassion for the swine but have been inclined to the view that Jesus ought to have saved them from their fate. But modern historical criticism, by depriving Jesus of the omnipotence and omniscience with which the traditional Christian theology endowed Him, has also relieved Him of any responsibility for the fate of the swine.

The number of the swine as given by Mk., where it comes in rather awkwardly, does not appear in the narratives of Mt. and Lk., which are dependent upon Mk. It may therefore have been no part of the original Marcan narrative but a marginal gloss. Lk. makes the demons request that they may not be sent into the abyss, which appears to have been the term for a cleft in the darkest and hottest portion of Gehenna especially assigned for the torment of demons, but that they may have a respite in the bodies of the swine. (Lk. 8^{31}.)

JAIRUS'S DAUGHTER AND THE WOMAN WITH THE ISSUE OF BLOOD

MK. 5^{21-43}

5 21 And when Jesus had crossed over again
in the boat unto the other side, a great
multitude was gathered unto him: and
22 he was by the sea. And there cometh one
of the rulers of the synagogue, Jaïrus by
name; and seeing him, he falleth at his
23 feet, and beseecheth him much, saying,
My little daughter is at the point of death:
I pray thee, that thou come and lay thy
hands on her, that she may be made
24 whole, and live. And he went with him;
and a great multitude followed him, and
they thronged him.
25 And a woman, which had an issue of
26 blood twelve years, and had suffered many
things of many physicians, and had spent
all that she had, and was nothing bettered,
27 but rather grew worse, having heard the
things concerning Jesus, came in the crowd
28 behind, and touched his garment. For
she said, If I touch but his garments, I
29 shall be made whole. And straightway
the fountain of her blood was dried up:
and she felt in her body that she was
30 healed of her plague. And straightway
Jesus, perceiving in himself that the power
proceeding from him had gone forth, turned
him about in the crowd, and said, Who
31 touched my garments? And his disciples
said unto him, Thou seest the multitude
thronging thee, and sayest thou, Who
32 touched me? And he looked round about
to see her that had done this thing.
33 But the woman fearing and trembling,
knowing what had been done to her, came
and fell down before him, and told him all
34 the truth. And he said unto her,
Daughter, thy faith hath made thee whole;
go in peace, and be whole of thy plague.
35 While he yet spake, they come from the
ruler of the synagogue's *house*, saying, Thy
daughter is dead: why troublest thou the
36 Master any further? But Jesus, not heed-
ing the word spoken, saith unto the ruler
of the synagogue, Fear not, only believe.
37 And he suffered no man to follow with
him, save Peter, and James, and John the
38 brother of James. And they come to the
house of the ruler of the synagogue; and
he beholdeth a tumult, and *many* weeping
39 and wailing greatly. And when he was
entered in, he saith unto them, Why make
ye a tumult, and weep? the child is not

MT. 9^{18-26}

9 18 While he spake these things unto them,
behold there came a ruler, and worshipped
him, saying, My daughter is even now
dead: but come and lay thy hand upon
19 her, and she shall live. And Jesus arose,
and followed him, and *so did* his disciples.
20 And behold, a woman, who had an issue
of blood twelve years, came behind him,
and touched the border of his garment:
21 for she said within herself, If I do but
touch his garment, I shall be made whole.
22 But Jesus turning and seeing her said,
Daughter, be of good cheer; thy faith hath
made thee whole. And the woman was
23 made whole from that hour. And when
Jesus came into the ruler's house, and saw
the flute-players, and the crowd making a
24 tumult, he said, Give place: for the damsel
is not dead, but sleepeth. And they
25 laughed him to scorn. But when the
crowd was put forth, he entered in, and
took her by the hand; and the damsel
26 arose. And the fame hereof went forth
into all that land.

LK. 8^{40-56}

8 40 And as Jesus returned, the multitude
welcomed him; for they were all waiting
41 for him. And behold, there came a man
named Jaïrus, and he was a ruler of the
synagogue: and he fell down at Jesus' feet,
and besought him to come into his house;
42 for he had an only daughter, about twelve
years of age, and she lay a dying. But as
he went the multitudes thronged him.
43 And a woman having an issue of blood
twelve years, which had spent all her
living upon physicians, and could not be
44 healed of any, came behind him, and
touched the border of his garment: and
immediately the issue of her blood
45 stanched. And Jesus said, Who is it that
touched me? And when all denied, Peter
said, and they that were with him, Master,
the multitudes press thee and crush thee.
46 But Jesus said, Some one did touch me:
for I perceived that power had gone forth
47 from me. And when the woman saw that
she was not hid, she came trembling, and
falling down before him declared in the
presence of all the people for what cause

40 dead, but sleepeth. And they laughed
him to scorn. But he, having put them
all forth, taketh the father of the child and
her mother and them that were with him,
41 and goeth in where the child was. And
taking the child by the hand, he saith unto
her, Talitha cumi; which is, being interpreted, Damsel, I say unto thee, Arise.
42 And straightway the damsel rose up, and
walked; for she was twelve years old.
And they were amazed straightway with
43 a great amazement. And he charged them
much that no man should know this: and
he commanded that *something* should be
given her to eat.

she touched him, and how she was healed
48 immediately. And he said unto her,
Daughter, thy faith hath made thee whole;
go in peace.
49 While he yet spake, there cometh one
from the ruler of the synagogue's *house*,
saying, Thy daughter is dead; trouble not
50 the Master. But Jesus hearing it, answered him, Fear not: only believe,
51 and she shall be made whole. And when
he came to the house, he suffered not any
man to enter in with him, save Peter, and
John, and James, and the father of the
52 maiden and her mother. And all were
weeping, and bewailing her: but he said,
Weep not; for she is not dead, but sleepeth.
53 And they laughed him to scorn, knowing
54 that she was dead. But he, taking her by
the hand, called, saying, Maiden, arise.
55 And her spirit returned, and she rose up
immediately: and he commanded that
56 *something* be given her to eat. And her
parents were amazed: but he charged
them to tell no man what had been done.

When Jesus had again crossed over from Gergesa to the western side of the Lake, a great crowd met Him on the shore; and a ruler of the synagogue, named Jairus (Mt. omits his name), prostrates himself at His feet.

A ruler of the synagogue would have much about the same status as an English churchwarden. It required ten adult male Jews to constitute a synagogue and these became its rulers. The synagogue in this case was possibly that of Capernaum, built by the centurion who loved the Jewish nation. Jairus beseeches Jesus fervently to come and heal his little daughter who is at the point of death. Mt. states that she had just died, and Lk. that she was dying, and that she was his only child. So Jesus went off with him: a great crowd following and pressing upon Him.

In the crowd was a woman who had suffered from an issue of blood for twelve years, who in her efforts to be healed had endured much from many physicians and had spent all her money and was in no way bettered but rather grew worse. Mt. omits this sardonic comment on medical skill, and Lk., with becoming restraint, merely states that no one had been able to heal her.

The woman was possessed of the conviction that if she could but grasp the tassel (*zizith*) of the *tallith* of Jesus she would be healed. The *tallith* was a sacred symbolical garment worn by every adult male Jew and had tassels of white and blue wool at its four corners. It was so worn that one of these hung down behind. It was this the woman grasped. Jesus, conscious of her action, turned round and asked: 'Who touched me?'

The disciples regard His question as absurd, with the crowd pressing upon Him, and tell Him so. He, however, takes no notice, but scrutinises the crowd in order to detect the culprit.

The woman, conscious that she has been healed, with fear and trembling comes forward, and tells Him the whole truth. He says to her: 'Daughter, thy faith hath healed thee, go in peace.' Mk. says: Jesus knew that He had been touched because He felt power go forth from Him. In Lk.'s narrative this is further developed, by making Jesus say to Peter: Someone did touch me, for I am conscious that power went forth from me.

Neither of these statements of the Evangelists is in agreement with that of Jesus: that it was the woman's faith that had healed her.

Whilst Jesus was still speaking to the woman, people came from the Ruler of the Synagogue's house and say to him: 'Thy daughter is dead. Why "worry" the Teacher further?'

Mt. naturally omits this incident, since he has stated that the child was dead. Lk. naturally follows Mk. at this point. Obviously Mk. was quite correct in the first instance, when he stated that when Jairus set out from his home his daughter was not dead. The announcement of her death is made to Jairus privately, but Jesus 'overhears it'—that is most probably the meaning of the better variant, although it may mean 'takes no notice of it'—and says to Jairus: 'Don't be afraid, only have faith.' Then Jesus permitted no one to go with Him except Peter and James and John. And they come into Jairus's house where the weeping and wailing for the dead has begun. [Mt. adds: that the flute players (whose pipes were used at funerals to give the note for the dirge (*qīnāh*)) had already arrived.]

Jesus, no doubt with the purpose of strengthening the faith of Jairus and that of His own disciples, asks: 'Why do you weep and make all this fuss? The little child is not dead but sleeps.' They begin to laugh at Him, but He puts them all outside and, taking with Him the father and the mother of the little child and His selected disciples, He enters into the room where the little girl was, and grasping her hand, He says to her in the Aramaic tongue: 'Little maid, get up,' as though she had only been sleeping. And immediately the little girl stood upright and began to walk about; for she was twelve years old. [Lk., after the manner of physicians, states her age at the outset of his narrative (8^{42}.)]

Mk. adds: That they were all astonished with a great astonishment and that Jesus charged them strongly not to let anyone know about it, and also that He directed that something should be given to the child to eat.

Lk., like a good physician, puts this order about the patient before the general injunction not to talk about the matter.

That Mk.'s narrative represents in detail an actual Petrine reminiscence we have no doubt. Whether the little girl was dead or in a trance is not clear. Perhaps the most amazing detail in this astonishing, yet actual, occurrence is the command of Jesus—not to talk about the matter. Yet how entirely it fits in with His whole attitude towards the miraculous and the vulgar misuse of it.

THE VISIT TO NAZARETH

MK. 6^{1-6a}

6 1 And he went out from thence; and he
cometh into his own country; and his dis-
2 ciples follow him. And when the sabbath
was come, he began to teach in the synagogue: and many hearing him were
astonished, saying, Whence hath this man
these things? and, What is the wisdom that

MT. 13^{53-58}

8 53 And it came to pass, when Jesus had
finished these parables, he departed
54 thence. And coming into his own country
he taught them in their synagogue, insomuch that they were astonished, and said,
Whence hath this man this wisdom, and
55 these mighty works? Is not this the

is given unto this man, and *what mean* such
3 mighty works wrought by his hands? Is
not this the carpenter, the son of Mary,
and brother of James, and Joses, and
Judas, and Simon? and are not his sisters
here with us? And they were offended in
4 him. And Jesus said unto them, A prophet
is not without honour, save in his own
country, and among his own kin, and in his
5 own house. And he could there do no
mighty work, save that he laid his hands
upon a few sick folk, and healed them.
6 And he marvelled because of their unbelief.

carpenter's son? is not his mother called
Mary? and his brethren, James, and
56 Joseph, and Simon, and Judas? And his
sisters, are they not all with us? Whence
57 then hath this man all these things? And
they were offended in him. But Jesus said
unto them, A prophet is not without
honour, save in his own country, and in his
58 own house. And he did not many mighty
works there because of their unbelief.

LK. 4^{16-30}

4 16 And he came to Nazareth, where he had
been brought up: and he entered, as his
custom was, into the synagogue on the
17 sabbath day, and stood up to read. And
there was delivered unto him the book of
the prophet Isaiah. And he opened the
book, and found the place where it was
written,

18 The Spirit of the Lord is upon me,
Because he anointed me to preach
good tidings to the poor:
He hath sent me to proclaim release
to the captives,
And recovering of sight to the blind,
To set at liberty them that are
bruised,
19 To proclaim the acceptable year of
the Lord.

20 And he closed the book, and gave it back
to the attendant, and sat down: and the
eyes of all in the synagogue were fastened
21 on him. And he began to say unto them,
To-day hath this scripture been fulfilled in
22 your ears. And all bare him witness, and
wondered at the words of grace which
proceeded out of his mouth: and they
23 said, Is not this Joseph's son? And he
said unto them, Doubtless ye will say unto
me this parable, Physician, heal thyself:
whatsoever we have heard done at Capernaum, do also here in thine own country.
24 And he said, Verily I say unto you, No
prophet is acceptable in his own country.
25 But of a truth I say unto you, There were
many widows in Israel in the days of
Elijah, when the heaven was shut up three
years and six months, when there came a
26 great famine over all the land; and unto
none of them was Elijah sent, but only to
Zarephath, in the land of Sidon, unto a
27 woman that was a widow. And there
were many lepers in Israel in the time of
Elisha the prophet; and none of them was
cleansed, but only Naaman the Syrian.
28 And they were all filled with wrath in the
29 synagogue, as they heard these things; and
they rose up, and cast him forth out of the
city, and led him unto the brow of the hill
whereon their city was built, that they
30 might throw him down headlong. But he
passing through the midst of them went
his way.

Cf. JN. 4^{44}

4 44 For Jesus himself testified, that a prophet
hath no honour in his own country.

Jesus now leaves the vicinity of the Sea of Galilee and taking His band of disciples with Him, like some notable Rabbi, He pays a visit to Nazareth, whose ridge commands magnificent views of the Mediterranean Sea and the Syrian coast. Neither in Mk. nor Mt. is Nazareth mentioned in connexion with this incident; they simply state that it occurred in the *patris* (native place) of Jesus. It is to Lk. (4^{16}) that we owe the designation Nazareth. Lk. omits the term *patris* in designating Nazareth and states that it was where Jesus had been brought up. But a little lower down, in his account of the visit to Nazareth, he relates that Jesus said of Himself to the Nazarenes in their synagogue:

'I say unto you that no prophet is acceptable in his *patris*.' (Lk. 4^{24}.)

Patris must mean either (1) native place, or (2) ancestral home—the place from which one's family draws its origin. If Jesus was of Davidic descent, as there seems good reason to believe He was (cf. Rom. 1³), then Bethlehem, and not Nazareth, was His ancestral home. In that case *patris* must be used of Nazareth as the birthplace of Jesus. The Mother of Jesus, his brothers and sisters are residents of Nazareth, and on the Sabbath Jesus visited the synagogue which He had often attended in years gone by. He had developed not a little since He was last there. Mk. relates that He began to teach in the synagogue and His audience are amazed at His wisdom, asking whence He derived it. 'Is not this,' said they, 'the carpenter, the son of Mary and the brother of Jacob and Joseph and Judas and Simon, and are not his sisters here with us?'

[Mt. has 'the son of the carpenter' and Lk. has 'the son of Joseph.' There is little doubt, however, that 'carpenter' and 'the son of the carpenter' in Oriental idiom mean the same thing.

The great Christian scholar, Origen, writing early in the third century, in reply to the attack made on Christianity by the pagan Celsus, asserted that he did not know of any passage in Scripture where Jesus is called a carpenter. On the other hand, the Christian philosopher, Justin Martyr, who was himself born in Shechem, writing about A.D. 150, says that he had actually seen yokes and ploughs (these in Palestine are of wood) which had been made by Jesus. There seems to be little doubt that Jesus was a carpenter, although some have taken the term *tektōn* to mean a builder (so Frenssen, the German novelist).

The pagan sneerer who asked of a Christian of Antioch at the moment when Julian the Apostate was expiring in Parthia, 'What is your son of a carpenter doing now?' and received the reply: 'Perhaps our son of a carpenter is making a coffin'—indicates that the term *tektōn* was taken in the case of Jesus, at any rate, to mean, not a builder but a joiner.]

Mk. relates that the congregation of His townspeople took offence at Jesus, but it is difficult from Mk.'s narrative to see why they should do so. Wisdom and eloquence and gifts of healing should be no cause of offence, but rather of pride to the fellow-townsmen of Jesus. When, however, we turn to Lk.'s account, which is very much fuller than that of Mk. and Mt., we see why they were offended.

Jesus, so Lk. tells us, went into the synagogue, as was His wont on Sabbath days, and stood up (this was the usual attitude) to read the Scriptures. There was put into His hand by the *Chazzan*, or synagogue attendant, a roll of the Prophet Isaiah. Jesus unrolls it and reads out the famous passage (61¹, ²) which describes the gracious Mission of the Servant of the Lord, anointed by the Divine Spirit to preach glad tidings to Israel. Jesus then sat down (the attitude of the preacher) and began His sermon with the words:

'This day hath this Scripture been fulfilled in your ears.'

It was doubtless this Messianic claim, for it was surely nothing less, made by one who had been the village carpenter which excited hostile and contemptuous comment on the part of the congregation.

Criticism passes into a challenge: We have heard of your wonderful works of healing at Capernaum; how is it we have seen none of them here in your own town? Deeply wounded, Jesus retorts with two apt illustrations from the Old Testament,

Elijah in the days of a notable famine provided support, not for an Israelite woman, but for a Sidonian widow of Zarephath. Elisha cleansed a leper, but the leper was not an Israelite, but a Syrian. Prophets do not always minister to the needs of their fellow-nationals nor are they always acceptable in their native place.

Infuriated by His satire, the Nazarenes, according to Lk., seek to throw Him down the precipice on the edge of which their city was built, but He escapes from them.

This very full and illuminating statement by Lk., which seems so vivid and characteristic as to make it deserving of credit, is lacking from Mk. Why is this? Is it possible that Simon Peter was not present in the synagogue of Nazareth? Undoubtedly the mother and sisters of Jesus were present, and it is possible that from this feminine source Lk. derived his special information. Mk. relates, however, what is absent from Lk., that Jesus was unable in Nazareth to do any powers except that He laid His hands on a few sick folk, and that He was astonished at the lack of faith of the Nazarenes. This remarkable statement, which indicates clearly what Jesus Himself so often taught, that without faith healing was impossible, is altered, characteristically, by Mt. into, 'He did not there many powers on account of their lack of faith'—as though Jesus were punishing the Nazarenes for their lack of faith by refusing to heal many of their sick people.

THE MISSION OF THE TWELVE

MK. 6^{6b-13}

6 6 And he went round about the villages
teaching.
7 And he called unto him the twelve,
and began to send them forth by two and
two; and he gave them authority over the
8 unclean spirits; and he charged them that
they should take nothing for *their* journey,
save a staff only; no bread, no wallet, no
9 money in their purse; but *to go* shod with
sandals: and, *said he*, put not on two coats.
10 And he said unto them, Wheresoever ye
enter into a house, there abide till ye
11 depart thence. And whatsoever place
shall not receive you, and they hear you
not, as ye go forth thence, shake off the
dust that is under your feet for a testimony
12 unto them. And they went out, and
13 preached that *men* should repent. And
they cast out many devils, and anointed
with oil many that were sick, and healed
them.

MT. 4^{23}, 9^{35}, 10^{1-15}

4 23 And Jesus went about in all Galilee,
teaching in their synagogues, and preaching the gospel of the kingdom, and healing
all manner of disease and all manner of
sickness among the people.

9 35 And Jesus went about all the cities and
the villages, teaching in their synagogues,
and preaching the gospel of the kingdom,
and healing all manner of disease and all
manner of sickness.

10 1 And he called unto him his twelve disciples, and gave them authority over
unclean spirits, to cast them out, and to
heal all manner of disease and all
manner of sickness.
2 Now the names of the twelve apostles
are these: The first, Simon, who is called
Peter, and Andrew his brother; James
the *son* of Zebedee, and John his brother;
3 Philip, and Bartholomew; Thomas, and
Matthew the publican; James the *son* of
4 Alphæus, and Thaddæus: Simon the
Cananæan, and Judas Iscariot, who
5 also betrayed him. These twelve Jesus
sent forth, and charged them, saying,
Go not into *any* way of the Gentiles,
and enter not into any city of the
6 Samaritans: but go rather to the lost

7 sheep of the house of Israel. And as ye
go, preach, saying, The kingdom of
8 heaven is at hand. Heal the sick, raise
the dead, cleanse the lepers, cast out
devils: freely ye received, freely give.
9 Get you no gold, nor silver, nor brass in
10 your purses; no wallet for *your* journey,
neither two coats, nor shoes, nor staff:
for the labourer is worthy of his food.
11 And into whatsoever city or village ye
shall enter, search out who in it is
worthy; and there abide till ye go forth.
12 And as ye enter into the house, salute it.
13 And if the house be worthy, let your
peace come upon it: but if it be not
worthy, let your peace return to you.
14 And whosoever shall not receive you, nor
hear your words, as ye go forth out of
that house or that city, shake off the dust
15 of your feet. Verily I say unto you, It
shall be more tolerable for the land of
Sodom and Gomorrah in the day of
judgement, than for that city.

LK. 9^{1-6}

9 1 And he called the twelve together, and
gave them power and authority over all
2 devils, and to cure diseases. And he sent
them forth to preach the kingdom of God,
3 and to heal the sick. And he said unto
them, Take nothing for your journey,
neither staff, nor wallet, nor bread, nor
4 money; neither have two coats. And into
whatsoever house ye enter, there abide,
5 and thence depart. And as many as
receive you not, when ye depart from that
city, shake off the dust from your feet for a
6 testimony against them. And they departed, and went throughout the villages,
preaching the gospel, and healing everywhere.

The following parallel passages from Lk. 10 are extracted from the Charge of Jesus to the Seventy Disciples—an incident peculiar to Lk.

LK. 10^{1-10}

10 1 Now after these things the Lord appointed seventy others, and sent them
two and two before his face into every
city and place, whither he himself was
2 about to come. And he said unto them,
The harvest is plenteous, but the
labourers are few: pray ye therefore the
Lord of the harvest, that he send forth
3 labourers into his harvest. Go your
ways: behold, I send you forth as lambs
4 in the midst of wolves. Carry no purse,
no wallet, no shoes: and salute no man on
5 the way. And into whatsoever house ye
shall enter, first say, Peace *be* to this house.
6 And if a son of peace be there, your peace
shall rest upon him: but if not, it shall
7 turn to you again. And in that same
house remain, eating and drinking such
things as they give: for the labourer is
worthy of his hire. Go not from house to
8 house. And into whatsoever city ye
enter, and they receive you, eat such
9 things as are set before you: and heal
the sick that are therein, and say unto
them, The kingdom of God is come nigh
10 unto you. But into whatsoever city ye
shall enter, and they receive you not, go
11 out into the streets thereof and say, Even
the dust from your city, that cleaveth to
our feet, we do wipe off against you: howbeit know this, that the kingdom of God
12 is come nigh. I say unto you, It shall
be more tolerable in that day for Sodom,
than for that city.

As the calling of the disciples and Apostles marked a special stage in the Messianic Mission of Jesus; as another stage in that mission was marked by the change from popular to parabolic teaching; so another stage is marked by the sending out of the Twelve Apostles on a special mission. Hitherto they had accompanied Jesus on His preaching tours: their headquarters had apparently been Peter's house in Capernaum and they used his fishing boat for their expeditions across the Lake.

The visit to Nazareth had proved a failure. Mk. 6^{6b} seems to indicate that Jesus spent some time preaching in the villages which surrounded Nazareth. He then summoned the Twelve and began to send them out, two by two, apparently throughout the tetrarchy of Herod Antipas, since their activity appears to have excited the attention of that ruler. Before dismissing them on their mission, Jesus gave them authority (Lk. adds ' and power ') over demons.

The distinction between these two words authority (*exousia*) and power (*dunamis*) is important. The former signifies ' official right ' the latter ' personal force.'

The precise meaning is well brought out by a saying of Archbishop Benson: that what was wrong with the Church in so many instances was that the men who possessed the *exousia* had not the *dunamis* and that the men who possessed the *dunamis* had not the *exousia.* Lk. provides that the Twelve Apostles shall have both.

The Charge to the Twelve which follows differs in various points as given by the Synoptists. These differences, it is held, can best be accounted for by supposing that the original charge has been altered and enlarged to meet the needs of, or to conform with, the customs of missionary work in the primitive Church.

Lk. has a Second Charge to Missionaries, supposed to have been delivered by Jesus to the Seventy Disciples before sending them out (Lk. 10). And it will be observed that a number of the directions which Lk. there records are parallel to those which Mk. records (followed by Mt.) as having been delivered to the Twelve on this occasion.

In *The Teaching of the Twelve Apostles* (a very primitive Christian document) a most interesting body of directions is provided for the Church's itinerant ministry of apostles and prophets, e.g. they are not allowed to ask for money; they must not remain more than three days in one place; they are to have complete freedom in the prayers they offer up at the Eucharist, etc.

Mk.'s directions do not permit the missionaries to make any provision for their journey; not even food or money or a change of linen, not even two shirts. (The *chitōn* or tunic was not a coat but an undergarment worn next to the skin.) According to Mk. the Twelve were commanded to take a staff and to wear sandals. The Apostles are not allowed to take bronze (or coppers) in their belts. (It is in the cummerbund that the Oriental carries his money.) Mk. is very primitive here.

Mt. writes that they are not to provide ' gold or silver or bronze ' for their journey, and Lk. that they are not to provide ' silver '; but these departures from Mk. belong to a later period.

St. Peter said to the lame beggar at the Beautiful Gate of the Temple: ' Silver and gold have I none ' (Acts 3^{6}). The primitive Apostles of Jesus were not accustomed to handle either gold or silver. A few coppers covered their financial transactions.

What Mk. meant by a wallet (*pēra*) is not clear. It is plainly not a purse here; possibly it may have been a provision basket or 'valise' for clothes. Some have suggested that it was a receptacle intended for alms, like the copper basin carried by mendicant Buddhist monks. In that case Jesus forbids his missionaries to be mendicants.

Lk. in his directions for the Seventy (10^4), we may note, forbids not only a *pēra* but also a *ballantion* (R.V. 'purse'). What this precisely signified in this connexion is also uncertain. They might, indeed must, receive hospitality, but they must not beg for alms. When staying as guests in a house they are not to change their quarters while in that locality. Such a direction is very significant: the missionary would probably at first be entertained by some very poor and humble person. If the missionary proved to be an influential evangelist he would soon be proffered hospitality by wealthy people of considerable social standing, but he was to decline it and to stay with his poor host. Mt. adds, and it is obviously a later addition, that he was to show discrimination in the selection of his host in the first instance—he was to look out for someone who was 'worthy.'

It was so very easy for those early missionaries to get into touch, at the outset, with the wrong kind of people in the locality and so prejudice the whole prospects of the mission.

Mt. definitely restricts the mission of the Twelve to the Jews. The Apostles are forbidden to go either to the Samaritans or to the Gentiles. This is probably a very early addition to the words of Jesus. It is very unlikely that the primitive disciples, who were Jews, would dream of going to Samaritans and Gentiles, unless definitely commanded to do so. There would certainly be no need for Jesus to forbid them. Only at a much later stage would the question of preaching to Gentiles arise.

Another point to be noted here is a tendency evident in Mt.'s Charge, as elsewhere in his Gospel, to emphasise asceticism. The primitive missionaries in their travels are forbidden the help of sandals and staff: they must go, like the mediæval friars, barefooted. Mt., after his fashion, makes their preaching apocalyptic. 'The Kingdom of the Heavens is at hand': 'it shall be more tolerable . . . in the day of judgement.' Both these phrases are absent from Mk. The Apostles are to give the Jewish salutation to those they visit, 'Peace be to this house.' If not courteously received, the Apostles are directed to exhibit their disapproval by shaking off the dust of their feet against the inhospitable community as they depart from it. This is to be a witness to the community that by their refusal to receive the evangelical missionaries they have invoked judgement on themselves. We really wonder if Jesus could have commanded this insulting gesture.

Mk. relates that the Apostles went forth and proclaimed that men should repent (i.e. turn over a new leaf), and that they cast out many demons and anointed many sick people with oil and healed them. This anointing the sick with oil has its parallel in the directions given in the *Epistle of St. James* (5^{14}): 'Is any among you sick? Let him call for the elders of the Church and let them pray over him, anointing him with oil in the name of the Lord.'

HEROD ANTIPAS, JESUS, AND JOHN THE BAPTIST

MK. 6^{14-29}

6 14 And king Herod heard *thereof*; for his
name had become known: and he said,
John the Baptist is risen from the dead,
and therefore do these powers work in him.
15 But others said, It is Elijah. And others
said, *It is* a prophet, *even* as one of the
16 prophets. But Herod, when he heard
thereof, said, John, whom I beheaded, he is
17 risen. For Herod himself had sent forth
and laid hold upon John, and bound him
in prison for the sake of Herodias, his
brother Philip's wife: for he had married
18 her. For John said unto Herod, It is not
lawful for thee to have thy brother's wife.
19 And Herodias set herself against him, and
desired to kill him; and she could not;
20 for Herod feared John, knowing that he
was a righteous man and a holy, and kept
him safe. And when he heard him, he
was much perplexed; and he heard him
21 gladly. And when a convenient day was
come, that Herod on his birthday made a
supper to his lords, and the high captains,
22 and the chief men of Galilee; and when
the daughter of Herodias herself came in
and danced, she pleased Herod and them
that sat at meat with him; and the king
said unto the damsel, Ask of me whatsoever thou wilt, and I will give it thee.
23 And he sware unto her, Whatsoever thou
shalt ask of me, I will give it thee, unto the
24 half of my kingdom. And she went out,
and said unto her mother, What shall I
ask? And she said, The head of John the
25 Baptist. And she came in straightway
with haste unto the king, and asked, saying, I will that thou forthwith give me in a
26 charger the head of John the Baptist. And
the king was exceeding sorry; but for the
sake of his oaths, and of them that sat at
27 meat, he would not reject her. And
straightway the king sent forth a soldier of
his guard, and commanded to bring his
head: and he went and beheaded him in
28 the prison, and brought his head in a
charger, and gave it to the damsel; and
29 the damsel gave it to her mother. And
when his disciples heard *thereof*, they came
and took up his corpse, and laid it in a tomb.

MT. 14^{1-12a}

14 1 At that season Herod the tetrarch
2 heard the report concerning Jesus, and
said unto his servants, This is John the
Baptist; he is risen from the dead; and
therefore do these powers work in him.
3 For Herod had laid hold on John, and
bound him, and put him in prison for the
sake of Herodias, his brother Philip's
4 wife. For John said unto him, It is not
5 lawful for thee to have her. And when
he would have put him to death, he
feared the multitude, because they
6 counted him as a prophet. But when
Herod's birthday came, the daughter of
Herodias danced in the midst, and
7 pleased Herod. Whereupon he promised with an oath to give her whatsoever
8 she should ask. And she, being put
forward by her mother, saith, Give me
here in a charger the head of John the
9 Baptist. And the king was grieved; but
for the sake of his oaths, and of them
which sat at meat with him, he com-
10 manded it to be given; and he sent, and
11 beheaded John in the prison. And his
head was brought in a charger, and given
to the damsel: and she brought it to her
12 mother. And his disciples came, and
took up the corpse, and buried him.

LK. 9^{7-9}, $3^{19, 20}$

9 7 Now Herod the tetrarch heard of all that
was done: and he was much perplexed,
because that it was said by some, that
8 John was risen from the dead; and by
some, that Elijah had appeared; and by
others, that one of the old prophets was
9 risen again. And Herod said, John I beheaded: but who is this, about whom
I hear such things? And he sought to
see him.

3 19 but Herod the tetrarch, being reproved
by him for Herodias his brother's wife,
and for all the evil things which Herod
20 had done, added yet this above all, that
he shut up John in prison.

Here Mk. uses the words 'King Herod.' That was what Peter and his other Galilean subjects called him. (Mt. and Lk. describe him correctly as Tetrarch, the ruler of the quarter of a kingdom.) King Herod became aware of the existence of Jesus because He was becoming a public personage. It was this Herod Antipas (one of the sons of Herod the Great) who had beheaded John the Baptist. He said therefore to his courtiers: 'Jesus is John, the Baptiser, whom I beheaded; he is risen from the dead.' This remark indicates how widespread the Pharisaic belief in the Resurrection had become.

There were others, however, who did not share Herod's view, and they asseverated that Jesus was Elijah; others that He was a prophet, or more cautiously, that 'He was as one of the prophets' ('ancient prophets,' Lk.). But Herod said: 'It is John whom I beheaded, he is risen from the dead, and that is why he does such miracles.'

It is related of John the Baptist in the Fourth Gospel that he worked no miracles. It was apparently Herod's view that his resurrection endowed him with this power.

Cardinal Newman complained on one occasion that bad men had no more difficulty in believing in the creeds than had good men. The religious beliefs of Herod Antipas provide an illustration of this. Antipas had arrested John because he had condemned him for marrying Herodias, his brother Philip's wife, her former husband being still alive. (He was not the Herod Philip who Lk. tells us was Tetrarch of Ituræa, etc., but another of the same name who lived as a private citizen in Rome.)

John's rebuke caused Herodias to harbour a deep grudge against him, and she wished to have him executed, but Herod refused because he reverenced John's character. So he protected him.

Mk. states that Antipas was much affected and perplexed by John's preaching. Like Felix, when he listened to St. Paul, the Tetrarch's conscience recognised the truth of the prophetic message but he lacked the moral strength to obey. The statement in the Authorised Version (Mk. 6^{20}) that Antipas 'did many things' on account of John's preaching is based upon a textual variant for which 'was much perplexed' has been rightly substituted by the Revisers.

John would not have been executed if Antipas had not been entrapped by his wife's plot. Antipas, on his birthday more probably than on his accession day, gave a dinner for his courtiers, magnates, military commanders, and the chief citizens of Galilee. After dinner the daughter of Herodias (Mk. blunders in calling Herodias *his* daughter) came in and danced before the guests. It was an extraordinary condescension on the part of a princess of the reigning house. Indeed, it transgressed the limits of propriety. Antipas and his guests were delighted and he said to the girl, 'Ask from me whatever thou wilt, and I will give it thee,' and he added with an oath, 'even unto the half of my kingdom.' Herodias went out and said to her mother: 'What shall I ask?' And her mother said: 'The head of John the Baptiser.' Returning immediately to the dining-hall with haste, she made her request to Antipas, saying: 'I wish that you should give me immediately on a large dish the head of John the Baptist.' And Antipas was very grieved, but on account of his oath, and his guests, he would not refuse her. And he sent immediately one of his body-guard (literally a 'scout') and commanded him to bring John's head. And departing he beheaded him in the prison and brought his head in a large dish, and he gave it to the maiden and the maiden gave it to her mother. And when the disciples of John heard, they came and took up the corpse and placed it in a sepulchre.

Mk.'s account is more primitive than that of Mt. and the brief notice given by Lk. This is seen in its favourable attitude towards Antipas. He has good in him and might have done much better but for his Jezebel of a wife who induced him to kill the second Elijah even as Jezebel had tried to kill the first.

Lk. merely asserts that Antipas, enraged by the Baptist's prophetic rebukes, imprisoned him. Mt. asserts that, stung by John's rebuke of his adultery, Antipas imprisoned John and wished to execute him but was afraid to do so on account of the populace who held him to be a prophet. But he was entrapped by Herodias into beheading John, an act which his political judgement condemned.

The tendency, and it should be noted of later writers, is to blacken the bad characters and to whiten the good ones, e.g. Judas Iscariot and here Herod Antipas. Mk. in presenting Antipas in a less unfavourable light indicates the primitive character of his narrative.

John's fate is also related by the Jewish historian Josephus, writing about half a century after his execution. It differs seriously from Mk.'s account. According to Josephus, Antipas put John to death because he feared he might stir up a political rising. Josephus tells the story of Antipas's scandalous marriage with his brother's wife whom he persuaded to desert her husband. He tells also what Mk. does not tell, that in order to marry Herodias, Antipas had to undertake to divorce his own wife, the daughter of Aretas (King of the Nabatæan Arabians), which led to a disastrous war between Herod and his father-in-law. Josephus gives the name of Herodias' daughter as Salome, and states that John was imprisoned and presumably executed at Machærus—a combined palace and fortress situated near the Dead Sea, on the borders of Antipas's Peræan territory. Mk.'s account of the death of the Baptist is much earlier than that given by Josephus. It undoubtedly preserves a primitive local tradition, as is evident from the many vivid details it contains, e.g. the birthday feast, the classes of the guests, the King's rash oath, the Queen's plot, the public dancing of the princess, the guardsman-executioner, the eagerness of the girl, the dish for the head.

We should suppose from Mk.'s account that the King's birthday feast was celebrated at Tiberias, his Galilean capital. If, however, we try to reconcile Mk. and Josephus on this point, the festival took place at Machærus and all the executioner would have to do would be to behead the prisoner in the palace dungeon and bring the head upstairs to the banqueting-hall.

The account given by Josephus is colourless and general, compared with that of Mk. There is good historical reason for believing also that it is chronologically confused.

THE FEEDING OF THE FIVE THOUSAND

MK. 6[30-44]	MT. 14[13-21]
6 30 And the apostles gather themselves together unto Jesus; and they told him all things, whatsoever they had done, and	14 13 Now when Jesus heard *it*, he withdrew from thence in a boat, to a desert place apart: and when the multitudes heard

31 whatsoever they had taught. And he
saith unto them, Come ye yourselves
apart into a desert place, and rest a while.
For there were many coming and going,
and they had no leisure so much as to eat.
32 And they went away in the boat to a
33 desert place apart. And *the people* saw
them going, and many knew *them*, and
they ran there together on foot from all
34 the cities, and outwent them. And he
came forth and saw a great multitude, and
he had compassion on them, because they
were as sheep not having a shepherd: and
35 he began to teach them many things. And
when the day was now far spent, his disciples came unto him, and said, The place
is desert, and the day is now far spent:
36 send them away, that they may go into
the country and villages round about, and
37 buy themselves somewhat to eat. But he
answered and said unto them, Give ye
them to eat. And they say unto him,
Shall we go and buy two hundred pennyworth of bread, and give them to eat?
38 And he saith unto them, How many loaves
have ye? go *and* see. And when they
39 knew, they say, Five, and two fishes. And
he commanded them that all should sit
down by companies upon the green grass.
40 And they sat down in ranks, by hundreds,
41 and by fifties. And he took the five loaves
and the two fishes, and looking up to
heaven, he blessed, and brake the loaves;
and he gave to the disciples to set before
them; and the two fishes divided he among
42 them all. And they did all eat, and were
43 filled. And they took up broken pieces,
twelve basketfuls, and also of the fishes.
44 And they that ate the loaves were five
thousand men.

thereof, they followed him on foot from
14 the cities. And he came forth, and saw
a great multitude, and he had compas-
15 sion on them, and healed their sick. And
when even was come, the disciples came
to him, saying, The place is desert, and
the time is already past; send the multitudes away, that they may go into the
16 villages, and buy themselves food. But
Jesus said unto them, They have no need
17 to go away; give ye them to eat. And
they say unto him, We have here but five
18 loaves, and two fishes. And he said,
19 Bring them hither to me. And he commanded the multitudes to sit down on
the grass; and he took the five loaves,
and the two fishes, and looking up to
heaven, he blessed, and brake and gave
the loaves to the disciples, and the dis-
20 ciples to the multitudes. And they did
all eat, and were filled: and they took up
that which remained over of the broken
21 pieces, twelve baskets full. And they
that did eat were about five thousand
men, beside women and children.

LK. 9^{10-17}

9 10 And the apostles, when they were returned, declared unto him what things
they had done. And he took them, and
withdrew apart to a city called Bethsaida.
11 But the multitudes perceiving it followed
him: and he welcomed them, and spake
to them of the kingdom of God, and them
12 that had need of healing he healed. And
the day began to wear away; and the
twelve came, and said unto him, Send the
multitude away, that they may go into the
villages and country round about, and
lodge, and get victuals: for we are here in
13 a desert place. But he said unto them,
Give ye them to eat. And they said, We
have no more than five loaves and two
fishes; except we should go and buy food
14 for all this people. For they were about
five thousand men. And he said unto his
disciples, Make them sit down in com-

JN. 6^{1-13}

6 1 After these things Jesus went away to
the other side of the sea of Galilee, which
2 is *the sea* of Tiberias. And a great multitude followed him, because they beheld
the signs which he did on them that were
3 sick. And Jesus went up into the mountain, and there he sat with his disciples.
4 Now the passover, the feast of the Jews, was
5 at hand. Jesus therefore lifting up his
eyes, and seeing that a great multitude
cometh unto him, saith unto Philip,
Whence are we to buy bread, that these
6 may eat? And this he said to prove
him: for he himself knew what he would
7 do. Philip answered him, Two hundred
pennyworth of bread is not sufficient for
them, that every one may take a little.
8 One of his disciples, Andrew, Simon
9 Peter's brother, saith unto him, There is a
lad here, which hath five barley loaves,

15 panies, about fifty each. And they did so,
16 and made them all sit down. And he
took the five loaves and the two fishes, and
looking up to heaven, he blessed them, and
brake; and gave to the disciples to set
17 before the multitude. And they did eat,
and were all filled: and there was taken
up that which remained over to them of
broken pieces, twelve baskets.

and two fishes: but what are these among
10 so many? Jesus said, Make the people sit
down. Now there was much grass in the
place. So the men sat down, in number
11 about five thousand. Jesus therefore took
the loaves; and having given thanks, he
distributed to them that were set down;
likewise also of the fishes as much as they
12 would. And when they were filled, he
saith unto his disciples, Gather up the
broken pieces which remain over, that
13 nothing be lost. So they gathered them
up, and filled twelve baskets with broken
pieces from the five barley loaves, which
remained over unto them that had eaten.

The Twelve return from their missionary expedition and report to Jesus all that they had done and taught. We learn from Lk. 10^{17-20} that they took a most optimistic view of their achievements, especially in the sphere of exorcism. Jesus, characteristically, bids them not to value this power over demons too highly but rather to rejoice that they are sons of the Kingdom. As always, He stresses the moral and spiritual aspect of His mission. Recognising their need for rest, He bids them to come apart and rest awhile in some desert place, for so great was the pressure of the multitude, says Mk., that they had no convenient opportunity to take their meals. So they went off in a boat to seek privacy in a desert place—some uninhabited spot, according to Mk. But according to Lk., they withdrew to the city of Bethsaida (Lk. 9^{10}).

This was plainly Bethsaida Julias, situated north of the Lake, and east of the Jordan. Jn. describes the locality as ‘ the mountain,’ i.e. the high land on the other side of the Lake from Capernaum.

The crowd saw them departing in the boat but were resolved not to be forsaken. So, going round the Lake on foot, they outwent them and by hard running arrived first at the landing-place. When, therefore, they disembarked the crowd was there awaiting them. Jesus was moved, not with irritation but with compassion, for they seemed to him like sheep without a shepherd, and He began to teach them.

Mk. now relates the feeding of the five thousand men by Jesus. (Mt. adds not reckoning women and children.)

This miracle is the only one in the Gospels recorded by all four evangelists. Many explanations have been offered of it.

(1) Traditionalist commentators interpret it as entirely miraculous.

(2) Extreme critics view it as pure myth created in imitation of the story of the miraculous feeding by Elisha recorded in 2 Kings 4^{42-44}:

‘ And there came a man from Baal-shalishah, and brought the man of God bread of the first fruits, twenty loaves of barley, and fresh ears of corn in his sack. And he said, Give unto the people, that they may eat. And his servant said, What, should I set this before an hundred men? But he said, Give the people, that they may eat: for thus saith the Lord, They shall eat, and shall leave thereof. So he set it before them, and they did eat, and left thereof, according to the word of the Lord.’

(3) Others have avoided the antithesis of miracle or myth and have interpreted the story allegorically. Jesus, having first satisfied the spiritual and moral needs of men, then more than satisfies their economic needs. It thus enshrines the Gospel of the Christian Socialist. Others would allegorise the narrative differently. The five loaves are the ' five-fifths of the Torah,' the two fishes are the Prophets and the Hagiographers, which together constitute the three classes of the Jewish Canonical Scriptures. Although possessed of these, the vast multitude of the simple people were suffering moral and spiritual starvation until Jesus, in contrast to the scribes, imparted, by His vital use of those Scriptures, the moral and spiritual sustenance of which the multitude stood in need.

The earliest allegorical interpretation of the Feeding of the Five Thousand is of course to be found in Jn. 6, where Jesus compares Himself to the Heavenly Manna, ' the Bread which came down from Heaven to give life unto the world,' of which they who partake shall never die. By this bread Jesus means His teaching—' the words which I have spoken unto you are Spirit and are Life ' (Jn. 6^{63}).

(4) There is a fourth school of interpreters who feel unable to adopt the solely miraculous interpretation: as they doubt, in the light of modern knowledge, whether the miraculous is a divine method of operation. On the other hand, they recognise that, if the feeding of the five thousand be a purely mythical narrative, the claim that any part of the Gospel narratives is historical becomes extremely precarious.

These exegetes would attempt what some would call a rationalist interpretation. They recognise that there is a core of fact. There was a hungry multitude and their physical hunger was satisfied under the influence of Jesus: satisfied, by means of five loaves and two small fishes—but how? Did Jesus by the magnetic force of His personality induce those who partook of the tiny fragments of bread and fish to feel that their physical pangs were satisfied? Or did the generous action of Jesus and His disciples in surrendering their small store of provisions to the hungry multitude induce some among the multitude to produce their own stores of food to be distributed? Or is there some other, better exposition on these lines? This was the line taken by the late Professor Sanday, who said:

> That he was inclined to regard the account as fact, save in one particular, that they were all ' filled.'

Mk.'s narrative is of a very vivid character. It opens with a dialogue in which, when Jesus refuses to dismiss the fasting crowds, the disciples ask satirically if they shall buy 200 *denarii* worth of bread for them (6^{37}). (The *denarius* was a small silver coin, a little larger than a sixpence but with a purchasing power of at least ten times that amount.) Next there is the command of Jesus to go and see how much provisions they have. These no doubt were in the boat. Then when they had learnt (Gk., i.e. by actual experience) they tell him. Then follows the arrangement of the multitude in separate feeding (literally, ' drinking ') parties, hundreds and fifties, in which, to take the Greek literally, they appeared like beds of herbs in a field as they reclined on the *green* grass. (The grass is green in Palestine only in the spring, and Mk.'s statement about the grass agrees with that of Jn. that the feeding of the five thousand took place shortly before the

Feast of the Passover which falls in March–April. Jn. also states that there was *much grass* in the place (6^{10}).

Next we have recorded the gesture of Jesus: ‘ taking the five loaves and two fishes He looked up into heaven and blessed and brake up the bread into fragments.’ Jn. here uses the word *eucharistēsas* for ‘ give thanks,’ as he sees in this incident the institution of the Eucharist, which in consequence he deliberately omits from his account of the Last Supper. Lk.’s statement that Jesus was made known to His two disciples at Emmaus ‘in the breaking of bread’ would seem to indicate that there was something very characteristic in this action of Jesus.

Then there is the imparting of the fragments to His disciples who, like the Deacons in the primitive Church, distributed to the faithful the elements which had been blessed by the presiding presbyter or bishop.

The whole concludes with the gathering up of the fragments, which fill twelve small luncheon baskets. Were these the luncheon baskets of the twelve Apostles? In the later account of the feeding of the four thousand, the seven baskets filled by the fragments are different; they are ‘ kits ’ in which, for instance, a workman would carry his tools.

Jn. states that the loaves were of barley. This was not only the cheapest kind of bread, but it is the bread of the early spring, as we see in the Elisha narrative already referred to. This supports incidentally the season of the feeding. Jn. corrects the synoptic narrative in two particulars. The loaves and fishes used did not belong to Jesus and the Apostles, but were contributed by a little boy who gave them up to St. Andrew. In Jn. Jesus Himself distributes the food (both bread and fish) to the multitudes.

WALKING ON THE LAKE

MK. 6^{45-52}

6 45 And straightway he constrained his disciples to enter into the boat, and to go
before *him* unto the other side to Bethsaida,
while he himself sendeth the multitude
46 away. And after he had taken leave of
them, he departed into the mountain to
47 pray. And when even was come, the boat
was in the midst of the sea, and he alone
48 on the land. And seeing them distressed
in rowing, for the wind was contrary unto
them, about the fourth watch of the night
he cometh unto them, walking on the sea;
and he would have passed by them;
49 but they, when they saw him walking on
the sea, supposed that it was an appari-
50 tion, and cried out: for they all saw him,
and were troubled. But he straightway
spake with them, and saith unto them, Be
51 of good cheer: it is I; be not afraid. And
he went up unto them into the boat; and
the wind ceased: and they were sore
52 amazed in themselves; for they understood
not concerning the loaves, but their heart
was hardened.

MT. 14^{22-33}

14 22 And straightway he constrained the
disciples to enter into the boat, and to go
before him unto the other side, till he
23 should send the multitudes away. And
after he had sent the multitudes away, he
went up into the mountain apart to pray:
and when even was come, he was there
24 alone. But the boat was now in the
midst of the sea, distressed by the waves;
25 for the wind was contrary. And in the
fourth watch of the night he came unto
26 them, walking upon the sea. And when
the disciples saw him walking on the sea,
they were troubled, saying, It is an apparition; and they cried out for fear.
27 But straightway Jesus spake unto them,
saying, Be of good cheer; it is I; be not
28 afraid. And Peter answered him and
said, Lord, if it be thou, bid me come
29 unto thee upon the waters. And he said,
Come. And Peter went down from the
boat, and walked upon the waters, to
30 come to Jesus. But when he saw the
wind, he was afraid; and beginning to

sink, he cried out, saying, Lord, save me.
31 And immediately Jesus stretched forth
his hand, and took hold of him, and saith
unto him, O thou of little faith, wherefore
32 didst thou doubt? And when they were
gone up into the boat, the wind ceased.
33 And they that were in the boat worshipped him, saying, Of a truth thou art the Son of God.

JN. 6^{15-21}

6 15 Jesus therefore perceiving that they were about to come and take him by force, to make him king, withdrew again into the mountain himself alone.
16 And when evening came, his disciples
17 went down unto the sea; and they entered
into a boat, and were going over the sea unto Capernaum. And it was now dark, and Jesus had not yet come to them.
18 And the sea was rising by reason of a great
19 wind that blew. When therefore they had
rowed about five and twenty or thirty furlongs, they behold Jesus walking on the sea, and drawing nigh unto the boat:
20 and they were afraid. But he saith unto
21 them, It is I; be not afraid. They were
willing therefore to receive him into the boat: and straightway the boat was at the land whither they were going.

Mk. relates that, after the Feeding, *immediately* Jesus *compelled* His disciples to embark in the boat and go ahead across the Lake to Bethsaida whilst He dismisses the multitude.

When He had said farewell to them (the term for a courteous leave-taking is used) He departed into ‘ the mountain ’ to pray. Although the insistent needs of the multitude had compelled Jesus to sacrifice the leisure He was seeking, He does not Himself hurry away from them as soon as His ministration is over. He does, however, provide for immediate quietude for His disciples by compelling them to leave Him with the multitude and to go off in the boat.

Mk.'s statement about the disciples going ahead to Bethsaida conflicts with Jn. 6^{17}, that the disciples went across to Capernaum. Commentators have been much concerned by this apparent contradiction, but the matter is of no real importance. *Prima facie* there seems more to be said for Capernaum than for Bethsaida as the destination of the Apostles.

When evening fell (Mk. 6^{47}) the Apostles in the boat were in the midst of the Lake and Jesus alone on the land. The note of time here has caused difficulty because, already before the feeding of the five thousand (Mk. 6^{35}), it has been stated that the hour was late.

The word ‘late’ might refer to any time ‘ between the evenings,’ three to five in the afternoon. Out on the Lake the apostles were ‘tormented’ by a head wind and had to row. Jesus, Mk. states, saw them on the Lake, apparently from the mountain where He was praying, and in the fourth watch of the night, i.e. between 3 a.m. and 6 a.m., came to them, walking on the sea. Then Mk. makes the extraordinary statement (omitted by Mt.) that He wished to pass them by. The disciples, however, saw Him walking upon the sea and supposed it was a phantasm—a psychical appearance—and they cried out. And then Mk. adds, to make assurance doubly sure (unless it be a marginal gloss which has crept into the text), ‘for they all saw Him and were troubled.’ Immediately Jesus spoke to them and said: ‘ Take courage, it is I, don't be afraid.’ And He went into the boat and the wind ceased, and they were extraordinarily astonished, for they had not understood about the loaves; for their heart (i.e. their consciousness, moral and spiritual) was insensitive (literally, had been made callous).

A PROBLEM IN LITERARY CRITICISM

Mt. inserts into Mk.'s account an extraordinary story of St. Peter challenging the apparition of Jesus to bid him come to Him on the water. Peter attempts to do so and losing faith would have sunk, but was saved by the help of Jesus.

Mt. also adds that when Jesus came into the boat all the disciples worshipped Him saying: 'Truly thou art the Son of God.' As the Apostles had not yet confessed Jesus to be the Messiah, Mt. is surely mistaken in making them here worship Him as the Messiah.

Jn.'s account also differs from Mk.'s in important respects. The difference between Capernaum and Bethsaida as the destination of the Apostles has already been noted. Jn. does not relate that Jesus entered the boat, but that when the disciples were willing to receive Him into the boat, then the boat was immediately at the shore whither they went, although at the moment of their sighting Jesus they were some twenty-five or thirty furlongs out from the eastern side of the Lake; which it is supposed must mean that they were a considerable distance from the western shore.

Jesus walking on the Lake has no parallel in Lk., who omits from now onwards, until Peter's confession at Cæsarea Philippi, every incident which Mk. records. Some have supposed that this was owing to Luke having access to a shorter and earlier form of Mk.'s Gospel—a hypothetical document which used to be named *Ur-Marcus*.

This theory is discredited by Dr. Streeter's view that Lk., unlike Mt., did not use Mk. as a primary source for his Gospel, but coming across Mk. after he (Lk.) had made a first draft of the Third Gospel, he then intercalated a certain number of passages from Mk. into the Third Gospel. If this be so, then the omission from Lk. of this series of sections from Mk. would not necessarily indicate that they were absent from Lk.'s text of Mk., but simply that he (Lk.) did not think these Marcan sections worthy to be included in his own Gospel. The fact that Mt.'s Gospel, which is probably as old as our present Lk., contains all these omitted sections (save two) would seem to point to their having been part of Mk.'s original Gospel. The sections Lk. omits are:

(1) Jesus walking on the Lake.

(2) The landing at Gennesaret.

(3) The real uncleanness.

(4) The healing of the Syrophœnician woman's daughter.

(5) The healing of the deaf-mute.

(6) The feeding of the four thousand.

(7) Warnings against signs and against the leaven of the Pharisees. (There are references to these in the Lukan teaching—Lk. $11^{16, 29}$, 12^{1}.)

(8) The blind man of Bethsaida who saw men like trees walking.

Mt. omits (5) and (8) of the above.

It is possible to perceive a reason for Luke's omission in every case.

(1) He probably regarded this as an hallucination.

(2) If (1) goes, then (2) must naturally go also.

(3) Luke invariably omits all controversies which concern Jewish ritual as of no interest to his Gentile readers.

(4) This incident might easily be interpreted as indicating that Jesus despised the Gentiles and that He had not come to be their Saviour.

(5) The method of the healing of this man is unusual for Jesus, and Luke may easily have viewed the account with suspicion.

(6) This Luke may have regarded as merely a doublet of the feeding of the five thousand or as not demanding to be included since he had already recorded the feeding of the five thousand.

(7) Luke has references to these warnings, but they probably come from Q, not from Mk.

(8) In the case of this miracle also the method is unusual. Moreover, Jesus appears to be unsuccessful at the first attempt and only succeeds completely at the second. Professor Percy Gardner has said: 'Luke dearly loves a good miracle,' and this plainly is not a good miracle.

If these omitted sections seemed to present difficulties to Luke which precluded their insertion into his Gospel, they are not without difficulties for the modern reader. And these difficulties, we shall see, are of various kinds: not the least of them being historical credibility, at least in the walking on the water, the healing of the deaf-mute, the feeding of the four thousand and the healing of the blind man at Bethsaida.

Their literary style is sufficiently like that of Mk. to allow of their being regarded as part of the original Gospel. But if, following the universal tradition of the primitive Church, we accept as generally reliable the theory that Mark's Gospel contains the Roman preaching of Peter, it may yet be possible that these sections were not derived from the original Petrine source. This would seem to be the case with the eschatological discourse in Mk. 13, and it may be the case here. It we were to accept such a conclusion, the question of style would not come in, since *ex hypothesi*, if part of the original gospel of Mk., the style would be Marcan.

It is the conflict of certain of the contents of some of these sections with the rest of the Gospel which makes us insecure as to their Petrine origin, and would forbid their being regarded as crucial for the interpretation of the mission and methods of Jesus and as tests of the historical credibility of the Marcan-Petrine tradition.

There is, however, a third possibility that these sections, or at least some of them, although part of the original Roman Petrine preaching, may yet relate incidents which Peter had on hearsay, and which were not his actual experience.

What we should wish the reader to realise here is something of the nature of the problems presented by these sections, but not to assume that these problems have been solved, or indeed can be solved.

St. Augustine said of Holy Scripture that whilst it contained pools at which lambs might drink it also contained depths in which elephants must swim.

It is not surprising that those who attack the essentially historical character of Mk. should make their assault on those sections which Lk. omits, but whilst it is not surprising it is also significant. These sections, with chapter 13, are most open to doubt as to whether they constituted part of the original Mk., or at least part of the original Petrine preaching.

THE LANDING AT GENNESARET

MK. 6^{53-56}

6 53 And when they had crossed over, they
came to the land unto Gennesaret, and
54 moored to the shore. And when they
were come out of the boat, straightway
55 *the people* knew him, and ran round about
that whole region, and began to carry
about on their beds those that were sick,
56 where they heard he was. And wheresoever he entered, into villages, or into cities,
or into the country, they laid the sick in
the marketplaces, and besought him that
they might touch if it were but the border
of his garment: and as many as touched
him were made whole.

MT. 14^{34-36}

14 34 And when they had crossed over, they
came to the land, unto Gennesaret.
35 And when the men of that place knew
him, they sent into all that region round
about, and brought unto him all that
36 were sick; and they besought him that
they might only touch the border of his
garment: and as many as touched were
made whole.

Gennesaret was the name of the small fertile plain on the edge of which the town of Capernaum was situated. The phrase 'moored to the shore' (R.V.) does not occur elsewhere in Mk. The word for 'beds' is Marcan and means mattresses or perhaps sleeping-rugs, such as the paralytic carried off when Jesus said to him, 'Take up thy bed.'

'Marketplaces' seems strange in connexion with the country, but a rural market-place would consist of nothing more than cross-roads.

'The border of his garment,' the *zizith* of the *tallith*, has already been explained in connexion with the healing of the woman with the issue of blood.

THE REAL UNCLEANNESS

MK. 7^{1-23}

7 1 And there are gathered together unto
him the Pharisees, and certain of the
scribes, which had come from Jerusalem,
2 and had seen that some of his disciples ate
their bread with defiled, that is, un-
3 washen, hands. For the Pharisees, and all
the Jews, except they wash their hands
diligently, eat not, holding the tradition
4 of the elders: and *when they come* from the
marketplace, except they wash themselves,
they eat not: and many other things there
be, which they have received to hold,
washing of cups, and pots, and brasen
5 vessels. And the Pharisees and the
scribes ask him, Why walk not thy disciples according to the tradition of the
elders, but eat their bread with defiled

MT. 15^{1-20}

15 1 Then there come to Jesus from Jerusa-
2 lem Pharisees and scribes, saying, Why
do thy disciples transgress the tradition
of the elders? for they wash not their
3 hands when they eat bread. And he
answered and said unto them, Why do
ye also transgress the commandment of
4 God because of your tradition. For God
said, Honour thy father and thy mother:
and, He that speaketh evil of father or
5 mother, let him die the death. But ye
say, Whosoever shall say to his father or
his mother, That wherewith thou
mightest have been profited by me is
6 given *to God*; he shall not honour his
father. And ye have made void the
word of God because of your tradition.

6 hands? And he said unto them, Well did
Isaiah prophesy of you hypocrites, as it is
written,
This people honoureth me with their
lips,
But their heart is far from me.
7 But in vain do they worship me,
Teaching *as their* doctrines the precepts of men.
8 Ye leave the commandment of God, and
9 hold fast the tradition of men. And he
said unto them, Full well do ye reject the
commandment of God, that ye may keep
10 your tradition. For Moses said, Honour
thy father and thy mother; and, He that
speaketh evil of father or mother, let him
11 die the death: but ye say, If a man shall
say to his father or his mother, That
wherewith thou mightest have been profited by me is Corban, that is to say,
12 Given *to God*; ye no longer suffer him to do
13 aught for his father or his mother; making
void the word of God by your tradition,
which ye have delivered: and many such
14 like things ye do. And he called to him
the multitude again, and said unto them,
15 Hear me all of you, and understand: there
is nothing from without the man, that
going into him can defile him: but the
things which proceed out of the man are
17 those that defile the man. And when he
was entered into the house from the multitude, his disciples asked of him the
18 parable. And he saith unto them, Are ye
so without understanding also? Perceive
ye not, that whatsoever from without goeth
19 into the man, *it* cannot defile him; because
it goeth not into his heart, but into his
belly, and goeth out into the draught?
This he said, making all meats clean.
20 And he said, That which proceedeth out
21 of the man, that defileth the man. For
from within, out of the heart of men, evil
22 thoughts proceed, fornications, thefts,
murders, adulteries, covetings, wicked-
nesses, deceit, lasciviousness, an evil eye,
23 railing, pride, foolishness: all these evil
things proceed from within, and defile the
man.

7 Ye hypocrites, well did Isaiah prophesy
of you, saying,
8 This people honoureth me with their
lips;
But their heart is far from me.
9 But in vain do they worship me,
Teaching *as their* doctrines the precepts of men.
10 And he called to him the multitude, and
said unto them, Hear, and understand:
11 Not that which entereth into the mouth
defileth the man; but that which proceedeth out of the mouth, this defileth
12 the man. Then came the disciples, and
said unto him, Knowest thou that the
Pharisees were offended, when they
13 heard this saying? But he answered and
said, Every plant which my heavenly
Father planted not, shall be rooted up.
14 Let them alone: they are blind guides.
And if the blind guide the blind, both
15 shall fall into a pit. And Peter answered
and said unto him, Declare unto us the
16 parable. And he said, Are ye also even
17 yet without understanding? Perceive
ye not, that whatsoever goeth into the
mouth passeth into the belly, and is cast
18 out into the draught? But the things
which proceed out of the mouth come
forth out of the heart; and they defile the
19 man. For out of the heart come forth
evil thoughts, murders, adulteries, forni-
20 cations, thefts, false witness, railings: these
are the things which defile the man: but
to eat with unwashen hands defileth not
the man.

The R.V., following the best manuscripts, omits Mk. 7^{16}, 'If any man hath ears to hear, let him hear.'

This section of Mk. is a very mixed one. It consists of three attacks made by Jesus upon Pharisaic legalism and scribal casuistry. (A, 1–8; B, 9–13; C, 14–23.)

A. The first deals with religious ablutions.

B. The second deals with the Corban casuistry.

C. The third deals with clean and unclean foods.

Although these three criticisms of contemporary Judaism were probably delivered on separate occasions by Jesus, they have all been welded into one body of teaching by Mk. as pointing to the essential difference between the teaching of Jesus and that of the Pharisees on the crucial issue of what God requires from man.

(*a*) Religious Ablutions (1–8)

The Pharisees, who were the self-constituted guardians of religious observance in their localities, accompanied by certain of the experts of their party whom presumably they had summoned to their aid from Jerusalem in their organised opposition to the mission of Jesus in Galilee, observed that some of the disciples of Jesus, following the example of their Master (as we see from Lk. 11^{38}), were eating with 'common' or unwashed hands.

Mk. asserts that the Jews practised these ritual ablutions in obedience to the Tradition of the Elders (i.e. the extra-legal ritual regulations developed by successive generations of Jewish scribes for the protection of the great precepts of the Law). There was an obvious tendency among the less discerning Jews to give to the regulations of the scribes more thought than they devoted to the principles of the Law. Jesus regarded the Tradition of the Elders as detrimental to moral and spiritual religion and even as hostile to the Law which it sought to protect. Yet Jesus, although He regarded the Law as possessed of Divine authority in comparison with the human authority of the Tradition of the Elders, did not view even the Law itself as perfect. As Messiah He interpreted its precepts in the light of moral and spiritual principles which went beyond the letter of the Law, and sometimes even against it. It was said to them of old time—but, 'I say unto you.'

The Jews of this period attached great religious importance to ablutions. Jesus, in the spirit of the great eighth-century prophets of Israel, and the fourth-century poet-philosophers of Greece, attached no religious value to ablutions.

To the pure precincts of Apollo's fountain
Come, pure in heart, and touch the lustral wave.
One drop sufficeth for the guiltless mortal,
All else, e'en Ocean's billows cannot lave.

So wrote Euripides of the Delphic Spring—the most sacred baptismal laver of the Hellenic world.

And when Isaiah wrote (1^{16}) 'Wash you, make you clean,' his exhortation is directed not to washing the body but to moral reformation.

In criticism of the emphasis placed by the scribes on the Tradition of the Elders, Jesus cites Is. 29^{13}, in which the prophet complains of the verbal honour given to God by those whose hearts are far from Him. The quotation comes short of the aptness which characterises our Lord's citations from the Old Testament.

[Mk. explains the term 'common,' or 'defiled,' hands for his Gentile readers. (Mt., who is writing for Jewish readers, omits Mk.'s explanation.) The term 'diligently' (R.V.) is either meant to be the translation of an inferior textual variant 'frequently' or of a better textual variant 'with the fist.' Possibly some ritual prescription for rubbing one hand over the other in washing. Others interpret the phrase as 'washing up to the elbow.' Mk. states erroneously that all Jews observed these ritual ablutions, prescribed by the Tradition of the Elders. It was only the Pharisees who observed them all.]

(*b*) Casuistry and Corban (9–13)

Jesus finds an example of the scribal tendency to observe the Tradition of the Elders at the expense of the Law in the way in which they allow their Corban casuistry to override the Fifth Commandment. Apparently a son, asked by his father to support him, could escape the financial obligation by saying to his father that the money asked for was Corban, that is to say, dedicated for presentation to the Corban or Temple treasury. It is even alleged that having made this statement he could escape fulfilling it. There seems grave doubt as to whether this could really have been the case.

The Jewish Mishna, which preserves the Tradition of the Elders, was codified a good deal later than the Ministry of Jesus, but it may reflect Rabbinical teaching which was contemporary with Him. The Mishna is in agreement with the teaching of Jesus: that no vows or dedications could release a man from the obligation to support his parents. There may, however, have been some scribes, contemporary with Jesus, who taught that Corban vows and dedications could release a man from his filial obligations. Also it is possible that Christian criticism of such Jewish casuistry may account for the Mishna's teaching on this point.

(*c*) Can Food Defile? (14–23)

Here Jesus reverts to the question of uncleanness, but addresses not the Pharisees but the multitude.

Jesus has already declared that eating with unwashed hands does not make a man unclean in the sight of God. He now declares that even eating unclean foods cannot do it. Nothing that enters into a man through his mouth can make him really unclean. It is only that which comes forth from his heart (i.e. from his moral and spiritual consciousness, not from his body) which makes him unclean in God's sight. What are these things? Mk. gives a list of them, probably an elucidatory expansion of the teaching of Jesus provided by the primitive Christian Church in Rome. In this list occurs the curious phrase, 'an evil eye.' This does not refer to magical practices but to a spirit of hardness, meanness, grudging, as in Mt. 6^{23}, 20^{15}. This is illustrated by the following Old Testament passages: Dt. 15^{9}; Prov. 23^{6}; Ecclus. 14^{10}.

Mk. 7^{19b}, 'making all meats clean' should be 'making all *foods* clean': meat being the Tudor English for food. This passage is lacking from Mt. and may be a marginal gloss explaining the bearing of this teaching of Jesus upon the legal distinction between clean and unclean foods.

It is impossible not to ask why, if St. Peter had heard this teaching of Jesus, he should have required the vision on the housetop of Simon the Tanner at Joppa. (Acts 10 and 11^{1-23}.)

In that vision the Divine voice says: 'Rise, Peter, kill and eat,' but Peter replies: 'Not so, Lord, for nothing common or unclean hath at any time entered my mouth.'

To which the Divine voice makes reply: 'What God hath made clean, call not thou common. (Acts 10^{15}, 11^{9}.)

This narrative in Acts suggests either that Peter had never heard this teaching of Jesus about the real uncleanness, or else had failed entirely to understand it.

Of course Mk.'s Gospel emphasises again and again the lack of understanding on the part of the Apostles, and this no doubt does represent in some measure Peter's accusing conscience as, looking back, he reflected on his failure to realise the significance of his beloved Master's teaching, which at a later date had become clear to him.

It should be added, however, that the significance of the vision on the housetop is interpreted in Acts, not as vouchsafed in order to obliterate the Jewish distinction between clean and unclean foods but to obliterate the distinction between clean and unclean men—i.e. Jews and Gentiles. St. Peter, according to his critic St. Paul in the Epistle to the Galatians ($2^{12f.}$), would seem to have eaten unclean foods with unclean men—i.e. Gentile Christians at Antioch; but, apprehensive of criticism from Jewish Christians, he gave up the practice, at least on that occasion, and in consequence incurred the well-merited rebuke of the Apostle of the Gentiles.

Yet another difficulty is created by Acts in its accounts of the Council of Jerusalem and the letter issued by that Council. That Council was concerned, among other things, with the food question as it affected Gentile Christians. Yet in the discussion in the Council where James, the brother of Jesus, presided, no reference is made to the teaching of Jesus on the food question, though we should naturally expect it if such teaching of Jesus were known. Lk., in writing Acts 13, may have had apologetic reasons for an omission here, yet *prima facie* the most natural explanation of the omission is that the teaching of Jesus on the food question was not in the possession of the Church of Jerusalem over which James presided. But as against this, there is the attitude of St. Paul.

St. Paul, most certainly, regarded Jesus, not simply as a liberator from the Tradition of the Elders but even as a liberator from the Law itself. St. Paul seems to have had no doubt that in ignoring the ceremonial distinction between clean and unclean foods he had the authority of Jesus behind him.

(Cf. Rom. 14^{20}, 'All things indeed are clean'; 1 Cor. 8^{8}, 'But food will not commend us to God'; and possibly Titus 1^{15}, 'All things are clean to the clean.')

B. THE FLIGHT OF JESUS FROM GALILEE

JESUS IN EXILE: THE SYROPHŒNICIAN WOMAN

MK. 7^{24-30}

7 24 And from thence he arose, and went
away into the borders of Tyre and Sidon.
And he entered into a house, and would
have no man know it: and he could not
25 be hid. But straightway a woman, whose
little daughter had an unclean spirit,
having heard of him, came and fell down
26 at his feet. Now the woman was a Greek,
a Syrophœnician by race. And she

MT. 15^{21-28}

15 21 And Jesus went out thence, and withdrew into the parts of Tyre and Sidon.
22 And behold, a Canaanitish woman came
out from those borders, and cried, saying,
Have mercy on me, O Lord, thou son of
David; my daughter is grievously vexed
23 with a devil. But he answered her not a
word. And his disciples came and besought him, saying, Send her away; for

besought him that he would cast forth the
27 devil out of her daughter. And he said
unto her, Let the children first be filled:
for it is not meet to take the children's
28 bread and cast it to the dogs. But she
answered and saith unto him, Yea, Lord:
even the dogs under the table eat of the
29 children's crumbs. And he said unto her,
For this saying go thy way; the devil is
30 gone out of thy daughter. And she went
away unto her house, and found the child
laid upon the bed, and the devil gone out.

24 she crieth after us. But he answered and
said, I was not sent but unto the lost
25 sheep of the house of Israel. But she
came and worshipped him, saying, Lord,
26 help me. And he answered and said, It
is not meet to take the children's bread
27 and cast it to the dogs. But she said,
Yea, Lord: for even the dogs eat of the
crumbs which fall from their masters'
28 table. Then Jesus answered and said
unto her, O woman, great is thy faith:
be it done unto thee even as thou wilt.
And her daughter was healed from that
hour.

The story of the Syrophœnician woman relates that the incident took place on the borders (Mt. has 'regions') of Tyre and Sidon. Some texts omit 'and Sidon.'

Both towns were situated on the Syrian coast—Tyre being just level with the northern boundary of Galilee, and Sidon some thirty miles north of it.

Jesus has become an exile—a refugee. Mk. relates that He entered into a house and He wished no one to know it; and He was not able to be concealed, for a woman, hearing about Him, immediately came. . . . Mt. omits this very significant statement by Mk. Obviously Jesus has not gone into Phœnicia (the home of the great sea-race who contended with Rome for the mastery of the ancient world) in order to evangelise it. He appears to have fled from Galilee because of the growing opposition of the ecclesiastical and political authorities. Some assume, and perhaps correctly, that He had not fled but was merely seeking that quiet and privacy for His disciples and Himself which He had failed to secure in Galilee. The effort fails.

A Syrophœnician woman—that is to say (as Mk. explains), she was Syrophœnician by race but probably Greek-speaking. This should be noted, because it seems to indicate that although our Lord undoubtedly used Aramaic as the language of His Ministry, yet it is possible that He conversed with this woman in Greek. Of course if the woman had spoken the Punic language of the Phœnician race, Jesus might well have understood her, as it is a Semitic language, not so very different from Aramaic and Hebrew, but Mk.'s statement that, although Syrophœnician by race, the woman was a Greek, seems to point to Greek as her language.

Since the Oriental campaigns of Alexander the Great (*circa* 333 B.C.) Greek had become the *lingua franca* of the East. Mt. calls the woman a Canaanite and says nothing about her being Greek-speaking.

The woman's little daughter was ill. The nature of the illness is not described. It is said to be due to possession by an unclean demon—the ancient equivalent for a modern microbe. The woman comes into the house and throws herself at the feet of Jesus, begging Him to heal her daughter. He refuses; plainly because He does not desire the immediate publicity and thronging which must follow on an act of healing. He had tried to heal in private, but it was all in vain. He had sternly charged those whom He had healed not to talk about it, but they had disregarded His injunctions.

Jesus replies to the woman's supplication: ' Allow the children to be fed first, it is not fair to throw the children's bread to the house dogs.' The woman retorts: ' True, O Lord, yet the little dogs under the table do eat of the children's crumbs.' Jesus recognises the aptness of the woman's reply and then, in a spirit of chivalrous humour, does that which He had not intended to do. He answers: ' On account of this saying, go thy way, the demon has gone forth from thy daughter '; and she departing to her home found the child laid on a bed and the demon gone forth.

There can be no doubt that we have here the record of an actual incident. We have many examples of our Lord's readiness of retort in controversy: this incident alone records His appreciation of it in the case of another.

The word for dog used in the dialogue with the Syrophœnician woman is a double diminutive and does not occur elsewhere in the Gospels. It describes a little dog, kept in the house, in contrast to the pariah dog of the streets. These pariah or scavenger dogs were regarded by the Jews as unclean. Hence the term ' dog ' became one of contempt applied to unclean persons (Gentiles; sodomites, cf. Dt. 23^{18}; those unfit to be citizens of the New Jerusalem, Rev. 22^{15}).

Among the ancient Jews the dog was not the companion and friend of man. The only case in which the dog appears in this capacity is in the Apocryphal *Book of Tobit*—Tobit's little dog accompanies him on his journey. Perhaps the Phœnicians in contrast to the Jews made pets of dogs; this may have led to our Lord's comparison between children and pet dogs.

It must not therefore be argued that our Lord is here adopting the common Jewish attitude of comparing Gentiles to dogs, since, as we have pointed out, the term dog used here is not the ordinary term for scavenger dogs.

Mt.'s account, which is plainly based on Mk., omits or alters much that is significant and makes some notable but hardly convincing additions. We have seen that Mt. omits all reference to our Lord as a refugee and His inability to secure privacy; also the fact that the woman, although she belonged to one race, spoke the language of another. Again, Mt. omits that the woman actually came into the house. He represents her as following Jesus and His disciples on the road, crying out: ' Have mercy upon me, O Lord, thou Son of David.' It is curious that a Phœnician should apply the Messianic title to Jesus, for even His own disciples (according to Mk.) had not yet confessed Him to be the Messiah. Mt. states that Jesus remained silent—' He answered her not a word.' His disciples then intervene and beg Him to send the woman off. He tells her, for plainly the statement must be addressed to her: ' I am not sent but unto the lost sheep of the House of Israel.' She comes forward and worships Him, saying: ' Lord, help me.' Then the Marcan dialogue follows, but Mt. changes ' children's crumbs ' into ' masters' crumbs '—suggesting the superiority of the Jew to the Gentile. Jesus replies: ' O woman, great is thy faith, may it be unto thee even as thou wilt.' It is the greatness of the woman's faith, not the aptness of her retort which in Mt. secures the healing of her daughter.

C. RETURN TO GALILEE *VIA* DECAPOLIS

THE DEAF-MUTE

MK. 7^{31-37}

7 31 And again he went out from the borders
of Tyre, and came through Sidon unto the
sea of Galilee, through the midst of the
32 borders of Decapolis. And they bring
unto him one that was deaf, and had an
impediment in his speech; and they be-
33 seech him to lay his hand upon him. And
he took him aside from the multitude
privately, and put his fingers into his ears,
34 and he spat, and touched his tongue; and
looking up to heaven, he sighed, and saith
unto him, Ephphatha, that is, Be opened.
35 And his ears were opened, and the bond
of his tongue was loosed, and he spake
36 plain. And he charged them that they
should tell no man: but the more he
charged them, so much the more a great
deal they published it.
37 And they were beyond measure astonished,
saying, He hath done all things well: he
maketh even the deaf to hear, and the
dumb to speak.

It would seem that our Lord left the Phœnician territory quickly. Mk. here gives us a very interesting but somewhat obscure geographical note:

'And again going forth from the Tyrian territory He passed through Sidon unto the Sea of Galilee travelling along the borders of the region of Decapolis.'

'Through the midst of' (R.V.) is a wrong translation. It should be 'between' or 'along the edge.' Our Lord's route, as here given by Mk., is circuitous. He first goes north through Sidon, then turns east and south and passes along where the Galilean territory of Antipas borders on the region of Decapolis and so reaches the Lake, presumably on its eastern side.

It has been ingeniously suggested that Sidon is a corruption for Bethsaida. If this be sound, then Jesus arrived at the north-east corner of the Lake in the locality where (according to Lk.) it would seem the feeding of the five thousand took place.

Mk.'s geographical note would seem to support the view that Jesus is a refugee, and that in His resolve to visit the Lake once again He cautiously skirts the territory of Antipas in order to do so.

When He gets to the Lake, He is naturally recognised, and a deaf-mute is brought to Him (literally carried) to be healed. The usual crowd has assembled. The deaf-mute is probably the right description of the patient. (Cf. Is. 35^{6}.)

Jesus puts his fingers in the man's ears and touches his tongue with saliva; no doubt with the intention of awakening faith. He then looked up to heaven and groaned and said in Aramaic: 'Be opened.' The cure proves effective. Again He charges them not to talk about it, but in vain.

The use of saliva by Jesus occurs also in the healing of the blind man of Bethsaida: another act of healing peculiar to Mk. (8^{22-26}). Saliva was generally believed to have curative properties and the action of Jesus would suggest to the invalid that he was being cured. The significance of the groaning, which may be compared to Jn.'s account of the raising of Lazarus, can be interpreted in many ways. Perhaps Jesus sees in the sufferings of the patient the power of evil in human life. No doubt the primitive Church regarded this act of healing as a fulfilment of Is. $35^{5,6}$.

THE FEEDING OF THE FOUR THOUSAND

MK. 8^{1-10}

8 1 In those days, when there was again a
great multitude, and they had nothing to
eat, he called unto him his disciples, and
2 saith unto them, I have compassion on the
multitude, because they continue with me
now three days, and have nothing to eat:
3 and if I send them away fasting to their
home, they will faint in the way; and some
4 of them are come from far. And his disciples
ciples answered him, Whence shall one be
able to fill these men with bread here in a
5 desert place? And he asked them, How
many loaves have ye? And they said,
6 Seven. And he commandeth the multitude to sit down on the ground: and he
took the seven loaves, and having given
thanks, he brake, and gave to his disciples,
to set before them; and they set them
7 before the multitude. And they had a
few small fishes: and having blessed them,
he commanded to set these also before
8 them. And they did eat, and were filled:
and they took up, of broken pieces that
9 remained over, seven baskets. And they
were about four thousand: and he sent
10 them away. And straightway he entered
into the boat with his disciples, and came
into the parts of Dalmanutha.

MT. 15^{32-39}

15 32 And Jesus called unto him his disciples,
and said, I have compassion on the
multitude, because they continue with
me now three days and have nothing to
eat: and I would not send them away
fasting, lest haply they faint in the way.
33 And the disciples say unto him, Whence
should we have so many loaves in a
desert place, as to fill so great a multi-
34 tude? And Jesus saith unto them, How
many loaves have ye? And they said,
35 Seven, and a few small fishes. And he
commanded the multitude to sit down on
36 the ground; and he took the seven loaves
and the fishes; and he gave thanks and
brake, and gave to the disciples, and the
37 disciples to the multitudes. And they
did all eat, and were filled: and they took
up that which remained over of the
38 broken pieces, seven baskets full. And
they that did eat were four thousand
39 men, beside women and children. And
he sent away the multitudes, and entered
into the boat, and came into the borders
of Magadan.

It has often been discussed whether the feeding of the four thousand is merely a doublet (or second account) of the feeding of the five thousand.

Mk. undoubtedly regards it as a separate occurrence. The account opens with the word 'again.' In Mk. 8^{19} Jesus is cited as definitely referring to both miracles of the feeding—five loaves among five thousand with twelve baskets (*kophinoi*) of fragments: seven loaves among four thousand and seven baskets (*spurides*) of fragments. It should be noted that the word having given thanks in *v.* 6 is that from which 'Eucharist' is derived.

There is great difficulty in understanding how the disciples, after the feeding of the five thousand, could have put the question to Jesus in *v.* 4: 'Whence shall one be able to fill these men with bread here in a desert place?' Really, they must have been dense beyond words: unless the feeding of the five thousand was not miraculous but was susceptible of some entirely natural explanation known to the Apostles, but which they did not regard as able to happen on this occasion. The account ends with a reference to the boat, which, if these events are in chronological order, had not been used for some time.

Dalmanutha (Mk. 8^{10}) is an enigma. Mt.'s parallel has Magadan (which has support in some codices of Mk.) with a variant reading Magdala: no doubt the place whence came Mary the Magdalene. Magdala may probably be identified with *El Mejdel* and is situated on the west side of the Lake, between Tiberias and Capernaum. It has been suggested that Dalmanutha is the Aramaic for 'into the parts of'—the phrase which occurs just before it in the text. Others have suggested that Dalmanutha is a corruption of *Migdol-nunia.* At any rate no such place as Dalmanutha is known in the locality.

THE SIGN FROM HEAVEN CONDEMNED

MK. 8^{11-12}

8 11 And the Pharisees came forth, and began
to question with him, seeking of him a sign
12 from heaven, tempting him. And he
sighed deeply in his spirit, and saith, Why
doth this generation seek a sign? verily I
say unto you, There shall no sign be given
unto this generation.

MT. 16^{1-4}

16 1 And the Pharisees and Sadducees came,
and tempting him asked him to shew
2 them a sign from heaven. But he
answered and said unto them, When it is
evening, ye say, *It will be* fair weather:
3 for the heaven is red. And in the morning,
It will be foul weather to-day: for the
heaven is red and lowring. Ye know
how to discern the face of the heaven;
but ye cannot *discern* the signs of the
4 times. An evil and adulterous generation
seeketh after a sign; and there shall
no sign be given unto it, but the sign of
Jonah. And he left them, and departed.

MT. 12^{38-42}

12 38 Then certain of the scribes and Pharisees
answered him, saying, Master, we
39 would see a sign from thee. But he
answered and said unto them, An evil
and adulterous generation seeketh after a
sign; and there shall no sign be given to
40 it but the sign of Jonah the prophet: for
as Jonah was three days and three nights
in the belly of the whale; so shall the Son
of man be three days and three nights in
41 the heart of the earth. The men of
Nineveh shall stand up in the judgement
with this generation, and shall condemn
it: for they repented at the preaching of
Jonah; and behold, a greater than Jonah
42 is here. The queen of the south shall
rise up in the judgement with this generation,
and shall condemn it: for she came
from the ends of the earth to hear the
wisdom of Solomon; and behold, a
greater than Solomon is here.

LK. 11^{16-32}

11 16 And others, tempting *him*, sought of
17 him a sign from heaven. But he, knowing
their thoughts, said unto them, Every
kingdom divided against itself is brought
to desolation; and a house *divided* against
18 a house falleth. And if Satan also is
divided against himself, how shall his
kingdom stand? because ye say that I
19 cast out devils by Beelzebub. And if I
by Beelzebub cast out devils, by whom do
your sons cast them out? therefore shall
20 they be your judges. But if I by the
finger of God cast out devils, then is the
21 kingdom of God come upon you. When
the strong *man* fully armed guardeth his
22 own court, his goods are in peace: but
when a stronger than he shall come upon
him, and overcome him, he taketh from
him his whole armour wherein he
23 trusted, and divideth his spoils. He that
is not with me is against me; and he that
24 gathereth not with me scattereth. The
unclean spirit when he is gone out of the
man, passeth through waterless places,
seeking rest; and finding none, he saith,
I will turn back unto my house whence I
25 came out. And when he is come, he
26 findeth it swept and garnished. Then
goeth he, and taketh *to him* seven other
spirits more evil than himself; and they
enter in and dwell there: and the last
state of that man becometh worse than
the first.
27 And it came to pass, as he said these
things, a certain woman out of the multitude
lifted up her voice, and said unto
him, Blessed is the womb that bare thee,

and the breasts which thou didst suck.
28 But he said, Yea rather, blessed are they
that hear the word of God, and keep it.
29 And when the multitudes were gathering together unto him, he began to say,
This generation is an evil generation: it
seeketh after a sign; and there shall no
sign be given to it but the sign of Jonah.
30 For even as Jonah became a sign unto
the Ninevites, so shall also the Son of
31 man be to this generation. The queen
of the south shall rise up in the judgement with the men of this generation,
and shall condemn them: for she came
from the ends of the earth to hear the
wisdom of Solomon; and behold, a
32 greater than Solomon is here. The men
of Nineveh shall stand up in the judgement with this generation, and shall condemn it: for they repented at the preaching of Jonah; and behold, a greater than
Jonah is here.

The Pharisees (Mt. adds 'and Sadducees') are now on the track of Jesus and demand from Him, in order to prove Him a deceiver, a sign from heaven. The word 'tempting' has the sinister meaning of putting to the test in order to prove that something is not what it seems to be. They were sure He could not give them a sign from heaven.

Moses had given divinely appointed signs of his commission to Pharaoh: lightning had supported the spiritual authority of Samuel and Elijah. Jesus condemns the demand, and groaning in spirit asks: Why does this generation seek a sign? Verily I say, there shall no sign be given to this generation. This attitude of Jesus towards the demand for signs is treated more fully in Mt. and Lk. In the sections which they cite from Q Jesus teaches emphatically that moral and spiritual teaching are self-authenticating and do not require the support of miracles. Jonah converted Nineveh by his preaching: yet he worked no miracle. Solomon, by his wisdom, won the Queen of Sheba: but he also worked no miracle. Jesus is conscious that His moral and spiritual teaching stands on a higher level than that of Jonah and Solomon and it needs no miracles to affirm its truth.

In Mt. those who seek a sign from Jesus are described by Him as evil and adulterous. By 'evil' is probably meant, so hardened as to be lacking in moral and spiritual perception: by 'adulterous' is meant 'disloyal to God.' Ever since the days of the prophet Hosea, adultery had had this second sense of spiritual infidelity. The dictum with which Jesus concludes the parable of the rich man and Lazarus: 'If they hear not Moses and the prophets, neither will they be persuaded though one rose from the dead' also exhibits the attitude of Jesus towards miracles. His statement, 'Verily I say, no sign shall be given to this generation,' caused perplexity to Christians even in very early days and is in acute conflict with the Fourth Gospel, which makes Jesus attach supreme importance to the evidence of miracles.

Mt. feels that one exception must be made to this declaration by Jesus, namely, the miracle of the Resurrection which he wrongly understands to be meant by the sign of Jonah. But the Resurrection was no sign given to that generation; only those who already believed in the Messiahship of Jesus experienced it.

In His attitude towards miracles, the teaching of Jesus is extremely modern. But it is only of very recent years that its real significance has been understood.

THE LEAVEN OF THE PHARISEES

MK. 8^{13-21}

8 13 And he left them, and again entering
into *the boat* departed to the other side.
14 And they forgot to take bread; and they
had not in the boat with them more than
15 one loaf. And he charged them, saying,
Take heed, beware of the leaven of the
16 Pharisees and the leaven of Herod. And
they reasoned one with another, saying,
17 We have no bread. And Jesus perceiving
it saith unto them, Why reason ye, because
ye have no bread? do ye not yet perceive,
neither understand? have ye your heart
18 hardened? Having eyes, see ye not? and
having ears, hear ye not? and do ye not
19 remember? When I brake the five loaves
among the five thousand, how many
baskets full of broken pieces took ye up?
20 They say unto him, Twelve. And when
the seven among the four thousand, how
many basketfuls of broken pieces took ye
up? And they say unto him, Seven.
21 And he said unto them, Do ye not yet
understand?

MT. 16^{5-12}

16 5 And the disciples came to the other
6 side and forgot to take bread. And Jesus
said unto them, Take heed and beware
of the leaven of the Pharisees and
7 Sadducees. And they reasoned among
themselves, saying, We took no bread.
8 And Jesus perceiving it said, O ye of
little faith, why reason ye among your-
9 selves, because ye have no bread? Do
ye not yet perceive, neither remember
the five loaves of the five thousand, and
10 how many baskets ye took up? Neither
the seven loaves of the four thousand,
11 and how many baskets ye took up? How
is it that ye do not perceive that I spake
not to you concerning bread? But
beware of the leaven of the Pharisees and
12 Sadducees. Then understood they how
that he bade them not beware of the
leaven of bread, but of the teaching of
the Pharisees and Sadducees.

LK. 12^{1}

12 1 In the mean time, when the many
thousands of the multitude were gathered
together, insomuch that they trode one
upon another, he began to say unto his
disciples first of all, Beware ye of the
leaven of the Pharisees, which is hypocrisy.

On one of their voyages across the Lake, the disciples having forgotten to lay in a store of bread and having but one loaf on board, misinterpret as a reproof of their forgetfulness a saying of Jesus that they should beware of the leaven of the Pharisees and of Herod (Mt. substitutes Sadducees for Herod).

Jesus reproves them for their misinterpretation by a reference to the feeding of the five thousand and the four thousand.

Mt. recognises the obscurity of Mk.'s account and adds an explanation that by His warning against leaven Jesus did not refer to bread at all but to the teaching of the Pharisees and Sadducees ($16^{11, 12}$).

Lk. records a warning by Jesus against the leaven of the Pharisees which that Evangelist understands to be hypocrisy (12^{1}). If the leaven of the Pharisees be interpreted as hypocrisy, the leaven of the Sadducees and the Herodians may well be interpreted as worldliness and materialism.

THE BLIND MAN OF BETHSAIDA

MK. 8^{22-26}

8 22 And they come unto Bethsaida. And
they bring to him a blind man, and
23 beseech him to touch him. And he took
hold of the blind man by the hand, and
brought him out of the village; and when
he had spit on his eyes, and laid his hands
upon him, he asked him, Seest thou aught?
24 And he looked up, and said, I see men;
25 for I behold *them* as trees, walking. Then
again he laid his hands upon his eyes; and
he looked stedfastly, and was restored, and
26 saw all things clearly. And he sent him
away to his home, saying, Do not even
enter into the village.

Jesus visits Bethsaida and a blind man is brought to Him to be healed. Jesus, as in the last act of healing recorded by Mk. (the deaf-mute), seeks to cure the patient in private. He makes use of saliva and touch. Jesus asks him, and the question is an unusual one: 'Seest thou aught?' The patient answers that he sees men as trees walking about. Again Jesus places His hands on his eyes and his sight is restored.

Nothing is said about faith in this act of healing. In this it is similar to the healing of the deaf-mute—the only other miracle of healing peculiar to Mk.

THE MESSIANIC SECRET CONFESSED BY ST. PETER

MK. 8^{27-30}

8 27 And Jesus went forth, and his disciples,
into the villages of Cæsarea Philippi: and
in the way he asked his disciples, saying
unto them, Who do men say that I am?
28 And they told him, saying, John the
Baptist: and others, Elijah; but others,
29 One of the prophets. And he asked them,
But who say ye that I am? Peter
answereth and saith unto him, Thou art
30 the Christ. And he charged them that
they should tell no man of him.

MT. 16^{13-20}

16 13 Now when Jesus came into the parts
of Cæsarea Philippi, he asked his disciples, saying, Who do men say that the
14 Son of man is? And they said, Some *say*
John the Baptist; some Elijah: and others,
15 Jeremiah, or one of the prophets. He
saith unto them, But who say ye that I
16 am? And Simon Peter answered and
said, Thou art the Christ, the Son of the
17 living God. And Jesus answered and
said unto him, Blessed art thou, Simon
Bar-Jonah: for flesh and blood hath not
revealed it unto thee, but my Father
18 which is in heaven. And I also say unto
thee, that thou art Peter, and upon this
rock I will build my church; and the
gates of Hades shall not prevail against it.
19 I will give unto thee the keys of the kingdom of heaven: and whatsoever thou
shalt bind on earth shall be bound in
heaven: and whatsoever thou shalt loose
20 on earth shall be loosed in heaven. Then
charged he the disciples that they should
tell no man that he was the Christ.

LK. 9^{18-21}

9 18 And it came to pass, as he was praying
alone, the disciples were with him: and he
asked them, saying, Who do the multitudes
19 say that I am? And they answering said,
John the Baptist; but others *say*, Elijah;
and others, that one of the old prophets is
20 risen again. And he said unto them, But
who say ye that I am? And Peter
21 answering said, The Christ of God. But
he charged them, and commanded *them* to
tell this to no man.

JN. 6^{66-69}

6 66 Upon this many of his disciples went
67 back, and walked no more with him. Jesus
said therefore unto the twelve, Would ye
68 also go away? Simon Peter answered
him, Lord, to whom shall we go? thou
69 hast the words of eternal life. And we
have believed and know that thou art the
Holy One of God.

As they are travelling on the road in the neighbourhood (Mk., villages; Mt., regions) of Cæsarea Philippi (the ancient Dan, situated in the northernmost point of Palestine), Jesus puts to His disciples the question : Who do men say that I am? The Apostles reply: John the Baptist; others, Elijah; others, one of the prophets. (Lk. has, 'one of the ancient prophets risen again,' and Mt. has, 'Jeremiah, or one of the prophets.') Jesus asks them : But who do ye say that I am? Peter answers him: Thou art the Messiah (the Anointed One, the Christ). Jesus charges the disciples that they should tell this to no man.

Lk., who here rejoins Mk., having left him immediately after the feeding of the five thousand, makes no reference to Cæsarea Philippi nor to the incident as taking place on the road, but states that Jesus was praying privately when His disciples came to Him and He put the question to them. Lk. gives Peter's confession in a form more understandable by his Gentile readers—'the Christ of God.'

Jn. is in agreement with Lk. in making Peter's confession follow immediately after the feeding of the five thousand. He relates that the teaching of Jesus, in exposition of that event, was so difficult that certain of His disciples left Him. Jesus then addresses the Twelve, saying: surely ye also do not wish to go away? Peter answers: O Lord, to whom shall we go away? Thou hast words (sayings) of eternal life and we have believed and know (from experience) that thou art the Holy One of God.

Mt.'s account is almost identical with Lk. but gives Peter's confession in a fuller form: 'Thou art the Christ, the Son of the Living God.' Mt.'s account is notable for the blessing which Jesus here bestows upon Peter. This blessing would seem to explain how Simon got the name of Peter (Petros) or the Rock man. It is because Jesus declares to Simon that He will found His Church (*ekklesia*) upon the rock (*petra*) of Simon's confession of Him as the Christ. This must be the meaning of this much-disputed passage. It cannot mean, unless it is to conflict with other New Testament teaching, that the Church is to be founded on Peter to the exclusion of the other Apostles and of Christ Himself.[1]

To the blessing, Christ adds the declaration that the Church so founded will never perish. The gates of Hades—the forces of death and destruction—shall not prevail against it. Then there follows the famous promise of the Keys of the Kingdom of Heaven: the statement that whatsoever Simon Bar-Jonah shall bind on earth shall be bound in heaven and whatsoever he shall loose on earth shall be loosed in heaven. These words are taken to signify the endowment of the Church with authority to legislate and order its constitution in accordance with the faith which confesses Jesus as the Messiah. Of course many Roman Catholic controversialists have interpreted this declaration as conferring a special privilege on Peter to the exclusion of the other Apostles. This, however, conflicts with Mt. (18^{18}): 'Verily I say unto you, whatsoever ye shall bind on earth shall be bound in heaven; and whatsoever ye shall loose on earth shall be loosed in heaven.' Compare also the declaration of the risen Christ in the Fourth Gospel, who, having breathed on His disciples, says: 'Receive ye the Holy Ghost. Whosesoever sins ye remit they are remitted unto them, and whosesoever sins ye retain

[1] Cf. my *Roman Church and the Modern Man.*

they are retained.' (Jn. 20^{23}.) The form of these promises to the whole apostolic body forbids the view that an exclusive authority and privilege is here conferred on St. Peter.

Mt.'s addition to the Marcan account of Peter's confession of the Messianic secret constitutes one of that interesting cycle of Petrine stories which characterise Mt. The historicity of these sections certainly seems to stand on a lower level than Mk. and Q. They indicate the very high estimation in which St. Peter was held in the Church (probably Antioch) in which Mt. originated.

Peter, not James, nor Paul, nor John, nor Thomas, is the apostolic saint and hero of this Church: and so legends which exalt him begin to cluster round his name. The fact that the phrase ' my church ' is put into the lips of Jesus in the promise of Jesus to Peter, a phrase which occurs nowhere else in the Gospel, suggests a late date for the dialogue.

THE FIRST PREDICTION OF THE PASSION

MK. 8^{31-33}

8 31 And he began to teach them, that the
Son of man must suffer many things, and
be rejected by the elders, and the chief
priests, and the scribes, and be killed, and
32 after three days rise again. And he spake
the saying openly. And Peter took him,
33 and began to rebuke him. But he turning
about, and seeing his disciples, rebuked
Peter, and saith, Get thee behind me,
Satan: for thou mindest not the things of
God, but the things of men.

MT. 16^{21-23}

16 21 From that time began Jesus to shew
unto his disciples, how that he must go
unto Jerusalem, and suffer many things
of the elders and chief priests and scribes,
and be killed, and the third day be raised
22 up. And Peter took him, and began to
rebuke him, saying, Be it far from thee,
23 Lord: this shall never be unto thee. But
he turned, and said unto Peter, Get thee
behind me, Satan: thou art a stumbling-
block unto me: for thou mindest not the
things of God, but the things of men.

LK. 9^{22}

9 22 The Son of man must suffer many
things, and be rejected of the elders and
chief priests and scribes, and be killed,
and the third day be raised up.

The Apostles having learnt the Messianic secret and having been charged by Jesus to keep it secret, He proceeds to teach them the true significance of His Messiahship. His Messiahship, He explains, will not be accepted by His nation. It must involve His rejection and death. It is at this point that the Passion teaching of Jesus begins.

It is here that Mk. undoubtedly uses the term Son of Man as a Messianic title, though whether it is to be understood of Jesus individually or of Himself together with the elect remnant which come unto God through Him, is open to dispute.

Jesus is to be rejected, not by the ignorant multitude, but by the elders, chief priests, and scribes, that is to say by the Sanhedrin, the official religious assembly which represented the nation. The melancholy declaration of the rejection and death of the Messiah is united to the inspiring statement that after three days He will rise again.

When Jesus proclaimed His rejection and death *with boldness* (this probably is the correct meaning, and not *publicly*), Peter began to rebuke Him semi-privately, but He rebuked Peter, saying unto him: Get thee behind me, Satan, for thou thinkest not the things of God but those of men.

Mt. makes the interesting addition to His declaration of suffering Messiahship that He must go up to Jerusalem. Mt. adds that Jesus described Peter as a stumbling-block to Him: that is to say, one who would lead Him to offend against the Divine Will.

THE DUTY OF CROSS-BEARING

MK. 8^{34}–9^{1}

8 34 And he called unto him the multitude
with his disciples, and said unto them, If
any man would come after me, let him
deny himself, and take up his cross, and
35 follow me. For whosoever would save his
life shall lose it; and whosoever shall lose
his life for my sake and the gospel's shall
36 save it. For what doth it profit a man, to
gain the whole world, and forfeit his life?
37 For what should a man give in exchange
38 for his life? For whosoever shall be
ashamed of me and of my words in this
adulterous and sinful generation, the Son
of man also shall be ashamed of him,
when he cometh in the glory of his Father
9 1 with the holy angels. And he said unto
them, Verily I say unto you, There be
some here of them that stand *by*, which
shall in no wise taste of death, till they see
the kingdom of God come with power.

MT. 16^{24-28}

16 24 Then said Jesus unto his disciples, If
any man would come after me, let him
deny himself, and take up his cross, and
25 follow me. For whosoever would save
his life shall lose it: and whosoever shall
lose his life for my sake shall find it.
26 For what shall a man be profited, if he
shall gain the whole word, and forfeit his
life? or what shall a man give in exchange
27 for his life? For the Son of man shall
come in the glory of his Father with his
angels; and then shall he render unto
28 every man according to his deeds. Verily
I say unto you, There be some of them
that stand here, which shall in no wise
taste of death, till they see the Son of
man coming in his kingdom.

LK. 9^{23-27}

9 23 And he said unto all, If any man would
come after me, let him deny himself, and
24 take up his cross daily, and follow me. For
whosoever would save his life shall lose it;
but whosoever shall lose his life for my
25 sake, the same shall save it. For what is a
man profited, if he gain the whole world,
26 and lose or forfeit his own self? For
whosoever shall be ashamed of me and of
my words, of him shall the Son of man be
ashamed, when he cometh in his own
glory, and *the glory* of the Father, and of
27 the holy angels. But I tell you of a truth,
There be some of them that stand here,
which shall in no wise taste of death, till
they see the kingdom of God.

MT. 10^{32-33}

10 32 Every one therefore who shall confess
me before men, him will I also confess
before my Father which is in heaven.
33 But whosoever shall deny me before men,
him will I also deny before my Father
which is in heaven.

LK. 12^{8-9}

12 8 And I say unto you, Every one who
shall confess me before men, him shall
the Son of man also confess before the
9 angels of God: but he that denieth me in
the presence of men shall be denied in
the presence of the angels of God.

MT. 10^{38-39}

10 38 And he that doth not take his cross and
follow after me, is not worthy of me.
39 He that findeth his life shall lose it; and
he that loseth his life for my sake shall
find it.

LK. 17^{33}

17 33 Whosoever shall seek to gain his life
shall lose it: but whosoever shall lose *his
life* shall preserve it.

In close connexion with the teaching that He is to be a Suffering Messiah, Jesus inculcates what loyalty to a Suffering Messiah must entail for His followers. If He is to bear the Cross, they also will be called upon to bear it in their turn. The Cross for Him is, as we have pointed out, not the Cross of an expiatory sacrifice but the Cross of perfect obedience to His Father's Will. This perfect obedience entails vicarious suffering for Him who would lead others along the narrow path to Eternal Life. The Cross for the followers of Jesus means loyalty to Him and to His principles. Shame and persecution must be the inevitable lot of these primitive Jewish disciples who should dare to affirm their conviction that the crucified Jesus was the Messiah. Many would shrink from such a confession, but Jesus points to that future time when the about-to-be-rejected-and-crucified Messiah will be hailed as triumphant and divine, and affirms that in that day He will be ashamed of those who are now ashamed of Him.

Closely connected with the duty of Cross-bearing is the teaching that the seeking to preserve one's life is the way to lose it: while the willingness to sacrifice one's life is the way to gain it. This is undoubtedly what is meant by these sayings of Jesus. More is meant than that if a man is willing to sacrifice his physical life in this world he shall secure a blessed immortality for his spirit in the world to come. The lesson that Jesus is teaching is the enrichment of a life which is lived in a spirit of social self-sacrifice, and the impoverishment and even dissolution of a life which is lived in the spirit of individualist selfishness.

The heroic self-sacrificing type of life secures, not only an enrichment of the personal life of the individual, but also an enrichment of the social life of the community. 'Except a grain of wheat fall into the earth and die, it abideth by itself alone, but if it die, it beareth much fruit' (Jn. 12^{24}) is a saying of Jesus in the Fourth Gospel which is united to the dictum: 'He that loveth his life loseth it: and he that hateth his life in this world shall keep it unto life eternal.'

The essence of the Christian life is not found in self-renunciation, nor in self-realisation, but in self-consecration to the Divine Will; and this self-consecration is no more selfish for the Christian than it was for Jesus Himself. 'For their sakes I consecrate myself that they themselves also may be consecrated in truth.' (Jn. 17^{19}.)

It is in His teaching about Cross-bearing that Jesus stresses the duty of loyalty to Himself. There is nothing egotistical in this demand for personal loyalty. It is not His own any more than He is His own. It is God's.

This theo-centric egoism is the very core of the Messianic consciousness of Jesus. Its justification is found in the profundity and permanence of the impact which His personality has made and is making on human history.

Mk. and Lk. record this teaching as being delivered publicly. It could hardly have been so at this stage in the Ministry. Mt. more correctly states that it was delivered to the disciples. Lk. domesticates the Cross as the symbol of self-discipline in the Christian life by inserting the word 'daily' here.

In Mk. 8^{38} and 9^{1}, the future triumph of the Messiah and His Kingdom is portrayed in apocalyptic imagery. It should be noted that Mt. heightens this apocalyptic element by equating Mk.'s coming of the Kingdom of God with the Son of Man coming in His Kingdom (Mt. 16^{28}).

The statement that there be some standing here who shall not taste of death, etc., suggests that Jesus, as certainly was the case with His early disciples, anticipated a more rapid advance of the Kingdom of God than has actually taken place. The prediction, however, may refer to the destruction of the Temple and the overthrow of Judaism which took place within the lifetime of many who heard Jesus.

THE TRANSFIGURATION

MK. 9^{2-8}

9 2 And after six days Jesus taketh with him
Peter, and James, and John, and bringeth
them up into a high mountain apart by
themselves: and he was transfigured before
3 them: and his garments became glistering,
exceeding white; so as no fuller on earth can
4 whiten them. And there appeared unto
them Elijah with Moses: and they were
5 talking with Jesus. And Peter answereth
and saith to Jesus, Rabbi, it is good for us
to be here: and let us make three tabernacles; one for thee, and one for Moses,
6 and one for Elijah. For he wist not what
to answer; for they became sore afraid.
7 And there came a cloud overshadowing
them: and there came a voice out of the
cloud, This is my beloved Son: hear ye him.
8 And suddenly looking round about, they
saw no one any more, save Jesus only with
themselves.

MT. 17^{1-8}

17 1 And after six days Jesus taketh with him
Peter, and James, and John his brother,
and bringeth them up into a high moun-
2 tain apart: and he was transfigured before
them: and his face did shine as the sun,
and his garments became white as the
3 light. And behold, there appeared unto
them Moses and Elijah talking with him.
4 And Peter answered, and said unto Jesus,
Lord, it is good for us to be here: if thou
wilt, I will make here three tabernacles;
one for thee, and one for Moses, and one
5 for Elijah. While he was yet speaking,
behold, a bright cloud overshadowed
them: and behold, a voice out of the cloud,
saying, This is my beloved Son, in whom
6 I am well pleased; hear ye him. And
when the disciples heard it, they fell on
7 their face, and were sore afraid. And
Jesus came and touched them and said,
8 Arise, and be not afraid. And lifting up
their eyes, they saw no one, save Jesus
only.

LK. 9^{28-36a}

9 28 And it came to pass about eight days
after these sayings, he took with him Peter
and John and James, and went up into
29 the mountain to pray. And as he was
praying the fashion of his countenance
was altered, and his raiment *became* white
30 *and* dazzling. And behold, there talked
with him two men, which were Moses and
31 Elijah; who appeared in glory, and spake
of his decease which he was about to
32 accomplish at Jerusalem. Now Peter and
they that were with him were heavy with
sleep: but when they were fully awake,
they saw his glory, and the two men that
33 stood with him. And it came to pass, as
they were parting from him, Peter said
unto Jesus, Master, it is good for us to be
here : and let us make three tabernacles;
one for thee, and one for Moses, and one
for Elijah: not knowing what he said.
34 And while he said these things, there
came a cloud, and overshadowed them:
and they feared as they entered into the
35 cloud. And a voice came out of the
cloud, saying, This is my Son, my chosen:
36 hear ye him. And when the voice came,
Jesus was found alone.

Most appropriately, in close succession upon the unveiling of the doctrine of the Suffering Messiah by Jesus, follows the vision of the Transfiguration.

The Transfiguration comes in the same class as the narratives of the Baptism, the Temptation, and the Resurrection. It is neither myth nor legend but mystical experience: perhaps it is best described by the word vision (Mt. 17^9, *horama*). By a vision is not meant to be understood a mere hallucination induced by phantasy. A true vision is not the result of chance or accident or some unprepared-for experience. It is a product of a psychical state. It may be a very prolonged one.

The psychical state which precedes the vision is one of intense strain induced it may be by fear or doubt or difficulty or desire. The vision (or it may be the audition, as in the case of St. Augustine or John Bunyan or Lord Herbert of Cherbury) ends the strain and comes as an emotional relief—the fear is removed: the doubt is solved: the desire is satisfied: the mental or moral anguish is replaced by a state of calm and assurance.

There are a number of such visions recorded which have had extraordinary influence in determining the course of human history.

There is the vision of Saul on the Damascus Road which determined for him his attitude to the crucified Jesus from which the call of the Gentiles into the Christian Church ensued.

There is Constantine's vision of the Cross, bearing the motto: 'In this sign conquer'; and as a result the Roman Empire became a Christian State.

There is Joan of Arc's vision of the Virgin among the apple blossom in the orchard at Domrémy; and as a consequence England ceased to be a Continental power and began to look westward across the Atlantic Ocean, and her oversea dominions came into being.

In each of these cases, those who experienced these visions were in deep perplexity. Saul, as to whether Stephen was right in claiming Jesus to be the Messiah; Constantine, as to whether he ought not to throw in his lot with the persecuted Christian Church which Diocletian had failed to extirpate; Joan of Arc was afflicted by the problem of the sufferings of her country and how deliverance might be achieved.

The Transfiguration comes into this class of vision. Peter had, in a moment of intuition, hailed Jesus as the Messiah. His intuition was accepted as sound, and then he had experienced the horror of being told that Messiahship involved repudiation, disgrace, and death for his Master. For a week or more (Mk. and Mt. six days, Lk. eight days) he brooded on this horror. No doubt he discussed with his two old fishing partners, the sons of Zebedee, the problem: How could the crucified Jesus be God's Messiah?

Then Jesus takes the three apart into a mountain. Commentators have been much concerned to identify this mountain: some would make it Mt. Tabor (quite impossible because inhabited), others would make it Mt. Hermon. (Lk. says He went there in order to pray, and that as the chosen three watched Him pray the vision came.) Jesus assumes a glorified appearance and is seen talking to Moses and Elijah, the two greatest personalities in ancient Israel. Lk.'s account of the Transfiguration, like his account of the visit to Nazareth, is superior to Mk.'s. It is fuller and more illuminating and narrates the subject of the conversation of Jesus with Moses and Elijah: it is the martyr's death (*exodos*) which Jesus is about to accomplish at Jerusalem.

Then it seems as though Jesus and Moses and Elijah are about to withdraw. Peter, in order to retain them, suggests that he and his companions shall construct three booths (such as the Jews were accustomed to build at the feast of tabernacles and on the flat roofs of their houses in the hot season). Then a luminous cloud

(*Shekinah*), the age-long symbol to the devout Israelite of the Divine Presence, overshadows them all. Peter experiences an overwhelming sense of the numinous as the cloud enshrouds him. Then a Divine Voice (known to the Jews as the *Bath-Qôl*) is heard proclaiming: This is my Son, the Beloved (Lk., my elect One), hear ye him.

The vision of the Transfiguration thus comes to St. Peter as the solution of the problem of the Suffering Messiah. The testimony of the law-giver and the prophet witnesses to these Messianic sufferings: both predict them and realise their significance. The Divine Father, although the angels in the words of Bishop Heber's hymn,

> " *Look down with sad and wondering eyes*
> *To see the approaching sacrifice*,"

yet Himself recognises the Sufferer, not as an executed impostor or suicidal fanatic, but as His own Anointed Son.

The declaration from the *Shekinah*: This is my Son, the Beloved, solves Peter's doubt as to whether one who was to be rejected and crucified by Judaism could possibly be God's Messiah.

Modern psychologists may hesitate to accept the statement that James and John shared Peter's psychical experience: we may hesitate also. The vision of the Transfiguration is Peter's. He is undoubtedly its first narrator. It was his confession that created the crisis which was the first step in inducing the vision. Peter, in the account of it, is the only spokesman of the apostolic body. He no doubt assumed that James and John must have shared the experiences which were his. Interpreted in this way the vision of the Transfiguration is in line with a very real and influential type of psychical experience.

Just as Jesus after Peter's confession of the Messiahship had forbidden the disciples to reveal the Messianic secret to others, so He forbids Peter and his companions to talk about their recent experience until the Son of Man be risen from the dead. This statement does undoubtedly create difficulties for the interpretation just advanced, because it does assume that John and James had shared the same experience as Peter. We cannot deny that they may have done so, though we think it improbable. On the other hand, it may be that the prohibition to speak about the Transfiguration Vision came into existence as an explanation of the fact that it was not until a much later date that the apostolic body received an account of this Vision on the Mount. According to Mk. (omitted by Mt. and Lk.), the disciples begin to speculate as to what the phrase ' rising from the dead ' can mean. There is no doubt that ' rising from the dead ' was a perfectly familiar phrase and idea in contemporary Pharisaic Judaism. Many supposed that even Jesus Himself was John the Baptist raised from the dead, or one of the ancient prophets. The difficulty no doubt was in connexion with the rising from the dead of the Messiah. How could the Messiah come again from the grave, for it was not possible that the Messiah should die? Believers in the Apocalypses expected His advent from Heaven to reign on earth for ever and ever. It is no doubt because Matthew realises the difficulty, and has no solution to offer, that he omits this Marcan statement.

THE PROBLEM OF ELIJAH'S SECOND ADVENT

MK. 9^{9-13}

9 9 And as they were coming down from
the mountain, he charged them that they
should tell no man what things they had
seen, save when the Son of man should
10 have risen again from the dead. And
they kept the saying, questioning among
themselves what the rising again from the
11 dead should mean. And they asked him,
saying, The scribes say that Elijah must
12 first come. And he said unto them, Elijah
indeed cometh first, and restoreth all
things: and how is it written of the Son of
man, that he should suffer many things
13 and be set at nought? But I say unto
you, that Elijah is come, and they have
also done unto him whatsoever they
listed, even as it is written of him.

MT. 17^{9-13}

17 9 And as they were coming down from
the mountain, Jesus commanded them,
saying, Tell the vision to no man, until
the Son of man be risen from the dead.
10 And his disciples asked him, saying, Why
then say the scribes that Elijah must first
11 come? And he answered and said, Elijah
indeed cometh, and shall restore all
12 things: but I say unto you, that Elijah
is come already, and they knew him not,
but did unto him whatsoever they listed.
Even so shall the Son of man also suffer
13 of them. Then understood the disciples
that he spake unto them of John the
Baptist.

LK. 9^{36b}

9 36 And they held their peace, and told no
man in those days any of the things which
they had seen.

The two concluding verses of the Old Testament Canon contain a prediction of Malachi ($4^{5,6}$) : 'Behold I will send you Elijah the prophet before the great and terrible day of the Lord come. And he shall turn the heart of the fathers to the children, and the heart of the children to their fathers; lest I come and smite the earth with a curse.'

If, as the disciples believe, the Messiah has come in the person of Jesus, how is it that Elijah has not preceded Him? Jesus solves their doubt by saying that Elijah has come in the person of John the Baptist, but no one recognised him as Elijah and so they treated him as they did. Critics believe that the original text of Mk. has suffered some dislocation here and that it should run in the following order: verses 10, 12*b*, 11, 12*a*, 13*b*, 13*a*, reading as follows:

'And they kept the saying, questioning among themselves what the rising again from the dead should mean, and how it was written of the Son of man that he should suffer many things and be set at nought. And they asked him, saying, How is it that the scribes say that Elijah must first come? And he said unto, them Elijah indeed cometh first, and restoreth all things as it has been written of him. But I say unto you, that Elijah is come, and they have also done unto him whatsoever they listed.'

It should be noted that Mt. is closer to our present Mk. than to the proposed rearrangement of the Marcan text.

Mt. in his parallel clarifies the obscurity of Mk. and states definitely that the prophecy of Malachi was fulfilled in the coming of John the Baptist.

THE HEALING OF THE EPILEPTIC LAD

MK. 9^{14-29}

9 14 And when they came to the disciples,
they saw a great multitude about them,
15 and scribes questioning with them. And
straightway all the multitude, when they
saw him, were greatly amazed, and
16 running to him saluted him. And he
asked them, What question ye with them?
17 And one of the multitude answered him,
Master, I brought unto thee my son, which
18 hath a dumb spirit; and wheresoever it
taketh him, it dasheth him down: and he
foameth, and grindeth his teeth, and pineth
away: and I spake to thy disciples that
they should cast it out; and they were not
19 able. And he answereth them and saith,
O faithless generation, how long shall I be
with you? how long shall I bear with you?
20 bring him unto me. And they brought
him unto him: and when he saw him,
straightway the spirit tare him grievously;
and he fell on the ground, and wallowed
21 foaming. And he asked his father, How
long time is it since this hath come unto
22 him? And he said, From a child. And
oft-times it hath cast him both into the
fire and into the waters, to destroy him:
but if thou canst do anything, have com-
23 passion on us, and help us. And Jesus
said unto him, If thou canst! All things
are possible to him that believeth.
24 Straightway the father of the child cried
out, and said, I believe; help thou mine
25 unbelief. And when Jesus saw that a
multitude came running together, he rebuked the unclean spirit, saying unto him,
Thou dumb and deaf spirit, I command
thee, come out of him, and enter no more
26 into him. And having cried out, and torn
him much, he came out: and *the child*
became as one dead; insomuch that the
27 more part said, He is dead. But Jesus
took him by the hand, and raised him up;
28 and he arose. And when he was come
into the house, his disciples asked him
privately, *saying*, We could not cast it out.
29 And he said unto them, This kind can
come out by nothing save by prayer.

MT. 17^{14-20}

17 14 And when they were come to the
multitude, there came to him a man,
15 kneeling to him, and saying, Lord, have
mercy on my son: for he is epileptic, and
suffereth grievously: for oft-times he
falleth into the fire, and oft-times into
16 the water. And I brought him to thy
disciples, and they could not cure him.
17 And Jesus answered and said, O faithless
and perverse generation, how long shall I
be with you? how long shall I bear with
18 you? bring him hither to me. And
Jesus rebuked him; and the devil went
out from him: and the boy was cured
19 from that hour. Then came the disciples to Jesus apart, and said, Why
20 could not we cast it out? And he saith
unto them, Because of your little faith:
for verily I say unto you, If ye have faith
as a grain of mustard seed, ye shall say
unto this mountain, Remove hence to
yonder place; and it shall remove; and
nothing shall be impossible unto you.

LK. 9^{37-43a}

9 37 And it came to pass, on the next day,
when they were come down from the
mountain, a great multitude met him.
38 And behold, a man from the multitude
cried, saying, Master, I beseech thee to
look upon my son; for he is mine only
39 child: and behold, a spirit taketh him, and
he suddenly crieth out; and it teareth him
that he foameth, and it hardly departeth
40 from him, bruising him sorely. And I
besought thy disciples to cast it out; and
41 they could not. And Jesus answered and
said, O faithless and perverse generation,
how long shall I be with you, and bear
42 with you? bring hither thy son. And as
he was yet a coming, the devil dashed him
down, and tare *him* grievously. But Jesus
rebuked the unclean spirit, and healed the
boy, and gave him back to his father.
43 And they were all astonished at the
majesty of God.

When Jesus rejoins the rest of the disciples after His descent from the Mount of Transfiguration He finds them being heckled by the scribes in the presence of a large crowd. The crowd are astonished at seeing Jesus and run to Him and salute Him. (This graphic incident is omitted by Mt. and Lk.)

Jesus enquires the cause of the dispute with the scribes. One of the crowd replies: 'O teacher, I brought unto thee my son who is possessed by a dumb spirit, and wheresoever it takes him it throws him down and he foams at the mouth and grinds his teeth and is shrivelled up.' The symptoms related plainly point to epilepsy, which was held to be due to demonic possession. (Mt. describes the patient as 'moon-struck,' which the R.V. renders 'epileptic.')

The father of the epileptic proceeds: 'They (indicating the disciples) were not strong enough.' Jesus exclaims: 'O faithless and perverse generation, how long shall I be with you, how long shall I endure you? Bring him to me.'

The use of the plural by Jesus suggests that the epileptic's father had come forward by himself and had left his son in the hands of the crowd, who are now bidden to bring (carry) the boy forward. They then bring the lad to Jesus, and as he comes forward he has an epileptic seizure and is convulsed; and falling on the ground he begins to wallow, foaming at the mouth. Jesus asks his father: 'Since when has he been like this?'

The father replies: 'From boyhood, and very often the demon throws him into the fire and into the water, in order to kill him. But if thou art able, have compassion upon us and help us.' (The father includes himself with his son in his supplication.) Jesus said to him: 'What do you mean by saying, "If thou art able"? All things are possible for him who has faith.' Immediately the father of the lad cries out, saying repeatedly: 'I believe: help thou mine unbelief.' Jesus, seeing that the crowd is running round them, charges the unclean spirit, saying: 'Thou dumb and deaf spirit, I charge thee come forth from him and no more enter into him.' The lad experiences a series of convulsions, and with a cry the spirit comes forth. The lad seems to be dead, which leads many to say: 'He is dead.' But Jesus takes him by the hand and raises him up and he stands on his feet.

When Jesus has come into the house (the phrase 'house' is indefinite, some house in the vicinity), the disciples ask Him privately: 'Why could we not cast him out?' And He said to them: 'This kind can come out by nothing save by prayer.' Certain codices add 'and fasting'; but there is no doubt that this is one of those later additions to the text that stresses the value of asceticism. Both Mt. and Lk. compress Mk.'s narrative greatly and deprive it of much of its vividness by doing so.

Lk. says that Jesus, when He had healed the lad, an only child, delivered him to his father; just as Lk. says that, having raised the widow's son (an only child) at Nain, He delivered him to his mother. This may refer to some customary medical gesture. Lk. also adds: that all were astonished at the majesty of God. Mt. makes Jesus rebuke the disciples for their lack of faith and tells them that if they had faith as a grain of mustard seed they could remove even a mountain.

The reference to the grain of mustard seed as a symbol of vital and effective faith refers to what Jesus has already emphasised in His teaching: that although the mustard seed is the smallest of seeds sown by farmers, yet its vitality is such that it produces much the largest growth.

The healing of the epileptic lad in Mk. ranks in vividness of detail and dramatic quality with such other Marcan narratives of healing as the paralytic, the Gergesene maniac, the woman with the issue of blood, Jairus's daughter, and blind Bartimæus.

Once again it has to be asked: Is this descriptive quality due to the reminiscence of an eye-witness or is it the product of dramatic literary creation? When we note the way in which Mt. and Lk., who seem possessed of greater literary power than Mk., omit some of the most striking of Mk.'s details, we are convinced that the vividness of Mk.'s narrative preserves the reminiscences of an eye-witness which, even if they could have been created, would not have been thought worth creating.

THE SECOND PREDICTION OF THE PASSION

MK. 9^{30-32}

9 30 And they went forth from thence, and
passed through Galilee; and he would not
31 that any man should know it. For he
taught his disciples, and said unto them,
The Son of man is delivered up into the
hands of men, and they shall kill him;
and when he is killed, after three days he
32 shall rise again. But they understood not
the saying, and were afraid to ask him.

MT. $17^{22, 23}$

17 22 And while they abode in Galilee,
Jesus said unto them, The Son of man
shall be delivered up into the hands of
23 men; and they shall kill him, and the
third day he shall be raised up. And
they were exceeding sorry.

LK. 9^{43b-45}

9 43 But while all were marvelling at all the
things which he did, he said unto his dis-
44 ciples, Let these words sink into your ears:
for the Son of man shall be delivered up
45 into the hands of men. But they understood not this saying, and it was concealed
from them, that they should not perceive
it: and they were afraid to ask him about
this saying.

Jesus continues his furtive progress through Galilee. Mk. states that He did not wish anyone to know it—a statement omitted by Mt. and Lk.

Whilst travelling with His disciples He teaches them. Mk. suggests by his use of the word 'for' (5^{31}) that His desire for privacy was that He might have the opportunity to teach His disciples. The subject of the teaching, and it is constantly reiterated, is the painful theme of the coming Passion. The Passion is so near and so certain that Jesus describes it as already proceeding: 'The Son of man is betrayed into the hands of men and they shall kill him, and when he is killed, after three days he shall rise again.' Mk. adds that the disciples 'understood not the saying, and that they were afraid to ask Him.' Mt. omits this statement about the failure of the disciples to understand Jesus and substitutes for it: They were very grieved.

Lk., on the other hand, follows Mk. in stating that the disciples did not understand Jesus—evidently by a Divine intervention—and explains that the meaning was hidden from them in order that they should not perceive it. Lk., however, agrees with Mk. in concluding with the statement that they were afraid to ask Him about it.

THE DISPUTE ABOUT GREATNESS

MK. 9^{33-37}

9 33 And they came to Capernaum: and
when he was in the house he asked them,
What were ye reasoning in the way?
34 But they held their peace: for they had
disputed one with another in the way, who
35 *was* the greatest. And he sat down, and
called the twelve; and he saith unto them,
If any man would be first, he shall be last
36 of all, and minister of all. And he took a
little child, and set him in the midst of
them: and taking him in his arms, he said
37 unto them, Whosoever shall receive one of
such little children in my name, receiveth
me: and whosoever receiveth me, receiveth not me, but him that sent me.

MT. 18^{1-5}

18 1 In that hour came the disciples unto
Jesus, saying, Who then is greatest in the
2 kingdom of heaven? And he called to
him a little child, and set him in the midst
3 of them, and said, Verily I say unto you,
Except ye turn, and become as little children, ye shall in no wise enter into the
4 kingdom of heaven. Whosoever therefore
shall humble himself as this little child,
the same is the greatest in the kingdom of
5 heaven. And whoso shall receive one
such little child in my name receiveth me.

LK. 9^{46-48}

9 46 And there arose a reasoning among
them, which of them should be greatest.
47 But when Jesus saw the reasoning of their
heart, he took a little child, and set him by
48 his side, and said unto them, Whosoever
shall receive this little child in my name
receiveth me: and whosoever shall receive
me receiveth him that sent me: for he that
is least among you all, the same is great.

MT. 10^{40}, $23^{11, 12}$

10 40 He that receiveth you receiveth me,
and he that receiveth me receiveth him
that sent me.
23 11 But he that is greatest among you shall
12 be your servant. And whosoever shall
exalt himself shall be humbled; and
whosoever shall humble himself shall be
exalted.

LK. 10^{16}, 22^{24-27}

10 16 He that heareth you heareth me; and
he that rejecteth you rejecteth me; and
he that rejecteth me rejecteth him that
sent me.
22 24 And there arose also a contention
among them, which of them is accounted
25 to be greatest. And he said unto them,
The kings of the Gentiles have lordship
over them; and they that have authority
26 over them are called Benefactors. But
ye *shall* not *be* so: but he that is the
greater among you, let him become as
the younger; and he that is chief, as he
27 that doth serve. For whether is greater,
he that sitteth at meat, or he that
serveth? is not he that sitteth at meat?
but I am in the midst of you as he that
serveth.

Jesus returns to Peter's house at Capernaum and asks His disciples what they disputed about on the road. They remain silent, because on the road they had disputed which of them should be the greatest. Jesus, being seated, summons the Twelve and says to them: 'If anyone wishes to be first he shall be last of all and the servant of all.' And taking a little child He stands him in the midst of them, and taking him up in His arms He says to them: 'Whosoever receives one such little child in my name receives me, and whosoever receives me, receives not me, but Him that sent me.'

The words of Jesus in Mk. teach that the true disciple achieves greatness not by seeking to hold great offices but by doing service to unimportant people.

Mt. seems to miss this point in Mk. and makes Jesus say: 'Verily I say unto you, except ye turn and *become* as little children, ye shall in no wise enter into the kingdom of heaven. Whosoever therefore shall humble himself as this little child, the same is the greatest in the kingdom of heaven' (18^{1-4}).

Lk. also ($22^{24 f.}$), in relating 'the contention' among the Apostles who should be the greatest, does not give the corrective teaching of Jesus in the Marcan form, but pointing to pagan conceptions of greatness He indicates that those standards are reversed for His disciples. Service and humility alone constitute greatness.

The action of Jesus in showing such a high and tender regard for a little child in the presence of His Apostles, as recorded in Mk., was no doubt intended to teach them that He valued and loved the child-like nature, in its simplicity and lack of worldly ambition, above any of those qualities of leadership and courage upon the possession of which the Apostles may have prided themselves.

THE STRANGER WHO EXORCISED IN THE NAME OF JESUS

MK. 9^{38-40}

9 38 John said unto him, Master, we saw one casting out devils in thy name: and we forbade him, because he followed not us.
39 But Jesus said, Forbid him not: for there is no man which shall do a mighty work in my name, and be able quickly to speak
40 evil of me. For he that is not against us is for us.

LK. $9^{49, 50}$

9 49 And John answered and said, Master, we saw one casting out devils in thy name; and we forbade him, because he followeth
50 not with us. But Jesus said unto him, Forbid *him* not: for he that is not against you is for you.

The sons of Zebedee were surnamed by Jesus, Sons of Thunder: no doubt because of their rigour and vigour. A strain of intolerance appears as one of their characteristics. It is related that when a certain Samaritan village refused to accept Jesus with hospitality, the Sons of Thunder desired to call down fire upon them from heaven after the example of Elijah (Lk. 9^{54}). So here, John seeing an exorcist making use of the name of Jesus, forbids him to do so since he is not one of the acknowledged disciples of Jesus. Jesus, in His reply to John, teaches the lesson of a large-minded and sympathetic tolerance and points out to His Apostle that one who exorcises in His name may be regarded as, at least, not hostile.

Neutrality may on occasions be friendly. The attitude of Jesus here will remind the reader of the attitude of Moses. When it had been announced to him that Eldad and Medad were prophesying in the camp, and Joshua answered and said, 'My lord Moses, forbid them,' Moses said unto him: 'Art thou jealous for my sake? Would God that all the Lord's people were prophets, that the Lord would put his spirit upon them!' (Num. 11^{27-29}.)

There is no evidence that during the lifetime of Jesus His disciples exorcised in His name, but they certainly did so in the period of the Acts of the Apostles, which relates the humiliating and painful experience of certain Jewish non-Christian exorcists, the sons of Sceva, who made use of the name of Jesus.

The exorcised maniac retorted: 'Jesus I know, and Paul I know, but who are ye?' and so handled them that they fled from the house naked and wounded. (Acts 19^{16}.)

A COLLECTION OF SAYINGS OF JESUS

MK. 9^{41-50}

9 41 For whosoever shall give you a cup of
water to drink, because ye are Christ's,
verily I say unto you, he shall in no wise
42 lose his reward. And whosoever shall
cause one of these little ones that believe
on me to stumble, it were better for him if
a great millstone were hanged about his
43 neck, and he were cast into the sea. And
if thy hand cause thee to stumble, cut it
off: it is good for thee to enter into life
maimed, rather than having thy two hands
to go into hell, into the unquenchable fire.
45 And if thy foot cause thee to stumble, cut
it off: it is good for thee to enter into life
halt, rather than having thy two feet to be
47 cast into hell. And if thine eye cause thee
to stumble, cast it out: it is good for thee
to enter into the kingdom of God with one
eye, rather than having two eyes to be
48 cast into hell; where their worm dieth not,
49 and the fire is not quenched. For every
50 one shall be salted with fire. Salt is good:
but if the salt have lost its saltness, wherewith will ye season it? Have salt in yourselves, and be at peace one with another.

MT. 10^{42}, 18^{6-10}, 5^{13}

10 42 And whosoever shall give to drink unto
one of these little ones a cup of cold water
only, in the name of a disciple, verily I
say unto you, he shall in no wise lose his
reward.
18 6 But whoso shall cause one of these little
ones which believe on me to stumble, it is
profitable for him that a great millstone
should be hanged about his neck, and
that he should be sunk in the depth of the
7 sea. Woe unto the world because of
occasions of stumbling! for it must needs
be that the occasions come; but woe to
that man through whom the occasion
8 cometh! And if thy hand or thy foot
causeth thee to stumble, cut it off, and
cast it from thee: it is good for thee to
enter into life maimed or halt, rather
than having two hands or two feet to be
9 cast into the eternal fire. And if thine
eye causeth thee to stumble, pluck it out,
and cast it from thee: it is good for thee
to enter into life with one eye, rather than
having two eyes to be cast into the hell of
10 fire. See that ye despise not one of
these little ones; for I say unto you, that
in heaven their angels do always behold
the face of my Father which is in heaven.
5 13 Ye are the salt of the earth: but if the
salt have lost its savour, wherewith shall
it be salted? it is thenceforth good for
nothing, but to be cast out and trodden
under foot of men.

LK. $17^{1, 2}$

17 1 And he said unto his disciples, It is
impossible but that occasions of stumbling should come: but woe unto him,
2 through whom they come! It were well
for him if a millstone were hanged about
his neck, and he were thrown into the
sea, rather than that he should cause one
of these little ones to stumble.
14 34 Salt therefore is good: but if even the
salt have lost its savour, wherewith shall
it be seasoned?

The R.V., following the best manuscripts, omits Mk. $9^{44, 46}$, where their worm dieth not and the fire is not quenched.

(*a*) A Cup of Water

Mk. contains a number of small collections of Sayings of Jesus. There is no evidence that these Sayings are arranged in chronological order. Their presence and arrangement appear to be prompted by some significant theme or word. ' Because ye are Christ's ' seems to be the reason for inserting the saying about the cup of cold water here, in succession to the incident of the exorcist, who in a technical sense was not Christ's although he exercised in Christ's name.

Æsop's fable of 'The Mouse and the Lion' with its moral, 'Small service is great service while it lasts,' teaches the same lesson as Jesus teaches in His saying about the cup of cold water.

(*b*) Offending Christ's 'Little Ones'

The following Saying (9^{42}), about those who cause Christ's little ones to offend, may perhaps have been suggested for insertion here by the thought that those who are Christ's are His 'little ones.'

'A great mill-stone'; literally a mill-stone turned by an ass, i.e. too large a mill-stone to be worked by hand.

(*c*) Self-mutilation

The next set of Sayings (9^{43-49}) was suggested for insertion here by the thought of 'causing offence.' Here the cause of offence is a man's own hand, foot, eye—the hand, which steals; the foot, which trespasses; the eye, which lusts or covets. Each of these may bring about the perdition of the whole man. In hyperbolical language Jesus teaches here the need for rigorous and unflinching self-discipline, where such discipline is needful to save the personality itself from absolute ruin. The phrase Gehenna, which is used here symbolically, is derived from a notable passage with which Isaiah concludes (66^{24}).

In this passage the Old Testament prophet predicts the abhorred fate of the apostates. Having been slain, their bodies shall lie amidst heaps of corrupting refuse in the desecrated Valley of Hinnom. This valley, which had formerly been used in the period of the later kings of Judah as the scene of child sacrifice, had been deliberately desecrated in the period after the return from the Exile. The sewage of Jerusalem was cast there. There the corrupting worm crawled and fires were kept continually burning for the purpose of destroying the refuse.

The word Gehenna is an actual transliteration of the Hebrew phrase, Valley of Hinnom. Unquenchable fire does not mean fire which burns for ever, but fire which cannot be extinguished until that which it has taken hold of is utterly consumed. The undying worm is not the symbol of a soul which cannot die, but is the symbol of corruption which cannot be purged.

It is of great interest to note in this set of Sayings that 'the Kingdom of God' (9^{47}) is equated with 'the Life' (*zoe*) (*vv.* 43, 45). The word 'life' here, in the idiom of the New Testament, is not used of life which man has in common with the animals (*psyche*), but of the higher life. It is the life of the Kingdom of God. Hence Jn. seems almost always to use the word *zoe* (usually united to the word eternal (*aiōnios*) instead of the phrase Kingdom of God; but the point of supreme interest is that, here, Mk. has anticipated Jn.'s equation of them.

(*d*) Salt

Next follow three Sayings about salt.

The first is suggested by the preceding Sayings about fire. 'Everyone shall be salted with fire.' Here certain codices add, 'and every sacrifice shall be salted with salt.' The reference is to the ceremonial law which prescribed the use of salt in the case of all food offerings. (Lev. 2^{13}.)

The lesson taught is that self-oblation made to God must involve suffering, not the suffering which ends in death but in fuller and higher life. It is the suffering, not of mortification, but of purgation.

The next Saying about salt is in the spirit of the Latin proverb: 'The worst corruption is that of the best'; or that of the Greek saying: 'Who shall guard the guards?' If the disciples of Jesus, whom He describes in the Sermon on the Mount as the salt of the earth, that which preserves human society from corruption and decay, become themselves corrupt—the situation is hopeless. Salt that is not salt is good for nothing; it is not even good for manure.

Some commentators of the literalist type, who feel it a duty to compress Oriental hyperbole within the strait waistcoat of scientific fact, have pointed out that salt can never cease to be salt, though it may suffer from the presence of non-saline elements, e.g. sand.

The third Saying about salt compares salt to those elements in human character which make for social peace.

Nietzsche stigmatised the Christian ethic as slave morality, because it laid supreme emphasis on those aspects of love which make its possessor patient, forgiving, gentle, and humble. These may not be the virtues upon which a noble, adventurous, progressive society can be built, nevertheless without these virtues a society will lack cohesion and permanence. They constitute the cement which binds the stones of the building together.

It is because the Christian religion is essentially social, not individualist, that the salt of the social virtues, which make pre-eminently for social peace, is needed. It is this salt which purges the Christian soul of personal ambition, emulation, self-conceit, envy, malice, and hatred.

D. ASCENT TO JERUSALEM *VIA* JORDAN VALLEY, PERÆA, AND JERICHO

MARRIAGE AND DIVORCE

MK. 10^{1-12}

10 1 And he arose from thence, and cometh
into the borders of Judæa and beyond
Jordan: and multitudes come together
unto him again; and, as he was wont, he
2 taught them again. And there came
unto him Pharisees, and asked him, Is it
lawful for a man to put away *his* wife?
3 tempting him. And he answered and
said unto them, What did Moses com-
4 mand you? And they said, Moses
suffered to write a bill of divorcement,
5 and to put her away. But Jesus said
unto them, For your hardness of heart he
6 wrote you this commandment. But
from the beginning of the creation, Male
7 and female made he them. For this
cause shall a man leave his father and
8 mother, and shall cleave to his wife; and
the twain shall become one flesh: so that
they are no more twain, but one flesh.
9 What therefore God hath joined together,
10 let not man put asunder. And in the

MT. 19^{1-12}, $5^{31, 32}$

19 1 And it came to pass when Jesus had
finished these words, he departed from
Galilee, and came into the borders of
2 Judæa beyond Jordan; and great multitudes followed him; and he healed them
there.
3 And there came unto him Pharisees,
tempting him, and saying, Is it lawful
for a man to put away his wife for every
4 cause? And he answered and said, Have
ye not read, that he which made *them*
from the beginning made them male and
5 female, and said, For this cause shall a
man leave his father and mother, and
shall cleave to his wife; and the twain
6 shall become one flesh? So that they
are no more twain, but one flesh. What
therefore God hath joined together, let
7 not man put asunder. They say unto
him, Why then did Moses command to
give a bill of divorcement, and to put *her*
8 away? He saith unto them, Moses for

house the disciples asked him again of
11 this matter. And he saith unto them,
Whosoever shall put away his wife, and
marry another, committeth adultery
12 against her: and if she herself shall put
away her husband, and marry another,
she committeth adultery.

your hardness of heart suffered you to
put away your wives: but from the be-
9 ginning it hath not been so. And I say
unto you, Whosoever shall put away his
wife, except for fornication, and shall
marry another, committeth adultery:
and he that marrieth her when she is put
10 away committeth adultery. The disciples say unto him, If the case of the man
is so with his wife, it is not expedient to
11 marry. But he said unto them, All men
cannot receive this saying, but they to
12 whom it is given. For there are eunuchs,
which were so born from their mother's
womb: and there are eunuchs, which
were made eunuchs by men: and there
are eunuchs, which made themselves
eunuchs for the kingdom of heaven's
sake. He that is able to receive it, let
him receive it.

5 31 It was said also, Whosoever shall put
away his wife, let him give her a writing
32 of divorcement: but I say unto you, that
every one that putteth away his wife,
saving for the cause of fornication,
maketh her an adulteress: and whosoever
shall marry her when she is put away
committeth adultery.

LK. 16^{18}

16 18 Every one that putteth away his wife,
and marrieth another, committeth adultery: and he that marrieth one that is
put away from a husband committeth
adultery.

Jesus having traversed Galilee on His way up to Jerusalem reaches the Judæan border in the Jordan valley. He then turns east and crosses the Jordan, coming into the region of Peræa. Further effort to secure privacy ceases and once more He begins to be thronged with expectant crowds and He resumes His public teaching.

Mk. alone stresses this resumption of His public teaching. Mt. simply refers to His healing ministry.

Immediately His ecclesiastical opponents are on His track. The Pharisees come to Him and ask Him if it is lawful for a husband to divorce his wife. Mk. (followed by Mt.) says that in putting this question to Him they were tempting Him, that is, trying to entrap Him. They had evidently heard reports that He had been teaching that divorce was wrong. In reply to the question He enquires: What did Moses command you? They reply in accordance with Dt. $24^{1, 2}$.

'When a man hath taken a wife, and married her, and it come to pass that she find no favour in his eyes, because he hath found some unseemly thing in her: then let him write her a bill of divorcement, and give it into her hand and send her out of his house.

'And when she is departed out of his house, she may go and be another man's wife.'

Jesus comments, ' on account of the hardness of your hearts Moses wrote this commandment for you.'

In the light of modern historical criticism of the Pentateuchal legislation it is hardly possible to maintain this position. The Deuteronomic Code, the product of the moral and spiritual teaching of the great eighth-century prophets, was an advance on the earlier legal codes. It is conspicuous for the humanity and tenderness of its precepts, particularly towards those classes of the population who were peculiarly liable to be the victims of injustice and oppression. Dt. 24^{1} comes in this class of enactment. Undoubtedly the Deuteronomic precept which required a legal document as a preliminary to divorce of a wife was intended to protect her from hasty and unjust treatment to which in earlier times she had been liable. If, however, the Pentateuch be viewed in the pre-critical way, and of course it was so viewed by our Lord and His contemporaries, then the reply which He makes is extraordinarily cogent. The Pharisees had cited a Pentateuchal passage, authorising divorce: Jesus cites another Pentateuchal passage, and from Genesis, which can be interpreted as prohibiting divorce. The Creator Himself had united the first pair of human beings in matrimony. No subsequent human legislation had the power to dissolve this Divine institution. To-day, particularly for the evolutionary mind, that which is latest possesses greater authority than that which is earlier; but for the pre-evolutionary type of mind, that which is earlier possesses the greater authority Hence, the passages in Genesis (1^{27} and 2^{24}) would be regarded as having a primary and absolute authority which could not be claimed for the later Pentateuchal enactment of Dt. 24^{1}. Dt. 24^{1}, therefore, could not be interpreted rightly as constituting a reversal of Gen. 1^{27} and 2^{24}, but merely as a subsidiary concession due to the difficulty of enforcing the primary law. This is the case as presented by Jesus against divorce, and His Pharisaic opponents found it unanswerable.

Mk.'s account here should be carefully compared with Mt. Mt. alters the question which the Pharisees put to Jesus. Mk. has: Is it lawful for a husband to divorce his wife? Mt. has: Is it lawful for a husband to divorce his wife *for every cause*?

By being asked the question in this Matthæan form, Jesus is required to give a decision on a point of dispute between the disciples of the Rabbi Hillel and the disciples of the Rabbi Shammai. Both of these great Jewish teachers recognised the rightfulness of divorce, but they differed about the causes for which a divorce might rightly be granted—Shammai, who took the stricter view, interpreted the phrase in Dt. 24^{1}, ' some unseemly thing in her ' (literally in the Hebrew, ' a matter of indecency '), as having reference only to conjugal infidelity and therefore permitted a man to divorce his wife only for unfaithfulness.

Hillel took the phrase as covering anything in a man's wife which caused him displeasure, even putting too much salt into his soup, and therefore allowed divorce for the most trivial reasons.

Jesus, in Mt., is made to decide for the school of Shammai as against the School of Hillel.

The argument of Jesus as presented in Mt. lacks the cogency of Mk. and also the originality. In Mt. Jesus forbids divorce except for *porneia* (' fornication ').

This word, as Archdeacon Charles has pointed out, has at least seven different meanings and may cover every form of sexual offence and perversion, and therefore could include both fornication before marriage and adultery afterwards.

Mt., in the Sermon on the Mount ($5^{31, 32}$), records Jesus as giving the same teaching there. For a man to divorce his wife except for infidelity is tantamount to committing adultery; and for a man to marry a woman so divorced is to commit adultery.

Mt. records (10–12) that the decision of Jesus created consternation in the minds of His disciples. They ask: If a man may not divorce his wife except for infidelity, is it expedient for him to marry? Jesus replies: It is not only not expedient for all men to marry: for some it is even impossible.

Mk. relates that after the public reply of Jesus to the Pharisees His disciples approach and question Him privately about His decision. We have already noted that teaching attributed to Jesus as having been given privately to His disciples cannot command the same authority as His public teaching. It comes in the class of later ecclesiastical exposition and expansion. This will apply to the answer which Jesus gives privately to His disciples here.

Jesus in His public teaching in Mk. pronounces marriage indissoluble and absolute. This is reiterated in His private teaching to His disciples, but it is expanded. The Pharisees who put their question to Jesus had only in view the right of a husband to divorce his wife. They had not raised the issue of the right of a wife to divorce her husband. It is maintained that in Judaism, notwithstanding the action of some of the women of the Herodian family, it was impossible for a woman to divorce her husband, although she might desert him. In Rome, however, where at this time it was the frequent practice of wives to divorce their husbands, it seemed necessary to provide an explicit prohibition of such action, and so Mk. (the Gospel of the Church of Rome) expands the teaching of Jesus on this point.

There remains a crucial question to be answered. Can the teaching of Jesus on divorce, as given in Mt., claim more authority than the teaching of Jesus as given in Mk.?

Mk. must be accepted as a reliable authority for the following reasons:

(1) There is no doubt that Mk.'s account is older than Mt.'s and that Mt. is dependent upon it here.

(2) In Mk. the attitude of Christ is more original and daring than in Mt.

(3) Lk. supports (16^{18}) Mk. as against Mt.

(4) St. Paul supports Mk. as against Mt. in 1 Cor. $7^{10f.}$. He writes:

'Those that have been married I charge, yet not I but the Lord. Let not the wife be separated from her husband—but if she be separated let her remain unmarried or else let her be reconciled to her husband—and let not the husband desert his wife.'

Here St. Paul refers to actual teaching of Jesus, and to teaching which is in agreement with Mk., as is also Rom. 7^3:

'She shall indeed be designated an adulteress if, while her husband be yet living, she be married to another man.'

In the face of this evidence there can be no doubt that Mt.'s version represents the attempt to adjust the absolute teaching of Jesus on the indissolubility of marriage to the existing practice in the Jewish Church. St. Paul himself also permitted an exception to the absolute teaching of Jesus when he allowed Christians who had (presumably on account of their religion) been divorced or deserted by their pagan partners to marry again, but this time to a Christian (1 Cor. 7^{15}).

These two notable New Testament exceptions to Christ's absolute teaching on the indissolubility of marriage indicate that this teaching was taken as expressing a principle or an ideal of marriage rather than as a legislative enactment.

JESUS AND LITTLE CHILDREN

MK. 10^{13-16}

10 13 And they brought unto him little children, that he should touch them: and the
14 disciples rebuked them. But when Jesus
saw it, he was moved with indignation,
and said unto them, Suffer the little
children to come unto me; forbid them
not: for of such is the kingdom of God.
15 Verily I say unto you, Whosoever shall
not receive the kingdom of God as a
little child, he shall in no wise enter
16 therein. And he took them in his arms,
and blessed them, laying his hands upon
them.

MT. 19^{13-15}

19 13 Then were there brought unto him
little children, that he should lay his
hands on them, and pray: and the dis-
14 ciples rebuked them. But Jesus said,
Suffer the little children, and forbid them
not, to come unto me: for of such is the
15 kingdom of heaven. And he laid his
hands on them, and departed thence.

LK. 18^{15-17}

18 15 And they brought unto him also their
babes, that he should touch them: but
when the disciples saw it, they rebuked
16 them. But Jesus called them unto him,
saying, Suffer the little children to come
unto me, and forbid them not: for of such
17 is the kingdom of God. Verily I say
unto you, Whosoever shall not receive
the kingdom of God as a little child, he
shall in no wise enter therein.

To judge by certain precepts in the Wisdom Literature the attitude of Jews to children was disciplinary and severe. That of Jesus was tender and sympathetic. He was undoubtedly interested in children and fond of them. His reference to their playing at marriages and funerals in the market-place; His refusal to order them to be silent when they sang Hosanna in His honour in the Temple; His citation of the words of the psalmist: 'Out of the mouths of babes and sucklings hast thou perfected praise'; His selection of a little child as an example to His Apostles; and also the incident related here support the view that Jesus may be justly acclaimed as the lover of little children.

The indignation of Jesus at His disciples forbidding little children to be brought to Him is omitted by both Mt. and Lk. It should be noted that according to the accounts of the three synoptists, it was the fathers (not the mothers) of the children who brought them to Jesus. Jesus welcomes the little children (Lk. babes) as those whom God would wish to have in His Kingdom. Indeed, those who had not the child-like spirit, Jesus declared, could not share in that Kingdom.

After saying this He embraced the little children and blessed them fervently. Mt. and Lk. both omit Mk.'s reference to these affectionate gestures of Jesus. Possibly it was regarded as unbecoming for such a religious personage to be so affectionate to children. Mt. also on a former occasion omits Mk.'s statement that Jesus took the little child in His arms whom He presented as an example to His disciples. (Mk. 9^{36}; Mt. 18^{2}; Lk. 9^{47}.)

LOVE OF RICHES AND LOVE OF THE KINGDOM

MK. 10^{17-31}

10 17 And as he was going forth into the
way, there ran one to him, and kneeled
to him, and asked him, Good Master,
what shall I do that I may inherit eternal
18 life? And Jesus said unto him, Why
callest thou me good? none is good save
19 one, *even* God. Thou knowest the commandments, Do not kill, Do not commit
adultery, Do not steal, Do not bear false
witness, Do not defraud, Honour thy
20 father and mother. And he said unto
him, Master, all these things have I ob-
21 served from my youth. And Jesus looking upon him loved him, and said unto
him, One thing thou lackest: go, sell
whatsoever thou hast, and give to the
poor, and thou shalt have treasure in
22 heaven: and come, follow me. But his
countenance fell at the saying, and he
went away sorrowful: for he was one
that had great possessions.
23 And Jesus looked round about, and
saith unto his disciples, How hardly shall
they that have riches enter into the king-
24 dom of God! And the disciples were
amazed at his words. But Jesus answereth again and saith unto them,
Children, how hard is it for them that
trust in riches to enter into the kingdom
25 of God! It is easier for a camel to go
through a needle's eye, than for a rich
man to enter into the kingdom of God.
26 And they were astonished exceedingly,
saying unto him, Then who can be saved?
27 Jesus looking upon them saith, With men
it is impossible, but not with God: for all
28 things are possible with God. Peter
began to say unto him, Lo, we have left
29 all, and have followed thee. Jesus said,
Verily I say unto you, There is no man
that hath left house, or brethren, or
sisters, or mother, or father, or children,
or lands, for my sake, and for the gospel's
30 sake, but he shall receive a hundredfold
now in this time, houses, and brethren,
and sisters, and mothers, and children,
and lands, with persecutions; and in the
31 world to come eternal life. But many
that are first shall be last; and the last first.

MT. 19^{16-30}

19 16 And behold, one came to him and said,
Master, what good thing shall I do, that
17 I may have eternal life? And he said
unto him, Why askest thou me concerning that which is good? One there is
who is good: but if thou wouldest enter
18 into life, keep the commandments. He
saith unto him, Which? And Jesus said,
Thou shalt not kill, Thou shalt not commit adultery, Thou shalt not steal, Thou
19 shalt not bear false witness, Honour thy
father and thy mother: and, Thou shalt
20 love thy neighbour as thyself. The
young man saith unto him, All these
things have I observed: what lack I yet?
21 Jesus said unto him, If thou wouldest be
perfect, go, sell that thou hast, and give
to the poor, and thou shalt have treasure
22 in heaven: and come, follow me. But
when the young man heard the saying,
he went away sorrowful: for he was one
that had great possessions.
23 And Jesus said unto his disciples,
Verily I say unto you, It is hard for a rich
man to enter into the kingdom of heaven.
24 And again I say unto you, It is easier for
a camel to go through a needle's eye,
than for a rich man to enter into the
25 kingdom of God. And when the disciples heard it, they were astonished exceedingly, saying, Who then can be
26 saved? And Jesus looking upon *them*
said to them, With men this is impossible; but with God all things are possible.
27 Then answered Peter and said unto him,
Lo, we have left all, and followed thee;
28 what then shall we have? And Jesus
said unto them, Verily I say unto you,
that ye which have followed me, in the
regeneration when the Son of man shall
sit on the throne of his glory, ye also shall
sit upon twelve thrones, judging the
29 twelve tribes of Israel. And every one
that hath left houses, or brethren, or
sisters, or father, or mother, or children,
or lands, for my name's sake, shall
receive a hundredfold, and shall inherit
30 eternal life. But many shall be last *that
are* first; and first *that are* last.

LK. 18^{18-30}

18 18 And a certain ruler asked him, saying,
Good Master, what shall I do to inherit
19 eternal life? And Jesus said unto him,
Why callest thou me good? none is good,
20 save one, *even* God. Thou knowest the
commandments, Do not commit adultery, Do not kill, Do not steal, Do not
bear false witness, Honour thy father
21 and mother. And he said, All these
things have I observed from my youth
22 up. And when Jesus heard it, he said
unto him, One thing thou lackest yet:
sell all that thou hast, and distribute unto
the poor, and thou shalt have treasure in
23 heaven: and come, follow me. But
when he heard these things, he became
exceeding sorrowful; for he was very rich.
24 And Jesus seeing him said, How hardly
shall they that have riches enter into the
25 kingdom of God! For it is easier for a
camel to enter in through a needle's eye,
than for a rich man to enter into the
26 kingdom of God. And they that heard
27 it said, Then who can be saved? But he
said, The things which are impossible
28 with men are possible with God. And
Peter said, Lo, we have left our own,
29 and followed thee. And he said unto
them, Verily I say unto you, There is no
man that hath left house, or wife, or
brethren, or parents, or children, for the
30 kingdom of God's sake, who shall not
receive manifold more in this time, and
in the world to come eternal life.

The incident of the little children had evidently taken place when Jesus was resting in a house by the roadside. On resuming His journey a certain man (Mt. a 'young man' and Lk. a 'ruler') approached, and kneeling, said to Him: 'O good Teacher, what shall I do that I may inherit eternal life?' Jesus asks: 'Why callest thou me good? There is no one good except God.' Lk., who states that the man was a ruler, gives his question and the reply of Jesus in the same form as Mk. does; but Mt. makes him say to Jesus: O Teacher, what good thing shall I do that I may have eternal life? To which Jesus replies: Why dost thou enquire from me concerning the good? One there is who is good.

Undoubtedly Mk. preserves the original form of the dialogue. Mt. has altered it to escape the difficulty presented by our Lord seeming to resent being addressed as good.

At the time Mt. wrote evidently attacks were being made, by Jewish antagonists, on the moral character of Jesus. For instance, they were saying: If Jesus were not a sinful man why should He have come to John's Baptism for the remission of sins? Mt. makes a special insertion into his Gospel to meet that hostile question. So undoubtedly his alteration of Mk. here has the same purpose. Mk. and Lk. do not seem to feel that the rebuke of Jesus because He was addressed as good indicates that He was not good. Jesus may have felt that this stranger had no right to address Him in this way. It is doubtful whether he was patronising Jesus as some have supposed: more probably he was ingratiating himself, by flattery. The reply of Jesus makes it clear that He felt that no one except God should be addressed absolutely as good.

This attitude to the Divine Father, so appropriate on the part of the Messianic Son, cannot be reasonably construed as proving that Jesus was conscious of His own sinfulness. Probably He was conscious of His imperfection, but that is quite another matter. Such consciousness of imperfection is essential for moral and spiritual progress, and Jesus, so Lk. relates, increased in wisdom, which included not merely intellectual but moral and spiritual qualities.

Many will feel that the ideal moral and spiritual state of one whose consciousness was truly and perfectly human is reflected in the attitude of Jesus, both to God and to man, on this occasion.

The man's question about eternal life refers to his share, or inheritance, in the life of the coming Kingdom of God. His attitude is that of an individualist seeking a personal good. The reply of Jesus is not a snub. For Jesus, obedience to the Decalogue as He interpreted it—wholehearted love of God and wholehearted love of man—constituted eternal life, the life of the Kingdom. The man's declaration that from his youth he had kept all the Commandments attracts Jesus to him.

Mk. says that Jesus, looking upon him, loved him. Mt. and Lk. omit this, probably in view of what followed. The man presses Jesus further: What lack I yet? Jesus replies: Go away, sell whatsoever thou hast and give to the poor and thou shalt have treasure in heaven, and come, follow me. At that word, says Mk., the man's face fell (became gloomy), and he went away sorrowful, having great possessions.

The command: Sell all that thou hast, has been described as a 'Counsel of Perfection' because in Mt. Jesus prefaces His command with the words: If thou wishest to be perfect. The command, however, was intended partly as a test of sincerity, and partly because Jesus felt that this man possessed qualities which would make him a good disciple. But the man failed to respond. Possibly he had hoped that Jesus would tell him that he lacked nothing morally and spiritually; that he had already attained and was already perfect. Jesus, who resented the title 'good' being bestowed on Himself, has no mind to bestow it upon this man. He only asked him to do what some of His own disciples had already done.

The man's refusal to renounce his possessions and to become the disciple of Jesus leads Jesus to remark on the difficulty which rich men have in entering the Kingdom. His disciples, so Mk. relates, were astonished at His statement. The Jews of this period viewed the possession of wealth as a mark of the Divine favour. 'The blessing of the Lord maketh rich, and He addeth no sorrow to it,' was a saying of the wise.

On the other hand, it was the families of evil men who were supposed to fall into poverty in Israel.

Abraham the Father of the Faithful, the righteous Job, the wise Solomon, were all wealthy men. Good and rich men in Judaism gave liberally to those in need, but there was no thought that God desired or required them to renounce their riches. Their poverty, besides suggesting the disfavour of God, would increase for them the difficulties of the good life. Agur, the son of Jakeh, if the oracle be his, had taught that great wealth tempted men into materialism and atheism, but this did not lead him to hold that poverty was an assistance to virtue.

> Give me neither poverty nor riches:
> Feed me with the food that is needful for me,
> Lest I be full and deny thee, and say, Who is the Lord?
> Or lest I be poor and steal, and use profanely the name of my God.
> (Prov. $30^{8, 9}$.)

Just as Jesus had shocked contemporary Jewish morality by teaching the indissolubility of marriage, so He shocked it again by His statement that it was easier for a poor man to enter the Kingdom than for a rich man. Peter, who heard this utterance of Jesus, recollected and recorded the shock which it gave him and his fellow-disciples. Mt. and Lk., written years later, when the ideal of Christian poverty was a commonplace in the Christian Church, do not regard the apostolic surprise as edifying, and so omit Mk.'s statement.

The Apostles' amazement leads Jesus to repeat His dictum, but with a significant difference: How hard is it for those who *trust* in riches to enter into the Kingdom of God. (This phrase, 'for them that trust in riches,' since it is omitted by some important codices, has been thought to be an early Christian gloss.)

The metaphor of the needle's eye has given trouble to commentators who have supposed that it may be the name for a postern gate in a city wall intended for foot-passengers and through which a camel could only be forced with much difficulty after stripping it of its baggage. Others have attempted to translate the word camel by 'cable,' but linguistic justification for this is lacking.

Jesus is speaking in hyperbole and can no more be taken literally here than when on another occasion He speaks of a man swallowing a camel. The way in which this rich man, although evidently a zealous seeker of virtue, has rejected the invitation to discipleship leads Jesus to emphasise the intensity of the conflict between the claims of material wealth and the spiritual ideals of the Kingdom. These claims can only be harmonised by those who seek the Kingdom of God first, and who possess and use their wealth in the spirit of God's stewards. This is well brought out in a sermon entitled, *Who is the rich man who is being saved?* by Clement of Alexandria about A.D. 200.

When Jesus declares that the salvation of a rich man is a possibility, because with God all things are possible, His utterance is not to be understood as teaching that God is able to save any man against his will. St. Luke, who evinces on a number of occasions not only his medical interests and his literary gifts but also a power of philosophical thought, deftly alters Mk.'s parallel into 'the things which are impossible with men are possible with God,' thus making Jesus agree with Aristotle, who cites the poet Agathon with approval when he writes:

> That it is not possible even for the Gods to make that which has been as though it had not been.

Divine omnipotence is not the power to do all things but the power to do all possible things.

Peter's prompt contrast between the rich man who refused to give up his riches in order to be a disciple, and the disciples who had surrendered all their possessions to follow Jesus, draws from Matthew Henry the quaint comment: 'What did you leave, Peter? A fishing boat and a few old nets.' This is hardly just. St. Peter seems to have been a man of substance: the head of a considerable fishing industry, and the possessor of a large house. Mt. gives Peter's naïve remark a more materialistic turn: 'What then shall we have?' The reply of Jesus is full of deep significance. He declares that no sacrifice made on behalf of Himself and the Gospel will be without its compensations. The disciples' reward shall be a hundredfold, and that not in some future life, but here and now, and in the age to come, eternal life.

Those who surrendered their individualism and material possessions to enter the Christian fellowship exchanged a life of narrow self-interest, and limited outlook, for the full and many-sided social activities and wider and higher interests of the Christian religion. A soldier who marched with Napoleon into Italy, when the ideals of liberty, equality, and fraternity were still strong, wrote of the experience: ' We were as men marching into the dawn.' No reader of the Lukan Acts of the Apostles and of the Pauline Epistles can fail to detect the same joyous and vital enthusiasm palpitating in the life of the primitive Christian community.

In one of his Epistles St. Paul sends greeting to a certain Rufus, ' his mother and mine ' (Rom. 16^{13}). A modern commentator remarks on this greeting: ' Paul had a hundred dear old mothers in those churches of his.'

Those who, as the result of becoming Christians—and they were many in those days—were disowned and despised by their relations, became, as a result of their conversion, possessed of a host of new relations. Our Lord adds, not sardonically, or ironically, that these new possessions will bring with them persecutions. What He asserts is of necessity part of the experience of all those who exchange a small life for a great one: small joys and small cares are exchanged for great joys and great cares. That is the law of true human progress.

(The phrases ' now in this season ' and ' with persecutions ' are both omitted by Mt. and the second by Lk. It is significant that wives are omitted from those possessions surrendered for the sake of the Gospel. New Testament scribes have striven to include them, but the best codices support the omission.

The saying ' many that are first shall be last,' etc., may be understood as predicting the admission into the Kingdom of the irreligious classes in Judaism rather than the priests and scribes. Probably Gentile Christians saw here their call predicted, and the rejection of the Jews.)

THE THIRD PREDICTION OF THE PASSION

MK. 10^{32-34}

10 32 And they were in the way, going up to
Jerusalem; and Jesus was going before
them: and they were amazed; and they
that followed were afraid. And he took
again the twelve, and began to tell them
the things that were to happen unto him,
33 *saying*, Behold, we go up to Jerusalem;
and the Son of man shall be delivered
unto the chief priests and the scribes;
and they shall condemn him to death,
and shall deliver him unto the Gentiles:
34 and they shall mock him, and shall spit
upon him, and shall scourge him, and
shall kill him; and after three days he
shall rise again.

MT. 20^{17-19}

20 17 And as Jesus was going up to Jerusalem, he took the twelve disciples apart,
18 and in the way he said unto them, Behold, we go up to Jerusalem; and the
Son of man shall be delivered unto the
chief priests and scribes; and they shall
19 condemn him to death, and shall deliver
him unto the Gentiles to mock, and to
scourge, and to crucify: and the third
day he shall be raised up.

LK. 18^{31-34}

18 31 And he took unto him the twelve, and
said unto them, Behold, we go up to
Jerusalem, and all the things that are
written by the prophets shall be accom-
32 plished unto the Son of man. For he
shall be delivered up unto the Gentiles,
and shall be mocked, and shamefully
33 entreated, and spit upon: and they shall
scourge and kill him: and the third day
34 he shall rise again. And they understood
none of these things; and this saying was
hid from them, and they perceived not
the things that were said.

The journey up to Jerusalem proceeds, but Mk. records what Mt. and Lk. omit. Jesus strides on ahead, and the amazed and terrified disciples follow Him at a distance. Then Jesus takes them again into His society but only to emphasise once more the fate which must await Him at Jerusalem. This, He gives with fuller details than on previous occasions. Lk. records Him as saying that these sufferings are to be fulfilled in accordance with the predictions of the prophets. Lk. also adds that the Apostles did not understand Jesus because the significance of His utterances had been concealed from them, presumably by Divine overruling.

THE AMBITIOUS REQUEST OF JAMES AND JOHN

MK. 10^{35-45}

10 35 And there come near unto him James
and John, the sons of Zebedee, saying
unto him, Master, we would that thou
shouldest do for us whatsoever we shall
36 ask of thee. And he said unto them,
What would ye that I should do for you?
37 And they said unto him, Grant unto us
that we may sit, one on thy right hand,
and one on *thy* left hand, in thy glory.
38 But Jesus said unto them, Ye know not
what ye ask. Are ye able to drink the
cup that I drink? or to be baptized with
the baptism that I am baptized with?
39 And they said unto him, We are able.
And Jesus said unto them, The cup that
I drink ye shall drink; and with the
baptism that I am baptized withal shall
40 ye be baptized: but to sit on my right
hand or on *my* left hand is not mine to
give: but *it is for them* for whom it hath
41 been prepared. And when the ten heard
it, they began to be moved with indigna-
42 tion concerning James and John. And
Jesus called them to him, and saith unto
them, Ye know that they which are
accounted to rule over the Gentiles lord
it over them; and their great ones exercise
43 authority over them. But it is not so
among you: but whosoever would become
44 great among you, shall be your minister:
and whosoever would be first among you,
45 shall be servant of all. For verily the
Son of man came not to be ministered
unto but to minister, and to give his life
a ransom for many.

MT. 20^{20-28}

20 20 Then came to him the mother of the
sons of Zebedee with her sons, worshipping him, and asking a certain thing of
21 him. And he said unto her, What
wouldest thou? She saith unto him,
Command that these my two sons may
sit, one on thy right hand, and one on thy
22 left hand, in thy kingdom. But Jesus
answered and said, Ye know not what ye
ask. Are ye able to drink the cup that I
am about to drink? They say unto him,
23 We are able. He saith unto them, My
cup indeed ye shall drink: but to sit on
my right hand, and on *my* left hand, is not
mine to give, but *it is for them* for whom it
24 hath been prepared of my Father. And
when the ten heard it, they were moved
with indignation concerning the two
25 brethren. But Jesus called them unto
him, and said, Ye know that the rulers of
the Gentiles lord it over them, and their
great ones exercise authority over them.
26 Not so shall it be among you: but whosoever would become great among you shall
27 be your minister; and whosoever would
be first among you shall be your servant:
28 even as the Son of man came not to be
ministered unto, but to minister, and to
give his life a ransom for many.

LK. 22^{24-27}

22 24 And there arose also a contention
among them, which of them is accounted
25 to be greatest. And he said unto them,
The kings of the Gentiles have lordship
over them; and they that have authority
26 over them are called Benefactors. But
ye *shall* not *be* so: but he that is the
greater among you, let him become as
the younger; and he that is chief, as he
27 that doth serve. For whether is greater,
he that sitteth at meat, or he that
serveth? is not he that sitteth at meat?
but I am in the midst of you as he that
serveth.

Cf. LK. 12^{50}

12 50 But I have a baptism to be baptized
with; and how am I straitened till it be
accomplished!

Mk. has already related that the Apostles had disputed among themselves who should be the greatest. He now indicates that our Lord's reproof on that occasion had plainly failed in the case of the sons of Zebedee. They request Jesus to give them the two positions of highest authority in His Kingdom. The grand vizier stood at his sovereign's right hand, the commander-in-chief at his left. When Jesus asks them if they are able to drink the cup of suffering which He has to drink, and to endure the Baptism of martyrdom which He is about to endure, the Sons of Thunder, true to their character, declare that they are able. The reply of Jesus is usually taken as predicting the martyrdom of them both. (That of St. James took place in A.D. 44 (see Acts 12^2). There is no undoubted record of the actual martyrdom of his brother John.)

The declaration of Jesus that it is not within His authority to assign to His Apostles the places for which they ask, is very significant. It is desert, not favour, merit, not self-seeking, which secures promotion in the Kingdom of God.

The remainder of the disciples, on whom James and John had hoped to steal a march, were naturally indignant when the action of John and James came to their ears. Again Jesus explains to them the difference between the mundane order and the spiritual order. In 'the world,' rulership is the mark of greatness: in the Kingdom, service is the mark of greatness. Even the Son of Man, the vicegerent of the Kingdom, comes, not to be served but to serve, and consummates His service by His self-sacrifice.

The Kingdoms of the earth go by
In purple and in gold;
They rise, they flourish, and they die,
And all their tale is told.

One Kingdom only is Divine,
One banner triumphs still,
Its King a servant, and its sign
A gibbet on a hill.

G. F. BRADBY.

Mt. seeks to save the faces, or rather protect the sacred memories, of St. James and St. John, by narrating that their mother, inspired by maternal love, made the ambitious request for them. This is one of many instances in the Bible where the weaker sex gets the blame which has been incurred by the stronger.

It should be noted that, although Lk. cites our Lord as saying to His disciples that He is among them as one that serveth, yet he does not cite our Lord's statement as given in Mk. and Mt., that the Son of Man came to give His life a ransom for many.

Lk.'s account of the institution of the Eucharist seems to indicate that he did not share the Jewish Christian view of the death of Jesus as a propitiatory sacrifice. Yet those words of Jesus, omitted by Lk., do not present His death as a propitiatory sacrifice but His life as one of vicarious service and suffering. The phrase 'for many' seems to be derived from the description of the Suffering Servant in Is. 53.

E. BLIND BARTIMÆUS

MK. 10^{46-52}

10 46 And they come to Jericho: and as he
went out from Jericho, with his disciples
and a great multitude, the son of Timæus,
Bartimæus, a blind beggar, was sitting
47 by the way side. And when he heard
that it was Jesus of Nazareth, he began
to cry out, and say, Jesus, thou son of
48 David, have mercy on me. And many
rebuked him, that he should hold his
peace: but he cried out the more a great
deal, Thou son of David, have mercy on
49 me. And Jesus stood still, and said,
Call ye him. And they call the blind
man, saying unto him, Be of good cheer:
50 rise, he calleth thee. And he, casting
away his garment, sprang up, and came
51 to Jesus. And Jesus answered him, and
said, What wilt thou that I should do
unto thee? And the blind man said
unto him, Rabboni, that I may receive
52 my sight. And Jesus said unto him, Go
thy way; thy faith hath made thee whole.
And straightway he received his sight,
and followed him in the way.

MT. 20^{29-34}

20 29 And as they went out from Jericho, a
30 great multitude followed him. And
behold, two blind men sitting by the way
side, when they heard that Jesus was
passing by, cried out, saying, Lord, have
31 mercy on us, thou son of David. And
the multitude rebuked them, that they
should hold their peace: but they cried
out the more, saying, Lord, have mercy
32 on us, thou son of David. And Jesus
stood still, and called them, and said,
What will ye that I should do unto you?
33 They say unto him, Lord, that our eyes
34 may be opened. And Jesus, being
moved with compassion, touched their
eyes: and straightway they received their
sight, and followed him.

Cf. MT. 9^{27-31}.

LK. 18^{35-43}

18 35 And it came to pass, as he drew nigh
unto Jericho, a certain blind man sat by
36 the way side begging: and hearing a
multitude going by, he inquired what
37 this meant. And they told him, that
38 Jesus of Nazareth passeth by. And he
cried, saying, Jesus, thou son of David,
39 have mercy on me. And they that went
before rebuked him, that he should hold
his peace: but he cried out the more a
great deal, Thou son of David, have
40 mercy on me. And Jesus stood, and
commanded him to be brought unto him:
and when he was come near, he asked
41 him, What wilt thou that I should do
unto thee? And he said, Lord, that I
42 may receive my sight. And Jesus said
unto him, Receive thy sight: thy faith
43 hath made thee whole. And immediately he received his sight, and followed
him, glorifying God: and all the people,
when they saw it, gave praise unto God.

Jesus has now completed His journey through Peræa: He has recrossed the Jordan a short distance above the Dead Sea, and has reached Jericho. On going out from Jericho with a great multitude He passes Timæus Bartimæus, a blind beggar. (Lk. records this incident as taking place before Jesus enters Jericho, but that is because Lk. has the story of Zacchæus to record as Jesus goes out from Jericho.)

The story of the healing of Timæus is very dramatic. The beggar is seated by the roadside. Hearing the throng pass by, he enquires the cause and is told that it is due to Jesus the Nazarene. Thereupon he begins to cry out: 'O Jesus, thou Son of David, have pity on me.' Many in the crowd tell him to be silent. The reason of this is not lack of sympathy, but the beggar is talking treason. 'Son of David' is a Messianic title, and to hail Jesus publicly as the Son of David might easily suggest to the Roman authorities the signal of revolt. It would seem that the advance of Jesus with His disciples on Jerusalem is beginning to be interpreted as having a political and revolutionary significance. Possibly, some of the disciples of Jesus, by the utterance of injudicious phrases, are themselves responsible for the creation of this idea in the public mind. Whatever many in the crowd may feel about the advance of Jesus on Jerusalem, at least they recognise the folly of the action of Timæus. Timæus, no doubt, is prompted to use the Messianic title because he hopes by so doing to please Jesus and secure His compassion. At any rate, he is acute enough to recognise that the more disturbance he makes the more likely he is to have his needs attended to.

The attention of Jesus is attracted: the procession comes to a halt. Jesus says to the crowd: ' Call him.' The crowd, now full of curiosity and eager sympathy, say to Timæus, ' Cheer up! Get up! He is calling thee.' The beggar flings away his cloak and springing up comes to Jesus and presents his petition. It is to be noted that in doing so he drops the title Son of David and substitutes for it Rabboni (my dear great one)—the affectionate and reverent title used by a pupil to his master (it is used by Mary Magdalene in addressing the risen Saviour).

The declaration of Jesus: ' Go off, thy faith has healed thee,' anticipates the immediate recovery of his sight: but like so many whom Jesus healed, he pays no attention to the command of Jesus to depart, but follows Him on the road.

As usual, when Mk.'s account is compared with those of Mt. and Lk., it is seen to be superior in dramatic presentation, although Lk., as is not uncommonly the case with him, does add an explanatory phrase or two which heightens the vividness of the scene.

Mt., as elsewhere, with a false sense of economy, combines two cases of healing (' two blind men ') and states that Jesus *touched* their eyes (possibly their eyeballs; cf. the healing of the blind man at Bethsaida). (Mk. 8^{23}.)

F. THE TRIUMPHAL ENTRY

MK. 11^{1-11}

11 1 And when they draw nigh unto
Jerusalem, unto Bethphage and Bethany,
at the mount of Olives, he sendeth two of
2 his disciples, and saith unto them, Go
your way into the village that is over
against you: and straightway as ye enter
into it, ye shall find a colt tied, whereon
no man ever yet sat; loose him, and
3 bring him. And if any one say unto you,
Why do ye this? say ye, The Lord hath
need of him; and straightway he will send
4 him back hither. And they went away,
and found a colt tied at the door without
in the open street; and they loose him.
5 And certain of them that stood there said
unto them, What do ye, loosing the colt?
6 And they said unto them even as Jesus
7 had said: and they let them go. And
they bring the colt unto Jesus, and cast
on him their garments; and he sat upon
8 him. And many spread their garments
upon the way; and others branches,
which they had cut from the fields.
9 And they that went before, and they that
followed, cried, Hosanna; Blessed *is* he

MT. 21^{1-11}

21 1 And when they drew nigh unto Jerusalem, and came unto Bethphage, unto
the mount of Olives, then Jesus sent two
2 disciples, saying unto them, Go into the
village that is over against you, and
straightway ye shall find an ass tied, and
a colt with her: loose *them*, and bring
3 *them* unto me. And if any one say aught
unto you, ye shall say, The Lord hath
need of them; and straightway he will
4 send them. Now this is come to pass,
that it might be fulfilled which was
spoken by the prophet, saying,
5 Tell ye the daughter of Zion,
Behold, thy King cometh unto thee,
Meek, and riding upon an ass,
And upon a colt the foal of an ass.
6 And the disciples went, and did even as
7 Jesus appointed them, and brought the
ass, and the colt, and put on them their
8 garments; and he sat thereon. And the
most part of the multitude spread their
garments in the way; and others cut
branches from the trees, and spread them
9 in the way. And the multitudes that

that cometh in the name of the Lord:
10 Blessed *is* the kingdom that cometh, *the*
kingdom of our father David: Hosanna
in the highest.
11 And he entered into Jerusalem, into
the temple; and when he had looked
round about upon all things, it being
now eventide, he went out unto Bethany
with the twelve.

went before him, and that followed,
cried, saying, Hosanna to the son of
David: Blessed *is* he that cometh in the
name of the Lord; Hosanna in the
10 highest. And when he was come into
Jerusalem, all the city was stirred, saying,
11 Who is this? And the multitudes said,
This is the prophet, Jesus, from Nazareth
of Galilee.

LK. 19^{28-44}

19 28 And when he had thus spoken, he went
on before, going up to Jerusalem.
29 And it came to pass, when he drew
nigh unto Bethphage and Bethany, at the
mount that is called *the mount* of Olives,
30 he sent two of the disciples, saying, Go
your way into the village over against
you; in the which as ye enter ye shall find
a colt tied, whereon no man ever yet sat:
31 loose him, and bring him. And if any one
ask you, Why do ye loose him? thus shall
ye say, The Lord hath need of him. And
32 they that were sent went away, and found
33 even as he had said unto them. And
as they were loosing the colt, the owners
thereof said unto them, Why loose ye the
34 colt? And they said, The Lord hath
35 need of him. And they brought him to
Jesus: and they threw their garments
upon the colt, and set Jesus thereon.
36 And as he went, they spread their gar-
37 ments in the way. And as he was now
drawing nigh, *even* at the descent of the
mount of Olives, the whole multitude of
the disciples began to rejoice and praise
God with a loud voice for all the mighty
38 works which they had seen; saying,
Blessed *is* the King that cometh in the
name of the Lord: peace in heaven, and
39 glory in the highest. And some of the
Pharisees from the multitude said unto
40 him, Master, rebuke thy disciples. And
he answered and said, I tell you that, if
these shall hold their peace, the stones
will cry out.
41 And when he drew nigh, he saw the
42 city and wept over it, saying, If thou
hadst known in this day, even thou, the
things which belong unto peace? but
43 now they are hid from thine eyes. For
the days shall come upon thee, when
thine enemies shall cast up a bank about
thee, and compass thee round, and keep
44 thee in on every side, and shall dash thee
to the ground, and thy children within
thee; and they shall not leave in thee one
stone upon another; because thou
knewest not the time of thy visitation.

JN. 12^{12-19}

12 12 On the morrow a great multitude that
had come to the feast, when they heard
13 that Jesus was coming to Jerusalem, took
the branches of the palm trees, and went
forth to meet him, and cried out,
Hosanna: Blessed *is* he that cometh in the
name of the Lord, even the King of
14 Israel. And Jesus, having found a
young ass, sat thereon; as it is written,
15 Fear not, daughter of Zion: behold, thy
King cometh, sitting on an ass's colt.
16 These things understood not his disciples
at the first: but when Jesus was glorified,
then remembered they that these things
were written of him, and that they had
17 done these things unto him. The multitude therefore that was with him when
he called Lazarus out of the tomb, and
raised him from the dead, bare witness.
18 For this cause also the multitude went
and met him, for that they heard that he
19 had done this sign. The Pharisees therefore said among themselves, Behold how
ye prevail nothing: lo, the world is gone
after him.

Jesus approaches the environs of Jerusalem. Bethphage (the House of Figs) was probably a suburb of Jerusalem situated outside the walls of the city. Bethany

(House of Dates) was a village to the south-east of Jerusalem situated on the slopes of the Mount of Olives, which is separated from Jerusalem by the valley of the Kidron.

It would seem that Jesus halted at Bethany and sent the two disciples into Bethphage to secure the ass on which He proposed to make His entry into Jerusalem. It is difficult to view what follows otherwise than as a deliberate symbolic action of Jesus intended to proclaim publicly the real character of His Messiahship to the inhabitants of Jerusalem. The prophet Zechariah had predicted the entry of the Messianic King into Jerusalem as one who should come, not as a triumphant military conqueror (cf. Psalm 24[7], Lift up your heads), but as a man of peace, the ideal civic governor riding, not in a chariot nor on a war-horse, but on an ass.

Rejoice greatly, O daughter of Zion; shout, O daughter of Jerusalem: behold, thy king cometh unto thee: he is just, and having salvation; lowly, and riding upon an ass, even upon a colt the foal of an ass. (Zech. 9[9].)

This is the first of a series of enigmatic but deeply significant indications given by Jesus of the real character of His Messianic mission—of the kind of Messiah He really is.

The cry Hosanna (Mk., Mt., Jn.) is the equivalent of our English 'God save the King.' The word occurs in Ps. 118[25], and means literally, 'Save now, we beseech Thee.' It could only be used in saluting a sovereign or his vice-gerent.

Lk.'s statement, that the ecclesiastical authorities requested Jesus to check the acclamations of the populace, indicates (although on account of his Gentile readers Lk. omits the word 'Hosanna') the effect which the use of this royal salutation might be expected to have on the Roman authorities. Lk. adds that Jesus retorted to their request: 'If these [the disciples] should hold their peace, the stones would cry out.' (Lk. 19[40].)

The acclamations recorded by Mk. bring out clearly the expectation of the multitude that Jesus was about to re-establish the Davidic Kingdom.

Hosanna:
Blessed is he that cometh in the name of the Lord:
Blessed is the Kingdom that cometh, the Kingdom of our father David:
Hosanna in the Highest. (*vv.* 9 and 10.)

Mt. omits entirely the reference to the Kingdom and Lk. does likewise. Mt.'s use of Hosanna seems to indicate that he does not understand Hebrew or Aramaic.

In Mk. the account of the borrowing of the ass by the two disciples, as directed by Jesus, is of a more normal character than in Mt. Going into the village over against them they will find, on their entering, a colt tied up. They are to untie it and bring it to Jesus. If any object, the disciples are to reply: The Lord (not Jehovah, but the Master) has need of it, and that after He has used it He will return the animal immediately to this place.

According to Mt., however, the owner of the colt, as soon as he is told that the Lord has need of it, will send it immediately.

The two disciples find the colt tied to a door, on the outside, where two ways met. Some commentators think that the phrase for the meeting of the ways is the Greek equivalent for Bethphage. Others think that it may be a corruption of the phrase 'to the vine,' and connect the tying up of the colt with the famous Messianic prophecy of Gen. 49^{8-11}.

> Judah, thee shall thy brethren praise:
> Thy hand shall be on the neck of thine enemies;
> Thy father's sons shall bow down before thee.
> Judah is a lion's whelp ;
> From the prey, my son, thou art gone up:
> He stooped down, he couched as a lion,
> And as a lioness; who shall rouse him up?
> The sceptre shall not depart from Judah,
> Nor the ruler's staff from between his feet,
> Until Shiloh come;
> And unto him shall the obedience of the peoples be.
> Binding his foal unto the vine,
> And his ass's colt unto the choice vine;
> He hath washed his garments in wine,
> And his vesture in the blood of grapes:

Mt., no doubt in order to secure precise fulfilment of a Messianic prophecy, doubles the animals. He does not realise the significance of parallelism in Hebrew poetry, which expresses the same thought in two different ways. The Hebrew poetry of this passage in Genesis and of the oracle of Zech. 9^9 refers to only one animal, but Mt. interprets it as referring both to an ass and to its foal: and furthermore makes Jesus ride on both of them at once. This instance of the straining by Mt. of a fact (recorded in Mk.) in order to secure the precise fulfilment of an Old Testament prediction is very significant because it indicates that there was a type of primitive Christian mentality for which the truth of Old Testament predictions was more certain than the truth of recorded fact.

Mk. (followed by Mt. and Lk.) states that no one had ever yet sat on the colt on which Jesus rode.

For the Jews (in common with other Semitic peoples) there was a quality of sacredness attached to newness (e.g. the sacred festivals of the first fruits, the new moon, the first year of married life, etc.). Hence, the newness of the colt on which Jesus rides, the newness of the tomb in which He is buried, the newness of the linen grave clothes which enwrap His body.

The Gospel narratives indicate that Jesus was treated as a royal person by those who spread their garments on the way. The development in the account of the greenery used is significant. Mk. merely states that green stuff, litter, cut by the disciples from the fields, was spread on the road: Mt., that branches were cut from the trees: Jn., that a procession with palm branches came forth to meet Jesus. Lk. omits all reference to the use of vegetation.

When Jesus had entered the city and visited the Temple, scrutinising all things, He returned with the Twelve to Bethany.

THE COMMERCIALISED TEMPLE AND THE FRUITLESS FIG TREE

MK. 11^{12-25}

11 12 And on the morrow, when they were
come out from Bethany, he hungered.
13 And seeing a fig tree afar off having
leaves, he came, if haply he might find
anything thereon: and when he came to
it, he found nothing but leaves; for it was
14 not the season of figs. And he answered
and said unto it, No man eat fruit from
thee henceforward for ever. And his
disciples heard it.
15 And they come to Jerusalem: and he
entered into the temple, and began to
cast out them that sold and them that
bought in the temple, and overthrew the
tables of the money-changers, and the
16 seats of them that sold the doves; and he
would not suffer that any man should
carry a vessel through the temple.
17 And he taught, and said unto them, Is it
not written, My house shall be called a
house of prayer for all the nations? but
18 ye have made it a den of robbers. And
the chief priests and the scribes heard it,
and sought how they might destroy him:
for they feared him, for all the multitude
was astonished at his teaching.
19 And every evening he went forth out
of the city.
20 And as they passed by in the morning,
they saw the fig tree withered away from
21 the roots. And Peter calling to remembrance saith unto him, Rabbi, behold,
the fig tree which thou cursedst is with-
22 ered away. And Jesus answering saith
23 unto them, Have faith in God. Verily I
say unto you, Whosoever shall say unto
this mountain, Be thou taken up and cast
into the sea; and shall not doubt in his
heart, but shall believe that what he
saith cometh to pass; he shall have it.
24 Therefore I say unto you, All things
whatsoever ye pray and ask for, believe
that ye have received them, and ye shall
25 have them. And whensoever ye stand
praying, forgive, if ye have aught against
any one; that your Father also which is in
heaven may forgive you your trespasses.

MT. 21^{12-22}

21 12 And Jesus entered into the temple of
God, and cast out all them that sold and
bought in the temple, and overthrew the
tables of the money-changers, and the
13 seats of them that sold the doves; and he
saith unto them, It is written, My house
shall be called a house of prayer: but ye
14 make it a den of robbers. And the blind
and the lame came to him in the temple:
15 and he healed them. But when the chief
priests and the scribes saw the wonderful
things that he did, and the children that
were crying in the temple and saying,
Hosanna to the son of David; they were
16 moved with indignation, and said unto
him, Hearest thou what these are saying?
And Jesus saith unto them, Yea: did ye
never read, Out of the mouth of babes
and sucklings thou hast perfected praise?
17 And he left them, and went forth out of
the city to Bethany, and lodged there.
18 Now in the morning as he returned to
19 the city, he hungered. And seeing a fig
tree by the way side, he came to it, and
found nothing thereon, but leaves only;
and he saith unto it, Let there be no fruit
from thee henceforward for ever. And
immediately the fig tree withered away.
20 And when the disciples saw it, they
marvelled, saying, How did the fig tree
21 immediately wither away? And Jesus
answered and said unto them, Verily I
say unto you, If ye have faith, and doubt
not, ye shall not only do what is done to
the fig tree, but even if ye shall say unto
this mountain, Be thou taken up and cast
22 into the sea, it shall be done. And all
things, whatsoever ye shall ask in prayer,
believing, ye shall receive.

LK. 13^{6-9}, $17^{5, 6}$, 19^{45-48}, 21^{37}

13 6 And he spake this parable; A certain
man had a fig tree planted in his vineyard; and he came seeking fruit thereon,
7 and found none. And he said unto the
vinedresser, Behold, these three years I
come seeking fruit on this fig tree, and
find none: cut it down; why doth it also
8 cumber the ground? And he answering
saith unto him, Lord, let it alone this year

JN. 2^{13-16}, $14^{13, 14}$, 16^{23}

2 13 And the passover of the Jews was at
hand, and Jesus went up to Jerusalem.
14 And he found in the temple those that sold
oxen and sheep and doves, and the
15 changers of money sitting: and he made a
scourge of cords, and cast all out of the
temple, both the sheep and the oxen; and
he poured out the changers' money, and
16 overthrew their tables; and to them that

also, till I shall dig about it, and dung it:
9 and if it bear fruit thenceforth, *well*; but
if not, thou shalt cut it down.

17 5 And the apostles said unto the Lord,
6 Increase our faith. And the Lord said,
If ye have faith as a grain of mustard
seed, ye would say unto this sycamine
tree, Be thou rooted up, and be thou
planted in the sea; and it would have
obeyed you.

19 45 And he entered into the temple, and
46 began to cast out them that sold, saying
unto them, It is written, And my house
shall be a house of prayer: but ye have
made it a den of robbers.

47 And he was teaching daily in the
temple. But the chief priests and the
scribes and the principal men of the
48 people sought to destroy him: and they
could not find what they might do; for
the people all hung upon him, listening.

21 37 And every day he was teaching in the
temple; and every night he went out, and
lodged in the mount that is called *the
mount* of Olives.

sold the doves he said, Take these things
hence; make not my Father's house a
house of merchandise.

14 13 And whatsoever ye shall ask in my
name, that will I do, that the Father may
14 be glorified in the Son. If ye shall ask
me anything in my name, that will I do.

16 23 And in that day ye shall ask me nothing.
Verily, verily, I say unto you, If ye shall
ask anything of the Father, he will give
it you in my name.

(*a*) The Commercialised Temple

On the next day Jesus, with the Twelve, goes again into Jerusalem and again visits the Temple. He finds the outer court of the Temple—the Court of the Gentiles—a centre of eager commercialism, as was the nave of St. Paul's in the sixteenth century. Traders, licensed by the Sadducean high-priesthood, are selling animals and birds required for sacrifice: others are engaged in exchanging pagan money for the sacred coinage which alone could be given to the Temple treasury. Jesus overturns the tables of the money-changers and commands the traders with their animal sacrifices to depart. The Court of the Gentiles, which was commonly used as a thoroughfare by porters, He closes against them.

Jn., who places the cleansing of the Temple at the beginning of the Messianic ministry of Jesus (2^{13-16}), relates that He made a scourge of cords (possibly rushes) which He used on this occasion. According to Mk., Mt., and Lk., Jesus enforces the lesson of His action by calling attention to the Divine ideal for the Temple (as voiced by an unknown post-Exilic prophet), ' My House shall be called a House of Prayer for all the Gentiles ' (Is. 56^7), and complains with Jeremiah that the Temple had become a cave of brigands (Jer. 7^{11}).

Some have seen in the cleansing of the Court of the Gentiles a deep concern on the part of Jesus for the religion of the Gentile world, and have held that His action foreshadows the Call of the Gentiles and the extension of the true religion of the Divine Father to all mankind. It is more probable that we have, in the cleansing of the Temple, a deliberate symbolic action by Jesus, setting forth an aspect of His Messianic office: the purging of contemporary Jewish religion from commercialism and materialism.

Mt. has the prophecy of Malachi in mind when relating the cleansing of the Temple. This is shown by his making Jesus cleanse the Temple immediately on His entry into Jerusalem on Palm Sunday, and not waiting to do it until the next day, as recorded by Mk., and Mt. thus secures the minute fulfilment of the words of Malachi:

'The Lord whom ye seek shall *suddenly* come to his Temple; the messenger of the covenant whom ye delight in, behold he cometh, saith the Lord of hosts . . . and he shall purify the sons of Levi . . . and they shall offer unto the Lord offerings in righteousness.' (Mal. 3^{1-3}.)

The action of Jesus, which was an obvious and public affront to the ecclesiastical rulers, excited their deepest hostility. They desired to destroy Him, but were afraid to do so on account of His extraordinary popularity, 'for the people all hung upon him, listening '(Lk. 19^{48}), 'being amazed at His teaching '(Mk. 11^{18}).

(*b*) The Fruitless Fig Tree

Mk. relates that on the morning when leaving Bethany to cleanse the Temple, Jesus was hungry. This suggests the earliness of the hour, or the failure, owing to the multitude of the Passover pilgrims, to secure provisions. He sees a fig tree some distance away (afar off) (Mt. 'beside the road') in full leaf. This promises figs. When He goes over to it He finds nothing but leaves. Seeing in the fig tree's leaves without fruit a symbol of hypocrisy—the vice He most detested—and a picture of contemporary Jewish religion—outwardly flourishing but actually barren—He says to the fig tree: 'May no man henceforth eat fruit from thee for ever.' Next morning, when again passing along that road, the disciples, who had heard the word which Jesus addressed to the fig tree, observe that it is withered, or dried up from the roots. They immediately assume that this is a miraculous fulfilment of the words of Jesus and call His attention to it. He replies: That if they have faith, greater things will be produced by their words than the withering of a barren fig tree. This saying of Jesus gives Mk. the opportunity to include, after his manner, several other sayings about effective prayer which must be combined with both the spirit of faith and the spirit of forgiveness.

The incident of the fig tree has caused much difficulty to commentators, Some have doubted whether it is really historical and have thought that the Parable of the Barren Fig Tree as given by Lk. has been transmuted by primitive Christian scribes into the Miracle of the Withered Fig Tree. It might well ease the situation if this view could be accepted, but Mk.'s account is altogether too circumstantial to admit of this solution. For the spirit of divine forbearance which is emphasised in Lk.'s parable, we find in Mk.'s narrative a spirit of dramatic judgement, accentuated, some have argued, by the irritability due to hunger and disappointment. Certainly the 'gentle Jesus' of the sentimentalists is not in evidence in this incident. It is the Jesus whom we hear reproving His disciples for their lack of faith and spiritual insight: the Jesus who reduces to impotent fury the ecclesiastical casuists and formalists who will neither themselves enter into the Kingdom nor allow others to do so. Jesus can and does show, on occasions, extraordinary forbearance and self-restraint, but the refusal to exhibit a divine indignation He no more regards as a virtue than do the great Christian moralists. Anger, said one of them, is not a weed to be extirpated but a wild plant to be cultivated. Another wrote: It is not a good thing to consort with such as cannot be angry. And it was St. Augustine who justly remarked: We ought not to exclaim with surprise that such a good man is angry, but rather we ought to enquire—Why is he angry?

Any student of Bishop Joseph Butler's famous sermon on Anger would be far more concerned to doubt the perfection of our Lord's moral character if evidence of the capacity for righteous anger were absent from it, than if He might seem at times too prone to righteous indignation. It is in those matters in which ordinary men show severity that our Lord is sympathetic and forgiving: and it is in those matters in which ordinary men are lax and tolerant, or even seem to commend, that our Lord is unflinchingly severe. Hardness of heart, lack of generosity and chivalry, mean selfishness, spiritual pride, religious formalism and self-complacency, and above all hypocrisy, drew from Jesus the sternest condemnation.

Much sympathy has been bestowed upon the fig tree, as also upon the Gadarene swine: but where the suffering must have been so slight, the sympathy is best reserved for more heart-rending cases.

Mt. emphasises the miraculous character of the withering of the fig tree by making it take place immediately after Jesus addresses it and by making the disciples exclaim: How did the fig tree immediately wither away! (Mt. 21^{20}.)

As Mk. tells the story, the incident is not necessarily miraculous. The fig tree's barrenness suggests some weakness: a hard frost on a cold night in the early spring, followed by hot sunshine, might naturally have accomplished its decease. Mk. complicates his narrative by writing: The season of figs was not yet. Mk. was himself an inhabitant of Jerusalem and he may have meant that it was unusual to get figs before the Passover there. On the other hand: If the fig tree were in full leaf, as he states, figs might normally be expected, though not ripe ones. The writer has seen natives in Galilee eating small, hard, unripe figs. Jerusalem is some 4,000 feet above the level of Jericho and as a consequence the Jericho season is several weeks ahead of that of Jerusalem. When in the Jordan valley Jesus had probably eaten figs and may not have realised that the season for figs had not yet come in Jerusalem.

FIVE QUESTIONS

(*a*) The Source of Authority

MK. $11^{27\text{-}33}$

11 27 And they come again to Jerusalem:
and as he was walking in the temple,
there come to him the chief priests, and
28 the scribes, and the elders; and they said
unto him, By what authority doest thou
these things? or who gave thee this
29 authority to do these things? And Jesus
said unto them, I will ask of you one
question, and answer me, and I will tell
you by what authority I do these things.
30 The baptism of John, was it from
31 heaven, or from men? answer me. And
they reasoned with themselves, saying, If
we shall say, From heaven; he will say,
32 Why then did ye not believe him? But
should we say, From men—they feared
the people: for all verily held John to be

MT. $21^{23\text{-}27}$

21 23 And when he was come into the
temple, the chief priests and the elders of
the people came unto him as he was
teaching, and said, By what authority
doest thou these things? and who gave
24 thee this authority? And Jesus answered
and said unto them, I also will ask you
one question, which if ye tell me, I likewise will tell you by what authority I do
25 these things. The baptism of John,
whence was it? from heaven or from
men? And they reasoned with themselves, saying, If we shall say, From
heaven; he will say unto us, Why then
26 did ye not believe him? But if we shall
say, From men; we fear the multitude;
27 for all hold John as a prophet. And they

33 a prophet. And they answered Jesus
and say, We know not. And Jesus saith
unto them, Neither tell I you by what
authority I do these things.

answered Jesus, and said, We know not.
He also said unto them, Neither tell I
you by what authority I do these things.

LK. 20^{1-8}

20 1 And it came to pass, on one of the days,
as he was teaching the people in the
temple, and preaching the gospel, there
came upon him the chief priests and the
2 scribes with the elders; and they spake,
saying unto him, Tell us: By what
authority doest thou these things? or who
3 is he that gave thee this authority? And
he answered and said unto them, I also
4 will ask you a question; and tell me: The
baptism of John, was it from heaven, or
5 from men? And they reasoned with
themselves, saying, If we shall say, From
heaven; he will say, Why did ye not
6 believe him? But if we shall say, From
men; all the people will stone us: for they
be persuaded that John was a prophet.
7 And they answered, that they knew not
8 whence *it was*. And Jesus said unto them,
Neither tell I you by what authority I do
these things.

The Sanhedrin, feeling that something must be done, come to Jesus when He is walking in the Temple and ask Him by what kind of right He acts as He does?

Jesus says He will answer if they will tell Him whether the Baptism of John was from heaven or of men. They dared not answer, 'from heaven,' because the Sanhedrin had ignored John's Baptism; they dared not say 'of men,' because the nation at large held the martyr John to be a 'prophet indeed.'

The question of Jesus makes it plain that He regarded the source of His authority as the same as John's. Both came from God.

Mt., when he makes the Sanhedrin say, 'we fear the multitude,' goes beyond probability. No body of rulers would dare to make such a confession to one another.

Lk., with more probability than Mt., makes them say: 'that people will stone us.'

The Parable of the Vine-Dressers and the Heir

MK. 12^{1-12}

12 1 And he began to speak unto them in
parables. A man planted a vineyard,
and set a hedge about it, and digged a pit
for the winepress, and built a tower, and
let it out to husbandmen, and went into
2 another country. And at the season he
sent to the husbandmen a servant, that
he might receive from the husbandmen
3 of the fruits of the vineyard. And they
took him, and beat him, and sent him
4 away empty. And again he sent unto
them another servant; and him they
wounded in the head, and handled
5 shamefully. And he sent another; and
him they killed: and many others; beat-
6 ing some, and killing some. He had yet
one, a beloved son: he sent him last unto
them, saying, They will reverence my
7 son. But those husbandmen said among
themselves, This is the heir; come, let us
kill him, and the inheritance shall be
8 ours. And they took him, and killed
him, and cast him forth out of the vine-

MT. 21^{33-46}

21 33 Hear another parable: There was a
man that was a householder, which
planted a vineyard, and set a hedge about
it, and digged a winepress in it, and built
a tower, and let it out to husbandmen,
34 and went into another country. And
when the season of the fruits drew near,
he sent his servants to the husbandmen,
35 to receive his fruits. And the husbandmen took his servants, and beat one, and
killed another, and stoned another.
36 Again, he sent other servants more than
the first: and they did unto them in like
37 manner. But afterward he sent unto
them his son, saying, They will reverence
38 my son. But the husbandmen, when
they saw the son, said among themselves,
This is the heir; come, let us kill him,
39 and take his inheritance. And they took
him, and cast him forth out of the vine-
40 yard, and killed him. When therefore
the lord of the vineyard shall come, what
will he do unto those husbandmen?

9 yard. What therefore will the lord of the
vineyard do? he will come and destroy
the husbandmen, and will give the vine-
10 yard unto others. Have ye not read
even this scripture;

The stone which the builders
rejected,
The same was made the head of the
corner:
11 This was from the Lord,
And it is marvellous in our eyes?

12 And they sought to lay hold on him;
and they feared the multitude; for they
perceived that he spake the parable
against them: and they left him, and
went away.

41 They say unto him, He will miserably
destroy those miserable men, and will let
out the vineyard unto other husbandmen, which shall render him the fruits in
42 their seasons. Jesus saith unto them,
Did ye never read in the scriptures,

The stone which the builders
rejected,
The same was made the head of the
corner:
This was from the Lord,
And it is marvellous in our eyes?

43 Therefore say I unto you, The kingdom
of God shall be taken away from you, and
shall be given to a nation bringing forth
44 the fruits thereof. And he that falleth on
this stone shall be broken to pieces; but
on whomsoever it shall fall, it will scatter
45 him as dust. And when the chief priests
and the Pharisees heard his parables,
they perceived that he spake of them.
46 And when they sought to lay hold on
him, they feared the multitudes, because
they took him for a prophet.

LK. 20^{9-19}

20 9 And he began to speak unto the people
this parable: A man planted a vineyard,
and let it out to husbandmen, and went
into another country for a long time.
10 And at the season he sent unto the husbandmen a servant, that they should give
him of the fruit of the vineyard: but the
husbandmen beat him, and sent him
11 away empty. And he sent yet another
servant: and him also they beat, and
handled him shamefully, and sent him
12 away empty. And he sent yet a third:
and him also they wounded, and cast
13 him forth. And the lord of the vineyard
said, What shall I do? I will send my
beloved son: it may be they will reverence
14 him. But when the husbandmen saw
him, they reasoned one with another,
saying, This is the heir: let us kill him,
15 that the inheritance may be ours. And
they cast him forth out of the vineyard,
and killed him. What therefore will the
16 lord of the vineyard do unto them? He
will come and destroy these husbandmen, and will give the vineyard unto
others. And when they heard it, they
17 said, God forbid. But he looked upon
them, and said, What then is this that is
written,

The stone which the builders
rejected,
The same was made the head of the
corner?

18 Every one that falleth on that stone shall
be broken to pieces; but on whomsoever
it shall fall, it will scatter him as dust.
19 And the scribes and the chief priests
sought to lay hands on him in that very
hour; and they feared the people: for
they perceived that he spake this parable
against them.

Having declared in Jerusalem His Messianic Mission by two symbolic acts (the entry on an ass and the cleansing of the Temple), Jesus now proclaims it by the parable of the evil vine-dressers who not only refused to pay their dues to the absent owner of the vineyard, but insult, maltreat, and even murder the successive messengers whom the owner of the vineyard sends to them on his behalf. The climax of their iniquity is reached by the murder of the heir of the vineyard, the beloved son of its owner. The point of the parable is stressed by the concluding question: What shall be the fate of these evil men? They shall be destroyed and the vineyard given to others.

The Jews were accustomed, as we see from the beautiful song of the vineyard in Isaiah ($5^{1ff.}$) and from a number of the Psalms, to think of Israel as Jehovah's vineyard. The servants in the parable are obviously ' the goodly fellowship of the prophets ' so badly treated at the hands of the priests and civic rulers of Jerusalem. The son in the parable is obviously the Messiah, and His rejection and death are here predicted.

Lk. and less probably Mt. conclude the parable by making Jesus refer to two passages from the Old Testament which present the Messiah as ' the stone.' The first refers to ' the stone which the builders rejected ' (Ps. 118^{22}). It would seem that some notable stone in the Temple structure, intended by the architect to constitute the head corner-stone or some ornamental pinnacle, was rejected by the builders of the Temple as something for which they could find no place in the structure. This stone, for the poet, becomes a symbol of Israel itself: despised and rejected by the world's builders. The sovereigns of the great empires of Assyria, Babylonia, Persia, and Greece could find no place for Israel in their schemes of mundane civilisation. Nevertheless, the Architect of the Universe (Jehovah) has designed Israel for the very highest place in His cosmogony. For the primitive Christian Church ' the stone which the builders rejected ' is not Israel, but Jesus, the Messiah. (Cf. Acts 4^{11}; Eph. 2^{20}; 1 Pet. $2^{6f.}$.)

The second passage refers to ' the stone cut out without hands ' (Dan. $2^{34f.}$), which smites the image composed of gold and silver and brass and iron and clay, representing the great world empires, and reduces it to powder, which is blown away by the wind. The stone itself becomes a great mountain which fills all the earth. This, according to the interpretation of the Book of Daniel, is the Kingdom of the saints of the Most High—the idealised Maccabæan State which in the end is to conquer the whole world and last for ever. As cited in the Gospels, ' the stone cut out without hands ' is Jesus the Messiah.

(*b*) The Question about Tribute to Cæsar

MK. 12^{13-17}

12 13 And they send unto him certain of the
Pharisees and of the Herodians, that they
14 might catch him in talk. And when they
were come, they say unto him, Master,
we know that thou art true, and carest
not for any one: for thou regardest not
the person of men, but of a truth teachest
the way of God: Is it lawful to give
15 tribute unto Cæsar, or not? Shall we
give, or shall we not give? But he,
knowing their hypocrisy, said unto them,
Why tempt ye me? bring me a penny,
16 that I may see it. And they brought
it. And he saith unto them, Whose is
this image and superscription? And
17 they said unto him, Cæsar's. And Jesus
said unto them, Render unto Cæsar the
things that are Cæsar's, and unto God
the things that are God's. And they
marvelled greatly at him.

MT. 22^{15-22}

22 15 Then went the Pharisees, and took
counsel how they might ensnare him in
16 *his* talk. And they send to him their disciples,
with the Herodians, saying,
Master, we know that thou art true, and
teachest the way of God in truth, and
carest not for any one: for thou regardest
17 not the person of men. Tell us therefore,
What thinkest thou? Is it lawful to give
18 tribute unto Cæsar, or not? But Jesus
perceived their wickedness, and said,
19 Why tempt ye me, ye hypocrites? Shew
me the tribute money. And they
20 brought unto him a penny. And he
saith unto them, Whose is this image and
21 superscription? They say unto him,
Cæsar's. Then saith he unto them,
Render therefore unto Cæsar the things
that are Cæsar's; and unto God the
22 things that are God's. And when they
heard it, they marvelled, and left him,
and went their way.

LK. 20^{20-26}

20 20 And they watched him, and sent forth
spies, which feigned themselves to be
righteous, that they might take hold of
his speech, so as to deliver him up to the
rule and to the authority of the governor.
21 And they asked him, saying, Master, we
know that thou sayest and teachest
rightly, and acceptest not the person *of*
any, but of a truth teachest the way of
22 God: Is it lawful for us to give tribute
23 unto Cæsar, or not? But he perceived
24 their craftiness, and said unto them, Shew
me a penny. Whose image and superscription
hath it? And they said,
25 Cæsar's. And he said unto them, Then
render unto Cæsar the things that are
Cæsar's, and unto God the things that
26 are God's. And they were not able to
take hold of the saying before the people:
and they marvelled at his answer, and
held their peace.

The Zealots regarded as unpatriotic the payment of tribute to Cæsar and declared it to be unlawful for a Jew to pay it. There were many Jews who dared not refuse payment of the tribute who yet secretly sympathised with the Zealots. Even pious heads wondered at times whether the Zealots might not be right. Pharisees and Herodians (Mk. alone has the latter here) come to Jesus to resolve their doubts. Their action is basely hypocritical: their whole purpose is to entrap Him, and secure if possible, as Lk. points out, His arrest by the Roman Governor (20^{20}). Had Jesus declared that it was unlawful to give tribute, He would have been at once arrested by the Roman authorities. Had He declared that it was lawful, He would thereby have seemed to many, not only to have forfeited any claim to be the Messiah, but even to be regarded as a brave, loyal, patriotic Jew.

His answer not only defeats the plot to entrap Him, but lays down the fundamental principles which must guide His disciples in those future crises in which human authority and divine authority—State and Church—make conflicting claims.

Jesus, as we also see from His refusal to intervene in the case of a disputed inheritance, had little sympathy with those who wished to support their materialistic claims by securing His moral and spiritual authority. (Lk. $12^{13, 14}$.)

(Mk. makes Jesus say: 'Bring to me' a denarius (a small Roman silver coin a little larger than a sixpence). Mt. and Lk. have 'shew me.' Mk.'s phrase seems to indicate that Jesus must at this time have been teaching in the Court of the Gentiles, since it was not lawful to bring a denarius, because of its idolatrous effigy, into the inner courts of the Temple. The request of Jesus to the crowd suggests that some of them ran outside the Temple and brought a denarius to Him—a Petrine reminiscence.)

(*c*) A Question about the Resurrection

MK. 12^{18-27}

12 18 And there come unto him Sadducees,
which say that there is no resurrection;
19 and they asked him, saying, Master,
Moses wrote unto us, If a man's brother
die, and leave a wife behind him, and
leave no child, that his brother should
take his wife, and raise up seed unto his
20 brother. There were seven brethren:
and the first took a wife, and dying left no
21 seed; and the second took her, and died,

MT. 22^{23-33}

22 23 On that day there came to him Sadducees,
which say that there is no resurrec-
24 tion: and they asked him, saying, Master,
Moses said, If a man die, having no children, his brother shall marry his wife,
25 and raise up seed unto his brother. Now
there were with us seven brethren: and
the first married and deceased, and having no seed left his wife unto his brother;
26 in like manner the second also, and the

leaving no seed behind him; and the
22 third likewise: and the seven left no seed.
23 Last of all the woman also died. In the
resurrection whose wife shall she be of
them? for the seven had her to wife.
24 Jesus said unto them, Is it not for this
cause that ye err, that ye know not the
25 scriptures, nor the power of God? For
when they shall rise from the dead, they
neither marry, nor are given in marriage;
26 but are as angels in heaven. But as
touching the dead, that they are raised;
have ye not read in the book of Moses,
in *the place concerning* the Bush, how God
spake unto him, saying, I *am* the God of
Abraham, and the God of Isaac, and the
27 God of Jacob? He is not the God of the
dead, but of the living: ye do greatly err.

27 third, unto the seventh. And after them
28 all the woman died. In the resurrection
therefore whose wife shall she be of the
29 seven? for they all had her. But Jesus
answered and said unto them, Ye do err,
not knowing the scriptures, nor the power
30 of God. For in the resurrection they
neither marry, nor are given in marriage,
31 but are as angels in heaven. But as
touching the resurrection of the dead,
have ye not read that which was spoken
32 unto you by God, saying, I am the God
of Abraham, and the God of Isaac, and
the God of Jacob? God is not *the God of*
33 the dead, but of the living. And when
the multitudes heard it, they were
astonished at his teaching.

LK. 20^{27-38}

20 27 And there came to him certain of the
Sadducees, they which say that there is
no resurrection; and they asked him,
28 saying, Master, Moses wrote unto us, that
if a man's brother die, having a wife, and
he be childless, his brother should take
the wife, and raise up seed unto his
29 brother. There were therefore seven
brethren: and the first took a wife, and
30 died childless; and the second: and the
31 third took her; and likewise the seven
32 also left no children, and died. After-
33 ward the woman also died. In the
resurrection therefore whose wife of them
shall she be? for the seven had her to wife.
34 And Jesus said unto them, The sons of
this world marry, and are given in
35 marriage: but they that are accounted
worthy to attain to that world, and the
resurrection from the dead, neither
36 marry, nor are given in marriage: for
neither can they die any more: for they
are equal unto the angels; and are sons
of God, being sons of the resurrection.
37 But that the dead are raised, even Moses
shewed, in *the place concerning* the Bush,
when he calleth the Lord the God of
Abraham, and the God of Isaac, and the
38 God of Jacob. Now he is not the God
of the dead, but of the living: for all live
unto him.

The Sadducees, although no doubt deeply disappointed at the failure of the Pharisees and Herodians to entrap Jesus, must yet have felt a certain secret satisfaction at the defeat of their clever rivals. They now propound to Jesus a question concerning the Resurrection from the dead. The Sadducees (who were mainly members of the high priestly clan) were the most conservative of the Jewish religious schools. They restricted the Canon of Scripture to the five Books of Moses (as did the Samaritans) and since, in their judgement, these Scriptures did not teach any doctrine of a future life, they refused to believe in it, or in the existence of angels. Their rivals, the Pharisees, held the doctrine of the Resurrection from the dead, which had become an article of faith in Judaism in the second century B.C.

The question put by the Sadducees arises out of the Levirate law of Deuteronomy ($25^{5, 6}$, cf. Gen. 38^{8}), which runs as follows:

'If brethren dwell together, and one of them die, and have no child, the wife of the dead shall not marry without unto a stranger: her husband's brother shall go in unto her, and take her to him to wife, and perform the duty of an husband's brother unto her. And it shall be, that the first-born which she beareth shall succeed in the name of his brother which is dead, that his name be not put out of Israel.'

Jesus dismisses the matrimonial problem of their question, somewhat contemptuously declaring that in the resurrection they neither marry nor are given in marriage but are as the angels in heaven. He then proceeds to say that there are two causes for the Sadducees not believing in a future life: (1) their failure to realise the power of God; (2) their ignorance of their Scriptures.

Jesus then cites the most famous passage in the Sadducean Canon of Scripture (Exod. $3^{6f.}$), entitled 'The Bush.' The Jewish Scriptures were at this time divided into sections, the most notable of which had distinctive titles. The chapters and verses of our Bibles belong to a much later date.

The passage cited by Jesus narrates the call of Moses by Jehovah. In that call Jehovah declares Himself to be the God of Abraham and of Isaac and of Jacob. These patriarchs had died several hundreds of years before the Divine Vision to Moses. But inasmuch as God is not the God of the dead but of the living (His distinctive title in Israel was, The Living God), it must follow that although the Patriarchs had died so far as this world was concerned, they must now be alive in God's presence. Jesus thus teaches, not only a doctrine of the future life, but one which is not dependent upon a materialistic doctrine of the Resurrection as was the contemporary Pharisaic doctrine. For at the time of Moses, the bodies of the patriarchs were well known to be resting in their ancestral sepulchres, yet they themselves were enjoying the resurrection life in God's presence.

Lk. has some remarkable variations.

A. 'They that are accounted worthy to attain to that world and the resurrection from the dead,' sounds like an echo of a Pauline passage: 'If by any means I may attain unto the resurrection from the dead.' (Phil. 3^{11}.)

B. 'For neither can they die any more but are equal unto the angels and are sons of God, being sons of the resurrection.' The phrase 'equal unto the angels' only occurs here in the New Testament. St. Paul seems to have held that Christians, even in this life, were, in knowledge and privilege, superior to the angels, and that in a future life they would sit in judgement on the evil angels. (This view is rabbinical.)

C. 'For all live unto him,' suggests the Pauline declaration: 'Whether we live, we live unto the Lord, or whether we die, we die unto the Lord, so that whether living or dying, we are the Lord's.' (Here the 'we' refers only to Christians.) (Rom. 14^{8}.)

(*d*) The Question about the Great Commandment

MK. 12^{28-34}

12 28 And one of the scribes came, and heard
them questioning together, and knowing
that he had answered them well, asked
him, What commandment is the first of
29 all? Jesus answered, The first is, Hear,
O Israel; The Lord our God, the Lord is

MT. 22^{34-40}

22 34 But the Pharisees, when they heard
that he had put the Sadducees to silence,
35 gathered themselves together. And one
of them, a lawyer, asked him a question,
36 tempting him, Master, which is the great
37 commandment in the law? And he said

30 one: and thou shalt love the Lord thy
God with all thy heart, and with all thy
soul, and with all thy mind, and with all
31 thy strength. The second is this, Thou
shalt love thy neighbour as thyself.
There is none other commandment
32 greater than these. And the scribe said
unto him, Of a truth, Master, thou hast
well said that he is one; and there is none
33 other but he: and to love him with all the
heart, and with all the understanding,
and with all the strength, and to love his
neighbour as himself, is much more than
all whole burnt offerings and sacrifices.
34 And when Jesus saw that he answered
discreetly, he said unto him, Thou art not
far from the kingdom of God. And no
man after that durst ask him any question.

unto him, Thou shalt love the Lord thy
God with all thy heart, and with all thy
38 soul, and with all thy mind. This is the
39 great and first commandment. And a
second like *unto it* is this, Thou shalt love
40 thy neighbour as thyself. On these two
commandments hangeth the whole law,
and the prophets.

LK. 10^{25-28}, $20^{39, 40}$

10 25 And behold a certain lawyer stood up
and tempted him, saying, Master, what
26 shall I do to inherit eternal life? And he
said unto him, What is written in the law?
27 how readest thou? And he answering
said, Thou shalt love the Lord thy God
with all thy heart, and with all thy soul,
and with all thy strength, and with all
thy mind; and thy neighbour as thyself.
28 And he said unto him, Thou hast
answered right: this do, and thou shalt
live.
20 39 And certain of the scribes answering
40 said, Master, thou hast well said. For
they durst not any more ask him any
question.

A certain scribe who had listened to the discussion with the Sadducees and had recognised the acuteness of our Lord's reply asked Him: Of what kind is the first of all the Commandments? The point at issue would appear to be whether the greatest commandment is of the nature of a positive precept, like the observance of the Sabbath or circumcision or sacrifice, or whether it is of the nature of a moral principle. This was one of the points at issue between priestly legalists and prophetic moralists. Jesus answers in the spirit of the great prophets of Israel, although His citations are actually taken from the Law. The First and the Great Commandment is from Dt. $6^{4, 5}$, and the second, which is like unto it, is from Lev. 19^{18}.

The Commandment to love God begins by stressing the unity of the Godhead and then insists on the worship of God with the whole personality. Mk. presents this worship as fourfold, as does Lk.: ' with all thy heart ' (moral consciousness); ' with all thy soul ' (vital emotion); ' with all thy mind ' (intellect); and ' with all thy strength ' (the full exercise of all the powers of the personality). In Mt. the exercise of this love is threefold, as also in the Septuagint, and as in the Hebrew Massoretic Text. There are some variants in the order and description of these three constituents.

There is good reason (so that great scholar Archdeacon Charles thought) for regarding Jesus as responsible for adding intellectual love (i.e. love with all the intelligence) as the fourth factor, or element, in His four-square love of God, as given in Mk. and Lk.

Lk. is responsible for making a scribe the author of the question about the two great commandments which leads Jesus, according to Lk., to deliver the parable of the Good Samaritan in answer to the scribe's question: Who is my neighbour? If Jesus, as we believe, is responsible for the expansion of the First great commandment by adding intelligence, He is no less responsible for the expansion of the Second great commandment. In the original context of the Second commandment the term neighbour means 'thy fellow-Israelite.' Jesus interprets neighbour to mean any human being with whom we come into contact who is in need of our help.

The scribe's reply in Mk. indicates that he also holds the prophetic, rather than the priestly, conception of righteousness and so wins the ready appreciation of Jesus. Jesus, recognising that the scribe had answered with real perception (literally, as having a mind) replies: Thou art not far from the Kingdom of God.

This delightful interlude in which the scribe is deeply appreciative of the teaching of Jesus, and Jesus warmly commends the insight of the scribe, is absent from Mt. and Lk., who represent the scribe as hostile and as putting his question to Jesus in order to entrap Him. The primitive Christian disciples had suffered or were suffering too much from the bitter attacks of Jewish scribes to be able to believe that one of this class could ever have appreciated Jesus or have been appreciated by Him. This omission by Mt. and Lk. is like their omission of the statement that Jesus loved the rich young ruler who refused to sell all and follow Him. These omissions are indications that Mt. and Lk. are later than Mk.

It is of profound importance to recognise in this connexion that although the Second commandment is like unto the First in that it demands the development and exercise of the spirit of love, yet it comes second, not first.

Love of man can exist without the conscious love of God, as Leigh Hunt's popular poem, *Abou Ben Adhem*, emphasises, but it is the love of God which can alone universalise and moralise and spiritualise the love of man. In short, the love of God is the only secure and permanent basis for a love of man which strives to secure the well-being, both temporal and eternal, of the object of its love.

A love of man which is not based on the love of God is always liable to succumb to the temptations of self-gratification, self-interest, and sentimentality.

(*e*) The Question about the Messiah's Descent

MK. 12[35-37]

12 35 And Jesus answered and said, as he taught in the temple, How say the scribes that the Christ is the son of
36 David? David himself said in the Holy Spirit,

The Lord said unto my Lord,
Sit thou on my right hand,
Till I make thine enemies the footstool of thy feet.

37 David himself calleth him Lord; and whence is he his son? And the common people heard him gladly.

MT. 22[41-46]

22 41 Now while the Pharisees were gathered together, Jesus asked them a question,
42 saying, What think ye of the Christ? whose son is he? They say unto him,
43 *The son* of David. He saith unto them, How then doth David in the Spirit call him Lord, saying,
44 The Lord said unto my Lord,
Sit thou on my right hand,
Till I put thine enemies underneath thy feet?
45 If David then calleth him Lord, how is
46 he his son? And no one was able to answer him a word, neither durst any man from that day forth ask him any more questions.

LK. 20^{41-44}

20 41 And he said unto them, How say they
42 that the Christ is David's son? For
David himself saith in the book of
Psalms,
The Lord said unto my Lord,
Sit thou on my right hand,
43 Till I make thine enemies the footstool of thy feet.
44 David therefore calleth him Lord, and
how is he his son?

The Messiah, in accordance with popular views, was expected to be a scion of the House of David. A number of passages from the prophets predict this. Jesus, citing the opening words of Ps. 110, asks the scribes: If David call him (the Messiah) Lord, How is he then David's son? It is difficult to be sure of the precise purpose of our Lord's question.

A. Some hold that He is attacking the popular view that the Messiah must be of Davidic descent. In that case it is assumed that He is making His claim to the Messiahship, though not Himself of Davidic descent. There seems, however, to be evidence, which cannot be ignored, that Jesus was of Davidic descent. St. Paul, an extremely well-informed Jew, plainly states that Jesus was of Davidic descent according to the flesh (Rom. 1^3). And the two genealogies in Mt. and Lk. respectively trace the descent of Jesus through David. If, then, Jesus was of Davidic descent, it seems improbable that He would challenge the popular view that the Messiah must be of Davidic descent.

B. Others hold that Jesus, by His question, seeks to indicate that though the Messiah be of Davidic descent, yet, since David calls him Lord, he must be of much more than Davidic descent—that is to say of Divine descent. This would not mean that Jesus as Messiah identifies Himself with the spiritual pre-existent Son of Man of the Apocalypses, still less with the Eternal Logos of the Prologue of the Fourth Gospel. His consciousness of His anointing with the Spirit at His baptism when He heard the Divine voice say to Him: 'Thou art my Son, to-day have I begotten thee,' would constitute for Jesus Divine Sonship.

A greater difficulty for many is caused by Jesus attributing to David a Psalm which was much later than David—probably Maccabæan. It was this fact which led Charles Gore, and other members of the *Lux Mundi* School, to realise that Jesus had intellectual limitations and that the knowledge of the Old Testament possessed by modern scholars was not possessed by Jesus. This led to the formulation of the theory of *kenosis* or self-limitation of the knowledge of Jesus during the period of His earth-life.

Quite apart from the soundness or otherwise of the doctrine of the *kenosis*, it is clear that Jesus did experience in many respects the limitations of knowledge common to His age and country.

WARNINGS AGAINST PHARISAISM

Cf. Lk. 11^{37}–12^{2}; Mt. 23^{11-36}

MK. 12^{38-40}

12 38 And in his teaching he said, Beware of
the scribes, which desire to walk in long
robes, and *to have* salutations in the
39 marketplaces, and chief seats in the
synagogues, and chief places at feasts:

MT. 23^{1-10}

23 1 Then spake Jesus to the multitudes
2 and to his disciples, saying, The scribes
3 and the Pharisees sit on Moses' seat: all
things therefore whatsoever they bid you,
these do and observe: but do not ye after

40 they which devour widows' houses, and
for a pretence make long prayers; these
shall receive greater condemnation.

their works; for they say, and do not.
4 Yea, they bind heavy burdens and
grievous to be borne, and lay them on
men's shoulders; but they themselves will
5 not move them with their finger. But all
their works they do for to be seen of
men: for they make broad their phylacteries, and enlarge the borders *of their gar-*
6 *ments*, and love the chief place at feasts,
and the chief seats in the synagogues,
7 and the salutations in the marketplaces,
8 and to be called of men, Rabbi. But be
not ye called Rabbi: for one is your
9 teacher, and all ye are brethren. And
call no man your father on the earth: for
one is your Father, which is in heaven.
10 Neither be ye called masters: for one is
your master, *even* the Christ.

LK. 20^{45-47}

20 45 And in the hearing of all the people he
46 said unto his disciples, Beware of the
scribes, which desire to walk in long robes,
and love salutations in the marketplaces,
and chief seats in the synagogues, and
47 chief places at feasts; which devour
widows' houses, and for a pretence make
long prayers: these shall receive greater
condemnation.

The condemnation by Jesus of the formalism, legalism, self-complacency, and hypocrisy of the scribes and Pharisees finds an important place in the Gospels.

Montefiore, Herford, Abrahams, and other eminent students of first century Judaism, hold that the condemnation of these religious people by Jesus is much too severe. It is argued that the Pharisees and scribes were excellent people, as we know not only from their recorded sayings (see Taylor's *Sayings of the Jewish Fathers*), but also from the anecdotes told of many of their Rabbis. This may be granted. It may also be allowed that there were probably many good men, according to their lights, in the communities condemned, in so wholesale a manner, by the great prophets of Israel. What has to be remembered is that in both these cases you have two entirely different types of religion in conflict: the lower and the higher, and that in such a case neither side can afford to show quarter.

It cannot be ignored that good, conscientious, diligent, and religious as Pharisaism was, it crucified the Lord, and bitterly persecuted the primitive Church, as St. Paul, a Pharisee of Pharisees, would have been the first to acknowledge. (Cf. 1 Thess. 2^{15-16}.)

It is not improbable, however, that there has been some amount of heightening and development of the teaching ascribed to Jesus on this point, due to the bitter and prolonged controversies between Jews and Christians. The scribes saw in Jesus one who would destroy the Temple, weaken the Law, and abolish the authority of the Tradition of the Fathers. Jesus saw in them men who would not enter into the Kingdom and were engaged in using all their influence to keep other men out.

In this connexion it is important to realise (1) that whilst sympathy possesses insight, so also does antipathy; and (2) that though men differ about small things, yet the causes of their differences are never small,

THE WIDOW'S MITE

MK. 12^{41-44}

12 41 And he sat down over against the
treasury, and beheld how the multitude
cast money into the treasury: and many
42 that were rich cast in much. And there
came a poor widow, and she cast in two
43 mites, which make a farthing. And he
called unto him his disciples, and said
unto them, Verily I say unto you, This
poor widow cast in more than all they
which are casting into the treasury:
44 for they all did cast in of their superfluity;
but she of her want did cast in all that
she had, *even* all her living.

LK. 21^{1-4}

21 1 And he looked up, and saw the rich
men that were casting their gifts into the
2 treasury. And he saw a certain poor
3 widow casting in thither two mites. And
he said, Of a truth I say unto you, This
4 poor widow cast in more than they all: for
all these did of their superfluity cast in
unto the gifts: but she of her want did
cast in all the living that she had.

The Corban or Temple Treasury was situated in the Court of the women of Israel. A number of chests with trumpet-shaped mouths received the monetary gifts of devotees. As Jesus sat watching those who gave, He observed a certain poor widow casting in two mites: little copper scale-like coins equivalent in value to a farthing (i.e. a quadrans, the fourth part of a Roman as).

Jesus turned to His disciples and said: ' This poor woman has cast in more than all the rest, for they have given of their abundance but she of her poverty—everything that she possesses."

The greatest gift is that which costs the giver most.

THE DESTRUCTION OF THE TEMPLE

MK. 13^{1-37}

13 1 And as he went forth out of the temple,
one of his disciples saith unto him,
Master, behold, what manner of stones
2 and what manner of buildings! And
Jesus said unto him, Seest thou these
great buildings? there shall not be left
here one stone upon another, which shall
not be thrown down.
3 And as he sat on the mount of Olives
over against the temple, Peter and James
and John and Andrew asked him
4 privately, Tell us, when shall these things
be? and what *shall be* the sign when these
things are all about to be accomplished?
5 And Jesus began to say unto them, Take
6 heed that no man lead you astray. Many
shall come in my name, saying, I am *he*;
7 and shall lead many astray. And when
ye shall hear of wars and rumours of
wars, be not troubled: *these things* must
needs come to pass; but the end is not
8 yet. For nation shall rise against
nation, and kingdom against kingdom:
there shall be earthquakes in divers
places; there shall be famines: these
things are the beginning of travail.
9 But take ye heed to yourselves: for they
shall deliver you up to councils; and in

MT. 24^{1-44}

24 1 And Jesus went out from the temple,
and was going on his way; and his disciples
came to him to shew him the
2 buildings of the temple. But he answered
and said unto them, See ye not
all these things? verily I say unto you,
There shall not be left here one stone
upon another, that shall not be thrown
down.
3 And as he sat on the mount of Olives,
the disciples came unto him privately,
saying, Tell us, when shall these things
be? and what *shall be* the sign of thy
coming, and of the end of the world?
4 And Jesus answered and said unto them,
Take heed that no man lead you astray.
5 For many shall come in my name, saying,
I am the Christ; and shall lead many
6 astray. And ye shall hear of wars and
rumours of wars: see that ye be not
troubled: for *these things* must needs come
7 to pass; but the end is not yet. For
nation shall rise against nation, and
kingdom against kingdom: and there
shall be famines and earthquakes in
8 divers places. But all these things are
9 the beginning of travail. Then shall
they deliver you up unto tribulation, and

synagogues shall ye be beaten; and before
governors and kings shall ye stand for my
10 sake, for a testimony unto them. And
the gospel must first be preached unto all
11 the nations. And when they lead you
to judgement, and deliver you up, be not
anxious beforehand what ye shall speak:
but whatsoever shall be given you in that
hour, that speak ye: for it is not ye that
12 speak, but the Holy Ghost. And
brother shall deliver up brother to death,
and the father his child; and children
shall rise up against parents, and cause
13 them to be put to death. And ye shall
be hated of all men for my name's sake:
but he that endureth to the end, the
same shall be saved.
14 But when ye see the abomination of
desolation standing where he ought not
(let him that readeth understand), then
let them that are in Judæa flee unto the
15 mountains: and let him that is on the
housetop not go down, nor enter in, to
16 take anything out of his house: and let
him that is in the field not return back to
17 take his cloke. But woe unto them that
are with child and to them that give suck
18 in those days! And pray ye that it be not
19 in the winter. For those days shall be
tribulation, such as there hath not been
the like from the beginning of the creation
which God created until now, and never
20 shall be. And except the Lord had
shortened the days, no flesh would have
been saved: but for the elect's sake, whom
21 he chose, he shortened the days. And
then if any man shall say unto you, Lo,
here is the Christ; or, Lo, there; believe *it*
22 not: for there shall arise false Christs and
false prophets, and shall shew signs and
wonders, that they may lead astray, if
23 possible, the elect. But take ye heed:
behold, I have told you all things
beforehand.
24 But in those days, after that tribulation, the sun shall be darkened, and the
25 moon shall not give her light, and the
stars shall be falling from heaven, and
the powers that are in the heavens shall
26 be shaken. And then shall they see the
Son of man coming in clouds with great
27 power and glory. And then shall he
send forth the angels, and shall gather
together his elect from the four winds,
from the uttermost part of the earth to
the uttermost part of heaven.
28 Now from the fig tree learn her
parable: when her branch is now become
tender, and putteth forth its leaves, ye
29 know that the summer is nigh; even so ye
also, when ye see these things coming to
pass, know ye that he is nigh, *even* at the
30 doors. Verily I say unto you, This

shall kill you: and ye shall be hated of all
10 the nations for my name's sake. And
then shall many stumble, and shall deliver up one another, and shall hate one
11 another. And many false prophets shall
12 arise, and shall lead many astray. And
because iniquity shall be multiplied, the
13 love of the many shall wax cold. But he
that endureth to the end, the same shall
14 be saved. And this gospel of the kingdom shall be preached in the whole world
for a testimony unto all the nations; and
then shall the end come.
15 When therefore ye see the abomination
of desolation, which was spoken of by
Daniel the prophet, standing in the holy
place (let him that readeth understand),
16 then let them that are in Judæa flee unto
17 the mountains: let him that is on the
housetop not go down to take out the
18 things that are in his house: and let him
that is in the field not return back to take
19 his cloke. But woe unto them that are
with child and to them that give suck in
20 those days! And pray ye that your flight
be not in the winter, neither on a sabbath:
21 for then shall be great tribulation, such as
hath not been from the beginning of the
world until now, no, nor ever shall be.
22 And except those days had been shortened, no flesh would have been saved:
but for the elect's sake those days shall be
23 shortened. Then if any man shall say
unto you, Lo, here is the Christ, or,
24 Here; believe *it* not. For there shall
arise false Christs, and false prophets,
and shall shew great signs and wonders;
so as to lead astray, if possible, even the
25 elect. Behold, I have told you before-
26 hand. If therefore they shall say unto
you, Behold, he is in the wilderness; go
not forth: Behold, he is in the inner
27 chambers; believe *it* not. For as the
lightning cometh forth from the east, and
is seen even unto the west; so shall be
28 the coming of the Son of man. Wheresoever the carcase is, there will the eagles
be gathered together.
29 But immediately, after the tribulation
of those days, the sun shall be darkened,
and the moon shall not give her light,
and the stars shall fall from heaven, and
the powers of the heavens shall be
30 shaken: and then shall appear the sign
of the Son of man in heaven: and then
shall all the tribes of the earth mourn,
and they shall see the Son of man coming
on the clouds of heaven with power and
31 great glory. And he shall send forth his
angels with a great sound of a trumpet,
and they shall gather together his elect
from the four winds, from one end of
heaven to the other.

generation shall not pass away, until all
31 these things be accomplished. Heaven
and earth shall pass away: but my words
32 shall not pass away. But of that day or
that hour knoweth no one, not even the
angels in heaven, neither the Son, but the
33 Father. Take ye heed, watch and pray:
34 for ye know not when the time is. *It is*
as *when* a man, sojourning in another
country, having left his house, and given
authority to his servants, to each one his
work, commanded also the porter to
35 watch. Watch therefore: for ye know
not when the lord of the house cometh,
whether at even, or at midnight, or at
36 cockcrowing, or in the morning; lest
coming suddenly he find you sleeping.
37 And what I say unto you I say unto all,
Watch.

32 Now from the fig tree learn her
parable: when her branch is now become
tender, and putteth forth its leaves, ye
33 know that the summer is nigh; even so
ye also, when ye see all these things,
know ye that he is nigh, *even* at the doors.
34 Verily I say unto you, This generation
shall not pass away, till all these things
35 be accomplished. Heaven and earth
shall pass away, but my words shall not
36 pass away. But of that day and hour
knoweth no one, not even the angels of
heaven, neither the Son, but the Father
37 only. And as *were* the days of Noah, so
shall be the coming of the Son of man.
38 For as in those days which were before
the flood they were eating and drinking,
marrying and giving in marriage, until
the day that Noah entered into the ark,
39 and they knew not until the flood came,
and took them all away; so shall be the
40 coming of the Son of man. Then shall
two men be in the field; one is taken,
41 and one is left: two women *shall be* grinding
at the mill; one is taken, and one is
42 left. Watch therefore: for ye know not
43 on what day your Lord cometh. But
know this, that if the master of the house
had known in what watch the thief was
coming, he would have watched, and
would not have suffered his house to be
44 broken through. Therefore be ye also
ready: for in an hour that ye think not
the Son of man cometh.

LK. 21^{5-36}

21 5 And as some spake of the temple, how
it was adorned with goodly stones and
6 offerings, he said, As for these things
which ye behold, the days will come, in
which there shall not be left here one
stone upon another, that shall not
7 be thrown down. And they asked him,
saying, Master, when therefore shall these
things be? and what *shall be* the sign
when these things are about to come to
8 pass? And he said, Take heed that ye
be not led astray: for many shall come in
my name, saying, I am *he*; and, The time
9 is at hand: go ye not after them. And
when ye shall hear of wars and tumults,
be not terrified: for these things must
needs come to pass first; but the end is
not immediately.
10 Then said he unto them, Nation shall
rise against nation, and kingdom against
11 kingdom: and there shall be great earthquakes,
and in divers places famines and
pestilences; and there shall be terrors and
12 great signs from heaven. But before all
these things, they shall lay their hands on
you, and shall persecute you, delivering
you up to the synagogues and prisons,
bringing you before kings and governors
13 for my name's sake. It shall turn unto
14 you for a testimony. Settle it therefore
in your hearts, not to meditate beforehand
15 hand how to answer: for I will give you
a mouth and wisdom, which all your
adversaries shall not be able to withstand
16 or to gainsay. But ye shall be delivered
up even by parents, and brethren, and
kinsfolk, and friends; and *some* of you
17 shall they cause to be put to death. And
ye shall be hated of all men for my
18 name's sake. And not a hair of your
19 head shall perish. In your patience ye
shall win your souls.
20 But when ye see Jerusalem compassed
with armies, then know that her desola-
21 tion is at hand. Then let them that are
in Judæa flee unto the mountains; and
let them that are in the midst of her depart out; and let not them that are in the
22 country enter therein. For these are
days of vengeance, that all things which
23 are written may be fulfilled. Woe unto
them that are with child and to them
that give suck in those days! for there
shall be great distress upon the land, and

24 wrath unto this people. And they shall
fall by the edge of the sword, and shall be
led captive into all the nations: and
Jerusalem shall be trodden down of the
Gentiles, until the times of the Gentiles
25 be fulfilled. And there shall be signs in
sun and moon and stars; and upon the
earth distress of nations, in perplexity for
the roaring of the sea and the billows;
26 men fainting for fear, and for expectation
of the things which are coming on the
world: for the powers of the heavens shall
27 be shaken. And then shall they see the
Son of man coming in a cloud with power
28 and great glory. But when these things
begin to come to pass, look up, and lift
up your heads; because your redemption
draweth nigh.
29 And he spake to them a parable:
Behold the fig tree, and all the trees:
30 when they now shoot forth, ye see it and
know of your own selves that the summer
31 is now nigh. Even so ye also, when ye
see these things coming to pass, know ye
32 that the kingdom of God is nigh. Verily
I say unto you, This generation shall not
pass away, till all things be accomplished.
33 Heaven and earth shall pass away: but
my words shall not pass away.
34 But take heed to yourselves, lest haply
your hearts be overcharged with surfeiting, and drunkenness, and cares of this
life, and that day come on you suddenly
35 as a snare: for *so* shall it come upon all
them that dwell on the face of all the
36 earth. But watch ye at every season,
making supplication, that ye may prevail
to escape all these things that shall come
to pass, and to stand before the Son of
man.

It is one of the extraordinary features of Jewish religion that three times it was predicted that its Temple on Mt. Zion should be destroyed: the first time by Micah (3^{12}), when the prediction was not fulfilled; the second time by Jeremiah ($26^{6,\ 16-18}$), when it was fulfilled by the Babylonians under Nebuchadnezzar; the third time by Jesus, when it was fulfilled by the Romans under Vespasian and Titus in A.D. 70.

One of the charges made against St. Stephen before the Sanhedrin was, ' we have heard him say that this Jesus of Nazareth shall destroy this place, and shall change the customs which Moses delivered unto us ' (Acts 6^{14}). In Jn. 2^{19}, Jesus challenges the Jews to ' destroy this Temple and in three days I will raise it up,' which Jn. interprets, not of the destruction of the Temple but of the resurrection of Jesus. Mk. (followed by Mt. and Lk.) narrates that Jesus made His prediction in the week before His crucifixion.

After Jesus has uttered His prediction and is seated upon the Mount of Olives, which commands a magnificent view of the Temple Courts, His four chief disciples ask Him privately: When shall these things be, and what shall be the sign when all these things shall be fulfilled?

Lk. has the question in very much the same form as Mk., but Mt. puts two questions into the mouth of the disciples:

(1) When shall these things be?

(2) What shall be the sign of Thy coming (literally, ' presence '—*parousia*) and of the consummation of the age?

Mt., by doubling the query, is plainly creating an opportunity for the introduction of his favourite apocalyptic teaching, much if not all of which is derived, not from Jesus, but from Jewish Apocalyptic literature and contemporary Christian speculation.

' *THE LITTLE APOCALYPSE* '

So far, then, as Mk. is concerned, what follows *v.* 4 purports to be an answer to the question: When shall the Temple be destroyed? The fact that Mk. states this information was communicated privately by Jesus to His Apostles places it under suspicion. There has been much doubt as to whether this discourse consists solely of utterances of Jesus. Many have thought that we have here, intermixed with a number of genuine sayings of Jesus, extracts from a written document (commonly spoken of as ' The Little Apocalypse ')—an oracle circulated among the Christians in Jerusalem shortly before the siege and destruction of the city; and which led the Christian Church of Jerusalem to flee from the doomed city and to escape across the Jordan to the mountains of Gilead (the highlands of Peræa), to the little city of Pella, where the Church remained in safety during the terrible Roman war in Palestine.

The great Church historian Eusebius refers to such an oracle in his *Ecclesiastical History* (Bk. iii, v, 3). There is much to be said for the view that this document is actually cited in the following passage attributed to Jesus by Mk.: 'But when ye see " the abomination of desolation " standing where he ought not (let him that readeth understand), then let them that are in Judæa flee into the mountains: and let him that is on the housetop not go down, nor enter in, to take anything out of his house: and let him that is in the field not " return back " to take his cloke,' etc.

The phrase ' let him that readeth ' indicates, not the reader of the Book of Daniel but the reader of this Christian oracle. This oracle refers to the abomination of desolation spoken of in Dan. 9^{27}. This abomination in Daniel is usually taken to be the small altar of Zeus, which Antiochus Epiphanes placed upon the great altar of sacrifice in the Court of the Priests in the Temple at Jerusalem about 168 B.C. This was one of the many outrages perpetrated by this Greek King of Syria who strove in vain, by education and persecution, to induce the Jews to give up their religion.

What the Christian oracle meant by the phrase ' abomination of desolation standing where he ought not ' is difficult to determine. Some interpret it as a prophecy of a future attempt (like that made by the Emperor Caligula in A.D. 38) to introduce the Roman imperial cultus into the Temple.

Among the Jews the word ' abomination ' means an idol or idolatrous symbol. It is a curious fact that whilst the word for ' abomination ' used here is neuter, the word ' standing ' is masculine, and would seem to indicate that some man will present himself in Jerusalem for divine adoration. Some would take the phrase ' that maketh desolate ' to mean either the herald or the agent of the desolation of the city or the Temple. Others understand it to mean something horrifying—an idolatrous act of the most dreadful character, such as the placing of a statue of a Roman emperor in the Holy of Holies. Others have supposed that it was the silver eagles of the Roman invaders under Vespasian, which all devout Jews regarded as idolatrous.

Josephus relates that terrifying signs appeared in Jerusalem just before the siege, the most conspicuous being a great comet shaped like a sword which hung over the city for nearly a year.

' Let them that are in Judæa flee into the mountains,' certainly suggests that the oracle was addressed to Jewish Christians; and the phrase ' the mountains ' is no doubt Mk.'s rendering of Ramoth (Gilead), which means the mountains or heights. It is clear that the mountains are situated to the east of the Jordan; which it is hoped the Jewish Christians will not have to cross in the winter when it is a raging torrent. So sudden will the flight be, that he who is on the flat roof of his house will have no time to go into his house to secure provisions for his journey but will descend by the outside staircase. He also who is working in his field will have no time even to secure his cloak which he has laid aside before beginning his work, but will take to immediate flight. For some women the flight may prove to be a disaster.

All this seems plainly to consist of extracts from the 'Little Apocalypse,' since it makes no reference at all to the destruction of the Temple but is concerned with warnings to the Christians of Judæa to fly from their homes when they see the sign. It could not therefore have formed part of our Lord's original reply to His Apostles as to when the destruction of the Temple was to take place.

There are many indications that the opening paragraph of the reply attributed to Jesus (Mk. 13^{5-13}) belongs to the most primitive stage of Christian history when Christians are little more than a Jewish sect being beaten in synagogues and tried before Jewish law courts. The kings and governors are no doubt Jewish Tetrarchs and Roman governors of Judæa. The false Christs and the false prophets are of course Jewish pretenders. The phrase, 'the beginning of travail,' or 'the beginning of birth pangs' (*v.* 8), was a well-known Rabbinical phrase for the various troubles, domestic, political, physical, which it was taught must precede the Messianic Age. Christians are also warned that there is much to be suffered and much to be done before the crisis comes. The Gospel has to be proclaimed first to all nations.

St. Paul asserts in his Epistles that this has already taken place in his day. (Rom. 1^{8}; Col. $1^{5, 6}$.)

Possibly the reference to 'hated of all men' may refer to actual persecution of Christians by the Roman authorities. Only those who have the faith and courage to hold out to the last will secure salvation. Watchfulness, sobriety, fidelity, prayerfulness are inculcated in the concluding paragraphs of this discourse as the qualities especially required of loyal disciples.

Verses 24–27 plainly undertake to answer the question: When may the Apocalyptic return of Jesus be anticipated? which the Apostles themselves in Mk. had not asked. This passage looks like an interpolation into, or an expansion of, the original reply of Jesus. It is expressed in the commonplaces of Apocalyptic imagery.

The meaning of *v.* 29 (which occurs at the conclusion of the Parable of the Fig Tree) is ambiguous: it may be translated 'he [the Messiah] is nigh' or 'it [the destruction of the Temple] is nigh.' Lk., however, takes it as meaning 'the Kingdom of God is nigh.'

The concluding sections, *vv.* 30–37, like the Parable of the Fig Tree, on which they follow, are very primitive and have strong claims to be regarded as utterances of Jesus, although not necessarily uttered on this occasion or in answer to the question about the destruction of the Temple. They do not attempt to fix the precise time, save that the crisis will come within the lifetime of some who have heard the prediction. The stress upon the limitation of the Messiah's knowledge of the future is very striking. He knows not the day nor the hour of the crisis. The crisis may befall in any one of the four watches of the night. That is only known to the omniscient Father.

The phrase ‘ the Son,’ ‘ the Father,’ to describe Jesus in His relation to God, which is so frequent in the Fourth Gospel, occurs only here in Mk. It should be noted, however, that it occurs in one very important passage in Q: ‘ No man knoweth the Son but the Father,’ etc. (Lk. $10^{21, 22}$; Mt. 11^{25-27}). Since this usage occurs in Q it may safely be assumed that it is primitive.

In reading Mk. 13, it must be borne in mind that the Christian readers for whom the Gospel was intended were intensely interested in the question of the Apocalyptic return of Jesus which formed part of the Gospel of St. Paul and, so far as we know, of all the primitive Apostles. It was the return of Jesus with power and great glory which, the Christians of that age felt, could alone justify their faith in Him and secure their triumph over their Jewish and pagan persecutors. As a consequence there was a great temptation to attribute to Jesus Himself predictions of this event.

We may feel assured that Jesus believed in the triumph of His Gospel: we may feel equally assured that He believed in the coming of the Kingdom of God. It would seem that He looked forward to a blessed reunion with His loyal disciples after His passion. But it cannot be a matter of certainty that He predicted His future advent as an Apocalyptic Messiah. The writer of the Fourth Gospel conceives of His Second Advent as a Divine spiritual indwelling in the personalities of His disciples.

THE PLOT OF THE HIGH PRIESTLY PARTY IN JERUSALEM

MK. 14^{1-2}

14 1 Now after two days was *the feast of* the
passover and the unleavened bread: and
the chief priests and the scribes sought how
they might take him with subtilty, and kill
2 him: for they said, Not during the feast,
lest haply there shall be a tumult of the
people.

MT. 26^{1-5}

26 1 And it came to pass, when Jesus had
finished all these words, he said unto his
2 disciples, Ye know that after two days the
passover cometh, and the Son of man is
3 delivered up to be crucified. Then were
gathered together the chief priests, and
the elders of the people, unto the court of
the high priest, who was called Caiaphas;
4 and they took counsel together that they
might take Jesus by subtilty, and kill him.
5 But they said, Not during the feast, lest
a tumult arise among the people.

LK. 22^{1-2}

22 1 Now the feast of unleavened bread drew
2 nigh, which is called the Passover. And
the chief priests and the scribes sought
how they might put him to death; for
they feared the people.

It had become clear to the High Priestly clan in Jerusalem that they must somehow get rid of Jesus. His teaching was too popular and too provocative to allow of its continuance. Yet every attempt to stop it had ended in failure. Action must be swift and secret: swift because things were rapidly approaching a crisis; secret because any disturbance of public order caused by the open arrest of Jesus would bring the High Priests into conflict with the Roman authorities—a result to be avoided at all costs.

The High Priest at this time was Joseph Caiaphas (A.D. 18–36), but his father-in-law, Annas (A.D. 6–15) was still alive, and he was the real, though not the official, head of the priesthood. At least five of his sons, and sons-in-law, had held the High Priesthood during his lifetime. The family had their palace in Jerusalem—apparently both Annas and Caiaphas occupying different parts of it; and it was here that the Council was held which decided on the death of Jesus.

THE BLOOD-MONEY

MK. $14^{10, 11}$

14 10 And Judas Iscariot, he that was one of
the twelve, went away unto the chief
priests, that he might deliver him unto
11 them. And they, when they heard it,
were glad, and promised to give him
money. And he sought how he might
conveniently deliver him *unto them.*

MT. 26^{14-16}

26 14 Then one of the twelve, who was
called Judas Iscariot, went unto the chief
15 priests, and said, What are ye willing to
give me, and I will deliver him unto you?
And they weighed unto him thirty pieces
16 of silver. And from that time he sought
opportunity to deliver him *unto them.*

LK. 22^{3-6}

22 3 And Satan entered into Judas who was
called Iscariot, being of the number of the
4 twelve. And he went away, and communed with the chief priests and captains,
5 how he might deliver him unto them. And
they were glad, and covenanted to give
6 him money. And he consented, and
sought opportunity to deliver him unto
them in the absence of the multitude.

It is more than doubtful whether Caiaphas could have carried out his plot if one of the disciples of Jesus had not turned traitor. Judas, called Iscariot, went to the High Priests and offered to betray Jesus to them. It was arranged that His arrest should take place secretly. The delighted High Priests agree to pay him. So Mk. and Lk., but Mt. states that they did pay him: they ' weighed ' for him thirty pieces of silver. Here it would seem Mt. is unhistorical. He has again been led astray by his conviction that the Old Testament oracles have higher historical value than the Marcan document. Zech. 11^{12} contained the statement, ' And they weighed my fee, thirty pieces of silver.' Later, Mt. relates, after the arrest and condemnation of Jesus, Judas repented and brought the thirty pieces of silver back to the High Priests, who, however, refused to receive them. Judas then flung them down in the Temple Courts and went and hanged himself; and the High Priests with the thirty pieces of silver bought the Potter's Field to be used as a burial-place for strangers: thus fulfilling a second oracle of Zech. 11^{13}: ' And I took the thirty pieces of silver, and cast them unto the potter, in the house of the Lord.' Lk., however (Acts 1^{18}), relates that Judas bought a field with the blood-money (' the reward of iniquity '), thus indicating that Judas did receive money for the betrayal of Jesus, although presumably it was not paid until after the deed was done.

What did Judas Betray?

(*a*) The general view has been that he betrayed the place where Jesus encamped on the Mount of Olives every night.

Possibly, to avoid arrest, or because He was too poor, Jesus did not lodge within the City, where nocturnal arrest would have been easy. It would have caused a great disturbance for the authorities to seek for Him after dark amid the vast multitude of pilgrims encamped outside Jerusalem. All our sources (including Acts 1^{16}) describe Judas as acting as guide to the officials who arrested Jesus. Therefore the view, that what Judas betrayed to the High

Priests for money was the spot where Jesus encamped after dark, has strong support.

(*b*) A more recent view is that what Judas betrayed to the High Priests was the Messianic secret.

By informing the High Priestly authorities that Jesus definitely claimed to be the Messiah, he provided them with the evidence needful for a capital charge. To claim to be Messiah, 'the King of the Jews,' was treason, and once the Roman authorities were convinced that Jesus made this claim they would undoubtedly execute Him.

The objection to this view is, that the evidence provided by the witnesses at His trials fails to secure the conviction of Jesus. In order to secure His conviction, why is not Jesus confronted by Judas?

There is no statement that Judas was used as a witness at the trials. It is only when the High Priest himself adjures Jesus in the most solemn fashion: 'If thou be the Messiah, tell us plainly,' that Jesus convicts Himself out of His own mouth. It is argued that the only reason why Caiaphas dares to put the question to Jesus is because he already possesses definite knowledge that Jesus does claim to be the Messiah.

It is more reasonable to regard Caiaphas as possessed of much circumstantial evidence but not enough to secure conviction. There were many things in the public actions and speeches of Jesus which suggested that He claimed to be the Messiah, but there was nothing absolutely definite. Hence the dramatic appeal of Caiaphas to Jesus to convict Himself. Had Jesus refused to comply, He would have discredited Himself with His own followers. But He also would have deprived Caiaphas of the power to secure His crucifixion by the Roman authorities.

On the whole, (*a*) has more claims to be regarded as probable than (*b*).

Judas Iscariot's Motive

The motive of Judas has been much discussed.

(1) Some have thought that he was simply tempted by love of money. This is the view of the Fourth Gospel—he was not only avaricious but dishonest. (Mt. 26^{14}, $27^{4\,f.}$; Jn. $12^{4\,ff.}$, cf. Mt. 26^{4}.) This is the motive exhibited in the Passion Play at Oberammergau.

(2) Others suppose that Judas was moved by a spirit of malice and hatred. It is thought, but this is not certain, that whilst all the other Apostles were Galileans, Judas was a Judæan and felt himself to be superior to them and in the end became alienated from them. He had been the leader of the Apostolic band, but was replaced by Peter. The evidence for this theory is of the slightest.

(3) Others think that the motive of Judas was not base. That he wished to force the hand of Jesus and make Him declare His Messiahship openly before the heads of His nation, feeling sure that if Jesus did so He would win the day and carry the nation with Him. Judas never dreamt, when he betrayed Jesus, that it would actually lead to the crucifixion of Jesus. It was because it did so that Judas hanged himself (according to Mt.).

Judas, it is urged, was probably not a Judæan. It is doubtful whether 'Iscariot' means Man of Kerioth: it much more probably means a left-wing

Zealot (*sicarius*). What more natural than for such an one to take an extreme course?

'. . . put it to the touch,
To win or lose it all.'

THE ANOINTING OF JESUS

MK. 14^{3-9}

14 3 And while he was in Bethany in the
house of Simon the leper, as he sat at
meat, there came a woman having an
alabaster cruse of ointment of spikenard
very costly; *and* she brake the cruse, and
4 poured it over his head. But there were
some that had indignation among themselves, *saying*, To what purpose hath this
5 waste of the ointment been made? For
this ointment might have been sold for
above three hundred pence, and given to
the poor. And they murmured against
6 her. But Jesus said, Let her alone; why
trouble ye her? she hath wrought a good
7 work on me. For ye have the poor always
with you, and whensoever ye will ye can
do them good: but me ye have not always.
8 She hath done what she could: she hath
anointed my body aforehand for the bury-
9 ing. And verily I say unto you, Wheresoever the gospel shall be preached throughout the whole world, that also which this
woman hath done shall be spoken of for a
memorial of her.

MT. 26^{6-13}

26 6 Now when Jesus was in Bethany, in the
7 house of Simon the leper, there came
unto him a woman having an alabaster
cruse of exceeding precious ointment, and
she poured it upon his head, as he sat
8 at meat. But when the disciples saw it,
they had indignation, saying, To what
9 purpose is this waste? For this *ointment*
might have been sold for much, and given
10 to the poor. But Jesus perceiving it said
unto them, Why trouble ye the woman?
for she hath wrought a good work upon
11 me. For ye have the poor always with
12 you; but me ye have not always. For in
that she poured this ointment upon my
body, she did it to prepare me for burial.
13 Verily I say unto you, Wheresoever this
gospel shall be preached in the whole
world, that also which this woman hath
done shall be spoken of for a memorial
of her.

Cf. LK. 7^{36-50}

7 36 And one of the Pharisees desired him that
he would eat with him. And he entered
into the Pharisee's house, and sat down to
37 meat. And behold, a woman which was
in the city, a sinner; and when she knew
that he was sitting at meat in the Pharisee's house, she brought an alabaster cruse
38 of ointment, and standing behind at his
feet, weeping, she began to wet his feet
with her tears, and wiped them with the
hair of her head, and kissed his feet, and
39 anointed them with the ointment. Now
when the Pharisee which had bidden him
saw it, he spake within himself, saying,
This man, if he were a prophet, would
have perceived who and what manner of
woman this is which toucheth him, that
40 she is a sinner. And Jesus answering said
unto him, Simon, I have somewhat to say
unto thee. And he saith, Master, say on.
41 A certain lender had two debtors: the one
owed five hundred pence, and the other
42 fifty. When they had not *wherewith* to
pay, he forgave them both. Which of
them therefore will love him most?
43 Simon answered and said, He, I suppose,
to whom he forgave the most. And he

JN. 12^{1-8}

12 1 Jesus therefore six days before the passover came to Bethany, where Lazarus was,
2 whom Jesus raised from the dead. So
they made him a supper there: and
Martha served; but Lazarus was one of
3 them that sat at meat with him. Mary
therefore took a pound of ointment of
spikenard, very precious, and anointed the
feet of Jesus, and wiped his feet with her
hair: and the house was filled with the
4 odour of the ointment. But Judas
Iscariot, one of his disciples, which should
5 betray him, saith, Why was not this ointment sold for three hundred pence, and
6 given to the poor? Now this he said, not
because he cared for the poor; but because
he was a thief, and having the bag took
7 away what was put therein. Jesus therefore said, Suffer her to keep it against the
8 day of my burying. For the poor ye
have always with you; but me ye have not
always.

said unto him, Thou hast rightly judged.
44 And turning to the woman, he said unto
Simon, Seest thou this woman? I entered
into thine house, thou gavest me no water
for my feet: but she hath wetted my feet
with her tears, and wiped them with her
45 hair. Thou gavest me no kiss: but she,
since the time I came in, hath not ceased
46 to kiss my feet. My head with oil thou
didst not anoint: but she hath anointed
47 my feet with ointment. Wherefore I say
unto thee, Her sins, which are many, are
forgiven; for she loved much: but to whom
48 little is forgiven, *the same* loveth little. And
he said unto her, Thy sins are forgiven.
49 And they that sat at meat with him began
to say within themselves, Who is this that
50 even forgiveth sins? And he said unto
the woman, Thy faith hath saved thee;
go in peace.

When not in Jerusalem, Jesus would seem, during these last days, to have spent His nights either on the Mount of Olives or in Bethany. In Bethany He stayed with one Simon, the leper, so called not because he was a leper, but because he had been one. Quite probably he was one of the lepers healed by Jesus.

One evening at dinner a woman anointed Jesus by breaking an alabaster flask of very precious spikenard ointment and pouring it upon His head. Who the woman was does not appear in Mk. or in Mt. In Jn., who relates that the incident took place in the house of Lazarus and Martha and Mary, Mary is the woman who anoints Jesus. This dramatic and emotional action seemed very extravagant to some who were present (Mt. says they were disciples: Jn. says Judas Iscariot).

The ointment was exceedingly costly and it was argued that it might have been sold for three hundred denarii (equal to £100 to-day) and have been distributed among the poor.

Jesus, who was Himself very poor and whose teaching emphasises the duty of compassionate generosity, did not agree with this argument. He took the side of the woman, as on certain other notable occasions. What she had done He declared to be a good deed literally—a fair and beautiful action. The poor, said He, are always at hand for their needs to be relieved, but it is not so in my case. My ministry is drawing to a close, and she hath anointed my body as a preparation for its entombment.

Several motives may have prompted the speech of Jesus. The primary one was no doubt a spirit of kindness towards the woman whose devotion to Him had moved her to make so costly an offering. Again, there are many indications that Jesus resented conventional, pietistic platitudes. To urge the claims of the poor in His presence was superfluous. Moreover, those claims might be pressed to such a degree as to render every other form of self-sacrificing activity impossible. The Ministry of Jesus was itself a form of the most intense and costly self-sacrifice, but it was directed, not to the relief of the economic needs of the poor, but to the preaching of the Gospel to them, in short, to the advancement of the Kingdom of God.

His Ministry was about to end: the woman's act was an expression of its value: it was therefore not misjudged or ill-timed. This incident, like so many others in the Gospels, possesses a distinction and quality of significant form, which reflects, not the creative imagination of primitive Christian teachers, but the actual reminiscences of eye-witnesses. We seem to see, in conflict here, the claims of two kinds of service; that of utilitarian philanthropy and that of religious devotion. Each has its place and its right. The self-sacrifice concentrated in the creation of a cathedral is not to be regarded as without moral and spiritual justification because of the pressing claims to support a hospital. The moral, spiritual, and æsthetic nature of man is as worthy of self-sacrificing service as are the needs of his physical being.

The words of Jesus recorded in Mk. and Mt., ' Wheresoever the Gospel shall be preached throughout the whole world, that also which this woman hath done shall be spoken of for a memorial of her,' seem to show that He recognised in this woman's action the essential spirit of His Gospel: that upon which He Himself was acting—a spirit which gives to the uttermost and counts not the cost.

[Jn. states that Mary anointed the feet of Jesus and wiped them with her hair. This connects the story with Lk.'s account of an incident in the Galilean ministry of Jesus, when as He was in the house of a Pharisee, named Simon (cf. Mk. and Mt.), at dinner on the Sabbath, a penitent woman wept over the feet of Jesus and wiped them with her hair, anointed them and kissed them.

The horrified host felt that Jesus ought not to have allowed the woman, considering her character, to behave in this way. Jesus, however, in a pointed speech, contrasts the behaviour of the woman with the behaviour of his host, and tells a parable, the moral of which is, that they who are forgiven little, love little.

The Mediæval Church identified this woman, with her abundant hair and many tears, with Mary Magdalene; but there is no historical basis for this identification.

In Jn.'s account we have a coalescence of the two distinct incidents of Mk. and Lk.]

DIRECTIONS TO PREPARE THE PASSOVER

MK. 14^{12-16}

14 12 And on the first day of unleavened
bread, when they sacrificed the passover,
his disciples say unto him, Where wilt
thou that we go and make ready that
13 thou mayest eat the passover? And he
sendeth two of his disciples, and saith
unto them, Go into the city, and there
shall meet you a man bearing a pitcher
14 of water: follow him; and wheresoever he
shall enter in, say to the goodman of the
house, The Master saith, Where is my
guest-chamber, where I shall eat the
15 passover with my disciples? And he will
himself shew you a large upper room
furnished *and* ready: and there make
16 ready for us. And the disciples went
forth, and came into the city, and found
as he had said unto them: and they made
ready the passover.

MT. 26^{17-19}

26 17 Now on the first *day* of unleavened
bread the disciples came to Jesus, saying,
Where wilt thou that we make ready for
18 thee to eat the passover? And he said,
Go into the city to such a man, and say
unto him, The Master saith, My time is
at hand; I keep the passover at thy house
19 with my disciples. And the disciples did
as Jesus appointed them; and they made
ready the passover.

LK. 22^{7-13}

22 7 And the day of unleavened bread
came, on which the passover must be
8 sacrificed. And he sent Peter and John,
saying, Go and make ready for us the
9 passover, that we may eat. And they
said unto him, Where wilt thou that we
10 make ready? And he said unto them,
Behold, when ye are entered into the
city, there shall meet you a man bearing
a pitcher of water; follow him into the
11 house whereinto he goeth. And ye shall
say unto the goodman of the house, The
Master saith unto thee, Where is the
guest-chamber, where I shall eat the
12 passover with my disciples? And he will
shew you a large upper room furnished:
13 there make ready. And they went, and
found as he had said unto them: and
they made ready the passover.

This section of Mk. raises chronological difficulties which have a bearing upon the historical accuracy of the Gospels and the precise significance of the Lord's Supper, or Eucharist. Mk. begins by stating that on the first day of unleavened bread, 'when they sacrificed the Passover,' His disciples ask Jesus where He wishes them to prepare for the Passover. Here Mk. makes a blunder and is followed by Lk. According to our best rabbinical scholars the Passover lamb was not killed on the first day of unleavened bread but the day after. Mt. evidently recognises Mk.'s blunder and omits the offending clause 'when they sacrificed the Passover.'

The Passover (*pascha*, Greek and Aramaic), the greatest of the Jewish religious festivals, being pastoral, agricultural, and historical in its character, commemorated the deliverance of Israel from Egyptian slavery. It fell on the 14th Nisan. The Paschal lamb was sacrificed between the evenings (somewhere between three and five o'clock) of the 13th Nisan, and the Passover actually began at sunset of that day.

It is very important to realise that the Jewish day began at sunset and ended at sunset: hence five minutes before sunset would be the 13th Nisan and five minutes after sunset would be the 14th Nisan.

The Synoptic Gospels seem to be agreed in relating that Jesus kept the Passover; was arrested late the same night; condemned to death in the early morning; crucified; and died on the Cross before sunset the same day. That is, according to the Synoptists, Jesus was crucified on the day of the Passover.

The Fourth Gospel puts everything twenty-four hours earlier, making Jesus die on the Cross on the 13th Nisan at the time when the Paschal lambs were being slain. If Jn. is right, then Jesus did not keep the Passover, and the Eucharist was not instituted at the Paschal meal. There is no doubt that Jn., on this point of the date of the crucifixion of Jesus, as on many other points, deliberately sets out to correct the Synoptists. Whether Jn. is right in this correction is not easy to decide owing to our uncertainty as to what were the precise customs in Judaism at this time, and also as to whether an unscrupulous and violent hierarchy, intent on judicial murder, might not, on the plea of necessity, override hampering ritual regulations. Modern-minded persons would feel that a sacred day or religious festival was desecrated by a public execution; but more primitive peoples felt that an additional sacredness and solemnity was contributed by such an event.

Simon, the Cyrenian, was coming from his farm when he met the execution procession on its way to Calvary, and so it is argued that it could not possibly have been the day of the Passover. On the other hand, Simon may only have been arriving late from the country and so was seized upon by the soldiers, with a crude sense of humour, and forced to retrace his steps.

The more the problem is studied the more difficult it is to decide as to which is the correct solution. What is clear, however, is that Jn. corrects the Synoptists, but whether he does it on historical grounds is not certain. He is a symbolist and a mystic and Jesus is for him the Lamb of God which beareth away the sin of the world. Jesus is also the Paschal Lamb of which a bone may not be broken, and this may have led Jn. to place the death of Jesus at the time when the Paschal lambs were being slain.

Jesus, according to Mk., sends two disciples (Lk.: Peter and John) into Jerusalem to make preparation for the Passover. The directions given to them are evidently intended to preserve the secret of the precise place where the Passover is to be celebrated, no doubt in order to avoid the danger of nocturnal arrest. The directions themselves have an Oriental quality redolent of the *Arabian Nights*. The two disciples (as prearranged) will meet in the city a man bearing a pitcher of water—quite an unusual sight, for in the East it is women who bear pitchers of water: men carry water-skins. The two disciples are to follow him and into whatsoever house he enters they are to enter and say to the householder: The teacher says, Where is my guest chamber where I may eat the Passover with my disciples? Thereupon the householder himself will show them a large upper room furnished and ready. They (the two disciples) will then make the necessary further preparation by providing such things as are needful for the Feast.

We do not know whose house it was. Could it have been the house of Mary, the mother of Mark, which became later the assembly place of the primitive Church in Jerusalem? And could it have been that Mark, her son, was the householder who showed the two disciples the large upper chamber prepared?

The details which Mk. gives here (followed by Lk.), are omitted by Mt. as too trivial for preservation. But if Mark himself were the householder, these details would not seem trivial to him.

PREDICTION OF THE BETRAYAL

MK. 14^{17-21}

14 17 And when it was evening he cometh
18 with the twelve. And as they sat and
were eating, Jesus said, Verily I say unto
you, One of you shall betray me, *even* he
19 that eateth with me. They began to
be sorrowful, and to say unto him one
20 by one, Is it I? And he said unto them,
It is one of the twelve, he that dippeth
21 with me in the dish. For the Son of
man goeth, even as it is written of him:
but woe unto that man through whom the
Son of man is betrayed! good were it for
that man if he had not been born.

MT. 26^{20-25}

26 20 Now when even was come, he was
sitting at meat with the twelve disciples;
21 and as they were eating, he said, Verily
I say unto you, that one of you shall
22 betray me. And they were exceeding
sorrowful, and began to say unto him
23 every one, Is it I, Lord? And he
answered and said, He that dipped his
hand with me in the dish, the same shall
24 betray me. The Son of man goeth, even
as it is written of him: but woe unto that
man through whom the Son of man is
betrayed! good were it for that man if he
25 had not been born. And Judas, which
betrayed him, answered and said, Is it I,
Rabbi? He saith unto him, Thou hast
said.

LK. $22^{14, 21-23}$

22 14 And when the hour was come, he sat
down, and the apostles with him.
21 But behold, the hand of him that
betrayeth me is with me on the table.
22 For the Son of man indeed goeth, as it
hath been determined: but woe unto that
23 man through whom he is betrayed! And
they began to question among themselves, which of them it was that should
do this thing.

JN. 13^{21-27}

13 21 When Jesus had thus said, he was
troubled in the spirit, and testified, and
said, Verily, verily, I say unto you, that
22 one of you shall betray me. The disciples looked one on another, doubting
23 of whom he spake. There was at the
table reclining in Jesus' bosom one of his
24 disciples, whom Jesus loved. Simon
Peter therefore beckoneth to him, and
saith unto him, Tell *us* who it is of whom
25 he speaketh. He leaning back, as he
was, on Jesus' breast saith unto him,
26 Lord, who is it? Jesus therefore answereth, He it is, for whom I shall dip the
sop, and give it him. So when he had
dipped the sop, he taketh and giveth it to
27 Judas, *the son* of Simon Iscariot. And
after the sop, then entered Satan into
him. Jesus therefore saith unto him,
That thou doest, do quickly.

In the evening of the same day (i.e. the next day according to Jewish modes of reckoning) Jesus assembles in the Upper Room with His disciples, and at the meal declares that one of those eating with Him will betray Him. When pressed further He asserts that the traitor is one of the Twelve: one who is dipping his hand with Him into the bowl.

Lk. makes Jesus merely assert, that the hand of the betrayer 'is with me on the table.' Mt. goes so far as to make Judas ask the question: 'Is it I?' To which Jesus replies: 'Thou hast said.' Jn. makes the identification of Judas as explicit as does Mt. by asserting that Jesus, having told the beloved disciple that the traitor is he to whom He shall give the sop, dips the sop and gives it to Judas Iscariot. This development by Mt. and Jn. in the precision of the prediction of Jesus is significant. Mk.'s vagueness indicates that he writes primarily as a chronicler, not as an apologist.

INSTITUTION OF THE EUCHARIST

MK. 14^{22-26}

14 22 And as they were eating, he took
bread, and when he had blessed, he
brake it, and gave to them, and said,
23 Take ye: this is my body. And he took
a cup, and when he had given thanks, he
gave to them: and they all drank of it.
24 And he said unto them, This is my blood
of the covenant, which is shed for many.
25 Verily I say unto you, I will no more
drink of the fruit of the vine, until that
day when I drink it new in the kingdom
of God.
26 And when they had sung a hymn, they
went out unto the mount of Olives.

MT. 26^{26-30}

26 26 And as they were eating, Jesus took
bread, and blessed, and brake it; and he
gave to the disciples, and said, Take, eat;
27 this is my body. And he took a cup,
and gave thanks, and gave to them,
28 saying, Drink ye all of it: for this is my
blood of the covenant, which is shed for
29 many unto remission of sins. But I say
unto you, I will not drink henceforth of
this fruit of the vine, until that day when
I drink it new with you in my Father's
kingdom.
30 And when they had sung a hymn, they
went out unto the mount of Olives.

LK. 22^{15-21}

22 15 And he said unto them, With desire I
have desired to eat this passover with you
16 before I suffer: for I say unto you, I will
not eat it, until it be fulfilled in the king-
17 dom of God. And he received a cup,
and when he had given thanks, he said,
Take this, and divide it among your-
18 selves: for I say unto you, I will not
drink from henceforth of the fruit of the
vine, until the kingdom of God shall
19 come. And he took bread, and when he
had given thanks, he brake it, and gave
to them, saying, This is my body [which
is given for you: this do in remembrance
20 of me. And the cup in like manner after
supper, saying, This cup is the new covenant in my blood, *even* that which is
poured out for you].

I COR. 11^{23-25}

11 23 For I received of the Lord that which
also I delivered unto you, how that the
Lord Jesus in the night in which he was
24 betrayed took bread; and when he had
given thanks, he brake it, and said, This
is my body, which is for you: this do in
25 remembrance of me. In like manner
also the cup, after supper, saying, This
cup is the new covenant in my blood:
this do, as oft as ye drink *it*, in remembrance of me.

Cf. JN. $6^{35, 48}$

6 35 Jesus said unto them, I am the bread of
life: he that cometh to me shall not
hunger, and he that believeth on me shall
never thirst.
48 I am the bread of life.

Cf. I COR. 10^{14-22}

10 14 Wherefore, my beloved, flee from
15 idolatry. I speak as to wise men; judge
16 ye what I say. The cup of blessing which
we bless, is it not a communion of the
blood of Christ? The bread which we
break, is it not a communion of the body
17 of Christ? seeing that we, who are many,
are one bread, one body: for we all par-
18 take of the one bread. Behold Israel
after the flesh: have not they which eat
the sacrifices communion with the altar?
19 What say I then? that a thing sacrificed
to idols is anything, or that an idol is any-
20 thing? But *I say*, that the things which
the Gentiles sacrifice, they sacrifice to
devils, and not to God: and I would not
that ye should have communion with
21 devils. Ye cannot drink the cup of the
Lord, and the cup of devils: ye cannot
partake of the table of the Lord, and of
22 the table of devils. Or do we provoke
the Lord to jealousy? are we stronger
than he?

ACT 2^{46}, $20^{7, 11}$

2 46 And day by day, continuing stedfastly
with one accord in the temple, and breaking bread at home, they did take their
food with gladness and singleness of
heart.
20 7 And upon the first day of the week,
when we were gathered together to break
bread, Paul discoursed with them, in-
tending to depart on the morrow; and
prolonged his speech until midnight.
11 And when he was gone up, and had
broken the bread, and eaten, and had
talked with them a long while, even till
break of day, so he departed.

Besides the roasted lamb and the bitter herbs and sauce at the Paschal meal there was also unleavened bread and cups of wine mixed with water. Jesus takes one of the loaves and blesses it, breaks it, and gives it to His disciples, saying: Take ye, this is my body. Jesus then takes a cup, and when He has given thanks (Gr., *eucharistēsas*) He gives it to them and they all drink from it. And He says to them: This is my covenant-blood which is shed on behalf of many.

Jn. omits the Institution of the Eucharist from his account of the Last Supper and substitutes Jesus washing the feet of His disciples. It is the discourse which follows the feeding of the five thousand in Jn. 6 which presents the eucharistic teaching of Jesus in the Fourth Gospel.

St. Paul's account in 1 Cor. $11^{23 f.}$ is the earliest written account of the Institution of the Eucharist. And it is best therefore to consider it at the outset.

St. Paul claims that he delivered to the Corinthians 'that which he also received from the Lord.' Of course, by the phrase 'from the Lord' he could not mean by the actual narration of Jesus, nor hardly by His inspiration. It seems more probable that he means that he received it from the Lord through the Apostles.

The points to be noted in St. Paul's account are:

(1) The Eucharist was instituted by Jesus on the night of His betrayal.

(2) That He took a loaf and blessed (*eucharistēsas*) and brake it and said: This is my body 'which is on your behalf,' or, 'is broken for you.'

(3) The command: Do ye this in my remembrance. (The word *anamnēsis* means *remembrance*, not memorial sacrifice, which is *mnēmosunon.*)

(4) The cup is taken after supper.

(5) The cup is the *new* covenant 'in my blood.'

(6) The Eucharist is given an apocalyptic significance by St. Paul's concluding sentence, 'as often as ye drink this cup ye proclaim the Lord's death till He come.'

St. Paul's account differs from Mk.'s in the following points:

(1) The covenant is the *new* covenant. It is thus a fulfilment of the prophecy in Jer. $31^{31 f.}$, which promises a new covenant to Israel the terms of which are to be written, not on stone or parchment, but in the heart. This covenant carried with it forgivenness of sins.

(2) Paul alone records the words which make the Eucharist a Christian *institution.* The command, 'do ye this,' does not occur in any of the Gospel accounts, but only in St. Paul. ('Do ye' means what it seems to mean, 'perform' or 'practise this,' not 'make this sacrifice,' which is an impossible rendering.)

(3) The Eucharist is to be a remembrance or a remembering of Jesus, and particularly a remembering of His death.

Are these three points part of the original Institution or are they additions made by St. Paul, as an ecclesiastical organiser? The general view is, that they are Pauline additions but entirely in harmony with the spirit of the Eucharist.

In its Marcan form and in its Pauline form the Eucharist is dramatic and symbolical but not miraculous or magical. It is not the commemoration in Mk. of an expiatory sacrifice, nor in St. Paul; still less is it the actual offering of such an expiatory sacrifice. It is the making or the renewal of a Divine covenant. Among Semitic peoples, covenants were made with blood which was sprinkled or smeared on the witnesses of, and participants in, the covenant.

In Exod. 24^{6-8} the first covenant was instituted by the sprinkling of blood upon the Israelites and the altar of the sanctuary.

The original idea of the Eucharist, as the making of a covenant and the renewal of that covenant by a sacred meal, was altered under the influence of Jewish sacrificial beliefs which identified Jesus with the Paschal Lamb since the Eucharist itself was instituted at the Passover season. This was done by St. Paul and Jn.

The significance of the Eucharist was also influenced by the figure of the Suffering Servant of the Lord with whom Jesus was identified. In Is. 53^{10} the Servant's soul is made an offering for sin. In *v.* 11 he is said to 'bear their iniquities.' In *v.* 12, 'he bare the sin of many.'

The phrase, 'on behalf of many,' in Mk., occurs more than once in the Septuagint of Is. 53. It is under the influence of these passages, no doubt, that Mt. adds to Mk.'s words of Institution, 'unto the remission of sins.'

The text of Lk.'s account has suffered much alteration in order to harmonise it, either with the accounts of the other Gospels, or with St. Paul's account, or in order to bring it into harmony with the liturgical practice of the Church. There is good reason for holding that the original account of Lk. ran as follows:

And when He received the cup, He blessed it (*eucharistēsas*) and said: Take ye this and divide it among yourselves, for I say to you that I will by no means drink from now onwards of the fruit of the vine until the Kingdom of God is come: and taking a loaf He blessed it and gave it to them, saying: This is my body.

It is obvious that Lk. reverses the order of the Institution; also that he makes it clear that our Lord did not partake of either the wine or bread; and thirdly, he makes no reference at all to the Eucharist as a covenant. [Lk. elsewhere calls the Eucharistic rite the 'Breaking of Bread' (Lk. 24^{35}; Acts $2^{42, 46}$, $20^{7, 11}$). St. Paul calls the rite the Lord's Supper, or the Communion of the Body and of the Blood of Christ (1 Cor. 11^{20}, 10^{16}).]

The declaration of Jesus in Lk., that He will not drink of the fruit of the vine until the Kingdom of God be come, appears in Mk. as, 'until I drink it new in the Kingdom of God.' Mt. has, 'until I drink it new with you in my Father's Kingdom,' thus pointing forward to a Eucharist which will be, for Him and for them, a festival both of reunion and of victory—when the Kingdom for which He is about to die will be a triumphant reality.

If the Institution of the Eucharist did not take place at the Paschal meal, then it is assumed that it took place at the *Kiddush.* This was a sacred meal, celebrated weekly in Jewish households on Friday afternoons to inaugurate the Sabbath, when bread is eaten; mixed cups of wine and water are drunk; prayers are said at table and hymns are sung. It ought to be added that Kiddush was also celebrated before each of the great festivals. If, however, the Passover fell on this occasion on the Sabbath, then the Paschal-Sabbath *Kiddush* would be held on the Thursday afternoon, and not on the Friday afternoon when the Paschal lambs were being slain (and when, according to Jn., Jesus was dying on the cross.

On the other hand, although no mention is made of the Paschal Lamb in our accounts of the Last Supper, two things are mentioned, besides the bread and wine, which may refer to Paschal customs.

(1) The bowl or dish in which the disciples dipped with Jesus may have held the sauce called *charoseth,* compounded of dates, raisins, and vinegar, in which the bitter herbs and unleavened bread were dipped.

(2) The hymn, sung by Jesus and His disciples before leaving the Upper Chamber for the Mount of Olives, may have been the Hallel, the six psalms of thanksgiving (Ps. 113–118) sung by Jewish households at the Paschal meal in celebration of the deliverance from Egypt.

PREDICTIONS OF DESERTION AND DENIAL

MK. 14^{27-31}

14 27 And Jesus saith unto them, All ye shall
be offended: for it is written, I will smite
the shepherd, and the sheep shall be
28 scattered abroad. Howbeit, after I am
raised up, I will go before you into
29 Galilee. But Peter said unto him,
Although all shall be offended, yet will
30 not I. And Jesus saith unto him, Verily
I say unto thee, that thou to-day, *even*
this night, before the cock crow twice,
31 shalt deny me thrice. But he spake
exceedingly vehemently, If I must die
with thee, I will not deny thee. And in
like manner also said they all.

MT. 26^{31-35}

26 31 Then saith Jesus unto them, All ye shall
be offended in me this night: for it is
written, I will smite the shepherd, and
the sheep of the flock shall be scattered
32 abroad. But after I am raised up, I will
33 go before you into Galilee. But Peter
answered and said unto him, If all shall
be offended in thee, I will never be
34 offended. Jesus said unto him, Verily I
say unto thee, that this night, before the
cock crow, thou shalt deny me thrice.
35 Peter saith unto him, Even if I must die
with thee, *yet* will I not deny thee.
Likewise also said all the disciples.

LK. 22^{31-34}

22 31 Simon, Simon, behold, Satan asked to
have you, that he might sift you as
32 wheat: but I made supplication for thee,
that thy faith fail not: and do thou, when
once thou hast turned again, stablish thy
33 brethren. And he said unto him, Lord,
with thee I am ready to go both to prison
34 and to death. And he said, I tell thee,
Peter, the cock shall not crow this day,
until thou shalt thrice deny that thou
knowest me.

JN. 13^{36-38}

13 36 Simon Peter saith unto him, Lord,
whither goest thou? Jesus answered,
Whither I go, thou canst not follow me
now; but thou shalt follow afterwards.
37 Peter saith unto him, Lord, why cannot I
follow thee even now? I will lay down
38 my life for thee. Jesus answereth, Wilt
thou lay down thy life for me? Verily,
verily, I say unto thee, The cock shall not
crow, till thou hast denied me thrice.

After having finished their hymns and left the Upper Chamber, Jesus and His disciples went out of Jerusalem across the brook Kidron to the Mount of Olives.

According to Mk. (followed by Mt.), it would appear that Jesus announced to His disciples that they would desert Him, citing a passage from Zech. 13^7, predicting the smiting of the shepherd with the sword. According to Lk. (possibly proto-Luke) and Jn., this prediction by Jesus takes place at supper time in the Upper Chamber.

Peter's stout resentment of our Lord's prediction is followed by the explicit declaration that before the cock crow twice (Mk.) Peter will thrice have denied Him. In the other three Gospels the prediction is slightly different. It is 'Before the cock crow: thou shalt have denied me thrice.'

Cocks crow in the early dawn. The last watch of the night was called the cock-crowing. According to Mk.'s text Jesus states that *before the second dawn*, that is some thirty hours hence, Peter will have denied Him three times. In the other form the prediction means that Peter will have denied Him before dawn. The form in which Lk. has the prediction: Simon, Simon, behold, Satan has begged hard for you (all the disciples) that he may sift you as wheat, but I have made supplication for thee (Peter) that thy faith fail not, etc., is very striking, and is in style characteristic of the more impressive utterances of Jesus. Why is this special supplication for Simon, and not for the others? Presumably not because he was weaker than the other disciples, but because as leader of the Twelve more depended on him.

The inclusion of this prediction in the Gospel tradition and its subsequent fulfilment is a testimony to the historical truth of that tradition. It is impossible to imagine that such a story could have been circulated in the primitive Church about its chief Apostle unless the story were true. It would seem probable, from its inclusion in Mk., that Peter himself was the first to recite it fully in his public preaching. In this respect it is parallel to Paul's public confession to Christian converts that he himself had been formerly a persecutor of the Christian Church.

The repentance of St. Peter and St. Paul may be compared with that of Judas, 'I have sinned in that I have betrayed the innocent blood.' In the case of the two first, their sin was followed by a sense of forgiveness and hope: in the case of the other, by despair.

GETHSEMANE

MK. 14^{32-42}

14 32 And they come unto a place which was
named Gethsemane: and he saith unto
his disciples, Sit ye here, while I pray.
33 And he taketh with him Peter and James
and John, and began to be greatly
34 amazed, and sore troubled. And he
saith unto them, My soul is exceeding
sorrowful even unto death: abide ye here,
35 and watch. And he went forward a
little, and fell on the ground, and prayed
that, if it were possible, the hour might
36 pass away from him. And he said,
Abba, Father, all things are possible unto
thee; remove this cup from me: howbeit
37 not what I will, but what thou wilt. And
he cometh, and findeth them sleeping,
and saith unto Peter, Simon, sleepest
thou? couldest thou not watch one hour?
38 Watch and pray, that ye enter not into
temptation: the spirit indeed is willing,
39 but the flesh is weak. And again he
went away, and prayed, saying the same
40 words. And again he came, and found
them sleeping, for their eyes were very
heavy; and they wist not what to answer
41 him. And he cometh the third time,
and saith unto them, Sleep on now, and
take your rest: it is enough; the hour is
come; behold, the Son of man is betrayed
42 into the hands of sinners. Arise, let us
be going: behold, he that betrayeth me
is at hand.

MT. 26^{36-46}

26 36 Then cometh Jesus with them unto a
place called Gethsemane, and saith unto
his disciples, Sit ye here, while I go
37 yonder and pray. And he took with him
Peter and the two sons of Zebedee, and
began to be sorrowful and sore troubled.
38 Then saith he unto them, My soul is exceeding
sorrowful, even unto death:
39 abide ye here, and watch with me. And
he went forward a little, and fell on his
face, and prayed, saying, O my Father,
if it be possible, let this cup pass away
from me: nevertheless, not as I will, but
40 as thou wilt. And he cometh unto the
disciples, and findeth them sleeping, and
saith unto Peter, What, could ye not
41 watch with me one hour? Watch and
pray, that ye enter not into temptation:
the spirit indeed is willing, but the flesh is
42 weak. Again a second time he went
away, and prayed, saying, O my Father,
if this cannot pass away, except I drink
43 it, thy will be done. And he came again
and found them sleeping, for their eyes
44 were heavy. And he left them again,
and went away, and prayed a third time,
45 saying again the same words. Then
cometh he to the disciples, and saith unto
them, Sleep on now, and take your rest:
behold, the hour is at hand, and the Son
of man is betrayed into the hands of
46 sinners. Arise, let us be going: behold,
he is at hand that betrayeth me.

LK. 22^{39-46}

22 39 And he came out, and went, as his
custom was, unto the mount of Olives;
and the disciples also followed him.
40 And when he was at the place, he said
unto them, Pray that ye enter not into

JN. $18^{1, 2, 11b}$

18 1 When Jesus had spoken these words,
he went forth with his disciples over the
brook Kidron, where was a garden, into
the which he entered, himself and his
2 disciples. Now Judas also, which be-

41 temptation. And he was parted from
them about a stone's cast; and he
42 kneeled down and prayed, saying,
Father, if thou be willing, remove this
cup from me: nevertheless not my will,
43 but thine, be done. And there appeared
unto him an angel from heaven, strength-
44 ening him. And being in an agony he
prayed more earnestly and his sweat
became as it were great drops of blood
45 falling down upon the ground. And
when he rose up from his prayer, he came
unto the disciples, and found them sleep-
46 ing for sorrow, and said unto them, Why
sleep ye? rise and pray, that ye enter not
into temptation.

trayed him, knew the place: for Jesus oft-
times resorted thither with his disciples.
11 The cup which the Father hath given
me, shall I not drink it?

Gethsemane means an oil-press—the oil being obtained, no doubt, from the neighbouring grove of olive trees after which the Mount of Olives was named.

According to Jn., Gethsemane was a walled garden, and was well known to Judas because Jesus often resorted thither with His disciples. Jesus is conscious of His imminent arrest and prepares for it. Leaving the main body of His disciples, He takes with Him Peter and James and John, saying to them amid signs of the deepest depression (the phrases of Mk. here are exceedingly strong: 'greatly amazed,' 'sore troubled'), 'My soul is exceeding sorrowful even unto death; abide ye here, and watch.'

Leaving the three disciples, He goes on farther (Lk., 'as it were a stone's throw'). He prostrates Himself on the earth and begins to pray.

The two Lukan additions, the agony of Jesus in which His sweat was like great drops of blood falling on the ground, and that an angel was seen strengthening Him, are not to-day regarded by many as historical. They are omitted by a certain number of important codices of the Gospels, but critics of great judgement regard them as part of the original Lucan text.

The form of the prayer in Mk. which Jesus utters should be noted: Father (Abba), all things are possible for Thee. 'All things are possible for Thee' is omitted by Mt. In Lk. the prayer takes the form: Father, if Thou wishest, remove this cup from me; nevertheless, not as I will but as Thou wilt.

Mk.'s statement that 'all things are possible to God' would seem to have created difficulties in view of what followed. Lk., we have noted elsewhere, seems to have held the Greek philosophical view that it was not possible even for God to do all things. If, as textual criticism demands, the agony, sweat, and angel be omitted from Lk.'s account of Gethsemane, the spirit in which Jesus (in Lk.) faces His doom is that of a philosopher. The intense struggle portrayed in Mk. by which Jesus brings Himself to accept the Divine Will has become obliterated in the Lucan account, yet in this matter the Marcan account is undoubtedly historical. It is reflected in the notable passage in the Epistle to the Hebrews, where the writer referring to Jesus says:

'Who in the days of his flesh, when he had offered up prayers and supplications with strong crying and tears unto him that was able to save him from death and had been heard for his piety, yet, though a Son, from the things which he suffered he learned obedience.' (Heb. $5^{7,8}$.)

Here, as in so many other cases in Mk., we have the 'full humanity' of Jesus preserved by an eye-witness.

If Jesus went up to Jerusalem prepared to suffer death in the assertion of His Messianic claim, how is it possible to account for Gethsemane?

Socrates, so far as our records go, passed through no such crisis: neither did many of the Christian martyrs. *A priori*, we should have expected Jesus to face the crisis in a triumphant and majestic manner, as He does in the Fourth Gospel: The cup which my Father hath given me, shall I not drink it? Yet, it is not so in Mk. Psychologically, our Lord was emotional and highly strung: His temperament was not one of philosophic calm. There were, if we may use the mystic's phrase, dark nights of the soul in His human experience, and Peter recorded such an one in Gethsemane. It was in the garden, rather than on the Cross, that the full surrender was made by Jesus to the Father's Will, and His perfection as the Author and Captain of our Salvation achieved. The self-restraint and heroic courage with which He faced His accusers and judges was secured by His prayer and self-surrender in Gethsemane. As the writer of the Hebrews affirms, 'He was heard.'

The words which Jesus addresses to His somnolent disciples when He comes to them the third time are something of an enigma. 'Sleep on now, and take your rest: it is enough.' They would appear to be sardonic. 'It is enough,' is the formula used in giving receipts. It is as though Jesus said: 'Well, you've had it after all, and now those who would arrest me are at hand.'

Why Jesus desired His disciples to watch with Him would seem to be that He sought the strength which their prayers united to His might give them all, in the approaching crisis. Their failure to watch and pray on this occasion may have been responsible for the sorry figure which they cut in the subsequent events.

THE ARREST OF JESUS

MK. 14^{43-52}

14 43 And straightway, while he yet spake,
cometh Judas, one of the twelve, and with
him a multitude with swords and staves,
from the chief priests and the scribes and
44 the elders. Now he that betrayed him
had given them a token, saying, Whomsoever I shall kiss, that is he; take him,
45 and lead him away safely. And when he
was come, straightway he came to him,
46 and saith, Rabbi; and kissed him. And
they laid hands on him, and took him.
47 But a certain one of them that stood by
drew his sword, and smote the servant of
the high priest, and struck off his ear.
48 And Jesus answered and said unto them,
Are ye come out, as against a robber,
49 with swords and staves to seize me? I
was daily with you in the temple teaching, and ye took me not: but *this is done*
that the scriptures might be fulfilled.
50 And they all left him, and fled.
51 And a certain young man followed

MT. 26^{47-56}

26 47 And while he yet spake, lo, Judas, one
of the twelve, came, and with him a great
multitude with swords and staves, from
the chief priests and elders of the people.
48 Now he that betrayed him gave them a
sign, saying, Whomsoever I shall kiss,
49 that is he: take him. And straightway
he came to Jesus, and said, Hail, Rabbi;
50 and kissed him. And Jesus said unto
him, Friend, *do* that for which thou art
come. Then they came and laid hands
51 on Jesus, and took him. And behold,
one of them that were with Jesus stretched
out his hand, and drew his sword, and
smote the servant of the high priest, and
52 struck off his ear. Then saith Jesus unto
him, Put up again thy sword into its
place: for all they that take the sword
53 shall perish with the sword. Or thinkest
thou that I cannot beseech my Father,
and he shall even now send me more than
54 twelve legions of angels? How then

with him, having a linen cloth cast about
him, over *his* naked *body*: and they lay
52 hold on him; but he left the linen cloth,
and fled naked.

should the scriptures be fulfilled, that
55 thus it must be? In that hour said Jesus
to the multitudes, Are ye come out as
against a robber with swords and staves
to seize me? I sat daily in the temple
56 teaching, and ye took me not. But all
this is come to pass, that the scriptures of
the prophets might be fulfilled. Then
all the disciples left him, and fled.

LK. 22^{47-53}

22 47 While he yet spake, behold, a multitude, and he that was called Judas, one
of the twelve, went before them; and he
48 drew near unto Jesus to kiss him. But
Jesus said unto him, Judas, betrayest
49 thou the Son of man with a kiss? And
when they that were about him saw what
would follow, they said, Lord, shall we
50 smite with the sword? And a certain
one of them smote the servant of the high
51 priest, and struck off his right ear. But
Jesus answered and said, Suffer ye thus
far. And he touched his ear, and healed
52 him. And Jesus said unto the chief
priests, and captains of the temple, and
elders, which were come against him,
Are ye come out, as against a robber,
53 with swords and staves? When I was
daily with you in the temple, ye stretched
not forth your hands against me: but this
is your hour, and the power of darkness.

JN. 18^{3-11}

18 3 Judas then, having received the band
of soldiers, and officers from the chief
priests and the Pharisees, cometh thither
with lanterns and torches and weapons.
4 Jesus therefore, knowing all the things
that were coming upon him, went forth,
and saith unto them, Whom seek ye?
5 They answered him, Jesus of Nazareth.
Jesus saith unto them, I am *he*. And
Judas also, which betrayed him, was
6 standing with them. When therefore he
said unto them, I am *he*, they went back-
7 ward, and fell to the ground. Again
therefore he asked them, Whom seek ye?
8 And they said, Jesus of Nazareth. Jesus
answered, I told you that I am *he*: if
therefore ye seek me, let these go their
9 way: that the word might be fulfilled
which he spake, Of those whom thou hast
10 given me I lost not one. Simon Peter
therefore having a sword drew it, and
struck the high priest's servant, and cut
off his right ear. Now the servant's
11 name was Malchus. Jesus therefore said
unto Peter, Put up the sword into the
sheath: the cup which the Father hath
given me, shall I not drink it?

We have discussed what it was that Judas betrayed to the High Priest. Was it the Messianic secret or was it the place outside the walls of Jerusalem where Jesus spent His nights amid the multitudes of Jewish pilgrims? Undoubtedly it was the latter which Judas betrayed. He was, in St. Peter's phrase, 'guide to them that took Jesus (Acts 1^{16}; cf. Jn. 18^{2}).

The account of the words spoken by Jesus on His arrest differs in each of the four Gospels.

In Mk. Jesus is not recorded to have said anything to the traitor when he hailed Him as Rabbi, and kissed Him.

In Mt. Jesus says: 'Friend [my good fellow], do that for which thou art come.'

In Lk., 'Judas, betrayest thou the Son of Man with a kiss?'

In Jn. Jesus does not address Judas, but the band of officials, saying: 'Whom seek ye?' They answered Him, 'Jesus, the Nazarene.' He says to them: 'I am he. . . .'

Lk. relates that the disciples possessed two swords (Lk. $22^{36, 38}$). Mk., that when they laid hands on Jesus one of those present (Mt., 'one of those with them'; Lk., 'those about Jesus'; Jn., 'Simon Peter') makes use of a sword and cuts off the ear (Lk. and Jn., ' right ear ') of the slave of the High Priest. Jn. gives the name of the slave as Malchus. Jesus commands His supporter to sheathe his sword. Lk. makes the extraordinary statement that Jesus restored the severed ear. It has been suggested that the restoration of the severed ear is due to a mistranslation of his Aramaic source by Luke. The command of Jesus to *restore* the sword to its sheath Lk. takes as addressed to the ear. Hence the miracle.

This incident of the armed resistance of the disciples of Jesus has again been the subject of much discussion since the discovery of a Slavonic edition of Josephus (the Jewish historian) which presents Jesus as the leader of an armed insurrection in Jerusalem. This narrative, attributed to Josephus, has been rejected as spurious by our best English scholars, including the learned Jewish scholar, Dr. Montefiore. All the evidence from the teaching of Jesus indicates strongly that He was utterly opposed to the policy of armed insurrection fomented by the Zealots and Sicarii.

His command, in Lk., at the Last Supper, to buy a sword is undoubtedly symbolical. It is the equivalent of saying to His disciples: ' When you went out on your missionary tour you found the people friendly: they shewed you hospitality and kindness: now all is changed. With the arrest and execution of your Master you will find all men hostile.' When the disciples indicate, by showing Him the two swords which they have in their possession, that they are taking Him literally He replies: ' It is enough.' Probably the very same phrase as He used later to His sleeping disciples, although rendered by a different Greek phrase.

Mk. alone relates an incident which appears at first sight to be hardly worth relating.

' And there followed him a certain young man, having a linen cloth cast about his naked body: and the young men laid hold on him; and he left the linen cloth, and fled from them naked. (Mk. $14^{51, 52}$.)

If, however, the young man was Mark himself, the incident is worthy of record. It is personal experience. The same young man is perhaps mentioned once again in Mk.'s Gospel (16^{5}). It is a young man who addresses the amazed women at the sepulchre on the first Easter Day, telling them that Jesus is not there, but is risen. It is only in these two places that the term young man (*neaniskos*) occurs in Mk.

It should be noted that Jesus regards His arrest, as also His Passion and Death, as a fulfilment of the Scriptures. No doubt the special passages in His mind are Is. 53 and Pss. 22 and 69.

JESUS TRIED BY THE ECCLESIASTICAL AUTHORITIES

MK. 14^{53-65}

14 53 And they led Jesus away to the high
priest: and there come together with him
all the chief priests and the elders and the
54 scribes. And Peter had followed him
afar off, even within, into the court of the
high priest; and he was sitting with the

MT. 26^{57-68}

26 57 And they that had taken Jesus led him
away to *the house of* Caiaphas the high
priest, where the scribes and the elders
58 were gathered together. But Peter followed him afar off, unto the court of the
high priest, and entered in, and sat with

officers, and warming himself in the light
55 *of the fire*. Now the chief priests and the
whole council sought witness against
Jesus to put him to death; and found it
56 not. For many bare false witness against
him, and their witness agreed not
57 together. And there stood up certain,
and bare false witness against him, say-
58 ing, We heard him say, I will destroy this
temple that is made with hands, and in
three days I will build another made
59 without hands. And not even so did
60 their witness agree together. And the
high priest stood up in the midst, and
asked Jesus, saying, Answerest thou
nothing? what is it which these witness
61 against thee? But he held his peace,
and answered nothing. Again the high
priest asked him, and saith unto him, Art
thou the Christ, the Son of the Blessed?
62 And Jesus said, I am: and ye shall see
the Son of man sitting at the right hand
of power, and coming with the clouds of
63 heaven. And the high priest rent his
clothes, and saith, What further need
64 have we of witnesses? Ye have heard
the blasphemy: what think ye? And
they all condemned him to be worthy of
65 death. And some began to spit on him,
and to cover his face, and to buffet him,
and to say unto him, Prophesy: and the
officers received him with blows of their
hands.

59 the officers, to see the end. Now the
chief priests and the whole council sought
false witness against Jesus, that they
60 might put him to death; and they found
it not, though many false witnesses came.
61 But afterward came two, and said, This
man said, I am able to destroy the temple
of God, and to build it in three days.
62 And the high priest stood up, and said
unto him, Answerest thou nothing? what
is it which these witness against thee?
63 But Jesus held his peace. And the high
priest said unto him, I adjure thee by the
living God, that thou tell us whether
thou be the Christ, the Son of God.
64 Jesus saith unto him, Thou hast said:
nevertheless I say unto you, Henceforth
ye shall see the Son of man sitting at the
right hand of power, and coming on the
65 clouds of heaven. Then the high priest
rent his garments, saying, He hath
spoken blasphemy: what further need
have we of witnesses? behold, now ye
66 have heard the blasphemy: what think
ye? They answered and said, He is
67 worthy of death. Then did they spit in
his face and buffet him: and some smote
68 him with the palms of their hands, saying,
Prophesy unto us, thou Christ: who is he
that struck thee?

LK. $22^{54,\ 55,\ 63-71}$

22 54 And they seized him, and led him
away, and brought him into the high
priest's house. But Peter followed afar
55 off. And when they had kindled a fire
in the midst of the court, and had sat
down together, Peter sat in the midst of
them.
63 And the men that held *Jesus* mocked
64 him, and beat him. And they blind-
folded him, and asked him, saying,
Prophesy: who is he that struck thee?
65 And many other things spake they against
him, reviling him.
66 And as soon as it was day, the assembly
of the elders of the people was gathered
together, both chief priests and scribes;
and they led him away into their council,
67 saying, If thou art the Christ, tell us.
But he said unto them, If I tell you, ye
68 will not believe: and if I ask *you*, ye will
69 not answer. But from henceforth shall
the Son of man be seated at the right
70 hand of the power of God. And they all
said, Art thou then the Son of God?
And he said unto them, Ye say that I am.
71 And they said, What further need have
we of witness? for we ourselves have
heard from his own mouth.

JN. $18^{12-14,\ 19-24}$ (cf. JN. 2^{19})

18 12 So the band and the chief captain, and
the officers of the Jews, seized Jesus and
13 bound him, and led him to Annas first;
for he was father in law to Caiaphas,
14 which was high priest that year. Now
Caiaphas was he which gave counsel to
the Jews, that it was expedient that one
man should die for the people.
19 The high priest therefore asked Jesus
20 of his disciples, and of his teaching. Jesus
answered him, I have spoken openly to
the world; I ever taught in synagogues,
and in the temple, where all the Jews
come together; and in secret spake I
21 nothing. Why askest thou me? ask them
that have heard *me*, what I spake unto
them: behold, these know the things
22 which I said. And when he had said
this, one of the officers standing by struck
Jesus with his hand, saying, Answerest
23 thou the high priest so? Jesus answered
him, If I have spoken evil, bear witness
of the evil: but if well, why smitest thou
24 me? Annas therefore sent him bound
unto Caiaphas the high priest.
2 19 Jesus answered and said unto them,
Destroy this temple, and in three days I
will raise it up.

According to the four Evangelists Jesus underwent four judicial trials before (1) Annas (Jn. 18^{12-14, 19-24}), (2) Caiaphas (Mk. and Lk. have 'the High Priest,' Mt. and Jn. have Caiaphas), (3) Pilate (Mk., Mt., Lk., Jn.), (4) Herod Antipas (Lk. 23^{6-12}).

Mk. relates only two trials (*a*) before the Sanhedrin (presided over by Caiaphas), and (*b*) before Pilate. But since we have reason to believe that Jn. possesses a special source derived from his acquaintance with the High Priest's household, and that Lk. possesses a special source connected with the Court of Herod Antipas, possibly derived from Manaen of Antioch, Herod's foster-brother, there is no good reason for rejecting these additional trials in Jn. and Lk. as legendary. Both trials seem in their circumstances to be *a priori* credible.

It is generally assumed that the Sanhedrin, during the period that Judæa was under the government of the Roman procurators, had no power to inflict capital sentences. On the other hand, the trial of Stephen and the infliction of the legal capital sentence—death by stoning—seems to conflict with this conclusion. It is argued, however, that the action of the Sanhedrin in the case of Stephen was *ultra vires*.

Jesus is led away to the Palace of the High Priest in Jerusalem. The High Priest at this time was Joseph Caiaphas who ruled from A.D. 18 to 36. He was the son-in-law of Annas, who had been High Priest, and a number of whose sons and sons-in-law filled the office.

According to Jn. (18^{12, 13}), Jesus underwent a preliminary examination before Annas, who probably occupied apartments in the same palace. Jesus was then brought before a full session of the Sanhedrin presided over by Caiaphas. A great number of witnesses were heard, but their evidence broke down under cross-examination. Under Jewish law, a capital conviction was impossible unless the testimony of at least two witnesses was in agreement. This the accusers failed to secure. The accusation that Jesus had declared that He would replace the material shrine by a spiritual shrine should be noted.

During His trial, according to the Synoptists, Jesus remained silent and only at last when solemnly adjured by the High Priest: 'Art thou the Christ, the Son of the Blessed One?' did Jesus answer in the affirmative: 'I am, and ye shall see the Son of Man seated at the right hand of Power and coming in the clouds of heaven.'

In Mk. the affirmation of His Messiahship by Jesus is positive and explicit. Whether it went beyond the words 'I am' may be doubted. The primitive Christian Church would naturally expand the affirmation of Jesus in terms which reflected the current, popular, apocalyptic, Messianic expectations.

Mt. gives the answer of Jesus in a somewhat different form, though not less positive and explicit, if the Oriental idiom, 'Thou hast said it,' be rightly understood as a definite acceptance of the charge.

Lk.'s account of the way in which Jesus responded to the High Priest's question, although differing considerably in form, and no doubt derived from another source, is yet in agreement on the main issue with Mk. and Mt.: 'If I tell you, ye will not believe: and if I ask you, ye will not answer. But from now onwards shall the Son of Man be seated at the right hand of the Power of God.

And they all said, Art thou then the Son of God? And he said unto them, Ye say that I am.'

Jn. represents Jesus as declining to furnish any direct evidence to the High Priest.

The term 'henceforth' or 'from now onwards' in Mt. (*v.* 64) and in Lk. (*v.* 69) would seem to indicate, not some future, apocalyptic advent of Jesus, but a progressive, spiritual ascendancy, beginning with His crucifixion—the equivalent of the Johannine 'now is the Son of Man glorified' (Jn. 13^{31}). 'From this very moment,' Jesus would seem to say to His High Priestly judge, 'I shall become, as you will see, the supreme, moral and spiritual judge of mankind.'

Of course the metaphor, Coming in, or on, the clouds of heaven, means with Divine power and authority. The imagery is derived from Dan. 7^{13}.

The dramatic gesture of the High Priest with which he receives the Confession of Jesus is expressive of horror and indignation. What he tore were his under-garments—his shirts (Mk.), not his outer garments (Mt.).

It was only usual to wear one shirt, but when he rent them it appeared that he was wearing several, due no doubt to the coldness of the night—suggested also by St. Peter warming himself by the fire in the courtyard.

PETER'S THREEFOLD DENIAL

MK. 14^{66-72}

14 66 And as Peter was beneath in the court,
there cometh one of the maids of the high
67 priest; and seeing Peter warming himself, she looked upon him, and saith,
Thou also wast with the Nazarene, *even*
68 Jesus. But he denied, saying, I neither
know, nor understand what thou sayest:
and he went out into the porch; and the
69 cock crew. And the maid saw him, and
began again to say to them that stood by,
70 This is *one* of them. But he again denied
it. And after a little while again they
that stood by said to Peter, Of a truth
thou art *one* of them; for thou art a
71 Galilæan. But he began to curse, and to
swear, I know not this man of whom ye
72 speak. And straightway the second
time the cock crew. And Peter called to
mind the word, how that Jesus said unto
him, Before the cock crow twice, thou
shalt deny me thrice. And when he
thought thereon, he wept.

MT. 26^{69-75}

26 69 Now Peter was sitting without in the
court: and a maid came unto him, saying, Thou also wast with Jesus the
70 Galilæan. But he denied before them
all, saying, I know not what thou sayest.
71 And when he was gone out into the
porch, another *maid* saw him, and saith
unto them that were there, This man
72 also was with Jesus the Nazarene. And
again he denied with an oath, I know not
73 the man. And after a little while they
that stood by came and said to Peter, Of
a truth thou also art *one* of them; for thy
74 speech betrayeth thee. Then began he
to curse and to swear, I know not the
man. And straightway the cock crew.
75 And Peter remembered the word which
Jesus had said, Before the cock crow,
thou shalt deny me thrice. And he
went out, and wept bitterly.

LK. 22^{56-62}

22 56 And a certain maid seeing him as he
sat in the light *of the fire*, and looking
stedfastly upon him, said, This man also
57 was with him. But he denied, saying,
58 Woman, I know him not. And after a
little while another saw him, and said,
Thou also art *one* of them. But Peter

JN. $18^{17, 18, 25-27}$

18 17 The maid therefore that kept the door
saith unto Peter, Art thou also *one* of this
man's disciples? He saith, I am not.
18 Now the servants and the officers were
standing *there*, having made a fire of
coals; for it was cold; and they were
warming themselves: and Peter also was

59 said, Man, I am not. And after the
space of about one hour another confidently affirmed, saying, Of a truth this
man also was with him: for he is a
60 Galilæan. But Peter said, Man, I know
not what thou sayest. And immediately,
61 while he yet spake, the cock crew. And
the Lord turned, and looked upon Peter.
And Peter remembered the word of the
Lord, how that he said unto him, Before
the cock crow this day, thou shalt deny
62 me thrice. And he went out, and wept
bitterly.

with them, standing and warming
himself.
25 Now Simon Peter was standing and
warming himself. They said therefore
unto him, Art thou also *one* of his disciples? He denied, and said, I am not.
26 One of the servants of the high priest,
being a kinsman of him whose ear Peter
cut off, saith, Did not I see thee in the
27 garden with him? Peter therefore denied
again: and straightway the cock crew.

Mk.'s account of Peter's threefold denial is extremely circumstantial. This is no doubt due to that account having been derived directly from Peter himself. It differs in a number of points from the other three accounts.

The points in which Mt. differs from Mk. are of no particular interest. It is otherwise in the case of the difference of Lk. and Jn. from Mk. Here both Lk. and Jn. seem to be drawing on special sources of their own.

The First Denial

Peter alone follows Jesus 'afar off' to the High Priest's palace. In Jn. he is admitted by a portress at the introduction of the 'beloved disciple' who was an acquaintance of the High Priest, and it is this portress who first charges Peter with being a disciple of Jesus. Peter denies, with the words 'I am not.' In Mt., Peter is outside the palace when a 'maidservant' makes the charge, and Peter answers: 'I know not what thou sayest.' In Lk., Peter is within the palace, 'seated against the light,' when a maidservant charges him. Peter answers: 'O woman, I know him not.' In Mk., Peter is 'beneath' with the High Priest's servants in the palace warming himself by the fire with his face against the light, and a maidservant charges him, and Peter replies 'I neither know nor understand what thou sayest.' In all four cases the words of the maidservant's charge and the words of St. Peter's denial differ, but not to such a degree as to alter the sense.

The Second Denial

In Mk., Peter, after his first denial, goes out into the courtyard in front of the palace and the maidservant who had made the first charge comes and repeats it; not, however, to Peter, but to the bystanders, and Peter denies again, but his actual words are not recorded. Mt. places the second denial in the porch or portico of the palace, and says that another maidservant makes the charge. This time Peter denied 'with an oath' saying: 'I know not the man.' Lk. says, 'another man' made the second charge. Peter replied: 'O man, I am not.'

Jn. says: While Peter was warming himself those present charge him and he answers: 'I am not.' In Jn., the second denial takes place within the palace. Mk.'s statement (followed by Mt.), that it took place outside, seems more probable.

The Third Denial

On the third occasion the bystanders in Mk. charge Peter, who 'began to curse and to swear,' saying: 'I know not this man of whom ye speak.' Mt. is here in almost entire agreement with Mk., but adds, as a reason for the third charge, 'For thy speech betrays thee.' The Galilean dialect was broader and rougher than that of Jerusalem. Lk. relates that about an hour had elapsed since the second charge, when another man charges Peter, and Peter replies: 'O man, I know not what thou sayest.' In Jn., the third charge is made by one of the slaves of the High Priest, a relation of Malchus, whose ear Peter had cut off. Peter again denies. No words are given. Immediately after the third denial it is stated in all four Gospels that the cock crowed, but Mk. has 'for the second time' (which is omitted by the *Codex Sinaiticus*). When Peter hears the cock crow he recalls the saying of Jesus. (Mk., Mt.) According to Mt. and Lk. he went forth and wept bitterly.

The meaning of Mk. here is very obscure—possibly the text is corrupt or defective. Some think that the phrase rendered 'when he thought thereon,' should be 'covered his head with his cloak'; others that 'he rushed outside'; others, that he responded to the cock's crowing by weeping.

Lk. alone states that at the third denial 'the Lord turned and looked upon Peter,' which suggests that Peter was able to witness what took place at the trial before the Sanhedrin. This point is of importance if Mk.'s account of the trial be that of Peter.

The numerous differences and small contradictions in the four accounts of Peter's denials will seem to some to discredit the historicity of the whole story. Such criticism is as unsound as it is sceptical. The conflicts in detail are not of such a kind as to discredit the essential historicity of the narrative. They seem indeed to suggest better reasons for regarding it as historical than if all accounts were in exact verbal agreement. Obviously, there is no collusion here.

JESUS BEFORE PILATE

MK. 15^{1-15}

15 1 And straightway in the morning the
chief priests with the elders and scribes,
and the whole council, held a consulta-
tion, and bound Jesus, and carried him
away, and delivered him up to Pilate.
2 And Pilate asked him, Art thou the King
of the Jews? And he answering saith
3 unto him, Thou sayest. And the chief
4 priests accused him of many things. And
Pilate again asked him, saying, Answerest
thou nothing? behold how many things
5 they accuse thee of. But Jesus no more
answered anything; insomuch that Pilate
marvelled.
6 Now at the feast he used to release
unto them one prisoner, whom they asked
7 of him. And there was one called
Barabbas, *lying* bound with them that
had made insurrection, men who in the
insurrection had committed murder.
8 And the multitude went up and began
to ask him *to do* as he was wont to do unto
9 them. And Pilate answered them, saying, Will ye that I release unto you the

MT. 27^{1-26}

27 1 Now when morning was come, all the
chief priests and the elders of the people
took counsel against Jesus to put him to
2 death: and they bound him, and led him
away, and delivered him up to Pilate the
governor.
3 Then Judas, which betrayed him,
when he saw that he was condemned,
repented himself, and brought back the
thirty pieces of silver to the chief priests
4 and elders, saying, I have sinned in that
I betrayed innocent blood. But they
said, What is that to us? see thou *to it*.
5 And he cast down the pieces of silver into
the sanctuary, and departed; and he
6 went away and hanged himself. And
the chief priests took the pieces of silver,
and said, It is not lawful to put them into
the treasury, since it is the price of blood.
7 And they took counsel, and bought with
them the potter's field, to bury strangers
8 in. Wherefore that field was called, The
9 field of blood, unto this day. Then was
fulfilled that which was spoken by Jere-

10 King of the Jews? For he perceived that
for envy the chief priests had delivered
11 him up. But the chief priests stirred up
the multitude, that he should rather re-
12 lease Barabbas unto them. And Pilate
again answered and said unto them,
What then shall I do unto him whom ye
13 call the King of the Jews? And they
14 cried out again, Crucify him. And
Pilate said unto them, Why, what evil
hath he done? But they cried out ex-
15 ceedingly, Crucify him. And Pilate,
wishing to content the multitude, released unto them Barabbas, and delivered
Jesus, when he had scourged him, to be
crucified.

miah the prophet, saying, And they took
the thirty pieces of silver, the price of him
that was priced, whom *certain* of the
10 children of Israel did price; and they
gave them for the potter's field, as the
Lord appointed me.
11 Now Jesus stood before the governor:
and the governor asked him, saying, Art
thou the King of the Jews? And Jesus
12 said unto him, Thou sayest. And when
he was accused by the chief priests and
13 elders, he answered nothing. Then saith
Pilate unto him, Hearest thou not how
many things they witness against thee?
14 And he gave him no answer, not even to
one word: insomuch that the governor
15 marvelled greatly. Now at the feast the
governor was wont to release unto the
multitude one prisoner, whom they
16 would. And they had then a notable
17 prisoner, called Barabbas. When therefore they were gathered together, Pilate
said unto them, Whom will ye that I
release unto you? Barabbas, or Jesus
18 which is called Christ? For he knew
that for envy they had delivered him up.
19 And while he was sitting on the judgement-seat, his wife sent unto him, saying,
Have thou nothing to do with that
righteous man: for I have suffered many
things this day in a dream because of
20 him. Now the chief priests and the
elders persuaded the multitudes that they
should ask for Barabbas, and destroy
21 Jesus. But the governor answered and
said unto them, Whether of the twain
will ye that I release unto you? And
22 they said, Barabbas. Pilate saith unto
them, What then shall I do unto Jesus
which is called Christ? They all say,
23 Let him be crucified. And he said,
Why, what evil hath he done? But they
cried out exceedingly, saying, Let him be
24 crucified. So when Pilate saw that he
prevailed nothing, but rather that a
tumult was arising, he took water, and
washed his hands before the multitude,
saying, I am innocent of the blood of this
25 righteous man: see ye *to it*. And all the
people answered and said, His blood *be*
26 on us, and on our children. Then released he unto them Barabbas: but Jesus
he scourged and delivered to be crucified.

LK. 23^{1-25}

23 1 And the whole company of them rose
2 up, and brought him before Pilate. And
they began to accuse him, saying, We
found this man perverting our nation,
and forbidding to give tribute to Cæsar,
and saying that he himself is Christ a
3 king. And Pilate asked him, saying,

JN. 18^{28-40}, 19^{4-16}

18 28 They lead Jesus therefore from Caiaphas into the palace: and it was early;
and they themselves entered not into the
palace, that they might not be defiled,
29 but might eat the passover. Pilate
therefore went out unto them, and saith,
What accusation bring ye against this

Art thou the King of the Jews? And he
answered him and said, Thou sayest.
4 And Pilate said unto the chief priests and
the multitudes, I find no fault in this
5 man. But they were the more urgent,
saying, He stirreth up the people, teaching throughout all Judæa, and beginning
6 from Galilee even unto this place. But
when Pilate heard it, he asked whether
7 the man were a Galilæan. And when he
knew that he was of Herod's jurisdiction,
he sent him unto Herod, who himself also
was at Jerusalem in these days.
8 Now when Herod saw Jesus, he was
exceeding glad: for he was of a long time
desirous to see him, because he had
heard concerning him; and he hoped to
9 see some miracle done by him. And he
questioned him in many words; but he
10 answered him nothing. And the chief
priests and the scribes stood, vehemently
11 accusing him. And Herod with his
soldiers set him at nought, and mocked
him, and arraying him in gorgeous
12 apparel sent him back to Pilate. And
Herod and Pilate became friends with
each other that very day: for before they
were at enmity between themselves.
13 And Pilate called together the chief
14 priests and the rulers and the people, and
said unto them, Ye brought unto me this
man, as one that perverteth the people:
and behold, I, having examined him
before you, found no fault in this man
touching those things whereof ye accuse
15 him: no, nor yet Herod: for he sent him
back unto us; and behold, nothing
worthy of death hath been done by him.
16 I will therefore chastise him, and release
18 him. But they cried out all together,
saying, Away with this man, and release
19 unto us Barabbas: one who for a certain
insurrection made in the city, and for
20 murder, was cast into prison. And
Pilate spake unto them again, desiring to
21 release Jesus; but they shouted, saying,
22 Crucify, crucify him. And he said unto
them the third time, Why, what evil hath
this man done? I have found no cause
of death in him: I will therefore chastise
23 him and release him. But they were
instant with loud voices, asking that he
might be crucified. And their voices
24 prevailed. And Pilate gave sentence
that what they asked for should be done.
25 And he released him that for insurrection
and murder had been cast into prison,
whom they asked for; but Jesus he
delivered up to their will.

30 man? They answered and said unto
him, If this man were not an evil-doer,
we should not have delivered him up
31 unto thee. Pilate therefore said unto
them, Take him yourselves, and judge
him according to your law. The Jews
said unto him, It is not lawful for us to
32 put any man to death: that the word of
Jesus might be fulfilled, which he spake,
signifying by what manner of death he
should die.
33 Pilate therefore entered again into the
palace, and called Jesus, and said unto
him, Art thou the King of the Jews?
34 Jesus answered, Sayest thou this of thyself, or did others tell it thee concerning
35 me? Pilate answered, Am I a Jew?
Thine own nation and the chief priests
delivered thee unto me: what hast thou
36 done? Jesus answered, My kingdom is
not of this world: if my kingdom were of
this world, then would my servants fight,
that I should not be delivered to the
Jews: but now is my kingdom not from
37 hence. Pilate therefore said unto him,
Art thou a king then? Jesus answered,
Thou sayest that I am a king. To this
end have I been born, and to this end
am I come into the world, that I should
bear witness unto the truth. Every one
that is of the truth heareth my voice.
38 Pilate saith unto him, What is truth?
And when he had said this, he went
out again unto the Jews, and saith unto
39 them, I find no crime in him. But ye
have a custom, that I should release unto
you one at the passover: will ye therefore
that I release unto you the King of the
40 Jews? They cried out therefore again,
saying, Not this man, but Barabbas.
Now Barabbas was a robber.
19 4 And Pilate went out again, and saith
unto them, Behold, I bring him out to
you, that ye may know that I find no
5 crime in him. Jesus therefore came out,
wearing the crown of thorns and the
purple garment. And *Pilate* saith unto
6 them, Behold, the man! When therefore
the chief priests and the officers saw him,
they cried out, saying, Crucify *him*,
crucify *him*. Pilate saith unto them,
Take him yourselves, and crucify him:
7 for I find no crime in him. The Jews
answered him, We have a law, and by
that law he ought to die, because he made
8 himself the Son of God. When Pilate
therefore heard this saying, he was the
9 more afraid; and he entered into the
palace again, and saith unto Jesus,
Whence art thou? But Jesus gave him
10 no answer. Pilate therefore saith unto
him, Speakest thou not unto me?
knowest thou not that I have power to

release thee, and have power to crucify
11 thee? Jesus answered him, Thou wouldest have no power against me, except it were given thee from above: therefore he that delivered me unto thee hath greater
12 sin. Upon this Pilate sought to release him: but the Jews cried out, saying, If thou release this man, thou art not Cæsar's friend: every one that maketh himself a king speaketh against Cæsar.
13 When Pilate therefore heard these words, he brought Jesus out, and sat down on the judgement-seat at a place called The Pavement, but in Hebrew, Gabbatha.
14 Now it was the Preparation of the passover: it was about the sixth hour. And he saith unto the Jews, Behold, your
15 King! They therefore cried out, Away with *him*, away with *him*, crucify him. Pilate saith unto them, Shall I crucify your King? The chief priests answered,
16 We have no king but Cæsar. Then therefore he delivered him unto them to be crucified.

They took Jesus therefore.

[The R.V., following the best manuscripts, omits Lk. 23[17], Now he must needs release unto them at the feast one *prisoner*.]

The Sanhedrin were not allowed to pronounce a capital sentence after dark; they had therefore to wait for the dawn to do so. As soon as this was done, it being still very early, the whole Sanhedrin took Jesus before Pilate.

Here, the difference of twenty-four hours in the chronology of Jn. and the Synoptists accounts for Jn.'s statement that the Sanhedrin would not go into Pilate's palace lest they should be rendered unclean and so unable to keep the Passover. Consequently, in Jn. we have the curious scene of the trial of Jesus being conducted in two places at once. The trial concludes with Pilate pronouncing sentence when seated outside his palace on the pavement called in Aramaic, *Gabbatha*.

(In Aldborough, Yorks, there is still to be seen a Roman tessellated pavement which marks the place of judicial proceedings in the little Roman town of Isurium. It is so constructed that when the judge took his seat, his eye was bound to fall on the Greek phrase 'Have mercy' inscribed in the mosaic of the pavement. Roman officials are recorded in certain cases to have taken their pavements with them into the Provinces.)

The dialogue between Jesus and Pilate has no parallel in the Synoptists.

In Mk. Pilate asks Jesus: Art thou the King of the Jews? He puts this question because the Sanhedrin had brought this accusation against Jesus as the reason for delivering Him up to the Procurator. Jesus made no reply to the accusation, which astonished Pilate greatly.

The Synoptists' accounts of the trial by Pilate clearly indicate that Pilate was favourably impressed by Jesus and was most unwilling to sentence Him to death on the charge of treason: perceiving that on account of envy (Mk. 15[10]) they had handed Jesus over as a prisoner.

Pilate, in view of the overwhelming evidence in support of the charge and the silence of the prisoner, is compelled to pronounce sentence. He bethinks him, however, of a device by which he may escape doing so. It was a custom on great Jewish feasts for the Roman Governor to pardon some notable prisoner, selected by the Jews to receive mercy. Pilate proposes, in accordance with this custom, to pardon Jesus, but the Jews insist on his pardoning a certain Jesus Bar-abbas, a notable (Mt.) revolutionary; and so Pilate, wishing to do 'the right thing' (Mk. 15^{15}), released Barabbas and delivered up Jesus, after He had been scourged, to be crucified.

Jesus is scourged. This punishment in Jn. is deliberately inflicted by Pilate as a substitute for crucifixion, but the Jews are implacable and demand the death sentence.

In Mk. and Mt. the scourging of Jesus is merely the cruel preliminary to His crucifixion and was often so practised by the Romans.

A theory has been recently put forth that it was not the Romans but the Jews who actually put Jesus to death, Pilate handing Him over to them. The evidence in support of such a contention is extremely weak.

Mt. alone relates an extraordinary story, that when Pilate was seated in judgement, his wife sent to him, bidding him to have nothing to do with this righteous man because that day she had suffered many things, on his account, in a dream. Mt. also relates that, in consequence, Pilate showed such repugnance to condemning Jesus that he actually washed his hands in the presence of the Jews as a sign to them that he refused to accept moral responsibility for passing the sentence of condemnation which they demanded. Whereupon all the Jews cried out: 'His blood be on us and on our children.'

It is difficult not to regard this incident as the product of dramatic imagination which viewed the terrible bloodshed of the Roman-Jewish war, which culminated in the destruction of Jerusalem in A.D. 70, as the Divine judgement visited on the Jews for the crucifixion of Jesus. It is scarcely credible historically that a Roman governor imbued with the principles of Roman justice could behave in this way in the presence of a subject population.

JESUS BEFORE HEROD ANTIPAS

Lk. alone relates, as we have noted, that Pilate, learning that Jesus was a Galilean, sent Him for trial to Herod Antipas, who at that time was in Jerusalem, no doubt for the Paschal feast. The Herod family, although in many cases bad men, seem to have been scrupulous in the observance of Jewish religious customs. Lk.'s statements that Herod had never seen Jesus, and was delighted to have the opportunity to become acquainted with Him, hoping to see some notable miracles done by Him: that Pilate's act of courtesy led to the ending of a difference which had formerly existed between Pilate and Herod, seem to possess the quality of historic probability.

The mocking of Jesus by Herod's soldiers and the arraying of Him in gorgeous apparel constitutes Lk.'s parallel to the mockery of Jesus by the Roman soldiers and is therefore of little historical value, as it seems hardly probable that the mockery by soldiers should have taken place twice.

The Mockery of Jesus by Roman Soldiers

MK. 15^{16-20a}

15 16 And the soldiers led him away within
the court, which is the Prætorium; and
17 they call together the whole band. And
they clothe him with purple, and plaiting
a crown of thorns, they put it on him;
18 and they began to salute him, Hail, King
19 of the Jews! And they smote his head
with a reed, and did spit upon him, and
20 bowing their knees worshipped him. And
when they had mocked him, they took
off from him the purple, and put on him
his garments.

MT. 27^{27-31a}

27 27 Then the soldiers of the governor took
Jesus into the palace, and gathered unto
28 him the whole band. And they stripped
him, and put on him a scarlet robe.
29 And they plaited a crown of thorns and
put it upon his head, and a reed in his
right hand; and they kneeled down before
him, and mocked him, saying, Hail,
30 King of the Jews! And they spat upon
him, and took the reed and smote him on
31 the head. And when they had mocked
him, they took off from him the robe, and
put on him his garments.

LK. OMITS

JN. 19^{2-3}

19 2 And the soldiers plaited a crown of
thorns, and put it on his head, and arrayed
3 him in a purple garment; and they came
unto him, and said, Hail, King of the
Jews! and they struck him with their
hands.

After being condemned to death Jesus is handed over to the Roman soldiers charged with His execution. Before crucifying Him they lead Him away into the palace, probably the Castle of Antonia which was occupied by the Roman garrison of Jerusalem at this time. Mt. has ' prætorium '—the usual term for the headquarters of a Roman military commander or provincial governor.

Mk.'s 'led Him away into the Palace' (*v.*16) indirectly supports Jn.'s statement that the actual condemnation of Jesus took place in the open, outside the palace.

Mk. and Mt. have ' the whole band,' [probably *cohort* (600 soldiers) or *maniple* (200 soldiers)] learning that Jesus has been condemned to death for claiming to be the Emperor of the Jews, proceed to mock Him. [The word *basileus* (in Greek, king) was at this time used of the Roman Emperor.]

The soldiers dress Him in a scarlet military cloak (*chlamys*), a part of their own uniform (Mt.). Mk. has ' the purple ' and Jn. has ' a purple cloak.' Ancient writers seem to us very confused in their description of colours compared with ourselves. Mt.'s statement fits the circumstances best. Then, having plaited a wreath from some thorny creeper, in cruel imitation of the laurel wreath worn by the Roman Emperor (see Roman coins), they place it on His brow. [The translation ' crown of thorns ' is inaccurate. Oriental monarchs wore crowns, Roman emperors wreaths.]

Then they put a reed in His hand in imitation of the sceptre. The reed may have been the very reed which was used later to give Him drink on the Cross. They then saluted Him in military fashion (raising the right hand), saying, Hail, Emperor of the Jews. (*Ave, Imperator!*) (Mk.) Mt. adds: they bowed the knee before Him in mockery. This seems unlikely. The soldiers then treated Jesus with brutal insult and violence.

It is important to compare this mocking of Jesus by the soldiers with the mocking of Him by the officials and servants of the Sanhedrin after His condemnation by that body. Whilst the former is characteristically Roman, the latter is characteristically Jewish. The Jewish officials salute Jesus as Messiah, not as Emperor. They cover His head and bid Him prophesy; because as Messiah He would be possessed of the prophetic spirit. (Mk. 14^{65}.)

It will be observed that the Evangelists record six mockings of Jesus by (1) the High Priest's servants, (2) Herod Antipas and his soldiers, (3) the soldiers of the Roman garrison, (4) the general public, (5) priests and scribes, (6) the two crucified brigands.

THE CRUCIFIXION

MK. 15^{20b-41}

15 20 And they lead him out to crucify him.
21 And they compel one passing by,
Simon of Cyrene, coming from the
country, the father of Alexander and
Rufus, to go *with them*, that he might
22 bear his cross. And they bring him unto
the place Golgotha, which is, being inter-
23 preted, The place of a skull. And they
offered him wine mingled with myrrh:
24 but he received it not. And they crucify
him, and part his garments among them,
casting lots upon them, what each should
25 take. And it was the third hour, and
26 they crucified him. And the superscription of his accusation was written over,
27 THE KING OF THE JEWS. And with him
they crucify two robbers; one on his right
29 hand, and one on his left. And they
that passed by railed on him, wagging
their heads, and saying, Ha! thou that
destroyest the temple, and buildest it in
30 three days, save thyself, and come down
31 from the cross. In like manner also the
chief priests mocking *him* among themselves with the scribes said, He saved
32 others; himself he cannot save. Let the
Christ, the King of Israel, now come
down from the cross, that we may see
and believe. And they that were crucified with him reproached him.
33 And when the sixth hour was come,
there was darkness over the whole land
34 until the ninth hour. And at the ninth
hour Jesus cried with a loud voice, Eloi,
Eloi, lama sabachthani? which is, being
interpreted, My God, my God, why hast
35 thou forsaken me? And some of them
that stood by, when they heard it, said,
36 Behold, he calleth Elijah. And one ran,
and filling a sponge full of vinegar, put
it on a reed, and gave him to drink, saying, Let be; let us see whether Elijah
37 cometh to take him down. And Jesus
uttered a loud voice, and gave up the
38 ghost. And the veil of the temple was
rent in twain from the top to the bottom.
39 And when the centurion, which stood by
over against him, saw that he so gave up

MT. 27^{31b-56}

27 31 And led him away to crucify him.
32 And as they came out, they found a
man of Cyrene, Simon by name: him
they compelled to go *with them*, that he
33 might bear his cross. And when they
were come unto a place called Golgotha,
34 that is to say, The place of a skull, they
gave him wine to drink mingled with
gall: and when he had tasted it, he would
35 not drink. And when they had crucified
him, they parted his garments among
36 them, casting lots: and they sat and
37 watched him there. And they set up
over his head his accusation written, THIS
38 IS JESUS THE KING OF THE JEWS. Then are
there crucified with him two robbers, one
on the right hand, and one on the left.
39 And they that passed by railed on him,
40 wagging their heads, and saying, Thou
that destroyest the temple, and buildest it
in three days, save thyself: if thou art the
Son of God, come down from the cross.
41 In like manner also the chief priests
mocking *him*, with the scribes and elders,
42 said, He saved others; himself he cannot
save. He is the King of Israel; let him
now come down from the cross, and we
43 will believe on him. He trusteth on
God; let him deliver him now, if he
desireth him: for he said, I am the Son
44 of God. And the robbers also that were
crucified with him cast upon him the
same reproach.
45 Now from the sixth hour there was
darkness over all the land until the ninth
46 hour. And about the ninth hour Jesus
cried with a loud voice, saying, Eli, Eli,
lama sabachthani? that is, My God, my
47 God, why hast thou forsaken me? And
some of them that stood there, when they
heard it, said, This man calleth Elijah.
48 And straightway one of them ran, and
took a sponge, and filled it with vinegar,
and put it on a reed, and gave him to
49 drink. And the rest said, Let be; let us
see whether Elijah cometh to save him.
50 And Jesus cried again with a loud voice,
51 and yielded up his spirit. And behold,

the ghost, he said, Truly this man was
40 the Son of God. And there were also
women beholding from afar: among
whom *were* both Mary Magdalene, and
Mary the mother of James the less and
41 of Joses, and Salome; who, when he was
in Galilee, followed him, and ministered
unto him; and many other women which
came up with him unto Jerusalem.

the veil of the temple was rent in twain
from the top to the bottom; and the earth
52 did quake; and the rocks were rent: and
the tombs were opened; and many bodies
of the saints that had fallen asleep were
53 raised; and coming forth out of the tombs
after his resurrection they entered into
the holy city and appeared unto many.
54 Now the centurion, and they that were
with him watching Jesus, when they saw
the earthquake, and the things that were
done, feared exceedingly, saying, Truly
55 this was the Son of God. And many
women were there beholding from afar,
which had followed Jesus from Galilee,
56 ministering unto him: among whom was
Mary Magdalene, and Mary the mother
of James and Joses, and the mother of
the sons of Zebedee.

LK. 23^{26-49}

23 26 And when they led him away, they
laid hold upon one Simon of Cyrene,
coming from the country, and laid on
him the cross, to bear it after Jesus.
27 And there followed him a great multitude of the people, and of women who
28 bewailed and lamented him. But Jesus
turning unto them said, Daughters of
Jerusalem, weep not for me, but weep for
29 yourselves, and for your children. For
behold, the days are coming, in which
they shall say, Blessed are the barren,
and the wombs that never bare, and the
30 breasts that never gave suck. Then shall
they begin to say to the mountains, Fall
31 on us; and to the hills, Cover us. For if
they do these things in the green tree,
what shall be done in the dry?
32 And there were also two others, malefactors, led with him to be put to death.
33 And when they came unto the place
which is called The skull, there they
crucified him, and the malefactors, one
on the right hand and the other on the
34 left. And Jesus said, Father, forgive
them; for they know not what they do.
And parting his garments among them,
35 they cast lots. And the people stood
beholding. And the rulers also scoffed
at him, saying, He saved others; let him
save himself, if this is the Christ of God,
36 his chosen. And the soldiers also mocked
him, coming to him, offering him vinegar,
37 and saying, If thou art the King of the
38 Jews, save thyself. And there was also a
superscription over him, THIS IS THE KING
OF THE JEWS.
39 And one of the malefactors which were
hanged railed on him, saying, Art not
thou the Christ? save thyself and us.
40 But the other answered, and rebuking
him said, Dost thou not even fear God,

JN. 19^{17-30}

19 17 And he went out, bearing the cross for
himself, unto the place called The place
of a skull, which is called in Hebrew
18 Golgotha: where they crucified him, and
with him two others, on either side one,
19 and Jesus in the midst. And Pilate wrote
a title also, and put it on the cross. And
there was written, JESUS OF NAZARETH,
20 THE KING OF THE JEWS. This title therefore read many of the Jews: for the place
where Jesus was crucified was nigh to the
city: and it was written in Hebrew, *and* in
21 Latin, *and* in Greek. The chief priests of
the Jews therefore said to Pilate, Write
not, The King of the Jews; but, that he
22 said, I am King of the Jews. Pilate
answered, What I have written I have
written.
23 The soldiers therefore, when they had
crucified Jesus, took his garments, and
made four parts, to every soldier a part;
and also the coat: now the coat was
without seam, woven from the top
24 throughout. They said therefore one to
another, Let us not rend it, but cast lots
for it, whose it shall be: that the scripture
might be fulfilled, which saith,

They parted my garments among
them,
And upon my vesture did they cast
lots.

These things therefore the soldiers did.
25 But there were standing by the cross of
Jesus his mother, and his mother's sister,
Mary the *wife* of Clopas, and Mary
26 Magdalene. When Jesus therefore saw
his mother, and the disciple standing by,
whom he loved, he saith unto his mother,
27 Woman, behold, thy son! Then saith he
to the disciple, Behold, thy mother!
And from that hour the disciple took her
unto his own *home*.

seeing thou art in the same condemna-
41 tion? And we indeed justly; for we
receive the due reward of our deeds: but
42 this man hath done nothing amiss. And
he said, Jesus, remember me when thou
43 comest in thy kingdom. And he said
unto him, Verily I say unto thee, To-day
shalt thou be with me in Paradise.
44 And it was now about the sixth hour,
and a darkness came over the whole land
45 until the ninth hour, the sun's light failing: and the veil of the temple was rent
46 in the midst. And when Jesus had cried
with a loud voice, he said, Father, into
thy hands I commend my spirit: and
having said this, he gave up the ghost.
47 And when the centurion saw what was
done, he glorified God, saying, Certainly
48 this was a righteous man. And all the
multitudes that came together to this
sight, when they beheld the things that
were done, returned smiting their breasts.
49 And all his acquaintance, and the women
that followed with him from Galilee,
stood afar off, seeing these things.

28 After this Jesus, knowing that all things
are now finished, that the scripture
might be accomplished, saith, I thirst.
29 There was set there a vessel full of
vinegar: so they put a sponge full of the
vinegar upon hyssop, and brought it to
30 his mouth. When Jesus therefore had
received the vinegar, he said, It is
finished: and he bowed his head, and
gave up his spirit.

[The R.V., following the best manuscripts, omits Mk. 15^{28}, And the scripture was fulfilled which saith, And he was reckoned with transgressors.]

A centurion was in charge of the four Roman soldiers who were to act as executioners.

They lead Jesus, possibly along the modern *Via Dolorosa*, outside Jerusalem (cf. Heb. 13^{12}, 'Jesus . . . suffered without the gate'). No satisfactory location of Golgotha (Aramaic) or Calvary (Latin) has been achieved. Whether it was called 'the place of the skull' because it was a knoll shaped like a man's head or whether because it was littered with the skulls of executed criminals, is uncertain. Jerome's legend that it was the burial-place of 'the skull of Adam' is, of course, purely fictitious.

On the road out, the soldiers 'commandeer' Simon the Cyrenian to carry the cross (Lk. says behind Jesus). [The word used here is Persian and refers to the *compelling* of civilians to perform official duties. It is the same word as is used in the saying of Jesus: If a man *compel* you to go a thousand paces, go with him two thousand.]

Simon was a member of that great Jewish dispersion (*diaspora*) perhaps most numerous in North Africa. Cyrene is situated on the coast west of Alexandria.

Mk. alone states that Simon was the father of Alexander and Rufus. This no doubt is because Alexander and Rufus were known to the Roman Church, for which the Gospel was primarily written.

It is possible that this Rufus and his mother (who would be the widow of Simon the Cyrenian) are included in St. Paul's greetings to the Church in Rome (Rom. 16^{13}). He is here called 'chosen in the Lord.' It is not without significance that they should have become converts to the Christian religion.

The reason for the 'commandeering' of Simon (who was coming into Jerusalem from the country) is, that Jesus was physically unable to bear the Cross.

They 'bring him' may be translated they 'carry' or 'bear him.' In other words: whilst Simon carries the Cross, the four soldiers carry Jesus who is in a state of physical collapse.

It should be noted that Jn. contradicts all this. He states: that Jesus went forth 'bearing the Cross for himself' (19^{17}). Lk. asserts that a great multitude of women bewailed Jesus, but He bids 'the daughters of Jersualem' to weep for themselves and for their children in view of the horrors which are to overtake the city.

When they get to the place of execution Jesus is offered myrrhed wine. This was an anæsthetic mercifully prepared by the women of Jerusalem for criminals condemned to death. Jesus, however, refuses to receive it.

Mt. changes 'myrrhed wine' into wine mingled with gall in order to secure a fulfilment of what he regards as a Messianic prophecy in Ps. 69^{21}.

> '*They gave me also gall for my food*
> *And in my thirst they gave me vinegar to drink.*'

Two robbers are crucified with Him, one on the right hand and the other on the left. These were probably Zealot revolutionaries reduced to brigandage. The Apocryphal Gospels assign them names: Zoathan and Cain, Disnas and Gestas, Titus and Dumachus.

Before Jesus is crucified, His garments are stripped off and divided by lot among his four executioners.

Jn. adds, that his undergarment, being woven without seam, was not torn into pieces. This detail of the clothes of Jesus, distributed by lot, has probably been inserted in the narrative of the Crucifixion as a fulfilment of Ps. 22^{18}.

'They parted my garments among them and on my vesture did they cast lots.'

An inscription (*titlos*) was set over the Cross of Jesus, possibly written with gypsum on a black board, indicating the reason for his execution. The inscription is given differently in each of the four Gospels:

Mk., The Emperor of the Jews.

Mt., This is Jesus, the Emperor of the Jews.

Lk., This is the Emperor of the Jews.

Jn., Jesus, the Nazarene, Emperor of the Jews.

Jn. relates that the Jewish authorities objected to the inscription (indeed they had already affirmed, 'We have no Emperor but Cæsar') and tried to get Pilate to alter it, but he gruffly replied: What I have written, I have written. Jn. also relates that the inscription was in Hebrew, Latin, and Greek, the languages respectively of Religion, Empire, and Culture.

Mk. states that Jesus was crucified at the third hour, i.e. 9 a.m. Jn. asserts that 'it was about the sixth hour.'

According to the Synoptists, Jesus hung on the Cross some six hours before He died, but according to Jn., only three.

Strange Portents accompanied the Passion

1. According to Mt., an earthquake rent the rocks in the neighbourhood of Jerusalem, and dead saints came forth from their sepulchres and appeared in the streets of Jerusalem to many.

This will remind the reader of Shakespeare's account of the death of Julius Cæsar: 'when ghosts did gibber in the streets of Rome.'

2. The sun was eclipsed, so Lk. This is an impossibility as the sun cannot be eclipsed when the moon is at the full, as it is at the Paschal season. (Hence later scribes have changed 'eclipsed' into 'was darkened.'

3. Mk., followed by Mt., says, there was darkness over the whole land (or earth) from the sixth to the ninth hour—12 noon to 3 p.m. This may have been due to heavy clouds. History records certain remarkable 'dark days' on which no eclipse occurred.

4. Mk., Mt., and Lk. relate that, as Jesus died, the veil of the shrine of the Temple was rent in twain from the top to the bottom. [The Temple had two veils—the outer veil which separated the Holy Place from the Court of the Priests, and the inner veil which separated the Holy Place from the Holy of Holies.] No doubt it was the inner veil that is meant, because that suits the symbolism of the Epistle to the Hebrews which sees in this veil that which separates man from God but which was removed by the sacrificial death of Jesus by which all men possess a new and living way of access to God. (Heb. 6^{19}, 9^{3}, 10^{20}.)

It seems not unreasonable to doubt whether all these portents are actual historical occurrences and not merely symbolical narratives expressing the terror and mystery which surrounded the death of Jesus. Man was dismayed: nature convulsed.

While hanging on the Cross Jesus is 'mocked' again and by three classes:

1. By the passers by: 'Ah, thou that destroyest the temple, and buildest it in three days, Save thyself, and come down from the cross.'

2. By the priests and scribes: 'He saved others: himself he cannot save. Let Christ the King of Israel descend now from the cross that we may see and believe.'

3. By the brigands who were crucified with Him.

Lk. alone relates that only one brigand reviled him and the other brigand rebuked the reviler.

All these mockings stress the Messianic claim of Jesus as does the title on the Cross and the incidents connected with the four trials.

'Words' from the Cross

Much difference exists as to the 'words' uttered from the Cross by Jesus. There are seven in all. Mk. and Mt. have only one 'word'—*Eloi, Eloi, lama sabachthani.*

Lk. has three 'words':

1. Father, forgive them, for they know not what they do.
2. To-day shalt thou be with me in Paradise.
3. Father, into thy hands I commend my spirit.

Jn. has three ' words ' :

1. Woman, behold thy Son; [then said he to the disciple] behold thy mother.
2. I thirst.
3. It has been fulfilled or it is finished.

Eloi, Eloi

This ' word ' from the Cross bristles with difficulties: critical, exegetical, Christological.

What is the evidence for it having been spoken by Jesus?

(1) Although Mk. and Mt. alone give it, yet Mt. relies here on Mk. According to universal Church tradition Mk.'s Gospel is St. Peter's, yet there is no evidence that Peter was present at the Crucifixion, or sufficiently near to hear anything said by Jesus. Yet he may have been among the crowd watching afar off, and have heard the words, since Mk. relates (possibly to explain this very point) that Jesus ' cried with a loud voice ' (so also Mt.).

(2) The words are in Aramaic or a mixture of Aramaic and Hebrew. We can generally feel secure that the words given in Aramaic in Mk.'s Gospel are the actual utterances of Jesus.

(3) Lk. seems to have known of it, but he interprets it as relating the eclipse of the sun or the sun's desertion. [The Greek *heliou* (of the sun) and *eloi* (my God) might be confused with each other]. The account of the sun's eclipse in Lk. occupies exactly the same position as Eloi, Eloi in Mk. and Mt.

Is this deliberate apologetic on Lk.'s part akin to that which has led him to give us the parable of the barren fig tree for the narrative of the cursing of the barren fig tree? We cannot decide whether Lk. is deliberately apologetic here, but in view of the impossibility of an eclipse we cannot regard him here as historical.

What do the ' words ' signify?

1. Those nearest to the cross supposed that Jesus was calling on Elijah to help Him.

2. Primitive Christians understood that Jesus was calling on God.

3. The early Gnostic heretics interpreted the utterance as ' My strength, my strength,' etc., and believed that the man Jesus was calling on the Æon, Christ, who left him at that moment. (The Gnostics held that the Æon, Christ, entered into Him at His baptism, but deserted Him at His crucifixion.)

4. Calvin interpreted this utterance as indicating that Jesus, as the expiatory sacrifice for the sins of the world, was experiencing the despair of a lost soul who feels himself to be deserted by God.

Are the words, ' Eloi, Eloi,' etc., a quotation or are they original? The utterance is usually taken to be the opening words of Ps. 22, which describes the suffering of one of God's saints who makes his supplication to God, and in the end, experiences a happy issue out of all his afflictions.

Primitive Christians regarded Ps. 22 as Messianic, and its fulfilment by Jesus would be for them a proof of His Messiahship. This belief of theirs may have led the earliest Christians to interpret the loud, but perhaps not very articulate, cry of the dying Saviour in this way. Whatever difficulties the utterance of these words by Jesus may have created for later Christians, they would seem to have had none for Mk. and Mt. The utterance of them would seem to be entirely in keeping with the Messianic character and claim of Jesus. All that had been written in the Scriptures concerning Himself Jesus, the Christ, must fulfil to the letter.

If Lk. omitted the words deliberately and not through misunderstanding, it might well be because Gentile Christians at this period (it was different later) were not as interested in and impressed by fulfilments of Messianic prophecy by Jesus as were the Jewish Christian readers of Mt.

Jn. (who must have known of the Eloi, Eloi) omits it possibly because in his day it was being used by the Gnostics in support of their curious and heretical views, and the Gospel of John is in some respects strongly anti-Gnostic.

If this utterance be a quotation from Ps. 22[1], then, although it expresses a sense of desertion by God, yet that experience may have been, in view of the tenor of Ps. 22, the prelude to the restoration of the sense of communion between the Divine Father and His Messianic Son. To assert, as some do, on the strength of this utterance, that Jesus died in despair, is to go too far. Calvin's interpretation is theological rather than critical, and can only be maintained by those who accept the Calvinist theology. But the difficulties in the way of accepting this utterance of Jesus as historic are very considerable. They are in conflict both with the Lukan as well as the Johannine accounts of the death of Jesus. The conflict with Jn. may not trouble us much, as his Gospel is dominated by a spirit of symbolism and mysticism. But it is otherwise with Lk.

The three words from the Cross which Jn. records are not prayers to God; but two, of the three words from the Cross, recorded by Lk., are prayers, and seem to provide sound reasons for regarding them as historical.

(*a*) They both begin with the word Father, which is typical of the prayers of Jesus. We may well doubt whether any prayer ascribed to Him which has not the word Father in it, can be His.

(*b*) The words of dying Stephen, who ' prayed for his murderers,' plainly reflect the influence of Lk.'s account of the prayer of Jesus for his executioners.

(*c*) Lk.'s Gospel, undoubtedly, makes use of much original material drawn from feminine sources. It was women followers of Jesus who stood nearest to the Cross, and doubtless Luke owes to them these words from the Cross which are not recorded in the other Gospels.

(*d*) Lk.'s Passion narrative is not, like Mt.'s, dependent upon Mk. He draws on other sources (Herodian, feminine, etc.) which appear to be of high historic value.

Lk.'s account, in contrast to that of Mk., certainly reflects the impression which the Passion of Jesus made upon the Primitive Christian disciples. He set His disciples an example how to suffer ' as Christians.' This is taught explicitly in the First Epistle of Peter, a letter intended to prepare Christians to face pagan persecution:

For even hereunto were ye called: because Christ also suffered for you, leaving you an example, that ye should follow his steps: who did no sin, neither was guile found in his mouth: who, when he was reviled, reviled not again: when he suffered he threatened not: but committed himself to him that judgeth righteously. (1 Pet. 2^{21-23}.)

The manner of His dying, so the three Synoptists relate, impressed profoundly the pagan centurion, but only Lk.'s account records those things in the dying of Jesus which would create such an impression. And that account would seem to have come, not from all the disciples, who forsook Him and fled, but from his women-followers, some of whom stood near the Cross.

The precise interpretation of the Eloi, Eloi is a difficult matter. This is indicated by the number of variants in the text and in the versions.

Of the many variants the following should be noted:

(1) Lamsa, in his translation, *The Gospels according to the Eastern Version*, renders the passage, 'My God, my God, for this I was kept' (i.e. 'destined').

(2) 'My God, my God, how hast thou glorified me.' This is a very improbable rendering, but possibly it is the source of Jn. $12^{27, 28}$:

Now is my soul troubled: and what shall I say? Father, save me from this hour: but for this cause came I unto this hour. Father, glorify thy name. Then came there a voice from heaven, saying, I have both glorified it, and will glorify it again.

(3) Why didst thou put me to shame (or revile me)? Of course, if the words uttered by Jesus are a quotation from Ps. 22, there is no doubt that they mean 'forsake' or 'desert' me.

There is no doubt that Mk.'s and Mt.'s 'word' from the Cross did create much difficulty for the Christian Church and particularly the Christian Church of modern times. And that is one reason why historical critics have felt that the 'word' must be a genuine one. No modern Christian could possibly fictitiously put such words into the mouth of the dying Saviour. They voice for us feelings of intolerable anguish: they suggest the breakdown of faith in God and therefore we feel sure that they must be genuine. Nevertheless, we do well to remember that the impression made on the Primitive Church was quite different from that which these words make on the modern mind. The Primitive Church felt that by His utterance of these words the Saviour identified Himself with the sufferer in Ps. 22, and that the drama of His Passion fulfilled that Scripture.

THE BURIAL

MK. 15^{42-47}

15 42 And when even was now come,
because it was the Preparation, that is,
43 the day before the sabbath, there came
Joseph of Arimathæa, a councillor of
honourable estate, who also himself was
looking for the kingdom of God; and he
boldly went in unto Pilate, and asked for
44 the body of Jesus. And Pilate marvelled
if he were already dead: and calling
unto him the centurion, he asked him
whether he had been any while dead.

MT. 27^{57-61}

27 57 And when even was come, there came
a rich man from Arimathæa, named
Joseph, who also himself was Jesus' dis-
58 ciple: this man went to Pilate, and asked
for the body of Jesus. Then Pilate com-
59 manded it to be given up. And Joseph
took the body, and wrapped it in a clean
60 linen cloth, and laid it in his own new
tomb, which he had hewn out in the
rock: and he rolled a great stone to the
61 door of the tomb, and departed. And

45 And when he learned it of the centurion,
46 he granted the corpse to Joseph. And
he bought a linen cloth, and taking him
down, wound him in the linen cloth, and
laid him in a tomb which had been hewn
out of a rock; and he rolled a stone against
47 the door of the tomb. And Mary
Magdalene and Mary the *mother* of Joses
beheld where he was laid.

Mary Magdalene was there, and the other Mary, sitting over against the sepulchre.

LK. 23^{50-56}

23 50 And behold, a man named Joseph,
who was a councillor, a good man and a
51 righteous (he had not consented to their
counsel and deed), *a man* of Arimathæa,
a city of the Jews, who was looking for
52 the kingdom of God: this man went to
Pilate, and asked for the body of Jesus.
53 And he took it down, and wrapped it in
a linen cloth, and laid him in a tomb that
was hewn in stone, where never man had
54 yet lain. And it was the day of the Pre-
55 paration, and the sabbath drew on. And
the women, which had come with him
out of Galilee, followed after, and beheld
the tomb, and how his body was laid.
56 And they returned, and prepared spices
and ointments. And on the sabbath
they rested according to the commandment.

JN. 19^{38-42}

19 38 And after these things Joseph of
Arimathæa, being a disciple of Jesus, but
secretly for fear of the Jews, asked of
Pilate that he might take away the body
of Jesus: and Pilate gave *him* leave. He
came therefore, and took away his body.
39 And there came also Nicodemus, he who
at the first came to him by night, bringing
a mixture of myrrh and aloes, about a
40 hundred pound *weight*. So they took the
body of Jesus, and bound it in linen
cloths with the spices, as the custom of
41 the Jews is to bury. Now in the place
where he was crucified there was a
garden; and in the garden a new tomb
42 wherein was never man yet laid. There
then because of the Jews' Preparation
(for the tomb was nigh at hand) they
laid Jesus.

Jesus died on the Preparation of the Sabbath (so Mk. relates). The Preparation was the name given to the Friday before the weekly Sabbath. The Preparation of course ended at sunset when the Sabbath began. It was contrary to the Jewish law (Dt. 21^{22-23}) that the bodies of impaled criminals should remain unburied after sunset. No such rule applies in the case of the victims of Roman justice. The bodies of the crucified remained on the cross, like the bodies of mediæval criminals on the gallows, until they rotted away. The Romans, however, may well have been sensitive to Jewish religious feeling, especially at an important religious festival when Jerusalem was crowded with thousands of Jewish fanatics, and so have allowed the bodies of the crucified to be taken down at sunset. Such a concession to Jewish religious feeling must, however, have entailed in many cases the violent death of the crucified by their executioners, for it was not unusual for the victims of crucifixion to take days in dying.

Jn. relates that accordingly the legs of the brigands were broken and the side of Jesus pierced with a lance.

The Synoptists relate nothing of this. All four Evangelists state that a certain Joseph who belonged to Arimathæa (Ramathaim = the two Peaks) undertook the burial of the body of Jesus. Joseph (according to Mt. and Jn.) was a disciple of Jesus. He was also an 'honourable councillor,' that is, a member of the Sanhedrin. Mt. alone states that he was rich. This statement is no doubt due to the influence of Old Testament prophecy. In Is. 53^9 it is written of the Suffering Servant, that 'they made his grave with the wicked, and with the rich in his death.'

Jn. adds that Joseph was accompanied by Nicodemus, evidently another member of the Sanhedrin. Mk. stresses, however, the courage of Joseph, who it would appear dared alone to go in to Pilate and ask for the body. Pilate was surprised that Jesus had already died. Mk.'s narrative of the Passion, which relates that Jesus was in a state of physical collapse on the road to Calvary, does not surprise us when he relates the sudden decease of Jesus on the cross. Mk. has already related the terrible strain of the week before the Passion—the long hours, the incessant controversy, possibly insufficient food, the anguish at Gethsemane, the preceding night of judicial examinations, insult, and violence. That death should ensue rapidly in such a case was natural enough. Commentators have been concerned to account for it. Stroud in his volume, *The Physical Causes for the Death of Christ*, believes it to have been due to the rupture of the heart. This he regards as borne out by the loud cry at the moment of death, and the 'water and blood' incident related in Jn.

Although Joseph was sprung from Ramathaim (possibly the Ramathaim-Zophim of 1 Sam. 1^1, or from another Ramathaim near Lydda, 1 *Macc.* 11^{34}), he would seem to have been a resident of Jerusalem and the possessor of a rock-hewn sepulchre outside the walls of Jerusalem near Calvary. Many such rock-hewn sepulchres may be seen to-day in the vicinity of Jerusalem.

Jn. states that the tomb was in a garden, no doubt a walled enclosure, and that it was close to the place of crucifixion.

Mt.'s remark that the women sat 'over against' it, suggests that the sepulchre was situated on a hillside in a valley, on the other side of which (presumably the Jerusalem side) the women sat. This opinion that the sepulchre was hewn on a hillside is also supported by Mk.'s statement (16^4) that the women on approaching it looked up. These points are small, but they do seem to indicate a definite primitive Christian tradition of a particular sepulchre.

Mt. states that it was a new tomb, and Lk. 'a tomb . . . where never man had yet lain.' (We have already indicated the sacredness of 'newness' in Judaism.) When Joseph had removed the body from the cross, he placed it in his rock-hewn sepulchre, and rolled a stone in front of its entrance. East of the Jordan there exist to-day doors and shutters of solid stone (basalt). Presumably the stone which closed the doorway of Joseph's sepulchre was shaped like one of our modern grindstones and was rolled in a rock groove in front of the doorway. This rolling of the stone required considerable physical force: 'the women' are represented as unable themselves to roll the stone, and Joseph in his task of burial was no doubt assisted by his servants. (Mt. would appear to have regarded the stone as a great block or boulder, for he represents the Angel of the Resurrection as sitting upon it.) Mk. relates that Mary Magdalene and Mary, the wife or mother of Joses, beheld the place where Jesus was buried. Mt. has 'Mary Magdalene was there and the other Mary, sitting over against the sepulchre.' Lk. indicates that a number of women from Galilee watched the interment and states that they returned and prepared spices and ointments, but were not able to take them at once, when prepared, to the sepulchre, as the Sabbath ensued immediately, on which they were compelled to rest.

Jn., on the other hand, relates that Joseph and Nicodemus brought with them 'about a hundred pound weight' mixture of myrrh and aloes, which they bound up in the linen cloths in which they wrapped the corpse.

It seems impossible to reconcile Lk. and Jn. on this point. Mk. and Mt. say nothing about 'spices,' and it seems very unlikely that in the very short period before the Sabbath began they could have been used in this most hurried entombment.

A number of modern critics have cast doubt on the whole story of the entombment, and have assumed that the body of Jesus (like that of the prophet Urijah) was cast into the grave of the common people. All four Evangelists, however, are agreed, that the body of Jesus was laid in the sepulchre of Joseph of Arimathæa, and if, as there is good reason to believe, the Gospel narratives are in the main historical, there is no sound reason for rejecting the story of the entombment.

On the other hand, Mt.'s story (peculiar to himself) relating the official sealing of the sepulchre by Pilate and the setting of a guard of Roman soldiers, at the request of the Jewish authorities and with the purpose of preventing the body of Jesus being stolen by His disciples (in order that they might thereby be enabled to propagate the story of the Resurrection of Jesus), would seem to be entirely unhistorical. It is plainly apologetic in its motive. It is intended to contradict, by adducing what is regarded as indubitable evidence, the Jewish slander that the disciples of Jesus stole His body from the sepulchre preparatory to their spreading abroad the falsehood of His resurrection.

Obviously, this invention belongs to a later period, when Judaism was making strenuous efforts to discredit the Gospel of the Resurrection as proclaimed by the primitive Christian Church.

Only more improbable than that Roman soldiers should sleep on guard, is that, for any sum of money offered to them by the Jews, they should confess to the Roman authorities that they had done so, since the penalty for such an offence was death.

RESURRECTION NARRATIVES

MK. 16^{1-8}

16 1 And when the sabbath was past, Mary
Magdalene, and Mary the *mother* of
James, and Salome, bought spices, that
2 they might come and anoint him. And
very early on the first day of the week,
they come to the tomb when the sun was
3 risen. And they were saying among
themselves, Who shall roll us away the
4 stone from the door of the tomb? and
looking up, they see that the stone is rolled
5 back: for it was exceeding great. And
entering into the tomb, they saw a young
man sitting on the right side, arrayed in a
6 white robe; and they were amazed. And
he saith unto them, Be not amazed: ye
seek Jesus, the Nazarene, which hath been
crucified: he is risen; he is not here: be-
7 hold, the place where they laid him! But
go, tell his disciples and Peter, He goeth
before you into Galilee: there shall ye see
8 him, as he said unto you. And they went
out, and fled from the tomb; for trembling
and astonishment had come upon them:

MT. 28

28 1 Now late on the sabbath day, as it
began to dawn toward the first *day* of the
week, came Mary Magdalene and the
2 other Mary to see the sepulchre. And
behold, there was a great earthquake;
for an angel of the Lord descended from
heaven, and came and rolled away the
3 stone, and sat upon it. His appearance
was as lightning, and his raiment white
4 as snow: and for fear of him the watchers
did quake, and became as dead men.
5 And the angel answered and said unto
the women, Fear not ye: for I know that
ye seek Jesus, which hath been crucified.
6 He is not here; for he is risen, even as he
said. Come, see the place where the
7 Lord lay. And go quickly, and tell his
disciples, He is risen from the dead; and
lo, he goeth before you into Galilee;
there shall ye see him: lo, I have told
8 you. And they departed quickly from
the tomb with fear and great joy, and ran
9 to bring his disciples word. And behold,

and they said nothing to any one; for
they were afraid.

LONG ENDING OF MK. (MK. 16^{9-20})

16 9 Now when he was risen early on the
first day of the week, he appeared first to
Mary Magdalene, from whom he had
10 cast out seven devils. She went and told
them that had been with him, as they
11 mourned and wept. And they, when
they heard that he was alive, and had
been seen of her, disbelieved.
12 And after these things he was manifested in another form unto two of them,
as they walked, on their way into the
13 country. And they went away and told
it unto the rest: neither believed they
them.[1] [And they defended themselves
saying, This age of lawlessness and unbelief is under Satan who through the
unclean spirits suffereth not the true
power of God to be apprehended: wherefore reveal thy righteousness now. *So*
spake they to Christ, and Christ said
unto them, The term of the years of the
authority of Satan had been fulfilled, but
there draw near other terrible things.
And on behalf of them that had sinned
was I delivered up unto death, that they
might turn unto the truth and sin no
more, that they might inherit the
heavenly, spiritual and incorruptible
glory of righteousness.]
14 And afterward he was manifested unto
the eleven themselves as they sat at meat;
and he upbraided them with their unbelief and hardness of heart, because they
believed not them which had seen him
15 after he was risen. And he said unto
them, Go ye into all the world, and
preach the gospel to the whole creation.
16 He that believeth and is baptized shall
be saved; but he that disbelieveth shall be
17 condemned. And these signs shall follow
them that believe: in my name shall they
cast out devils; they shall speak with new
tongues; they shall take up serpents, and
18 if they drink any deadly thing it shall in
no wise hurt them; they shall lay hands
on the sick, and they shall recover.
19 So then the Lord Jesus, after he had
spoken unto them, was received up into
heaven, and sat down at the right hand
20 of God. And they went forth, and
preached everywhere, the Lord working
with them, and confirming the word by
the signs that followed. Amen.

SHORT ENDING OF MK.

But all that had been commanded them
they briefly reported to Peter and those

[1] The bracketed passage occurs only in the Washington manuscript.

Jesus met them, saying, All hail. And
they came and took hold of his feet, and
10 worshipped him. Then saith Jesus unto
them, Fear not: go tell my brethren that
they depart into Galilee, and there shall
they see me.
11 Now while they were going, behold,
some of the guard came into the city, and
told unto the chief priests all the things
12 that were come to pass. And when they
were assembled with the elders, and had
taken counsel, they gave large money
13 unto the soldiers, saying, Say ye, His
disciples came by night, and stole him
14 away while we slept. And if this come
to the governor's ears, we will persuade
15 him, and rid you of care. So they took
the money, and did as they were taught:
and this saying was spread abroad
among the Jews, *and continueth* until this
day.
16 But the eleven disciples went into
Galilee, unto the mountain where Jesus
17 had appointed them. And when they
saw him, they worshipped *him*: but some
18 doubted. And Jesus came to them and
spake unto them, saying, All authority
hath been given unto me in heaven and
19 on earth. Go ye therefore, and make
disciples of all the nations, baptizing
them into the name of the Father and of
20 the Son and of the Holy Ghost: teaching
them to observe all things whatsoever I
commanded you: and lo, I am with you
alway, even unto the end of the world.

who were with him. And after these things
Jesus himself also appeared to them, and
from the East even to the West sent forth
through them the holy and incorruptible
proclamation of eternal salvation.

LK. 24

24 1 But on the first day of the week, at
early dawn, they came unto the tomb,
bringing the spices which they had pre-
2 pared. And they found the stone rolled
3 away from the tomb. And they entered
in, and found not the body of the Lord
4 Jesus. And it came to pass, while they
were perplexed thereabout, behold, two
men stood by them in dazzling apparel:
5 and as they were affrighted, and bowed
down their faces to the earth, they said
unto them, Why seek ye the living
6 among the dead? He is not here, but is
risen: remember how he spake unto you
7 when he was yet in Galilee, saying that
the Son of man must be delivered up into
the hands of sinful men, and be crucified,
8 and the third day rise again. And they
9 remembered his words, and returned
from the tomb, and told all these things
10 to the eleven, and to all the rest. Now
they were Mary Magdalene, and Joanna,
and Mary the *mother* of James: and the
other women with them told these things
11 unto the apostles. And these words appeared in their sight as idle talk; and they
12 disbelieved them. But Peter arose, and
ran unto the tomb; and stooping and
looking in, he seeth the linen cloths by
themselves; and he departed to his
home, wondering at that which was
come to pass.
13 And behold, two of them were going
that very day to a village named Emmaus, which was three-score furlongs
14 from Jerusalem. And they communed
with each other of all these things which
15 had happened. And it came to pass,
while they communed and questioned
together, that Jesus himself drew near,
16 and went with them. But their eyes
were holden that they should not know
17 him. And he said unto them, What
communications are these that ye have
one with another, as ye walk? And they
18 stood still, looking sad. And one of them,
named Cleopas, answering said unto
him, Dost thou alone sojourn in Jerusalem and not know the things which are
19 come to pass there in these days? And
he said unto them, What things? And
they said unto him, The things concerning Jesus of Nazareth, which was a
prophet mighty in deed and word before
20 God and all the people: and how the
chief priests and our rulers delivered him

JN. 20, 21

20 1 Now on the first *day* of the week cometh
Mary Magdalene early, while it was yet
dark, unto the tomb, and seeth the stone
2 taken away from the tomb. She runneth
therefore, and cometh to Simon Peter,
and to the other disciple, whom Jesus
loved, and saith unto them, They have
taken away the Lord out of the tomb,
and we know not where they have laid
3 him. Peter therefore went forth, and
the other disciple, and they went toward
4 the tomb. And they ran both together:
and the other disciple outran Peter, and
5 came first to the tomb; and stooping and
looking in, he seeth the linen cloths lying;
6 yet entered he not in. Simon Peter
therefore also cometh, following him, and
entered into the tomb; and be beholdeth
7 the linen cloths lying, and the napkin,
that was upon his head, not lying with
the linen cloths, but rolled up in a place
8 by itself. Then entered in therefore the
other disciple also, which came first to
9 the tomb, and he saw, and believed. For
as yet they knew not the scripture, that
10 he must rise again from the dead. So
the disciples went away again unto their
own home.
11 But Mary was standing without at the
tomb weeping: so, as she wept, she
12 stooped and looked into the tomb; and
she beholdeth two angels in white sitting,
one at the head, and one at the feet,
13 where the body of Jesus had lain. And
they say unto her, Woman, why weepest
thou? She saith unto them, Because
they have taken away my Lord, and I
know not where they have laid him.
14 When she had thus said, she turned herself back, and beholdeth Jesus standing,
15 and knew not that it was Jesus. Jesus
saith unto her, Woman, why weepest
thou? whom seekest thou? She, supposing him to be the gardener, saith unto
him, Sir, if thou hast borne him hence,
tell me where thou hast laid him, and I
16 will take him away. Jesus saith unto
her, Mary. She turneth herself, and
saith unto him in Hebrew, Rabboni;
17 which is to say, Master. Jesus saith to
her, Touch me not; for I am not yet
ascended unto the Father: but go unto
my brethren, and say to them, I ascend
unto my Father and your Father, and
18 my God and your God. Mary Magdalene cometh and telleth the disciples, I

up to be condemned to death, and cruci-
21 fied him. But we hoped that it was he
which should redeem Israel. Yea and
beside all this, it is now the third day
22 since these things came to pass. Moreover certain women of our company
amazed us, having been early at the
23 tomb; and when they found not his
body, they came, saying, that they had
also seen a vision of angels, which said
24 that he was alive. And certain of them
that were with us went to the tomb, and
found it even so as the women had said:
25 but him they saw not. And he said
unto them, O foolish men, and slow of
heart to believe in all that the prophets
26 have spoken! Behoved it not the Christ
to suffer these things, and to enter into his
27 glory? And beginning from Moses and
from all the prophets, he interpreted to
them in all the scriptures the things con-
28 cerning himself. And they drew nigh
unto the village, whither they were going:
and he made as though he would go
29 further. And they constrained him,
saying, Abide with us: for it is toward
evening, and the day is now far spent.
30 And he went in to abide with them. And
it came to pass, when he had sat down
with them to meat, he took the bread
and blessed it, and brake, and gave to
31 them. And their eyes were opened, and
they knew him; and he vanished out of
32 their sight. And they said one to
another, Was not our heart burning
within us, while he spake to us in the
way, while he opened to us the scrip-
33 tures? And they rose up that very hour,
and returned to Jerusalem, and found the
eleven gathered together, and them that
34 were with them, saying, The Lord is
risen indeed, and hath appeared to
35 Simon. And they rehearsed the things
that happened in the way, and how he was
known of them in the breaking of the
bread.

36 And as they spake these things, he
himself stood in the midst of them, and
37 saith unto them, Peace *be* unto you. But
they were terrified and affrighted, and
38 supposed that they beheld a spirit. And
he said unto them, Why are ye troubled?
and wherefore do reasonings arise in your
39 heart? See my hands and my feet, that
it is I myself: handle me, and see; for a
spirit hath not flesh and bones, as ye
40 behold me having. And when he had
said this, he shewed them his hands and
41 his feet. And while they still disbelieved
for joy, and wondered, he said unto them,
42 Have ye here anything to eat? And
they gave him a piece of a broiled fish.
43 And he took it, and did eat before them.

have seen the Lord; and *how that* he had
said these things unto her.

19 When therefore it was evening, on that
day, the first *day* of the week, and when
the doors were shut where the disciples
were, for fear of the Jews, Jesus came and
stood in the midst, and saith unto them,
20 Peace *be* unto you. And when he had
said this, he shewed unto them his hands
and his side. The disciples therefore
21 were glad, when they saw the Lord. Jesus
therefore said to them again, Peace *be*
unto you: as the Father hath sent me,
22 even so send I you. And when he had
said this, he breathed on them, and saith
unto them, Receive ye the Holy Ghost:
23 whose soever sins ye forgive, they are
forgiven unto them; whose soever *sins* ye
retain, they are retained.

24 But Thomas, one of the twelve, called
Didymus, was not with them when Jesus
25 came. The other disciples therefore said
unto him, We have seen the Lord. But
he said unto them, Except I shall see in
his hands the print of the nails, and put
my finger into the print of the nails, and
put my hand into his side, I will not
believe.

26 And after eight days again his disciples
were within, and Thomas with them.
Jesus cometh, the doors being shut, and
stood in the midst, and said, Peace *be* unto
27 you. Then saith he to Thomas, Reach
hither thy finger, and see my hands; and
reach *hither* thy hand, and put it into my
side: and be not faithless, but believing.
28 Thomas answered and said unto him,
29 My Lord and my God. Jesus saith unto
him, Because thou hast seen me, thou
hast believed: blessed *are* they that have
not seen, and *yet* have believed.

30 Many other signs therefore did Jesus
in the presence of the disciples, which are
31 not written in this book: but these are
written, that ye may believe that Jesus is
the Christ, the Son of God; and that
believing ye may have life in his name.

21 1 After these things Jesus manifested
himself again to the disciples at the sea of
Tiberias; and he manifested *himself* on
2 this wise. There were together Simon
Peter, and Thomas called Didymus, and
Nathanael of Cana in Galilee, and the
sons of Zebedee, and two other of his dis-
3 ciples. Simon Peter saith unto them, I
go a fishing. They say unto him, We
also come with thee. They went forth,
and entered into the boat; and that night
4 they took nothing. But when day was
now breaking, Jesus stood on the beach:
howbeit the disciples knew not that it
5 was Jesus. Jesus therefore saith unto

44 And he said unto them, These are my
words which I spake unto you, while I
was yet with you, how that all things
must needs be fulfilled, which are written
in the law of Moses, and the prophets,
45 and the psalms, concerning me. Then
opened he their mind, that they might
46 understand the scriptures; and he said
unto them, Thus it is written, that the
Christ should suffer, and rise again from
47 the dead the third day; and that repentance and remission of sins should be
preached in his name unto all the
48 nations, beginning from Jerusalem. Ye
49 are witnesses of these things. And behold, I send forth the promise of my
Father upon you: but tarry ye in the
city, until ye be clothed with power from
on high.
50 And he led them out until *they were*
over against Bethany: and he lifted up
51 his hands, and blessed them. And it
came to pass, while he blessed them, he
parted from them, and was carried up
52 into heaven. And they worshiped him,
and returned to Jerusalem with great
53 joy: and were continually in the temple,
blessing God.

ACTS $1^{1\text{-}13a}$

1 1 The former treatise I made, O Theophilus, concerning all that Jesus began
2 both to do and to teach, until the day in
which he was received up, after that he
had given commandment through the
Holy Ghost unto the apostles whom he
3 had chosen: to whom he also shewed himself alive after his passion by many proofs,
appearing unto them by the space of forty
days, and speaking the things concerning
4 the kingdom of God: and, being assembled
together with them, he charged them not
to depart from Jerusalem, but to wait for
the promise of the Father, which, *said he*,
5 ye heard from me: for John indeed baptized with water; but ye shall be baptized
with the Holy Ghost not many days
hence.
6 They therefore, when they were come
together, asked him, saying, Lord, dost
thou at this time restore the kingdom to
7 Israel? And he said unto them, It is not
for you to know times or seasons, which the
Father hath set within his own authority.
8 But ye shall receive power, when the Holy
Ghost is come upon you: and ye shall be
my witnesses both in Jerusalem, and in all
Judæa and Samaria, and unto the uttermost part of the earth. And when he
9 had said these things, as they were looking,
he was taken up; and a cloud received him
10 out of their sight. And while they were

them, Children, have ye aught to eat?
6 They answered him, No. And he said
unto them, Cast the net on the right side
of the boat, and ye shall find. They cast
therefore, and now they were not able to
7 draw it for the multitude of fishes. That
disciple therefore whom Jesus loved saith
unto Peter, It is the Lord. So when
Simon Peter heard that it was the Lord,
he girt his coat about him (for he was
naked), and cast himself into the sea.
8 But the other disciples came in the little
boat (for they were not far from the land,
but about two hundred cubits off),
9 dragging the net *full* of fishes. So when
they got out upon the land, they see a fire
of coals there, and fish laid thereon, and
10 bread. Jesus saith unto them, Bring of
the fish which ye have now taken.
11 Simon Peter therefore went up, and drew
the net to land, full of great fishes, a
hundred and fifty and three: and for all
there were so many, the net was not rent.
12 Jesus saith unto them, Come *and* break
your fast. And none of the disciples
durst inquire of him, Who art thou?
13 knowing that it was the Lord. Jesus
cometh, and taketh the bread, and
14 giveth them, and the fish likewise. This
is now the third time that Jesus was
manifested to the disciples, after that he
was risen from the dead.
15 So when they had broken their fast,
Jesus saith to Simon Peter, Simon, *son* of
John, lovest thou me more than these?
He saith unto him, Yea, Lord; thou
knowest that I love thee. He saith unto
16 him, Feed my lambs. He saith to him
again a second time, Simon, *son* of John,
lovest thou me? He saith unto him,
Yea, Lord; thou knowest that I love thee.
17 He saith unto him, Tend my sheep. He
saith unto him the third time, Simon, *son*
of John, lovest thou me? Peter was
grieved because he said unto him the
third time, Lovest thou me? And he
said unto him, Lord, thou knowest all
things; thou knowest that I love thee.
Jesus saith unto him, Feed my sheep.
18 Verily, verily, I say unto thee, When thou
wast young, thou girdedst thyself, and
walkedst whither thou wouldest: but
when thou shalt be old, thou shalt
stretch forth thy hands, and another shall
gird thee, and carry thee whither thou
19 wouldest not. Now this he spake, signifying by what manner of death he should
glorify God. And when he had spoken
20 this, he saith unto him, Follow me. Peter,
turning about, seeth the disciple whom
Jesus loved following; which also leaned
back on his breast at the supper, and said,
Lord, who is he that betrayeth thee?

looking stedfastly into heaven as he went,
behold, two men stood by them in white
11 apparel; which also said, Ye men of
Galilee, why stand ye looking into
heaven? this Jesus, which was received
up from you into heaven, shall so come in
like manner as ye beheld him going into
heaven.
12 Then returned they unto Jerusalem
from the mount called Olivet, which is
nigh unto Jerusalem, a sabbath day's
13 journey off. And when they were come
in, they went up into the upper chamber,
where they were abiding.

Cf. Acts 1^{22}, $2^{24, 31f}$, $3^{15, 26}$, $4^{10, 33}$, 5^{30}, 10^{40f}, 13^{30ff}, $17^{3, 18, 31}$, 26^{23}.

I COR. 15^{3-8}

15 3 For I delivered unto you first of all that
which also I received, how that Christ died
for our sins according to the scriptures;
4 and that he was buried; and that he hath
been raised on the third day according to
5 the scriptures; and that he appeared to
6 Cephas; then to the twelve; then he appeared to above five hundred brethren at
once, of whom the greater part remain
until now, but some are fallen asleep;
7 then he appeared to James; then to all
8 the apostles; and last of all, as unto one
born out of due time, he appeared to me
also.

Cf. Rom. 1^{4}, 4^{24f}, $6^{4f, 9}$, 7^{4}, $8^{11, 34}$, 10^{7ff}, 14^{9}; 1 Cor. 6^{14}, 15^{1-58}; 2 Cor. 4^{14}, 5^{15}, 13^{4}; Gal. 1^{1}; Eph. 1^{20}, 2^{6}; Phil. 3^{10}; Col. 1^{18}, 2^{12}, 3^{1}; 1 Thess. 1^{10}, 4^{14}; 2 Tim. 2^{8}.

Cf. also Heb. 13^{20}; 1 Pet. $1^{3, 21}$, 3^{21}; Rev. $1^{5, 18}$, 2^{8}.

21 Peter therefore seeing him saith to Jesus,
Lord, and what shall this man do?
22 Jesus saith unto him, If I will that he
tarry till I come, what *is that* to thee?
23 follow thou me. This saying therefore
went forth among the brethren, that
that disciple should not die: yet Jesus said
not unto him, that he should not die;
but, If I will that he tarry till I come,
what is *that* to thee?
24 This is the disciple which beareth witness of these things, and wrote these
things: and we know that his witness is
true.
25 And there are also many other things
which Jesus did, the which if they should
be written every one, I suppose that even
the world itself would not contain the
books that should be written.

When the Sabbath was over and it began to grow light on the first day of the week, three women (Mary Magdalene and Mary the Mother of Jesus, and Salome) came to the sepulchre bearing spices, in order to anoint the body. Mk. adds that the sun had risen. This seems to conflict with Lk.'s statement that it was 'deep dawn' and it does definitely contradict Jn.'s statement that it was still dark. It seems quite possible, since Mk. states that it was 'very early,' that a 'not' may have dropped out of his original text.

Mt. names only two women—'Mary Magdalene and the other Mary.'

Lk. has 'Mary Magdalene, and Joanna, and Mary the Mother of James.'

Jn. names only Mary Magdalene, but as he makes her say 'we' it may be inferred that other women were present on that occasion.

St. Paul, to whom we owe what is perhaps the earliest account of the Resurrection, in 1 Cor. 15, makes no reference to any women in connexion with the Resurrection appearances of Jesus.

When the women arrive they are surprised to find the stone rolled away from the door of the sepulchre. The question has been asked in a recent volume: 'Who rolled away the stone?'

Mt. answers the question quite definitely, that the Angel of Jehovah descended from Heaven and rolled it away. He connects the action with a preceding earthquake. The other Evangelists give no answer to the question. An eighteenth-century English bishop, more acutely, enquires, ' Why was the stone rolled away from the sepulchre ? ' and answers that it was not in order to let the Lord out but to let the women in. If the body of Jesus had already assumed that spiritual form which it is represented as possessing in the Fourth Gospel, where it passes into rooms through locked doors, this is undoubtedly the correct answer.

When the women in Mk. enter the sepulchre, they find there a young man, in a white robe, seated on the right side of the sepulchre, who tells them the Lord has risen and is on His way into Galilee to join His disciples there, in accordance with His former prediction. The women are bidden to inform the disciples and Peter of this. This prediction about Galilee is recorded in Mk. 14^{28} and in Mt. 26^{32} as having been made by Jesus just after the Last Supper, when He and His disciples were on the way to Gethsemane. It indicates that (in what was perhaps the most primitive tradition of the Resurrection) the first resurrection appearances of Jesus to His disciples were in Galilee.

Mt.'s angel of the Resurrection and Mk.'s young man at the sepulchre are both in agreement that the Risen Jesus will meet His disciples in Galilee. Mt., true to this prediction, relates that Jesus did appear to His disciples in Galilee, although he also relates that He first appeared to the women in Jerusalem.

Lk. makes Galilee refer to the place where Jesus predicted His Resurrection (24^{6}), not to the place where He is to meet His disciples, for Lk. records no resurrection appearances of Jesus in Galilee.

Lk. only relates the Judæan resurrection appearances of Jesus. While Jn. relates a number of Judæan appearances (20) he also relates in the Epilogue to his Gospel (21) a Galilean appearance to Peter and other disciples when fishing on the Lake.

The accounts of what happened at the sepulchre on the first Easter morning are conflicting. Mk. relates, as has been noted, that the women saw a young man there. There has been much conjecture as to who this young man was. Could it have been the same young man who followed Jesus on the night of His arrest? It is the same phrase *neaniskos* which is used in Mk. in these two instances alone.

If so, it is possible that the young man at the sepulchre was Mark himself, and in that case, it was possibly he who rolled away the stone. And the Risen Jesus must have appeared first to him. All this is very conjectural. The tendency has been to make the young man an angel, thus identifying him with the angel of the Lord who addresses the women in Mt. and with one of the two men ' in dazzling apparel ' who in Lk. asked the women: Why seek ye the Living One among the dead?

Jn. makes no reference to anyone at the empty sepulchre.

Not only have we this conflict of evidence with regard to those whom the women met at the sepulchre but also as to what was said to them. In substance what is said is in each case the same, but the phrases in which it is expressed differ widely.

Mk. relates that the women, after they had received the message, fled from the sepulchre ' for they were afraid.'

It is with these words that the Gospel of Mk. concludes in our two most precious and reliable codices—the *Codex Vaticanus*, the great Biblical treasure of the Vatican Library at Rome, and the *Codex Sinaiticus*, the lately acquired Biblical treasure of the British Museum.

Scholars have been much perplexed as to whether the original Gospel of Mark ended thus. The ending is abrupt, but it is not impossible. It must, however, have appeared inadequate and perhaps unnatural to a number of early Christian scribes, since two different endings (with which we shall deal later) have been composed and attached to the Marcan Gospel.

Eusebius relates that ' the accurate copies ' of Mk. ended with the words ' for they were afraid.'

The scribe of the *Codex Vaticanus*, however, leaves the rest of the column blank (after the subscription), which would seem to indicate that he was aware that an addition had been made to the Gospel at this point.

Two Endings of St. Mark's Gospel

But this is not all. In heraldry it is not rare to find lions blazoned with two tails. The Lion of St. Mark is such a creature. Mk.'s Gospel has two endings, and in a number of manuscripts both the endings appear side by side.

(1) *The Longer Ending*

The longer ending is well known to readers of the Authorised Version, as it was printed in that version as the conclusion of the last chapter (16) of Mk.'s Gospel.

It occurs in by far the greater number of the existing manuscripts of Mk. and in all the ancient versions. It is quoted by important Christian writers as St. Mark's in the second half of the second century. The literary style and vocabulary of the longer ending indicate that it was not composed by the writer of the Second Gospel.

In 1891 F. C. Conybeare discovered in the Patriarchal Library of Edschmiatzin an Armenian MS. of the Gospels written in A.D. 986, in which the last twelve verses are said to have been written by the hand of the Presbyter Aristion (no doubt the Aristion mention by Papias as one of the disciples of the Lord).

The twelve verses which constitute the longer ending begin by narrating the appearance of Jesus, not to the women as we should expect if the narrative were continuous with the original Mk., but to Mary Magdalene (as in the Fourth Gospel).

Next the longer ending relates the appearance of Jesus to the two disciples on their walk into the country. This incident is plainly a compression of St. Luke's account of the appearance of Jesus to the two disciples on the road to Emmaus ($24^{13 f.}$).

The longer ending next relates the appearance of Jesus to the eleven. He reproaches them for their unbelief and charges them to preach the Gospel to all creation. After these resurrection appearances of Jesus, the longer ending relates the Ascension and states that the Apostles fulfil the command of Jesus, and that He confirmed their preaching by signs.

The Baptismal command may be derived from the conclusion of St. Matthew, although it contains no Triune Formula.

The Ascension is no doubt derived from St. Luke (Acts 1), as is also the account of the primitive apostolic preaching and the accompanying signs. It should be noted that the word sign is used in a bad sense in Mk. as that which Jesus refused to give as a testimony to the truth of His Gospel, but in the longer ending it is used in the good sense which it has in the Fourth Gospel.

In the teaching of Jesus in the Synoptic Gospels there is no equivalent to the words:

'He that believeth and is baptized shall be saved, but he that disbelieveth shall be condemned.'

The emphasis upon Baptism is, however, apostolic, as we see from Lk.'s account of St. Peter's sermon on the Day of Pentecost and the baptising which followed it. It is very plain that when the longer ending was written, what are called miracles were taking place in the Christian Church—the successful exorcising of demons, the *glossolalia* or speaking with tongues, the recovery of the sick by the laying on of hands. The taking up of serpents is probably a reference to St. Paul's experience in the Island of Melita (Acts 28^{3}), but it may also be a reference to the words of our Lord's charge to the Seventy in Lk. 10^{19}:

'Behold, I have given you authority to tread upon serpents and scorpions, and over all the power of the enemy, and nothing shall in any wise hurt you.'

The drinking of any deadly thing is possibly a reference to an experience of Barsabbas related by Papias, as cited by Eusebius, or it may be a reference to the story of St. John and the cup of poison narrated in the *Acts of John*.

The classical word for 'any deadly thing' occurs only here in Biblical Greek.

Plainly, what we have in the longer ending of Mk. is a striking summary of primitive Church tradition gathered from a variety of sources.

A curious addition to the longer ending is found in a Greek manuscript of the Gospels purchased in 1906 from an Arab who claimed to have found it in the ruins of an Egyptian monastery. The MS., which is believed to date from the fifth century, was purchased by an American (Freer) and is usually spoken of as the Freer MS. It is at present in Washington, and hence is represented by the symbol W. This addition takes the form of a long interpolation at the end of *v.* 14. Part of the text is very corrupt and untranslatable. Conjecturally emended, the interpolation may be rendered as follows:

And they [the disciples] replied saying: This age of lawlessness and faithlessness is under Satan. . . . therefore reveal thy righteousness now. [Jesus says to them], The span of the years of the authority of Satan has been fulfilled, but other terrible things draw nigh, and on behalf of sinners I have been delivered over unto death that they might turn unto the truth and sin no more: that they might inherit the spiritual and incorruptible glory of righteousness which is in heaven.

(Here *v.* 15, etc., follows from the longer ending.)

(2) *The Shorter Ending*

The shorter ending of St. Mark's Gospel runs as follows:

But all that was enjoined them they reported briefly to those who were about Peter. And after this Jesus Himself [appeared to them and] from the East even to the West sent forth through them the holy and incorruptible proclamation of eternal salvation.

This ending occurs in several Greek MSS., also in the Ethiopic and two Egyptian versions, also in the Syriac version and the Old Latin. It is usually combined with the longer ending, but does occur by itself. It is possible that it is almost as old as the longer ending. Some critics think by its reference to the West that it originated in Rome. This is supported by the reference to Peter and by the magisterial brevity of the document. Its object plainly is to indicate that the women to whom Jesus appeared after His Resurrection fulfilled His command and that the subsequent extension of the Gospel throughout the world was in accordance with His expressed will.

It ought to be noted that the style and diction of the shorter ending is even less like the original Mk. than is the longer ending.

Reconstruction of Lost Ending of Mk.

In view of the evidence it seems very improbable that Mk.'s Gospel could have ended with the words 'for they were afraid.' The *codex* of Mk. from which all our existing copies would seem to have been ultimately derived must have experienced mutilation at this point. Possibly this mutilation occurred in the terrible persecution to which the Church of Rome was subjected by the Emperor Nero (A.D. 64). If, then, Mk. did not end originally at the words 'for they were afraid,' have we any means of concluding with assurance what followed these words in the original Mk.?

We have observed that the style and vocabulary of the two existing endings are undoubtedly not Marcan and that they belong to a later date than Mk.'s Gospel.

There yet remains, however, a source of information of the greatest importance for the solution of the mystery.

Mt., as we have seen, incorporates into his Gospel a very large portion of Mk., and is largely dependent upon Mk. for the order and structure of his narrative.

It is true that Mt. adds much to Mk. and also alters in a conscientious and consistent manner, mainly by compression and elucidation, a number of the Marcan narratives. It would seem probable, therefore, that Mt.'s account of the post-Resurrection period should contain, though treated in the Matthæan fashion, the lost ending of Mk.

When we turn to Mt. 28[8], which constitutes the parallel to our last verse of Mk., and examine carefully the rest of chapter 28 we are presented with facts which justify the inference that the lost ending of Mk. has been preserved in Mt. The first step towards securing this lost ending is to eliminate all portions of the narrative which are definitely Matthæan. These sections are easily recognised as they contain the story of the subsequent experience of the Roman guard which fled from the sepulchre at the descent of the Angel of the Resurrection—the circumstances of the posting of the guard having already been related by Mt. in an earlier section which is peculiar to himself. This subsequent experience consists of the bribing of the guard and is related in Mt. 28^{11-15}. When this section is eliminated we are left with two incidents: (1) the appearance of Jesus to the women in the vicinity of the sepulchre, *vv.* 9, 10, and (2) the appearance of Jesus to His disciples on a mountain in Galilee, *vv.* 16–20.

When we examine these two narratives, although we cannot say that they are definitely Marcan, yet we are precluded from saying, as in the case of the longer and the shorter endings, that they are definitely non-Marcan.

When we examine the first of these Matthæan resurrection narratives we observe, that after the women's 'quick departure' from the sepulchre (Mt. $28^{8, 9}$), it relates, that while they ran to deliver the angel's message, Jesus Himself met them and said, 'Rejoice.' And they came and held His feet, and worshipped Him. Jesus then repeats to them the charge of the angel.

Archdeacon W. C. Allen, to whom many students of the Gospels of Matthew and Mark owe much, is of opinion that a portion, if not the whole, of this narative is derived from the Marcan source. But he is also of opinion that, between the meeting of the women with Jesus as recorded in Matthew and the meeting of Jesus with His disciples in Galilee, there were several incidents related in the lost ending of Mk. which have been deliberately omitted by Mt.

These omitted verses related 'that the women brought Christ's message to the disciples, that the disciples disbelieved, and that, therefore, Christ Himself appeared to them and probably also to St. Peter.' (*Commentary on Matthew*, p. 303.)

But how can Matthew's omission of these incidents be accounted for? The reasons for Matthew's omission here are in agreement with a great number of similar omissions which he makes from Mk.'s narrative in the earlier part of his Gospel. Matthew deliberately excises, when using his Marcan source, statements which reflect upon the character of the apostles: their obtuseness, their self-seeking, their lack of faith. The omitted Marcan incidents do reflect seriously on the lack of faith of the Apostles in regard to the crucial miracle of the Gospel—the Resurrection of Jesus from the dead. It is of interest to note that Mt. omits Mk. 9^{10}, which records that the disciples disputed about the rising from the dead. (Cf. Allen's *Commentary*, pp. xxxiii. f.)

The second Matthæan Resurrection narrative recording the appearance of Jesus on the mountain in Galilee, not only fits in with Mt. 28^7, but also with the young man's statement to the women at the sepulchre in Mk. 16^7: 'Go tell His disciples and Peter, He goeth before you into Galilee: there shall you see Him, as He said unto you.'

This statement of the young man refers back to Mk. 14^{28}, 'Howbeit, after I am raised up, I will go before you into Galilee': which also appears in Mt. 26^{32}.

The phrase 'the mountain,' as we know, is characteristic of Mark, but whether it means a particular mountain, as seems most likely, or the high land above the Lake, we cannot be certain. The 'some who doubted' in this narrative of Mt.

are not the Apostles, who had been already convinced by the Lord's appearance to them and to St. Peter, but certain other persons.

There is no difficulty about accepting what follows as derived from Mk., with the exception of the Trinitarian baptismal formula, which is a liturgical development belonging to a later period of the Christian religion. The primitive Apostles baptised converts into the name of the Lord Jesus, as did also St. Paul. Outside our St. Matthew's Gospel the Trinitarian baptismal formula first occurs in the *Didache* composed in the second century.

The Lost Ending of St. Mark as Reconstructed

The lost ending of St. Mark, as reconstructed in accordance with this theory, will run somewhat as follows:

And while the women were going to bring His disciples word, Jesus met them and said: Rejoice, and Mary Magdalene held Him by the feet and worshipped Him (cf. Jn. 20^{17}), and Jesus said unto the women: Fear not, go tell my brethren, that they go into Galilee, and there shall they see me. And when the women announced these things to the disciples and to Peter, their words seemed to them as idle tales (cf. Lk. 24^{8-11}).

And after these things Jesus appeared unto Peter (cf. Lk. 24^{34}, The Lord is risen indeed, and hath appeared unto Simon) (cf. also 1 Cor. 15^{5}, He appeared to Cephas). And when Peter beheld Jesus he fell down at His feet and said: Depart from me: for I am a sinful man, O Lord (cf. Lk. 5^{8}), and Jesus said unto him: Strengthen thy brethren (cf. Lk. 22^{31}, 'Sift you like wheat'). After this Jesus appeared unto the eleven and rebuked them for their slowness of heart to believe. And when the eleven disciples went into Galilee as Jesus had appointed them, they saw Jesus, and worshipped Him, but some doubted. And Jesus came to them and spake to them saying: All authority hath been given unto me in heaven and on earth. Go ye therefore unto all the nations, and make disciples of them, teaching them to observe all things whatsoever I have commanded you. And behold I am with you all the days. (The phrase, 'the consummation of the age,' which occurs in the last verse of Mt. is in style Matthæan, not Marcan.)

This conjectural reconstruction of the lost ending of Mk.'s Gospel fulfils certain essential conditions.

(1) It contains an account of the Resurrection of Jesus, which had been predicted at least five times in the preceding portion of the Gospel.

(2) It gives an account of the appearance of Jesus to St. Peter, which is cited by St. Paul to the Corinthians as having been received by him as part of the primal Christian tradition (cf. 1 Cor. $15^{1f.}$).

It is almost inconceivable that the Petrine Gospel should not have related this appearance, although Mt. omitted it because it contained something disparaging to Peter.

(3) It gives an account of the appearance of Jesus to the disciples in Galilee which had been promised them in the preceding portion of Mk. This appearance is possibly to be identified with the appearance to the five hundred brethren at

once, of whom the greater part remain unto this present, related by St. Paul in 1 Cor. 15^6.

The Marcan narrative requires no Ascension: the Risen Christ is spiritually with His faithful disciples all the days.

THE RESURRECTION OF JESUS CHRIST

I

The most ancient extant account of the Rising again of Jesus Christ from the dead is that contained in St. Paul's First Epistle to the Corinthians ($15^{1f.}$).

It is precise and authoritative in tone, and runs as follows:

Now I make known unto you, brethren, the gospel which I preached unto you, which also ye received, wherein also ye stand, by which also ye are saved: *I make known, I say,* in what words I preached it unto you, if ye hold it fast, except ye believed in vain. For I delivered unto you first of all that which also I received, how that Christ died for our sins according to the scriptures: and that he was buried, and that he hath been raised on the third day according to the scriptures, and that he appeared to Cephas: then to the twelve: then he appeared to above five hundred brethren at once, of whom the greater part remain until now, but some are fallen asleep: then he appeared to James: then to all the apostles: and last of all, as unto one born out of due time, he appeared to me also.

This was written in the early fifties of the first century: that is to say, within twenty-five years of the events which it narrates. It was written before any of our existing Canonical Gospels. It claims, however, to go back a long period, presumably to the time of St. Paul's own conversion, which may have taken place within ten years of the Crucifixion. At any rate, at the time when St. Paul wrote the account, there were several hundred people alive who could testify to their experience of the Risen Jesus.

The accounts of the Resurrection appearances in the four Gospels may be summarised as follows:

Mk.'s Gospel, as we have it, does not actually contain an appearance of the Risen Jesus, although, as we have seen, it undoubtedly did, in its unmutilated form, contain such an account, since the Resurrection is predicted by Jesus at least five times in the earlier portion of that Gospel.

In Mt. we have two Resurrection appearances recorded:

(1) To the women who had visited the sepulchre.

(2) To the eleven apostles on the mountain in Galilee.

The account of these appearances, it is highly probable, Mt. derived from Mk. Although it is possible that he omitted to incorporate from Mk. other appearances.

Lk., in his Gospel, records three appearances of the Risen Jesus.

(1) To the two disciples on the road to Emmaus, one of them being named Cleopas or Clopas.

(2) To St. Peter.

(3) To 'the eleven.'

All these appearances take place in Jerusalem or in its vicinity on the day of the Resurrection.

The appearance to the eleven is followed by an account of the Ascension, which takes place at Bethany. Whether this follows immediately on the appearance to the eleven is not clear in Luke's Gospel, but in the Acts (1^3) it takes place on the Mount of Olives forty days after the Resurrection and was apparently preceded by many Resurrection appearances of Jesus to His disciples. At one or more of these appearances Jesus ate and drank in their presence and allowed Himself to be handled by His disciples, as a proof that He was not an apparition (Acts 1^4, 10^{41}).

In the Fourth Gospel (20) three appearances are recorded:

(1) To Mary Magdalene at the sepulchre.

(2) To the ten Apostles (Thomas being absent) behind closed doors. An open-minded study of Jn. 20 will suggest that the Resurrection, Ascension, and the Outpouring of the Holy Spirit all took place on the same day.

(3) To the eleven disciples (Thomas being present) eight days after the Resurrection.

The Epilogue of this Gospel (21) relates an appearance of Jesus to the disciples while fishing on the Lake of Galilee (Peter, James, John, Thomas, and Nathanael being among them).

Outside the Gospels we have three Resurrection appearances of Jesus recorded:

(1) To St. Stephen at his martyrdom (Acts 7^{55}).

(2) To St. Paul on the Damascus road. (There are three accounts of this in the Acts, and St. Paul refers to it himself in 1 Cor. 15^8.)

(3) To John, the Apocalyptic Seer in the Isle of Patmos (Rev. 1^{9-19}).

The accounts of the Resurrection appearances in the four Gospels are fragmentary and conflicting.

Mt. would seem only to know of the Resurrection appearances to the Apostles in Galilee.

Lk. would seem only to know of the Resurrection appearances to the Apostles in Judæa.

For Jn., the main Resurrection appearances are in Jerusalem: but his Gospel contains in its Epilogue an additional Resurrection appearance in Galilee.

To harmonise these accounts is far from easy. St. Paul's account, although not detailed, is the fullest we have, since he records six appearances, including the one to himself. It cannot escape notice, however, that although Mt., Lk., and Jn. (and no doubt the missing ending of Mk.) relate a Resurrection appearance to Mary Magdalene (accompanied by other women), St. Paul makes no reference to this at all, although he claims to be transmitting the Resurrection tradition of the Apostolic Church.

Yet it is the women who are the primary witnesses to the emptiness of the sepulchre. It is true that their statement is verified by a visit of Peter (and another) according to Jn. 20^{3-10}, and by a passage of doubtful genuineness in Lk. (24^{12}). (This verse is omitted by certain important ancient manuscripts, and is therefore possibly a later harmonising insertion summarising Jn. 20^{3-10}.)

Some may be disposed, in view of the conflicting and fragmentary character of the documentary evidence for the Resurrection, to discredit it altogether. But they are faced by formidable historical difficulties if they do so. The whole body of the New Testament writings is radiant with the light of the Resurrection.

I am the Resurrection and the Life.
I am He that liveth and was dead, and behold I am alive for evermore.

represent what Jesus is to the Church of the New Testament.

II

We possess four undoubted witnesses to the belief of the most primitive Christians in the Resurrection of Jesus.

(1) There is the evidence derived from the existence of the Christian Church itself. Had the crucifixion of Jesus ended His disciples' experience of Him, it is hard to see how the Christian Church could have come into existence. That Church was founded on faith in the Messiahship of Jesus. A crucified Messiah was no Messiah at all. He was one rejected by Judaism and accursed of God. It was the Resurrection of Jesus, as St. Paul declares in Rom. 1^4, which proclaimed Him to be the Son of God with power.

(2) There is the evidence derived from the existence of the New Testament writings. Who would have troubled to write these documents if Jesus had ended His career as a crucified revolutionary? Each of these writings attests the belief of its writer that Jesus had triumphed over death and was reigning in the spiritual world from which He would shortly return to judge the living and the dead. The New Testament could no more have come into existence, if the early Christians had not believed in the Resurrection of Jesus, than could the Christian Church.

(3) There is the evidence furnished by the observance of the First Day of the week as the sacred day of the Christian Church. All the early Christians had been Jews. For the Jew, the sacred day was the Sabbath, or Seventh Day of the week. The stupendous importance and sacredness of the Sabbath is attested by Jewish legal and rabbinical writings. Yet those who had been Jews changed the sacred day from the seventh to the first day of the week. Their reason for doing so is, that they believed that Jesus rose from the dead on that day and manifested Himself to His Apostles. All four Gospels are agreed that it was on the first day of the week that the Resurrection of Jesus took place, and we have evidence both from the First Epistle to the Corinthians (16^2) and from the Acts of the Apostles (20^7, Troas), and possibly also from the Book of the Revelation (1^{10}) that the first day of the week was being kept as their sacred day by Christians between the years A.D. 50 and 80.

(The *Epistle of Barnabas*, written possibly as early as the year A.D. 80, testifies to the observance of this day by Christians in contrast to the observance of the seventh day by Jews.)

It seems impossible to account for the observance of the first day of the week (the Lord's Day) except for the reason which Christian tradition gives, that it was due to the belief that Jesus rose from the dead on that day.

(4) There is the evidence derived from the existence of the primitive Christian

rite, variously known in the New Testament as the Breaking of the Bread, the Lord's Supper, the Communion of the Body and Blood of Christ. This rite commemorates the death of Jesus. Yet it is a rite in which there is no mourning for the dead. On the contrary, its note is one of grateful joyousness.

In the post-New Testament Church, its favourite designation was the Eucharist or Thanksgiving. (This is frequent in the *Epistles of Ignatius*, written about A.D. 110.) If the death of Jesus on the Cross had not been followed by the belief in His Resurrection, it would be impossible to account either for the existence of the Eucharistic rite or for its joyous character.

These four Christian institutions—the Church, the New Testament, the Lord's Day, the Eucharist—constitute irrefragable testimony to the universal primitive Christian belief in the Resurrection of Jesus.

III

Apart from this evidence of the Resurrection of Jesus, His triumph over death, there is the evidence which is based upon the affirmations of our rational, moral, and religious consciousness.

If Jesus did not triumph over death, it may be argued that the Creative Process denies our rational, moral, and religious affirmations which assert that if Jesus did not triumph over death, then no human being has done so, or can do so, and that in that case the Creative Process is neither rational nor moral nor spiritual.

These considerations belong to the wider sphere of the Philosophy of Religion, and are only referred to here as a reminder of the cogency of these considerations as constituting a basis upon which the historical argument for the Resurrection of Jesus can firmly rest.

IV

Whilst, therefore, the evidence for the *fact* of the Resurrection of Jesus is undoubtedly very strong, the same cannot be said of the evidence for any particular *mode* of the Resurrection.

We have noted the fragmentary and conflicting character of the Gospel evidence for the Resurrection, and yet we cannot have the slightest doubt of the sincere belief of the writers of these Gospels in the Resurrection of Jesus. They are agreed as to the sepulchre, in which the body of Jesus was placed in the vicinity of Calvary, being found vacant on the third day by certain women-followers of Jesus, although, as has been pointed out, St. Paul does not refer to the evidence of the women. They are agreed that Jesus was seen, and even conversed with, by His disciples after His crucifixion. But beyond that their agreement does not seem to extend.

Some critics have pointed out that the stress upon the third day and the unanimous agreement that on it Jesus rose from the dead is not based upon historic fact but is the product of the prevalent primitive Christian belief that the Old Testament was full of divine oracles to be fulfilled by the Messiah. Hence it may be the words in Hosea (6^2), 'on the third day he will raise us up, and we shall live in his sight,' or the experience of Jonah who was egurgitated after three days, that have led to the Resurrection of Jesus being assigned to the third day after His death by crucifixion.

The evidence for the empty sepulchre is certainly weak: not simply because St. Paul makes no reference to the witness of the women, but also because of the conflicting character of the testimony as to what occurred at the sepulchre on the first Easter morning.

In Mk., the women see a young man.

In Lk., two men in shining apparel.

In Mt., the majestic angel of the Lord.

In Jn., no one (save Jesus only).

We need not dwell upon the differences, they are but minor, in what is said at the sepulchre as recorded by the Evangelists.

Some critics, assuming the historic truth of the visit of the women to the sepulchre, and their finding it empty, have held it probable that in their confusion and anxiety the women visited the wrong sepulchre. This kind of argument seems to us to have little to commend it. Those more radical critics who doubt entirely the entombment of the body of Jesus in the sepulchre of Joseph of Arimathæa, and opine that the corpse of Jesus was cast into the grave of the common people (like that of the prophet Urijah) seem to us to be on firmer ground. At the bar of historical criticism, it is impossible to refute these critics, although their conjectures are not entirely convincing. It may be that the story of the empty sepulchre only came into existence after belief in the Resurrection of Jesus was firmly established in the Christian Church, and that it was only invented to give verisimilitude to a physical form of that Resurrection, possibly in order to confute the Gnostics.

V

There would seem to be three possible ways of conceiving of the *mode* of the Resurrection of Jesus.

(1) That His physical body was resuscitated and that in this physical body, which retained the actual marks of the crucifixion, Jesus manifested Himself to His disciples. That He actually invited His disciples to feel these wounds and thereby to assure themselves that it was He, their crucified Messiah, who was present with them. He even went so far as to eat with them. There is much *prima facie* evidence, as we have seen, in the Gospels and Acts for this view of the *mode*.

But if the Resurrection body of Jesus was His actual physical body, it becomes no easy matter to dispose of that body. St. Luke disposes of it by translating it into the sky, but this is not a view easily accepted by the modern mind, although the primitive and mediæval mind would seem to have welcomed it. A physical body has no proper place in the spiritual world and translation into the sky is not for modern thinking the equivalent for passing from the mundane to the spiritual stage of existence.

(2) That the physical body of Jesus was at His Resurrection transmuted into a spiritual body. This is undoubtedly the view of the writer of the Fourth

Gospel. As Latham points out with convincing lucidity in his book *The Risen Master*: what convinced Peter and John of the miracle of the Resurrection was that they recognised on visiting the empty sepulchre that the body of Jesus had passed forth from the grave-clothes without disturbing them, which only a spiritualised body could do. It is in this spiritualised body that Jesus passes through closed doors. In this spiritualised body Jesus is able to make Himself visible or invisible at will and so to be present, as He was when Thomas made his denial of the Resurrection, although none realised that He was present.

There is much to commend this *mode* as appropriate to the Resurrection, except the evidence for it. The Fourth Gospel is the latest of the Gospels, and this view of the transmutation of the physical body of Jesus into a spiritual body does not seem to have been the view of the earlier Evangelists, although, on the other hand, there seems reason to believe that St. Paul's belief in the *mode* of the Resurrection of Christians was of this kind.

We shall not all sleep, but we shall all be changed, in a moment, in the twinkling of an eye, at the last trump: for the trumpet shall sound and the dead shall be raised incorruptible, and we shall be changed. (1 Cor. $15^{51, 52}$.)

He shall change the body of our humiliation so that it may be like unto the body of His glory by the mighty working whereby He is able to subdue all things unto Himself. (Phil. 3^{21}.)

(3) That Jesus appeared to His disciples, not in a physical body resuscitated nor in a spiritual body into which His physical body had been transmuted, but, in a form similar to that in which the discarnate spirits of the dead manifest themselves to-day to those who have such psychical experiences as have been recorded by F. W. H. Myers and a host of other writers on psychical research.

This would not mean that Jesus did not manifest Himself to His disciples in a spiritual body, but only that the spiritual body was not His physical body transmuted into a spiritual body.

There are other ways of accounting for the existence of a spiritual body than by supposing it to be a transmuted physical body. St. Paul in 2 Cor. $5^{1f.}$ expresses belief in the existence of a spiritual body, but it would not seem that he identified that spiritual body 'which is from heaven' with the physical body in which he then 'groaned, being burdened.' The statements in the New Testament and other early Christian writers that Jesus affirmed that He was not an apparition but that He possessed a body composed of flesh and bones are to be accounted for as the primitive Christian reply to Gnostic heretical teachers who were affirming that Jesus was no real human being with a material body of flesh and blood but a celestial being who had not, and could not have, because He was Divine, any contact with matter.

It is maintained that it was this Gnostic spiritualising which accounts for the gross materialism of some of the early Christian accounts of the Resurrection of Jesus. These materialistic narratives of the Resurrection are apologetic: they are not historic. Furthermore, they are not primitive in the sense of being the first in the field. It is maintained that the psychical mode of the Resurrection was the first in the field. This is demonstrated by St. Paul in his argument in the opening of 1 Cor. 15. All the resurrection appearances of Jesus there recorded are introduced by the Greek phrase: *ōphthē*, equal to 'He appeared.'

This phrase is appropriately used of psychical appearances, and it is noticeable that in this passage St. Paul speaks of the appearance of the Lord to the various apostles and disciples in exactly the same way in which he speaks of the appearance of the Lord to himself. Now it is perfectly clear that the appearance of Jesus to Paul on the Damascus road was a psychical appearance, and therefore it is maintained that the earliest written account which we have of the Resurrection of Jesus presents it as psychical in its mode. Nevertheless this psychical theory has its difficulties. It is doubtful how far more than one person at a time can see a vision or apparition. How Jesus could have been seen after His crucifixion by more than five hundred brethren at once is a psychical problem of some magnitude.

It will be urged by some that the solution of the problem of the Resurrection is not to be solved by the acceptance of any one of these three objective modes of the Resurrection—physical, 'transmuted,' psychical.

For the modern mind the solution of the mode of the Resurrection must be psychological and subjective. The belief in the Resurrection of Jesus was created, not by an objective experience of His disciples after His crucifixion, but by a subjective experience created by the impact of His personality upon their personalities in the preceding period. Those who had become the disciples of Jesus had become so as the result of the influence of His personality. That influence was so powerful that it had convinced them that He was not simply a prophet but the Messiah.

It was their conviction that He was the Messiah which compelled them to believe in His Resurrection. God's Messiah, though crucified, could not die. 'Thou wilt not leave my soul to Sheol: Neither wilt thou suffer thy Holy One to see corruption' (Ps. 16^{10}), was the conviction of the Apostles of Jesus as soon as they had recovered from the terror and horror of His crucifixion. They were convinced that so vital, so transcendent, so Divine a personality could not be conquered by death or rejected by God: this personality came from God and must go to God. This explanation, as we have said, demands no resurrection acts of an objective kind, whether historical or psychical, to prove it. It has its foundation in the impression which the personality of Jesus made upon His disciples and the power and permanence of that impression constituted the impulse which created the Christian Church. It was this which gave the Apostles the Pentecostal experience of being the recipients of the Spirit of Jesus and enabled them to transmit that Spirit to later ages and to many lands.

It is this which is reflected in Arthur Hugh Clough's poem, 'Easter Day at Naples':

Though dead, not dead:
Not gone, though fled:
Not lost, though vanishéd.
In the great gospel and true creed,
He is yet risen indeed:
Christ is yet risen.

It is not clear that we can go farther than this, nor does it seem necessary that we should. Christian faith rests firmly on the *fact* of the Resurrection of Jesus, and regards the *mode* of that Resurrection as secondary and as having no particular value for the Christian religion. St. Paul's exhortation to his converts—

'If ye be risen with Christ, seek those things which are above where Christ sitteth at the right hand of God'

does not depend for its cogency upon belief in any particular *mode* of the Resurrection.

No doubt it would give intellectual satisfaction to know precisely by what mode or method Jesus triumphed over death, but it is doubtful if such knowledge is possible for us in the present stage of our existence.

It must be recognised, however, that if this psychological explanation of the origin of the faith in the Resurrection of Jesus be accepted, then our Gospel narratives of the Resurrection are more of the nature of myth than history. Myth, let it be understood, is not falsehood, but truth which expresses itself in the form of imaginative narrative.

Origin and Character of St. Matthew's Gospel

THE primitive Christian bishop, Papias of Hierapolis in Asia Minor, an ardent collector of apostolic traditions, wrote (probably not later than A.D. 140) in his lost volume, *Exegesis of the Oracles of the Lord*, cited by Eusebius in his *Ecclesiastical History* (iii. 39):

'Matthew therefore composed in the Hebrew language the sayings (*Logia*). But each translated them as he was able.'

Irenæus, Bishop of Lyons and Vienne in A.D. 178, and pupil of St. Polycarp of Smyrna, wrote in his great work against the Gnostics, as cited by Eusebius in his *Ecclesiastical History* (v. 8, 2):

'But Matthew indeed produced for the Hebrews a Gospel written in their own language, whilst Peter and Paul in Rome were preaching the Glad Tidings, and founding the Church.'

Origen, the third head of the Catechetical School of Alexandria, writing in the first half of the third century, is quoted by Eusebius in his *Ecclesiastical History* (vi. 25) as saying:

'But first was written the [Gospel] according to Matthew, formerly the tax-gatherer, but afterwards an apostle of Jesus Christ, who, having published it for the Jewish converts, composed it in the Hebrew language [letters].'

Eusebius himself writes in his *Ecclesiastical History* (iii. 24, 6):

'For Matthew first of all preached his Gospel to the Hebrews, when indeed on the point of going to other [nations], and committed it to writing in his native tongue, and thus supplied the lack of his presence to them, by his writings.'

Eusebius also writes in the same work of Pantænus, the first head of the Catechetical School of Alexandria (v. 10, 3):

'Of these [ardent missionaries] Pantænus is said to have been one, and to have come as far as the Indies. And the report is, that he there found that the Gospel of Matthew had anticipated his own arrival with some who had learned Christ there, to whom Bartholomew, one of the apostles, had preached, and had left them the writing of Mt. in Hebrew, which was also preserved until this time.'

These passages indicate that there was general agreement in the Christian Church in the second and third centuries that the First Gospel had been written by Matthew, the Apostle, in the Hebrew language. And this view has been universal in the Christian Church until quite recent times. Christian tradition is uniform on this point. In other words, what is called the external evidence asserts unanimously that our First Gospel is the composition of Matthew the Apostle in the Hebrew or Aramaic language.

Internal evidence, however (that is, the evidence derived from the study of the Gospel itself), contradicts these assertions. We have already seen in studying Mk.'s Gospel with parallel passages from the First Gospel, that the First Gospel makes large use of Mk.'s Gospel both in respect of contents and order.

It is hardly credible that a primitive apostle of Jesus in writing a Gospel should make use of another Gospel, and that not written by an Apostle. Surely a primitive apostle who undertook to write a Gospel would write his own reminiscences and not be dependent upon a written source for his narrative.

It is generally agreed that the writers of the First and Third Gospels have each made use of the same collection of the Sayings of Jesus, called by the critics Q. Although it is more credible that a primitive apostle of Jesus, not possessed of a very good verbal memory, should make use of a primitive collection made by someone else of the sayings of his Master, yet this seems unlikely.

When we examine the Gospel, the internal evidence points to its having been written originally in Greek and not in Hebrew. Much of its narrative, as we have observed, is dependent upon Mk. and upon our present Greek text of Mk. It is difficult to suppose a Hebrew writing for Hebrews in the Hebrew language should make use of Greek documents in writing an account of his own experiences.

It is, however, more difficult to believe that this Hebrew gospel when translated into Greek should coincide in a large number of Greek phrases with a Greek Gospel composed by Mark. Furthermore, the writer of the First Gospel does not seem to have understood the Hebrew language. It is doubtful by his use of the word *Hosanna* as to whether he knows what it means literally. Also, in his citation of the famous passage from Isaiah (7^{14}) he does not seem to be aware that the Hebrew word rendered 'virgin' means in the original Hebrew 'a young woman, either married or unmarried.'

It is observable in this case, as in most of the other Old Testament quotations in his Gospel, that they are derived, not direct from the Hebrew, but from the Greek translation of the Old Testament, known as the Septuagint. This is also in a measure true of the genealogy of our Lord furnished by this Gospel. This genealogy gives strong evidence of being dependent upon the Septuagint version of 1 Chronicles (1–3).

In view of these considerations, it is as difficult to believe that the First Gospel was written in the Hebrew language as that it was written by Matthew the Apostle.

All the internal evidence seems to point to its being a compilation from a number of Greek documents by one who had no first-hand knowledge either of the ministry of Jesus or of the Hebrew language.

It is very disconcerting to find such widespread and reputable external evidence in conflict with the internal evidence, and the question naturally arises: Is it possible that we have misinterpreted or misrepresented the external evidence?

There are two linguistic ambiguities in the evidence.

(1) The first concerns the word translated 'Hebrew.' This might equally well be translated 'Aramaic.' Although the Old Testament Scriptures (with inconsiderable exceptions [1]) were written in Hebrew, yet the ordinary Jew in Palestine, except for religious purposes, had ceased to make use of Hebrew in our Lord's day.

After the return from the Exile, Aramaic, a North-Arabian Semitic dialect, closely akin to Hebrew, replaced Hebrew as the language of everyday life. Aramaic was the language in which our Lord and His Apostles undoubtedly taught, and we have actual sayings of His in this language preserved in our Gospels. It was this use of Aramaic by the Jews which led to the composition of the Targums, i.e. Aramaic interpretations of the Old Testament which were recited in the synagogues after the reading of the Old Testament Lessons in Hebrew. The fact that Jesus read the Lessons in the synagogue on occasions certainly indicates that He understood Hebrew. When, however, our external evidence uses the term Hebrew of Matthew's composition it may be taken as pretty well certain that Aramaic is meant.

(2) The second ambiguity concerns the word translated 'sayings.' This is the word *logia*. This word may mean, and usually does mean, a saying, an utterance, an apophthegm. But it may also mean a testimony. In this sense it was applied in early Christian circles to those passages in the Old Testament which were regarded as Messianic predictions and as therefore fulfilled in the Messiah's life and ministry, His death and resurrection, His ascension and giving of the Spirit.

Now, in the case of the First Gospel, the word *logia* may be used in either or in both of these senses. For in that Gospel we have five collections of the Sayings of Jesus, and we also have a collection of twelve oracles from the Old Testament which are explicitly cited in that Gospel as having been fulfilled in connexion with Jesus.

It is possible that though Matthew the Apostle did not write our First Gospel, yet he may have made a collection (in Aramaic or Hebrew) of the Sayings of Jesus or a collection of Old Testament oracles fulfilled in the life of Jesus, or both.

Where our external evidence has probably gone wrong has been in the identification of the First Gospel with Matthew's *logia*. The writers of the external evidence knew of this Gospel as the Gospel 'according to Matthew.' Now 'according to Matthew' does not mean necessarily that Matthew was its author. It would much more probably mean that the work in question contained the preaching or good news as delivered by Matthew—no doubt at first orally. Hence it may well be that the First Gospel got its designation because it incorporated, and with a completeness that no other Gospel had done, Matthew's collection of *logia*.

SOURCES OF MT.

We have already had reason to refer to the composer of the First Gospel as having made use of a number of literary sources. What were these sources?

[1] Ezra 4^{7}–6^{18}, 7^{12-26}; Daniel 2^{4b}–7. These are in Aramaic.

(1) First in importance comes the Gospel of Mark, of which 606 verses out of 661 (in the Revised Version) are included in Mt.'s 1,068 verses.

(2) Hardly less important as a source comes Q, a collection of the Sayings of Jesus, possibly combined with such accounts of incidents as explain or give point to the Sayings. This source was used also as a primary source by St. Luke in the Third Gospel.

The Jews had a literary habit of dividing their collections into five. For instance, there are five Books of the Law (hence the term Pentateuch), and there are five Books of Psalms in the Psalter, each concluding with its Doxology. In the Old Testament there are five books called the Rolls (*megilloth*). There is a famous collection of the Sayings of the Jewish Fathers which consists of five books, and it is perhaps not without significance that Papias' *Exegesis of the Oracles of the Lord* also consisted of five books.

It can hardly be accidental that the collections of the Sayings of Jesus in the First Gospel number five, and each collection terminates with the same formula.

These five collections are:

(1) The Sermon on the Mount (5, 6, 7).

(2) The Charge to the Twelve (10^{5} to end).

(3) The seven parables of the Kingdom (13^{3-52}).

(4) Various sayings about little ones, repentance, forgiveness (18).

(5) (*a*) Denunciation of scribes and Pharisees (seven woes, 23). (*b*) Eschatological predictions (24). (*c*) Three parables of Judgement, Ten Virgins, the Talents, the Sheep and the Goats (25).

The formula with which each of the collections terminates runs as follows:

'And it came to pass when Jesus had ended. . . .'

This occurs in 7^{28a}, 11^{1a}, 13^{53}, 19^{1a}, 26^{1}.

This remarkable collection of the teaching of Jesus opens with the eight Beatitudes and concludes with the parable of the Judgement of the Nations, usually known as the Sheep and the Goats.

(3) Thirdly, there is a collection of proof texts (*testimonia*) from the Old Testament which are cited as being fulfilled in the life and ministry of Jesus. These proof texts are twelve in number and are introduced in each case by a characteristic formula.

The formula with slight variations runs as follows:

'This [took place] in order that it might be fulfilled which was spoken by the Lord [through the prophet . . .] saying.'

This formula occurs in the following places: $1^{22, 23}$, $2^{5, 6, 15, 17-18, 23}$, 4^{14-16}, 8^{17}, 12^{17-21}, 13^{35}, 21^{4-5}, 27^{9}.

Some of these Old Testament quotations come from the Septuagint; some seem to be direct translations from the Hebrew, others are in their origin mixed and doubtful.

(4) A genealogy of Jesus traced from Abraham through King David.

(5) A body of apologetic material made use of for confuting various contemporary Jewish slanders directed against the primitive Christian presentation of Jesus, and against the integrity of the Apostles. Such slanders as that Mary, the Mother of Jesus, was an immoral woman and that Jesus Himself was illegitimate; that Jesus knew Himself to be sinful and that is why He came to John to be baptised for the remission of sins; that Jesus was recognised by the Roman authorities as a criminal and therefore justly crucified; that Jesus never rose from the dead, but that His Apostles stole His body from the sepulchre and then fraudulently proclaimed His Resurrection.

Whether this source, like the other five cited, is a written source is open to question.

It is possibly partly written and partly oral, or it may be that what some would regard as the oral portion of the source is really the production of the compiler of the Gospel himself.

This source is a very important feature of the first two chapters of the Gospel. In these first two chapters God is represented as making His will known in dreams as in the Elohist sections of the *Pentateuch*.

Now the phrase 'in a dream' (*kat' onar*) occurs five times in the first two chapters (Mt. 1^{20}, $2^{12, 13, 19, 22}$), and it occurs nowhere else in the New Testament except in a later section of the First Gospel (27^{19}) which relates Pilate's wife's dream. This would seem to indicate that the narrative of Pilate's wife's dream belongs to the same literary source as those sections in chapters 1 and 2, which contain the phrase *kat' onar*.

SOME CHARACTERISTICS OF MT.

The First Gospel has been aptly described as the second edition of St. Mark's Gospel enlarged and revised.

Reading these two Gospels, side by side, it is of great interest and importance for the understanding of the mind and outlook of the writer of the First Gospel, to notice the way in which he handles St. Mark. Anything in Mk. which seems to reflect upon the Divine character of Jesus the Messiah, Mt. omits or alters. For example, where we are told on two occasions by Mk. (one at Nazareth, the other in Phœnicia) that Jesus was not *able* to do certain things, Mt. omits the 'was not able' in both cases. Also Mk.'s version of the reply of Jesus to the young man: Why callest thou me good? is altered by Mt. into: Why askest thou me concerning the good? (Mk. 10^{18}; Mt. 19^{17}.)

Again, the writer of the First Gospel is very sensitive with regard to the good reputation of the Apostles of Jesus, and although he cannot shield them from every possible criticism, he does strive, when he can, to defend them. For instance, where Mk. tells us that James and John came with their ambitious request to Jesus that they might be given seats, one on His right hand and the other on His left hand in His Kingdom, Mt., by altering Mk.'s narrative, makes the mother of the sons of Zebedee the author of the petition.

The reason for these alterations of Mk. by Mt. is that Mt. is acting on the defensive: the result of the author's living in an atmosphere of controversy.

He is anxious that his Gospel shall not contain anything which will give the bitter Jewish opponents of the Christian religion any possible ground of attack.

We have already noted how much the author of the First Gospel is interested in the fulfilment of Old Testament prophecies in the life and ministry of Jesus. This leads him in certain cases to alter Mk.'s narrative in order to secure a precise Old Testament fulfilment.

For instance, Mk. 14^{11} relates that Judas betrayed Jesus for money, but Mt. 26^{15} adds that the Jewish authorities paid Judas thirty pieces of silver, thus securing a fulfilment of Zech. 11^{12}. Or to take another instance: Mk. says that Jesus was offered myrrhed wine (15^{23}) before His crucifixion, but Mt. (27^{34}), in order to secure a fulfilment of Ps. 69^{21}, says that Jesus was offered wine mingled with gall.

In describing our Lord's entry into Jerusalem on Palm Sunday, Mt., in order to secure a literal fulfilment of Zech. 9^{9}, makes Jesus ride on both the ass and its colt at the same time; thus indicating not only that he does not understand the significance of duplication in Hebrew poetry, but also that he is willing to go to almost any lengths in his narrative to secure the precise fulfilment of an Old Testament oracle.

Mt. besides in some cases altering the event to fit the prophecy, in other cases would seem to have altered the prophecy to fit the event. This way of treating Mk. brings out strongly the definitely apologetic character and purpose of Mt.

Again, although Mt. is undoubtedly deeply interested in the Sayings of Jesus, and provides us with a most precious collection of them in his Gospel, yet he is not interested in the conversations of Jesus, which for modern readers are even more precious than the Sayings; so we find Mt. on a number of occasions compressing or excising these conversations as given by Mk. For example, the vivid dialogue between Jesus and the father of the epileptic lad whom Jesus encounters after His descent from the Mount of Transfiguration disappears from Mt. (Mk. 9^{14-29}; Mt. 17^{14-20}.) This habit of abbreviation, practised by Mt., leads him to omit a great number of extraordinarily interesting details contained in Mk. For instance, in the story of our Lord's blessing little children, Mt. omits that Jesus was 'indignant' with the disciples for forbidding the children to be brought to Him. Mt. also omits that Jesus took them into His arms and blessed them. He merely states that Jesus placed His hands upon them and went away. (Mk. 10^{13-16}; Mt. 19^{13-15}.)

In another case Mt. excises Mk.'s statement that Jesus took a little child in His arms. (Mk. 9^{36}.) Mt. evidently regarded this affectionateness to children as unbecoming in a great spiritual personage: details which seem to us to indicate that in some sections of Mk., at least, we have the narrative of an eye-witness.

Again, when Mk. uses, as he does on rare occasions, words of ambiguous meaning, Mt. omits or explains them. For instance, Mk.'s rare term for what was probably a pillow, or cushion, on which the head of Jesus rested when He slept through the storm is omitted by Mt. as strange.

This explanation also extends to sayings of Jesus hard to be understood:

such as His warning against the leaven of the Pharisees in Mk., which Mt. says meant the *teaching* of the Pharisees and Sadducees (Mt. 16^{12}); or when Mk. relates that Jesus spoke of the Elijah which was for to come, Mt. explains that Jesus is here referring to John the Baptist (Mt. 17^{13}).

Again, on several occasions Mk. seems to have blundered in reference to the Old Testament. For instance, Mk. 1^{2} assigns a prophecy to Isaiah which comes from Malachi: Mk. 2^{26} states that a certain event happened in the days of Abiathar the High Priest, whereas the High Priest was Abimelech or Ahimelech: Mk. 14^{12} asserts that the Paschal Lamb was slain on the first day of the Unleavened Bread. All these Mt. omits, which indicates, by the way, that he was a serious student of Judaism and its Scriptures.

Again, Mt. exhibits a tendency to darken the characters of the opponents of the Gospel. For example, Mk. says that Herodias entrapped Herod Antipas into beheading John the Baptist, and that Antipas was very sorry, as he revered John. Mt. says, Antipas was very sorry because the act would diminish his popularity with his subjects (Mk 6^{20}; Mt. 14^{5}).

Also Mk. relates that Jesus loved the rich young man whom He invited to follow Him, but who turned away because he would not renounce his wealth. Mt. omits the statement that Jesus loved one who would not accept His call (Mk. 10^{21}; Mt. 19^{21}).

Mt., it may be said, is harsher towards the Jewish opponents of Jesus than is Mk.

Mt. is an ardent apocalyptist. He not only believes that Jesus is the pre-existent celestial Son of Man of the *Book of Enoch*, but that He will return to earth as the apocalyptic judge of mankind in the near future. His apocalyptic beliefs lead him to introduce the title 'Son of Man' where it is not in the Marcan parallel: and sayings of Jesus about the Kingdom, he alters in certain cases to make it clear to the reader that the Kingdom is apocalyptic. Mt.'s attitude towards those who fail to enter the Kingdom is marked by the cruel severity of the Apocalyptists. These offenders, he reiterates, are to be 'cast' into the outer darkness, where shall be weeping and gnashing of teeth.

Mt.'s collection of the Sayings of Jesus when compared with that in Lk. indicates that Mt. has in view Jewish-Christian and possibly Jewish readers who are deeply interested in the contemporary controversies between these two bodies. As a consequence, he relates particular points of conflict of Jesus with Jewish opponents in the spheres of ceremonial and legalist casuistry which Lk. omits as of no interest or value for his Gentile-Christian readers.

Another characteristic of Mt. is his inclusion of the cycle of incidents relating to St. Peter. Of course St. Peter is a prominent figure in the other Gospels, but he is peculiarly exalted in Mt. Jesus and he seem to stand apart from the rest of the Apostles. Mt. alone relates the famous words, 'Thou art Peter and on this rock I will found my Church' (16^{16-18}); the walking of Peter on the water ($14^{28, 29}$); and the catching of the fish with the half-shekel in its mouth which is to pay the temple-tax for Jesus and Peter (17^{24-27}).

Another characteristic of Mt. is his stress on the relation of Jesus to the Jewish Law. Jesus is not the destroyer of that Law. He seeks its perfect fulfilment: not one minutest fragment—no jot nor tittle—shall pass from that Law till all be fulfilled: even scribes and Pharisees ‘ who sit on Moses’ seat ’ are to be heard and obeyed. On the other hand, Jesus Himself is the new law-giver who, like a second Moses on the Mount, delivers His law—the law of the Kingdom—to His disciples. His authority, as the Messianic law-giver, is greater than that of Moses. ‘It was said to them of old time . . . but I say unto you . . .’ (Mt.$5^{21, 27, 33, 38, 43}$).

While Jn. sees the Gospel of Jesus as Spirit and Life, Mt. sees it, as does St. James in his Epistle, as the perfect law.

Another feature of Mt. is, that it alone of all the Gospels refers to the Church. The word church (*ekklesia*) does not even occur in the other Gospels, but it is found in two passages in Mt: (1) in which Jesus declares, ‘ On this rock I will found my Church ’ (16^{18}), (2) and the other the passage in which Jesus lays down the way in which the erring disciple should be excommunicated (18^{17}).

Mt. definitely teaches that Jesus founded the Church and provided authority and principles for its government. In this connexion it should be noted that Mt. alone records Jesus as commanding the practice of Baptism.

What has been written will indicate that Mt. is arbitrary in the use of his literary sources, but he is arbitrary in a conscientious way: he always acts according to principles and seems to adhere very firmly to them. Where his principles and purposes do not demand the alteration of his sources, he transmits them unimpaired, save that, as a good editor, he seeks to improve Mk.’s style and is also compelled, on account of the mass of his material, to compress and excise.

Some of the other characteristics of Mt. to which we have referred will indicate to modern readers that his Gospel is of late date.

This is particularly clear in the narratives which are peculiar to him: especially those which are of an apologetic and controversial kind and are intended to protect the Christian religion against Jewish attacks. It should be recognised that in many of these characteristics of Mt. we see a reflection of the teaching, practice, and spirit of the Christian Church of Palestine and Syria of which he was a member.

AUTHORSHIP, PLACE, AND DATE

It is clear that the author of this Gospel cannot be the tax-gatherer Matthew or Levi, the Apostle of Jesus. Who the author was cannot be determined.

Internal evidence would seem to indicate conclusively that he was a Greek-speaking Jewish-Christian who gives to his readers the Gospel of Jesus as it was generally received in the great Jewish-Christian churches of Palestine and Syria, where Judaism was fiercest in its attacks and St. Peter highly honoured. Mt.’s great regard for St. Peter would seem to indicate that Antioch was the place of the origin of this Gospel and not Jerusalem, where St. James, the Lord’s brother, was the head of the Church (about A.D. 44–68).

As Mk.’s Gospel was in all probability not written earlier than A.D. 65 and, as Mt. uses it as a primary source, it is clear that Mt. could not have been written before A.D. 65.

The fuller references in Mt. to the destruction of Jerusalem by Vespasian and Titus in A.D. 70, would seem to indicate that this Gospel was written after that event. In Mk. 13 (*vv.* 1 and 2), where Jesus predicts the coming destruction of the Temple, the disciples ask: 'When shall these things come to pass?' But in the parallel passage in Mt. the disciples are made to ask, not only when shall these things come to pass? but also, 'What shall be the sign of thy coming (*parousia*) and of the consummation of the age?' (Mt. 24^3.)

This would seem to indicate clearly that the destruction of the Temple had already taken place when Mt. wrote, and that the great event of interest now to which Christians were looking forward was the Advent of the Son of Man.

The inclusion of the Trinitarian Baptismal formula (assuming that it is a part of the original text of Mt.) in the last charge of Jesus, 'to make disciples o all nations,' indicates also the late date of this Gospel, since the Trinitarian Baptisma formula was not used until the Christian Mission had passed out beyond the boundaries of Judaism into the Pagan world. It is usual, therefore, to place the date of Mt. about the year 80.

The only sections of St. Matthew's Gospel dealt with here are: (1) Those which have not been referred to as parallel passages in the exposition of Mk., and (2) Those which are not expounded by Dr. Manson.

Incidents in St. Matthew's Gospel not Found in St. Mark's

THE GENEALOGY OF JESUS

MT. 1^{1-17}

1 1 The book of the generation of Jesus
Christ, the son of David, the son of
Abraham.
2 Abraham begat Isaac; and Isaac begat
Jacob; and Jacob begat Judah and his
3 brethren; and Judah begat Perez and
Zerah of Tamar; and Perez begat Hezron;
4 and Hezron began Ram; and Ram begat
Amminadab; and Amminadab begat
Nahshon; and Nahshon begat Salmon;
5 and Salmon begat Boaz of Rahab; and
Boaz begat Obed of Ruth; and Obed
6 begat Jesse; and Jesse begat David the
king.
And David begat Solomon of her *that*
7 *had been the wife* of Uriah; and Solomon
begat Rehoboam; and Rehoboam begat
8 Abijah; and Abijah begat Asa; and Asa
begat Jehoshaphat; and Jehoshaphat be-
9 gat Joram; and Joram begat Uzziah; and
Uzziah begat Jotham; and Jotham begat
10 Ahaz; and Ahaz begat Hezekiah; and
Hezekiah begat Manasseh; and Manasseh
11 begat Amon; and Amon begat Josiah; and
Josiah begat Jechoniah and his brethren,
at the time of the carrying away to
Babylon.
12 And after the carrying away to Babylon,
Jechoniah begat Shealtiel; and Shealtiel
13 begat Zerubbabel; and Zerubbabel begat
Abiud; and Abiud begat Eliakim; and
14 Eliakim begat Azor; and Azor begat
Sadoc; and Sadoc begat Achim; and
15 Achim begat Eliud; and Eliud begat
Eleazar; and Eleazar begat Matthan; and
16 Matthan begat Jacob; and Jacob begat
Joseph the husband of Mary, of whom was
born Jesus, who is called Christ.
17 So all the generations from Abraham
unto David are fourteen generations; and
from David unto the carrying away to
Babylon fourteen generations; and from
the carrying away to Babylon unto the
Christ fourteen generations.

Mt.'s Gospel opens with the roll of the pedigree of Jesus. The purpose of this pedigree is to prove that Jesus the Messiah is a true Jew of noblest descent—not only from Abraham, the Father of the Faithful, through all the patriarchs, but also a member of the Royal House of David. The pedigree is intended, not only to prove that Jesus, since He was sprung from the Royal House of David, could rightly claim to be that Son of David whose coming the Prophets had predicted but also to confute aspersions cast upon our Lord's legitimacy.

The Jewish Talmud slanderously asserts that Jesus was a bastard (*mamzer*), whose father Pantherus, a Roman soldier, seduced a Jewish girl named Miriam. There is no historical evidence for this assertion, although Pan-Teutonists and Anti-Semites have been eager to claim it as historical. In our records of Him, Jesus is characteristically Jewish.

There can be little doubt that Mt.'s genealogy and infancy narrative are intended to discredit this aspersion upon our Lord's legitimacy and the purity of His Jewish descent. This aspersion, besides being reflected in the opening chapters of Mt.'s Gospel, reappears in the Fourth Gospel in the Jewish retort to Jesus: 'We were not born of fornication' (Jn. 8^{41}).

It is for this reason that Mt.'s pedigree contains, what is most unusual in

Jewish pedigrees, the names of five women. These five women, three of whom are the ancestresses of King David, and the fourth, the mother of King Solomon, were all open to criticism, as not conforming to the Hebrew ideal of wifehood.

The first is Tamar, the widow of a deceased elder brother and later the mother of an incestuous child.

The second is Rahab, a Canaanite by birth, a 'sacred woman' or prostitute who afterwards married into a noble Israelite family.

The third is Ruth, a Moabitess, who as a widow married the aged Boaz.

The fourth was the daughter of Sheba, who became the wife of Uriah, the Hittite whose story is too well known to be related here.

Fifth and last we have Mary, the Mother of our Lord.

She, by the Divine overruling, is one of an illustrious line of mothers in Israel whom God selected in accordance with His purpose. Those Jews who maliciously and blindly criticised the Mother of the 'Son of David' would do well to remember that the ancestresses of King David himself were open to criticism by those who in these matters could not discern the Divine purpose.

The pedigree is divided into three sections, each of which consists of fourteen names; the first fourteen being from Abraham to David, the second fourteen from Solomon to Jeconiah, the third fourteen from Shealtiel to Jesus. [It should be noted that in the Gospel text of the pedigree a name appears to have been lost from this section which only contains thirteen names.]

In Hebrew each consonant has a numerical value and the consonants of the name David (*dwd*, $4 + 6 + 4$) make the number fourteen. Thus each section of the pedigree enshrines the Davidic descent of Jesus. The names in the first two sections would seem to have been derived from the Septuagint version of 1 Chron. 1^{34}–3^{19}. The pedigree traces the line of the ancestry of Jesus from David through Solomon and through all the kings of Judah down to the Babylonian exile. This conflicts with Lk.'s pedigree, which traces the ancestral line of Jesus through Nathan, a younger son of David and his descendants. Mt.'s pedigree and Lk.'s having parted company after David, meet again in Shealtiel or Salathiel and his son Zerubbabel. The latter was the Davidic prince who acted as Persian Vicegerent in Jerusalem at the Restoration.

The pedigrees of Mt. and Lk. again part company and only meet in Matthan, two generations before Joseph. Although this conflict between the two genealogies may reflect on their historical accuracy, at least it attests their historical independence: each genealogist is convinced of the Davidic descent of Jesus although he differs in his method of proving it.

Numerous erudite and intricate attempts have been made to reconcile these genealogies.

(*a*) Some have maintained that Mt. gives us the genealogy of Joseph, the husband of Mary: while Lk. gives us the genealogy of Mary herself. This is an impossible solution, since Joseph is hailed in Mt. (1^{20}) as the Son of David, which is confirmed by the Angel's message to Mary in Lk. 1^{27} (cf. 1^{32}), and also by the words of the *Benedictus*: 'and hath raised up a horn of salvation for us in the House of his servant David' (Lk. 1^{69}), whereas we are nowhere told that Mary was of Davidic descent. Lk.'s statement in his infancy narrative that she was the cousin of Elisabeth (Lk. 1^{36}), who was a member of the tribe of Levi, would seem to suggest that Mary herself was a member of the priestly tribe.

(*b*) Another attempt at reconciliation has been to maintain that Mt. gives us the legal descent of Jesus whereas Lk. gives us his natural or physical descent. Many eminent modern critics take this view. It is true that different terms are used in each genealogy: Mt. has 'begat' and Lk. has 'the son of,' but is it certain that these terms are used in different senses?

The older theory of Levirate marriage, according to which the actual descent might differ at several points from the legal descent so that there might be two equally valid genealogies running side by side, is regarded as much too artificial and speculative a solution to be acceptable to modern criticism.

It is perfectly clear, however, that both genealogies were intended by their authors to trace the descent of Joseph from David: Mt. deriving the ancestral line from Abraham, and Lk. carrying it back to 'Adam the son of God.'

Quite apart from these genealogies, there is strong evidence for the Davidic descent of Jesus. St. Paul, a learned Rabbi, and at one time a bitter persecutor of Christians, asserts in his Epistle to the Romans that Jesus 'was born of the seed of David, according to the flesh' (Rom. 1^{3}), and the very able Hellenistic Jew who wrote the Epistle to the Hebrews affirms that it is evident 'that our Lord hath sprung out of Judah' (Heb. 7^{14}).

The question in the Synoptists: 'If David calleth him Lord, how is he then his son?' put with regard to the interpretation of the opening words of Ps. 110 would also seem to point to a primitive belief in the Davidic descent of Jesus. Jn., who is aware of it, regards it as valueless to prove the Messianic claim of Jesus ($7^{41, 42}$).

Perhaps the greatest crux of Mt.'s genealogy is contained in its concluding clause:

'Jacob begat Joseph the husband of Mary, of whom was born Jesus, who is called Christ' (1^{16}).

In certain ancient Syriac, Old Latin, and Greek codices a number of variants occur which indicate that the original text was in a form which seemed to demand alteration. It is impossible to produce positive proof as to what was the original form of the passage, but there are strong indications that it may have been—

'Jacob begat Joseph the husband of Mary, Joseph begat Jesus who is called Christ.'

This is the conclusion of Dr. Vincent Taylor, *The Virgin Birth*, pp. 111, 112.

Those eminent critics (Burkitt, Taylor, Allen, etc.) who maintain that the term 'begat' in Mt.'s genealogy is used of legal descent would not understand the original form of 1^{16} as asserting that Joseph was the natural father of Jesus, but merely His legal father.

THE NATIVITY OF THE CHRIST

MT. 1^{18-25}

1 18 Now the birth of Jesus Christ was on
this wise: When his mother Mary had
been betrothed to Joseph, before they
came together she was found with child of
19 the Holy Ghost. And Joseph her husband, being a righteous man, and not
willing to make her a public example, was
20 minded to put her away privily. But
when he thought on these things, behold,
an angel of the Lord appeared unto him in
a dream, saying, Joseph, thou son of David,
fear not to take unto thee Mary thy wife:
for that which is conceived in her is of the
21 Holy Ghost. And she shall bring forth a
son; and thou shalt call his name JESUS;
for it is he that shall save his people from
22 their sins. Now all this is come to pass,
that it might be fulfilled which was spoken
by the Lord through the prophet, saying,
23 Behold, the virgin shall be with child,
and shall bring forth a son.
And they shall call his name Immanuel;
which is, being interpreted, God with us.
24 And Joseph arose from his sleep, and did
as the angel of the Lord commanded him,
25 and took unto him his wife; and knew her
not till she had brought forth a son: and
he called his name JESUS.

Mt. now relates the birth or begetting of Jesus. The fact that the same word (*genesis*) is used here (1^{18}) in the sense of a birth or begetting as is used in 1^{1}, for genealogy or pedigree, would seem to indicate that the genealogy and the nativity sections are by different hands. It is possible that the Gospel originally began here (1^{18}) and that the genealogy was prefixed as an afterthought.

The account which follows is very Jewish in tone and indicates an accurate knowledge of Jewish life. Betrothal constituted in Jewish law a legal relationship which could only be dissolved by legal means.

The word 'righteous' has the technical meaning of a strict observer of the Jewish Law. Legally Joseph could, of course, have secured the disannulment of the betrothal and severe penalties could have been inflicted on Mary. This step, however, he was unwilling to take and proposed to dissolve the relationship but without going to the law courts. His problem is solved for him, however, by an angelic apparition in a dream. In ancient Israel the Divine Being was believed to make His will known in various ways—by prophets, by sacred lots manipulated by the priest, by visions and voices, and by dreams.

In what are called the Elohist sections of the Pentateuch, God makes His will known pre-eminently in dreams, and Joseph 'the dreamer of dreams' is one who is particularly favoured by God with this form of revelation. It is possible that the Old Testament Joseph is in this respect regarded as the precursor of the New Testament Joseph.

The reference to the Holy Spirit as the creative agency in the future Saviour's nativity should be noted here. It reminds the reader of the genesis of creation itself, in which, according to Gen. 1^{2}, the Spirit of God is the creative agent.

In the great conciliar creeds of the Christian Church it is the primal action of the Holy Spirit operating in the Incarnation which is stressed—'conceived of the Holy Ghost.'

Jesus is a Greek form of the Hebrew name Joshua and means 'he shall save.' The ancient saviours of Israel saved their people from foreign oppressors but Jesus shall save His people from a more disastrous and deep-seated evil—moral failure and weakness. The word for people here means Israel, God's people, and the word for sin means 'missing the mark.'

The virgin birth of Jesus is stated by Mt. to be in fulfilment of an Old Testament oracle. Mt. cites twelve of these oracles as having been fulfilled in the life and mission of the Messiah, and he always calls attention to this fulfilment in a formula with which he introduces his Old Testament citation.

'This was done that it might be fulfilled which was spoken by the Lord through the prophet.'

The citation from Is. 7^{14} is taken from the Septuagint, which translates the Hebrew word *'almāh*, which means strictly a young woman of marriageable age, by *parthenos*, which means a virgin. The other Greek versions, more correctly, translate *'almāh* by *neanis*, a young person.

Why the Septuagint used *parthenos* here, which can only be rightly used to translate the Hebrew word *bethûlāh*, is a mystery. No one, however, can maintain on philological grounds that the rendering is other than inaccurate.

Hence in the Is. 7^{14} citation, in the original Hebrew, there is no prediction of a virgin birth for Him who was to be called 'Immanuel, God with us.' Of course Isaiah's prophecy is not concerned with a distant future. Had it concerned a distant future, it would have had little interest or value for Isaiah's contemporaries, who were terrified at an imminent danger from which the prophet predicted deliverance—the sign of this deliverance being the birth and early childhood of Immanuel.

What particular person, if any, Isaiah had in mind when he made this prediction, is a problem unsolved by Old Testament scholars.

Jewish Christians who made use of the Septuagint as their Bible and who believed it to be full of oracles relating to the life and mission of the Messiah seized upon this passage as being a prediction of the *mode* of the Messiah's birth and so came to believe, as it was written in the Scriptures, that Jesus must have been born in this way. This would seem to be in all probability the origin of the primitive Christian belief in the virgin birth of Jesus.

When, however, Jewish Christians began to proclaim the virgin birth of Jesus, it was not unnatural that the unbelieving and hostile Jews should attack what they regarded, not only as a monstrous fiction but also a most impudent misrepresentation of the true text of their Scriptures, by retorting that if Jesus had no known human father that was not because his mother was a virgin, but because she was an immoral woman.

The Jewish Christians who used the Septuagint were not without defence. They were able to maintain that the word *'almāh*, although it meant a young woman either married or unmarried, must be taken in this particular passage to mean unmarried and that the Holy Spirit, who was believed to have guided the seventy Jewish elders who translated the Hebrew Scriptures into Greek, must be believed to have guided them rightly in their selection of the word *parthenos* to render *'almāh*. Those who do not believe in the plenary verbal inspiration of the Septuagint translators—and no modern scholar who has studied the Septuagint can believe in this—are forced to regard the early Christian argument as futile,

No scholar to-day regards the story of the translation of the Septuagint related in the *Epistle of Aristeas* as historical. This 'Scripture-proof' of the virgin birth of Jesus, like a number of other Scripture proofs which Mt. makes use of, has no value as testimony to historic fact.

Joseph, as the result of the Divine oracle vouchsafed to him in his dream, terminates the betrothal by taking Mary to live in his house. Verse 25 indicates that the *semper virgo* or perpetual virginity of Mary has no foundation in Scripture.

THE VISIT OF THE MAGI

MT. 2^{1-12}

2 1 Now when Jesus was born in Bethlehem
of Judæa in the days of Herod the king,
behold, wise men from the east came to
2 Jerusalem, saying, Where is he that is
born King of the Jews? for we saw his star
in the east, and are come to worship him.
3 And when Herod the king heard it, he
was troubled, and all Jerusalem with him.
4 And gathering together all the chief priests
and scribes of the people, he inquired of
them where the Christ should be born.
5 And they said unto him, In Bethlehem of
Judæa: for thus it is written by the
prophet,
6 And thou Bethlehem, land of Judah,
Art in no wise least among the
princes of Judah:
For out of thee shall come forth a
governor,
Which shall be shepherd of my people
Israel.
7 Then Herod privily called the wise men,
and learned of them carefully what time
8 the star appeared. And he sent them to
Bethlehem, and said, Go and search out
carefully concerning the young child; and
when ye have found *him*, bring me word,
that I also may come and worship him.
9 And they, having heard the king, went
their way; and lo, the star, which they saw
in the east, went before them, till it came
and stood over where the young child was.
10 And when they saw the star, they rejoiced
11 with exceeding great joy. And they came
into the house and saw the young child
with Mary his mother; and they fell down
and worshipped him; and opening their
treasures they offered unto him gifts, gold
12 and frankincense and myrrh. And being
warned *of God* in a dream that they should
not return to Herod, they departed into
their own country another way.

Mt., like Lk., records that Jesus was born at Bethlehem, but the circumstances connected with the birth and what follows differ greatly in the two narratives.

In Mt., Jesus is born in the home of Joseph (2^{11}), but in Lk. He is born in a manger because Joseph and Mary, whose home is in Nazareth and who had come up to Bethlehem to be enrolled there, can find no lodging in the inn. Lk. records the visit of the local shepherds to the infant, but says nothing of the visit of the Magi. Mt. records the visit of the Magi, but says nothing of the visit of the shepherds. Mt. records the flight into Egypt; Lk. says nothing of a flight to Egypt, but states that after the Circumcision and Purification, Joseph and Mary having—

'accomplished all things that were according to the law of the Lord, . . . returned into Galilee, to their own city Nazareth.' (Lk. 2^{39}.)

This conflict of evidence attending the circumstances of the birth of Jesus at Bethlehem has raised suspicions as to the accuracy of the statement that He was born at Bethlehem. It is argued that it was natural that primitive Jewish Christians, in view of the prediction of Micah (5^{2}) that from Bethlehem 'should come forth one who shall rule my people Israel,' should feel convinced that Jesus, the Messiah, the son of David, must have been born in Bethlehem, David's town.

[The oracle cited by the Jewish authorities in answer to Herod's question is not a correct quotation either of the Hebrew or of the Septuagint, but reproduces freely the sense of the passage.]

Suspicion as to the historical accuracy of the statements of Mt. and Lk. that Jesus was born at Bethlehem is increased by the fact that in our Gospels He is always spoken of as the Nazarene, Jesus of Nazareth, and in the Acts His early followers are called Nazarenes. Moreover, the Roman official inscription on His cross described Him as the Nazarene. If, however, He had been born in Bethlehem at the time of the taking of the imperial census, one might perhaps expect that the Roman official statement would have described Him as from Bethlehem.

In the story of the visit of Jesus to Nazareth recorded in Mk., Mt., and Lk., Jesus declares, in the Synagogue of Nazareth, that a prophet is not without honour save in his *patris*. The word *patris* means either one's native place or the place in which one's ancestors lived. If Joseph was, as the evidence indicates, a descendant of David, then Bethlehem was the *patris* of Jesus in that sense, and Nazareth was not. In that case the only sense in which Nazareth could be called the *patris* of Jesus would be that it was His birthplace.

New Testament scholars have felt the seriousness of accepting the conclusion that Nazareth, and not Bethlehem, was the birthplace of Jesus, for if Nazareth was His birthplace then no historical weight can be attached to the story of the virgin birth and the attendant circumstances related by Mt. and Lk. in their opening chapters.

Renan, no mean historian, in his *Vie de Jésus* ignores the birth of Jesus at Bethlehem as undeserving of discussion and opens his account of the life of Jesus by saying that He was born at Nazareth, in support of which statement he appends a footnote consisting of numerous New Testament references.

On the other hand, Sir Wm. Ramsay, hardly less eminent as a scholar and archæologist than Renan, argues with great erudition and acumen for the birth of Jesus at Bethlehem in his most readable volume, *Was Christ born in Bethlehem?*

It ought, however, to be mentioned, that facts which have come to light since Ramsay wrote have greatly weakened his argument for a universal Roman census in the reign of Herod the Great.

The King to whom Mt. refers is Herod the Great, who was sovereign, under the Roman imperial rule, of the whole of Palestine and died in the spring of 4 B.C. His character as depicted here by Mt. is true to life. He was cruel, crafty, capable, passionate, and intensely suspicious. There is no record outside Mt. of his massacre of young children in Bethlehem and its neighbourhood, but various murders and massacres were committed by him, and a man who could execute a beloved and beautiful wife and two of his sons because he suspected them of treason would not be likely to hesitate about a slaughter of provincial infants.

The wrath (literally rage) of Herod when he finds himself outwitted by the Magi was a striking feature in the mediæval miracle plays and one much appreciated by the audience. Shakespeare refers to it in *Hamlet*, where he speaks of tearing a passion to tatters and out-Heroding Herod.

Astrology, the predecessor of our modern astronomy, originated in Mesopotamia many centuries before Christ. Sometime before 500 B.C., the Babylonian astrologers had learnt to predict eclipses. Astrology was an important element in Mesopotamian religion. (See Cumont's *Astrological Religions of Babylonia.*) It was also used for the purpose of predicting events in human history, particularly the birth and death of princes. That certain Babylonian astrologers should come to the conclusion that some great personage was to be born in the West Land and that they should set out to seek him, was natural enough.

Classical writers (Suetonius, Pliny the Elder, Dio Cassius) relate that a certain Tiridates, accompanied by other Magi in seeking a world's deliverer, paid a visit to Nero. This of course was some sixty years later than the incident related here by Mt., but we know, from Vergil especially, that there were in the age of the Natitivy widespread pagan messianic expectations.

That when they come as far as it is possible for them to travel overland to the Palestinian coast they should visit the King of the country and ask his assistance in their mission, is what might be expected. Their statement to Herod is more correctly rendered ' We saw his star at its rising ' (*v.* 2). (It differs from the phrase translated ' the East ' in *v.* 1.)

That Jerusalem should be troubled when Herod was troubled is entirely characteristic. Josephus relates that in order to secure national mourning for his own death, Herod collected and imprisoned a large number of prominent citizens and ordered that when he died all of them should be executed.

Again, the phrase, ' in the East ' in *v.* 9 should be translated ' at its rising.' That the star actually stood over the place may be regarded as a dramatic or poetic expression intended to give vividness to the narrative.

The gifts are typically Eastern and were regarded as symbolical by later Christian commentators. Gold it was said symbolised Christ's royalty; incense, His priesthood; myrrh, His entombment. (For the gifts, compare Is. 60^{6}; Ps. $72^{10, 11, 15}$; Cant. 3^{6}.) In mediæval legend those who offer the gifts are kings, thus fulfilling the prophecy of Isaiah:

' Kings shall see and arise; princes, and they shall worship.' (49^{7}.)

' Gentiles shall come to thy light, and kings to the brightness of thy rising.' (60^{3}.)

In the apocryphal Armenian *Gospel of the Infancy* the number of the Magi is given as three, and they are named Melkon (Melchior, King of Persia), Caspar (King of India), and Balthazar (King of Arabia).

THE FLIGHT INTO EGYPT AND THE MASSACRE OF THE INNOCENTS

MT. 2^{13-18}

2 13 Now when they were departed, behold,
an angel of the Lord appeareth to Joseph
in a dream, saying, Arise and take the
young child and his mother, and flee into
Egypt, and be thou there until I tell thee:
for Herod will seek the young child to

14 destroy him. And he arose and took the
young child and his mother by night, and
15 departed into Egypt; and was there until
the death of Herod: that it might be fulfilled which was spoken by the Lord
through the prophet, saying, Out of
16 Egypt did I call my son. Then Herod,
when he saw that he was mocked of the
wise men, was exceeding wroth, and sent
forth, and slew all the male children that
were in Bethlehem, and in all the borders
thereof, from two years old and under,
according to the time which he had care-
17 fully learned of the wise men. Then was
fulfilled that which was spoken by Jeremiah the prophet, saying,
18 A voice was heard in Ramah,
Weeping and great mourning,
Rachel weeping for her children;
And she would not be comforted,
because they are not.

Nowhere else in the Gospels do we find any reference to the Flight into Egypt.

Celsus, the philosopher who attacked the Christian religion most bitterly in the second century, states that Jesus worked as a labourer in Egypt, and there learnt magic which He used when He returned to Palestine in support of His claim to divinity. This charge by Celsus is not regarded as original, but as derived from earlier Jewish accusations which are reflected in the Talmud. There can be no doubt that it is with the object of meeting these accusations that Mt. records the Flight into Egypt.

The passage from Hosea (11^1) which is cited as being fulfilled by the return of Jesus from Egypt cannot be regarded as a fulfilment. Hosea in this passage is not predicting the future. He is making an historical reference to the past. He refers to Jehovah's deliverance of Israel out of Egypt which began its national life. Israel is spoken of as Jehovah's son in the Old Testament as is also at a later date the Messianic King of Israel.

The words of Hosea are therefore not, from the historical point of view, fulfilled by Jesus. The primitive Christians seem to have been for the most part entirely lacking in the power to interpret their Scriptures historically. Their interpretation was allegorical, dramatic, poetic and, above all, predictive. This is seen in Mt.'s citation from Jeremiah (31^{15}) (following for the most part the Septuagint) which he regards as being fulfilled by Herod's massacre of the babes of Bethlehem. The context in Jeremiah indicates clearly that the passage Mt. cites makes no reference whatsoever to the slaughter of children. The passage pictures Nebuchadnezzar's captives from Jerusalem, filing along the road, past Ramah, on their way into captivity in Babylon. Rachel's tomb was at Ramah, and she, a mother in Israel, is finely represented by Jeremiah as standing by the roadside weeping for her children who are being driven into exile.

The massacre at Bethlehem is not recorded by Josephus nor by any classical writer.

THE RETURN TO PALESTINE

MT. 2^{19-23}

2 19 But when Herod was dead, behold, an
angel of the Lord appeareth in a dream to
20 Joseph in Egypt, saying, Arise and take
the young child and his mother, and go
into the land of Israel: for they are dead
21 that sought the young child's life. And
he arose and took the young child and his
mother, and came into the land of Israel.
22 But when he heard that Archelaus was
reigning over Judæa in the room of his
father Herod, he was afraid to go thither;
and being warned *of God* in a dream, he
23 withdrew into the parts of Galilee, and
came and dwelt in a city called Nazareth:
that it might be fulfilled which was spoken
by the prophets, that he should be called
a Nazarene.

Herod the Great, who died 4 B.C., was succeeded by three sons.

According to Jewish custom, Herod's inheritance was divided into four portions. Archelaus, the eldest son, received two portions, represented by Judæa, with the title Ethnarch. The two other sons, Antipas and Philip, received one portion each, with the title of Tetrarch: Galilee and Peræa (a district east of the Jordan) constituted the Tetrarchy of Antipas ; Philip's Kingdom consisted of Ituræa and Trachonitis (see Lk. 3^{1}).

Archelaus turned out to be a very tyrannical and incompetent ruler and after ten years was deposed by the Romans. He is probably referred to as the nobleman who went away to receive a Kingdom but was withstood by a protest of his citizens (Lk. $19^{12\text{f.}}$). The Jews sent an embassy to the Roman Emperor to protest against the appointment of Archelaus, but were unsuccessful.

The Old Testament oracles referred to by Mt. have caused much difficulty. There is no Old Testament oracle which affirms that the Messiah, or indeed anyone else, shall be called the Nazarene (*Nazoraios*).

Jewish writers are fond of assonances or puns, and the reference to Nazarene here is taken to be of that character.

In Hebrew there is a word *nêtser*, which means a branch or sprout. This is used in the Messianic prophecy of Is. 11^{1}:

'And there shall come forth a shoot out of the stem of Jesse,
And a Branch shall grow out of his roots.'

In Jeremiah 23^{5}, 33^{15} the Messiah is described as a branch (although a different Hebrew word is used here).

Archdeacon Allen, a very competent Semitic scholar, writes:

'If the play on the words *nêtser* = branch, and Nazara be thought too artificial for the Evangelist, his statement that the prophets had foretold that Christ should be called a Nazorean must remain unexplained.'

There is a collection of a number of just as feeble assonances or bad puns to be found in Micah $1^{10\text{-}12}$.

If the incidents related by Mt. in connexion with the birth of Jesus are not historical, how are they to be accounted for? The impulse which produced them would appear to be twofold.

(1) The desire to find in the life of the Messiah fulfilments of certain Old Testament oracles. The Old Testament, not the New Testament, was 'the Scriptures' of the primitive Christian Church throughout the first century of the Christian era. These Scriptures were in the early Christian view divinely inspired and infallible and were full of predictions divinely intended to be fulfilled in the life and mission of the Messiah. It was by pointing to the fulfilment of these predictions by Jesus that He was proved, to the Jews especially, to be the Messiah, although they had been blind enough to reject and crucify Him.

(2) The need for the defence of the Christian faith in Jesus as the Messiah against the slanderous attacks of Judaism.

(*a*) The virgin-birth story is not only a miraculous fulfilment of the Divine oracle in Is. 7^{14}, but also a refutation of the Jewish slander that Jesus was a bastard and His mother an immoral woman. No bastard could be the Messiah, still less one who had a Gentile father; therefore if the Jewish slander was not confuted the Christian claim for the Messiahship of Jesus lapsed.

Modern Christian scholars can decisively defeat the charge that Jesus was a bastard and Mary an immoral woman, but by quite different arguments from those which Mt. employs.

(*b*) The birth at Bethlehem is not only a fulfilment of the Divine oracle in Micah 5^{2}, but it is also an evidence that Jesus was of the House of David, both of which primitive Christian claims were denied by the unbelieving Jews. Jesus, they asserted, was born in 'poor despiséd Nazareth' and had come forth from Galilee whence ariseth no prophet. As for His Davidic descent, they regarded it as an impudent fiction.

(*c*) The visit of the Magi was not only a fulfilment of Old Testament oracles (though these are not cited by Mt.) but it also foreshadowed the adoration of the Messiah by the Gentiles. (E.g. 'The Gentiles shall come to thy light and kings to the brightness of thy rising' (Is. 60^{3}). 'To him shall be given the gold of Arabia: incense shall be offered unto him.' (Ps. 72^{15}.))

Gentile wise men inspired, not by the oracles of the Old Testament (and perhaps that is why they are not cited here) but inspired by their astrological researches, are led to seek out and worship the infant Messiah, long before He is recognised as Messiah by the Jews. The massacre of infants which the visit of the Magi caused was not their fault. It is a fulfilment of a Divine oracle in Jeremiah (31^{15}).

(*d*) The flight into Egypt followed by the return to Palestine is not only a fulfilment of the Divine oracle in Hosea 11^{1}, but is a confutation of the Jewish slander that Jesus was a magician, who had received His training in Egypt, the home of magic, and was thus able to perform remarkable miracles, but not by the power of the Spirit of God. The story of the Flight into Egypt admits that Jesus was in Egypt, but shows that He went there in obedience to Divine providence and left the country long before He was able to be instructed by its magicians.

(*e*) The residence in despised Nazareth was not only the fulfilment of Divine oracles which had declared that the Messiah should be called a Nazarene (or human shoot from the great trunk of David), but also an act of obedience to a Divine warning vouchsafed to Joseph, which forbad Him to reside in Judæa.

Without denying that there is any historical basis for these early narratives of Mt., save the undoubted fact that Jesus lived in Nazareth and began His religious mission in Galilee, it does seem possible to explain their origin as the product of the double motive of the fulfilment of Old Testament oracles and the necessity for confuting Jewish attacks upon the primitive Christian faith in Jesus.

These narratives, unhistorical though they may be, are seen when viewed in this way to be sincere. They are not forgeries or deliberate fictions, but are the products of a mind which, being absolutely convinced of the Divine truth of the Scriptures and of the Messiahship of Jesus, creates out of these convictions a series of narratives with which to confute the falsehoods of Jewish opponents.

JOHN HESITATES TO BAPTISE JESUS

MT. 3^{13-15}

3 13 Then cometh Jesus from Galilee to the
Jordan unto John, to be baptized of him.
14 But John would have hindered him, saying,
I have need to be baptized of thee, and
15 comest thou to me? But Jesus answering
said unto him, Suffer it now: for thus it
becometh us to fulfil all righteousness.
Then he suffereth him.

[MT. 3^{1-12} is explained in connexion with its Marcan parallel.]

This section constitutes Mt.'s defence against the Jewish charge that Jesus was a sinner and conscious of His sin, and therefore He came to Jn.'s baptism. The Baptist is represented by Mt. as recognising the moral superiority of Jesus and confessing that he, the Baptist, ought to be baptised by Jesus. Jesus, however, explains that His purpose in coming to the baptism is not that He may be washed from His sins but that He may fulfil all righteousness, by which is meant perform every duty. It is in short, not as a sinner, but as an example to others, that Jesus is baptised.

There is no parallel to this in Mk. and Lk., but in Jn. the spirit of the incident, though not the incident itself, is reflected in the words of Jesus: Which of you convicteth me of sin? (Jn. 8^{46}.)

Many modern critics regard this dialogue between Jesus and the Baptist as unhistorical, and as created solely for apologetic reasons. Even though the dialogue be an apologetic creation it may yet represent truly the spirit in which Jesus came as one loyal to John's prophetic mission, his proclamation of the need for a new heart and a new mind by Israel. Adhesion to this mission was symbolised and consecrated by the public act of Baptism.

JESUS BEGINS HIS MINISTRY AT CAPERNAUM

MT. 4^{12-17}

4 12 Now when he heard that John was
delivered up, he withdrew into Galilee;
13 and leaving Nazareth, he came and dwelt
in Capernaum, which is by the sea, in the
14 borders of Zebulun and Naphtali: that it
might be fulfilled which was spoken by
Isaiah the prophet, saying,
15 The land of Zebulun and the land of
Naphtali
Toward the sea, beyond Jordan,
Galilee of the Gentiles,
16 The people which sat in darkness
Saw a great light,
And to them which sat in the region
and shadow of death,
To them did light spring up.
17 From that time began Jesus to preach,
and to say, Repent ye: for the kingdom of
heaven is at hand.

Mt. is dependent upon Mk. for the date when Jesus begins His Galilean mission. It was after the arrest of John the Baptist. The phrase 'withdrew into Galilee' might seem to suggest that Jesus Himself was apprehensive of arrest. This, however, could not be the motive for His action, since Galilee was a part of the territory of Herod Antipas who had arrested the Baptist.

The Baptist's arrest opened the way for Jesus to carry on the religious mission which the arrest of the Baptist had checked. That no doubt was the reason why Jesus left the region of the Lower Jordan or the desert of Judæa to begin His mission in Galilee. Mt. clearly indicates that He did not begin the mission in

His native Nazareth, but began it on the other side of Galilee in Capernaum, which He made His permanent home.

The word 'dwelt' is a translation of a Greek word which means, not to sojourn temporarily, but to dwell permanently. Mt. is here fuller and more precise than Mk. Mt. 3^2 has already stated that the preaching of the Baptist was, 'Repent ye, for the Kingdom of Heaven is at hand.' Hence in Mt. Jesus is made to begin His mission by repeating the message of the Baptist. Mk., however, in his account of the Baptist's preaching says nothing of the proclamation of the Kingdom of God. John preaches repentance to be followed by Baptism, but predicts the advent of One who shall baptise 'not with water but with the Spirit.'

In Mk., it is Jesus, not John, who declares that the Kingdom of Heaven is at hand, and that men should repent and believe the glad tidings. No doubt Mk. is to be preferred to Mt. on this point.

Mt. finds in Jesus dwelling at Capernaum on the seashore of the Lake of Galilee a fulfilment of Is. $9^{1,\,2}$. In its original context, Isaiah here predicts deliverance for the people of Northern Israel who had suffered grievously from the terrible Assyrian invasions of the early eighth century B.C. Zebulun and Naphtali are the names of two of the northern tribes. The 'way of the sea' refers either to the Syrian coast road from Egypt right up to and beyond Beirut and the Dog River—a great military road used from 2,000 B.C. down to modern times, or else the road from Megiddo to Damascus which ran near the Lake of Galilee.

Jewish prejudice against the Galilean character of the Messiah and His mission is reflected by Mt.'s citation. There can be little doubt that the Jewish opponents maintained that the true Messiah would make Jerusalem, the sacred city, the originating centre of His mission.

> 'For out of Zion shall go forth the Law
> And the Word of the Lord from Jerusalem.' (Is. 2^3; Micah 4^2.)

We cannot but admire the acumen and ingenuity of the Jewish-Christian scribe who confutes his opponents with an Isaianic prophecy of the evangelisation of Galilee by the Messiah.

THE HEALING OF THE CENTURION'S SERVANT

MT. 8^{5-13}

8 5 And when he was entered into Capernaum, there came unto him a centurion,
6 beseeching him, and saying, Lord, my servant lieth in the house sick of the palsy,
7 grievously tormented. And he saith unto
8 him, I will come and heal him. And the centurion answered and said, Lord, I am not worthy that thou shouldest come under my roof: but only say the word, and my
9 servant shall be healed. For I also am a man under authority, having under myself soldiers: and I say to this one, Go, and he goeth; and to another, Come, and he cometh; and to my servant, Do this, and

LK. 7^{1-10}

7 1 After he had ended all his sayings in the ears of the people, he entered into Capernaum.
2 And a certain centurion's servant, who was dear unto him, was sick and at the
3 point of death. And when he heard concerning Jesus, he sent unto him elders of the Jews, asking him that he would come
4 and save his servant. And they, when they came to Jesus, besought him earnestly, saying, He is worthy that thou
5 shouldest do this for him: for he loveth our nation, and himself built us our synagogue.
6 And Jesus went with them. And when he

10 he doeth it. And when Jesus heard it, he
marvelled, and said to them that followed,
Verily I say unto you, I have not found so
11 great faith, no, not in Israel. And I say
unto you, that many shall come from the
east and the west, and shall sit down with
Abraham, and Isaac, and Jacob, in the
12 kingdom of heaven: but the sons of the
kingdom shall be cast forth into the outer
darkness: there shall be the weeping and
13 gnashing of teeth. And Jesus said unto
the centurion, Go thy way; as thou hast
believed, *so* be it done unto thee. And
the servant was healed in that hour.

was now not far from the house, the centurion sent friends to him, saying unto
him, Lord, trouble not thyself: for I am
not worthy that thou shouldest come
7 under my roof: wherefore neither thought
I myself worthy to come unto thee: but
say the word, and my servant shall be
8 healed. For I also am a man set under
authority, having under myself soldiers:
and I say to this one, Go, and he goeth;
and to another, Come, and he cometh;
and to my servant, Do this, and he doeth
9 it. And when Jesus heard these things,
he marvelled at him, and turned and said
unto the multitude that followed him, I
say unto you, I have not found so great
10 faith, no, not in Israel. And they that
were sent, returning to the house, found
the servant whole.

Although the healing of the Capernaum centurion's servant is recorded both in Mt. and Lk., there are important differences in the two accounts. Lk. relates that the humility of the centurion was so great that he sent a delegation to Jesus of Jewish elders. They, in preferring the centurion's request, emphasise his love for Judaism as shown by his having built them their synagogue.

If Capernaum is rightly identified with Tel-Hum (and not with Khan-Minyeh), then it is quite possible that the remains of a stately building in the Græco-Roman style to be seen there to-day are those of the synagogue built by the centurion. In that case it would be the synagogue in which Jesus began His Galilean ministry and was hailed as Messiah by a demoniac.

A second delegation, this time consisting of the friends of the centurion, meets Jesus as He is approaching the house, deprecating that He should trouble to come any farther. The centurion is convinced that Jesus has only to command and the demon of sickness will leave his servant. Jesus is amazed at the centurion's faith and declares that He has not found its equal in Israel. The rest of the saying which Matthew records as being said by Jesus on this occasion Lk. has got in 13^{28-30} in answer to the question put to Jesus on His journey through Peræa: Are there few that be saved?

The Greek word used in *v.* 10 should be translated *slave* not *servant.* Besides his great faith and extreme humility, the centurion deserves to be remembered for his humanity to his sick slave.

Mt. omits both delegations, but the likeness between Mt. and Lk. in relating this incident is so close that it is plain they are using the same literary source.

The comment of Jesus on the centurion's faith as given by Lk. is to be preferred historically to that of Mt. At this stage in His ministry Jesus could hardly have pronounced the rejection of Israel and the call of the Gentiles.

THE TWO ASPIRANTS

(MT. 8^{18-22})

See Lk. 9^{57-62}, p. 277.

THE HEALING OF TWO BLIND MEN

MT. 9^{27-31}

9 27 And as Jesus passed by from thence,
two blind men followed him, crying out,
and saying, Have mercy on us, thou son of
28 David. And when he was come into the
house, the blind men came to him: and
Jesus saith unto them, Believe ye that I
am able to do this? They say unto him,
29 Yea, Lord. Then touched he their eyes,
saying, According to your faith be it done
30 unto you. And their eyes were opened.
And Jesus strictly charged them, saying,
31 See that no man know it. But they went
forth, and spread abroad his fame in all
that land.

Mt. has a habit of duplicating. That Jesus in this early stage of His ministry should have been addressed by the Messianic title, Son of David, which in Mk. is only used in addressing Jesus on the last stage of His final journey to Jerusalem, suggests that Mt. has got this incident out of its right order. It is to be noted that blind Bartimæus uses this title in addressing Jesus, as does the Syro-Phœnician woman in Mt.

THE HEALING OF A DUMB DEMONIAC

MT. 9^{32-34}

9 32 And as they went forth, behold, there
was brought to him a dumb man possessed
33 with a devil. And when the devil was
cast out, the dumb man spake: and the
multitudes marvelled, saying, It was never
34 so seen in Israel. But the Pharisees said,
By the prince of the devils casteth he out
devils.

The house in which the healing is related to have taken place is no doubt St. Peter's in Capernaum. Nothing is here said of the faith of the dumb man, probably because being dumb he was not able to express it.

THE BAPTIST IN PRISON SENDS TO JESUS

MT. 11^{2-6}

11 2 Now when John heard in the prison the
works of the Christ, he sent by his dis-
3 ciples, and said unto him, Art thou he that
4 cometh, or look we for another? And
Jesus answered and said unto them, Go
your way and tell John the things which
5 ye do hear and see: the blind receive their
sight, and the lame walk, the lepers are
cleansed, and the deaf hear, and the dead
are raised up, and the poor have good
6 tidings preached to them. And blessed is
he, whosoever shall find none occasion of
stumbling in me.

LK. 7^{18-23}

7 18 And the disciples of John told him of all
19 these things. And John calling unto him
two of his disciples sent them to the Lord,
saying, Art thou he that cometh, or look
20 we for another? And when the men were
come unto him, they said, John the Baptist hath sent us unto thee, saying, Art thou
he that cometh, or look we for another?
21 In that hour he cured many of diseases
and plagues and evil spirits; and on many
22 that were blind he bestowed sight. And
he answered and said unto them, Go your
way, and tell John what things ye have
seen and heard; the blind receive their
sight, the lame walk, the lepers are
cleansed, and the deaf hear, the dead are
raised up, the poor have good tidings
23 preached to them. And blessed is he,
whosoever shall find none occasion of
stumbling in me.

If John the Baptist had himself witnessed the theophany at the Baptism of Jesus and had received the special testimony to His Messiahship to which the Baptist himself bears witness in Jn. 1^{32-33}, it would be no easy matter to explain the embassy of John's disciples to Jesus enquiring whether He is the Messiah. (The Coming One was a Messianic title.)

If, however, the experience of Jesus at His Baptism was purely subjective, as in Mk., then the Baptist's embassy and question are quite comprehensible, although they conflict acutely with the Baptist's protest of his unworthiness to baptise Jesus in Mt. $3^{14, 15}$.

When the Baptist baptised Jesus, we may assume, following Mk., that John was not aware that Jesus was the Messiah, but John, hearing when in prison from his own disciples of the extraordinary success attending the mission of Jesus, sent to enquire if Jesus were the Messiah. (Lk. states that the disciples sent were two in number.)

Jesus in harmony with His reticence about His Messianic claim makes no direct reply, but points to the beneficent results attending His mission, using language which will remind the Baptist of the description of the effect of the mission of the Servant of the Lord as described in Is. $61^{1f.}$.

Lk. would seem to indicate that Jesus actually wrought miracles in the presence of the Baptist's disciples in order to prove His Messiahship. This is extremely improbable in view of our Lord's refusal on other occasions to give proofs of His Messianic mission by working a 'sign.'

The Beatitude, 'Blessed is he whosoever shall not be offended by me,' is intended to console John the Baptist. The Baptist would seem to have expected the advent of a successor of extraordinary majesty and severity; one who would utterly destroy all the evil. Jesus with His mission of preaching the Glad Tidings to the poor and performing deeds of pity and beneficence must strike one of the Baptist's temper and expectations as a very disappointing Messiah.

The attitude of Jesus towards the ascetic and apocalyptic Baptist here is one of sympathetic reverence, yet He recognises, notwithstanding the splendour of the Baptist's personality, the limitations of his religious message. He who is but a little one (a minor) in the Kingdom is greater than he. God's Kingdom of love and life, as Jesus conceived of it, is beyond the Baptist's ken.

Mt. and Lk. are evidently making use of the same literary source here.

ST. PETER WALKING ON THE WATER

MT. 14^{28-31}

14 28 And Peter answered him and said,
Lord, if it be thou, bid me come unto thee
29 upon the waters. And he said, Come.
And Peter went down from the boat, and
walked upon the waters, to come to
30 Jesus. But when he saw the wind, he
was afraid; and beginning to sink, he
31 cried out, saying, Lord, save me. And
immediately Jesus stretched forth his
hand, and took hold of him, and saith
unto him, O thou of little faith, wherefore
didst thou doubt?

This incident of St. Peter's walking on the water is one of a series of Petrine stories which have for their purpose the exaltation of St. Peter and are peculiar to Mt. They have, on the whole, a low historical value.

The obvious lesson of the incident is that, by the power of faith, things can be accomplished which would otherwise be impossible.

THE COIN IN THE FISH'S MOUTH

MT. 17^{24-27}

17 24 And when they were come to Capernaum they that received the half-shekel
came to Peter, and said, Doth not your
25 master pay the half-shekel? He saith,
Yea. And when he came into the house,
Jesus spake first to him, saying, What
thinkest thou, Simon? the kings of the
earth, from whom do they receive toll or
tribute? from their sons, or from stran-
26 gers? And when he said, From strangers,
27 Jesus said unto him, Therefore the sons
are free. But, lest we cause them to
stumble, go thou to the sea, and cast a
hook, and take up the fish that first cometh
up; and when thou hast opened his mouth,
thou shalt find a shekel: that take, and
give unto them for me and thee.

This is another Petrine incident. Those who receive the didrachma are not the publicans or tax-gatherers who collected taxes, often by oppressive means, for the Roman government. They are the eminently respectable persons who collected the Temple tax of half a shekel which every adult male Jew was required to pay annually for the maintenance of the Temple and its worship. According to Jewish legal tradition this tax was instituted by Moses:

'And the Lord spake unto Moses, saying, When thou takest the sum of the children of Israel after their number, then shall they give every man a ransom for his soul unto the Lord, when thou numberest them: that there be no plague among them, when thou numberest them. This they shall give, every one that passeth among them that are numbered, half a shekel after the shekel of the sanctuary: (a shekel is twenty gerahs:) an half shekel shall be the offering of the Lord.' (Exod. 30^{11-13}.)

The coin which is here called a didrachma or double drachma was the exact equivalent in Antioch to the Jewish half-shekel. It is said that Antioch was the only place in the Roman Empire where this was so. This is a reason, albeit a minor one, for identifying the place of origin of Matthew with Antioch.

The Temple tax-gatherers, it is of interest to note, come to Peter's house in Capernaum which Jesus had made the headquarters of His mission in the vicinity of the Galilean lake. The fact that the tax-gatherers come there to collect the tax from Jesus suggests that He must have resided with Peter a considerable time, as well as suggesting that Jesus was not a permanent resident of Capernaum or they would have known what His custom was in the matter of the Temple tax. The incident also suggests that there must have been some popular feeling that the religious movement preached by Jesus might be continued as a revolt against the Jewish ecclesiastical authorities in Jerusalem.

The question of Jesus to Peter, 'How seems it to thee, Simon, do the kings of the earth receive tax or tribute from natives (their own sons) or from foreigners?' reflects the practice of the ancient East, that members of the victorious and ruling race were not subject to taxation. It was their privilege to levy taxes on their subject races. The disciples of Jesus therefore who are the Sons of the Kingdom, the adherents of the Messiah, are free from an obligation to pay the Jewish Temple tax. Yet because our Lord desires that there should be no cause of needless offence between His disciples and the Jews, He consents to the payment of the tax, and indicates to Peter the means by which it may be paid. This payment is made by catching a fish with a stater in its mouth. The stater was a silver coin equal in value to the shekel or two didrachmas, the amount due to the Temple from Jesus and Peter.

Some have regarded this incident as frankly miraculous, others as a coincidence. Jesus, it is supposed, had said to Peter: You will have to go and catch some fish to pay this tax. Peter went, and the first fish he caught had a stater in its mouth. As a consequence, Peter assumed, that when Jesus had directed him to go and catch fish he had foreseen what was to take place.

It is possible that the incident may be explained in this way. Rix in *Tent and Testament* (p. 119) relates that there is a fish (*Coracinus*) in the Lake of Galilee, the male of which has the curious habit of carrying the young in its mouth till in some cases they are three or four inches long. It is possible that a fish of such habits might carry a coin in this way.

Others see in this whole incident a reflection of a problem with which, years after the Crucifixion of Jesus, the Jewish Christian Church was faced. Ought Jews, who had become Christians, to pay the Temple tax or were they not morally and spiritually free to cease payment? This story sought to solve their doubts by the authority of Jesus Himself. They were morally and spiritually free not to pay, but if by non-payment they gave offence to Jewish relations and neighbours, then they had better pay.

Josephus states that after the destruction of Jerusalem and the Temple in A.D. 70, the Romans insisted on the Jews paying the Temple tax to the maintenance of the Pagan Temple of Jupiter Capitolinus, erected on the ancient Temple site. If this be so, then the story must have arisen before A.D. 70.

THE FATE OF JUDAS ISCARIOT

MT. 27 3-10

27 3 Then Judas, which betrayed him,
when he saw that he was condemned,
repented himself, and brought back the
thirty pieces of silver to the chief priests
4 and elders, saying, I have sinned in that
I betrayed innocent blood. But they
said, What is that to us? see thou *to it*.
5 And he cast down the pieces of silver into
the sanctuary, and departed; and he
6 went away and hanged himself. And
the chief priests took the pieces of silver,
and said, It is not lawful to put them into
the treasury, since it is the price of blood.
7 And they took counsel, and bought with
them the potter's field, to bury strangers
8 in. Wherefore that field was called, The
9 field of blood, unto this day. Then was
fulfilled that which was spoken by
Jeremiah the prophet, saying, And they
took the thirty pieces of silver, the price
of him that was priced, whom *certain* of
10 the children of Israel did price; and they
gave them for the potter's field, as the
Lord appointed me.

ACTS 1 18-19

1 18 (Now this man obtained a field with the
reward of his iniquity; and falling headlong, he burst asunder in the midst, and
19 all his bowels gushed out. And it became
known to all the dwellers at Jerusalem;
insomuch that in their language that field
was called Akeldama, that is, The field of
blood.)

There are two accounts of the fate of Judas Iscariot in the New Testament. But they are in disagreement on many points.

Mt. alone relates the repentance or rather the remorse of Judas when he saw that his act of betrayal must lead to the death of his Master. This would seem to indicate that when Judas betrayed his Master he did not intend to cause the death of Jesus. He hoped possibly that it would lead Jesus to vindicate His Messiahship by some act of power, possibly by invoking a Divine intervention.

Peter's speech, as recorded in Acts, makes no suggestion of the repentance of Judas. Both accounts, however, are agreed that the death of Judas was violent. Mt. definitely states that it came about by suicide.

Acts would seem to suggest that possibly when going to view his newly acquired field Judas fell over a precipice with fatal results. Both Mt. and Acts know of a Field of Blood (Akeldama) connected with the memory of Judas, but give different reasons for it being so called. Mt. relates that it was called the Field of Blood because purchased with the blood money which Judas received for betraying Jesus. Acts relates that it was called the Field of Blood because the blood of Judas was poured out on it.

Mt.'s statement that Judas cast the thirty pieces of silver into the very shrine of the Temple itself suggests his desperate mood. To cast the money into the shrine, Judas would have to traverse the Court of the Priests which it was not lawful for him to do. The refusal of the Jerusalem priesthood to place the money in the Corban or sacred treasury was in accordance with the Deuteronomic law which prohibited money obtained by base means being given to the House of the Lord. (Dt. 23^{18}.)

Mt. sees in the purchase of the Potter's Field as a cemetery for strangers, with the money for which Jesus was betrayed, the fulfilment of a passage in Zech. 11^{13}. The prophet Zechariah narrates the meagre sum (thirty pieces of silver) paid to the true shepherd of Israel. What he sardonically calls ' the goodly price ' at which he was valued—the price of a male slave—the shepherd, by Divine command, cast into the treasury of the Temple.

There is some doubt about the true text of Zechariah here, which has ' potter ' for ' treasury.' The two words are very much alike in the Hebrew. It suits Mt.'s fulfilment of prophecy to read ' potter,' which fits in with the purchase of the Potter's Field. On the other hand ' treasury ' suits the context in Zechariah.

The early Christian Church, which shows a tendency to paint in ever darker colours the characters of its enemies, and in certain cases to depict with gratification their horrible fates—exemplified in the great work of Lactantius *On the Death of the Persecutors*—developed in disgusting detail the end of Judas Iscariot. Papias tells of the swelling of the body of Judas, which even while he was yet alive became a mass of putrefaction. This is further developed by a later Christian writer. (See Article on Judas Iscariot in Hastings' *Dictionary of the Bible*.)

PILATE'S WIFE'S DREAM

MT. 27^{19}

27 19 And while he was sitting on the judgement seat, his wife sent unto him, saying, Have thou nothing to do with that righteous man: for I have suffered many things this day in a dream because of him.

Mt.'s record of this incident is intended to stress the fact that Jesus was not regarded as a criminal by the Roman authorities. It was the Jews who forced Pilate, against his will and better judgement, to crucify Jesus. Pilate's wife is unknown to history, save for this incident. What she suffered on account of Jesus is not recorded; artists have sought to depict her dream, which they have imagined to be a vision of Jesus, as the King of humanity, receiving the adoration of all mankind. In the New Testament the phrase 'in a dream' occurs six times in Mt. alone, five of these being in chapters 1 and 2. God was believed by pagans to reveal His will in dreams. This was also the belief of the Jews.

Pilate's wife is named Procla, or Claudia Procula, in the apocryphal *Gospel of Nicodemus* (*Acts of Pilate*). Later she was canonised.

PILATE WASHING HIS HANDS

MT. $27^{24, 25}$

27 24 So when Pilate saw that he prevailed
nothing, but rather that a tumult was
arising, he took water, and washed his
hands before the multitude, saying, I am
innocent of the blood of this righteous
25 man: see ye *to it*. And all the people
answered and said, His blood *be* on us,
and on our children.

This incident is intended to demonstrate that Pilate refused to take responsibility for condemning Jesus to death and that the responsibility for the death of Jesus was deliberately accepted by the Jewish leaders and people. No doubt the early Christian Church saw in the terrible bloodshed which accompanied the capture of Jerusalem by the Romans under Vespasian and Titus the exacting of Divine vengeance for the death of the Messiah.

It has seemed very doubtful whether this incident can be historical. It is impossible to imagine that a Roman procurator, the symbol in his region of Roman justice, could openly, by a symbolic action, declare his failure to face the responsibility to see justice done.

'It is not the custom of the Romans,' was the firm reply, with some touch of superiority in it, with which Festus, a successor of Pilate, declined to yield to Jewish pressure to act unjustly. (Acts 25^{16}.)

Pontius Pilate (fifth procurator of Judæa A.D. 26–36) appears in a much more favourable light in the Gospel accounts of him than in Jewish accounts. In Jewish accounts he is described as hard, merciless, cruel, obdurate, unjust. He made no effort apparently either to understand or to conciliate Jewish feeling. His governorship was marked by various acts of insult and outrage. He was deprived finally of his governorship on account of his cruel massacre of the Samaritans.

Pilate's efforts, as related in the Gospels, to conciliate the Jews and to deliver Jesus from the death sentence are so unlike the Pilate of secular history, as to suggest a Christian apologetic motive having influenced our Gospel accounts. Undoubtedly the cruel persecution of the primitive Christian Church by the Jews, in contrast to the general attitude of the Roman imperial officials towards the Christians, led primitive Christian writers to stress the implacable persistency of the Jews in their demand for the death of Jesus and also led to this being contrasted with the mild and humane attitude of the Roman governor. It is not surprising to find that in later Christian legend, Pilate himself becomes a Christian penitent, and in the Coptic Church was elevated to the rank of saint and martyr.

In the Greek Orthodox Church, as well as in the Coptic Church, his wife is honoured as a saint.

RESURRECTION OF JEWISH SAINTS

MT. 27^{51b-53}

27 51 And the earth did quake; and the
52 rocks were rent; and the tombs were
opened; and many bodies of the saints
53 that had fallen asleep were raised; and
coming forth out of the tombs after his
resurrection they entered into the holy
city and appeared unto many.

Mt. alone relates the earthquake at the death of Jesus and the rending of the rocks. He alone relates the opening of the sepulchres in the vicinity of Jerusalem and the actual coming forth from these sepulchres of the bodies of the saints which slept therein and their entrance into the Holy City and their appearance to many after the resurrection of Jesus Himself.

It is difficult to regard these incidents as historical, though easy enough to account for their creation. They are doubtless due to the desire to secure the precise fulfilment of an oracle in Isaiah.

'Thy dead men shall live, together with my dead body shall they arise. Awake and sing, ye that dwell in dust; for thy dew is as the dew of herbs, and the earth shall cast out the dead.' (Is. 26^{19} A.V.)

The Rabbi Gamaliel, the teacher of St. Paul, had maintained that this oracle (Is. 26^{19}) proved the truth of the doctrine of the Resurrection of the Dead. Its literal fulfilment, so primitive Christians must have felt, required, not only the resurrection of Jesus, but also the resurrection of others with Him.

The phraseology of these Matthæan incidents is strongly Jewish, e.g. 'the Saints' for the pious Jewish dead; 'sleeping' as a description of death; the 'Holy City' as the name for Jerusalem. On contemporary Jewish coins we have the inscription 'Jerusalem, the Holy.'

THE SEALED TOMB AND THE ROMAN GUARD

MT. 27^{62-66}, $28^{1-8, 11-15}$

27 62 Now on the morrow, which is *the day*
after the Preparation, the chief priests
and the Pharisees were gathered together
63 unto Pilate, saying, Sir, we remember
that that deceiver said, while he was yet
alive, After three days I rise again.
64 Command therefore that the sepulchre be
made sure until the third day, lest haply
his disciples come and steal him away,
and say unto the people, He is risen from
the dead: and the last error will be worse
65 than the first. Pilate said unto them, Ye
have a guard: go your way, make it *as*
66 sure as ye can. So they went, and made
the sepulchre sure, sealing the stone, the
guard being with them.
28 1 Now late on the sabbath day, as it
began to dawn toward the first *day* of the
week, came Mary Magdalene and the
2 other Mary to see the sepulchre. And behold, there was a great earthquake; for
an angel of the Lord descended from
heaven, and came and rolled away the
3 stone, and sat upon it. His appearance
was as lightning, and his raiment white
4 as snow: and for fear of him the watchers
did quake, and became as dead men.
5 And the angel answered and said unto

the women, Fear not ye: for I know that
ye seek Jesus, which hath been crucified.
6 He is not here; for he is risen, even as he
said. Come, see the place where the
7 Lord lay. And go quickly, and tell his
disciples, He is risen from the dead; and
lo, he goeth before you into Galilee; there
shall ye see him: lo, I have told you.
8 And they departed quickly from the
tomb with fear and great joy, and ran to
bring his disciples word.
11 Now while they were going, behold,
some of the guard came into the city, and
told unto the chief priests all the things
12 that were come to pass. And when they
were assembled with the elders, and had
taken counsel, they gave large money
13 unto the soldiers, saying, Say ye, His disciples came by night, and stole him away
14 while we slept. And if this come to the
governor's ears, we will persuade him,
15 and rid you of care. So they took the
money, and did as they were taught: and
this saying was spread abroad among the
Jews, *and continueth* until this day.

Mt. alone refers to the Roman guard. This incident, like a number of other incidents peculiar to Mt., is plainly apologetic. It is intended to refute a slanderous statement of Jewish controversialists that Jesus did not rise from the dead, but that His disciples stole away His body from the sepulchre as a preliminary to proclaiming His resurrection. Various features of the story of the Roman guard suggest that it is unhistorical.

(*a*) It is unlikely that the Jewish authorities, who were strictly Sabbatarian, would have gone to Pilate on the Sabbath day. For the day after the Preparation (Friday) can mean nothing else than Saturday.

(*b*) It is most unlikely that the Jewish authorities at the time of the Crucifixion could have been aware of, or have attached any importance to, a prediction of Jesus that He would rise again on the third day, or that they should have interpreted such a saying as foretelling His physical resurrection from the sepulchre.

(*c*) It is extremely unlikely that the truculent and contemptuous Pilate, especially if the Jewish authorities had opposed his wishes by securing the death of Jesus, should grant their request and provide them with a military guard.

(*d*) It is even more unlikely that Roman soldiers, however large the bribe offered to them, would confess that they had slept on guard, and so had failed to perform the special duty for which they had been appointed. Nor is it in the least likely that they would have believed in the promises or the ability of the Jewish officials to protect them from the consequences of their dereliction of duty.

(*e*) The story of the Angel of the Lord, who terrified the Roman guard into a death-like torpor, is difficult to harmonise with the other accounts of what happened at the sepulchre on the first Easter morning.

These considerations make it very difficult to accept Mt.'s story of the Roman guard as historical.

Some commentators assume that the sealing was done by Pilate. It was the Roman custom to seal houses and property, which by this act passed into official custody. It was equivalent to placing the 'broad arrow' upon them. Other commentators assume that the sealing was done by the Jewish authorities, and cite the sealing of the den of lions by the Persian authorities after Daniel had been cast into it.

There is something sardonic, or rather ironical, in the remark attributed to Pilate—'Make it as sure as ye can.' It may be compared with Pilate's 'What I have written, I have written,' when he refused, at the request of the Jewish authorities, to alter the inscription, 'The King of the Jews,' which he had had inscribed on the Cross over the head of Jesus.

THE RESURRECTION APPEARANCE OF JESUS IN GALILEE

MT. 28^{16-20}

28 16 But the eleven disciples went into
Galilee, unto the mountain where Jesus
17 had appointed them. And when they
saw him, they worshipped *him*: but some
18 doubted. And Jesus came to them and
spake unto them, saying, All authority
hath been given unto me in heaven and
19 on earth. Go ye therefore, and make
disciples of all the nations, baptizing
them into the name of the Father and the
20 Son and of the Holy Ghost: teaching
them to observe all things whatsoever I
commanded you: and lo, I am with you
alway, even unto the end of the world.

This incident of the appearance of Jesus to His eleven disciples on the mountain in Galilee is treated in my notes on the Resurrection appearances. The mountain may possibly be the Mount of the Beatitudes. The command of Jesus that His disciples should go to all the nations, although doubtless in entire harmony with the principles and spirit of His Gospel, is yet hard to reconcile with their slowness in carrying out this commission, and the evident apprehension and repugnance with which the Jewish-Christian authorities in Jerusalem viewed the expansion of the Christian Church to include Gentile adherents.

The Trinitarian baptismal formula, possibly introduced into the text of this Gospel because it was used in baptizing in the Church where this Gospel circulated, could hardly have been uttered by Jesus Himself, since the Christian Church for many years after the death of Jesus never used that baptismal formula at all, but was satisfied to baptize converts into the name of the Lord Jesus alone. The parting charge of Christ, which has been rightly named 'The Charter of Foreign Missions,' stresses, not only the universality, but also the eternal and final quality of His Gospel.

Introduction to St. Luke's Gospel

STYLE and language offer convincing proof that the Third Gospel and the Acts of the Apostles are from the same hand. Universal Church tradition attributes the authorship of these two volumes to Luke the Physician, the travelling companion of St. Paul. As Luke is not precisely named in Church tradition until the second half of the second century as the author of the Third Gospel, some have cast doubt upon the ascription of the authorship to him. But it is very difficult, if Luke was not the author, to account for his being considered its author, as he was not a prominent person in the Apostolic Church. He is only mentioned three times by name in the New Testament.

(1) In Col. 4^{14}, where he is described as Luke, the beloved physician. The way in which he is mentioned suggests that he was of Gentile birth. Cf. *v.* 11, where those of St. Paul's companions who are ' of the circumcision ' are named together.

(2) In Philem. *v.* 24, where Luke is referred to as one of St. Paul's fellow-workers. Both these Epistles of St. Paul were written during his imprisonment at Rome, and these references to Luke indicate that he was with St. Paul during that imprisonment which is described in the last chapter of the Acts of the Apostles. Whether St. Paul was released from this imprisonment and visited the churches of the Lycus valley, Colossæ, Hierapolis, and Laodicea, as he expresses the hope of doing in these Epistles, is one of the unsolved problems of Pauline biography.

The references to St. Luke suggest that he was known to these churches, although St. Paul, when he wrote these Epistles, was himself personally unknown to them.

(3) In 2 Tim. 4^{11}, St. Paul writes, ' only Luke is with me.' Whether we take the view that the whole of the Pastoral Epistles (1 Timothy, Titus, 2 Timothy) were composed by St. Paul or whether we hold that these Pastoral Epistles consist of two primitive Christian Church Orders of Ephesus and Crete, combined with five brief personal letters of the Apostle, will make no difference to our conclusion that here (2 Tim. 4^{11}) we have a passage in a last extant letter of the Apostle, written just before his execution at Rome. Whether this execution took place at the end of his second imprisonment, if such befell him, or at the end of his first imprisonment, as others hold, does not affect the conclusion that Luke, so far as we know, was the last of his fellow-Christians to be with St. Paul before his execution.

But perhaps hardly less important than these three direct references to St. Luke in the New Testament are three passages in the Acts of the Apostles known as the ' We ' sections, in which the narrative in Acts, having related events in the third person, suddenly uses instead the first person plural. This change of person suggests one of two hypotheses, either that the writer of Acts is himself taking part with St. Paul in the events which he describes, or else that he is citing from a document written by one who was himself associated with St. Paul in these undertakings. The former hypothesis has much the most to support it, since a very precise examination of the style and language of these ' We ' sections proves, it may be said almost beyond doubt, that the author of the 'We' sections is also the author of the Third Gospel and the Acts. These 'We' sections are: (1) Acts 16^{10-18}, (2) 20^{5}–21^{17}, (3) 27^{1}–28^{16}.

The perusal of these three 'We' sections indicates that the author of Acts becomes associated with St. Paul at Troas on his second missionary journey. Some have even supposed that it was St. Luke himself who first proposed to St. Paul the evangelisation of Europe and induced him to preach the Gospel in Philippi.

It has even been suggested that the man of Macedonia who appeared to St. Paul, in the vision of the night, and besought him saying: 'Come over into Macedonia and help us,' possessed the features and voice of St. Luke.

The first 'We' section concludes with St. Paul's encounter at Philippi with the girl possessed of the spirit of the Delphic Python.

The second 'We' section relates St. Paul's arrival at Philippi several years later on his third missionary journey, after passing through Macedonia on his last visit to Jerusalem. This clearly indicates that St. Luke, who was at Philippi when St. Paul came there, accompanied him on his sea voyage to Cæsarea, the Roman port of Palestine, and thence travelled with the Apostle on the land journey up to Jerusalem.

The third 'We' section opens with St. Paul's departure from Cæsarea as a prisoner, to make his appeal to Cæsar in Rome. This 'We' section concludes with the account of St. Paul's entry into Rome after his perilous sea voyage. From this we learn that St. Luke accompanied St. Paul on his notable journey from Cæsarea to Rome.

These 'We' sections are remarkably detailed and vivid in their descriptions of events and support the view that they are the narratives of an eye-witness who would seem to have kept a diary of his experiences.

The curious point is that these 'We' sections are almost entirely concerned with travel.

It is possible that there is a fourth 'We' section in Acts 11^{28}, but it is of doubtful genuineness. It relates the joy which 'we,' the Christians of Antioch, experienced when visited by certain prophets from Jerusalem.

This 'We' section has its main support from the *Codex Bezae*, the great Biblical treasure of the University of Cambridge, but this support is lacking in the other great codices of the New Testament. It has, however, a very special bearing on St. Luke.

Two of the most learned men of the ancient Church, Eusebius and Jerome, state that Luke was an inhabitant of Antioch. That assertion is supported by this possible fourth 'We' section, and it would account for Luke's precise knowledge of the origin, membership, and early history of the second great Church of Christendom, the Church of Antioch.

A primitive Christian document, the *Anti-Marcionite Prologue to St. Luke's Gospel*, preserves a tradition about Luke and his Gospel as held in the Church between 150 and 180 A.D. It runs as follows:

Luke is a Syrian of Antioch, a physician by calling, who has become a disciple of the apostles and afterwards, having followed Paul until his martyrdom, and having served the Lord without remission, wifeless and childless, in the eighty-fourth year of his age he, full of the Holy Spirit, fell asleep in Bœotia.

This man, when there were already Gospels in existence, namely that according to Matthew which was recorded in Judæa and that according to Mark in Italy, having been moved by the Holy Spirit in the district of Achaia, composed the whole of this Gospel, making clear by means of the preface this very fact that before him others had been written and that it was necessary to publish for the faithful among the Gentiles the accurate narrative of the ministry in order that they might not be distracted by Jewish myths nor, being deceived by schismatic and empty fabrications, miss the truth. As being therefore most necessary we have received [from him] immediately at the beginning the birth of John, who is the beginning of the Gospel, having become a forerunner of the Lord and partner in the fashioning of the Gospel and in the inauguration of Baptism and in the participation in the Passion. A prophet among the Twelve recalls this ministration.

Moreover, the same Luke afterwards wrote the *Acts of the Apostles;* and afterwards John the Apostle, one of the Twelve, wrote the *Apocalypse* in the Island of Patmos and after this the Gospel.

Another piece of evidence in favour of St. Luke being the author of the Third Gospel and Acts is the medical language and interest in medical cases which characterise these writings. The argument that the medical language used indicates that the author was a physician has been seriously discredited in recent years. It has been pointed out that medical terminology, as we have it in the modern world, did not exist in the ancient Greek world. Greek physicians used the language of their fellow-citizens. The case for this contention is very strong. Nevertheless, there are passages in the Lucan writings, which although they cannot be said to prove, yet do support the hypothesis, that the author was a physician.

For instance, Mk. relates of the woman with an issue of blood that she—

'had suffered many things of many physicians and had spent all that she had and was nothing bettered, but rather grew worse.' (Mk. 5^{26}.)

Lk. omits this reflection on the medical profession and merely states that the woman 'could not be healed by anyone.' Lk. states that when the woman touched the tassel of the *tallith* worn by Jesus, immediately her flow of blood was 'stayed' or 'stood.' This is undoubtedly a technical term used by Greek physicians, and we observe that Mk.'s narrative, which Lk. has rewritten, has here the 'fountain of her blood was dried up.'

In Lk.'s account of the raising of Jairus' daughter he states her age at the outset, after the manner of a physician (she was about twelve years old), whereas Mk., whose narrative Lk. is using, puts her age at the conclusion.

Mk. also states that after the little girl had been raised the spectators were astonished, and that Jesus immediately charged them not to make the matter known. Mk. then adds that Jesus said that 'something should be given to her to eat.' Lk., true to his medical training, makes Jesus give His directions about the patient first, and then later relates the astonishment of the parents at the miracle and the charge to keep silence.

There are a number of little points in Lk.'s account of cases of healing which do suggest a medical interest and knowledge. For instance, he states that Peter's mother-in-law suffered from a 'great' fever. Mk. does not so describe it, but Greek physicians did classify fevers as great and small.

Again, the author of Acts states that the father of Publius of Melita was laid up with dysentery and fever, and adds, that after Paul had healed him many in consequence also came to receive medical attention, who 'honoured us with many honours,' which seems to suggest that Luke, as a physician, co-operated with St. Paul. (Acts 28^{8}.)

These instances, and others which might be cited, do not, as we have said, prove that the author of these writings was a physician, but they do support the universal Church tradition that Luke, 'the beloved physician,' was their author.

SOURCES AND THEIR TREATMENT

Like Mt., the author of the Third Gospel makes use of Mk. and Q. It is, however, maintained by eminent scholars that, while Mk. is a primary source for Mt., it is but a secondary source for Lk.

What is called the proto-Luke hypothesis alleges that Luke had composed a Gospel which had made use of Q and a number of other sources, literary and oral, but had not made use of Mk. When, however, somewhat later, Lk. came across Mk., recognising its value, he inserted extracts from it into various portions of his Gospel. Lk. contains 455 of Mk.'s 661 verses in his own Gospel of 1,149 verses. Where, however, he had already treated a Marcan incident, he left it unaltered, and only inserted passages from Mk. dealing with incidents which he had not already recorded in his proto-Luke. This use of Mk. as a secondary source in Lk., although not accepted by certain other eminent scholars, does yet explain among other things the peculiar distribution of Marcan and non-Marcan sections in Lk., which is otherwise inexplicable.

Proto-Luke, according to Dr. Streeter, who is mainly responsible for this hypothesis, began with Lk. 3, the preaching of John the Baptist. Streeter supposes it to have been written some twenty years before our present Gospel of Lk. It would thus be earlier than Mk., but of course later than Q.

There can be little doubt that our present Lk. was written after the destruction of Jerusalem. The following predictions, peculiar to his Gospel, seem to indicate this :

'And when he was come near, he beheld the city, and wept over it, saying, If thou hadst known, even thou, at least in this thy day, the things which belong unto thy peace! but now they are hid from thine eyes. For the days shall come upon thee, that thine enemies shall cast a trench about thee, and compass thee round, and keep thee in on every side. And shall lay thee even with the ground, and thy children within thee: and they shall not leave in thee one stone upon another: because thou knewest not the time of thy visitation.' (Lk. 19^{41-44}.)

'And they shall fall by the edge of the sword, and shall be led away captive into all nations: and Jerusalem shall be trodden down of the Gentiles, until the times of the Gentiles be fulfilled.' (Lk. 21^{24}.)

'But Jesus turning unto them said, Daughters of Jerusalem, weep not for me, but weep for yourselves, and for your children. For, behold, the days are coming, in the which they shall say, Blessed are the barren, and the wombs that never bare, and the paps which never gave suck. Then shall they begin to say to the mountains, Fall on us: and to the hills, Cover us.' (Lk. $23^{28\,f.}$.)

But perhaps even more significant than these three predictions is the way in which Lk. 21^{20} alters the parallel passage in Mk. 13^{14}. Mk. runs thus :

'Whensoever ye see the abomination of desolation standing where he ought not (let him that readeth understand), then let those that are in Judæa flee unto the mountains.'

This Lk. alters into:

'Whensoever ye see Jerusalem encompassed by armies, then know ye that her desolation has drawn nigh. Then let those that are in Judæa flee unto the mountains.'

For the mysterious 'abomination of desolation' Lk. substitutes the encompassing Jerusalem with armies. He could hardly have interpreted this phrase in this way unless the siege of Jerusalem, which preceded its desolation, had taken place.

We have already noted that, besides Q and Mk., Lk. has used many other sources for the material peculiar to his Gospel. These sources were probably both oral and written. Some of them are so feminine in their interest that it is supposed that Lk. derived them from Christian women known to him. Possibly the prophetic virgin daughters of Philip the Evangelist, whom he mentions, may have contributed. Lk. alone mentions the number of women disciples who followed Jesus and ministered to Him of their substance; among them being Joanna, the wife of Chuza, Herod's steward.

It seems possible that Joanna also may have imparted special information to Luke concerning the relations of Herod Antipas with Jesus, since Lk. alone relates that Pilate sent Jesus for trial to Herod, and that this led to the reconciliation of Pilate and Herod, who had formerly been on bad terms. Joanna may also have told Luke of the message sent by Jesus to 'that fox' Herod, as this too is peculiar to his Gospel.

It should, however, be borne in mind that Luke seems to have known a certain Manaen, a prominent primitive Christian of Antioch (Acts 13^{1}), who was a 'foster-brother' of Herod, and who therefore may have imparted to him this information. The term foster-brother is somewhat ambiguous and may mean confidential friend or adviser. The Herod named is Herod Antipas. But whether Luke's informant was Joanna or Manaen or someone else, it seems clear that Luke was able to draw upon a source which furnished him with special information about the relations of Herod Antipas to Jesus.

It is clearly observable that the very beautiful narratives of the birth and infancy of John the Baptist and Jesus are written from a woman's point of view. Hence it has been supposed that some who were among the acquaintances of Mary, the Mother of Jesus, may have related these narratives to Luke—not, however, Mary herself, since Lk. seems to stress her unwillingness to speak of memories which she had treasured. (Lk. $2^{19, 51}$.)

Elisabeth and Anna, who are there mentioned with Mary, had passed away long before Luke wrote his Gospel. Some have supposed that the virgin daughters of Philip may have been his informants, but this seems very improbable. Luke mentions a number of prominent Christian women in his writings; Mary the mother of Mark, Tabitha or Dorcas, Martha and Mary of Bethany, Priscilla, Lydia, and others, but we cannot assign with any security the source of Luke's feminine narrative to any one of them in particular.

Ernest Renan described Luke's Gospel as 'the most beautiful book in the world.' The idyllic charm, domestic tenderness, purity and simplicity, the deeply devotional spirit which mark its opening chapters, are unequalled even in the Old Testament, which has served in some measure as a model to Luke here.

It is to Luke's Gospel we owe that remarkable collection of primitive Christian hymns known as the *Magnificat*, *Nunc Dimittis*, *Benedictus*, and the Hymn of the Angels, so precious to the Christian worshipper.

It might not be amiss to describe Luke's Gospel as the most Christian of the Gospels. It alone preserves so much which is rightly regarded as characteristically Christian. For instance, the parables of the Prodigal Son, the Good Samaritan, Dives and Lazarus, and the Pharisee and the Publican are peculiar to Lk.

Lk. alone gives us those three words from the Cross—the most treasured of the seven—'Father, forgive them, for they know not what they do; To-day shalt thou be with me in Paradise; Father, into Thy hands I commend my spirit.'

Luke's Gospel is pre-eminently the Gospel of Prayer. There are some twenty references to prayer in it. On every great occasion in His Ministry he represents Jesus as praying. He alone states that Jesus was praying when the Spirit came upon Him at His Baptism (3^{21}); that He prayed all night before choosing the twelve Apostles (6^{12}); that He was praying just before He put to St. Peter the question which drew from that Apostle his great confession of the Messiahship of Jesus (9^{18}); that it was when He was praying that Jesus was transfigured (9^{29}); that it was seeing Him pray which led one of the disciples to ask Him to teach them to pray—a request which secured the Lord's prayer (11^{1}).

Luke alone relates the parables of the Importunate Widow and the Unjust Judge (18^{1-8}), and the Friend at Midnight (11^{5-8}), in order that from them men should learn always to pray and not to grow slack.

Luke's Gospel is pre-eminently the Gospel of Thanksgiving. On every occasion in the Gospel when the Divine power is manifested, and the goodness of God realised, men offer thanksgiving to God. Closely akin to this spirit of thanksgiving is the spirit of joyousness which marks this Gospel. When the Gospel closes with the departure of Jesus from His disciples they are not left in sadness or fear, but—

'returned to Jerusalem with great joy: and were continually in the Temple blessing God.'

Luke would seem, more than do the other Evangelists, to stress the value of penitence. It is to him we owe the saying of Jesus:

'There shall be joy in heaven over one sinner that repenteth, more than over ninety and nine righteous persons which need no repentance.' (Lk. 15^{7}; cf. *v.* 10.)

He alone relates that the penitent publican who prayed: 'God be merciful to me a sinner,' went back to his home justified.

Luke alone relates the story of the penitent robber, and the story of the penitent prostitute, and the parable of the prodigal son and the parable of the lost coin; all of which stress the blessedness of penitence.

Luke's Gospel has been called by a modern preacher the Gospel of Democracy. He sees in Luke the Christian democrat, and the Gospel of Christian Democracy heralded in the words of the *Magnificat*.

'He has put down the mighty from their seat and has exalted the humble and meek; he has filled the hungry with good things and the rich he has sent empty away.'

Certainly Luke has little love or respect for the ruling classes. He, alone, in the account of the Temptation of Jesus, makes Satan declare that the kingdoms of this world and the glory of them are entrusted to him and that he gives them to whomsoever he will—a very different view from that of St. Paul, who regarded governors and kings as the ministers of God. Luke's cynical remark that the rulers of the pagans who exercise lordship over them are called Benefactors—presumably by the rulers themselves—is only equalled by the cynicism of his statement that Pilate and Herod who had formerly been at enmity became friends over the trial of Jesus.

Luke sees true greatness in service.

'He that is greatest among you shall be the servant of all. And he that is least among you all shall be great.'

Another note of Luke's Gospel is its universalism. Jesus for him is not only, as in Mt., the 'Son of David, the Son of Abraham' (Mt. 1^{1}). He is also 'the Son of Adam, the Son of God' (Lk. 3^{38}).

Jesus is destined to be not only 'the glory of his people Israel,' but also 'a light to lighten the Gentiles.'

The universalism of Lk. is seen in what it omits as well as in what it contains. Much that is distinctively Jewish in Mt.'s Sermon on the Mount is absent from Lk.'s Sermon on the Plain (6^{17-49}).

Mt.'s reinterpretation of the Mosaic law, 'It was said to them of old time . . . but I say unto you,' is not found in Lk. So also directions as to the right way to pray, fast, and give alms, in contrast to the wrong way as practised by the Pharisees. The controversy with the Jews about 'eating with unwashen hands' found in Mk. and Mt. is lacking in Lk. (Mt. $15^{1-11, 15-20}$; Mk. 7^{1-23}.)

Lk. also omits the story of the Syrophœnician woman, where Jesus declares Himself unwilling to give the children's bread to the dogs, i.e. Gentiles. (Mt. $15^{21, 22, 26-28}$; Mk. 7^{24-30}.)

Just as Lk. alone records the Parable of the Good Samaritan, so it is to him we owe the story of the grateful Samaritan who alone returned to give glory to God when his nine Jewish fellow-lepers were healed (17^{11-19}).

Lk. also relates Christ's rebuke of the sons of Zebedee for wishing to call down fire from heaven upon an inhospitable Samaritan village (9^{51-56}).

In these characteristics of the contents of Luke's Gospel we see reflected undoubtedly the spirit of that great Gentile mission in which Luke was himself an ardent worker, the spirit which went forth conquering and to conquer, unsupported by material resources and confiding only in the quality of that which it had to give and in the power of Him from whom it came.

There is no historic foundation for the tradition that Luke was an artist. That, however, St. Luke was a gifted literary man there is plenty of evidence. His selection of his materials and their arrangement indicate this. To judge from his Preface to his Gospel, he had a vast mass of material from which to select. But how little of what he has given us is less than first class in quality. We could perhaps dispense with the genealogy of Jesus without loss, but of how little else? It is his sense of artistic fitness which has led him to rearrange much of his material and to sacrifice, probably in a number of cases, historic accuracy to his artistic sense of the fitness of things.

The facts and sayings which are peculiar to Luke have high historic value, but where his Gospel differs from the Marcan order, Mk. is to be preferred. Lk. gives us, what no other Gospel gives us, a chronological table which relates the ministry of Jesus to secular history. (Cf. Lk. $2^{1, 2}$, $3^{1, 2}$.)

Lk.'s Gospel is primarily a gospel for the Roman Empire. It is not intended primarily for Palestinian Christians, but for Greek-speaking Pagans and Pagan proselytes to Judaism who formed an important section of the Jewish Dispersion (*Diaspora*) in all the great cities of the Roman Empire.

Circulating widely among the great Pauline churches, St. Luke's Gospel does not reflect certain characteristic doctrines of the Pauline theology. Although Luke had undoubtedly the highest admiration for St. Paul as a man and a missionary, he would appear to have dissented from some of St. Paul's doctrines, and where he dissented to have been nearer to the teaching of Jesus than was St. Paul himself.

St. Paul's doctrine that the death of Jesus was a propitiatory sacrifice intended to secure the Divine forgiveness of human sin, Luke will have nothing to do with. Divine forgiveness he presents as dependent upon human penitence, human willingness to forgive the sins of others, the presence of love in the human heart.

Lk. omits the saying ascribed to Jesus in Mk. 10^{45} (contained also in Mt. 20^{28}), 'The son of man came not to be ministered unto but to minister, and to give his life a ransom for many.' Yet Luke undoubtedly knew of it, and he cites the substance of the saying of Jesus which precedes it, that service, not lordship, is the true ideal of life.

Also Lk.'s original account of the institution of the Eucharist (22^{17-19}) contains no reference to the shedding of the blood of Jesus for the remission of sins which we have in Mt. 26^{28}.

Jesus appears to us in this Gospel pre-eminently as 'the Saviour'—a title which Lk. alone of the Synoptists gives to Him (Lk. 1^{47}, 2^{11}; Acts. 5^{31}, 13^{23}). (Jn. has it only in 4^{42}.) Jesus in Lk. is 'the Good Physician' who delivers men from demons, sin, and suffering, and fills them with love and joy.

TEXT AND COMMENTARY

Incidents Peculiar to St. Luke's Gospel

PREFACE TO ST. LUKE'S GOSPEL

LK. 1[1-4]

1 1 Forasmuch as many have taken in hand
to draw up a narrative concerning those
matters which have been fulfilled among us,
2 even as they delivered them unto us, which
from the beginning were eyewitnesses and
3 ministers of the word, it seemed good to me
also, having traced the course of all things
accurately from the first, to write unto thee
4 in order, most excellent Theophilus; that
thou mightest know the certainty concerning the things wherein thou wast instructed.

In the Preface to his Gospel, modelled on those of classical writers, reflecting, it is said, the influence of several prefaces to ancient medical works, St. Luke sets forth the purpose of his Gospel.

The Preface is addressed to a certain most excellent Theophilus. ' Most Excellent ' could properly be used in addressing high officials, and it may be that Theophilus is an actual person occupying such a position. On the other hand, since the name Theophilus means a ' lover of God,' Theophilus may be intended to represent the Christian readers for whom the Gospel is composed.

The purpose of the Gospel is to assure Theophilus of the certainty of those things in which he has been orally instructed. The Greek word rendered by ' orally instructed ' is that from which our English word ' catechised ' is derived. The most primitive Christians received, of course, the Glad Tidings, not in documentary form, but as a spoken message—the utterance of ' a living and abiding voice,' as Papias described it.

Lk. gives four reasons which should justify his effort :

(1) That although many had written accounts of Jesus, he had striven to go back to the very earliest origins.

(2) That he had made use of *all* available material as far as it would serve his purpose.

(3) That he had recognised the need for a high standard of accuracy.

(4) That he had tried to present events in their chronological order and relations.

These are the methods and ideals which would guide a sound historical writer to-day. The study of Luke's Gospel will indicate that it has much in it to justify his claims for it.

Lk.'s Preface to his Gospel should be compared to his Preface to the Acts, which is also dedicated to Theophilus.

Lk.'s reference to ' eye-witnesses ' who handed down their accounts to ' us ' does not necessarily suggest that Luke was acquainted with these eye-witnesses, as the ' us ' refers to the whole Christian body, recipients of the Christian tradition. Luke indicates that these first eye-witnesses were also the primitive preachers of the Gospel. He knew at least one of them, for in a ' we ' section (Acts 21^{16}) he relates that he stayed a night with Mnason, ' an archaic disciple,' which description seems certainly to indicate that his discipleship went back to the days of Jesus, and, of course, St. Luke, as the companion of St. Paul, must almost certainly have met St. James, the Lord's brother, and St. Peter.

THE PROMISE OF THE BIRTH OF JOHN THE BAPTIST

LK. 1^{5-25}

1 5 There was in the days of Herod, king of
Judæa, a certain priest named Zacharias,
of the course of Abijah: and he had a wife
of the daughters of Aaron, and her name
6 was Elisabeth. And they were both
righteous before God, walking in all the
commandments and ordinances of the
7 Lord blameless. And they had no child,
because that Elisabeth was barren, and
they both were *now* well stricken in years.
8 Now it came to pass, while he executed
the priest's office before God in the order
9 of his course, according to the custom of
the priest's office, his lot was to enter into
the temple of the Lord and burn incense.
10 And the whole multitude of the people
were praying without at the hour of in-
11 cense. And there appeared unto him an
angel of the Lord standing on the right
12 side of the altar of incense. And Zacharias was troubled when he saw *him*, and
13 fear fell upon him. But the angel said
unto him, Fear not, Zacharias: because
thy supplication is heard, and thy wife
Elisabeth shall bear thee a son, and thou
14 shalt call his name John. And thou shalt
have joy and gladness; and many shall
15 rejoice at his birth. For he shall be great
in the sight of the Lord, and he shall drink
no wine nor strong drink; and he shall be
filled with the Holy Ghost, even from his
16 mother's womb. And many of the children of Israel shall he turn unto the Lord
17 their God. And he shall go before his
face in the spirit and power of Elijah, to
turn the hearts of the fathers to the children, and the disobedient *to walk* in the
wisdom of the just; to make ready for the
18 Lord a people prepared *for him*. And
Zacharias said unto the angel, Whereby
shall I know this? for I am an old man,
19 and my wife well stricken in years. And
the angel answering said unto him, I am
Gabriel, that stand in the presence of God;
and I was sent to speak unto thee, and to
20 bring thee these good tidings. And behold, thou shalt be silent and not able to
speak, until the day that these things shall
come to pass, because thou believedst not
my words, which shall be fulfilled in their
21 season. And the people were waiting for
Zacharias, and they marvelled while he
22 tarried in the temple. And when he came
out, he could not speak unto them: and
they perceived that he had seen a vision
in the temple: and he continued making
signs unto them, and remained dumb.
23 And it came to pass, when the days of his
ministration were fulfilled, he departed
unto his house.
24 And after these days Elisabeth his wife
conceived; and she hid herself five months,
25 saying, Thus hath the Lord done unto me
in the days wherein he looked upon *me*, to
take away my reproach among men.

Whilst the Preface is in the style of a classical Greek writer, the style of the series of idyllic narratives which follow is that of the Old Testament. Possibly it will remind readers most of the Book of Ruth, or some of the Elisha narratives in 2 Kings, or the opening chapters of 1 Samuel.

John the Baptist, although Jesus called him a prophet, yea, and more than a prophet, was, like Jeremiah and Ezekiel, of priestly descent. Both his father and his mother were of the tribe of Levi, and both were eminently strict observers of the Mosaic ordinances. After the return from the Captivity, the priests were divided into twenty-four classes, of which the eighth was Abijah (1 Chron. 24^{10}).

Each class came up in turn for a week's service in the Temple. 'The priests were required by the Law (Lev. 21^{14}) to marry virgins of Israelite birth, but they were not restricted to the priestly families.' Childlessness was regarded as a great affliction by the Jews, and even as a Divine punishment. Possibly that is why the righteousness of the parents is stressed in this connexion. Invariably in the Bible it is the wife who is regarded as the cause of childlessness.

The offering of incense was made in the Holy Place twice a day, before the morning sacrifice and before the evening sacrifice. The later Jews regarded the offering of incense as symbolical of prayer. The priest who performed this duty, which was regarded as a great honour, was chosen by lot. It is said that some priests never enjoyed this privilege. The occasion was no doubt a very notable one for Zacharias. His receiving a Divine oracle during his performance of this act has its parallel in the case of the Maccabean high priest, John Hyrcanus, who, according to Josephus the Jewish historian, received a Divine oracle while he was offering incense, that his son had conquered the Greek tyrant Antiochus, and who immediately came forth from the Holy Place and announced it to the worshippers.

It has been noted that in Mt. God is regarded as making His will known in dreams, which is the belief of the Elohist writer in the Hexateuch, but Lk. believes that God makes His will known by angels or Divine messengers, which is the belief of the Yahwist writer in the Hexateuch. No doubt the particular belief held by the individual in this matter would determine for him the way in which God's will would be made known to him.

Zacharias' childlessness had been much on his mind. He had made it a matter of prayer, presumably on this special occasion, and the vision came as the solution of his problem. He shall not only have a son, but his son shall fulfil his profoundest religious aspirations. The Old Testament Canon (Mal. 4^{6}) closed with the prediction that God would send Elijah before the great Day of the Lord to turn the hearts of the fathers to the children and the hearts of the children to their fathers. Zacharias' son shall be this Elijah.

The news seems to Zacharias to be too good to be true, and his subsequent speechlessness or aphasia he regards as the punishment of his lack of faith.

Gabriel (the hero of God), one of the four great archangels, is represented as being justly incensed at the incredulity of the old priest. It was the archangels alone who, according to Jewish angelology, had the right of entrance to the Divine Presence.

THE ANNUNCIATION TO MARY

LK. I^{26-38}

1 26 Now in the sixth month the angel
Gabriel was sent from God unto a city of
27 Galilee, named Nazareth, to a virgin
betrothed to a man whose name was
Joseph, of the house of David; and the
28 virgin's name was Mary. And he came
in unto her, and said, Hail, thou that art
highly favoured, the Lord *is* with thee.
29 But she was greatly troubled at the saying,
and cast in her mind what manner of
30 salutation this might be. And the angel
said unto her, Fear not, Mary: for thou
31 hast found favour with God. And behold, thou shalt conceive in thy womb,
and bring forth a son, and shalt call his
32 name Jesus. He shall be great, and shall
be called the Son of the Most High: and
the Lord God shall give unto him the

33 throne of his father David: and he shall
reign over the house of Jacob for ever; and
34 of his kingdom there shall be no end. And
Mary said unto the angel, How shall this
35 be, seeing I know not a man? And the
angel answered and said unto her, The
Holy Ghost shall come upon thee, and the
power of the Most High shall overshadow
thee: wherefore also that which is to be
born shall be called holy, the Son of God.
36 And behold, Elisabeth thy kinswoman, she
also hath conceived a son in her old age:
and this is the sixth month with her that
37 was called barren. For no word from
38 God shall be void of power. And Mary
said, Behold, the handmaid of the Lord;
be it unto me according to thy word.
And the angel departed from her.

As the Archangel Gabriel announces to Zacharias the birth of John the Baptist, so he announces to the maiden Mary, who is espoused to Joseph of the House of David, the birth of Jesus. As John the son of Zacharias is divinely destined to be the Elijah of the new era, so the son of Mary is destined to be the Messiah, the 'Son of God,' who shall receive the throne of his father David.

Vv. 34, 35, the question which Mary puts to the Archangel, is regarded by many critics as an interpolation. The reason for this view is that the narrative having stated that Joseph is of the House of David proceeds to state that the Son to be born of Mary shall possess the throne of David. This would seem, *prima facie*, to suggest that although as Messiah, He is Son of God, yet He will be, in the natural course of events, the son of Joseph. If this be so it must then be presumed that shortly afterwards Joseph and Mary were married, and that it was as his wife she travelled with him to Bethlehem where Jesus was born.

This is taken to be the original form of the Lucan narrative, but it is maintained that, in the interests of the miracle of the Virgin Birth, it has been interpolated by a later hand. Assuming that all these narratives of the annunciation, birth, and childhood of John the Baptist and Jesus are from the same source as the similarities of their style and background suggest, there is much to be said for the theory of interpolation and alteration, since in their present form they exhibit various discrepancies. Nevertheless, there are great difficulties in regarding this interpolation as being the act of some unknown Christian scribe and not the act of Luke himself. Luke is a lover of the miraculous. It constitutes for him an impressive manifestation of the Divine activity and presence in human affairs.

The doubt of Mary expressed in 1^{34} may be regarded as the literary parallel of the doubt of Zacharias in 1^{18}, but Gabriel's treatment of it in her case is not censure, but reassurance and explanation.

If *v.* 34 formed no part of the Lucan Gospel, but is the interpolation of a later hand, there is good reason to believe that some evidence of this interpolation would have been preserved in the textual history of the passage, but there is practically none. Only two old Latin MSS. exhibit displacement here. All the Greek texts of Luke and all the other versions (translations) contain it.

Luke would seem, when all the evidence is reviewed, to have believed in the Virgin Birth, and to have included it in his Gospel. He failed, however, as we shall see, to alter his original narratives with such deftness and consistency as to obliterate the fact that they did not contain an account of the Virgin Birth, but regarded Joseph as the father of Jesus.

It should be noted that in Luke's narrative the Annunciation takes place at

Nazareth, and that both Mary and Joseph are regarded as belonging to that town. In Mt. they are regarded as belonging to Bethlehem, where they have a house.

'In the sixth month' (*v.* 26) is intended to state that Gabriel's visit to Mary took place six months after his announcement to Zacharias. (Cf. *v.* 36.) This indicates clearly that we have the same source for the annunciation to Mary as for the annunciation to Zacharias.

The command, that the son to be born shall be named Jesus, has its parallel in Mt. 1^{21}.

'Reign over the House of Jacob for ever' presents the son to be born as a purely Jewish Messiah. Later we have the prediction that He shall be a light to lighten the Gentiles.

The Holy Spirit, who is represented as the Agent of the Creation in Gen. 1^{2}, is declared here to be the Agent of the Incarnation.

'Elisabeth, thy kinswoman,' would suggest, as Elisabeth was one of the daughters of Aaron, that Mary herself was also of priestly descent. We are nowhere told that Mary was of the House of David. This is only said of Joseph.

MARY'S VISIT TO ELISABETH (*The* MAGNIFICAT)

LK. 1^{39-56}

1 39 And Mary arose in these days and went
into the hill country with haste, into a city
40 of Judah; and entered into the house of
41 Zacharias and saluted Elisabeth. And it
came to pass, when Elisabeth heard the
salutation of Mary, the babe leaped in her
womb; and Elisabeth was filled with the
42 Holy Ghost; and she lifted up her voice
with a loud cry, and said, Blessed *art* thou
among women, and blessed *is* the fruit of
43 thy womb. And whence is this to me,
that the mother of my Lord should come
44 unto me? For behold, when the voice of
thy salutation came into mine ears, the
45 babe leaped in my womb for joy. And
blessed *is* she that believed; for there shall
be a fulfilment of the things which have
46 been spoken to her from the Lord. And
Mary said,
My soul doth magnify the Lord,
47 And my spirit hath rejoiced in God
my Saviour.
48 For he hath looked upon the low
estate of his handmaiden:
For behold, from henceforth all generations shall call me blessed.
49 For he that is mighty hath done to
me great things;
And holy is his name.
50 And his mercy is unto generations
and generations
On them that fear him.
51 He hath shewed strength with his
arm;
He that scattered the proud in the
imagination of their heart.
52 He hath put down princes from *their*
thrones,
And hath exalted them of low degree.
53 The hungry he hath filled with good
things;
And the rich he hath sent empty
away.
54 He hath holpen Israel his servant,
That he might remember mercy
55 (As he spake unto our fathers)
Toward Abraham and his seed for
ever.
56 And Mary abode with her about three
months, and returned unto her house.

The hill country undoubtedly refers to the mountainous highland of Judah which stretches from Jerusalem to Hebron. The 'City of Judah,' where Elisabeth lived, is not further described; presumably it was one of the cities assigned to the priests.

Mary's visit to Elizabeth is not to be regarded as exhibiting lack of faith on her part—a desire to find out whether Gabriel had been speaking the truth—

but a wish to discuss the wonderful event with Elisabeth, to whom an experience hardly less wonderful had been vouchsafed.

The *Magnificat* (*vv.* 46 f.) is known to the Christian Church as the Hymn of Mary, but New Testament textual criticism creates doubt on this point. Codices of the Old Latin version read Elisabeth, not Mary, and Church Fathers of great eminence and erudition (Irenæus, Origen, Jerome) knew of this variant. It is very difficult to imagine, that if Mary were in the original text, any scribe could have altered it to Elisabeth. Possibly the original form of the text was ‘ she said,’ and some scribes substituted Mary and others Elisabeth for the word ‘ she.’ In that case the point to be determined critically, is whether the *Magnificat* is more suitable to Elisabeth or to Mary. The *Magnificat* is similar in many points to the Song of Hannah. (1 Sam. 2^{1-10}.)

Hannah's Song voices the triumphant thankfulness of one who having long endured the reproach of childlessness is at last, by the Divine power, blessed with a son. This is exactly parallel to the case of Elisabeth, and therefore the *Magnificat* would seem to be more rightly assigned to her than to Mary, whose case was entirely different.

The first half of the *Magnificat* is an expression of personal thankfulness; the second half takes the form of national thanksgiving for the birth of one who is to be the Saviour of Israel. This twofold character of the *Magnificat* has its parallel in the Song of Hannah. It is of interest to note that while in the Old Testament we have the inspired hymns of Miriam, Deborah, and Hannah, we have in the New Testament this hymn of Elisabeth.

There is of course a third explanation, namely, that St. Luke, having become possessed of the wonderful collection of Christian hymns included in his opening chapters, assigned them to his characters in accordance with his own judgement of their appropriateness and not because he had any historic basis for his action.

THE BIRTH OF THE BAPTIST (*The* BENEDICTUS)

LK. I$^{57-80}$

1 57 Now Elisabeth's time was fulfilled that
she should be delivered; and she brought
58 forth a son. And her neighbours and
her kinsfolk heard that the Lord had
59 magnified his mercy towards her; and
they rejoiced with her. And it came to
pass on the eighth day, that they came to
circumcise the child; and they would have
called him Zacharias, after the name of
60 his father. And his mother answered and
said, Not so; but he shall be called John.
61 And they said unto her, There is none of
thy kindred that is called by this name.
62 And they made signs to his father, what
63 he would have him called. And he asked
for a writing tablet, and wrote, saying, His
name is John. And they marvelled all.
64 And his mouth was opened immediately,
and his tongue *loosed*, and he spake, bless-
65 ing God. And fear came on all that dwelt
round about them: and all these sayings
were noised abroad throughout all the hill
66 country of Judæa. And all that heard
them laid them up in their heart, saying,
What then shall this child be? For the
hand of the Lord was with him.
67 And his father Zacharias was filled with
the Holy Ghost, and prophesied, saying,
68 Blessed *be* the Lord, the God of Israel;
For he hath visited and wrought
redemption for his people,
69 And hath raised up a horn of salvation
for us
In the house of his servant David
70 (As he spake by the mouth of his holy
prophets which have been since
the world began),
71 Salvation from our enemies, and from
the hand of all that hate us;
72 To shew mercy towards our fathers

And to remember his holy covenant;
73 The oath which he sware unto Abraham our father,
74 To grant unto us that we being delivered out of the hand of our enemies
Should serve him without fear,
75 In holiness and righteousness before him all our days.
76 Yea and thou, child, shalt be called the prophet of the Most High:
For thou shalt go before the face of the Lord to make ready his ways;
77 To give knowledge of salvation unto his people
In the remission of their sins,
78 Because of the tender mercy of our God,
Whereby the dayspring from on high shall visit us,
79 To shine upon them that sit in darkness and the shadow of death;
To guide our feet into the way of peace.
80 And the child grew, and waxed strong in spirit, and was in the deserts till the day of his shewing unto Israel.

Having heard that the Lord had ' magnified his mercy ' towards Elisabeth in giving her a son, the relations and friends assemble at the circumcising of the child, which takes place on the eighth day after birth. At Circumcision, as at Baptism, the personal name is given to the child, and he was called John, in accordance with the command of the angel.

Wonders accompanying the birth and infancy of a child were regarded in ancient times as foreshadowing his coming greatness.

The *Benedictus* is known to the Church as the Hymn of Zacharias, but the assigning of it to him is not without difficulty. The hymn does not seem to celebrate the birth of the Second Elijah but that of the Messiah Himself. The *Benedictus* opens by thanking God for having raised up a horn of salvation in the house of His servant David. This is not appropriate to John the Baptist, who was of Levitical descent. The Messiah, on the other hand, was expected to be of the House of David.

The holy prophets referred to go back to Nathan, David's Seer, with whom the ' sure mercies of David ' originated. (2 Sam. 7^{13-16}; cf. Is. 55^{3} and Acts 13^{34}.) Among the later prophets who make similar predictions are Amos and Isaiah.

Although in *v.* 76 the new-born infant is hailed as the prophet of the highest, and one who is to go before the face of the Lord to prepare His ways, which no doubt led to the infant being identified with John the Baptist, yet in *v.* 78 the infant is hailed as the ' Dayspring,' which is the title given to the Messiah in Jeremiah and Zechariah.

Behold the days come, saith the Lord, that I will raise unto David a righteous *Branch*, and he shall reign as King, etc. (Jer. 23^{5}.)

Behold, I will bring forth my servant the *Branch*. (Zech. 3^{8}.)

Behold the man whose name is the *Branch* . . . shall bear the glory and shall sit and rule upon his throne. (Zech. 6^{12}.)

In these three passages in the Septuagint the English word ' Branch ' is the rendering of the same Greek word (*anatolē*) as is rendered ' Dayspring ' in the *Benedictus*.

' Shine on them that sit in darkness and in the shadow of death ' is an echo of the Messianic prophecy of Is. $9^{1, 2}$, which refers to the coming ideal ruler whose name shall be called Wonderful Counsellor, Mighty God, Everlasting

Father, Prince of Peace. It would seem, therefore, that the *Benedictus* heralds or acclaims the birth of the Messiah, not the birth of His forerunner.

The concluding verse of this chapter, which describes the growth of John, is a model on the Old Testament summaries of the growth of Samson and Samuel. (Judges 13^{24}; 1 Sam. 2^{26}.)

Cf. the account of the growth of our Saviour in Lk. $2^{40, 52}$.

BIRTH OF JESUS

The Census : Visit to Bethlehem : Angels and Shepherds

LK. 2^{1-20}

2 1 Now it came to pass in those days, there
went out a decree from Cæsar Augustus,
2 that all the world should be enrolled. This
was the first enrolment made when
3 Quirinius was governor of Syria. And all
went to enrol themselves, every one to his
4 own city. And Joseph also went up from
Galilee, out of the city of Nazareth, into
Judæa, to the city of David, which is called
Bethlehem, because he was of the house
5 and family of David; to enrol himself with
Mary, who was betrothed to him, being
6 great with child. And it came to pass,
while they were there, the days were ful-
7 filled that she should be delivered. And
she brought forth her firstborn son; and
she wrapped him in swaddling clothes, and
laid him in a manger, because there was
no room for them in the inn.
8 And there were shepherds in the same
country abiding in the field, and keeping
9 watch by night over their flock. And an
angel of the Lord stood by them, and the
glory of the Lord shone round about them:
10 and they were sore afraid. And the angel
said unto them, Be not afraid; for behold,
I bring you good tidings of great joy which
11 shall be to all the people: for there is born
to you this day in the city of David a
12 Saviour, which is Christ the Lord. And
this *is* the sign unto you; Ye shall find a
babe wrapped in swaddling clothes, and
13 lying in a manger. And suddenly there
was with the angel a multitude of the
heavenly host praising God, and saying,
14 Glory to God in the highest,
And on earth peace among men in
whom he is well pleased.
15 And it came to pass, when the angels
went away from them into heaven, the
shepherds said one to another, Let us now
go even unto Bethlehem, and see this thing
that is come to pass, which the Lord hath
16 made known unto us. And they came
with haste, and found both Mary and
Joseph, and the babe lying in the manger.
17 And when they saw it, they made known
concerning the saying which was spoken
18 to them about this child. And all that
heard it wondered at the things which
were spoken unto them by the shepherds.
19 But Mary kept all these sayings, pondering
20 them in her heart. And the shepherds
returned, glorifying and praising God for
all the things that they had heard and
seen, even as it was spoken unto them.

Christian Art has rightly delighted to reproduce with a wealth of colour and imagination the events attendant on our Lord's birth derived from Mt. and Lk. Rightly has Christian Art attempted this, because one of the functions of Art is to capture and preserve the fleeting aspects of significant form and in that significant form to present ideas and ideals which the recital of historic facts fails to transmit to ordinary minds.

Whether these nativity scenes be the actualities of history, or the creation of prophetic imagination and of adoring love, has vexed, and is vexing, many devout Christians to-day. Yet ought it to do so? It is a matter of extreme difficulty to determine to-day beyond all possibility of doubt what is historical and what is not historical in these narratives.

If the view be adopted that they are very largely the creation of the primitive Christian imagination, it must be recognised that, in that case, they embody in most perfect literary form the attitude of the primitive Christian Church towards its Head, and that this attitude constitutes reality of the most precious kind. Angelic songs proclaim His birth, prophetic voices foretell His significance.

In these Gospel scenes the infant Jesus is presented as not only human but Divine: He constitutes a link between the world of history and the spiritual sphere which is the originating centre of the creative process. The events recorded in Lk. as attending His birth symbolise the sacredness of His personality and the scope and quality of His mission.

Lk.'s reference to the decree (*dogma*) of Cæsar Augustus, the first Roman Emperor (30 B.C.–A.D. 14), in whose reign Jesus was born, has caused much difficulty for those who believe in the historical infallibility of Lk.

There seems to be no convincing evidence that the imperial enrolment (*apographē*) to which Lk. refers took place in Palestine during the reign of Herod the Great 37–4 B.C. It is difficult to believe that whilst Herod was King any imperial enrolment could take place in his kingdom. When Lk. states that the 'whole world,' i.e. the whole Roman Empire, was enrolled, as the result of the decree, it is hardly less than amazing that it has proved impossible to secure any direct evidence for it. Indirect evidence in connexion with the appointment of juries in Cyrene indicates that at a period subsequent to the date suggested by Sir Wm. Ramsay for Lk.'s enrolment, the Roman authorities were not in possession of the names of Greek citizens in that region. If there had been a universal imperial enrolment at this time this official ignorance would be incomprehensible.

There was an imperial enrolment in Palestine in A.D. 6, and this led to a rebellion headed by Judas of Galilee, the Zealot, because the enrolment was resented as an act of imperial tyranny. This could hardly have been the case had it been the second enrolment. Gamaliel refers to it in his speech in Acts 5^{37}. For this imperial enrolment adequate evidence exists. It took place, as we have already noted, in A.D. 6–8 after Judæa had become a Roman province. It constituted a preliminary to taxation, and Josephus, the Jewish historian, writes of it as an innovation and of the rebellion which it aroused (*Ant.*, xvii. 13, 5; xviii. 1, 1).

This enrolment took place when Quirinius was Governor of Syria. Sir Wm. Ramsay, in his book, *Was Christ born at Bethlehem?* maintains with great archæological erudition that Quirinius had held an earlier official administrative post in Syria and that it was under him 8–6 B.C. that the first enrolment took place, which Luke relates in his Gospel. It is maintained that this first enrolment was not connected with imperial taxation and was carried out with such consideration for local susceptibilities that it aroused no opposition.

A critical examination of the evidence supports the view that Quirinius occupied an official position in Syria at this earlier date, but reduces the supposed evidence for the earlier imperial enrolment to little more than apologetic conjecture.

If we are to rely upon conjecture, then it is possible that there may have been some local census instituted by Herod the Great and that Luke wrongly supposed that it had imperial authority. On the other hand, we have to admit, that there is no evidence for this. Josephus does not relate it.

Another kind of difficulty is that presented by Mt.'s narrative of the nativity. He makes no reference to Nazareth as the original home of Joseph and Mary, or of any journey by them to Bethlehem. He clearly thinks of Bethlehem as their home, and relates that it was in response to a Divine oracle vouchsafed to Joseph and in fulfilment of Old Testament prophecy that Joseph and Mary, with the infant Jesus, made their second home in Nazareth.

According to Christian tradition, the stable of the inn or caravanserai was a cave, and in this cave, which at present constitutes the crypt of a Church, the Saviour was born.

St. Jerome, the great Biblical scholar of the fourth century, lived in this cave.

The Song of the Angels occurs in two forms, either:

(1) ' Glory to God in the Highest,
Peace on Earth,
Goodwill towards men,'

or

(2) ' Glory to God in the Highest,
And Peace on Earth among men of good will.'

The second is the better attested form.

The phrase ' of good will ' may perhaps be more correctly translated ' with whom God is well pleased.'

According to Lk., this Nativity incident did receive some amount of publicity and did attract considerable attention, but Mary herself was silent about it (2^{19}). This taciturnity combined with reflective recollection Lk. represents as characteristic of her (2^{51}).

It is hard to reconcile Mary's reflections on the incidents of the Nativity with Mk's statement, that in the days of the Galilean ministry of Jesus she, with other members of His family, sought to restrain Him. (See Mk. $3^{21,\ 31\text{-}35}$.)

THE CIRCUMCISION OF JESUS

LK. 2^{21}

2 21 And when eight days were fulfilled for
circumcising him, his name was called
JESUS, which was so called by the angel
before he was conceived in the womb.

The Jewish rite of Circumcision was practised on the eighth day after the birth of all male infants. It was practised in the home. By this rite the infant was brought into covenant with the God of Israel. The personal name was given on this occasion, as we see in the case of John, the son of Zacharias.

THE PURIFICATION AND PRESENTATION

SIMEON, *NUNC DIMITTIS*, ANNA

LK. $2^{22\text{-}39}$

2 22 And when the days of their purification
according to the law of Moses were fulfilled, they brought him up to Jerusalem,
23 to present him to the Lord (as it is written
in the law of the Lord, Every male that
openeth the womb shall be called holy to
24 the Lord), and to offer a sacrifice according
to that which is said in the law of the Lord,
25 A pair of turtledoves, or two young pigeons.
And behold, there was a man in Jerusalem,

whose name was Simeon; and this man
was righteous and devout, looking for the
consolation of Israel: and the Holy Spirit
26 was upon him. And it had been revealed
unto him by the Holy Spirit, that he
should not see death, before he had seen
27 the Lord's Christ. And he came in the
Spirit into the temple: and when the
parents brought in the child Jesus, that
they might do concerning him after the
28 custom of the law, then he received him
into his arms, and blessed God and said
29 Now lettest thou thy servant depart,
O Lord,
According to thy word, in peace;
30 For mine eyes have seen thy salvation,
31 Which thou hast prepared before the
face of all peoples;
32 A light for revelation to the Gentiles,
And the glory of thy people Israel.
33 And his father and his mother were
marvelling at the things which were
34 spoken concerning him; and Simeon
blessed them, and said unto Mary his
mother, Behold, this *child* is set for the
falling and rising up of many in Israel;
and for a sign which is spoken against;
35 yea and a sword shall pierce through thine
own soul; that thoughts out of many hearts
36 may be revealed. And there was one
Anna, a prophetess, the daughter of
Phanuel, of the tribe of Asher (she was of
a great age, having lived with a husband
37 seven years from her virginity, and she had
been a widow even for fourscore and four
years), which departed not from the
temple, worshipping with fastings and
38 supplications night and day. And coming
up at that very hour she gave thanks unto
God, and spake of him to all them that
were looking for the redemption of
39 Jerusalem. And when they had accomplished all things that were according
to the law of the Lord, they returned into
Galilee, to their own city Nazareth.

Lk. relates two further sacred rites but does not separate clearly between them. The Jewish Law (Lev. 12^{2-4}) enacted that the mother of a male child should be regarded as unclean for forty days after its birth. This is a survival in the religion of Israel of the birth taboo of primitive religions. Her uncleanness was terminated by a sacrificial service in the Temple when offerings were made. In the case of a wealthy mother, she is directed to bring a lamb; in the case of a poor mother, a pair of turtledoves or two young pigeons (Lev. 12^{8}). Mary is in the latter class.

'Their purification'—those referred to are plainly Mary and her babe—not Joseph and Mary. 'Their' has created difficulty for those who regard the entail of human guilt, inherited from Adam, as being broken in the case of Jesus by the virgin birth. In consequence, some codices have substituted 'her' for 'their.'

The Presentation, with which St. Luke combines the Purification, has no ritual connexion with it. Mary, like Hannah, presents her child to God in recognition of her having received her child from Him. In Israel the eldest male was regarded as belonging to God, and if not given to Him, had to be redeemed by an offering. Lk. refers to this Jewish law: 'Sanctify unto me all the firstborn, whatsoever openeth the womb among the children of Israel, both of man and of beast: it is mine' (Exod. 13^{2}).

Simeon, a strict observer of the Law, and a man of personal piety, belonged to the class of those who waited for 'the consolation of Israel.' This, no doubt, refers to his Messianic expectations. Speaking under Divine inspiration, he recognises the babe as the future Messiah—not only the Messiah of Israel, but a light to lighten the Gentiles as well.

The statement that Joseph and Mary 'were marvelling' at the things spoken by Simeon would seem to indicate that in its original form, the cycle of Lucan Nativity narratives, of which this is one, knew nothing of the virgin birth.

The blessing of Joseph and Mary by Simeon may be compared with the blessing of Hannah and her husband Elkanah, by Eli. There, the blessing takes the form of an expressed desire that God will grant to Hannah and her husband further offspring in return for the loan which was lent unto the Lord (1 Sam. 2[20]).

In mystical language, Simeon proclaims the mission of Jesus to His people. Like the mission of Isaiah (6), the Messiah's mission will not prove an unqualified and popular triumph—not all will be saved, but all will be affected. Some, by rejecting Him, will sink into the depths of separation from God; others by accepting Him will be raised to the newness of moral and spiritual life.

The term 'rising again' (*anastasis*) is invariably used of the resurrection from the dead in the New Testament. As in the Fourth Gospel, the mission of Jesus will separate those who love the darkness from those who love the light, and so will make clear the essential character of each. Nevertheless, the Messiah's mission will not be accomplished without suffering. He will meet with opposition, rebuke, and scorn. He will be a sign to be spoken against and His sufferings will constitute the sword which will pierce His Mother's heart.

The 'sorrows of Mary' play a large part in Roman Catholic devotion, but a very small part in the Gospels. Her relation to her Son is veiled in mystery. In Mk. she hardly appears at all, and even then as apparently lacking in sympathy with Him. The words of Jesus which required His disciples to place loyalty to Him above the love of relations, reflect perhaps the way in which His own loyalty to His Messianic Mission had separated Him from the family of Nazareth.

THE GROWTH OF JESUS

LK. 2[40]

2 40 And the child grew, and waxed strong, filled with wisdom: and the grace of God was upon him.

Like a good physician, Lk. is interested in the growth of the child.

'And the child grew, and waxed strong, filled with wisdom; and the grace of God was upon him.'

This account is supplemented in *v.* 52.

'And Jesus advanced in wisdom and stature, and in favour with God and men.'

This may be compared with Lk.'s account of the growth of John the Baptist,

'And the child grew, and waxed strong in spirit' (1[80]).

These accounts of ideal development are perhaps modelled on narratives in the Old Testament of the growth of Samuel,

'And the child Samuel grew before the Lord' (1 Sam. 2[21]);

and that of Samson,

'And the child grew and the Lord blessed him' (Judges 13[24]).

JESUS WITH THE RABBIS IN THE TEMPLE

LK. 2[41-52]

2 41 And his parents went every year to Jerusalem at the feast of the passover.
42 And when he was twelve years old, they went up after the custom of the feast;
43 and when they had fulfilled the days, as they were returning, the boy Jesus tarried behind in Jerusalem; and his parents knew
44 it not; but supposing him to be in the

company, they went a day's journey; and
they sought for him among their kinsfolk
45 and acquaintance: and when they found
him not, they returned to Jerusalem, seek-
46 ing for him. And it came to pass, after
three days they found him in the temple,
sitting in the midst of the doctors, both
hearing them, and asking them questions:
47 and all that heard him were amazed at
48 his understanding and his answers. And
when they saw him, they were astonished:
and his mother said unto him, Son, why
hast thou thus dealt with us? behold, thy
49 father and I sought thee sorrowing. And
he said unto them, How is it that ye sought
me? wist ye not that I must be in my
50 Father's house? And they understood not
the saying which he spake unto them.
51 And he went down with them, and came
to Nazareth; and he was subject unto
them: and his mother kept all *these* sayings
in her heart.
52 And Jesus advanced in wisdom and
stature, and in favour with God and men.

At the age of twelve, the Jewish boy was admitted to the status of a Son of the Law (*Ben-Torah*), when he became responsible henceforth for the discharge of his religious duties, which as a circumcised Jew he was bound to discharge.

By the Mosaic law, all adult male Jews were required to present themselves three times a year in the Temple at Jerusalem—on the Feast of the Passover, the Feast of Tabernacles, and the Feast of the Harvest Home. Apparently the visit to Jerusalem by Joseph and Mary at the Feast of the Passover coincided with Jesus becoming a son of the Law. The incident which follows indicates His interest and progress in the religion of His nation.

Many sayings of the Jewish Rabbis are preserved which show that they valued the study of the Jewish Law (*Torah*) above every other occupation, and felt that any day which was passed without the study of *Torah* was lost. For this study the Jewish father was primarily responsible, according to the Deuteronomic precept:

'And these words, which I command thee this day, shall be in thine heart; and thou shalt teach them diligently unto thy children, and shalt talk of them when thou sittest in thine house, and when thou walkest by the way, and when thou liest down, and when thou risest up. And thou shalt bind them for a sign upon thine hand, and they shall be as frontlets between thine eyes. And thou shalt write them upon the posts of thy house, and on thy gates' (Dt. 6^{6-9}).

In the period after the return from the Babylonian exile the synagogue system provided, in every Jewish community of any size, a synagogue school in which all male children were taught the Law. As a result, the level of popular education in the Judaism of our Lord's time was intellectually, morally, and spiritually much above the level of any other ancient civilisation, with the possible exception of that of Athens.

The word 'company' (*v.* 44) would be better translated 'caravan.' The pilgrims from different localities travelled up in great caravans to the sacred feasts. It is said, that the fifteen Psalms of Degrees (120–134) were chanted by these pilgrim caravaners at different stages of their ascent to the House of the Lord.

'After three days' (*v.* 46) may mean on the third day.

Jesus was not engaged in examining the Rabbis in order to discover how much they knew with the purpose of correcting their ignorance and supplementing their knowledge, as some, who regarded Him as omniscient, have supposed. No doubt His intention, as became a child of His intelligence deeply interested in His religion, was to take the opportunity to learn from them. Doubtless He had found that there were many of His questions which his teacher in the synagogue school of Nazareth had been unable to answer.

'His parents' (*vv.* 41, 43), as also the phrase 'thy father' (*v.* 48, used of Joseph), would seem to indicate that this narrative does not presuppose the virgin birth. Various MSS. have, in consequence, altered 'his parents' into 'Joseph and His Mother.'

The reply of Jesus to Mary and Joseph ought to be translated, 'Wist ye not that I must be in my Father's house?' i.e. the Temple.

Of course there is in these words no tacit rebuke of Mary by Jesus. He is not rebuking her for calling Joseph his father, and recalling to her memory 'the awful secret of his birth' which she had momentarily forgotten, as some commentators have supposed.

The reply of Jesus indicates His consciousness at this early age of Divine Sonship, which at a later stage becomes a definitely Messianic consciousness. His words also indicate His deep reverence for the Temple. Possibly this was the first occasion on which He had seen it. How changed was His attitude towards it in the later days of His ministry!—'Ye have made it a cave of robbers.'

THE GENEALOGY OF JESUS

LK. 3^{23-38}

3 23 And Jesus himself, when he began *to teach,* was about thirty years of age, being
the son (as was supposed) of Joseph, the
24 *son* of Heli, the *son* of Matthat, the *son* of
Levi, the *son* of Melchi, the *son* of Jannai,
25 the *son* of Joseph, the *son* of Mattathias,
the *son* of Amos, the *son* of Nahum, the *son*
26 of Esli, the *son* of Naggai, the *son* of Maath,
the *son* of Mattathias, the *son* of Semein,
27 the *son* of Josech, the *son* of Joda, the *son* of
Joanan, the *son* of Rhesa, the *son* of Zerubbabel, the *son* of Shealtiel, the *son* of Neri,
28 the *son* of Melchi, the *son* of Addi, the *son*
of Cosam, the *son* of Elmadam, the *son* of
29 Er, the *son* of Jesus, the *son* of Eliezer, the
son of Jorim, the *son* of Matthat, the *son* of
30 Levi, the *son* of Symeon, the *son* of Judas,
the *son* of Joseph, the *son* of Jonam, the *son*
31 of Eliakim, the *son* of Melea, the *son* of
Menna, the *son* of Mattatha, the *son* of
32 Nathan, the *son* of David, the *son* of Jesse,
the *son* of Obed, the *son* of Boaz, the *son* of
33 Salmon, the *son* of Nahshon, the *son* of
Amminadab, the *son* of Arni, the *son* of
Hezron, the *son* of Perez, the *son* of Judah,
34 the *son* of Jacob, the *son* of Isaac, the *son* of
Abraham, the *son* of Terah, the *son* of
35 Nahor, the *son* of Serug, the *son* of Reu,
the *son* of Peleg, the *son* of Eber, the *son* of
36 Shelah, the *son* of Cainan, the *son* of
Arphaxad, the *son* of Shem, the *son* of
37 Noah, the *son* of Lamech, the *son* of
Methuselah, the *son* of Enoch, the *son* of
Jared, the *son* of Mahalaleel, the *son* of
38 Cainan, the *son* of Enos, the *son* of Seth,
the *son* of Adam, the *son* of God.

Lk.'s genealogy of Jesus does not, like Mt.'s, stop at Abraham, but goes right back to Adam, who was the son of God. He thus draws a Divine descent for Jesus through the long line of His human ancestry—a reminder of the profound declaration in the Genesis creation narrative, that man is created in the Divine image and after the Divine likeness. (Gen. 1^{26}.)

Lk.'s genealogy does not, as in Mt., run through Solomon and all the Kings of Judah down to the Exile; but is taken through Nathan, a younger son of David, and through his descendants. The only points at which the genealogy coincides with that of Mt. between Joseph and David, is Matthat, Zerubbabel, and Shealtiel.

(The word *Rhesa* (*v.* 27) is not the proper name of a person but the title 'a Prince,' borne presumably by Zerubbabel.)

The names, where derived from the Old Testament, are taken, not from the Hebrew but from the Septuagint, as in Mt.

Lk.'s phrase 'the son of' is usually taken by expositors to have a different significance from Mt.'s phrase, 'begat.' The former is taken to express natural descent and the latter legal descent. It is very doubtful if this distinction would have been made, or at least recognised, if it were not required by the attempt to harmonise the two genealogies.

Whether Luke himself composed the genealogy or derived it, there is nothing to indicate. Perhaps the phrase 'the son, *as was supposed*, of Joseph' (3^{23}) would favour the view that Luke did not compose it, but inserted the phrase to prevent it clashing with the story of the virgin birth. It is hardly possible that the phrase 'as was supposed' could have been in the original genealogy.

The purpose of the genealogy is like that of Mt., to prove the Davidic descent of Jesus. This descent, as in Mt., is traced through Joseph, not Mary. The theory that Lk. gives us here the genealogy of Mary, not Joseph, can only be traced back to the fifth century.

'Thirty years of age' (*v.* 23) was the time when Jewish priests began their ministrations. A comparison of the dates in 3^{1-2} indicates that John the Baptist began his ministry not earlier than A.D. 26, nor later than A.D. 33.

THE WIDOW'S SON AT NAIN

LK. 7^{11-17}

7 11 And it came to pass soon afterwards,
that he went to a city called Nain; and his
disciples went with him, and a great
12 multitude. Now when he drew near to
the gate of the city, behold, there was
carried out one that was dead, the only
son of his mother, and she was a widow:
and much people of the city was with her.
13 And when the Lord saw her, he had compassion on her, and said unto her, Weep
14 not. And he came nigh and touched the
bier: and the bearers stood still. And he
said, Young man, I say unto thee, Arise.
15 And he that was dead sat up, and began
to speak. And he gave him to his mother.
16 And fear took hold on all: and they glorified God, saying, A great prophet is arisen
among us: and, God hath visited his
17 people. And this report went forth concerning him in the whole of Judæa, and
all the region round about.

Nain or Nein is a little town situated between Gilboa and Shunem on the hillside above the great Galilean plain of Esdraelon. Visiting it, I was much impressed by the knowledge of the locality exhibited by the Lucan account. There seemed to be only one road to it, and this road ran past an ancient cemetery situated some distance from the city gate. This is indicated indirectly by Lk.'s statement, that as Jesus approached the city He met the corpse being carried on a bier.

The miracle is singular, since there is no prayer of faith on the part of the poor mother. The motive for the action is pure compassion.

The phrase 'gave him to his mother' recalls Lk.'s statement, 'He gave him back to his father,' used of the epileptic boy (Lk. 9^{42}). The phrase would seem to suggest some gesture or formal act with which the physician in this ancient world presented his patient, after his recovery, to his relations.

Besides the raising of Jairus' daughter (Mt., Mk., Lk.), this is the only other account in the Synoptic Gospels of raising from the dead. Jn., which relates neither of these cases, narrates the raising of Lazarus.

Lk. states that the young man was an only child; this he also asserts to have been the case with the daughter of Jairus.

The phrase ' the Lord ' (*v.* 13) should be noted. It here refers to Jesus, not to God, and is characteristic of some sections of Lk.

JESUS AND THE WOMAN WHO LOVED MUCH

LK. 7^{36-50}

7 36 And one of the Pharisees desired him
that he would eat with him. And he
entered into the Pharisee's house, and sat
37 down to meat. And behold, a woman
which was in the city, a sinner; and when
she knew that he was sitting at meat in the
Pharisee's house, she brought an alabaster
38 cruse of ointment, and standing behind at
his feet, weeping, she began to wet his feet
with her tears, and wiped them with the
hair of her head, and kissed his feet, and
39 anointed them with the ointment. Now
when the Pharisee which had bidden him
saw it, he spake within himself, saying,
This man, if he were a prophet, would
have perceived who and what manner of
woman this is which toucheth him, that
40 she is a sinner. And Jesus answering said
unto him, Simon, I have somewhat to say
unto thee. And he saith, Master, say on.
41 A certain lender had two debtors: the one
owed five hundred pence, and the other
42 fifty. When they had not *wherewith* to
pay, he forgave them both. Which of
them therefore will love him most?
43 Simon answered and said, He, I suppose,
to whom he forgave the most. And he
said unto him, Thou hast rightly judged.
44 And turning to the woman, he said unto
Simon, Seest thou this woman? I entered into thine house, thou gavest me no
water for my feet: but she hath wetted my
feet with her tears, and wiped them with
45 her hair. Thou gavest me no kiss: but she,
since the time I came in, hath not ceased
46 to kiss my feet. My head with oil thou
didst not anoint: but she hath anointed
47 my feet with ointment. Wherefore I say
unto thee, Her sins, which are many, are
forgiven; for she loved much: but to
whom little is forgiven, *the same* loveth
48 little. And he said unto her, Thy sins are
49 forgiven. And they that sat at meat with
him began to say within themselves, Who
is this that even forgiveth sins? And he
50 said unto the woman, Thy faith hath
saved thee; go in peace.

This incident recorded by Lk. has been identified, but wrongly, with the anointing of Jesus by Mary of Bethany a few days before His crucifixion.

The woman of Lk.'s narrative, 'who was a sinner', that is, a member of the unfortunate class, is certainly not to be identified with Mary of Bethany, the sister of Martha and Lazarus. Nor is she to be identified, as she was by mediæval artists, with Mary Magdalene, out of whom the Lord cast seven demons. This woman, like the woman taken in adultery, is rightly nameless.

The incident occurs in Galilee in the early days of the Lord's Ministry. It is doubtful if, in the later days of our Lord's Galilean Ministry, a Pharisee would have invited Him to dinner. It is a curious coincidence that His host's name was Simon, as in the case of the other anointing. But Simon was a very common name in Palestine at this time, and anointing was a very frequent act, almost as frequent as washing, as we see by our Lord's injunction :

' But thou, when thou fastest, anoint thy head, and wash thy face.' (Mt. 6^{17}.)

Alabaster boxes or flasks containing ointment, though rare with us, were the normal receptacles of unguents in the East.

It was the words of Jesus and the circumstances of the anointing, in Bethany as on this occasion, which made the anointings memorable.

The Sabbath was a day of hospitality, and devout Jews, having fasted and attended the synagogue and given alms, returned to their houses to dine. Simon does not seem to have known our Lord. He may, however, have heard Him read or speak in the synagogue, and recognising Him to be a stranger and a man of prophetic personality, have invited Him to his house—perhaps almost as an act of religious charity. From what follows the Pharisee would appear to have treated Jesus as a social inferior.

In the East, in times of festivity, open house is literally kept and people from the street look in to see what is going on. The woman, although not an invited guest, came in, doubtless with others, from the street and stooped down behind Jesus where He reclined in Oriental fashion on a sofa at the table. She was deeply penitent, no doubt as the result of some recent words of Jesus, and her tears fall on His feet; she wipes them with her hair and kisses them, and then in Oriental fashion, His feet having been washed in this way, she anoints them. Jesus appears to have taken no notice, but the Pharisee recognising her character was affronted by her action.

Either some gesture or some word of the Pharisee led Jesus to defend the woman. He contrasted her kindness with His host's neglect and declared that the woman's sins were forgiven her because she loved much. This is one of the many golden sayings enshrined in the Gospels. Love and penitence are the two qualifications for Divine forgiveness, and Jesus recognises that the woman has both.

The attached Parable of the Two Debtors does not teach that those who love much are forgiven much, but that those who are forgiven much will love much. The Pharisee here who, in his own estimation, had little to be forgiven, had a correspondingly small amount of love in his heart.

What we observe outstandingly exhibited here, as in the case of the anointing by Mary of Bethany and the incident of the adulterous woman, is the courageous chivalry of Jesus. It would have been so much safer to have remained silent, and no doubt in the estimation of many, so much more judicious.

There is a silence which is golden, such as Jesus exhibited at His trial, but there is also a silence which is cowardly and cruel.

WOMEN DISCIPLES OF JESUS

LK. 8^{1-3}

8 1 And it came to pass soon afterwards, that
he went about through cities and villages,
preaching and bringing the good tidings of
the kingdom of God, and with him the
2 twelve, and certain women which had been
healed of evil spirits and infirmities, Mary
that was called Magdalene, from whom
3 seven devils had gone out, and Joanna the
wife of Chuza Herod's steward, and
Susanna, and many others, which ministered unto them of their substance.

Lk. alone preserves for us the names of certain women disciples of Jesus. In this class are Joanna the wife of Chuza, and Susanna. Of them we know nothing except what is told us here: that they followed Jesus and ministered to Him and His Apostles.

Lk. would seem to have derived much of the special information in his Gospel from women. It is thought that his special information about Herod Antipas may have been derived from Joanna.

The seven demons who came forth from Mary of Magdala are more likely to have been demons of disease than demons of vice, although Jesus does cite the case of a demon who being cast out of a man takes to himself seven demons *more wicked* than himself. Magdala would seem to have been a village in the vicinity of the Lake of Galilee, and the term Magdalene, like Nazarene, would mean one that came from that locality.

THE LAST JOURNEY TO JERUSALEM

Lk. 9^{51}–19^{28} relates incidents in the last journey of Jesus from Galilee to Jerusalem.

This section in Lk. is sometimes called the Lucan ' Travel Document,' sometimes the ' Peræan Ministry,' sometimes ' the Great Interpolation,' sometimes the ' Central Third of Lk.' Considerable portions of it are derived from Q. Those portions of it which have parallels in Mk. are probably not derived from Mk. but from Q, which would seem to have contained a certain amount of material common to Mk. There is also much in it peculiar to Lk., which he has derived from other sources. Whether all that he relates as having occurred on this last journey to Jerusalem actually occurred then, is open to question. For instance, the sending out of the Seventy Disciples would seem more naturally to belong to an earlier period. It is difficult to see how the Seventy could have accomplished their mission in the brief period in which Jesus was proceeding from Galilee through Peræa *via* Jericho to Jerusalem. Other incidents, such as Herod's hostility and the disputes with the Pharisees, seem to suggest the background of the Galilean Ministry.

The *order* of events in Lk., between 9^{51} and 18^{14}, has no parallel in Mk. Whilst the acts and sayings of Jesus recorded in Lk. 9^{51}–18^{14} would seem to have high historic value, the order of events in this section of Lk., and the precise connexion in which he places parables and sayings, would seem to be mainly conjectural.

THE INHOSPITABLE SAMARITANS

LK. 9^{51-56}

9 51 And it came to pass, when the days
were well-nigh come that he should be
received up, he stedfastly set his face to go
52 to Jerusalem, and sent messengers before
his face: and they went, and entered into
a village of the Samaritans, to make ready
53 for him. And they did not receive him,
because his face was *as though he were* going
54 to Jerusalem. And when his disciples
James and John saw *this*, they said, Lord,
wilt thou that we bid fire to come down
55 from heaven, and consume them? But he
56 turned, and rebuked them. And they
went to another village.

This incident, peculiar to Lk., constitutes the opening paragraph in Lk.'s Travel Document.

The Samaritan village is unnamed, but is traditionally identified with Engannim (modern Jenin), a village situated just at the point where the mountainous Samaritan territory descends to the plain of Esdraelon.

The incident referred to in the life of Elijah (2 Kings 1^{10}) is the least attractive of all the stories told of him. It exhibits him as a ruthless and merciless fanatic. Jesus will have none of that Spirit in His disciples. The memorable words—

'Ye know not what manner of Spirit ye are of; for the Son of man came not to destroy men's lives but to save them,'

although omitted here by a number of important codices, breathe the spirit of Jesus, and are hardly likely to have been invented by a Jewish-Christian scribe.

This incident, like a number of others, would seem to indicate that Jesus was accompanied by a great band of followers on His last journey to Jerusalem. Lk. alone mentions the messengers sent ahead by Jesus to prepare the way for His reception.

They went to another village, plainly a Jewish village. The word 'other' in Greek means 'of another kind.' It is said that the Samaritans were very hostile in their attitude towards Jewish pilgrims going up to the great feasts at Jerusalem and would not allow them to pass through their territory.

It is possible that John and James, the sons of Zebedee, may have been nicknamed 'Sons of Thunder' from this incident.

THE THREE ASPIRANTS

LK. 9^{57-62}

9 57 And as they went in the way, a certain
man said unto him, I will follow thee
58 whithersoever thou goest. And Jesus said
unto him, The foxes have holes, and the
birds of the heaven *have* nests; but the Son
of man hath not where to lay his head.
59 And he said unto another, Follow me.
But he said, Lord, suffer me first to go and
60 bury my father. But he said unto him,
Leave the dead to bury their own dead;
but go thou and publish abroad the king-
61 dom of God. And another also said, I will
follow thee, Lord; but first suffer me to bid
farewell to them that are at my house.
62 But Jesus said unto him, No man, having
put his hand to the plough, and looking
back, is fit for the kingdom of God.

(Cf. MT. 8^{18-22})

8 18 Now when Jesus saw great multitudes
about him, he gave commandment to
19 depart unto the other side. And there
came a scribe, and said unto him, Master,
I will follow thee whithersoever thou goest.
20 And Jesus saith unto him, The foxes have
holes, and the birds of the heaven *have*
nests; but the Son of man hath not where
21 to lay his head. And another of the disciples said unto him, Lord, suffer me first
22 to go and bury my father. But Jesus
saith unto him, Follow me; and leave the
dead to bury their own dead.

Lk. next relates the way in which Jesus treated three aspirants to discipleship, or possibly apostleship. Mt. relates the first and second of these incidents, but puts them early in the Ministry—presumably in the days when Jesus was popular. Lk. has them here on the last journey to Jerusalem when the popularity of Jesus revived again as a flash in the pan. The manner in which Jesus treats the three aspirants would seem to fit in better with the situation into which Lk. inserts them. For Jesus, the time was short, and decisions must be made rapidly. Moreover, the decision involved the resolution to take part in what all must regard as a desperate adventure, some as a forlorn hope. It should also be noted that, according to Lk., the incidents take place, not when Jesus is staying in a locality, but 'as they were going on the road' (9^{57}).

Mt., who seems to have a particular interest in scribes, makes the first aspirant a scribe. There are two indications that the reply of Jesus belongs to the later period of His Ministry: (1) His description of Himself as the Son of man, (2) the declaration that He has no fixed abode.

In all the earlier period of the Galilean Ministry Jesus had a home in the house of Peter at Capernaum. It was only after He had aroused the opposition of both the ecclesiastical and political authorities in Galilee that He became a refugee.

The first aspirant offers to follow Jesus, but Jesus repels him. The second aspirant Jesus commands to follow Him, but the man finds a reason for delay. Here we have a conflict of loyalties : loyalty to a Divine call and loyalty to a human relationship. Jesus, there is good reason to believe, had faced this conflict in His own experience and had decided, at what emotional cost we know not, to follow unflinchingly the Divine call. Whether this man did the same we cannot tell.

Commentators have felt uncertain as to whether the man's father had actually died and his corpse was awaiting interment—a sacred duty imposed by custom on his son—or whether the man meant that his father was old and dependent on him and that he wished to remain at home with him until he died. Again we have no means for deciding which is the right answer.

Jesus did not favour disregard of filial obligations, as is shown by his condemnation of the casuistry by which a son might excuse himself from helping his father. (Cf. Mk. $7^{11f.}$.) Nevertheless, the claim of the Kingdom came first in His own life, and he felt it must come first in the life of all others who heard its call.

The words 'Let the dead bury their dead' are, of course, epigrammatic. 'Let the spiritually dead'—those who have not been raised to a new life by the call of the Kingdom—'bury the physically dead.' More pressing duties demand the devotion of the sons of the Resurrection.

The 'grave-diggers' was a secret designation used by Egyptian Christians of themselves in the persecutions of the third century, as we see from an extant papyrus letter. Could this name have come from the Roman Catacombs?

The case of the third aspirant is peculiar to Lk. The man asks only for a brief delay. Courtesy and kindness ought, it might seem, to have granted his request. Jesus abruptly refuses it. Possibly the man's manner suggested hesitancy and indecision. The situation and its claims demanded both urgency and absolute devotion. Jesus, like the Old Testament Gideon (Judges 7), desires in His following, not quantity, but quality. He demands from those whom He calls, even more than Elijah required from Elisha. (1 Kings 19^{16-21}.) His motto is 'now or never; now for ever.'

THE MISSION OF THE SEVENTY

LK. 10^{1-20}

10 1 Now after these things the Lord appointed seventy others, and sent them two and two before his face into every city and place, whither he himself was
2 about to come. And he said unto them, The harvest is plenteous, but the labourers are few: pray ye therefore the Lord of the harvest, that he send forth

3 labourers into his harvest. Go your
ways: behold, I send you forth as lambs
4 in the midst of wolves. Carry no purse,
no wallet, no shoes: and salute no man
5 on the way. And into whatsoever house
ye shall enter, first say, Peace *be* to this
6 house. And if a son of peace be there,
your peace shall rest upon him: but if not,
7 it shall turn to you again. And in that
same house remain, eating and drinking
such things as they give: for the labourer
is worthy of his hire. Go not from house
8 to house. And into whatsoever city ye
enter, and they receive you, eat such
9 things as are set before you: and heal the
sick that are therein, and say unto them,
The kingdom of God is come nigh unto
10 you. But into whatsoever city ye shall
enter, and they receive you not, go out
11 into the streets thereof and say, Even the
dust from your city, that cleaveth to our
feet, we do wipe off against you: howbeit
know this, that the kingdom of God is
12 come nigh. I say unto you, It shall be
more tolerable in that day for Sodom,
13 than for that city. Woe unto thee,
Chorazin! woe unto thee, Bethsaida! for
if the mighty works had been done in
Tyre and Sidon, which were done in you,
they would have repented long ago,
14 sitting in sackcloth and ashes. Howbeit
it shall be more tolerable for Tyre and
Sidon in the judgement, than for you.
15 And thou, Capernaum, shalt thou be
exalted unto heaven? thou shalt be
16 brought down unto Hades. He that
heareth you heareth me; and he that
rejecteth you rejecteth me; and he that
rejecteth me rejecteth him that sent me.
17 And the seventy returned with joy,
saying, Lord, even the devils are subject
18 unto us in thy name. And he said unto
them, I beheld Satan fallen as lightning
19 from heaven. Behold, I have given you
authority to tread upon serpents and
scorpions, and over all the power of the
enemy: and nothing shall in any wise
20 hurt you. Howbeit in this rejoice not,
that the spirits are subject unto you; but
rejoice that your names are written in
heaven.

The Mission of the Seventy is peculiar to Lk. Lk. has related in common with Mk. and Mt. the sending out of the Twelve on their Mission of proclaiming the Kingdom and healing disease. (Lk. 9^{1-6}.) While the number twelve symbolises the Mission of Jesus to Israel, the twelve-tribed nation, the number seventy, or seventy-two (both variants occur in the Lucan text), symbolises the nations of mankind, and it is no doubt because Luke, the companion of St. Paul, the Apostle to the Gentiles, wishes to indicate the Mission of Jesus to mankind, that we have this sending forth of the Seventy related by him.

It is to be observed, however, that the actual narrative of the Mission of the Seventy does not fit in with the symbolism. The Seventy are sent, not to the Gentiles, but to those places in Palestine into which Jesus Himself proposes to come. Of course, these places may include, and apparently did include, Samaritan communities and possibly the pagan or semi-pagan cities of Decapolis, which constituted the north-easterly section of Peræa.

The directions given to the Seventy have much in common with those given to the Twelve, and when, in Lk. 22^{35}, Jesus refers the Apostles to their being sent out, and the conditions imposed upon them, He actually cites conditions which Lk. relates Him as prescribing to the Seventy.

The opening words (10^{2}), with reference to the greatness of the harvest, are reflected in our Lord's conversation with His disciples at Jacob's Well in Jn. 4^{35-38}.

'Lift up your eyes and behold, the fields are white already to harvest, and he that reapeth receiveth wages and gathereth fruit unto life eternal.'

The saying about sending them forth as sheep into the midst of wolves (10^{3}) has a curious sequel attributed to it in the most ancient Christian sermon (*circa* A.D. 140) preserved outside those contained in the New Testament. In what was wrongly called the *Second Epistle of Clement* (really a homily) Peter is related to have said to the Lord: 'What therefore if the wolves should rend asunder the sheep (lambs)?"

To which Jesus replies to Peter: 'Let not the sheep, after they are dead, fear the wolves.'

This dialogue, though interesting, is in all probability apocryphal.

MARTHA AND MARY

LK 10^{38-42}

10 38 Now as they went on their way, he
entered into a certain village: and a
certain woman named Martha received
39 him into her house. And she had a sister
called Mary, which also sat at the Lord's
40 feet, and heard his word. But Martha
was cumbered about much serving; and
she came up to him, and said, Lord, dost
thou not care that my sister did leave me
to serve alone? bid her therefore that she
41 help me. But the Lord answered and
said unto her, Martha, Martha, thou art
anxious and troubled about many things:
42 but one thing is needful: for Mary hath
chosen the good part, which shall not be
taken away from her.

Martha is only mentioned here and in the Fourth Gospel (Jn. 11^{1}–12^{2}), where we are told that Lazarus of Bethany is their brother. Martha is evidently the elder sister on whom the responsibility for the household management falls.

Lk. apparently does not think of Martha's house as being situated in Bethany, but in Peræa.

Codices give the reply of Jesus in variant forms, either: 'There is need of few things' or 'There is need of one thing.'

Whether Jesus here pleads for domestic simplicity, as some have supposed, or for the claims of the spiritual above the material, is not easily determined. If He said 'There is need of one thing' then He may certainly be taken as asserting the claim of the Kingdom as against the claim of all material needs.

Mary, sitting at the feet of Jesus, indicates her recognition of this supreme claim.

If Jesus said 'There is need of few things' then He may be regarded as pleading for a simple meal—'a dry morsel and quietness therewith.'

This incident has been used to stress the superiority of the life of religious contemplation over that of practical activity, but if that practical activity be devotion to the service of others, even though it be only directed to the relief of their physical needs, it has much to justify it in the teaching of Jesus. The Christian religion, in contrast to Buddhism, is essentially a life of practical service inspired by Divine love rather than a life of mystical contemplation in search of the Beatific Vision.

The reduplication of the personal name is characteristic of Jesus, e.g. Simon, Simon; Saul, Saul; etc. The rebuke of Martha might be rendered: Thou art worried and flurried; or hustle and bustle is your way. Martha was not wrong in her dedication of herself to practical service but in the method of her discharging it.

PILATE'S MASSACRE OF GALILEANS AND THE SILOAM DISASTER

LK. 13^{1-5}

13 1 Now there were some present at that
very season which told him of the Galilæans, whose blood Pilate had mingled with
2 their sacrifices. And he answered and
said unto them, Think ye that these
Galilæans were sinners above all the
Galilæans, because they have suffered
3 these things? I tell you, Nay: but, except
ye repent, ye shall all in like manner
4 perish. Or those eighteen, upon whom
the tower in Siloam fell, and killed them,
think ye that they were offenders above all
5 the men that dwell in Jerusalem? I tell
you, Nay: but, except ye repent, ye shall
all likewise perish.

This massacre of Galileans by Pilate is peculiar to Lk. There is no reference to it in Josephus or any other author. It must have taken place in the Temple at Jerusalem during some religious festival. The Galilean Zealots were notoriously turbulent, and Pilate was ruthlessly cruel. Many massacres marked his administration. Some have thought that this particular massacre may have caused the bad feeling between Pilate and Herod Antipas, to which Lk. alone refers. Others have connected Barabbas with the incident.

Nothing outside Lk. is known of the fall of the Tower in Siloam. Siloam, like Bethesda, was a pool situated in Jerusalem. It is referred to in Nehemiah's account of the rebuilding of the walls of Jerusalem (Neh. 3^{15}), and the Tower is no doubt one of the towers of the city wall. Siloam or Shiloah is referred to in the Fourth Gospel as the pool in which the man who was born blind washed (Jn. $9^{7, 11}$).

Presumably these incidents had only recently occurred. Jesus, in contrast to the popular belief which regarded all suffering as caused by sin, refuses to take this view. Physical disasters, like physical advantages, are no indication that those who experience them are either worse or better than their fellow-men.

In this respect, as in many others, the teaching of Jesus is in harmony with the conclusions of modern thought, but it conflicted acutely with the convictions of the ancient world.

THE HUNCH-BACKED WOMAN STRAIGHTENED

LK. 13^{10-17}

13 10 And he was teaching in one of the
11 synagogues on the sabbath day. And
behold, a woman which had a spirit of
infirmity eighteen years; and she was
bowed together, and could in no wise lift
12 herself up. And when Jesus saw her, he
called her, and said to her, Woman, thou
13 art loosed from thine infirmity. And he
laid his hands upon her: and immediately she was made straight, and glorified
14 God. And the ruler of the synagogue, being moved with indignation because Jesus
had healed on the sabbath, answered
and said to the multitude, There are six
days in which men ought to work: in
them therefore come and be healed, and
15 not on the day of the sabbath. But the
Lord answered him, and said, Ye hypocrites, doth not each one of you on the
sabbath loose his ox or his ass from the
stall, and lead him away to watering?
16 And ought not this woman, being a
daughter of Abraham, whom Satan had
bound, lo, *these* eighteen years, to have
been loosed from this bond on the day of
17 the sabbath? And as he said these
things, all his adversaries were put to
shame: and all the multitude rejoiced for
all the glorious things that were done by
him.

This miracle is peculiar to Lk. Here Jesus, moved by compassion, takes the initiative. Nothing is said of the woman's faith, though it must have been there. The command and touch of Jesus effect the cure.

Her spinal weakness is regarded as due to Satanic influence. Satan had bound her: Jesus looses her on the Sabbath day, just as a man looses his beast and leads it away to water it on the Sabbath.

The ruler of the synagogue was a lay official; no doubt the chief member of the council of ten adult males who regulated the local synagogue.

Though some have criticised the logic of the retort of Jesus, its cogency is irrefutable, which asserts that if the Sabbath rest may be broken to minister to the needs of beasts, how much more may this be done in order to minister to the needs of men.

JESUS AND HEROD ANTIPAS

LK 13^{31-33}

13 31 In that very hour there came certain
Pharisees, saying to him, Get thee out,
and go hence: for Herod would fain kill
32 thee. And he said unto them, Go and
say to that fox, Behold, I cast out devils
and perform cures to-day and to-
morrow, and the third *day* I am per-
33 fected. Howbeit I must go on my way
to-day and to-morrow and the *day* following: for it cannot be that a prophet perish
out of Jerusalem.

This incident, in common with several others which concern Herod and his entourage, is peculiar to Lk. It is supposed to be derived from some special Herodian source to which Lk. had access. The source may have been Joanna, the wife of Chuza, Herod's steward, or possibly Manaen, Herod's foster-brother, a very early Antiochene Christian. The incident is obviously misplaced in Lk. It clearly refers, not to Peræa, but to the later days of our Lord's Galilean Ministry, before He took refuge in the coasts of Tyre and Sidon.

The Pharisees have no desire to save Jesus from the fate which had befallen John the Baptist. They desire to frighten Him or discredit Him, but, above all, to get rid of Him. The reply of Jesus indicates the contempt in which He held Herod, the murderer of the Baptist. It also indicates that Jesus will act according to plan: not Herod's, but God's.

Howbeit, in the end, Jesus must leave Galilee, for it is to be His fate, like other great prophets, to die in Jerusalem.

Perhaps the phrase rendered 'I am perfected' should be compared with Jn.'s last Word from the Cross—'It has been completed' (Jn. 19^{30}).

HEALING OF THE MAN WITH THE DROPSY

LK. 14^{1-6}

14 1 And it came to pass, when he went into
the house of one of the rulers of the Pharisees on a sabbath to eat bread, that they
2 were watching him. And behold, there
was before him a certain man which had
3 the dropsy. And Jesus answering spake
unto the lawyers and Pharisees, saying, Is
it lawful to heal on the sabbath, or not?
4 But they held their peace. And he took
5 him, and healed him, and let him go. And
he said unto them, Which of you shall have
an ass or an ox fallen into a well, and will
not straightway draw him up on a sabbath
6 day? And they could not answer again
unto these things.

This incident of the healing of a dropsical man in a Pharisee's house on the Sabbath would seem in all probability to belong to the Galilean Ministry of Jesus.

As in the account of the healing of the hunch-backed woman, nothing is said of the faith of the person healed. Of course the significance of each of these miracles of Luke is that Jesus performed them on the Sabbath.

THE GRATEFUL SAMARITAN LEPER

LK 17^{11-19}

17 11 And it came to pass, as they were on
the way to Jerusalem, that he was passing
through the midst of Samaria and
12 Galilee. And as he entered into a certain
village, there met him ten men that were
13 lepers, which stood afar off: and they
lifted up their voices, saying, Jesus,
14 Master, have mercy on us. And when
he saw them, he said unto them, Go and
shew yourselves unto the priests. And it
came to pass, as they went, they were
15 cleansed. And one of them, when he
saw that he was healed, turned back,
16 with a loud voice glorifying God; and he
fell upon his face at his feet, giving him
17 thanks: and he was a Samaritan. And
Jesus answering said, Were not the ten
18 cleansed? but where are the nine? Were
there none found that returned to give
19 glory to God, save this stranger? And
he said unto him, Arise, and go thy
way: thy faith hath made thee whole.

The geographical note with which this section opens is ambiguous. The text gives evidence of alterations. The passage may have originally meant 'along the border between Galilee and Samaria.' This would certainly suit the conditions of a leper colony consisting of nine Jews and one Samaritan.

The leper colony inhabited an isolated house situated outside the entrance to the village. The lepers would come out of their house and stand near the road in order to beg. The command of Jesus that they should show themselves to the priests suggests, as does the proportion of Jews in the leper colony, that the village, although on the Samaritan border, was yet situated in Galilean territory. The priests at Jerusalem were the official officers of health, and without their certificate that he was healed, no leper could return to live with his relations.

The Samaritan on his way to the priests, recognising that he is healed, apparently discontinues his journey to Jerusalem and returns to give thanks to Jesus. Jesus tells him that his faith has healed him and bids him go his way.

Here Lk. presents to his readers a Samaritan, in contrast to nine Jews, as a noble example of gratitude, as elsewhere He presents another Samaritan, in contrast to a Jewish priest and Jewish Levite, as the ideal neighbour.

ZACCHÆUS

LK. 19^{1-10}

19 1 And he entered and was passing
2 through Jericho. And behold, a man
called by name Zacchæus; and he was
3 a chief publican, and he was rich. And
he sought to see Jesus who he was; and
could not for the crowd, because he was
4 little of stature. And he ran on before,
and climbed up into a sycomore tree to
see him: for he was to pass that way.
5 And when Jesus came to the place, he
looked up, and said unto him, Zacchæus,
make haste, and come down; for to-day
6 I must abide at thy house. And he
made haste, and came down, and re-
7 ceived him joyfully. And when they
saw it, they all murmured, saying, He is
gone in to lodge with a man that is a
8 sinner. And Zacchæus stood, and said

unto the Lord, Behold, Lord, the half of
my goods I give to the poor; and if I have
wrongfully exacted aught of any man, I
9 restore fourfold. And Jesus said unto
him, To-day is salvation come to this
house, forasmuch as he also is a son of
10 Abraham. For the Son of man came to
seek and to save that which was lost.

Zacchæus is only mentioned here, and in order to find a place for this incident, Lk. transfers the healing of Blind Bartimæus to the entrance of Jesus into Jericho. In Mk. the incident of Bartimæus takes place as Jesus leaves Jericho.

The whole scene is extraordinarily vivid and is full of grace, not without a touch of humour. Although his fellow-countrymen, because Zacchæus is a tax-gatherer, refuse to regard him as a fellow-Israelite, Zacchæus shows himself on this occasion in the presence of Jesus to be a true son of Abraham by his conduct. Love of God was shown by love to the poor to whom Zacchæus now gives half his wealth. His promise to restore fourfold anything which he had taken unjustly from any man was in accordance with the Mosaic Law, which demanded, as the penalty for theft, fourfold restoration of the things stolen. (Exod. 22^{1}; 2 Sam. 12^{6}.)

JESUS CHECKS EXPECTATION OF AN IMMINENT PAROUSIA

LK. 19^{11}

19 11 And as they heard these things, he
added and spake a parable, because he
was nigh to Jerusalem, and *because* they
supposed that the kingdom of God was
immediately to appear.

This Lucan note on the expectation by the followers of Jesus that the Kingdom of God 'was immediately to appear,' and that Jesus expressly spoke a parable on the last stage of His journey up to Jerusalem to refute this expectation, is significant. There is no doubt that their conception of the Kingdom is political and nationalist. It reappears in Acts 1, where the Apostles asked Jesus, just before the Ascension: 'Dost thou at this time restore the Kingdom to Israel?'

The reply of Jesus: 'It is not for you to know the times and seasons which the Father hath placed in His own power,' is, we believe, typical of the teaching of Jesus. The interval may be long or it may be short; what is needful in the interval is the spirit which is dutiful, sober, watchful.

In the parable of the Pounds (19^{12-27}), the phrase 'went into a *far* country' is intended to suggest that the Parousia is not imminent.

There is thought by some to be a historic reference here ($19^{14, 27}$) to the journey made by Archelaus, the son of Herod the Great, who went to Rome in order to secure from Augustus the succession to his father's kingdom. Josephus relates that the Jews, on account of his evil character, protested against his claim, but in vain.

JESUS WEEPING OVER JERUSALEM

LK. 19^{41-44}

19 41 And when he drew nigh, he saw the
42 city and wept over it, saying, If thou
hadst known in this day, even thou, the
things which belong unto peace! but now
43 they are hid from thine eyes. For the
days shall come upon thee, when thine
enemies shall cast up a bank about thee,
and compass thee round, and keep thee
44 in on every side, and shall dash thee to
the ground, and thy children within thee;
and they shall not leave in thee one stone
upon another; because thou knewest not
the time of thy visitation.

Lk. relates that when Jesus came within sight of the city He wept over it because it failed to recognise the time of its visitation and the things which belonged to its peace. Subsequent events were to indicate how true this was. The weeping of Jesus over Jerusalem may be appropriately connected with the pathetic passage preserved in Q. (Mt. 23^{37} = Lk. 13^{34}.)

'O Jerusalem, Jerusalem, which killest the prophets, and stonest them that are sent unto thee: how often would I have gathered thy children together, as a hen doth gather her brood under her wings, and ye would not!

'Behold, your house is left unto you desolate: and verily I say unto you, Ye shall not see me, until the time come when ye shall say, Blessed is he that cometh in the name of the Lord.'

When Jesus had entered the city and visited the Temple, scrutinising all things, He returned with the Twelve to Bethany.

Mk. relates that on the next day Jesus again visits Jerusalem.

SATAN'S REQUEST, THE TWO SWORDS, ETC.

LK. 22^{31-38}

22 31 and the Lord said, Simon, Simon,
behold, Satan asked to have you, that
32 he might sift you as wheat; but I made
supplication for thee, that thy faith
fail not: and do thou, when once thou
hast turned again, stablish thy brethren.
33 And he said unto him, Lord, with thee I
am ready to go both to prison and to
34 death. And he said, I tell thee, Peter,
the cock shall not crow this day, until
thou shalt thrice deny that thou knowest
me.
35 And he said unto them, When I sent
you forth without purse, and wallet, and
shoes, lacked ye any thing? And they
36 said, Nothing. And he said unto them,
But now, he that hath a purse, let him
take it, and likewise a wallet: and he that
hath none, let him sell his cloke, and buy
37 a sword. For I say unto you, that this
which is written must be fulfilled in me,
And he was reckoned with transgressors:
for that which concerneth me hath fulfil-
38 ment. And they said, Lord, behold,
here are two swords. And he said unto
them, It is enough.

In Lk.'s account of the entry of Jesus into Jerusalem and His subsequent teaching before His crucifixion, Lk. follows Mk., his only important omission being the incident of the withered fig tree. Lk. also omits Mk.'s question of the scribe about ' the first commandment of all ' (Mk. $12^{28\,f.}$; cf. Lk. 20^{39}). This is no doubt due to Lk. having recorded, what is apparently the same incident, although much altered, to serve as his introduction to the parable of the Good Samaritan. (Lk. 10^{25-29}.)

Lk. also omits Mk.'s account of the anointing of Jesus in Bethany in the house of Simon the Leper (Mk. 14^{3-9}). This is no doubt due to Lk.'s having recorded an anointing of Jesus by a woman much earlier in the days of His Galilean Ministry (cf. Lk. $7^{36\,f.}$).

In 22^{31-38} Lk. is making use of a source or sources not used by Mk. or Mt.

(*a*) Satan's request to God for the disciples reflects the character of the Satan of earlier Jewish tradition as we have him depicted in the Book of Job. (Job 1^{12}, 2^{6}.)

There Satan asks the Lord for Job that he may test his virtue, and the Lord grants his request. Jesus tells Peter that Satan has made request for them that he may separate in them the husk from the grain. Jesus has prayed to God for Peter that he may come through this period of testing without loss of faith.

The phrase ' when thou art converted ' predicts Peter's fall, but not his perdition. The command to strengthen his brethren reminds us of the scene in the Epilogue of the Fourth Gospel, ' Feed my sheep.' (Jn. $21^{15f.}$.) The whole incident attests the leadership of St. Peter and his prominence in the primitive Church.

(*b*) The incident of the two swords has been very variously interpreted. The discovery and exposition by Dr. Eisler of the Slavonic Josephus has been taken as offering historical support to the view that we have in this incident of the two swords a survival of the true view of the last visit of Jesus to Jerusalem—that He really went there to lead an armed revolution against the authorities. Hence His words about the necessity for the sword are to be interpreted, not as symbolic, or ironic, but literally. His bids the disciples arm in preparation for the rising. Quite apart from the question of the genuineness of the peculiar element in the Slavonic Josephus which excellent scholars, Jewish and Christian, discredit, it is extremely difficult, in view of all we have recorded of Jesus and His Mission, to believe that He could possibly have either advocated or sanctioned a militarist undertaking on behalf of the Kingdom. Whilst the Jews of the first and second centuries of the Christian era were conspicuous for their militarism on behalf of their religion, the Christians were equally conspicuous for their pacifism. This attitude is consistently taught (save, perhaps, in that not generally accepted canonical book, *The Revelation of St. John*) throughout the whole of the New Testament, particularly in 1 Peter, where the example of Jesus Himself is cited.

The action of the proto-martyr Stephen, who prayed for his executioners, ' Lord, lay not this sin to their charge ' (Acts 7^{60}), is undoubtedly modelled on the example of Jesus, who at His execution prayed: ' Father, forgive them, for they know not what they do.'

That Jesus was intensely opposed to Zealot militarism is not only indicated by His utterance: ' They that take the sword shall perish by the sword,' but also by His general teaching on the duty of non-resistance, and of submission to the Roman authorities.

' If a man compel thee to go with him one mile, go with him two,' refers, as the technical word translated ' compel ' indicates, to official, not to private compulsion.

His saying: ' Render to Cæsar the things that are Cæsar's and to God the things that are God's,' indicates that in His view it was possible to be a loyal son of the Kingdom and yet at the same time to accept the Roman rule as it was then exercised in Palestine. His riding into Jerusalem on an ass was undoubtedly a deliberate symbolic action intended to make it clear that His Messiahship was peaceful, not militarist.

In view of such facts it is impossible to regard the incident of the two swords, if historic, as indicating that Jesus was bidding His disciples to prepare for and play their part in a military rising on His behalf. On the other hand, it is quite possible, even probable, that some of His Apostles, and possibly many of His disciples, believed that He intended to overthrow the authorities in Jerusalem and that He would acquiesce in their use of the sword. Undoubtedly His refusal on the occasion of His arrest in Gethsemane to sanction armed resistance disheartened His Apostles and led to their flight. His saying on that occasion, as recorded in Mt. $26^{53, 54}$:

'Thinkest thou that I cannot now pray to my Father, and He shall presently give me more than twelve legions of angels? But how then shall the scriptures be fulfilled, that thus it must be?'

indicates that not even the swords of angels, still less those of men, were to be used on behalf of the Kingdom.

What the words of Jesus, as recorded in Lk. 22^{35-38}, are meant to teach His disciples is, that in the light of what is about to happen to Him—His execution by the ecclesiastical and political authorities—the attitude of the community, which on a former occasion had been markedly friendly to His followers, would now be changed to one of bitter hostility. No longer in their missionary travels would they be able to rely on the hospitality of those to whom they went.

When He finds that His Apostles—even St. Peter—misunderstand His saying about buying a sword and show Him that they have already forestalled His command, He cuts the discussion short by saying, 'It is enough.'

The phrase 'it is enough' is an ambiguous one, but papyrus documents indicate that it was the formula used in giving a receipt which concluded a business transaction.

In the Middle Ages the two swords were interpreted as symbolising the power of the Holy Roman Church and the Holy Roman Empire. These, in co-operation, which was seldom the case, must prove sufficient for every emergency.

These words, it should be noted, were uttered by Jesus in the Upper Chamber in which The Last Supper had been eaten.

THE BLOODY SWEAT

LK. $22^{43, 44}$

22 43 And there appeared unto him an angel
44 from heaven, strengthening him. And
being in an agony he prayed more
earnestly: and his sweat became as it
were great drops of blood falling down
upon the ground.

The incidents of the bloody sweat and the Strengthening Angel, peculiar to Lk., are omitted by a number of important codices.

If this omission be accepted as proving that these incidents were not in Luke's original text, then Lk.'s account of what happened in Gethsemane comes mid-way between Mk. and Jn.

In Mk., Jesus suffers extreme emotional and mental anguish. He is intensely human, as the writer of the Epistle to the Hebrews states:

'Who in the days of his flesh, when he had offered up prayers and supplications with strong crying and tears unto him that was able to save him from death.' (Heb. 5^{7}.)

In Lk., omitting the Agony, Jesus, in His calm acceptance of the Divine Will, reminds us of Plato's account of the dying Socrates.

In Jn., the prayer for strength to accept the Divine Will is altogether omitted. (Cf. Jn. 18^{1-4}.)

If the bloody sweat be regarded as part of the original text of Lk., it is not necessarily to be interpreted that Jesus actually sweated blood, although such a phenomenon is recorded to have taken place on rare occasions. The French King responsible for the Massacre of St. Bartholomew, and a thief condemned to death in a papal court of justice in the sixteenth century, are both said to have had a bloody sweat.

The passage may be correctly interpreted as saying no more than that the sweat of Jesus was so heavy that it dripped from Him like blood dripping from a wound. The incident of the angel strengthening Him, we may regard as a later mythical addition to the narrative. It is absent from a number of important manuscripts and may be compared with a passage, which is probably an interpolation, in the Fourth Gospel where it is stated that the troubling of the waters of the pool of Bethesda when they became effective for healing was due to the descent of an angel into them. (Jn. 5^4.)

THE HEALING OF THE SEVERED EAR

LK. 22^{49-51}

22 49 And when they that were about him
saw what would follow, they said, Lord,
50 shall we smite with the sword? And a
certain one of them smote the servant of
the high priest, and struck off his right
51 ear. But Jesus answered and said, Suffer
ye thus far. And he touched his ear,
and healed him.

Lk. alone of the Synoptists relates that it was the *right* ear that was severed and he alone relates the healing of the ear by Jesus—one of the most difficult of the miracles of healing to regard as historic.

It has been ingeniously suggested that his ' miracle of surgery ' is due to Luke's misunderstanding of his source, and that he understood the command of Jesus ' to restore ' (that is, the sword to its sheath) as addressed to the severed ear. (Cf. Mt. 26^{52}.) Lk. has a mind prone to believe the miraculous and to interpret non-miraculous events in a miraculous manner. We see this in his alteration of Mk.'s statement, that at the baptism of Jesus the Spirit descended as a dove. Lk. writes, ' in the bodily form of a dove.'

Professor Percy Gardner has expressed this Lucan tendency in the phrase, ' Luke dearly loves a good miracle.'

JESUS BEFORE HEROD ANTIPAS

LK. 23^{4-16}

23 4 And Pilate said unto the chief priests
and the multitudes, I find no fault in this
5 man. But they were the more urgent,
saying, He stirreth up the people, teaching throughout all Judæa, and beginning
6 from Galilee even unto this place. But
when Pilate heard it, he asked whether
7 the man were a Galilæan. And when he
knew that he was of Herod's jurisdiction,
he sent him unto Herod, who himself also
8 was at Jerusalem in these days. Now
when Herod saw Jesus, he was exceeding
glad: for he was of a long time desirous
to see him, because he had heard con-

cerning him; and he hoped to see some
9 miracle done by him. And he questioned
him in many words; but he answered
10 him nothing. And the chief priests and
the scribes stood, vehemently accusing
11 him. And Herod with his soldiers set
him at nought, and mocked him, and
arraying him in gorgeous apparel sent
12 him back to Pilate. And Herod and
Pilate became friends with each other
that very day: for before they were at
enmity between themselves.
13 And Pilate called together the chief
priests and the rulers and the people, and
14 said unto them, Ye brought unto me this
man, as one that perverteth the people:
and behold, I, having examined him
before you, found no fault in this man
touching those things whereof ye accuse
15 him: no, nor yet Herod: for he sent him
back unto us; and behold, nothing
worthy of death hath been done by him.
16 I will therefore chastise him, and release
him.

This sending of Jesus by Pilate to Herod Antipas is peculiar to Lk. and is no doubt derived by him from his particular source connected with Herod's entourage. As Lk. relates the mockery of Jesus by Herod and his soldiers, he omits the purple (scarlet) robe and wreath of thorns and the mockery by the Roman soldiers. No doubt, in the silence of Jesus in the presence of His accusers, the primitive Christians recognised a fulfilment of the words of Is. 53:

'As a sheep before her shearers is dumb, so he opened not his mouth.'

Nothing is known of the cause of the enmity between Pilate and Herod Antipas. Herod seems to have held that Jesus was John the Baptist, raised from the dead. It would appear that it was the reputation of Jesus as a worker of miracles rather than as a prophetic preacher which had aroused the curiosity of Herod.

DAUGHTERS OF JERUSALEM

LK. 23^{27-31}

23 27 And there followed him a great multitude of the people, and of women who
28 bewailed and lamented him. But Jesus
turning unto them said, Daughters of
Jerusalem, weep not for me, but weep for
29 yourselves, and for your children. For
behold, the days are coming, in which
they shall say, Blessed are the barren,
and the wombs that never bare, and the
30 breasts that never gave suck. Then shall
they begin to say to the mountains, Fall
on us; and to the hills, Cover us. For if
31 they do these things in the green tree,
what shall be done in the dry?

Lk. records more of the ministry of women than do the other Evangelists. Lk. tells us that numbers of women followed Jesus up from Galilee, but it is here the women of Jerusalem who are referred to.

The mourning for Him by the women of Jerusalem would seem to indicate that His preaching there in the last days of His Ministry had had no little effect. The words of Jesus are a prediction of the horrors which will overtake the inhabitants of the city in its approaching destruction.

The phrase: 'For if they do these things in the green tree, what shall be done in the dry,' is equivalent to saying: 'If green wood burns so fiercely, how much more fiercely will dry wood burn?' If I, the guiltless, suffer so much, what will be the sufferings of the guilty? It is an *a fortiori* argument.

THREE WORDS FROM THE CROSS

LK. 23^{34-46}

23 34 And Jesus said, Father, forgive them;
for they know not what they do. And
parting his garments among them, they
35 cast lots. And the people stood beholding. And the rulers also scoffed at him,
saying, He saved others; let him save

himself, if this is the Christ of God, his
36 chosen. And the soldiers also mocked
him, coming to him, offering him vinegar,
37 and saying, If thou art the King of the
38 Jews, save thyself. And there was also
a superscription over him, THIS IS THE
39 KING OF THE JEWS. And one of the malefactors which were hanged railed on him,
saying, Art not thou the Christ? save
40 thyself and us. But the other answered,
and rebuking him said, Dost thou not
even fear God, seeing thou art in the
41 same condemnation? And we indeed
justly; for we receive the due reward of
our deeds: but this man hath done noth-
42 ing amiss. And he said, Jesus, remember
me when thou comest in thy kingdom.
43 And he said unto him, Verily I say unto
thee, To-day shalt thou be with me in
44 Paradise. And it was now about the
sixth hour, and a darkness came over the
whole land until the ninth hour, the
45 sun's light failing: and the veil of the
46 temple was rent in the midst. And when
Jesus had cried with a loud voice, he said,
Father, into thy hands I commend my
spirit: and having said this, he gave up
the ghost.

Lk., like Jn., records three utterances of Jesus on the Cross which are not recorded by any other Evangelist. Why they are not recorded, if Jesus really uttered them, may well cause conjecture; but there is no satisfactory solution of the problem.

Although His disciples forsook Him, many women were present at His crucifixion, and it may well be that Lk. derived his three Words from some feminine source.

In literary form, and in essential spirit, the first and the third Words are in harmony with the teaching of Jesus. They both address God as Abba, even as Jesus taught His disciples to do: they both breathe the spirit of forgiveness and of faith so characteristic of His Gospel. The prayer of the dying Stephen is plainly modelled on the first: the third is an echo of Ps. 31^{5}:

'Into thy hand I commend my spirit: thou hast redeemed me, O Lord, thou God of truth.'

Cf. also 1 Peter 2^{23}:

'Who when he was reviled, reviled not again: when he suffered he threatened not, but committed himself to Him that judgeth righteously.'

Lk. alone relates the penitence of the crucified brigand. The brigand's utterance shows that he recognises Jesus as the Messiah. Quite possibly the brigand had been a Zealot patriot, who looked for a Messiah like a Maccabean warrior-prince. His association with Jesus on the Cross has changed his conception both of the Kingdom and its Messiah. Jesus, though rejected and crucified, is the Messiah and He is coming into His Kingdom.

There is no indication what the brigand thought to be the nature of that Kingdom. It suffices that for him Jesus is its King, and Jesus promises him that he shall not be separated from Him in that mysterious future into which He is entering.

Paradise is a Persian word and means a walled park such as surrounded a royal palace. It presents a picture of delight. The care of the dying Jesus for the brigand in Lk. may be compared with His care for His Mother in Jn. $19^{26, 27}$.

We see reflected in Lk.'s three Words from the Cross a picture of Jesus which is more in harmony with what the Christian Church has believed Him to be in His personal character than we have in the four Words from the other Gospels.

It ought to be added, however, that a certain number of important codices omit the words, 'Father, forgive them, for they know not what they do.' Some have supposed that this omission in these codices is due to their representing an earlier text of Lk.'s Gospel which he himself afterwards revised, adding this Word from the Cross.

Others have supposed that the omission is due to the persecution of Christians and the deep resentment aroused in Christian circles against their persecutors. The fiery Tertullian, about A.D. 200, so far from praying for the persecutors of Christians, anticipates satisfaction at witnessing in a future life their torment.

The first reason given for this omission is more probable than the second. Unless, however, there were a very strong and early tradition in favour of these words as actually uttered by Jesus, it is hard to account for their preservation in Lk.

THE ECLIPSE OF THE SUN

LK. 23^{45}

23 45 the sun's light failing: and the veil of the temple was rent in the midst.

Lk.'s statement that the darkness at the time of the Crucifixion was due to an eclipse of the sun (for it is difficult to see how his statement can mean anything else), has given much trouble to Christian apologists, since the Crucifixion having taken place at the Passover, when the moon is full, an eclipse of the sun is astronomically impossible.

As a consequence, the original text of Lk. has suffered alteration here—the phrase ' the sun being darkened ' being substituted for ' the sun was eclipsed.'

Some have thought, as we have pointed out in commenting on Mk.'s Word from the Cross, Eloi, Eloi, etc., that Lk has misinterpreted this utterance as a statement that an eclipse took place—the Aramaic word for ' my God ' sounding something like the Greek phrase ' of [the] sun.' If, however, the words which Jesus uttered were taken by the spectators, as we are told they were, to refer to Elias, then, the two words become practically identical in sound and Lk.'s confusion of the two is easily accounted for.

THE SPECTATORS SMITE THEIR BREASTS

LK. 23^{48}

23 48 And all the multitudes that came together to this sight, when they beheld the things that were done, returned smiting their breasts.

The mourning of the spectators, like the weeping of the daughters of Jerusalem, is peculiar to Lk. Several codices (Old Syriac and Old Latin) make various additions at this point:

' Woe unto us, since these things have been done to-day on account of our sins, for the desolation of Jerusalem has drawn nigh.'

Sources of Lk.'s Passion Narrative

A much-debated point is whether Lk., in his account of the Passion, makes use of Mk. as his main source. Although Lk. does not contain some Marcan incidents and has himself given to his readers a large number of incidents which are not in Mk., yet in the main, the framework of his Passion narrative and that of Mk. are the same.

Of course this does not necessarily mean that Lk. is dependent upon Mk. for this framework, since this framework may reflect the universal tradition of the primitive Church.

WOMEN BUY SPICES ON GOOD FRIDAY

LK. 23^{56}

23 56 And they returned, and prepared spices and ointments. And on the sabbath they rested according to the commandment.

The conflict of evidence with regard to the spices used for the burial of the Lord's body should be noted. Mt. says nothing at all about spices for the burial. He states that the women came 'In the end of the Sabbath, as it began to dawn toward the first day of the week . . . to behold the Sepulchre.' (Mt. 28^{1}.)

Jn. states that the spices were brought by Nicodemus and used by him and Joseph of Arimathæa at the Lord's interment on Good Friday evening. (Jn. $19^{39, 40}$.)

Lk. states that the women bought spices late on Good Friday evening, i.e. before 6 p.m., but had no time to bring them to the Sepulchre as the Sabbath began at 6 p.m. They therefore rested on the Sabbath day (i.e. Saturday), and very early on Easter Sunday brought the spices to the Sepulchre and found it empty. (Lk. $24^{2f.}$.)

Mk. relates that when the Sabbath was passed the women 'bought spices in order that they should come and anoint him.' (Mk. 16^{1}.) This presumably was sometime after six o'clock on Saturday evening, when the Sabbath was completed. He then goes on to say that early in the morning on the first day of the week they set out for the Sepulchre. (Mk. $16^{1, 2}$.)

PETER'S VISIT TO THE SEPULCHRE

LK. 24^{12} (Cf. JN. 20^{3-10})

24 12 But Peter arose, and ran unto the tomb; and stooping and looking in, he seeth the linen cloths by themselves; and he departed to his home, wondering at that which was come to pass.

Important codices omit this passage. It reads very much like an insertion. It is probably derived from Jn. 20^{3-10}, which relates a visit of Peter to the Sepulchre.

THE APPEARANCE OF JESUS ON THE ROAD TO EMMAUS

LK. 24^{13-35}

24 13 And behold, two of them were going
that very day to a village named Emmaus, which was threescore furlongs
14 from Jerusalem. And they communed
with each other of all these things which
15 had happened. And it came to pass,
while they communed and questioned
together, that Jesus himself drew near,
16 and went with them. But their eyes were
holden that they should not know him.
17 And he said unto them, What communications are these that ye have one with
another, as ye walk? And they stood
18 still, looking sad. And one of them,
named Cleopas, answering said unto
him, Dost thou alone sojourn in Jerusalem and not know the things which are
19 come to pass there in these days? And
he said unto them, What things? And
they said unto him, The things concerning Jesus of Nazareth, which was a prophet mighty in deed and word before
20 God and all the people: and how the
chief priests and our rulers delivered him
up to be condemned to death, and cruci-
21 fied him. But we hoped that it was he
which should redeem Israel. Yea and
beside all this, it is now the third day
22 since these things came to pass. Moreover, certain women of our company
amazed us, having been early at the
23 tomb; and when they found not his body,
they came, saying, that they had also
seen a vision of angels, which said that he
24 was alive. And certain of them that
were with us went to the tomb, and
found it even so as the women had said:
25 but him they saw not. And he said unto
them, O foolish men, and slow of heart to
believe in all that the prophets have
26 spoken! Behoved it not the Christ to
suffer these things, and to enter into his
27 glory? And beginning from Moses and
from all the prophets, he interpreted to
them in all the scriptures the things con-
28 cerning himself. And they drew nigh
unto the village, whither they were
going: and he made as though he would
29 go further. And they constrained him
saying, Abide with us: for it is toward
evening, and the day is now far spent.
And he went in to abide with them.
30 And it came to pass, when he sat down
with them to meat, he took the bread,
and blessed it, and brake, and gave to
31 them. And their eyes were opened, and
they knew him; and he vanished out of
32 their sight. And they said one to another,
Was not our heart burning within us,
while he spake to us in the way, while he
33 opened to us the scriptures? And they
rose up that very hour, and returned to
Jerusalem, and found the eleven gathered
together, and them that were with them,
34 saying, The Lord is risen indeed, and
35 hath appeared to Simon. And they
rehearsed the things *that happened* in the
way, and how he was known of them in
the breaking of the bread.

Lk.'s account of the appearance of Jesus after His crucifixion to two disciples as they are walking to Emmaus on the first Easter Day is, from the literary point of view, the most perfect of all our Resurrection narratives.

Emmaus presents great difficulties because it is situated 176 stades, or twenty English miles, from Jerusalem. It is hardly possible that the two disciples having arrived there at sunset should afterwards have walked all the way back again to Jerusalem and have found the Apostles assembled together.

In consequence of the difficulties presented by the location of the well-known Emmaus, an attempt has been made to alter the distance in the text by inserting one hundred before sixty in some MSS.

Another attempted solution has been to identify the Lucan Emmaus with Kolonieh, whose ancient name was Emmaus, which is situated about four miles from Jerusalem, in the direction of Joppa.

Of Cleopas, the only one named of the two wayfarers, we know nothing. Some Latin MSS. give the name as Cleophas, and in Jn. 19^{25} one of the women who stood by the Cross was His Mother's sister, Mary of Clopas. If Cleopas be identified with Clopas, then he would be our Lord's uncle by marriage and the father of the Simeon who succeeded St. James (our Lord's brother) as head of the Church in Jerusalem. This identification suggests that the Emmaus Resurrection narrative was an important element in the Resurrection tradition of the Church in Jerusalem.

Some have even supposed that the unnamed wayfarer is Simeon himself.

The failure of the wayfarers to recognise Jesus at first may be compared with Mary Magdalene's identification of Him with the gardener in Jn. $20^{14, 15}$.

'A vision of angels' (*v.* 23) indicates that the women at the Sepulchre regarded the two men (Lk. 24^{4}) as angels.

The primitive Church was convinced that its belief that the Old Testament was full of oracles, predicting particulars about the Messiah and His Mission, went back to Jesus Himself, who first taught them to study the Old Testament in this way. It seems probable that the figure of the Suffering Servant in Is. 53 did suggest to Jesus that it was the rôle of the Messiah to suffer, but it may be assumed that it was more probably the primitive Christian Church, and not Jesus Himself, who pointed to many other passages in the Old Testament as having been fulfilled by His sufferings. Just as all the laws in the Old Testament are attributed to Moses, and all the Psalms to David, and all the Wisdom literature to Solomon, so it would be natural in the New Testament to attribute to Jesus the identification of all the Old Testament passages which the primitive Christian Church regarded as predicting His Passion.

The Breaking of the Bread is the name given in the early chapters of the Acts of the Apostles and in the account of St. Paul's visit to the Church at Troas (Acts $20^{7, 11}$) to the primitive Christian common meal—a combination of the *Agapē* or Love-Feast, and the Lord's Supper or Eucharist. The statement that the Lord was made known to them in the breaking of the bread may be a mystical reference to the experience of the early Christian Church at the Eucharist. It was no doubt pre-eminently at that rite that they were conscious of their Lord's presence, and as not only crucified, but also, as risen from the dead.

It is strange that although the appearance of the Risen Lord to St. Peter is referred to in Lk.'s narrative (*v.* 34), and also by St. Paul in 1 Cor. 15^{5}, yet we have no actual account of that Resurrection appearance to Peter except in the Epilogue of the Fourth Gospel (Jn. 21^{7}).

RESURRECTION APPEARANCE TO THE DISCIPLES IN JERUSALEM

LK. 24^{36-49}

24 36 And as they spake these things, he
himself stood in the midst of them, and
37 saith unto them, Peace *be* unto you. But
they were terrified and affrighted, and
supposed that they beheld a spirit.
38 And he said unto them, Why are ye
troubled? and wherefore do reasonings
39 arise in your heart? See my hands and
my feet, that it is I myself: handle me,
and see: for a spirit hath not flesh and
40 bones, as ye behold me having. And
when he had said this, he shewed them
41 his hands and his feet. And while they
still disbelieved for joy, and wondered,
he said unto them, Have ye here any-
42 thing to eat? And they gave him a

43 piece of a broiled fish. And he took it,
and did eat before them.
44 And he said unto them, These are my
words which I spake unto you, while I
was yet with you, how that all things
must needs be fulfilled, which are written
in the law of Moses, and the prophets,
45 and the psalms, concerning me. Then
opened he their mind, that they might
46 understand the scriptures; and he said
unto them, Thus it is written, that the
Christ should suffer, and rise again from
47 the dead the third day; and that repentance and remission of sins should be
preached in his name unto all the
48 nations, beginning from Jerusalem. Ye
49 are witnesses of these things. And behold, I send forth the promise of my
Father upon you: but tarry ye in the
city, until ye be clothed with power
from on high.

This Resurrection appearance presumably takes place very late in the night of the first Easter Day, and in that case is to be identified with the Resurrection appearance narrated in Jn. 20^{19-25} to the ten Apostles. It differs from it, however, in important particulars. Jn.'s account includes the Insufflation or the Breathing of the Holy Spirit into the disciples.

Lk., on the other hand, contains a statement that the Lord ate in their presence. Some MSS. add to the broiled fish, 'and of a honeycomb,' but it is most improbable that this was part of the original text of Lk. The manifest purpose of this account is to confute the very early Docetic heresy which taught that Jesus possessed no body of flesh and blood but appeared to men only as a phantasm.

The same purpose is manifest in Jn.'s account of the Resurrection appearance of Jesus to Thomas Didymus, bidding him to handle Him (Jn. 20^{26-29}).

St. Ignatius, about A.D. 110, refers to this appearance in his *Epistle to the Smyrnæans*, when he writes that Jesus came to those around Peter and said to them: 'Take, handle me, because I am not a bodiless demon.' The rare word translated 'handle' here is the same as that used in Lk. 24^{39}, and is also the same as is used in 1 Jn. 1^{1} (the Word of Life 'which our hands have handled').

All of these passages undoubtedly refer to the same incident.

In the Acts also, Luke states that Jesus ate with His disciples after His Resurrection.

The declaration of Jesus that His Apostles are to be His witnesses, beginning in Jerusalem and unto all mankind, is also stressed in the opening of the Acts.

THE ASCENSION

LK. 24^{50-53}

24 50 And he led them out until *they were*
over against Bethany: and he lifted up
51 his hands, and blessed them. And it
came to pass, while he blessed them, he
parted from them, and was carried up
52 into heaven. And they worshipped
him, and returned to Jerusalem with
53 great joy: and were continually in the
temple, blessing God.

ACTS 1^{1-13a}

1 1 The former treatise I made, O Theophilus, concerning all that Jesus began both
2 to do and to teach, until the day in which he
was received up, after that he had given
commandment through the Holy Ghost
unto the apostles whom he had chosen:
3 to whom he also shewed himself alive after
his passion by many proofs, appearing
unto them by the space of forty days, and
speaking the things concerning the king-
4 dom of God: and, being assembled together with them, he charged them not to
depart from Jerusalem, but to wait for the
promise of the Father, which, *said he*, ye

5 heard from me: for John indeed baptized
with water; but ye shall be baptized with
the Holy Ghost not many days hence.
6 They therefore, when they were come
together, asked him, saying, Lord, dost
thou at this time restore the kingdom to
7 Israel? And he said unto them, It is not
for you to know times or seasons, which the
Father hath set within his own authority.
8 But ye shall receive power, when the Holy
Ghost is come upon you: and ye shall
be my witnesses both in Jerusalem, and in
all Judæa and Samaria, and unto the utter-
9 most part of the earth. And when he
had said these things, as they were looking,
he was taken up; and a cloud received him
10 out of their sight. And while they were
looking stedfastly into heaven as he went,
behold, two men stood by them in white
11 apparel; which also said, Ye men of
Galilee, why stand ye looking into
heaven? this Jesus, which was received up
from you into heaven, shall so come in like
manner as ye beheld him going into
heaven.
12 Then returned they unto Jerusalem
from the mount called Olivet, which is
nigh unto Jerusalem, a sabbath day's
13 journey off. And when they were come
in, they went up into the upper chamber
where they were abiding.

The Ascension is not narrated in Mt., nor in what remains to us of Mk., and although referred to at least thrice in Jn., is not narrated there (3^{13}, 6^{62}, 20^{17}).

Luke alone gives an account of the Ascension, both in his Gospel and in the Acts. The Acts' account is fuller and makes the Ascension take place at Bethany on the Mount of Olives forty days after the Resurrection. Had it not been for this precise statement in Acts 1, it would probably have been assumed that the Ascension took place on the day of the Resurrection.

In Jn. Jesus bids Mary Magdalene not to cling to Him because he is not yet ascended and speaks as though that Ascension were to take place immediately. Indeed, it might be assumed from Jn. that Jesus ascended between the time of His appearance to Mary Magdalene and to his ten Apostles that same night.

In the *Epistle of Barnabas*, written probably before the end of the first century, there is a passage which seems to make the Ascension take place on the same day as the Resurrection: 'Wherefore also we keep the eighth day for rejoicing, in the which also Jesus rose from the dead, and having been manifested ascended into the heavens' (15).

It will not be forgotten that the Longer Ending of Mk. (possibly composed by the primitive Christian, Aristion) relates the Ascension as follows:

'So then the Lord Jesus, after he had spoken unto them, was received up into heaven, and sat down at the right hand of God' (Mk. 16^{19}).

Some have seen in the Old Testament story of Elijah and the chariot of fire the anticipation of the New Testament episode. In the New Testament, however, St. Paul cites the words of Psalm 68^{18}:

'When he ascended up on high, he led captivity captive and *gave* gifts unto men'

as referring to the Ascension of Christ (Eph. $4^{8f.}$).

For modern Christians, who live in the days of the Copernican astronomy, the Ascension of Christ signifies, not His elevation into the sky, but His transition from this world of sense and space into the eternal invisible sphere.

'While he blessed them he was parted from them.' This parting is well made. To use Shakespeare's phrase; there is nothing here for tears. The disciples rejoice in the triumph of Jesus. They worship Him, as does the dying Stephen, and as do the hosts of the redeemed in the *Revelation of St. John.*

The conclusion reflects St. Luke's attitude and the whole spirit of his Gospel.

'And they worshipped him, and returned to Jerusalem with great joy: and were continually in the Temple praising and blessing God.'

END OF BOOK I

SELECT BIBLIOGRAPHY FOR BOOK I

The following books present a body of assured results of modern study, and their conscientious readers will gain from them a sound understanding of the many problems with which the modern student of the Gospels is faced.

W. Sanday: *Outlines of the Life of Christ.* T. & T. Clark, 1931, 8*s.*

T. R. Glover: *The Jesus of History.* S. C. M., 1917, 4*s.* 6*d.* (A popular life of Jesus.)

J. Klausner: *Jesus of Nazareth. His Times, His Life and His Teaching.* Allen & Unwin, 1929, 12*s.* 6*d.* (A Jewish life of Jesus.)

J. MacKinnon: *The Historic Jesus.* Longmans, Green, 1931, 16*s.* (A modern historian's life of Jesus.)

R. H. Charles: *Religious Development between the Old and New Testaments.* Home University Library, Thornton & Butterworth, 1934, 2*s.* 6*d.*

W. Fairweather: *The Background of the Gospels.* T. & T. Clark, 1926, 12*s.*

G. A. Smith: *The Historical Geography of the Holy Land.* Hodder & Stoughton, 1931, 25*s.*

F. C. Burkitt: *The Gospel History and its Transmission.* T. & T. Clark, 1925, 12*s.*

Kirsop Lake: *The Text of the New Testament.* Rivington, 1933, 2*s.* 6*d.* (Textual Criticism of the New Testament. Oxford Church Text Books.)

B. H. Streeter: *The Four Gospels.* Macmillan, 1930, 21*s.*

Vincent Taylor: *The Formation of the Gospel Tradition.* Macmillan, 1935, 7*s.* 6*d.*

BOOK II. THE SAYINGS OF JESUS

Introduction

I. *THE CHRISTIAN GOSPEL AND THE TEACHING OF JESUS*

HISTORIC Christianity is first and foremost a Gospel, the proclamation to the world of Jesus Christ and Him crucified. For the primitive Church the central thing is the Cross on the Hill rather than the Sermon on the Mount, and the characteristic Church act is the Communion rather than the conference. Christian doctrine and Christian ethics may be the inevitable corollaries of the Christian gospel; but they are corollaries. What is preached in the first instance is something that God has done for man in Christ. Only when this has been appropriated does the question arise how we are to think of the God who has done this great thing, or how we are now to order our lives as Christians.

Yet the problems of theology and ethics do arise very quickly in the Christian community. The earliest documents of the New Testament, the letters of St. Paul, are largely occupied with questions of Christian belief and Christian conduct. They presuppose groups of people who have already heard and responded to the preaching of the Gospel, who now require teaching about the truths implied in the Gospel, and the kind of life that ought to be lived by those who accept the gift of God in Christ. When such instruction has to be given the natural place to which the teacher turns is the source of the Gospel—Jesus Himself. In His life and words will be found the standard and norm of Christian behaviour.

The teaching of Jesus in the fullest and deepest sense is Jesus Himself, and the best Christian living has always been in some sort an imitation of Christ; not a slavish copying of His acts but the working of His mind and spirit in new contexts of life and circumstance. So we might be tempted to argue that all that is necessary is to have the Spirit and then all the details of belief and practice will settle themselves. The first epistle to the Corinthians is evidence that there were those in the Church there who took that view. It is also evidence that conversion did not at once make men and women infallible judges of what actually is the mind and spirit of Christ. Some objective test was required, and it was found in the recorded acts and words of Jesus.

Here, then, we have the chief motive for the preservation and collection of the sayings of Jesus: they were needed in the pastoral work, which followed necessarily on any successful missionary effort.

But while this was the principal factor, it was not the only one at work in the process which has given us the records of the teaching. It is possible to distinguish three other interests.

There is a personal interest in Jesus Himself. It is not a desire to write His biography—in the strict sense of the word there is no biography of Jesus—but rather a very natural instinct to treasure up characteristic words, words that revealed Him, sayings which, in their pointed brevity, told more about Him than many pages of description could tell. The interest of those who preserved and compiled these sayings is comparable to that which preserved the oracles of the Hebrew prophets long after the historical situations to which they were relevant were past. It is part of the devotion of the disciple to his Master, and it is not difficult to believe that there were many among those who followed Jesus and heard His teaching, who pondered His sayings in their hearts, not with an eye to the future needs of the Church, but simply because they had known the author of them and loved Him.

Again, the sayings had a use in Christian propaganda in the Græco-Roman world. They did not constitute the Gospel. The Gospel meant primarily the story of the Passion and the Resurrection. But they provided, increasingly as time went on, a way of approach to those people in the Roman Empire who were in earnest with religion and morals. And these were not few. The world to which St. Paul brought the Gospel had its full measure of vices and iniquities; but it had its own virtues and, more important still, it had men and women who were seriously concerned to find the truth and to live the good life. The Stoic propaganda found a ready hearing for its exacting moral demands, and the Jewish synagogues of the Dispersion gathered round themselves a fringe of 'God-fearers,' men and women who were attracted by the pure monotheism and the high moral standards of Judaism, and only deterred from embracing the faith of Israel by those other requirements—circumcision, for example—which were necessary for full membership of the Jewish community. It was the religious and moral teaching of Judaism that attracted these Gentiles. How much more would they be attracted by the teaching of Jesus, claiming to express a righteousness higher than that of the Scribes and Pharisees and free from those features in Judaism which were naturally repugnant to Greek and Roman. The teaching of Jesus was singularly adapted to prepare the way for the Gospel. Hence we find that, when the Apologists set about their task of commending Christianity to the educated and influential classes in the Roman Empire, it was to the teaching of Jesus that they turned for evidence of the value of the new religion.

Finally, the teaching was important to the Palestinian Church in its relation to Palestinian Judaism, and especially to the Jewish Law. The teaching of Jesus was not given as a new Law, yet it did at many points touch both the written Law and the scribal tradition. Jesus Himself had, more than once, taken up an attitude to these standards that, from the point of view of orthodox Judaism, could only be described as heretical. Those who followed Him and accepted His teaching inevitably came under suspicion of heresy. It might be pleaded that the Teacher came not to destroy the Law but to fulfil it; but this plea would not be seriously considered by those in authority. Further, the natural tendency of hostile criticism would be —as it commonly is—to single out those features in the teaching which could be most readily attacked or misconstrued and to pass by the elements which were attractive. It was even possible for the teaching to be misrepresented in order to discredit the new heresy. It was therefore the more necessary that the Palestinian community should have some reliable and authoritative compilation of the teaching, first as a defence against Jewish misrepresentation and secondly for propaganda among Jewish scholars who might show some sympathy towards Christianity. That misrepresentation of the teaching was a real danger is shown by the story of Imma Shalom and Gamaliel (Klausner, *Jesus of Nazareth*, pp. 44 ff.).

We have thus four motives at work in the compilation of the teaching: the pastoral care of the churches, the personal interest of the disciple in the Master, the apologetic value of such teaching in the Gentile world, and the need of the Palestinian community to defend itself against the charge of uttering subversive doctrines. Of these the first was probably the most powerful. All four might be expected to make themselves felt at a very early stage in the history of the Church, and this expectation is confirmed by literary criticism of the Gospels. For it appears that both Matthew and Luke used a document consisting entirely of teachings of Jesus, and this document has a fair claim to be as old as, if not older than, the earliest written Gospel—that of Mark. We have in fact to recognise that in the earliest stages of the Christian tradition there are two streams which eventually unite to form the Gospel as we see it in Matthew or Luke The one has its source in the Passion and Resurrection: its story is the story of Him who came not to be ministered unto but to minister and to give His life a ransom for many. The other is the record of the sayings of a Teacher who astonished the multitudes because He taught with authority and not as their Scribes. It is this second stream of tradition whose history we must now attempt to trace.

2. *THE HISTORY OF THE TRADITION*

The ultimate source of all genuine matter in the teaching is the spoken word of Jesus Himself. The two most certain facts in the gospel tradition are that Jesus taught and that He was crucified. In Mark the verb 'teach' occurs seventeen times, and in sixteen of these cases Jesus is the subject. In the same Gospel He is called 'teacher' twelve times—four times by His disciples, once by Himself, five times by persons not of His circle but not hostile to Him, and twice *by His opponents*. Four times also in Mark He is called 'Rabbi,' the usual name for a Jewish teacher. The narrative parts of the Synoptic Gospels portray Him preaching and teaching in the synagogues and in the open air, instructing His followers in private, and discussing questions of belief and practice with the Jewish religious authorities.

The question now arises: granting that Jesus did teach, was He a teacher in the proper Jewish sense? Was He, so to speak, academically qualified for the title of Rabbi? Popular fancy has generally preferred to think of the simple carpenter of Nazareth, who, by His superior insight, confounds the learned. But such information as we have points rather in the opposite direction. The fact that He was addressed by His opponents as 'Teacher' is difficult to explain unless He was in fact recognised by them as their equal in point of scholarship. The quotations from the Old Testament in His teaching show a close familiarity with the five books of the Law, most of the prophetic books, and Psalms, Job, and Daniel in the third division of the Hebrew canon. It is probable that He knew the Old Testament in Hebrew, and, I think, possible at least that He was acquainted with the Rabbinic Hebrew used in the schools of the Law. If Jesus used this language at all, it would be in His controversies with the learned. The impression left by the accounts of His dealings with these men is not that they saw in Him a village craftsman turned amateur theologian but rather a competent scholar who had developed heretical tendencies.

It may be taken as certain that the bulk of the teaching was spoken in Aramaic, the vernacular language of Palestine, and the only language in which the majority of the people were at home. It was their mother-tongue as it was the mother-tongue of Jesus, the language of His prayers—as is shown by His use of the word *Abba*—and the language which He used in speaking to ordinary folk—as we learn from the stories of the raising of Jairus' daughter and the healing of the deaf-mute (Mk. 5^{41}, 7^{34}). Besides this direct evidence we have the fact that many of the differences between Matthew and Luke in reporting the words of Jesus can be readily explained as due to translation—in a few cases, mistranslation—from Aramaic.

We have to think of the teaching being delivered in all kinds of circumstances to all kinds of people: in synagogues to congregations assembled for worship, or in the open air to crowds who had gathered, drawn by the reputation of Jesus, or again in chance encounters with individuals friendly or hostile, or in the intimate circle of the disciples, or in argument with more orthodox Jewish teachers. The scene constantly changes, and it can be shown that in some respects the form and content of the teaching vary with the kind of audience that is being addressed.[1]

There is no trace of evidence that Jesus Himself committed any of His teaching to writing. No book by Him has come down to us, nor any hint that such a book ever existed. All the evidence points in one direction, to the conclusion that in the earliest period we are dependent on oral tradition. The teaching was given by Jesus and passed on by word of mouth from those who first heard it. And at this time the number of such people must have been very great. In the second quarter of the first century there must have been literally thousands of people in Judæa and Galilee who had at one time or another seen Jesus, and could tell some story about Him or repeat some saying of His. The majority of these people would only have fragments of the whole story; but the tradition is made up by the piecing together of fragments. Some of these eye-witnesses must have become Christians and members of the Palestinian Church, and so their stories and sayings would find their way into the common stock of the community's story of its Founder.

Again, those who fell into argument with Jesus would carry away with them vivid memories of their encounters. His retorts to critics would not be easily forgotten, least of all by those who provoked them, and His counter-attacks on the scribal tradition may well have rankled in scribal memories. It has even been suggested, though it is never likely to be proved, that the criticisms made by Jesus may, at a later time when their origin was forgotten, have played some part in the development of the Jewish code as it took shape in the Mishnah and the Talmud.

The largest part of the tradition must, however, be credited to the disciples. They were most constantly with Jesus during the ministry. They heard what He said when He spoke to the multitudes or debated with Scribes and Pharisees, and they heard much besides that He taught them privately. They, more than any-one else, were in a position to know His mind on many points and to pass on their information to their fellow-Christians.

The importance of these considerations is that they remind us that in the first decades of the life of the original Palestinian community the tradition concerning the teaching of Jesus rested on a broader basis than we commonly imagine. We tend to think of it as being in the hands of a few distinguished persons who were

[1] For a fuller discussion of this point see my book *The Teaching of Jesus* (1931).

leaders of the Church, and to forget the common people who had heard Jesus gladly and who also had memories. When this is realised we can see that the Church's task in meeting the problems which arose in its own life and in its relations with the Jewish authorities was not that of creating words of Jesus applicable to these situations, but rather that of selecting what was relevant from the available mass of reminiscences.[1]

At this stage the tradition is still preserved in Aramaic and probably in the form of isolated sayings. Where sayings are already grouped together it will be because they happened to be spoken on the same occasion or on successive occasions; that is, the arrangement will be chronological. But when we consider the motives that led to the compilation of the teaching, it becomes obvious that a different kind of arrangement would be called for. For catechetical purposes what was required was a collection that would bring together all that Jesus had said on this or that important question of belief or practice: how far the Jewish Law was still binding on Christians, how one should think about demon-possession and exorcism, how members of the fellowship should behave towards one another, and the like. Study of the first three Gospels leads to the conclusion that such collections probably existed before the Gospels were written, and even before the compilation of the main sources used by the evangelists. Among such collections we should reckon the 'Little Apocalypse' (Mk. 13^{5-31}), which may well have had a separate existence before it came in to break the connexion between Mk. 13^{1-4} and 13^{32-37}.[2] Similarly, Lk. 11^{14-26} is a collection of sayings on demon-possession and exorcism. Strictly speaking, the reply to the charge of casting out demons by the aid of Beelzebul comes to an end at Lk. 11^{20}, and the essential refutation of the charge is given in Lk. $11^{17f.}$, which is parallel to Mk. 3^{23-26}. Now this section in Mk. is followed immediately by the saying about the 'strong man' (Mk. 3^{27}), and another version of this saying stands ($11^{21f.}$) immediately after the Lucan reply to the charge. The natural inference is that this collocation is earlier than Mk. and Q (Luke is here dependent on Q).[3] Again, in Matthew's Sermon on the Mount we have a long section (Mt. 5^{17-48}) dealing with the Jewish Law and contrasting it with the higher standard of righteousness demanded from followers of Jesus. As it stands, this section is composite; but here again it seems possible to separate out an original kernel older than the Gospel and probably older than the sources used by Matthew. To this original group of sayings we should probably assign *vv.* 17, 20; 21, 22*a*; 27, 28; 31, 32; 33, 34*a* (37*a*); 38, 39*a*; 43, 44*a*.[4]

In the cases just considered the grouping of the sayings is by subject. They are brought together by the fact that they give the answer to a single problem or show the mind of Jesus on a particular topic. This is not, however, the only method of grouping. We have also groups of sayings in which the connexion is not logical but simply by catchwords. This method, to which we can find parallels elsewhere in the New Testament, and frequently in the Talmud, is a simple way of ensuring that sayings will be remembered. Given the first link in

[1] See Vincent Taylor, *The Formation of the Gospel Tradition*, pp. 145 f.

[2] See my *Teaching of Jesus*, pp. 260–263.

[3] I think it possible to show that Mk. 3^{20-35} formed a separate whole before the Gospel was written.

[4] See below, pp. 445–455.

the series, the others can be recollected by association of ideas. We have such a group of sayings in Mk. $9^{49 f.}$, where the link between them is the word 'salt.' Another is Lk. 11^{33-36}, where the catchword is 'light.'

So far we are dealing with the tradition of an Aramaic-speaking community, and the teaching naturally remains in the mother-tongue of the members. But Christianity is a missionary religion, and it was not long before the new faith began to spread beyond the borders of Palestine. It may be conjectured that it was at Antioch (Acts $11^{19 ff.}$), where Gentiles began to come into the Church in considerable numbers, that the need for a Greek version of the teaching first became pressing. Such a document would have to be sufficiently comprehensive in its scope to meet the needs of converts who had not been brought up in the Jewish tradition. Here, then, we have the incentive to bring together the smaller groups and the scattered individual sayings and to frame a larger Aramaic document which could then be translated into Greek.

Nor is this the only way in which a large collection of teaching could have been formed. The Palestinian community may well have felt the need for a full and comprehensive statement of the teaching for use in controversy with orthodox Judaism, as well as for the instruction of converts from Judaism, whether natives of Palestine or Greek-speaking Jews of the Dispersion who came into touch with Christianity when on pilgrimage to Jerusalem.

Such considerable bodies of teaching were certainly in existence at an early date. St. Paul appears to have had such a collection at his disposal when he wrote his first letter to the Corinthians (1 Cor. 7^{10}, 9^{14}), which would suggest that these compilations were already being made as early as the middle of the first century, and perhaps even earlier, certainly before the earliest of our Gospels was written. This is the stage in the history of the tradition to which we should assign the source Q and the source that lies behind matter peculiar to Matthew. Whether the special matter of Luke is derived from a written document or from oral tradition is a difficult matter to determine. Again it is a question whether there were not other collections of teaching of which we now know nothing, because they did not happen to be incorporated in one of the canonical Gospels. It may be, as Dibelius suggests,[1] that we have a remnant from such a collection in *I Clement* 13.

The final stage in the process, which we have been tracing, is the amalgamation of these sayings-collections with other material to form the canonical Gospels. Here it is Matthew and Luke that come specially into prominence. Both have drawn on the collection which we call Q and each has in addition another source containing teaching. For convenience we may use the symbols M and L to designate matter peculiar to Mt. and Lk. respectively. When the process which gave us the Gospels of Matthew and Luke was completed is still a matter of dispute. In any case, they are probably later than the date which we assign to Mk.; but if Streeter's Proto-Luke theory [2] is correct, the union of Q and L may easily antedate the writing of Mk.

Of more importance for our present purpose is the recognition of the editorial

[1] *Die Formgeschichte des Evangeliums*,[2] pp. 243f.
[2] See *The Four Gospels*, ch. viii.

methods of Matthew and Luke. These can be determined with certainty from a study of their treatment of Mk., which both used and which itself survives for purposes of comparison. The main conclusion to be drawn from this comparison is that Matthew conflates his sources, while Luke selects from them. That is to say, where two sources overlap at a given point, Matthew makes a new story or a new version of a saying by combining the words and phrases of the original accounts. Good examples of this are Mt. $12^{31 f.}$. (Mk. + Q) and $13^{31 f.}$ (Mk. + Q). In like circumstances Luke follows one of his sources and leaves the other on one side. Another major difference between the two is that Matthew breaks up the material provided in his sources in order to compile long discourses. Mt. 10 is a good example of the method, containing, as it does, material drawn from Mk. 6 and 13, from various parts of Q, and from the special source M. Luke, on the other hand, tends to keep his sources separate, so that his Gospel consists of alternate layers of material from the different documents. This means that it is much easier to disentangle the sources in Lk. than in Mt.; and it also makes it probable that the order in which we find the fragments of a source in Lk. is nearer to the original order than is the sequence of the corresponding fragments in Mt. In the matter of verbal faithfulness to his sources Luke on the whole maintains a higher standard than Matthew. Bussmann,[1] who has recently studied the synoptic problem in great detail, comes to the conclusion that Luke's principal alterations are stylistic and that he is less prone to alter the spoken words of Jesus than to improve the style of the narrative portions. There are other more detailed differences between the two evangelists in their editorial methods: these will be noticed as occasion offers in the commentary.[2]

3. *THE SOURCES*

(*a*) The Document Q

For teaching of the sort with which we are here concerned, namely religious and moral instruction suitable for those who have embraced Christianity, our principal source is the document now usually known as Q. In the first instance Q is posited to account for the agreement of Mt. and Lk. in sections where they are not dependent on Mk., and on the whole this explanation of the phenomena has commended itself to scholars rather than the alternative hypotheses that Matthew has borrowed from Lk. or Luke from Mt. in these sections. The existence of a common source being granted, the next thing is to see what can be learnt about it, to attempt to restore it from the remains preserved in Mt. and Lk., to speculate about its probable date, authorship, place of origin, and the like.

From what has been said on the editorial methods of Luke it follows that his Gospel offers the most promising field for the restorer of Q, and it is usual now to make restorations in terms of Lk. rather than of Mt. In such attempts as have been made in recent years there is a large measure of agreement, though no two restorations correspond exactly. At the same time, the differences between scholars are on the fringes. If we take what are perhaps the three most important

[1] *Synoptische Studien*, ii. pp. 106–109.

[2] Valuable studies in Scholten, *Das älteste Evangelium* (1869)—Matthew's treatment of Mk.; Hawkins, *Horæ Synopticæ* [2]; Cadbury, *Style and Literary Method of Luke*.

of modern restorations, those of Harnack, Streeter, and Bussmann, we find a large measure of agreement between them. The matter common to all three restorations is Lk. 3^{7-9}, 4^{1-13}, $6^{20-23, 27-33, 35-44, 46-49}$, $7^{1-10, 18-20, 22-35}$, 9^{57-60}, $10^{2-16, 21-24}$, $11^{9-13, 29-35, 39, 41, 42, 44, 46-52}$, $12^{2-10, 22-31, 33, 34, 39, 40, 42-46, 51, 53, 58, 59}$, $13^{18-21, 24, 28, 29, 34, 35}$, $14^{26, 27, 34, 35}$, $16^{13, 16-18}$, $17^{1, 3, 4, 6, 23, 24, 26, 27, 33-35, 37}$. This represents the minimum to be assigned to Q. What more we shall add depends on the nice balancing of probabilities in particular cases. My reconstruction of Q is as follows. Brackets indicate doubt. Lk. $3^{7-9, 16, 17}$, 4^{1-13}, 6^{20-49}, $7^{(1-6a), 6b-9(10), 18-35}$, 9^{57-62}, $10^{2, 3, 8-16, 21-24}$, $11^{9-26\ (27, 28), 29-36, (37-41), 42-52}$, $12^{(1), 2-12, 22-34, (35-38), 39-46, (47-50), 51-59}$, $13^{18-30, 34, 35}$, $14^{15-24, 26, 27, (34, 35)}$, $16^{13, 16-18}$, $17^{1-6, 22-37}$. This document begins and ends with the thought of the coming judgement. Its first sentences contain the eschatological preaching of John the Baptist; its closing paragraph consists mainly of a poem about the coming of the Son of Man. Is this deliberate? If it is, it is a strong argument in favour of the view, which I think antecedently probable, that in Mt. and Lk. we have preserved for us substantially all that Q ever contained.

An examination of the material shows that it consists entirely, or almost entirely, of teaching. The amount of narrative is negligible, and what there is shows so little agreement in the parallel versions of Mt. and Lk. that we may well doubt whether it is part of the original document.[1] Along with this goes the fact that there is no account of the Passion. Various reasons have been suggested for this remarkable omission. To Sir William Ramsay [2] it is an indication that the document was composed during the lifetime of Jesus. Professor Burkitt [3] thinks that Q did contain a Passion narrative in spite of the absence of non-Marcan material common to Mt. and Lk. in the relevant sections of those gospels. The most probable explanation is that there is no Passion-story because none is required, Q being a book of instruction for people who are already Christians and know the story of the Cross by heart.

A third striking feature in Q is the exceedingly small quantity of polemical matter which it contains. It records no disputes with Scribes and Pharisees such as we find in Mk. (2^{1}–3^{6}; 11^{27}–12^{34}). At the same time, it contains a denunciation of Pharisaism (Lk. $11^{(37-41), 42-52}$). But ninety per cent. of the document is positive religious and moral teaching. This fact again is explicable on the assumption that the work was intended for use within the Christian community as a manual of instruction in the duties of the Christian life. If, as is possible, it was also intended to show the true nature of Christian beliefs and practices to the Jews, it may well be that the compiler thought that this purpose too would be better served by positive statement than by mere disputation.

So much we can learn from the document itself. The question now arises whether there is any external evidence which will throw light on its origin and history, and here we have to consider a much-discussed sentence from Eusebius. In his *Ecclesiastical History* (III. xxxix. 16), after quoting (§ 15) a tradition set forth by Papias, bishop of Hierapolis, concerning Mark the evangelist, he goes on:

[1] See my *Teaching of Jesus*, pp. 29 ff.
[2] *Luke the Physician*, p. 89.
[3] *Earliest Sources for the Life of Jesus*, pp. 103–106.

'Such then is Papias' account of Mark. But the following is the statement concerning Matthew: "So then, Matthew compiled the oracles in the Hebrew language; but everyone interpreted them as he was able."' (Lawlor and Oulton's translation.)

Eusebius is here quoting from a work written by Papias early in the second century.[1] In this book he gave not only his own views, but also traditions which he had collected at an earlier date from leading men in the Church. The first point to be decided, therefore, is whether 'the statement concerning Matthew' is Papias' own opinion or a piece of earlier tradition. The latter alternative is the more probable for the following reasons: (1) The immediately preceding statement about Mark is expressly said to be a tradition. We should expect Eusebius to give more of the same kind. (2) The form of the statement, its brevity, its categorical statements without argument, suggest that Papias is reporting evidence rather than airing his views. (3) Eusebius himself in this same chapter (§ 13) gives his opinion of Papias: 'He evidently was a man of exceedingly small intelligence, as one might say judging from his discourses.' It does not seem likely that Eusebius would have troubled to record the private opinion of Papias on such a question as this, if he had so poor an opinion of the bishop's mental powers. We may therefore conclude that the statement of Papias is material which he derived from an earlier generation. In that case, the statement is thrown back into the first century.

The next question is: if someone about A.D. 100 told Papias what Eusebius has reported, what did the statement mean? Before we discuss this question it should be noted that the Greek word rendered 'interpreted' by Lawlor and Oulton could equally well mean 'translated,' and that this is the more probable rendering, as we shall see.

Short as it is, the Papias fragment makes four separate assertions:

(*a*) That a collection of oracles (*logia*) was put together.

(*b*) That it was composed in the Hebrew language. (This probably means the spoken language of the Palestinian Jews of the time, i.e. Aramaic[2]).

(*c*) That the composer of this work was named Matthew—presumably the Apostle is meant.

(*d*) That various people translated it as best they could—doubtless into Greek.

As applied to the Gospel of Matthew two of these propositions are demonstrably false (*b* and *d*); (*c*) is in the last degree improbable; and (*a*) a collection of oracles is a singularly inept description of the Gospel. It is true that the late Professor Bacon [3] argued that 'the Oracles' was a perfectly legitimate designation of Mt., having regard to its five great discourses; but when it is observed that the discourses in question amount to scarcely more than one-third of the gospel the explanation becomes extremely forced. Further, the argument of Donovan [4] that

[1] The date of Papias is discussed by C. J. Cadoux in the *London Quarterly and Holborn Review*, July 1933, pp. 289–292. His conclusions demand careful consideration.

[2] Parallels for this use of 'Hebrew' where 'Aramaic' is meant in Dalman's *Grammatik* ² § 1.

[3] *Studies in Matthew.*

[4] *The Logia in Ancient and Recent Literature* (1924).

the Greek *ta logia*, ' the oracles,' must in this context mean the canonical gospel of Matthew, rests on a series of misinterpretations of the term as used in the Septuagint, New Testament, and contemporary Jewish and early Christian writings. The use of the term ' oracles ' in the LXX can be very simply defined. In a general sense it means direct communications of God to man, notably those made through prophetic inspiration; and in particular it is applied to these communications considered as Divine commands or Divine promises. The ' oracles ' is the name, not of Scripture as a whole, but of certain things contained in Scripture, the things that God has said for the guidance or encouragment of Israel. It can be shown that this meaning for ' oracles ' fits perfectly in the places where the term occurs in the New Testament and other primitive Christian writings. Later the word came to be used in the sense ' Scripture,' and there is no doubt that Eusebius understood the statement of Papias to refer to the Gospel of Matthew; but at the time to which we refer the tradition (end of the first century) the original sense was still the proper and natural sense, as can be shown from the first epistle of Clement (*c.* A.D. 96).

The importance of this point is that it shows that the statement of Papias which cannot be made to fit the Gospel of Matthew except by a forced and unnatural interpretation, does, when taken in its simple and natural meaning, fit a document such as Q like a glove. For Q is a collection of Dominical oracles given for the guidance and encouragement of the New Israel. Just as to the Hebrew saints, whose piety found expression in the Psalter, ' the oracles ' meant the commands and promises of God under the Old Covenant, so to the Church ' the oracles ' meant the commands and promises of God under the New Covenant.

The statement that ' the oracles ' were composed in Hebrew (= Aramaic) and that various people translated them as best they could can be shown to be true in respect of Q. We have already seen that the tradition of the teaching circulated at first in Aramaic, and that probably the first considerable collections of it would be made in the original language. There is nothing improbable in the supposition that several Greek versions of such a document might be made. We know that at least four Greek versions of the Old Testament were made at various times and for various reasons. These, however, are possibilities: we must look now at the facts. We have two versions of Q—Q according to Matthew and Q according to Luke. The differences between them can be explained in part as editorial—stylistic or other ' improvements ' carried out by the Evangelists. But after we have allowed for these there is still a certain amount of difference in wording, and some of it at least can be explained on the supposition that we have before us two different renderings of a single Aramaic original. Such cases will be noted in the Commentary; here the point may be illustrated by a single example.

The Golden Rule is given by Matthew and Luke in almost identical words. The main difference is at the beginning. Here we have:

> Mt. 7^{12}. All things therefore whatsoever ye would that men . . .
> Lk. 6^{31}. And as ye would that men . . .

Now in the LXX version of Genesis 44^{1} the Greek expression of Mt. rendered here by ' whatsoever ' is used to translate the Hebrew word *ka'ăsher*; and in

Genesis 41^{18} the Greek word behind ' as ' in Lk. translates the same Hebrew word. In Aramaic the equivalent of the Hebrew *ka'ăsher* is *kmā dĕ*. We may therefore legitimately regard Mt.'s ' whatsoever ' and Lk.'s ' as ' as alternative renderings of a common Aramaic original. This leaves Mt.'s ' all things ' in the air. This, however, is easily explained. In eleven places where Mt. is dependent on Mk. we find the word ' all ' in Mt. with nothing corresponding to it in the source. For example, in the Marcan account of the feeding of the 4,000 we read (8^8): ' And they ate and were satisfied ': the Matthæan reproduction of this (15^{37}) is: ' And they *all* ate and were satisfied.' That is to say, one of the literary habits of Matthew is to heighten the effects by inserting the word ' all ' from time to time. Finally, we have ' therefore ' in Mt. against ' and ' in Lk. Here we have to take account of Matthew's tendency to build up his material into discourses. The probability is that ' therefore ' is an attempt to provide a logical connexion between the Golden Rule and what has preceded it in the Sermon on the Mount. Luke's ' and ' represents the earlier state of the tradition. The result is that of the three differences between Mt. and Lk. in these few words, two can be put down to the editorial work of Matthew, while the third points to an Aramaic original behind the two variant renderings. There is a sufficient number of such translation variants to justify the belief that Q was originally an Aramaic document and that in Mt. and Lk. we have two renderings of it.

Thus three out of the four propositions contained in the Papias tradition tally with what can be discovered about Q. The tradition fits Q as it does not fit Mt.

The fourth proposition that ' the oracles ' were compiled by Matthew cannot be proved or disproved. All that can be said is that if at three points out of four this early tradition fits Q, there is a reasonable probability in favour of the fourth. If we wish to put an author's name on the title-page of Q, Matthew is the only candidate in the field: the tradition as we interpret it favours him, and there is nothing against the identification. It may be objected that if Q was a document of apostolic authorship, it is almost inconceivable that it should have been allowed to perish. To this it may be replied that the primitive Church was probably very little concerned about making archives for the use of scholars in the twentieth century. A community living in daily expectation of the end of the world does not pause to consider the literary requirements of a remote posterity. The wonder is not that some documents have perished, but that so many have been preserved. Further by the end of the first century an Aramaic original would be of interest only to a fraction of the Christian community. For the great majority the apostolic document *was* preserved in the only form in which it was of any use to them, in the Greek language. Again, the preservation or destruction of important documents is all too often determined by circumstances outside the control of the persons chiefly interested. Who can tell how much priceless evidence for the history of primitive Christianity perished in A.D. 70? Or, to come nearer home, it is to us almost inconceivable that the autographs of Shakespeare's plays should have been allowed to perish. Yet they were. Doubtless by about the middle of the second century an Aramaic document of apostolic origin giving the words of Jesus would have been a prized possession at Rome or Alexandria; but by that time it was probably too late. And even if such a document had survived till then its chances of falling into the hands of someone who would be able to identify it and appreciate its value are very remote. The history of priceless manuscripts in Eastern monasteries is a melancholy commentary on the survival-value of ancient documents, even in what might be considered favourable circumstances.[1]

Concerning the date and place of origin of Q we can do no more than make more or less probable conjectures. If it had its origin as a book of instruction for converts from Gentile paganism, it would be natural to connect it with Antioch, the first headquarters of the Gentile mission, and to date it about the middle of the first century, probably rather before than after A.D. 50. It is a point slightly in favour of this connexion with Antioch that Q, more than any other of the synoptic sources, shows a friendly attitude towards Gentiles. The Roman centurion, whose faith could not be paralleled in Israel; the people of Tyre and Sidon; the men of Nineveh, who were readier to repent than the Chosen People; and the Queen of Sheba, who was more eager for the wisdom of Solomon than the Jewish contemporaries of Jesus for the Kingdom of God—these are all Q characters: and to Q belongs the statement that people from all the ends of the earth will find their way into the Kingdom.

Additional Note

Dr. W. Bussmann, in the course of a very elaborate and painstaking study of the synoptic problem, has put forward the view (*Synoptische Studien*, ii) that Q can really be split up into two distinct sources. He starts from the fact that in some Q sections the agreement between Mt. and Lk. is very close while in others there is considerable difference. He lists the passages as follows:

I. Passages showing close agreements: Lk. 3^{7-9}, 4^{1-13}, $6^{31, 37-42}$, $7^{1-10, 18-35}$, 9^{57-62}, $10^{2-16, 21-24}$, 11^{33}, $12^{22-46, 51-56}$, 13^{18-35}, 16^{13}. This document he calls T.

II. Passages showing considerable variation: Lk. $6^{20-30, 32-36, 43-49}$, $11^{1-4, 9-13, 29-32, 34-36}$, 11^{37}–12^{12}, 12^{57-59}, $14^{5, 6, 16-27, 34, 35}$, 15^{3-7}, 16^{16-18}, $17^{1-6, 22-37}$. This he calls R.

Working on this basis he finds a certain number of linguistic differences between R and T. These are given in *Synoptische Studien*, ii, pp. 124–126. In further investigation he thinks that he can detect differences of thought as well as of language between the two documents. Bussmann draws the conclusion that Matthew and Luke are dependent on the same Greek document for T. For R, on the other hand, they had (or made) separate Greek versions of an Aramaic original. R is the older of the two and is probably the *logia* of the Papias tradition.

An adequate treatment of this view will require as detailed and painstaking an examination of the material as Bussmann's own, and this cannot be undertaken here. But a few general observations may be made.

First, the outstanding feature of T is close agreement in wording between Mt. and Lk. Another characteristic of T, according to Bussmann, is that it contains a certain amount of narrative. But one of the features of the narrative settings of

[1] See, for example, the story of the discovery of *Codex Sinaiticus*, of which Tischendorf rescued portions from the monastic waste-paper basket.

sayings in Q is wide divergence between Mt. and Lk. In the story of the Centurion at Capernaum (Mt. 8^{5-13}; Lk. 7^{1-10}) the agreement between Mt. and Lk. begins and ends with the spoken words. The differences in the narrative setting are so great that it is difficult to suppose that the two evangelists are drawing on a common source in Greek or any other language; while the agreements in the dialogue are so close that here a common source seems to be necessary. This means that the two characteristics of T, close verbal agreement and the presence of narratives, are mutually inconsistent.

Further, the theory that only R shows unmistakable signs of being before us in two versions from Aramaic is seriously open to question. There are numerous examples in T of variants between Mt. and Lk. which are most probably to be regarded as translation variants. Not only so, but the general character of Bussmann's T sections is not inconsistent with the theory that they are translations from Aramaic. It is possible to compare theory with fact at this point. Certain chapters of the book of Daniel are written in Aramaic, and of this book we have two Greek versions, the LXX and the translation of Theodotion. Taking a passage at random from Daniel (Dan. 7^{9-14}), we find that it is turned into Greek by the LXX in 166 words, by Theodotion in 157. Comparing the two versions, we find complete agreement between them in 105 words and partial agreement in 12. Taking a passage of approximately equal length from Bussmann's T (Lk. $7^{24-28,\ 31-35}$ = Mt. $11^{7-11,\ 16-19}$), we get in Lk. 170 Greek words, in Mt. 158. There is complete agreement in 115 words and partial agreement in 20. That is to say, the features presented by Mt. and Lk. in a passage from T are very similar to those presented by LXX and Theodotion in what we know to be two translations from a common Aramaic original. Whether the similarity will hold over a larger range of passages is a matter for investigation.

So far as one can judge, Bussmann's case is not convincing, and if our view of Q is to be modified, it seems more likely that it will be in another direction, namely by recognition of the possibility of the overlapping of sources and so transferring passages, where verbal agreement between Mt. and Lk. is small, from Q to M or L. For the problem, which Bussmann tries to solve by his two-source hypothesis, namely the considerable difference in the measure of agreement between Mt. and Lk. in Q passages, is a real problem; and if we reject his solution, we are still left with the task of finding a better.

(*b*) The Matter peculiar to Mt.

The matter peculiar to Mt. falls into four groups: (i) Editorial additions and formulas; (ii) narratives; (iii) testimonia; (iv) teaching. Our chief concern will be with (iv); but we may note in passing that almost the whole of the narrative matter can be collected under two heads: birth and infancy stories and stories about the events in Jerusalem from the triumphal entry to the Resurrection. The fact that the special narrative contribution of Mt. to the story of the Ministry is mainly concerned with events in and about Jerusalem may well have some bearing on the question of the origin both of this material and of the special teaching peculiar to this Gospel. The testimonia, or illustrations of the fulfilment of Old

Testament prophecies in the life of Jesus, number eleven and are distributed through the Gospel from the birth narratives to the account of the arrest (Mt. $1^{22f.}$, $2^{5f., 15, 17f., 23}$, 4^{13-16}, 8^{17}, 12^{17-21}, 13^{35}, $21^{4f.}$, 27^{9}). The teaching proper is all contained in chapters 5–25 and is mostly arranged topically. The main sections are: Jesus' preaching (5–7), Mission charge to the disciples (10), Parables bearing on missionary work (13), Nature of the Christian fellowship (18), Conditions of service and reward (19, 20), The Refusers (21, 22), Against Pharisaism (23), Eschatology (25). Comparing this scheme with that of Q, it is important to note that the arrangement of this teaching material, which we shall call M, as given in Mt. corresponds at four points with the arrangement of the Q material *in Luke's order.*

Q	M
1. John's Preaching	——
2. The Temptations	——
3. Jesus' Preaching . . .	1. Jesus' Preaching
4. Centurion of Capernaum	——
5. Jesus and John the Baptist	——
6. Mission Charge	2. Mission Charge
7. Beelzebul controversy	——
8. Refusal of a sign	——
——	3. Parables of missionary work
——	4. Nature of the Christian fellowship
——	5. Conditions of service and reward (cf. Q 10)
——	6. The Refusers (cf. Q 11)
9. Against Pharisaism . . .	7. Against Pharisaism
10. Service, sacrifice, and reward (12) (cf. M 5)	——
11. Refusers (13, 14) (cf. M 6)	——
12. Eschatology	8. Eschatology

(*N.B.*—This table takes account only of considerable blocks of material. To avoid complication small pieces are omitted.)

The four points are Jesus' preaching, the mission charge, the speech against Pharisaism, and the eschatological speech. From this fact the inference is either that there is a scheme of the teaching older than M and Q, to which both conform, or that the M material has been incorporated into Q. The latter alternative would involve a kind of Proto-Matthew hypothesis; but the former seems the more probable view.

More than this coincidence in the general structure, there are also traces of coincidence in the structure of some of the speeches. If we compare the structure of the Q preaching of Jesus (Lk. 6^{20-49}) with those portions of the Sermon on the Mount that can most probably be assigned to M, we find a certain parallelism at four points.

	Q	M
Lk. 6^{20-23}	Beatitudes . . .	Beatitudes Mt. 5^{7-10}
6^{24-26}	Woes	——
	——	(Salt and Light 5^{13-16})
6^{27-36}	The Law of the Christian life	The old Law and the new $5^{17-24,\ 27-39a,\ 43\ (44a)\ (44b-48)}$
6^{37-42}	Against censoriousness	——
6^{42-45}	The test of true religion—character and life	The old piety and the new $6^{1-4,\ 5-8,\ (9-15),\ 16-18}$
	——	Some isolated sayings 6^{34}, $7^{6,\ 13f.,\ 15,\ (16-20)}$
6^{46}	Why do you call me Lord, Lord . . .?	Self-deceivers and their fate 7^{21-23}
6^{47-49}	Parable of the two builders	——

(Brackets indicate a certain doubt as to whether the verses so enclosed belong to M.)

In the Mission Charge there are coincidences between Q and M at Lk. $10^{8f.}$‖ Mt. $10^{7f.}$ and Lk. 10^{16}‖Mt. $10^{40f.}$. In the speech against Pharisaism we may compare Lk. 11^{43} with Mt. 23^{7b}; Lk. 11^{44} with Mt. $23^{27f.}$; Lk. $11^{47f.}$ with Mt. 23^{30}. Similar in purport, though far apart in expression, are Lk. 11^{42} and Mt. 23^{24}.

We should not attempt to build too much on these parallelisms; but, such as they are, they allow us at least to entertain the supposition that there was a rough outline of the essentials of the teaching at an earlier stage of the tradition than is represented by Q and M. This outline, if it had a separate existence, dealt with essentials: the substance of the Christian life, the principles of Christian missionary propaganda, the defence of the new religion against Jewish attacks, and the hope of the future.[1]

The question whether there are any traces of earlier compilation within the sections, which go to make up M, is a difficult one. The most we can do is to indicate possibilities or probabilities. The most likely case occurs in the Sermon on the Mount. Here we have in Mt. 5^{21-48} a series of contrasts between the old Law and the new. Each is in the form ' Ye have heard that it was said . . . But I say to you . . .' This form is most clearly displayed in the pronouncement on divorce ($5^{31f.}$). Here the old rule is concisely stated in *v.* 31, and the new with similar brevity in *v.* 32. Passing from this to the cases of the *lex talionis* (5^{38-42}) and love of neighbour (5^{43-48}), we find that, while the old is still shortly stated, the new is considerably expanded, and that the extra matter is similar to matter given by Luke in the Q version of the Sermon. Thus we read ($5^{38,\ 39a}$):

You have heard that it was said: An eye for an eye and a tooth for a tooth.
But I tell *you* not to resist the evil (person or act).

[1] It may be no more than a coincidence, at any rate an interesting one, that the *Didache* in its general outline is very near to this scheme. I, The substance of the Christian life (1^1–10^6), divided into two parts, (*a*) morality (1^1–6^2), (*b*) piety (7^1–10^6); II, the Christian Mission and its workers (11^1–13^7); III, Church life and organisation (14^1–15^4) (cf. Mt. 18. Has the scheme been modified to meet new needs?); IV, Eschatology (16^{1-8}). In three out of four heads the *Didache* agrees with the scheme.

Then the exhortation continues: 'But whoever strikes *thee* on the right cheek . . .' This is parallel to Lk. $6^{29\,f.}$: 'To him who strikes thee on the cheek . . .' The change from 'you' to 'thee' is another sign that we are now dealing with a new source; and the conclusion is that the original antithesis ended with the word 'evil.' In that case it is similar to the saying on divorce. The same holds of Mt. 5^{43-48}, though not so obviously, because the overlapping with Q begins earlier.[1] Again, in 5^{27-30} we have a saying ($5^{27\,f.}$), which is true to the type, followed by a further exhortation, which has a parallel in Mk. 9^{43-48}. The conclusion of the whole matter is that the original kernel of the passage 5^{21-48} was a series of six brief antithetical statements comprising verses 21–22a, 27–28, 31–32, 33–34a, 38–39a, 43–44a.

A similar group of sayings can be extracted from Mt. 6^{1-18}. Here three acts of piety—almsgiving, prayer, and fasting—are described antithetically. The antithesis is between 'the hypocrites' and the believer. The form is well marked: 'When thou doest alms do not . . . as the hypocrites do . . . and thy Father who sees in secret will reward thee.' This series occupies Mt. $6^{2-4,\ 5-6,\ 16-18}$.

Concerning the date and place of origin of M we cannot do more than make reasonable conjectures. If the hypothesis of a group of antitheses in Mt. 5^{21-48} is sound, we can fix a probable lower limit for the compilation of the Sermon on the Mount in its M form and perhaps for the whole M collection. In Mt. 5^{21-22a} we have the first antithesis proper. What follows in 22b may be part of it also, or an expansion of it. Then in 23 f. comes the exhortation beginning 'If then thou art offering thy gift on the altar . . .' This presupposes that the Temple is still standing. It is extremely unlikely that such a word would be incorporated in a collection of maxims for practical use after A.D. 70, when the Temple was destroyed. And probably we should go farther and say not later than about 65, since in the last few years before the Jewish war relations between Jewish Christians and Jews became increasingly strained. Now on our theory $5^{23\,f.}$ has been inserted into an already existing document—the six antitheses. If this insertion took place in the process of the compilation of what we now call M, it is evidence that the compilation took place not later than about A.D. 65.

At the same time there is some reason for thinking that the date cannot be much before 65. In Mt. 5^{17-20} we have a passage purporting to give the attitude of Jesus to the Jewish Law. In this section *vv.* 18 f. are very significant. 'For verily I say unto you, Till heaven and earth pass away, one jot or one tittle shall in no wise pass away from the law, till all things be accomplished' (5^{18}). This verse has a parallel in Q (Lk. 16^{17}): 'But it is easier for heaven and earth to pass away, than for one tittle of the law to fall.' This Q version of the saying stands between two sayings which in effect contradict it: 'The law and the prophets (were) *until John*: from that time the gospel of the Kingdom of God is preached, and every man entereth violently into it' (Lk. 16^{16}); and 'Every one that putteth away his wife, and marrieth another, committeth adultery: and he that marrieth one that is put away from a husband committeth adultery' (Lk. 16^{18}). Lk. 16^{16} implies that since the appearance of John a new thing has come into the world to take the place of the Law. Lk. 16^{18} is a flat contradiction of the provision of the Law relating to

[1] On this see the Commentary below, p. 453.

divorce. The solution of this problem is, I venture to think, that the saying (Lk. 16^{17}) was originally ironical: it was a comment, not on the eternity of the provisions of the Law, but on the obstinate conservatism of the Scribes. The Matthæan form of the saying shows no trace of this. Here the Law in all its details is represented as absolutely binding, at all events, till the end of the world. Coupled with this is the saying (5^{19}): 'Whosoever therefore shall break one of these least commandments, and shall teach men so, shall be called least in the kingdom of heaven: but whosoever shall do and teach them, he shall be called great in the kingdom of heaven.' It may well be thought that we have here a reflection of the disputes which arose out of the Gentile mission (Acts 15) and of the deep suspicion with which Paul was regarded by the more extreme Jewish Christians (Acts 21^{15-25}). These two verses (Mt. $5^{18 f.}$) will then point to a time after A.D. 50 as the time for the compilation of M, and probably nearer 60 than 50. If 5^{19} be thought to refer to Paul, it may be doubted whether it would have been added after the news of his martyrdom was known in the East. For it might well be that his martyr's death would be regarded as atoning for his laxity in matters of the Law. In that case we should have a further small confirmation of the date 65 as the lower limit.

In the light of this discussion of the date of M it is not difficult to guess its place of origin. Its most striking characteristics all point in one direction, and far the most probable conjecture is that which connects M with the Jewish Christians of Judæa, with their headquarters at Jerusalem. Such sayings as Mt. 10^{6} reflect the interests of a community which felt that its mission was to the circumcision (cf. Gal. $2^{7 f.}$). The extreme respect for the Law coupled with a violent antagonism to the lawyers is best understood in a community at once proud of its Jewish heritage and at loggerheads with the official guardians of that heritage. This can only be the churches of Judæa—or a section of them—in the years before the fall of Jerusalem.

The general character of the source agrees with these inferences from particular passages. The 'atmosphere' is more definitely Palestinian Jewish than in any other of the gospel documents. It is in M that we get reminiscences of Rabbinic terminology most widespread. Here also the sayings are often closely parallel to the sayings of the Rabbis. The whole passage Mt. 22^{11-14}, the Matthæan appendix to the parable of the Great Feast, is very similar to a parable preserved in the Talmud.[1]

But M is not merely Christianised Rabbinism. There are other and characteristic strains in its composition. It shows clear traces of the influence of the teaching of John the Baptist. The burden of John's teaching as given in Q is the impending judgement and the sharp division between the righteous and the wicked. This feature reappears with great force in many of the parables peculiar to M. (Mt. $13^{24-30, 47-50}$, 22^{11-14}, $25^{1-13, 31-46}$). Characteristic teaching of the Baptist is put into the mouth of Jesus; and that this is no accident is shown by the fact that John's phrase 'offspring of vipers' (Mt. 3^{7} = Lk. 3^{7}, Q) reappears in the mouth of Jesus in Mt. 12^{34}, 23^{33} (M) and nowhere else in the New Testament. These facts are the more impressive if, as I think very probable, the M parable of the

[1] *The Teaching of Jesus*, p. 35, n. 3.

Wheat and Tares (13^{24-30}) is an adaptation of Mark's parable of the Seed growing secretly (Mk. 4^{26-29}); and if the parable of the Dragnet is an expansion of a genuine saying of Jesus preserved in Mt. 13^{47} and meaning that the Kingdom of God takes hold of all sorts of people.[1] In this connexion it is worth remembering that the scene of John's activity was Judæa, and that his influence was exerted most fully on the population of Judæa and Jerusalem (Mk. 1^{5}).

Again, we may note in M the strong Church-interest, the feeling that Christians are a compact body of believers sharing a common body of doctrine, a common rule of life, a common discipline and organisation, and a common hope. Of the teaching in M two-thirds is represented as addressed to the disciples, a quarter is polemical, and only a small fraction—less than one-tenth—is public preaching. The document reflects the situation of a community which is not only compact but also self-contained, we might almost say driven in upon itself, facing a rather hopeless task as a missionary body, and bitterly conscious of the strength of the opposition; yet holding on grimly to its rule of faith and life and hoping for its speedy vindication at the final consummation of the present evil age.

From what has been said it will be evident that M is a source to be treated with caution. Doubtless it preserves much authentic teaching of Jesus; but there are good grounds for suspecting that there has been a considerable amount of adulteration from the Jewish side and from the teaching of John the Baptist. Each piece of teaching must be considered on its merits and in comparison with what is given in the earlier and more reliable source Q.

(*c*) The Matter peculiar to Lk.

The question how Lk. was put together is still under discussion, which centres round what is known as the Proto-Luke hypothesis. This hypothesis was stated by Dr. Streeter in the *Hibbert Journal* for October 1921, and, more fully, in *The Four Gospels* (1924), ch. viii. It rests on an analysis of the text of Lk. from which it appears that this Gospel falls into two main parts, one dependent on Mk., the other almost entirely independent. This latter part consists, according to Streeter, of: 3^{1}–4^{30}, 5^{1-11}, 6^{14-16}, 6^{20}–8^{3}, 9^{51}–18^{14}, 19^{1-27}, 19^{37-44}, $21^{18,\ 34-36}$, 22^{14}–24^{53}. This part is an amalgam of Q and the matter peculiar to Lk., which includes both narratives and teaching. The essence of the Proto-Luke theory is that this Q + L makes up a short gospel by itself and that it had a separate existence as Luke's first draft of his work, being subsequently expanded by the addition of the sections derived from Mk., and finally by the prefixing of the narratives of the birth and infancy.[2] The alternative to this is to suppose that Mk. or some more primitive document, from which Mk. is descended, is the foundation document into which the Q and L material has been inserted. However this question may be settled, the fact remains that in what is called Proto-Luke we have solid blocks of material made up, so far as one can see, of alternate layers of Q and L.

[1] R. Otto, *Reich Gottes und Menschensohn*, p. 47.

[2] For an elaboration and defence of the Proto-Luke theory see Vincent Taylor. *Behind the Third Gospel; The First Draft of St. Luke's Gospel; The Formation of the Gospel Tradition;* and *The Gospels: a Short Introduction.*

This stratified structure extends as far as 17^{37}, which is the end of the last section from Q.[1] Thereafter all the non-Marcan material seems to be derived from L.

What remains, when we take away from 'Proto-Luke' the sections derived from Q, is a mixture of narrative and teaching. The teaching from this source is as follows. Brackets indicate cases where it is doubtful whether the passage should be given to Q or L.

Lk. 3^{10-14}, 9^{51-56}, $10^{1, 4-7, 17-20, 25-42}$, $11^{(1-4), 5-8, 37-41, 53-54}$, $12^{(1), 13-21}$, $13^{1-9, (15), (31-33)}$, $14^{(5), 7-14, 28-33}$, 15^{1-32}, $16^{1-12, 14-15, 19-31}$, $17^{7-10, 20-21}$, 18^{1-14}, $19^{11-27, 39-44}$, $21^{12-15, 18-26, 28, 34-36}$, $22^{24-30, 31-33, 35-38}$, 23^{27-31}.

It will be observed that in ch. 21 somewhat more is allowed to L than Streeter assigns to Proto-Luke. On this point see the Commentary *ad loc.*

Surveying this material, one is struck by the fact that there is little or no sign of the topical arrangement which we found in Q and M. L begins with a fragment of the preaching of John (3^{10-14}), and this is followed a little later by $10^{1, 4-7, 17-20}$, which belongs to the Mission charge. But in both cases the probable explanation is that this L material stands where it does because it has been attracted to corresponding material in Q. Towards the end of the L teaching we have a series of parables and sayings (15^{11-32}, 16^{14-15}, 17^{20-21}, 18^{9-14}, and possibly also 16^{19-31}, and 19^{11-27}) with a considerable amount of common interest; but this group is broken up by other matter and does not form a compact whole. Its present position may reflect what is no doubt the historical truth that the opposition between Jesus and the Jewish religious authorities came to a head towards the end of the ministry. Still later in the collection comes a group of sayings roughly corresponding to the eschatological sections in Q and M; but with this striking difference that in L the reference is largely to the impending downfall of Jerusalem. This group includes 19^{39-44}, $21^{12-15, 18-26, 28, 34-36}$, 23^{27-31}, and possibly 22^{35-38}. One way of explaining this difference is to say that the matter in Lk. 21 is a rewriting by Luke of the corresponding matter in Mk. 13 in the light of the fall of Jerusalem in A.D. 70. But as it happens Luke has kept in 21^{25-28} a plain reference to the final consummation, which is closely connected with the other events; and Goguel makes the good point that 'Luke might have transmitted, but he cannot have created, an unfulfilled prophecy whereby the fall of Jerusalem and the final cataclysm were combined.'[2] Moreover, we have the evidence of Mk. $13^{1f.}$ and of L sections quite independent of Mk. 13 (Lk. 19^{41-44}, 23^{27-31}) that Jesus did prophesy the fall of Jerusalem—just as, eight centuries before, Amos had prophesied the fall of Samaria. And, lastly, such drastic rewriting of his sources is not in Luke's manner, especially where the words of Jesus are concerned. It may well be, therefore, that Luke found this prophecy of the fall of Jerusalem in his sources. This does not, of course, mean that the section as it stands is necessarily or even probably a faithful report of what Jesus may have said on this subject.

The unsystematic character of the L teaching compared with Q and M suggests that we are not here dealing with a more or less official compilation for

[1] Harnack assigned Lk. 19^{12-27}, 22^{28-30} to Q; Streeter also gives 19^{11-27} to Q; Bussmann, I think rightly, does not go beyond 17^{37}.

[2] *Harvard Theological Review*, xxvi. 28.

the instruction of Church members, but with oral tradition. This supposition gains some support from the fact that a large proportion of the matter is in the form of parables. There are fourteen in this source, several of them of considerable length. Now we are explicitly told that the parable was constantly used by Jesus in His public preaching. We are therefore entitled to assume that the parables would be the most widely known, as they would certainly be the most easily remembered utterances of Jesus. Further, many of them are of the sort that would have a special appeal to the common people who heard Him gladly, showing, as they do, the sympathy and friendliness of Jesus towards those whom a more rigid piety tended to despise.

At this point we may take account of another fact, the high proportion of polemical matter in L. Almost two-fifths of the whole is polemic, just over one-third is public preaching, and only about a quarter private instruction to the disciples. The polemic is different from that of the other sources in this respect, that in place of open attack we find the subtler method of rebuke by means of parables such as the Prodigal Son or the Pharisee and the Publican. This is the kind of thing that would not easily slip the memory of anyone, least of all those publicans and sinners who found a friend in Jesus.

If, then, the L material is derived from oral tradition, we must ask: when, where, and by whom? To these questions the most probable answer is: about A.D. 60, by Luke at Cæsarea during Paul's detention there. If we are right in thinking that Q is an earlier document connected with the Church at Antioch, it is quite possible that Luke had a copy of it by this time, and that he expanded it by addition of stories and sayings collected from Christians with whom he would certainly come into contact during his long stay at Cæsarea.

4. *THE FORM OF THE TEACHING*

The most important distinction to be made here is that between utterances which are an integral part of a story and those which are independent of any narrative setting, between *ad hoc* utterances and considered statements. It is to be expected *a priori* that in the teaching of Jesus we shall find both kinds and that in general the former kind of saying will occur most often in polemical contexts, where a quick and effective reply to criticism has to be made; the latter in more leisurely talk for the instruction of friends and disciples. It is not probable that highly elaborated poetical utterances like Lk. 17^{26-30} on the Day of the Son of Man or Lk. 12^{24-48} on the loving care of the Father were improvised on the spur of the moment; whereas the retort of Jesus in Mk. 2^{17} has all the appearance of spontaneity. The Gospels furnish a good number of these brief stories whose point is a saying of Jesus. Taylor [1] recognises some thirty-two such 'pronouncement-stories,' and it is noteworthy that nineteen of them are polemical. The distinction between these pronouncement-stories and sayings which do not have a narrative setting is not that the more circumstantial pronouncement-story is historically more reliable; for the difference in form is most probably the result of difference in the circumstances of their origin. The word of Jesus is in the one

[1] *The Formation of the Gospel Tradition*, pp. 63–84.

case repartee and in the other pure teaching. But the distinction is useful in exposition when we have to deal with short detached sayings like the three in Mk. $9^{49 f.}$, where a convincing interpretation becomes very difficult if not impossible. In such cases it may well be that our difficulties arise from the fact that we are dealing with pronouncements stripped of the narrative setting which would make them intelligible.

The material presented by Q, M, and L consists mainly of the second sort of teaching, deliberate religious and moral instruction which can be understood by itself without any narrative context; and within this class we are presented with all kinds of utterances, from the stark simplicity of the Golden Rule to the high elaboration of the parable of the Prodigal Son.

The simplest form of the teaching is provided by such sayings as Lk. 6^{39}, 'Can one blind man act as guide to another? Will not both fall into the ditch?'; Lk. 10^{7b}, 'The labourer is worthy of his hire'; Lk. 10^{16}, 'He who hearkens to you, hearkens to me, and he who rejects you, rejects me; and he who rejects me rejects Him that sent me.' It should be noted that the first of these sayings is called, in the text, a parable (*parabolē*). Now *parabolē* is the Greek equivalent of the Hebrew word *māshāl*, which commonly means what we should call a proverb, as well as what we understand by parable. That is to say, the Hebrew *māshāl* (Aramaic *mathlā*) covers both proverb and parable, a point which is very important when we come to consider the nature of parable.[1]

A special class of these brief sayings comprises the Beatitudes and Woes. Both are common in the Old Testament and later Jewish writings, the former especially in the Psalms and Wisdom literature, the latter in the prophetic books. It is important to remember that these exclamations are *not* blessings and curses. A great deal of nonsense is written and spoken about Jesus cursing the Pharisees. A blessing or a curse in the proper sense of the words implies a wish that good or evil may come upon the person blessed or cursed. The beatitude and the woe are highly emotional statements of fact, and not wishes at all; and it would be more accurate to say, 'Alas for you Pharisees . . .' than 'Woe unto you Pharisees . . .' as a translation of the words of Jesus in these passages. There are no beatitudes in Mk., but they are found in Q (Lk. 6^{20-22}, 7^{23}, 10^{23}, (11^{28}), $12^{(37, 38), 43}$), M (Mt. $5^{5, 7-10}$, 16^{17}), and L (Lk. 14^{14}, 23^{29}). Woes appear in Mk. (13^{17}, 14^{21}), Q (Lk. 6^{24-26}, 10^{13}, 11^{39-52}, 17^{1}), M (Mt. 23^{15-16}), but none in L.

Very numerous and important are the precepts, both commands and prohibitions, covering various aspects of the Christian life: the disciple's relation to God, to his neighbour, to property, to the chances and changes of human existence. Usually these are stated simply and left to carry conviction by their own power of self-authentication to anyone who has a heart that will understand. Occasionally the way of Jesus is put in contrast with current rules or practice, notably in the collection of antitheses (Mt. 5^{21-48}) and in the directions concerning works of piety (Mt. 6^{1-18}) and ranks and titles (Mt. 23^{6-12}).

Or the teaching may be given in the form of dialogue, and here we must distinguish between conversations with disciples, e.g. Lk. 9^{51-56}, with friendly disposed persons other than disciples, e.g. Lk. $11^{27 f.}$, and with opponents, e.g. Mk. 3^{22-26}.

[1] See *The Teaching of Jesus*, pp. 57–81.

The special value of dialogue for the interpretation of the teaching is that by presenting the sayings of Jesus in their context it enables us to gather the original sense of the sayings with greater ease and certainty than might otherwise be the case. The uncertainty which sometimes attends the interpretation of the isolated saying is well illustrated by the Q passage Lk. 12^{57-59}||Mt. $5^{25 f.}$: 'And why even of yourselves judge ye not what is right? For as thou art going with thine adversary before the magistrate, on the way give diligence to be quit of him; lest haply he hale thee unto the judge, and the judge shall deliver thee to the officer, and the officer shall cast thee into prison. I say unto thee, Thou shalt by no means come out thence, till thou have paid the very last mite.' The context of this saying in Lk., which is presumably its Q context, shows that it has to do with the coming judgement: and it is probably to be regarded as a parable —just as a wise citizen does his utmost to settle an action out of court, so the wise man will be well advised to escape what is coming by timely repentance. In the Sermon on the Mount, however, the context is changed and the eschatological parable has become an ordinary rule of everyday life: and if we had not the Lucan version, we should probably never suspect that it was anything else. Even with the hint given by the Q context the interpretation given here cannot be regarded as more than highly probable, because we cannot be absolutely certain that the Q context is the original context. If we knew with some certainty the circumstances in which the words were spoken, we should feel more confidence about the interpretation of them.

It is otherwise with the immediately following section in Lk. (13^{1-5}). There the other side of the conversation is indicated, and this furnishes the clue to what is the most likely interpretation of the saying of Jesus.[1]

A common form of the dialogue is that in which Jesus is asked a question and replies. Here again we have to distinguish the questioners. There is the disciple who brings his question to the Master because he wants instruction, e.g. Lk. 11^{1-4}. Or there is the friendly outsider who comes to see what Jesus has to say on some problem in which he is interested. Such a case is the question concerning the chief commandment, of which we have two independent versions (Mk. 12^{28-34} and Lk. 10^{25-28}). Or again the questioners may be hostile to Jesus and their questions trap questions, e.g. Mk. 12^{13-17}. In dealing with documents where large masses of teaching have been collected it is necessary to consider carefully in every case where the reply of Jesus really ends, and how far matter not originally part of the reply, but nevertheless bearing upon the subject under discussion, has been attracted to it. This seems to have happened in the Q version of the Beelzebul controversy (Lk. 11^{14-26}), where at least one saying (Lk. 11^{24-26}), which has nothing to do with the original charge, has been tacked on to the reply of Jesus, because it has a bearing on the general subject of demon-possession.

Two important features of the teaching remain for consideration: our Lord's use of poetic form and His practice of teaching in parables.

It is now generally recognised that a large part of the teaching is, like the oracles of the Hebrew prophets, cast into poetic form. Such passages will be noticed in the Commentary, and here it will be necessary only to make a few

[1] See the Commentary, *ad loc.*

observations on the nature of Hebrew poetry.[1] The characteristic feature of this kind of poetry is what is known as ' parallelism ' or the rhyming of thoughts. In an English heroic couplet we look for a correspondence in the two lines first in the number of stressed syllables and then in the sound of the final syllables. In a pair of Latin hexameters we expect a certain amount of correspondence in the arrangement of long and short vowels. In a Hebrew couplet there is a certain correspondence of rhythm and, most important, a correspondence in thought. Bishop Lowth, the pioneer in this field, recognised three kinds of parallelism or correspondence in thought, to which he gave the names synonymous, antithetic, and synthetic. The first two kinds of parallelism are easily recognised and understood. For example, in Ps. 18[25 ff.].

With the merciful thou wilt show thyself merciful;
With the perfect man thou wilt show thyself perfect;
With the pure thou wilt show thyself pure;
And with the perverse thou wilt show thyself froward.
For thou wilt save the afflicted people;
But the haughty eyes thou wilt bring down.

Here the first two lines are in synonymous parallelism and the last two are antithetic. The middle lines show a mixture of both kinds. Considered as wholes, they are in synonymous parallelism; but if we take the separate terms, those are antithetic. Hebrew parallelism is not a cast-iron system, but is capable of immense variety in the application of the fundamental principles. The weak point in Lowth's classification is the ' synthetic.' Synthetic parallelism is really just a name to cover pairs of lines which are somehow connected but not by way of strict synonymous or antithetic parallelism. In this class we should probably recognise that there are some couplets which display *partial* synonymous or antithetic parallelism, and others where there is no parallelism at all in the strict sense but rather *continuation* of the thought of the first line in the second.[2] In other words, we must not expect to find Hebrew poetry constructed on a rigorous system of couplets each consisting of a pair of strictly parallel lines; rather we must look for infinite flexibility in the use of this form, strict parallelism alternating with partial, and with what may be called ' continuation.' To this we have an analogy in the English use of rhyme. Any four lines of verse may be rhymed in a variety of patterns: 1 with 2 and 3 with 4—heroic couplets; or 1 with 3 and 2 with 4; or 2 with 4, 1 and 3 being unrhymed; or 1 with 2 and 4, 3 being unrhymed, as in Fitzgerald's *Omar Khayyam* stanzas; or 1 with 4 and 2 with 3 as in Tennyson's *In Memoriam*. There is the same variety in the Hebrew use of parallelism as in the English use of rhyme.

Parallelism can be employed on a still larger scale. Just as in Spenser's *Prothalamion* we have the same scheme of rhymes repeated with but slight variation

[1] The best treatment of the subject in English is G. B. Gray's *The Forms of Hebrew Poetry*. For the application of the principles to the Gospels see, above all, *The Poetry of our Lord*, by C. F. Burney. Reference may also be made to *The Teaching of Jesus*, pp. 50–56.

[2] See Gray, *op. cit.*, pp. 49 ff.

in each of the ten stanzas of eighteen lines, and as in the choruses of Greek drama we have strophe and antistrophe answering line for line in metrical structure, so in Hebrew poetry it is possible to have whole strophes parallel to one another. This complex parallelism is to be seen in a tentative shape, and not yet fully carried out, in the Old Testament, for example in the series of oracles in the book of Amos (1^{3}–2^{16}). Perfect specimens are to be found in the poetry of Jesus.

With this much by way of explanation, we may give a few out of the many examples of poetic structure in the teaching, reserving fuller treatment of them till a later stage.

1. Simple synonymous parallelism:

He causeth His sun to rise upon evil and good
And raineth upon just and unjust. (Mt. 5^{45}.)

2. Simple antithetic parallelism:

Every good tree bringeth forth good fruits,
But the corrupt tree bringeth forth evil fruits. (Mt. 7^{17}.)

3. Slightly more elaborated, producing a parallelism between two short strophes of three lines each:

Ask, and it shall be given you;
Seek, and ye shall find;
Knock, and it shall be opened to you.
For every asker receiveth;
And the seeker findeth;
And to the knocker it shall be opened. (Lk. $11^{9\,f.}$ = Mt. $7^{7\,f.}$.)

4. Still more complex strophic parallelism:

And as it happened in the days of Noah,
So shall it be in the days of the Son of Man:
They ate, they drank,
They married, they gave in marriage,
Till the day when Noah went into the ark
And the Deluge came and destroyed them all.

Likewise as it happened in the days of Lot:
They ate, they drank,
They bought, they sold,
They planted, they built.
But in the day when Lot went forth from Sodom,
Fire and brimstone rained from heaven and destroyed them all.
Just so shall it be in the day when the Son of Man is revealed. (Lk. 17^{26-30}.)

Closely related to the use of poetic form in the teaching is the use of metaphor, simile, parable, and allegory. Both alike are products of the poet's mind; and just as in poetic form we find all degrees of elaboration, so in the use of pictorial imagery we find a similar variation from the simple metaphor 'You are the light of the world' (Mt. 5^{14}) to the complexity of the great parables.

The distinction between metaphor and simile is that in the simile the comparison is explicit, e.g. 'I send you forth *as* sheep in the midst of wolves; therefore be wise *as* serpents and harmless *as* doves' (Mt. 10^{16}). In the metaphor the compared object actually takes the place of the object to be illustrated, e.g. 'I came to cast fire upon the earth' (Lk. 12^{49}), 'Strive to enter in by the narrow door' (Lk. 13^{24}). It is clear that the metaphor presupposes the simile. The metaphor 'I came to cast fire upon the earth' is only intelligible if 'fire' stands for something else which may well be compared to fire.

The parable rests upon this basis and in its simplest forms it is obvious that it is nothing but an extended simile or metaphor. In the parables of the mustard seed and the leaven we have extended simile. 'To what is the kingdom of God like . . .? It is like a mustard seed . . .' Then the parable goes on to point out those characteristics in the mustard seed which make it a good illustration of the nature of the Kingdom. In the parable of the lamp (Lk. 11^{33}||Mt. 5^{15}) we have an extended metaphor. We are told certain things about the lamp, and it is left to our own common sense or insight to discover what the lamp stands for. A more highly elaborated example of the same sort is the parable of Dives and Lazarus (Lk. 16^{19-31}). We are given the stories of the rich man and the poor beggar, but we are not told who or what they represent.

What is essential to the parable is that there should be a real analogy between what is narrated in the parable and that which the parable is intended to explain or illustrate. The mustard seed grows from small beginnings to something great, and so does the Kingdom. The kindled lamp must light the way into the house; then so—let us say—must the enlightened disciple guide others into the Kingdom of God. In the simpler parables there is one such point to be set before the hearers with the utmost possible clearness and convincing power. But there need not be only one. It is the mark of mastery in the construction of parables that the story told can be made to illustrate and illuminate the truth at several points. The parable of the Prodigal Son has one main point—the outgoing love of God. This is not the only one. The parable has several subsidiary points, and it is a more perfect parable for having them. For these subsidiary points do not destroy the unity of the parable: on the contrary, they serve to throw the central point into stronger relief.

The characteristic feature of the true parable is that this central point is always an appeal to the insight of the hearers. It demands a moral judgement on the behaviour of the characters in the story; and, on the basis of that judgement, it issues its challenge to faith and life. A human father, with all his faults and follies, will not mock his hungry children with stones for bread. Then if you believe in a heavenly Father at all, you must believe that in Him is all that is best in human fatherhood and more besides. Even an unscrupulous judge will give a righteous judgement for the sake of peace and quietness: and shall not the Judge of all the earth do right? The Good Samaritan is good? Then go and do likewise. You admire the business acumen of the Dishonest Steward? Then see whether you cannot apply your own wits with equal assiduity to better purposes. Where the parable succeeds, it succeeds by inspiring faith and by stimulating conscience: where it fails, it fails because men cannot or will not see the point or, if they see it, will not respond.

This enables us to distinguish properly between parable and allegory. For the difference between the two is not one of form or construction, but one of inner meaning and purpose. This is clear from the etymology of the two words. Parable signifies essentially a comparison, a setting of two facts or sets of facts side by side, so that an analogy between them may be established. Allegory is essentially a mode of speech, the description of a fact or set of facts in terms appropriate to another fact or set of facts. Allegory had its beginnings among the Greeks at the time when the old tales about the Olympian gods were falling into discredit for the excellent reason that they 'ascribed to the gods all things that are a shame and a disgrace among mortals, stealings and adulteries and deceivings of one another.' [1] One way of saving the old myths was to maintain that they were not to be taken literally, but as figurative accounts of something else. This is the allegorical method. It was employed, for example, by one Heraclitus, who undertook to show that the stories told by Homer about the doings of the gods in the Iliad were in reality picturesque descriptions of natural phenomena. Then all that the reader of Homer needs is a sort of dictionary which will tell him that when the poet mentions Apollo he really is speaking about the sun, that Apollo shooting arrows is a poetic way of describing the sun's rays, and so on. So interpreted the Iliad becomes the first example of 'Natural Science without tears.' Philo of Alexandria applied the same method to the Old Testament and found his own philosophy concealed in the patriarchal narratives. St. Paul found the secret of the Law and the Gospel adumbrated in the story of Hagar and Sarah. In all these cases we have old traditional material allegorically interpreted: the new meaning is read into the old story. The allegorist may, however, not find anything suitable at hand: he must then try to make a story of his own, which will embody the doctrine he wishes to impart. Then we get such masterpieces of allegory as the *Pilgrim's Progress* and the *Holy War*. Here again there is no obvious and inevitable connexion between the story told and the doctrine to be conveyed. The connexion is made by Bunyan himself, who furnishes the characters and scenes of his story with significant names. These names are at once an indication that the story is not to be taken at its face value, and the code by which its real meaning may be discovered. Now what is common to all these examples is the fact that the story is regarded as the means for conveying correct information or true doctrine about matters with which the story as such has no apparent connexion; and the other fact that the discovery of the true meaning depends on being able to translate the terms used in the story into the terms of the doctrine. The allegory is thus a conventional form by which information may be conveyed to the reader in an interesting and attractive way. This information may be anything from a system of natural science to a body of religious dogma. The point is that what is offered is information claiming to be true.

This discussion is necessary because it has been claimed that there are among the parables of Jesus some which are not parables at all, but allegories. It has

[1] Xenophanes of Colophon, fr. 11 (Diels).

further been suggested that only the true parables—not the allegories—should be regarded as genuine creations of Jesus. If we are to make this distinction between parables and allegories, it is essential that we should make it on the right basis; and in the light of this discussion we must look at the purpose of the stories rather than at the outward form. The ultimate difference between a parable and an allegory is that the parable is meant to create trust in God and love to man by an appeal to conscience and insight, while the allegory is meant to convey information, stimulating interest by an appeal to the imagination. If this test be applied to the parables in the Synoptic Gospels, it will be found that they are for the most part genuine parables, and that in the few cases where we have an allegory, as, for example, in Matthew's parable of the Wheat and Tares, it is probably to be explained as a later allegorising of what was originally a parable.

5. *THE MEANING AND PERMANENT VALUE OF THE TEACHING*

'My yoke is easy and my burden is light.' Easy and light are not the epithets that one would spontaneously apply to the teaching, particularly to its moral demands. Indeed, the criticism most commonly levelled at it is that it is magnificent but impracticable, a beautiful dream which can never come true in such a world as this. This criticism may mean anything or nothing. If it means that the demands of Jesus are of such a kind that no Parliament would enact them and that no police force could enforce them, it is doubtless correct; but it may be questioned whether Jesus ever contemplated such a consummation. Or again, it is suggested that while the teaching may have been all very well for simple first-century Palestine, it is not adequate to our complex twentieth-century civilisation. To which it may be replied that the supposed greater complexity of modern life is largely a myth. Greater ease and rapidity of communication have made more obvious the complexity that has been there all the time. The Egyptian grain harvest affected Rome and, through Rome, the whole Roman Empire as really in the first century as the American grain harvest affects the world in the twentieth. Only then it took somewhat longer for the results to appear than it does now. More than that, the matters with which Jesus was concerned are not affected by the alleged complexity of modern life. What He thought and said about marriage and divorce has to do with realities that are not touched by the fact that the first-century Jewish husband could divorce his wife by writing out a document that would go comfortably on a half-sheet of notepaper, while the twentieth-century husband must go through a long, complicated, and expensive legal process.

It will simplify the discussion if we admit the truth at the outset: that the teaching of Jesus is difficult and unacceptable because it runs counter to those elements in human nature which the twentieth century has in common with the first—such things as laziness, greed, the love of pleasure, the instinct to hit back, and the like. The teaching as a whole shows that Jesus was well aware of this and recognised that here and nowhere else lay the obstacle that had to be surmounted. The question is: how?

We may construe what Jesus said as the enunciation of a new Law, simpler and at the same time more searching and more exacting than the old. The propounder of such a Law would, of course, be open to the practical objection that if people had found the old Law too difficult, they would be still more liable to fail under the new with its more drastic requirements. 'If thou hast run with the footmen, and they have wearied thee, then how canst thou contend with horses?' Further, it may be objected to this legal interpretation that, in the last resort, Jesus reduces the whole Law to a pair of commandments, love towards God and love towards neighbour, and that love cannot be the subject of legislation; for it is of the very essence of love that it should be freely given, spontaneous, and not the laboured response to an external requirement.

Recognising this difficulty, we may try the opposite course and suggest that the teaching is not the promulgation of a new set of rules of piety and morality, but rather the inculcation of a certain temper and spirit which should govern man's attitude to God and neighbour. This interpretation is at once met by the practical objection that 'temper' and 'spirit' are vague terms; that the thing they stand for can easily degenerate into mere sentimentalism; and that the sentimentalist, in spite of his fine feelings, is often singularly ruthless and cruel in action. Moreover, the teaching does not confine itself to the spirit and temper of man, but goes on to specify definite kinds of action and to approve or condemn them.

The way out of this impasse is seen when we take account of the following facts:

(*a*) To the Jew the Law was not merely a set of rules of conduct such as might have been evolved by human wisdom considering the pros and cons of different lines of action and carefully working out the greatest happiness of the greatest number. It was a revelation of God's will and therefore of God Himself. Jesus stands in this tradition, and where He criticises or amends the existing Law it is in order to express more adequately what is for Him the will of God.

(*b*) Jesus is not concerned with the academic analysis of conduct into act, intention, motive, and so on. He *is* concerned with the whole character which expresses itself in life and action. The interest and importance of acts are that they reveal persons.

(*c*) Jesus is not the mere theorist in theology and ethics, but Himself the embodiment of His teaching. In the Gospels the life illuminates the teaching and the teaching the life, just because they are all of a piece.

This means that the teaching must be regarded in a new light. It has to do not with mere acts and motives but with the fundamental relation of man's will to God's. Repentance is not a striving to bring one's conduct into line with the Law or with the higher righteousness demanded by Jesus. Neither is it a painful scrutiny of one's motives with a view to substituting, let us say, unselfish for selfish motives. It is a return of the whole personality to God, a submission of the will to His will, the acceptance of His sovereignty. Now it is by this act of submission that the Kingdom of God is entered, and it is this decisive change that is presupposed in the detailed teaching of Jesus. The change itself is made possible by the new experience of God as Jesus reveals Him, that is, as the merciful loving Father who seeks and saves the lost. This tranforming experience bears fruit in life and conduct; and the examples of the higher righteousness given by Jesus in

His teaching are, so to speak, samples of this fruit. The word 'fruit' is used advisedly, for there is a certain spontaneity and inevitableness about this new behaviour that cannot be attained by mechanical obedience to rules or by meticulous scrutiny of one's motives.

It should thus be apparent that the teaching of Jesus has to do not with the rightness of actions and motives or with the academic discussion of the *summum bonum*, but with the achievement of good living. This means the identification of human wills with the will of God so that one's life becomes part and parcel of the purpose of God in the world. Such life is as difficult and arduous as the composition of a Beethoven symphony is difficult, even for a Beethoven, and as spontaneous and inevitable. We cannot legislate in advance for such life: it creates its own rules in the light of the unfolding purpose of God. Nor can we judge it, for the only final criterion is the whole purpose of God, which is known to God alone. Such life is inspired, creative, adventurous. It is movement towards a goal: and for the purposes of that pilgrimage the teaching of Jesus is a compass rather than an ordnance map. He who grasps it in its wholeness and simplicity is sure of his direction: he must pick his own steps.

At this point we may consider one other difficulty that may be raised concerning the teaching, this namely, that the whole teaching and the whole life of the early Church was dominated by the belief that the end of the existing world-order was close at hand. Then it may be urged that in His teaching Jesus was not laying down rules for the permanent use of mankind, but only issuing a kind of emergency legislation to cover the short interval before the final consummation. The teaching is in fact an interim ethic. Granting the point that Jesus and His first followers believed the end of the existing world-order to be imminent, we must still reject the conclusions drawn with regard to the teaching.

In the first place 'interim-ethic' for such teaching in such circumstances is a misnomer. If, in the belief that the whole monetary system of the world is going to be abolished next week, someone advises me to withdraw all my money from the bank and distribute it in charity, he may be giving me the best advice in the circumstances; but to dignify his advice with the name of 'ethic' or even 'interim-ethic' is to make a virtue of necessity with a vengeance.

But further, and this is the vital point, if the object of the teaching is to give direction rather than directions, to point to the goal of all good living rather than to legislate for particular cases, then the important thing is not whether the goal is near or far away, but whether the direction is correct. If the object of Jesus was so to guide His followers that their lives should fit into the great purpose of God, the question whether that purpose would be realised in ten years or ten thousand became a minor consideration. Now we must maintain that this was precisely the object of Jesus. Where Kant says: 'Act so that the maxims of your will may be in perfect harmony with a universal system of laws,' Jesus says: Live so that your will may be in perfect harmony with the purpose of God. That is the purport of 'Thy will be done on earth as it is in heaven' or 'Be ye merciful, even as your Father is merciful.' It means: live so that your life is a fulfilment, in part at least, of God's purpose. Whether that purpose in its completeness is to have immediate or ultimate fulfilment is a secondary consideration.

The teaching in its inmost nature is thus bound up with faith, the conviction that the world has meaning which can be expressed in terms of the wise and loving purpose of God; that man's sin and misery can be explained in terms of his opposition to that purpose, and cured by a new submission of man's will to God's; and that by this submission man's life acquires new unity, new meaning, new direction, and new hope.

TEXT AND COMMENTARY

I.—The Document Q

A. JOHN THE BAPTIST AND JESUS

(*Note.—In this reconstruction the order of Lk. is followed. For the convenience of readers who may use the commentary with a synopsis before them, the numbers of the paragraphs in Huck's* Synopse *(8th ed.) are added in brackets at the head of each section. References in the commentary are, unless otherwise stated, to the text of Lk.*)

1. *THE PREACHING OF JOHN THE BAPTIST* (2, 4)

MT. 3^{7-12}

3 7 But when he saw many of the Pharisees
and Sadducees coming to his baptism, he
said unto them, Ye offspring of vipers,
who warned you to flee from the wrath to
8 come? Bring forth therefore fruit worthy
of [1] repentance: and think not to say
9 within yourselves, We have Abraham
to our father: for I say unto you, that
God is able of these stones to raise up
10 children unto Abraham. And even
now is the axe laid unto the root of
the trees: every tree therefore that
bringeth not forth good fruit is hewn
11 down, and cast into the fire. I indeed
baptize you [2] with water unto repentance:
but he that cometh after me is mightier
than I, whose shoes I am not [3] worthy to
bear: he shall baptize you [2] with the Holy
12 Ghost and *with* fire: whose fan is in his
hand, and he will throughly cleanse his
threshing-floor; and he will gather his
wheat into the garner, but the chaff he
will burn up with unquenchable fire.

[1] Or, *your repentance.*
[2] Or, *in.*
[3] Gr. *sufficient.*

LK. $3^{7-9,\ 16,\ 17}$

3 7 He said therefore to the multitudes that
went out to be baptized of him, Ye offspring of vipers, who warned you to flee
8 from the wrath to come? Bring forth
therefore fruits worthy of [1] repentance, and
begin not to say within yourselves, We
have Abraham to our father: for I say
unto you, that God is able of these stones
9 to raise up children unto Abraham. And
even now is the axe also laid unto the root
of the trees: every tree therefore that
bringeth not forth good fruit is hewn
down, and cast into the fire.
15 And as the people were in expectation,
and all men reasoned in their hearts concerning John, whether haply he were the
16 Christ; John answered, saying unto them
all, I indeed baptize you with water; but
there cometh he that is mightier than I,
the latchet of whose shoes I am not
[2] worthy to unloose: he shall baptize you
17 [3] with the Holy Ghost and *with* fire: whose
fan is in his hand, throughly to cleanse
his threshing-floor, and to gather the
wheat into his garner; but the chaff he
will burn up with unquenchable fire.

[1] Or, *your repentance.*
[2] Gr. *sufficient.*
[3] Or, *in.*

There is another, probably independent, account of John's preaching in Mk. $1^{7f.}$. As is commonly the case in Q sections, the verbal agreement between Mt. and Lk. begins with the words of the preacher. 'Pharisees and Sadducees' (Mt. 3^{7}) is a favourite phrase with Matthew (cf. Mt. $16^{1,\ 6,\ 11,\ 12}$). From Mk. 11^{27-33} we learn that 'the High priests, scribes, and elders' had rejected the baptism of John, and the same is reported of 'the Pharisees and lawyers' in Lk. $7^{29f.}$. These two passages suggest that John's converts were drawn from the common people; and, so far, Luke's introduction is preferable to Matthew's, though it may perhaps be doubted whether either stood in Q. Lk. 3^{15} is another piece of narrative setting introduced by the evangelist. It has no parallel in Mt., and it breaks the unity of the address.

Traces of the original Aramaic are to be seen in '*begin* not to say' (Lk. 3^{8}, cf. 13^{25}), a literal translation of a common Aramaic idiom (Mt. 3^{8} has 'think not to say,' which represents a better Greek, but a less faithful rendering of the original); and in the saying about raising up children to Abraham from stones, where there is probably a play upon words, the Aramaic words for 'children' and 'stones' being almost identical. Probably also in the phrase 'bring forth fruits,' lit. 'make fruits.' A single Aramaic verb may also lie behind 'bear' (Mt. 3^{11}) and 'unloose' (Lk. 3^{16}).

7, 8, 9, 17. John addresses his audience as 'offspring of vipers' in sharp contrast to their own thought of themselves as children of Abraham. The serpent is the type of evil cunning: and at a later date we find 'the old serpent' as a description of Satan (Rev. 12^{9}). Cf. John 8^{44}, 'Ye (Jews) are of your father the devil.' Here 'offspring of vipers' may well have much the same force as 'children of Satan.' Signs of repentance from such people are so amazing that they must have learned somewhere of the coming judgement. Here we come to the main theme of John's preaching, the wrath to come. John thinks of it as an essential part of the rule of God. There is to be a settling of accounts, and at it strict justice will be the order of the day. Evildoers will by no means escape the penalty of their misdeeds. Repentance is necessary, and this repentance must be real; it must issue in amendment of life. The fact that the guilty are of the Chosen People will not avail them—as many thought—in the day of judgement. Here John takes up a position that is as old as Amos, 'You only have I known of all the families of the earth: therefore I will visit upon you all your iniquities' (Am. 3^{2}). There will be no most favoured nation in the day that is coming. And that day is imminent. Already the axe is resting on the tree root, ready to be raised for the first blow. As nothing can save the unfruitful tree from the fire, so nothing will save an unrepentant and unreformed Israel from the judgement. The judgement may also be pictured in terms of the threshing-floor. Here only what is good is preserved: all that is worthless is destroyed in the fire. There is no doubt as to what is meant by the fire. We may compare *Psalms of Solomon* $15^{6f., 10\text{-}15}$: 'Flaming fire and the wrath against the ungodly . . . when it goeth forth against the sinners from before the face of the Lord, to destroy all the substance of the sinners. . . . For the mark of destruction is upon their forehead, and the inheritance of the sinners is destruction and darkness: and their iniquities shall pursue them as far as hell beneath. . . . And the sinners shall perish in the day of the Lord's judgement for ever, when God visiteth the earth with His judgement to recompense the sinners unto everlasting. But they that fear the Lord shall find mercy therein: and shall live in the righteousness of their God' (trans. Ryle and James).

16. This brings us to what is the crucial point in the interpretation of the passage—the two baptisms. The coming baptism is described by both Mt. and Lk. as a baptism 'with the Holy Ghost and with fire.' In Mk. (1^{8}) and John (1^{33}) it is baptism 'with the Holy Ghost.' In Acts 1^{5} the risen Lord says to His followers: 'John baptized with water; you will soon be baptized with the Holy Ghost.' In Acts 11^{16}, Peter, explaining his dealings with Cornelius, says: 'I remembered the word of the Lord,' referring back to Acts 1^{5}. From Acts itself it is clear how

this word of the Lord was understood, namely as a prophecy fulfilled at Pentecost, when a baptism with the Holy Spirit was symbolised by tongues of fire descending on the disciples' heads. Now in Acts 19^{1-6} we meet with disciples of John who have not even heard of a baptism with the Holy Spirit. But this is very strange if John did in fact teach that his own baptism was only a preliminary to another and richer baptism with the Spirit. These conflicting data are explicable on the hypothesis that the experience of the early Church led them to interpret 'baptism with fire' as baptism with the Holy Spirit, and that this interpretation has already affected the passages in Acts 1 and 2 and also the form of John's saying in Mk. 1^{8}. It is then open to us to say that in Mt. and Lk. we have the original form of the saying as recorded in Q plus the interpretation put upon it by the early Church. This original Q form, which is also the better tradition of John's saying, had no reference to the Spirit. It ran: 'He will baptize you with fire.' So long as the Holy Spirit is retained, John's words are a promise: my baptism is a prelude to a better. When the reference to the Spirit is dropped, the true nature of the saying is apparent. It falls into line with the rest of John's preaching. The baptism with fire is parallel to the other references to fire and to be understood in the same way. The sense of the saying is not that John's baptism is the preliminary to something better, but that it is the last chance of escaping something very much worse, namely the coming judgement.

The agent in this coming crisis is not God. The language of *v.* 16 is not the kind that John would have used of God. 'He that is mightier than I' means the Messiah. Might is one of the attributes of the Messiah (Is. 9^{6}, *Ps. Sol.* 17^{44}). There is no indication that John thinks of the Messiah as a supernatural being. The description given here would be appropriate to a human Messiah endowed with supernatural power and authority and similar to the judge and ruler foretold in *Ps. Sol.* 17^{23-31}. To look after the footgear of such a Person, which is normally a slave's job, would be for John a high honour.

The preaching of John as a whole belongs to the same strain as the preaching of the greatest Old Testament prophets. Like them, he has his message of doom for a sinful nation. But he goes farther. His task is not merely to proclaim the coming wrath, but also (again in the words of Amos) to prepare Israel to meet her God, to show a way of repentance and amendment whereby some at least may be delivered before it is too late. In this setting the baptism of John can perhaps be most readily understood by reference to the Jewish baptism of proselytes. As the baptism of the proselyte was part of the ceremony of dedication by which a Gentile was incorporated into Israel, so John's baptism is an act of rededication by which Israelites, who through sin have lost their right to the name, may be incorporated afresh into the true Israel.

2. *THE TEMPTATIONS OF JESUS* (8)

MT. 4^{1-11}

4 1 Then was Jesus led up of the Spirit into
the wilderness to be tempted of the devil.
2 And when he had fasted forty days and
3 forty nights, he afterward hungered. And

LK. 4^{1-13}

4 1 And Jesus, full of the Holy Spirit, returned from the Jordan, and was led [1] by
the Spirit in the wilderness during forty
2 days, being tempted of the devil. And

the tempter came and said unto him, If
thou art the Son of God, command that
4 these stones become [1] bread. But he
answered and said, It is written, Man shall
not live by bread alone, but by every
word that proceedeth out of the mouth of
5 God. Then the devil taketh him into the
6 holy city; and he set him on the [2] pinnacle
of the temple, and saith unto him, If thou
art the Son of God, cast thyself down: for
it is written,

He shall give his angels charge concerning thee:
And on their hands they shall bear thee up,
Lest haply thou dash thy foot against a stone.

7 Jesus said unto him, Again it is written,
Thou shalt not tempt the Lord thy God.
8 Again, the devil taketh him unto an exceeding
high mountain, and sheweth him
all the kingdoms of the world, and the
9 glory of them; and he said unto him, All
these things will I give thee, if thou wilt
10 fall down and worship me. Then saith
Jesus unto him, Get thee hence, Satan:
for it is written, Thou shalt worship the
Lord thy God, and him only shalt thou
11 serve. Then the devil leaveth him; and
behold, angels came and ministered unto
him.

[1] Gr. *loaves*.
[2] Gr. *wing*.

he did eat nothing in those days: and
when they were completed, he hungered.
3 And the devil said unto him, If thou art
the Son of God, command this stone that
4 it become [2] bread. And Jesus answered
unto him, It is written, Man shall not live
5 by bread alone. And he led him up, and
shewed him all the kingdoms of [3] the world
6 in a moment of time. And the devil said
unto him, To thee will I give all this
authority, and the glory of them: for it
hath been delivered unto me; and to
7 whomsoever I will I give it. If thou therefore
wilt worship before me, it shall all be
8 thine. And Jesus answered and said unto
him, It is written, Thou shalt worship the
Lord thy God, and him only shalt thou
9 serve. And he led him to Jerusalem, and
set him on the [4] pinnacle of the temple, and
said unto him, If thou art the Son of God,
10 cast thyself down from hence: for it is
written,

He shall give his angels charge concerning thee, to guard thee:

11 and,

On their hands they shall bear thee up,
Lest haply thou dash thy foot against a stone.

12 And Jesus answering said unto him, It is
said, Thou shalt not tempt the Lord thy
God.
13 And when the devil had completed
every temptation, he departed from him
[5] for a season.

[1] Or, *in*.
[2] Or, *a loaf*.
[3] Gr. *the inhabited earth*.
[4] Gr. *wing*.
[5] Or, *until*.

Mk. ($1^{12f.}$) records the fact that Jesus was tempted, but does not specify the nature of the temptations. In the narrative setting of the Q account there is little agreement between Mt. and Lk. apart from words which they have in common with Mk. They agree against Mk. in calling the adversary 'devil' rather than 'Satan,' and in introducing the name Jesus at the beginning of the story. This latter agreement does not amount to much, since Luke, by introducing the genealogy between the Baptism and the Temptations, makes a fresh start necessary. If the name Jesus did stand in Q at this point, it would be an indication that the Q account of the Temptations was a self-contained section. Mt. and Lk. also agree in describing Jesus' fast; but the wording of the two accounts is different except for the verb 'hungered.' The fast and the hunger are the necessary prelude to the first temptation.

The most striking difference between Mt. and Lk. is in the order of the temptations. Matthew's arrangement works up to a fine dramatic climax, so fine that it is difficult to imagine what could have induced Luke to alter it, if it had stood so in his source. It is probable that the order in Lk. is the original Q order.

1 f. *Narrative introduction.* Mk. ($1^{12 f.}$) tells us that Jesus was in the wilderness —the home of evil spirits—for forty days and that during that period He was tempted by Satan. Mt. ($4^{1 f.}$) says that He was led into the wilderness to be tempted, that the forty days were spent in fasting, and that then the temptations began. (Similarly, in the story of the Baptism Mt. converts Mk.'s statement that Jesus came and was baptised into a statement that He came to be baptised.) Lk. has a combination of the two versions. With Mk. he makes the temptation continue throughout the forty days. With Mt. he describes the fast, and then commences a new set of temptations at the end of the forty days. It does not seem possible to determine how much of this is Q matter; but there must have been some reference to the fast and the hunger in order to make the first temptation intelligible. For the fast cf. Ex. 34^{28}, Moses' fast on Mt. Sinai. Forty days is the Jewish conventional figure for a considerable time. Mt. has ' forty days and forty nights ' as in Ex. 34^{28}.

3 f. *The first temptation.* This and the temptation on the Temple are introduced by the words ' If thou art the Son of God.' The fact that this formula is not used in the temptation where Jesus is offered the kingdoms of the world, is a clue to its meaning here; for it may be safely conjectured that the reason why the tempter does not use the formula in that case is that if Jesus is the Son of God, the things which Satan is about to offer are already His by right, the right of the Messiah. But the term Son of God for Messiah is curiously rare in Hebrew and Jewish literature. In the Old Testament angels are called ' sons of God ' and the name Son of God is given to Israel as a whole and to the king of Israel. In the Septuagint and the Apocrypha and Pseudepigrapha the name is given to Israel, to the godly and upright in Israel, and to the Messiah. (This last probably only in 4 *Ezra*.) In the Rabbinical literature it is used for Israel and for the Davidic Messiah. Here again the cases where it is used of the Messiah are few, and Billerbeck points out that they only occur where a Messianic interpretation of an Old Testament text is unavoidable. It may be, as he suggests, that the Rabbis deliberately avoided the expression because of its use by Christians as a designation of Christ. In any case, it is difficult to see what else Son of God can mean in the present context.

The challenge to the Messiah to transform stone into bread may best be explained by reference to the current belief that the Messianic Age would be marked by a miraculous abundance of material goods. Satan says in effect: If you are the Messiah, produce one of the recognised signs of the Messiah's coming. Jesus replies by quoting from Dt. 8^3, ' Man shall not live by bread alone.' Mt. (4^4) has the addition ' but by every word that proceedeth out of the mouth of God,' which cannot have stood in Q, because it is a quotation from the Septuagint. The force of the quotation appears when we take in the immediately preceding words in Dt. : ' And He humbled thee, and suffered thee to hunger, and fed thee with manna, which thou knowest not, neither did thy fathers know; that He might make thee know that man doth not live by bread only but by every thing that proceedeth out of the mouth of the Lord doth man live.' It was God who fed the people miraculously in the wilderness with food of His own providing; and not even the Messiah can usurp God's place, Even the Messiah is only God's servant. It is not his to command, but only to obey.

5–8. *The second temptation.* The differences between Mt. and Lk. are here considerable. Luke's 'led him up' without specification of place, and the words 'in a moment of time' suggest a visionary experience. Mt. (4^8) makes the place of the temptation a very high mountain from whose summit the whole inhabited world is actually visible. Such a mountain is mentioned in the *Apocalypse of Baruch* 76^3, and another in *Enoch* 24 f. The summit of the latter is like a throne, and it is here that God will sit when He comes down to visit the earth with goodness (*Enoch* 25^3). This mountain would be a very suitable scene for Satan's offer. The wording of the offer is fuller in Lk. than in Mt. The words 'and the glory of them' are awkwardly placed in Lk. 4^6, for 'of them' clearly refers back to the kingdoms of the world and what Satan is offering is the authority. The words may be accidentally misplaced or they may have crept into the text of Lk. from Mt. The claim of the tempter that the sole right of disposing of the authority is his does not appear in Mt. In the Q passage Mt. 11^{27} = Lk. 10^{22} similar words are used by Jesus. Does Mt. suppress them here as false and blasphemous in the mouth of Satan? The speech of Satan in Lk. is subtle: (*a*) the unqualified promise 'I will give it to you': (*b*) the claim 'It is mine to do with as I please'; (*c*) the trap 'I will let you have it on very easy terms.' In Mt. we have only the bald statement of the offer and the condition. This offer is rejected, again in terms borrowed from the Old Testament (Dt. 6^{13}) and slightly adapted to the situation. The original runs: 'Thou shalt fear the Lord thy God; and Him shalt thou serve.' Here 'worship'—better 'do homage to'—is substituted for 'fear,' and 'only' is added after 'Him.' Satan has said: 'I will make you ruler of the world, if you will do homage to me.' Jesus replies 'Homage is to be done to God, who is the sole object of man's loyalty and obedience.' Even the Messiah is only God's servant.

9–12. *The third temptation.* This takes place in Jerusalem. 'The holy city' (Mt.) is a common Jewish designation of the capital. What is meant by 'the pinnacle of the temple' is uncertain. The Greek word here translated 'temple' means the whole complex of buildings within the sacred enclosure, including the temple proper. In this case the pinnacle may be what was known as the 'Royal colonnade' on the south side of the outer court. This cloister overlooked a deep ravine, and Josephus (*Ant.*, xv. 11, 5) says that to look down from the roof made one giddy. The Jewish tradition that the Messiah would appear on the roof of the Temple and there proclaim deliverance to the people has no real connexion with this temptation; for there is no hint that the Messiah was expected to prove his title by leaping from the roof. The tempter, twice repulsed with scripture texts, tries a text himself. This is quoted from Ps. $91^{11f.}$, which is obviously intended to be understood messianically. The challenge is: God has made this promise to the Messiah: if you are the Messiah, let Him fulfil it. This challenge is met by Jesus with words taken from Dt. 6^{16}. There the full text runs: 'Ye shall not tempt the Lord your God, as ye tempted Him in Massah.' 'Tempt' is hardly the right word either in Dt. 6^{16} or here: it is really a case of 'putting

God to the test.' The reference to Massah is explained by Ex. 17^{1-7}, where it is related how the Israelites by their complaints forced God's hand when they should have trusted His promises. To test God's good faith is to show one's own lack of faith. Again, the Messiah is only God's servant. It is not for him to dictate to God, but only to trust and obey. If the way of obedience means leaping over a precipice—or going to the Cross—that is another matter; but to thrust oneself into peril, merely to provide God with the occasion for a miracle, is not faith but presumption.

13. *Narrative Conclusion.* Mt. and Lk. both tell of the departure of the tempter, though in different words. Mt. adds the detail of the ministry of angels to Jesus from Mk. 1^{13}. Lk. says that the tempter left after he had tried every kind of temptation. This doubtless means both the three here described and the others alluded to in *v.* 2. Lk. adds that the respite from temptation was only for a time. He may be thinking of the Passion, Satan's final attack, using Judas as his tool (Lk. 22^{3}); though the kind of temptation pictured in this section is present throughout the ministry.

Concerning the temptation narrative Origen said: 'Two kings are struggling together to reign—the king of sin, the devil, and the king of righteousness, Christ.' It would, of course, be easy to take a much simpler line and interpret all the temptations in a moral sense as appeals to such universal human characteristics as the physical appetites, the lust for power, and the thirst for admiration; but, when we look at the narrative as a whole, it is clear that such an interpretation is inadequate. The temptations are fully intelligible only when they are taken in connexion with Jesus' sense of His divinely appointed mission to Israel. It is, however, argued that the temptations cannot be Messianic, because the primitive Church found in the miracles of Jesus one of the principal proofs of His Messiahship. To this it may be replied that even for the early Church miracles did not prove Messiahship; for miracles are recorded of the Apostles, who made no Messianic claims, and, moreover, it was believed that even the Antichrist could and would perform miracles (Mk. 13^{22}, 2 Thess. 2^{9}). Further, the supreme proof that Jesus was the 'son of God' was found in a miracle wrought by God and not by Jesus, the Resurrection (Rom. 1^{4}). But even if the ground alleged were sound, it would prove, not that the temptations are not Messianic, but, what is antecedently probable, that the early Church could not have invented them.

Again it is urged against these stories that similar tales are told of the Buddha, of Zarathustra, and of numerous Christian saints. This argument, so far as it means anything at all, would appear to mean:

> All temptation stories told about great religious leaders of antiquity are legendary.
>
> Mt. 4^{1-11} = Lk. 4^{1-13} is such a story.
>
> Therefore it is legendary.

We may venture to doubt the major premiss.

The first and third temptations in Lk.'s order recur in the course of the ministry in the repeated demand for a sign (Mk. 8^{11-13}; Mt. 12^{38-42}||Lk. 11^{29-32}; Lk. 12^{54-56}, 23^{8}; Mk. 15^{32}, and parallels). That is, they correspond to something real in the experience of Jesus. The same is true of the second temptation. The whole history of the Jewish people from 200 B.C. to A.D. 130 is solid testimony to the fact that if Jesus had wished to raise a revolt against Gentile domination, He would have found a following without difficulty. The temptations as a whole picture the clash between what Jesus knew Himself called by God to do, and what popular expectation demanded. And here we may note that Jesus does not set forth the positive features of His own conception of His ministry. He rejects a number of proposals quite decisively, as much as to say: Whatever else God may have appointed me to do, it is not this or this. This fact suggests that the experience recorded in the stories belongs to the early part of His work.

Granted that the stories report a genuine experience of Jesus, He must Himself be the narrator of them. It may be conjectured that they were told to the disciples after He had been recognised by them as Messiah and began to inform them of what Messiahship had come to mean for Him. In that case the present position of the section becomes highly significant, following as it does close upon the Messianic prophecies of John the Baptist. For, as we have seen, John's preaching represents the Jewish messianic expectation in its purest and highest form, the picture of a king who will reign in absolute righteousness. Even this is not good enough, much less the vulgar hope of a potentate who would, with God's assistance, restore the vanished glories of the kingdom of David and Solomon. Here is the characteristic of the temptation stories which it is difficult to attribute to anyone except Jesus Himself, the violence with which He flings behind His back the common Jewish notion of messiahship, and says: 'This is not the will of God, but the wiles of the Devil.' [1]

3. *THE PREACHING OF JESUS*

(*a*) The Beatitudes and Woes (73, 74)

MT. $5^{1-3, 4, 6, 11, 12}$

5 1 And seeing the multitudes, he went up
into the mountain: and when he had sat
2 down, his disciples came unto him; and he
opened his mouth and taught them,
saying,
3 Blessed are the poor in spirit; for theirs is
the kingdom of heaven.
4 Blessed are they that mourn; for they
shall be comforted.
6 Blessed are they that hunger and thirst
after righteousness; for they shall be filled.
11 Blessed are ye when *men* shall reproach
you, and persecute you, and say all manner of evil against you falsely, for my sake.
12 Rejoice, and be exceeding glad: for great is
your reward in heaven: for so persecuted
they the prophets which were before you.

LK. 6^{20-26}

6 20 And he lifted up his eyes on his disciples,
and said, Blessed *are* ye poor: for yours is
21 the kingdom of God. Blessed *are* ye that
hunger now: for ye shall be filled. Blessed
are ye that weep now: for ye shall laugh.
22 Blessed are ye, when men shall hate you,
and when they shall separate you *from
their company*, and reproach you, and cast
out your name as evil, for the Son of man's
23 sake. Rejoice in that day, and leap *for
joy*: for behold, your reward is great in
heaven: for in the same manner did their
24 fathers unto the prophets. But woe unto
you that are rich! for ye have received
25 your consolation. Woe unto you, ye that
are full now! for ye shall hunger. Woe
unto you, ye that laugh now! for ye shall
26 mourn and weep. Woe *unto you*, when all
men shall speak well of you! for in the
same manner did their fathers to the false
prophets.

[1] So Karl Holl, *Gesammelte Aufsätze*, ii. 16 f.

20. The sermon as given in Mt. is much longer than that in Lk. The explanation is that in Mt. material from another source or sources is combined with the sermon as given in Q. This Q form is probably preserved in Lk. 6^{20-49}. In both Mt. and Lk. the sermon is addressed to the disciples. Mt. $5^{1f.}$ suggests that it is the disciples alone, Jesus having gone away with them to the hills to avoid the crowds. Cf. 8^{1} and 8^{18}. The Lucan context, on the other hand, suggests the presence of the crowd as well as of the disciples . Cf. 6^{12-19}.

Lk. gives four beatitudes followed by four corresponding woes. In Mt. 5^{3-12} there are nine beatitudes, of which four—given above—correspond to those in Lk., four (Mt. 5^{7-10}) may be assigned to M., and one—'Blessed are the meek . . .'—seems to be an adaptation of Ps. 37^{11}; it may, however, also belong to M. In Lk. beatitudes and woes are in the second person throughout; in Mt. all except the last ($5^{11f.}$) are in the third person. In utterances of this sort the third person is much the commonest in the Old Testament, though the second person is also found occasionally there and quite frequently in other Semitic literature. The second person is probably the original here. In Mt. the phrasing of the beatitudes has been given a more edifying turn than in Lk. Here also it is likely that the stark simplicity of Lk. is the original. This simpler form is strongly eschatological. It paints in vivid colours the contrast between things as they are and things as they will be in the good time that is coming.

The first beatitude states the contrast in general terms. The meaning of the word 'poor' is given by such passages as Ps. 69^{29-36}. In the Judaism of the last two centuries B.C. the term was practically a synonym for *Ḥāsīd*, i.e. 'saintly' or 'pious,' in the best sense. So, for example, *Ps. Sol.* 10^{7} : 'The saints also shall give thanks in the assembly of the people : and God will have mercy on the poor in the (day of) gladness of Israel.' Here 'the saints' and 'the poor' stand in synonymous parallelism. Again in the Talmud they are treated as synonyms (*Ber.* 6^{b}). The use of the word 'poor' in this way goes back to the days of the Seleucid rule in Palestine. Then it was the poor above all who remained faithful to their religion and the Law. The well-to-do upper classes in Jerusalem allowed themselves to be tainted with heathenism. Hence 'rich' tends to mean 'worldly' and 'irreligious,' and 'poor' the opposite. In this specialised sense the word is used here. In Mt. the paraphrase 'poor in spirit' is an attempt to make this fact clear. The Kingdom of God belongs to these simple devoted souls, because they belong to it, having accepted God's will as the only rule of their lives. As they submit themselves to the obligations of the Kingdom, so they become heirs of its privileges.

21. This is now drawn out in more detail. The contrast between the present and the future lot of the godly is that between a famine and a feast. In Jewish and Christian imagery the good time coming is likened to a great feast. Cf. Is. 49^{10-12}; Ps. 107^{1-9}; Mt. $8^{11f.}$||Lk. 13^{28-30}; Mt. 22^{1-10}||Lk. 14^{15-24}; Lk. 22^{30}. It is obvious that this imagery is not to be taken literally. Cf. Amos $8^{11ff.}$—'a famine in the land, not a famine of bread, nor a thirst for water, but of hearing the words of the Lord.' For the Rabbis the Law is bread and wine. So here in Mt. we have the paraphrase 'hunger and thirst after righteousness,' which gives something near the sense of the bare statement in Lk. The righteousness in question

is not just the conformity of human conduct to a divinely appointed standard. It is the fulfilment by man of God's will *and* the fulfilment by God of His own purposes of grace and mercy (cf. Dodd, *Romans*, p. 12). In that fulfilment those who are now dissatisfied with themselves and with life as it is, will find complete satisfaction.

This contrast between the present and the future is as sharp as the difference between weeping and laughter, sorrow and joy. In Mt. the strong words are softened down, unnecessarily. For the sentiment and wording cf. Ps. 137^{1-4} and 126. There the exiles sit by the waters of Babylon and weep ; and when God turns again the captivity of Zion, their mouth is filled with laughter and their tongue with singing. Just so the saints are homesick for the Kingdom of God ; and their joy cannot be perfected till it comes. Cf. Phil. 3^{20}.

22. But the present hardship of the godly does not consist only in the fact that what they hope for lies still in the future : there is also the fact that they live in a world where they and the thing for which they stand must inevitably be hateful to many. Hence they must be prepared to face hostility, opposition, and persecution for the sake of the Kingdom. Mt. 5^{10} may be regarded as the M version of this beatitude. Cf. also Jas. 2^{7}; 1 Pet. $4^{14, 16}$; Mk. 13^{9-13}. There are some important differences between Mt. and Lk. in this beatitude. Lk. mentions four kinds of persecution, Mt. only three; and the wording is not the same. Lk. supplies the subject ' men ' ; it is probably not part of the original text of Q. These opponents ' hate.' They exclude the objects of their hatred from their society, and ' reproach ' them. It has been suggested that the separation or exclusion here referred to is a form of synagogue discipline, but this is unlikely (Billerbeck iv. 331). Corresponding to these three activities we have in Mt. ' reproach ' and ' persecute.' If we take ' persecute ' in the sense of ' drive away ' (cf. Mt. 10^{23}, 23^{34}), it will be roughly equivalent to ' separate ' or ' exclude ' in Lk. The fourth kind of persecution is slander. The Lucan phrase ' cast out your name as evil ' is best explained as an attempt to translate a phrase found both in Hebrew and Aramaic. Literally translated the phrase runs ' send out an evil name upon,' and it means ' issue an evil report about.' Mt. gives the sense of the phrase correctly in the words ' speak evil against you.' The words ' all manner of ' and ' falsely ' are added by the writer of the Gospel. The former is a well-known editorial device of his, and the latter is an example of his somewhat pedantic way of making sweeping statements more precise. These hardships are borne ' for the sake of the Son of Man ' (Lk.) or ' for my sake ' (Mt.). Here the original wording is probably preserved by Lk. Mt. alters ' Son of Man ' to the personal pronoun elsewhere (Mt. 16^{21}), and may well have done so here. The Son of Man is the embodiment of all that the persecuted saints hold sacred. On the meaning of ' Son of Man ' see my *Teaching of Jesus*, pp. 211–234.

23. The experience of opposition and persecution is no occasion for discouragement or complaint, rather for rejoicing. For it is a proof that those who endure it stand in the succession of the great servants of God in past ages, who received like treatment in their day. Moreover, it is only for a time. The fulfilment of God's purpose is sure, and in that consummation God's servants will find their reward with joy. The difference between Lk.'s ' for in the same manner did

their fathers unto the prophets ' and Mt.'s ' for so persecuted they the prophets which were before you ' may be explained by a slight confusion of the original Aramaic. It is probable that Lk. has the sense correctly in this case. Cf. Mt. $23^{29ff.}$ ||Lk. $11^{47ff.}$.

The fourth beatitude should almost certainly be assigned to a late date in the ministry. It differs in tone from the other three. We feel that we are no longer concerned with the saints and their destiny in general terms, but with the fate of a definite group of people in a particular situation. Here Jesus is speaking to His chosen helpers about the things that actually threaten Him and them. Now in the Mission Charge (Lk. 10^{1-16}) the tone is still hopeful. Opposition there will be ; but, on the whole the messengers may expect a friendly reception. For a parallel to the fourth beatitude we have to go to passages like Mk. 10^{38-40}; Lk. 19^{41-44} ; Mk. 13^{9-13}, 8^{34-38} ; and a number of others, all of which fall after Peter's confession. (Cf. *The Teaching of Jesus*, pp. 205 f.)

24–26. After the beatitudes Lk. has a corresponding set of four woes. These have no parallel in Mt., and it can be urged against them (*a*) that they are hardly in place in an address to *disciples* (but cf. Jas. 4^{13}–5^{6}), and (*b*) that they necessitate a fresh start in *v.* 27. On these grounds it has been suspected that they did not stand in Q, but have been brought in by Luke from another source, or else are his own composition. There is no entirely satisfactory solution of the problem. It might, however, be conjectured that the earliest form of the section consisted of the first three beatitudes with the corresponding woes ; that the fourth beatitude—a genuine saying of Jesus—was added later; and that finally the fourth woe was produced to round off the whole.

24, 25. The rich in the first woe are the opposite of the poor in the first beatitude. That is, they are the worldly people who care for and trust in material goods, money and the things that money can buy; who serve Mammon rather than God. They have their satisfaction now in the way they choose, and that is all. They lack nothing except the things that really matter. They have unlimited pleasure, but not lasting joy. When the day of reckoning comes, the things that now satisfy and please them will have an end and they will have nothing to put in their place.

26. This verse is the counterpart to *vv.* 22 f. Here again we are aware of a change of tone. It is the disciples who are being warned to beware of popularity. A ready welcome for themselves and their message may well be the first sign that they are being unfaithful to Him who sent them, forgetting the Kingdom of God, and coming to terms with the world. If this is a genuine saying of Jesus, it also must belong to the later period of the ministry.

(*b*) The Law of Love (75)

MT. $5^{44, 39, 40, 42}$, 7^{12}

5 44 But I say unto you, Love your enemies, and
39 pray for them that persecute you. But
whosoever smiteth thee on thy right
40 cheek, turn to him the other also. And if
any man would go to law with thee, and

LK. 6^{27-31}

6 27 But I say unto you which hear, Love
your enemies, |do good to them that hate
28 you, ||bless them that curse you, |pray for
29 them that despitefully use you. ||To him
that smiteth thee on the *one* cheek |offer

take away thy coat, let him have thy cloke
42 also. Give to him that asketh thee, and
from him that would borrow of thee turn
not thou away.
7 12 All things therefore whatsoever ye would
that men should do unto you, even so do
ye also unto them: for this is the law and
the prophets.

also the other; ||and from him that taketh
away thy cloke |withhold not thy coat also.
30 ||Give to every one that asketh thee; ||and
of him that taketh away thy goods ask
31 them not again.||And as ye would that
men should do to you, |do ye also to them
likewise.||

The Lucan form of this piece of teaching appears to be the original. In Mt. the precepts and examples have been broken up and rearranged to fit into the ethical Antitheses from M. (see below, p. 451); and the Golden Rule has been transferred to the end of a long section in the Sermon on the Mount. The Lucan version, on the other hand, is in strict poetic form, showing parallelism and—on retranslation into Aramaic—rhythm and rhyme. See C. F. Burney, *The Poetry of our Lord*, p. 169. In the text above the ends of lines and half-lines are marked || and | respectively.

27a. A fresh start is made with the words ' But I say unto you which hear.' Those who think that the woes are an insertion here explain the words as an attempt to restore the connexion which has been broken. But see below on Mt. 5^{43-48}, p. 453.

27b, 28. A general exhortation carrying a stage farther the commandment ' Thou shalt love thy neighbour as thyself.' In Mk. 12^{28-34} Jesus puts love to neighbour as an obligation second only to love to God. In the parable of the Good Samaritan He tacitly declines to set any limit to the scope of the term ' neighbour.' Here He carries His attitude to its logical conclusion: ' neighbour ' includes everyone, even enemies. That this love is not mere sentiment is shown by the remaining injunctions. It involves active beneficence, unfailing courtesy, and a goodwill so genuine that it will stand the test of being brought into the presence of God in prayer. It does not involve countenancing anything that is false or cruel or unjust. And it leaves room for a prophetic indignation against things which are clearly contrary to the will of God, and for maintaining unflinchingly what one sees to be true and good. In these two verses we have the completest expression of the ideal personal relation between man and man. And it is put forward primarily as that and nothing else. At a very early date it comes to be claimed that it is also the best policy: 'Love those that hate you, and you will have no enemy ' (*Didache* 1^3). This may be true—it is very optimistic—but it is not the reason assigned by Jesus. The kind of love of which He is here speaking would cease to be what it is if any ulterior motive, however excellent, entered into it. It must be the spontaneous self-manifestation of a human nature that has been touched by the love of God and must now reproduce that love in itself in all relations with other men and women. In setting up this absolute ideal Jesus neither quotes nor contradicts Jewish principles. He brings to sharp and decisive expression ideals which show themselves in Judaism at its best; and He clears away much in Jewish teaching that was inconsistent with those ideals. He says in effect to the Judaism of His day : This and this alone is the will of the God of our fathers and our God. His originality lies in the way in which He goes to the very heart of the prophetic religion, and sets free a spirit which was in danger of being stifled by Rabbinic fundamentalism on the one hand, and, on the other, by the very natural resentment and hatred of the Gentile, engendered by centuries of foreign oppression. It is necessary to remember that this ideal was set up before Jews whose land at that very moment was occupied, and not for the first time, by a foreign army; that among the theologians the question whether the word ' neighbour ' in Lev. 19^{18} could apply to a non-Jew was a matter for serious debate; that in the popular Apocalyptic literature there was little love wasted on the Gentile nations. It was in this context that Jesus gave to Judaism, and to the world, this unqualified and uncompromising statement of the true Israelite ideal.

29 f. The change from plural to singular indicates that we have here a separate saying. The sermon consists of such utterances on various occasions brought together and topically arranged to show the general character of the preaching of Jesus. The purport of the injunctions in *vv.* 29 f. is, in Paul's words (Rom. 12^{21}), ' Be not overcome of evil, but overcome evil with good,' which is more than non-resistance. It is the requiting of active enmity with active love. Lk. has first two cases of personal violence. (*a*) The slap on the face. Mt. here is more precise—' the right cheek.' But with a right-handed assailant the first blow would normally be on the left cheek of the victim. What is probably meant is a buffet with the back of the hand, which, according to the Mishnah (*Baba Ḳamma* 8^{6}, Danby, p. 343), was a peculiarly insulting assault and punishable by a specially heavy fine. (*b*) Robbery of a garment. Here Mt. pictures a very different case—a legal action. The plaintiff claims the defendant's shirt. According to Jewish law the actual possessor is deemed to have the legal right to the article possessed, and the onus of proof is on the claimant. The injunction given by Jesus then means that the defendant is not to insist on possessor's right, but to surrender the shirt. He is to go farther than that. He is also to give the plaintiff what he has not claimed, and apparently could not claim (Ex. $22^{25\text{f.}}$, Dt. $24^{12\text{f.}}$), the outer garment, a sort of blanket or plaid, which served as clothing by day and bedding by night. G. Kittel thinks that the Mt. version is original, and Lk. an adaptation for Gentile readers who would not understand the technicalities of Jewish law. In Lk. we have the picture of the footpad who snatches the outer garment, and is to be presented with the shirt as well. In either case the issue would be nudism, a sufficient indication that it is a certain spirit that is being commended to our notice —not a regulation to be slavishly carried out. But this fact does not entitle us to evade the demand, which is here put forward in an extreme case. What Jesus here says is seriously, even if not literally, meant; and His followers have the task of manifesting the spirit of the injunction in the varied situations which arise in actual life.

In *v.* 30 two fresh cases are dealt with, the beggar and the borrower. The followers of Christ are to be sensitive to the plight of the poor and needy, and their sympathy is to be practical. Lk.'s ' everyone ' may be his own. It does not appear in Mt.; and, as it is a favourite word with that evangelist, it is unlikely that he would have left it out, had it stood in Q. The second half of the injunction is a little obscure. In Mt. 5^{42} we have a command not to repulse a borrower. This looks like an attempt to interpret what is given in Lk. It may be that the meaning here is: When someone has borrowed your property, do not be constantly dunning him to let you have it back. In all these transactions delicacy and consideration of the feelings of the other man are essential. Cf. *Ecclus.* 20^{15}: ' To-day he lendeth, to-morrow he will demand it back : hateful is such an one.'

31. All that has been said so far can be summed up in the Golden Rule, which is now given in its positive form. The change from singular to plural is to be noted. The Lucan form is more original than that in Mt. 7^{12} (see above, pp. 310 f.). Mt. adds the comment : ' For this is the law and the prophets.' He does the same kind of thing in Mt. 20^{40}||Mk. 12^{31}. The Rule appears in the negative form in *Tobit* 4^{15} : ' What thou hatest, do to no man.' Hillel, who belonged to the generation before Jesus, gave as the essence of the Jewish Law the precept : ' What is hateful to thee do not to anyone else,' adding ' this is the whole Law and the rest is commentary ; go and study.' This negative form also appears in some MSS. in Acts 15^{28} and in the *Didache* (1^2). In the *Letter of Aristeas* § 207 we have advice to a king in these terms: ' As thou desirest that evils should not befall thee, but to partake of all that is good, thou shouldst act in this spirit to thy subjects and to offenders, and shouldst very gently admonish such as are virtuous; for God draws all men (to Him) by gentleness ' (Thackeray's transl.). Here we approach the positive form. The question whether the positive form states a higher moral ideal than the negative is one of little moment. The Rule as Jesus gives it is a rule of thumb for the purpose of guiding those who already accept the fundamental principles of love to God and love to neighbour when they are puzzled about what to do for the best in particular cases. What is important is that for Jesus these two great principles and this rule supersede all other rules and regulations, and are a complete and sufficient equipment for the adventure of good living. (See further my *Teaching of Jesus*, pp. 302–308.)

Additional Note

In his *Rabbinic Literature and Gospel Teachings*, pp. 103 f., Dr. C. G. Montefiore says : ' I would not cavil with the view that Jesus is to be regarded as the first great Jewish teacher to frame such a sentence as : " Love your enemies, do good to them who hate you, bless them that curse you, and pray for them who ill-treat you " (Lk. $6^{27, 28}$). Yet how much more telling his injunction would have been if we had had *a single story* about his doing good to, and praying for, a single Rabbi or Pharisee! One grain of practice is worth a pound of theory. . . . But no such deed is ascribed to Jesus in the Gospels. Towards his enemies, towards those who did not believe in him, whether individuals, groups, or cities (Matt. 11^{20-24}), only denunciation and bitter words! The injunctions are beautiful, but how much more beautiful would have been a *fulfilment* of those injunctions by Jesus himself.'

This criticism raises the whole question of Jesus' consistency, how far His life answers to His own demands. This question cannot be properly discussed or finally settled on historical grounds, because we have not the materials. But on the point raised by Dr. Montefiore the following observations may be made:

(1) The bulk of the material which has gone to make our Gospels was collected together at a time when the relation between the Jewish religious leaders and the

Church was one of hostility. The former recognised in the new faith a threat to all that they held dear, and they did their utmost to put down what was, from their point of view, a dangerous heresy. There was thus everything to induce collectors of traditions about Jesus to select those stories which showed Rabbis and priests in an unfavourable light, and to leave on one side tales which showed Jesus in a benevolent attitude towards the enemies of the Church. Indeed, it is not, I think, improbable that sayings of Jesus have been made sharper and more bitter in the process of tradition by reason of this bitterness between Synagogue and Church.

(2) Much of the denunciation in the Gospels comes under the heading of prophetic indignation. Much of it is directed, not so much against persons as against abuses in the system. In trying to find the personal attitude of Jesus to the Rabbi or Pharisee from the Gospels, we are in much the same position as if we had to discover from Hansard's reports of debates on matters of critical importance the personal relation of statesmen to one another.

(3) From what we are told in the Gospels it appears that Jesus found that the most urgent need was among another class of people than the Rabbis and Pharisees. He was known as the friend of publicans and sinners, doubtless because He gave them the first claim on His time and strength.

(4) While it is true that Jesus defended Himself with vigour when He was attacked, it must be admitted that many of His denunciations are the answer, and we must maintain the proper answer, to criticisms levelled from the Pharisaic point of view at His teaching and practice. Where a scribe came to Him in a friendly spirit and with a desire to find truth, he received friendly and generous treatment (Mk. 12^{28-34}). If we have a story of how Jesus publicly rebuked one synagogue-ruler (Lk. 13^{15-17}), we read also of the raising of the daughter of Jairus.

(5) If it is right to quote Mt. 11^{20-24} as showing the indignation of Jesus at the refusal of the Galilean towns to receive His message, it is equally legitimate to quote Lk. 13^{34} and Lk. $19^{41\,ff.}$ as evidence of the real feelings of Jesus in the face of opposition and enmity.

To sum up, I should say that, taking such evidence as we have, it suggests that the opportunities for the kind of thing that Dr. Montefiore desiderates were few, partly because Jesus gave Himself so much to the service of those who needed help more than the Rabbis and Pharisees, partly because when He did come into contact with the Rabbis and Pharisees, His first task was commonly to defend Himself against their criticisms. Secondly, even if there were stories of friendly contacts, their chance of survival in the formative period of the tradition would be small. And thirdly, we have evidence that behind the indignation of Jesus at the rejection of His message there is a deep disappointment and sorrow.

(*c*) Imperfect and Perfect Love (75)

MT. $5^{46,\,47,\,44,\,45,\,48}$

5 46 For if ye love them that love you, what
reward have ye? do not even the[1] publicans
47 the same? And if ye salute your brethren
only, what do ye more *than others*? do not
even the Gentiles the same?

LK. 6^{32-36}

6 32 And if ye love them that love you, |what
thank have ye? |for even sinners love those
33 that love them.||And if ye do good to them
that do good to you, | what thank have ye?
34 |for even sinners do the same.||And if ye

44 Love your enemies. . . .
45 that ye may be sons of your Father which
is in heaven : for he maketh his sun to rise
on the evil and the good, and sendeth rain
48 on the just and the unjust. Ye therefore
shall be perfect, as your heavenly Father is
perfect.

[1] That is, *collectors or renters of Roman taxes:* and so elsewhere.

lend to them of whom ye hope to receive, |
what thank have ye? |even sinners lend to
35 sinners, to receive again as much.||But
love your enemies, and do *them* good, and
lend, [1] never despairing ;||and your reward
shall be great, |and ye shall be sons of the
Most High: |for he is kind toward the un-
36 thankful and evil.||Be ye merciful, even as
your Father is merciful.

[1] Some ancient authorities read *despairing of no man.*

In this passage the kind of love demanded by Jesus is further defined. First it is distinguished from the kind of human affection and benevolence which rests largely upon a more or less enlightened self-interest, and finds its proverbial expression in such sayings as ‘ Dog does not eat dog ’ or ‘ Honour among thieves ’ (32–34). Genuine love is purged of selfishness and considers only the need of its objects, not their attitude to the giver, nor their deserts. In this respect it is akin to God's love (35 f.). In Lk. the poetic structure is again visible. In Mt. the sayings have been rearranged and abbreviated, and other matter has been incorporated with them. It is quite possible that the amount of other matter in Mt. outweighs what has been taken from Q.

32–34. Three verses with a recurring refrain in the middle of each. The ordinary sort of relation established on the level of ‘ One good turn deserves another ’ is all very well, but there is nothing in it to deserve the special approval of God. The word rendered ‘ thank ’ in R.V. is the regular word in the LXX for the approbation and goodwill of a superior, especially the approval and favour of God. ‘ Sinners ’ is a term of wide application in later Judaism. The opposites ‘ righteous ’ and ‘ sinners ’ are common in the Psalms and later literature. The ‘ righteous ’ are those who know and keep the Law: ‘ sinners ’ are those who either do not know it (e.g. the Gentiles, cf. Gal. 2^{15}) or who, knowing it, cannot or will not obey its provisions. For ‘ sinners ’ Mt. has ‘ publicans ’ (5^{46}) and ‘ Gentiles ’ (5^{47}). The word here translated ‘ Gentiles ’ occurs three times in Mt., but not in Mk. or Lk.; and the collocation of ‘ publican ’ and ‘ Gentile ’ is found again in Mt. 18^{17}.

35. The new standard of goodness must rise above the ‘ fifty-fifty ’ level. Love must be given where none is given in return, benefits conferred where none are deserved, loans must be made when lending seems to be throwing good money after bad. The words ‘ never despairing ’ do not mean ‘ never despairing of getting your money back.’ They apply to all three injunctions and mean the same thing as Paul's ‘ Let us not be weary in well-doing ’ (Gal. 6^{9}), or ‘ Be ye stedfast, unmoveable, always abounding in the work of the Lord, forasmuch as ye know that your labour is not in vain in the Lord ’ (1 Cor. 15^{58}). The way of Jesus may seem to be useless, even futile, when judged by immediate results; but it must be persevered with in the faith that it is God's way. Those who so persevere will have their reward in the approval of God, if not in the thanks of men. More than that, they will have that approval in its highest form; God will recognise them as His sons, for something of His own nature will be reflected in them. The name here used for God ‘ The Most High ’ is, as a Divine proper

name, peculiar to Lk. ($1^{32, 35, 76}$, 6^{35}) and Acts (7^{48}). It is used as an adjective 'the most high God' in Mk. 5^7 = Lk. 8^{28}; Acts 16^{17}; Heb. 7^1. It is common in later Jewish writings—Ecclesiasticus (about 50 times), Daniel, *Enoch*, *Jubilees*, and 4 *Ezra* (68 times in chs. 3–14). It was a term admirably fitted to form a bridge between Judaism and the higher Greek religion, between the one Lord of Jewish monotheism and the First Principle of Greek thought. To the Jew it expressed the ideas of the supremacy and omnipotence of God. The corresponding verse in Mt. has 'your Father which is in heaven' a characteristic Matthæan and Jewish term. Of the two Lk. is the more likely to be original. On the verse as a whole cf. *Ecclus* 4^{10} (Hebrew).

> 'Be as a father to orphans, and in place of a husband to widows;
> Then God will call thee "son," and will be gracious to thee, and deliver thee from the Pit.'

For 'Then God will call thee "son"' the Greek version has 'And thou shalt be as a son of the Most High.'

36. The motive and driving power for this way of living is now stated. It is the imitation of God. This way is right and good because it is God's way. He is kind to those who deserve no kindness. (Mt. 5^{45} expresses this in a different and probably independent form.) But it is not mere imitation of a Divine standard set up, so to speak, in heaven. It is the reproduction, in daily life and in relations with other men, of something which has come down to earth and touched our own lives. We are to copy this god-like way—and are able to do so—just because we have experienced its working ourselves. We love, because He first loved us (1 John 4^{19}). For 'merciful' (Lk.) Mt. has 'perfect.' In favour of the former is the fact that in the Old Testament the epithet 'merciful' is given to God, hardly ever to man; and the epithet 'perfect' to man, never to God. As God is the standard of comparison, we expect a recognised *Divine* attribute to be mentioned. On the Merciful as a name for God see Dalman, *Words of Jesus*, p. 204. On the imitation of God as a Jewish ideal see Abrahams, *Studies in Pharisaism and the Gospels*, ii. 138 ff.

(*d*) Justice and Mercy (76)

MT. $7^{1, 2}$	LK. $6^{37, 38}$
7 1 Judge not, that ye be not judged. 2 For with what judgement ye judge, ye shall be judged: and with what measure ye mete, it shall be measured unto you.	6 37 And judge not, and ye shall not be judged :| and condemn not, and ye shall not be condemned:||release, and ye shall 38 be released:|give, and it shall be given unto you;||good measure,|pressed down, shaken together,||running over,|shall they give into your bosom.||For with what measure ye mete| it shall be measured to you again.||

37, 38. On the rhythmical structure of Lk. $6^{37 f.}$ see Burney, *The Poetry of our Lord*, pp. 114 and 123. The parallel in Mt. is shorter; but the longer version in Lk. shows the poetic form and is probably the original. It also links up better with the thought of the preceding passage. The singling out of God's mercy as the attribute which is to be the model for human conduct leads naturally to the question how the misdeeds of others are to be treated. We are to return good for evil; but surely we are not to condone the evil. Even if we forgive the offence, we must surely condemn it. Jesus says it is not our business to sit in judgement on our neighbours. The whole business of judging persons is in God's hands, for He alone knows the secrets of men's hearts. This does not mean that we are not to use all the moral insight we possess in order to discover what is right and wrong; but that we are to confine ourselves to that field and refrain from passing judgement on persons. For our judgement is itself a factor in shaping their lives, and a harsh judgement may help a fellow-creature on the road to perdition. ' Give a dog a bad name—and hang him.' ' Release ' in this context may mean ' acquit ' or ' forgive.' The former sense is scarcely appropriate since man is not to sit in judgement at all, either to condemn or to acquit. For the sense ' forgive ' we may compare Mt. 18^{27}, where the verb is used of remitting a debt. And as debt is a common figure for sin, the transition from the idea of cancelling a debt to forgiving an offence is an easy one. And this brings us back to the positive demand to give. Not content with cancelling the debt, the merciful man makes a further gift to the debtor: so the merciful man not only forgives the wrong, he goes farther and shows kindness to the wrongdoer. And in so doing he finds favour with God. ' They ' is probably—as in the Rabbinic literature—a way of referring to God. ' Good measure, pressed down, shaken together, running over ' is a figure drawn from the corn-market where corn is being sold by measure. We are told that the corn-merchants in Egypt still use Arabic terms corresponding to those in Lk., when commending their wares to a prospective customer. They offer corn at so much a measure ' shaken, pressed together, overflowing.'[1] ' Bosom ' means the fold formed by a loose garment overhanging a girdle. This was often used as a pocket (Plummer). There is in the picture of the packed and overflowing measure the idea of a kindness on God's part that will go far beyond the kindness of man, so that even a little kindness on man's part meets with a lavish reward from God. For the measure that man uses with his fellows is the measure that God will use with him. (Another version of this saying, Mk. 4^{24}.)

These illustrations are drawn from the law-court and the market-place; but the thing they illustrate is not a legal or a commercial relation between God and man or between man and man. What underlies all that Jesus here says is a simple and fundamental spiritual law. ' Forgive and you will be forgiven: condemn and you will be condemned ' is not tit for tat, but the expression of the truth that nothing more surely shuts out a man from love than a censorious and unforgiving disposition. He who will not forgive closes his own heart against God's forgiveness. He who despises and hates his fellow-man closes his own heart against God's love.

[1] I am indebted for this information to Mr. G. Swan, Superintendent of the Egypt General Mission.

(*e*) A Collection of Parables (76–78)

MT. 15^{14}, $10^{24, 25a}$	LK. $6^{39, 40}$
15 14 Let them alone: they are blind guides. And if the blind guide the blind, both shall fall into a pit. **10** 24 A disciple is not above his [1] master, 25*a* nor a [2] servant above his lord. It is enough for the disciple that he be as his [1] master, and the [2] servant as his lord. [1] Or, *teacher*. [2] Gr. *bondservant*.	**6** 39 And he spake also a parable unto them, Can the blind guide the blind? shall they 40 not both fall into a pit? The disciple is not above his [1] master: but every one when he is perfected shall be as his [1] master. [1] Or, *teacher*.

The section Lk. 6^{39-49} consists of a series of parables all of which, except these first two, have parallels in Mt.'s Sermon on the Mount. The fact that Mt.'s parallels to Lk. $6^{39\,f.}$ are in a different context casts some doubt on the right of these verses to a place here, the more so as they come somewhat awkwardly between the exhortations about judging and the parable bearing on the same topic (Lk. $6^{41\,f.}$). On the other hand, it may be said that Mt. 15^{14} is an obvious insertion in the place where it stands. It is not even connected with the M material which immediately precedes it. And Mt. $10^{24\,f.}$ equally is part of an artificial construction made by the first evangelist; and, where it stands the point of the saying is that the disciple need not expect to fare any better than his master. It is possible that both Mt. 15^{14} and $10^{24\,f.}$ belong to M rather than Q. The question whether Lk. $6^{39\,f.}$ should be regarded as Q or L will then depend on whether it can be shown to fit into its present context.

39, 40. The question form (Lk.) is probably the original rather than the assertion (Mt.). In Mt. the saying is made to refer to the Pharisees. Cf. Mt. 23^{16} (M) where the Scribes and Pharisees are called 'blind guides.' This reference is not necessarily implied in the saying as it stands in Lk. It is perhaps better to make the connexion with what has gone before in this way: No man is free from sin, and therefore no man has the right to condemn another. But equally no man has the right to dictate to another what is his duty. For one sinner to judge another is a piece of presumption. For one sinner to legislate for another is to court disaster. The only person who is fit to guide others is one who has himself seen the light. The only true teacher is he who has first been taught of God. This prepares the way for the claim that where such a teacher appears he is to be heard with respect. One who is thus inspired is not on the same level as other men. He is not there to be argued with, but to reveal spiritual truth. Those who hear him are not superiors to whom he submits his opinions for approval, but pupils to whom he declares truth, which they reject at their peril. The most that the pupil can do is, by humbly receiving the truth, and applying it in faith to his own life, to come to see it as truth with something of the same clearness and certainty that the master sees it. This is, in fact, the justification for the authority with which Jesus teaches. He does not say, 'I will undertake to demonstrate,' but 'I tell you; and if you accept what I tell you in humility and trust, you will find for yourselves that it is true.' This verse is then the statement in general terms of a principle, which is presently to be more particularly applied in $6^{46,\ 47-49}$.

(i) *The Mote and the Beam* (76)

MT. 7^{3-5}

7 3 And why beholdest thou the mote that is in thy brother's eye, but considerest not
4 the beam that is in thine own eye? Or how wilt thou say to thy brother, Let me cast out the mote out of thine eye; and
5 lo, the beam is in thine own eye? Thou hypocrite, cast out first the beam out of thine own eye; and then shalt thou see clearly to cast out the mote out of thy brother's eye.

LK. $6^{41, 42}$

6 41 And why beholdest thou the mote that is in thy brother's eye, but considerest not
42 the beam that is in thine own eye? Or how canst thou say to thy brother, Brother, let me cast out the mote that is in thine eye, when thou thyself beholdest not the beam that is in thine own eye? Thou hypocrite, cast out first the beam out of thine own eye, and then shalt thou see clearly to cast out the mote that is in thy brother's eye.

This parable takes up the thoughts just enunciated. It is directed to those who, themselves sinners, presume to sit in judgement on and to correct their fellows. The agreement in language between Mt. and Lk. is close. The parable is frankly hyperbolical. One utter absurdity is exposed by another. Cf. Mk. 10^{25} (Camel and eye of needle) and Mt. 23^{24} (Gnat and camel). The mote and beam recur in another connexion in a saying of R. Tarphon (*c.* A.D. 100), who said: 'I should be surprised if there were anyone in this generation who would accept correction. If one says to a man, "Remove the spelk from your eye," he will reply, "Remove the beam from yours."' The figure may belong to a Jewish proverbial saying, which has been used independently by Jesus and Tarphon, or it may be that the saying of Tarphon is a piece of anti-Christian polemic, with this parable in view. We know that Tarphon was a strong opponent of the Palestinian Christians. (See Schürer, ii. 444 f.)

41, 42. The mote. The Greek word means any small dry object, a splinter or chip of wood, small twig or the like. The parable starts from the fact that man is by nature quick to perceive and arraign wickedness in other people. The contemplation of human folly and sin, with the aid of a looking-glass, is a less congenial occupation; but very salutary. This truth is a commonplace both in Greek and Hebrew thought. 'It is better to condemn one's own faults than those of others' (Democritus (5th cent. B.C.) fr. 60). Having perceived the shortcomings of our neighbours, we now proceed to put them right. The blind will lead the blind. This zeal for the reformation of others coupled with a serene complacency about one's own life is stigmatised by Jesus as hypocrisy. If the desire for social reformation were really sincere, the reformation would begin at home. It is still the case that our natural inclination is to make ourselves happy and our neighbours virtuous: and the conjecture may be hazarded that the world would be a better and a happier place if we attempted instead to make ourselves better and our neighbours happier. The followers of Jesus certainly have the task of showing the right way to others; but to do that they must first find it themselves. And an essential preliminary to that is to discover where they themselves are at fault. 'First cast the beam out of thine own eye.' A reformed character is the most effective instrument for effecting the reformation of others.

(ii) *Character and Life* (77)

MT. 7^{16-20}

7 16 By their fruits ye shall know them. Do
men gather grapes of thorns, or figs of
17 thistles? Even so every good tree bringeth
forth good fruit; but the corrupt tree
18 bringeth forth evil fruit. A good tree
cannot bring forth evil fruit, neither can a
corrupt tree bring forth good fruit.
19 Every tree that bringeth not forth good
fruit is hewn down, and cast into the fire.
20 Therefore by their fruits ye shall know
them.

MT. 12^{33-35}

12 33 Either make the tree good, and its fruit
good; or make the tree corrupt, and its
fruit corrupt: for the tree is known by its
34 fruit. Ye offspring of vipers, how can ye,
being evil, speak good things? for out of
the abundance of the heart the mouth
35 speaketh. The good man out of his good
treasure bringeth forth good things: and
the evil man out of his evil treasure
bringeth forth evil things.

LK. 6^{43-45}

6 43 For there is no good tree|that bringeth
forth corrupt fruit;||nor again a corrupt
44 tree|that bringeth forth good fruit.||For
each tree is known by its own fruit.||
For of thorns men do not gather figs,| nor
of a bramble bush gather they grapes.||
45 The good man out of the good treasure of
his heart bringeth forth that which is good;
|and the evil *man* out of the evil *treasure*
bringeth forth that which is evil:||for out
of the abundance of the heart his mouth
speaketh.||

The material here given by Lk. is split up and incorporated with other material in Mt. Lk. 6^{43}||Mt. 7^{18}; Lk. 6^{44a}||Mt. 12^{33b}, cf. Mt. $7^{16a, 20}$; Lk. 6^{44b}||Mt. 7^{16b}; Lk. 6^{45}||Mt. $12^{35, 34b}$. Mt. 7^{16-20} is attached to a warning against false prophets (7^{15}) and indicates how they may be distinguished from true. Mt. 12^{33-35} is inserted into Jesus' defence against the charge of casting out demons by Beelzebul. It is curious that in both cases we find expressions borrowed from the preaching of John the Baptist: Mt. 7^{19} = Mt. 3^{10b}, and in Mt. 12^{34} 'Ye offspring of vipers' from Mt. 3^{7}. It is difficult to resist the conclusion that the Q material given here in Lk. has been freely adapted in Mt. to other purposes.

The passage as it stands in Lk. makes a good connexion with what precedes. The influence of a man on his fellows, for better or worse, depends on his life; and the quality of his life depends on his character.

43, 44. The word translated 'corrupt' means properly 'rotten,' 'putrid,' 'rancid.' This cannot be the meaning here, for the fruit of even the worst trees is ripe before it is rotten. Moreover, the same adjective is used in Mt. 13^{48} to describe freshly-caught fish, which would certainly not be rotten, though they might well be unfit for food. It seems therefore that we must understand 'corrupt' to mean something like 'useless,' 'worthless.' This curious use of the Greek word (*sapros*) may be influenced by the fact that the Aramaic verb 'to be evil' (*b'ēsh*) is etymologically identical with the Hebrew verb *bā'ash*, 'to stink.' Also the wild grapes in Isaiah's parable of the Vineyard (Is. $5^{2, 4}$) have a name in Hebrew, which means literally 'stinking things.' We may then perhaps think of the 'corrupt tree' as a wild tree producing fruit—not rotten—but unsuitable for eating because it is harsh and bitter. The transition from this to the next verse is then easy and straightforward. If we cannot distinguish the crab tree from Cox's

Orange by inspection, we have only to try the fruit. The fig and the grape, two of the most highly prized fruits of Palestine, are not gathered from thorn bushes and brambles. So Luke. Mt. 7^{16} has grapes from thorns and figs from thistles. It is worth noting in favour of Mt. that the word translated ' thorn ' here is the word used in the LXX for the ' wild grapes ' of Is. $5^{2, 4}$; and also that the fruit of the thistle bears at least a faint resemblance to a fig. The plants mentioned are typical weeds (Gen. 3^{18}, Hos. 10^{8}), from which no useful produce can be expected.

45. The obvious application of the parable. From the good man a good influence will come. The words ' bringeth forth ' in Mt. and Lk. represent two different Greek words, which are themselves alternative translations of a single Aramaic word, which in this context can best be rendered by ' utters.' The utterances of the man express his character, for speech is the outpouring of what is in the heart. So the Rabbis use the expressions ' What is in the heart is in the heart ' and ' What is in the heart is in the mouth ' for feelings repressed and feelings expressed respectively. The parable has a special application to the man who admonishes and instructs others. If he is not a good man himself, his instruction is worthless, as useless for its purpose as the produce of thorns and thistles for food. If his own character is good, then his words will be the bread of life to others, who receive them and live by them. But given such a teacher, will men act upon his teaching? The experience of Jesus is given in the next verse.

MT. 7^{21}

7 21 Not every one that saith unto me, Lord, Lord, shall enter into the kingdom of heaven; but he that doeth the will of my Father which is in heaven.

LK. 6^{46}

6 46 And why call ye me, Lord, Lord, and do not the things which I say?

The form in Mt. is fuller, but that in Lk. is probably the original. It is more direct and personal, and it links up both with what precedes and what follows. Mt. takes the saying as if it meant that true piety consists in producing good actions, as a good tree produces good fruit. But the tree parable here is not the same as the tree parable in the preaching of John the Baptist. As we have seen, the point here is that good teaching can come only from one who is good at heart. Now Jesus says to His contemporaries: ' You recognise my right to teach, and you pay respect to me by calling me " Lord, Lord "; but you do not act on my teaching.' There are few sadder words in the New Testament than Lk. 6^{46}: and all the pathos has gone in the version given by Mt.

(iii) *Wise and Foolish Building* (78)

MT. 7^{24-27}

7 24 Every one therefore which heareth these words of mine, and doeth them,|shall be likened unto a wise man, which built
25 his house upon the rock:||and the rain descended,|and the floods came,|and the winds blew,| and beat upon that house;| and it fell not:| for it was founded upon
26 the rock.|| And every one that heareth these words of mine, and doeth them not,|

LK. 6^{47-49}

6 47 Every one that cometh unto me, and heareth my words, and doeth them, I will
48 shew you to whom he is like: he is like a man building a house, who digged and went deep, and laid a foundation upon the rock: and when a flood arose, the stream brake against that house, and could not shake it: [1] because it had been well
49 builded. But he that heareth, and doeth

shall be likened unto a foolish man,
27 which built his house upon the sand:||and
the rain descended,|and the floods came,|
and the winds blew,|and smote upon that
house;|and it fell:|and great was the fall
thereof.||

not, is like a man that built a house upon the earth without a foundation; against which the stream brake, and straightway it fell in; and the ruin of that house was great.

[1] Many ancient authorities read *for it had been founded upon the rock;* as in Matt. vii. 25.

This section, which concludes the Sermon both in Mt. and Lk., contains a double parable. The two characters, the wise builder and the foolish, are described in turn and in parallel terms. This duplication is a common feature of the teaching of Jesus. Cf. Mk. $2^{21\,f.}$, 9^{43-48}; Lk. 12^{24-28} = Mt. 6^{26-30}; Lk. 13^{18-21} = Mt. 13^{31-33}; Lk. 10^{13-15} = Mt. 11^{21-23}; Lk. 4^{25-27}, 13^{2-5}, 14^{28-33}, 15^{4-10}; Mt. 13^{44-46}, 23^{16-21}. The parallelism of structure in the two parts of the parable is better preserved in Mt. than in Lk. In Lk. this feature has been sacrificed to the Greek style of the evangelist.

A similar parable is attributed to Elisha ben Abuya (*c.* A.D. 120). It is to the effect that a Jew, who has much knowledge of the Law and many good works, is like a man who lays stone foundations for his house and builds thereon with sun-dried brick. Though floods may come, the house is not affected because its foundations are sound. But the man who has much knowledge of the Law and no good works is like a man who lays foundations of sun-dried brick, and builds thereon with stone. If only a small flood comes, the house collapses because the foundations are not sound.

47–49. Lk.'s ' every one that cometh unto me ' is not strictly relevant to the parable, which is concerned only with hearing and doing. On the other hand, ' a man ' seems better than Mt.'s ' a wise man ' (*v.* 24) and ' a foolish man ' (*v.* 26). The issue shows plainly enough that one is wise and the other foolish; and Mt. is apt to paint the lily. Lk. appears to have elaborated the laying of the foundation. His builder takes great pains to get down to rock. But the point is not the amount of labour expended, but the choice of a suitable foundation. The simpler statement of Mt. is to be preferred, as is also Mt.'s dramatic description of the tempest. ' Because it had been well builded ' (Lk.) misses the point. We are to imagine both houses as equally well built. The only difference is that correctly given by Mt.: one was founded on rock and the other on sand. In his description of the second house and its fate Lk. is briefer. The fuller form in Mt. is more likely to be the original.

The point of the parable lies in the difference between the two foundations: the one sure and stedfast, the other shifting and unstable. All the other features in the two cases are identical. The rock is ' hearing and doing.' The teaching is heard, and accepted, and becomes a firm conviction issuing in action. Such solid conviction makes a stable foundation; it gives unity and consistency to life. The sand is ' hearing without doing.' The teaching is heard; but it is only one among many interests and motives, and there is no solid centre of conviction in the man's life. So in the day of stress and crisis the one man stands firm and the other goes under. What this crisis is we can only conjecture. It may mean one of those times of severe testing, which constantly recur in human history, when men's loyalty to their professed beliefs is tried to the uttermost. Or it may mean the final judgement (cf. 1 Cor. $3^{13\,ff.}$). In favour of the former view are such sayings as Mt. $10^{32\,f.}$ = Lk. $12^{8\,f.}$ (Q); Mk. 13^{13}, etc.

We have already seen reason for thinking that the Temptations are placed in Q after the Messianic prophecy of John in order to bring out the difference between John's conception of the Messiah and that which Jesus held. When we consider the Sermon as a whole, we may well think that its position is also significant, and again by way of contrast with John's preaching. John's sermon begins with a denunciation of his hearers: 'Ye offspring of vipers, who warned you to flee from the wrath to come?' Jesus begins: 'Blessed are ye poor: for yours is the kingdom of God.' Thus at the outset the contrast is stated. For John the coming kingdom means primarily judgement; for Jesus it means primarily deliverance, salvation. For John the God, whose kingdom it is, is inflexible righteousness; for Jesus He is the Father whose nature is to be merciful ($6^{35\,f.}$). The demand of John is for repentance coupled with such reformation of conduct as will satisfy the Judge in the coming assize; the demand of Jesus is that men should show in their hearts and lives that merciful love that is characteristic of God. The most that John can hold out to his followers is escape from the coming wrath; Jesus speaks of the coming kingdom as a gift from God to man, a gift bringing satisfaction and joy to the sons of God.

It is thus quite wrong to say, as is sometimes said, that Jesus merely takes up and carries on the mission of John. His preaching has much in common with John's. There is the same insistence on moral issues in both, the same demand that men should turn from sin to righteousness, from the service of self and Mammon to the service of God, the same sense of the urgency of the message. These things are extremely important; but they are not so important as the points where Jesus differs from John and goes far beyond him. These positive and characteristic features are brought out plainly in the Sermon, and John's preaching, the Temptations, and Jesus' preaching are so placed at the beginning of Q that a reader cannot fail to see the contrast between the best that could be offered under the old order and the new thing that has come into the world with Christ.

4. *THE CENTURION OF CAPERNAUM* (79)

MT. $8^{5-10,\,13}$

8 5 And when he was entered into Caper-
6 naum, there came unto him a centurion,
beseeching him, and saying, Lord, my
[1] servant lieth in the house sick of the palsy,
7 grievously tormented. And he saith unto
8 him, I will come and heal him. And the
centurion answered and said, Lord, I am
not [2] worthy that thou shouldest come
under my roof: but only say [3] the word,
9 and my [1] servant shall be healed. For I
also am a man [4] under authority, having
under myself soldiers: and I say to this
one, Go, and he goeth; and to another,
Come, and he cometh; and to my [5] servant,

LK. 7^{1-10}

7 1 After he had ended all his sayings in the
ears of the people, he entered into
Capernaum.
2 And a certain centurion's [1] servant, who
was [2] dear unto him, was sick and at the
3 point of death. And when he heard concerning Jesus, he sent unto him elders of
the Jews, asking him that he would come
4 and save his [1] servant. And they, when
they came to Jesus, besought him earnestly, saying, He is worthy that thou
5 shouldest do this for him: for he loveth our
nation, and himself built us our synagogue.
6 And Jesus went with them. And when he

10 Do this, and he doeth it. And when
Jesus heard it, he marvelled, and said to
them that followed, Verily I say unto you,
[6] I have not found so great faith, no, not
13 in Israel. . . . And Jesus said unto the centurion, Go thy way; as thou hast believed,
so be it done unto thee. And the [1] servant
was healed in that hour.

[1] Or, *boy.*
[2] Gr. *sufficient.*
[3] Gr. *with a word.*
[4] Some ancient authorities insert *set*: as in Luke vii. 8.
[5] Gr. *bondservant.*
[6] Many ancient authorities read *With no man in Israel have I found so great faith.*

was now not far from the house, the centurion sent friends to him, saying unto
him, Lord, trouble not thyself: for I am
not [3] worthy that thou shouldest come
7 under my roof: wherefore neither thought
I myself worthy to come unto thee: but
[4] say the word, and my [5] servant shall be
8 healed. For I also am a man set under
authority, having under myself soldiers:
and I say to this one, Go, and he goeth;
and to another, Come, and he cometh;
and to my [1] servant, Do this, and he doeth
9 it. And when Jesus heard these things,
he marvelled at him, and turned and said
unto the multitude that followed him, I
say unto you, I have not found so great
10 faith, no, not in Israel. And they that
were sent, returning to the house, found
the [1] servant whole.

[1] Gr. *bondservant.*
[2] Or, *precious to him.* Or, *honourable with him.*
[3] Gr. *sufficient.*
[4] Gr. *say with a word.*
[5] Or, *boy.*

Cf. John 4^{46-53}.

This section raises a number of peculiar problems. (1) It is the only narrative in Q. (2) The agreement between Mt. and Lk. is confined to the dialogue. In the narrative setting the only verbal agreements are in the three words ‘ entered,’ ‘ Capernaum,’ and ‘ centurion.’ (3) The dialogue is a complete and self-contained story apart from the narrative: and the point of it is the saying of Jesus, ‘ I have not found so great faith, no, not in Israel.’ (4) This statement of Jesus implies a ministry that has already lasted some time. Such words are hardly appropriate at the beginning of His mission. (5) Immediately after this saying Mt. has another Q oracle (Mt. $8^{11 f.}$) which has a parallel in Lk. $13^{28 f.}$. These facts suggest some inferences which may now be given in descending order of probability. (1) It is almost certain that the dialogue alone belongs to Q. The narrative framework is supplied independently by Mt. and Lk. (2) The fact that in their narrative settings Mt. and Lk. agree on the place Capernaum suggests that, either in Q or in the tradition of the Palestinian Church, the incident was definitely located in that town. (3) It is possible that this fact is responsible for the present position of the whole story (dialogue + narrative) in Mt. and Lk. A story about a centurion at Capernaum must be placed in the Capernaum period of the ministry. (4) It is possible that the original unexpanded dialogue stood later in Q. (5) It may be conjectured that Mt. $8^{11 f.}$ is, for once, not conflation, but an indication of the original context of the dialogue. If this were so, we should have an excellent connexion between the first three sections of Q and what is now the fifth: John's question to Jesus and Jesus' testimony to John (Lk. 7^{18-35}), where the difference between John and Jesus, which is implicit in the first three sections of Q, is made quite clear and definite.

1–5. Lk. begins by making the connexion between the conclusion of the Sermon and this incident. Mt. inserts the cleansing of the leper (Mk. 1^{40-45})

between the departure from the mountain and the arrival in Capernaum. Mt. makes the centurion approach Jesus in person and state his trouble. Lk. begins with a narrative of the circumstances, describing the illness of the servant and the regard in which he was held by his master. The word used by Lk. means 'slave.' In Mt. 8^{6} the Greek word may mean 'servant' or 'son,' much the same as the English word 'boy.' In John (4^{46}) the invalid is definitely the 'son' of the petitioner. In Lk. 7^{7} the 'slave' of *v.* 2 has become 'boy' as in Mt.: and in *v.* 8 the centurion speaks of his 'slave' as if the slave were another person than his 'boy.' Taking all these facts into consideration, the balance of probability is in favour of 'son' rather than 'slave.' For the phrase 'who was dear to him' (R.V.) offers two alternatives in the margin. The papyri provide numerous examples where the adjective is used to describe soldiers with long and distinguished service, and it has even been suggested that in Lk. 7^{2} the epithet means 'honourable,' and originally belonged to the centurion. As the text stands it doubtless means that the centurion held his slave in high esteem. Lk. having understood 'boy' in the sense 'slave' rather than 'son' produces a reason for the remarkable concern of the master, a concern which would be perfectly natural and would need no explanation, if it was a case of father and son. The centurion does not, as in Mt., come himself to Jesus, but sends first a deputation of Jewish elders with the request that Jesus will come and heal the slave. The elders here are the local magistrates, the leading citizens of the town. It may be noted that the participation of the Jewish elders is hardly consistent with the subsequent statement, 'I have not found such faith in Israel.' The elders come to Jesus and add their own pleas to the centurion's request. The reason for their friendly attitude to the heathen soldier is now given. He has shown a friendly disposition towards Jews and Judaism, and proved his goodwill by building the local synagogue. He is portrayed as one of a very numerous class in this period, Gentiles who were attracted by Jewish monotheism and by the high moral standard of Judaism. Such people were adherents of the synagogue without actually becoming proselytes to Judaism. There are inscriptions from Egypt showing that synagogues were occasionally built by non-Jews; and the Palestinian Talmud has a story of the presentation of a synagogue lamp by a Roman emperor. The ruins of a synagogue at Tell Hum, the probable site of Capernaum, belong to a later period.

6–10. Jesus accedes to the request of the elders and proceeds with them. Near the house they are met by a second deputation, this time composed of the centurion's friends. They are charged with a message from the centurion practically identical with what, in Mt., the centurion himself says to Jesus. The second deputation is an expression of the humility of the man, and this is made explicit in *v.* 7, which has no parallel in Mt. and is not to be regarded as original. The power of Jesus is such that it will be sufficient if He gives the command that the boy should recover. The word 'only' in Mt. 8^{8} is editorial: cf. Mk. 2^{26}, Mt. 12^{4}; Mk. 11^{13}, Mt. 21^{19}; Mk. 13^{32}, Mt. 24^{36}. Lk.'s 'and my servant shall be healed' is literally 'and let my boy be healed,' imperative followed by a jussive, a construction found in Hebrew. The words 'for I also am a man set under authority' are difficult; for the centurion goes on at once to say that he has men under him to whom he gives orders, whereas the opening phrase means one who receives orders. Torrey (*The Four Gospels*, p. 292) tries to get over the difficulty by supposing that the word ' set ' is a misrendering of an Aramaic original, and that the true rendering would be something like ' exercising authority.' This is not convincing, because the word ' set ' occurs only in Lk. Another and perhaps more likely explanation is that there has been confusion of the two senses of the Aramaic preposition *tĕḥōth*. This word means both ' under ' and ' in place of.' What the centurion really said was, ' I am the representative of the government ' or ' the deputy of the commander-in-chief.' This makes sense with what follows and also makes clear the analogy between the centurion's position and that of Jesus. Both are representatives of the king, the centurion of Antipas (probably) and Jesus of God; and both have such authority as belongs to their respective offices. Jesus is deeply impressed by the centurion's saying and utters the comment, ' I have not found such faith, no, not in Israel.' It is now clear what the faith in question is: it is the recognition by the centurion of Jesus as the representative of God, endowed with Divine power and authority. With this comment the original Q section closes. Mt. adds another saying from Q (Mt. $8^{11 \text{f.}}$), which *may* be part of the original context of the passage. Lk. goes on immediately to report the cure. He does not mention any command of Jesus that the cure should take place, unless the comment ' I have not found such faith ' is meant to effect the cure. All that happens is that the messengers have their conversation with Jesus, and, on their return, find the ' slave ' in good health. Mt. (8^{13}) makes Jesus speak the word asked for: ' As thou hast believed, so be it done unto thee,' and the cure takes place forthwith.

The miracle has several features in common with the story of the Syro-Phœnician woman (Mk. 7^{24-30}||Mt. 15^{21-28}). In the one case we have mother and daughter, in the other father and son (probably). In both cases the petitioner is a Gentile; in both Jesus is persuaded to perform the miracle by an apt saying of the petitioner; in both the healing is performed in the absence of the patient (the only two cases of this sort in the Synoptic Gospels); and, curiously, in both the accounts differ widely in the narrative part and agree closely in the dialogue. It is possible, as Dibelius suggests, that the original form of the incident in Mk. 7^{24-30} also contained little more than the conversation between Jesus and the woman.

A similar miracle is related of R. Ḥanina ben Dosa (*c.* A.D. 70). Here the son of Rabban Gamaliel was ill and the Rabban sent two scholars to Hanina to request his prayers. Hanina saw them coming, went up on to the roof of his house and prayed. When he came down he said to the messengers: ' Go, for the fever has left him. . . .' They took careful note of the time, and, on returning home, learned that that was the exact moment at which the fever had left the patient (b. *Berach*, 34b.). Cf. Mt. 8^{13}, ' in that hour,' and John 4^{50-53}.

The most probable conclusion of the whole matter would seem to be that the dialogue is the original kernel, which belonged to Q and probably stood later in the document. This original has been furnished with two different narrative settings, which appear in Mt. and Lk. These narrative settings agree in stating that the cure was effected; and this was probably implied in the original Q story. But the interest of the compiler of Q was not in the cure of the boy, but in the contrast between the faith of the Gentile and the unbelief of Israel. Now if the dialogue with the centurion is out of place here, we again get a good connexion between the Sermon of Jesus and the next Q section, which is John's enquiry from prison and the reply of Jesus. This will give one large block of Q material: (1) the preaching of John comprising exhortation to repentance and Messianic prophecy; (2) the temptations of Jesus in which the current Messianic idea is rejected; (3) the preaching of Jesus displaying a higher morality than John's; and (4) a final settlement of accounts between Jesus and John, in which it is made clear how great John was, and how much greater is the new thing that has come into the world with Jesus.

5. *JOHN AND JESUS: THE FINAL RECKONING*

(*a*) John's Challenge to Jesus (81)

MT. 11^{2-6}

11 2 Now when John heard in the prison the
3 works of the Christ, he sent by his disciples,
and said unto him, Art thou he that
4 cometh, or look we for another? And
Jesus answered and said unto them, Go
your way and tell John the things which
5 ye do hear and see: the blind receive their
sight, and the lame walk, the lepers are
cleansed, and the deaf hear, and the dead
are raised up, and the poor have [1] good
6 tidings preached to them. And blessed is
he, whosoever shall find none occasion of
stumbling in me.

[1] Or, *the gospel*.

LK. 7^{18-23}

7 18 And the disciples of John told him of all
19 these things. And John calling unto him
[1] two of his disciples sent them to the Lord,
saying, Art thou he that cometh, or look
20 we for another? And when the men were
come unto him, they said, John the Baptist
hath sent us unto thee, saying, Art thou he
21 that cometh, or look we for another? In
that hour he cured many of diseases and
[2] plagues and evil spirits; and on many
22 that were blind he bestowed sight. And
he answered and said unto them, Go your
way, and tell John what things ye have
seen and heard; the blind receive their
sight|the lame walk,||the lepers are
cleansed,|and the deaf hear,||the dead are
raised up,|the poor have [3] good tidings
23 preached to them.||And blessed is he,
whosoever shall find none occasion of
stumbling in me.||

[1] Gr. *certain two*.
[2] Gr. *scourges*.
[3] Or, *the gospel*.

The narrative introduction is much longer than in Lk. than in Mt. As Mt. is apt to cut down redundant detail (cf. his treatment of Mk. 5^{21-43}, Mt. 9^{18-26}), it is possible that Lk. 7^{18-20} is original. The words 'in prison' (Mt. 11^{2}) may also belong to Q. Lk. could leave them out because he had already reported the imprisonment of John ($3^{19\,f.}$). Lk. 7^{21} is an editorial insertion to provide the messengers with first-hand evidence. The answer in *vv.* 22 f. is poetry, which Lk. has treated as if it were prose.

18. 'All these things.' If *vv.* 18–20 belong to Q, and if our interpretation of Lk. 7^{1-10} is correct, 'these things' can only be the contents of the Sermon (6^{20-49}). The contrast between that and the preaching of John is sufficiently violent to call forth the question: 'Art thou he that cometh?' The coming one, according to John, was to execute judgement: Jesus comes preaching mercy and loving-kindness. This is the falsification of John's predictions.

19–23. The two disciples have a parallel in Mk. 6^{7}, 11^{1}, and in the story of R. Hanina (above, p. 357). It may be doubted whether 'the Lord' stood in Q. It is a favourite title of Jesus in Lk. 'He that cometh' refers back to John's own preaching (Lk. 3^{16}||Mt. 3^{11}). The implication of the question is that John has already entertained the idea that Jesus may be the fulfilment of his prophecy; but that what he now hears causes him to have serious doubts. The kind of Messiah that John has in mind would not behave like this. The messengers bring the question to Jesus, who at once, according to Lk., proves His title by performing a series of miracles. This is just the sort of sign which Jesus elsewhere refuses to give. In Mt. this section from Q is brought into the story at a later stage when a sufficient number of miracles have already been related in the ordinary course of the narrative. It is difficult to believe either that *v.* 21 stood in Q or that it corresponds to the facts. The real answer of Jesus is not a sign, but a reiteration of what He stands for. It is cast in poetic form (cf. Burney, *The Poetry of our Lord*, p. 117); and is expressed in terms reminiscent of the great promises in Isaiah (cf. Is. 26^{19}, $29^{18f.}$, $35^{5f.}$, 61^{1}). The point of this declaration lies in the deliberate contrast between it and the preaching of John. John looked for the destruction of the morally unfit. Jesus affirms that His business is not the destruction of such people, but their restoration to moral health. 'They that are whole need not the physician, but they that are sick.' Jesus thus in effect answers John's question by saying: 'Yes—but not the kind that you expected.' He adds to this words which mean: 'Do not be distressed if things are not turning out in accordance with your plan.'

(*b*) Jesus' Testimony to John (82) (65)

MT. $11^{7-11, 16-19}$

11 7 And as these went their way, Jesus
began to say unto the multitudes concerning John, What went ye out into the
wilderness to behold? a reed shaken with
8 the wind? But what went ye out for to
see? a man clothed in soft *raiment*? Behold,
they that wear soft *raiment* are in kings'
9 houses. [1] But wherefore went ye out? to
see a prophet? Yea, I say unto you,
10 and much more than a prophet. This is
he, of whom it is written,

Behold, I send my messenger before thy face,
Who shall prepare thy way before thee.

11 Verily I say unto you, Among them that
are born of women there hath not arisen
a greater than John the Baptist: yet he
that is [2] but little in the kingdom of
heaven is greater than he.
16 But whereunto shall I liken this generation? It is like unto children sitting
in the marketplaces, which call unto
17 their fellows, and say, We piped unto
you, and ye did not dance; we
18 wailed, and ye did not [3] mourn. For
John came neither eating nor drinking,

LK. 7^{24-35}

7 24 And when the messengers of John were
departed, he began to say unto the multitudes concerning John, What went ye out
into the wilderness to behold? a reed
25 shaken with the wind? But what went ye
out to see? a man clothed in soft raiment?
Behold, they which are gorgeously apparelled, and live delicately, are in kings'
26 courts. But what went ye out to see? a
prophet? Yea, I say unto you, and much
27 more than a prophet. This is he of whom
it is written,

Behold, I send my messenger before thy face,
Who shall prepare thy way before thee.

28 I say unto you, Among them that are born
of women there is none greater than John:
yet he that is [1] but little in the kingdom of
29 God is greater than he. And all the
people when they heard, and the publicans, justified God, [2] being baptized with
30 the baptism of John. But the Pharisees
and the lawyers rejected for themselves the
counsel of God, [3] being not baptized of
31 him. Whereunto then shall I liken the
men of this generation, and to what are

19 and they say, He hath a [4] devil. The
Son of man came eating and drinking,
and they say, Behold, a gluttonous man,
and a winebibber, a friend of publicans
and sinners! And wisdom [5] is justified
by her [6] works.

[1] Many ancient authorities read *But what went ye out to see? a prophet?*
[2] Gr. *lesser.*
[3] Gr. *beat the breast.*
[4] Gr. *demon.*
[5] Or, *was.*
[6] Many ancient authorities read *children*: as in Luke vii. 35.

32 they like? They are like unto children
that sit in the marketplace, and call one
to another; which say, We piped unto you,
and ye did not dance; we wailed, and ye
33 did not weep. For John the Baptist is
come eating no bread nor drinking wine;
34 and ye say, He hath a [4] devil. The Son
of man is come eating and drinking; and
ye say, Behold, a gluttonous man, and a
winebibber, a friend of publicans and
35 sinners! And wisdom [5] is justified of all
her children.

[1] Gr. *lesser.*
[2] Or, *having been.*
[3] Or, *not having been.*
[4] Gr. *demon.*
[5] Or, *was.*

This section is marked by close verbal agreement between Mt. and Lk. It falls into two parts: (i) Lk. 7^{24-28}, containing the testimony proper, and (ii) 7^{31-35} grim comment on the reception given to John and Jesus. These two parts are separated in Lk. by a statement that John was accepted by the common people and rejected by the recognised exponents of piety and morality ($7^{29 f.}$). In Mt. there is at this point a passage about John (Mt. 11^{12-15}). The first half of it is perhaps Q; it has a parallel in Lk. (Mt. $11^{12 f.}$||Lk. 16^{16}). The rest appears not to belong to this source. It is of course possible that Mt. 11^{12-15} comes from M. What is reasonably certain is that it did not stand in Q at this point. For Lk. 16^{16} stands in a group of disconnected oracles, and it is not credible that Lk. would have removed it from its place here, where it would fit admirably, to another place, where it has no proper context at all. It is much more likely that Mt. has provided the detached saying with an appropriate setting.

24–26. 'Were departed' (Lk.), 'went their way' (Mt.), is a very common translation variant. Jesus, having justified His own way to John, now proceeds to justify John to the people. The wilderness was the place of John's preaching (Mk. 1^4). 'What did you go out into the wilderness to see? A reed shaken by the wind? Surely not.' The point of this first suggestion may be understood in the light of a Rabbinical saying (b. *Ta'anith* 20a): 'Man should strive to be tender like the reed and not hard like the cedar.' The meaning is that the reed gives to every wind that blows, the cedar does not. The question then means: 'Did you expect to find the Baptist a complaisant, easy-going person? Of course you did not. Indulgence was the last thing you would expect from him.' Then the reference to soft apparel becomes clear. (The wearers of it are in kings' courts; but John is in the king's prison.) Just as John had no mercy on others, so he had no mercy on himself. His austerity was austerity all round. He was neither self-indulgent nor indulgent to other people. He was a prophet of the same kind as Amos.

27. But John is more than a prophet. He is a prophet in the fullest sense, and something more. This is explained by the quotation from the Old Testament, which follows. Under the influence of statements, such as Mt. 11^{14}, which identify John with Elijah, the text quoted here is usually taken to be from Mal. (3^1), where the return of Elijah is prophesied ($4^{5 f.}$). The quotation re-

appears in Mk. 1^{2} in almost identical words. There it is combined with Is. 40^{3}. The text of Malachi, however, differs considerably from the text quoted in Q:

Mal. 3^{1}. Behold I send my messenger, and he shall prepare *the* way before *me*.

Lk. 7^{27}. Behold I send my messenger *before thy face*, who shall prepare *thy* way before *thee*.

Ex. 23^{20} (LXX). And behold I send my messenger before thy face, that he may guard thee in the way.

In Malachi, and in *Ecclesiasticus* (48^{1-11}), the messenger (= Elijah) is the forerunner of God Himself, and there is no idea of a Messiah. In John's preaching John is the forerunner of the Messiah, and there is no suggestion that John identifies himself with Elijah. In the Pseudepigrapha the place of Elijah in the last days is taken by others, and he plays no distinctive part. In the popular expectation in the days of Jesus, as reflected in Mk. 8^{28}, 9^{11-13}, John 1^{21}, the return of Elijah was looked for; but Mk. 8^{28} is clear evidence that John was not identified with Elijah. In Rabbinic speculation[1] there are three Elijah doctrines: (*a*) Elijah belongs to the tribe of Gad. He prepares the way for God and is the redeemer of Israel. This view is a development of that in *Ecclus.* 48. It does not have much influence on Rabbinic thought. (*b*) Elijah belongs to the tribe of Benjamin. He is the forerunner of the Messiah, and his principal task appears to be the announcement of the good news of the Messiah's coming. (*c*) Elijah belongs to the tribe of Levi. He is the High Priest of the Messianic age. He is thus a colleague of the Messiah rather than his forerunner. In the early Christian speculation both Elijah and Moses have a rôle in the last days. The belief in a return of Moses could be based on Dt. $18^{15, 18}$, 34^{10}. Moses appears with Elijah in the Transfiguration scene; and the two witnesses in Rev. 11^{3-13} are probably Moses and Elijah (see Charles, *Revelation*, i. 281). 'The prophet' (John 6^{14}, 7^{40}) is perhaps a reference to the second Moses promised in Dt. 18. Cf. also John 1^{21}, where the Baptist is asked, 'Art thou Elijah?' and 'Art thou the prophet'; and Mk. 8^{28}, 'one of the prophets.' In this maze of conflicting views it is difficult to arrive at any satisfactory conclusion. The identification of John with Elijah is stressed especially in Mt. It is denied absolutely in John, where the Baptist himself is made to reject the identification (John 1^{21}). This is very strange if the identification was known to have been made by Jesus Himself. It is also very strange that Jesus should make a quotation which agrees word for word with the LXX version of Ex. 23^{20} in its first part, and with nothing in the Old Testament in its second part. One solution, proposed by J. Weiss and accepted by Merx, is that *v.* 27 is an interpolation in Lk. For this there is a certain amount of textual evidence. Its removal still leaves an excellent connexion between *v.* 26 and *v.* 28. It would then be likely that it did not stand in Q. Its place in Mt., which is textually secure, could be explained by the supposition that it belonged to the collection of 'testimonies' of which Mt. made use. Its presence in the MSS. of Lk. would be due to early assimilation to Mt. In favour of this hypothesis is the fact that the same text has found its way into Mk. 1^{2}, where it makes nonsense. The reason why the identification of John with Elijah

[1] See the account given by Billerbeck, *Kommentar*, iv. pp. 781–798.

was stressed, and that particularly in Mt., may be found in Justin's *Dialogue with Trypho* (§§ 8, 49, 110), where Justin has to meet the objection from the Jewish side that the true Messiah must be anointed and proclaimed as such by Elijah.

If, then, *v.* 27 does not belong to Q, what is meant by saying that John is a 'prophet—and more'? The natural interpretation appears when we look at John's work. For he did not only prophesy: he also acted. He announced the coming of 'the stronger one,' and he actively prepared a people for the approaching crisis. He is John the Baptist rather than John the prophet.

28. 'Verily' in Mt. 11^{11} is probably original, and perhaps also 'prophet' in Lk. John is the greatest man that ever lived—outside the Kingdom of God. This saying implies that the kingdom is in some real sense a present reality, and bound up with Jesus and His followers. For we cannot suppose that the words are meant to exclude John from the coming Kingdom altogether. There is a distinction between the Kingdom as it is revealed in the present age in Jesus and those who follow Him, and the Kingdom as it is to be fully realised in the future. John does not belong to the former; but he has his share in the latter. The least in the Kingdom—in its present manifestation—is greater than John, not by what the least in the Kingdom does for God. John set up a record of devotion and self-sacrifice not easy to be equalled, much less surpassed. Where the least in the Kingdom has the advantage is in what God does for him here and now. The real parallel to John in the Old Testament is not Elijah but Moses. Just as Moses led the children of Israel to the borders of the Promised Land, but could not himself enter, so John led his followers up to the verge of the new order initiated by Jesus, but could not himself enter. He was the last and greatest of the heroes of faith, who looked for 'the city that hath foundations, whose builder and maker is God,' who died without receiving the promises.

29 f. These verses are not part of the testimony of Jesus to John, nor of Q. They may be from Lk.'s special source or they may be comment of his own. Cf. Mk. 11^{27-33} and parallels, and Mt. 21^{28-32}. For the collocation of Pharisees and lawyers see Lk. 11^{37-52}. The curious expression 'justified God' occurs frequently in the *Psalms of Solomon* (2^{16}, 3^{5}, 4^{9}, $8^{7, 27, 31}$, 9^{3}). It means that they acknowledged God to be in the right, when they confessed their sins and were baptized. The Pharisees and lawyers, who rejected John's baptism, tried to put themselves in the right against God. 'For themselves': perhaps the Aramaic ethic dative, best left untranslated.

31 f., 33–35. The whole matter is rounded off with a parable, whose point is the unresponsiveness of men to any sort of high religious appeal. The way of John is too strait and the way of Jesus too lax for their taste. The parable of the children in the market-place, who will play neither weddings nor funerals, is perfectly simple and obvious. The ascetic discipline of John is rejected as madness. The same criticism was also passed on Jesus Himself (Mk. 3^{22}), and, at a later date, on Mohammed (cf. Muir, *The Life of Mohammad* (1923), p. 48). It is a quick and easy way of dealing with such troublesome persons. 'The Son of Man' here is obviously meant to refer to Jesus Himself. It is probable that the phrase here, both in Mt. and Lk., rests on a misunderstanding of an Aramaic idiom in which the phrase 'that son of man' = 'that man' is used as a periphrasis for the

first personal pronoun (see *The Teaching of Jesus*, pp. 217 f.). 'Glutton and winebibber' need not be understood in the sense that the life of Jesus was a round of feasting. So far as the Gospels go, they do not suggest anything of the sort. Possibly the real offence was not the occasional feasts, but the failure to observe the fasts prescribed by Pharisaic piety (cf. Mk. $2^{18\,ff.}$). 'Friend of publicans and sinners' was true enough. But the quality of the friendship was determined by Jesus and not by the publicans and sinners. It raised them without lowering Him. Nevertheless there were doubtless many in that generation who were prepared to be convinced that a man is known by the company he keeps; and could not perceive that this very friendship lay at the heart of the Gospel (Mk. $2^{15\,ff.}$). Yet in spite of indifference and opposition, both John and Jesus had found a response from the common people, who regarded John as a prophet (Mk. 11^{32}) and heard Jesus gladly (Mk. 12^{37}). They repented at the preaching of John (Lk. 7^{29}; Mt. $21^{31\,f.}$) and they accepted the friendship of Jesus. The wisdom of God was justified by results. As the text stands in Mt. and Lk., the results may be thought of as things accomplished, 'works' (Mt.), or as the people who have been changed for the better, 'children' (Lk.). It is, however, possible, as Lagarde suggested, that behind the two words lies a common Aramaic original. The point of the saying is not affected in any case; for it is simply that while the failure of both John and Jesus with one section of the community is a fact, it is also a fact that both John and Jesus found a response in another section, and that this response is itself a proof that the work of both was part of God's plan. The baptism of John *was* from heaven, and so is the good news, for which it paved the way and by which it is superseded.

With this testimony to John the first main section of Q comes to an end. In it the contrast is drawn, not between the Law and the Gospel, but between Prophecy and the Gospel. For John is not a scribe, but the greatest of the prophets. And, like most of the prophets, he is a lonely figure. He was admired, respected, reverenced, and feared. One wonders whether he was loved. He made every effort and every sacrifice in the service of his calling. He achieved much, yet somehow not enough. 'The least in the Kingdom of God is greater than he.' It is only on the background of the Gospel that we can see the magnificence of his failure. As against those who rejected him John was in the right. He was justified by those who repented at his call. But his message was not the Gospel, and in these Q passages the difference between John's prophetic message and the Gospel of Jesus is set forth. John's Messianic ideal is rejected; instead of the ruler and judge of his expectation there comes one who is first and foremost God's servant among men. John's message is 'Save yourselves from him that cometh.' He comes, and it appears that His business is to save men from themselves. With that something better than righteousness is given, and this is set out in the Sermon, with its insistence on the merciful love of God as the ground of man's hope and the norm of man's life. With the manifestation of this love in the world the Kingdom has in a real sense come and John's prediction is at once fulfilled and falsified.

B. JESUS AND HIS DISCIPLES

1. *CANDIDATES FOR DISCIPLESHIP* (138)

MT. 8^{19-22}

8 19 And there came [1] a scribe, and said unto
him, [2] Master, I will follow thee whither-
20 soever thou goest. And Jesus saith unto
him, The foxes have holes, and the birds
of the heaven *have* [3] nests; but the Son of
21 man hath not where to lay his head. And
another of the disciples said unto him,
Lord, suffer me first to go and bury my
22 father. But Jesus saith unto him, Follow
me; and leave the dead to bury their own
dead.

[1] Gr. *one scribe.*
[2] Or, *Teacher.*
[3] Gr. *lodging-places.*

LK. 9^{57-62}

9 57 And as they went in the way, a certain
man said unto him, I will follow thee
58 whithersoever thou goest. And Jesus said
unto him, The foxes have holes, and the
birds of the heaven *have* [1] nests; but the
Son of man hath not where to lay his head.
59 And he said unto another, Follow me.
But he said, Lord, suffer me first to go and
60 bury my father. But he said unto him,
Leave the dead to bury their own dead;
but go thou and publish abroad the king-
61 dom of God. And another also said, I
will follow thee, Lord; but first suffer me
to bid farewell to them that are at my
62 house. But Jesus said unto him, No man,
having put his hand to the plough, and
looking back, is fit for the kingdom of God.

[1] *Gr. lodging-places.*

The next five sections of Q all have to do with discipleship: its conditions, its duties, its privileges. The conditions are defined in this section by particular examples of would-be disciples who come to Jesus. Only two of Lk.'s three cases have parallels in Mt. It is therefore possible that Lk. $9^{61f.}$ comes from L rather than from Q. Where Mt. and Lk. are parallel the agreement is close in the dialogue, but not in the narrative setting.

57, 58. The scene is the road with Jesus and others making a journey by land. In Mt. the interview takes place when Jesus is on the point of embarking on a boat. For Lk.'s 'a certain man' Mt. has the more definite 'a scribe'; and this scribe addresses Jesus as 'Master.' The differences serve to show that most probably the dialogue is the whole of the original tradition. The would-be disciple anticipates a possible 'Follow me' (cf. Mk. $1^{17, 20}$, 2^{14}) by himself offering to follow Jesus. The reply of Jesus is in effect: 'Count the cost.' It is metaphorically expressed, and opinions differ as to the meaning of the terms employed. The view that *v.* 58 is a popular proverb put into the mouth of Jesus may be dismissed. Proverbs, in order to survive, must contain some element of truth: and this proverb is required to say that man, in contrast to foxes and birds, has no home; which is plain nonsense. For man, of all the living creatures, has provided himself with the most elaborate and permanent lodgings. A second possibility is that 'Son of Man' is here, as in Lk. 7^{34}, a periphrasis for 'I.' This is not, I think, likely. We require an interpretation which will give point to the strange conjunction of foxes and birds, as well as to the phrase 'Son of Man.' Now as an apocalyptic symbol the birds of the air stand for the Gentile nations, and the phrase is used again in this sense by Jesus in the parable of the Mustard Seed (see below, p. 415). In *Enoch* (89) 'foxes' is a symbol for Ammonites, a people racially akin to, but politically enemies of Israel. Jesus Himself uses the epithet 'fox' of Herod (Lk. 13^{32}). Then the sense of the saying may be: everybody is at home in

Israel's land except the true Israel. The birds of the air—the Roma
the foxes—the Edomite interlopers, have made their position secur
Israel is disinherited by them: and if you cast your lot with me and m
the ranks of the dispossessed, and you must be prepared to serve God
conditions.

59, 60. Mt. and Lk. again differ over the setting of the saying.
gives His call, and the prospective disciple asks for a short postponem
a disciple asks leave to go first and bury his father. The word ' first
awkwardly in Mt.'s account. Of the two, Lk.'s account is to be pref
duty of giving decent burial to the dead ranked high among the Jews
and more especially in the case of near relatives. But the claims of t
of God take precedence of all others. Mt. gives the words ' Follow m
reply to the request. They are more in place where Lk. has them.
' Leave the dead to bury their own dead ' seems harsh, and it has been
get over this by supposing a mistaken rendering of the Aram
Jesus really said was something like ' Leave the dead to the bu
(see Abrahams, *Studies in Pharisaism and the Gospels*, ii. 183 f.).
this is that the son himself would be the natural and proper pers
burial of his father. Nor is it likely that there is a distinction in
the dead who are to bury and those who are to be buri
spiritually dead, the latter the physically dead. The u
way of saying: ' That business must look after itself; y
work to do.' What the more important work is is exp
clause, which has no parallel in Mt., probably does no
mand is ' Follow me,' not—or at any rate not yet—' Go

61 f. With this third case compare the call of Elisha (1 Kings 19[19-]
was less exacting than Jesus. The position is that the business of the K
God is urgent (Lk. 10[2]). The little parable about the plough would b
an agricultural community. ' Fit for the Kingdom of God ' means he
tasks, rather than worthy of its rewards.

In all three cases it is emphasised that the way of discipleship, or th
the Kingdom, is not an easy thing. It offers no obvious advantages, a
extremely exacting demands. Those, therefore, who would attach th
Jesus must count the cost of their allegiance; they must be prepared
hardship; they must be willing to sacrifice their own feelings; they
absolute priority to the work of the Kingdom, and give themselves
perfect singleness of purpose.

2. *THE MISSION CHARGE* (139) 109 5

The mission of the disciples is one of the best-attested facts in the li
There is an account of the sending out of the Twelve in Mk. (6^{6-13}); it is
the agreements of Mt. and Lk. that Q contained a mission charge; the
the long composite address in Mt. 9^{37}-10^{42} shows that it contains ma
from Mk. and Q, and also from M, which must also have had a ver
mission charge. Lk. has two missions and two mission charges. T

derived from Mk. 6^{6-13}. The second (10^{1-16}) contains matter which
, be assigned to Q, and other matter which we shall see reason to
The mission charge is thus attested by all the sources. For the
analysis it will be convenient to consider the whole block, Lk. 10^{1-20}.
-point is the observation (Bussmann, *Synoptische Studien*, ii. 64) that the
2^{35} refers back to the mission charge. Now 22^{35} stands in a context
1 Luke's special source. The inference is that this source also con-
count of the mission charge. If Lk. has preserved anything of the L
hould expect to find it in 10^{1-20}. We should not expect to find any
erial in this section, since that is already used fully in Lk. 9^{1-6}. If, then,
reason to suppose that Lk. 10^{1-20} is composite, it will be a compound of

Lk. 22^{35} we read: 'When I sent you forth without purse, and wallet,
acked ye anything?'; and here in 10^{4} 'carry no purse, no wallet, no
rrespondence in the two lists is very striking, the more so as
...ent. Moreover, the word here translated 'purse' occurs
New Testament, all in Lk. Next we observe that Lk. 10^{8} is
of *vv.* 6 f., and that *vv.* 8–12 form a unity by themselves. The
from these facts, coupled with what we otherwise know of
t *vv.* 4–7 form an extract from L. We need have no
and 13–16 to Q; and probably *vv.* 8–12 are also from
...her L or an editorial introduction by Lk., with the
in favour of the former alternative; for in 17–20
, and, as 17–20 most probably comes from L, it
There seems no good reason why Lk. should have
e mission ... ty-two. It is more probable that he found the
o in his source L and that the fact that seventy-two missioners were
was an indication to him that this was a separate mission from that
Mk. This does not, of course, dispose of the question whether there was
re than one mission. It still remains possible that the mission of the
o in L is a doublet of the mission of the Twelve in the other sources.
of the analysis then is that we assign to Q *vv.* 2, 3, 8–12, 13–16, and to
, 17–20. It may be ...ed that the amount of agreement between Mt.
the ground covered by Lk. 10^{4-7} is exceedingly small.

(*a*) The Commission

MT. $9^{37\,f.}$, 10^{16a}.	LK. $10^{2\,f.}$
1 saith he unto his disciples, The t truly is plenteous, but the ers are few. Pray ye therefore the f the harvest, that he send forth ers into his harvest. 1, I send you forth as sheep in the of wolves.	**10** 2 And he said unto them, The harvest is plenteous, but the labourers are few: pray ye therefore the Lord of the harvest, that he send forth labourers into his harvest. 3 Go your ways: behold, I send you forth as lambs in the midst of wolves.

introductory words in Mt. are more likely to represent Q than those in
as 'he said unto them,' because the audience has already been described
. The saying is the best explanation of the sayings in the preceding

section of Q. The seeming harshness of Jesus and His almost brutal thrusting into the background of natural feelings and obligations are due to the overwhelming urgency of His task. The King's business requires haste. He leaves no room for the kind of selfishness that takes shelter behind the plea that charity begins at home. Moreover, the demands which He makes are not His only: they are God's. The right to demand such sacrifices and the power to make them can come only from God. It is God who must send out the labourers to do God's work. And that the messengers chosen by Jesus are bidden to pray is an indication that the prayer is to be, in the first instance, one of self-dedication to God's will, cf. Is. 6[8].

3. The figure is abruptly changed. In the Apocalyptic literature (*Enoch* 90[6-17]) the lambs are a symbol for the *Ḥăsīdīm*, those in Israel who, in times of persecution and defection, had remained loyal to the Faith. 'Sheep' in Mt. 10[16] is a translation variant (see the Greek versions of Lev. 3[7], 2 Sam. 6[13]). 'Go
your ways' is probably original, perhaps omitted by Mt. be[illegible]aic, and that what
discourse he has a great deal more to say, and the dism[illegible]ier of their dead'
The task of the disciples is not going to be easy. The king[illegible] The objection to
belong is one to which the kingdoms of the world are hostile. [illegible]n to see to the
expect better treatment from the Herods and the Cæsars [illegible] meaning between
from Antiochus. [illegible]d, the former being the
[illegible]terance is a paradoxical
[illegible]ou have more important
[illegible]ained by Lk. This extra
[illegible]t belong to Q. The com[illegible]
[illegible] and preach.' [illegible]

(*b*) Missionary M[illegible]

Cf. Mt. 10[11a, 7, 8, 14, 15].
Cf. Mk. 6[10f].

MT. 10[15].

10 15 Verily I say unto you, It shall be more tolerable for the land of Sodom and Gomorrah in the day of judgement, than for that city.

10 8 they [illegible]
9 s[illegible] that are
th[illegible] them, The kingdom
10 of God is come nigh unto you. But into whatsoever city ye shall enter, and they receive you not, go out into the streets
11 thereof and say, Even the dust from your city, that cleaveth to our feet, we do wipe off against you: howbeit know this, that
12 the kingdom of God is come nigh. I say unto you, It shall be more tolerable in that day for Sodom, than for that city.

8 f., 10 f., 12. Mt. at this point is an elaborate conflation of material borrowed from Mk., Q, and M, and parallels with Lk. are confined to single words and phrases, except for Mt. 10[15]. The directions fall into two parts. (i) Procedure where the reception is friendly: accept their hospitality in the spirit in which it is offered. This is not the time to raise questions about whether, for example, tithe has been given from the food offered, or whether it is ritually clean. There are more important things to do. Then also do for them what lies in your power—heal their sick. And, what is the *raison d'être* of the mission, proclaim the Kingdom as a present reality, which has come near and touched them in the person of its members, in their power to help and heal, and in the message itself. The whole of the dealings of the messengers with the people, to whom they come, are to be a manifestation of the Kingdom in its grace and saving power. (ii) Where the reception is unfriendly, no time is to be wasted. The disciples are to pass on to

more promising fields. But before going away they will publicly and solemnly disclaim all responsibility for the consequences of that city's refusal to hear their message. The significance of the ritual of wiping the feet before leaving the city is that the city is reckoned as heathen, and its inhabitants as no part of the true Israel, even though it is a city of Israel and its people Jews by birth. Cf. the notes on John's baptism (Lk. 3^{16}, above, pp. 332 f.). The Kingdom has come near to them and they have rejected it. Their blood will be upon their own heads in the coming judgement, and the disciples are relieved from responsibility. Cf. Ezek. 3^{16-21}. For ' that day ' Mt. 10^{15} has ' the day of judgement,' a phrase which does not occur in Mk. or Lk. It is probably an editorial explanation. For ' Sodom ' (Lk.) Mt. has ' land of Sodom and Gomorrah,' which is doubtless an editorial expansion to bring the saying into closer agreement with the Old Testament story. In Rabbinical usage it is Sodom alone that is singled out as a type of obstinate wickedness. (See the passages collected by Billerbeck, *Komm.* i. 572 ff.) Rabbinical belief excluded the people of Sodom and Gomorrah from any part in the life to come.

The instructions given in this section are clearly coloured by the belief that the final crisis is imminent. This is why the missionaries are not to waste time. They are few, and the ground to be covered is great, and the time is short. It is greatly to be feared that with the abandonment of the belief in the imminent end of the world, the sense of the urgency of the preaching of the Kingdom has been lost; that, hypnotised by the idea of progress, we should forget that there is such a thing as repentance.

(*c*) The Woes on the Galilean Cities

MT. 11^{20-24}

11 20 Then began he to upbraid the cities
wherein most of his [1] mighty works were
21 done, because they repented not. Woe
unto thee, Chorazin! woe unto thee,
Bethsaida!||for if the [1] mighty works had
been done in Tyre and Sidon which were
done in you,||they would have repented
22 long ago in sackcloth and ashes.||Howbeit I say unto you, it shall be more tolerable for Tyre and Sidon in the day of
23 judgement, than for you.||And thou,
Capernaum, shalt thou be exalted unto
heaven? thou shalt [2] go down unto
Hades:||for if the [1] mighty works had
been done in Sodom which were done
in thee,|| it would have remained until
24 this day.||Howbeit I say unto you, that it
shall be more tolerable for the land of
Sodom in the day of judgement, than
for thee.||

[1] Gr. *powers*.

[2] Many ancient authorities read *be brought down*.

LK. 10^{13-15}

10 13 Woe unto thee, Chorazin! woe unto
thee, Bethsaida! for if the [1] mighty works
had been done in Tyre and Sidon, which
were done in you, they would have repented long ago, sitting in sackcloth and
14 ashes. Howbeit it shall be more tolerable for Tyre and Sidon in the judge-
15 ment, than for you. And thou, Capernaum, shalt thou be exalted unto heaven?
thou shalt be brought down unto Hades.

[1] Gr. *powers*.

The woes on the Galilean towns are not strictly relevant to the work of the disciples, and it is noteworthy that Mt. does not include them in his account of

the mission charge. In his arrangement they come between the testimony of Jesus to John (11^{7-19}) and the Doxology (11^{25-27}). In Lk. also the next Q section is the Doxology ($10^{21f.}$). It is therefore possible that the original order of Q was Lk. $10^{2f., 8-12, 16, 13-15, 21f.}$, and that *v.* 16 and *vv.* 13–15 have changed places in Lk.'s editing. The saying about the fate of recalcitrant cities in *v.* 12 would tend to attract *vv.* 13–15; and it may be urged that *v.* 16 would come more effectively after *v.* 12. than after *v.* 15. If that is so, then the introduction in Mt. 11^{20} may be from Q. The fuller form of the second oracle as given in Mt. $11^{23f.}$ deserves the preference over the shorter form in Lk. It preserves the strophic parallelism, which is so characteristic a feature of the teaching.

13, 14. 'Woe unto thee,' rather 'Alas for thee.' Chorazin is not mentioned elsewhere in the Bible, nor in Josephus. The solitary reference in the Talmud is textually uncertain. The place is identified with the present-day *Chirbet kerāze*, about 3 miles N. of *Tell ḥūm* (Capernaum). Bethsaida on the E. side of the Jordan, near its entry into the Sea of Galilee, christened Julias by Herod Philip in honour of the daughter of Augustus. It is identified with *et-tell*, about 5 miles from Capernaum. The mention of the mighty deeds done in these two places shows vividly what gaps there are in the story of the ministry. There is no account whatever in the Gospels, apart from this mention, of any visit of Jesus to Chorazin. Yet activity there must have been, and that of such a sort that it would have brought the heathen cities, Tyre and Sidon, to repentance. Sackcloth is mourners' garb. The ashes were either sprinkled on the head of the mourner (so apparently Mt.), or the mourner sat in them (so Lk.). Tyre and Sidon will be more leniently dealt with in the judgement, because they have not had the opportunity which Chorazin and Bethsaida have had and rejected.

15. Capernaum was a centre of the Galilean ministry of Jesus. It had had a better chance than most of accepting the message. The rhetorical question and its answer are reminiscent of the taunt-song against the king of Babylon (Is. 14^{13-15}):

'And thou saidst in thy heart, I will ascend into heaven,
I will exalt my throne above the stars of God;
And I will sit upon the mount of Assembly in the uttermost north:
I will ascend above the heights of the clouds; I will be like the Most High.
Yet thou shalt be brought down to Sheol, to the uttermost parts of the pit.'

Unbridled ambition and brazen self-confidence close the door to the messengers of God and open the way to destruction. Capernaum has stood firm, where even Sodom would have wavered in its wicked ways, and this will be in favour of Sodom in the day of judgement.

(*d*) Conclusion of the Mission Charge

(MT. 10^{40})	LK. 10^{16}
10 40 He that receiveth you receiveth me, and he that receiveth me receiveth him that sent me.	**10** 16 He that heareth you heareth me; and he that rejecteth you rejecteth me; and he that rejecteth me rejecteth him that sent me.

Cf. Mk. 9^{37}. Whosoever shall receive one of such little children in my name, receiveth me : and whosoever receiveth me, receiveth not me, but him that sent me.

I am inclined to think—Mk. 9^{36} notwithstanding—that these three are all forms of one and the same original saying. There are certain sayings about the treatment of children (see notes on Lk. 17^{1}, p. 430), and others about the treatment of disciples of Jesus; and there has been a certain amount of confusion in the tradition owing to the fact that Jesus spoke of His disciples as 'children.' It will be observed that these three sayings are all in the same poetic form, which Burney called climactic parallelism. Lk. 10^{16} is to be assigned to Q. About Mt. 10^{40} one may have doubts whether it should be labelled Q or M. It is possible that the original form of the saying was fuller than any of the three existing versions. Perhaps it ran:

He that heareth you heareth me;
[And he that heareth me heareth him that sent me:]
And he that rejecteth you rejecteth me;
And he that rejecteth me rejecteth him that sent me.

The conclusion that all three passages go back to a common original is further strengthened by the observation that the Aramaic verb *qabbēl* means both 'to receive' and 'to hear' in the sense of 'obey.' (Cf. Gen. 3^{17}, Heb. LXX, and Peshiṭta 'hear': Targums 'receive'; similarly Gen. 21^{12}, $23^{6, 8, 13}$). Likewise 'rejecteth' here may be the opposite of 'receive' or 'hear,' that is, it may signify the rejection either of the persons or of their message. (It may be that in Mk. 6^{11} we have side by side alternative renderings of the one Aramaic original in 'not receive you' and 'nor hear you.')

The messengers are, in a sense, the Kingdom of God itself. The solidarity is impressive. The disciple represents in the fullest sense Jesus, and Jesus represents in the fullest sense the Kingdom of God. What they offer is God's offer and what they claim is God's claim. Cf. Mk. 8^{38} where the true text is probably 'me and mine,' i.e. 'me and my disciples,' rather than 'me and my words' [1]; and Mt. 25^{31-46}.

3. *THE PRIVILEGES OF DISCIPLESHIP*

(*a*) The Knowledge of God (141)

MT. 11^{25-27}

11 25 At that season Jesus answered and said,
I [1] thank thee, O Father, Lord of heaven
and earth, that thou didst hide these
things from the wise and understanding,
26 and didst reveal them unto babes: yea,
Father, [2] for so it was well-pleasing in
27 thy sight. All things have been delivered
unto me of my Father: and no one
knoweth the Son, save the Father;
neither doth any know the Father, save
the Son, and he to whomsoever the Son
willeth to reveal *him*.

[1] Or, *praise*.
[2] Or, *that*.

LK. $10^{21f.}$

10 21 In that same hour he rejoiced [1] in the
Holy Spirit, and said, I [2] thank thee, O
Father,|Lord of heaven and earth,|that
thou didst hide these things from the wise|
and understanding, and didst reveal
them unto babes:|yea, Father;|[3] for so it
22 was well-pleasing in thy sight.|All things
have been delivered unto me of my
Father:|and no one knoweth who the
Son is, save the Father;| and who the
Father is, save the Son,|and he to whomsoever the Son willeth to reveal *him*.

[1] Or, *by*.
[2] Or, *praise*.
[3] Or, *that*.

[1] On the text of Mk. 8^{38} see C. H. Turner in *Journal of Theol. Stud.*, xxix. 2 f. Mk. does not use the possessive adjective in the sense 'my,' but always the genitive of the pronoun.

The differences between Mt. and Lk. are very few. The most important is 'knoweth the Son (Father)' (Mt.) and 'knoweth who the Son (Father) is' (Lk.). The phrase 'in the Holy Spirit' is probably Lk.'s own. The clause about the Father's knowledge of the Son is rejected by Harnack and Wellhausen as a very early interpolation. Burney (*The Poetry of our Lord*, 133, 171 f.) found that in Aramaic retranslation the passage 'forms a rhythmical poem which rhymes regularly couplet by couplet.' To carry out the scheme he has to delete the words 'and understanding,' and to add the words 'I give glory to thee' after 'Yea, Father.' The rhythm is three stresses to the line. The passage is full of Semitic turns of phrase, and certainly Palestinian in origin. There is no good reason for doubting its authenticity. (See *The Teaching of Jesus*, pp. 109–112.)

21. 'In that same hour' corresponds exactly to the Rabbinic phrase *bĕʾōthāh shāʿāh*. The phrase 'at that season' in Mt. is one of Mt.'s editorial phrases (cf. Mk. 2^{23} with Mt. 12^{1}, and Mk. 6^{14} with Mt. 14^{1}). 'Thank' here signifies glad acknowledgement of God's goodness and wisdom in ordering His revelation as He ordered it. 'Father' *Abba* without any qualification is Jesus'—not the Jewish—way of speaking to God. (See note on Mt. 6^{9}, below, p. 460.) 'Lord of heaven and earth' is an alternative to the very common Jewish title for God, 'Lord of the world.' What is meant by 'these things' depends on how we understand 'all things' in *v.* 22, and on what we make of the following clauses of that verse. What has been revealed so far in Q is the nature of the Kingdom of God and His righteousness. In Palestine 'the wise' means primarily the learned in the Law. Actually the Rabbis preferred to call themselves 'disciples of the wise'; but that was due to their modesty. 'Understanding': the Greek word here is frequently used in the LXX to translate a Hebrew word meaning 'intelligent,' 'discerning.' So far as it is possible to distinguish between the two words, 'understanding' seems to refer to a quality of mind, a capacity which one has or has not; 'wise' implies the natural gift plus something more added as the result of exercise. The revelation here spoken of has passed by the learned and the clever, and come to the babes, the simple and childlike, the followers of Jesus drawn from the relatively uneducated and unsophisticated. 'For so it was well-pleasing in thy sight' corresponds to a common Jewish phrase.

22. 'All things have been delivered unto me.' The verb 'deliver' is that commonly used of the handing down of knowledge from teacher to pupil (Mk. 7^{13}; Lk. 1^{2}; 1 Cor. $11^{2, 23}$). It can also be used of the handing over of power and authority (Lk. 4^{6}). Here the whole context is in favour of the former sense. The revelation, the complete revelation of God and His purpose, has been entrusted to Jesus. One immediate result is that He holds the revelation not as 'from God' merely, but 'from my Father.' Another result is that He is conscious of being God's chosen instrument for the disclosure of this revelation to others. Nobody knows the Father as He knows Him, and all who are to come to a like knowledge must learn of Jesus. The knowledge of God here spoken of is not abstract theology, the learning of a set of propositions about the nature and attributes of the Deity. It is knowledge of the Father, a new personal relation between God and man, in which all that the Old Testament writers mean by 'knowledge of God' finds full scope and expression. For in Old Testament

ways of speech ' knowledge of God ' stands for a religious activity of man, the joyful discovery and recognition of God and all that God means for man and his life. This is the knowledge that Jesus claims to possess and impart. And if this is right interpretation, it is clear that the text of Mt. ' knows the Father ' is to be preferred to Lk.'s ' knows who is the Father.' It is also probable that the clause about the Father knowing the Son is an interpolation. It is not relevant to the things that are being stated here. The whole passage is concerned with a glorious revelation of God, and the only significance of the Son in this connexion is that He is the first recipient of this revelation and the sole mediator of it to the rest of the world.

(*b*) The Joy of the Kingdom (142)

MT. $13^{16\,f.}$	LK. $10^{23\,f.}$
13 16 But blessed are your eyes, for they see; 17 and your ears, for they hear. For verily I say unto you, that many prophets and righteous men desired to see the things which ye see, and saw them not; and to hear the things which ye hear, and heard them not.	**10** 23 And turning to the disciples, he said privately, Blessed *are* the eyes which see 24 the things that ye see: for I say unto you, that many prophets and kings desired to see the things which ye see, and saw them not; and to hear the things which ye hear, and heard them not.

Mt. has taken this saying and inserted it in a new context, where the understanding of parables is under discussion. This has involved small changes in Mt. 13^{16}, which completely alter the sense. There can be no doubt that Lk. is here more faithful to Q. The alterations made by Mt. bring the saying into closer agreement with the text from Is. $6^{9\,f.}$ quoted in Mt. $13^{14\,f.}$

23, 24. Lk.'s introductory words would seem to belong to Q. They can scarcely be editorial, seeing that almost the same formula is used to introduce the immediately preceding verse. The formula ' Blessed are the eyes . . .' is just a striking way of saying ' Blessed are you.' Cf. Lk. 11^{27}, 23^{29}. The blessedness consists not in the fact that their eyes are open (as in Mt.), but in the fact that there is something to be seen by the open-eyed, the manifestation, namely, of the kingdom of God. This is where the disciples have the advantage over the prophets and the righteous kings of old. They also were looking for something; but they looked in vain, because it was not yet come. In this sense the least of the followers of Jesus is greater than the greatest of the prophets (Lk. 7^{28}). ' Prophets and kings ' (Lk.) is preferable to ' Prophets and righteous men ' (Mt.). The latter collocation is characteristic of Mt. Cf. Mt. 10^{41} (M), 23^{29}.

The point of the saying is that what for all former generations lay still in the future is now a present reality. What was for the best men of the past only an object of faith and hope is now matter of present experience. Anyone who has his eyes open can see the unmistakable signs that the Kingdom has drawn near: anyone who has ears to hear can hear the proclamation of the good news. With this beatitude compare and contrast another, which belongs to the middle of the first century B.C. (*Ps. Sol.* 17^{50}).

> Blessed are they that shall be born in those days,
> To behold the good things which God shall bring to pass in the gathering together of the tribes.

Lk. $10^{23\,f.}$ says that ' those days ' have come; God is bringing the good things to pass, and all who now turn to Him will prove for themselves that it is so. This makes the transition to the next section of Q.

(*c*) Free Access to God (148)

MT. 7^{7-11}

7 7 Ask, and it shall be given you; seek, and
ye shall find; knock, and it shall be
8 opened unto you: for every one that
asketh receiveth; and he that seeketh
findeth; and to him that knocketh it shall
9 be opened. Or what man is there of you,
who, if his son shall ask him for a loaf, will
10 give him a stone; or if he shall ask for a
11 fish, will give him a serpent? If ye then,
being evil, know how to give good gifts
unto your children, how much more shall
your Father which is in heaven give good
things to them that ask him?

LK. 11^{9-13}

11 9 And I say unto you, Ask, and it shall
be given you;|seek, and ye shall find;|
knock, and it shall be opened unto you.||
10 For every one that asketh receiveth;|and
he that seeketh findeth;|and to him that
11 knocketh it shall be opened.||And of which
of you that is a father shall his son ask [1] a
loaf, and he give him a stone?|or a fish,
and he for a fish give him a serpent?|
12 Or *if* he shall ask an egg, will he give him
13 a scorpion?||If ye then, being evil, know
how to give good gifts unto your children,
||how much more shall *your* heavenly
Father give the Holy Spirit to them that
ask him?||

[1] Some ancient authorities omit *a loaf, and he give him a stone? or.*

This passage, which shows close agreement between Mt. and Lk., is in poetic form (cf. Burney, *op. cit.*, pp. 67, 82, 114). The three short (two-stress) lines in *v.* 10 answer to the three lines in *v.* 9; and the triple form is carried into the short parable which follows (*vv.* 11 f.), though here there is serious doubt about the text. The clause about the loaf and the stone is omitted in Lk. by B 1241 Sahidic, MSS. of the Old Latin, Sinaitic Syriac, Armenian, Marcion, and Origen. Many scholars regard it as an assimilation of the text of Lk. to that of Mt. But the question whether it stood in Lk. is distinct from the question whether it stood in Q; and, leaving the text of Lk. on one side, we have three points in the parable. The first is attested by Mt. (and Lk.?), the second by Mt. and Lk., the third by Lk. alone. The evidence for the place of the first point in Q is at least as good as that for the third; and the fact that the poem is in a triple form favours a threefold parable. The only other important difference between Mt. and Lk. is in Lk. 11^{13}, where Lk. has ' the Holy Spirit ' and Mt. ' good things.' The latter is surely the original.

9, 10. The giver is God; and the opener is God. The parallelism requires us to suppose that the finding is also possible only by God's grace. The blessings of the new age are not the fruits of ' progress ' or ' evolution ': they are the result of an act of God in history, His response to human needs and longings. The repetition of the particular injunctions in the form of general truths is another way of saying that this is God's will; this is how God chooses to bestow His benefits. The gifts are not just what may be called spiritual gifts, but all things that the Father sees His children need (cf. Lk. 12^{22-34} Q). The thing to be sought is the Kingdom of God, which, being found, is the satisfaction of all needs (Lk. 12^{31}). The door to be knocked at is the door which gives entrance into the Kingdom of God.

11 f., 13. The situations supposed in the parable are deliberately and frankly

absurd. Each question demands the answer, 'Of course not.' Then follows the conclusion: 'If you, bad as you are, know how to love your children, *a fortiori* God will know how to treat His children.' This is one of Jesus' favourite methods of instruction. He takes human nature at its best and then says: 'God is all that and far more.' The implication, which Jesus here leaves His hearers to draw for themselves, is that if you weak and sinful men are such that your children can bring their requests to you with confidence, how much more can you bring your requests to a Father who is perfect. R.V. in this verse has '*your* heavenly Father,' which is a paraphrase. The Greek text of most MSS. is, literally translated, 'the Father from heaven' where the words 'from heaven' go with 'Father' and not with 'give.' This text can hardly be right, and there is something to be said for Merx's idea that the insertion of the article before 'from heaven' in the Greek MSS. is a Marcionite interpolation. In my opinion the true text of Lk. is 'How much more will the Father give from heaven a Holy Spirit to those who ask Him.' The text of Q was the same except that it had 'good things' as in Mt., which Lk. altered to 'a Holy Spirit.' For the idea of good gifts from heaven, cf. James 1^{17}, 'Every good gift and every perfect boon is from above, coming down from the Father of lights.' It may be added that 'the Father,' which we take as the true text of Lk. and Q here, is true to Jesus' way of speaking about God, and to God.

The conclusion of the whole matter is that disciples may trust God absolutely for all their needs. This trust rests on a twofold basis: the knowledge that God is perfect love, and the knowledge that they are God's servants for whom He takes responsibility. Both these grounds for trust are intimately bound up with the disciples' relation to Jesus. It is through Him that they know the Father, and it is through Him that their call to the service of the Kingdom comes.

Looking back over this second main block of Q material, one feature of it is very striking. That is the order in which the material is presented. It begins by stressing the hardships and difficulties of discipleship, goes on to enlarge upon the tasks, and only at the end does it speak of the privileges and joys. Whatever else Q may be, it is a very honest document.

C. JESUS AND HIS OPPONENTS

1. *THE BEELZEBUL CONTROVERSY* (149) 86

(*a*) THE CHARGE

MT. 12^{22-24}

12 22 Then was brought unto him [1] one possessed with a devil, blind and dumb: and he healed him, insomuch that the
23 dumb man spake and saw. And all the multitudes were amazed, and said, Is
24 this the son of David? But when the Pharisees heard it, they said, This man doth not cast out [2] devils, but [3] by Beelzebub the prince of the [2] devils.

[1] Or, *a demoniac*. [2] Gr. *demons*. [3] Or, *in*.

LK. 11^{14-16}

11 14 And he was casting out a [1] devil *which was* dumb. And it came to pass, when the [1] devil was gone out, the dumb man spake; and the multitudes marvelled.
15 But some of them said, [2] By Beelzebub the prince of the [3] devils casteth he out
16 [3] devils. And others, tempting *him*, sought of him a sign from heaven.

[1] Gr. *demon*. [2] Or, *In*. [3] Gr. *demons*.

Cf. Mk. 3^{20-22}.

This is one of the rare occasions on which Mt. and Lk. show a certain amount of agreement about the narrative setting of a Q passage. They agree that the debate followed on an exorcism performed by Jesus, that the patient was dumb, that the cure was proved by the fact that he could afterwards speak, and that the crowds were astonished. Mt. adds that the man was blind and is then committed to the awkward statement that 'the dumb man spake and saw.' He also has the question of the crowd which is lacking in Lk. In Lk. those who make the accusation are not particularly specified: in Mt. they are the Pharisees: in Mk. 3^{22} they are scribes who have come down from Jerusalem. Mk. does not have the story of the exorcism at all. Instead, the charge is linked up with another story that the opinion was abroad that Jesus was insane. In Mk. 3^{22} these two points are kept distinct: the insult 'He's mad,' and the accusation 'He is in league with Beelzebul'; and the two charges are answered separately, the first in Mk. 3^{28-30} and the second in Mk. 3^{23-27}. In Q the question of Jesus' sanity is not raised at this point, and consequently Mt. in 12^{31-36} is answering a charge that has not, in his account, been made. Lk. in *v.* 16 has the statement that Jesus was also asked for a sign. This request is not dealt with until 11^{29}, an indication that it is not editorial. For Lk. would hardly have inserted here introductory matter to something which was not going to be treated until 13 verses later. Lk. has here been faithful to his source, even though it involved a certain awkwardness in the flow of the narrative. Mt., on the other hand, deserts Q here and makes a fresh start with an introduction of his own at Mt. 12^{38}.

14. The statement that the demon was dumb is more primitive than Mt.'s description (cf. Mk. $9^{17, 25}$). The symptoms of the patient are transferred to the demon who is believed to cause them. When the demon goes out he carries his dumbness away with him.

15. The indefinite subject 'some of them' seems to be the original. The temptation to make the indefinite definite is stronger than that to make the definite indefinite. The terms of the charge are almost identical in all three gospels. That Jesus used black magic continued to be urged from the Jewish side for centuries after this first promulgation of the charge. (Cf. Justin, *Dial.* § 69; Klausner, *Jesus of Nazareth*, pp. 18–54). The name of the chief of the demons offers a complete set of problems of its own. There are three forms in the MSS.: Beelzebub, Beelzebul, and Beezebul. This last is the reading of the Vatican and Sinaitic MSS. and is accepted by W. Foerster as representing the Palestinian pronunciation of the name Beelzebul. The form Beelzebul is the most generally accepted. The name does not occur in Jewish literature, which is surprising. The meaning of the name is disputed (cf. Billerbeck, *Komm.*, i. 631–635). Jewish imagination showed a certain fertility in devising names for the arch-fiend. Thus we get Mastema in *Jubilees*, Sammael in Rabbinic literature, Asmodaeus in *Tobit*, Beliar in *Jubilees*, *Sibylline Oracles*, *Test. XII Patriarchs*, *Ascens. Isaiah*. 'By Beelzebul' is literally 'in Beelzebul,' i.e. 'in the power of' or 'empowered by,' analogous to the phrase 'in the Holy Spirit.'

16. The seekers after a sign did not regard the casting out of demons as convincing; for others besides Jesus could perform this feat (*v.* 19). They ask for something more startling by way of proof. Proof of what? His messiahship?

Or His right to speak and act as He did? The popular view (Mk. 8^{28}) was that He was a prophet, and this is the view that is doubted by the Pharisee in Lk. 7^{39}. Possibly some sign that He was a prophet was asked for, such as was related of Elijah (1 Kings 18^{30-39}) or Isaiah (2 Kings 20^{8-11}).

(*b*) The Reply of Jesus

This is given by all three Synoptics. The disposition of the material is shown in the following table; which, for reasons which will appear, is carried beyond the limits of the reply proper.

MT. 12^{25-37}		MK. 3^{23-30}		LK. 11^{17-23}	
25 f.	Divided kingdom, etc.	23–26.	Divided kingdom, etc.	17 f.	Divided kingdom.
27.	How do your sons do it?		—	19.	How do your sons do it?
28.	If I by the spirit of God . . .		—	20.	If I by the finger of God . . .
29.	The strong man bound.	27.	The strong man bound.	21 f.	The strong man bound.
30.	He who is not with me . . .		—	23.	He who is not with me . . .
31 f.	The unforgivable sin.	28–30.	The unforgivable sin.		—
33.	Tree and fruits.		—		—
34–37.	Character and speech.		—		—
	—		—	24–26.	Return of the ejected demon.
	—	[31–35.	Jesus' true relatives.]	27 f.	Compliment to Jesus' mother.
38.	Demand for a sign (cf. Lk. 11^{16}).		—		—
39 f.	The sign of Jonah.		—	29f.	The sign of Jonah.
41 f.	Men of Nineveh and Queen of Sheba.		—	31 f.	Queen of Sheba and men of Nineveh.
43–45.	Return of the ejected demon (cf. Lk. $11^{24ff.}$).		—		—
46–50.	Jesus' true relatives.	31–35.	Jesus' relatives.	[8^{19-21}.	Jesus' true relatives.]

Lk. 11^{17-26} is, I think, a Q collection of sayings on demons and demon-possession. Verses 17–23 are all more or less relevant to the charge made against Jesus, though actually the first piece (*vv.* 17 f.) is an effective and sufficient reply. *V.* 19 is also a counter to the charge. Verses 20 and 21 f. are relevant, but have more to do with the positive aspects of Jesus' activity against the demons and their head, than with the rebuttal of the accusation. The saying in *v.* 23 winds up the whole series of utterances, *vv.* 17–22, and was doubtless regarded by the compiler of Q as the close of Jesus' reply. Mk. has two elements in common with Q: *vv.* 23–26 and *v.* 27. This is all the Marcan reply to the charge; for *vv.* 28–30 deal with the statement that Jesus was mad. The implication is that the collocation of ' Divided kingdom ' and ' Strong man bound ' is older than Mk. or Q. There is enough agreement of Mt. and Lk. against Mk. in Mt. $12^{25f.}$ and Lk. $11^{17f.}$ to make it probable that this item stood in Q; and the Lucan version of the ' Strong man bound ' is so completely different in wording from the Marcan that the two must be independent. Lk. *vv.* 21 f. may, of course, come from L. It is very remarkable that Mt. 12^{29} shows no trace of agreement with Lk. $11^{21f.}$ against Mk. 3^{27} in a context where Mt. is borrowing freely from Q. If Lk. $11^{21f.}$ is assigned to L, it raises a difficulty. For we have then to assume either that Lk.

by a happy accident hit on this exact point in Q for the insertion of the L passage, or that the arrangement of the material has been influenced by that of Mt. The latter supposition is as near to incredible as makes no matter; and the invocation of happy accidents is to be deprecated. We may therefore, though with some hesitation, assign Lk. $11^{21f.}$ to Q, and assume that the two replies had got together at a stage in the tradition anterior to Mk. and Q.

An interesting point which emerges from the comparison of Mk. and Lk. (i.e. Q) is that 3^{31-35} in Mk. and Lk. $11^{27f.}$ in Q occupy the same relative positions. Both come at the end of a series of sayings on demon-possession. Moreover, they have a common sentiment. 'Whosoever shall do the will of God, the same is my brother, and sister, and mother' (Mk. 3^{35}): 'Blessed are they that hear the word of God and keep it.' This suggests the possibility that Mk. 3^{20-35} was already a closed section before it was incorporated in the Gospel; and that Lk. 11^{17-28} is a similar complete section.

MT. 12^{25-30}

12 25 And knowing their thoughts he said unto them, Every kingdom divided against itself is brought to desolation; and every city or house divided against
26 itself shall not stand: and if Satan casteth out Satan, he is divided against himself;
27 how then shall his kingdom stand? And if I [1] by Beelzebub cast out [2] devils, [1] by whom do your sons cast them out?
28 therefore shall they be your judges. But if I [1] by the Spirit of God cast out [2] devils, then is the kingdom of God come upon
29 you. Or how can one enter into the house of the strong *man*, and spoil his goods, except he first bind the strong
30 *man*? and then he will spoil his house. He that is not with me is against me; and he that gathereth not with me scattereth.

[1] Or, *in*.
[2] Gr. *demons*.

LK. 11^{17-23}

11 17 But he, knowing their thoughts, said unto them, Every kingdom divided against itself is brought to desolation; [1] and a house *divided* against a house
18 falleth. And if Satan also is divided against himself, how shall his kingdom stand? because ye say that I cast out
19 [2] devils [3] by Beelzebub. And if I [3] by Beelzebub cast out [2] devils, by whom do your sons cast them out? therefore shall
20 they be your judges. But if I by the finger of God cast out [2] devils, then is the
21 kingdom of God come upon you. When the strong *man* fully armed guardeth his
22 own court his goods are in peace: but when a stronger than he shall come upon him, and overcome him, he taketh from him his whole armour wherein he
23 trusted, and divideth his spoils. He that is not with me is against me; and he that gathereth not with me scattereth.

[1] Or, *and house falleth upon house*.
[2] Gr. *demons*.
[3] Or, *in*.

17 f. First refutation of the charge. Mk. calls it a parable. Mt. $12^{25f.}$ is a conflation of Mk. and Q. 'Knowing their thoughts' belongs to Q. It does not imply thought-reading; for they had spoken their views (*v.* 15). Jesus saw what they meant: and it was something like this. The sending away of demons is nothing. It could be done by arrangement with their chief. To convince us you must do something which requires *Divine* power. (Cf. Ex. 7^8–8^{19}.) The statement that demons can be cast out in alliance with Satan is answered by the contention that Satan is not such a fool. He has his kingdom; and, like all kingdoms, its strength lies in its unity. Why should Satan raise civil war in his own realm? Lk. appears to have only the one picture. The kingdom in the throes of civil war is laid waste and the houses fall in ruins together (R.V. margin is the literal rendering of the Greek). Mk. and Mt. have the picture of the divided

kingdom and the divided household. There are three possibilities: (1) Supply the word 'divided' as in the R.V. text; (2) assume that R.V. mg. is correct, that there was only one parable, as in Lk., and that the second parable in Mk. and Mt. is a mistaken expansion of a detail in the first; (3) assume that there were two parables and that Lk., by a misunderstanding, has reduced the second to a detail of the first. We have no means of arriving at a sure decision; I prefer (2). Happily the decision of this point does not affect the interpretation of the passage as a whole.

19 f. A further objection, carrying the war into the enemies' camp. Jesus is not the only one who casts out demons. There were also Jewish exorcists. Cf. Josephus, *Ant.* VIII, ii. 5; Billerbeck, *Komm.*, iv. 533 ff.; Acts 19[13] with Lake and Cadbury's notes (*Beginnings of Christianity*, iv. 240). Will the critics of Jesus offer the same explanation of the exorcisms performed by members of their own party? ('Your sons' = your adherents. So the adherents of Hillel are called the 'household of Hillel' = 'school of Hillel'). Jesus does not stay to discuss this point, but goes on to give the true significance of His own exorcisms. They are a manifestation of the Kingdom of God. So far from being signs of an alliance with Satan, they are signs of warfare against him. They are part of the struggle between the Kingdom of God and the kingdom of Satan. 'Finger of God' (Lk.) is the true Q text altered by Mt. to 'spirit of God.' See *The Teaching of Jesus*, 82. For an interesting archæological illustration of this passage and of Ex. 8[19], on which this saying ultimately depends, see Flinders Petrie in *Ancient Egypt*, Sept. 1932, p. 69: 'A wood carving of a finger, springing from a falcon's head. That head was the emblem of Ra and of Horus. . . . Such a symbol as a finger for divine action was familiar in Egypt. . . . No doubt the wooden finger . . . was used in ceremonial and magical acts by the priests.' The finger of God is here a symbol for the might of the Kingdom of God revealed as saving helpless men and women, and destroying the power of Satan. Jesus Himself is the medium through which the power of the Kingdom becomes operative. 'He does not "bring" the Kingdom—a notion entirely strange to Jesus Himself—but the Kingdom brings Him with it' (Otto, *Reich Gottes und Menschensohn*, 80). In one other respect this saying is extremely important. Arbesmann (*Das Fasten bei den Griechen u. Römern*, p. 20) describes the elaborate preparations necessary to fit men for intercourse with the Deity, quoting Porphyry: 'that when they (the evil demons) have departed the Parousia of the god may take place.' This is in sharp contrast with our text, where the exit of the evil spirits is the *result* of the Divine presence, not the *preparation* for it. This is the difference between the Gospel and other religions.

21 f. Another picture of the war between the two opposing kingdoms. It is based on Is. 49[24ff.], an oracle describing Jehovah's deliverance of His people from an enemy, who is described as 'the mighty one.' As retold here the strong man is Satan, who claims sway over the world (Lk. 4[6]). His 'goods' and his 'spoils' (*v.* 22) are his human victims. His 'whole armour' represents the hosts of demons. The stronger one who comes upon him and defeats him is Jesus Himself, as God's representative, armed with divine power. Cf. *Ps. Sol.* 5[4] and the note of Ryle and James.

23. The concluding verse goes closely with *vv.* 21 f. The situation is one where no man can be neutral. It is war to the knife between the Kingdom of God and the kingdom of Satan. Jesus is God's chosen instrument for the waging of that war. He who takes his place by the side of Jesus, takes his place in the army of God. He who ignores the summons, is reckoned to the enemy. Cf. Lk. $9^{49 f.}$ for the other side of the picture. On gathering and scattering, cf. *Ps. Sol.* 17^{28}, 'And he (the Messiah) shall gather together a holy people, whom he shall lead in righteousness'; and 4^{13} 'He (the wicked) never ceaseth to scatter and bereave.' The Kingdom of God is the one constructive unifying redemptive power in a distracted world; and every man has to choose whether he will take sides with it or against it.

(*c*) A Saying on Demon-possession (150)

MT. 12^{43-45}

12 43 But the unclean spirit, when [1] he is gone out of the man, passeth through waterless places, seeking rest, and findeth
44 it not. Then [1] he saith, I will return into my house whence I came out, and when [1] he is come, [1] he findeth it empty,
45 swept, and garnished. Then goeth [1]he, and taketh with [2] himself seven other spirits more evil than [2] himself, and they enter in and dwell there: and the last state of that man becometh worse than the first. Even so shall it be also unto this evil generation.

[1] Or, *it*.
[2] Or, *itself*.

LK. 11^{24-26}

11 24 The unclean spirit when [1] he is gone out of the man, passeth through waterless places, seeking rest; and finding none, [1] he saith, I will turn back unto my house
25 whence I came out. And when he is come, [1] he findeth it swept and garnished.
26 Then goeth [1] he, and taketh *to him* seven other spirits more evil than [2] himself; and they enter in and dwell there: and the last state of that man becometh worse than the first.

[1] Or, *it*.
[2] Or, *itself*.

The charge of casting out demons by Beelzebul has been more than adequately dealt with in the foregoing verses. This piece stands here in Q because it deals with exorcism, and presumably it was convenient for purposes of instruction to have it along with kindred matter. Mt., who doubtless saw that it was not strictly relevant to the Beelzebul controversy, has removed it to a place after the speech against the sign-seekers; and his closing words 'Even so shall it be also unto this evil generation' are modelled on phrases in the Q passage on sign-seeking, e.g. Lk. 11^{30}. The agreement between Mt. and Lk. is close.

24–26. 'Unclean spirit' represents one of the Jewish synonyms for 'demon.' The whole description is in terms of Jewish beliefs about demons and demon-possession which Jesus shared with His contemporaries. The waterless places, i.e. the desert, are the natural home of demons. But the ejected demon is no longer content with a bedouin life. He wishes himself back in his old quarters enjoying a settled life. A visit of inspection shows that they have been cleaned and decorated. Mt. has the further detail that they are vacant. This ascertained the demon collects seven others, worse than himself, and together they take possession. It may be assumed that the demon does not bring the seven others out of sheer benevolence. The idea is rather that the eight of them will be better able to resist a second exorcism than one alone.

The meaning of the whole seems to be that exorcism by itself is not sufficient. The expulsion of the demon and the restoration of the victim to his normal condition leaves things exactly as they were before the demon first took possession. If the demon is to be kept out something more must be done than can be done by a mere exorcist. Now Jesus claims that His ejection of demons is not mere exorcism, but a manifestation of the Kingdom of God. It is the power of God that expels the demon. Then God must take possession of the vacant dwelling. The former house of the demon must become God's property, what Paul calls (1 Cor. 3^{16}) 'a temple of God,' the dwelling-place of the Holy Spirit. Cf. 2 Cor. 6^{16}; Eph. 2^{22}. In modern language the old obsessions, complexes, morbid fears and desires, and so on must be replaced by new loyalties and affections. The man whom God has delivered must give himself, body, soul, and spirit, to God and the service of His Kingdom.

2. *FLATTERY REBUKED* (151)

LK. $11^{27 f.}$

No parallel in Mt.

Cf. Mt. 12^{46-50} = Mk. 3^{31-35}.

11 27 And it came to pass, as he said these things, a certain woman out of the multitude lifted up her voice, and said unto him, Blessed is the womb that bare thee, and the breasts which thou didst suck.
28 But he said, Yea rather, blessed are they that hear the word of God, and keep it.

27, 28. On the relation of this section to the foregoing see above, p. 377. The introductory words in *v.* 27 are editorial. The formula is characteristically Lucan. It connects this incident in time and place with the preceding controversy; but the probability is that we have here a separate incident, and that such connexion as there is is topical rather than real. The exclamation of the woman is a common form of compliment when one wishes to be specially complimentary. Cf. Gen. 49^{25}; Mishnah, *Aboth*, 2^{8} (Danby, p. 448); other Rabbinic examples are given by Billerbeck (ii. 187 f.). In particular it is said of the Messiah that when he comes people will say 'Blessed is the womb from which he came forth' (*Pesiḳta*, ed. Buber, 149*a*). The response of Jesus is curt. For 'yea rather' 'Nay rather' would be better. The force of the Greek is something like 'So *you* say: (but) I say.' For the thought cf. Mk. $3^{34 f.}$; Lk. 6^{46}||Mt. 7^{21}; Lk. $6^{47 ff.}$||Mt. 7^{24-27}; Rom. 2^{13}; John 13^{17}. Jesus was not deluded by people who made pious noises, and He brought them back to realities by the shortest possible route. A similar case is Lk. 14^{15} and the following parable of the Great Feast. (See below, pp. 420 ff.)

The incident has a certain connexion with what has gone before, in particular with *v.* 23. There Jesus makes His demand for decision for or against Him, which is the same thing as for or against the cause of God's Kingdom. Here He is offered fine words. But fine words are not an adequate response to His demands. Decision is not just saying 'Lord, Lord,' but doing what He says.

3. *AGAINST SIGN-SEEKERS* (152)

(*a*) The Sign of Jonah

Mt. 12^{38-40}

12 38 Then certain of the scribes and Pharisees answered him, saying, [1] Master, we
39 would see a sign from thee. But he
answered and said unto them, An evil
and adulterous generation seeketh after
a sign; and there shall no sign be given
to it but the sign of Jonah the prophet:
40 for as Jonah was three days and three
nights in the belly of the [2] whale; so
shall the Son of man be three days and
three nights in the heart of the earth.

[1] Or, *Teacher*.
[2] Gr. *sea-monster*.

Lk. $11^{29 f.}$

11 29 And when the multitudes were gathering together unto him, he began to say,
This generation is an evil generation: it
seeketh after a sign; and there shall no
sign be given to it but the sign of Jonah.
30 For even as Jonah became a sign unto
the Ninevites, so shall also the Son of
man be to this generation.

Cf. Mk. 8^{11-13}||Mt. 16^{1-4}.

In Mk. $8^{11ff.}$ the request for a sign comes from the Pharisees, whom Mt. (16^1) turns into Pharisees and Sadducees. Here Mt. gives an introduction in which certain of the scribes and Pharisees are the petitioners. The true Q introduction is most probably to be found in Lk. 11^{16}. Then Mt. 12^{38} may be regarded as editorial; and the narrative introduction in Lk. 11^{29} comes under suspicion.

29, 30. The desire for a sign is a desire for something stupendous. This demand for a convincing display of supernatural power is said by Paul to be the characteristic feature of Judaism (1 Cor. 1^{22}). The construction in Lk. suggests that this seeking after a sign is an indication of the wickedness of the generation. In Mt. it seems rather that such an evil generation has no right to expect a sign. Mt. describes the generation as 'evil and adulterous' (Lk. 'evil' alone) which may be original. 'Adulterous' is used, as often in Old Testament prophecy, in the sense of 'unfaithful to God,' 'apostate.' This meaning would be unfamiliar to Gentile readers, and Lk. may have dropped the word for that reason. In Mk. the request for a sign is met by a flat refusal. In Q a sign is offered—from ancient history. Jonah was a sign to the Ninevites: so the Son of Man will be a sign to this generation. How? This question arises for us on the assumption that Lk. 11^{30} is genuine Q and a genuine word of Jesus. One answer to the question is offered in Mt. 12^{40}. The analogy between Jonah and the Son of Man is that Jonah prefigures the descent of Christ to Hades and His return from the abode of the dead. Or so it seems. It is then possible to object that Mt. 12^{40} is prophecy after the event and represents not a word of Jesus, but a reflection of the Christian community on the word more accurately preserved in Lk. 11^{30}. In support of this it is urged that the Ninevites knew nothing of Jonah's submarine adventures, and that he appeared before them as a preacher of repentance in face of coming judgement. The preaching of Jonah is the sign. This criticism of Mt. 12^{40} is at first sight plausible: it is, however, open to one very serious objection. Jonah was certainly inside the great fish for three days and three nights (Jon. 1^{17}). But the whole early Christian tradition (Mt. included) is unanimous on the point that Jesus was buried on a Friday afternoon and rose again on a Sunday morning. He was in the grave for three days—if we count Friday and Sunday as days—and *two* nights. We are thus faced with a supposed prophecy after the event, which begins by falsifying the event—a somewhat strange phenomenon.[1] It may, however, be pointed out that in Mt. 4[13] Capernaum, which lay in the old tribal territory of Naphtali, is assigned to Zebulun and Naphtali in order to give point to the following quotation from Isaiah. It is possible that the author of Mt. 12[40] thought that his account was near enough to the facts. If then we dismiss Mt. 12[40] as early Christian explanation of Lk. 11[30] (= Q), we have to seek an interpretation of the latter passage. It is suggested by Bultmann [2] that the meaning is: as Jonah came from a distant land to the Ninevites, so will the Son of Man come from heaven to this generation. The sign asked for is the Son of Man himself, when he comes in judgement (cf. Mt. 24[30]). The objection to this view is that the analogy is not close. For Jonah came preaching repentance; the Son of Man comes to execute judgement. The sign of Jonah was of some use to the Ninevites: it gave them opportunity to repent. The sign of the Son of Man will be of no use to this generation; for when it comes, it will be too late to repent. Such a sign is hardly worthy of the name of sign. Another solution proposed is that the original saying of Jesus did not go beyond Lk. 11[29], and that both Lk. 11[30] and Mt. 12[40] are interpretative glosses. But even glosses have a meaning; and we should only be free to call Lk. 11[30] or 12[40] a gloss if the meaning were such that it could not reasonably be supposed to be the thought of Jesus. Yet another proposal is that 'Jonah' in Lk. 11[29] and Mt. 12[39] was originally 'John' (the Baptist). That the confusion of the two names was possible is shown by Mt. 16[17] compared with John 21[15]. The only sign to be given is, then, John the Baptist. In this case it would be impossible to regard Lk. 11[30] and Mt. 12[40] as anything but glosses on the corrupted text. Against this solution is the fact that it would deprive the ministry of Jesus of significance.

Before we can hope to solve the problem we must ask what those who asked for a sign wanted. The answer is that they wanted something that would authenticate Jesus to them, prove to them that He was indeed God's messenger to them. Then presumably the Ninevites might have put the same demand before Jonah; and if Jonah had produced some miracle to prove his bona fides, that would be Jonah's sign. But in the story of Jonah no such sign is either asked by the Ninevites or given by Jonah. Jonah himself was the only sign to the people. That can only mean that he and his message were such that of themselves they carried conviction to the Ninevites. People listening to Jonah recognised the voice of God. That, and only that, is what will be given to this generation. Once more God is speaking through the 'Son of Man.' For those who are not wilfully deaf to the message it is self-authenticating. The 'Son of Man' is the sign in exactly the same way that Jonah was. Cf. Is. 8[18].

It remains to determine the meaning of 'Son of Man' in this saying. If the interpretation just given is correct, 'Son of Man' here is used, as in Lk. 7[34], in the sense 'a certain man' i.e. 'I who speak.' Jesus Himself is the sign, the only sign, that will be given. The Q passage is then in real agreement with Mk. 8[11f.]. It

[1] G. Kittel, *Rabbinica*, pp. 36 f.
[2] *Geschichte der Synoptischen Tradition*,[2] p. 124.

refuses just as definitely as Mk. 8^{12} the request for a supernatural vindication of Jesus. It is to be noted that Jesus as His own sign differs from Jonah in one respect. Jonah only preached. Jesus both preaches and acts. His ministry is the manifestation of the Kingdom of God; He Himself is the manifestation of the Kingdom. And in Him the Kingdom is self-authenticating. The progress of His ministry will be the proof of His mission from God.

This interpretation is confirmed by the following verses, in which Jesus contrasts the response of the Gentiles with the unresponsiveness of Israel. We may compare the case of the centurion of Capernaum and the woes on the towns of Galilee.

(*b*) Gentile Responsiveness and Israelite Obstinacy

MT. $12^{41f.}$

12 41 The men of Nineveh shall stand up in the judgement with this generation, and shall condemn it: for they repented at the preaching of Jonah; and behold, [1] a
42 greater than Jonah is here. The queen of the south shall rise up in the judgement with this generation, and shall condemn it: for she came from the ends of the earth to hear the wisdom of Solomon; and behold, [1] a greater than Solomon is here.

[1] Gr. *more than.*

LK. $11^{31f.}$

11 31 The queen of the south shall rise up in the judgement with the men of this generation, and shall condemn them: for she came from the ends of the earth to hear the wisdom of Solomon; and behold,
32 [1] a greater than Solomon is here. The men of Nineveh shall stand up in the judgement with this generation, and shall condemn it: for they repented at the preaching of Jonah; and behold, [1] a greater than Jonah is here.

[1] Gr. *more than.*

The two cases are stated in closely parallel terms. The difference in order between Mt. and Lk. is best explained on the supposition that Lk.'s order is that of Q, which Mt. has reversed in order to bring together the sayings about Jonah. The Lucan order is chronological. The two gospels are almost identical in the wording.

31. The queen of the south (1 Kings 10^{1-13}) is the queen of Sheba. She plays a great part in Arabic legend, where her name is given as Bilkîs. 'The South,' i.e. the Southern land, corresponds to the Arabic name of the territory, *Al-Yaman*, the modern Yemen, in S. Arabia. This heathen princess will be raised from the dead to appear at the final judgement along with the Jewish contemporaries of Jesus. Rabbinical eschatology distinguishes between those who are so bad that they are not raised at all, but are left in Gehenna, where they have been since death; and those who are raised for the judgement. The latter may be awarded bliss or torment in the judgement. See Mishnah, *Sanhedrin*, 10^3 (Danby, 397 f.); Moore, *Judaism*, ii. 287–322, 377–395. Jesus says that in the coming judgement the fact that the queen of the South responded to such revelation as was available in her day will be damning evidence against those who fail to respond to the fuller revelation given by Himself. The phrase 'a greater than Solomon' is literally translated in R.V. mg. The adjective is neuter in both verses here, and in Mt. 12^6, where a similar expression occurs. In Mt. 11^9 = Lk. 7^{26} the adjective should be regarded as masculine. The neuter adjective here and in Mt. 12^6 refers not to

Jesus personally, but to that which is manifested in Him, the Kingdom of God, which is a greater thing than the wisdom of Solomon or the preaching of Jonah.

In *v.* 31 Lk. has ‘ the men of this generation ’ against Mt.’s ‘ this generation.’ The latter is to be preferred. Lk. has a weakness for the Greek word here represented by ‘ men.’ (Cf. Cadbury, *Style and Literary Method of Luke*, p. 189.) In *v.* 32 Lk. has refrained from inserting it, perhaps on account of ‘ the men of Nineveh.’

In both examples the effect on the Gentiles is produced, not by some violent breach of natural laws, but by the demonstration of spiritual power. The queen is fascinated by Solomon’s God-given wisdom (1 Kings 3^{5-15}); the Ninevites are convinced by Jonah’s divinely inspired preaching. Now God is revealing Himself again to His own people in the ministry—preaching, teaching, healing—of Jesus; and the response is miserably inadequate. This concludes the speech against sign-seekers; but not all that Jesus has to say about signs. For the next section deals with the true sign, under the figure of light.

(*c*) The True ‘ Sign from Heaven ’—Light (153)

MT. 5^{15}, $6^{22f.}$

5 15 Neither do *men* light a lamp, and put it
under the bushel, but on the stand; and
it shineth unto all that are in the house.
6 22 The lamp of the body is the eye:||if
therefore thine eye be single,||thy whole
23 body shall be full of light.||But if thine eye
be evil,||thy whole body shall be full of
darkness.||If therefore the light that is in
thee be darkness,||how great is the dark-
ness!||

LK. 11^{33-36}

11 33 No man, when he hath lighted a lamp,
putteth it in a cellar, neither under the
bushel, but on the stand, that they which
34 enter in may see the light. The lamp of
thy body is thine eye:||when thine eye is
single,||thy whole body also is full of
light;||but when it is evil,||thy body also
35 is full of darkness.||Look therefore
whether the light that is in thee be not
36 darkness. If therefore thy whole body
be full of light, having no part dark, it
shall be wholly full of light, as when the
lamp with its bright shining doth give
thee light.

Mt. by putting these sayings into the Sermon on the Mount (though Mt. 5^{15} may be from M) indicates his belief, which is no doubt correct, that they were originally addressed to the disciples. That they are in their proper place in Q in the Lucan order is obvious as soon as we see that they have to do with the one true sign. Just as the first sign of God’s creative activity was the command ‘ Let there be light,’ so the sign that God is at work for the salvation of men is the shining of the spiritual light in the lives of men.

33. There are two distinct sayings in this section, *v.* 33 and *vv.* 34–36. The former has a parallel in Mk. $4^{21f.}$: ‘ And he said unto them, Is the lamp brought to be put under the bushel, or under the bed (and) not to be put on the stand? For there is nothing hid, save that it should be manifested; neither was (anything) made secret, but that it should come to light.’ Mk.’s question form of the saying may well be original. There are three Old Testament ideas involved in the verse. (i) The source and creator of light is God. (ii) The spirit of man is the lamp of the Lord (Prov. 20^{27}). (iii) The Servant of the Lord is a light to the Gentiles (Is. 42^{6}). It is God who kindles the lamp (Ps. 18^{28}) in giving new spiritual power to a man.

And when this happens it cannot and ought not to be hidden. The transformed character is to be a beacon to those who are still in darkness to draw them to God. Cf. Mt. 5^{14} ‘ Ye are the light of the world ’ and 5^{16} ‘ Even so let your light shine before men.’ There is a small but significant point of difference between Lk. 11^{33} and Mt. 5^{15}. In Lk. the light is placed on the lamp-stand ‘ that they which enter in may see the light ’: in Mt. to give light to those who are in the house. The latter contemplates a reformation within Judaism, the former conversions from outside. Mt. 5^{15} is akin to the M version of the Mission Charge (Mt. $10^{5f.}$): Lk. 11^{33} shows the wider interest characteristic of Q. Those who have the light, those who have been kindled by God, inherit the task of the Servant of Jehovah. They are to be a light to the Gentiles. On the whole saying cf. 2 Cor. 4^{6}.

34 f. The second saying is a distinct parable in poetic form. Burney (p. 131) maintains that the version given in Mt. is rhythmically superior to that in Lk. In describing the diseased eye Lk. has certainly sacrificed the parallelism to brevity. The conclusion (Mt. 6^{23b}) seems to be better than Lk. 11^{35}. For a retranslation into Aramaic see Burney *loc. cit.*

As this is a parable based on physical facts, the description of the facts must not be mixed up with other considerations. It is not relevant to the interpretation of the saying that ‘ a good eye ’ is used in Jewish teaching as a synonym for a generous disposition and ‘ an evil eye ’ for a covetous disposition. We are not here concerned with the business of the moralist, but with that of the oculist. The lamp of the body is the eye. The condition of the eye determines whether the whole man is a blind man or a seeing man. If the eye is ‘ single ’—i.e. clear, sound, healthy—the man himself will be a seeing man. If the eye is ‘ evil ’—i.e. diseased—the man himself will be blind. (For dark = blind cf. Ps. 69^{23} and Targum Onkelos to Dt. 28^{65}.) ‘Thy whole body ’ is a literal rendering of an Aramaic expression which means ‘ you yourself ’ (Dalman, *Gramm.* [2], §17^{12}, p. 115). The saying then comes to this:

> The lamp of the body is the eye (or *Your* lamp is your eye).
> If your eye is healthy, you yourself will see:
> If your eye is diseased, you yourself will be blind.

The conclusion drawn from these facts is differently expressed in Mt. and Lk. In Lk. it is a caution: Beware lest the light that is in thee be darkness. In Mt. it is an exclamation: If the light that is in thee be darkness, what a darkness! We pass here from the parable to the moral. If what you imagine to be clear-sightedness is really blindness; if your supposed cleverness and penetration are really dullness and stupidity; if when you think you are facing the realities of your situation, you are really ignoring the vital facts—what then? Sure and certain disaster for yourself and all who are influenced by you. (I suspect that the force of this conclusion was enhanced in the original utterance by the fact that in Palestinian Aramaic the word ‘ light ’ was used euphemistically for ‘ blindness.’) Cf. Lk. 6^{39} ‘ Can the blind lead the blind? Will not both of them fall into the pit? ’

36. This verse has no parallel in Mt., and as it stands the only sense which it offers is a dull and obvious platitude. That is most probably why Mt. omits it. Lk., faithful to his source, has left it in even though he could make little or nothing

of it. The verse is omitted by D, and also by 7 MSS of the old Latin version, and the Curetonian Syriac, doubtless because of the difficulty of turning senseless Greek into sensible Latin or Syriac. In the Sinaitic Syriac and 2 old Latin MSS. there appears a version differing from the Greek text. This is an attempt to get over the difficulty by emendation. What appears to be the true solution is offered by Torrey, who suggests (*The Four Gospels*, p. 309) that the Greek text, translated in R.V. ' it shall be wholly full of light,' ' renders (incorrectly) *nahīr leh'wē kōllā*. This last word, rendered correctly as the adjective in the first clause of the verse, is here unquestionably *the noun*, " the whole, everything." The man who is full of light lights the world about him.' Torrey accordingly translates *v.* 36: ' If however your whole body is lighted up, with no part dark, then all about you will be light; just as the lamp lights you with its brightness.' This brilliant suggestion clears up in the simplest way the worst difficulty of the Greek text. It should be added that here again, as in *v.* 34 ' your whole body ' means ' you yourself.' If you yourself are illuminated, have an eye for spiritual things, you will be like a lamp in the darkness to all around you. This verse is then the Q equivalent of Mt. 5^{14} ' you are the light of the world.' It is also the other side of the picture drawn in *v.* 35. The disciple who really sees the truth is the opposite of the blind guide.

So then we have the true and only sign from heaven, the light of God's revelation. This light shines in Jesus, and through Him in His followers. Its shining beacon is a guide to those who are in darkness. If they follow the light, they too will come to their desired haven.

4. *AGAINST PHARISAISM* (154)

Lk. 11^{37-52} contains a series of woes, three addressed to the Pharisees and three to the lawyers. The whole series is preceded by an introductory narrative leading up to a dispute between Jesus and a Pharisee on the subject of hand-washing. The group of woes against the lawyers is furnished with a short introduction. The woes are followed by a short narrative describing the reactions of the scribes and Pharisees. Mk. (12^{38-40}) has a speech against the scribes. This brief utterance contains no woes, and is not directly addressed to the scribes. The Pharisees are not even mentioned. The Marcan speech is a warning against the practices of the scribes, and is apparently uttered in public teaching. Mt. (23^{1-36}) presents a long discourse, addressed to the crowds and Jesus' own disciples. This discourse is, like all the great speeches in Mt., a conflation. It uses matter from Mk. 12^{38-40}; it has other matter in common with Lk. 11^{37-52}, and therefore presumably from Q; and it has sayings peculiar to Mt. and probably derived from M. Mt. 23 has seven woes, six of which are addressed to the scribes and Pharisees by name. The discourse is concluded with the lament over Jerusalem (23^{37-39}) from Q (cf. Lk. $13^{34f.}$), and there is no account of its effect on the scribes and Pharisees. Mt. goes straight on to the eschatological discourse.

We now turn to the arrangement in detail, to see what can be surmised about the composition of the discourses. We begin with a table of contents in parallel columns.

MT. 23		MK. 12		LK. 11	
2 f.	Moses' seat.			37 f.	Narrative introduction.
4.	Heavy burdens.			39–41.	External purity.
5.	Show of piety.			42.	I. Woe, Tithes.
6 f.	Pride of place.	38 f.	Scribal pride.	43.	II. Woe, Pride of place.
8–12.	Warning against pride.	40.	Scribal fraud and sham piety.	44.	III. Woe, Hidden tombs.
13.	I. Woe, Closing Kingdom.			45.	The lawyer's protest.
15.	II. Woe, Proselyte hunters.			46.	IV. Woe, Heavy burdens.
16–22.	III. Woe, Oaths and vows.			47 f.	V. Woe, Tombs of the prophets.
23 f.	IV. Woe, Tithes.				
25 f.	V. Woe, External purity.			49–51.	Blood of the prophets.
27 f.	VI. Woe, Whited sepulchres.			52.	VI. Woe, Key of knowledge.
29–32.	VII. Woe, Tombs of the prophets.			53 f.	Anger of scribes and Pharisees.
33.	Threat of judgement.				
34–36.	Blood of the righteous.				

The discrepancies in order between Mt. and Lk. are very striking, and equally striking is the wide divergence in language between the two Gospels in passages which they have in common. The following verses of Mt., which have no parallel in Mk. or Lk., may be provisionally assigned to M: *vv.* 2 f., 5, 7^b–12, 15–22, 24, 28, 32 f. From Mk. *vv.* 6, 7^a seem to be derived. The remaining verses have contacts with Lk., and if any part of Mt. 23 is derived from Q, it is here that we must look for it in the first instance. It may be noticed that the great bulk of the matter common to Mt. and Lk. comes from the woes. But taking the woes as a whole the correspondence in order between Mt. and Lk. is not striking. This may be shown by two tables. The first (A) is based on the Mt. order of woes; the second (B) on Lk. In either case the second column gives the number of the answering woe in the order of the other Gospel.

A. Mt.	Lk.
I	VI
II	—
III	—
IV	I
V	*vv.* 39–41 (not a woe)
VI	III
VII	V

B. Lk.	Mt.
I	IV
II	*vv.* 6 f. (not a woe)
III	VI
IV	*v.* 4 (not a woe)
V	VII
VI	I

The only coincidence in order here is that woes IV, VI, VII in Mt. correspond to I, III, V in Lk. If we now turn to the possible Q matter in Mt. we find what may be displayed in the following table.

Mt.	Lk.
v. 4	*v.* 46 (woe IV)
v. 13 (woe I)	*v.* 52 (woe VI)
v. 23 (woe IV)	*v.* 42 (woe I)
vv. 25 f. (woe V)	*vv.* 39–41
v. 27 (woe VI)	*v.* 44 (woe III)
vv. 29–31 (woe VII)	*vv.* 47 f. (woe V)
vv. 34–36	*vv.* 49–51

Mt. 23^{4} and Lk. 11^{46} deal with the same subject. But Lk. 11^{46} is a woe and Mt. 23^{4} is not. The agreements in wording are insignificant beside the differences. And 23^{4} comes in the middle of a section which seems to be solid M. For these reasons we may regard it as more probably M than Q. The same considerations apply to Mt. 23^{13}. Mt. 23^{23} is the first verse in the chapter than can be assigned with any real confidence to Q. There is identity of subject-matter and considerable agreement in wording with Lk. 11^{42}. Mt. $23^{25\,f.}$ is a woe: Lk. 11^{39-41} is not. The subject-matter is the same; but the agreements in wording are not very numerous. In Mt. 23^{27} and Lk. 11^{44} the subject is the same; but the treatment of it is different and the verbal agreement is practically nil. Mt. 23^{29-31} and Lk. $11^{47\,f.}$ deal with the same point but again the measure of agreement in wording is small, though not negligible. The same is true of Mt. 23^{34-36} compared with Lk. 11^{49-51}. The result is that Mt. 23^{23} is the only verse that can be given to Q with any sort of confidence.

The conclusion to which these facts seem to point is that in the main Mt. 23 is derived from M. In places—notably *vv.* 23, 25 f., 29–31, 34–36—the M material may well have been conflated with Q; but it remains likely that the backbone of the chapter is M. The coincidences in order between Mt. and Lk. will then be coincidences between M and Q and point to a stage in the tradition anterior to these two sources. At that stage, we may surmise, the woes concerning meticulous tithing, the whited sepulchres (or hidden tombs), and the tombs of the prophets, together with the saying about the blood of the prophets (or righteous men) were already fixed in that order.

The question remains whether the Lucan version of the speech is to be assigned to Q or L. So far we have assumed that it is Q, which is the general opinion. Streeter assigns Lk. 11^{9-52} to Q; Bussmann gives 11^{34}–12^{1} to his source R, which for our purposes is the same as giving it to Q; Harnack recognised *vv.* 39, 41, 42, 44, 46–52 as belonging to Q. Bultmann thinks that Q contained originally seven woes, corresponding to *vv.* 43, 46, 52, 42, (39), 44, 47 in Lk. and *vv.* (4, 6), 13, 23, 25, 27, 29 in Mt.; and that Lk. has made a larger composition by setting them in a narrative frame (37–39*a*), by the little piece of dialogue (*v.* 45), and the narrative conclusion (53 f.). That is, the passage is Q with the editorial additions of Lk.

The crucial question is whether the division of the woes between Pharisees and lawyers in Lk. is original or the creation of Lk. himself. My own feeling is that Lk. found it and did not create it, though he may have written *v.* 45 to help the transition from the one set of woes to the other. In that case we have as the nucleus of the Q version of the speech six woes, three against Pharisees and three against lawyers. (Cf. the four beatitudes and four woes in Lk.'s version of the preaching of Jesus.) Lk. 11^{49-51} was already firmly attached to the fifth woe in the source as Lk. had it. It is then possible to suppose that Lk. 11^{37-41} is a separate section (from L?), which Lk. has used as the introduction to the six woes; and that $11^{53\,f.}$ (with or without 12^{1}) is the conclusion of the story told in *vv.* 37–41. The coincidences in language between Lk. 11^{39-41} and Mt. $23^{25\,f.}$ would then be explained as due to the overlapping of M and L. To Q I should assign with considerable confidence *vv.* 42–44 and 46–52 of Lk.

(*a*) The Woes against Pharisees

LK. 11^{42-44}

Cf. Mt. 23^{23}.

Cf. Mk. $12^{38\,f.}$; Mt. $23^{6\,f.}$; Lk. 20^{46}.

Cf. Mt. 23^{27}.

11 42 But woe unto you Pharisees! for ye tithe mint and rue and every herb, and pass over judgement and the love of God: but these ought ye to have done,
43 and not to leave the other undone. Woe unto you Pharisees! for ye love the chief seats in the synagogues, and the saluta-
44 tions in the marketplaces. Woe unto you! for ye are as the tombs which appear not, and the men that walk over *them* know it not.

The first three woes are spoken to Pharisees. The Pharisees may be described as ' practising Jews ' using the word ' practising ' in somewhat the same sense as in the phrase ' practising Catholics.' Their origin can be traced back to the days when the Seleucid overlords of Palestine attempted to force Greek religion and culture upon the Jewish people, with some success. Those who, in that crisis, remained faithful to the religion of Israel—often at the cost of their lives—received the name *Hăsîdîm*, ' the saints ' or ' the godly.' Later, when their object had been attained by arms, and religious freedom was assured, they refused to join in the further military and political plans of the Maccabean leaders and received the nickname *Pĕrûshîm* or ' Separatists.' This name they accepted and construed in their own way as meaning separateness from everything ungodly as judged by the Law of God. (See further, *The Teaching of Jesus*, pp. 184–188 and literature there cited.)[1] From the beginning their concern is essentially with the practice of religion. The interpretation of the Law and the working out of the theology and morals of Judaism they left to experts, the scribes. These belonged largely, though not entirely, to the Pharisaic party, and were its intellectual leaders. The scribes are thus a group within the much larger body of Pharisees. It was not necessary to be learned in order to be a Pharisee. The essence of the Pharisaic life was strict obedience to the Law as interpreted by the scribes. It is in accord with this definition that the woes against Pharisees are all concerned with the practice rather than with the interpretation of the Law. As the Greek text stands the sweeping denunciations are directed against the whole Pharisaic party. Whether this was the case in the original Aramaic is a question which cannot be answered. All that can be said is that ' Woe unto you Pharisees! for ye tithe . . . ' represents Aramaic which could equally well be rendered ' Woe unto you Pharisees who tithe . . .' (compare the beatitudes and woes, Lk. 6^{20-26}). The reference could then be not to the whole body of Pharisees, but to those among them who were Pharisees only on the surface. That such people existed is confirmed by Jewish evidence (Billerbeck, iv. 336–339, gives the passages); and it is at least possible that Jesus had them in mind rather than the whole body of the Pharisees.

42. ' Woe unto you ' better ' Alas for you.' See Introduction, p. 321. The payment of tithe was an essential part of the religious obligation of the Jew, and

[1] I am not entirely satisfied with this explanation of the origin of the name ' Pharisee.' It is, I think, possible that the name originally meant ' Persianizers ' and referred to characteristic Pharisaic beliefs, which had close affinities with the religion of Zarathustra. But this theory must be reserved for fuller discussion elsewhere.

the question whether any given kind of farm or garden produce was subject to tithe was one for experts. The really important things in this connexion were of course the main crops; but scribal conscientiousness saw to it that rules were laid down for all kinds of produce. The question in this woe is whether the assertion is that the Pharisees observe these rules in the minutest detail or whether in their zeal to appear righteous they go beyond the rules and give tithe where none is required. In Lk. the specified kinds are mint and rue. There is no evidence that mint was subject to tithe, and definite evidence that rue was not subject (*Shebi'ith* 9^1, Danby, p. 49). And certainly not every kind of herb was subject to tithe. The Lucan version of the woe thus asserts that more is done, in the matter of trifles, than even the scribal interpretation of the Law requires. This suggests that it is only some of the Pharisees who are here accused. It is unlikely that all Pharisees would go to such lengths and equally unlikely that Jesus would make an accusation against the whole body, which any member of it could immediately disprove. Mt. 23^{23} gives a different list: mint, dill, and cummin. Dill was liable to tithe (*Ma'aseroth* 4^5, Danby, p. 72) and so was cummin (*Demai* 2^1, Danby, p. 21). It is possible that Lk.'s rue and Mt.'s dill both go back to a single Aramaic original. The Aramaic names of these two plants could easily be confused in writing. As it stands Mt.'s text is not clear. It gives mint, which was not tithed, and dill and cummin, which were. This is explicable on the assumption that it is a conflation of M and Q. The M text perhaps contained dill and cummin and understood the saying as pillorying the meticulous observance of the tithe laws by the Pharisees. The mint is then an intrusion from the Q version, which asserts that some Pharisees in order to gain a reputation for piety pay tithe where no tithe is due. The Q version as given by Lk. seems to be on all grounds preferable. It may be paraphrased 'Alas for you hypocritical members of the Pharisaic party, who simulate piety by paying tithes where none are required.' That their piety is a sham is proved by the fact that along with their extreme conscientiousness in trifles goes a remarkable indifference in the really vital matters, 'judgement and the love of God.' 'Judgement' is here, as often in the Old Testament, the quality which fits one to be a judge, i.e. a keen sense of right and wrong, an inward rectitude, an unshakeable determination to uphold what is right and true and good. The love of God is the essence of true religion. It is to be noted that in the Jewish account the Pharisee who is a Pharisee from the motive of love is set in contrast with six other sorts of Pharisee to their disadvantage. (Billerbeck, iv. 339.) Mt. has a different list of weightier matters of the law—'judgement and mercy and faith' —again probably a conflation of M and Q.

'But these (judgement and the love of God) ought ye to have done, and not to leave the other (the tithing of mint, etc.) undone.' This sentence cannot belong to Q. For the tithing of mint, etc., was a thing that could very well be left undone, seeing that it was not required by the Law or by the scribal tradition. In Lk. it is omitted by Marcion and by the Codex Bezae; and it may be a very early interpolation from Mt. 23^{23}.

43. This occupation with the details of religion, the successful performance of the minor pieties, produces spiritual pride. Concentration on the central things would produce humility. This is true of Christianity as well as Judaism.

Those who are meticulous in the payment of their religious taxes expect others to show a proper appreciation of their exemplary piety. Having no inner assurance of God's approval, their need of human recognition is all the greater. The danger is that they will be satisfied with the latter and never even feel their need of the former. The charge of seeking this human recognition is made independently in Mk. $12^{38f.}$, but not in the form of a woe. 'The chief seats in the synagogues,' cf. Mt. 23^{2}, 'Moses' seat' and notes thereon (below, p. 520). 'Salutations'—we might almost say 'salaams.' The regular salutation was 'Peace upon thee' and the principle laid down in the Palestinian Talmud (*Berachoth*, II. 4^{b}. 24; Billerbeck, i. 382) is that a man must salute his superior in the knowledge of the Law. But in practice we find that distinguished Rabbis preferred to waive the right, and be themselves the first to make the salutation. We may suspect that in Pharisaism, as in other circles, those whose title to respect was shaky were foremost in insisting on their dignity. And again we may think that the indictment of Jesus is not directed against the whole body of Pharisees, but only against a section.

44. This woe appears in Mt. 23^{27}; but there the treatment is different. Mt.'s point is that the tomb which outwardly looks fine and clean is full of rottenness: so the Pharisee who is outwardly a model of piety and morality is a mass of corruption within. The Lucan form of the saying depends on the law in Num. 19^{16} that contact with a grave defiles a man for seven days. There are Pharisees like unmarked graves. Other people come in contact with them and are defiled thereby. The Lucan form appears to be the original. Whited sepulchres (Mt.) is not a good simile for hypocrites. For the point of the whitening is that it advertises the fact that the grave is what it is (see Abrahams, *Studies*, ii. 29–32), and warns the passer-by of the risk of defilement. The Lucan form asserts that there are Pharisees who have nothing about them to warn the unsuspecting that they are really bad men whose influence will be thoroughly evil.

These three woes are all concerned with character and conduct. There is in them no polemic against Pharisaism as a system. Nor, I think, does Jesus arraign the whole body of the scribes and Pharisees. The impression that He did so is given by Mt. If we read these woes in Lk.'s version, keeping out of our minds any ideas derived from Mt. 23, it seems that here we have a condemnation of bad Pharisees such as could be made, and was made, from the Pharisaic side. The Pharisaic ideal was a genuine religious ideal; and the men who gave themselves to it were mostly sincere and earnest. To maintain that all Pharisees were *ipso facto* hypocrites is as absurd as to claim that they were all saints. The truth is that some of them were men of eminent saintliness, many kept a worthy standard both in piety and morality, and some were complete frauds. It is to this last class that the woes really apply. Note that Jesus does *not* say: 'You ought to concentrate on the love of God and drop tithes' or 'It is time that these marks of respect were done away with.' He is not here attacking the system, but those who abuse it for their own advantage. And those who loved the system and believed in it were always ready to do the same. The real Pharisee, the 'Pharisee from love' would agree with Jesus, though certainly not with all the explanations of what Jesus is supposed to have meant.

(*b*) The Woes against Scribes

LK. 11^{45-52}

11 45 And one of the lawyers answering saith
unto him, [1] Master, in saying this thou
46. Cf. Mt. 23^{4}.
46 reproachest us also. And he said, Woe
unto you lawyers also! for ye lade men
with burdens grievous to be borne, and
ye yourselves touch not the burdens with
47 f. Cf. Mt. $23^{29\ 31}$.
47 one of your fingers. Woe unto you! for
ye build the tombs of the prophets, and
48 your fathers killed them. So ye are
witnesses and consent unto the works of
your fathers: for they killed them, and ye
49–51. Cf. Mt. 23^{34-36}.
49 build *their tombs*. Therefore also said the
wisdom of God, I will send unto them
prophets and apostles; and *some* of them
50 they shall kill and persecute; that the
blood of all the prophets, which was shed
from the foundation of the world, may
51 be required of this generation; from the
blood of Abel unto the blood of Zachariah, who perished between the altar and
the [2] sanctuary: yea, I say unto you, it
52. Cf. Mt. 23^{13}.
52 shall be required of this generation. Woe
unto you lawyers! for ye took away the
key of knowledge: ye entered not in
yourselves, and them that were entering
in ye hindered.

[1] Or, *Teacher*.
[2] Gr. *house*.

45. The transition from the woes against Pharisees to the three woes against scribes is effected in *v.* 45. It may be doubted whether it stood in Q. If it is the editorial work of Lk., that is an indication that he found the two sets of woes distinguished in his source, and felt himself called upon to make a link between the two. The connexion is not particularly good since the foregoing woes do not touch the scribes as such, but only in so far as they belong to the Pharisaic party. Lk. uses the word 'lawyer' rather than scribe. 'Lawyer' would certainly convey the true sense better to a Gentile reader, to whom 'scribe' would suggest a clerk or secretary rather than an expert in Jewish religion and law. 'Reproachest' is too weak a translation; better 'insultest.'

46. The three woes against scribes deal with their attitude to the Law, the prophets, and the Kingdom of God. The first concerns their interpretation of the Law. It is important to realise what Jesus does *not* say. He does not say that the scribes make one law for themselves and another for the ordinary people. The most stringent interpreters among the Rabbis were commonly themselves most particular in their observance. For the Rabbis there was only one Divine Law, written in the Old Testament or handed down by oral tradition from Mt. Sinai; only one true interpretation of it; only one proper application of it in any given case. And that Law rightly interpreted and applied was absolutely binding on all Jews, scribes included. Moreover, as lawyers the scribes could not do otherwise than they did. They were neither inspired prophets nor higher critics. They were the guardians of what they believed to be a God-given rule of faith and morals, every syllable of which was divinely inspired. Their business was

merely to expound. The business of Israel, themselves included, was to obey. That this mass of legislation formed a burden which few were able to bear cannot be disputed. The result was that in the days of Jesus there was a sharp division between those who were bearing the burden with more or less success and those who failed, between the righteous and sinners.

Jesus does not suggest that the requirements should be relaxed in favour of the weaker brethren, that the heavy burdens should be borne exclusively by scribes and Pharisees, and a lighter one prepared for the publicans and sinners. His complaint is that the scribes will not lift a finger to help those who break down under the burden. The scribe, as such, expounds the Law; he may himself keep it; but he has nothing to say to the Israelite who fails to keep it, except 'You have sinned: you must repent and begin again.' This is the point of Jesus' accusation. It comes with all the greater force because He lavished so much love on the Law's failures, so much that He became known as 'the friend of publicans and sinners.' The Law is the expression of God's will. But ultimately God's will must be the working out of the Father's love for His children; and there is something wrong with an interpretation of the Law which results constantly in God's children being estranged from Him because they cannot keep the Law. There is something wrong with scribal labours which multiply the number of ways in which a man may offend God, but cannot help him to please God.

47 f. In the second woe the attitude of the scribes to prophecy is challenged. Put in a word the criticism is: The only prophet you honour is a dead prophet. In the parallel in Mt. 23^{29} the characteristic Matthæan 'prophets and righteous men' appear. The reference to the building of tombs for the prophets may be bitter irony. Outwardly you seem to pay honour to the great prophets of the past; but your real object is to make permanent the work of your fathers. They killed the prophets: you make sure that they stay dead. It is possible that here Jesus is hitting at the absolute supremacy given by the scribes to the Law. If we may judge from the Scripture quotations ascribed to Him in the Gospels, He turned rather to the prophetic books and the psalter. Out of 94 quotations in the Synoptic Gospels, only 24 are from the Law; 46 are from the prophetic books; and 24 from the third division of the Hebrew canon, 23 of them from Psalms and Daniel. But in the scribal view the Law was supreme. Prophecy could confirm, but could not reform, it; and the book of Ezekiel was at one time in danger of exclusion from the Old Testament, because it was thought to be at variance with the Law. If the great prophetic figures of the past had thus to play second fiddle to the Law, what chance was there that the living voice of prophecy would receive a hearing? John the Baptist supplied the answer to that question. The whole attitude of the scribes to prophecy, past or present, is according to Jesus proof that they agree with those who killed the prophets.

49–51. The second woe is followed by a passage which has been a fruitful field for discussion and conjecture. (*a*) It is commonly held that these verses are a quotation from a Jewish apocryphal book; and that the quotation has been put into the mouth of Jesus in the process of tradition. The upholders of this theory are unable to verify the quotation, as the book in question cannot be produced. They think it must have been lost. The main reason for thinking that the verses are a quotation is the fact that in Lk. they open with the words 'Therefore also said the wisdom of God'; but, so far as the usage of the gospels is anything to go by (cf. Mt. 22^{24}; Mk. 7^{10}, 12^{36}; John 1^{23}, $12^{39, 41}$), this would imply that the wisdom of God wrote the supposed book, as Moses was believed to have written the Law, or David the Psalms, or Isaiah the book of Isaiah. A much better way of taking the Lucan introductory formula is to regard it as equivalent to 'God, in His wisdom, said.' It is a commonplace that Jewish thought tended to personify the attributes of God. In the Rabbinical literature the attributes of Justice (*middath had-dîn*) and Mercy (*middath hā-raḥămîm*) are constantly personified and represented as speaking. When we read in these writings that 'The attribute of Justice said,' we realise that this is a picturesque way of saying 'God, in His justice, said.' For the orthodox Jew the wisdom of God was an attribute of God. As revealed to men it was the Law, the Torah, which is also sometimes personified. But this personification is only a mode of speech. It makes for greater vividness; but it does not imply that God's justice, mercy, wisdom, and so on, are separate personal entities. (See Moore, *Judaism*, i. 414 ff.) (*b*) Along with the view that these verses are a quotation goes a further theory that Mt. 23^{37-39} is a continuation of the same quotation, which Lk. has transferred to another place (Lk. $13^{34 f.}$). This is very unlikely, for two reasons. First, it does not appear to be Lk.'s practice to break up his sources in this way. If Lk. 11^{51} marked the end of a block of Q material in Lk. and Lk. 13^{34} the beginning of the next block of Q, there would be something to be said for the theory; but this is not the case. Secondly, a comparison of Mt. and Lk. in the passages in question is strongly against the theory. Mt. 23^{34-36} contains (in Greek) 72 words, Lk. 11^{49-51} contains 58. The two versions of the saying agree in 22 words and partly agree in 7. Taking Lk.'s shorter version as standard the amount of agreement between Mt. and Lk. is under 50 per cent. Now Mt. 23^{37-39} contains 56 words and Lk. $13^{34 f.}$ 53. There is agreement between the two in 45 words and partial agreement in 4. Again taking Lk. as the standard, the amount of agreement between Mt. and Lk. is near 90 per cent. It is difficult to believe that this wide divergence followed by almost word-for-word agreement could have taken place in the quotation of a single short passage of little more than a hundred words.

49, 50 f. All that has happened in the past and is happening in the present to the messengers of God is foreseen and provided for by God in His wisdom. He sends out His prophets and messengers knowing the fate that awaits them. For 'prophets and messengers' Mt. (23^{34}) has 'prophets, and wise men, and scribes,' generally regarded as more original than Lk. But see below, pp. 530 f. The 'apostles' of R.V. is better rendered 'messengers.' The term 'apostles' has a technical ecclesiastical sense, which ought not to be read into the text here. Jesus used the Aramaic equivalent of the word, and—as I think—gave it as a name to certain of His disciples; but He used it in a wide sense to designate anyone who had a mission from God to men. Cf. Lk. 13^{34} = Mt. 23^{37}, 'Jerusalem, which killeth the prophets, and stoneth them that are sent unto her.' 'Messengers' is a wider term than 'prophets': and in this sense all prophets are messengers, though all messengers are not necessarily prophets. The fate of these representatives of God is death and persecution. It is described in greater detail in Mt. 23^{34}. The result of this behaviour to the men of God is that the persecutors will have to answer for their misdeeds. The 'that' which stands at the beginning of the verse represents the common Semitic idiom by which the result of an action is spoken of as if it were the purpose of the action. 'The blood of all the prophets' is difficult, for the text goes on to give as examples two men who were not prophets. Abel in Jewish tradition is a type of righteousness; but I do not know that he is anywhere called a prophet. Zachariah, on the most probable interpretation, is the Zechariah whose death is described in 2 Chron. $24^{20 f.}$; and he was not a prophet, but a priest. Mt. (23^{35}) has 'all the righteous blood,' which fits better with what follows. The righteous blood is what is called in the Old Testament 'innocent blood,' i.e. blood unrighteously shed. That such blood clamours for vengeance is a common idea in the Old Testament (Gen. 4^{10}; Jb. 16^{18}; Is. 26^{21}; Ezek. $24^{7 f.}$; 2 Ki. 9^{26}) and in Jewish thought (Billerbeck, i. 940 ff.). Compare and contrast Heb. 12^{24}. It should be noted that the blood of Abel is represented as crying for vengeance (Gen. 4^{10}); and that in the account of the death of Zechariah (1 Chron. 24^{22}) the dying priest says, 'The Lord look upon it and require it': also that in Jewish legend the blood of this Zechariah refused to soak into the ground until vengeance was exacted by Nebuzaradan (Billerbeck, *loc. cit.*) Cf. Robertson Smith, *Religion of the Semites,*^{2} p. 417. n. 5. 'This generation' will have to answer for all the crimes of its predecessors because it will not break with the past in the only possible way—by repentance and submission to the will of God.

52. The third woe against the scribes. The statement of the charge in Mt. 23^{13} is different. There the scribes and Pharisees are accused of closing the Kingdom against those who wished to enter. This may refer to their opposition to John the Baptist and Jesus. But then it does not appear that their opposition prevented those who really wished to enter the Kingdom from doing so. It can hardly mean that they prevented Gentiles from being converted to Israel, for that is contradicted by *v.* 15. The Matthean form looks like an attempt to clarify the more difficult form of the saying in Lk. The 'knowledge' here meant is the knowledge of God as revealed in the Old Testament. Of this revelation the scribes were the custodians, and the charge against them is that by their method of interpretation they have obscured the simple and central truths there given. The knowledge of God as Father and King and of His rule of love and mercy has been buried under an ever-increasing mass of traditions and precedents and pettifogging rules. Continually busied with the details of the Law they forgot the great principles of the prophetic religion; and the finished product of their expert labours was not so much a revelation of God as of their own ingenuity, calculated to make men despair of themselves rather than trust in God, to turn men away from the Kingdom rather than bring them into it.

Additional Note: The Death of Zachariah

In commenting on Lk. 11^{51} we have assumed that the Zachariah there mentioned is the Zechariah whose fate is described in 2 Chron. $24^{20 ff.}$. This view is by no means universally accepted; and, at one time or another, other identifications have been proposed. As the matter is of importance for the dating of the New Testament documents, the point must be discussed in detail. In Lk. the name is Zachariah simply: in Mt. 23^{35} it is Zachariah the son of Barachiah. The following identifications have been made.

(1) Zacharias the father of John the Baptist. The story of his murder in the Temple appears in early Christian apocryphal literature. It is referred to by Epiphanius (*Haer.* xxvi. 12), quoting from a Gnostic work called 'The Birth of Mary' (*Trans.* M. R. James, *Apocryphal New Testament*, p. 19). It is also found in the *Protevangelium*, xxiii f. (James, *op. cit.*, p. 48), in the Coptic conclusion of the *Apocalypse of Paul* (James, *op. cit.*, p. 554), and in the *Latin Infancy Gospels* (ed. James), pp. 90 ff. Another version of the story was known to Origen and Peter of Alexandria (H. Smith, *Ante-Nicene Exegesis of the Gospels*, iv. 75; v. 85–96). Origen identified this Zacharias with the Zachariah of Mt. 23^{35} and Lk. 11^{51}.

(2) Zechariah the prophet (*c.* 520 B.C.) son of Berechiah and grandson of Iddo (Zech. $1^{1, 7}$), of priestly descent (Neh. $12^{4, 16}$), co-worker with the prophet Haggai (Ezra 5^{1}, 6^{14}—in both places called Zechariah son of Iddo). Concerning the death of this prophet nothing is known. In late Jewish tradition he was confused with the Zechariah mentioned in 2 Chron. $24^{20\,ff.}$. The passages are: Targum on Lam. 2^{20} and Josippon 80.

(3) Zechariah son of Jehoiada a priest, stoned 'in the court of the house of the Lord' by the people at the command of Joash (2 Chron. $24^{20\,ff.}$). 'And when he died he said, The Lord look upon it and require it' (24^{22}). According to Rabbinic tradition, his blood would not dry up, but remained till the time of the destruction of Solomon's Temple, when it was avenged by Nebuzaradan. Rabbinical passages in Billerbeck, i. 940 ff.

(4) Zechariah son of Baris, murdered in the Temple in A.D. 67 by two Zealots. The story is told by Josephus (*BJ* iv. 334–344). The name of his father is differently given in the MSS. of Josephus as Baris, Baruch, and Bariscaeus. Baris is the reading adopted by Niese and Thackeray. The latter says (note on *BJ*, iv. 335) that the reading Baruch is negligible. The identification of this Zechariah with the Zachariah of our text is as old as Chrysostom. It was also held by Grotius. For these it meant that the words of the text were a prediction made by Jesus and duly fulfilled in A.D. 67. The same identification is made by Wellhausen and Meyer; but for them it is prophecy after the event and proves that the saying is later than A.D. 67.

It may be assumed that our text is from Q. The first question then concerns the name of the victim. Is the Q text (*a*) Zechariah son of Barachiah (Mt.) or (*b*) Zachariah (Lk.)? If (*a*), then who is meant?

(i) There is no evidence that the prophet Zechariah was martyred; but there is evidence that in late Judaism there was a confusion between Zechariah the prophet and Zechariah the priest who was killed in the Temple. It is possible that this confusion was already made when Q was compiled or still earlier.

(ii) Zacharias the father of John hardly comes into account. The legend of his death looks like an attempt to make the facts fit the saying.

(iii) Zechariah the son of Baris might be meant, but:

(α) Baris or even Bariscaeus is not the same as Barachias.

(β) There is no suggestion that this man was a prophet: all that Josephus tells us is that he was a respectable law-abiding citizen of Jerusalem, who was the victim of the illegal violence of the Zealots.

(γ) The legend of the death of Zacharias the father of John is so far evidence against this identification. For there would be no need to invent a death for Zacharias the father of John, if there was already a murdered Zechariah provided by Josephus.

(δ) If Zechariah the son of Baris were meant, it would bring the date of Q down later than 67, which is on other grounds improbable.

If (*b*), then the words ' son of Barachiah ' are an editorial expansion in Mt.

(i) Mt. might have confused Zechariah the priest with Zechariah the prophet.

(ii) The legend of the death of Zechariah the father of John is not likely to have been in circulation when the Gospel of Mt. was compiled.

(iii) Assuming a date later than 67 for the compilation of Mt. it is just possible that Mt. knew of the fate of Zechariah son of Baris and supposed that this was the Zachariah referred to in Q, and that Jesus had prophesied his fate. As Chrysostom and Grotius were able to believe this, it is possible that Mt. believed it too.

But if Zachariah alone is the text of Q we have to ask whether it is a correct report of the words of Jesus; and if so, what *He* meant.

Here we have a further complication. It is argued that the Lucan form of the saying indicates that it is a quotation from a written source. This view is to be rejected for the reasons given above. If the words were a quotation from a Jewish prophetic-apocalyptic writing, that document would be earlier than Q, and the objection raised against Zechariah the son of Baris in iii(δ) becomes still stronger. If the words are a genuine utterance of Jesus, He can only have meant Zechariah the priest or have confused that Zechariah with Zechariah the prophet. In either case the incident referred to is that recorded in 2 Chron. 24.

(*c*) Conclusion of the Speech against Pharisaism

Lk. $11^{53f.}$ is the conclusion of Lk.'s narrative setting of the speech against Pharisaism. It is followed by a short self-contained anecdote (12^{1}), giving another saying of Jesus again Pharisaism. Lk. 12^{1} has an independent parallel in Mk. 8^{14-21}, which is probably the more original setting of the saying. It does not seem likely that Lk. 12^{1} is derived from Q. More probably it is a fragment of Lk.'s separate tradition (L), inserted here in what seemed to him an appropriate context. Actually Lk. 11^{53}–12^{1} breaks the connexion between 11^{52} and 12^{2-3}. Lk. $12^{2f.}$ I take to be the conclusion of the speech against Pharisaism. In 12^{4} a new beginning is made with the words ' And I say unto you, my friends.'

MT. $10^{26f.}$	LK. 12^{2-3}
10 26 Fear them not therefore: for there is nothing covered, that shall not be revealed; and hid, that shall not be known. 27 What I tell you in the darkness, speak ye in the light: and what ye hear in the ear, proclaim upon the housetops.	**12** 2 But there is nothing covered up,| that shall not be revealed:||and hid,|that shall 3 not be known.||Wherefore whatsoever ye have said in the darkness|shall be heard in the light;||and what ye have spoken in the ear in the inner chambers|shall be proclaimed upon the housetops.||

Cf. Mk. 4^{22}||Lk. 8^{17}

4 22 For there is nothing hid, save that it should be manifested; neither was *anything* made secret, but that it should come to light.

2. The sayings are in poetical form. Mk. 4^{22} appears in a context which makes it refer most probably to the coming manifestation of the Kingdom in power. In Mt. the sense is different: the saying prepares the way for an exhortation to the disciples to utter publicly the things that Jesus has confided privately to them. This is inevitable, since Mt. has incorporated the section of Q represented by Lk. 12^{2-9} in his Mission Charge to the Twelve. If our analysis of the text is correct these verses in Lk.—and in Q—are really a warning to the opponents of Jesus that a time is coming when their doings will be exposed. Bultmann argues that the saying was originally no prophetic word of encouragement, but a popular warning against entrusting secrets to anyone, and so purely secular. He maintains that in Q it is already interpreted as a promise, for only so could it be used in the Christian tradition. Mt. carries the process farther in the same direction. It may, however, be doubted whether the original form of the saying is a proverb of worldly wisdom. It belongs rather to the order of things represented by Mt. 6^{1-18}. The things which are said and done in secret are not concealed from God; and in the Judgement all will be brought to light. There are scribes and Pharisees who may well dread this coming exposure.

3. The original form of the saying is preserved by Lk. Mt. has adapted it to its context in the Mission Charge. 'Wherefore' would be better translated 'because.' Darkness is a figure for secrecy (cf. Sophocles, *Antigone*, 692), and light for publicity. The words 'in the inner chambers' do not appear in Mt., and are probably added by Lk. They spoil the parallelism, which is between 'spoken in the ear' and 'proclaimed upon the housetops.' 'Spoken in the ear,' i.e. whispered, stands for secret communications; 'proclaimed upon the housetops' means public announcement. (Cf. Billerbeck, i. 580.)

5. *DISCIPLES UNDER PERSECUTION* (155, 157)

In the preceding sections the nature of the opposition to Jesus and His message has been exposed. The remainder of this portion of Q (Lk. $12^{4-12, 22-34}$) is a series of exhortations to the disciples concerning their behaviour in face of this situation. The first part (12^{4-12}) deals with conduct when persecuted, and its keynotes are loyalty and trust. Verses 4–9 have a parallel in Mt.'s Mission Charge (10^{28-33}). Mt. here borrows from Q. Besides this there is an independent parallel to *v.* 9 in Mk. 8^{38}||Lk. 9^{26}. Lk. 12^{10} has an independent parallel in Mk. $3^{28f.}$. Mt. $12^{31f.}$ is a conflation of Mk. and Q. Lk. $12^{11f.}$ has an independent parallel in Mk. 13^{11}, and what is probably another in Lk. $21^{14f.}$ (L?). Mt. $10^{19f.}$ is a conflation of Mk. and Q.

(*a*) Fearlessness

MT. 10^{28-31}	LK. 12^{4-7}
10 28 And be not afraid of them which kill the body, but are not able to kill the soul: but rather fear him which is able to	**12** 4 And I say unto you my friends, Be not afraid of them which kill the body, and after that have no more that they can do.

29 destroy both soul and body in [1] hell. Are
not two sparrows sold for a farthing? and
not one of them shall fall on the ground
30 without your Father: but the very hairs
31 of your head are all numbered. Fear
not therefore; ye are of more value than
many sparrows.

[1] Gr. *Gehenna.*

5 But I will warn you whom ye shall fear:
Fear him, which after he hath killed hath
[1] power to cast into [2] hell; yea, I say unto
6 you, Fear him. Are not five sparrows sold
for two farthings? and not one of them is
7 forgotten in the sight of God. But the
very hairs of your head are all numbered.
Fear not: ye are of more value than many
sparrows.

[1] Or, *authority.*
[2] Gr. *Gehenna.*

4, 5. The beginning of a new section is marked by the words ' And I say unto you my friends,' dropped by Mt. because the whole passage is incorporated in the Mission Charge. This is the only place in the Synoptic Gospels where Jesus calls His disciples ' My friends.' Cf. John $15^{14\text{f.}}$. Mt. 10^{28} ' but are not able to kill the soul ' looks like an attempt to make the words ' after that have no more that they can do ' more precise. As the text stands in Lk. it gives a perfectly good sense. The disciples are not to fear men; for man's extreme penalty is a mere nothing compared with the consequences of apostasy. Cf. 4 *Macc.*, $13^{14\text{f.}}$, ' Let us not fear him who thinketh he kills; for a great struggle and peril of the soul awaits in eternal torment those who transgress the ordinance of God.' What is to be dreaded is now stated. It is the condemnation of God. The Lucan form of the saying is the more original. Mt. 10^{28b} is abbreviation. With Lk.'s ' cast into Gehenna ' compare Mk. $9^{43, 45, 47}$. The destruction of body and soul in Gehenna (Mt. 10^{28}) is an alteration of the general statement to bring it into more exact agreement with Jewish belief. This belief is stated in *Tos. Sanhedrin* 13^{3}: ' The wicked of Israel in their bodies, and the wicked of the nations of the world in their bodies go down to hell and are punished in it for twelve months. After twelve months their souls become extinct, and their bodies are burned up, and hell casts them out, and they turn to ashes, and the wind scatters them and strews them beneath the soles of the feet of the righteous ' (Moore, *Judaism*, ii. 387). The expression ' Yea, I say unto you ' (Lk.) is characteristic of Q. Cf. Lk. 7^{26}||Mt. 11^{9}; Lk. 11^{51}. It is omitted in Mt.'s abbreviated form of the saying. The R.V. translation ' hell ' stands for Gehenna, the Græcised form of the Hebrew Gehinnom. The idea of Gehenna as a place of punishment for the godless after the final Judgement first appears in the second century B.C. Originally it is a place of punishment for the godless Israelites only; but this restriction was soon dropped, and in the days of Jesus it was thought of as prepared for all sinners, who were to be sent to it after the Judgement. Soon after the middle of the first century A.D. Gehenna began to be conceived as the place where sinners would be punished in the period between death and the Judgement. In this passage Gehenna means the place of torment for those who are condemned in the final Judgement. (Cf. Billerbeck, iv. 1029 ff. and Abrahams, *Studies*, ii. 41–49.)

6, 7. If God the Judge is to be feared, God the King is to be trusted. No human persecution is to be allowed to corrupt the loyalty of the disciples to God or to diminish their trust in Him. The duty of trusting God is illustrated first by the case of sparrows sold for food. Mt. and Lk. differ here. Mt. has ' two for a farthing': Lk. 'five for two farthings.' More correct equivalents in English money would be a halfpenny and a penny respectively. Lk. may be the more original: five is used in Jewish reckoning in much the same way as we use 'half a dozen.' At the end of the third century A.D. an edict of the Emperor Diocletian fixed the maximum price of ten sparrows at a sum equivalent to threepence-halfpenny. The sparrow's is the cheapest life in the market; but it is not outside God's care. A similar saying is ascribed to Rabbi Simeon ben Jochai (*c.* A.D. 150): 'No bird perishes without God—how much less a man!' 'Not one of them shall fall on the ground without your Father' (Mt.) is to be preferred to Lk.'s 'not one of them is forgotten in the sight of God.' For it makes clearer the connexion between the illustration of the sparrows and the reference to the hairs of the head, which is inserted between the illustration and the conclusion to be drawn from it. The force of the saying that the hairs of your head are all numbered is 'Not one hair of your head shall fall to the ground without your Father.' Cf. 1 Sam. 14^{15}. The sparrow cannot be killed apart from God's will; but you cannot suffer the smallest injury apart from God's will. God cares for the sparrow: he cares still more for you. 'Ye are of more value than many sparrows' correctly translates the Greek; but the Greek is most probably a mistranslation of the Aramaic. The conclusion required is 'Ye are of much more value than sparrows.' The difference is qualitative, not quantitative. So Wellhausen.

(*b*) Loyalty

MT. 10^{32-33}, 12^{32}

10 32 Every one therefore who shall confess
[1] me before men, [2] him will I also confess
before my Father which is in heaven.
33 But whosoever shall deny me before
men, him will I also deny before my
Father which is in heaven.
12 32 And whosoever shall speak a word
against the Son of man, it shall be forgiven him; but whosoever shall speak
against the Holy Spirit, it shall not be
forgiven him, neither in this [3] world, nor
in that which is to come.

Lk. $12^{11f.}$. Cf. Mt. $10^{19f.}$

[1] Gr. *in me.*
[2] Gr. *in him.*
[3] Or, *age.*

LK. 12^{8-12}

12 8 And I say unto you, Every one who
shall confess [1] me before men, [2] him shall
the Son of man also confess before the
9 angels of God: but he that denieth me in
the presence of men shall be denied in
the presence of the angels of God.
10 And every one who shall speak a word
against the Son of man, it shall be forgiven him: but unto him that blasphemeth against the Holy Spirit it shall not
11 be forgiven. And when they bring you
before the synagogues, and the rulers,
and the authorities, be not anxious how
or what ye shall answer, or what ye shall
12 say: for the Holy Spirit shall teach you
in that very hour what ye ought to say.

[1] Gr. *in me.*
[2] Gr. *in him.*

8 f. The duty of loyalty to God does not remain an abstraction. Jesus Himself is the object of it. It is as if He said: 'He that is faithful to me is faithful to Him that sent me.' The Jewish martyrs of the Maccabean age showed their loyalty to God by their obedience to the Law: the disciples will show the same loyalty to God in their devotion to Jesus. In Him the Kingdom of God is manifested. There are only two alternatives, acknowledgement or denial: there is no middle position. The second half of the saying is reported independently in Mk. 8^{38}:

8 38 For whosoever shall be ashamed of me and of my words in this adulterous and sinful generation, the Son of man also shall be ashamed of him, when he cometh in the glory of his Father with the holy angels.

It is to be noted that Mk. here agrees with Lk. in distinguishing between Jesus and the Son of Man. The substitution of 'I' for 'the Son of man' in Mt. is editorial work. The original Q form of the saying is that of Lk. What, then, is the meaning of this distinction between Jesus and the Son of Man? It may be that Jesus in His earthly ministry is only Son of Man designate. The force of 'him shall the Son of man also confess' will then be 'him will I also confess when I become Son of man'; and the text of Mt. will be a correct interpretation of the saying. It is, I think, more probable that the distinction is a real one, and that the 'Son of man' here stands for the Remnant, the true Israel of which Jesus is the head. This view is fortified if we accept what is probably the true reading in Mk. 8^{38} 'me and mine' rather than 'me and my words.' The idea that the community—Christ plus those that are His—will confess or deny people at the final consummation may seem strange; but it seems also to be implied in Mt. 25^{31-46} (M); Mt. 19^{28} (M); Lk. 22^{30} (L). Cf. also 1 Cor. $6^{2f.}$, and the discussion in my *Teaching of Jesus*, pp. 263–270. Moreover, the solidarity of Jesus and His followers is stressed in such sayings as Lk. 10^{16} (Q), 'He that heareth you heareth me; and he that rejecteth you rejecteth me.' So 'Whosoever shall be ashamed of me and mine' (Mk. 8^{38}) is really equivalent to the Lucan 'he that denieth me' (12^{9}). In the final consummation the confessors and deniers on earth will be confessed or denied by the Son of Man, that is, by the true spiritual Israel speaking through Christ its King.

The R.V. mg. 'confess in me' 'confess in him' gives the literal translation of the Greek text, which is itself a literal rendering of the Aramaic idiom. For 'the angels of God' (Lk.) Mt. has 'my Father which is in heaven.' The latter is a favourite Matthæan expression and probably editorial here. It has been suggested (Dalman, *Words of Jesus*, 209 f.) that 'the angels of God' is a pious periphrasis for God. There is, however, no Jewish example of such a usage, and it would be very unlikely that Jesus spoke thus or that Luke made Him speak thus. More likely we should take the words in Lk. as they stand, and regard 'before the angels of God' as another way of saying 'in heaven' or 'in the presence of God.' Cf. Lk. 15^{7} and 15^{10}.

10. This saying also has an independent parallel in Mk. $3^{28ff.}$.

3 28 Verily I say unto you, All their sins shall be forgiven unto the sons of men, and their blasphemies wherewith soever
29 they shall blaspheme: but whosoever shall blaspheme against the Holy Spirit hath never forgiveness, but is guilty of an
30 eternal sin: because they said, He hath an unclean spirit.

In the Marcan context it is Jesus' reply to the charge that He was mad; and it is probable that this is the original. It is to be noted that in Mk. there is no word about blasphemy against the Son of Man; but there is a reference to the blasphemies of the sons of men, i.e. the blasphemies which men utter against one another. Such insults, it is said, are forgivable; it is only blasphemy against the

Holy Spirit that is unforgivable. Here we have the original form of the saying. In Q the saying is detached from its context, and the blasphemies of men have become blasphemies against the Son of Man. This makes an impossible situation. For it has just been said that he who denies Christ will be denied in the Judgement. Now it is said that he who speaks a word (= blasphemes) against the Son of Man will be forgiven. The difficulties disappear when it is recognised that 'the Son of Man' in Lk. 12[10] should be 'a man.' The compiler who brought the saying into its present Q context in Aramaic may have been aware of this and understood it to mean that slanders against the disciples would put the slanderers in gravest peril, since the same Holy Spirit that worked in Jesus worked also in His followers. But if this was the case in the Aramaic Q, it has been obscured in the Greek.

Blasphemy against the Holy Spirit is not merely a matter of bad language. It is far more deadly than that. It is the extremest form of opposition to God. He who blasphemes against the Holy Spirit has identified himself so completely with the kingdom of evil that for him evil is good, ugliness beauty, and falsehood truth; and so the workings of the Holy Spirit appear to him as madness.

11 f. This saying is reported independently in Mk. 13[11] with a parallel, which may be independent (L?) in Lk. 21[14f.].

MK. 13[11]

13 11 And when they lead you to *judgement*, and deliver you up, be not anxious beforehand what ye shall speak: but whatsoever shall be given you in that hour, that speak ye: for it is not ye that speak, but the Holy Ghost.

Mt. 10[19f.] is a conflation of Mk. 13[11] and Lk. 12[11f.] (Q). In the persecution of the disciples the forms of law will be invoked. They will be prosecuted before Jewish courts (synagogues) and Gentile tribunals (the rulers and the authorities cf. Lk. 20[20]). In Rabbinic Hebrew the word 'authority' (*rāshūth*) is similarly used of the Gentile government. When the disciples—many of them simple and unlearned men—find themselves in this position, their defence will be provided for them by Divine inspiration. Cf. Acts 4[8, 13]. In Lk. 12[12], Mk. 13[11] it is 'the Holy Spirit' that inspires the defence: in Mt. 10[20] this has been changed to 'the Spirit of your Father': in Lk. 20[15] it is Christ Himself who will supply what has to be said. 'The Holy Spirit' is no doubt the original.

In all the campaign of defamation and persecution to which they will be exposed the disciples are to keep the faith, keep faith with God, and faith in God. Their first duty is to obey God at all costs; and their chief reliance is to be upon God, whom they serve and who will see them through. This is only possible if all worldly advantages and selfish ambitions are put in the background. You cannot serve God and mammon; and equally you cannot trust God and mammon. The concluding section of this part of Q sets forth this principle.

(*c*) Freedom from Worldly Cares

Lk. 12[22-31] begins with an exhortation not to be anxious about material things. The force of the exhortation in this context is obvious. Such anxiety is a hindrance to the single-minded service of God. The disciple is in danger of having business of his own to which he must attend before he can give himself to God's work. It also undermines trust in God. 'Trust in God and keep your powder dry' very soon reduces itself to 'keep your powder dry' or to 'God is on the side of the big battalions' or to 'Heaven helps those who help themselves'—in more senses than one. Material things are not, however, despised or rejected. They are put in their place. 'Seek the Kingdom, and these things shall be added unto you.' Material things have a place in the Kingdom both among its benefits (12^{31}) and in its service ($12^{33 f.}$). They can be used and enjoyed for the glory of God, but only by those who give first place to God.

MT. 6^{25-33}

6 25 Therefore I say unto you, Be not
anxious for your life, what ye shall eat, or
what ye shall drink; nor yet for your body,
what ye shall put on. Is not the life more
than the food, and the body than the
26 raiment? Behold the birds of the heaven,
that they sow not, neither do they reap,
nor gather into barns; and your heavenly
Father feedeth them. Are not ye of
27 much more value than they? And which
of you by being anxious can add one cubit
28 unto his [1] stature? And why are ye
anxious concerning raiment? Consider
the lilies of the field, how they grow; they
29 toil not, neither do they spin: yet I say
unto you, that even Solomon in all his
glory was not arrayed like one of these.
30 But if God doth so clothe the grass of the
field, which to-day is, and to-morrow is
cast into the oven, *shall he* not much more
31 *clothe* you, O ye of little faith? Be not
therefore anxious, saying, What shall we
eat? or, What shall we drink? or, Where-
32 withal shall we be clothed? For after all
these things do the Gentiles seek; for your
heavenly Father knoweth that ye have
33 need of all these things. But seek ye first
his kingdom, and his righteousness; and
all these things shall be added unto you.

[1] Or, *age*.

LK. 12^{22-31}

12 22 And he said unto his disciples, Therefore I say unto you, Be not anxious for
your [1] life, what ye shall eat;| nor yet for
your body, what ye shall put on.||For
23 the [1] life is more than the food,|and the
24 body than the raiment.||Consider the
ravens,| that they sow not, neither reap;
||which have no store-chamber nor barn;|
and God feedeth them:|of how much
25 more value are ye than the birds!||And
which of you by being anxious can add a
26 cubit unto his [2] stature? If then ye are
not able to do even that which is least,
why are ye anxious concerning the rest?
27 Consider the lilies, how they grow;|they
toil not, neither do they spin;||yet I say
unto you, Even Solomon in all his glory
28 was not arrayed like one of these.||But if
God doth so clothe the grass|in the field,
which to-day is,|and to-morrow is cast
into the oven;||how much more *shall he*
29 *clothe* you, O ye of little faith?||And seek
not ye what ye shall eat, and what ye
shall drink, neither be ye of doubtful
30 mind. For all these things do the
nations of the world seek after: but your
Father knoweth that ye have need of
31 these things. Howbeit seek ye [3] his
kingdom, and these things shall be added
unto you.

[1] Or, *soul*.
[2] Or, *age*.
[3] Many ancient authorities read *the kingdom of God*.

The whole of this Q section has been embodied by Mt. in his Sermon on the Mount. The verbal agreement between Mt. and Lk. is high.

22 f., 24, 27. 'And he said unto his disciples' marks the beginning of a new section. Mt. has altered the introductory formula in the interests of his continuous discourse. Verses 22 f. state the theme of the paragraph. Jesus is not preaching asceticism. He does not suggest that there is any religious value in starvation or nakedness. What He demands is a sense of proportion and a true valuation of things. Food is not an end in itself, but only a means to an end, the maintenance of life. Similarly dress is necessary for the protection of the body. Life and health

are more important than food and clothing. It is possible that there is here a tacit criticism of the multitude of scribal regulations about permitted and forbidden foods and articles of clothing—whether an egg laid on a Feast-day might be eaten or not, and the like. But the main point is the more general one that God has given man life and that He may be trusted to give also what is necessary for the maintenance of life. This is enforced by two illustrations. These two short pieces are an excellent example of what I have called compound parallelism (*Teaching of Jesus*, pp. 54 ff.). The two illustrations as wholes answer to one another; and the several parts of each are also in parallelism. This can best be shown by setting the two pieces out in lines.

I. Consider the ravens, (*a*)
That they neither sow nor reap; (*b*1)
They have no barn or storehouse; (*b*2)
And God feeds them: (*d*)
How much better are you than the birds! (*f*)

II. Consider the lilies, (*a*)
How they neither toil nor spin, (*b*)
Yet I tell you that Solomon in all his glory
was not arrayed like one of these. (*c*)
But if God so clothe the grass (*d*)
Which to-day is in the field (*e*1)
And to-morrow is cast into the oven; (*e*2)
How much more you, O ye of little faith? (*f*)

In the first strophe the Lucan text is better than that in Mt. ‘ Ravens ’ (Lk.) is generalised by Mt. to ‘ birds.’ Then when ‘ birds ’ appears in the last line Mt. has to alter it to ‘ them.’ The parallelism of lines 2 and 3 in Lk. is destroyed in Mt.’s ‘ they sow not, neither do they reap, nor gather into barns ’ which is more logical but less poetical. In the second strophe the words ‘ they grow ’ are omitted by some important authorities for the text of Lk. They are probably an intrusion from Mt.; and the true text of Q is as given in line 2. It is closely parallel in form to the corresponding line in strophe I. The original text of Lk. is: ‘ How they neither spin nor weave ’; that of Mt.: ‘ How they grow; they toil not, neither do they spin.’ The form of the line in Lk. is preferable to that in Mt.; but the verbs of Mt. are more likely to be original than those of Lk. Lk.’s ‘ spin ’ and ‘ weave ’ is more logical; but the ‘ toil ’ and ‘ spin ’ of Mt. probably represents a play upon words in Aramaic (*‘ămal* and *‘ăzal*). So the original Q form of the line may be reconstructed: ‘ How they neither toil nor spin.’ The translation given in strophe II, line 5 is preferable to that of R.V.

Jesus here appeals to the wild birds and the wild flowers, which owe nothing to human care. God gives them existence and life, and God provides for them. If He does that for the lower forms of life, He will do no less for man. In the second strophe by ‘ the lilies ’ may be meant the purple anemone, which would be contrasted with the royal purple of Solomon (so Dalman). It should be noted how Jesus here makes use of an old motif (Job 8^{12}, 14^{2}; Ps. 37^{2}, $90^{5f.}$, $103^{15f.}$; Is. 37^{27},

40[6-8]), in which the brief life of the plant is used as an illustration of the shortness of human life. To-day the wild plants are a brave show: to-morrow they will be withered and dried up, so much fuel for the oven. But Jesus gives the old motif an original and characteristic turn. For Him the moral of the tale is not 'These things pass, and so must we,' but 'God lavishes infinite pains on these things, brief though their span of life is: how much more will He care for His children.'

25 f. Between the two illustrations a further argument is introduced. The translation of *v.* 25 presents a difficulty; for the Greek word translated 'stature' in R.V. commonly means 'age.' The question is whether the words mean 'Which of you by being anxious can increase his height?' or 'Which of you by being anxious can prolong his life?' Commentators are divided on this point. In the present context the former alternative is the more likely. The section is concerned with food and clothing; and for first-century Palestine food and clothing depended mainly on the growth of crops and the produce of the farm generally. These are the very things about which the small farmer is constantly worrying. Jesus says: if it were possible to stimulate growth by worrying, you ought to be able to do it in your own persons. If you cannot make yourself grow, how can you expect to make the corn grow by worrying? All growth depends on God. Verse 26 has no parallel in Mt.

29, 30. The version of the saying in Mt. (*v.* 31) appears to be the more original. Compare the saying of the first-century Rabbi Eleazar: 'Whoever has bread in his basket and asks, What shall I eat to-morrow, is none other than those of little faith' (*Sotah*, 48*b*). The true attitude of man towards God in these matters is given in the Lord's Prayer. The constant anxiety about material things is characteristic of the Gentiles. One is reminded of the pagan fertility cults and other magical devices to secure material goods. Since the days of Hosea it had been a dogma in Israel that it is God alone who gives the corn and the wine and all the other produce of nature. The knowledge that these things come from the Father as His gifts to His children, that they come not capriciously but out of His perfect knowledge of man's needs and His perfect love for His children, this is the true antidote to anxiety and fear and to the superstition that follows in their train.

31. Life is more important than food; but there is something more important than life itself—the Kingdom of God. This comes first and disciples must place it first. They must pray 'Thy Kingdom come: Thy will be done' *before* they say 'Give us our daily bread.' Jesus establishes a hierarchy of values; and at the head stands the Kingdom. His claim is that nothing else can be understood or valued aright until this is given its rightful place. Once men have done this, they will know the true value of their own lives and of all other things: and in that knowledge they will find deliverance from fear and anxiety. The Lucan form of the saying is the more original. 'And his righteousness' and 'all' in Mt. 6[33] are characteristic Matthæan touches.

(*d*) Confidence in God

LK. 12[32]

12 32 Fear not, little flock; for it is your Father's good pleasure to give you the kingdom.

32. This verse has no parallel in Mt. Compare Lk. $22^{29\text{ f.}}$ (L); Mt. 21^{43}. The little flock is a handful of lambs in the midst of wolves (10^{3}); a seemingly hopeless position. The search for the Kingdom seems to be a fool's errand. But in the last resort success in this quest does not depend on human power or wisdom, but upon God. It is God who gives the Kingdom, as He gives all else. The Kingdom, as here conceived, is the Kingdom that is to be, the perfect condition of existence for God's children.

(*e*) Independence of Worldly Goods

Cf. Mt. 6^{19-21} (M?)	LK. 12^{33-34}
	12 33 Sell that ye have, and give alms;‖make for yourselves purses which wax not old, ‖a treasure in the heavens that faileth not,‖where no thief draweth near, neither 34 moth destroyeth.‖For where your treasure is, there will your heart be also.‖

33, 34. Mt. 6^{19-21} is similar to these verses; but the differences are large. It is possible, as Bussmann suggests (*Syn. Stud.*, ii. 82 f.) that Mt. is here drawing from his special source (M) and that Lk. 12^{32-34} is the Q version of the saying. The voluntary poverty here recommended depends chiefly on the recognition that all the world's goods are of little value in comparison with the good things of the Kingdom. Further, there is the conviction that the coming of the Kingdom with all its benefits is very near. This conviction is dominant in the early Church, and certainly goes back to Jesus Himself. The fact that the attempt was made in the earliest days of the Jerusalem community to put this precept into practice (Acts $2^{44\text{ f.}}$, 4^{32-37}) is strong evidence for the authenticity of the saying. The motive for hoarding is gone, if that is at hand which will demonetise all existing wealth. But that is not all. The saying has to do with the belief, common in every age, that wealth is power, and the consequent temptation to trust mammon rather than God. Jesus here asserts that in reality money is a very weak thing. So far from being a protection it requires to be protected. The millionaire spends one half of his life in acquiring his million and the other half in trying to keep it. So material goods, which should serve man, become his master; and the thought, strength, and love that should be devoted to God and His Kingdom are given instead to mammon.

D. THE FUTURE

In the preceding sections the message and mission of Jesus have been set out in relation to the best that had been thought and achieved before Him (section A), in relation to those who hear His call (section B) and those who reject and oppose Him (section C). The interest now turns more definitely to the future and the fulfilment of what has been prepared for by John and revealed in Jesus. In this concluding section of Q there are four main divisions: (1) The present time a time of crisis in view of the approaching end. (2) The peril of neglect and refusal of the message. (3) The demands of discipleship in view of the end. (4) The final consummation. There is no sharp division between the present section and the preceding. The thought of the disciples under persecution and opposition leads naturally to the thought that this present state is but the prelude to another condition in which faithfulness will receive its reward.

The view which dominates the whole of this section is that the existing order is coming to an end, and that the end will come soon and suddenly. It will break into the normal order of human existence like a thunderbolt out of a clear sky. This is the earliest form of the Christian expectation, as appears from 1 Thess. 5^{1-10}. It is also the view of Lk. 21^{34-36} (L) and Mk. 13^{32-37}. This view stands in sharp contrast to the programme outlined in Mk. 13^{5-31}. There the end is led up to by a series of catastrophes. There can be little doubt that the teaching of Jesus is more accurately represented by Q and its allies than by Mk. 13^{5-31}; and it seems probable that the solution of the contradiction is that Mk. 13^{5-31} is a document made up, in the main, of genuine sayings of Jesus, but so arranged that the total impression is wrong. Cf. *The Teaching of Jesus*, pp. 260 ff.

The first part of this eschatological section of Q may be divided up somewhat as follows. The present time is a time of crisis: (*a*) for the disciples (12^{35-48}); (*b*) for Jesus Himself (12^{49-53}); (*c*) for Israel (12^{54-59}). This is so because (*d*) forces have been set in motion which lead inevitably to one result (13^{18-21}). With the coming of Jesus something has happened which marks the end of the old order and the beginning of the new. Soon the change will be complete. The call to men and women is a call to repent while there is still time. To those who have already accepted the yoke of the Kingdom it is a call to be watchful and faithful in the time that remains. It is the old challenge that is set before the people: 'Choose you this day whom ye will serve.' But it comes with a new urgency because it is backed by a new revelation of the nature of God and of His Kingdom. In the light of that revelation to refuse the challenge is to take a terrible responsibility.

1. *THE TIME OF CRISIS*

(*a*) For the Disciples (158, 159)

Cf. Mt. 25^{1-13} (M).

LK. 12^{35-38}

12 35 Let your loins be girded about, and
36 your lamps burning; and be ye yourselves
like unto men looking for their lord,
when he shall return from the marriage
feast; that, when he cometh and knocketh, they may straightway open unto him.
37 Blessed are those [1] servants, whom the
lord when he cometh shall find watching:
verily I say unto you, that he shall gird
himself, and make them sit down to
meat, and shall come and serve them.
38 And if he shall come in the second watch,
and if in the third, and find *them* so,
blessed are those *servants*.

[1] Gr. *bond-servants*.

35-38. Lk. 12^{35-38} has no parallel in Mt.; but Mt. 25^{1-13} has several features in common with this passage. The girt loins signify readiness and the lighted lamp watchfulness. The time when the servants will be required is uncertain. 'Men' (*v.* 36) means servants (Preuschen-Bauer, col. 108); and the 'looking for' their master is a looking with eager expectancy, a waiting to welcome Him. For the disciples the consummation is the consummation of their *hopes*. The significance of the marriage feast may be left an open question for the moment. See below, p. 517. The point is that the master of the servants is absent and the exact time of his return is unknown to them. They will not even see him coming. The first intimation of his presence will be his knock at the door. Those who are prepared for his appearance will find that it spells the highest happiness for them. Hitherto they have given of their best to their master: now he will give to them service for service and benefit for benefit. We must compare Lk. 17^{7-10}. There the point is that the very thing that is here promised is the last thing that servants would dare to expect. So the point here is that the reward of watchfulness and faithfulness will be something beyond all expectation. The saying ends with a fresh emphasis on the uncertainty of the time of the Parousia. The reference to second and third watch implies the Jewish division of the night into three periods. Roman practice divided the night into four watches. The latter system appears in Mk. 13^{35}. The servants must be prepared to stay awake all night if necessary. So the disciples must continue watchful, even after their first expectations have been disappointed. 'Blessed are those servants' is an exclamation: 'How happy are those servants!' Compare Philip Doddridge's paraphrase of this passage in his hymn beginning

'Ye servants of the Lord,
Each in his office wait.'

MT. 24^{43-44}

24 43 [1] But know this, that if the master of the house had known in what watch the thief was coming, he would have watched, and would not have suffered
44 his house to be [2] broken through. Therefore be ye also ready: for in an hour that ye think not the Son of man cometh.

[1] Or, *But this ye know.*
[2] Gr. *digged through.*

LK. 12^{39-40}

12 39 [1] But know this, that if the master of the house had known in what hour the thief was coming, he would have watched, and not have left his house to
40 be [2] broken through. Be ye also ready: for in an hour that ye think not the Son of man cometh.

[1] Or, *But this ye know.*
[2] Gr. *digged through.*

A second parable stressing the unexpectedness of the end. The agreement between Mt. and Lk. is close. 'Hour' (Lk. 12^{39}) should perhaps be preferred to 'watch' (Mt. 24^{43}). Cf. Lk. 12^{40} = Mt. 24^{44}; Lk. 12^{46} = Mt. 24^{50}. Several early and important authorities omit the words 'have watched and' in Lk. 12^{39}. This shorter text may be the original in Lk. and Q, and the added words an editorial gloss in Mt., which has crept into MSS. of Lk. 'Left' (Lk.) and 'suffered' (Mt.) are translation variants. Cf. the Greek versions of Dan. $4^{12, 23}$.

39 f. This second parable makes the same point as the preceding. The figure here employed appears again in 1 Thess. $5^{2ff.}$, 'The day of the Lord so cometh as a thief in the night.' Cf. 2 Pet. 3^{10}; Rev. 3^{3}, 16^{15}. 'Digged through' (R.V. mg.) is a more literal rendering of the Greek than 'broken through.' Cf. Mt. 6^{19}; Job. 24^{16}. The expression depends on the fact that in Palestine the walls of houses were commonly made of clay. The practice of digging through the wall

rather than forcing the door of the house may have been due to superstitious motives. Cf. Trumbull, *The Threshold Covenant*, pp. 260 f. For those who are not prepared the coming of the Son of Man means disaster. This coming of the Son of Man, which Paul, using a term borrowed from the Old Testament, calls 'the day of the Lord,' stands for the Judgement, the final vindication of righteousness and the end of evil. It is the full manifestation of the Kingdom of God in power and glory; and this means, among other things, the vindication of all who have accepted the Kingdom and been faithful. The origin of the idea is in Dan. 7.

MT. 24^{45-51}

24 45 Who then is the faithful and wise
[1] servant, whom his lord hath set over his
household, to give them their food in due
46 season? Blessed is that [1] servant, whom
his lord when he cometh shall find so
47 doing. Verily I say unto you, that he
48 will set him over all that he hath. But if
that evil [1] servant shall say in his heart,
49 My lord tarrieth; and shall begin to beat
his fellow-servants, and shall eat and
50 drink with the drunken; the lord of that
[1] servant shall come in a day when he
expecteth not, and in an hour when he
knoweth not, and shall [2] cut him
asunder, and appoint his portion with
51 the hypocrites: there shall be the weeping
and gnashing of teeth.

[1] Gr. *bondservant*.
[2] Or, *severely scourge him*.

LK. 12^{41-46}

12 41 And Peter said, Lord, speakest thou
this parable unto us, or even unto all?
42 And the Lord said, Who then is [1] the
faithful and wise steward, whom his lord
shall set over his household, to give them
their portion of food in due season?
43 Blessed is that [2] servant, whom his lord
when he cometh shall find so doing.
44 Of a truth I say unto you, that he will set
45 him over all that he hath. But if that
[2] servant shall say in his heart, My lord
delayeth his coming; and shall begin to
beat the menservants and the maidservants, and to eat and drink, and to be
46 drunken; the lord of that [2] servant shall
come in a day when he expecteth not,
and in an hour when he knoweth not,
and shall [3] cut him asunder, and appoint
his portion with the unfaithful.

[1] Or, *the faithful steward, the wise* man *whom, etc.*
[2] Gr. *bondservant*.
[3] Or, *severely scourge him*.

The task of the disciples is not confined to watchfulness. They have positive duties to perform and those who stand nearest to Jesus have the heaviest responsibility. The work is the work of the Kingdom as already defined in the Mission Charge. And at the end this work will be examined. Cf. 1 Cor. 4^{1-5}. The agreement between Mt. and Lk. is close.

41. This verse has no parallel in Mt., which is curious since Mt. is following Q from 24^{43} to 24^{51}. If the verse stood in Q, Mt. has omitted it. It is commonly regarded as the work of Lk. On the other hand, Mt. may have omitted it because it was difficult to understand what it meant. It certainly is difficult. When Peter asks whether 'this parable' refers to 'us,' he presumably means the Twelve; and the most natural interpretation of 'this parable' is the immediately preceding parable of the thief in the night. But it is impossible to see what special reference this parable could have to the Twelve rather than to anyone else. Possibly 'this parable' means the whole passage Lk. 12^{35-40}, with the promise of *v.* 37 specially in view. Peter is then asking whether the privileges there mentioned are for the Twelve alone or for all disciples. If *v.* 41 is genuine, this seems to be the only suitable interpretation. There is now the further difficulty that *vv.* 42–46 do not give an answer to the question put in *v.* 41. We can only conclude that if Lk.

invented *v.* 41, he did so for some purpose which he succeeded in concealing from his readers. Editorial glosses are usually more transparent than this. Perhaps the truth is that the verse stood in Q and that Mt. omitted it because it was as obscure to him as it is to us

42–44. The reply of Jesus is another parable. The subject of the story is the servant who, in the absence of the master, is made responsible for the welfare of his fellow-servants. From the contrasting *v.* 45 it is clear that *v.* 42 is very much compressed. It begins by asking who is to be chief among the servants, and immediately goes on to explain this headship in terms not of rule, but of service. This is in entire agreement with the principle laid down in Mk. 10^{42-45}, 9^{35}; Mt. 23^{11}. Cf. John $21^{15ff.}$ We might venture to paraphrase: ' If anyone deserves the name of wise and faithful steward, it is he, who being left in charge of his fellow-servants, devotes himself to their welfare.' This makes a good connexion with *v.* 43. Such a servant will have the approval of his master and will be amply rewarded—with larger duties and responsibilities. Compare the parable of the Talents. The good time that is coming at the end of the present age is not described in the teaching of Jesus, save in figurative terms. But there is here a definite hint that it is not passive enjoyment, but a larger and more satisfying activity that is promised; a more abundant and fruitful life with fuller opportunities of service.

45. The other side of the picture. The servant who conceives his position as an opportunity to gratify the lust for power and authority and to satisfy his own selfish desires. Mt. (24^{48}) designates him as ' evil,' explaining the obvious. ' Say in his heart ' is the common Hebrew idiom for ' think.' ' Begin to beat ' is another Semitism. The use of ' begin ' as a kind of auxiliary verb with no special significance is a common Aramaic idiom.

46. The servant who acts in this way will have a rude awakening. The return of his master will be sudden and unexpected; and it will mean deposition and punishment for him. As the Greek text stands the punishment is death. There is no authority for the marginal alternative ' severely scourge.' The method of execution is the antique one of cutting the victim in two or hewing him in pieces. (Homer. *Od.* 18^{339}; 2 Sam. 12^{31}; Heb. 11^{37}, etc.) But it may be questioned whether the Greek text is reliable at this point. For (1) if the master has cut the servant in two, the appointing of his portion among the unfaithful is a superfluous anticlimax; and (2) *vv.* 47 f. in Lk. go on to describe the punishment for unsatisfactory servants in detail, and in the worst case it is only severe scourging. Perhaps we have here a mistranslation of the Aramaic. It may be pointed out that the Hebrew word for ' to cut in pieces ' is *nittach*, and that the corresponding Aramaic verb *nattach* means to ' take away,' ' separate.' The original sense here may therefore have been ' he will separate him [from the rest] '; cf. Mt. 25^{32}. ' Appoint his portion ' is a Jewish idiom. ' Unfaithful ' (Lk.) is preferable to ' hypocrites ' (Mt.): it stands in contrast to ' faithful ' in Lk. *v.* 42. Mt. (*v.* 51) adds ' there shall be the weeping and gnashing of teeth,' a favourite expression in that gospel; cf. Mt. $13^{42, 50}$, 22^{13}, 25^{30}; and 8^{12} with the parallel in Lk. 13^{28}.

47 f. The nature of the punishment is now described in Lk. $12^{47f.}$. These verses have no parallel in Mt. It may be conjectured that Matthew omitted them

because he realised the finality of ' cut him asunder.' Luke will have kept them, being, as usual, faithful to his source.

LK. 12^{47-48}

12 47 And that [1] servant, which knew his lord's will, and made not ready, nor did according to his will, shall be beaten with
48 many *stripes*; but he that knew not, and did things worthy of stripes, shall be beaten with few *stripes*. And to whomsoever much is given, of him shall much be required: and to whom they commit much, of him will they ask the more.

[1] Gr. *bondservant*.

The punishment of unfaithful servants depends on whether the offence was wilful disobedience or mere stupidity and folly. The distinction is the same as that made in the Old Testament between sins of ignorance and sins committed ' with a high hand.' And ignorance in this connexion does not necessarily mean absolute ignorance: it can mean the peculiar human tendency to forget the rule at the critical moment. So the Rabbis in the Mishnah (*Sabbath* 7^1): ' A great general rule have they laid down concerning the Sabbath: whosoever, forgetful of the principle of the Sabbath, committed many acts of work on many Sabbaths, is liable only to one sin-offering; but if, mindful of the principle of the Sabbath, he yet committed many acts of work on many Sabbaths, he is liable for every Sabbath [which he profaned] ' (Danby, p. 106). Similarly here: he who knowingly flouts the will of his master will have the severer punishment; he who is forgetful of it, the lighter. This is applicable especially to the disciples. They, more than anyone else, have been admitted to the confidence of Jesus. Accordingly, a greater faithfulness will be expected of them, than of the less intimate of the hearers and followers of Jesus. This principle is stated in general terms (*v.* 48^b). With the whole passage (Lk. 12^{41-48}) cf. 1 Cor. 4^{1-5}.

We may now see a connexion with *v.* 41. Peter asks whether the fine promises made in *v.* 37 are for the Twelve specially. The reply of Jesus is in effect: ' I make no promises to you: I give you tasks. Your reward depends on the spirit and manner in which you perform those tasks. He who would be great in the Kingdom of God must be the servant of all.'

(*b*) For Jesus Himself (160)

MT. 10^{34-36}

10 34 Think not that I came to [1] send peace on the earth: I came not to [1] send peace,
35 but a sword. For I came to set a man at variance against his father, and the daughter against her mother, and the daughter in law against her mother in
36 law: and a man's foes *shall be* they of his own household.

[1] Gr. *cast*.

LK. 12^{49-53}

12 49 I came to cast fire upon the earth;||and
50 what will I, if it is already kindled?||But I have a baptism to be baptized with;|| and how am I straitened till it be ac-
51 complished!||Think ye that I am come to give peace in the earth?||I tell you, Nay;
52 but rather division:||for there shall be from henceforth five in one house divided,||three against two, and two
53 against three.||They shall be divided, father against son, and son against father;||mother against daughter, and daughter against her mother;||mother in law against her daughter in law, and daughter in law against her mother in law.||

This section is in poetical form (cf. Burney, p. 90). The first two verses of Lk. are absent from Mt. Perhaps he dropped them as not strictly relevant in the context in which he was incorporating the rest of the Q passage. Verse 36 of Mt. does not appear in Lk.: it is the end of the prophetic oracle (Micah 7[6]), upon which the saying is based. Whether it stood in Q or has been supplied in Mt. from the Old Testament it is difficult to say. The latter seems the more probable alternative.

49 f. These two verses express in poignant terms the heavy burden which His mission lays upon Jesus. He, who above all others wishes to establish friendship and brotherly love among men, must create strife and division. For the Kingdom of God comes to cut across all the natural relations of men. Its absolute demands take precedence of all human claims, friendships, family affection. Jesus cannot speak smooth and comfortable words to His generation. And in these lines we see the desperate tension in the kindest of all hearts between His own tenderness and the hardness of His task. The nearest parallel to this tragedy is to be found in the 'Confessions' of Jeremiah, where there is a similar struggle in the prophet's mind 'between fidelity to his prophetic commission and the natural feelings and impulses of his heart' (Skinner, *Prophecy and Religion*, p. 210; see the whole chapter, XI). This tension is given expression in Jer. 20[9] (Skinner's translation):

If I said, 'I will seek to forget Him,
  And speak no more in His name,'
'Twas like glowing fire in my breast,
  Shut up in my bones.
I was weary with keeping it under;
  I could not hold out.

We should probably translate Lk. 12[49]:

I came to cast fire upon the earth;
And how I wish that it was now kindled!

The natural shrinking from a terrible necessity, and the clear vision that the task must be carried out. Along with this goes the sense that the fulfilment of the mission means extreme suffering for Himself, and that not merely as something incidental. The 'baptism' is an essential, the essential part of His work. He is hampered and handicapped until it is accomplished. For this use of 'baptism' cf. Mk. 10[38]. The idea can be traced back to the Old Testament (Ps. 42[7], 69[2, 15]); and there is perhaps an echo of it in the Pauline phrase 'baptized into His death.'

51, 52 f. The remainder of the section has a parallel in Mt. 10[34-36]. It dwells further on the point made in *v.* 49. The manifestation of the Kingdom means warfare to the bitter end against evil; and evil is so firmly entrenched in human life and human relations that much suffering and heartbreak are inevitable before it can be cast out. Those who think that the Messiah will come and transform the world by a wave of the magic wand are sadly mistaken. The coming of Jesus brings tension: it brings to sharpest issue the struggle between the Kingdom of

God and the forces of evil. It compels men to take sides; and members of the same family may be in opposite camps. This is expressed in terms borrowed from Micah 7[6]. Cf. *Jubilees* 23[16, 19], 'and in that generation the sons will convict their fathers and their elders of sin and unrighteousness. . . . And they will strive one with another, the young with the old, and the old with the young.' Mishnah, *Soṭah* 9[15], 'with the footprints of the Messiah presumption shall increase and dearth reach its height. . . . Children shall shame the elders and the elders shall rise up before the children, "for the son dishonoureth, etc." (Micah 7[6]). The face of this generation is as the face of a dog, and the son will not be put to shame by his father' (Danby, p. 306). The division 'three against two and two against three' is a division of old and young. The household consists of the father and mother on the one side and the son and his wife and the daughter on the other. It is the new generation against the old. Cf. Mk. 2[21 f.], 3[31-35]; Lk. 9[59-62], 11[27 f.], 14[26]. The picture here drawn by Jesus of the results of His work is in startling contrast to the kind of expectation shown in the rôle assigned to Elijah in Malachi 4[5 f.]. Here again Jesus reverses current expectations about the coming of the Kingdom.

(*c*) For Israel (160, 161)

LK. 12[54-56]

12 54 And he said to the multitudes also, When ye see a cloud rising in the west, straightway ye say, There cometh a
55 shower; and so it cometh to pass. And when *ye see* a south wind blowing, ye say, There will be a [1] scorching heat; and it
56 cometh to pass. Ye hypocrites, ye know how to [2] interpret the face of the earth and the heaven; but how is it that ye know not how to [2] interpret this time?

[1] Or, *hot wind*.
[2] Gr. *prove*.

54 f., 56. This passage has no parallel in Mt. The similar saying in Mt. 16[2 f.] is an early interpolation in that Gospel. It is said that the Lucan form of the saying agrees with the facts in Palestine, where rain comes from the West (cf. 1 Kings 18[44]), and wind from the East and South is accompanied by heat-waves. (Cf. G. A. Smith, *Historical Geography of the Holy Land* [20], pp. 66 ff.) These things are important to the Palestinian farmer, and he makes it his business to understand the significance of the weather signs. This meteorological sensitiveness stands in sharp contrast to the religious insensitiveness of the people. Things are happening in their midst, under their noses, of far greater significance; and they cannot or will not see the meaning of them. They cannot or will not realise that this is for them a time of crisis, when decisions must be made which are of supreme importance. The work of Jesus is the sign of the time. From it they ought to infer that the Kingdom of God has come upon them and that the final consummation is near. But they refuse to know the things that belong to their peace. If they did, they would hasten to repent and seek entrance into the Kingdom while there is still time.

This parable is followed by what is now rightly regarded as another parable bearing upon the same point. In Mt. it has been incorporated in the Sermon on the Mount and transformed into a moral rule. The Q context shows clearly that it is originally an eschatological parable.

MT. 5^{25-26}

5 25 Agree with thine adversary quickly, whiles thou art with him in the way; lest haply the adversary deliver thee to the judge, and the judge [1] deliver thee to the
26 officer, and thou be cast into prison. Verily I say unto thee, Thou shalt by no means come out thence, till thou have paid the last farthing.

[1] Some ancient authorities omit *deliver thee.*

LK. 12^{57-59}

12 57 And why even of yourselves judge ye
58 not what is right? For as thou art going with thine adversary before the magistrate, on the way give diligence to be quit of him; lest haply he hale thee unto the judge, and the judge shall deliver thee to the [1] officer, and the [1] officer shall
59 cast thee into prison. I say unto thee, Thou shalt by no means come out thence, till thou have paid the very last mite.

[1] Gr. *exactor.*

57, 58 f. Verse 57 effects the transition from the preceding parable to this one. It pillories the moral and spiritual blindness of the people. They can see what is to their advantage in any sphere except the most important of all. If they would take stock of their lives they would see that there was only one decent, honest course open to them—to come to God in the deepest humility, confessing their moral and spiritual bankruptcy and casting themselves on His mercy while there is still time. If they were in the same strait financially, they would know what to do. The shrewd Galilean peasant would not go to court with a hopeless case. He would use every persuasion, every artifice to come to terms before the hearing, and so avoid the possibility of being imprisoned for the debt with no prospect of release until all is paid. The ' mite ' is the smallest copper coin, equivalent to about one-sixteenth of a penny. It corresponds to the Jewish coin known as the *pĕruṭah*. Mt. has ' farthing,' the Roman *quadrans*, a coin equal to two mites. In the Mishnah the *quadrans* is not mentioned, and in the New Testament ' mite ' is the regular word for a very small amount of money. The only other place in the New Testament where ' farthing ' is used is Mk. 12^{42}, where it is introduced by the evangelist to explain the meaning of ' mite ' to his Gentile readers. It is therefore probable that ' mite ' is the original reading of Q.

The moral of the parable is sufficiently obvious. Men are even now on their way to the court, where they must give account of their lives. For the comparison of a sinner to an insolvent debtor see Mt. 18^{23-35}; Lk. 7^{41-43}. The only hope for men is to come to terms by repentance while there is still time.

The reason why the present time is a time of crisis is now stated in a double parable in which the Kingdom of God is likened sucessively to Mustard Seed and Leaven. The obvious point in these two parables is the fact that a small beginning is made whose consequences are great and far-reaching. Not only so, but once the beginning has been made, the result is inevitable. The Kingdom has begun to come in the mission of Jesus; and now it must run its course to the final consummation. This means that Jesus and His little group of followers represent the vital factor in the whole situation, the sign of the times. To understand the mission of Jesus, to come to terms with what He represents, is a life and death matter for men.

MT. 13^{31-33}

13 31 Another parable set he before them, saying, The kingdom of heaven is like unto a grain of mustard seed, which a

LK. 13^{18-21} (164)

13 13 He said therefore, Unto what is the kingdom of God like? and whereunto
19 shall I liken it? It is like unto a grain of

32 man took, and sowed in his field: which indeed is less than all seeds; but when it is grown, it is greater than the herbs, and becometh a tree, so that the birds of the heaven come and lodge in the branches thereof.

33 Another parable spake he unto them; The kingdom of heaven is like unto leaven, which a woman took, and hid in three [1] measures of meal, till it was all leavened.

[1] The word in the Greek denotes the Hebrew seah, a measure containing nearly a peck and a half.

mustard seed, which a man took, and cast into his own garden; and it grew, and became a tree; and the birds of the heaven lodged in the branches thereof.
20 And again he said, Whereunto shall I
21 liken the kingdom of God? It is like unto leaven, which a woman took and hid in three [1] measures of meal, till it was all leavened.

[1] See marginal note on Matt. xiii. 33.

MK. 4^{30-32}

4 30 And he said, How shall we liken the kingdom of God? or in what parable shall
31 we set it forth? [1] It is like a grain of mustard seed, which, when it is sown upon the earth, though it be less than all the
32 seeds that are upon the earth, yet when it is sown, groweth up, and becometh greater than all the herbs, and putteth out great branches; so that the birds of the heaven can lodge under the shadow thereof.

[1] Gr. *As unto.*

18, 19. The parable of the Mustard Seed is reported independently in Mk. 4^{30-32}. The version of it in Mt. is a conflation of Mk. and Q. The introduction in question form (Mk. and Lk.) corresponds to Jewish ways of introducing parables, and is surely original. It has disappeared in Mt. The grain of mustard seed is a proverbial Jewish expression for a minute quantity. Cf. Mt. 17^{30} = Lk. 17^{6} (Q); *Niddah* 5^{2} (Danby, p. 750); also *Koran* 21^{48}. According to Jewish rule the mustard plant is sown in the field and not in the garden; and so Mt.'s ' field ' is probably the original. In Palestine the mustard plant attains a height of eight and twelve feet and birds come to it for the seeds (*Encyclopædia Biblica*, col 3244). The reference to the ' birds of the heaven ' is probably significant. Both in apocalyptic and Rabbinical literature ' the birds of heaven ' stand for the Gentile nations. (Cf. *The Teaching of Jesus*, p. 133, n. 1); and an interest in the Gentiles is characteristic of Q. It is possible that we have here in parable what is said openly in a later Q passage (Lk. 13^{28-30}).

There are two points in the parable. The first and most important is that mentioned above, that a process has been started which *must* go on to its inevitable end. Whether it will take a short time or long does not enter into the calculation. It is the same as in the seed parable in Mk. 4^{26-29}. There also, once the seed is sown, each subsequent stage till the harvest follows inevitably. The second point lies in the contrast between the small and seemingly insignificant beginnings and the final realisation. The preaching and healing mission of the Carpenter of Nazareth hardly seems to usher in the new age. Yet it does.

20 f. These two points again come to expression in the companion parable of the Leaven. Once the leaven has been put into the dough the leavening process goes on inevitably till the whole is leavened; and this although there is no comparison between the mass of dough and the small quantity of leaven.

The passages considered so far are all heavy with the sense of terrible urgency. We see Jesus Himself tasting the full bitterness of the conflict between the claims of His mission and the natural instincts and affections of the human heart. We see the constant demand for loyalty, courage, watchfulness. We hear the summons to repent while there is yet time. Obedience to this call is costly, only less costly than disobedience. There are those who will not hear the call; and our document now turns to speak of their fate.

2. *THE FATE OF THE UNREPENTANT*

(*a*) The Closed Door (165)

Lk. $13^{23 f.}$ Cf. Mt. $7^{13 f.}$

Lk. 13^{25}. Cf. Mt. 25^{10-12}.

Lk. $13^{26 f.}$ Cf. Mt. $7^{22 f.}$

Lk. 13^{28-30}. Cf. Mt. $8^{11 f.}$

MT. 8^{11-12}

8 11 And I say unto you, that many shall come
from the east and the west, and shall [1] sit
down with Abraham, and Isaac, and
12 Jacob, in the kingdom of heaven: but the
sons of the kingdom shall be cast forth into
the outer darkness: there shall be the
weeping and gnashing of teeth.

[1] Gr. *recline.*

LK. 13^{22-30}

13 22 And he went on his way through cities
and villages, teaching, and journeying on
23 unto Jerusalem. And one said unto him,
Lord, are they few that be saved?
24 And he said unto them, Strive to enter in
by the narrow door: for many, I say unto
you, shall seek to enter in, and shall not
25 be [1] able. When once the master of the
house is risen up, and hath shut to the
door, and ye begin to stand without, and
to knock at the door, saying, Lord, open
to us; and he shall answer and say to
26 you, I know you not whence ye are; then
shall ye begin to say, We did eat and
drink in thy presence, and thou didst
27 teach in our streets; and he shall say, I
tell you, I know not whence ye are; depart from me, all ye workers of iniquity.
28 There shall be the weeping and gnashing
of teeth, when ye shall see Abraham, and
Isaac, and Jacob, and all the prophets,
in the kingdom of God, and yourselves
29 cast forth without. And they shall come
from the east and west, and from the
north and south, and shall [2] sit down in
30 the kingdom of God. And behold, there
are last which shall be first, and there are
first which shall be last.

[1] Or, *able, when once.*
[2] Gr. *recline.*

The Matthæan parallels to this section are scattered about in Mt. With the exception of Mt. 8^{11-12} they are probably all to be assigned to M. The first is hardly a parallel at all. For Mt. $7^{13 f.}$ is concerned with *two* ways, one leading to life and the other to death; while Lk. $13^{24 f.}$ is concerned with *one* door, and the question is which side of the door a man is on. Mt. 25^{10-12} belongs to the parable of the Ten Virgins, which is derived from M. Mt. $7^{22 f.}$ shows very little verbal agreement with Lk. $13^{26 f.}$; and what there is is confined to the quotation from Ps. 6^{8}. Mt. $8^{11 f.}$, which is inserted into Mt.'s account of the Centurion of Capernaum, may be derived from Q: it has considerable resemblance to Lk. 13^{28-30}.

22 f., 24. These verses provide the setting for the speech of Jesus which follows. Whether *v.* 22 belonged to Q may be doubted. On the other hand, *v.* 23 may well be part of Q. Cf. Lk. 9^{57-62} for similar openings. The question put to Jesus was one often discussed in Judaism, both with reference to Israel and to the Gentile nations. A great variety of answers is given showing all degrees of optimism and pessimism. The most despairing is that of 4 Ezra 8^{1-3}: 'This age the Most High

has made for many, but the age to come for few. . . . Many have been created, but few shall be saved.' The question and the answers given presuppose that salvation depends in some way on the favouritism rather than the love of God. But it is not a matter of saying light-heartedly, 'We have Abraham to our father' or of abandoning all hope for mankind. The reply of Jesus begins by asserting that the way of salvation is a door which God opens and man enters. The entry cannot be made without God. The gate of heaven opens only from the inside. But also man has to make his own way in, once the door is opened. And this is not easy. The entrance is narrow, and it is a case of struggling through rather than strolling in. If men fail to enter, it is not that God is unwilling to admit them, but that they will not enter on the only terms on which entrance is possible.

25–27. Moreover, the door does not stand open indefinitely. A time is coming, and soon, when the door will be shut. Here again the eschatological motive is clear. The discourse moves in a sphere that is strange to us with our ideas of progress and evolution. The notion that the world may come to an end to-morrow or next week is repugnant to us in a way in which it was not repugnant to Palestinian Jews of the first century. They believed that such a thing could happen, and many were convinced that it would come to pass in their own day. This means that there is only a limited time for repentance. When that time is up, it will be too late. Those who often passed by the open door will knock in vain at a door now shut. The words 'I do not know you' mean 'I do not acknowledge you': cf. Is. 63^{16}; 2 Tim. 2^{19}; and the general principle laid down in Mk. 8^{38}; Mt. 10^{33}; Lk. 12^{9}. In Mt. 7^{23} the words are 'I never knew you,' a phrase which, in Rabbinical circles, seems to have meant 'I don't wish to have anything to do with you.' Cf. Billerbeck, iv. 293. In face of this chilly reception all that the late-comers can claim is superficial contact with Jesus. They have sat at the same table with Him or have heard Him preach. They say in effect, 'You are one of us.' To which the answer is, 'You are none of mine.' The words are clearly addressed in the first instance to the Jewish contemporaries of Jesus; but their application can be extended to a much wider circle now. The quotation which follows, 'Depart from me all ye workers of iniquity,' is from Ps. 6^{8}.

28 f. These verses describe in vivid contrast what is going on inside and outside the closed door. Inside is light and joy. The patriarchs and prophets—the godly of every generation in Israel's history—and men from every quarter of the world—such as are spoken of elsewhere in Q: repentant Gentiles—sit down to the Messianic banquet in the Kingdom of God. (Cf. Is. 49^{12}; Mal. 1^{11}.) Outside darkness and despair, made deeper by the realisation of what has been missed. It may be noted that there is no mention here of special punishment for the unrepentant. They suffer enough in the loss of what might have been theirs.

30. Thus the Kingdom of God turns things upside down. Most of all, it upsets the calculations of those who believe that they have a prescriptive right to the favour of God, the kind of assurance expressed often in the apocalyptic literature, e.g.:

'Thou didst choose the seed of Abraham before all the nations

'And didst set Thy name upon us, O Lord; and Thou wilt abide among us for ever' (*Psa. Sol.* $9^{17f.}$). Cf. Rom. $9^{4f.}$ As Jesus sees it, all this counts for nothing. In the last issue the fate of a man depends not on whether he is of the seed of Abraham, but on his response to the manifestation of the Kingdom of God. Judged by that criterion, 'they are not all Israel, which are of Israel: neither, because they are Abraham's seed, are they all children' (Rom. $9^{6\,ff.}$). Publicans and harlots go into the Kingdom of God before the high priests and elders of the people (Mt. 21^{31}). Gentiles show faith and insight such as cannot be found in Israel. Privilege is at an end: and the only passports to the Kingdom are repentance and submission to God.

(*b*) Lament over Jerusalem (167)

MT. 23^{37-39}

23 37 O Jerusalem, Jerusalem, which killeth
the prophets, and stoneth them that are
sent unto her! how often would I have
gathered thy children together, even as a
hen gathereth her chickens under her
38 wings, and ye would not! Behold, your
39 house is left unto you [1] desolate. For I
say unto you, Ye shall not see me henceforth, till ye shall say, Blessed *is* he that cometh in the name of the Lord.

[1] Some ancient authorities omit *desolate.*

LK. 13^{34-35}

13 34 O Jerusalem, Jerusalem, which killeth
the prophets, and stoneth them that are
sent unto her! how often would I have
gathered thy children together, even as a
hen *gathereth* her own brood under her
35 wings, and ye would not. Behold, your
house is left unto you *desolate*: and I say unto you, Ye shall not see me, until ye shall say, Blessed *is* he that cometh in the name of the Lord.

The warning given in the preceding passage is followed by a passage of deep pathos. According to Burney (*Poetry of our Lord*, p. 146), it is in the poetical form known as *Kīnā*, i.e. the rhythm of the old Hebrew dirge or elegy. The nature of the poem can best be shown by giving Burney's translation and arrangement of the passage. Burney's rendering follows the text of Mt.

Jerúsalem, Jerúsalem, that sláyeth the próphets,
  and stóneth her méssengers,
How mány tímes have I lónged
  to gáther thy chíldren,
Like a hén that gáthereth her chícks
  beneáth her wíngs:
Yet ye would not.
  Behóld there remaíneth to yoú
   your hoúse a desolátion.

The remainder of the passage does not fall into this rhythmical scheme.

Many scholars regard these verses as the continuation of Lk. 11^{49-51} and as part of the extract from a lost Jewish book. On this theory the speaker here is the Wisdom of God. Reasons have been given above for rejecting this view. If Burney is right, we have a further reason for maintaining that these verses are independent of Lk. 11^{49-51}; for there is no suggestion of *Kīnā* rhythm about that passage.

34. The repetition of the name in address is extremely common in Jewish literature. The reputation of Jerusalem as a place where prophets are murdered is difficult to understand. There is the case of the prophet Uriah (Jer. $26^{20\,ff.}$) in the Old Testament; and there are other murders of prophets (1 Kings $18^{4,\,13}$, 19^{10})

not connected with Jerusalem; also the attempted murder of Jeremiah. In Jewish legend there is the murder of Isaiah. Further, the Zechariah whose murder is recorded in 2 Chron. $24^{20\,ff.}$ came to be identified with Zechariah the prophet. We should perhaps make allowance for a certain amount of poetic licence here, and take Jerusalem as typical of Israel as a whole. The present participles of the Greek text may then be taken to mean something like 'ever ready to slay the prophets and stone her messengers.' On the stoning of messengers it may be noted that Josephus (*Ant.* ii. 327), paraphrasing Exod. 14^{10-12}, says that the Israelites wished to stone Moses.

The words 'How often would I . . .' have been taken to imply more activity in Jerusalem on the part of Jesus than is recorded in the Synoptics. There is nothing impossible in the suggestion that He had visited Jerusalem and worked there on other occasions than the final one. The Synoptic Gospels imply a ministry lasting a year at least; but the Synoptic narrative accounts for less than half of this period. And there are other indications in the Synoptics pointing, though not in a decisive way, to the possibility that Jesus was no stranger to the capital when He came up for the last time. At the same time this text cannot be pressed. It says, 'How often have I longed,' not 'How often have I tried.' And we cannot be certain that 'Jerusalem' is to be taken literally. The figure of the bird gathering her brood under her wings is found in the Old Testament: Dt. 32^{11}; Ps. 17^{8}, 36^{7}; and the Jew who converts a Gentile is said to bring him under the wings of the *Shekhinah* (the presence of God). It is not necessary to seek for any mystical meaning here. The sense is the quite simple one of bringing men into the Kingdom of God, it being remembered that for all practical purposes entry into the Kingdom is equivalent to becoming a disciple of Jesus. This, the central purpose of the ministry, has been frustrated by the fact that the people would not have anything to do with it. They are wedded to things as they are. In particular they still believe in their own doctrine of the Kingdom of God, which means the vindication of themselves by the power of God, the establishment of Jerusalem as the capital of the world, and the Temple of Jerusalem as the central and only sanctuary of mankind.

35. The inevitable issue of this doctrine and of the policy based upon it is ruin. These grandiose dreams of world-dominion will surely end in destruction for Jerusalem and the Temple. Cf. Mk. $13^{1\,f.}$. Against the interpretation of 'your house' as the Temple it is urged that in Jewish speech the Temple is invariably God's house and no one else's. (Billerbeck, i. 944.) (Yet in Is. 64^{11} we have the expression 'Our holy and beautiful house' with reference to the First Temple.) The meaning then assigned to the words 'your house' is 'your commonwealth.' This is possible. On the other hand, the words may well be spoken in bitter irony '*your* Temple—so much more yours than God's.' In any case, the Temple and the Jewish commonwealth stand and fall together. Much more difficult is the interpretation of the next sentence. The chief problem is what is meant by the words 'until ye shall say . . .' Is the time here thought of some future visit of Jesus to Jerusalem, or is it the final consummation? According to Mk. 11^{9}, when Jesus made His entry into Jerusalem 'they that went before, and they that followed, cried, Hosanna; blessed is he that cometh in the name of the Lord.'

Mt. evidently does not regard the triumphal entry as a fulfilment of the saying, since he places the saying after his report of the entry. M. Goguel suggests that the words are spoken by Jesus at the time of the Feast of Tabernacles. Jesus has gone up to Jerusalem and worked there without much response. The force of the saying then is 'I am leaving Jerusalem and you will not see me again until Passover.' But it seems a very high-falutin way of conveying a very prosaic piece of information. The words 'Blessed is he . . .' are a quotation from Ps. 118^{26}, a psalm which has connexions with the great pilgrim feasts of Judaism, but especially with the Feast of Tabernacles. (Thackeray, *The Septuagint and Jewish Worship*, pp. 74 ff.) Now in the Jewish liturgy the prophetic lesson appropriated to Tabernacles is Zech. 14, which begins with a prophecy of the desolation of Jerusalem (Zech. $14^{1 f.}$), followed by the promise that God will then appear to establish His Kingdom over the whole earth (Zech. 14^{9}). That appearance will be a coming of God with all the saints (Zech. 14^{5}). There is also a piece of Rabbinical evidence connecting Ps. 118 with the final deliverance of Israel (Billerbeck, i. 850). It seems probable, therefore, that the time referred to in this saying is the time of the final consummation. The preceding passages suggest that the meaning is: 'The time will come when you will be ready to say to me, "Blessed is he that cometh in the name of the Lord"; but then it will be too late.'

(*c*) The Great Feast (170)

MT. 22^{1-10}

22 1 And Jesus answered and spake again in
2 parables unto them, saying, The kingdom
of heaven is likened unto a certain king,
which made a marriage feast for his son,
3 and sent forth his [1] servants to call them
that were bidden to the marriage feast:
4 and they would not come. Again he
sent forth other [1] servants, saying, Tell
them that are bidden, Behold, I have
made ready my dinner: my oxen and my
fatlings are killed, and all things are
5 ready: come to the marriage feast. But
they made light of it, and went their
ways, one to his own farm, another to his
6 merchandise: and the rest laid hold on
his [1] servants, and entreated them shame-
7 fully, and killed them. But the king was
wroth; and he sent his armies, and destroyed those murderers, and burned
8 their city. Then saith he to his [1] servants, The wedding is ready, but they
that were bidden were not worthy.
9 Go ye therefore unto the partings of the
highways, and as many as ye shall find,
10 bid to the marriage feast. And those
[1] servants went out into the highways, and
gathered together all as many as they
found, both bad and good: and the
wedding was filled with guests.

[1] Gr. *bondservants*.

LK. 14^{15-24}

14 15 And when one of them that sat at meat
with him heard these things, he said unto
him, Blessed is he that shall eat bread in
16 the kingdom of God. But he said unto
him, A certain man made a great supper;
17 and he bade many: and he sent forth his
[1] servant at supper time to say to them
that were bidden, Come; for *all* things
18 are now ready. And they all with one
consent began to make excuse. The first
said unto him, I have bought a field, and
I must needs go out and see it: I pray
19 thee have me excused. And another
said, I have bought five yoke of oxen, and
I go to prove them: I pray thee have me
20 excused. And another said, I have
married a wife, and therefore I cannot
21 come. And the [1] servant came, and told
his lord these things. Then the master of
the house being angry said to his [1] servant, Go out quickly into the streets and
lanes of the city, and bring in hither the
poor and maimed and blind and lame.
22 And the [1] servant said, Lord, what thou
didst command is done, and yet there is
23 room. And the lord said unto the
[1] servant, Go out into the highways and
hedges, and constrain *them* to come in,
24 that my house may be filled. For I say
unto you, that none of those men which
were bidden shall taste of my supper.

[1] Gr. *bondservant*.

This parable again has to do with those who reject the Kingdom of God. And again it is made clear that those who are excluded from the Kingdom exclude themselves. The invitation is issued by God; but God will not drag the recipients of the invitation into the feast against their will.

The superiority of the Lucan version of the parable is obvious. It is clear, consistent, and straightforward. In Mt., on the other hand, the story as told by Lk. has been severely cut down, and new features introduced, which make nonsense of it. The most glaring case is Mt. 22^6 f.. There we are suddenly introduced to a group of persons called ' the rest,' who behave like the wicked husbandmen in Mk. 12^1-12. Their shameful treatment of the messengers causes the king to send a punitive expedition against them to destroy them and their city. The amazing thing is that the feast, which was ready before these things happened, is still ready, and apparently fit to eat, when all is over. It is plain that *vv.* 6 f. are an interruption of the story; and most scholars regard them as an interpolation, an *ex post facto* reference to the destruction of Jerusalem in A.D. 70. This explanation would serve if *vv.* 6 f. were the only peculiarity in the Matthæan version of the parable. But we note that *v.* 6 recalls Mk.'s parable of the wicked husbandmen, and that Mt. 22^3 f. tells of two summonses to the feast, a feature which again recalls Mk. 12^1-12. The true solution of the problem may be that Mt. has here combined the Q parable of the great feast with another parable, now lost, which was originally a companion parable to Mk. 12^1-12. For a fuller discussion see *The Teaching of Jesus*, pp. 83–86. Mt. further joins on yet another parable—or a fragment of a parable—from his special source (Mt. 22^11-14: see below, pp. 518 f.).

15. The introductory verse is peculiar to Lk. There is therefore no certainty that it stood in Q. It does, however, make an excellent introduction to what follows, probably too good to be invented. One of Jesus' fellow-guests at a meal gives utterance to a characteristic piece of apocalyptic piety. The comparison of the realised Kingdom of God to a banquet is well known both in Rabbinical teaching and in the Gospels. The exclamation is apt to the circumstances of its utterance and impeccable in its sentiment. The reply of Jesus does not challenge the sentiment, but the sincerity of the speaker. He says in effect: 'You talk beautifully about the Kingdom of God; but you do not mean a word of it. If you had the opportunity for which you profess to crave, you would unhesitatingly reject it.' This is the essential point of the parable.

16, 17, 18 ff., 21, 22 f. 'A certain man' is God, and the feast is the Kingdom of God, considered as a great blessing which God is prepared to bestow. The double invitation is in accordance with Jerusalem custom, according to the Rabbinical commentary (*midrash*) on Lam. 4^2. The invited guests are in the first instance the righteous Jews; and the first invitation is a reference to the promises in the Old Testament. The servant who comes to announce that the feast is ready is Jesus Himself. But the guests who had accepted the invitation in the first instance, now wish to withdraw their acceptance. Cf. Mt. 21^30. The Greek phrase translated ' with one consent ' is probably a literal rendering of an Aramaic expression meaning ' immediately,' ' at once.' (So Wellhausen, Torrey.) The different excuses are offered with varying degrees of politeness; but they all come to the same thing: ' we have other and more important business to attend to.' The claims of Mammon take precedence of the claims of God; and treasure on earth is more valuable than treasure in heaven. The report of the servant angers the master, who despatches the servant on a new errand. He is to bring in other inhabitants of the city, the despised and neglected members of the community: ' the poor ' who have no wealth or status to recommend them, and ' the maimed ' who are unattractive through physical defects. The word here rendered ' maimed ' is used in Greek to cover physical defects of all kinds. Strictly speaking, the blind and lame are sub-classes of the class ' maimed.' (Cf. Plato, *Crito*, 53A.) The fact that these guests are to be found in the same city as the original guests, suggests that they represent Jews of another class. If the first guests are the righteous Jews, the religious aristocracy, men of the Pharisaic type, these may well be the religious lower classes, the publicans and sinners: Israelites like the Pharisees, but bad Israelites from the Pharisaic standpoint. Even after these have been brought in, there is still room for others; so a new command is issued. The servant is to go beyond the city boundaries out on to the main roads. This is doubtless meant to suggest a mission beyond the borders of Israel to the Gentiles. ' Constrain ' here does not mean ' compel.' It expresses rather an insistent hospitality. Cf. Gen. 19^{3}. Here we have another example of that interest in the Gentile mission which is so characteristic of Q. The order of events corresponds to the Pauline dictum, 'To the Jew first, and also to the Greek' (Rom. 1^{16}, $2^{9f.}$). 'That my house may be filled': the purpose of God is wider than Israel. The necessary corollary to the prophetic doctrine of God's universal rule is here drawn. Cf. Heb. $11^{39f.}$ The whole parable might be regarded as a *midrash* on Is. 49^{6}.

24. The closing word excludes from the feast those, and those only, who have already excluded themselves. The only people who do not enter are those who do not wish to enter.

The issue in this parable, as in the preceding passages, is set out with the utmost clearness. Jesus does not here teach either a mechanically operating predestination, which determines from all eternity who shall or shall not be brought into the Kingdom. Neither does He proclaim that man's entry into the Kingdom is purely his own affair. The two essential points in His teaching are that no man can enter the Kingdom without the invitation of God, and that no man can remain outside it but by his own deliberate choice. Man cannot save himself; but he can damn himself. And it is this latter fact that makes the preaching of Jesus so urgent. For He sees the deepest tragedy of human life, not in the many wrong and foolish things that men do, or the many good and wise things that they fail to accomplish, but in their rejection of God's greatest gift.

3. *DISCIPLESHIP IN A TIME OF CRISIS*

The discourse is now turned back to the conditions of discipleship in such a time of crisis. It is very easy to remain outside the Kingdom of God: not so easy to enter. It is true that salvation is free: but it is not cheap. God gives the Kingdom: but the accepting of God's gift means the rejection of many other things. The Kingdom of God offers the greatest gifts: but it demands exclusive loyalty and whole-hearted devotion. The great feast is a feast and not a distribution of free rations. Those who wish to enjoy it must come in. They cannot have portions sent out for them to enjoy, while they busy themselves with other things. Consequently the closing sections of Q are devoted mainly to a reiteration in uncompromising terms of the conditions of discipleship.

(*a*) The Absolute Claims of the Kingdom (171)

MT. 10^{37-38}

10 37 He that loveth father or mother more
than me is not worthy of me: and he that
loveth son or daughter more than me is
38 not worthy of me. And he that doth
not take his cross and follow after me, is
not worthy of me.

LK. 14^{25-27}

14 25 Now there went with him great multitudes: and he turned, and said unto
26 them, If any man cometh unto me, and
hateth not his own father, and mother,
and wife, and children, and brethren,
and sisters, yea, and his own life also, he
27 cannot be my disciple. Whosoever doth
not bear his own cross, and come after
me, cannot be my disciple.

25. This verse, which is probably editorial, effects the transition from the preceding parable to the following exhortations.

26 f. One of the most uncompromising statements of the claims of the Kingdom in the New Testament. There are considerable differences between Mt. and Lk. in the form of the statement; but there are also signs of an Aramaic original underlying the variants. These are (i) 'hateth not' (Lk.) 'loveth more' (Mt.). In the Old Testament (e.g. Gen. $29^{31 ff.}$; Dt. $21^{15 ff.}$) 'love' and 'hate' stand side by side in contexts where it is obvious that 'hate' is not to be taken in the literal sense, but in the sense 'love less.' The same idiom appears in the Talmud (*Ta'anith* 7^b), where it is said of handsome Rabbis that 'if they hated their beauty, they would be more learned' than they are. That is, if they thought less of their personal appearance, they would be better scholars. So here Lk.'s version is a literal rendering of the original; but the meaning is not that a disciple's relatives are to be hated by him, but that they must take second place in his regard. The first place in his affections must be given to the Kingdom manifested in Jesus. For an Old Testament parallel to this exclusive loyalty see Dt. $33^{8 f.}$; and for the other side of this tremendous demand Mk. $10^{28 ff.}$. (ii) The phrases 'is not worthy of me' (Mt.) and 'cannot be my disciple' (Lk.) may go back to a common original in Aramaic. See *The Teaching of Jesus*, pp. 237–240. (iii) The words 'bear' (Lk.) and 'take' (Mt.) are translation variants. Cf. the Greek versions of Num. $14^{33 f.}$. Verse 27 has a parallel in Mk. 8^{34}.

8 34 And he called unto him the multitude
with his disciples, and said unto them, If
any man would come after me, let him
deny himself, and take up his cross, and
follow me.

The taking up of the cross is the voluntary acceptance of martyrdom at the hands of the Roman Empire. Crucifixion is the typical Roman punishment; and the implication of the words is that Jesus is aware of an irreconcilable hostility between the Kingdom for which He stands and the Empire represented by Pontius Pilate.

Discipleship means the risk of being reckoned undutiful sons, bad husbands, dangerous agitators; and he who becomes a disciple accepts these risks with his eyes open, and is prepared to accept all the consequences that may follow. And this is not just a matter of a single moment of decision in a burst of enthusiasm. It demands a dogged endurance, the maintenance of the first enthusiasm right through to the end. This is enforced in:

(*b*) The Parable of the Salt (171)

MT. 5^{13}

5 13 Ye are the salt of the earth: but if the salt have lost its savour, wherewith shall it be salted? it is thenceforth good for nothing, but to be cast out and trodden under foot of men.

LK. 14^{34-35}

14 34 Salt therefore is good: but if even the salt
have lost its savour, wherewith shall it be
35 seasoned? It is fit neither for the land
nor for the dunghill: *men* cast it out.
He that hath ears to hear, let him hear.

Cf. Mk. 9^{50}.

9 50 Salt is good: but if the salt have lost its saltness, wherewith will ye season it?

34 f. The saying occurs independently in a small collection in Mk. It is possible that the form in Mt. is independent of the other two, and derived from M. The opening words of Mt. 5^{13} (cf. Mt. 5^{14}) are correct interpretation of the meaning of the saying for Christians. The disciples are like salt, with its many uses in the house and in the field. And like salt they are of use only so long as they retain their characteristic quality. A disciple who has lost his zeal and devotion is like salt that has become insipid. Such salt is completely useless. The agricultural use of salt is well known in Egypt and Palestine. 'Fit neither for the land nor for the dunghill' is difficult, for the use of salt on the land is as manure. A very attractive solution is that of Perles, that 'land' is a mistaken rendering of an Aramaic word which ought to be translated 'seasoning.' It is a further point in favour of this restoration that it gives a play upon the two Aramaic words *tabbālā* (seasoning) and *zabbālā* (manure). It is possible that the saying was originally not just an exhortation to the disciples, but primarily a warning to Israel. Israel ought to be the salt of mankind; but the savour has gone out of Judaism. Let the disciples, the new Israel, beware lest they go the same way. In favour of this interpretation is the fact that the Talmud preserves an anecdote concerning R. Joshua ben Chananiah (*c.* A.D. 90) in which he makes fun of this saying. He is asked: 'If the salt becomes savourless, with what will it be salted?' He replies: 'With the after-birth of a mule.' It is retorted that the mule (which is barren) cannot have an after-birth, to which his answer is: 'Neither can the salt become savourless.' The natural interpretation of this is that in the Rabbi's view Israel is a salt that does not become insipid, and therefore stands in no need of seasoning, least of all by Jesus or His followers. (Billerbeck, i. 236; cf. G. Kittel, *Probleme*, p. 123.) The casting out of the useless salt into the street, the common refuse-tip in the East, follows on the recognition of its utter worthlessness. The additional words in Mt. 'trodden under foot of men' indicate that the street is the destination of the salt. The rejection of men from the Kingdom of God is described in similar terms in an earlier passage in Q (Lk. 13^{28}||Mt. 8^{12}).

The upshot of the matter is that men must choose whom they will serve; and, having chosen, they must be prepared to abide by their choice. The whole matter can be put in a single word, which is given in the next Q verse :

(*c*) The Last Word on Discipleship (174)

MT. 6^{24}	LK. 16^{13}
6 24 No man can serve two masters: for either he will hate the one, and love the other; or else he will hold to one, and despise the other. Ye cannot serve God and mammon.	**16** 13 No [1] servant can serve two masters: for either he will hate the one, and love the other; or else he will hold to one, and despise the other. Ye cannot serve God and mammon. [1] Gr. *household-servant.*

The two versions of the saying are identical except that Lk. has the word for 'domestic servant,' which is absent in Mt. Similar expressions are found outside the New Testament: Plato, *Rep*. viii. 555C. 'It is impossible for the citizens of a state to honour wealth, and at the same time acquire a proper amount of temperance; because they cannot avoid neglecting either the one or the other.' Persius, *Sat*. v. 154 ff., to one torn between avarice and extravagance: 'You have two hooks pulling you different ways—are you for following this or that? You must needs obey your masters by turns and shirk them by turns, by a division of duty.' Philo, *frag*. II, 649: 'It is impossible for love of the world to coexist with the love of God.' [1] *Poimandres*, IV. 6 : 'It is not possible, my son, to attach yourself both to things mortal and to things divine.' For the disciple of Jesus the irreconcilable alternatives are God and mammon. Mammon is the Aramaic word *māmōn*. Its derivation is disputed, but its meaning certain: it is wealth of every kind. The service of God *and* mammon is impossible, because their demands on man are irreconcilable. God calls for the utmost of self-dedication and self-sacrifice: mammon for self-assertion and self-aggrandisement. The only way for disciples is complete devotion to God, and this is not possible unless they are prepared to sit loose to all the things that human selfishness counts as goods.

These sayings on the absolute claims of the Kingdom are now followed by a number of utterances bearing upon special problems which arise in the life of the disciple. What is his relation to the old order given in the Jewish scriptures? How is he to act when he feels himself wronged by a fellow-disciple? In what way is he to face the difficulties of his task as a disciple? The sayings do not appear to be arranged in any systematic way. Indeed it seems probable that we have here a small collection of sayings linked together by the fact that they answer questions which arise in the community of the disciples.

(*d*) The Old and the New (176)

MT. 11^{12-13}	LK. 16^{16}
11 12 And from the days of John the Baptist until now the kingdom of heaven suffereth violence, and men of violence 13 take it by force. For all the prophets and the law prophesied until John.	**16** 16 The law and the prophets *were* until John: from that time the gospel of the kingdom of God is preached, and every man entereth violently into it.

[1] Cf. Billerbeck, *Komm*. i. 435.

The differences between Mt. and Lk. are considerable and striking; and Mt. is generally held to preserve the saying in a more original, because more difficult, form than Lk. The Lucan form is then explained as an attempt to clarify the obscurity of the original saying. It is, however, probable that the principal alterations are due to Mt. Thus the order of the clauses in Lk. is to be preferred: Mt. has reversed this order on transferring the saying to another context. In Mt. 11^{13} the word ' all ' is a typical Matthæan gloss; and the word ' prophesied ' is a clumsy attempt to fill up the gap in the original statement. In order to get in his favourite word ' all,' Mt. has reversed the natural order ' the law and the prophets.' On the other hand it is probable that Mt. has kept the original wording in the statement that the Kingdom of God ' suffereth violence, and men of violence take it by force.' The question now arises as to the meaning of this difficult saying. ' Suffereth violence ' represents the Greek *biazetai*, which may be either passive, as R.V. takes it, or middle. In the latter case the meaning will be ' exercises force,' ' shows its power,' or the like. ' Take it by force ': the Greek verb used here (*harpazousin*) may have this meaning; but it may equally well mean no more than ' snatch at,' ' seize.' The Greek word translated ' men of violence ' (*biastai*) is exceedingly rare, and the meaning to be assigned to it in this passage is uncertain. The sense which we give to ' men of violence ' depends on the sense in which we take *harpazousin*. If the verb is regarded as signifying hostile action, then the ' men of violence ' will be the enemies of the Kingdom—demonic or worldly powers. If we suppose the verb to mean ' snatch at ' in the sense of making every effort to obtain what is seen to be a supreme blessing, then the ' men of violence' will be ordinary men who are roused to make great efforts by the prospect of securing a place in the Kingdom. Such are the possibilities. The most satisfactory interpretation of the saying is that given by Otto (*Reich Gottes und Menschensohn*, pp. 84–88). It involves rendering the saying as follows:

> ' The Law and the prophets were until John:
> From that time the Kingdom of God exercises its power and men of violence snatch at it.'

How does the Kingdom of God exercise its power? By overcoming those forces of evil which degrade and destroy man. ' If I by the finger of God cast out devils, then is the Kingdom of God come upon you ' (Lk. 11^{20}||Mt. 12^{28}). ' And into whatsoever city ye enter . . . heal the sick that are therein, and say unto them, The Kingdom of God is come nigh unto you ' (Lk. $10^{8f.}$; cf. Mt. $10^{7f.}$). The Kingdom shows its power in the work of Jesus and His messengers. Otto explains ' men of violence ' as the kind of men described in Mk. 9^{42-48}; Lk. 9^{57-62}, $13^{23f.}$, 14^{26}. They are men who will take every risk and make every sacrifice in order to have their share in the Kingdom. It then appears that Lk. has, on the whole, interpreted the saying rightly. ' The Kingdom of God is proclaimed as good news, and everyone presses into it ' is not far from what we take to be the original sense of the saying. It is further to be noticed that the saying contrasts two periods in history: the period of the Law and prophets and the period of the Kingdom of God. The former is one of promise, the latter of fulfilment; and the ministry of the Baptist is the dividing line between the two. It is involved in this idea that the new era in some sense supersedes the old: the Law and the prophets take second place to the fuller manifestation of the Kingdom of God in its saving power, as delivering us from evil; whereas they could only warn against evil. This idea of the supersession of the Law by the fuller revelation of God is developed by Paul; but it has its roots here in Q. In the light of this interpretation the immediately following verse in Lk. becomes perplexing.

MT. 5^{18}	LK. 16^{17}
5 18 For verily I say unto you, Till heaven and earth pass away, one jot or one tittle shall in no wise pass away from the law, till all things be accomplished.	**16** 17 But it is easier for heaven and earth to pass away, than for one tittle of the law to fall.

This verse seems, at first sight, to assert the absolute eternity of the Law in its minutest details. The form in Mt. does not go so far: it only maintains the Law in full force until the final consummation. The Jewish view was that the Law remains in full validity throughout the present age and the Messianic period. Whether it was expected to be in force in the world to come is a question much more difficult to answer. (See Moore, *Judaism*, i. 269 ff.) The text as given in Mt. conforms exactly to the Rabbinical doctrine of the perpetuity of the Law. But is this what Jesus meant to say? It is difficult to believe so, when in the preceding verse we have a saying which implies that the Law is already in some measure superseded; and when in the next verse we have a saying on divorce, which, as we shall see, is inconsistent with the Law; to say nothing of other passages in the Gospels where Jesus treats the letter of the Law in a very revolutionary way.

If now we look at the Lk. version of the saying, bearing in mind the possibility that Mt. 5^{18} is a revision of it to bring it explicitly into line with Rabbinical doctrine, another possibility at once emerges: that the saying in its original form asserts not the perpetuity of the Law but the unbending conservatism of the scribes. This interpretation is fortified when we take into account the true meaning of the word 'tittle.' This has usually been regarded as meaning the serif which distinguishes certain letters of the Hebrew alphabet, as it distinguishes G from C in English. But this is not so. The 'tittle' most probably stands for certain scribal ornaments added to certain letters in the Hebrew Scriptures (Billerbeck, i. 248 f.). These were no part of the Law itself, but an addition to it. The fact that they were placed on the tops of the letters, and that another name for them was 'crowns,' may have some bearing on the use of the word 'fall' in Lk. The tittle then is part of that scribal tradition which Jesus so often criticised The saying thus comes to mean: It is easier for heaven and earth to pass away than for the scribes to give up the smallest bit of that tradition by which they make the Law of none effect. The saying in its original form is not sound Rabbinical dogma but bitter irony. Lk. has faithfully preserved it; and it is only because we constantly read the verse through Mt.'s Jewish-Christian spectacles that we are misled as to its true purport.

The way in which Jesus feels free to revise the Law is illustrated by the next verse in Lk. This has to do with divorce and remarriage, and we must take into account the parallels in Mt. 5^{32} (M) and Mk. $10^{11 f.}$||Mt. 19^{9}.

LK. 16^{18}

Cf. Mt. $5^{31f.}$ (M), Mk. $10^{11f.}$||Mt. 19^{9}.

16 18 Every one that putteth away his wife, and marrieth another, committeth adultery: and he that marrieth one that is put away from a husband committeth adultery.

Mt. $5^{31f.}$ runs:

'It was said also, Whosoever shall put away his wife, let him give her a writing of divorcement: but I say unto you, That every one that putteth away his wife, saving for the cause of fornication, maketh her an adulteress: and whosoever shall marry her when she is put away committeth adultery.'

The other relevant passages are:

MT. 19^{9}

19 9 And I say unto you, Whosoever shall put away his wife, [1] except for fornication, and shall marry another, committeth adultery: [2] and he that marrieth her when she is put away committeth adultery.

[1] Some ancient authorities read *saving for the cause of fornication, maketh her an adulteress*: as in ch. v. 32.

[2] The following words, to the end of the verse, are omitted by some ancient authorities.

MK. 10^{11-12}

10 11 And he saith unto them, Whosoever shall put away his wife, and marry another, committeth adultery against
12 her: and if she herself shall put away her husband, and marry another, she committeth adultery.

The discussion of these passages is usually undertaken with a view to finding from the words of Jesus some clear rule for the Church in dealing with the question of divorce and remarriage. But for critical purposes, especially in the present context, the primary question is not what rules Jesus lays down concerning divorce and remarriage, but how the formulations here given compare with Jewish legislation about the offence of adultery. And here the essential point is that in Jewish Law adultery is *always* intercourse between a married woman and a man other than her husband. (In construing the law formal betrothal is regarded as equivalent to marriage.) Hence while a woman can commit adultery against her husband, a man cannot commit adultery against his wife. He can only commit adultery against another married man. In the light of this the following observations may be made.

(*a*) The principle that a man cannot commit adultery against his own wife is flatly contradicted in Mk. 10^{11}, where the words 'against her' can only refer to the first wife.

(*b*) The dictum Mk. 10^{11} is taken over by Mt. in the parallel 19^{9} with two alterations, both highly significant. (i) Mt. introduces the excepting clause 'except for fornication,' and so brings the rule into agreement with the interpretation of the Jewish Law favoured by the school of Shammai. (ii) He omits the words 'against her.' This does not remove the contradiction between the dictum of Jesus and the Jewish definition of adultery; but it makes it somewhat less obvious.

(*c*) Mk. 10^{12} flatly contradicts Jewish Law, in which the wife could not divorce her husband. In certain cases (*not* including infidelity on his part) she could compel him to divorce her; but in Jewish Law it is not proper to speak of a wife divorcing her husband. It is true that in two early Aramaic Jewish documents from Elephantine (*Aramaic Papyri of the Fifth Century B.C.*, ed. Cowley, Nos. 9 and 15) divorce of the husband by the wife is a legal possibility; but the community in Elephantine was eccentric in other respects, and can hardly be cited as an example of orthodox Jewish practice. A possible explanation of Mk. 10^{12} is that given by Burkitt (*Gospel History and its Transmission*, pp. 98–101), that the verse is a direct reference to Herodias (Mk. 6$^{17 \text{ff.}}$). The weak point in this explanation is that there is no evidence that Herodias *divorced* her husband.

(*d*) Lk. 16^{18} agrees substantially in its first half with Mk. 10^{11} save that it has nothing corresponding to ‘ against her ’ in Mk. In its second half it proceeds ‘ and he who marries a woman divorced from her husband commits adultery.’ It is possible that this is the correct rendering of an original Aramaic which has been misunderstood and mistranslated in Mk. 10^{12}. If that be so we are dealing with the case in which a husband divorces his wife and both remarry. The dictum of Jesus is that the husband commits adultery against his divorced wife. This is involved in Lk. 16^{18a}, and explicit in Mk. 10^{11}. Further, in the case of the divorced wife who remarries, the man who marries her commits adultery against her first husband. So Lk. 16^{18b}, which is to be preferred to Mk. 10^{12}.

(*e*) There remains the formulation in Mt. 5$^{31 \text{f.}}$. Here we have the same exception as in Mt. 19^{9}. It is differently phrased, but its purport is the same. It makes the condition of divorce the same as that laid down by the Rabbinical school of Shammai. This Matthæan form differs from all the others in this, that it does not deal with the situation created if the divorcing husband remarries. What it does say is that a man who divorces his wife makes her become an adulteress, presumably if she marries again; and that the man who marries a divorced woman commits adultery. That is, if a divorced woman remarries, she and her second husband are both guilty of adultery; and the first husband is morally responsible for this state of affairs. This is perfectly consistent with the Jewish doctrine of adultery. And it is an extension of what is implied in Lk. 16^{18b}.

(*f*) The conclusion to be drawn is that the Q form of the saying (Lk. 16^{18}) is the original. Mk. 10^{11a} gives the sense of Lk. 16^{18a} and makes it more precise by the addition of the words ‘ against her.’ Mk. 10^{12} is a misunderstanding of the Aramaic underlying Lk. 16^{18b}. Mt. 19^{9} is Mk. 10^{11} modified in the direction of Shammaite legal doctrine by the addition of the excepting clause. Mt. 5^{32} is an expanded version of the part of the dictum represented by Lk. 16^{18b}. It may be the M version of the saying. It contains the excepting clause (as in Mt. 19^{9}), which here *may* belong to the original text of M.

(*g*) The characteristic and original feature in our Lord’s teaching on this subject is stated in Q and underlined in Mk.:—that a husband can commit adultery against his wife. This means that in respect of marriage after divorce both parties are put on a footing of absolute equality. For either to marry again is adultery. This fact is a strong argument against the genuineness of the excepting clauses in Mt. For the privilege there accorded is granted to the husband only, and it is not likely that Jesus, after correcting the one-sidedness of the Jewish

Law, would stultify what He had just done, by according to the husband a privilege withheld from the wife.

The passages just considered give the opinion of Jesus on the Jewish Law of divorce and remarriage. His positive teaching on the nature of marriage is given in Mk. 10^{2-9}. Cf. *The Teaching of Jesus*, pp. 292 f.

(*e*) Stumbling-blocks (178)

MT. 18^{6-7}

18 6 But whoso shall cause one of these little ones which believe on me to stumble, it is profitable for him that [1] a great millstone should be hanged about his neck, and *that* he should be sunk in the depth of the sea.
7 Woe unto the world because of occasions of stumbling! for it must needs be that the occasions come; but woe to that man through whom the occasion cometh!

[1] Gr. *a millstone turned by an ass.*

LK. 17^{1-2}

17 1 And he said unto his disciples, It is impossible but that occasions of stumbling should come: but woe unto him, through
2 whom they come! It were well for him if a millstone were hanged about his neck, and he were thrown into the sea, rather than that he should cause one of these little ones to stumble.

MK. 9^{42}

9 42 And whosoever shall cause one of these little ones that believe [1] on me to stumble, it were better for him if [2] a great millstone were hanged about his neck, and he were cast into the sea.

[1] Many ancient authorities omit *on me.*
[2] Gr. *a millstone turned by an ass.*

Compare also Mk. 9^{37}|| Mt. 18^{5}||Lk. 9^{48}, Mt. 10^{40}||Lk. 10^{16}, Mk. 9^{41}||Mt. 10^{42}, Mk. 6^{11}|| Mt. 10^{14}||Lk. 9^{5}.

A comparison of these passages shows how complicated, not to say confused, these sayings have become in the course of tradition. We may attempt to disentangle them; but it must be emphasised that any results attained cannot be more than probable conjectures. The root of the confusion is that Jesus said certain things about little children and certain things about His own disciples in their missionary work; and that He was accustomed to address His disciples as 'children.' See, for example, Mk. 10^{24} and compare Mt. 11^{25} = Lk. 10^{21}. Now the early Church was more interested in the original disciples than in children; and we should expect the tendency of the tradition to be to transfer sayings concerning 'children' or 'little ones' to the disciples. The result is that in every case we have to ask whether a saying about 'children' or 'little ones' is to be taken literally or understood of the disciples.

Mk. 9^{33-42} is a passage in which this problem is at its most acute. In this passage there are three verses which we must consider: 37, 41, 42. Mk. 9^{37} has already been discussed above (p. 370) on Lk. 10^{16}. It may be suspected that Mk. $9^{41f.}$ were originally sayings concerning children. There is a steady movement in the direction of turning 'little ones' into 'disciples':

Lk. 17^{2} 'one of these little ones.'

Mk. 9^{42} 'one of these little ones that believe.'

Mt. 18^{6} 'one of these little ones that believe on me.'

With Mk. 9^{41} we can compare Mt. 10^{42}:

Mk. 9^{41} 'For whosoever shall give you a cup of water to drink . . .'

Mt. 10^{42} 'And whosoever shall give to drink unto one of these little ones a cup of cold water only . . .'

Mt. 10^{42} shows considerable agreement with Mk. 9^{41}; but it contains elements which are perhaps to be attributed to M. In any case 'one of these little ones' seems to me to be more original than 'you.' It may therefore be supposed that the original saying was to this effect:

He who shows the smallest kindness to a child will surely be rewarded (Mk. 9^{41}|| Mt. 10^{42}).

He who harms a little child will surely be severely punished (Mk. 9^{42}||Lk. 17^{2}).

Such harm is inevitable; but woe to him who is responsible for it (Mt. 18^{7}||Lk. 17^{1}).

The first two sentences are in antithetic parallelism. This interpretation of the saying suggests that the order of verses in Mt. is the original. It may be added that the great rewards and punishments are more appropriate on this interpretation. The disciple can look after himself; but the child is weak and helpless: and we do, in fact, feel more strongly about the treatment of children than of adults.

(*f*) Differences within the Fellowship (179)

LK. 17^{3-4}

Cf. Mt. $18^{15, 21, 22}$ (M).

17 3 Take heed to yourselves: if thy brother sin, rebuke him; and if he repent, forgive
4 him. And if he sin against thee seven times in the day, and seven times turn again to thee, saying, I repent; thou shalt forgive him.

The parallel passage in Mt. is much more elaborate than Lk. $17^{3f.}$. The whole of Mt. 18^{15-22} is probably to be assigned to M. Cf. Streeter, *The Four Gospels*, pp. 257 f., and see below, pp. 501 ff. The saying, as it stands in Lk. (= Q), does not go into the question of the jurisdiction of the fellowship in disputes between its members. The injunction supposes that all such cases may be decided in a spirit of brotherhood by the parties concerned. The fact that the parallel in Mt. prescribes a quasi-legal procedure in such cases is itself evidence that it is a later development.

3, 4. 'Take heed to yourselves' is followed immediately by an address in the second person singular. This does not create any difficulty. 'Thy brother' means 'the brother of any one of you.' Does 'take heed to yourselves' mean 'each of you take heed to himself' or 'take heed to one another'? In view of Lk. 21^{34} we should probably take the former alternative. 'If thy brother sin': we must supply 'against thee' as in *v.* 4. 'Rebuke him.' The advice is by no means superfluous, for the natural tendency is either to harbour a secret grudge or to complain to some third party. The nature of the Christian fellowship requires a certain frankness in the dealings of its members with one another. Repentance on the part of the offender and forgiveness by the injured party together make an end of the matter. The duty of the injured party to forgive is Jewish as well as Christian doctrine. 'In the case of man as well as God the condition of forgiveness is repentance and confession—in that of man, reparation also. When the wrongdoer makes this amends, it is the duty of the injured party to forgive him: "When thou hast mercy upon thy fellow, thou hast One to have mercy on thee; but if thou hast not mercy upon thy fellow, thou hast none to have mercy on thee" (*Tanḥuma*)' (Moore, *Judaism*, ii. 154). And this readiness to forgive is not limited. Seven times is not to be taken literally: it means that forgiving is to go on indefinitely, so long as there is a sign of genuine repentance. The spirit here inculcated is that which is celebrated by Paul in 1 Cor. $13^{4, 5, 7}$.

(*g*) The Power of Faith (180)

MT. 17^{20} (M)

17 20 And he saith unto them, Because of your little faith: for verily I say unto you, If ye have faith as a grain of mustard seed, ye shall say unto this mountain, Remove hence to yonder place; and it shall remove; and nothing shall be impossible unto you.

LK. 17^{5-6}

17 5 And the apostles said unto the Lord,
6 Increase our faith. And the Lord said, If ye have faith as a grain of mustard seed, ye would say unto this sycamine tree, Be thou rooted up, and be thou planted in the sea; and it would have obeyed you.

Cf. Mk. 11^{23}

11 23 Verily I say unto you, Whosoever shall say unto this mountain, Be thou taken up and cast into the sea; and shall not doubt in his heart, but shall believe that what he saith cometh to pass; he shall have it.

Here again we have a complicated and confused tradition. Mk. 11^{23} occurs in the story of the withering of the barren fig tree. Mt. 17^{20}, which is generally held to be derived from Q, is inserted by Mt. in the story of the cure of the epileptic boy. There it takes the place of the original reply of Jesus (as given in Mk. 9^{29}) to the disciples' question why they could not cast out the demon. Mk. 11^{23} and Mt. 17^{20} both have 'mountain' against Lk.'s 'sycamine tree,' and in this they have support from 1 Cor. 13^{2}. Now 1 Cor. 13^{2} is in close agreement with Mt. 17^{20}. Both speak of a faith that will transfer a mountain from one place to another, but not of casting a mountain into the sea. 1 Cor. is thus proof that the saying in a form similar to Mt. 17^{20} was current before about A.D. 55. Lk. 17^{6} is quite different. It speaks of uprooting a tree and planting it in the sea. Mk. 11^{23} has features from both pictures. Like Mt. 17^{20} it has the removal of the mountain; and, as in Lk., the destination of the removed object is the sea. There is a *prima facie* case for the hypothesis that originally there were two independent sayings on the power of faith, one preserved in Mt. 17^{20} and the other in Lk. 17^{6}; and that Mk. 11^{23} is a mixture of the two in the process of tradition.

It is, however, commonly held that Lk.'s version of the saying is not original, that he has substituted the tree for the mountain of the original saying, and that his version of the saying is an echo of the story of the cursing of the fig tree, which he omits in his Gospel. This view is open to the following objections:

(1) The tree that was cursed in Mk. 11 is a fig tree, not a 'sycamine.'

(2) When Lk. means 'fig tree' he uses the proper Greek word for it. Lk. 17^{6} is the only place in the New Testament where the 'sycamine tree' is mentioned.

(3) There is Rabbinical evidence that the 'sycamore' (Heb. *shikmāh*) was very deep-rooted. A rule of the Mishnah (*Baba Bathra* 2^{11}, Danby, p. 368) required it to be planted 50 cubits from a neighbour's cistern as against 25 cubits for other trees. 'Sycamine' in Greek properly means the mulberry tree; but the Hebrew *shikmāh* in the Old Testament is translated by 'sycamine' in the Septuagint. 'Sycomore' appears in Lk. 19^{4}; but this is from a different source, L. The conclusion is that 'sycamine' in 17^{6} is a mistranslation *in Q* of the Aramaic *shikmā*, and that here, as elsewhere, Lk. has faithfully copied what was in his source.

We may therefore regard Lk. 17^{6} as a saying from Q, similar in meaning to the other saying preserved in Mt. 17^{20} (M), and independent of it. This Q saying is introduced by Lk. 17^{5}, a verse which is commonly regarded as Lk.'s own composition. Bussmann (*Synoptische Studien*, ii. 90) thinks that it is the connecting verse in Q between *vv.* 3 f. and *v.* 6. The disciples, faced by the demand for unlimited readiness to forgive wrongs, see that this needs a great amount of faith; and so ask that their faith may be increased. Jesus replies that it is not a matter of quantity of faith. The smallest quantity, provided that it is genuine, is capable of accomplishing the seemingly impossible. The grain of mustard seed is a common Jewish expression for a minute quantity. It should be noted that the idea of *planting* a tree in the sea is frankly absurd. It is a plain warning against taking the saying in a sense that was never intended. The saying is a paradox of the same kind as the camel passing through the eye of a needle. Neither the one nor the other is meant to be attempted in the literal sense. But by faith men can do things that seem to be as absurd and impossible as transplanting trees and making them grow in the sea. This word of Jesus does not invite Christians to become conjurers and magicians, but heroes like those whose exploits are celebrated in the eleventh chapter of Hebrews.

4. *THE DAY OF THE SON OF MAN* (184)

(*a*) Longings and False Alarms

MT. 24^{26-27}

24 26 If therefore they shall say unto you,
Behold, he is in the wilderness; go not
forth: Behold, he is in the inner cham-
27 bers; believe [1] *it* not. For as the lightning cometh forth from the east, and is
seen even unto the west; so shall be the
[2] coming of the Son of man.

[1] Or, them. [2] Gr. *presence*.

LK. 17^{22-25}

17 22 And he said unto the disciples, The
days will come, when ye shall desire to
see one of the days of the Son of man, and
23 ye shall not see it. And they shall say to
you, Lo, there! Lo, here! go not away,
24 nor follow after *them*: for as the lightning,
when it lighteneth out of the one part
under the heaven, shineth unto the other
part under heaven: so shall the Son of
25 man be [1] in his day. But first must he
suffer many things and be rejected of this
generation.

[1] Some ancient authorities omit *in his day*.

Cf. Mk. 13^{21-23}.

13 21 And then if any man shall say unto
you, Lo, here is the Christ; or, Lo, there;
22 believe [1] *it* not: for there shall arise false
Christs and false prophets, and shall shew
signs and wonders, that they may lead
23 astray, if possible, the elect. But take ye
heed: behold, I have told you all things
beforehand.

[1] Or, him.

Mk. and Q combine in testifying that Jesus prophesied the coming of bogus prophets and bogus messiahs, who would appeal to the Jewish hope of deliverance, by Divine help, from the oppressions of their enemies. Such people will represent the Messianic ideal which Jesus Himself has utterly rejected. See above, pp. 337 f. His disciples must also reject it and have nothing to do with it. The promised deliverance is not of the earth earthy, but from heaven. It is not a human movement, but a Divine intervention.

22–24. The opening formula marks the change of audience from that in Lk. $17^{20\,f.}$. The saying which follows has no parallel in Mt. or Mk. 'The days will come' is a common formula in Old Testament prophecy. The difficulty of the saying lies in the words 'one of the days of the Son of Man.' For 'the day of the Son of Man' in the Gospels, like 'the day of the Lord' in the Old Testament, is a point of time and not a period. It is what divides the present age from the age to come. Strictly speaking, therefore, it is not proper to speak of 'the days of the Son of Man'; and though the words occur in 17^{26} they have there a different sense. See notes *ad loc.* A most ingenious and attractive explanation is offered by Torrey (*The Four Gospels*, p. 312). The present text depends on a misunderstanding of the Aramaic adverb *lachdā* meaning 'very much,' as the numeral 'one' with the sign of the accusative. The true meaning is then 'you will greatly desire to see the day of the Son of Man.' The disciples will be longing for the Parousia, and this hope deferred will expose them more than others to the dangers arising from false prophets and false Messiahs. Lk.'s 'Lo there! Lo here!' has the support of Mk. Mt. gives a more circumstantial picture: the Messiah is in the wilderness—the mobilisation place of rebellions—don't go to join him; he is in the inner chambers—the places of intrigues and plots—put no trust in all that. Whence Mt. obtained these additional details we cannot say. It is unlikely that they come from Q; for if they had stood there Lk. would not have altered them to what is a mere repetition of *v.* 21^{a}. 'Go not away, nor follow after' is a command to observe strict neutrality. These manifestations should rouse neither fear nor hope. They have nothing to do with the true deliverance which is to come from God. This, when it comes, will come without any preliminary plottings and skirmishings. It will be like the lightning—from above, and lighting up the whole world from horizon to horizon. Mt. makes the lightning come forth from the east and be seen even unto the west, which is not true to fact. 'Shineth' (Lk.) and 'is seen' (Mt.) are translation variants. Cf. the Greek versions of Dan. 12^{3}.

25. This verse, which has no parallel in Mt., is commonly regarded as an insertion by Lk. (cf. 24^{25-27}) influenced perhaps by the three passages in Mk. where the Passion of the Son of Man is predicted (Mk. 8^{31}, 9^{31}, $10^{33\,f.}$). It should be noted, however, that the predictions in Mk. have in view a condemnation and execution at the hands of the leaders and rulers of the people, whereas this verse speaks of the Son of Man suffering many things and being rejected by this generation. Further, 'suffer many things and be rejected' is very vague, if it is an *ex post facto* reference to the Crucifixion. An interpolator would surely have given something more precise, something which left the reader in no doubt that it was His own death on the Cross that Jesus was predicting. If, as I think, the verse is from Q and a genuine utterance of Jesus, we have to ask what is meant by the sufferings

and rejection of the Son of Man. On the view which I take of the meaning of the name 'Son of Man,' the answer is that it is the Remnant that must suffer and be rejected by this generation: and that means Jesus and His disciples. This idea of an inevitable period of suffering before the final vindication is not strange to Q. We may refer to Lk. 11^{47-51}, $12^{4-12, 49-53}$, $13^{34 f.}$.

(*b*) The Eschatological Poem

MT. 24^{37-39}

24 37 And as *were* the days of Noah, so shall
38 be the [1] coming of the Son of man. For
as in those days which were before the
flood they were eating and drinking,
marrying and giving in marriage, until
the day that Noah entered into the ark,
39 and they knew not until the flood came,
and took them all away; so shall be the
[1] coming of the Son of man.

[1] Gr. *presence.*

LK. 17^{26-30}

17 26 And as it came to pass in the days of
Noah, even so shall it be also in the days
27 of the Son of man. They ate, they drank,
they married, they were given in marriage, until the day that Noah entered
into the ark, and the flood came, and
28 destroyed them all. Likewise even as it
came to pass in the days of Lot; they ate,
they drank, they bought, they sold, they
29 planted, they builded; but in the day
that Lot went out from Sodom it rained
fire and brimstone from heaven, and
30 destroyed them all: after the same
manner shall it be in the day that the
Son of man is revealed.

The poetic form of the passage is preserved in Lk. In Mt. the whole of the second strophe is sacrificed in the interests of brevity. On the structure of the poem, see above, p. 324. The Matthæan version of the first strophe is a prosaic paraphrase of what is given in Lk. The most striking feature about the poem as a whole is the discrepancy between the view of the final consummation here and that in Mk. 13^{5-31}. In Mk. 13^{5-31} the end is the last member of a series of predicted events. There is a gradual crescendo of catastrophes until we come to the appearance of the Son of Man. In Q the picture is very different. The world is going about its ordinary affairs; everything is normal. 'When they are saying, Peace and safety, then sudden destruction cometh upon them.' There can be little doubt that the Q account is to be preferred to the Marcan. It appears in a poetic form which is specially characteristic of the genuine teaching of Jesus; and it is supported by 1 Thess. 5^{1-10}; Mk. 13^{32-37}; Lk. 21^{34-36} (L). Mk. 13^{5-31} is probably to be regarded as a catena containing genuine sayings of Jesus so arranged that they give an incorrect impression of His teaching on this subject. (Cf. *The Teaching of Jesus*, pp. 260 ff.)

26, 27. The first strophe, *vv.* 26–27 compares the day of the Son of Man to the Deluge. 'The days of Noah' in this context must mean the period which came to an end with the Flood. Then 'the days of the Son of Man' is a similar expression formed for the sake of parallelism, and meaning the period which will be terminated by the 'Day of the Son of Man,' that is, the Parousia. 'Days of the Son of Man' is not the plural of 'Day of the Son of Man,' but a poetical way of describing the last days of the existing order. This is perceived in Mt.'s version, where the Q passage is rewritten in this sense, and the strange expression 'days of the Son of Man' avoided. The emphasis in the description is not on the sinfulness of the people, but on the fact that they were living in complete disregard of what was coming, immersed in their daily occupations and pleasures, planning and arranging their lives with no thought beyond their immediate interests, self-sufficient and self-satisfied, until sudden calamity overwhelmed them and their civilisation (Gen. $6^{11ff.}$, $7^{21ff.}$).

28 f., 30. The second strophe, *vv.* 28–30. The inhabitants of Sodom are described in similar terms to the generation of the Flood. The sins of Sodom were notorious; but it is not their sins that are mentioned. It is their indifference to the seriousness of their situation that proves their undoing. Noah in the Old Testament story is no paragon of the virtues, much less Lot. But both realised that the catastrophe must come, and both took means to save themselves. The Christian message is not for those who think that they deserve a better fate than their neighbours, but for those who, in the midst of universal indifference and complacency, realise the desperateness of their situation, and ask, 'What must I do to be saved?' The things that happened in the remote past have a real bearing on the present. The most dangerous of all theological errors is that which says, 'He's a good fellow, and 'twill all be well,' rashly assuming that our indifference and carelessness have their counterparts in heaven and that God's holy purpose must inevitably come to terms with our shallow optimism.

(*c*) Closing Sayings

LK. 17^{31-32}

17 31 In that day, he which shall be on the housetop, and his goods in the house, let him not go down to take them away: and let him that is in the field likewise
32 not return back. Remember Lot's wife.

Cf. Mk. 13^{14-16}.

13 14 But when ye see the abomination of desolation standing where he ought not (let him that readeth understand), then let them that are in Judæa flee unto the
15 mountains: and let him that is on the housetop not go down, nor enter in, to
16 take anything out of his house: and let him that is in the field not return back to take his cloke.

The saying Lk. $17^{31f.}$ has no Q parallel in Mt.: it has an independent parallel in Mk. It can hardly be considered relevant to its present context. For the advice given in the two verses is appropriate in the case of war—the siege of Jerusalem, for example. Then there is at least a chance of escape. But in the day of the Son of Man it is idle to think of flight. There is no place to which one may escape. The verses in Lk. are therefore commonly explained as an insertion by Lk. On the other hand, it can be urged that Lk. was sufficiently intelligent to see that such an insertion would be inappropriate at this point; and that it is much more likely that he has kept the unsuitable verses because they were in his source. This means that they belong to Q. Then how did they come to take this place in Q? The answer lies in *v.* 32 with its reference to Lot's wife. The name of Lot provides the connexion with the preceding poem: and this connexion is not logical but mnemonic. The conjunction of *vv.* 28–30 and *vv.* 31 f. goes back to the time of oral tradition: it is probably older than Q.

Verses 31 f. have nothing to do with the Parousia. They belong to another circle of ideas. Jesus prophesied the fall of Jerusalem as the Old Testament prophets had prophesied the fall of Samaria and Jerusalem before Him (Mk. $13^{1f.}$; Lk. $13^{34f.}$). The natural tendency was for these two things—the fall of Jerusalem and the end of the existing world order at the Parousia—to be confused in the tradition. This has happened in Mk. 13. It may be that we have the beginnings of this confusion in this Q passage.

The picture is one of precipitate flight in face of imminent peril. In such circumstances the refugees dare not take time to collect their belongings. They must go as they are, and consider themselves fortunate if they escape with their lives. The story of Lot's wife (Gen. 19^{26}) serves to give point to the warning.

MT. 10^{39}

10 39 He that [1] findeth his [2] life shall lose it; and he that [3] loseth his [2] life for my sake shall find it.

[1] Or, *found*. [2] Or, *soul*. [3] Or, *lost*.

LK. 17^{33}

17 33 Whosoever shall seek to gain his [1] life shall lose it: but whosoever shall lose *his* [1] *life* shall [2] preserve it.

[1] Or, *soul*. [2] Gr. *save it alive*.

Cf. Mk. 8^{35}.

8 35 For whosoever would save his [1] life shall lose it; and whosoever shall lose his [1] life for my sake and the gospel's shall save it.

[1] Or, *soul*.

This verse, as is shown by the context in which it is preserved independently by Mk., and by the context into which it is inserted by Mt. (Mission Charge), has to do originally with the loyalty of disciples to their calling and task. To save one's life at the cost of treachery to Jesus and His mission is to lose it; and to sacrifice one's life in the service of the Kingdom of God is to save it. We may conjecture that the saying was well known in the primitive community, and that it was commonly understood in this sense. Lk., who has a doublet of the saying in the Marcan context (Lk. 9^{24}), must also have known this original and presumably correct interpretation of the saying. The inference is that he has it here a second time because it stood here in Q. Why does it stand here in Q? The answer may perhaps be furnished by the thought of Lk. $17^{31f.}$ There the disciples are told that in certain circumstances they must save their lives by flight. Verse 33 then comes in as a reminder that there are cases in which this course is not open. Wherever running away would involve disloyalty to Jesus and the Kingdom of God, it is better to stay and die.

MT. 24^{40-41}

24 40 Then shall two men be in the field;
41 one is taken, and one is left: two women *shall be* grinding at the mill; one is taken, and one is left.

LK. 17^{34-35}

17 34 I say unto you, In that night there shall be two men on one bed; the one shall be
35 taken, and the other shall be left. There shall be two women grinding together; the one shall be taken, and the other shall be left.[1]

[1] Some ancient authorities add ver. 36. *There shall be two men in the field; the one shall be taken, and the other shall be left.*

The first problem here concerns the text of Lk. As appears from the R.V. mg., there are two forms of the saying. The shorter, *vv.* 34 and 35 only, is the reading of the majority of the most ancient Greek MSS. and the Egyptian versions: the longer, *vv.* 34–36, is supported by two uncial MSS. (D and U) and the Latin, Syriac, and Armenian versions. In modern critical editions of the text *v.* 36 is omitted and commonly explained as an intrusion from Mt. 24^{40}. If this be so, the interpolator did his job thoroughly. For he not only borrowed Mt. 24^{40} here: he also rewrote it in the style of Lk. $17^{34 f.}$. It is more probable that *v.* 36 was omitted by some intelligent scribe or reviser, who saw the words ' in that night ' in *v.* 34, and reflected that agriculture is not a nocturnal pursuit. He did not know, or forgot, that in Palestine farming does involve night work for shepherds (cf. Lk. 2^{8}) and for watchmen set to guard fields, gardens, and orchards against thieves. (Cf. Feldman, *Parables and Similes of the Rabbis*, pp. 132 f.) ' The field ' in Palestinian thought is not restricted to arable land: it can be used for any kind of agricultural land whether cultivated or not. If we accept *v.* 36 as genuine, we have a complete picture of a Palestinian household consisting of husband and wife, two maidservants, and two menservants. The number of the male servants is determined by the fact that one is to be taken and one left in each case. Two is the normal number of persons to work a hand-mill.

34. The words ' in that night ' suggest that the saying is a continuation of the line of thought represented by the early Pauline ' the day of the Lord so cometh as a thief in the night ' (1 Thess. 5^{2}). It is not to be taken literally as a prophecy that the Parousia will occur at night. R.V. translates ' two men on one bed.' The word ' men ' has no equivalent in the Greek text: and the Revisers' rendering depends on the fact that the numeral ' two ' and the pronouns ' the one ' and ' the other ' are all masculine. But it could not be otherwise if, as is probable, husband and wife are meant. Two persons are together (male *and* female): one (male *or* female) will be taken, and the other (male *or* female) will be left. In each case the masculine gender is inevitable. We have then the household with its master and mistress. One is taken, that is, gathered into the number of those destined to a share in the new age that is now coming in.

35 f. Two maids are working at the hand-mill. The same happens in their case. Two men are working in the fields. The same happens to them. The day of the Son of Man cuts across all human relations: it has no regard for ties of blood or marriage, for economic or social distinctions. It has its own principle of division and on that principle it makes a clean cut, separating mankind into two classes.

MT. 24^{28}

24 28 Wheresoever the carcase is, there will the [1] eagles be gathered together.

[1] Or, *vultures*.

LK. 17^{37}

17 37 And they answering say unto him, Where, Lord? And he said unto them, Where the body *is*, thither will the [1] eagles also be gathered together.

[1] Or, *vultures*.

The question ' where? ' and the related question ' when? ' have always had a fascination for those who let their imaginations play upon the apocalyptic hope. Thus in Zech. 14^{4} the appearance of God for the deliverance of His people takes place on the Mount of Olives. Jesus declines to give details of time and place. 'Of that day or that hour knoweth no one, not even the angels in heaven, neither the Son, but the Father' (Mk. 13^{32}) is the answer to the question 'When shall these things be?' (Mk. 13^{4}). And here the question 'Where, Lord?' is met by a saying, probably proverbial, which does not answer the question, but says something else. R.V. mg. 'vultures' is more accurate than the text 'eagles.' But 'vulture' for the Palestinian does not have the unpleasant associations which it has for us. When the vulture is mentioned in the Old Testament it is usually thought of as a noble bird: e.g. Exod. 19^{4}; Dt. 32^{11}; Is. 40^{31}. One characteristic of the vulture is the almost incredible swiftness with which it discovers and makes its way to its prey. This swiftness on the prey is mentioned in Job 9^{26} and Hab. 1^{8}. Cf. also 2 Sam. 1^{23}; Jer. 4^{13}; Lam. 4^{19}. The saying here draws attention to what has already been emphasised—the swiftness and suddenness of the coming of the day of the Son of Man. Jesus says in effect: 'The whole present order of things is nearing its end. Civilisation as you know it is dying. The important thing is not to know the answers to questions about the exact time and place of the end; but to be prepared for it. It is useless to ask for signs of the end, when the first sign of the passing of the present age will be the arrival of the new order.'

Mt. has inserted the saying in a context in his eschatological discourse (chaps. 24 f.) which makes the introductory question superfluous. In the saying itself the words 'body' (Lk.) and 'carcase' (Mt.) are translation variants. See the Greek versions of Num. 14^{33}.

EPILOGUE

We may pause here to ask what is the total impression made upon us by this very early attempt at a systematic account of the teaching of Jesus. And we must bear in mind that the work is not the preached Gospel of the primitive Church, but a supplement to the Gospel (see above, p. 302). If our division of the book is approximately correct, it represents Jesus to us under three main aspects.

First it shows His connexion with the past. John the Baptist is the last and greatest representative of the prophetic order: and John's preaching is all within the framework of the old Covenant. It has to do with what God requires of Israel and with what God will do for Israel; with the demands and promises of God. The focal points of John's preaching are his call to repentance and reformation of life, and his Messianic predictions. Jesus starts from this point; but He goes far beyond John. He rejects the Messianic ideal of John and puts in its place the ideal of the Kingdom of God. What this means to Him is shown in the Temptation story and in the Great Sermon. In its essence it is God overcoming evil with good, the love of God triumphant. Those who submit to it find that it is deliverance and new life; but a new life turned to the service of God's Kingdom by the imitation of God. So we come to a more perfect righteousness than that of John. It is no longer the bringing of one's life into conformity with a given standard of conduct, but the reproduction in human nature of the creative merciful love of God.

Secondly, this determines the task of Jesus and His disciples in the present. It is a mission, in the first instance to Israel, and through Israel to the world. To this mission all other interests must be subservient. Jesus gives to God and demands from His followers unqualified trust and complete devotion. No earthly good may seduce them from their allegiance to the Kingdom; no opposition or persecution may daunt them. This is the main theme of the two middle sections of Q.

Thirdly, Q gives us the expectation of Jesus concerning the future. The essence of it is that the existing world-order based upon selfishness is the exact contrary to the Kingdom of God. The economic structure of society, the social organisations, the political methods of the nations—these things flatly contradict all that Jesus means by the Kingdom of God. Therefore they are doomed to perish. It is clear from the Synoptic Gospels that Jesus expected the end of the existing order and the establishment of the new to come quickly, suddenly, and completely. But it is also clear that He regarded the question of times and seasons as something which God kept in His own hands. For Jesus and His disciples the immediate and urgent business was the service of the Kingdom.

The Gospel is the record of how Jesus gave Himself to that business, and how it took Him to the Cross. There the world seemed to say 'No' to His call: and God to His hopes. Defeated and discredited, deserted by His friends, and forsaken by God, He died alone. And overcame sin and death. In His bitter humiliation, in His lonely agony, He was the realisation of His own demands and the fulfilment of His own hopes. In the light of the Easter experience the men of the primitive Church knew it, and all who know and love Jesus Christ crucified know it too. To the Jews a stumbling-block, to the Greeks foolishness, to us Jesus Christ in His helplessness and humiliation is the very power and wisdom of God.

II.—Teaching Peculiar to Matthew

WE have already seen that the teaching matter peculiar to Mt. falls into large blocks, and that the arrangement of the blocks corresponds at four points with that of Q (see Introd., p. 314). In dealing with this material we shall follow the scheme shown in the Introduction, at the same time taking account of smaller fragments, which do not fit into it. In considering these smaller fragments it is necessary to ask the question whether they belong to Mt.'s special source and have been removed by Mt. from their original context to a more suitable place in the chronological scheme of his Gospel, or whether they are editorial additions, or again whether they are fragments of floating tradition not previously incorporated in a collection. The problem is posed by the first piece of special Matthæan matter.

A FRAGMENT ON THE BAPTISM OF JESUS (6)

MT. 3^{14-15}

3 14 But John would have hindered him, saying, I have need to be baptized of thee,
15 and comest thou to me? But Jesus answering said unto him, Suffer [1] *it* now: for thus it becometh us to fulfil all righteousness. Then he suffereth him.

[1] Or, me.

In the account of the baptism Mk. narrates the bare fact: Jesus came and was baptised. Mt. (3^{13}) emphasises that it was the purpose of Jesus: He came to be baptised. This alteration is necessary to prepare the way for Mt. $3^{14f.}$. The tendency of this passage is obvious. It emphasises the subordination of John to Jesus, identifying Jesus at once with ' the stronger one ' prophesied by John: and it attempts an answer to the question why Jesus undergoes a repentance baptism if He is without sin. That this was a problem in the early Church is shown by a fragment of the apocryphal Gospel according to the Hebrews preserved by Jerome (James, *Apocryphal New Testament*, p. 6). ' Behold the mother of the Lord and his brethren said unto him: John the Baptist baptizeth unto the remission of sins; let us go and be baptized of him. But he said unto them: wherein (what) have I sinned, that I should go and be baptized of him? unless peradventure this very thing that I have said is (a sin of) ignorance.' The dialogue Mt. $3^{14f.}$ can hardly be historical. The words ' I have need to be baptized of thee ' will not fit into John's conception of the Messianic baptism, which is a baptism of fire, i.e. judgement. See on Lk. 3^{16}, above, p. 332. The fragment is early Christian apologetic and doubtless originated in circles where it was necessary to maintain that John the Baptist was the forerunner of the Messiah Jesus and that Jesus Himself was sinless; that is, in Jewish-Christian circles. It is not necessary to suppose that Matthew composed these verses. More probably they are a fragment of Palestinian Christian oral tradition which Matthew incorporated in his account of the baptism. The ' fulfilling of all righteousness ' (*v.* 15) is explicable if the interpretation of John's baptism given above (p. 333) be accepted. Jesus recognises in John's effort to create a new Israel the purpose of God; and willingly enters into it. The baptism of John is from heaven (Mk. $11^{29f.}$). That is sufficient for Jesus.

The question is not whether Jesus has or has not sins to confess, but whether He is to obey the call of God which comes through the last and greatest of the prophets.

We come now to the first large section of the M teaching.

A. THE PREACHING OF JESUS

This is the M parallel to the Q section A3 (above, pp. 338–354). A certain amount of similarity in structure between M and Q has been noticed above (Introd., p. 314). As in Q, the Sermon opens with a collection of beatitudes.

1. *THE BEATITUDES* (19)

MT. 5^{7-10}

5 7 Blessed are the merciful: for they shall obtain mercy.
8 Blessed are the pure in heart: for they shall see God.
9 Blessed are the peacemakers: for they shall be called sons of God.
10 Blessed are they that have been persecuted for righteousness' sake: for theirs is the kingdom of heaven.

7. This beatitude is characteristic of the teaching of Jesus. It is the theme of the parable in Mt. 18^{23-35} (M); and it has parallels in thought in the other sources: e.g. Lk. $17^{3f.}$ (Q); Mk. 11^{25}. In Jewish teaching about God's forgiveness the start is made from the consideration of the case of the offender; and the principle is that if I have injured my neighbour in any way I must first make reparation to him and seek his forgiveness, and then ask forgiveness of God. Jesus thinks rather of the injured party. He must be ready to forgive the offender. That is to say, for Jesus the essential requisite for receiving God's forgiveness is to have a forgiving spirit oneself. This thought is also to be found in Judaism, *Ecclus.* 28^{2-5}:

> 'Forgive thy neighbour the injury (done to thee),
> And then, when thou prayest, thy sins will be forgiven.
> Man cherisheth anger against another;
> And doth he seek healing from God?
> On a man like himself he hath no mercy;
> And doth he make supplication for his own sins?
> He, being flesh, nourisheth wrath;
> Who will make atonement for his sins?'

Similarly, the Jewish Patriarch Gamaliel II (*c.* A.D. 90) says: 'So long as thou art merciful, the Merciful (i.e. God) is merciful to thee' (*Tos. B.Q.* 10^{30}). Other Jewish parallels, Billerbeck, i. 203 ff. Such difference as there is between Jesus and Judaism is a difference of emphasis. Jesus lays great stress on the fact that he who will not forgive is thereby unfitted to receive God's forgiveness. It is not a matter of outward words or acts. Nor is it as if God offered a *quid pro quo*: 'You forgive your neighbour and I will forgive you.' It is a matter of inward character and disposition. The Christian who has not learned how to overcome evil with good, has not learned the first thing about the nature of God: he does not know God as a Christian ought to know God. If he did, he would see his offending neighbour, as it were, through God's eyes, and forgive him.

8. Cf. Ps. $24^{3\,f.}$:

'Who shall ascend into the hill of the Lord?
And who shall stand in his holy place?
He that hath clean hands and a pure heart;
Who hath not lifted up his soul unto vanity,
And hath not sworn deceitfully.'

'Pure in heart' is not to be construed as absolutely sinless. The meaning of the expression may be gathered from the promise attached. To 'see God' is in Palestinian speech another way of saying 'appear before God'; and this has special reference to attending the Temple worship, especially that of the great Festivals. The Jewish Law recognises various kinds of bodily defilement, which disqualify a person from joining in the Temple worship, that is, from 'seeing God' in this sense. The purifications prescribed in the Law serve to remove this physical disqualification. From this it is a simple matter to take the step that is taken in Ps. 24 and to think of an inward cleansing as the qualification for communion with God. The difference between Jesus and the Rabbis is that while they admit the necessity for both outward (levitical) purity and inward cleanness of heart, Jesus throws all the emphasis on the latter. For Him *the* condition of having fellowship with God, here or hereafter, is a clean heart, a heart that loves goodness and hates evil.

9. The peacemakers are not those who merely practise the negative virtue of non-resistance to evil. They are the people who overcome evil with good, and establish peace where there is discord and strife, who make up quarrels and reconcile enemies. This positive virtue is inculcated in the Rabbinical literature. There is a famous saying of Hillel (*Aboth* 1^{12}): 'Be of the disciples of Aaron, loving peace and pursuing peace, loving mankind and bringing them nigh to the Law.' Further citations in Montefiore, *Rabb. Lit. and Gospel Teachings*, pp. 27 ff. To be called sons of God means to be so called by God Himself, acknowledged and adopted by Him. Hence to be called sons of God is to be sons of God. In the Old Testament and in Jewish belief the title belongs to Israel (Dt. 14^{1}; Hos. 1^{10}; *Ps. Sol.* 17^{30}). Rabbi Aḳiba (martyred A.D. 135) used to say: 'Beloved are Israel for they were called children of God; still greater was the love in that it was made known to them that they were called children of God, as it is written (Dt. 14^{1}), "Ye are the children of the Lord your God"' (*Aboth* 3^{15}; Danby, p. 452). The title is specially appropriated to the godly in Israel (*Wisdom* $2^{13,\,18}$; other passages in Billerbeck, i. 219). The peacemakers are the true Israel and acknowledged by God as His children.

10. This may be regarded as the M version of the saying which closes the Q set of beatitudes, Lk. $6^{22\,f.}$||Mt. $5^{11\,f.}$. (See above, p. 340). In the Q version it is persecution as followers of Christ that is thought of: here it is persecution 'for righteousness' sake.' Righteousness is a favourite word in Mt., where it occurs seven times (not in Mk; once in Lk., in a poetical passage, 1^{75}). It gives to the beatitude a characteristically Jewish-Christian flavour. For in Jewish speech the words 'righteous' and 'righteousness' always have a reference, open or implied, to obedience to the Law. (See *Teaching of Jesus*, pp. 324 f.) The persecuted for

righteousness' sake would thus include the Jewish martyrs as well as the Christian, as in Heb. 11; whereas the Q form has reference only to persecuted followers of Jesus. The reward of those who endure persecution is a share in the Kingdom of heaven. 'Heaven,' as regularly in Mt., is not the future state of the righteous, but a substitute for the Divine name. This substitution of 'Kingdom of heaven' for 'Kingdom of God' is another touch of Jewish-Christian piety. It corresponds to a common Jewish usage.

5. It is possible that Mt. 5^{5}:

> Blessed are the meek: for they shall inherit the earth

should be added to this group of beatitudes. It is open to some suspicion on two grounds: (*a*) Its place in the series is not clear. In some MSS. it precedes 'Blessed are they that mourn . . .,' and in others it follows. This uncertainty about the place of a verse is often a sign of interpolation. (*b*) The thought is not very original. The saying looks as if it had been manufactured out of Ps. 37^{11}, 'The meek shall inherit the land.' The 'meek' in Mt. 5^{5} are the same people who are called the 'poor' in Lk. 6^{20} (Q). The promise of inheriting the earth implies the expectation of a Messianic kingdom to be established on earth in the future. But it may be doubted whether Jesus contemplated the establishment of such a kingdom. The day of the Son of Man appears to be the day of the final judgement rather than the day when the Messianic kingdom is to be established on earth: and after that day the place of the godly seems to be in heaven. On the whole it seems best to treat Mt. 5^{5} as a Jewish-Christian interpolation.

2. *SALT AND LIGHT* (20)

MT. 5^{13-16}

5 13 Ye are the salt of the earth: but if the
salt have lost its savour wherewith shall it
be salted? It is thenceforth good for
nothing, but to be cast out and trodden
14 under foot of men. Ye are the light of the
world. A city set on a hill cannot be hid.
15 Neither do *men* light a lamp, and put it
under the bushel, but on the stand; and it
shineth unto all that are in the house.
16 Even so let your light shine before men,
that they may see your good works, and
glorify your Father which is in heaven.

The opening phrases, 'Ye are the salt of the earth' and 'Ye are the light of the world,' suggest that both verses 13 and 14 are from one source. And since *v.* 14 has no parallel in Lk. we may perhaps assign both verses to M. Again, *v.* 16, which has no parallel in Lk., and is therefore presumably M, presupposes *v.* 15. Verse 15 has a parallel in Lk.; but the parallel is only partial. It may well be that the whole passage *vv.* 13–16 is to be assigned to M.

13. See Lk. $14^{34f.}$ (Q), above, p. 424.

14. The disciples of Jesus are the light of the world. So, in Is. 42^{6}, 49^{6}, is the Servant of the Lord. In the Rabbinical literature the title 'light of the world' is given to God, Adam, Israel, the Law and the Temple, Jerusalem. In Rom. 2^{19} the Jews are represented as thinking of themselves as 'a light of them that are in darkness,' and in Phil. 2^{15} Christians are described as 'lights in the world.' In John 8^{12} it is Jesus Himself who is the light of the world. The sense in which the saying is to be taken is given in *vv.* $15^{f.}$.

The saying about the city seems to be irrelevant to the present context. It has a parallel in the Oxyrhynchus fragment I, 7. (Grenfell and Hunt, *New Sayings of Jesus* (1904), p. 38): 'Jesus saith, A city built upon the top of a high hill and stablished, can neither fall nor be hid.' It is probable that the saying is originally a piece of worldly wisdom. There are two ways of obtaining safety. One is to take up a commanding situation; the other is to hide oneself. It is not possible to do both. In its present position the saying appears to be meant to convey the same meaning as 'Ye are the light of the world.' All eyes are upon the disciples, who must show to the best advantage.

15. See on Lk. 11^{33} (Q), above, p. 384.

16. The disciples are to shine by their behaviour, which must be astonishingly good. So good that men will see the disciples as living examples of God's power and grace, and praise Him, who can so transform human lives.

3. *THE NEW LAW* (21–27)

The kernel of this passage is a series of six brief antithetical statements, in which the provisions of the old Law are contrasted with the higher righteousness demanded by Jesus. This original nucleus has been expanded by the addition of relevant material from various sources. See above, Introd., pp. 315 f.

(*a*) Introduction. The Attitude of Jesus to the Law (21)

MT. 5^{17-20}

5 17 Think not that I came to destroy the
law or the prophets: I came not to destroy,
18 but to fulfil. For verily I say unto you,
Till heaven and earth pass away, one jot
or one tittle shall in no wise pass away
from the law, till all things be ac-
19 complished. Whosoever therefore shall
break one of these least commandments,
and shall teach men so, shall be called
least in the kingdom of heaven: but whosoever shall do and teach them, he shall be
20 called great in the kingdom of heaven. For
I say unto you, that except your righteousness shall exceed *the righteousness* of the
scribes and Pharisees, ye shall in no wise
enter into the kingdom of heaven.

The plain purpose of this preamble is to prevent misunderstanding of the provisions which follow. There was no point on which devout Palestinian Jews were more sensitive than on any attempt to tamper with the Law, which was for them something given directly by God Himself, and therefore perfect and irreformable. Conservative Palestinian Christians were not only themselves sympathetic towards this high doctrine of the Law, but also under the necessity of defining the Jewish-Christian attitude to their national heritage. They had to live in the midst of an orthodox—at times fanatically orthodox—Jewish community: and, more than that, they had to carry on the Christian mission among these very people (Gal. 2^{9}). For them it was essential that the positive teaching of Jesus should not appear to be an overthrowng of all that was most sacred to the devout Jew. The differences between the teaching of Jesus and orthodox Jewish doctrine must be shown to be due not to heresy on the part of Jesus but to His deeper and fuller understanding of the Law. His pronouncements, so far from upsetting the Law, bring out its true meaning and purpose. In this way, it might be hoped, the new wine would settle down in the old wine-skins.

17. The formula 'Think not that I came to . . . I came not to . . . but to . . .' recurs (Mt. 10^{34}). There is no reason why Jesus should not have uttered this

saying. It is best understood in the light of Mk. 7^{6-13} and the Q sayings against the scribes (Lk. 11^{45-52}, above, pp. 392–395). Jesus accuses the scribes of stultifying the Law by their interpretation of it, and claims that His way brings to light the true meaning, the will and purpose of God in framing it. Cf. the treatment of marriage and divorce (Mk. 10^{1-12}). As against scribal interpretation of the Law and priestly conduct of the Temple worship (Mk. 11^{15-19}), Jesus says: 'It is not I who make the Law of none effect, but you.' Something of this sort may well have been the original meaning of this saying: in its present context it makes Jesus sound too sympathetic towards orthodox Judaism.

18. This saying has a parallel in Q (Lk. 16^{17}, see above, p. 427). In its present form and context the saying is an affirmation of the permanent validity of the Law in its minutest details. But such an affirmation by Jesus is hardly thinkable in view of such a passage as Mk. 10^{1-12}. It is most probable that the Q form is the original, and that the meaning was as suggested in the notes on Lk. 16^{17}. The words 'Till heaven and earth pass away' maintain the Law in full force until the final consummation. Whether the whole Law would be necessary in the sinless and perfect life of the world to come is another question. 'One jot or one tittle': on 'tittle' see notes on Lk. 16^{17}. The 'jot' is the Hebrew letter '*yod*,' the smallest consonant in the Hebrew alphabet. 'Till all things be accomplished' is probably to be understood in the light of 'Till heaven and earth pass away.' The Law is given to man in the present world and is a complete revelation of God's will for man in his present situation. In the next world, after God's purpose in this has been completed, the situation may well be different; and man may no longer require the kind of revelation of God's will that was necessary for him in this world.

19. 'Break' in this verse should be translated 'relax.' The Greek verb is used elsewhere in M as the equivalent of the Hebrew verb *hittīr*. The person in view here is one who permits less than the Law requires either by allowing what it forbids or by exempting men from some of its positive requirements. In the phrase 'one of these least commandments' the word 'these' is literal translation of the Greek, which is in its turn literal translation of a common Aramaic idiom. The idiomatic rendering would be 'one of the least commandments.' The relaxing of the Law begins first in the practice of the man himself and then is taught by him as the true way for others. It has already been suggested above (Introd., p. 317) that it is St. Paul who is thought of in this verse. Such a man will be called—i.e. he will be—least in the Kingdom. Aramaic has no special form for the superlative of adjectives. So far as an Aramaic original is concerned 'little' would be the same as 'least'; but no doubt 'least' gives the accepted sense of the original in the circles where the saying was at home. The opposite to this character, the Jewish Christian who maintains the Law in its full stringency, demanding from others (and practising himself) strict obedience to the dietary laws, circumcision of Gentile converts to Christianity, and the like—such a man will be great in the Kingdom. We have in this verse the convictions of people like those who appear in Gal. $2^{12f.}$; Acts 15^{5}. These sentiments are put into the mouth of Jesus: it is in the last degree unlikely that He thought or said such a thing.

20. The righteousness required for entrance into the Kingdom is that which is about to be explained in the antitheses which follow. The scribes and Pharisees, it is implied, have their interpretation of the meaning of the Law; and it is the wrong one. The right interpretation, which will be the true fulfilment of the Law, will penetrate below the surface and bring to light the fundamental principles, the spirit of the Law. A righteousness based on those first principles and not on mechanical obedience to precept and tradition is the condition of entry into the Kingdom. So the compiler seems to understand the saying.

(*b*) Murder (22)

MT. 5^{21-24}

5 21 Ye have heard that it was said to them of old time, Thou shalt not kill; and whosoever shall kill shall be in danger of the
22 judgement: but I say unto you, that every one who is angry with his brother [1] shall be in danger of the judgement; and whosoever shall say to his brother, [2] Raca, shall be in danger of the council; and whosoever shall say, [3] Thou fool, shall be
23 in danger [4] of the [5] hell of fire. If therefore thou art offering thy gift at the altar, and there rememberest that thy brother
24 hath aught against thee, leave there thy gift before the altar, and go thy way, first be reconciled to thy brother, and then come and offer thy gift.

[1] Many ancient authorities insert *without cause.*
[2] An expression of contempt.
[3] Or, *Moreh*, a Hebrew expression of condemnation.
[4] Gr. *unto* or *into.*
[5] Gr. *Gehenna of fire.*

To this passage Mt. adds *vv.* 25–26 derived from Q. See above, p. 414.

21, 22. 'Ye have heard'—often, in the reading of the Law in the Synagogue. Those 'of old time' are the generation who were alive when the Law was given from Sinai. 'Thou shalt not kill' (Exod. 20^{13}; Dt. 5^{17}) the sixth commandment of the Decalogue. The following clause: 'and whosoever . . . judgement' is likewise based on the written Law. Cf. Exod. 21^{12}; Lev. 24^{17}; Dt. 17^{8-13}. 'In danger of the judgement' clearly means liable to trial and punishment as prescribed in the Law. All that is given in *v.* 21 is thus a concise and simple statement of the law concerning murder, as it stands in the Old Testament. Now comes the comment of Jesus. In its original form it probably did not go beyond the word 'judgement.' What follows is, then, to be regarded as later expansion of the saying. The point of the antithesis lies in the contrast between the outward act, of which an earthly court can take cognisance, and the inward disposition, which may or may not produce the act; but which is known to God and judged by Him. The judgement in the second case must be the judgement of God: no earthly tribunal can deal with the crime of hatred. The marginal note 1 of R.V. draws attention to an important variant in the text. The authorities against the words 'without a cause' are weighty; and those which insert the words are also early and important. In favour of the latter is the fact that qualifying additions of this sort are quite in Mt.'s manner. It is probable that the addition is part of the true text of Mt.; and not part of the original saying, but a gloss inserted by the Evangelist himself. The insistence on the inward disposition can be paralleled from Judaism and from Gentile thought. A saying attributed to R. Eliezer (*c.* A.D. 90) runs: 'He who hates his neighbour, lo he belongs to the shedders of blood' i.e. he is classed with the murderers. The early Greek philosopher Democritus says: 'An enemy is not one who wrongs (us), but one who would like (to do so)' (Fr. 89).

The meaning of the terms of abuse in the second half of the verse is still disputed. Raca is not a Greek word. It is perhaps best explained as a transliteration of the Aramaic *rêkā*, meaning 'empty,' and so 'empty-headed,' 'stupid,' 'blockhead.' *Mōre* can be taken as Greek. It then means, as in R.V., 'fool.' But this will hardly do, if the saying is seriously meant. There is no point in threatening a man with the Sanhedrin for saying 'blockhead' and with hell-fire for saying 'fool.' It is therefore probable that *Mōre* represents the Rabbinic word *mōrā* with a shade of meaning contributed by the Hebrew word *Mōreh*. This last means more than merely 'stupid': it means 'stubborn,' 'rebellious,' and so 'obstinately wicked.' The distinction between the two words will then be that *Raca* suggests a defect of intelligence, while *Mōre* makes the much more serious charge of moral defect. The 'council' is the Sanhedrin, the supreme court in the Jewish legal system. On Gehenna see notes on Lk. 12^{5}, above, p. 399. It may be doubted whether *v.* 22^{b} is a genuine saying of Jesus.

23 f. These verses do not belong to the original antithesis. They are brought in at this point as being more or less relevant to the subject. The duty of establishing peace takes precedence even of the Temple worship. The Jewish rule in such cases, where a man has begun to carry out one religious obligation and remembers another, which he ought to carry out, is that the more important obligation takes precedence of the less important (Billerbeck, i. 284). This saying to a Jew would mean that reconciliation was more important than sacrifice. Further, it is sound Jewish doctrine that a man must seek forgiveness from his neighbour whom he has wronged before he asks God's forgiveness for doing the wrong. 'For transgressions that are between man and God the Day of Atonement effects atonement, but for transgressions that are between a man and his fellow the Day of Atonement effects atonement only if he has appeased his fellow' (*Yoma* 8^{9}, Danby, p. 172). (Cf. Hos. 6^{6}.) Mt. $5^{23 f.}$ has nothing to do with Mk. $11^{25-(26)}$; see Mt. $6^{14 f.}$, below, p. 463.

(*c*) Adultery (23)

MT. 5^{27-30}

5 27 Ye have heard that it was said, Thou
28 shalt not commit adultery: but I say unto you, that every one that looketh on a woman to lust after her hath committed adultery with her already in his heart.
29 And if thy right eye cause thee to stumble, pluck it out, and cast it from thee: for it is profitable for thee that one of thy members should perish, and not thy whole body
30 be cast into [1] hell. And if thy right hand causeth thee to stumble, cut it off, and cast it from thee: for it is profitable for thee that one of thy members should perish, and not thy whole body go into [1] hell.

[1] Gr. *Gehenna*.

Cf. MK. 9^{43-48}

9 43 And if thy hand cause thee to stumble, cut it off: it is good for thee to enter into life maimed, rather than having thy two hands to go into [1] hell, into the unquench-
45 able fire.[2] And if thy foot cause thee to stumble, cut it off: it is good for thee to enter into life halt, rather than having
47 thy two feet to be cast into [1] hell. And if thine eye cause thee to stumble, cast it out: it is good for thee to enter into the kingdom of God with one eye, rather than having two eyes to be cast into [1] hell;
48 where their worm dieth not, and the fire is not quenched.

[1] Gr. *Gehenna*.

[2] Ver. 44 and 46 (which are identical with ver. 48) are omitted by the best ancient authorities.

The original antithesis is given in *vv.* 27 f. The two verses which follow are additional relevant matter, of which we have an independent version in Mk. As the Marcan passage is reproduced in Mt. $18^{8f.}$, we may regard Mt. $5^{29f.}$ as the M version of the saying.

27. The Law as given to Israel (Exod. 20^{14}; Dt. 5^{17}), the seventh commandment of the Decalogue. For the Jewish definition of adultery, see on Lk. 16^{18}, above, p. 428.

28. The comment of Jesus. As in the case of murder, He distinguishes between the act and the inward disposition that produces the act. The lustful look is not actionable as adultery is; but it shows just as clearly the kind of character that is within. And the character is that of an adulterer in God's sight, even though there has been no adulterous act for which the man might be made to answer to an earthly court. The same line is taken by the Rabbis. Thus we have the Rabbinic dictum 'He who looks at a woman with desire is as one who has criminal intercourse with her' (*Kalla*, § 1). For other sayings to the same effect see Montefiore, *Rabb. Lit. and Gospel Teachings*, pp. 41 ff.; Abrahams, *Studies*, ii. 205 f.

29 f. These verses are linked to the preceding by the offending eye. In Mk. the eye is dealt with last. It may be that Mt. has reversed the order to make a better connexion. But there is no real connexion. What is given in these verses is very strongly worded advice to tame the natural desires and passions at all costs. The point is the same as in 1 Cor. 9^{27}: 'I buffet my body, and bring it into bondage: lest by any means, after that I have preached to others, I myself should be rejected.'

(*d*) DIVORCE (24)

MT. 5^{31-32}

5 31 It was said also, Whosoever shall put away his wife, let him give her a writing of
32 divorcement: but I say unto you, that every one that putteth away his wife, saving for the cause of fornication, maketh her an adulteress: and whosoever shall marry her when she is put away committeth adultery.

Here we have an antithesis in something like its original form, without any accretions of teaching from elsewhere. There are parallels to the saying in Mk. $10^{11f.}$ and Q (Lk. 16^{18}).

31. The reference is to Dt. 24^{1}. In Jewish law marriage was a partnership which could be dissolved by the husband himself without having recourse to the courts. The divorce was effected by serving on the wife a document, properly drawn up and attested, declaring that she was no longer his wife. The rules governing the preparation and delivery of such 'writings of divorcement' are codified in the Mishnah tractate *Gittin* (Danby, pp. 307–321). The form of the document is given in Lightfoot's *Horæ Hebraicæ* (ed. Gandell, Oxford, 1859) ii. 124, and in Billerbeck, i. 311 f.

32. Jesus forbids divorce. His reasons are given in Mk. 10^{6-9} and are founded, not on the Mosaic regulations for divorce, but on the purpose of God in instituting marriage. The excepting clause 'saving for the cause of fornication' is an interpolation, as is the similar excepting clause in Mt. 19^{9}. The question on what grounds a man might divorce his wife was debated in Jesus' day by the

schools of Hillel and Shammai. The Matthæan form of the saying brings Jesus into agreement with the school of Shammai. But Jesus agreed with neither school. His attitude to the whole question is quite different from theirs. (See notes on Lk. 16[18], above, pp. 428 ff., and *Teaching of Jesus*, pp. 292 f.)

(*e*) Vows and Oaths (25)

MT. 5[33-37]

5 33 Again, ye have heard that it was said to them of old time, Thou shalt not forswear thyself, but shalt perform unto the Lord
34 thine oaths: but I say unto you, Swear not at all; neither by the heaven, for it is the
35 throne of God; nor by the earth, for it is the footstool of his feet; nor [1] by Jerusalem, for it is the city of the great King.
36 Neither shalt thou swear by thy head, for thou canst not make one hair white or
37 black. [2] But let your speech be, Yea, yea; Nay, nay: and whatsoever is more than these is of [3]the evil *one*.

[1] Or, *toward*.
[2] Some ancient authorities read *But your speech shall be*.
[3] Or, *evil*: as in ver. 39; vi. 13.

Parallels: Mt. 23[16-22]; James 5[12]. It is to be noted that in both cases the parallel is with the latter part of this section, beginning 'Swear not at all.' The difficulty in these verses lies in the fact that *v.* 33, as it stands, has to do with vows, while *vv.* 34–37 have to do with oaths. There are two possibilities: (*a*) *V.* 33 really is about vows. The natural conclusion will then be that the original antithesis ended with the words 'Swear not at all'; and the sense will be: The Law says, Do not break your vows, but perform what you have promised: but I say, Make no vows at all. (*b*) The antithesis is not concerned with vows at all, but with speaking the truth. In that case the words in *v.* 33 'but shalt perform unto the Lord thine oaths' are an intrusion. The sense of the passage would be: The Law forbids perjury: but I say, Do not take oaths at all, etc. This second alternative is to be preferred for the following reasons: (i) All the other antitheses are concerned with my duty to my neighbour. It is therefore probable that this one will be concerned with the social duty of truthfulness, rather than with vows, which are a concern between God and man. (ii) The second interpretation enables us to take the principal verbs in their most natural and obvious sense. (iii) It has the support of James 5[12].

33. As the result of the preceding discussion, we reject the clause 'but shalt perform . . . oaths' as a mistaken attempt to explain 'thou shalt not forswear thyself.' The prohibition of perjury goes back to Lev. 19[12]: 'And ye shall not swear by my name falsely, so that thou profane the name of thy God.' Cf. Exod. 20[7]; Dt. 5[11]: the third commandment of the Decalogue. The Law does not forbid oaths; but it does forbid perjury, which is regarded as a profanation of the name of God.

34, 35, 36. The comment of Jesus forbids the use of oaths altogether. And this prohibition covers not only such ancient and solemn forms of oath as 'As the Lord liveth,' or that recorded in Mt. 26[63]. It forbids also those milder forms, which, since they did not involve an explicit mention of God, might be thought not to involve profanation of the Name. The argument of *vv.* 34–36 is that these apparently harmless oaths do involve a reference to God. Heaven is His throne, earth His footstool, Jerusalem His city—'the great King' = God—man himself and every part of him is God's handiwork. It is God who ordains the black hair of youth and the white of old age.

37. What is required is something that cannot be supplied by oaths, however solemn—a disposition to speak the truth. Given that inward honesty all oaths become superfluous. Indeed, the plain Yes or No of an honest man is more reliable than the word of a liar, even though that word be supported by the most solemn oath. For 'Let your speech be, Yea, yea; Nay, nay' James (5^{12}) has 'let your yea be yea, and your nay, nay.' The form in Mt. can be explained as mistranslation due to following an Aramaic original word by word. There can be little doubt that James 5^{12} here gives the correct rendering. This is confirmed by the fact that in Jewish teaching the doubled yes or no is regarded as a form of oath.

There is ample evidence that the fortifying of statements by oaths of various kinds was a common Jewish practice, and also that the Rabbis disliked and condemned idle swearing. There are also Rabbinic parallels to the saying 'Let your yea be yea, and your nay, nay.' R. Huna said, 'The yea of the righteous is a yea; their no is a no.' (For this and other examples, cf. Montefiore, *op. cit.*, pp. 48 ff.) But the Rabbis never prohibited entirely the taking of oaths.

(*f*) Retribution (26)

MT. 5^{38-42}

5 38 Ye have heard that it was said, An eye
39 for an eye, and a tooth for a tooth: but I say unto you, Resist not [1] him that is evil: but whosoever smiteth thee on thy right
40 cheek, turn to him the other also. And if any man would go to law with thee, and take away thy coat, let him have thy cloke
41 also. And whosoever shall [2] compel thee to go one mile, go with him twain.
42 Give to him that asketh thee, and from him that would borrow of thee turn not thou away.

[1] Or, *evil*. [2] Gr. *impress*.

This passage is composite. The original antithesis is contained in *vv.* 38, 39^a. Verses 39^b, 40, 42 have a parallel in Lk. $6^{29 f.}$, and are probably from Q. *V.* 41 is a saying of the same kind as those which precede it, and may be assigned to M.

38. The *lex talionis*: Exod. 21^{22-25}; Lev. $24^{19 f.}$; Dt. 19^{21}. The law governing cases of injury to the person. What is prescribed is equivalence of injury and punishment. It is important to remember than when this rule is first instituted, it is a great advance; for it puts an end to the vendetta, the interminable blood-feud, as well as to the system of repaying injuries with interest. Cf. Gen. $4^{23 f.}$.

39. The comment of Jesus cancels this rule by which injury to the person is punished by the infliction of an exactly similar injury on the aggressor. In its place He lays down the principle 'Resist not him that is evil' (R.V.) or 'Resist not evil' (R.V. mg.). The Greek words may mean 'the evil person' or 'the evil thing.' Which is originally meant must be determined, if at all, on other grounds. In favour of the former view is the fact that the Greek word translated 'resist' commonly means to fight against. It is not 'passive resistance' but active hostility that is implied in the word; and hostility of this sort is more naturally thought of as directed against persons. Further, it is part of the Christian life to resist evil and overcome it with good. The Christian warfare, according to Paul, is not against men but against the forces of evil. The saying

may then be taken to mean that the violence of the wrongdoer is not to be met by violence, either by way of revenge or by way of getting one's own blow in first. This conclusion must not, however, be taken in isolation. It forms part of the whole collection of antitheses; and it is to be understood in the light of the other members of the series. This means that it is not just an amendment of the existing law on humanitarian grounds. It is a demand for such a change in the character and disposition of the disciples that they will rather endure than inflict injury, and go on enduring injury rather than inflict it. Cf. 1 Cor. 6^{7}, 13^{4-7}. Further, we must take into account those passages in which Jesus speaks of the persecution of His followers, and invites them to rejoice when they are persecuted. This implies a radical alteration of their estimate of the dreadfulness of physical suffering, just as His sayings on wealth involve a radical change in the estimation of worldly goods. The attitude to those who wrong and injure us, required in the principle of Jesus, is thus only possible if we have come to the point at which we learn, so to speak, to despise suffering. But this point is only reached when we care so much for the Kingdom of God that we care very little about pleasure and pain; and that implies a radical change of character and disposition.

39^{b}, 40, 42. On these verses see above, pp. 341–344.

41. The word translated 'compel' is properly a technical term meaning to impress a person or his draught animals for the public service. The practice can be traced back to the institution, under the Persian empire, of a system of state couriers for the purpose of rapid communication between the central government and its subordinates. Speed was achieved by working the couriers in relays: and for the efficient working of the system it was essential that a courier should be able to requisition a horse if necessary. Under the Roman empire the same word is used for the requisition of similar services from civilians by the army (Dittenberger, *O.G.I.S.*, $665^{21, 24}$). Cf. Epictetus, IV. i. 79. 'If there is a requisition and a soldier seizes it (your ass), let it go. Do not resist or complain, otherwise you will be first beaten, and lose the ass after all.' The same word is used for the requisitioning of personal service in Mk. 15^{21}, where the Roman troops in charge of the Crucifixion impress Simon to carry the cross. It is therefore natural to suppose that Mt. 5^{41} is concerned with the situation which would arise if a Jewish civilian is impressed as a baggage-carrier by a Roman soldier of the army of occupation. If the victim is a follower of Jesus, he will give double what is demanded. The first mile renders to Cæsar the things that are Cæsar's; the second mile, by meeting oppression with kindness, renders to God the things that are God's.

(*g*) Love of Neighbour (27)

MT. 5^{43-48}

43 Ye have heard that it was said, Thou
shalt love thy neighbour, and hate thine
44 enemy: but I say unto you, Love your
enemies, and pray for them that persecute
45 you; that ye may be sons of your Father
which is in heaven: for he maketh his sun
to rise on the evil and the good, and
sendeth rain on the just and the unjust.
46 For if ye love them that love you, what
reward have ye? do not even the [1] publicans
47 the same? And if ye salute your brethren
only, what do ye more *than others*? do not
48 even the Gentiles the same? Ye therefore
shall be perfect, as your heavenly Father
is perfect.

[1] That is, *collectors or renters of Roman taxes*: and so elsewhere.

In this section we have again a parallel in Lk.; and it begins unusually early, with *v.* 44. Lk. 6^{27} begins 'But I say unto you which hear, Love your enemies ...' But in what follows, while there is a good deal of agreement between Mt. and Lk. in thoughts, there is surprisingly little either in the order in which they are presented or in the wording. It may, therefore, be the case that Mt. and Lk. are independent in this passage, and that Mt. draws on M, and Lk. on Q. Further, the opening words of Lk. 6^{27} suggest that in Q a fragment of this antithesis has been preserved. There would be nothing surprising in this; for the fragment in question gives one of the most striking and characteristic of the teachings of Jesus.

43 f. The existing law. 'Thou shalt love thy neighbour' from Lev. 19^{18}. It is perfectly clear what Lev. 19^{18} means by 'neighbour,' namely fellow-Israelite. The Rabbis gave to 'neighbour' the widest possible meaning by including under the term not only born Israelites but also converts to Judaism from the Gentile nations. There was nothing in Lev. 19^{18} to indicate to a Jew in the days of Jesus that he ought to love Pontius Pilate. Indeed there was a great deal in the Pentateuch to justify an opposite attitude. And the Pentateuch was regarded as in the fullest sense inspired. There would have been nothing surprising if any Jew had inferred from Lev. 19^{18} that his duty was to love his fellow-Jews and hate his Roman enemies. But Jewish literature is ransacked in vain for evidence that such a conclusion is explicitly drawn. 'Thou shalt love thy neighbour and hate thine enemy' cannot be found. Now if we look at the other antitheses in this section, we find that the first member of the antithesis usually contains a bare statement of the existing rule: 'Thou shalt not commit adultery,' or 'an eye for an eye and a tooth for a tooth.' In Mt. 5^{33} we have in addition to 'Thou shalt not forswear thyself' the further clause 'but shalt perform unto the Lord thine oaths'; and it is precisely this additional clause that makes nonsense of the passage. The inference is that the words 'and hate thine enemy' are an interpolation. The moment they are removed the true force of the antithesis springs to light. It is not a matter of loving some and hating others. The antithesis in its stark simplicity is:

> The Law says, Thou shalt love thy neighbour.
> I say, Love your enemies.

Whether the original antithesis went on to give the rest of *v.* 44, or even the fuller version in Lk. $6^{27 f.}$ it is not possible to say. It is not probable that it had more than this, because the characteristic feature of these sayings is their pointed epigrammatic brevity. That the true meaning of the saying is 'Love your enemies as well as your friends' and not 'Love your enemies rather than hate them' is shown by the examples which follow.

45. First, an appeal to God's way. In the order of nature He grants sunshine and rain to friend and foe alike.

46 f. Second, a demonstration that the 'higher righteousness' required of a disciple requires something more than the sort of kindness and affection to be found among publicans and Gentiles, to say nothing of scribes and Pharisees.

48. Third, by a statement of the goal of all disciples, to be like God.

For further comment on these verses see notes on Lk. 6^{27-36}, above, pp. 341–347.

On the basis of the preceding discussion we may conjecture that the original, unexpanded form of the antitheses was somewhat as follows:

Introduction 17 Think not that I came to destroy the Law or the prophets:
I came not to destroy but to fulfil.

20 For I say unto you, that except your righteousness shall exceed that of the scribes and Pharisees, ye shall in no wise enter into the Kingdom of heaven.

I 21 Ye have heard that it was said to them of old time,
Thou shalt not kill; and whosoever shall kill shall be in danger of the judgement:

22 But I say unto you, that every one who is angry with his brother shall be in danger of the judgement.

II 27 Ye have heard that it was said,
Thou shalt not commit adultery:

28 But I say unto you, that everyone that looketh on a woman to lust after her hath committed adultery with her already in his heart.

III 31 And it was said also,
Whosoever shall put away his wife, let him give her a writing of divorcement:

32 But I say unto you, that everyone that putteth away his wife maketh her an adulteress: and whosoever shall marry her when she is put away committeth adultery.

IV 33 Again, ye have heard that it was said to them of old time,
Thou shalt not forswear thyself:

34 But I say unto you, Swear not at all.

V 38 Ye have heard that it was said,
An eye for an eye, and a tooth for a tooth:

39 But I say unto you, Resist not him that is evil.

VI 43 Ye have heard that it was said,
Thou shalt love thy neighbour:

44 But I say unto you, Love your enemies (and pray for them that persecute you).

(Conclusion 48 Ye shall be perfect, as your heavenly Father is perfect.)

The main question arising out of this passage may be put thus: What is the precise difference between the righteousness of scribes and Pharisees, and the higher righteousness here demanded and exemplified? It is common ground that the Law is not to be destroyed but fulfilled. We do the scribes and Pharisees a monstrous injustice if we imagine that they did not conscientiously strive to carry out what was for them a divinely appointed rule of life. Indeed if any criticism is to be made, it is that they were too conscientious; that in their zeal for the minutest details of Law and tradition they were apt to lose sight of the larger moral purposes which the Law as a whole was meant to serve; that they made the Law an end in itself and forgot that the Law was made for man and not man for the Law. For the Pharisee fulfilment of the Law means obedience to everything that the Law commands; and since man can only obey the rules that he knows, perfect obedience involves study of the Law. These things, painstaking study and meticulous obedience, are fundamental in the position of the scribes and Pharisees. More than that: there is abundant evidence in the Rabbinical literature that Pharisaism included more than an elaborate casuistry issuing in a mechanical fulfilment of legal precepts. The adulterous eye is condemned in the Talmud as well as in the Sermon on the Mount; and Pharisaic legalism was adorned by what has been well named Pharisaic delicacy. It could hardly be otherwise with men who consecrated their lives to the study of the Old Testament prophecy and piety as well as its laws. The difference between the righteousness of the scribes and Pharisees and the righteousness here demanded by Jesus is not correctly stated by saying off-hand that the one is external and the other inward; that the one is concerned merely with the letter of the Law, the other with its spirit.

It becomes possible to see where the difference lies when we realise that neither the Law nor the moral requirement of the Sermon on the Mount is an ethical system in our sense. Both are fundamentally eschatological; that is to say, both are concerned primarily with the judgement of God, and not with the formulation of an ethical ideal, or the planning of a better social order, or with any of the things that interest the Western mind. To both the subscription may be added: This do and thou shalt live. The difference between Jesus and the scribes is that whereas they maintain that the issue of the judgement depends on a man's record, on what he has done or omitted to do, Jesus insists that the final test is the character of the man himself. It remains true, of course, that actions reveal character. 'By their fruits ye shall know them.' But actions do not fully reveal the whole nature and disposition of man, which can be known only to God Himself. Hence the injunction: Judge not, that ye be not judged.

The more abundant righteousness called for in the Sermon is thus not to be attained by having a larger total of good deeds and a smaller total of bad deeds than the scribes and Pharisees. Rather it requires a radical transformation of character and disposition. And it is surely significant in this connexion that when the 'Pharisee of the Pharisees' really got into difficulties with the Law, it was with the one commandment in the Decalogue that does not have to do with overt acts (Rom. 7^{7-12}). The things here demanded in the six antitheses are not put forward as the outline of a new and more rigorous interpretation of the Law, still less as the skeleton constitution for yet another Utopia, but as samples of the kind of fruit that will be produced in lives transformed by the Grace of God.

4. *THE NEW PIETY* (28–31)

The antitheses were occupied with the relations of man and man. The sections which follow deal with the relation of man to God, with what we might call religious exercises. There are three heads: almsgiving, prayer, and fasting. The passage extends over the first 18 verses of Chap. 6; and seems to have consisted originally of an introduction (*v.* 1), and three short sections: *vv.* 2–4, 5–6, 16–18. The middle section has been expanded by the addition of *vv.* 7–8 on wrong ways of praying, 9–13, the Lord's Prayer, and 14–15 on prayer for forgiveness. The three original sayings are antithetical in form. The antithesis is between those who engage in these exercises for show and those who do so from more worthy motives. There is a corresponding contrast in the manner of the exercise in the two cases, and also in the response of God. The form of the sayings is:

> Be not like the hypocrites with their ostentatious piety. They have their reward.
>
> You (the truly pious) will be unostentatious in your piety. And God will reward you.

The group of sayings is startling in what it includes and in what it omits. Almsgiving occurs to us as a good deed rather than an act of worship. Yet here it stands at the head of the religious exercises. The omission of any reference to the Temple and its worship is equally striking. These two things taken together remind us of the text quoted elsewhere by Jesus: ' I desire mercy and not sacrifice ' (Hos. 6^{6}).

(*a*) Almsgiving (28)

MT. 6^{1-4}

6 1 Take heed that ye do not your righteousness before men, to be seen of them: else ye have no reward with your Father which is in heaven.
2 When therefore thou doest alms, sound not a trumpet before thee, as the hypocrites do in the synagogues and in the streets, that they may have glory of men. Verily I say unto you, They have received their reward.
3 But when thou doest alms, let not thy left hand know what thy right hand doeth:
4 that thine alms may be in secret: and thy Father which seeth in secret shall recompense thee.

1. This verse forms the introduction to what follows. If that is so, ' righteousness ' must be a comprehensive term for the three activities which follow: almsgiving, prayer, and fasting. The Aramaic equivalent means both ' righteousness ' or ' piety ' and ' beneficence,' ' charity.' But the latter meanings are excluded in this verse by the fact that in *v.* 2, where almsgiving is specifically mentioned, another word is used. We must therefore understand by ' righteousness ' something like ' religious obligation ' or ' work of piety.' Such works of piety are to be done without ostentation, if they are to earn the approval of God. The superficial inconsistency between this verse and 5^{16} disappears when we take note of the motive in the two cases. In 5^{16} disciples are to let their light (their good deeds) shine before men for the glory of God: here it is a case of performing works of piety for self-glorification. The Rabbis speak in similar terms. R. Zadok (1st century A.D.) says: ' Make them (the words of the Law) not a crown wherewith to magnify thyself or a spade wherewith to dig. And thus used Hillel to say: He that makes worldly use of the crown shall perish. Thus thou mayest learn that he that makes profit out of the words of the Law removes his life from the world ' (*Aboth* 4^{5}, Danby, p. 453).

2. On private and public charity in Judaism see Moore, *Judaism*, ii. 162–179. There is abundant evidence both of the importance of almsgiving in Jewish religious life, and of the Pharisaic demand that the giving of charity should be as unostentatious as possible. The Rabbis recognised that alms could be given in

such a way that they served merely to gratify the vanity of the giver and to humiliate the recipient. On this point they are in complete agreement with Jesus. It follows that unless Jesus was being gratuitously unjust to the Pharisees, He cannot have equated 'hypocrites' and Pharisees in this connexion. The hypocrites of this saying are not any party or class in Judaism. They are such people as answer to the description which follows, whether they be Pharisees or Sadducees or rank and file Jews or Gentiles or—for that matter—Christians. The sounding of the trumpet is to be taken as a metaphor, meaning that the hypocrites take steps to give the fullest publicity to their benefactions in order to obtain the greatest possible kudos. They spend their money not to relieve distress but to buy public admiration. They get what they pay for. The Greek verb translated 'they have received' is found in business documents, where it is used of the settlement of accounts. The hypocrite's charity is a business transaction. He gives so much money; and, in return, he gets so much public admiration. The transaction is closed: he is paid in full.

3. The almsgiving of disciples is to be a strictly private affair. The relation of the right hand to the left is used by the Arabs as a type of the closest fellowship. So the verse may be taken to mean: do not let your nearest friend know about your charitable gifts. There are again abundant parallels in the Rabbinical literature. 'There were two chambers in the Temple: one the Chamber of Secrets and the other the Chamber of Utensils. Into the Chamber of Secrets the devout used to put their gifts in secret and the poor of good family received support therefrom in secret' (*Shekalim* 5^6, Danby, p. 158).

4. This charity, which is unknown to men, is known to God. 'Thy Father which seeth in secret' is probably a misunderstanding of a Semitic idiom: the sense is: 'Thy Father which seeth that which is secret'—the secret almsgiving—'will reward thee.' Cf. Rom. 2^{16}; 1 Cor. 4^5, 14^{25}. This does not mean that a business transaction with God is substituted for a business transaction with men. It is not a case of saying 'private charity, which buys God's favour, is a better bargain than public charity, which only buys human admiration.' It means that secret almsgiving is the kind of which God approves, and that because the giver seeks nothing for himself. His sole motive is to relieve the distress of his neighbour. Just because the motive is unselfish, the deed wins the approval of God; but if the motive is to secure that approval, it ceases to be unselfish. True charity will receive the approval of God; but charity done to earn approval—even God's approval—is not true charity.

(*b*) Prayer (29)

Mt. 6^{5-6}

6 5 And when ye pray, ye shall not be as the hypocrites: for they love to stand and pray in the synagogues and in the corners of the streets, that they may be seen of men. Verily I say unto you, They have received
6 their reward. But thou, when thou prayest, enter into thine inner chamber, and having shut thy door, pray to thy Father which is in secret, and thy Father which seeth in secret shall recompense thee.

5. In addition to the public services of Temple and Synagogue there were a number of private acts of worship which were obligatory on the individual Jew.

Concerning these there is a good deal of material in the Mishnah Tractate *Berakoth* (Danby, pp. 2–10). See also Moore, *Judaism*, ii. 212–238; Abrahams, *Studies in Pharisaism*, ii. 72–93. These regular times of prayer could be a wholesome spiritual discipline for the devout: they could also be an opportunity to the hypocrite to make parade of his sham piety. Here again we are not to make the equation hypocrites = Pharisees. Doubtless there were hypocrites among the Pharisees; but the Pharisees had no monopoly in the matter. And there were a great many Pharisees who were obviously and genuinely sincere in their piety. For the Pharisee as for Jesus the important thing in prayer is the direction of the soul towards God. For the 'hypocrite' it is the admiration of his piety by men. He loves to be 'alone with God,' surrounded by a crowd of admirers. He gets what he works for.

6. In contrast to this sham piety the prayer of the disciples is to be a genuine communion with God. The 'inner chamber' is not meant literally: it is, as in Lk. 12[3]; Mt. 24[26], a figure for complete privacy, whether in a closed room or out on the hillside. Everything is to be shut out that would distract the soul: the whole man is to be turned towards God. Such prayer is approved by God. 'Thy Father which is in secret': it is doubtful whether the words 'which is' belong to the true text. The analogy of *v.* 4 would suggest that it is the praying that is in secret rather than God; and this is supported by some ancient authorities for the text of Mt. Probably we should render: 'pray in secret to thy Father, and thy Father who seeth that which is secret shall recompense thee.' Cf. notes on *v.* 4. The saying does not disparage public worship or discourage disciples from joining in the service of the Synagogue with their neighbours. Jesus Himself used both Temple and Synagogue; and His first followers did the same without any apparent sense that they were disobeying any precept of their Master. What Jesus insists on here is that private devotions should be private. The reward of true prayer is not specified. It is sufficient that such prayer has the approval of God: how that approval is expressed is a secondary consideration.

The original saying on prayer ends here. It is followed by a brief saying in which a fresh contrast is set up with heathen forms of prayer. This saying (*vv.* 7–8) then forms a kind of introduction to Mt.'s version of the Lord's Prayer.

MT. 6[7-8]

6 7 And in praying use not vain repetitions, as the Gentiles do: for they think that they shall be heard for their much speaking. 8 Be not therefore like unto them: for [1] your Father knoweth what things ye have need of, before ye ask him.

[1] Some ancient authorities read *God your Father*.

7. The Greek word translated 'use vain repetitions' is exceedingly rare. Its etymology is disputed; but its meaning seems to be 'chatter' or 'gabble.' It is not the length of time spent in praying or persistency in prayer that is criticised. Jesus Himself gave long periods to prayer; and he explicitly recommends persistent prayer, for example in the parable of the Importunate Widow. In the prayers of Gentiles the point where there is 'much speaking' is in the address to the god or gods. In a polytheistic religion it is necessary to invoke the right deity, and in order to make sure it is advisable to call upon all who may be concerned.

Again, even if one knows the right god or goddess, it is equally important that the correct epithet should be employed in conjunction with the name. If the right deity is not invoked in the proper terms, the prayer may be ineffective. The difficulty is commonly met by the heaping up of names and epithets in prayer; and it may be this verbosity that is criticised in the saying.

8. In contrast to the Gentile the disciple of Jesus has to deal with one God, who is his Father. And there is no need to ransack the dictionary for the appropriate password; for this God already knows what the petitioner needs. The one word that serves for name and epithet in one is the name Father.

So far the exposition has largely been by negatives: how not to pray. Now Mt. gives the positive side: a concrete example of how to pray.

(i) *The Lord's Prayer* (30)

MT. 6^{9-13}

6 9 After this manner therefore pray ye:
Our Father which art in heaven, Hallowed
10 be thy name. Thy kingdom come. Thy
will be done, as in heaven, so on earth.
11, 12 Give us this day [1] our daily bread. And
forgive us our debts, as we also have for-
13 given our debtors. And bring us not into
temptation, but deliver us from [2] the evil
one.[3]

[1] Gr. *our bread for the coming day.*
[2] Or, *evil.*
[3] Many authorities, some ancient, but with variations, add *For thine is the kingdom, and the power, and the glory, for ever. Amen.*

Another version of this prayer appears in Lk. 11^{2-4}, which is probably to be assigned to L. In Lk.'s account the prayer was given by Jesus to His disciples in response to a request from them that He would teach them to pray as John the Baptist taught his disciples. The form in Mt. early became the form for liturgical use in the Church. In the *Didache* $8^{2f.}$ we read: 'And do not pray as the hypocrites, but as the Lord commanded in His Gospel, pray thus.' Then follows the Lord's Prayer almost exactly as in Mt., with the doxology 'for thine is the power and the glory for ever,' and the injunction: 'Pray thus three times a day.' The prayer has very much in common with Jewish piety. Numerous parallels are given by Montefiore (*Rabb. Lit. and Gospel Teachings*, pp. 125 ff.) and Abrahams (*Studies*, ii. 94–108). The amount of agreement may be estimated by comparing the following made-up parallel, which is constructed entirely from materials drawn from Jewish sources (cf. Abrahams, *op. cit.*, pp. 98 f.):

> 'Our Father, who art in Heaven. Hallowed be Thine exalted Name in the world which Thou didst create according to Thy will. May Thy Kingdom and Thy lordship come speedily, and be acknowledged by all the world, that Thy Name may be praised in all eternity. May Thy will be done in Heaven, and also on earth give tranquillity of spirit to those that fear thee, yet in all things do what seemeth good to Thee. Let us enjoy the bread daily apportioned to us. Forgive us, our Father, for we have sinned; forgive also all who have done us injury; even as we also forgive all. And lead us not into temptation, but keep us far from all evil. For thine is the greatness and the power and the dominion, the victory and the majesty, yea all in Heaven and on earth. Thine is the Kingdom, and Thou art lord of all beings for ever. Amen.'

The originality of the Lord's Prayer lies in the composition as a whole, in the choice of just these petitions and no others, in the arrangement of them, in its brevity and completeness. It may be said that the teaching of Jesus on the fatherhood of God is summarised in the Lord's Prayer. 'This prayer is in fact a complete statement of what God's children should desire and ask of their Father in heaven: and since what we ask of God is the surest indication of the kind of God we believe in, this prayer may justly be taken as a sketch of what, in the thought of Jesus, the Father is.'

'The prayer falls into two main divisions, the first concerned with what may be called world issues, the second with the affairs of individuals. Both alike are conceived as being in the hands of the Father: the same God who orders the course of history with sovereign power also ministers to the daily needs, material and spiritual, of His individual children' (*Teaching of Jesus*, p. 113).

9. 'After this manner' is not to be pressed so as to exclude the use of the prayer itself. The disciples are to use the original and also to make other prayers of their own in the same spirit. 'Ye' is emphatic: the disciples in contrast to Gentiles. For 'Our Father which art in heaven' Lk. has simply 'Father.' Mt.'s phrase is an adaptation of the original 'Father' to conform to Jewish liturgical usage. The originality of Lk. is shown by the recorded prayer of Jesus Himself (Mk. 14^{36}) and the testimony of Paul (Rom. 8^{15}; Gal. 4^{6}). The word which Jesus used in speaking to God, and which He taught His disciples to use, is the Aramaic word *abba*. The importance of this fact is well brought out by G. Kittel (*Die Religionsgeschichte und das Urchristentum*, pp. 92–95). In Aramaic the place of the possessive adjectives 'my,' 'thy,' etc., is taken by suffixes attached to the noun. So 'father' is *abba*; but 'my father' is *abī*, 'our father' is *abīnū*, and so on. Kittel maintains that the Jewish usage is that in speaking of an earthly father the suffixes are used of anybody's father except one's own. That is, one says 'thy father' or 'their father,' but not 'my father.' For 'my father' one says 'father' simply, i.e. *abba*. But this way of speaking of one's earthly father does not hold when speaking of the Father in heaven. Jewish piety felt it unfitting to speak of God or to God in the same familiar and intimate way in which one spoke of or to one's earthly father. Therefore when 'my Father' means God the form with the suffix, *abī*, takes the place of the simple *abba*. Jesus abolished this distinction. He used *abba* of God and taught His followers to do the same. This is an indication of the depth and intensity of His realisation of the Fatherhood of God, a realisation in which He would have His disciples share.

'Hallowed be thy name.' For Hebrew thought the name is not a mere word. It is in a sense the person so named. To know God's name is in a real sense to know God. When God acts 'for His name's sake' it is practically equivalent to saying that He acts for His own sake. To hallow (make holy) the name of God is to regard Him as God, to give Him the worship and obedience that are due to Him. When God hallows His name it is by acting so that men are led to acknowledge Him as God and reverence Him accordingly. 'And as it is God's supreme end that all mankind shall ultimately own and serve Him as the true God, so it is the chief end of Israel . . . to hallow His name by living so that men shall see and say that the God of Israel is the true God. That is the meaning of . . .

the hallowing of the Name, as the supreme principle and motive of moral conduct in Judaism' (Moore, *Judaism*, ii. 103). In this petition 'may Thy name be hallowed' seems to mean both that God should hallow His name by His mighty acts and that men should hallow it by their acknowledgement of Him as the one true God, and by living in accordance with His will. So when the disciples live in such a way that men see their good works and glorify God (Mt. 5^{16}), they hallow the name of God.

10. Above all God hallows His name by bringing in His Kingdom. So the petition: 'Thy Kingdom come' is intimately connected with 'Hallowed be thy name.' The coming of the Kingdom here asked is certainly the final consummation, the 'coming of the Kingdom of God in power' (Mk. 9^{1}). Cf. Mk. 8^{38}, 13^{32}; Lk. 12^{32}, 22^{29}. In the fullest sense the Kingdom is still future and an object of hope rather than experience. The petition is that the hope may be fulfilled. In the primitive Church this hope is bound up with the expectation of the return of the risen Lord: and the early Christian equivalent of 'thy kingdom come' is '*marana tha*—Come our Lord.'

The rest of this verse: 'Thy will be done, as in heaven, so on earth' does not appear in the Lucan version of the prayer. The petition certainly has an eschatological sense: the time when the Kingdom has come will be a time when God's will will be supreme on earth as in heaven. But it need not be an exclusively eschatological petition. There is a sense in which the Kingdom comes whenever and wherever God's will is acknowledged and obeyed on earth. And the prayer, if it is to be sincerely prayed, must have a reference to him who prays it. Thy will be done—and done by me. Cf. Mk. 14^{36}, which is the best commentary on the petition.

11. 'Give us this day our daily bread.' 'Daily' in this verse is a guess. The Greek word so rendered does not occur in Greek literature outside the Lord's Prayer. But it does appear in a papyrus account-book from the Fayum. The text of this document was published by Flinders Petrie in 1889 in the volume *Hawara, Biamu and Arsinoe*. The original now appears to be lost. The interpretation of this text is helped by a Latin wall-inscription at Pompeii (*CIL* IV, Suppl. 4000 g). It appears that our Greek word may be the equivalent of the Latin *diaria*, the daily rations issued to slaves, soldiers, and workmen, etc. The Greek word can then be connected etymologically with another word signifying 'the coming (day),' i.e. to-morrow. This reflects the social environment of the Gospels. The bread issued to-day is for consumption to-morrow, so that everyone has his food in his house overnight. This is the state of affairs reflected in the parable Lk. $11^{5ff.}$. and perhaps in Lk 12^{42}: cf. also James 2^{5}. This puts the petition in a new light. The disciples are God's servants, and what they ask is a sufficient provision from day to day to enable them to perform the tasks which God appoints them to do: enough to-day to face to-morrow's duties. (Further details: F. Stiebitz in *Philologische Wochenschrift*, 16 July 1927, cols. 889–892; Deissmann in *Reinhold-Seeberg-Festschrift* (1929), i. 299–306).

12. 'Forgive us our debts.' For 'debts' the Lucan version (11^{4}) has 'sins.' This is a translation variant. The one Aramaic word *ḥōbā* means 'debt,' 'sin,' and 'punishment for sin.' The use of 'debt' as a metaphor for 'sin' is common

in the teaching (Mt. 18^{23-35}; Lk. 7^{41-43}). In this petition we have the characteristic doctrine of Jesus that God's forgiveness can only come to those who themselves show a forgiving spirit. For the Jewish view see on Mt. $5^{23f.}$, above, p. 448. We have an anticipation of this petition in *Ecclus.* 28^{2}.

> 'Forgive thy neighbour the injury (done to thee),
> And then, when thou prayest, thy sins will be forgiven.'

There are also Rabbinical parallels (Billerbeck, i. 424 ff.). But generally the Jewish insistence is on the duty of the offender to seek forgiveness of the injured party; that of Jesus on the duty of the injured party to offer forgiveness. Jesus would not, we may presume, have condemned the Jewish doctrine: nor would the Pharisees perhaps have condemned that of Jesus. It is a matter of emphasis; and it is the characteristic teaching of Jesus that is emphasised in this petition.

13. 'And bring us not into temptation.' The word 'temptation' is ambiguous. It may mean 'trial' in the sense of suffering, persecution, martyrdom; or it may stand for the seductions of sin. It is likely enough that the former meaning is uppermost. Cf. 1 *Macc.* 2^{49-64}. Similarly *Ecclus.* $2^{1f.}$.

> 'My son, when thou comest to serve the Lord,
> Prepare thy soul for temptation.
> Set thy heart aright and endure fimly,
> And be not fearful in time of calamity.'

We may further compare Rom. 5^{3-5} with James $1^{2f.}$.

ROM.	JAMES
Let us also rejoice in our tribulations: knowing that tribulation worketh patience; and patience probation; and probation hope.	Count it all joy, my brethren, when ye fall into manifold temptations; knowing that the proof of your faith worketh patience.

For Judaism in the last two centuries B.C. as for the Church in the first three centuries A.D. temptation means above all religious persecution, persecution for righteousness' sake, for the Law or the Gospel. And in the last resort this is a moral temptation, as much as the temptations to theft or adultery. For persecution is the incentive to apostasy, the worst sin known to Judaism or the early Church. What this petition asks, therefore, is that disciples may not be exposed to trials so severe that their loyalty to God may be undermined. 'But deliver us from the evil (one).' Grammatically 'the evil' may be neuter, 'the evil state or condition,' or masculine, 'the evil one.' 'The evil (one)' is characteristically Matthæan. Cf. Mk. 4^{15} where Mk.'s 'Satan' is turned by Lk. (8^{12}) into 'the Devil,' and by Mt. (19^{19}) into 'the evil one.' Further, the preposition used with the verb 'deliver' suggests deliverance from a personal adversary rather than out of an evil condition. Finally, while the lot of the disciple may be evil in the present evil age (Gal. 1^{4}), it is evil, and the age is evil, only because the present age is dominated by Satan. The petition asks not for deliverance from distress or suffering, but for deliverance from the arch-enemy of God and man. That such a being existed and was the head of a kingdom hostile to the Kingdom of God was an unquestioned belief in Judaism and in the early Church.

The doxology: 'For thine is the kingdom . . . .' is omitted by three of the most important MSS. It appears to have been unknown to the early Fathers, Tertullian, Cyprian, and Origen. It is not in Lk.'s version of the prayer. Moreover, the text of the doxology is uncertain. The chief variants are:

For thine is the power for ever and ever (k).

For thine is the kingdom and the glory for ever and ever. Amen. (Old Syriac Cur.)

For thine is the power and the glory for ever. (*Didache* 8², Sahidic.)

The probability is that the doxology is no part of the original prayer, but came to be added when the prayer was used liturgically in the various churches. The current form may be the resultant of different local practices. It has some points in common with 1 Chron. 29¹¹ᶠ·.

(ii) *A saying on Forgiveness*

MT. 6¹⁴⁻¹⁵

6 14 For if ye forgive men their trespasses,
your heavenly Father will also forgive you.
15 But if ye forgive not men their trespasses,
neither will your Father forgive your
trespasses.

The first part of this saying has a parallel in Mk. 11²⁵:

And whensoever ye stand praying, forgive, if ye have aught against anyone; that your Father also which is in heaven may forgive you your trespasses.

Mk. 11²⁶, which is the equivalent of Mt. 6¹⁵, is rejected by modern editors on textual grounds.

The saying makes more explicit what is already contained in the petition for forgiveness in the Lord's Prayer. The form in Mk. looks more original. There there is exhortation to cultivate a forgiving spirit as the condition of receiving God's forgiveness. The disciples are almost to help God to forgive them. Here the thought is in process of being legalised. If you do this, God will do that. It is *quid pro quo*.

(*c*) Fasting (31)

MT. 6¹⁶⁻¹⁸

6 16 Moreover when ye fast, be not, as the
hypocrites, of a sad countenance: for they
disfigure their faces, that they may be seen
of men to fast. Verily I say unto you,
17 They have received their reward. But
thou, when thou fastest, anoint thy head,
18 and wash thy face; that thou be not seen
of men to fast, but of thy Father which is
in secret: and thy Father, which seeth in
secret, shall recompense thee.

The third antithesis on religious exercises. Fasting was a regular feature in the Jewish religious calendar. In addition to the solemn fasts of the Day of Atonement, New Year, and the anniversaries of great calamities in Jewish history, there were special public fasts proclaimed from time to time, for example in time of prolonged drought. On all these see Moore, *Judaism*, ii. 55–69. In addition to these public fasts there were those which were undertaken by individuals as a means of religious and moral self-discipline. Such regular private fasts were observed by the Pharisees (cf. Lk. 18^{12}; Mk. 2^{18}) and the disciples of John the Baptist (Mk. 2^{18}). Among the Pharisees Monday and Thursday were the customary days for keeping private fasts. These private fasts offered an opportunity to those who wished to gain a reputation for exemplary piety. They could not only fast but also let all the world know that they were fasting. See further, Moore, ii. 257–266; Abrahams, *Studies*, i. 121–128.

16 ff. The verse has to do with the voluntary private fasts. The disfiguring of the face is achieved by not washing or anointing and by strewing ashes on the head. These outward signs advertise the fact that a fast is taking place. The ensuing popular admiration is the only reward for the exercise. The disciples may fast; but their fast is to be private. There is to be no external sign of the fast: rather they are to appear as they normally do, or even as if prepared for a feast. The Father who sees what is in secret will approve and reward.

How easily this high doctrine could be corrupted appears from the precept in the *Didache* 8^1: 'Let not your fasts be with the hypocrites, for they fast on Mondays and Thursdays, but do you fast on Wednesdays and Fridays.'

This concludes the section of the Sermon dealing with religious exercises. The next section (6^{19-34}) has to do with the proper attitude of the disciple towards worldly possessions. The greater part of it appears to be drawn from Q; but there are a few verses which may be from M.

5. *WORLDLY WEALTH AND WORLDLY CARES* (32–35)

(*a*) Earthly and Heavenly Treasure (32)

MT. 6^{19-21}

6 19 Lay not up for yourselves treasures upon the earth,| where moth and rust doth consume,|and where thieves [1] break through
20 and steal:||but lay up for yourselves treasures in heaven,|where neither moth nor rust doth consume,|and where thieves
21 do not [1] break through nor steal:||for where thy treasure is, there will thy heart be also.||

[1] Gr. *dig through*.

On the poetic form of these verses see Burney, p. 115, n. 2. According to him the rhythm in Mt. is different from that in the Lucan parallel (Lk. $12^{33f.}$). If this is so, it is a further argument in favour of the view that Mt. here draws on M and Lk. on Q. Like the two preceding sections on the New Law and the New Piety this piece is cast in antithetic form. The wrong way is stated in *v.* 19, a short strophe of three three-beat lines: the right way in *v.* 20, which is similarly constructed. The whole is rounded off by the general truth in *v.* 21, which is a four-beat line. The agreement in wording between Mt. 6^{19-20} and Lk. 12^{33} is exceedingly small. On the other hand *v.* 21 in Mt. agrees closely with Lk. 12^{34}. It is possible, therefore, that only *vv.* 19–20 are from M and that *v.* 21 is from Q.

19. What lies behind the saying is the thought that the accumulation and hoarding up of worldly goods is due to the desire for security, the desire to be rid of anxiety about the future. Then it is argued: so far from removing anxiety, the possession of such goods is a source of anxiety. For they themselves are liable to

loss and decay. They deteriorate by the agency of 'moth and rust.' 'Rust' (lit. 'eating') signifies any kind of corrosion or decay. It would include the damage done by moth, and need not exclude other sorts of damage due to natural causes. Besides this natural deterioration there is the constant danger of theft.

20. In contrast to earthly possessions is the treasure in heaven. This heavenly wealth is a permanent possession exempt from the ravages of time, and beyond the reach of thieves. Mt. does not specify what it is or how it is obtained. According to the Q version of the saying, it is obtained by giving earthly goods in charity. He that giveth to the poor lendeth to the Lord. Perhaps the same holds good in this form of the saying, though it is not explicitly stated.

21. On this verse and *vv.* 19 f., see notes on Lk. $12^{33f.}$, above, p. 406.

Mt. 6^{22-23} (Q). See on Lk. 11^{34-36}, above, p. 385.

Mt. 6^{24} (Q). See on Lk. 16^{13}, above, p. 425.

Mt. 6^{25-33} (Q). See on Lk. 12^{22-31}, above, p. 403.

(*b*) Anxiety (35)

MT. 6^{34}

6 34 Be not therefore anxious for the morrow:
for the morrow will be anxious for itself.
Sufficient unto the day is the evil thereof.

This verse comes at the end of the passage on worldly wealth and worldly cares, which consists chiefly of extracts from Q. The verse itself has no parallel in Lk., and is probably not from Q. The question is whether it is a genuine saying of Jesus derived from M or a bit of secular proverbial wisdom, which had got mixed up with sayings of Jesus in the oral tradition of Palestinian Christians. It looks as if the verse contained two proverbial sayings.

The first, 'Be not anxious for the morrow: for the morrow will be anxious for itself' begins by giving the complement to Prov. 27^1: 'Boast not thyself of to-morrow; for thou knowest not what a day may bring forth' (cf. James 4^{13-17}). There there is a warning against undue confidence about the future; here against undue anxiety. There it is said that the morrow may falsify one's hopes; and here one might expect something that would suggest that the morrow may prove one's fears to be liars. Instead we have the cryptic statement that 'the morrow will be anxious for itself.' It is possible that 'itself' is a mistranslation of the Aramaic *dīleh*, meaning 'its own affairs'; but not very likely. The meaning appears to be that it is foolish to worry about to-morrow, because to-morrow will bring its own worries. That is, the morrow will bring its troubles; but quite probably they will not be the troubles about which we are gratuitously anxious to-day. This gives added force to the following sentence, which says, in effect, 'why worry about to-morrow? there's real trouble enough to-day, without bringing in to-morrow's possible troubles.' There is a very similar saying in *Ber.* 9b.

The saying, as a whole, breathes that pessimism which commonly goes with Oriental fatalism. The attempt to square it with Jesus' faith in the fatherly providence of God may be regarded as wasted labour.

6. *THE RIGHT ATTITUDE TO ONE'S NEIGHBOUR* (36–39)

Practically the whole of this section is drawn from Q.

Mt. 7^{1-5} (Q). See on Lk. $6^{37f., 41f.}$, above, pp. 347 f., 350.

Mt. 7^{7-11} (Q). See on Lk. 11^{9-13}, above, p. 373.

Mt. 7^{12} (Q). See on Lk. 6^{31}, above, p. 344.

The only verse in this section which has no parallel in Lk. is Mt. 7^6.

MT. 7^6

7 6 Give not that which is holy unto the dogs,
|neither cast your pearls before the swine,|
lest haply they trample them under their
feet,|and turn and rend you.|

On the poetical form—four three-beat lines with rhyme—see Burney, pp. 131 f., 169; and on the saying itself Abrahams, *Studies*, ii. 195 f.

The dog is reckoned, in Rabbinical literature, among the wild beasts; the pig is an unclean animal. In *Enoch* 89^{42} the enemies of Israel are figured as dogs, foxes, and wild boars: and dogs = Philistines, wild boars = Edomites. Rabbinical thought makes the further equation Edom = Rome. But if there is a tendency in Judaism to speak of Gentile nations as 'dogs' or 'swine,' it is not merely because they are Gentiles, but because they are the enemies of Israel, the deniers of Israel's religion, and so the enemies of Israel's God. If we were to interpret the saying from a strictly Jewish point of view, we should take it to mean: Do not reveal the holy things of our religion to the Gentiles; for, so far from reverencing them, they will only be roused to a more intense hatred and oppression of Israel. And this would truly represent the temper of some Jews, but not of all. For there is abundant evidence of strong missionary activity among the Gentiles in this period. The truth seems to be that there were differing attitudes within Judaism; and that we cannot make generalisations about the Jewish attitude to Gentiles. Some Jews adopted a narrow and exclusive attitude and tended to hate and despise the Gentile. Their views often come to expression in the Apocalyptic literature. Others entertained more generous sentiments, as can be shown from many passages in the Rabbinical literature. Something similar happened in the early Church, where we find a narrow, conservative, and exclusive party in Palestine, and a more generous, strongly missionary party with its headquarters at Antioch. The tension between these two parties, between Paul and those who called themselves followers of James, is evident in the letter to the Galatians. Mt. 7^6 looks very like a bit of apocalyptic Jewish exclusiveness, adopted by extreme Jewish Christians, and incorporated among the sayings of Jesus. Later the Gentile Church turned the saying to face the opposite way, interpreting the holy thing as the Eucharist, and the dogs and swine as Jews, heretics, and unbaptised persons. (Cf. Juster, *Les Juifs dans l'Empire Romain*, i. 320 f.) An early stage in this process is reflected in the *Didache* 9^5:

> But let none eat or drink of your Eucharist except those who have been baptised in the Lord's Name. For concerning this also did the Lord say, 'Give not that which is holy to the dogs.'

7. *THE MOTIVE OF CHRISTIAN BEHAVIOUR: THE JUDGEMENT* (40–43)

(*a*) The Two Ways (40)

MT. 7^{13-14}

7 13 Enter ye in by the narrow gate: ||for wide
[1] is the gate,|and broad is the way,|that
leadeth to destruction,|and many be they
14 that enter in thereby.||[2] For narrow is the
gate,|and straitened the way,|that leadeth
unto life,|and few be they that find it.||

[1] Some ancient authorities omit *is the gate*.
[2] Many ancient authorities read *How narrow is the gate, &c.*

This saying is very different from Lk. $13^{23f.}$ (Q). See above, p. 416. The structure is antithetical, as is so much of the M material in the Sermon. The figure of the two ways is found in the Old Testament (Jer. 21^{8}; Ps. 1^{6}; Prov. 14^{12}), in Jewish literature (*Ecclus.* 21^{10}; 4 *Ezra* 7^{1-9}; the Jewish tract incorporated in the *Didache*, cf. $1^{1f.}$, 5^{1}; the Rabbinical writings—Billerbeck i. 460 ff.), and in classical writings (Hesiod, *Works and Days*, 287–292; Cebes, *Tabula* 15; Maximus of Tyre, *Diss.* 39^{3}; Virgil, *Æn.* $6^{540-543}$, etc.). It is possible that M has preserved a saying of Jesus cast in this commonplace form. More probably it is the M version of the Q saying (Lk. $13^{23f.}$). The point of Lk. $13^{23f.}$ is the urgency of the Gospel message in view of the Judgement: go in at the door while it is still open. It may be conjectured that the saying has been moralised in the same way as Lk. 12^{57-59}, an eschatological parable which reappears in Mt. $5^{25f.}$ as a moral rule. In favour of this view is the fact that what Mt. has in common with Lk. is the injunction to enter in by the narrow gate.

13. The thought of this verse is the commonplace that vice is more attractive than virtue, and that the line of least resistance is commonly the way to disaster. The 'destruction' to which this way leads is something more than physical death. It is either complete annihilation or eternal punishment. The former seems more likely: it is complete death as opposed to eternal life; death with no hope of life as opposed to life with no fear of death.

14. The narrow way, the way of self-denial and self-sacrifice, is unattractive, and only firm determination and constant effort will keep a man on it; but at the end of it is life, eternal life, the life of the world to come.

The whole saying takes a very gloomy view of human life and destiny. In this respect it comes near to the spirit of 4 *Ezra*.

(*b*) False Prophets and their Fate (41)

This passage appears to be a combination of Q and M material. It begins (*v.* 15) with a warning about false prophets who are like wolves disguised in sheepskins. Then it is said that they will be known by their fruits (*v.* 16^{a}). This leads up to the Q passage on the tree and its fruits (16^{b}–18||Lk. $6^{43f.}$), which is followed by a saying of John the Baptist (*v.* 19 = Mt. 3^{10b}), and the repetition of *v.* 16^{a}. The only fresh matter in this passage is *v.* 15.

7 15 Beware of false prophets, which
come to you in sheep's clothing,
but inwardly are ravening wolves.

False prophets are prophesied in Mk. 13$^{22 f.}$: 'There shall arise false Christs and false prophets, and shall shew signs and wonders, that they may lead astray, if possible, the elect. But take ye heed: behold I have told you all things beforehand.' Also, independently of Mk., in Mt. 24^{11}: 'And many false prophets shall arise, and shall lead many astray.' 'False prophet' does not here mean one who prophesies what is false, though that is involved; but rather bogus prophet, one who pretends to be a prophet and is not. The figure of the wolf disguised as a sheep goes with the thought of the disciples as the flock and Jesus as their shepherd. Cf. Lk. 10^{3}||Mt. 10^{16} (Q), above, p. 367.

Mt. 7^{16a}. 'By their fruits ye shall know them' effects the transition from *v.* 15 to the Q passage.

Mt. 7^{16b-18} (Q). See on Lk. 6$^{43-44}$, above, p. 351.

Mt. 7^{19} is a repetition of Mt. 3^{10} (Preaching of John the Baptist, Q) See on Lk. 3^{9}, above, p. 332; and Introduction, p. 317.

Mt. 7^{20} repeats 16^{a}. Cf. Lk. 6^{44a}, above, p. 351.

(*c*) False Disciples and their Fate (42)

This section (Mt. 7$^{21-23}$) contains two sayings. The first (*v.* 21) is commonly assigned to Q, the second (*vv.* 22 f.) to M; but it is quite possible that both are from M. Mt. 7^{21} has a parallel in Lk. 6^{46}; but the verbal agreement between the two is confined to the words 'Lord, Lord' and the verb 'do.' Verbal agreement between Mt. 7$^{22 f.}$ and Lk. 13$^{26 f.}$ is confined to the words which they quote in common from Ps. 6^{9}.

7 21 Not every one that saith unto me, Lord, Lord, shall enter into the kingdom of heaven; but he that doeth the will of my Father which is in heaven.

This saying is given by Lk. (6^{46}) in what is undoubtedly the more original form. The Matthæan version has been moralised. Entry into the Kingdom is obtained by doing God's will, that is, by 'works of the Law,' even if we grant that it is by works of the new Law rather than the old. Salvation depends on conduct, not on Christology. This is in direct (conscious?) contrast to such a passage as Rom. 10^{9}: 'If thou shalt confess with thy mouth Jesus as Lord . . . . thou shalt be saved.' We may well think that the saying has been shaped by the controversy between Jewish and Pauline Christianity, the same controversy that appears in the Epistle of James. The original saying has been given an anti-Pauline turn in Mt.'s version. See further notes on Lk. 6^{46}, above, p. 352.

MT. 7$^{22-23}$

7 22 Many will say to me in that day, Lord, Lord, did we not prophesy by thy name, and by thy name cast out [1] devils, and by
23 thy name do many [2] mighty works? And then will I profess unto them, I never knew you: depart from me, ye that work iniquity.

[1] Gr. *demons*. [2] Gr. *powers*.

This saying has likewise been modified by controversy. The more original form is preserved by Lk. (13$^{26 f.}$). There the complaint is against unbelieving Jews who rejected the opportunity afforded them by the presence and work of

Jesus. Here it is against Christian false teachers. Moreover, the saying, as it stands in Mt., is in striking contrast to Mk. 9^{38-41}. There is also a significant point of difference from Lk. in the quotation of Ps. 6^{9}. Lk. has 'workers of unrighteousness' (*adikia*): Mt. has 'ye that work lawlessness' (*anomia*), in agreement with the LXX. 'Ye that work lawlessness' means 'ye whose acts are contrary to the Law'; and the Law in this connexion is the will of God as revealed to Moses and interpreted by Jesus, the new Law already expounded in Mt.'s Sermon. There is a distinct anti-Pauline bias in the M form of the saying. The M emphasis on conduct persists. We may compare the curious saying given in 2 *Clem.* 4^{5} and in a marginal note in the cursive MS. 1424.

2 CLEM.	1424 mg.
If ye be gathered together with me in my bosom, and do not my commandments, I will cast you out, and will say to you, Depart from me, I know not whence ye are, ye workers of lawlessness (*anomias*).	The Jewish has here: If ye be in my bosom and do not the will of my Father which is in heaven, out of my bosom will I cast you away.

22. 'In that day' is the day of judgement (Is. $2^{11, 17}$; Zech. 14^{6}). 'By thy name': R.V. suggests that 'the name' was used by these persons as a kind of charm or incantation, as in Acts 19^{13}: 'But certain also of the strolling Jews, exorcists, took upon them to name over them which had the evil spirits the name of the Lord Jesus, saying, I adjure you by Jesus whom Paul preacheth.' But equally it may mean simply 'in thy name,' that is, claiming to act on behalf of and with the authority of Jesus. The latter interpretation fits all three activities: the former fits exorcism and the doing of miracles, but not prophesying. The early Church soon discovered that not all who called themselves prophets were the genuine article. The *Didache* (11^{7-12}) lays down rules for distinguishing true prophets from impostors.

That demons could be exorcised and mighty works done in the name of the Lord was firmly believed in the primitive Church (cf. Acts 19^{13}; James $5^{14f.}$; Irenæus, *Haer.* (ed. Harvey), II. iv. 6).

23. It is not denied that the prophecies, exorcisms, and mighty works have taken place. Only they do not prove that those who performed them are true disciples. The test by which the Lord recognises those that are His is the test of obedience to the will of God (*v.* 21). Cf. *Didache* 11^{8}: 'But not every one who speaks in a spirit is a prophet, except he have the behaviour of the Lord. From his behaviour, then, the false prophet and the true prophet shall be known.' The rejection of the pretended disciples, 'I never knew you,' corresponds to the mildest form of ban as pronounced by the Rabbis (Billerbeck, iv. 293). As used by a Rabbi it meant something like 'I do not wish to have anything to do with you.' The words 'Depart from me . . . iniquity' are from Ps. 6^{9}.

(*d*) Closing Parable (43)

Mt. 7^{24-27}, the parable of the wise and foolish builders, is taken from Q (see notes on Lk. 6^{47-49}, above, p. 353).

The outstanding feature of the M teaching in the Sermon is its intense religious and moral earnestness. The Christians who made this collection had inherited the quality that is distinctive of Pharisaism at its best. And they had retained it when they embraced Christianity. They still revere the Law; but it is the Law as interpreted by Jesus and not as interpreted by the scribes. They have their forms of piety; but these are for use and not for display. Their religion is a secret communion of the soul with God, a dedication of themselves to unobtrusive service and quiet self-discipline. They sit loose to all worldly possessions and seek to be rich towards God. They are timid and conservative, distrusting any revolutionary departure from the ways that have been consecrated by the Jewish saints of former generations. The administration of the Gentile churches by a Paul is calculated to fill them with fear and dismay. Their task is to be the nucleus of a new and reformed Israel. And in carrying out that task they are blessed: blessed as they fulfil the Law of God in the way of mercy taught by Jesus, blessed as they attain purity of heart by prayer and fasting and self-giving, blessed as they live at peace with their people and make peace among them, blessed even when they have to endure persecution for the sake of the new righteousness taught and shown by Jesus. They are the scribes who have been made disciples unto the Kingdom of heaven and bring out of their treasures things new and old.

The antithetical character of the teaching is strongly marked throughout. The new interpretation of the Law is set in contrast to the old. The new piety is opposed to the sham religiosity of the hypocrites. The true wealth is contrasted with worldly gear. The way of life and the way of destruction are set side by side. The true disciple is set over against false prophets and Christians who have nothing of Christ save His name.

In all this it is made clear that what matters is character and conduct. Salvation comes to those who turn with a single mind to worship and obey God, walking in the way that has been opened up by Jesus.

Mt. adds his own comment on the Sermon as a whole ($7^{28 \text{f.}}$).

8. *THE EVANGELIST'S POSTSCRIPT TO THE SERMON* (44)

MT. 7^{28-29}

7 28 And it came to pass, when Jesus ended
these words, the multitudes were aston-
29 ished at his teaching: for he taught them
as *one* having authority, and not as their
scribes.

28 f. The first half of verse 28 is a regularly recurring editorial formula in Mt. (cf. 11^1, 13^{53}, 19^1, 26^1). It marks the close of the great discourses, which Mt. builds up in his Gospel. The remainder of the passage, from ' the multitudes ' to ' scribes ' is borrowed from Mk. 1^{22}. The authority of Jesus is not to be misunderstood. It does not mean that He was dogmatic in His pronouncements and that the scribes by contrast were wavering and undecided. The scribes were very dogmatic: they were the guardians of an infallible tradition. The difference between Jesus and the scribes was that He spoke with the assurance of first-hand knowledge, with no appeal to tradition or precedent. His attitude was: ' I know

that this is true; and if you look at it candidly and sincerely, you will see for yourselves that it is true.' His 'Verily I say unto you' and His 'He that hath ears to hear, let him hear' go together. His teaching is the fruit of His insight; and His appeal is to the insight of His hearers.

B. THE MISSION CHARGE (58)

This is the M parallel to the Q section B2, above, pp. 365–370. Mt.'s account of the sending out of the disciples extends from 9^{35} to 11^{1}, and is made up of materials derived from Mk., Q, and M. The analysis of the account into its components is exceedingly difficult in places owing to Mt.'s practice of conflating his sources. Nevertheless, a good deal of the structure can be made out with a fair degree of certainty.

The account begins with a narrative introduction (9^{35}–10^{5a}). This tells of Jesus' own activity as He went about the country preaching and healing (9^{35}). This verse is based on Mk. 6^{6}. Seeing the condition of the people He was sorry for them (9^{36} from Mk. 6^{34}). Then follows the saying about the harvest and the labourers (9^{37-38}||Lk. 10^{2}: from Q; see above, p. 366). In 10^{1} the summoning and commissioning of the Twelve is described in general terms. Here Mt. is dependent on Mk. 6^{7} and $3^{14f.}$. A list of the Twelve follows (10^{2-4}). This list does not agree exactly with any of the lists in the New Testament. (See the excursus by Lake in *Beginnings of Christianity*, v. 37–46). After this narrative introduction comes the mission charge proper.

1. *THE SCOPE AND METHOD OF THE MISSION*

MT. 10^{5-8}

10 5 These twelve Jesus sent forth, and charged them, saying,
Go not into *any* way of the Gentiles, and enter not into any city of the Samaritans:
6 but go rather to the lost sheep of the house
7 of Israel. And as ye go, preach, saying,
8 The kingdom of heaven is at hand. Heal the sick, raise the dead, cleanse the lepers, cast out [1] devils: freely ye received, freely give.

[1] Gr. *demons*.

5. The verse begins with what is perhaps an editorial link to join the following teaching with what has gone before. The charge begins with a command which restricts the activities of the Twelve to Israel, excluding the Gentiles and the half-Jewish population of Samaria. 'A way of the Gentiles' is probably a road leading to a Gentile city (cf. *Abodah Zarah* 1^{4}, Danby, p. 437). The reference in that case will be to the Hellenistic cities of Palestine, for example the Decapolis. In these cities the Greek religion was dominant. Among the Samaritans the religion of Israel was held with reservations. Only the Pentateuch was accepted as canonical by them; and they had their own Temple on Mt. Garizim with their own priesthood and ritual. To orthodox Jews they were schismatic. Moreover, they were not regarded as pure-blooded Israelites (2 Kings. $17^{24ff.}$). The Jewish attitude to them is expressed in *Ecclus.* 50^{25ff}:

> 'For two nations doth my soul feel abhorrence,
> (Yea), and (for) a third, which is not a people;

The inhabitants of Seir and Philistia,
And that foolish nation that dwelleth in Sichem.'

See, further, Moore, *Judaism*, i. 23–27; Billerbeck, i, 538–560.

6. Cf. Mt. 15^{24}, where Jesus says to the Canaanitish woman, 'I was not sent but unto the lost sheep of the house of Israel.' (This verse has no parallel in Mk.) These two sayings can scarcely be reconciled with Mt. 28^{19}. The ministry of Jesus was in fact a ministry to the Jews; and we find that the leaders of the Palestinian community in the early days of the Church felt that their duty was to work among their own people (Gal. 2^{6-10}). The conjecture may be hazarded that, with the number of missionaries available, the field of operations had to be restricted: and that whatever we may imagine Jesus' ultimate aim to have been, the obvious place to begin was with His own people. The danger in later times was that what had been a special arrangement to meet a definite situation should be turned into a dogma of general application.

7, 8. The content of the Mission preaching: The Kingdom is at hand. This is not merely an announcement about the future. The Kingdom is the future breaking into the present, and manifesting itself in the things which the disciples are to do in addition to their preaching. This combination of preaching and beneficent activity is their task as it is the task of their Master. The whole work is to be done without payment. This principle, it may be noted, governs the missionary work of Paul, who supported himself by manual labour in his evangelistic career.

MT. 10^{9-16}

10 9 Get you no gold, nor silver, nor brass
10 in your [1] purses; no wallet for *your*
journey, neither two coats, nor shoes, nor
staff: for the labourer is worthy of his
11 food. And into whatsoever city or
village ye shall enter, search out who in it
is worthy; and there abide till ye go
12 forth. And as ye enter into the house,
13 salute it. And if the house be worthy,
let your peace come upon it: but if it be
not worthy, let your peace return to you.
14 And whosoever shall not receive you, nor
hear your words, as ye go forth out of
that house or that city, shake off the dust
15 of your feet. Verily I say unto you, It
shall be more tolerable for the land of
Sodom and Gomorrah in the day of
judgement, than for that city.
16 Behold, I send you forth as sheep in
the midst of wolves: be ye therefore wise
as serpents, and [2] harmless as doves.

[1] Gr. *girdles*. [2] Or, *simple*.

This passage is a conflation containing material from Mk., Q, and M. Verses 9–13 seem to consist of Mk. and M material; verses 14–16 of material from all three sources.

9 f. Equipment. There is considerable variation between the accounts given in our sources.

(1) Things prohibited:

MT. $10^{9f.}$	MK. $6^{8f.}$	LK. $9^{3\cdot}$ (‖MK.)	LK. 10^{4} (L?), cf. 22^{35}
Money (gold, silver, or copper)	Money (copper)	Money (silver)	Purse
Wallet	Wallet	Wallet	Wallet
Second shirt	Second shirt	Second shirt	—
Sandals	—	—	Sandals
Staff	—	Staff	—
—	Bread	Bread	—

(2) Things allowed:

MT. $10^{9\text{ f.}}$	MK. $6^{8\text{ f.}}$	LK. $9^{3\cdot}$ (‖MK.)	LK. 10^{4} (L?), cf. 22^{35}
—	Staff	—	—
—	Sandals	—	—

Mk. is alone in permitting the staff and sandals, and in forbidding bread (for Lk. is here dependent on Mk.). In the list of prohibited things as given in Mt. and corroborated by the other accounts come money and the wallet (for carrying provisions). The natural inference is that the missionaries are to be like an invading army, and live on the country. They are to rely on the friendly hospitality of the people. (See further, notes on Lk. 22^{35}, below, p. 633.) The prohibition of staff and sandals is strange. One would have thought them most necessary on an undertaking of this sort. In the Mishnah (*Berakoth* 9^{5}, Danby, p. 10) it is ordained that a man 'may not enter the Temple Mount with his staff or his sandal or his wallet.' This is on account of the holiness of the place. It is possible that the mission of the disciples is meant to be regarded as a specially sacred undertaking, and that they are to set out upon it as if they were setting out to worship in the Temple. The saying 'the labourer is worthy of his food' appears in Lk. 10^{7} (L?) with 'hire' for 'food.' Cf. *Didache* 13^{1}: 'Every true prophet who wishes to settle among you is worthy of his food. In 1 Tim. 5^{18} the Lucan form is quoted, apparently as scripture. St. Paul seems to have known the saying, for he writes, 'Even so did the Lord ordain that they which proclaim the gospel should live of the gospel' (1 Cor. 9^{14}).

11–14. These verses describe the procedure to be adopted on arrival at a town or village. Verses 11 and 14 are based largely on Mk. $6^{10\text{ f.}}$; 12 & 13 appear to belong to M. These two verses have a parallel in Lk. $10^{6\text{ f.}}$ (L); but the verbal agreement is very small, and it seems probable that neither version is derived from Q. The Q account of the procedure to be adopted seems to me to be in Lk. $10^{8\text{-}12}$.

11. Mt. is alone in giving the first step, that of finding in a strange town someone 'worthy,' i.e. esteemed and respected by his fellow-citizens. Having found a suitable lodging they are to stick to it for the period of their stay. Here Mt. is in agreement with Mk. (6^{10}) and L (Lk. 10^{7}).

12 f. On coming to the house a greeting is to be uttered. The form of words is given in Lk. 10^{5} as 'Peace to this house.' The Aramaic *shĕlām* means both 'greeting' and 'peace.' It is the same thing as the Mohammedan *salaam*. This greeting is here thought of as no mere formality, but as a real benediction. If the household are really deserving people the greeting will take effect on them, they will have some good of it. Otherwise the benefit will accrue to the disciples themselves. There is here a feeling for the power of the spoken word in blessing or cursing. Once the word is uttered it is irrevocable. (Cf. Crawley, *Oath, Curse, and Blessing*.)

14. This verse is borrowed from Mk. 6^{11} with alterations necessitated by the insertion of Mt. $10^{12\text{ f.}}$. Mk. has 'whatever place does not receive you'; but Mt., having gone on to speak of greeting households, alters this to 'whoever does not receive you'; and is then committed to saying that the disciples are to leave that house or city. The verse seems to say: 'If anyone does not receive you, leave the place.' This can hardly be original. The Marcan version: 'If any place does not

receive you, leave it' is more likely to be correct. On the significance of the wiping of the feet before leaving, see notes on Lk. $10^{10\text{ f.}}$, above, p. 368. It may be added that the Mishnah (*Berakoth* 9^{5}) cited above on *vv.* 9 f. goes on to prohibit a man from entering the Temple mount 'with the dust on his feet.' This suggests that the disciples are to rid themselves of the dust of the unresponsive town before resuming their sacred mission.

15. From Q. See notes on Lk. 10^{12}, above, p. 367.

16. The first half of the verse is from Q. See notes on Lk. 10^{3}, above, p. 368.

The injunction 'be ye wise as serpents and harmless as doves' is peculiar to Mt. and may be assigned to M. Paul may have had it in mind when he wrote Rom. 16^{19}. The wisdom of the serpent was proverbial. Cf. Gen. 3^{1}. The Greek word translated 'harmless' means originally 'undamaged.' Then it comes to have the positive sense 'unblemished,' 'pure.' The disciples are to be clever enough to see through the frauds and shams of the world, but not so clever as to try such devices themselves. The same contrast between serpents and doves occurs in a saying of R. Jehuda b. Simon (*c.* A.D. 320). It is to the effect that Israel in relation to God is like a dove; in relation to the Gentiles like a serpent.

2. *THE MISSIONARIES UNDER PERSECUTION* (59)

Mt. 10^{17-22} is drawn from Mk. 13^{9-13}. See notes, *ad. loc.*

MT. 10^{23-25}

10 23 But when they persecute you in this city, flee into the next: for verily I say unto you, Ye shall not have gone through the cities of Israel, till the Son of man be come.
24 A disciple is not above his [1] master,
25 nor a [2] servant above his lord. It is enough for the disciple that he be as his [1] master, and the [2] servant as his lord. If they have called the master of the house [3] Beelzebub, how much more *shall they call* them of his household!

[1] Or, *teacher*.
[2] Gr. *bondservant*.
[3] Gr. *Beelzebul*: and so elsewhere.

23. These rather pessimistic verses are hardly in harmony with the other accounts of the sending out of the Twelve. It is assumed in the other sources that the missioners may expect a friendly reception. Their message may be rejected; but there is a difference between rejecting a message and persecuting those who bring it. See *Teaching of Jesus*, pp. 221 f. The motive for haste is the imminence of the coming of the Son of Man. But nowhere in the Gospels is there any suggestion on the part of Jesus that the coming of the Son of Man is to take place so quickly as this. The most that is said in Mk. is that the Kingdom will come with power within the lifetime of some of the contemporaries of Jesus (Mk. 9^{1}). And it is emphasised that the time of this great event is known only to God (Mk. $13^{32\text{ f.}}$). Now there is evidence in these three verses of Mt. that the evangelist is bringing together material that properly belongs elsewhere in the story. The idea that the disciples will be persecuted rather than hospitably received (*v.* 23) belongs to a later stage in the ministry (cf. Lk. $22^{35\text{ff.}}$.) Again in *v.* 25 there is a reference to calling the master of the house Beelzebul; and in Mt. the Beelzebul incident does not come in until Chap. 12. The conclusion seems to be that *v.* 23 is out of place in this context. It reflects the experience and the expectations of the primitive Palestinian Church.

24 f. There is a partial parallel in Lk. 6^{40} (Q). But there the point is different. See notes, above, p. 349. Here the force of the saying is that the disciple need not hope to fare any better than his master. That is, the disciples must expect to be treated very much as Jesus has been treated. It can hardly be doubted that the Q form is the original, and that the M version is the result of reading the Q form in the light of later events in the ministry and in the experience of the Jerusalem church. The shorter version of the saying in Lk., which refers only to the teacher-disciple relation, is probably to be preferred. The additional figure of servant and master may well come from the Jewish proverb 'It is enough for the servant to be like his master' (Billerbeck, i. 577 f.). Verse 25^b is clearly out of place in this context in Mt. There is nothing against it as a genuine saying of Jesus; but it belongs to a time when opposition has become definite and strong.

Mt. 10^{26-33} derived from Q. See notes on Lk. 12^{2-9}, above, pp. 397–401.

Mt. 10^{34-36} from Q. See notes on Lk. 12^{51-53}, above, pp. 412 f.

Mt. 10^{37-38} from Q. See notes on Lk. 14^{26-27}, above, pp. 423 f.

Mt. 10^{39} from Q. See notes on Lk. 17^{33}, above, p. 437.

3. *CONCLUSION OF THE MISSION CHARGE* (63)

MT. 10^{40}–11^{1}

10 40 He that receiveth you receiveth me, and he that receiveth me receiveth him
41 that sent me. He that receiveth a prophet in the name of a prophet shall receive a prophet's reward; and he that receiveth a righteous man in the name of a righteous man shall receive a righteous
42 man's reward. And whosoever shall give to drink unto one of these little ones a cup of cold water only, in the name of a disciple, verily I say unto you, he shall in no wise lose his reward.

11 1 And it came to pass, when Jesus had made an end of commanding his twelve disciples, he departed thence to teach and preach in their cities.

40. This verse has a parallel in Lk. 10^{16}, and it may belong to Q. But it is also possible that it is the M version of a saying that has not been completely preserved in any of our sources. See notes on Lk. 10^{16}, above, pp. 369 f. The Matthæan version emphasises the positive side and says nothing about the rejection of the divine message. The compiler of M seems to have wished to end the Mission Charge on an optimistic note.

41. Peculiar to Mt. The collocation of prophets and righteous men occurs again in Mt. 13^{17}, where Lk. (10^{24}) has 'prophets and kings.' To receive a prophet 'in the name of a prophet' is to receive a prophet as such, recognising him as God's messenger. Similarly, to receive a righteous man in the name of a righteous man is to receive him as one who shows the divinely appointed way in his life. In the one case it is the acceptance of the will of God proclaimed; in the other the acceptance of the will of God exemplified. Such treatment of the servants of the Kingdom is reckoned as service of the King Himself. (Cf. Mt. 25^{34-40}.)

42. There is a parallel to this verse in Mk. 9^{41}:

9 41 For whosoever shall give you a cup of water to drink in my name, that ye are Christ's, verily I say unto you, he shall in no wise lose his reward.

On the original form of the saying see notes on Lk. $17^{1f.}$, above, pp. 430 f. There it is argued that Jesus meant ' little children ' literally in these sayings (Lk. 17^{2}; Mk. $9^{41f.}$; Mt. 10^{42}). The tendency of the tradition was to turn ' children ' into 'disciples'; and that has clearly happened here. Whatever may have been the meaning of Jesus, the meaning of Mt. is that kindness shown to a disciple *qua* disciple will surely be rewarded. For the disciple represents the Kingdom of God and service done to a representative of the Kingdom is reckoned as service done to the King. Compare the Rabbinical saying (*Gen. Rabbah* on Gen. 23^{18}): ' Whoever gives a piece of bread to a righteous man, it is as though he had fulfilled the whole Law.'

Ed. Meyer in his work on the origin and beginnings of Christianity (i. 143 n. 1) saw in Mt. 10^{40-42} a reflection of the organisation of the Christian community into the Twelve or the Apostles (*v.* 40), the Christian Prophets, the members of outstanding piety and mature faith (the ' righteous ') (*v.* 41), and the rank and file members (the ' little ones ') (*v.* 42). It is unlikely that such a clear-cut division was present to the mind of the compiler of M or to the Evangelist. It is more probable that we have here collected together a number of sayings considered relevant to the business of the Christian mission. They are linked together not by the supposed organisation of the community, but by the catchwords ' receive ' and ' reward.'

11^{1}. The discourse is rounded off with the characteristic formula of the Evangelist. See on Mt. $7^{28f.}$, above, p. 470. The verse is editorial. It is noteworthy that Mt. has nothing further to say about the progress of the Mission. Contrast Mk. $6^{12f.}$; Lk. 10^{17-20}. For Mt. the discourse is the important thing; and its importance is in its bearing on the work of the Church in the Evangelist's own day. Its precepts are not confined in their application to the original Mission of the Twelve but are valid for all time.

The portions of the Mission Charge which may be assigned to M reflect the aims and aspirations of the Palestinian community. Their task is the evangelisation of ' the circumcision.' Their business is not with Samaritans or Gentiles but with the lost sheep of the house of Israel. The method is simple: start with the ' worthy,' the best characters that Judaism produces; and work outwards. The results are in God's hands. By some people the messengers will be hated and persecuted; by some they will be welcomed and helped. God will deal with all that in due time. The task of the disciples is not that of bringing in the Kingdom. That is God's work. Their business is to prepare Israel for the coming of the Son of Man; and that coming cannot be long delayed.

C. VARIOUS SAYINGS

1. *JOHN THE BAPTIST AND ELIJAH* (65)

Mt. 11^{14-15}

11 14 And if ye are willing to receive [1]*it*,
15 this is Elijah, which is to come. He that
hath ears [2] to hear, let him hear.

[1] Or, him.
[2] Some ancient authorities omit *to hear*.

These two verses come in the Matthæan account of Jesus' testimony to John the Baptist (Mt. 11^{7-19}), derived mainly from Q. It is possible that *vv.* $14^{f.}$ are from M—they have no parallel in Lk.—but more likely that they are an editorial comment, whether of the compiler of M or of the Evangelist. In favour of the view that the insertion is due to Mt. is the fact that a similar editorial comment occurs in Mt. 17^{13}, where there is nothing corresponding in Mk. (9^{9-13}). The fact is that the identification of John with Elijah is peculiarly at home in Mt.; and it may be conjectured that the identification was made by Jewish Christians who had to meet the objection from the Jewish side that the true Messiah would be anointed and proclaimed by the returned Elijah, that this had not happened in the case of Jesus, and that therefore Jesus was not the true Messiah. The obvious way of countering this argument was to say that Elijah had indeed come and prepared the way for Jesus—in the person of the Baptist. That Jesus Himself anticipated and met the objection, or indeed that He cared very much about fulfilling the current Jewish Messianic expectations, is most unlikely. See further Billerbeck, iv. 779–798; and the notes on Lk. 7^{24-35}, above, pp. 359–363.

2. *THE GOSPEL INVITATION* (68)

MT. 11^{28-30}

11 28 Come unto me, all ye that labour and are heavy laden, and I will give you rest.
29 Take my yoke upon you, and learn of me; for I am meek and lowly in heart: and ye shall find rest unto your souls.
30 For my yoke is easy, and my burden is light.

This invitation follows in Mt. immediately on the Q passage, Mt. 11^{25-27}||Lk. 10^{21-22}, above, pp. 370 ff. For an attempt to show that Mt. 11^{25-30} is a single piece consisting of three strophes, and that the whole passage stood in Q, see Norden, *Agnostos Theos*, pp. 277–308. But the absence of these verses from Lk. is a fatal objection to the theory that they stood in Q. It is hardly credible that Lk. would have omitted a saying so entirely after his own heart, if it had stood in his source. It must therefore be assigned to M. But even if it be assigned to M, its genuineness may be disputed. The view is quite widely held that the saying is a quotation from a Jewish wisdom book, and that it has been put into the mouth of Jesus. In support of this view many parallels from Jewish wisdom literature can be quoted, in which the Divine Wisdom personified speaks: Prov. 1^{20-33}, 8^{1-36}; *Ecclus.* 24^{19-22}, 51^{23-27}. In this last passage personified Wisdom says:

23 Turn in unto me, ye unlearned,
And lodge in my house of instruction.
24 How long will ye lack these things?
And (how long) shall your soul be so athirst?

Then the author himself testifies:

25 I open my mouth and speak of her,
Acquire Wisdom for yourselves without money.
26 Bring your necks under her yoke,
And her burden let your soul bear;

She is nigh unto them that seek her,
And he that is intent (upon her) findeth her.
27 Behold with your eyes that I laboured but (little) therein,
And abundance of peace have I found.

But under all this poetical eloquence it is plain enough what the author is really commending: it is the study of the Law. 'He that taketh hold of the Law findeth her' (i.e. Wisdom) 15^1, cf. 34^8, 21^{11}; Moore, *Judaism*, i. 263 ff. In fact, the identification of Wisdom and the Law is a commonplace in Judaism. It can then be argued that in Mt. 11^{28-30} it is not Jesus who speaks but Wisdom, and that therefore the passage is a quotation similar to the passages quoted above. It is true that the book from which the supposed quotation is taken is otherwise quite unknown; but this difficulty is not felt. Otto (*op. cit.*, pp. 137 ff.) admits that the words are a quotation; but holds that the quotation was made by Jesus Himself, speaking as the representative of the divine Wisdom, *in persona Sapientiæ*. But it does not seem necessary to assume that the words are a quotation. If the author of *Ecclesiasticus* could think of such words, so might Jesus. Further, it is not necessary to suppose that there is any reference to Wisdom in the text as it stands. The verbal similarities to *Ecclus.* $51^{23ff.}$ may suggest, but they do not necessitate, such a reference. It is surely more natural to suppose that Jesus is here speaking as the representative, not of the divine Wisdom, but of the Kingdom of God. This may be best seen if we begin with *vv.* 29 f.

29 f. 'Take my yoke upon you and learn of me.' *Ecclus.* 51^{26} says: 'Bring your necks under her yoke.' It is clear that what is meant there is the yoke of the Law; for the 'house of instruction' in *v.* 23 is nothing else but the *Beth ha-Midrash*, the school of the Law. The injunction of Ben Sirach can then be compared with the saying of R. Nehunya b. Ha-Kanah (*c.* A.D. 70): 'He that takes upon himself the yoke of the Law, from him shall be taken away the yoke of the kingdom (i.e. the oppression of worldly powers) and the yoke of worldly care' (*Aboth* 3^5; Danby, p. 450). Devotion to the Law of God sets a man free from the cares and troubles of the world. The Law in this sense is the written Law plus the interpretation given in the 'house of instruction.' Jesus says, Take *my* yoke upon you; and His yoke is not the same thing as the yoke of the Law. It is the yoke of the Kingdom. There is thus a contrast between the word of Jesus and the word of Ben Sirach as well as a similarity: and the contrast is more important than the similarity. To take upon oneself the yoke of the Kingdom is to accept the sovereignty of God and to give oneself to His service. And what that means is something to be learnt from Jesus, who is meek and lowly in heart. This learning is not merely receiving instruction, even such instruction as is conveyed in the Sermon on the Mount: it is learning from the example of Jesus Himself how to serve God and man in love. (See *The Teaching of Jesus*, pp. 237–240.) In this way of discipleship men find rest to their souls, which is substantially what Ben Sirach claims to have got from the Law: 'abundance of peace have I found' (51^{27}). It thus appears that Jesus claims to do for men what the Law claimed to do; but in a different way. In comparison with the yoke of the Law the yoke of the Kingdom is easy and light. Cf. Lk. 11^{46}. In comparison with

the way of the scribes the way of Jesus is simple: and His claim is that whereas the scribes load men with grievous burdens, His way gives rest to the weary and heavy-laden (*v.* 28). 'Come unto me' then means 'Become my disciples,' and that means in practice 'Enter the Kingdom of God.' 'Take my yoke upon you' means in effect 'Take the yoke of the Kingdom upon you,' and that means 'Enter the Kingdom of God.' There is thus no necessity to regard these verses as other than a genuine saying of Jesus.

3. *THE SABBATH* (69, 70)

MT. 12^{5-7}

12 5 Or have ye not read in the law, how
that on the sabbath day the priests in the
temple profane the sabbath, and are guilt-
6 less? But I say unto you, that [1] one
7 greater than the temple is here. But if ye
had known what this meaneth, I desire
mercy, and not sacrifice, ye would not
have condemned the guiltless.

[1] Gr. *a greater thing.*

These verses are inserted by Mt. into the Marcan account of the controversy provoked by the disciples' plucking and eating corn on the Sabbath. This plucking of corn was allowed by the Law (Dt. 23^{25}). But to do it on the Sabbath was not allowed. Plucking corn was a kind of harvesting, and harvesting was work, and work was forbidden. We may call this pettifogging if we please—and then go and ask what difference English law makes between the theft of a penny and the theft of a hundred pounds. Theft is theft whether the amount be small or great: and work is work whether it be done in a few minutes or many hours. So the Rabbis could justly argue. The act of the disciples was a serious matter from the point of view of strict Judaism. It meant a new attitude towards the Sabbath, an attitude which is bluntly stated in Mk. 2^{27}. The behaviour of the disciples is defended by Jesus first by the case of David and the shewbread. To this Mt. adds the present passage.

5. 'Have ye not read in the law?' The Law nowhere commands the violation of the Sabbath in so many words. But it contains rules for the Temple service, which cannot be carried out unless the priests work on the Sabbath. The general principle for the interpretation of the Law is that positive commandments for which a definite time is prescribed take precedence of the Sabbath law if the two happen to clash. Hence the rule of the scribes that 'The Temple service takes precedence of the Sabbath,' i.e. the priests are allowed to work on the Sabbath in order to carry out the ritual.

6. Jesus claims that something more important than the Temple and its ritual has come into the world. That something is the Kingdom of God. He does not break through the traditions of the scribes merely in order to be different, but in obedience to a higher obligation, the claims of the Kingdom.

The fact that these verses appear in the matter peculiar to Matthew is a strong argument in favour of the genuineness of the saying. The conservative Jewish Christians who gathered this material together were not the people to invent sayings of this kind.

7. If this verse goes with the preceding, it is an indication that the whole passage (*vv.* 5–7) originally had a narrative setting of its own other than that into

which it is now incorporated. There were doubtless other occasions on which the behaviour of Jesus and His disciples was condemned as a breach of the Sabbath. The text 'I desire mercy, and not sacrifice' is from Hosea 6^{6}, and as quoted it agrees with the Hebrew against LXX and Targum. Mt. inserts it again (9^{13}) in the Marcan narrative 2^{13-17}. The same text was used by the Rabbis, who interpreted 'mercy' in the sense of acts of loving-kindness (Billerbeck, i. 500). 'The guiltless' in the present context will be the disciples. But as the whole passage probably had a context of its own originally, we cannot say what the original reference of the word was.

MT. 12^{11-12}

12 11 And he said unto them, What man shall there be of you, that shall have one sheep, and if this fall into a pit on the sabbath day, will he not lay hold on it,
12 and lift it out? How much then is a man of more value than a sheep? Wherefore it is lawful to do good on the sabbath day.

Another saying which Mt. has inserted into a Marcan context, the story of the healing of a man with a withered hand in the synagogue on the Sabbath (Mk. 3^{1-6}). Mt. omits Mk. 3^{3}: 'And he saith unto the man that had his hand withered, Stand forth,' and puts this saying in its place. His interest is in the Sabbath question rather than in the details of the story. The argument in *vv.* 11, 12*a* is presumed by Mt. to settle the question, and consequently the first half of Jesus' question in Mk. 3^{4} becomes the conclusion of the argument in Mt. 12^{12b}. The same argument is used again in the story of the healing of a dropsical man on the Sabbath (Lk. 14^{1-6}, which is to be assigned to L). It is reasonable to suppose that the Lucan story gives the argument in its original narrative setting. In that case we may suppose that in the M compilation the argument alone was found, without any accompanying narrative (as in the case of Mt. 12^{5-7}), and that the evangelist inserted it in what he considered to be a suitable context. The alternative to this would be that in the case both of Mt. 12^{5-7} and $12^{11f.}$ the sayings had narrative settings in M, and that Mt., in the interest of brevity, suppressed these and incorporated the teaching in other suitable narratives.

The argument is introduced into the story of a healing on the Sabbath. The scribal answer to the question: 'Is it lawful to heal on the Sabbath?' would have been: 'If the life of the patient is in danger, Yes; if not, No' (Billerbeck, i. 623). They would have said that the man with the withered hand could safely wait till the Sabbath was past for his cure. Cf. Lk. 13^{14}.

11. On the point raised in this verse it is not possible to say with certainty what the scribes would have said in our Lord's day. Opinions were still divided in the Rabbinical schools at a much later time. Some said that if an animal fell into a pit on the Sabbath, it was lawful to bring food to it there. Others held that it was further permissible to place mattresses and cushions under it, so that it might get out by its own exertions. In the so-called '*Fragments of a Zadokite Work*' 13^{23} (Charles's edition) the rule is laid down: 'And if it (an animal) falls into a pit or ditch, he shall not raise it on the Sabbath.' But the regulations of this document do not represent normative Judaism. In view of the uncertainty in the Talmudic period it would be rash to assume that there was any fixed rule

in the time of Jesus. Further, the form of the question suggests that Jesus is not appealing to rule but to the actual practice of His hearers. Compare the form of question in Mt. 7^9||Lk. 11^{11}; Lk. 11^5. The question is addressed to men as men; and ordinary humanity is expected to supply the answer.

12*a*. The conclusion is drawn from the expected answer by the favourite Rabbinical argument known as ' light and heavy,' the equivalent of our *a fortiori*. If so much may be done for one of the lower animals, how much more ought to be done for a man. Here the argument ends. The following words ' Wherefore . . . day ' are no part of the saying, but borrowed from Mk. 3^4.

Additional Note: Jesus and the Sabbath Laws

Anyone who forms his views about the Jewish Sabbath from a study of the Rabbinical regulations alone will probably come to the conclusion that it is an elaborate bondage. Such a conclusion would be quite mistaken. It can be easily corrected by reading such a book as Mr. Loewe's *Mediæval Hebrew Minstrelsy*, where the joy of the devout Jew in the Sabbath finds poetical expression in many songs. Much that seems to the outsider to be an intolerable burden is custom that has been sanctified by long usage. In the first century A.D. the observance of the Sabbath had become the hall-mark of Judaism. It was something by which every Jew, without distinction of age or sex, was shown to belong to the Chosen People. And this observance had been maintained at no small cost. See the magnificent story told in 1 *Macc*. 2^{29-38}, or that related by Josephus (*Contra Apionem*, i. 209–211). The faithful Jew would keep the Sabbath even at the price of his life.

The keeping of the Sabbath was a direct commandment in the Decalogue; but it was a commandment in general terms. The great mass of detailed rules came not from the written Law, but from tradition. The Mishnah says (*Hagigah* 1^8; Danby, p. 212): ' The rules about the Sabbath . . . are as mountains hanging by a hair, for [teaching of] Scripture [thereon] is scanty and the rules many.' Here we have a plain hint that much of the Sabbatarian practice of Judaism was ancient custom hallowed by long observance.

Jesus cannot have been unaware of the great price which had been paid by His people for the right to keep the Sabbath. He cannot have been insensitive to the sacred associations of the observance in Jewish homes and in every department of Jewish life. Why then does He deal so drastically with the thing that was so sacred to His people, a thing which He had doubtless been taught in childhood to regard as sacred?

The answer to this question is given in principle in Mt. 12^{5f}. The requirements of the Temple worship override the Sabbath laws: and the Kingdom of God is a greater thing than the Temple worship. It is the tremendous importance and urgency of the service of the Kingdom that justifies for Jesus the way which He takes. In this connexion the prohibition of staff, sandals, and wallet in the Mission Charge may be very significant. These things were forbidden in Jewish law to one going up to the Temple: they are forbidden again by Jesus to men setting out on an undertaking more important than the Temple service. The service of the Kingdom overrides the Sabbath laws. It is a work that can and must be done even on the Sabbath. It is a task that goes on all seven days of the week.

At this point we may ask whether this has not a bearing on the incident related in Mk. 2^{23-28}. Surely what is described in *v.* 23 is not just a quiet Sabbath afternoon stroll. Should we not rather think of Jesus and His disciples really journeying from one place to another on the missionary work of the Kingdom? Should we not think of the plucking of the corn, not as an idle pastime, but as something done to satisfy real hunger?

Further light is thrown on the problem by the incident told in Lk. 13^{10-17}. There the affliction of the woman, who is healed on the Sabbath, is described as possession by a 'spirit of infirmity' and it is subsequently said by Jesus that she has been 'bound by Satan' for eighteen years. This brings out plainly the fact that the work of the Kingdom in the mind of Jesus, and indeed throughout the New Testament, is a warfare against the power of Satan. Every healing is a blow struck against the supreme enemy of the Kingdom of God. 'If I by the finger of God cast out demons, then has the Kingdom of God come upon you.' But Satan does not keep the Sabbath. Evil works seven days a week. And the warfare against Satan must go on on the Sabbath as well as on the other six days.

We therefore conclude that Jesus did not break through the Sabbath rules lightly or unadvisedly, but because 'the King's business required haste'; because the service of the Kingdom of God and the warfare against the kingdom of Satan must go on day in and day out; because the business on which God had sent Him was the most important business in the world.

4. *CHARACTER AND WORD* (86)

Mt. inserts into Mk.'s account of the Beelzebul controversy (Mk. 3^{20-30}) passages drawn from Q, and at the end he adds a section (Mt. 12^{33-37}) which seems to consist of Q and M material. Verses 33, 35, and 34^b, have a parallel in Lk. 6^{43-45} and a doublet in Mt. 7^{16-20}. See above, pp. 351 f. Verses 34^a, 36, and 37 are peculiar to Mt.

MT. 12^{34a}

12 34*a* Ye offspring of vipers, how can ye, being evil, speak good things?

'Offspring of vipers' appears in the account of the Baptist's preaching (Q). Mt. makes Jesus also use the expression; but he is alone in doing so. The expression occurs again Mt. 23^{33}. The sentence may be an editorial composition to make the transition from *v.* 33 to *v.* 34^b, or it may come from M. It reflects the peculiar feature of M—and Mt.—a fierce dislike of the scribes and Pharisees, which, curiously, goes with a tremendous veneration of the Law. Whether the saying is a genuine utterance of Jesus may be doubted.

MT. 12^{36-37}

12 36 And I say unto you, that every idle word that men shall speak, they shall give account thereof in the day of judgement.

37 For by thy words thou shalt be justified, and by thy words thou shalt be condemned.

36. The Greek word translated 'idle' means originally 'unemployed'; then 'lazy,' 'idle.' Here it means something like 'purposeless.' The 'idle' word is distinguished from the deliberate, purposeful utterance. The statement of *v.* 36 is now a commonplace in psychology. The whole technique of psycho-analysis is built upon the principle that the 'idle' word reveals character more truly and completely than the deliberate, considered statement. The things that a man says when he is 'off his guard,' when he does not stop to think, are commonly the things that also 'give him away.' The idle word reveals character, and character determines destiny.

37. The change of person from plural to singular suggests that the statement of *v.* 36 is being reinforced by the quotation of some proverbial saying. Such sayings are common in the East. 'If there goes forth good from the mouth of (men, it is well), and if a curse shall go forth (from) their mouth, the gods will curse them' (*Words of Ahikar* 123 f., Cowley, *Aramaic Papyri*, p. 224). There is Rabbinical evidence (Billerbeck, i. 639 f.) for the Jewish belief that the record of a man as kept in heaven included his words, even his harmless utterances, as well as his acts.

D. PARABLES OF MISSIONARY WORK

Mt. 13 is a composite structure containing materials drawn from Mk., Q, and M. The framework is supplied by Mk. 4^{1-34}; and the Q and M passages are inserted into this or appended to it.

Mt. 13^{1-9} = Mk. 4^{1-9}. The Parable of the Sower.

Mt. 13^{10-15} is based on Mk. 4^{10-12}, the discussion on the purpose of parabolic teaching. But Mt. makes two additions. At 13^{12} he inserts the saying which in Mk. does not come until 4^{25}. And he adds *vv.* 14 f. (= Is. $6^{9\,f.}$) from his collection of *Testimonia.*

Mt. 13^{16-17} are from Q. See on Lk. $10^{23\,f.}$, above, pp. 372 f.

Mt. 13^{18-23} = Mk. 4^{13-20}. Interpretation of the Parable of the Sower.

Mt. omits Mk. 4^{21-25} at this point. He has a parallel to Mk. 4^{21} in Mt. 5^{15}; to Mk. 4^{22} in Mt. 10^{26}; to Mk. 4^{24} in Mt. 7^{2}; and Mk. 4^{25} has already been inserted at Mt. 13^{12}.

Mt. 13^{24-30}, the Parable of the Wheat and Tares, takes the place of Mk. 4^{26-29}, the Parable of the Seed growing inevitably.

Mt. 13^{31-32}, the Parable of the Mustard Seed is a conflation of Mk. (4^{30-32}) and Q (Lk. $13^{18\,f.}$). See above, pp. 414 f.

Mt. 13^{33}, the Parable of the Leaven, from Q (Lk. $13^{20\,f.}$). See above, pp. 415 f.

Mt. 13^{34} from Mk. $4^{33\,f.}$.

Mt. 13^{35} (= Ps. 78^{2}) again probably from a collection of Testimonia. Cf. *vv.* $14^{f.}$.

Mt. 13^{36-43}. Interpretation of the Parable of the Wheat and Tares.

Mt. 13^{44-46}. Parables of the Treasure and the Pearl.

Mt. 13^{47-50}. Parable of the Net.

Mt. 13^{51-53}. Conclusion of the Parabolic Discourse.

The passages which may be assigned to M are *vv.* 24–30, 36–43, 44, 45 f., 47–50, 51 f.

I. *THE PARABLE OF THE WHEAT AND TARES* (96)

In chapter 13 Mt. is following Mk. closely. Except for two short passages he reproduces the whole of Mk. 4. The two passages are Mk. 4^{21-25}, for which he has parallels elsewhere; and Mk. 4^{26-29}. In place of Mt. 4^{26-29} he gives this parable; and a comparison of the language in detail strongly suggests that Mt. 13^{24-30} is an expansion of Mk. 4^{26-29}. (Cf. *The Teaching of Jesus*, p. 222.) The reason for this procedure can only be conjectured. Mk. 4^{26-29} is one of the most cryptic of all the parables. Even now there is no small difference of opinion as to its meaning. Lk. omits it altogether. It may be suggested that the reason for Lk.'s omission and Mt.'s remodelling is the same—the obscurity of the parable. It is hardly possible to determine whether the Evangelist himself produced the new version of Mk. 4^{26-29} or whether the work had already been done. There is a little evidence in favour of the former alternative. In Mk. 4^{31} the mustard seed is sown 'on the ground.' In Mt. 13^{31} this is altered to 'in his field'; and this may safely be regarded as Mt.'s editorial revision. Now in Mk. 4^{26} we have again 'on the ground,' and in Mt. 13^{24} 'in his field.' It is natural to assume that this change is the work of the same hand as the change in Mt. 13^{31}, and that possibly the same hand that made this change made all the rest. But that is no more than a guess.

MT. 13^{24-30}

13 24 Another parable set he before them,
saying, The kingdom of heaven is likened
unto a man that sowed good seed in his
25 field: but while men slept, his enemy
came and sowed [1] tares also among the
26 wheat, and went away. But when the
blade sprang up, and brought forth fruit,
27 then appeared the tares also. And the
[2] servants of the householder came and
said unto him, Sir, didst thou not sow
good seed in thy field? whence then hath
28 it tares? And he said unto them, [3] An
enemy hath done this. And the [2] servants say unto him, Wilt thou then that
29 we go and gather them up? But he
saith, Nay; lest haply while ye gather up
the tares, ye root up the wheat with them.
30 Let both grow together until the harvest:
and in the time of the harvest I will say
to the reapers, Gather up first the tares,
and bind them in bundles to burn them:
but gather the wheat into my barn.

[1] Or, *darnel*.
[2] Gr. *bondservants*.
[3] Gr. *A man* that is *an enemy*.

MK. 4^{26-29}

4 26 And he said, So is the kingdom of God,
as if a man should cast seed upon the
27 earth; and should sleep and rise night and
day, and the seed should spring up and
28 grow, he knoweth not how. The earth
[1] beareth fruit of herself; first the blade,
then the ear, then the full corn in the ear.
29 But when the fruit [2] is ripe, straightway he
[3] putteth forth the sickle, because the
harvest is come.

[1] Or, *yieldeth*.
[2] Or, *alloweth*.
[3] Or, *sendeth forth*.

24. The introductory formula reappears in Mt. 13^{31}, and, with change of verb, in 13^{33}. The three M parables in this chapter have no special introduction (Mt. $13^{44, 45, 47}$). The rest of the verse is the same as Mk. *v.* 26 except that in view of what is to follow Mt. specifies 'good' seed.

25. 'But while men slept,' cf. *v.* 27 of Mk. The sowing of the weeds takes place at night. 'Tares' (Gr. *zizania*); the Greek name is of Semitic origin. (Accadian *zizānu*.) The plant is now generally identified with the 'darnel'

(R.V. mg.), *Lolium temulentum*, which grows to a height of about two feet and closely resembles wheat. It produces grain similar to that of wheat in size, but of a dark colour. It appears in Rabbinical literature under the name *zūn*, Aram. *zūnā*.

26. This verse again is an adaptation of *v.* 28 in Mk. 'Appeared' means presumably that the darnel was recognisable as such. As it was sown at about the same time as the wheat, this cannot well be its first appearance above ground. Perhaps the darnel would now be distinguishable by the darker colour of the grain.

27, 28, 29. The Matthæan parable now goes its own way. It is not clear why the servants should be surprised at the appearance of darnel among the wheat, unless it was present in great quantity, which is not stated. The surprising thing would be a field that did not have some weeds. It is also not clear how the farmer knows that this is the work of an enemy. 'An enemy,' R.V. mg. 'a man that is an enemy,' lit. 'an enemy a man': probably a Semitism (Dalman, *Gramm.*[2], p. 122). The proposal of the servants to weed the cornfield at this stage is so absurd that it would hardly have been made in real life. It is required not because such things are done in farming, but for the sake of the interpretation which is to follow. We are dealing here not with parable but with allegory. The master gives the obvious reply to an absurd question.

30. The wheat and darnel will be sorted out at the harvest, when the wheat will be preserved and the darnel burned. The reapers are not identical with the farm-workers, but apparently special workers employed for the harvest. But again this does not square with real life. The farmer may employ extra men in harvest time; but his regular workers also do their share. This distinction between 'servants' and 'reapers' does not arise naturally out of the story. It is imported for the purposes of the interpretation: that is, it is allegory and not parable. The binding of the darnel into bundles corresponds to the binding of the wheat into sheaves. This verse is a clear reminiscence of the preaching of John the Baptist.

It is now clear what Mt. 13^{24-30} is. It is an allegory constructed out of material supplied by Mk.'s parable (4^{26-29}) combined with the eschatological teaching of the Baptist. The story, as it stands, is an allegory composed for the sake of the explanation which is to follow. It is not to be regarded as a genuine parable of Jesus.

The Interpretation of the Parable (100)

Mt. 13^{36-43}

13 36 Then he left the multitudes, and went
into the house: and his disciples came
unto him, saying, Explain unto us the
37 parable of the tares of the field. And he
answered and said, He that soweth the
38 good seed is the Son of man; and the
field is the world; and the good seed,
these are the sons of the kingdom; and
the tares are the sons of the evil *one*;
39 and the enemy that sowed them is the
devil: and the harvest is [1] the end of the
40 world; and the reapers are angels. As
therefore the tares are gathered up and
burned with fire; so shall it be in [1] the
41 end of the world. The Son of man shall
send forth his angels, and they shall
gather out of his kingdom all things that
cause stumbling, and them that do
42 iniquity, and shall cast them into the
furnace of fire: there shall be the weeping
43 and gnashing of teeth. Then shall the
righteous shine forth as the sun in the
kingdom of their Father. He that hath
ears, let him hear.

[1] Or, *the consummation of the age.*

The explanation of the parable follows the original story point by point. The correspondence is so exact that the suspicion is confirmed that the story has been made to fit the explanation. See the discussion on allegory (Introd., pp. 326 f.). This didactic device is found often in the Jewish Apocalypses. Compare, for example, Dan. 7. And similar detailed interpretations of passages of the Old Testament occur in the Rabbinical commentaries, the Midrash, especially in the homiletic parts. The explanation has as little claim to be considered authentic teaching of Jesus as the parable.

36. The explanation is given privately to the disciples. In the Marcan narrative the withdrawal of Jesus and His followers from the multitude takes place at an earlier stage, after the parable of the Sower. Mt. postpones it to this point, with the result that the following parables of the Treasure, Pearl, and Net, are represented as spoken to the disciples alone.

37. Mt. identifies Jesus with the Son of Man. He does the same elsewhere: cf. Mt. 16^{13} with Mk. 8^{27}. This identification was undoubtedly made by the early Church; but did Jesus Himself make it? Cf. Mk. 8^{38}. Do the Son of Man sayings in the Synoptics amount to the claim: I am that Son of Man who is spoken of in the *Similitudes of Enoch*? Or is Son of Man in the teaching a symbol, the name for an ideal which Jesus realised in His life and death? If we take, as I think we must, the latter view, then ' He that soweth the good seed is the Son of Man ' is primitive Church dogma, and not teaching of Jesus.

38, 39. ' The field is the world.' This does not agree with the facts. The field of the activity of Jesus was Palestine. It does not agree with the M programme of the Mission (Mt. $10^{5 f.}$), where the field is Israel in the narrowest sense of the word. It does agree with Mt. 28^{18-20}, that is, it is early Christian dogma. The good seed is not, as we might expect, on the analogy of the parable of the Sower, the teaching. It stands for ' the sons of the Kingdom.' These are the people who are qualified to enter the Kingdom, the true disciples. The expression is found only in Mt. It does not occur in the Rabbinical literature. In Mt. 8^{12} the parallel in Lk. is ' you '; and there it is clear that ' sons of the Kingdom ' means Jews, those who by birth were deemed to have a right to a place in the Kingdom. Here the sons of the Kingdom are qualified by discipleship rather than by birth. And their qualification stands good. Cf. Dalman, *Words of Jesus*, pp. 115 f.; Abrahams, *Studies*, ii. 187 f. The ' sons of the evil one ': the phrase is the equivalent of John the Baptist's ' offspring of vipers.' Cf. also John 8^{44}, ' Ye are of your father the devil,' and 1 John 3^{10}, ' the children of the devil.' The ' sons of the evil one ' are those who belong to the kingdom of Satan. He plants them in the world and they grow according to his plan. The harvest is the ' end of the world ' or the ' consummation of the age ' (R.V. mg.). Analogous expressions in Apocalyptic and Rabbinical literature suggest that the meaning is the end of the existing world-order. This does not, for the Hebrew mind, necessarily carry with it the abolition of the material world. It may mean a transformation of it. It is essentially the end of a period of history, that period in which Satan still has some power, a period which can consequently be described as ' the present evil age.' It will come to an end when Satan is finally overthrown, and God alone reigns in the world. The expression is peculiar to Mt. in the Gospels (Mt. $13^{39, 40, 49}$, 24^{3}, 28^{20}). The participation of angels in the Judgement is little mentioned in the Rabbinical literature. It appears more commonly in the Apocalypses. E.g. *Enoch* 53[3-5]: 'I saw all the angels of punishment abiding (there) and preparing all the instruments of Satan. And I asked the angel of peace who went with me: "For whom are they preparing these instruments?" And he said unto me: "They prepare these for the kings and the mighty of this earth, that they may thereby be destroyed."' Cf. *Enoch* 54[6], 55[3], 56[1ff.], 62[11], 63[1], 100[4f.]; *Ass. Mosis* 10[2].

40, 41. Verses 40–43 are the point of the whole matter. The parable itself and all the foregoing exposition of it only prepare the way for this. The problem is the problem of a mixed community; a Church which contains genuine Christians and others, a Church which contains strict observers of the Jewish Law, and others who are lax; a Church which knows the ascetic rigour of James the Just and the scandals of Corinth. And in these verses the Evangelist gives his solution of the problem. The false brethren will be separated from the true at the Judgement. The Son of Man, the returning Christ, will depute His angels to make the separation. 'The things that offend' is literally 'the scandals.' The corresponding Hebrew word means originally something which causes one to stumble, a stone in the path or the like. Then it gains a moral significance and becomes something which causes one to sin. Then since occasions to sin may be persons as well as things, it can be used of a person who tempts one to sin. It is so used in Mt. 16[23], 'He turned and said unto Peter, Get thee behind me, Satan: thou art a stumbling-block unto me.' In this last sense we should interpret the present passage. It is not things but persons here, those who by their teaching or example cause others to go wrong. Cf. Rom. 14[13-23]; 1 Cor. 8[9]. These, the worst offenders, are mentioned first. Then come those who 'do lawlessness.' See on Mt. 7[23], above, p. 469.

42, 43. The 'furnace of fire' occurs again in 13[50] and nowhere else in the Gospels. Cf. Rev. 1[15], 9[2]; IV *Ezra* 7[36]:

'And then shall the pit of torment appear,
  and over against it the place of refreshment;
The furnace of Gehenna shall be made manifest,
  and over against it the Paradise of delight.' (Box's translation.)

The Rabbis also described Hell as a furnace of fire. (Billerbeck i. 673.) 'There shall be weeping and gnashing of teeth.' Cf. *Enoch* 108[3]: 'Their names shall be blotted out of the book of life and out of the holy books . . . and they shall cry and make lamentation in a place that is a chaotic wilderness, and in the fire shall they burn.' The gnashing of teeth expresses the utter despair of the victims. This refrain is characteristic of Mt. Cf. 8[12], 13[50], 22[13], 24[51], 25[30]. The happy lot of the righteous stands out by comparison with the fate of the wicked. Cf. Dan. 12[2f.]: 'And many of them that sleep in the dust of the earth shall awake, some to everlasting life, and some to shame and everlasting contempt. And they that be wise shall shine as the brightness of the firmament.' The righteous will be clothed with a supernatural glory. Cf. Mt. 17[2]; *Enoch* 39[7], 104[2]: 'But now ye shall shine as the lights of heaven, ye shall shine and ye shall be seen, and the portals of heaven shall be opened to you.' The closing word, 'He that hath ears, let him hear,' goes back to Ezek. 3^{27}, where God says to the prophet: 'But when I speak with thee, I will open thy mouth, and thou shalt say unto them, Thus saith the Lord God: He that heareth, let him hear; and he that forbeareth, let him forbear: for they are a rebellious house.' It emphasises the Divine authority of the prophetic message and the personal responsibility of the hearer for what he makes of it. As used by Jesus the force of the saying is the same. He means: 'What I say to you is God's truth. If you will face it honestly, you will see that it is. The responsibility lies with you.' The Evangelist has used this word of Jesus to give force and impressiveness to his interpretation. 'Let every Church member look to himself and see how this parable fits his own case.'

This allegory and its interpretation we may regard as probably the free composition of the Evangelist himself. We now come to three genuine M parables. The first two form a pair and may be considered together.

2. *THE HIDDEN TREASURE AND THE VALUABLE PEARL* (101)

MT. 13^{44-46}

13 44 The kingdom of heaven is like unto a
treasure hidden in the field; which a
man found, and hid; and [1] in his joy he
goeth and selleth all that he hath, and
buyeth that field.
45 Again, the kingdom of heaven is like
unto a man that is a merchant seeking
46 goodly pearls: and having found one
pearl of great price, he went and sold all
that he had, and bought it.

[1] Or, *for joy thereof.*

These two parables have a direct bearing on the missionary work of the disciples. The thesis of both of them is that once a man sees the Kingdom of God as it really is, he will spare no effort and consider no sacrifice too great to attain to it. The object of all the preaching of the Kingdom is therefore to convince men that the Kingdom is the most precious thing conceivable, so precious that in comparison with it all other goods lose their value. It is wealth which demonetises all other currencies.

44. The treasure hidden in the field: cf. Mt. $25^{18, 25}$. The treasure is obviously not hidden by the present owner. The parable is not concerned with the question how the finder comes to discover the treasure, or who put it there originally. Still less does the question of the morality of the finder's behaviour arise. The point of the parable is that the finder realises that he has stumbled upon something of great value, and immediately sets about securing it for himself. If you will show such energy and determination in order to secure worldly wealth, how much more you should strive to secure the treasure of all treasures. There are Rabbinical parallels to the story (Billerbeck i. 674). The legal question as to the right of the buyer to the treasure would be governed by the rule laid down in the Mishnah (*Baba Bathra* $4^{8\,f.}$, Danby, p. 371).

45 f. The point of the second parable is the same as that of the first. Here the merchant's procedure is not open to criticism. The fact also that he is seeking for pearls of fine quality, while the hero of the former parable stumbles on the treasure by chance, is probably not to be unduly stressed. The point is that having found the pearl of pearls, he deems it good business to sell everything he

has in order to obtain it. The fact that he would presumably have to sell it again in order to live is also not relevant to the parable.

It is one of the curiosities of New Testament interpretation that the pearl in this parable came to be identified, not with the Kingdom, but with Christ Himself. (Cf. H. Usener in the *Festschrift* for Weizsäcker, pp. 203–213).

3. *THE PARABLE OF THE NET* (102)

MT. 13^{47-50}

13 47 Again, the kingdom of heaven is like
unto a [1] net, that was cast into the sea,
and gathered of every kind: which,
48 when it was filled, they drew up on the
beach; and they sat down, and gathered
the good into vessels, but the bad they
49 cast away. So shall it be in [2] the end of
the world: the angels shall come forth,
and sever the wicked from among the
50 righteous, and shall cast them into the
furnace of fire: there shall be the weeping
and gnashing of teeth.

[1] Gr. *drag-net*.
[2] Or, *the consummation of the age*.

In its present form this parable is a companion piece to the parable of the Wheat and Tares; but it may be doubted whether the present form is the original. The interpretation (*vv.* 49 f.) does not fit the parable. In the parable it is the fishermen themselves who sort the fish. That is, the missionary disciples of Jesus. But in the interpretation it is the angels who undertake this task. Further, in the parable the fishing presumably represents missionary work (cf. Mk. 1^{17}); but it is very curious missionary work which wins people only in order to reject them immediately they are won. As it stands, the parable does not make sense; and the interpretation does not arise out of the parable, but is an irrelevancy tacked on to it. These difficulties are met by the hypothesis of Otto (*op. cit.*, pp. 99–102) that the genuine parable of Jesus is contained in *v.* 47 and that the rest is later expansion.

47. On this view the original parable has nothing to do with good and bad Christians. It has to do with the fact that just as a net collects fish of many different species, so the preaching of the Kingdom brings in men of many different sorts and conditions, men from all levels of society and of all degrees of culture, and so on. The point then is clear that the thing which God offers to men in the proclamation of the Kingdom is offered to all men, high and low, rich and poor, wise and simple, Pharisee and publican. And it is also implicit that all alike need that which is offered. This simple truth is completely obscured by the additional verses.

48. The net is emptied and its contents sorted by the fishermen. Following the figure used in *v.* 47, this can only mean that the missionaries sit in judgement on their converts, thus usurping the task which Jesus elsewhere reserves for God or God's representative. Contrast Mt. 7^1. This, the plain meaning of the parable, is corrected in *v.* 49 by the introduction of the angels. But this correction is at the expense of the parable. The bad fish are rejected and the good retained. This also is very curious. For the object of the preaching is to save sinners (cf. Mk. 2^{17}); and there seems little point in throwing them out as soon as they are caught. But it is clear from *v.* 49 that the explanation is not in terms of missionary activity, but in terms of an existing Church which is a mixed body

already containing true Christians and false. The evangelist is occupied with the same problem as in the parable of the Tares; and he offers the same solution. Cf. 13^{41-43}. Verses 48–50 appear for what they are, a clumsy attempt to foist on to *v.* 47 a view identical with that expressed in the parable of the Tares. Verse 47 is a genuine parable of Jesus: the rest is Matthæan embroidery.

4. *CONCLUSION OF THE PARABOLIC DISCOURSE* (103)

MT. 13^{51-53}

13 51 Have ye understood all these things?
52 They say unto him, Yea. And he said
unto them, Therefore every scribe who
hath been made a disciple to the kingdom of heaven is like unto a man that is
a householder, which bringeth forth out
of his treasure things new and old.
53 And it came to pass, when Jesus had
finished these parables, he departed
thence.

51. This verse may be regarded as an editorial transition to the following saying. It refers to the whole collection of parables in chapter 13; and it is exceedingly unlikely that they were all delivered on one occasion, or indeed that they where all delivered by Jesus. The question and the answer of the disciples both belong to the artificial situation which Mt. has himself created in this chapter.

52. It is difficult to see what is the force of 'therefore' in this saying. Presumably it means that because the disciples understand the teaching just given in the parables, they are to be regarded as scribes who have been made disciples to the Kingdom of heaven. But the disciples, so far as we know, were not scribes, but fishermen and the like. Cf. Acts 4^{13}. The meaning of the saying itself is not obscure. The scribe, as scribe, knows the Law; as a disciple of the Kingdom he knows the Gospel. From the point of view of the Palestinian Jewish Christian, he knows all that is worth knowing. He has at command the best both of Judaism and Christianity. We find a similar idea among the Rabbis. R. Akiba is compared to a full treasury. Rab Chisda (late 3rd cent. A.D.) explained 'new and old' (Song of Songs 7^{13}) thus: the 'old' is the written Law; the 'new' is the words of the scribes. It may be that something similar is meant by old and new in this saying. The old will be the Law of Moses; the new will be the new interpretation given by Jesus. A concrete example of such a combination would be the Gospel of Mt. itself, or the composite work in the *Didache* produced by incorporating sayings of Jesus into the Jewish document of the 'Two Ways.' What, however, is not clear is how this saying is to be reconciled with such sayings as are given in Mk. $2^{21 f.}$, or with the collection of antitheses in Mt.'s Sermon, where Jesus puts his 'I say unto you' in contrast to prescriptions from the written Law. It is beyond doubt that the sharpest and most obvious conflict in the ministry of Jesus was that between His teaching and the scribal interpretation of the written Law. Mt., more than any other Gospel, emphasises this fact. But Mt. also attempts, here and elsewhere, to suggest that the conflict goes no deeper than that; that it is a dispute about the exegesis of the Law, and that the Law itself is not in question. Both Jesus and the scribes knew better than that. They knew that the teaching of Jesus was revolutionary; that if it was accepted, the Law as well as the scribal interpretation would be

put on a new footing. The bitter hostility of the scribes to Jesus is not mere professional jealousy. It is based on the recognition that the logical issue of Jesus' teaching is the end of the Law. They saw clearly from the Jewish side what Paul later saw with equal clearness from the Christian side. Jewish Christianity did its best to hold a mediating position; but it was an impossible task. This saying expresses perfectly the Jewish-Christian ideal: it may well be doubted whether it represents the convictions of Jesus Himself.

53. The closing formula of the Evangelist. See on $7^{28\,f.}$, above, p. 470.

E. VARIOUS SAYINGS

Between the close of the parabolic discourse and the beginning of the discourse on the Church (chap. 18) we have a series of sayings and comments inserted in Marcan contexts. The passages to be considered under this head are Mt. $15^{12\,f.,\ 22b-25}$, $16^{2b-3,\ 17-19}$, 17^{20}.

1. *A SAYING ON WEEDS* (115)

MT. 15^{12-13}

15 12 Then came the disciples, and said unto him, Knowest thou that the Pharisees were [1] offended, when they heard this
13 saying? But he answered and said, Every [2] plant which my heavenly Father planted not, shall be rooted up.

[1] Gr. *caused to stumble.*
[2] Gr. *planting.*

The verses 12–14 are inserted by Mt. into the Marcan record of the dispute about the washing of hands. Verse 14^{b} is derived from Q. See on Lk. 6^{39}, above, p. 349. Verse 14^{a} is the Evangelist's transition from *v.* 13 to *v.* 14^{b}. Verses 12 f. have no parallel.

12. The short narrative introduction is necessary to prepare the way for the saying which follows. It is to be regarded as the work of the Evangelist.

13. In the present context the weeds can only be the Pharisees who took offence at the preceding saying. In the Rabbinical literature Israel and especially the pious Israelites are thought of as a planting of God. The idea goes back to Is. 60^{21}: 'Thy people also shall be all righteous, they shall inherit the land for ever; the branch of my planting, the work of my hands, that I may be glorified.' In the Mishnah (*Sanh.* 10^{1}, Danby, p. 397) this text is quoted as proof of the proposition that 'All Israelites have a share in the world to come.' The doctrine that righteous Israelites are the planting of God is found in the *Psalms of Solomon* (1st cent. B.C.) $14^{2\,f.}$: 'The saints of the Lord shall live therein for ever: the garden of the Lord, even the trees of life, such are his saints. The planting of them is rooted for ever: they shall not be plucked out all the days of the heaven: for the portion and the inheritance of God is Israel.' The saying in Mt. is most naturally regarded as a warning against the thoughtless optimism of those who accepted such congenial doctrine as that expressed in the above passages. The saying could be applied in many ways. Mt. here applies it to the Pharisees. He could have used it with equal effect in the situation implied by the parable of the Tares. It is one of those general statements that are capable of many

applications. It may be a genuine saying of Jesus; but we have no guarantee that its present application in Mt. is the original application.

2. *JESUS AND THE GENTILE WORLD* (116)

MT. 15^{22-25}

15 22 And behold, a Canaanitish woman came out from those borders, and cried, saying, Have mercy on me, O Lord, thou son of David; my daughter is grievously
23 vexed with a [1] devil. But he answered her not a word. And his disciples came and besought him, saying, Send her
24 away; for she crieth after us. But he answered and said, I was not sent but unto the lost sheep of the house of Israel.
25 But she came and worshipped him, saying, Lord, help me.

[1] Gr. *demon.*

This passage occurs in the Mt. parallel to Mk.'s account of the Syro-Phœnician woman (Mt. 15^{21-28}||Mk. 7^{24-30}). The whole passage in Mt. is remarkable for its small amount of agreement with Mk. except in the dialogue, Mt. 15^{26-27}||Mk. 7^{27-28}. The Matthæan and Marcan accounts of this incident are in this respect surprisingly like the Matthæan and Lucan accounts of Jesus' dealings with the Centurion of Capernaum (above, pp. 354–358). It is even suggested by Dibelius that this story was originally delivered simply as a dialogue between Jesus and the woman; and that there may have been a common source of Mt. and Mk., which contained only the conversation and left the cure to be understood. Whatever the explanation, the divergence between Mt. and Mk. in the narrative setting of the conversation is very striking and demands explanation. It may, of course, be that Mt.'s special source contained an account of the incident, and that Mt. has conflated that account with Mk. In that case it would be reasonable to suppose that some part at least of *vv.* 22–25 comes from M.

22. ' Canaanitish ' occurs only here in the N.T. It reflects the old distinction between the Israelites and the previous occupants of the Holy Land. Mk. describes the woman as a ' Greek, a Syrophœnician by race,' where ' Greek ' probably refers to her religion. ' Came out from those borders ' can hardly be right, since in *v.* 21 Jesus has already entered the territory. Perhaps we should take the words ' from those borders ' with woman and render: ' a Canaanitish woman from those borders (i.e. belonging to that part of the country) came out.' Alternatively it could be argued that the discrepancy points to a change of source in Mt. The Marcan narrative represents Jesus as going into the territory of Tyre and Sidon, and Mt. follows it in *v.* 21. But perhaps the M account of the incident did not allow Jesus to enter this heathen land. Perhaps it represented the heathen woman as leaving her own country and coming over the frontier to lay her petition before Jesus. This would be consonant with the M version of the Mission Charge (Mt. $10^{5f.}$); and it would imply that the M insertion begins at *v.* 22.

The titles used by the woman, ' O Lord ' and ' Son of David,' both suggest that Jesus is the Jewish Messiah. ' Son of David ' is the title of the expected Messianic king in *Ps. Sol.* 17^{23}. ' Lord ' is the natural title by which to address such a personage. With the combination we may compare the commonly occurring 'My lord the King' in address to kings in the Old Testament. On these titles see Dalman, *Words of Jesus*, pp. 316–331.

23, 24, 25. The silence of Jesus is doubtless meant to be a tacit refusal of the request. The implication of 'she crieth after us' is that Jesus and the disciples are walking on and paying no heed to the woman. The disciples find the woman's pursuit annoying and ask Jesus to get rid of her. Jesus answers in terms similar to those of the Mission Charge ($10^{5f.}$): 'Go not into any way of the Gentiles, and enter not into any city of the Samaritans: but go rather to the lost sheep of the house of Israel.' While this piece of dialogue is taking place the woman comes forward, throws herself on the ground before Jesus and begs for His help. The subsequent dialogue follows the account in Mk.

The authenticity of this saying in its present context is open to doubt. It is quite possible that Jesus believed and said that His task lay among His own people, at any rate in the first instance. It is also possible that such a saying, like the similar injunction in the Mission Charge, was restricted in its application to the circumstances of the moment. See the notes on $10^{5f.}$, above, pp. 471 f. But that Jesus meant to lay this proposition down as a dogma and never looked beyond the borders of Israel is very unlikely. The generalisation of the saying is more probably the work of the Jewish-Christian community.

[The Signs of the Times] (119)

[MT. 16^{2-3}]

16 2 But he answered and said unto them,
[1] When it is evening, ye say, *It will be* fair
3 weather: for the heaven is red. And in
the morning, *It will be* foul weather to-day:
for the heaven in red and lowring. Ye
know how to discern the face of the
heaven; but ye cannot *discern* the signs of
the times.

[1] The following words, to the end of ver. 3, are omitted by some of the most ancient and other important authorities.

This passage from the words 'When it is evening' onwards is generally regarded as an interpolation, though a very early one, in the text of Mt. There is the strongest textual evidence against the passage. Cf. Streeter, *The Four Gospels*, pp. 241 f. Further, there is another saying on weather-signs in Lk. 12^{54-56} (Q), above, p. 413. The Lucan saying agrees with the observed facts about the weather of Palestine. The saying in Mt. agrees with English weather-saws; but how far it holds of Palestinian weather is not clear. Rabbinical sayings about the weather-signs (Billerbeck, i. 727 f.) are concerned, as in Lk., with cloud and wind, not with the appearance of the sky at dawn and sunset.

3. *THE PLACE OF PETER IN THE CHURCH* (122)

MT. 16^{17-19}

16 17 And Jesus answered and said unto
him, Blessed art thou, Simon Bar-Jonah:
for flesh and blood hath not revealed it
unto thee, but my Father which is in
18 heaven. And I also say unto thee, that
thou art [1] Peter, and upon this [2] rock I
will build my church; and the gates of
19 Hades shall not prevail against it. I will
give unto thee the keys of the kingdom of
heaven: and whatsoever thou shalt bind
on earth shall be bound in heaven: and
whatsoever thou shalt loose on earth
shall be loosed in heaven.

[1] Gr. *Petros*.
[2] Gr. *petra*.

Few passages in the New Testament have given rise to so much discussion as these three verses. The saying, particularly *vv.* 18 f., is one of the main proof-texts for the Roman Catholic doctrine of the Papacy. The critical questions raised by the passage come under two main heads: (*a*) Is it a part of the genuine text of Mt.? (*b*) If it is, is it a genuine saying of Jesus?

(*a*) It has been held that the passage, or at least part of it, is interpolated in Mt. The textual evidence for this view is of the slenderest. The strongest point against the passage is the fact that it is not mentioned by the Fathers of the second century. But this argument from silence loses much of its weight when we reflect that the matters with which these men were concerned were, for the most part, matters in which the assertion of the primacy of Peter would not be specially relevant. The primacy of Peter would not be a very useful weapon against Gnosticism, for example. There does not seem to be any good reason against regarding these verses as a genuine part of the Gospel.

(*b*) But if they are genuine Mt., are they a genuine saying of Jesus? They stand alone. Mk. knows nothing of this strong commendation of Peter. Indeed, the Marcan account, taken by itself, would not suggest that Peter's declaration was received with any great enthusiasm by Jesus. And, in any case, the absence of the saying from the Marcan account is very difficult to explain. The principal arguments against the genuineness of the saying are as follows:

(i) The word 'church' occurs only here and Mt. 18^{17} in the Gospels. Both passages are suspect. This suspicion does not rest merely on the fact that the word occurs only twice. There are many words in the Gospels which occur only once or twice, and are none the less reliable for that. The difficulty is that this word occurs in Mt. here in a saying which has no parallel in Mk., though Mk. records the incident. It occurs again (Mt. 18^{17}) in a passage which has a parallel in Q (Lk. $17^{3f.}$), and again the Q parallel knows nothing about the peculiar Matthæan details. (See above, p. 431.) Further, the author of Lk.–Acts knows the word 'church' and the thing signified by the word very well. He uses the word more than a score of times in Acts, but never in his Gospel, either in speech or narrative. Finally, the word as used in Mt. seems to reflect the conditions of a later time. In Mt. 18^{17} it can hardly mean anything but the local community: here it clearly means the whole Church. (Hort, *Christian Ecclesia*, pp. 9 ff.) But this state of affairs—a great Church, whose constituent members are smaller communities—belongs to the period of Acts. In the Gospels we have a body of disciples with Jesus at their head expecting the coming of the Kingdom of God.

(ii) The second argument arises out of the first. Jesus and His followers expect the coming of the Kingdom. Therefore, it is contended, Jesus cannot have founded a Church in the ordinary sense of the word, an institution which was to continue for centuries, and do the work that had been done by Temple and Synagogue in Judaism. To this it is replied that 'church' in the New Testament is really the Christian equivalent of the Old Testament *ḳāhāl*, and means not a new religious organisation but the new Israel. The followers of Jesus are the true spiritual Israel, the chosen people of God. At this point we can bring in a Jewish parable from the old homiletic Midrash, *Yelammedenu*. It is about a king who planned the building of a palace: 'He dug in several places seeking proper ground for a foundation; at last he struck rock beneath, and said, Here I will build, so he laid the foundations and built. Just so when God sought to create the world, He examined the generation of Enoch and the generation of the Flood, and said, How can I create the world when these wicked people will rise up and provoke me to anger? When He saw Abraham who was to arise, he said, Now I have found a rock (*petra*) on which to build and establish the world. For this reason He calls Abraham a rock (Is. $51^{1f.}$).' (Moore, *Judaism*, i. 538). On this analogy it can be contended that Peter is the foundation of the New Israel. But this does not carry with it the doctrine of the primacy of Peter. It is one thing to be the foundation and quite another to be the ruler of the New Israel. And it may be added that if the phrase Kingdom of God means anything, it means that God is sole ruler of the New Israel.

(iii) It is urged against the saying that if it were genuine, Peter must have enjoyed an authoritative position as ruler of the primitive Church, and that the earliest documents show that no such absolute status was accorded to him. In Acts $11^{2ff.}$ he has to justify his dealings with the centurion at Joppa; and at Antioch Paul 'resisted him to the face, because he stood condemned' (Gal. 2^{11}). There is no satisfactory answer to this objection.

(iv) It is argued that the description 'rock' is unsuitable to the somewhat unstable character of Peter. It might be suggested that 'live wire' would be a more apt description than 'rock.' To this it is replied that it is not the character of Peter that is the foundation. It is rather Peter as the recipient of Divine revelation and as proclaiming this revelation, that is the foundation. But again this will scarcely carry with it the primacy of Peter. For it can hardly be asserted that the reception of such revelations and the proclamation of them when received is in the New Testament the peculiar prerogative of Peter.

(v) It may be added that the idea of one of the Twelve being given a position of primacy is not consistent with other sayings of Jesus. Jesus commonly thinks and speaks in terms of the coming Kingdom; and there there is no primacy of any apostle. In Mt. 19^{28} (M)||Lk. 22^{30} (L) there are twelve thrones, apparently of equal importance. In Mk. 10^{35-45} the request of the sons of Zebedee for the leading places is rejected, not on the ground that the primacy belongs already to Peter, but on the ground that it is not in the power of Jesus to confer such rank. The M parable of the Labourers in the Vineyard (Mt. 20^{1-16}) goes even farther in this direction. It suggests that even the Twelve must not look for special reward or recognition in the end of the day.

For these reasons we should not regard the saying as a genuine utterance of Jesus. It is, however, of Palestinian origin; and it is possible at least to surmise how and when it became current. In 1 Cor. we get evidence of the existence of a Petrine party, whose influence was felt even in Corinth. There is nothing to show that Peter himself had worked there, and so gathered followers like Paul and Apollos. The Petrine party in Corinth seems to stand for claims made on behalf of Peter to have some kind of oversight of the Gentile churches. Against all such claims Paul defends his own position as father in Christ of the Corinthian community (1 Cor. 4^{15}). Moreover, in this epistle he identifies Christ Himself with the rock (*petra*), by a piece of Rabbinical exegesis (10^{4}). And in this epistle he insists on the fact that there is not and cannot be any foundation of the Church but Christ Himself. 'Other foundation can no man lay than that which is laid, which is Jesus Christ' (3^{11}). In view of these facts we may conjecture that the kind of claim for Peter which we have in Mt. $16^{18 f.}$ was being pressed in the fifties of the first century, and that Paul is resisting it in Corinth when he writes 1 Cor. It may also be conjectured that the challenge implied in the claim was directed against Paul himself. He was always suspect to the Palestinian Church; and it is possible that the elevation of Peter was meant to act as some kind of check upon Paul.

17. The first verse is in form a beatitude. Peter is given his full name Simon Bar-Jonah. *Bar* is the Aramaic word for 'son.' In John $21^{15 ff.}$ Peter is addressed as Simon son of John. The Semitic form of John is Jochanan. It is possible that Jonah is an abbreviation of Jochanan. There is no clear proof of this (Dalman, *Gram.*[2] 179, n. 5); but Jona appears as a variant in MSS. of the Septuagint, where the Hebrew has Jochanan. The exact form of the name of Peter's father must remain doubtful. 'Flesh and blood' is a characteristic Rabbinical phrase. It stresses humanity as opposed to divinity. The revelation is from heaven and not of men. As the saying stands, this revelation can only be the fact that Jesus is 'the Messiah, the Son of the living God.' Now it appears to be common ground in the early Church that it is the Resurrection which manifests this fact (Acts 2^{36}; Rom. 1^{4}). Peter's confession may therefore be regarded as an inspired utterance, prophetic in character. This is significant in view of the fact that Peter, who is the first to assert the Messiahship of Jesus, is also the first witness of the Resurrection (Lk. 24^{34}; 1 Cor. 15^{5}). These facts gave to Peter a special distinction; and the beatitude of this verse may well express the feelings of his Jewish fellow-Christians. In view of the silence of Mk. it must be considered doubtful whether it represents the response of Jesus to his Confession.

18. The play upon the name Petros and the word *petra* ('rock') indicates an earlier play on the Græcised Aramaic nickname Kephas, which is the same thing as the Aramaic noun *kêphā* meaning 'rock.' Cf. John 1^{43}. The Aramaic name is undoubtedly the original. Paul calls Peter Kephas regularly in Gal. and 1 Cor. ('Peter' only Gal. $2^{7 f.}$). The nickname was given to Peter by Jesus Himself, but whether in jest or earnest we cannot say. The similar nickname 'Sons of thunder' bestowed on James and John seems to be playful rather than serious, a gentle rebuke to their hasty temper. The possibility cannot be excluded that Jesus called Peter 'Rock' as a similar mild rebuke to Peter's instability. What, then, is the rock upon which the Church is to be built? The obvious intention of the verse is that we should understand Peter himself to be the rock. Other interpretations have been suggested: the rock is Peter's Confession, or the fact of the Messiahship just acknowledged by Peter, or other things even more fanciful. But they all have to be forced upon the text. They depend on bringing in another 'rock' and ignoring the 'rock' that is already there in the words, 'Thou art Kêphā,' 'Thou art the Rock.' On this rock, on Peter himself, the Church is to be built. This figurative use of the verb 'build' is specially characteristic of Jeremiah in the Old Testament. With him it has the sense of establishing and maintaining, and the object of the verb is Israel. Here and in 1 Cor. 2^{10-17} the same figure is employed and the object of the verb is the Church. But Paul is quite clear that the founda-

tion is Christ, not Peter. There is, however, a sense in which it might be said that the Church was built on Peter; and that depends on the fact that Peter is the first witness to the Resurrection. In this sense he is the first member of the Church, the first witness to the fact that Jesus has been made both Lord and Christ, and declared to be the Son of God with power by the resurrection of the dead. This would explain why the gates of Hades cannot prevail against it. It is the Church of a Messiah who has already triumphed over death. The expression ' the gates of Hades ' comes from Is. 38^{10}, where the words ' In the noontide of my days I shall go into the gates of Sheol ' are a poetical way of saying ' I shall die prematurely.' Cf. *Wisdom* 16^{13}; III *Macc.* 5^{51}; *Ps. Sol.* 16^{2}. Hades is the Greek equivalent of the Hebrew Sheol, the abode of the dead. To say that the gates of Hades will not prevail against the Church is the same thing as to say that death will not have any power over it. As ' death hath no more dominion over ' Christ (Rom. 6^{9}), so it will have no more dominion over the Church. The whole verse thus seems to belong to the post-Resurrection period, and to express the convictions founded upon the Resurrection appearances of which Peter is the first witness.

19. Cf. Is. 22^{22}, a prophecy concerning Eliakim the son of Hilkiah: ' And the key of the house of David will I lay upon his shoulder; and he shall open, and none shall shut; and he shall shut and none shall open.' Here the key is ' the symbol of unlimited authority over the royal household ' (Skinner, *ad loc.*). The meaning must be similar in Mt. Peter is to be God's vice-gerent in all the affairs of the Kingdom on earth. This means that he is the ruler of the Church. The kind of power which he is to exercise is further defined as binding and loosing. ' Bind ' and ' loose ' are Rabbinical technical terms meaning ' forbid ' and ' permit ' respectively. The authority of Peter is an authority to declare what is right and wrong for the Christian community. His decisions will be confirmed by God. That is, Peter is to have the same powers in the Church as were enjoyed by the scribes in Judaism. The grant of exclusive power to Peter is inconsistent with Mt. 18^{18}, where the same powers are given to the whole body of disciples. Of the two Mt. 16^{19} is less likely to be original.

The question remains whether we should regard these verses as part of Mt.'s special source M. We have already seen that they are not an interpolation into the text of Mt. It is also very unlikely that they are a free composition of Mt. himself; for we have seen reason to think that the doctrine expressed in them was current in Jewish-Christian circles in the fifties of the first century. It may therefore be presumed that they were a part of the Jewish-Christian tradition which Mt. incorporated in his gospel. That is, they probably belong to M.

4. *FAITH THAT REMOVES MOUNTAINS* (126)

MT. 17^{20}

Here again we have a verse inserted into a context where Mt. is following Mk. Mt. 17^{14-21} is an abbreviation of Mk. 9^{14-29}, the story of the healing of the epileptic boy. At the end the disciples ask Jesus privately why they were not able to effect the cure. The reply of Jesus in Mk. (9^{29}) is: ' This kind can come out by nothing, save by prayer.' In Mt. the answer to the same question is given (17^{20}) as follows:

17 20 And he saith unto them, Because of your little faith: for verily I say unto you, If ye have faith as a grain of mustard seed, ye shall say unto this mountain, Remove hence to yonder place; and it shall remove; and nothing shall be impossible unto you.

Following on this many MSS. add: 'But this kind goeth not out save by prayer and fasting.' But this addition is absent from the best authorities for the text of Mt. and is rejected by modern editors. Mt. 17^{20} has parallels in Lk. 17^{6} (Q); Mk. 11^{23}||Mt. 21^{21}. For a discussion of the various forms of the saying see above, pp. 432 f.

To 'remove mountains' is a Jewish proverbial expression for doing the seemingly impossible. In the Rabbinical literature the title 'Uprooter of mountains' is given to some scholars who have a gift for solving apparently insoluble problems in the exegesis of the Old Testament. The saying as given here agrees with 1 Cor. 13^{2}. It may therefore be regarded as early and assigned to M.

Why has Mt. substituted it here for the answer given in Mk.? No certain answer can be given to this question; but it may be noted that elsewhere Mt. writes in such a way as to suggest that he regards faith as the one essential for the performance of miracles. In 14^{31} it is implied that the only thing that prevents Peter from walking on the water is lack of faith; and in 16^{8} the suggestion is that if the disciples had faith they would not be worrying about a shortage of bread, presumably because faith could produce a supply miraculously.

F. THE NATURE OF THE CHRISTIAN FELLOWSHIP

In chapter 18 Mt. gives a discourse about the Church and the duties of its members towards one another. For the first part of the composition (*vv.* 1–9) he is dependent chiefly on Mk.: the remainder (*vv.* 10–35) is a solid block of M material. The Marcan basis of Mt. 18^{1-9} is Mk. $9^{33-37, 42-48}$. Bultmann thinks that behind the Marcan section 9^{33-50} lies a short didactic piece of tradition bearing on the duties of members of the Fellowship to one another and the like. This comprised *vv.* 35, 37, 41–50; and Mk. has turned it into a scene from the life of Jesus by prefixing the narrative verses 33 f. This is also the view of Dibelius (*Formgeschichte*^{2}, p. 260), though he leaves it an open question whether the narrative setting comes from Mk. or was already created in the process of tradition. This is not an impossible theory; but it may be noted that the real difficulty in Mk. 9^{33-37} is created by *v.* 36. It has already been suggested above (p. 370), in discussing Lk. 10^{16}, that Mk. 9^{37} really has to do with disciples and not with children. That is, it is part of the answer to the question, Who is greatest among the disciples? and it says that all are on the same footing, because all are representatives of the one Master and of the one God. Mk. 9^{36} is a mistaken attempt to provide a narrative preparation for the phrase 'one of such little children' in *v.* 37. The introduced child now takes the centre of the stage with results that can be clearly seen in Mt. and Lk. In Lk. the saying Mk. 9^{35b} is transferred to the end of the story. In Mt. more drastic alterations are made. For Mt. apparently sees, what we see, that the saying in Mk. 9^{37} is not really adequate to the situation created by Mk. 9^{36}. He therefore introduces at this point the more appropriate saying from Mk. 10^{15} and rewrites it to fit the existing situation. The result is Mt. $18^{3 f.}$:

MT. 18^{2-4}

18 2 And he called to him a little child, and set
3 him in the midst of them, and said, Verily
I say unto you, Except ye turn, and become as little children, ye shall in no wise
4 enter into the kingdom of heaven. Whosoever therefore shall humble himself as
this little child, the same is the [1] greatest
in the kingdom of heaven.

[1] Gr. *greater*.

This is not M material but a free adaptation of Mk. 10^{15}; and it may be noticed that when Mt. comes to the story of the blessing of the children in Mk. (10^{13-16}) = Mt. 19^{13-15}, he omits *v.* 15 of Mk., presumably because he has already made use of it in this context. Verse 3 is Mt.'s interpretation of Mt. 10^{15}: 'Whosoever shall not receive the kingdom of God as a little child, he shall in no wise enter therein.' Mt. understands this to mean that the disciples must become like little children. In what respect they are to resemble children is stated in *v.* 4. It is humility. There is no parallel in Rabbinical literature to the idea that the child is the type of humility, which is not surprising; for the natural child is not humble. But humility is the virtue required in the disciples and Mt. accordingly finds it in the child. He may have been helped by the saying given in Mt. 23^{12}; Lk. 14^{11}, 18^{14}, where it is taught that he who exalts himself will be humbled, and he who humbles himself will be exalted.

The first nine verses of Mt. 18 can now be allocated as follows:

1*a* Editorial; 1*b* from Mk. 9^{34}; the whole verse an editorial rewriting of Mk. $9^{33 f.}$ so as to save the face of the disciples.

2 from Mk. 9^{36}. 3 f. a free rewriting of Mk. 10^{15}. 5 from Mk. 9^{37}. 6 from Mk. 9^{42}. 7 from Q; see on Lk. $17^{1 f.}$, above, pp. 430 f. 8 f. from Mk. $9^{43, 47 f.}$ The rest of chapter 18 may be assigned to M.

1. *THE CHURCH AND THE OUTSIDER* (133)

MT. $18^{10, 12-14}$

18 10 See that ye despise not one of these little
ones; for I say unto you, that in heaven
their angels do always behold the face of
12 my Father which is in heaven.[1] How
think ye? if any man have a hundred
sheep, and one of them be gone astray,
doth he not leave the ninety and nine,
and go unto the mountains, and seek that
13 which goeth astray? And if so be that
he find it, verily I say unto you, he
rejoiceth over it more than over the
ninety and nine which have not gone
14 astray. Even so it is not [2] the will of
[3] your Father which is in heaven, that
one of these little ones should perish.

[1] Many authorities, some ancient, insert ver. 11, *For the Son of man came to save that which was lost.* See Luke xix. 10.
[2] Gr. *a thing willed before your Father*.
[3] Some ancient authorities read *my*.

For Mt. this passage is clearly a unity, for *v.* 14 refers back to *v.* 10. That being so, Mt. can hardly have understood the 'little ones' of *vv.* 10 and 14 to be children; for in *vv.* 3 f. it is necessary to become like a little child in order to enter the Kingdom, and in this section the 'little ones' are compared to lost sheep. It is therefore probable that Mt. understood 'the little ones' of *v.* 10 in some other sense than 'children.' Now Lk. has a parallel to Mt. $18^{12 f.}$ in

Lk. 15^{4-7}, which I assign to L. The context in which Lk.'s three parables are there set is instructive. All three parables are spoken to scribes and Pharisees who were shocked by Jesus' friendly reception of disreputable characters. Such men and women, publicans and sinners, attached themselves to Jesus, and some of them were doubtless disciples of His. As such He could call them 'little ones.' If, then, we assume the genuineness of the saying, it is possible that it was spoken in the first instance to scribes and Pharisees, who made the criticism that Jesus was collecting the dregs of society about Himself. Later this saying becomes a warning to the Church not to adopt the censorious attitude which Jesus had condemned in the scribes and Pharisees.

10. Cf. Lk. 18^{9}: 'Certain which trusted in themselves that they were righteous, and set all others at nought.' The 'little ones' are repentant sinners who are drawn into the circle of the disciples of Jesus. The belief that men are under the care of angels is found in Judaism. Cf. Ps. 91^{11}: 'He shall give his angels charge over thee, to keep thee in all thy ways'; *Tobit* $5^{6, 22}$; Rabbinical passages, Billerbeck, i. 781 ff.; iii. 437 ff. The statement that these angels always 'behold the face' of God is not to be taken literally. As in 2 Kings 25^{19} the phrase 'behold the face of' means 'have direct access to.' These angels can at any time report to God concerning their charges.

11. This verse is omitted by the leading authorities for the text and rejected by modern editors.

12 f. Cf. Lk. 15^{3-6}. The parable of the Lost Sheep clearly has to do with sinners and not with children. The numbers 'a hundred,' 'one,' and 'ninety-nine' are often used by the Rabbis: examples in Billerbeck, i. 784 f. 'Doth he not leave the ninety and nine and go unto the mountains . . . ?': another possible rendering of the Greek is 'Doth he not leave the ninety and nine upon the mountains, and go . . . ?' The hill-country is thought of as the grazing-place for the flock. Lk. has 'Doth he not leave the ninety and nine in the wilderness, and go . . . ?' The account of the shepherd's doings on finding the lost sheep is much fuller in Lk. than in Mt. This may be due to Mt.'s habit of abbreviating, or it may be that the details have been lost in the process of tradition.

14. The Matthæan conclusion differs widely in wording from the corresponding verse (7) in Lk. R.V. mg.: 'a thing willed before your Father' is a more literal rendering than R.V. text. It corresponds to a common Hebrew and Aramaic formula, which reflects the Jewish fear of anthropopathism in speaking about God. Lk. has 'there shall be joy in heaven.' It may be noted that the Hebrew and Aramaic words underlying R.V. mg. 'a thing willed' (*rāṣōn* and *ra'wā*) mean both 'decision' and 'pleasure.' The same ambiguity is in them as in the English word 'pleasure.' 'Pleasure' does not mean quite the same thing in 'It gives me great pleasure' and in 'His Majesty's pleasure.' In Lk. the underlying Aramaic is taken in the sense 'God is pleased'—though it is more cautiously expressed than that. In Mt. the other sense is taken: 'God wills.' These are not mere translation variants: there is a difference of interpretation, which is an indication that the saying has come down to us through two different lines of tradition. The authorities for the text of Mt. are divided between 'your Father' and my Father,' with a slight preponderance in favour of 'my.' If the word

Father occurred at all in the original form of the saying, it is probable that Jesus would say neither 'your Father in heaven' nor 'my Father in heaven' but simply 'the Father' (*abba*). More probably, however, He said none of these. The passage, as appears from the Lucan parallel, is originally polemical; and it is more likely that Jesus said 'Heaven' (= God, as often in Jewish speech) as in Lk., and that this has been expanded in M to 'my (your) Father in heaven.'

It would be rash to infer from *v.* 14 that the teaching of Jesus is that none of the 'little ones' will perish. God's good purpose is that they should be saved; but human freedom is a fact, and Jesus elsewhere recognises the fact that man can reject the salvation of God and so perish. The Lucan form of the saying is different and perhaps more original.

2. *LIFE WITHIN THE CHURCH* (134 f.)

MT. 18^{15-20}

18 15 And if thy brother sin [1] against thee,
go, shew him his fault between thee and
him alone: if he hear thee, thou hast
16 gained thy brother. But if he hear *thee*
not, take with thee one or two more, that
at the mouth of two witnesses or three
17 every word may be established. And if
he refuse to hear them, tell it unto the
[2] church: and if he refuse to hear the
[2] church also, let him be unto thee as the
18 Gentile and the publican. Verily I say
unto you, What things soever ye shall
bind on earth shall be bound in heaven:
and what things soever ye shall loose on
19 earth shall be loosed in heaven. Again
I say unto you, that if two of you shall
agree on earth as touching anything that
they shall ask, it shall be done for them
20 of my Father which is in heaven. For
where two or three are gathered together
in my name, there am I in the midst of
them.

[1] Some ancient authorities omit *against thee.*

[2] Or, *congregation.*

There is a parallel to *v.* 15 in Lk. 17^{3} (Q), and another to *vv.* 21 f. in Lk. 17^{4} (Q). The verbal differences between Mt. and Lk. are great; and the most natural interpretation of the evidence is that the two passages come through different lines of tradition. Lk. $17^{3\,f.}$ is from Q. Mt. 18^{15-22} gives us the same original saying that is preserved in Lk. $17^{3\,f.}$, but changed and enlarged by the addition of other matter in the process of the M tradition.

15. See notes on Lk. 17^{3} (Q), above, pp. 431 f. In the Q form the saying has to do with wrongs committed by one member of the community against another. This is made clear in Lk. 17^{4}. It can be argued that in Mt. the saying has been developed into a rule for dealing with any kind of sin in the community. It has become a rule of Church discipline. This interpretation involves deleting the words 'against thee' as an assimilation to Lk. 17^{4}. The words are rejected by Hort and Tischendorf. The procedure in dealing with a wrongdoer then falls into three stages. The person who knows of the offence is to reprove the offender. If that fails, he is to reprove him before witnesses. If this produces no effect the offence is to be published to the Church. These three stages all have in view the bringing of the offender to repentance. If they all fail, he is to be considered as no longer a member of the Church. The first step rests on the injunction in Lev. 19^{17}: 'Thou shalt not hate thy brother in thine heart: thou shalt surely rebuke thy neighbour, and not bear sin because of him.' There are many Rabbinic sayings on the duty both of giving and accepting reproof. R.

Tarphon claimed that disaster overtook the Jews in A.D. 70 because they did not know how to give or accept reproof rightly. 'Thou hast gained thy brother'—as such. For if the measures to be taken all fail, he is lost as a brother; he ceases to be a member of the community. In Jewish usage 'brother' stands for co-religionist, fellow-member of the Jewish community as a religious group. It is distinguished from 'neighbour,' which means fellow-member of the Jewish people as a nation (Billerbeck, i. 276). A similar usage is found in pagan religious communities (Deissmann, *Bible Studies*, pp. 87 f.; Lake and Cadbury, *Beginnings of Christianity*, v. 92, 378 f.). The Christian use of the term 'brother' depends on the knowledge of God as Father; but the term was already there to be filled with its Christian meaning.

16, 17. The second stage is preparatory to the third. If the offender will not hear friendly reproof the official discipline must be put in motion. Here, according to Mt., it is necessary to take account of the Law as laid down in Dt. 19^{15}: 'One witness shall not rise up against a man for any iniquity, or for any sin, in any sin that he sinneth: at the mouth of two witnesses, or at the mouth of three witnesses, shall a matter be established.' This principle is accepted here. No Church member is to be condemned by the Church on the evidence of one witness. By taking one or two members with him the person concerned ensures that if the offender has to be brought before the Church, there will be adequate evidence against him. Even at this stage it is still possible for the offender to avoid the next stage by mending his ways. But if he remains obstinate, there is no course open but to lay the matter before the Church. The Church here is clearly a body of no great size. If M is the Jerusalem tradition, 'the Church' may be the Jerusalem Church. It is in any case the local community. If the Church cannot obtain satisfaction, there is nothing for it but to regard the offender as no longer a brother. 'Gentile' stands in contrast to Israelite; and the Church regards itself as the true Israel. It is also practically synonymous with 'sinner': cf. Gal. 2^{15}. The use of the word 'Gentile' in this connexion is evidence that we are dealing with Jewish-Christian tradition. A Gentile-Christian community would have been strongly tempted to change the word. (Cf. Streeter, *The Four Gospels*, p. 258.) The same collocation of publican and Gentile occurs in Mt. $5^{46 f.}$, which is probably from M (see above, p. 453).

18. Cf. Mt. 16^{19}. The authority there given to Peter alone is here given to the Church. In the present context it may be argued, with Billerbeck (i. 738 ff., 792 ff.), that the binding and loosing have to do with the proceedings just described. If the Church puts the offender under a ban, or if it releases him from the ban, its verdict stands good before God. Josephus uses the verbs 'bind' and 'loose' in this way in his *Jewish War*, i. 111: 'They (the Pharisees) became at length the real administrators of the state, at liberty to banish and to recall, to loose and to bind, whom they would.' There 'loose' and 'bind' are used of persons so that 'bind' is practically equivalent to 'banish' and 'loose' to 'recall.' So here 'bind' may be equivalent to 'expel from the community' and 'loose' to 'restore to fellowship' (cf. 1 Cor. 5^{1-5}). But it is also probable that *v.* 18 did not always stand in this context. And the fact that it is things, and not persons, that are to be bound and loosed is an indication that originally the

saying had reference to the definition of right and wrong, and not to the discipline of Church members.

19, 20. 'Again I say unto you' introduces a fresh saying, only loosely connected with what has gone before. As the corporate decision is valid in God's sight, so corporate prayer is powerful with Him. Two is the smallest number that can constitute a brotherhood or community. And in this matter two is much more than twice one. The underlying thought is that where two—or more—Christians are in perfect agreement, the thing that brings them into agreement is the thing that is greater than themselves, the thing that makes them one, the Kingdom of God. It is only real Christian agreement that is covered by this saying—not compromise or conspiracy. It is only agreement about things that can honestly be asked for in prayer. The selfish desires of A plus the selfish desires of B do not constitute an agreement in the sense in which the word 'agree' is used here. What does constitute an agreement is shown by *v.* 20. It is the kind of thing that Christians can come to when they meet together in the name of Christ, and with His presence in their midst. The speaker is the risen and glorified Christ whose spiritual presence is a reality in the community of His followers (cf. Mt. 28^{20}). There is a similar Jewish saying in *Aboth* 3^{2}: 'R. Hananiah b. Teradion (died *c.* A.D. 135) said: If two sit together and words of the Law [are spoken] between them the Divine Presence rests between them, as it is written (Mal. 3^{16}), Then they that feared the Lord spake one with another: and the Lord hearkened, and heard, and a book of remembrance was written before him, for them that feared the Lord, and that thought upon his name.' Cf. *Aboth* 3^{6} (Danby, p. 450). Verse 20 appears in a rather different form in some old authorities (D, Syr. sin., with support from g, Sahidic, and Clement of Alexandria): 'For there are not two or three gathered together in my name, with whom I am not in the midst of them.' This is regarded as the more primitive form of the saying by Wellhausen and Klostermann; and this view may be right. The reading of the text may well be an attempt to produce a smoother version of the saying, which in its D form seems to show traces of its Aramaic origin.

MT. 18^{21-22} (135)

18 21 Then came Peter, and said to him, Lord, how oft shall my brother sin against me, and I forgive him? until
22 seven times? Jesus saith unto him, I say not unto thee, Until seven times; but, Until [1] seventy times seven.

[1] Or, *seventy times and seven.*

A dialogue on forgiveness of wrongs done by one member of the community to another member. There is a parallel in Lk. 17^{4} (Q), see above, pp. 431 f. According to Jerome there was yet another version in the apocryphal Gospel used by the Nazarenes. It is as follows: 'If thy brother (saith he) have sinned by a word and made thee amends, seven times in a day receive thou him. Simon his disciple said unto him: Seven times in a day? The Lord answered and said unto him: Yea, I say unto thee, unto seventy times seven times. For in the prophets also, after they were anointed by the Holy Spirit, the word of sin was found.' (James, *Apocryphal N.T.*, p. 6.) Here 'the word of sin' is a Semitism, meaning 'somewhat of sin.' This form of the saying has been regarded as the original; but it may equally be a compound of Mt. and Lk.

The form of the saying in Mt. differs from Lk. principally in that there is here no mention of the repentance of the offender. Possibly it is taken for granted in the Mt. version. Whether the question and answer form is true historical reminiscence or a creation of the Evangelist it is not possible to determine.

21 f. It is Jewish teaching that the offender must repent, apologise, and make reparation for the wrong done. It is then the duty of the injured party to forgive him. The finest statement of the doctrine is in the *Testaments of the XII Patriarchs*, Gad 6^{3-7}: 'Love ye one another from the heart; and if a man sin against thee, speak peaceably to him, and in thy soul hold not guile; and if he repent and confess, forgive him. . . . But if he be shameless and persisteth in his wrong-doing, even so forgive him from the heart, and leave to God the avenging.' 'Seven times' is a round number. Cf. Gen. 4^{15}; Lev. 26^{21}; Prov. 24^{16}. The taking of vengeance seven-fold represents the stage of desert justice anterior to the *lex talionis*—an eye for an eye, a life for a life. In this verse and the following we have a reminiscence of this old law of vengeance. In Gen. 4^{24} the song of Lamech runs:

If Cain shall be avenged seven-fold,
Truly Lamech seventy and seven-fold.

The blood-feud is to be carried on without mercy and without limit. The reply of Jesus in *v.* 22 says: Just as in those old days there was no limit to hatred and vengeance, so among Christians there is to be no limit to mercy and forgiveness. At what period the 77-fold vengeance of Lamech ($70 + 7$) became $70 \times 7 = 490$-fold is not clear; but it already appears in the *Testament of Benjamin*, chap. 7, and may be regarded as pre-Christian. It is possible that R.V. mg. is right in translating the Greek 'seventy times and seven'; but no good parallel is quoted for such a construction of the Greek, and the early versions are in favour of 70×7.

3. *THE PARABLE OF THE UNMERCIFUL STEWARD* (136)

MT. 18^{23-35}

18 23 Therefore is the kingdom of heaven
likened unto a certain king, which would
make a reckoning with his [1] servants.
24 And when he had begun to reckon, one
was brought unto him, which owed him
25 ten thousand [2] talents. But forasmuch
as he had not *wherewith* to pay, his lord
commanded him to be sold, and his wife,
and children, and all that he had, and
26 payment to be made. The [3] servant
therefore fell down and worshipped him,
saying, Lord, have patience with me,
27 and I will pay thee all. And the lord of
that [3] servant, being moved with compassion, released him, and forgave him
28 the [4] debt. But that [3] servant went out,
and found one of his fellow-servants,
which owed him a hundred [5] pence: and
he laid hold on him, and took *him* by the
29 throat, saying, Pay what thou owest. So
his fellow-servant fell down and besought
him, saying, Have patience with me, and
30 I will pay thee. And he would not: but
went and cast him into prison, till he
31 should pay that which was due. So
when his fellow-servants saw what was
done, they were exceeding sorry, and
came and told unto their lord all that
32 was done. Then his lord called him
unto him, and saith to him, Thou wicked
[3] servant, I forgave thee all that debt,
33 because thou besoughtest me: shouldest
not thou also have had mercy on thy
fellow-servant, even as I had mercy on
34 thee? And his lord was wroth, and
delivered him to the tormentors, till he
35 should pay all that was due. So shall
also my heavenly Father do unto you, if
ye forgive not every one his brother
from your hearts.

[1] Gr. *bondservants*.

[2] This talent was probably worth about £240.

[3] Gr. *bondservant*.

[4] Gr. *loan*.

[5] The word in the Greek denotes a coin worth about eight pence halfpenny.

The parable is introduced here, as the introductory 'therefore' shows, in order to illustrate the point made in *vv.* 21 f. This it does not quite do. For the point of *v.* 22 is not merely that one should be ready to forgive, but that one should be ready to forgive again and again. The point of the parable is just that one must be ready to forgive; and there is nothing in the parable about repeated forgiveness. It may therefore be assumed that the connexion of the parable with the saying is one which has been made in the tradition or by Mt. himself. The parable itself emphasises a characteristic feature in the teaching of Jesus—that only a forgiving spirit can receive forgiveness, that a mean and revengeful disposition shuts out God's forgiveness, that the wrath of God is kindled against the hard and relentless more than against the weak and foolish.

23, 24, 25, 26 f. 'A certain king,' lit. 'a man a King,' i.e. a human king in contrast to the divine King. The servants are probably not slaves or domestic servants but government officials. The term would cover court officials or ministers of state, and provincial governors, as well as people in lower positions. These persons are all to present their accounts to be audited. One shows a deficiency of ten thousand talents, a colossal sum equivalent to about two million pounds. The exaggeration may well be deliberate in order to heighten the contrast with the hundred pence of *v.* 28. Otherwise it might be conjectured that the numerical signs for 10 and 10,000 have been confused, and that originally the debt amounted to 10 talents, about £2,000. If the debt amounted to two millions, the sale of the debtor and his family would not suffice for 'payment to be made.' For the enslavement of children through the insolvency of the father cf. 2 Kings 4^{1}; Neh. 5^{5}; Is. 50^{1}. In Jewish law the wife is not sold into slavery; but if the husband is so sold, the wife may accompany him into bondage. The debtor asks for time to pay. The king goes far beyond this request by cancelling the whole debt. The word translated 'debt' means literally 'loan' (R.V. mg.). This may perhaps mean that the debtor had been working with capital lent for that purpose by his master; cf. $25^{14\,ff.}$ His deficiency could then be regarded as embezzlement. See on *v.* 30.

28, 29, 30. In sharp contrast to the generosity of the king is the subsequent behaviour of the steward. The fellow-servant is presumably a 'colleague' in the royal service as in Ezra $4^{9,\,17,\,23}$, etc. The amount of the debt is trifling in comparison with that which the king has just cancelled. A hundred 'pence' would hardly amount to £4. The drastic method of debt-collecting adopted here may be illustrated from the Mishnah (*Baba Bathra* 10^{8}, Danby, p. 382): 'If a man seized a debtor by the throat in the street . . .' The debtor asks for time to pay in much the same terms as were employed by his creditor a short time before. But his entreaties are in vain. He is not sold into slavery but imprisoned till the debt be paid. On imprisonment for debt, see Deissmann, *Light from the Ancient East*, p. 267. In Jewish law an Israelite could sell himself into slavery if he could not make a living as a free man, or he could be sold by order of the Court if he was convicted of theft and had not property sufficient to replace what he had stolen. But he could not be sold if he had stolen less than his own value in the slave-market (Billerbeck, iv. 698 ff.). Presumably, therefore, it was not in the power of the creditor here to sell his debtor. No doubt it is to be understood that the imprisonment of the debtor follows on legal action by the creditor; cf. Mt. $5^{25 f.}$.

31, 32 f., 34. The other servants are 'exceeding sorry.' The same expression occurs in Mt. 17^{23}, and in the LXX Neh. 5^{6}; Jonah $4^{4, 9}$, where the Greek verb translates a Hebrew verb meaning 'to burn with anger.' It is therefore probable that the servants were not so much distressed at the fate of the debtor as indignant at the disgraceful behaviour of the creditor. Consequently they do not raise a subscription to pay the debt but go and reveal what has happened to the king. The king shares their opinion and takes immediate action against the unmerciful steward. 'Thou wicked servant': cf. Mt. 25^{26}; Lk. 19^{22}. The king had set an example of mercy which the steward ought to have followed. Without this example his conduct might have been understood: with it, it is inexcusable. So in the last resort the command that Christians are to be merciful rests upon the fact that God is merciful, and not upon considerations of expediency such as that mercy is the best policy (Lk. 6^{36}). The behaviour of the king sets the standard for his subjects. The king is angry at the hard-heartedness of the steward as he was not angry about the original debt. He hands the steward over to the 'tormentors' (*basanistæ*); cf. *Ecclus.* 30^{35} (33^{27}): 'Yoke and thong bow down the neck, And for an evil servant (there are) stocks and chastisements (*basanoi*).' The punishment is to continue till the original debt is wiped out. Doubtless the thought here is of punishment after death. If so, the idea of torment is present, but not the idea of *eternal* torment. Cf. Lk. 12^{57-59} (Q).

35. The moral of the tale. Even the saved are not safe; and a harsh and unforgiving disposition in a Christian puts him back to where he was before he became a Christian. The forgiveness demanded is 'from your hearts' (cf. Is. 59^{13}; *Test. Gad* 6^{7}, quoted on $18^{21 f.}$ above). That is, it is not to be a mere form of words, but a genuine expression of sincere feeling; not forgiveness because forgiveness is a duty, but forgiveness as the natural self-expression of a merciful and forgiving disposition.

The discourse closes with the customary Matthæan formula.

MT. 19^{1}

19 1 And it came to pass when Jesus had finished these words, he departed from Galilee, and came into the borders of Judæa beyond Jordan.

G. SERVICE AND REWARD

This section consists of three pieces, Mt. 19^{10-12}, 19^{28}, and 20^{1-16}. The first is appended to the Marcan pericope on divorce (Mk. 10^{2-12}||Mt. 19^{1-9}); the second is inserted into the Marcan context (Mt. 19^{16-30}||Mk. 10^{17-31}); the third is inserted between two Marcan sections (Mk. 10^{17-31}||Mt. 19^{16-30} and Mk. 10^{32-34}||Mt. 20^{17-19}).

1. *MARRIAGE AND CELIBACY* (187)

MT. 19^{10-12}

19 10 The disciples say unto him, If the case
of the man is so with his wife, it is not
11 expedient to marry. But he said unto
them, All men cannot receive this saying,
12 but they to whom it is given. For there
are eunuchs, which were so born from
their mother's womb: and there are
eunuchs, which were made eunuchs by
men: and there are eunuchs, which made
themselves eunuchs for the kingdom of
heaven's sake. He that is able to receive
it, let him receive it.

10, 11, 12. This passage is added at the end of the section in which Jesus has stated the true ideal of marriage as a Divine ordinance and deprived the husband of the power to divorce his wife. (See notes on Lk. 16^{18} (Q), above, pp. 428 ff.) The upshot of this teaching is to strip the husband of all the onesided privileges which were his under the Jewish law. That being so, it is possible to explain *v.* 10, though not in any sense that is creditable to the disciples. For if *v.* 10 refers back to the foregoing teaching, it can only mean that the disciples say to Jesus: 'If that is your idea of marriage, we prefer to remain unmarried'; and it is somewhat hard on the disciples to have to suppose that they were not only spiritually blind but also insolent. There remain two possibilities. Either *v.* 10 is the composition of Mt. for the purpose of making the transition from the sayings on marriage to that on celibacy. In that case 'this saying' in *v.* 11 must point forward to *v.* 12. Or, what is perhaps more probable, we have in *vv.* 10–12 the conclusion of a passage, and what preceded *v.* 10 is lost. Comparison of this passage with 1 Cor. 6^{12}–7^{40} would suggest that it may have been a saying pointing out the possibility of a clash between the claims of matrimony and the claims of the Kingdom. (Cf. Lk. 9^{59-62}||Mt. $8^{21f.}$; Lk. $14^{26f.}$||Mt. $10^{37f.}$.) The reply of the disciples would then be the perfectly sensible one that such a clash of loyalties, with its possibilities of acute suffering, can be avoided by not marrying at all. 'This saying,' in *v.* 11, will then refer to the disciples' suggestion. Jesus says in effect: Celibacy all round would solve the problem; but celibacy all round is not practicable. The suggestion is well enough for those who can accept it; but there are many who cannot embrace a celibate life—a fact which Paul recognises in 1 Cor. 7. There are, however, those for whom the celibate life is the natural and inevitable thing. There are those for whom marriage in the full sense is an impossibility for physical reasons: either because they are 'eunuchs from their mother's womb,' i.e. sexually impotent from birth; or because they have been 'made eunuchs by men,' i.e. rendered sexually impotent by a surgical operation. This distinction is recognised in the Rabbinical treatment of the subject (Billerbeck, i. 805 f.) There is yet a third class—those who have 'made themselves eunuchs for the kingdom of heaven's sake.' Does this mean that they have voluntarily submitted to an operation whereby they become sexually impotent, or does it mean simply that they have voluntarily embraced a life of celibacy? The following considerations favour the latter alternative. (1) The whole sentiment of Judaism was against castration. The eunuch was disqualified for membership of the community (Deut. 23^1). A Jew simply would not understand how this operation could serve the ends of the Kingdom of God. (2) The word 'eunuch' and the abstract noun derived from it appear in early Christian literature with the sense, unknown to classical or Hellenistic Greek, of 'celibate' and 'celibacy' respectively. The classic example is Clement of Alexandria's definition (*Paed.* III, 4, 26): 'The true eunuch is not he who cannot but he who will not indulge himself.' (3) There is no evidence that Jesus had any sympathy with asceticism for asceticism's sake. He requires—and makes—the greatest sacrifices for the sake of the Kingdom. If the Kingdom requires the sacrifice of the happiness of marriage, the sacrifice is to be made. Self-mutilation cannot add anything to the fullness of such sacrifice. (4) The literal sense is as inappropriate here as it is in Mk. 9^{43-48} and

Mt. $5^{29 f.}$ (see notes, above, p. 449). (5) Jesus, John the Baptist, Paul, and probably some of the Twelve were unmarried; others of the Twelve sacrificed their home-life for the sake of the Kingdom. But that was all. There is no word of any becoming eunuchs in the literal sense of the word. The conclusion is that the three classes of eunuchs in this verse fall into two. The first class comprehends those who cannot marry; the second those who can but do not, who sacrifice their happiness, but not their manhood, for the sake of the Kingdom of God.

There is an excellent account of the early exegesis of this difficult passage by Bauer in the Heinrici *Festschrift*, pp. 234–244.

2. *THE REWARD OF THE TWELVE* (189)

MT. 19^{28}

19 28 And Jesus said unto them, Verily I say unto you, that ye which have followed me, in the regeneration when the Son of man shall sit on the throne of his glory, ye also shall sit upon twelve thrones, judging the twelve tribes of Israel.

28. This saying is introduced into the Marcan context between the question of Peter (Mk. 10^{28}||Mt. 19^{27}) and the answer of Jesus (Mk. 10^{29}||Mt. 19^{29}). It has a parallel in Lk. 22^{28-30}; but verbal agreement between the two is confined to the closing words of the saying. It is therefore most probable that Mt. 19^{28} belongs to M and Lk. 22^{28-30} to L. Cf. Streeter, *The Four Gospels*, p. 288. We may also compare the promise in Rev. 3^{21}: He that overcometh, I will give to him to sit down with me in my throne, as I also overcame, and sat down with my Father in his throne'; cf. 20^{4}; 2 Tim. $2^{11 f.}$.

'Ye which have followed me,' as the reference to twelve thrones shows, must be the twelve close companions of Jesus as distinct from the general body of those who heard and responded to His preaching. The original answer to Peter's question as given in Mk. $10^{29 f.}$ contains no such restriction to the Twelve. The 'regeneration' (*palingenesia*) is a technical term in Stoic philosophy, where it signifies the beginning of a new cycle in the cosmic process. But not new in the strict sense, for each new cycle is just a repetition of the old. 'Stoicism held that the whole universe, which had come into being by condensation out of the Divine Fire, would one day be resolved again into the Divine Fire, but that then, after a period, another universe, just like the present one, would be formed, run a precisely similar course, and be reabsorbed into the Fire, and so on, world after world for ever' (E. Bevan, *Christianity*, p. 11). The Jewish expectation was different. They also expected the end of the existing order and the beginning of a new one. But the new order would be really new and not a mere repetition of what had gone before. It would really be the second volume of the history of the world and not a reprint of volume one. So 'regeneration' or *palingenesia* in a Jewish or Jewish-Christian context means a new era that is really new, a new creation. Jewish views as to how this would happen differed considerably (Billerbeck, iii. 840 ff.). For some it meant a radical transformation of the existing world; for others it meant that the present world would revert to the condition described in Gen. 1^{2}, and that out of this formless mass God would create a new world;

for others again it meant that the existing world would be completely abolished and that God would create a new world absolutely *de novo*. The important thing is that it will be a new era that is new.

In this new age the Son of Man will 'sit on the throne of his glory.' The expression occurs again in Mt. 25^{31}. The 'throne of glory' is properly God's throne. In the Rabbinical view it is one of the things which were created before the world; and its place is in the seventh heaven. The notion that anyone except God could sit on this throne is foreign to Jewish thought, with one exception—the so-called *Similitudes of Enoch*. So *Enoch* 45^{3}: 'On that day Mine Elect One shall sit on the throne of glory and shall try their works, and their places of rest shall be innumerable.' Cf. 51^{3}: 'And the Elect One shall in those days sit on My throne'; 55^{4}, 61^{8}, 62^{2-5}, 69^{27}. The Lucan version of the saying has nothing of this, but: 'I appoint unto you a kingdom, even as my Father appointed unto me.'

'Ye also shall sit upon twelve thrones.' Bultmann and others regard this promise as put into the mouth of the Risen Lord by the primitive Christian community. But it is hard to see how the primitive Church could have invented a saying which promises a throne, amongst others, to Judas Iscariot. The saying surely belongs to a much earlier period, before the treachery of Judas was suspected, much less known. 'Judging' may be taken in the literal sense, in which case the saying means that the Twelve are to be assessors at the Last Judgement (cf. Mt. $25^{31ff.}$; 1 Cor. 6^{3}). Or the word may be taken in the wider sense, common in the Old Testament, of 'ruling,' 'administering' (cf. 1 Sam. 8^{5}; *Ps. Sol.* 17^{28}: 'And he (the Messiah) shall gather together a holy people, whom he shall lead in righteousness; and shall judge (= rule) the tribes of the people that hath been sanctified by the Lord his God.'). The former sense seems, on the whole, to be intended here; and the latter sense in the Lucan version of the saying. This suggests that there was doubt in the early Church as to the correct interpretation of what was meant by sitting on twelve thrones judging the twelve tribes of Israel. It is also uncertain what is meant by the twelve tribes of Israel: whether the words are to be taken literally as meaning the Jewish people, or metaphorically for the spiritual Israel, the Church. (Rev. 7^{4-8}; Rom. 2^{29}; Gal. 3^{29}, 6^{16}; Phil. 3^{3}; 1 Pet. 1^{1}; James 1^{1}; Hermas, *Sim.* 9^{17}.)

In the Rabbinical literature we find the idea that the righteous Israelites are to assist in the final Judgement (Billerbeck, iv. 1103 f.). This view is based on the text Dan. 7^{9} 'I beheld till thrones were placed, and one that was ancient of days did sit.' The plural 'thrones' is taken as meaning that God will have assessors at the Judgement. This interpretation may perhaps underlie the Septuagint version of Dan. 7^{22}, where it is said that God 'gave the judgement (*krisin*) to the saints of the Most High' (cf. *Wisdom* 3^{8}). It is possible that some such meaning as this is the original meaning of this saying, in which case it would be in substantial agreement with the description of the Judgement in Mt. $25^{31ff.}$. But the saying is obscure and certainty is probably unattainable.

3. *THE PARABLE OF THE LABOURERS IN THE VINEYARD* (190)

MT. 20^{1-16}

20 1 For the kingdom of heaven is like unto
a man that is a householder, which went
out early in the morning to hire labourers
2 into his vineyard. And when he had
agreed with the labourers for a [1] penny
a day, he sent them into his vineyard.
3 And he went out about the third hour,
and saw others standing in the market-
4 place idle; and to them he said, Go ye
also into the vineyard, and whatsoever is
right I will give you. And they went
5 their way. Again he went out about the
sixth and the ninth hour, and did like-
6 wise. And about the eleventh *hour* he
went out, and found others standing; and
he saith unto them, Why stand ye here all
7 the day idle? They say unto him, Because no man hath hired us. He saith
unto them, Go ye also into the vineyard.
8 And when even was come, the lord of the
vineyard saith unto his steward, Call the
labourers, and pay them their hire,
beginning from the last unto the first.
9 And when they came that *were hired* about
the eleventh hour, they received every
10 man a [1] penny. And when the first
came, they supposed that they would
receive more; and they likewise received
11 every man a [1] penny. And when they
received it, they murmured against the
12 householder, saying, These last have
spent *but* one hour, and thou hast made
them equal unto us, which have borne
the burden of the day and the [2] scorching
13 heat. But he answered and said to one
of them, Friend, I do thee no wrong:
didst not thou agree with me for a
14 [1] penny? Take up that which is thine,
and go thy way; it is my will to give unto
15 this last, even as unto thee. Is it not
lawful for me to do what I will with
mine own? or is thine eye evil, because
16 I am good? So the last shall be first,
and the first last.

[1] See marginal note on ch. xviii. 28.
[2] Or, *hot wind.*

In its present context this parable stands in sharp contrast to what has gone before. The promise of special pre-eminence to the Twelve is balanced by a strong affirmation of equality of reward in the Kingdom. The Twelve who have laboured with Jesus from the beginning of His Ministry will receive neither more nor less than any other disciple: and they may not expect or claim more. But if the parable be taken by itself, without reference to the context in which Mt. has placed it, other possible interpretations present themselves. For example, it may be regarded as an answer to the criticism that Jesus opened the Kingdom to the publicans and harlots. Cf. Mt. 21^{31}: 'Verily I say unto you that the publicans and harlots go into the Kingdom of God before you.' Or, again, it may be taken as a sketch of the whole history of Israel (cf. Mk. 12^{1-12}). The sense will then be that the disciples of Jesus will receive the same reward as the patriarchs and prophets (cf. Lk. 13^{28-30} (Q), above, pp. 417 ff.). In any case, the essential point of the parable is that the rewards of the Kingdom are not measured by man's desert but by God's grace. At the same time, the parable cannot be made to support the thoroughgoing Pauline and Lutheran doctrine of salvation by grace alone. There is not a shadow of suggestion that those who have worked in the vineyard all day have not earned their wages. All that is asserted is that it is God's good pleasure to pay full wages to those who have earned less than full wages. The parable does not attack the idea of merit in general, but only the notion that some people, be they the 'Fathers' or the Pharisees or the Apostles, have special merits which require special reward from God, and that others who have less to commend them ought to receive less from God. Indeed, the parable has nothing to do with the question of salvation by grace or works. It is concerned entirely with the question whether there are distinctions within the Kingdom; and what it says is that the love of God is such that He makes no such distinctions, but gives to all alike.

1 f. According to Jewish law a working day lasts from sunrise till the appearance of the stars at evening. A 'penny' is the Roman *denarius* equivalent to about 8½*d.* But the purchasing power of money was greater then than now. A good ox could be bought for 100 denars, a young bullock for 20, a ram for 8, and a lamb for 4 (Mishnah, *Menachoth* 13^8; Danby, p. 512). One denar per day was considered a good wage. The great Hillel did manual labour for half that sum; and R. Meir, who was an accomplished scribe, earned 2 denars a day as a writer of documents.

If we may think of the parable as covering the whole history of Israel, we may take these earliest workers to be the Fathers. Then perhaps the express stipulation of the payment may be a reference to the Covenant between God and Israel.

3 f., 5. The third hour is about 9 a.m. The market-place appears as the resort of the unemployed. No scale of wages is agreed in the case of the men hired on this occasion. They are promised a fair remuneration. The procedure is repeated at the sixth hour (about noon) and the ninth hour (about 3 p.m.). Is it fanciful to see in these successive excursions a reference to the summonses issued to Israel from time to time through the prophets?

6 f. The last stage, about the eleventh hour (about 5 p.m.). On the interpretation suggested, the eleventh hour is the period of John the Baptist and Jesus Himself. There are still many who have not found their places in the vineyard —the publicans and harlots for whom there seemed to be no place there (?). They also are taken in and given work to do.

8. The day comes to an end. It is the end of the present age. The time of labour is ended and the time of reward has come. According to the Law (Lev. 19^{13}, Dt. $24^{14f.}$) the labourer was entitled to have his wages at the end of the day's work. In this parable the actual payment is done not by the householder himself, but by his steward. We may compare the description of the Judgement in Mt. $25^{31ff.}$, where the verdicts and sentences are given not by God, but by the Son of Man (see below, p. 541). The payment begins with the last employed. It is possible that there was a view that those who survived till the Parousia would have some sort of advantage over those who did not. Paul is at pains to contradict such a view in 1 Thess. $5^{15f.}$.

9–12. Those who have worked for an hour receive a full day's pay. Those who have worked for longer periods up to the full day receive the same, though only those who have worked twelve hours are explicitly mentioned. They feel that they are unjustly treated. If payment is at the rate of one denar for an hour's work, surely they should get twelve denars. Alternatively they should get what they bargained for, and the last-comers should get a twelfth of the amount. It is not right that those who have put in so little work should be made equal to those who have laboured so abundantly under the most trying conditions. The 'scorching heat' is the midday heat: the 'hot wind' of the mg. is not in place here. The objection of the labourers is based on human ideas of justice between man and man.

13–15. The reply of the householder is based not upon these considerations, but upon his own generosity. So far as justice goes there is no ground for complaint. Those who worked all day received the full day's pay. What they call justice is really envy and covetousness. The 'evil eye' is a common Rabbinical name for a mean and envious disposition, as the 'good eye' is for a generous and unselfish character. If the master chooses to be generous he can be, for he has already been just. In giving extra to the late-comers he deprives the others of nothing to which they are entitled. They have their just payment: let them take it and go.

16. So human estimates are reversed. This closing comment does not fit the parable. For the essence of the parable is not that the last become first and the first last, but that such terms as first and last cease to have any meaning. This verse is probably a comment by the Evangelist. Cf. 19^{30}.

With all explanations made that can be made this parable leaves one with the sense that if we consider the services rendered by the various sets of workmen, the policy of the householder is neither strict justice nor sound economics. To this it can only be replied that it is fortunate for most of us that God does not deal with us on the basis of strict justice and sound economics. In the last resort the rewards of such poor service as men can give to the Kingdom are not an exact *quid pro quo*. They are an expression of God's love towards His servants; and God's love cannot be portioned out in quantities nicely adjusted to the merits of individuals. There is such a thing as the twelfth part of a denar. It was called a *pondion*. But there is no such thing as a twelfth part of the love of God.

On Jewish views of service and reward see Moore, *Judaism*, ii. 89–111; Montefiore, *Rabbinic Literature and Gospel Teachings*, pp. 285–299; Billerbeck, iv. 484–500.

H. THE REFUSERS

Cf. the Q passages collected under D2, above, pp. 416–422. The passages to be considered under this head are two parables: the Two Sons (21^{28-32}), and the Marriage Feast (22^{1-14}). The former is peculiar to Mt.; the latter has a parallel in Lk. 14^{16-24}, which is assigned to Q. In addition to these there is a saying connected with the cleansing of the Temple (21^{14-16}), which may be considered in this connexion; and a pair of comments, probably the Evangelist's own work (21^{43}, 22^{40}).

1. *THE OFFENCE OF ENTHUSIASM* (198)

MT. 21^{14-16}

21 14 And the blind and the lame came to him
15 in the temple: and he healed them. But
when the chief priests and the scribes saw
the wonderful things that he did, and
the children that were crying in the
temple and saying, Hosanna to the son
of David; they were moved with indigna-
16 tion, and said unto him, Hearest thou
what these are saying? And Jesus saith
unto them, Yea: did ye never read, Out
of the mouth of babes and sucklings thou
hast perfected praise?

With this passage we must compare Lk. $19^{39 f.}$ (L) where the enthusiasm of the crowd accompanying Jesus towards Jerusalem likewise comes under criticism:

LK. 19^{39-40}

19 39 And some of the Pharisees from the
multitude said unto him, Master, rebuke
40 thy disciples. And he answered and
said, I tell you that, if these shall hold
their peace, the stones will cry out.

The differences are considerable. In Lk. the incident takes place before the triumphal entry; in Mt. it comes after the cleansing of the Temple. In Mt. it is children who are full of enthusiasm; in Lk. the disciples. And the reply of Jesus in Mt. is quite different from that in Lk.

14, 15. The statement of this verse at once creates difficulties. For according to an ancient maxim the blind and the lame were excluded from the Temple. 'The blind and the lame shall not come into the house' (2 Sam. 5^8, R.V. mg.). How this maxim was understood is made plain by the Septuagint rendering: 'The blind and the lame shall not enter into the house of the Lord.' This rule is confirmed in the Mishnah (*Hagigah* 1^1; Danby, p. 211): 'All are subject to the command to *appear* [*before the Lord* (at the three great feasts)]; excepting a deaf-mute, an imbecile, a child, one of doubtful sex, one of double sex, women, slaves that have not been freed, a man that is lame or blind or sick or aged, and one that cannot go up [to Jerusalem] on his feet.' Cf. Acts $3^{2, 8}$. Further, Mk. records no healings in Jerusalem. This verse must consequently be regarded as untrustworthy. (See further, Dalman, *Sacred Sites and Ways*, pp. 288 ff.) The high priests and scribes take umbrage at the miracles and the shouting of the children. In Lk. it is 'some of the Pharisees' who object to the clamour of the disciples. It is to be noted that when the priests and scribes complain to Jesus, they say nothing about the miracles, but complain only about the shouting. This is a further indication that the reference to the healings is an insertion into the story.

16. 'Hearest thou what these are saying?' The implication is that Jesus ought to stop them. Their cries are seditious and revolutionary, calculated to lead to a breach of the peace. Besides, such behaviour in the Temple is far from reverent. If Jesus allows it to go on He must take responsibility for it. The answer of Jesus is 'Yes'—I do hear it and approve of it. This is fortified by an appeal to Scripture, Ps. 8^3. This quotation agrees with the LXX 'Out of the mouth of babes and sucklings thou hast prepared praise for thyself,' against the Hebrew: 'Out of the mouth of babes and sucklings thou hast established strength.' This fact tells strongly against the authenticity of the saying, and suggests that the scripture quotation has ousted the original reply as given in Lk. 19^{40}. The meaning of the quotation in this context is that the shouts of the children are by a kind of divine inspiration. Flesh and blood has not revealed to them that they should cry 'Hosanna to the son of David,' but the Father in heaven. Cf. Mt. 16^{17}. See further on Lk. $19^{39 f.}$, below, pp. 610 f.

2. *THE PARABLE OF THE TWO SONS* (203)

MT. 21^{28-32}

21 28 But what think ye? A man had two
sons; and he came to the first, and said,
29 [1] Son, go work to-day in the vineyard.
And he answered and said, I will not:
but afterward he repented himself, and
30 went. And he came to the second, and
said likewise. And he answered and
31 said, I *go*, sir: and went not. Whether
of the twain did the will of his father?
They say, The first. Jesus saith unto
them, Verily I say unto you, that the
publicans and the harlots go into the
32 kingdom of God before you. For John
came unto you in the way of righteousness, and ye believed him not: but the
publicans and the harlots believed him:
and ye, when ye saw it, did not even
repent yourselves afterward, that ye
might believe him.

[1] Gr. *Child*.

The passage falls into two parts: the parable proper and its meaning (28–31), and an explanation (32). The connexion between the two parts is artificial, for the explanation does not fit the parable. The religious authorities said 'No' to the call of John, and did not repent subsequently: the publicans and harlots said 'Yes,' and acted accordingly. Verse 32 has nothing to do with *vv.* 28–31, which form an independent and self-contained piece to be considered by itself.

Verses 28–31 present a very complicated textual problem, for they have come down to us in no fewer than three forms, each form supported by important manuscripts or versions. The three forms are as follows:

I. The first son says 'No' and repents: the second son says 'Yes' and does nothing. Who did the will of his father? The first.

II. The first son says 'No' and repents: the second son says 'Yes' and does nothing. Who did the will of his father? The second.

III. The first son says 'Yes' and does nothing: the second son says 'No' and repents. Who did the will of his father? The second.

I is the form adopted by Tischendorf and R.V. II is defended by Merx and Wellhausen. III is the text adopted by Westcott and Hort. There is no certain solution of the purely textual problem; but for the purposes of understanding the story the variations can be reduced to two: I and III against II. For I and III say the same thing in different words. They agree that it is the son who says 'No' and repents that does the father's will. Their version makes the priests and scribes condemn themselves. In II, on the other hand, the answer given is contrary to expectation. The son who says 'Yes' and does nothing is the one who does the father's will! Those who defend this text say that the priests and scribes see the point of the parable and deliberately give the wrong answer in order to avoid the inevitable application to themselves. The difficulty about this explanation is that Jesus goes on to make application as if they had given the right answer. This can only be met by arguing that the reply of Jesus is not the application of the parable but an outburst of indignation. The question whether the priests and scribes condemned themselves or not, which is the only question of interpretation, must remain an unsolved problem.

28–30. The words 'But what think ye?' link the parable on to the preceding section in Mt., in which the challenge to the authority of Jesus is met by the question about John's baptism: was it a divine institution or a human device

(Mt. 21^{23-27}||Mk. 11^{27-33})? The opening of the parable is similar to Lk. 15^{11}. The first son answers brusquely that he will not go. Afterwards he is sorry and goes. The father makes the same request to the other son. It has been argued against text III that the request to the second son is not necessary, if the first son has consented to go. But it would be a very small vineyard that had room only for one labourer. The second son answers very politely—in contrast to his brother—and does nothing further. The politeness is probably significant. The Greek word translated 'sir' is the same that is translated 'Lord' in Lk. 6^{46}: 'And why call ye me, Lord, Lord, and do not the things which I say?' Cf. Mt. 7^{21}.

31. The question is now put, and only one answer is possible to the question as put. For the question is who *did* the will of the father. The R.V. text (I) makes the priests and scribes give the correct answer. The reply of Jesus identifies the two sons. The son who first said 'No' and then repented stands for the 'publicans and harlots,' the typical representatives of the immoral and irreligious section of the community. The other son is the type of the priests and scribes, or of that section of them that maintained the outward appearance of piety without any real devotion to the will of God. There are several points of contact here with Mt. 7^{21}.

MT. 7^{21}

7 21 Not every one that saith unto me, *Lord, Lord,* shall *enter into the kingdom* of heaven; but he that *doeth the will of* my *Father* which is in heaven.

MT. $21^{30 f.}$

21 30 f. I go, *Sir.*

Publicans and harlots *go into the kingdom* of God before you.

Whether of the twain *did the will* of his *father*?

32. A separate saying which Mt. has made into a comment on the parable. Actually it is a saying about John the Baptist with a parallel in Lk. $7^{29 f.}$:

7 29 And all the people when they heard, and the publicans, justified God, being baptized with the baptism of John. But the Pharisees and the lawyers rejected for themselves the counsel of God, being not baptized of him.

'John came unto you in the way of righteousness' means 'he came with the way,' i.e. he brought it and showed it to you. The way of righteousness is the demand for repentance and reformation which John preached. In Lk. it is called 'the counsel of God.' But John's message found no response among the religious leaders. His converts were drawn from the publicans and harlots (Mt.) or 'the people and the publicans' (Lk.) And even the testimony of the amended lives of the outcasts was not enough to convince the priests and scribes that John was sent from God and had a message for them.

An Editorial Addition

MT. $21^{43, [44]}$

21 43 Therefore say I unto you, The kingdom of God shall be taken away from you, and shall be given to a nation bringing
44 forth the fruits thereof. [1] And he that falleth on this stone shall be broken to pieces: but on whomsoever it shall fall, it will scatter him as dust.

[1] Some ancient authorities omit ver. 44.

43. This verse is probably to be regarded as an editorial comment of Mt., making the application of the parable of the Wicked Husbandmen. It has no parallel in Mk. or Lk., and it does not fit the parable itself. For the parable threatens the wicked husbandmen with destruction, not merely with dispossession. Further, *v.* 43 clashes with *v.* 45. After the very pointed explanation of the parable given in *v.* 43, it seems superfluous to say that the priests and Pharisees perceived that the parable was directed at them. The 'nation' that is to succeed to the Kingdom is probably the Church, the new Israel.

44. This verse is generally regarded as an early interpolation into Mt. from Lk. 20^{18}. It is omitted by several early authorities for the text; and it is out of place here. It ought to stand before *v.* 43. See on Lk. 20^{18}, below, p. 614.

3. *THE PARABLE OF THE MARRIAGE FEAST* (205)

MT. 22^{1-14}

22 1 And Jesus answered and spake again
2 in parables unto them, saying, The kingdom of heaven is likened unto a certain
king, which made a marriage feast for
3 his son, and sent forth his [2] servants to call
them that were bidden to the marriage
4 feast: and they would not come. Again
he sent forth other [2] servants, saying, Tell
them that are bidden, Behold, I have
made ready my dinner: my oxen and my
fatlings are killed, and all things are
5 ready: come to the marriage feast. But
they made light of it, and went their
ways, one to his own farm, another to his
6 merchandise: and the rest laid hold on
his [1] servants, and entreated them shame-
7 fully, and killed them. But the king was
wroth; and he sent his armies, and destroyed those murderers, and burned their
8 city. Then saith he to his [1] servants, The
wedding is ready, but they that were
9 bidden were not worthy. Go ye therefore unto the partings of the highways,
and as many as ye shall find, bid to the
10 marriage feast. And those [1] servants
went out into the highways, and gathered
together all as many as they found, both
bad and good: and the wedding was
11 filled with guests. But when the king
came in to behold the guests, he saw
there a man which had not on a wedding-
12 garment: and he saith unto him, Friend,
how camest thou in hither not having a
13 wedding-garment? And he was speechless. Then the king said to the [2] servants,
Bind him hand and foot, and cast him
out into the outer darkness; there shall be
14 the weeping and gnashing of teeth. For
many are called, but few chosen.

[1] Gr. *bondservants*. [2] Or, *ministers*.

The first part of the parable (*vv.* 1–10) corresponds to Lk. 14^{15-24} (see above, pp. 420 ff.). Verses 11–14 are peculiar to Mt. They are best explained as part of another parable which Mt. has appended to *vv.* 1–10. But when we consider *vv.* 1–10, it is quite impossible to make a consistent story of it. The most glaring example is in *vv.* 4 and 8. In *v.* 4 the feast is ready, and in *v.* 8 it is still ready, although in the meantime armies have been mobilised, a punitive expedition sent against the city, murderers executed, and the city burned. On the other hand *vv.* 1–10 have definite points of contact with Lk. 14^{15-24}. These coincidences may be stated as follows: A man makes a feast. He sends for the guests, who will not come because they have other business to attend to. He cancels the original invitations and sends his servants to collect other guests from the streets. This is done and the feast takes place. The Matthæan story is shorter than the Lucan by the omission of the various excuses made by the first set of guests, and by giving only one expedition of the servants to collect new guests. The foundation of the Mt. parable is thus an abbreviated version of what is given in Lk.

The extra material in Mt. may now be considered. The feast is a marriage feast given by a king for his son. Servants are twice sent out to invite the guests. The first set are sent, it seems, to invite the guests before the feast is actually prepared. The second set go out when the feast is ready (as in Lk.); but the words of their message are peculiar to Mt. The servants are maltreated and killed. The king is angry and punishes the murderers.

Two explanations of this extra material are possible: interpolation or conflation. Against interpolation is the fact that when the supposed interpolations are put together they make the outline of a parable similar to Mk.'s parable of the Wicked Husbandmen (Mk. 12^{1-12}). It is therefore more probable that we have to do with the conflation of the original Q parable of the Great Feast with another parable of the same kind as Mk. 12^{1-12}. Cf. *The Teaching of Jesus*, pp. 83–86.

1. The words 'He spake in parables unto them' are characteristic of Mk. 'In parables,' Mk. 3^{23}, $4^{2, 11}$, 12^{1}.

2. The marriage feast for the king's son is a figure for the Messianic age with all its joys. Cf. Moore, *Judaism*, ii. 363 ff.; Rev. 19^{9}; 4 *Ezra* 2^{38-41}.

3 f. The twofold invitation is peculiar to Mt. We are told that it is still the custom in the East to issue a preliminary invitation to the guests, followed by a second when the feast is ready. If the detail may be pressed the first invitation will correspond to the mission of the great prophets, the second to that of Jesus and the Apostles. The invited guests are then the recalcitrant Jews. They reject both invitations. The plural 'servants' in both cases, as against Lk.'s 'servant' will correspond to the prophets and Apostles (both plural). For the terms of the message in *v.* 4 cf. Prov. 9^{1-6}. 'All things are ready': R. Akiba used to say, 'All is made ready for the banquet' in the world to come (*Aboth* 3^{16}; Danby, p. 452). Cf. Rev. 19^{17}.

5. This verse appears to summarise what is given in Lk. $14^{18f.}$.

6. Who are 'the rest'? The abrupt introduction of these persons suggests that we have here a change of sources. It may be surmised that the original parable told how the guests set upon the servants. But Mt. following the Q parable in *v.* 5 has already described the behaviour of the guests in that story. In the Q story the guests merely decline to come: in the M story they maltreat the messengers. Mt. adopts the simplest expedient. In the new composite parable some of the guests simply decline and 'the rest' maltreat the servants and kill them. Cf. Mt. 23^{29-36}, 5^{10-12}.

7. This verse is commonly taken to be an interpolation by the Evangelist, a prophecy after the event, referring to the downfall of Jerusalem in A.D. 70; but the statement is in quite general terms and is in agreement with such passages as Lk. $13^{34f.}$ (Q); Mk. 12^{9}, etc. The explanation that it is the continuation of *v.* 6, from another parable, is to be preferred.

8 f. Mt. now returns to the parable of the Feast as told in Q. These verses give in an abbreviated form what is told by Lk. in 14^{21-24}. 'They that were bidden were not worthy' corresponds to Lk. 14^{24}: 'For I say unto you, that none of those men which were bidden shall taste of my supper.' 'The partings of the highways' (Lat. *exitus uiarum*) may be the places where the main roads of the city issue into the country round about, or street-junctions within the city. As the city has already

been burned in *v.* 7, perhaps Mt. means us to understand that the servants are to collect the refugees as they escape from the catastrophe, the Jews who avoid the fate of their recalcitrant brethren and become Christians. Cf. Acts 2^{40}.

10. The wedding can now take place. The hall for the banquet is filled with guests. Here Lk.'s parable comes to an end; but Mt. has still more to add. There is to be a further sifting of the guests (11–14), and the way is prepared for this additional matter by the statement that the guests comprise 'both bad and good.' Cf. the parables of the Wheat and Tares (Mt. 13^{24-30}) and the Net (13^{47-50}).

11–14. The conclusion of Mt.'s parable is very similar to a parable of R. Johanan ben Zakkai on the necessity of timely repentance. The Jewish parable is as follows (*Shabb.* 153^{a}): 'Like a king who invited his servants to a feast, and did not specify a time for them. The astute ones among them adorned themselves and sat at the gate of the palace. They said, "There is no lack in the palace" (consequently the feast may begin at any time). The foolish ones among them went to their work. They said, "There is no feast without preparation" (consequently it will not occur immediately). Suddenly the king asked for his servants. The astute ones among them came into his presence as they were, adorned; and the foolish ones came into his presence as they were, dirty. The king was pleased with the astute ones and angry with the foolish ones. He said, "Let these who adorned themselves for the feast sit down and eat and drink. Let those who did not adorn themselves for the feast stand and look on."' The moral is that men should live in this world in such a way that they may always be ready for the next.

11. The king comes in to 'behold' the guests. The Greek verb probably means no more than 'look in on' in the sense 'visit.' Cf. Rom. 15^{24}. He finds a man without a wedding-garment. The question may be asked: how could people just brought in at a moment's notice be expected to be dressed for the feast? This difficulty is sometimes met by the supposition that wedding-garments were issued to hastily invited guests as they entered the feast. But the complaint against the offender in *v.* 12 is not that he refused a wedding-garment but that he came in without one. Nor is this the only inconsistency. In *v.* 10 we are told that both good and evil persons were brought into the feast. But here we have only one guest who is to be expelled from the company. Why only one? It cannot be for the sake of the dialogue, for the offender when questioned has nothing to say. One is tempted to surmise that the one man of the parable is meant for some one person—a Judas, or (if party feeling ran high enough) a Paul? As early as Irenæus the wedding-garment is understood to signify works of righteousness.

12. The guest when taxed with his discourtesy is 'speechless.' The Greek verb here is a strong one used elsewhere of 'muzzling' an animal.

13. The king turns to the servants (the Greek word used here is different from that in *vv.* 1–10) and commands them to bind the offender hand and foot and cast him into the outer darkness. An early form of the text (D, old Latin, old Syriac, Irenæus) reads: 'Take him up by the hands and feet, etc.' The binding hand and foot would be in place if the 'outer darkness' is another name for Hell. If, however, the offender is merely to be excluded from the feast, the latter reading might be preferred. The 'outer darkness' is a phrase peculiar to Mt. (8^{12}, 22^{13}, 25^{30}). In Jewish literature 'darkness' appears to stand for

Gehenna. Cf. *Enoch* 103^{5-8}: ‘Woe to you, ye sinners, when ye have died. . . . Into darkness and chains and a burning flame where there is grievous judgement shall your spirits enter.’ Also *Ps. Sol.* 14^{6}, 15^{11}; *Orac. Sib.* 4^{43}; Rabbinical parallels in Billerbeck, iv. 1076 ff. It is probable that Mt.'s ‘outer darkness’ means the same, and that the binding is part of the picture. ‘There there shall be weeping and gnashing of teeth’ is a characteristic refrain in Mt. (8^{12}, $13^{42, 50}$, 22^{13}, 24^{51}, 25^{30}). It occurs once in Lk. (13^{28} Q); see notes above, p. 417. Whether we are meant to think of this refrain as the remark of the king or of Jesus or of Mt. is not clear.

14. This verse does not fit with what has just preceded. For in *vv.* 11–14 many are called, and all but one are chosen. Nor does it fit with *vv.* 1–10; for there many are called and none are chosen. It can be made to fit the whole composition, *vv.* 1–14, since out of all who are invited at various times only a part sit down to the banquet in the end. This shows that the verse is a comment added by the Evangelist who put the separate parables together. Whether it is a genuine saying of Jesus or not cannot be surely determined. It agrees with a good deal of His other teaching to this extent at least, that He has occasion to lament the fact that there are only too many who are called and will not hear the call. There are Jewish parallels to the saying in 4 *Ezra* 8^{3}: ‘Many have been created, but few shall be saved’; 9^{15}: ‘There are more who perish than shall be saved.’ Cf. *Apoc. Baruch* (Syr.) 44^{15}.

Editorial Comment (208)

MT. 22^{40}

In the section 22^{34-40} Mt. is following the corresponding section in Mk. 12^{28-34}, the question about the greatest commandment. He records the answer of Jesus that the first commandment of all is to love God, and the second to love one's neighbour. After giving this answer Mk. continues (12^{31b}): ‘There is none other commandment greater than these.’ He then goes on to tell of further conversation between Jesus and the enquirer ($12^{32ff.}$). Mt. drops *vv.* 32–34 entirely, and for Mk. 12^{31b} substitutes a conclusion of his own:

22 40 On these two commandments hangeth the whole law, and the prophets.

The Marcan conclusion asserts that no other commandment can take precedence of these two. That is, these two stand in a class by themselves. Mt.'s conclusion says something different, that these two commandments are the fundamental principles upon which all other commandments in Scripture are based. Mt. thus tacitly excludes the possibility of a clash between the two great commandments and the rest, whereas Mk. reckons with such a possibility and declares how it is to be decided. The Marcan version is the more original of the two: the Matthæan alteration is dictated by Jewish-Christian reverence for the Law.

I. THE SPEECH AGAINST PHARISAISM (210)

On the Q version of this speech (Lk. 11^{37-52}) see above, pp. 386–397. There it is argued that the greater part of the material in Mt. 23 is derived from M, though something has been added from both Mk. and Q. The last verses of the chapter (37–39) are undoubtedly from Q; and *v.* 23 is also probably from this source. There has been conflation of M and Q in other verses. Again, *vv.* 6–7 appear to be borrowed from Mk. 12[38 f.]. But the backbone of the chapter is M. The chapter may be divided as follows: (1) Denunciation of the pride and hypocrisy of scribes and Pharisees (1–7). (2) Warning to the disciples not to be like them (8–12). (3) Seven woes against the scribes and Pharisees (13–36). Prophecy concerning Jerusalem (37–39).

1. *DENUNCIATION OF SCRIBES AND PHARISEES*

MT. 23[1-7]

23 1 Then spake Jesus to the multitudes and
2 to his disciples, saying, The scribes and the
3 Pharisees sit on Moses' seat: all things
therefore whatsoever they bid you, *these* do
and observe: but do not ye after their
4 works; for they say, and do not. Yea,
they bind heavy burdens [1] and grievous
to be borne, and lay them on men's
shoulders; but they themselves will not
5 move them with their finger. But all their
works they do for to be seen of men: for
they make broad their phylacteries, and
6 enlarge the borders *of their garments*, and
love the chief place at feasts, and the chief
7 seats in the synagogues, and the salutations in the marketplaces, and to be called of men, Rabbi.

[1] Many ancient authorities omit *and grievous to be borne.*

1. The opening part of the speech is addressed to the general public and the disciples. It is not spoken to the scribes and Pharisees but at them. Only at *v.* 13 does direct address to the religious leaders begin. Mk. 12[38] has: 'And in his teaching he said,' again speaking not to the scribes and Pharisees but to the general public. Mt.'s addition of the disciples is important. The rules laid down are to hold for the Church.

2. 'The scribes and Pharisees sit on Moses' seat.' This has hitherto been explained as a figure of speech, meaning that the scribes and Pharisees are the constituted authorities for determining the Law, just as Moses was in his day. They are the guardians of the tradition handed down from the days of Moses. Cf. *Aboth* 1[1-12], where the chain of tradition is traced from Moses to Hillel and Shammai (Danby, pp. 446 f.). Recent archæological work in Palestine shows that the 'Seat of Moses' was no mere figure of speech, but a part of the furniture of the Synagogue. "The first 'Seat of Moses' was unearthed at Hammath-by-Tiberias, and was followed by another at Chorazin. We know that whereas the congregation sat on the stone benches that are still found along the side walls of many of the ancient synagogues, or else on mats on the floor, 'the elders' sat 'with their faces to the people and their backs to the Holy (i.e. to Jerusalem).' It was evidently for the most distinguished among 'the elders' that the stone chair found *near the south wall* of the Hammath synagogue was reserved. This was no doubt 'the Seat of Moses'" (E. L. Sukenik, *Ancient Synagogues in Palestine and Greece*, pp. 58 f., where a most interesting account of these seats (with illustrations) is given). The Seat of Moses is thus the visible tangible sign of the authority which the scribes and Pharisees enjoyed.

3. This authority is here recognised as binding upon the disciples, who might well feel embarrassed by the number of authorities established in M—Peter

(16^{19}), the Church or the Twelve (18^{18}), and now the scribes and Pharisees. It is hardly possible to believe that if Jesus said to the scribes and Pharisees: ‘ Ye leave the commandment of God, and hold fast the tradition of men ’ and ‘ Ye reject the commandment of God that ye may keep your tradition ’ (Mk. $7^{8f.}$), He could also have set up the scribes and Pharisees as authorities for His disciples. ‘ Do not after their works,’ i.e. do not be like them. ‘ They say and do not ’ appears to be a proverbial expression in Aramaic (*Ber. Rabba* on Gen. 21^{1}, ed. Theodor, p. 555). The importance of ‘ doing ’ the Law is stressed also by the Rabbis. Simeon, the son of Gamaliel, says: ‘ Not the expounding [of the Law] is the chief thing but the doing [of it] ’ (*Aboth* 1^{17}, Danby, p. 447). R. Eleazar b. Azariah (*c.* 50–120) used to say: ‘ He whose wisdom is more abundant than his works, to what is he like? To a tree whose branches are abundant but whose roots are few; and the wind comes and uproots it and overturns it. . . . But he whose works are more abundant than his wisdom, to what is he like? To a tree whose branches are few but whose roots are many; so that even if all the winds in the world come and blow against it, it cannot be stirred from its place ’ (*Aboth* 3^{18}, Danby, p. 452). The question continued to be a live issue in Judaism. ‘ R. Tarphon and the Elders were once sitting in an upper chamber in the house of Nitzah in Lydda; the following question was propounded before them: Which is the greater, study or practice? R. Tarphon answered and said: “ Practice is the greater.” R. Akiba answered and said: “ Study is the greater.” All [the others] answered and said: “ Study is the greater, because study induces practice ” ’ (*Kidd.* 40b). In the case of Akiba that was certainly true: and in many other cases besides. But there is clear evidence in the Rabbinical literature itself that study did not always induce practice. Neither in Judaism nor in any other religion is theological learning a guarantee of sanctity. And there was always the danger in Judaism—and not in Judaism only—that men would be so engrossed in the *minutiæ* of the Law that they would have no time for the central principles which were its true *raison d'être*.

4. In Q (Lk. 11^{46}, above, p. 392) this verse appears as the first woe against the scribes. The Greek word translated ‘ grievous to be borne ’ is omitted by many ancient authorities for the text of Mt. It may be an intrusion from Lk. 11^{46}. The collocation ‘ heavy ’ and ‘ hard to bear ’ occurs in Prov. 27^{3}. ‘ Move ’ here probably = ‘ remove ’ (cf. Rev. 2^{5}, 6^{14}). See notes on Lk. 11^{46} (above, p. 392) and Lk. 16^{17} (above, p. 427). The charge against the scribes is that they are doctrinaire and conservative to the last degree. Precedents are more important to them than people.

5–7. These verses contain further charges, introduced by the statement that the scribes and Pharisees do all their works for show. Their ostentation is then described in terms which have a parallel in Mk. 12^{38-40}.

MK. 12^{38-40}

12 38 And in his teaching he said, Beware of
the scribes, which desire to walk in long
robes, and *to have* salutations in the
39 marketplaces, and chief seats in the
synagogues, and chief places at feasts:
40 they which devour widows' houses, and
for a pretence make long prayers; these
shall receive greater condemnation.

The common matter in the two accounts may be seen by a comparison in parallel columns.

MT.	MK.
(*a*) They make broad their phylacteries.	(1) They desire to walk in long robes.
(*b*) They enlarge the borders (of their garments).	(2) And (to have) salutations in the marketplaces.
(*c*) They love the chief place at feasts.	(3) And chief seats in the synagogues.
(*d*) And the chief seats in the synagogues.	(4) And chief places at feasts.
(*e*) And the salutations in the marketplaces.	(5) Who devour widows' houses.
(*f*) And to be called of men, Rabbi.	(6) And for a pretence make long prayers.

In these two lists there are obvious correspondences: (*c*), (*d*), (*e*) = (4), (3), (2). There are equally obvious differences: (*f*) has no parallel in Mk., and (5) has no parallel in Mt. The remaining cases are (*a*) and (*b*) in Mt. and (1) and (6) in Mk. It has been suggested that (*a*) and (6) really correspond (cf. Burney, *Aramaic Origin of the Fourth Gospel*, p. 10 n.; Abrahams, *Studies* ii. 203 ff.). This depends on the fact that the Late Hebrew and Aramaic name for phylacteries (*tephillīn*) also means, in Hebrew, prayers. There is a similar ambiguity in the Aramaic word for 'broaden.' So it is argued that the Aramaic which means 'they make broad their phylacteries' could be also translated 'they make long their prayers.' It is most probable that the version in Mt. gives the original sense of the saying. What, then, is meant by broadening the phylacteries? The phylactery consisted of: (*a*) a small leather box containing certain texts of the Old Testament written on parchment; (*b*) a leather strap to which this box was attached. Two phylacteries were worn, one on the head, the other on the left arm. (Full description in Billerbeck, iv. 250–276.) If 'make broad' is to be taken in the literal sense it must mean broadening the strap. But not very much could be done in this way. Alternatively the enlarging of the phylacteries might be understood to mean increasing, not the phylacteries themselves, but the wearing of them. The time to wear phylacteries, in the Rabbinical ideal, is all day and every day except Sabbaths and Festivals. But exceptions were allowed in certain cases. What was regarded as absolutely essential was that the pious Jew should wear them at the time of his morning and evening devotions; and it is significant that the *Letter of Aristeas* (§ 158) and Josephus (*Ant.* iv. 212 f.) mention them in the same context as these daily devotions. Along with this goes the fact (Billerbeck, iv. 264) that the Rabbis found the general mass of the people unwilling to rise to their demands in the matter of wearing phylacteries. This suggests that originally the time for wearing them may have been the times of morning and evening prayer, and that it was the Rabbis who extended the wearing to all day. In that case it may be this extension that is criticised in our text.

There remain two counts in the indictment: (*b*) 'They enlarge the borders (of their garments)' and (1) 'They desire to walk in long robes.' Again it is possible that these two are equivalent. The 'borders' (*kraspeda*) are usually taken to be the tassels (*ṣīṣīōth*) ordained in the Law (Num. $15^{38ff.}$; Dt. 22^{12}). These tassels were to be fixed at the four corners of the rectangular shawl used as an outer garment (Billerbeck, iv. 277–292). As no maximum length was prescribed for these decorations, those who wished to make a display of piety might make the tassels as long as they pleased. The 'long robe' in Mk. (*stolē*) is the Jewish *ṭallīth*, the outer garment of all classes of the community. The scribe was distinguished from ordinary people by the voluminousness of his *ṭallīth*, and the way he wore it. Properly the time to wear this garment was at prayer, and in the performance of certain other duties of the scribes (Billerbeck, ii. 31 ff.). The Marcan passage complains that the scribe *walks about* in his *ṭallīth*. The Matthæan version says that he 'enlarges the borders.' This may mean that he lengthens the tassels; but it is much more naturally understood of the enlargement of the garment itself. The common root of Mt. and Mk. might then be a saying against those ostentatiously pious who loved to parade their voluminous prayer-shawls.

If these suggestions are correct, (*a*) and (*b*) and (1) and (6) belong together. They are a protest against the Rabbinic tendency to make the wearing of the phylacteries and the prayer-shawl a constant practice outside the set times for prayer; a protest against the idea that a man becomes specially devout by perpetually wearing the uniform of devotion. It is suggested that this going about continually dressed as if for prayer is a kind of hypocrisy.

It may be further concluded that (*a*) and (*b*) in Mt. have come by a line of tradition independent of Mk. That is, they are assigned to M. The next three items in Mt.—(*c*), (*d*), (*e*)—may be derived from Mk.

'The chief places at feasts' were given, according to later Rabbinical rule, to the oldest guests. Precedence was by age. But the earlier practice gave precedence to the most learned. That precedence in banquets was highly esteemed is shown by Lk. 14^{7-11}. On the 'chief seats in the synagogues' see notes on *v.* 2, above, p. 520. 'Salutations in the marketplaces': see notes on Lk. 11^{43}, above, p. 391. 'To be called of men, Rabbi' may be regarded as a doublet of 'Salutations in the marketplaces.' It is the M equivalent of the Marcan phrase. Mt. has kept both the Marcan and M forms because the latter is necessary as the introduction to what follows in *v.* 8. 'Rabbi' is an honorific form of address equivalent to 'Sir.' The nearest parallel in English usage is the custom of addressing judges of the High Court, when on the bench, as 'My Lord,' although they are not usually peers. Later the word becomes the regular title of the Palestinian teachers of the Law.

2. *WARNING TO THE DISCIPLES*

MT. 23^{8-12}

23 8 But be not ye called Rabbi: for one is
your teacher, and all ye are brethren.
9 And call no man your father on the
earth: for one is your Father, [1] which is
10 in heaven. Neither be ye called masters:
for one is your master, *even* the Christ.
11 But he that is [2] greatest among you shall
12 be your [3] servant. And whosoever shall
exalt himself shall be humbled; and whosoever shall humble himself shall be
exalted.

[1] Gr. *the heavenly.*
[2] Gr. *greater.*
[3] Or, *minister.*

8. There is no room in the community of the disciples for the distinctions used in Judaism. The use of the passive rather than the active voice of the verb is

significant. What is forbidden is not the desire to show respect to a brother, but the desire to have it shown to oneself by the brethren. Such titles are a danger because they can so easily produce spiritual pride. That is the practical consideration. There is further—and this is the vital matter—a fundamental objection in principle. The community knows no human authorities: God is the teacher. The idea goes back to the Old Testament and in particular to the prophetic literature and the Psalms. It appears in the terms of the New Covenant: 'I will put my law in their inward parts, and in their heart will I write it; and I will be their God, and they shall be my people: and they shall teach no more every man his neighbour, and every man his brother, saying, Know the Lord: for they shall all know me, from the least of them unto the greatest of them, saith the Lord' (Jer. $31^{33f.}$). 'And all thy children shall be disciples of Jehovah' (Is. 54^{13}).

9. 'Father' (*abba*) as an honorific title belongs pre-eminently to the three patriarchs, Abraham, Isaac, and Jacob. Certain specially distinguished Rabbis are also called 'Fathers of the world,' e.g. Hillel and Shammai (*Eduyoth* 1^4, Danby, p. 422). Further, the title Abba is prefixed to the names of a considerable number of first- and second-century Rabbis (Billerbeck, i. 919). And we have the principle in *Sifre* Dt. § 34: 'As the disciples are called 'Sons,' so the teacher (*Rab*) is called 'Father' (*Ab*).' It is not certain how the saying is to be translated. Besides the R.V. rendering, the following is possible: 'Call no one of your number "Father" on earth.' '*Abba*' is the name for God, and is to be kept for Him. It is not to be given to members of the community. The words 'which is in heaven' (R.V. mg. 'the heavenly') are an unnecessary explanation by the Evangelist, who has also added the words 'on the earth' to complete the picture. The original form of the saying was, I think: 'Call no one of your number "Father": for one is your Father,' corresponding in form to *v.* 8. It is possible that the words 'And all ye are brethren,' at the end of *v.* 8, should stand at the end of *v.* 9; but the weight of MS. authority is against this change.

10. 'Masters': the Greek word (*kathēgētēs*) occurs only here in the New Testament. It means in the first instance 'guide' and then 'teacher' 'instructor.' In Modern Greek it means 'professor.' Its meaning in the present context may be elucidated by the fact that Josephus and Philo respectively use the cognate words *exēgētēs* and *hyphēgētēs* when speaking of the Rabbis as interpreters of the Law. What Mt. means to say may therefore be that Christ is the sole interpreter of the will of God to men. And Jesus certainly appears in that capacity in Mt.'s Sermon on the Mount, particularly in Mt. 5^{17-48} and 6^{1-18}. Many modern scholars reject *v.* 10 as a doublet of *v.* 8. It may be an attempt of Mt. or his source to find a place for Christ as an authority in the Church, seeing that *vv.* 8 f. refer to God alone. On the other hand, the Gospels are full of the authority with which Jesus taught, and there can be no doubt that He did claim the right to make known the will of God. It is therefore possible that *v.* 10 is a genuine saying of Jesus, except for the words 'the Christ,' which may be regarded as an explanatory comment.

11 f. These two verses have parallels elsewhere in the Gospels. They are brought in here as warnings against pride and rivalry within the community. With *v.* 11 cf. Mk. 9^{35}||Lk. 9^{48}; Mk. $10^{43f.}$||Mt. $20^{26f.}$; Lk. 22^{26} (L?). In all these

cases the saying is the answer of Jesus to manifestations of personal ambition among His disciples. With *v.* 12 cf. Mt. 18^4 (above, p. 499); Lk. 14^{11}, 18^{14} (below, pp. 571, 604). The saying, which is doubtless a genuine saying of Jesus, has excellent parallels in the Rabbinical literature: 'God will exalt him who humbles himself, God will humble him who exalts himself' (*Erubin* 13^b). Further examples in Montefiore (*op. cit.*, pp. 328 f.).

3. *THE WOES AGAINST SCRIBES AND PHARISEES*

(i) MT. 23^{13}

23 13 But woe unto you, scribes and Pharisees, hypocrites! because ye shut the kingdom of heaven [1] against men: for ye enter not in yourselves, neither suffer ye them that are entering in to enter.[2]

[1] Gr. *before.*

[2] Some authorities insert here, or after ver. 12, ver. 14, *Woe unto you, scribes and Pharisees, hypocrites! for ye devour widows' houses, even while for a pretence ye make long prayers: therefore ye shall receive greater condemnation.* See Mark xii. 40; Luke xx. 47.

This corresponds to the third Q woe against the lawyers (Lk. 11^{52}, above, p. 395). In spite of the difference of wording, the sense in both versions of the woe is the same. See the notes on Lk. 11^{52}.

Some MSS. insert either before *v.* 13 or after it an additional woe based on Mk. 12^{40}. The uncertainty in the placing of this extra verse is a sign that it is an interpolation. It is omitted by the leading authorities for the text, and rejected by modern editors.

(ii) MT. 23^{15}

23 15 Woe unto you, scribes and Pharisees, hypocrites! for ye compass sea and land to make one proselyte; and when he is become so, ye make him twofold more a son of [1] hell than yourselves.

[1] Gr. *Gehenna.*

The outstanding characteristics of Judaism, in contrast to contemporary pagan religion, were its strong monotheism and its high ethical standard. Social and political factors made it impossible for these things to be hid from the Gentile nations. The Jews were scattered all over the civilised world of those days; and wherever they were present in sufficient numbers they founded a synagogue. These synagogues of the Dispersion became the centres of strong Jewish propaganda, and inevitably attracted to themselves thoughtful Gentiles, who had become disgusted with the old myths and felt that if a God was to be adored, he must first be respected and reverenced. The synagogues drew those who were perplexed and disquieted by the moral laxity of the age. In Judaism they found a God who was Himself holy, who also demanded holiness of His votaries; who was righteous, and required righteousness; who was merciful, and demanded mercy. The result was that the synagogues of the Dispersion gathered round themselves a fringe of earnest and thoughtful Gentiles who came to be known as the 'God-fearing' (Gr. *Sebomenoi*; Lat. *Metuentes*). These people were not proselytes in the full sense. They were not members of the synagogue, but adherents, who worshipped the God of the Jews and tried to live up to the moral standards of Judaism. Full membership of the Jewish community required further steps to be taken. (1) The convert must be further instructed in the Jewish Law, and must accept it in its entirety. (2) A male convert must be circumcised. (3) All converts must submit to the proselyte bath. (4) The proselyte must offer sacrifice in the Temple at Jerusalem. Only a certain proportion of the God-fearers were prepared to take these final steps, and only those who did so were proselytes in the true sense of the word. The proselyte was thus a full Jew, and differed from other Jews in this only, that he was a Jew by conversion and not by birth. See Moore, *Judaism* i. 323–353; Juster, *Les Juifs dans l'Empire Romain* i. 253–290; Lake, *Beginnings of Christianity*, v. 74–96. Parkes, *The Conflict of the Church and the Synagogue*, pp. 23–26. The scribes and Pharisees make all efforts to obtain converts to Judaism.

'A son of Gehenna' should naturally mean one who is destined for Gehenna as 'son of the world to come' means one who is destined for heaven. It may be supposed that, as is often the case, the converts tended to be even more zealous than their teachers, more Pharisaic than the Pharisees.

(iii) MT. 23^{16-22}

23 16 Woe unto you, ye blind guides, which
say, Whosoever shall swear by the
[1] temple, it is nothing; but whosoever
shall swear by the gold of the [1] temple, he
17 is [2] a debtor. Ye fools and blind: for
whether is greater, the gold, or the
[1] temple that hath sanctified the gold?
18 And, Whosoever shall swear by the altar,
it is nothing; but whosoever shall swear
by the gift that is upon it, he is [2] a debtor.
19 Ye blind: for whether is greater, the gift,
or the altar that sanctifieth the gift?
20 He therefore that sweareth by the altar,
sweareth by it, and by all things thereon.
21 And he that sweareth by the [1] temple,
sweareth by it, and by him that dwelleth
22 therein. And he that sweareth by the
heaven, sweareth by the throne of God,
and by him that sitteth thereon.

[1] Or, *sanctuary*: as in ver. 35.
[2] Or, *bound* by his oath.

This woe is peculiar to Mt. The passage falls into two parts (*vv.* 16–19 and 20–22). The first part is criticism of the distinctions made between oaths; the second a positive assertion that all the forms of oath used are, in the last resort, swearing by God. This latter part has points in common with Mt. 5^{33-37}.

16. 'Blind guides': cf. Mt. 15^{14}, where the Pharisees are described as 'blind guides of the blind,' and Lk. 6^{39}, with notes, above, p. 349. The 'blind guides' here take the place of the 'scribes and Pharisees' of the other woes. It is possible that this passage was not a woe at all originally, but a piece of criticism which has been turned into a woe by Mt. or his source.

'Whosoever shall swear.' The Mishnah (*Nedarim* 1^{3}, Danby, p. 264) contradicts the statement in this verse. But the contradiction is only in appearance; for the Mishna is dealing with vows, and this passage is concerned with oaths. The vow and the oath are two quite distinct things, and are carefully distinguished in Jewish writings. The Greek verb translated 'swear' in Mt. is used in the LXX to translate the Hebrew verb *shāba'*, 'to swear,' but *never* to translate the Hebrew *nādar*, 'to take a vow.' There does not appear to be any Rabbinical testimony either to confirm or to contradict the statements in Mt. $23^{16, 18}$ concerning the validity of the various forms of oath there described. The gold of the temple might mean either the contents of the temple treasury or the golden utensils and decorations of the temple; probably the latter. The phrase 'it is nothing' and 'he is a debtor' signify 'the oath is not binding' and 'the oath is binding' respectively.

17. An oath 'by gold' is not binding: an oath 'by the gold of the temple' is. It is obvious that it is the temple that differentiates this gold from all other gold. The important thing is not that it is gold but that it is *temple* gold. That is, the temple matters more than the gold.

18 f. A similar case to that in *vv.* 16 f. There is nothing sacrosanct about a lamb or a bullock in itself. It acquires a certain sacredness by being laid upon the altar. So in the Mishnah (*Zebahim* 9[1], Danby, p. 481): 'The Altar makes holy whatsoever is prescribed as its due.' This again means that the altar is more important than the offering.

20. This verse goes with 21 f. The object of the two latter verses is to show that the mere fact that the name of God is not mentioned in taking an oath counts for nothing. The substitution of something else for the Divine name is an evasion, for all the time it is God who is thought of, though it is only something connected with God that is mentioned. That being so, it may be suspected that there is something wrong with *v.* 20. What we should expect is: 'He therefore that sweareth by the altar, sweareth by it, and by Him to whom offering is made thereon' or something else to the same effect. There is no point in the verse as it stands; for it has just been argued in *vv.* 18 f. that the things offered on the altar have no significance apart from the altar. It may be conjectured that the original form of the saying had something like 'sweareth by it, and by Him that is above it,' i.e. by God.

21 f. The significance of the temple in an oath is that it is thought of as the temple of God, the place where God dwells. Similarly, heaven is significant as the throne of God. The temple as God's house and heaven as His throne are Old Testament ideas. See further the notes on Mt. 5^{33-37}, above, pp. 450 f.

(iv) MT. 23^{23-24}

23 23 Woe unto you, scribes and Pharisees, hypocrites! for ye tithe mint and [1]anise and cummin, and have left undone the weightier matters of the law, judgement, and mercy, and faith: but these ye ought to have done, and not to have left the
24 other undone. Ye blind guides, which strain out the gnat, and swallow the camel.

[1] Or, *dill.*

23. This verse has a parallel in Lk. 11^{42} (Q). On the relation of the two versions of the woe see above, pp. 389 f. In Mt.'s list of things tithed the mint probably comes from Q, and the dill and cummin from M. Mint was not liable to tithe; dill and cummin were. In that case the M form of the woe is a protest against the meticulous fulfilment of legal trifles, and the neglect of vital matters. The 'weightier matters' are the more important matters. R. Judah the Patriarch said: 'Be heedful of a light precept as of a weighty one, for thou knowest not the recompense of reward of each precept' (*Aboth* 2[1], Danby, p. 447). The three essentials, judgement, mercy, and faith, are reminiscent of the classical statement of prophetic religion in Mic. 6[8]: 'He hath showed thee, O man, what is good; and what doth the Lord require of thee, but to do justly, and to love mercy, and to walk humbly with thy God?' Humble walking with God is just what in Judaism is meant by 'faith,' a combination of trustful obedience to God's commandments and humble confidence in His good promises. Such faith is the religious root of

the right relation to one's neighbour described as judgement and mercy. Faith puts man in the right relation to God; judgement and mercy put him in the right relation to his neighbour. And the exercise of judgement and mercy is, in a sense, an imitation of God; for the two great attributes of God in Jewish thought are the attributes of justice (*middath ha-dīn*) and the attribute of mercy (*middath hā-rachămīm*).

These, the weightier matters of the Law, you ought to have done, and not to have left the other, the lighter matters, undone. The tithing of dill and cummin was obligatory; but justice, mercy, and faith take precedence. The sentence appears in Lk. 11[42] (Q), but is probably an interpolation there. (See notes, above, p. 390.) Here it is more in place; but it may be doubted whether it is a genuine word of Jesus. It is rather an editorial attempt to let the polemic of Jesus have its full effect against the scribes and Pharisees, and at the same time save the Law and the tradition from attack. Jesus must not appear to be antinomian, however strongly he may attack the lawyers.

24. 'Blind guides,' as in *v.* 16. The straining out of gnats refers to the practice of straining wine through a cloth or fine wicker basket (Mishnah, *Shabbath* 20[2], Danby, p. 117). It appears from the Talmud (*Chullin* 67[a]) that an insect called by the Jews *Yabchush* was thus removed from the wine, and there is evidence that it was believed that this creature was generated in the dregs of wine and in the mass of pressed grapes in the wine-press (Bochart, *Opera*, iii. 562 ff.). The ground for filtering the wine so carefully is Lev. 11[41]: 'And every creeping thing that creepeth upon the earth is an abomination; it shall not be eaten.' But the camel also is an unclean beast (Lev. 11[4]). The saying then pillories the elaborate precautions taken in minor matters and the carelessness about big things. Like other sayings in the Gospels it is frankly hyperbolical.

Mt. 23[23 f.] differs from Lk. 11[42] (Q) in this, that the latter is a charge against some hypocritical Pharisees that they do things not required by the Law in order to gain a reputation for great piety; while the charge in Mt. is that hypocritical scribes and Pharisees devote themselves to the minutiæ of the Law and neglect the more important matters.

(v) MT. 23[25-26]

23 25 Woe unto you, scribes and Pharisees, hypocrites! for ye cleanse the outside of the cup and of the platter, but within they are full from extortion and excess.

26 Thou blind Pharisee, cleanse first the inside of the cup and of the platter, that the outside thereof may become clean also.

This woe has a parallel in Lk. 11[39-41] (L) where it is not a woe but a criticism of the Pharisees. The version in Mt. is the simpler of the two: it confines itself strictly to the question of the ritual cleanness of vessels. This vast and complicated subject is treated in the Mishnah tractate *Kelim*. In chapter 25 of this tractate (Danby, pp. 640 ff.) the distinction between the outside and the inside of utensils is made. The chief question in this woe is whether the whole is to be taken literally, or whether the cup and the platter are used figuratively of the scribes and Pharisees themselves. The latter view seems to be preferable (*a*) in view of the following woe in Mt. *vv.* 27 f.; and (*b*) in view of the context of the Lucan parallel (Lk. 11[37-41]).

25. The scribes and Pharisees are very particular about ritual purity, not only of vessels but also of their own persons. But just as a ritually clean vessel may be full of poison, so a ritually clean person may be full of ' extortion and excess.' The word translated ' excess ' means properly ' incontinence.'

26. Any effective cleansing must begin from within. Cf. Mk. 7^{18-23}. The figure of the cup is maintained as in the previous verse. The words ' and of the platter ' are omitted in this verse by important early authorities. It is probable that they are an interpolation to bring *v.* 26 into agreement with *v.* 25. See further on Lk. $11^{39ff.}$, below, p. 561.

(vi) MT. 23^{27-28}

23 27 Woe unto you, scribes and Pharisees, hypocrites! for ye are like unto whited sepulchres, which outwardly appear beautiful, but inwardly are full of dead
28 men's bones, and of all uncleanness. Even so ye also outwardly appear righteous unto men, but inwardly ye are full of hypocrisy and iniquity.

27. This woe has a parallel in Lk. 11^{44} (Q). See above, p. 391. The whitewashing of sepulchres took place in the spring. The date appointed in the Mishnah (*Shekalim* 1^1, Danby, p. 152) is 15th Adar (Adar approximately = March). The object of this was to guard the people, especially the priests, against accidental defilement by contact with the tombs. The coat of whitewash thus acted as a warning to passers-by to keep their distance. This was its real purpose; and it is merely incidental that it gave a smart appearance to the tombs. ' Dead men's bones and all uncleanness ': the words ' all uncleanness ' doubtless emphasise the fact that the uncleanness of a corpse was reckoned the most pervasive and contagious of all kinds of uncleanness (Mishnah, *Kelim* 1^4, Danby, pp. 604 f.).

28. The application of the comparison. The scribes and Pharisees make a brave display of piety and goodness; but behind this imposing façade there is nothing but hypocrisy and iniquity. But the comparison breaks down at the vital point. For in this verse the outward appearance of righteousness is assumed in order to *conceal* the evil condition within; whereas the whitewashing of the tombs *advertises* the fact that they are full of corruption. The simplest solution of the contradiction is to suppose that the word ' whited ' in *v.* 27 should be deleted as a piece of mistaken antiquarianism, supplied by Mt. or some other early authority; and that the original reference has nothing to do with the whitewashing of tombs, but rather with the fact that the sepulchres of famous or wealthy persons were often elaborately built and carved. Thus, for example, Josephus, speaking of the sepulchres of the Patriarchs at Hebron (*Jewish War*, iv. 532), says, ' Their tombs are shown in this little town to this day, of really fine marble and of exquisite workmanship.' The contrast between the outward attractiveness and the inward corruption would then be complete, and the parallel perfect.

The Lucan woe is quite different, and probably independent. It does not seem probable that the two woes can be traced back to a common root; nor is there any means of saying with absolute certainty which is the more original. The Lucan form has the merit of brevity and simplicity; and the Matthæan may be an attempt to elaborate it.

(vii) MT. 23^{29-36}

23 29 Woe unto you, scribes and Pharisees,
hypocrites! for ye build the sepulchres of
the prophets, and garnish the tombs of
30 the righteous, and say, If we had been in
the days of our fathers, we should not
have been partakers with them in the
31 blood of the prophets. Wherefore ye
witness to yourselves, that ye are sons of
32 them that slew the prophets. Fill ye up
33 then the measure of your fathers. Ye
serpents, ye offspring of vipers, how shall
34 ye escape the judgement of [1]hell? Therefore, behold, I send unto you prophets,
and wise men, and scribes: some of them
shall ye kill and crucify; and some of
them shall ye scourge in your synagogues,
35 and persecute from city to city: that
upon you may come all the righteous
blood shed on the earth, from the blood
of Abel the righteous unto the blood of
Zachariah son of Barachiah, whom ye
slew between the sanctuary and the altar.
36 Verily I say unto you, All these things
shall come upon this generation.

[1] Gr. *Gehenna*.

This section, except for *vv.* 32–33, has a parallel in Lk. 11^{47-51}; see above, pp. 393 ff.

29. The words ' and garnish the tombs of the righteous ' do not appear in Lk. The conjunction of prophets and righteous men is characteristic of Mt.: cf. 10^{41}, 13^{17}. The insertion of the words here may be prompted by the fact that neither of the examples given in *v.* 35 was a prophet. It may be noted that Mt. has ' Abel the righteous ' where Lk. has only ' Abel.'

30 f. They perceive and condemn the wickedness of their ancestors; and they recognise the outstanding merits of those whom their ancestors persecuted. They are quick to champion causes that no longer need championship, to stand up in defence of reputations that are already assured. But the prophets suffered because they challenged the accepted beliefs and standards of their day. Their heresies are now orthodoxy. And scribes and Pharisees are as tenacious in defence of this new orthodoxy as their ancestors were in defence of what was orthodoxy in their day. The prophets are canonised; but woe betide anyone who ventures farther along the way that they marked out. The very spirit that leads scribes and Pharisees to build the tombs of the old prophets will make them dig the graves of new prophets.

32 f. No parallel in Lk. ' Fill ye up then the measure of your fathers ' is to be regarded as bitter irony, if the imperative is the true reading. The injunction means most probably: continue and bring to completion the evil work which your ancestors began. Destroy the messengers of God in your generation, as they did in theirs. When you have made your contribution the cup of Israel's iniquity will be full, and the judgement will come. How can you hope to escape it? These verses make the introduction to what follows. It is unlikely that they are a genuine utterance of Jesus. Verse 33 is an imitation of the saying of John the Baptist (Mk. 3^{7}||Lk. 3^{7}, Q). The verses may have stood in M or they may be Mt.'s editorial work effecting the transition from *v.* 31 to *v.* 34.

34. Mt. does not have the reference to the wisdom of God (Lk. 11^{49}). The oracle, *vv.* 34–36, thus appears not as a decree of God in His wisdom but as a decree of Jesus. The word ' therefore ' is probably to be regarded as looking forward to *v.* 35: ' It is for this reason that I send . . . namely, in order that upon you may come all the righteous blood. . . .' The sending of prophets to a people who will not receive them has its parallel in the Old Testament: e.g.

Jer. $7^{25 f.}$, 'Since the day that your fathers came forth out of the land of Egypt unto this day, I have sent unto you all my servants the prophets, daily rising up early and sending them: yet they hearkened not unto me, nor inclined their ear, but made their neck stiff: they did worse than their fathers.' Cf. Jer. $25^{4ff.}$. The order prophets, wise men, scribes is a little puzzling. Rabbinical Judaism would almost certainly have given the order: prophets, scribes, wise men. In the Mishnah the title 'scribes' is used for the authorities of earlier times. The 'sages' or 'wise men' are the contemporary authorities. On the other hand, in the New Testament the contemporary Jewish authorities are called 'scribes.' If then the text here has a purely backward reference, there is no difficulty about the prophets. They are the men whose teachings appear in the second division of the Hebrew canon. The most natural interpretation of 'wise men' will be that they were teachers such as those who appear in Proverbs or *Ecclesiasticus*. And the 'scribes' will be such men as Ezra, 'the men of the Great Synagogue,' and others enumerated in *Aboth* 1. But it is possible that the reference is not entirely to the past, but that it has some bearing on contemporary conditions. In that case the term 'prophets' would be extended to include such a man as John the Baptist. 'Wise men' would have the meaning of teachers of wisdom such as is found in Proverbs, etc. 'Scribes' might then be taken in another meaning: not as referring to the great legal authorities of the past but to religious teachers in the present. This use of the term is found in a saying of R. Eliezer ben Hyrcanus (*Sotah* 9^{15}, Danby, p. 306), where the scribes are teachers of religion and of lower rank than the Sages. It might then be conjectured that Mt. has in mind the order of *didaskaloi* or teachers in the Church. The scribes are the teachers in the Jewish-Christian community. Cf. Mt. 13^{52}: 'Therefore every scribe who hath been made a disciple to the kingdom of heaven is like unto a man that is a householder, which bringeth forth out of his treasure things new and old.' In favour of this latter interpretation is the fact that the context of the verse is a woe against scribes and Pharisees. It is therefore not likely that 'scribes' and 'wise men' in the ordinary Jewish sense of Rabbis will be represented as the chosen messengers of God. The easiest interpretation is that the envoys are prophets, teachers of wisdom, and Jewish-Christian teachers. And in that case it is clear that the text of Mt. is less original than that of Lk. See on Lk. 11^{49}, above, pp. 394 f.

The fate of God's envoys is described in much greater detail here than in Lk. This detail supports the interpretation just given and strengthens the suspicion that Mt. is expanding the shorter Lucan version in the light of the experience of the early Church. At the same time it is to be remembered that Jesus elsewhere spoke of the certainty of persecution for His disciples, and claimed that disciples must be ready to take up the cross. Yet 'kill and crucify' is awkward, the more so as crucifixion was not a Jewish but a Roman form of execution. Jews could only get disciples crucified by denouncing them to the Roman authorities on some charge punishable in that way under Roman Law. Cf. Mk. 13^{9}: 'Before governors and kings shall ye stand for my sake, for a testimony unto them.' The scourging in synagogues is a regular Jewish punishment, prescribed in Deut. $25^{2 f.}$. There the number of stripes is fixed at forty. In actual practice the maximum number inflicted was thirty-nine for any one offence. St. Paul relates that he suffered this punishment five times (2 Cor. 11^{24}). The regulations governing the punishment by scourging are given in the Mishnah tractate *Makkoth*, Danby, pp. 401–408. On the persecution from city to city see Mt. 10^{23}, above, p. 474.

35 f. See on Lk. $11^{50f.}$, above, pp. 394 f. 'That upon you may come all the righteous blood.' Cf. Mt. 27^{25}. The meaning is that the judgement for all these murders will come upon this generation. On Zachariah son of Barachiah see above, pp. 395 ff.

37–39. These verses are from Q; see above, pp. 418 ff.

J. ESCHATOLOGY

The eschatological matter peculiar to Mt. consists of (1) two brief insertions in Marcan contexts (Mt. 24^{10-12} and 24^{30a}), and (2) a long appendix to the Marcan eschatological chapter (13), containing the parable of the Ten Virgins (25^{1-13}), the parable of the Talents (25^{14-30}) and the picture of the Last Judgement (25^{31-46}).

1. *THE INSERTIONS IN MARCAN CONTEXTS*

(*a*) MT. 24^{10-12} (215)

24 10 And then shall many stumble, and shall deliver up one another, and shall
11 hate one another. And many false prophets shall arise, and shall lead many
12 astray. And because iniquity shall be multiplied, the love of the many shall wax cold.

This passage is inserted in Mt.'s version of what has come to be known as the 'Little Apocalypse.' It has already been argued that the Little Apocalypse does not represent the genuine teaching of Jesus, which is given rather in Lk. 17^{26-30}, above, pp. 435 f. It may be further suggested that two factors have contributed to shape the expectations of the early Church as we find them set down in Mk. 13^{5-31}. One is the necessity of accounting for the delay of the Parousia. And here the simplest expedient is to assert that the forces of evil must make one more final effort before the Kingdom of God is manifested in power. We find this explanation in use as early as 2 Thess. 2^{1-12}. (I am inclined to regard 2 Thess. as a genuine epistle of Paul and prior in date to 1 Thess.) The other factor is the belief, widespread in Jewish Apocalypses, that the final consummation would be preceded by a period of trouble and distress, the so-called 'Woes of the Messiah,' the birth-pangs of the New Age. This Jewish belief goes back to Dan. 12^{1}: 'And at that time shall Michael stand up, the great prince which standeth for the children of thy people: and there shall be a time of trouble, such as never was since there was a nation even to that same time: and at that time thy people shall be delivered, every one that shall be found written in the book.' Further evidence in Billerbeck, iv. 977–986.

The feature of the Matthæan addition (24^{10-12}) is that it adds a prophecy of strife and apostasy within the Church to the predictions of woe given in Mk. 13. It is very unlikely that it is genuine teaching of Jesus.

10. Many will stumble, that is, they will take offence (cf. Mt. 11^{6}||Lk. 7^{23}) when their expectations are not immediately realised. They will be disillusioned and 'fed up.' The community will be divided by mutual suspicions and hatreds. This latter feature seems to be an adaptation of the genuine saying of Jesus preserved in Q (Lk. 12$^{51-53}$), where the reference is to divisions in Judaism caused by the mission of Jesus and not, as here, to divisions in the community caused by the delay of the Second Coming. Cf. Mk. 13^{12}, where the point is the same as in Lk. 12$^{51ff.}$.

11. This verse may be the M version of Mk. 13$^{21f.}$; Lk. 17^{23} (Q); cf. Rev. 19^{20}. *Apoc. Baruch* 48$^{30-37}$. Josephus (*Jewish War*, vi. 283–287) tells of a multitude of false prophets who arose during the siege of Jerusalem, 'suborned by the tyrants to delude the people'; and in particular of the destruction of six thousand refugees who had been misled by a false prophet.

12. In 4 *Ezra* 5$^{1f.}$ the signs of the end are thus described: 'Behold the days come when the inhabitants of earth shall be seized with great panic, and the way of truth shall be hidden, and the land of faith be barren. And iniquity (*iniustitia*) shall be increased above that which thou thyself now seest or that thou hast heard of long ago.' Cf. *Enoch* 91^{7}. Similarly in the Mishnah *Sotah* 9^{15} (Danby, p. 306): 'With the footprints of the Messiah presumption shall increase and dearth reach its height . . . and the empire shall fall into heresy and there shall be none to utter reproof. The council-chamber shall be given to fornication. . . . The wisdom of the Scribes shall become insipid and they that shun sin shall be deemed contemptible, and truth shall nowhere be found.' Such passages as these sufficiently explain the multiplying of iniquity or increase of lawlessness in this verse. We may, however, wonder whether there is not a further reference here to the controversy between Jewish and Gentile Christianity on the matter of the observance of the Law. The love which grows cold in these circumstances is doubtless brother love of Christians towards one another, as in Rev. 2^{4}.

(*b*) MT. 24^{30a} (219)

24 30 And then shall appear the sign of the Son of man in heaven: and then shall all the tribes of the earth mourn, and they shall see the Son of man coming on the clouds of heaven with power and great glory.

In *v.* 29 Mt. is following Mk. 13$^{24f.}$. In *v.* 30 the words 'and then' are derived from Mk. 13^{26}. The following words 'shall appear . . . mourn' have no parallel in Mk. With 'they shall see the Son of man . . .' Mt. resumes his transcription of Mk.

There are striking similarities between Mt. 24^{30} and Rev. 1^{7}: 'Behold, he cometh with the clouds; and every eye shall see him, and they which pierced him; and all the tribes of the earth shall mourn over him.' In both texts we have the combination of two Old Testament passages: Dan. 7^{13} and Zech. 12$^{10, 12}$. In both the reference is eschatological. Whether Rev. 1^{7} is dependent on Mt. 24^{30}, or both on a common source, it would be difficult to say. 'The sign of the Son of Man' may be the Son of Man Himself or, what is perhaps more probable, some supernatural appearance which heralds His coming. There is a great variety of opinions in early Christian literature on the nature of the sign. (See

Bousset, *The Antichrist Legend*, pp. 232 ff.) A very early belief was that the Cross had been taken up to heaven at the time of the Ascension, and that it was the sign that would appear in the sky at the time of the Parousia. Cf. *Gospel of Peter* x. 39 (James, *Apocryphal New Testament*, p. 92); *Epistle of the Apostles* xvi. (*op. cit.*, p. 490).

'All the tribes of the earth shall mourn.' The meaning is that the nations of the world which have not accepted the Gospel will now be without hope. The original sense of the passage in Zech. 12^{10-12} is that the Jews will mourn as a sign of repentance for past misdeeds. But that original sense has been abandoned; and the text of Mt., as it stands, shows the standpoint of Jewish Apocalyptic with its prophecies of woe for the Gentile nations.

The insertion is not to be regarded as a word of Jesus but as a piece of half-Christianised Jewish apocalyptic, inserted by Mt. at this point.

2. *THE ESCHATOLOGICAL PARABLES*

(*a*) The Ten Virgins (227)

MT. 25^{1-13}

25 1 Then shall the kingdom of heaven be
likened unto ten virgins, which took their
[1] lamps, and went forth to meet the
2 bridegroom. And five of them were
3 foolish, and five were wise. For the
foolish, when they took their [1] lamps,
4 took no oil with them: but the wise took
oil in their vessels with their [1] lamps.
5 Now while the bridegroom tarried, they
6 all slumbered and slept. But at midnight there is a cry, Behold, the bridegroom! Come ye forth to meet him.
7 Then all those virgins arose, and
8 trimmed their [1] lamps. And the foolish
said unto the wise, Give us of your oil;
9 for our [1] lamps are going out. But the
wise answered, saying, Peradventure
there will not be enough for us and you:
go ye rather to them that sell, and buy for
10 yourselves. And while they went away
to buy, the bridegroom came; and they
that were ready went in with him to the
marriage feast: and the door was shut.
11 Afterward come also the other virgins,
12 saying, Lord, Lord, open to us. But he
answered and said, Verily I say unto you,
13 I know you not. Watch therefore, for
ye know not the day nor the hour.

[1] Or, *torches*.

This parable is a curiously involved mixture of ideas drawn from various sources. The first part seems to present a parallel to the Q parable of the servants who wait for their master's return from the marriage (Lk. 12^{35-38}). The closing verses (10–12) seem to be derived from another parable in Q (Lk. 13^{23-27}). The division of the virgins into two classes, the one destined for bliss and the other for exclusion from the good time that is coming, reflects that characteristic Matthæan dichotomy found in other parables peculiar to Mt., and going back eventually to the preaching of John the Baptist. Along with this goes another idea, that of Christ as the heavenly bridegroom. This idea of the marriage of Christ and the Church is the New Testament equivalent of the Old Testament idea of God as the bridegroom of Israel (cf. Hos. 2^{16}; Is. 54^{6}; Ezek. $16^{7\,f.}$). In the New Testament cf. 2 Cor. 11^{2}; Eph. $5^{25,\,32}$; Rev. 19^{7}.

1, 2, 3 f. The procedure which seems to be implied in the parable is that the bride awaits the coming of the bridegroom at her own home. The virgins are her friends who are to meet the bridegroom when he comes with his friends, and then join in escorting the couple back to the bridegroom's home, where the wedding-feast will take place. And here comes the first difficulty. For the bride is not mentioned at all in the parable. By all the New Testament analogies the bride is the Church; but it is quite plain that the ten virgins represent the Church, and the Church as a mixed community containing good and bad members. There is no room for the bride in the story because her place has been taken by the bridesmaids. What is meant by the lamps and the oil is not clear. All have lamps and all the lamps have oil. The only fault of the foolish is that they have no reserve supply of oil. This means that they cannot keep their lamps going right through to the end. This would suggest that the moral of the lamps is perseverance in faith. 'He that endureth to the end, the same shall be saved' (Mk. 13^{13}||Mt. 24^{13}).

5, 6 f., 8, 9, 10, 11 f. The bridegroom tarries—the second Coming of Christ is delayed. Meanwhile all, wise and foolish alike, slumber and sleep. This is in strange contrast to the moral of the parable (*v.* 13): 'Watch therefore, for ye know not the day nor the hour.' At midnight the coming of the bridegroom is announced and all prepare to meet him. The lamps have apparently been burning all the time, for the wicks now require to be trimmed, and the oil in them is exhausted or nearly so. The foolish appeal to the wise for oil from their reserve stock. But the wise have no oil to spare, and advise the foolish to go and buy; though one would not expect that shops would be open at midnight. There is, however, no suggestion that the foolish virgins were unsuccessful in their quest for oil even at that late hour. But while they are on this errand the bridegroom comes, the party go in to the feast, and the door is shut. Those who were ready are inside; those who were not ready are outside. The qualification for entrance is readiness in all respects and at all times. This is confirmed when the foolish virgins arrive, having now provided themselves with the extra supply of oil. Their request for admission to the feast is refused point-blank. Admission, therefore, does not depend on having lamp or oil, but on having lamp and oil at the precise moment when these things are required. It may then be argued that the original and essential point of the story is that the ten maidens have one task and one only, to be ready with lamps burning brightly when the bridegroom appears. Those who fulfil that task enter the feast; those who fail are shut out. What is meant by keeping the lamp burning brightly may be understood by reference to another M saying, Mt. 5^{16}: 'Even so let your light shine before men, that they may see your good works, and glorify your Father which is in heaven.'

13. The moral of the story. If it is the moral of the story, it is clear that 'Watch' must be taken in another sense than 'keep awake': for (*a*) the maidens do not keep awake (*v.* 5), and (*b*) the point of the story is the necessity of being ready in all respects when the bridgroom arrives.

Additional Note on the text of Mt. 25^{1}

The commentary above assumes that the true text of the parable is substantially as given in R.V. There is, however, one important variant in *v.* 1; and in order to avoid complicating further what is already complicated enough, the bearing of it may be considered separately. In *v.* 1 the virgins go forth 'to meet the bridegroom.' A considerable number of early and important authorities have 'to meet the bridegroom and the bride.' The genuineness of this reading is defended by Prof. Burkitt (*Encyclopædia Biblica*, col. 4991; *Journ. Theol. Stud.*, xxx (1929), pp. 267–270).

If this is the true text, the ten virgins will not be bridesmaids waiting in the neighbourhood of the bride's home, but 'neighbours' children, fellow-townsmen of the bridegroom but not his particular friends,' and 'their plan is to light up the approach to the bridegroom's house as a welcome, in return for which they would hope to have some share in the rather promiscuous hospitality of an oriental festivity' (Burkitt, p. 269). The religious interpretation of this is then that the bridal party stands for the Son of Man and all His angels, and the ten girls stand for the disciples. This is the interpretation offered by Dr. Burkitt in his more recent exposition. In the earlier discussion of the parable in the *Encyclopædia Biblica* he suggested that the virgins were maidservants left in the bridegroom's house to keep watch while he went to bring the bride; and they stand for the Church.

The difficulty about Prof. Burkitt's latest interpretation is the fact that the disciples have to be equated with people who stand in no very close relation to the bridegroom or to the wedding-feast. Elsewhere Jesus speaks of the disciples as the sons of the bridechamber (Mk. 2^{19}), which seems more like what we should expect. If one had to choose between the two views put forward, one would incline to prefer the earlier.

Further, if the virgins represent disciples, they represent in some sense the Church. What then does the bride stand for? The answer is that bride, bridegroom, and the whole bridal retinue together stand for the Son of Man and His angels. But the New Testament usage is that the bridegroom is Christ and the bride the Church. This suggests a possible third interpretation, which is put forward with all reserve and as no more than a conjecture.

Jewish thought was at home with the idea of Israel as the bride of God. And Israel did not mean only the Jews of any one generation. It was Israel as a historical entity, a living unity through the ages. The early Church claimed to be the continuation of this true Israel; and this claim would be most cogent on the part of the Jewish-Christian branch of the Church. It is then possible to suggest that the bride in the parable is the true Israel, by which is meant the Israel of the patriarchs and prophets and Jewish Christians. The ten virgins stand for the Gentile converts. The wise among them are those who accept the Jewish-Christian standard of conformity to the Law. The foolish are those who do not. In support of this it may be urged that both lamp and oil are used as figures for the Law. Ps. 119^{105}; Prov. 6^{23}: 'The commandment is a lamp; and the law is light.' *Apoc. Baruch* 59^{2}; 4 *Ezra* $14^{20f.}$. For the comparison of the Law with oil cf. Feldman, *Parables and Similes of the Rabbis*, pp. 164 f.; Billerbeck, ii. 357: 'As oil is light for the world, so also are the words of the Law light for the world' (*Dt. Rabba* 7).

It must, however, be emphasised again that all this is conjecture. One is left at the end with the suspicion that the parable as presented in Mt. is the working up of something originally much simpler, in the same way that Mt.'s parable of the Wheat and Tares is the working up of Mk.'s parable of the Seed growing secretly.

What this original, and probably genuine, parable was like we have now no means of determining; but we may guess that its point was the necessity of being fully prepared for the coming of the day of the Son of Man.

(*b*) The Talents (228)

MT. 25^{14-30}

25 14 For *it is* as *when* a man, going into
another country, called his own [1] servants, and delivered unto them his goods.
15 And unto one he gave five talents, to
another two, to another one; to each
according to his several ability; and he
16 went on his journey. Straightway he
that received the five talents went and
traded with them, and made other five
17 talents. In like manner he also that
18 *received* the two gained other two. But
he that received the one went away and
digged in the earth, and hid his lord's
19 money. Now after a long time the lord
of those [1] servants cometh, and maketh a
20 reckoning with them. And he that received the five talents came and brought
other five talents, saying, Lord, thou
deliveredst unto me five talents: lo, I
21 have gained other five talents. His lord
said unto him, Well done, good and
faithful [2] servant: thou hast been faithful
over a few things, I will set thee over
many things: enter thou into the joy of
22 thy lord. And he also that *received* the
two talents came and said, Lord, thou
deliveredst unto me two talents: lo, I
23 have gained other two talents. His lord
said unto him, Well done, good and
faithful [2] servant; thou hast been faithful
over a few things, I will set thee over
many things: enter thou into the joy of
24 thy lord. And he also that had received
the one talent came and said, Lord, I
knew thee that thou art a hard man,
reaping where thou didst not sow, and
gathering where thou didst not scatter:
25 and I was afraid, and went away and hid
thy talent in the earth: lo, thou hast
26 thine own. But his lord answered and
said unto him, Thou wicked and slothful
[2] servant, thou knewest that I reap where
I sowed not, and gather where I did not
27 scatter; thou oughtest therefore to have
put my money to the bankers, and at my
coming I should have received back mine
28 own with interest. Take ye away therefore
the talent from him, and give it unto him
29 that hath the ten talents. For unto
every one that hath shall be given, and
he shall have abundance: but from him
that hath not, even that which he hath
30 shall be taken away. And cast ye out
the unprofitable [2] servant into the outer
darkness: there shall be the weeping
and gnashing of teeth.

[1] Gr. *bondservants*.
[2] Gr. *bondservant*.

This parable has a parallel in Lk.'s parable of the Pounds (Lk. 19^{12-27}) which is to be assigned to L. This means that the main outline of the story was already fixed before the M and L traditions took shape; and makes it probable that the parable, in its original form, goes back to Jesus Himself. The story itself is told with considerable detail in both versions; but much of the detail is artistic amplification, given to make the story, as a story, more vivid and lifelike. It is therefore the more important in all this wealth of detail to try to perceive what is the central and essential point. This does not lie in any of the details, as for example the significance of the talents, or of their distribution, but in the principle of Jewish Law assumed throughout the parable though nowhere expressly stated; the slave belongs to his master, and all that the slave produces or earns belongs to his master. For the legal texts see Billerbeck, i. 970 f. Translated into religious terms this means the absolute claim of God upon man. Man himself, all that he has, and all that he can produce, all belong to God. The purpose of man's existence is to serve God, and apart from such service his life is meaningless and worthless. The reward of such service is opportunity for further and larger service; and the worst punishment for failure to serve is just to be deprived of the opportunity to serve at all.

14. The master going into another country may be taken to represent God. In that case the other country is heaven. The servants—better rendered here ' bondservants ' (R.V. mg.) or ' slaves,' and so throughout the parable—are men, who are made responsible for the conduct of God's business on earth. The immediate application is of course to Israel and, within Israel, especially to the disciples of Jesus. The goods may be anything in the world, the whole raw material of man's work conceived as a service offered to God.

15. The talents have no special significance. They are introduced simply as a means of expressing the varied opportunities of the slaves in terms of a common denominator—money. The modern use of the word ' talent ' in the sense of a special kind of ability does not enter in at all. All that is implied is that in the distribution of ' the goods ' one slave receives goods to the value of five talents £1,000–1,200; another gets over £400 worth; another over £200 worth. The distribution is governed by the abilities of the servants. The most capable is given the largest responsibility; and it is assumed that no slave is allotted a task beyond his powers. The master now leaves the slaves to get on with the work. So far as the work is concerned they are as good as free. Possibly the master could have got more abundant results by staying and directing all the operations; but that, it would seem, is not his purpose. So doubtless the world might be better managed if there were more interference from heaven. But if the end in view is that men should become God's children rather than His puppets, it may be that non-interference is necessary.

16 f., 18. The first two slaves go to work and succeed in doubling what has been entrusted to them. The actual doubling is doubling of goods. As in the description of the distribution, so here the value of the work done and the results produced are reduced to the same common denominator—money. The third slave—it might equally have been one of the other two—makes no use of his opportunities. For the burying of valuables as a way of keeping them in safety cf. Mt. 13[44], above, p. 488.

19. In due course the master comes to see how the slaves have managed his property. The same situation occurs in Mt. 18[23 ff.] and the same expression, ' make a reckoning,' is used. In Mt. 18 the reference is clearly not to the final Judgement and here such a reference is only necessitated by *v.* 30, which is probably not part of the original parable. It is worth noting that in Jewish literature we have the idea of an annual Judgement, which takes place on the Jewish New Year's Day. So in the Mishnah (*Rosh ha-Shanah* 1[2], Danby, p. 188): ' On New Year's Day all that come into the world pass before him (God) like legions of soldiers, for it is written, He that fashioneth the hearts of them all, that considereth all their works (Ps. 33[15]).' Cf. Abrahams, *Festival Studies*, pp. 19–24; *Companion to the Daily Prayer Book*, pp. cxcvi–cxcix; *Authorised Daily Prayer Book* (ed. Singer), pp. 249–252; Billerbeck, iii. 230 f. At this time the doings of each man are reviewed and a verdict passed on them. The ensuing period from New Year's Day until the Day of Atonement is allowed for repentance; and on the Day of Atonement the sentence, whatever it may be, is pronounced.

20–23. The first two servants report in much the same terms (*vv.* 20, 22) and are commended in much the same terms (*vv.* 21, 23). The reward of faithful service is first the approval of the master, and second the opportunity for more abundant and more responsible service. So Ben Azzai says: 'The reward of a duty [done] is a duty [to be done]' (*Aboth* 4^2, Danby, p. 453). Cf. the passage quoted by Montefiore (*op. cit.*, p. 332): 'God does not give greatness to a man till He has proved him in a small matter: only then He promotes him to a great post. Two were proved and found faithful, and God promoted them to greatness. He tested David with the sheep . . . and God said, Thou wast found faithful with the sheep, I will give thee *my* sheep that thou shouldst feed them. And so with Moses, who fed his father-in-law's sheep. To him God said the same.' The words 'enter thou into the joy of thy lord' have nothing corresponding in Lk. They give a definitely eschatological cast to the scene. But this is not necessarily original. It may be that the fuller service is service in the world to come; but this is not necessarily implied in the story as a whole.

24 f. The third slave has now to justify himself if he can. The obvious course is to complain about the conditions of his service and to blacken the character of the master. He is a hard man, who enriches himself by the labours of other people. He reaps where he has not sown and gathers where he has not scattered. This latter clause should probably be translated 'garnering where thou hast not winnowed.' The Greek word translated 'scatter' in R.V. probably represents the Aramaic verb *dĕrā*, which means both to scatter and to winnow. The fear of the slave is to be understood as the fear of losing what had been entrusted to him in any enterprise which he might undertake. His argument appears to be: If I make a profit the master gets it; if I make a loss he will come upon me to make it good. Therefore the best course is to do nothing. 'Lo, thou hast thine own'—no more and no less.

26. The master makes no attempt to rebut the charge. As between master and slave the statement of the case is correct. That *is* the situation. The slave works and the master takes the results of his labours. The good and faithful slave accepts the situation and does his best in it. The slave who refuses to do his best is a bad slave. He ought to have been a good and faithful slave and trusted that the master would be kind and generous. It is to be noted that the master does not accept the designation 'hard man.' The point of this verse in religious terms is that it is insolence and presumption on man's part to question the terms on which God has created him and given him a place in the world. It is not man's business to sit in judgement upon God. It is his business to do his best in the situation in which he finds himself. It is his business to live and work and die for the glory of God. That is his privilege: and his highest reward is to be allowed to go on doing it. The well-known prayer of Ignatius Loyola is very much to the point here.

27. The law concerning deposits with bankers is given in the Mishnah (*Baba Metziah* 3^{11}, Danby, p. 352): 'If a man left money in the keeping of a money-changer and it was sealed up, he (the money-changer) may not make use of it and, therefore, if it was lost he is not answerable for it; if the money was loose he may make use of it and, therefore, if it was lost he is answerable for it.' That is, if the bank is used merely as a safe-deposit, it is so used at one's own risk. But if the money is put into the bank on a deposit account, the banker can use it for

his business, is bound to restore it in full, and will pay some interest for the use of it. Therefore in depositing the money at a bank the slave would not be risking the capital, and he would be ensuring some increase for his master.

28 f. The punishment for neglected opportunity is deprivation of opportunity. But God's work goes on; and the task which one man refuses is given to another who will do it. Verse 29 states the general principle. It is so briefly stated as to be cryptic. It may be expanded thus: To him who has added something of his own to what I entrusted to him, more of mine shall be entrusted and he shall have abundance. But from him who has added nothing of his own to what I entrusted to him, shall be taken away what I entrusted to him.

30. With this statement the parable reaches what ought to be its conclusion; and this is the last verse which has a parallel in Lk. Mt., however, has another verse describing further punishment for the slave. The verse is largely made up of phrases which are favourites with Mt.: 'cast into the outer darkness' (Mt. 8^{12}, 22^{13}, 25^{30}, and nowhere else in the New Testament); 'there shall be the weeping and gnashing of teeth' (Mt. 8^{12}, $13^{42, 50}$, 22^{13}, 24^{51}, 25^{30}; elsewhere only Lk. 13^{28}).

Eusebius in his *Theophany* discusses this verse with reference to an apocryphal gospel (the Gospel according to the Hebrews or the Gospel according to the Nazarenes), which he believed to be the Hebrew original of Mt. The passage is given in James, *Apocryphal New Testament*, p. 3. He informs us that in this gospel there were three servants, 'one who devoured his master's substance with harlots and flute-girls, another who multiplied it by trading, and another who hid the talent.' The second was accepted, the third only rebuked, and the first was shut up in prison. Eusebius then goes on to conjecture that *v.* 30 in Mt. may refer to the servant who 'ate and drank with the drunken,' apparently referring back to Mt. 24^{49}. It is more probable that the parable in the apocryphal gospel is an attempt to deal with *v.* 30 in Mt. That is, it was soon perceived that *v.* 30 did not really belong to the case of the man who buried his talent. He had been dealt with in *vv.* 28 f. The 'unprofitable servant' must be yet another, and so the servant who wastes his capital in debauchery is invented. The apocryphal gospel is thus evidence that at an early date the separateness of *v.* 30 from *vv.* 28 f. was felt. But the true explanation of that separateness is most probably that it is an editorial addition by Mt. and no part of the original parable.

(*c*) THE LAST JUDGEMENT (229)

MT. 25^{31-46}

25 31 But when the Son of man shall come
in his glory, and all the angels with him,
then shall he sit on the throne of his
32 glory: and before him shall be gathered
all the nations: and he shall separate
them one from another, as the shepherd
33 separateth the sheep from the [1] goats: and
he shall set the sheep on his right hand,
34 but the [1] goats on the left. Then shall
the King say unto them on his right hand,
Come, ye blessed of my Father, inherit
the kingdom prepared for you from the
35 foundation of the world: for I was an
hungred, and ye gave me meat: I was
thirsty, and ye gave me drink: I was a
stranger, and ye took me in; naked, and
36 ye clothed me: I was sick, and ye visited
me: I was in prison, and ye came unto
37 me. Then shall the righteous answer
him, saying, Lord, when saw we thee an
hungred, and fed thee? or athirst, and
38 gave thee drink? And when saw we
thee a stranger, and took thee in? or
39 naked, and clothed thee? And when
saw we thee sick, or in prison, and came
40 unto thee? And the King shall answer

and say unto them, Verily I say unto you,
Inasmuch as ye did it unto one of these
my brethren, *even* these least, ye did it
41 unto me. Then shall he say also unto
them on the left hand, [2] Depart from me,
ye cursed, into the eternal fire which is
prepared for the devil and his angels:
42 for I was an hungred, and ye gave me no
meat: I was thirsty, and ye gave me no
43 drink: I was a stranger, and ye took me
not in; naked, and ye clothed me not;
sick, and in prison, and ye visited me not.
44 Then shall they also answer, saying,
Lord, when saw we thee an hungred, or
athirst, or a stranger, or naked, or sick,
or in prison, and did not minister unto
45 thee? Then shall he answer them,
saying, Verily I say unto you, Inasmuch
as ye did it not unto one of these least,
46 ye did it not unto me. And these shall
go away into eternal punishment: but the
righteous into eternal life.

[1] Gr. *kids*.
[2] Or, *Depart from me under a curse*.

This word-picture of the Last Judgement has no parallel in the other Gospels. Whether or not it belongs as a whole and in all its details to the authentic teaching of Jesus, it certainly contains features of such startling originality that it is difficult to credit them to anyone but the Master Himself. The frame of the picture is the conventional Jewish Apocalyptic expectation; but many details of the picture would seem to be the creation of Jesus Himself. On the Jewish expectations see Moore, *Judaism*, ii. 279–395; Billerbeck, iv. 1199–1212. In Jewish accounts the Judge is always God, except in the one case (*Enoch* 61^{6}-63^{12}) where the Messiah (the Elect One) performs this office; and even here there are clear indications (62^{10-14}) that the Lord of Spirits (= God) has a decisive part in the proceedings, to say nothing of Messel's contention that the Elect One in this passage is a figure for Israel, and not for the Messiah. Mt.'s account of the Judgement differs from the usual Jewish view in this important respect that here the judge is not God but the Son of Man. In this respect it has some affinity with the passage in *Enoch* (61^{6}–63^{12}).

The principal characters in the drama are as follows: (1) the Son of Man accompanied by the angels, (2) all the Gentiles, (3) the King, (4) the King's Father, (5) the King's brethren. The identification of these characters is not easy in every case. It is, however, clear that the King's Father is God. It follows that God is not the Judge in this scene. It is then clear that the King is meant for Jesus Himself. Who, then, are the King's brethren? The obvious course is to suppose that they are the disciples of Jesus. This leads to an important conclusion: the King is not alone in the judgement, but is the representative and spokesman of a body of persons (' my brethren ') distinct from the other parties present. They are clearly not identical with those who are to be condemned; but neither are they identical with the righteous. For they have been the objects of neglect by the one party and of kindness and help by the other. We have thus three distinct parties: the King's brethren, and the two classes of Gentiles, those who helped (sheep) and those who did not help (goats). We must accordingly picture the scene thus: in the centre the King and his brethren; on the right hand of this party the good Gentiles; on the left hand the wicked Gentiles. What, then, is signified by the Son of Man? It would seem that there are two possibilities. Either the Son of Man is the same as the King, in which case ' Son of Man ' has the meaning commonly assigned to it in *Enoch*; or ' Son of Man ' stands for the body comprising the King and his brethren, in which case ' Son of Man ' approximates in meaning to ' Son of Man ' in Dan. 7^{13}, and the interpretation proposed by Messel for ‘ Son of Man ’ in *Enoch*. The latter is, in my opinion, the correct interpretation.

It may be noted that there is a similar threefold division of mankind in the eschatology of Mohammed (*Koran*, Sura 56): ‘ When the inevitable day of judgement shall suddenly come . . . it will abase some and exalt others . . . Ye shall be separated into three distinct classes: the companions of the right hand; (how happy shall the companions of the right hand be!) and the companions of the left hand; (how miserable shall the companions of the left hand be!) and those who have preceded others in the faith, shall precede them to paradise.’ But none of the three classes acts in a judicial capacity.

For further instances of the idea of the Judgement being carried out by a corporate body see notes on Mt. 19^{28}, above, pp. 508 f.

31. The coming of the Son of Man is spoken of in the Synoptic Gospels in Mk. 8^{38} and ||s; 13^{26} and ||s; 14^{62} and ||s; in Q: Lk. 12^{40}||Mt. 24^{44}; in M: Mt. 10^{23}, 25^{31}; in L: Lk. 18^{8}. Cf. also Lk. $17^{24, 26, 30}$ (Q). The angels are often pictured in Jewish literature as in attendance upon God at the Judgement, and as assisting in the execution of it; but there is, according to Billerbeck, no mention in early Jewish literature of angels accompanying the Messiah (Billerbeck, i. 973 f.). ‘ The throne of his glory ’ = His glorious throne. The throne of glory is one of the things which, according to Jewish belief, were created before the world. In Jewish thought it is essentially the throne of God. The only place in Jewish literature where anyone but God is said to sit on it is the *Similitudes of Enoch* (*Enoch* 37–71). There the Elect One sits on the throne or is set thereon by God (*Enoch* 45^{3}, 51^{3}, 55^{4}, 61^{8}, $62^{2, 3, 5}$, $69^{27, 29}$).

32 f. ‘ All the nations ’: the usage of Mt. elsewhere would suggest that ‘ all the Gentiles ’ is the rendering here. If it be asked where Israel comes into this scheme, it may be suggested that the true Israel is covered by the concept ‘ Son of Man,’ interpreted as ‘ the people of the Saints of the Most High.’ The Jews who have rejected the Kingdom as preached to them by Jesus and His disciples are reckoned among the Gentiles. See notes on Lk. $10^{10 ff.}$, above, pp. 367 f. The assembling of the people for judgement is done by the angels. Cf. Mt. 13^{41}. The separation takes place forthwith: the characters and records of the persons concerned are already known. It is judgement, not trial, for which the court is assembled. The right hand is the place of honour; and, in this connexion, the left hand the place of rejection. The same convention appears in the myth of Er (Plato, *Republic* x. p. 614). In the state after death Er saw judges ‘ who, after passing sentence, commanded the just to take the road to the right upwards through the heaven . . .; while the unjust were ordered to take the road downwards to the left.’ Cf. Virgil, *Æn.* vi. 540 ff.

34. The King speaks. He is the spokesman of Himself and His brethren; and He speaks in the name of His Father. He is clearly to be identified as Christ, the spokesman and representative of the ‘ Son of Man,’ the people of the Saints of the Most High. The favourable judgement which He has to deliver on those on the right hand is essentially the judgement of God, ‘ Come ye blessed *of my Father*.’ ‘ Inherit ’ means ‘ enter into the possession and enjoyment of.’ That the Kingdom is ‘prepared’ for them from the foundation of the world may mean

either that it was provided for in God's plan, though not actually created, or that it was actually created in the beginning and has been waiting for its inheritors till now. Cf. Dan 7[27]; Lk. 12[32]; 1 Cor. 2[9]. According to Jewish ideas, some things were created before the world. Various lists are given and the distinction is made between real creation and planning (Billerbeck, i. 981 ff.; ii. 334 f.). Other things were created in advance at the close of the sixth day of Creation (*Aboth* 5[6], Danby, p. 456).

35. The ground for the favourable decision. It is a striking feature of this and the following verses that those on the right are not commended for abstinence from the cruder sins, nor are those on the left condemned for indulgence in them. Again, it is not that one group have been kind-hearted and the other callous. Honesty, chastity, kindness, and the like are very important things and their importance is duly stressed in the teaching of Jesus elsewhere. But here the vital question is not whether a man has lived a moral life or whether he has been decently kind to other people. It is how he stood towards the Kingdom of God: was he on the side of the Kingdom or against it?

35 f. Consequently in these verses the emphasis is on 'I' and 'me,' and not on the verbs. The good deeds done were deeds done to help the cause of God. They were an acknowledgement of God's sovereignty as manifested in His representative Jesus Christ.

37–39. The righteous are not aware of having done any kindnesses to Jesus. They helped this or that good man in his need; but it was other people that they helped, not Him who speaks.

40. The answer of the King brings out clearly the solidarity of Christ and His brethren. He and His brethren are many, but together they are one—the Son of Man. Help given to one is help given to all, and above all to their Head. The same principle is laid down in Mk. 9[41]; Lk. 10[16]||Mt. 10[40] (Q), see notes above, pp. 369 f; Mt. 10[41 f.] (M), see above, pp. 475 f. The fact that the phrase 'in my name' is not used here probably signifies nothing. It is assumed that the help has been given to the disciples of Jesus, when they were engaged on their apostolic task, when they arrived in a strange town, hungry and thirsty, or when they were worn out and ill through toil and travel, when they were imprisoned for preaching the Gospel—why else should the brethren of Christ be in prison? Cf. 1 Pet. 4[14-16]. The deeds of the righteous are not just casual acts of benevolence. They are acts by which the Mission of Jesus and His followers was helped, and helped at some cost to the doers, even at some risk.

'One of these my brethren even these least' is a literal rendering of the Greek, which is probably a literal rendering of a misunderstood Aramaic idiom. Translate 'one of the least of my brethren' and cf. Mt. 5[19], above, p. 446.

41. The King now turns to the other group. The principle of judgement in their case is the same as in the case of the righteous. The question is whether a man is for or against the Kingdom of God. And there is no such thing as neutrality. 'He that is not with me is against me; and he that gathereth not with me scattereth' (Lk. 11[23]||Mt. 12[30] Q, above, p. 379). The Kingdom comes with definite claims upon every man. To ignore them is to reject them; and to reject them is to side with the enemy. Those on the left hand have chosen Satan

—by doing nothing—and to Satan they go. Their own choice puts them outside the pale of God's blessing; and to be outside is to be under the curse. The dreadful imagery of the eternal fire made ready for the Devil and his angels is doubtless appalling. Once it was terrifying to the ungodly. It is no longer terrifying because it is no longer believed by most people. But it corresponds to a spiritual reality, to the fact that God having given us freedom, has given us freedom to reject Him, to be rebels against His will, to cut ourselves off from our true life.

42–45. These verses present the other side of the case stated in *vv.* 35–40. In *v.* 44 the statement is abbreviated.

46. The conclusion of the matter. The destiny of both parties is unalterably fixed for ever. Before the righteous is everlasting bliss; for the others there is no prospect but endless torment. This is the conventional apocalyptic view. Cf. Dan 12[2]. The same remarks apply to this verse as are made on *v.* 41.

III.—Teaching Peculiar to Luke

AS there do not seem to be any signs of a special arrangement of the L material, the sections which follow are numbered consecutively as they occur in Lk.'s order. Where two or more consecutive passages are connected in subject-matter they are brought under the same number.

1. *TEACHING OF JOHN THE BAPTIST* (3)

LK. 3^{10-14}

3 10 And the multitudes asked him, saying,
11 What then must we do? And he answered
and said unto them, He that hath two
coats, let him impart to him that hath
none; and he that hath food, let him do
12 likewise. And there came also [1] publicans
to be baptized, and they said unto him,
13 [2] Master, what must we do? And he said
unto them, Extort no more than that
14 which is appointed you. And [3] soldiers
also asked him, saying, And we, what
must we do? And he said unto them, Do
violence to no man, neither [4] exact *anything* wrongfully; and be content with
your wages.

[1] See marginal note on Matt. v. 46.
[2] Or, *Teacher*.
[3] Gr. *soldiers on service*.
[4] Or, *accuse* any one.

This passage shows the real weakness of John's preaching. He is at his most powerful in exposing and denouncing the wickedness of his age. His mission is to prepare the way for one mightier than himself. Consequently, when he is asked for positive constructive teaching, he has nothing new to offer. That people should treat one another kindly, that publicans should abstain from extortion and soldiers from bullying, was doubtless useful advice, but not an epoch-making moral discovery. John's ethical teaching here is the real 'interim ethic'—do your best in the circumstances till the Messianic age comes. Then things will be put on a proper footing.

10. The fiery preaching of coming judgement has its effect and the common people respond (cf. Lk. 7^{29}). 'What must we do'—to be saved? Some MSS. add these words. They are a gloss, but a gloss that gives the correct sense. The call is 'Bring forth fruits worthy of repentance' (3^{8}). Then what will be considered worthy fruits?

11. John's answer in general terms is positive, even if not far-reaching. His demand for practical kindness to one's neighbour prepares the way for the more radical demand made by Jesus. For 'coats' read 'shirts.' Those who have more than the bare sufficiency for physical needs are to share with those who have not even a bare sufficiency; the poor are to help the destitute. Did the people who listened readily to John consist mainly of those to whom a spare change of underclothing meant comparative prosperity?

12. The publicans here are the collectors of customs as distinct from taxes. In Judæa at this time the taxes would be collected by Roman officials acting for the Procurator. The customs, however, were still farmed out. That is, the right to collect them was sold by the Roman authorities to the highest bidder, who then collected them through subordinate agents of his own. Any surplus remaining, after paying the sum offered to the Government and the cost of collection, went into the pocket of the contractor (publican). Such a system invited the collectors

to practise fraud and oppression in the exercise of their office, and fraud and oppression certainly took place. The result was that in Palestine and elsewhere the collectors of customs were despised and hated. In Judæa they were specially disliked for a further reason. The customs were collected for the Roman Emperor, and that by Jews. The publican thus appeared in the eyes of his patriotic fellow-countrymen as one who had sold his country for private gain. To the average Jew ' publican ' was synonymous with ' traitor and scoundrel,' and such collocations as 'publicans and sinners' or 'publicans and harlots' are taken as a matter of course.

For such people the day, whose approach John proclaimed, would be a day of reckoning; and it is not surprising that some, at any rate, of them were moved to repentance. They address John as 'Master' (Rabbi) and ask his advice. Are they to give up their occupation? Or are they to carry out their task in a new way?

13. John's reply is again interim ethic. Doubtless in the time that is coming Roman taxes and customs will be abolished. Meanwhile they are inevitable, and all that can be demanded is that those who collect the customs should be honest, and not use their position to enrich themselves at the expense of their neighbours. They are not to charge more than the amounts prescribed by law or custom. For an attempt to regulate the charges made by customs-collectors see the bilingual Palmyrene inscription of A.D. 137 in Bevan's *Commentary on Daniel*, pp. 214–219.

14. The question is put by soldiers. What kind of soldiers they were—Roman troops or mercenaries from the army of Herod Antipas—is not stated. It is unlikely that they were Roman in the strict sense, since ' the garrison of Judæa under the procurators was regularly composed of Syrian auxiliary cohorts ' (*Beginnings of Christianity*, v. 439). Such troops had not only to perform their proper military tasks. They were also largely employed in police duties. Here again there was large scope for violent and unscrupulous men to misuse their power.

15. John's reply does not suggest that they should give up their occupation. He tells them to abstain from oppressing the civil population, from extorting money from them by threats of violence or by blackmail. They have their wages: let them be content. This also is interim ethic—making the best of a bad job until the heaven-sent ' Stronger One ' comes, who will put all things right. John's positive teaching serves to mitigate the worst evils of an evil system; but it does not and cannot transform the system. It could relieve the sickness of society; but it was not the radical cure.

2. *OLD AND NEW WINE* (54)

LK. 5^{39}

5 39 And no man having drunk old *wine* desireth new: for he saith, The old is [1]good.

[1] Many ancient authorities read *better*.

This saying is appended by Lk. to the parable of the Wine-skins (Lk. $5^{37f.}$), which he has taken from Mk. (2^{22}). The fact that wines improve with age was a commonplace in ancient literature. Here it is used to illustrate the power of tradition, established belief and custom in religion. The old ways are congenial; and those who are schooled in them will have nothing to do with new movements.

They do not necessarily condemn the new: they just do not want to have anything to do with it.

The reading 'better' is to be rejected: and the adjective (*chrēstos*) would be better rendered by 'mellow' or 'fit for use.' Old and new wines alike may be good or bad. Their quality does not depend on their age. But even a good new wine requires time to make it fit for use. What our connoisseur says in effect is: 'No wine is fit to drink till it is old.' Hence no religious belief or practice which has not the sanctity of age is worth following. Jesus here says that a great obstacle to the reception of new revelation is the *pietas* of religious people. Just so Horace finds an obstacle to the progress of literature in the veneration of the classics, and uses the same illustration (*Epistles* II, i. 34 f.).

Cf. *Aboth* 4^{20} (Danby, p. 455), 'R. Jose b. Judah of Kefar ha-Babli said: He that learns from the young, to what is he like? To one that eats unripe grapes and drinks wine from his winepress. And he that learns from the aged, to what is he like? To one that eats ripe grapes and drinks old wine. Rabbi said: Look not on the jar but on what is in it; there may be a new jar that is full of old wine and an old one in which is not even new wine.'

3. *SAMARITAN UNFRIENDLINESS* (137)

LK. 9^{51-56}

9 51 And it came to pass, when the days [1] were well-nigh come that he should be received up, he stedfastly set his face to go
52 to Jerusalem, and sent messengers before his face: and they went, and entered into a village of the Samaritans, to make ready
53 for him. And they did not receive him, because his face was *as though he were* going
54 to Jerusalem. And when his disciples James and John saw *this*, they said, Lord, wilt thou that we bid fire to come down
55 from heaven, and consume them [2]? But
56 he turned, and rebuked them.[3] And they went to another village.

[1] Gr. *were being fulfilled.*

[2] Many ancient authorities add *even as Elijah did.*

[3] Some ancient authorities add *and said, Ye know not what manner of spirit ye are of.* Some, but fewer, add also *For the Son of man came not to destroy men's lives, but to save them.*

This passage would be more important for our present purpose if the marginal readings were genuine. As they are commonly rejected as later interpolations into the text of Lk., we have no teaching in the proper sense of the word beyond the fact that Jesus sternly rejects the suggestion of James and John

The paragraph is the opening of a long section of Lk. (9^{51}–19^{48}) purporting to describe the journey of Jesus from Galilee to Jerusalem. The greater part of the section (9^{51}–18^{14}) is independent of Mk. The incident described in Mk. 9^{33-37} (Lk. 9^{46-48}) takes place in Capernaum. The next note of place is Mk. 10^{1}, however it is to be understood . (Cf. Burkitt, *Gospel History and its Transmission*, p. 96 n.) At Mk. 10^{13} (Lk. 18^{15}) Lk. rejoins Mk. Mk. 10^{46} (Lk. 18^{35}) brings Jesus to Jericho. In the result Mk. gives two fixed points for the journey: Capernaum (9^{33}) and Jericho (10^{46}). The only intermediate point is Mk. 10^{1}, and there is no certainty how that is to be interpreted; and therefore no certainty what route was followed by Jesus. The Lucan itinerary is equally difficult to follow. It is thus summarised by Burkitt (*Beginnings of Christianity*, ii. 486): 'Jesus now sets His face to go to Jerusalem, and is consequently not received at a Samaritan village ($9^{51 ff.}$). The seventy-two are sent out and return ($10^{1, 17}$). On the way Jesus is received by

Martha and Mary at a certain village (10^{38}). A number of incidents follow, several of which involve the presence of crowds ($11^{14, 27, 29}$, $12^{1, 13, 54}$, 14^{25}), Pharisees ($11^{37, 53}$, 13^{31}, 14^{1}, 15^{2}, 16^{14}), and a synagogue (13^{10}), all on the way to Jerusalem (13^{22}). Presently Jesus is " journeying through the midst of Samaria and Galilee " (17^{11}), and so arrives at Jericho (18^{35}), from whence He goes up to Jerusalem (19^{28})'. What is to be made of these details is a still unsolved problem; but it is most unlikely that they mark stages in a journey through Samaria from Galilee to Judæa. Whatever else Lk. 9^{51}–18^{14} may be, it does not appear to be a chronicle.

51, 52. Lk. recognises that the close of the Galilean ministry is a turning-point in the life of Jesus. From now on events march inevitably towards His being ' received up,' i.e. most probably the Ascension. (Cf. Ryle and James on *Ps. Sol.* 4^{20}; Charles on *Apoc. Baruch* 46^{7}; 2 Kings 2^{11}; Mk. 16^{19}; Acts 1^{2}; 1 Tim. 3^{16}.) Jesus determines to go to Jerusalem. The route chosen is through Samaria. That this way was taken by Galilean pilgrims to Jerusalem is shown by Josephus (*Ant.* XX, vi. 1). In the *Life* (§ 269) Josephus says that this was the quickest route, the journey from Galilee to Jerusalem being possible in three days.

53. The Samaritans refuse hospitality to Jews going up to Jerusalem to the rival sanctuary. The refusal of hospitality was a serious matter. In the Palestinian Talmud a place is mentioned which has the name *Kefar Bīsh* (= evil village), and the name is explained as having been given because the inhabitants would not give hospitality to travellers.

54. James and John wish to take summary vengeance for this affront. Cf. 2 Kings $1^{9ff.}$. Their proposal is in keeping with their nickname ' Sons of Thunder.' We may wonder whether this was not the occasion on which the name was conferred. The addition ' even as Elijah did ' (R.V. mg.) is probably to be regarded as an interpretative gloss, establishing the parallel with 2 Kings $1^{9ff.}$.

55 f. The shortest text, usually regarded as the original, is that given in R.V. (text). The two additions in R.V. mg. are usually rejected as interpolations, probably of Marcionite origin. The second may be an adaptation of the saying in Lk. 19^{10} (cf. John 3^{17}). The first is a little better attested, and might conceivably be the original text of Lk.; but the weight of evidence is against both passages. Both, however, give correctly enough the sense of the rebuke. Evil is not overcome with evil but with good.

It is not clear whether the other village, to which Jesus and the disciples go, is another Samaritan village or not.

4. *THE MISSION OF THE DISCIPLES* (139)

LK. $10^{1, 4-7}$

10 1 Now after these things the Lord appointed seventy[1] others, and sent them two and two before his face into every city and place, whither he himself was about to come.
4 Carry no purse, no wallet, no shoes:
5 and salute no man on the way. And into whatsoever house ye shall[2] enter, first say,
6 Peace *be* to this house. And if a son of peace be there, your peace shall rest upon [3]him: but if not, it shall turn to you again.
7 And in that same house remain, eating and drinking such things as they give: for the labourer is worthy of his hire. Go not from house to house.

[1] Many ancient authorities add *and two*: and so in ver. 17.
[2] Or, *enter first, say.*
[3] Or, *it.*

1. For the reasons for regarding these verses as belonging to L see above, pp. 365–370. The doubt as to the exact number of missionaries goes back to a very early date, for seventy-two is given by the Sahidic and Old Syriac versions, while seventy is the reading of Irenæus. There can be little doubt that seventy-two is the correct reading. The mission is a mission to Israel and the number is determined, as is the number of the Apostles, by the thought of the twelve tribes. Later the number is reduced to seventy in accordance with the idea that there are seventy nations in the world. The smaller number reflects the interests of the Gentile mission. But the errand on which these disciples were sent out was certainly no Gentile mission. Lk. represents it as designed to prepare the way for the arrival of Jesus Himself; but if preparations were going on simultaneously in thirty-six different places, it is difficult to see how one person could overtake the work. Moreover, Jesus does not appear to follow up the preparations. In Lk. 10^{17} the seventy-two return to Him: He does not follow them. Further, Lk. $22^{35ff.}$ definitely seems to refer back to Lk. 10^{4}; and in Lk. $22^{35ff.}$ it is the Twelve who are addressed. This last point suggests very strongly that the mission of the seventy-two is a doublet of the mission of the Twelve. How the number seventy-two came into existence in the tradition is an unsolved problem.

4–6. See on Mt. $10^{9f.}$, above, p. 472. The injunction to abstain from greetings by the way is illustrated by the injunction of Elisha to Gehazi (2 Kings 4^{29}): ' Gird up thy loins, and take my staff in thine hand, and go thy way: if thou meet any man, salute him not; and if any salute thee, answer him not again: and lay my staff upon the face of the child.' In this case the matter is one of life and death: no greetings are to be exchanged on the way because the business is urgent. So in the charge to the disciples their mission is a sacred one, and it is very urgent. There is no time to waste in wayside pleasantries. The greetings withheld on the journey are to be offered on reaching the destination. Cf. Mt. 10^{12} and notes, above, p. 473. The greeting is no mere formula, as an exchange of compliments on the road might be. It is a manifestation of the Kingdom of God in word, the first intimation of the new grace and power that have come into the world, an announcement that ' the Kingdom of God is come nigh unto you.' This gives the meaning of ' a son of peace.' In Hebrew and Aramaic idiom ' son of ' may mean either ' possessor of ' or ' worthy of.' So ' son of peace ' may mean either a peaceable person or one worthy of peace. Since the peace in question here is the peace of God's Kingdom, the second meaning must be chosen. If there is anyone in the house worthy to receive this gift of God, he will receive it. Otherwise it will return to the messengers.

7. Where hospitality is received there the messengers are to stay. They are to accept the food and shelter of the household as a right. The labourer deserves his hire: and they who give up everything for the sake of bringing the good news to others are entitled to a subsistence while they do it. But they are also to be content with what is available. They are not to be seeking for better quarters and ampler rations. The labourer is worthy of his hire; but his hire is not the object of his labour.

On *vv.* 8–16, which I assign to Q, see above, pp. 367–370.

5. *THE RETURN OF THE MISSIONARIES* (140)

LK. 10^{17-20}

10 17 And the seventy returned with joy,
saying, Lord, even the [1] devils are subject
18 unto us in thy name. And he said unto
them, I beheld Satan fallen as lightning
19 from heaven. Behold, I have given you
authority to tread upon serpents and
scorpions, and over all the power of the
enemy: and nothing shall in any wise
20 hurt you. Howbeit in this rejoice not,
that the spirits are subject unto you; but
rejoice that your names are written in
heaven.

[1] Gr. *demons*.

17. Here, as in *v.* 1, the true reading is probably 'seventy-two.' The mission is clearly understood to have been successful, at any rate from the point of view of the missionaries. The thing that pleases them is the fact that they have been able to perform exorcisms in the name of Jesus. For the use of the name of Jesus for this purpose cf. Lk. $9^{49\text{ f.}}$; Acts 19^{13}. The power to overcome the demons is a cause for rejoicing because it is a sign of the presence of the Kingdom of God. See Lk. $11^{20\text{ff.}}$ (Q), above, p. 378. The same divine power which is manifested in the Master is now manifested in the disciples.

18, 20. This is confirmed by the reply of Jesus. The overcoming of the demons is the overthrow of their chief. The words of Jesus describe a visionary experience in which He watched Satan fall (Moulton, *Prolegomena*, p. 134) like lightning from heaven. There are two views about Satan in Judaism. According to one he had already been cast down from heaven in the beginning of time (Charles, *Revelation*, i. 323). According to the other, which has the support of the Old Testament passages Job. $1^{6\text{ f.}}$; Zech. $3^{1\text{ff.}}$, and perhaps also *Enoch* 40^{7}, he has at least access to heaven. The final overthrow of Satan was an integral part of the Jewish expectation of the good time coming, though there were different opinions as to who would be the agent: God Himself or the angels or the Messiah (Billerbeck, ii. 167 f.). It is significant that Jesus describes Himself as a spectator of Satan's downfall. The most natural inference is that He regards it as an act of God. This is a strong argument for the genuineness of the saying. Later Christology would not have assigned such a passive rôle to the Messiah. The fall of Satan is the beginning of the end of his kingdom. Something is achieved through the mission of Jesus and the disciples; and that which is thus begun must go on to its inevitable end in the complete subjection of the forces of evil and the full manifestation of the sovereignty of God. For the figure cf. Is. 14^{12} and Rev. $12^{8\text{ f.}}$. The natural sequel to *v.* 18 is *v.* 20; and *v.* 19 may be regarded as an intrusion here.

While it is legitimate to rejoice over the subjection of the forces of evil, it must be remembered that this is only a means to an end. The warfare of the Kingdom is to make way for the peace of the Kingdom. The destruction of evil is part and parcel of the salvation of man. So the true reason for joy is that salvation is being achieved. 'There is more joy in heaven . . .' The 'spirits' here = the demons. In Jewish speech 'spirit,' without further qualification, regularly signifies 'evil spirit.' The figure employed to describe the salvation of the disciples is that their names are inscribed in the burgess-roll of the Kingdom. Heavenly books appear in Jewish literature and are distinguishable into four kinds: (1) the Book of Life or of the Living (Ps. 69^{29}, 87^{4-6}; Exod. 32^{32}; Dan. 12^{1};

Phil. 4^{3}; Heb. 12^{23}; Rev. 3^{5}, 13^{8}, 17^{8}) containing the names of those who are members of God's Chosen People, and so destined for life, whether a life of prosperity in the Holy Land, or the life of the world to come; (2) the book containing the record of each man's deeds (Mal. 3^{16}; Is. 65^{6}; Rev. 20^{12}); (3) the book containing the earthly destiny of men; (4) the book containing the Divine plan for the history of the world and the destiny of Israel and the nations. (See Billerbeck, ii. 169–176). It is the first of these books that is thought of here. That the disciples have their names inscribed in it means that they are destined for the bliss of the coming Kingdom.

19. This verse, which breaks the connexion between *vv.* 18 and 20 resembles slightly the words ascribed to the Risen Christ in the spurious ending of Mk. ($16^{17 f.}$). Cf. also Ps. 91^{13}:

> Thou shalt tread upon the lion and the adder:
> The young lion and the serpent shalt thou trample under feet,

and Dt. 8^{15}. The serpents and scorpions may be thought of as semi-demonic creatures. The serpent in the story of the Fall is identified with Satan. Cf. notes on Lk. 3^{7}, above, p. 332. The 'enemy' is Satan; and the promise of the verse is that nothing that Satan can do will be able to harm the disciples.

Lk. 10^{21-24} (Q), above, pp. 370–373.

6. *THE WAY OF LIFE* (143)

LK. 10^{25-28}

10 25 And behold, a certain lawyer stood up
and tempted him, saying, [1] Master, what
26 shall I do to inherit eternal life? And
he said unto him, What is written in the
27 law? how readest thou? And he
answering said, Thou shalt love the Lord
thy God [2] with all thy heart, and with all
thy soul, and with all thy strength, and
with all thy mind; and thy neighbour as
28 thyself. And he said unto him, Thou
hast answered right: this do, and thou
shalt live.

[1] Or, *Teacher*.
[2] Gr. *from*.

This piece of dialogue is generally regarded as the Lucan (L) parallel to Mk. $12^{28-31,(34)}$. Actually the only point of resemblance is the fact that the two great commandments are conjoined in both accounts. In Mk. the question put to Jesus is, so to speak, an academic one and one that seems to have been debated a good deal among the scribes, since the answers of distinguished Rabbis have come down to us. In Lk. it is a very practical question; cf. Mk. 10^{17}. In Mk. Jesus gives the answer to the question: in Lk. it is given by the lawyer himself. In Mk. the comment of Jesus on the answer is: 'There is none other commandment greater than these.' Here it is: 'This do, and thou shalt live.' We are justified in assuming that the Lucan story is independent of Mk. Are they then different versions of the same incident? It might be argued that Lk. thought so, seeing that he omits the Marcan account from his Gospel. But if Lk. was interested chiefly in the point about the commandments, he may well have omitted the Marcan narrative on the ground that the essential point was already made in his own story, without staying to consider whether the two stories were different accounts of one and the same encounter. Further, the considerations which show the independence of the two accounts also suggest that they are accounts of two separate incidents. For the chief connecting link, the conjunction of the great commandments, is precisely the sort of thing that could appear over and over again. If a modern teacher of religion thought of such a thing as that, he would print it and it would make its way into the minds of the million. But in the first century A.D. in Palestine the only way of publishing great thoughts was to go on repeating them in talk or sermons.

It is thus quite possible, even probable, that when Jesus gave His famous answer to the scribe's question in the Marcan story, it was not the first time that He had expressed the whole duty of man by putting together those two texts. It must be emphasised that cases of this sort are not on all fours with the duplication of the miracles of feeding the multitude or with the two cleansings of the Temple. Great teachers constantly repeat themselves.

We may therefore entertain the hypothesis that the lawyer in the Lucan story gives the reply (*v.* 27) which he already knows to represent the opinion of Jesus, and that he does so in order to raise the further question: Who is my neighbour? That is to say, the Lucan story begins in earnest where the Marcan leaves off; and Lk. 10^{25-28} is really just introduction to what follows. It states what is common ground between Jesus and the lawyer, what Jesus teaches and what the lawyer is prepared to accept in principle, though he requires further definition in detail.

25. Lk. uses the word ' lawyer ' rather than ' scribe,' because the latter would be easily misunderstood by Gentile readers of his Gospel. The Greek word translated ' tempting ' does not necessarily have a hostile connotation. It may mean no more than ' questioning,' but questioning with the idea of testing the qualifications of the person questioned. The question itself contains no trap. It is the supreme religious question, and so the supreme test of a religious teacher. By their answers to just this question all religions are judged.

26. The questioner is referred to the Law, of which he is an accredited expositor, for the answer to his question. It is not expected that he will recite all its manifold commands and prohibitions, only that he should know the fundamental ends which these provisions are intended to secure.

27. The lawyer gives the answer which Jesus Himself gives in Mk. 12^{28-31}. This is not impossible or even improbable. It has already been suggested that Jesus may have been teaching this doctrine before, and that it was well known that this was the way in which He construed the Law. And, apart from that, there is the fact that in pre-Christian Jewish teaching the twin ideals of love to God and love to neighbour had been brought together in the *Testaments of the XII Patriarchs*. E.g. *Issachar* $5^{1f.}$.

> Keep, therefore, my children, the law of God,
> And get singleness, and walk in guilelessness,
> Not playing the busybody with the business of your neighbour.
> But love the Lord and your neighbour,
> Have compassion on the poor and weak.

Cf. *Iss.* 7^6; *Test. Dan.* 5^3: 'Love the Lord through all your life, and one another with a true heart.' The texts from the Old Testament here brought together are

Dt. 6^5 and Lev. 19^{18}. Philo, in his own way, makes the same conjunction when He describes the chief of the virtues as piety and philanthropy. (Cf. Drummond, *Philo Judæus*, ii. 315 f.). See further my *Teaching of Jesus*, pp. 302 ff.

28. The reply of Jesus gives complete approval to this solution of the problem. He says in effect: ' That is my answer to the question. It only remains to translate correct theory into regular practice, and you will find that it is the way of life for you.' There is nothing hypothetical about the sentence. Jesus says: 'This is the way to life, the life of the coming age; take it and you will find that it is so.' The moment this theory is put into practice, the question arises as to the scope of its application. This question is raised by the lawyer and answered by Jesus in

The Parable of the Good Samaritan (144)

LK. 10^{29-37}

10 29 But he, desiring to justify himself, said
unto Jesus, And who is my neighbour?
30 Jesus made answer and said, A certain
man was going down from Jerusalem to
Jericho; and he fell among robbers, which
both stripped him and beat him, and
31 departed, leaving him half dead. And
by chance a certain priest was going
down that way: and when he saw him, he
32 passed by on the other side. And in like
manner a Levite also, when he came to
the place, and saw him, passed by on the
33 other side. But a certain Samaritan, as
he journeyed, came where he was: and
when he saw him, he was moved with
34 compassion, and came to him, and bound
up his wounds, pouring on *them* oil and
wine; and he set him on his own beast,
and brought him to an inn, and took
35 care of him. And on the morrow he
took out two [1] pence, and gave them to
the host, and said, Take care of him; and
whatsoever thou spendest more, I, when
I come back again, will repay thee.
36 Which of these three, thinkest thou,
proved neighbour unto him that fell
37 among the robbers? And he said, He
that shewed mercy on him. And Jesus
said unto him, Go, and do thou likewise.

[1] See marginal note on Matt. xviii. 28.

29. The point of the lawyer's objection is that it is precisely when one begins to put such a rule as this into practice that difficulties arise. And they turn on the construction of the word ' neighbour.' ' Love God '—that goes without saying. Love one's family, or one's fellow-worshippers in the Synagogue, or one's colleagues in the Rabbinical school—that also is understood. But where does one draw the line between neighbour and not-neighbour, that is, between those who are entitled to this consideration from me and those who are not. All ancient civilisations drew the line somewhere, whether between Greek and Barbarian, Roman citizen and foreigner, freeman and slave, or Jew and Gentile. The context of Lev. 19^{18} shows plainly enough that ' neighbour ' there means fellow-Israelite. The concept might be enlarged by reckoning as neighbours those who, though not of Jewish race, embraced the Jewish faith; or it might be narrowed by excluding those who, though of Jewish blood, rejected or neglected the faith of their fathers. But at any rate the word ' neighbour ' ought to be definable; and it is for Jesus' definition that the lawyer asks.

It is often made a criticism of the parable of the Good Samaritan that it is no answer to the question posed. But this is a shallow criticism. Certainly no definition of ' neighbour ' emerges from the parable: and for a very good reason. The question is unanswerable, and ought not to be asked. For love does not begin by defining its objects: it discovers them. And failure in the observance of the great commandment comes not from lack of precise information about the application of it, but from lack of love. The point of the parable is that if a man has love in his heart, it will tell him who his neighbour is; and this is the only possible answer to the lawyer's question.

30. With the parable itself cf. 2 Chron. 28^{5-15}. It has been suggested that this story is not fiction but fact, that Jesus Himself was the 'certain man' who fell among thieves. In support of this hypothesis it could be urged that in Aramaic 'that man,' which is practically equivalent to 'a certain man,' is used as a polite periphrasis for the personal pronoun. But the theory cannot be proved, and should not be regarded as more than a possibility.

The road from Jerusalem to Jericho (about 17 miles) passes through country which is 'desert and rocky' (Josephus, *War*, iv. 474), and suited by nature for the operations of brigands. Jerome reports that raiding bands of Arabs were active on the road in his day. The Greek word translated 'both' in R.V. has rather the force of 'as you might expect,' or 'as their way is.' The evil work was thoroughly done, and when it was finished the victim was left without goods, without power to help himself or to follow his attackers, with very little between him and death.

31 f. Priest and Levite represented the national aristocracy of that period. It was to them that one might have looked for the manifestation of Judaism at its best. They above all others should have shown how to fulfil the commandment given in Lev. 19^{18}. Their callousness stands in sharp contrast to the ideal of which they were the official guardians. It is possible that they were on their way home after serving in the Temple.

33. The Samaritan—a layman and, from the Jewish standpoint, a schismatic—shows a better spirit than the official exponents of Jewish piety. He would appear to be a travelling trader. Some difficulty has been felt at the idea of a Samaritan appearing on business in Judæa, especially as relations between Jews and Samaritans were bad at this time; and it has been supposed that originally the parable told not of a good Samaritan, but of a good 'Israelite.' In this case 'Israelite' would mean a Jewish layman in contrast to the Priest and the Levite. This is not very likely; and if we have to deal with the difficulty of the Samaritan being on the road from Jerusalem to Jericho, it is simpler to suppose that originally the third to arrive on the scene was an *'am hā-āres*, i.e. a Jew who did not attend with proper strictness to the details of the legal system, a Jew who was not a 'practising' Jew. Such a conjecture would make the change to 'Samaritan' easily conceivable. But we should probably retain 'Samaritan' in spite of the unlikelihood of finding a Samaritan travelling from Jerusalem to Jericho. The parable is fiction, not history. See notes on *v.* 36. In any case the point is that mercy and kindness were displayed by the last person from whom one would have looked for these qualities.

34, 35. The Samaritan renders first aid to the victim. Oil and wine, either separately or mixed, were recognised as healing agents both in Palestine (Mishnah, *Shabbath*, 19^2; Danby, p. 116) and among the Greeks. Having made his man comfortable, the Samaritan brings him to an 'inn,' or rather caravanserai, where shelter and protection could be obtained for the night. More than that, on the following day, when he must continue his journey, the Samaritan pays in advance for such further care as his penniless protégé may require. The ‘ two pence ’ are two *denarii*, silver coins worth about 8½*d*., but with much greater purchasing power. In the Mishnah four denars is the price of a lamb fit for sacrifice (*Menahoth* 13^{8}; Danby, p. 512); and in Mt. 20^{2} one denar is the day's wage for a working man. The good Samaritan further promises that on his return journey he will pay any further debt that may have been incurred.

36. Having told the story Jesus asks the lawyer for his opinion. The question is not whether the victim of the robbers was neighbour in a legal sense to any or all of those who encountered him, but whether any of them showed a neighbourly spirit towards him. The principle underlying the question is that while mere neighbourhood does not create love, love does create neighbourliness. Supposing, as we may, that the man who fell among thieves was a Jew, he was in fact ‘ neighbour ’ in the technical Jewish sense to the Priest and the Levite; and he was not ‘ neighbour ’ to the Samaritan. Yet his lawful ‘ neighbours ’ were of no use to him in his extremity, and it was a man who was not his lawful ‘ neighbour ’ who helped him. Love created neighbourliness. Hence the conclusion implicit in the whole parable: it is wrong to construe Lev. 19^{18} in terms of ‘ neighbour ’; you must construe it in terms of ‘ love.’ For it is ‘ love ’ that is fundamental, not neighbourhood.

37. The lawyer gives the only possible answer to Jesus' question, and this is met by the command: Go, and do thou likewise. This is the final answer to the lawyer's original question (*v.* 25): What shall I do to inherit eternal life?

7. *MARTHA AND MARY* (145)

LK. $10^{38\text{-}42}$

10 38 Now as they went on their way, he
entered into a certain village: and a
certain woman named Martha received
39 him into her house. And she had a sister
called Mary, which also sat at the Lord's
40 feet, and heard his word. But Martha
was [1] cumbered about much serving;
and she came up to him, and said, Lord,
dost thou not care that my sister did leave
me to serve alone? bid her therefore that
41 she help me. But the Lord answered
and said unto her, [2] Martha, Martha,
thou art anxious and troubled about
42 many things: [3] but one thing is
needful: for Mary hath chosen the good
part, which shall not be taken away
from her.

[1] Gr. *distracted.*

[2] A few ancient authorities read *Martha, Martha, thou art troubled; Mary hath chosen, &c.*

[3] Many ancient authorities read *but few things are needful, or one.*

Beside the teaching on the way to eternal life Lk. places this incident, whose purport is to show that that way is the supreme interest of men. The parable of the Good Samaritan shows the one way to the goal; the story of Martha and Mary insists that there is only one goal worth seeking.

38–40. The setting of the incident is vague. Presumably Lk.'s source did not give further particulars; and the two sisters do not appear elsewhere in the Synoptics. In the fourth gospel (11^{1}) their home was in Bethany. Both Martha and Mary are Jewish names. Martha appears here as the head of the household: there is no mention of a brother Lazarus, as in John. She is the industrious capable housewife. Her sister Mary is more concerned to ‘ attend upon the Lord without distraction ’ (1 Cor. 7^{35}). To sit at the feet of a person is to be his pupil.

Cf. Acts 22[3], Paul brought up 'at the feet of Gamaliel'; *Aboth* 1[4] (Danby, p. 446): 'Let thy house be a meeting-house for the Sages and sit amid the dust of their feet and drink in their words with thirst.' Martha, up to the eyes in work, regards her sister's interest in theology with disapproval. Time enough to listen when the household work is finished. (Though we may suspect that Martha was one of those whose work is never finished.) She appeals to Jesus to send his new disciple about her proper business.

41 f. The sense of Jesus' reply is clear enough in the main; but the exact form of it is uncertain. As it has come down to us in MSS. and versions there are four main forms:

I. Martha, Martha, Mary hath chosen the good part, etc.

II. Martha, Martha, thou art anxious and troubled about many things: but one thing is needful: for Mary hath chosen the good part, etc.

III. Martha, Martha, thou art anxious and troubled about many things: but few things are needful: for Mary hath chosen the good part, etc.

IV. Martha, Martha, thou art anxious and troubled about many things: but few things are needful, or one: for Mary hath chosen the good part, etc.

Of these readings IV may be dismissed as a conflation of II and III. It is, however, in that case evidence for the antiquity of III. Some ancestor of the authorities, which have IV, had the reading III. Someone inserted in the margin of his copy the words 'or one,' which then found their way into the text. I do not consider it necessary to decide between 'but one thing is needful' and 'but few things are needful'; because I regard them as variant forms of an original gloss on the text. They probably correspond to early variations in the interpretation of the story. Such interpretations were already current in the time of Origen. For example, Martha is the type of Jewish Christianity, Mary of Gentile Christianity: or Martha is the type of the practical life, Mary of the contemplative: or again the 'many things' stand for the numerous commandments of the Law while the 'few things' are the Gospel commandments of love. If, however, we ask what the two clauses could mean in the original context, it would seem that 'few things' can only be in contrast to 'many things.' Martha is making great preparations; but something much simpler would be quite adequate. On the other hand 'one thing' can only anticipate 'the good part': the one thing needful is the good part which Mary has chosen.

It seems most likely to me that the original answer ran: Martha, Martha, thou art anxious and troubled about many things: but Mary hath chosen the good part, etc. Some such reading appears to lie behind the quotation of this text by Clement of Alexandria (ed. Stählin, iii. 166).

The contrast between Martha and Mary does not lie where the patristic commentators found it. It is something much simpler and more primitive. The good thing which Mary has chosen is not the contemplative life, or the ethic of the Sermon on the Mount, but the Kingdom of God. The true parallel in thought to this saying is Lk. 12[29-31]||Mt. 6[31-33] (Q), above, p. 405. The contrast is between Martha, immersed in the business of her little corner of the workaday world, and Mary, who is of the kind that leave all to follow Christ. It could be urged, and

Martha makes the point, that in leaving all Mary has mostly left her duties in the house. A similar criticism could, however, have been made by Peter's wife or the father of James and John; and it can be said that the progress of the Gospel in the world would not have been what it was if there had not been those who heard a call that cancelled all other obligations. As the story stands Mary belongs to those who take the Kingdom of God by storm, who put their hands to the plough and do not look back, who leave the dead to bury their dead.

8. *THE LORD'S PRAYER* (146)

LK. 11^{1-4}

11 1 And it came to pass, as he was praying
in a certain place, that when he ceased,
one of his disciples said unto him, Lord,
teach us to pray, even as John also taught
2 his disciples. And he said unto them,
When ye pray, say, [1] Father, Hallowed be
3 thy name. Thy kingdom come.[2] Give
us day by day [3] our daily bread. And
4 forgive us our sins; for we ourselves also
forgive every one that is indebted to us.
And bring us not into temptation.[4]

[1] Many ancient authorities read *Our Father, which art in heaven.* See Matt. vi. 9.
[2] Many ancient authorities add *Thy will be done, as in heaven, so on earth.* See Matt. vi. 10.
[3] Gr. *our bread for the coming day.*
[4] Many ancient authorities add *but deliver us from the evil* one (or, *from evil*). See Matt. vi. 13.

The Lord's Prayer, in the form familiar to us through liturgical use, appears in Mt. 6^{9-13} (above, pp. 459–463). The Lucan version, which we assign to L, is shorter and differs from Mt. in several particulars. The true text of the Lucan form is not easy to establish, because the tendency in the copying of MSS. has been to conform it to the Matthæan, which was the version in the liturgical use.

1. The Prayer is here provided with a narrative setting. In Mt. it is incorporated into a collection of teachings on the general subject of prayer as a part of religious observance. Here the origin of the Lord's Prayer is described. It is given in response to a request from one of the disciples; and the disciple is led to make his request through observing that John's disciples had forms of prayer prescribed by their master. Three early Christian practices seem thus to be derived from imitation of John's discipline: baptism, common prayer, and regular fasts.

2. 'Father' is undoubtedly the true text of Lk. The marginal reading is an instance of the tendency to conform MSS. to the text of Mt. 'Father' is almost certainly the original form of the address, see above, p. 460. The two following petitions agree with Mt. But there is a remarkable variant reading: 'Thy holy Spirit come upon us and cleanse us.' In the version of Lk. published by the second-century heretic Marcion this petition takes the place of 'Hallowed be thy name'; and in two cursive MSS. as well as in the writings of Gregory of Nyssa, and Maximus Confessor it takes the place of 'Thy kingdom come.' By some scholars it is regarded as the original text of Lk., though not necessarily the original language of the Prayer. The strongest argument in favour of this reading is the fact that in 11^{13} Lk. speaks of God giving the Holy Spirit to those who ask Him, where Mt. in the parallel passage (7^{11}) speaks of God giving 'good things.' Mt.'s 'good things' is almost certainly the true representation of the Q text. If Lk.

is responsible for 'Holy Spirit' in 11^{13}, it is the more likely that he is responsible for the clause asking for the Holy Spirit here, for the two things hang together. But even if the petition is inserted by Lk. himself, it is unlikely that it is part of the original Prayer. More probably it may be regarded as an old petition, used in connexion with the baptism of converts, which found its way into the Lord's Prayer. Or it may be that both the petition here and 'Holy Spirit' in 11^{13} are due to Marcionite revision. The addition in R.V. mg. 'Thy will be done, etc.,' is not genuine text of Lk., but assimilation to Mt.

3. See notes on Mt. 6^{11}, above, p. 461. The Lucan form of the petition is less original than the Matthæan. The request in Mt. asks for enough to-day to provide for to-morrow. In Lk. this is generalised into the request that every day we may have enough for the next day.

4. See notes on Mt. 6^{12}, above, p. 461. The L form of the petition is less concrete and definite than the Matthæan. In Mt. the prayer says 'we have forgiven'; and the thought is that definite known cases of offence have been disposed of in this way. Cf. Mt. $5^{23f.}$, above, p. 448. In Lk. it is rather a regular practice that is stated in general terms—and statements in general terms are dangerous in prayer. Mt.'s form is to be preferred.

5. See notes on Mt. 6^{13}, above, p. 462. The Lucan form omits the last petition for deliverance from the evil. The reading given in R.V. mg. is again a case of assimilation to the text of Mt.

The differences between the forms of the Prayer in Mt. and Lk. can be considered under two heads.

First, there are the differences in wording in the parts where Mt. and Lk. coincide; and here it must be said that in the main Mt.'s wording is to be preferred. The one case in which Lk. clearly deserves the preference is 'Father' for 'Our Father which art in heaven.'

Secondly, there is the fact that the genuine text of Lk. gives a shorter version of the prayer than Mt. Here it is important to remember that the tendency of liturgical forms is to grow rather than to shrink through use. There is thus some antecedent probability that the shorter form is the more original. This is strengthened if we regard the petition 'Thy will be done, etc.,' as exposition of the immediately preceding 'Thy kingdom come,' and take the petition 'but deliver us from the evil (one)' as commentary on 'Lead us not into temptation.'

We cannot do more than guess at the original form of the Prayer; but a tentative reconstruction on the basis of the evidence of Mt. and Lk. would be somewhat as follows:

Father, Hallowed be thy name.
Thy Kingdom come.
Give us this day our bread for the coming day.
And forgive us our sins, as we also have forgiven those who have wronged us.
And bring us not into temptation.

9. *THE PARABLE OF THE IMPORTUNATE FRIEND* (147)

LK. 11^{5-8}

11 5 And he said unto them, Which of you
shall have a friend, and shall go unto him
at midnight, and say to him, Friend, lend
6 me three loaves; for a friend of mine is
come to me from a journey, and I have
7 nothing to set before him; and he from
within shall answer and say, Trouble me
not: the door is now shut, and my children
are with me in bed; I cannot rise and give
8 thee? I say unto you, Though he will
not rise and give him, because he is his
friend, yet because of his importunity he
will arise and give him [1] as many as he
needeth.

[1] Or, *whatsoever things*.

Mt. follows the Lord's Prayer with a caution that God's forgiveness is conditional on a forgiving spirit in man; Lk. with a discourse (11^{5-13}, L + Q) on God's readiness to give to those who ask Him. The first part of the discourse is the present parable, which is peculiar to Lk. The second part is from Q, and has been treated above, pp. 373 f. This parable has a companion in the parable of the Importunate Widow (Lk. 18^{1-8}), which is also peculiar to this Gospel (below, p. 597). That parable may be regarded as comment on the petition 'Thy kingdom come'; this as comment on 'Give us this day our bread for the coming day.' The one looks forward to the final fulfilment of God's plan; the other has in mind the needs of God's servants while they wait and work for it. There is a certain superficial inconsistency between what is taught in this parable and the principle laid down in Mt. $6^{7 f.}$ (M), particularly the words 'Your Father knoweth what things ye have need of before ye ask him.' But the inconsistency is more apparent than real. Certainly, if we think of God's providence as a piece of supernatural machinery, which distributes with infallible accuracy what every man ought to have, it may seem superfluous to express our desires in prayer. But the teaching of Jesus is that we are not dealing with a mere combination of omniscience and omnipotence, but with a Father who cares for us as persons; and that therefore our desires are His concern as much as our needs. If we are dealing with a government department, there may be nothing for it but to apply on the printed form and sign on the dotted line; but if we are dealing with a father, we may exercise more freedom of speech. Prayer is the means of establishing agreement between God's will and man's desires: and it may well be that the best of all ways of educating our desires is to express them to God in prayer. It may be that it is only by telling God frankly what we want that we can learn what we truly need.

5 f. The situation described is a simple one. There is the arrival late at night of an unexpected guest and the discovery that the contents of the larder are inadequate to the claims of hospitality. The only thing to be done is to knock up a friend and borrow what is needed. This the householder proceeds to do as politely as possible. Note the 'Friend' in the request: it is absent from the reply. Also the explanation offered for disturbing the friend at that time of night.

7. There is an absence of cordiality in the reply from within. It is a nuisance to be roused from one's sleep, a nuisance to have to unlock the door, a nuisance to have the children disturbed. The conclusion of the matter is 'I cannot arise and give thee.' Here, as so often, 'I cannot' camouflages 'I will not.'

8. But the hero of the parable will not take No for an answer, and it soon appears that the only way for his friend to continue his night's rest is to come down and supply what is required.

The conclusion is not explicitly drawn; but it is sufficiently obvious. If a human friend, who is a prey to moods and tempers, can be persuaded even against his inclination to get up and oblige you, how much more will God your Father and your perfect friend be ready to supply all your needs. The disciple who has this confidence will be able to open his heart freely before God. He will also be able to accept whatever God sends him. He will know how to say: 'I have learned in whatsoever state I am, therein to be content. I know how to be abased, and I know also how to abound: in everything and in all things have I learned the secret both to be filled and to be hungry, both to abound and to be in want. I can do all things in him that strengtheneth me' (Phil. 4^{11-13}).

10. *OUTWARD AND INWARD PURITY* (154)

LK. $11^{37-41, 53, 54}$, 12^{1}

11 37 Now as he spake, a Pharisee asketh
him to [1] dine with him: and he went in,
38 and sat down to meat. And when the
Pharisee saw it, he marvelled that he had
39 not first washed before [1] dinner. And
the Lord said unto him, Now do ye
Pharisees cleanse the outside of the cup
and of the platter; but your inward part
40 is full of extortion and wickedness. Ye
foolish ones, did not he that made the
41 outside make the inside also? Howbeit
give for alms those things which [2] are
within; and behold, all things are clean
unto you.
53 And when he was come out from
thence, the scribes and the Pharisees
began to [3] press upon *him* vehemently,
and to provoke him to speak of [4] many
54 things; laying wait for him, to catch
something out of his mouth.
12 1 In the mean time, when [5] the many
thousands of the multitude were gathered
together, insomuch that they trode one
upon another, he began to [6] say unto his
disciples first of all, Beware ye of the
leaven of the Pharisees, which is hypocrisy.

[1] Gr. *breakfast.*
[2] Or, *ye can.*
[3] Or, *set themselves vehemently against him.*
[4] Or, *more.*
[5] Gr. *the myriads of.*
[6] Or, *say unto his disciples, First of all beware ye.*

On the composition of the whole passage 11^{37}–12^{1}, see above, pp. 386 ff. The conclusion there reached is that our present passage 11^{37-41}, 11^{53}–12^{1}, is the L framework into which Lk. has inserted the Q woes against scribes and Pharisees. This passage makes a complete and self-contained story whose subject is the same as that in Mk. 7^{1-23}, though the situation and the treatment of the topic are different. The central point (*vv.* 39–41) has a parallel in Mt.'s woes against scribes and Pharisees (Mt. $23^{25 f.}$, above, p. 528). But it is more likely that the woe has been extracted out of the story than that the story has been constructed round the woe.

37 f. The scene of the incident is a Pharisee's house, to which Jesus has been invited for a meal. The nature of the meal is uncertain. The ordinary Jewish practice was to have two meals per day (three on the Sabbath). These were taken in the morning and evening. But among that class of the community to which this Pharisee may well have belonged, the morning meal was not taken until about midday; and the practice was to take a little food, not a full meal, earlier in the

morning. It seems most probable that the meal in this case was a midday meal. Jesus shocked his host by sitting down to the meal without first washing. This 'washing' consisted in pouring water over the hands; and it was customary before and after the meal (Billerbeck, i. 695–704). We are not told how the Pharisee expressed his surprise, whether in speech or merely by a raising of the eyebrows; but we are clearly to understand that there was some indication. This indication, whatever it was, provoked the reply of Jesus.

39 ff. The M version of this saying seems in the main to give it more correctly. There the figure is maintained throughout. Here the Lucan version wavers between parable and interpretation. It is probable, I think, that Jesus spoke throughout in terms of pots and pans, and left His hearers to make the obvious application of the parable. The vessel may be perfectly clean; but that is no advantage if its contents are putrid.

There is nothing in Mt. corresponding to *v.* 40 in Lk.; and the verse as it stands is exceedingly difficult to interpret. If we take the R.V. translation, we must understand the verse: '"Did not God, who made the material universe, make men's souls also?" It is folly to be scrupulous about keeping material objects clean, while the soul is polluted with wickedness' (Plummer). But perhaps we ought to translate differently: 'He, who has dealt with the outside, has not thereby dealt with the inside.' This involves taking the verb 'make' not in the sense of 'create' but in the sense in which it is used when we speak of 'making a bed' i.e. putting it in order, making it fit for use.

Lk. *v.* 41 has a parallel in Mt. 23^{26}. But whereas Lk. has 'Give for alms those things which are within,' Mt. has 'Cleanse first the inside of the cup.' It is probable that Lk.'s 'give alms' is a mistaken rendering of an Aramaic original correctly translated by Mt. Then the verse may be taken to say: 'Purify the inside (the heart), and then all is pure for you.' The meaning seems to be that the heart is what counts. If the heart is pure the whole man is pure. Defilement is cut off at the source. 'All things are clean unto you' I take to mean 'The whole —outside and inside, the complete man—is clean, so far as you are concerned.' This agrees in substance with Mt. who says 'cleanse the inside, and you also cleanse the outside.' It is also in agreement with the teaching of Mk. 7^{18-23}. In this verse we have the application of the parable quite clearly in the mind of the speaker. For cleansing the inside of a vessel does not automatically cleanse the outside. But it can be said that if a man's heart is pure, he is pure.

We may compare the saying of Raba (died A.D. 352): 'A scholar (Rabbi) whose inward (thoughts) do not correspond to his outward (profession) is no scholar' (Billerbeck, ii. 188).

53 ff. These verses describe the effect of this attack upon the hearers. They began to make a dead set against Jesus and to 'heckle' him about all kinds of subjects. Every question was a trap by which they hoped to elicit a reply which might be turned against Him. Lk. seems to picture this contest as drawing a large crowd of the general public, all anxious to hear the dispute and jostling one another in their eagerness to get to the front. In the midst of the uproar Jesus turns to His disciples, who have not hitherto been mentioned, and says to His disciples first of all, 'Beware of the leaven of the Pharisees, which is hypocrisy.'

It is clear that Lk. must introduce the disciples at this point, because of the Q passage (12^{2-12}) which he is about to link on to this saying, and which is clearly addressed to disciples. It is therefore possible that in his source the words of *v.* 1 were addressed to the assembled crowd. This would explain the 'first of all.' The words, Lk. will have us understand, are meant to be heard by the crowd—as, presumably, in his source—but they are primarily for the disciples, to whom what immediately follows is addressed. If this is the correct explanation it becomes unnecessary to repunctuate the verse and translate, with some scholars, 'He began to say to His disciples: Before all beware of the leaven, etc.'

On the above interpretation 12^1 forms a dramatic climax to the whole incident. It may be noted that we have a point of contact with Mk.'s account of a similar dispute, with this difference that the charge of hypocrisy comes at the end of Lk.'s story, whereas in Mk. it is the first item in Jesus' reply (Mk. $7^{6 ff.}$).

On the 'leaven' of the Pharisees cf. Mk. 8^{15}: Take heed, beware of the leaven of the Pharisees and the leaven of Herod. This obscure saying was already a problem in the early days. Mt. in the parallel (Mt. 16^6) changes Mk.'s text to 'leaven of the Pharisees and Sadducees' and later interprets this (16^{12}) as the 'teaching of the Pharisees and Sadducees.' Here the leaven is hypocrisy. It is possible that the words 'which is hypocrisy' are an explanatory comment either of Lk. or his source. In the Rabbinical literature 'leaven' is used figuratively of the evil disposition in man (Billerbeck, i. 728 f.).

In spite of the skill with which Lk. has presented the story, it remains more than possible that 12^1 was originally a separate fragment, which has nothing to do with what precedes or follows.

11. *THE PERIL OF COVETOUSNESS* (156)

LK. 12^{13-21}

12 13 And one out of the multitude said unto
him, [1] Master, bid my brother divide the
14 inheritance with me. But he said unto
him, Man, who made me a judge or a
15 divider over you? And he said unto
them, Take heed, and keep yourselves
from all covetousness: [2] for a man's life
consisteth not in the abundance of the
16 things which he possesseth. And he
spake a parable unto them, saying, The
ground of a certain rich man brought
17 forth plentifully: and he reasoned within
himself, saying, What shall I do, because
I have not where to bestow my fruits?
18 And he said, This will I do: I will pull
down my barns, and build greater; and
there will I bestow all my corn and my
19 goods. And I will say to my [3] soul,
[3] Soul, thou hast much goods laid up for
many years; take thine ease, eat, drink,
20 be merry. But God said unto him, Thou
foolish one, this night [4] is thy [3] soul
required of thee; and the things which
thou hast prepared, whose shall they be?
21 So is he that layeth up treasure for himself, and is not rich toward God.

[1] Or, *Teacher.*
[2] Gr. *for not in a man's abundance consisteth his life, from the things which he possesseth.*
[3] Or, *life.*
[4] Gr. *they require thy soul.*

For Lk. this incident seems to be the continuation of what has gone before. Lk. 12^{2-12} form the continuation of the saying in 12^1; and the crowd *v.* 13 is the same as that in *v.* 1. But it is unlikely that the connexion is anything more than a literary device. The passage *vv.* 13–21 is a self-contained unit, which Lk. has skilfully inserted between two Q passages. It falls into two parts (*a*) a piece of dialogue between Jesus and a dissatisfied heir, leading up to (*b*) the parable of the Rich Fool. The first part has been supposed, for no very good reason, to be an artificial introduction to the parable. The connexion is good; and the most likely view is that the bit of dialogue, which is not in itself of vital importance, has been preserved by the fact that it was attached to the parable from the beginning.

13 f. The unknown person who appeals to Jesus is described by Lk. as 'one out of the multitude.' This description serves to link the incident to what has gone before. No doubt it replaces a still more indefinite phrase, such as, 'a certain man.' There is nothing odd in the man's bringing a question of this sort to Jesus. In Judaism the one Law covered everything. There was no sharp division between the secular and the sacred, between civil and ecclesiastical matters. The same authorities decided matters of religious belief and practice and matters of civil and criminal justice. The dictum 'This is a court of law, not a court of morals' would have had no meaning to a Jewish scribe in the first century. A 'teacher' (Rabbi) was the very person to decide both religious and, what we should call, legal questions. The rules of inheritance are given in the Mishnah (*Baba Bathra* 8–9, Danby, pp. 376–380). We are not told what the issue was in this particular case; and the details are irrelevant, since the reply of Jesus to the request makes it clear that he would refuse to adjudicate in any case. He refuses to be interested in the 'facts of the case,' because there is one outstanding fact which makes all the rest insignificant; the fact that two men, worshippers of the same God, members of the one Chosen People and of the same family, are separated and antagonised over the possession of a piece of property. What is needed is not a just settlement of the dispute by some third party, but that the parties themselves and all the multitude should feel the shame and disgrace of such a dispute. Cf. 1 Cor. $6^{7 ff.}$. If the brothers realise that, they will settle the matter amicably between themselves. Our Lord's curt refusal to have anything to do with the case is put in words reminiscent of Exod. 2^{14}.

15. The whole wretched business is in flat contradiction to the fundamental rule of life given in Lev. 19^{18}: Thou shalt love thy neighbour as thyself. And the active cause of the trouble is just plain greed. What is needed is not the decision of this or any other case, but the elimination of that which makes the dispute. 'All covetousness' means self-seeking in all its manifold shapes, both in the crude desire for material things and in the subtler forms which it can also take with those whose tastes are more refined. There is a twofold reason for avoiding it. First, it causes disunion and strife, as in the case which has given rise to this piece of teaching. And secondly, it leads nowhere. He who hopes to achieve fullness of life by increasing his possessions finds in the end that he has laboured for that which satisfieth not. It is true that a certain minimum of material goods is necessary for life; but it is not true that greater abundance of goods means greater abundance of life. Cf. Eccles. 2^{1-11}; Ps. 49; Job $31^{24 f.}$.

16, 17 f. This general principle is now driven home by the story of the Rich Fool (*vv.* 16–21). The parable has some affinity with the passage in *Ecclus.* $11^{18 f.}$:

> There is that waxeth rich from self-denial,
> And this is his allotted reward:

What time he saith: 'I have found rest,
And now I will enjoy my goods'—
He knoweth not what lot shall befall;
He shall leave (them) to others and die.

In the story as told by Jesus we are introduced to the hero when his ambitions are on the point of being realised. He already has abundance of material goods. The only problem remaining is that of storage. This is simply solved by demolishing the existing storehouses and building larger. Translated into modern terms—here is a man who has made a large fortune in business, and now wishes to retire. He realises his capital and invests all in trustee securities.

19. Having made all the necessary provision for the future the rich man will be able, he thinks, to spend the remainder of his days in enjoyment. Cf. Eccles. 8^{15}: 'A man hath no better thing under the sun, than to eat, and to drink, and to be merry.' *Tobit* 7^{10}; Euripides, *Alc.*, 788 f.

20. But the rich man's plans for the future are destined not to be carried out. In the midst of his scheming he hears the summons that cannot be ignored. The R.V. mg. gives the literal rendering of the Greek. This impersonal 3rd person plural has the effect of a passive. It is, of course, God who requires the man's soul. The sting of the words lies, however, not in the announcement that the man must die, but in the following question, which shows clearly the real poverty of his life. He is lonely and friendless in the midst of his wealth.

For a perfect modern parallel to the story see Jung, *Collected Papers on Analytical Psychology*, pp. 399 ff.

21. This verse supplies the comment on the story. Whether it comes from Jesus Himself or from some early Christian or from Lk. is doubtful. It can be connected with the closing words of *v.* 20 by the consideration that if the rich man had employed his riches in an unselfish way, he would have had both friends on earth and treasure in heaven.

12. *THE URGENCY OF THE GOSPEL* (162)

LK. 13^{1-9}

13 1 Now there were some present at that
very season which told him of the Galilæans, whose blood Pilate had mingled with
2 their sacrifices. And he answered and
said unto them, Think ye that these
Galilæans were sinners above all the
Galilæans, because they have suffered
3 these things? I tell you, Nay: but, except
ye repent, ye shall all in like manner
4 perish. Or those eighteen, upon whom
the tower in Siloam fell, and killed them,
think ye that they were [1] offenders above
5 all the men that dwell in Jerusalem? I
tell you, Nay: but, except ye repent, ye
shall all likewise perish.
6 And he spake this parable; A certain
man had a fig tree planted in his vineyard;
and he came seeking fruit thereon, and
7 found none. And he said unto the vinedresser, Behold, these three years I come
seeking fruit on this fig tree, and find
none: cut it down; why doth it also cumber
8 the ground? And he answering saith
unto him, Lord, let it alone this year also,
till I shall dig about it, and dung it:
9 and if it bear fruit thenceforth, *well*; but
if not, thou shalt cut it down.

[1] Gr. *debtors.*

This passage consists of two portions, both occupied with the same matter, the urgent necessity for timely repentance. The Gospel is good news, but only for those who will listen to it. It opens up a way of salvation for those who will leave the way of destruction. It is at once a warning and a promise: and in this passage, as in the immediately preceding Q section (12^{57-59}, above, p. 414), it is the warning note that is stressed.

1. The passage opens with a precise note of time; but the words ' at that very season ' do not really tell us anything. If Lk. himself inserted them in order to link this bit of L material to the preceding bit of Q, it can only be said that he did not show very much skill. The alternative is to suppose that the words were in the anecdote as it came to him, and that they refer to some context now lost. The Greek verb translated ' there were present ' can also mean ' there arrived,' and this rendering is to be preferred. The story which these persons told is not elsewhere recorded. The scene of the incident must be Jerusalem, for only there could sacrifice be offered. Galileans have come up to the Temple and are either slaughtering or assisting at the slaughtering of the victims when they are massacred by the Romans. There are evidences outside the New Testament of Pilate's brutality (e.g. Josephus, *Antiquities*, xviii. 60 ff., 85 ff.; *War*, ii. 175 ff.), but nothing that tallies with this story. The question at once arises whether this tale of Pilate's outburst is fact or fiction; and this goes with the further question why the story was brought to Jesus. Two answers may be given to this latter question. Either the story was told in the hope that it would rouse Jesus to lead a revolt against Rome, or in the hope that in His indignation He would say something about Pilate which might be used in evidence against Him on a charge of sedition. In the latter case the story did not even need to be true so long as it achieved its object. Those who came and told it would be, of course, enemies of Jesus. In the former case the tellers of the tale would presumably be ardent patriots. Their story would be the better of being true; but even if false, it would have served its purpose if it raised a revolt. For once started on a revolt there could be no going back. It is thus possible that the story was fiction from the beginning.

2 f. Whatever the motive may have been, the expected response did not materialise. Jesus was not to be drawn into criticism of the Roman governor or revolt against the Empire. Instead, He carries the whole matter out of the political into the religious sphere. Here it becomes another example of the kind of problem that created the book of Job. The easy solution would be to say, as Job's friends said, that the fate of the Galileans overtook them in the providence of God, and that it was doubtless a just punishment for some iniquity of which they were guilty. Jesus rejects this theory. If suffering were a punishment for sin, there would be a great deal more suffering than there is. While rejecting the retribution theory, Jesus does not put forward any alternative at this point. He leaves the ' problem of suffering ' and treats this story and another, which He brings forward Himself, as parables. And the point of the parables is the urgency of the Gospel.

Here are people going about their business in the Temple or the street, and suddenly death comes upon them. It is like the world in the days of Noah or Sodom and Gomorrah in the days of Lot. The fate of these people is a reminder not of their sins—they were neither better nor worse than many others—but of the urgency of the Gospel. Had they only known what was astir, been warned that Pilate was in a black mood or that the building was dangerous, they might have saved their lives. But there was nobody to warn them, and they perished. So this generation, says Jesus in effect, is walking—politically and religiously—straight for disaster. But the warning has been given, first by John the Baptist and now by Jesus. It is a warning to change direction before it is too late. 'Unless ye repent ye shall all likewise perish.'

4 f. The accident described in this verse is not mentioned elsewhere, which is not surprising, since it was an accident and not an 'incident.' It had no significance for the secular historian. The spring and reservoir of Siloam lay near the junction of the south and east walls of the city. The tower which collapsed may well have been some part of these ancient fortifications, and it is perhaps possible that the collapse was caused by the building operations carried out by Pilate to improve the water-supply of Jerusalem (Josephus, *Ant.* xviii. 60; *War*, ii. 175).

6. The lesson derived from the two incidents is further enforced by a parable. The parable is often regarded as having some relation to the incident of the fig tree narrated in Mk. $11^{12-14,\ 20-25}$ and Mt. 20^{18-22}, but not in Lk. Actually the two stories have nothing in common except the fact that the fig tree produces no fruit. They are so different that it is extremely unlikely that either could have arisen from the other. All that can be said with any confidence is that Lk. may have omitted the Marcan incident from his Gospel because he already had this story of a barren fig tree and did not wish to duplicate it. Various attempts have been made to interpret the details of the parable; for example: the vineyard = Israel; the fig tree = Jerusalem; the vinedresser = Jesus; the three years = the ministry of Jesus (so Zahn); or the vineyard = Israel and the fig tree represents the individual (Jew) (so Wellhausen). But the point of the parable does not lie in details. It is meant to teach one lesson only, the need for timely repentance; and there is no profit in turning it into an allegory, nor any sort of certainty in the proposed identifications. Others can be devised which have as much or as little probability. For example, in the Rabbinical literature the Law is compared to a fig tree and the righteous to figs (Feldman, *Parables and Similes of the Rabbis*, pp. 155 ff.). But it would, I think, be a mistake to argue that this parable is concerned with the failure of the Law to produce righteous men and that therefore the Law is to be abolished.

A parallel to the parable has been found in the *Story of Aḥikar*, 8^{35} (Syriac) (Charles, *Apoc. and Pseud.*, ii. 775). A comparison of the different versions, however, suggests that the Syriac version of *Aḥikar* may have been influenced by reminiscences of the New Testament.

It was the custom in Palestine to plant fruit trees of all kinds in vineyards. According to Krauss (Billerbeck, i. 873) there were no vineyards, in the strict sense of the word, in Palestine, but only orchards in which all kinds of fruit trees stood together. A Rabbinical parable speaks of such a garden containing a row of fig trees, a row of vines, a row of pomegranate-trees, and a row of apple trees.

7 f. In spite of its favourable situation the tree produces no fruit; and this is not just an accident. This is the third fruitless year. The owner of the garden accordingly instructs the vinedresser to cut it down. (Cf. Lk. 3^{9} = Mt. 3^{10}, Q.) It not only occupies space which might be used to better advantage. It is just a

glorified weed that exhausts the goodness of the land and yields nothing in return. The vinedresser will not, however, abandon hope of the tree, and pleads for another chance for it. He will loosen the earth round its roots and manure it. If it produces fruit in the following year, well and good. (The leaving of the apodosis to be understood, as here, is a common idiom in the Semitic languages.) If there is still no result, then the tree can go.

The central point in the parable is the need for repentance. Jesus says to His hearers: '*You* are in the same position as that fig tree.' The subsidiary point is the fact that God is both just and merciful. The conversation between the owner of the vineyard and his workman is reminiscent of Rabbinical passages in which the attributes of God debate, the attribute of justice with the attribute of mercy. If God dealt with Israel by strict justice, Israel would perish. But He does not. He gives another chance. And if it is madness to fly in the face of His justice, it is desperate wickedness to flout His mercy.

13. *SABBATH OBSERVANCE* (163)

LK. 13^{15-16}

This saying, from the story of the healing by Jesus of a crippled woman on the Sabbath, may be treated here as being allied to such sayings as Mt. $12^{11 f.}$ (above, pp. 480 f.) and Lk. 14^{5} (below, p. 569). It is Jesus' reply to the protest that the healing might easily have been postponed till the Sabbath was over.

13 10 And he was teaching in one of the
11 synagogues on the sabbath day. And
behold, a woman which had a spirit of
infirmity eighteen years; and she was
bowed together, and could in no wise lift
12 herself up. And when Jesus saw her, he
called her, and said to her, Woman, thou
13 art loosed from thine infirmity. And he
laid his hands upon her: and immediately
she was made straight, and glorified
14 God. And the ruler of the synagogue,
being moved with indignation because
Jesus had healed on the sabbath,
answered and said to the multitude,
There are six days in which men ought
to work: in them therefore come and be
healed, and not on the day of the sabbath.
15 But the Lord answered him, and said,
Ye hypocrites, doth not each one of you
on the sabbath loose his ox or his ass from
the [1] stall, and lead him away to water-
16 ing? And ought not this woman, being
a daughter of Abraham, whom Satan
had bound, lo, *these* eighteen years, to
have been loosed from this bond on the
17 day of the sabbath? And as he said
these things, all his adversaries were put
to shame: and all the multitude rejoiced
for all the glorious things that were done
by him.

[1] Gr. *manger*.

It is understood that cattle must be watered even on the Sabbath. The rules for their management on the Sabbath are given in the Mishnah (*Shabbath* 5^{1-4}, Danby, pp. 103 f.). The tying and loosing of knots were among the 39 kinds of 'work' forbidden on the Sabbath (*Shabbath* 7^{2}, Danby, p. 106); but certain knots and fastenings were exempted from the general prohibition (*Shabbath* $15^{1 f.}$, Danby, p. 113). Further rules for watering cattle on the Sabbath in *Erubin* 2^{1-4}, Danby, pp. 122 f.

On the point of the argument here, see the additional note on 'Jesus and the Sabbath Laws,' above, p. 482.

14. *THE HOSTILITY OF HEROD* (166)

LK. 13^{31-33}

13 31 In that very hour there came certain Pharisees, saying to him, Get thee out, and go hence: for Herod would fain kill
32 thee. And he said unto them, Go and say to that fox, Behold, I cast out [1] devils and perform cures to-day and to-morrow, and the third *day* I am per-
33 fected. Howbeit I must go on my way to-day and to-morrow and the *day* following: for it cannot be that a prophet perish out of Jerusalem.

[1] Gr. *demons.*

31. Here as in Lk. 13^{1-5} we are left to speculate on the motives of those who brought the message to Jesus. It may be that these Pharisees were friendly disposed and wished to give warning of a real danger which threatened Jesus, and so save Him from the fate which had overtaken John the Baptist. There is evidence in Mk. $6^{14 \text{ff.}}$ that Herod had his eye on Jesus, and it may well have been a hostile eye. On the other hand there is the possibility that the warning was inspired by Herod himself or by his officers, and was a device to get Jesus out of Herod's territory without resorting to open expulsion. (Cf. Amos 7^{10-17}.) Unfortunately the available evidence is too scanty to allow us to do more than state possibilities.

The story itself implies that Jesus is still in the territory of Herod, that is, either in Galilee or Peræa. In that case the question remains open whether we ought not to think of the incident as taking place in such a set of circumstances as we have described in Mk. 8, prior to the departure of Jesus to Cæsarea Philippi.

32 f. The answer of Jesus is defiant. It characterises Herod in one uncomplimentary word, and then goes on to say in effect: 'I will go when I am ready; and when I go it will be for another reason than fear of Herod.' This stiff and uncompromising reply, together with the fact that the messengers are told to convey it to Herod, may incline us to think that Jesus regarded these Pharisees as semi-official emissaries of the Tetrarch rather than sympathisers with Himself.

'Fox' in Jewish usage has a double sense. It typifies low cunning as opposed to straightforward dealing, and it is used in contrast to 'lion' to describe an insignificant third-rate person as opposed to a person of real power and greatness. To call Herod 'that fox' is as much as to say he is neither a great man nor a straight man; he has neither majesty nor honour.

The message goes on to say that the work which Jesus is doing for the souls and bodies of men will continue. It is not political agitation but a task of another kind to which God has sent Him; and He will continue with it, though only for a short time longer. 'To-day and to-morrow' seems to be used in the general sense of 'a short time.' The Greek verb rendered 'I am perfected' would be better translated by 'I am finished,' which has the same ambiguity as the original. It may mean 'my life is at an end' or 'my work here is at an end.' If the former meaning is the correct one, we should have here a prophecy of the Passion. The same Greek verb is used later of Christian martyrdom. If the latter sense is the original, as seems more probable, the message means: 'I shall continue my work here for a little while longer and then finish with it.' The mission will be carried to its end; but that will not be long now.

There is some difficulty in the following statement that the period just described is to be spent in going away (from Herod's territory); and it is possible that ' to-day and to-morrow and the day following ' is a mistaken repetition from the preceding verse. On the other hand it is to be remembered that the mission of Jesus is essentially a travelling mission. There is thus no fundamental inconsistency in saying ' I shall continue my work in Galilee for some time yet ' and ' In the next few days (or weeks) I shall be moving out of Galilee.' All that it amounts to is that Jesus will work His way towards Judæa and not flee thither. ' While I am finishing my work here I shall be making my way out of Herod's territory.' The reason for the move is not fear of Herod but what is expressed in the strange statement, ' It cannot be that a prophet perish out of Jerusalem.' The Greek words translated ' it cannot be ' can also bear the meaning ' it is not appropriate '; and in view of the case of John the Baptist, whom Jesus regarded as a prophet and who certainly perished out of Jerusalem, we should prefer the meaning ' it is not appropriate.' There is, then, a bitter irony in the words. Herod must not be greedy: for Jerusalem has first claim on the blood of God's messengers.

15. *SABBATH OBSERVANCE* (168)

LK. 14^{5}

There is a parallel to this saying in Mt. 12^{11}, where Mt. has inserted it into a Marcan narrative context, the story of the healing of the man with the withered hand (Mk. 3^{1-6}). Here the saying appears in a context of its own. The person healed is suffering from dropsy; and Jesus performs the cure first and gives His reasons afterwards. (Cf. Lk. 13^{10-17}.)

14 1 And it came to pass, when he went into
the house of one of the rulers of the Pharisees on a sabbath to eat bread, that they
2 were watching him. And behold, there
was before him a certain man which had
3 the dropsy. And Jesus answering spake
unto the lawyers and Pharisees, saying, Is
it lawful to heal on the sabbath, or not?
4 But they held their peace, And he took
him, and healed him, and let him go.
5 And he said unto them, Which of you
shall have [1] an ass or an ox fallen into a
well, and will not straightway draw him
6 up on a sabbath day? And they could
not answer again unto these things.

[1] Many ancient authorities read *a son*. See ch. xiii. 15.

The chief difficulty in the saying is textual. The marginal reading ' son ' is adopted by Tischendorf and Westcott and Hort. The evidence of MSS. and versions is remarkably divided; and, as Hort rightly urged (*Notes on Select Readings*), ' there is no intrinsic difficulty in either reading.' A child might fall into a well as easily as an ass. There are, however, considerations which seem to favour the reading ' ass.' First the fact that the speech of Jesus is greatly coloured by the Old Testament and the fact that ox and ass often occur together there. Secondly, the analogy of Lk. 13^{15}. Thirdly, the general sense of the argument. The most natural way of understanding it is that Jesus means to say: ' And how much more valuable is a man than an ox or an ass! ' (Cf. Mt. 12^{12}.) This conclusion is not possible if we substitute ' son ' for ' ass.' Not one of these arguments is decisive. For the general purport of the argument see notes on Mt. $12^{11f.}$, above, pp. 480 f.

16. *TABLE MANNERS* (169)

LK. 14^{7-11}

14 7 And he spake a parable unto those which were bidden, when he marked how they chose out the chief seats; saying unto
8 them, When thou art bidden of any man to a marriage feast, [1] sit not down in the chief seat; lest haply a more honourable
9 man than thou be bidden of him, and he that bade thee and him shall come and say to thee, Give this man place; and then thou shalt begin with shame to take the
10 lowest place. But when thou art bidden, go and sit down in the lowest place; that when he that hath bidden thee cometh, he may say to thee, Friend, go up higher: then shalt thou have glory in the presence
11 of all that sit at meat with thee. For every one that exalteth himself shall be humbled; and he that humbleth himself shall be exalted.

[1] Gr. *recline not.*

This passage along with *vv.* 12–14 provides rules for the receiving and giving of hospitality. There can be little doubt that *vv.* 12–14 are just what they seem to be—precepts concerning the using of material goods in a charitable way. But there is some reason for thinking that originally *vv.* 7–11 were a parable of the Kingdom. It may be noted that in *v.* 7 what follows is described as 'a parable.' Then we find that advice similar to that given in *vv.* 8–11 is given in the Rabbinical literature as a rule of etiquette. R. Akiba reports as teaching of R. Simeon ben Azzai (*c.* A.D. 110): 'Stay two or three seats below thy place' (i.e. the place to which thou art entitled), 'and sit until they say to thee, "Go (farther) up." Do not begin by going up because (in that case) they may say to thee, "Go (farther) down." It is better that they should say to thee "Go up, go up" than that they should say to thee "Go down, go down"' (*Leviticus Rabbah* 1). Moreover, if we take this passage as a parable, it has obvious affinities with other teaching, e.g. the Parable of the Labourers in the Vineyard (Mt. 20^{1-16}), and Jesus' treatment of the request of the Sons of Zebedee (Mk. 10^{35-45}).

It is therefore probable that Jesus has here taken a Jewish rule of etiquette and used it as a parable of the Kingdom. Greatness in the Kingdom, whether in its present manifestation or in its final consummation, is determined not by our opinion of our deserts but by God's judgement. And we know from other sayings how God will determine the question of precedence. He will be greatest who is servant of all. One thing is certain. Greatness in the Kingdom will not be attained by standing on one's dignity.

7, 8 f. It is possible that this introductory verse is the expansion of a simpler formula, with a view to bringing the parable into the context provided by *v.* 1. Insistence on precedence was not peculiar to Jewish dinner parties. Theophrastus (*Characters* 21^{2}) gives as one of the traits of the vain man that when he is invited out to dinner he does his utmost to secure the place of honour beside his host. The precise disposition of the places in a Jewish feast can hardly be determined with certainty (Billerbeck, iv. 618 ff.). In the time of Jesus the order of precedence seems to have been determined by the rank or distinction of the guests. Later (about A.D. 300) the rule came to be that precedence went with age. This parable certainly reflects the former rule since it supposes that the guest who has chosen the place of honour may have to vacate it in favour of a more distinguished guest. The displaced person must then go to the humblest place, presumably because all the other seats have, in the meantime, been occupied.

10. The wise course is to take the humblest place. If the host desires to give you honour, he will bring you to a more distinguished position. Then you will have honour, the real kind of honour which is conferred by others and not arrogated to yourself.

An independent version of the parable is given by some ancient MSS. after Mt. 20^{28}. The fact that it was interpolated just there is itself evidence that the parable was rightly understood in the early days of the Church. (See Streeter, *The Four Gospels*, pp. 241 f.) Yet another version is to be found in a papyrus fragment from Oxyrhynchus (Grenfell and Hunt, *New Sayings of Jesus*, p. 18; James, *Apocr. N.T.*, p. 26).

With the Jewish rule of etiquette we may compare Prov. $25^{6 f.}$:

Put not thyself forward in the presence of the king,
And stand not in the place of great men:
For better is it that it be said unto thee, Come up hither;
Than that thou shouldest be put lower in the presence of the prince,
Whom thine eyes have seen.

Also *Ecclus.* 3^{17-20}.

11. The whole is rounded off by a general statement, which seems to have been a favourite saying either with Jesus or His reporters. Cf. Mt. 18^{4}, 23^{12}; Lk. 18^{14}. Pride and self-assertion in ordinary human society may be bad manners and bad policy. In the Kingdom of God such things are a contradiction of the fundamental principle of God's rule. There inevitably 'pride goeth before destruction, and a haughty spirit before a fall': there there is only one kind of dignity, the kind that attaches itself to those who seek it not, but are content to serve God and man in love and humility.

17. *RULES OF HOSPITALITY* (169)

LK. 14^{12-14}

14 12 And he said to him also that had bidden him, When thou makest a dinner or a supper, call not thy friends, nor thy brethren, nor thy kinsmen, nor rich neighbours; lest haply they also bid thee again, and a recompense be made thee.
13 But when thou makest a feast, bid the poor, the maimed, the lame, the blind:
14 and thou shalt be blessed; because they have not *wherewith* to recompense thee: for thou shalt be recompensed in the resurrection of the just.

In this section there does not appear to be any parabolic intention. The rules given are meant to be taken simply as they stand, and acted upon in the plain and natural sense. At the same time the plain and natural sense is not an injunction to rob Peter to pay Paul. Nor does Jesus say that hospitality to the poor is a better investment than hospitality to the rich. He opposes two kinds of hospitality. The one sort exists to gratify the desire for a 'good time,' the other to satisfy urgent need. The one sort resolves itself into a fair exchange; the other must always be a free gift. The kind of hospitality for which Jesus asks is the latter kind. It will include in its scope the poor, the maimed, the lame, the blind; and it will not exclude friends or brethren or kinsmen or even rich neighbours. But it will always be hospitality that is given, not hospitality that is exchanged.

12. Dinner and supper are the midday and evening meals; see on Lk. $13^{37\text{ f.}}$, above, p. 560. 'Brethren' may perhaps mean the nearest relatives, the inner group in the wider circle of 'kinsmen.'

13 f. The guests to be invited to a feast are those who cannot return the hospitality; and the fact that they cannot is the best of all reasons for inviting them. Their inability to return the kindness is the measure of their need of it. In the mind of Jesus this principle goes far wider than food and drink. It lies behind His whole dealing with the morally bankrupt as well as with the economically depressed classes. For the besetting danger of the religious people of that day, as of every period, was that they tended to exchange hospitality in spiritual things, to enjoy the society of those who shared their beliefs and maintained with them the same standards of piety and morality. Their piety did not go out to the spiritually poor and maimed and lame and blind, as did that of 'the Friend of publicans and sinners.' So there is a sense in which this saying is also a parable; but that is only because with Jesus life is all of a piece, and it is the same spirit that prompts Him to give His food to the hungry and His love to the weaklings and failures.

The promise of reward for this kind of life is there as fact. You do not live in this way for the sake of the reward. If you do, you are not living in this way but in the old selfish way. Yet it is impossible to achieve, even for a moment, a pure unselfish kindness without knowing a blessedness that comes in no other way, a foretaste of something to be made perfect at the resurrection of the just.

With the injunction to invite the poor to the feast we may compare the saying of Jose ben Jochanan (*c.* 140 B.C.): 'Let thy house be opened wide and let the needy be members of thy household' (*Aboth* 1^{5}, Danby, p. 446).

18. *ON COUNTING THE COST* (171)

LK. 14^{28-33}

14 28 For which of you, desiring to build a
tower, doth not first sit down and count
the cost, whether he have *wherewith* to
29 complete it? Lest haply, when he hath
laid a foundation, and is not able to
finish, all that behold begin to mock him,
30 saying, This man began to build, and
31 was not able to finish. Or what king, as
he goeth to encounter another king in
war, will not sit down first and take
counsel whether he is able with ten
thousand to meet him that cometh
32 against him with twenty thousand? Or
else, while the other is yet a great way off,
he sendeth an ambassage, and asketh
23 conditions of peace. So therefore whosoever he be of you that renounceth not
all that he hath, he cannot be my
disciple.

These verses are attached by Lk. to the Q passage Lk. 14^{25-27} (see above, pp. 423 f.). They furnish a good example of a favourite teaching method of Jesus, that of the twin parables. The burden of them is to warn men against rash and unconsidered professions of discipleship. To become a disciple is much the same as joining the army in time of war. He who has not determined to venture all, even life itself, has no final defence against ignominious failure.

Epictetus issues a similar warning to those who think they can embrace his philosophy without much trouble to themselves. (*Discourses*, iii. 15): 'In every affair consider what precedes and follows, and then undertake it. Otherwise you will begin with spirit; but not having thought of the consequences, when some of them appear you will shamefully desist. . . . Consider first, man, what the matter is, and what your own nature is able to bear. . . . Do you think that you can act as you do, and be a philosopher? . . . You must watch, you must labour, you must get the better of certain appetites, must quit your acquaintance, be despised by your servant, be laughed at by those you meet; come off worse than others in everything, in magistracies, in honours, in courts of judicature. When you have considered all these things round, approach, if you please; if, by parting with them, you have a mind to purchase apathy, freedom, tranquillity. If not, do not come hither.'

28 ff. The first parable concerns the ordinary business of life. The ' tower ' might be a piece of fortification; but in that case it would be the work of a ruler; and rulers have generally contrived to find the money for such undertakings. More probably the Greek word translated ' tower ' means here a farm-building of some kind. The wise man will make a careful estimate of the cost of building before he begins, and not expose himself to ridicule by becoming the possessor of something which he can neither abandon nor complete.

31 f. In the second case we have high policy instead of private finance. When a king has a dispute with a neighbouring ruler, he does not at once resort to war to settle it. He first carefully considers what chance he has of success; and if his forces are hopelessly outnumbered by those of the enemy, he does his utmost to secure a peaceful settlement of the matter. It has been suggested (Thackeray, *Journal of Theol. Studies*, xiv. 389 f.) that Jesus had in mind the incident (2 Sam. $8^{9 f.}$) of the submission of Toi, king of Hamath, to David.

33. The farmer will certainly consider the cost of the building; and if he finds that he can afford it, he will not hesitate to spend all that may be necessary. The king will weigh carefully his chances of success in battle against a bigger army; and if he believes that he has a reasonable chance, he will fling all his forces and all his resources into the conflict. The object of these parables is not to scare possible disciples away, but to enlist men and women who are ready to stake all with enthusiasm on an issue which they have first considered in cold blood. Discipleship does not rest on a momentary burst of feeling, an enthusiasm that may wane as quickly as it blazed up. It is for those who have considered the worth of the enterprise of Jesus, and who are prepared to pay the price of sharing in it. The verb translated ' renounce ' means to say farewell to a person and to renounce or give up a thing. Later it becomes a technical term in the monastic life. There is not in the teaching of Jesus any idea that worldly goods are to be regarded as evil, and rejected as hindrances to the ' spiritual life.' The true analogy to the kind of sacrifice here demanded is that which a man makes when he enters upon any great enterprise in which he must risk the loss of everything, his life included. The pioneers in the therapeutic employment of X-rays are the kind of people who answer most nearly to the description here.

19. *GOD AND THE SINNER—THREE PARABLES*

(*a*) THE LOST SHEEP AND THE LOST COIN (172)

LK. 15^{1-10}

15 1 Now all the publicans and sinners were
drawing near unto him for to hear him.
2 And both the Pharisees and the scribes
murmured, saying, This man receiveth
sinners, and eateth with them.
3 And he spake unto them this parable,
4 saying, What man of you, having a
hundred sheep, and having lost one of
them, doth not leave the ninety and nine
in the wilderness, and go after that which
5 is lost, until he find it? And when he
hath found it, he layeth it on his shoul-
6 ders, rejoicing. And when he cometh
home, he calleth together his friends and
his neighbours, saying unto them, Rejoice with me, for I have found my sheep
7 which was lost. I say unto you, that
even so there shall be joy in heaven over
one sinner that repenteth, *more* than over
ninety and nine righteous persons, which
need no repentance.
8 Or what woman having ten [1] pieces of
silver, if she lose one piece, doth not light
a lamp, and sweep the house, and seek
9 diligently until she find it? And when
she hath found it, she calleth together her
friends and neighbours, saying, Rejoice
with me, for I have found the piece which
10 I had lost. Even so, I say unto you,
there is joy in the presence of the angels
of God over one sinner that repenteth.

[1] Gr. *drachma*, a coin worth about eight pence.

The L material in chapters 15–19 might be called in a special sense the Gospel of the Outcast. There is in this section a great concentration of teaching, chiefly in the form of parables, whose purpose is primarily to demonstrate God's care for those whom men despise and condemn. This appears very clearly in the three parables which together make up chap. 15, in the parables of the Poor Widow (18^{1-8}) and the Pharisee and the Publican (18^{9-14}), and in the story of Zacchæus (19^{1-10}). This Divine love for the unloved and unlovable is, indirectly, the condemnation of the harsh and censorious attitude taken towards these unfortunates by more righteous folk. That the righteous fail from lack of kindness and human sympathy, and spoil themselves by pride, is one of the lessons of such passages as Lk. $16^{1-8,\ 14f.,\ 19-31}$, 18^{9-14}. Again it is taught that even from the most unpromising people there can be a genuine response to kindness and understanding (17^{11-19}, 19^{1-10}). In Lk.'s arrangement this mass of material leads up to the account of Passion Week: it is as though the whole of Lk. from chap. 15 onwards were written to illustrate the Pauline text, 'God commendeth his own love toward us, in that, while we were yet sinners, Christ died for us.'

This 'Gospel of the Outcast' begins with the three parables of chap. 15; and the root of the matter is that it is God Himself who wills that the outcasts should be gathered in. The attitude of Jesus to publicans and sinners is not a mere humanitarian enthusiasm on His part: it is the manifestation of the will and purpose of God. The scribes and Pharisees cannot accept that without qualification. They are represented as criticising Jesus because He is too free and easy with disreputable people. He, in His turn, criticises them for being too stiff and censorious. On the one side is the conviction, born of long and possibly sad experience, that 'evil communications corrupt good manners,' that it is not easy to touch pitch and not be defiled, that the will of God is that His chosen ones should separate themselves from everything that is evil. On the other side is the equally firm conviction that God wills the restoration of the outcast, and that God's way of restoration is the way of merciful love going out to seek and save the lost.

The first two parables in chap. 15 form a pair. Doubtless Lk. found them together in his source; and most probably they stood together in the tradition because they were so given by Jesus in the first instance. The practice of teaching by means of twin parables is one frequently adopted by Jesus, and several examples have already been noted. In both parables the main point is the same: the endless trouble that men will take to recover lost property, and their deep satisfaction when they succeed. The inference is that the publicans and sinners really belong to God, despite all appearances to the contrary, and that God really wants them back and will take trouble to win them back to Himself.

The parable of the Lost Sheep (*vv.* 4–7) has a parallel in Mt. $18^{12\text{-}14}$ (above, pp. 499 ff.); and consequently Lk. $15^{4\text{-}7}$ is by many scholars assigned to Q. It is more likely that we have here a case of the overlapping of sources, and that the Matthæan version belongs to M and the Lucan to L.

1–3. The narrative setting of the parables is very similar to that of another incident, in Mk. $2^{13\text{-}17}$, especially *vv.* 15 f. (On this see my article, 'The Christology of the New Testament,' in the *Congregational Quarterly*, April, 1935, pp. 158 f.). It has been suggested that these introductory verses are Lk.'s own composition, which is possible; or that they are really the introduction to the parable of the Prodigal Son (note the singular 'this parable'), and that Lk. has inserted *vv.* 4–10 between the introduction and its proper sequel. The third possibility is that Lk. found the introduction and the three parables in his source as they stand. In view of the special characteristics of the section 15^{1}–19^{10} indicated above, one is inclined to think that a certain amount of gathering together of material had already taken place before Lk. set to work, and that this whole chapter was taken over by him substantially as we now have it.

The eagerness of the irreligious and immoral to listen to the most exacting of all teachers of religion and morality is very striking. They realised that He cared for them and believed in them enough to make His enormous demands upon them—and to bring His own perfect gift of understanding and sympathy. The scribes and Pharisees doubted the wisdom and propriety of such familiar friendship with publicans and sinners. (They are not the only religious people who have entertained such scruples.) Billerbeck quotes an old Rabbinical rule from *Mekhilta* on Exod. 18^{1}, 'Let not a man associate with the wicked, not even to bring him nigh to the Law.' This, no doubt, represents the strictest attitude, the attitude taken by the sharpest critics of Jesus. Whether every Pharisee would have maintained this rule in full strictness is another question. Jesus' reply to those who did criticise Him is given in the parables.

4–7. For these verses, cf. notes on Mt. $18^{12\text{-}14}$, above, pp. 499 ff. The 'wilderness' is not the sandy desert but open uncultivated pasture land where flocks and herds may be taken to graze. (Cf. *Enc. Bibl.*, col. 1076, and 1 Sam. 17^{28}). So in Mk. 6^{35} the place where the five thousand are assembled is 'desert,' but in *v.* 39 the multitude are directed to sit down on the 'green grass.' In the Lucan version of the parable stress is laid on the persistent seeking by the shepherd 'until he find' the lost sheep, and his joy at finding it is described much more fully than in Mt. For the picture of the shepherd carrying the exhausted animal on his shoulders, cf. Is. 40^{11}, 49^{22}; and the charming story from the Rabbinical commentary on Exodus, translated by Montefiore (*Rabb. Lit. and Gospel Teachings*, p. 259). The description of the shepherd summoning his friends and neighbours to share in his joy has no parallel in Mt. It is the kind of detail that Mt. readily omits. The conclusion drawn in Lk. (*v.* 7) differs entirely in wording from that in Mt. 18^{14}. The purport of Lk.'s conclusion is that it pleases God—in both senses of the word ' please '—that sinners should repent: in Mt. it pleases God in the sense that it is God's will. ' Joy in heaven ' and ' joy in the presence of the angels of God ' are probably just cautious ways of saying that God is glad. Rabbinical teaching lays great stress also on the value of repentance; and there is ample evidence that the repentant sinner was generously treated. Philo teaches that God holds penitence in as high esteem as guiltlessness; and R. Abahu (end of third century A.D.) argues that God gives a higher place to repentant sinners than to the completely righteous. (Cf. Moore, *Judaism*, iii. 157 ff.) But the characteristic feature of these two parables is not so much the joy over the repentant sinner as the Divine love that goes out to seek the sinner before he repents.

8–10. The companion parable runs on parallel lines to the first. The essential point is the unwearied search for what is lost and the joy when it is found. The ' piece of silver ' is the *drachma*, a coin approximately equal in value to the silver *denarius*. See note on 10^{35}, above, p. 555. The total amount suggests that we are to think of the savings of a poor woman rather than of housekeeping money. The lighting of a lamp is natural in the circumstances. Palestinian houses nineteen centuries ago were not too well provided with windows. A Rabbinical parable (Billerbeck, ii. 212) has a similar picture of a man lighting many lamps to search the house for a lost coin. The thorough and careful search goes on till the missing coin is found. Then there is rejoicing with friends and neighbours. The same conclusion is drawn from this parable as from the preceding, though in somewhat shorter form. If man will take such trouble to recover his lost property, how much more trouble will God take to secure the return of His wandering children: and if this is God's way, then the way of Jesus with publicans and sinners is amply justified.

The attitude of God to sinners is now further displayed in the third parable.

(*b*) The Two Sons (173)

LK. 15^{11-32}

15 11 And he said, A certain man had two
12 sons: and the younger of them said to his
father, Father, give me the portion of
[1] *thy* substance that falleth to me. And
13 he divided unto them his living. And
not many days after the younger son
gathered all together, and took his
journey into a far country; and there he
wasted his substance with riotous living.
14 And when he had spent all, there arose a
mighty famine in that country; and he
15 began to be in want. And he went and
joined himself to one of the citizens of
that country; and he sent him into his
16 fields to feed swine. And he would fain
have been filled with [2] the husks that the
swine did eat: and no man gave unto
17 him. But when he came to himself he
said, How many hired servants of my
father's have bread enough and to spare,
18 and I perish here with hunger! I will
arise and go to my father, and will say
unto him, Father, I have sinned against
19 heaven, and in thy sight: I am no more
worthy to be called thy son: make me as
20 one of thy hired servants. And he
arose, and came to his father. But while
he was yet afar off, his father saw him,

and was moved with compassion, and
ran, and fell on his neck, and [3] kissed
21 him. And the son said unto him,
Father, I have sinned against heaven,
and in thy sight: I am no more worthy to
22 be called thy son[4]. But the father said
to his [5] servants, Bring forth quickly the
best robe, and put it on him; and put a
ring on his hand, and shoes on his feet:
23 and bring the fatted calf, *and* kill it, and
24 let us eat, and make merry: for this my
son was dead, and is alive again; he was
lost, and is found. And they began to
25 be merry. Now his elder son was in the
field: and as he came and drew nigh to
the house, he heard music and dancing.
26 And he called to him one of the servants,
and inquired what these things might be.
27 And he said unto him, Thy brother is
come; and thy father hath killed the
fatted calf, because he hath received him
28 safe and sound. But he was angry, and
would not go in: and his father came out,
29 and intreated him. But he answered
and said to his father, Lo, these many
years do I serve thee, and I never transgressed
a commandment of thine: and
yet thou never gavest me a kid, that I
30 might make merry with my friends: but
when this thy son came, which hath
devoured thy living with harlots, thou
31 killedst for him the fatted calf. And he
said unto him, [6] Son, thou art ever with
32 me, and all that is mine is thine. But it
was meet to make merry and be glad:
for this thy brother was dead, and is alive
again; and *was* lost, and is found.

[1] Gr. *the*.
[2] Gr. *the pods of the carob tree*.
[3] Gr. *kissed him much*.
[4] Some ancient authorities add *make me as one of thy hired servants*. See ver. 19.
[5] Gr. *bondservants*.
[6] Gr. *Child*.

The attempt has been made to divide this parable into two at *v.* 24. The reasons in favour of this procedure are: (1) that in the two preceding parables nothing is said about the attitude of the ninety-nine sheep towards the stray, or about that of the nine pieces of silver towards the lost piece; and so it is an irrelevance to be told about the attitude of the elder brother: (2) that in *v.* 12 the father divides his property between the two sons, whereas in *vv.* 29–31 the father still seems to be himself in possession of the elder brother's share; and the elder brother is working for him on the land. With regard to the first it may be replied that the parables of the Lost Sheep and the Lost Coin are parables and not fables; and therefore we do not expect to hear about the feelings of the sheep or the coins. Further, there was no reason why Jesus having made two parables on this model should be compelled to make every other on the same pattern. To the second argument it may be replied that the inconsistency, if it be an inconsistency (see notes on *vv.* 11 f.), is not between *vv.* 11–24[a] and 24[b]–32; for the father is already giving orders to the elder brother's servants and disposing of his goods—in fact, acting as head of the household—in *vv.* 22 f. More than that, the younger son in the far country says, 'How many hired servants of my father's'—not 'my elder brother's.' If we are to cut the parable in two for inconsistency, the cut would have to be made at the end of *v.* 16, which is hardly a suitable place. There is, in fact, no good reason for supposing that the story is anything but a perfect unity.

The parable is distinguished from the other two by the fact that it makes two main points. The first, which it has in common with the others, is the care and patience of God towards the sinner and the joy with which the repentant sinner is received. The second is the rebuke to the harsh and censorious attitude taken up by the righteous towards sinners. The strength of this rebuke lies less in any formal charge brought against the elder brother than in the contrast between his attitude and that of the father.

Apart from these critical questions there is a further, and much more difficult, theological problem raised by the parable. This lies in the fact that there does not seem to be any place in it for the doctrine that God's forgiveness of sinners is made possible by the sacrificial death of Jesus. On this point it may be said first that the Christian doctrine of the Atonement is not based on this parable alone, but on the whole set of facts presented in the life and teaching of Jesus and in the experience of Christians. Secondly, this one parable does not offer, and was not meant by Jesus to offer, a complete compendium of theology. Its primary business is to justify the attitude of Jesus to sinners by showing that His way is the fulfilment of God's will concerning them, and that the way of the scribes and Pharisees is the wrong way. If the carrying out of the purpose of God leads, as in fact it did, to the Cross, then it becomes the business of Christians to include the Cross in the purpose of God and to think out, as best they can, how the death of Christ is involved in God's purpose of saving sinners. Christian theologians have in the past made this attempt, and various explanations have been offered. It is not our business here to discuss the question whether any one of these theories is completely satisfying. All that we have to do is to recognise that Jesus in this parable lays down the fundamental principle of God's relation to sinful men: that God loves the sinner while he is still a sinner, *before* he repents; and that somehow it is this Divine love that makes the sinner's repentance possible. This is the true point of the parable.

It is a fact of history and of Christian experience that this love of God becomes fully effective in the Cross; but this fact does not touch the basic principle laid down in the parable. It has to be explained in the light of that principle; and all that can be said is that any doctrine of the Atonement that explains the death of Jesus in such a way as to weaken the principle here laid down by Jesus Himself has no chance of ultimate survival.

11 f. The simplest explanation of the story is that the father represents God, the elder brother those scribes and Pharisees who criticised Jesus, and the younger brother the publicans and sinners whom Jesus befriended. Probably we should not attempt to go farther than this in the interpretation of the details. The Greek phrase rendered by 'the portion . . . that falleth to me' is common in the papyri. It can be used either of privileges to which one is entitled or of obligations which one is bound to meet. A corresponding Aramaic phrase is found in the Elephantine Papyri (ed. Cowley, No. 28). On the Jewish law of inheritance see the Mishnah, *Baba Bathra* 8 f., Danby, pp. 376 ff. The owner of property could dispose of it either by will or by gift during his lifetime. If by will, his testamentary dispositions had to conform to the Law as laid down in Dt. 21^{15-17} and Num. 27^{8-11}. (Cf. *Encycl. Bibl.*, cols. 2728 f.) If by gift, he could dispose of the property without regard to the Old Testament provisions, which covered bequests only and not gifts. If such a gift is made, it does not normally take full effect until the death of the donor. In the meantime the property is settled. It remains in the possession of the donor; but he has no power to dispose of it. All that he can do is to lease it for the indeterminate period which will end at his death, when the property will automatically revert to the person to whom he assigned it by gift. That is, he can only sell his own life-interest in the property. Likewise the beneficiary under the gift cannot

dispose of the property immediately; for it is still subject to the donor's life-interest. If he sells it, the purchaser can only take possession at the death of the donor. This is the normal procedure, and it is illustrated by the relation between the father and the elder son. Throughout the story the father still has complete use and enjoyment of what has been assigned to the elder son; yet he can say to him 'All that I have is thine.'

In the case of the younger brother it is necessary to suppose that a further step has been taken. The younger son does not merely desire that the shares of his brother and himself should be determined by a deed of gift, which would normally become effective at the death of the father. He wants immediate possession of his share. This requires that the father not only makes an assignment of the property to the two sons, but also grants to the younger son the immediate possession of his share. This he could do; but once it was done the younger son had, of course, no further right in the estate. What remained was irrevocably assigned to his brother. That parents could and actually did hand over their property to their heirs is shown by the fact that Ben Sirach advises against the practice (*Ecclus.* 33^{19-23}):

> To son or wife, to brother or friend,
> Give no power over thyself while thou livest;
> And give not thy goods to another
> So as to have to ask for them again. . . .
> For it is better that thy children ask of thee
> Than that thou shouldst look to the hand of thy sons. . . .
> When the days of thy life are ended,
> In the day of death, distribute thine inheritance.

We must therefore understand the words 'he divided unto them his living' as meaning that he executed a kind of deed of gift securing to either son his share of the inheritance, and then as a further act gave the younger son the immediate and absolute possession of what he would ordinarily have inherited in due course. The elder son having made no request, his share remains in the possession of the father, who has the use and enjoyment of it but not the right to dispose of it in any way that would infringe the elder son's sole right to inherit it. If that is the situation, there is no inconsistency between the two parts of the parable.

13–16. The younger son lost no time in setting about the enjoyment of his new freedom. He collected all together and, putting as large a distance as possible between himself and the paternal eye, he proceeded to lay out his money to what seemed to him the best advantage. The Greek adverb translated 'with riotous living' may mean that he spent his money 'extravagantly,' or that he spent it on dissolute pleasures, or both. The elder brother (*v.* 30) evidently took the third view. However that may be, it was not long until the funds were exhausted; and to crown his misfortunes the land of his adoption was visited by a serious famine, which doubtless provided the friends of his affluence with a good excuse for not helping him in the day of adversity. He was thus reduced to working for his living, and that at what was in Jewish estimation one of the most loathsome and degrading of all tasks. (Cf. the proverb preserved in the Talmud (*Baba*

Kamma 82^b): 'Cursed is the man who rears swine, and cursed is the man who teaches his son Greek philosophy.') But even this work would hardly produce a living: and the prodigal was reduced to such straits that he would gladly have shared the diet of the swine. R.V. 'He would fain have been filled: A.V. 'He would fain have filled his belly,' which is more vigorous and probably original. R.V. follows a large group of MSS. which here bowdlerise. The 'husks' are the seed-pods of the carob tree (*Ceratonia siliqua*), also called the locust tree. The tree still grows in Palestine and the Mediterranean lands, and the pods are used as fodder for animals. Their use for human food is a mark of deep poverty. Hence the Rabbinical saying: 'When the Israelites are reduced to eating carob-pods, then they repent.'

17. The restoration of the prodigal begins when he first realises the wretchedness of his condition, when he sees himself as he really is. Contrast Rev. 3^{17}. The expression 'he came to himself,' i.e. came to his senses, is found in Greek, Latin, and Hebrew. The son in poverty in the far country contrasts his own condition with that of the humblest members of his father's household at home. The Palestinian Rabbis had a saying: 'When a son (abroad) goes barefoot (through poverty), then he remembers the comfort of his father's house.'

18 f. But the prodigal does not stop at vain regrets for what he has lost. With the realisation of his folly goes the resolve to make an end of it in the only way open to him, by returning to his father's house and submitting to the father's discipline. This involves confession that he has behaved disgracefully, admission that he has by his behaviour forfeited all his rights as a son, and so becoming humble enough to accept orders where formerly he had demanded gifts. It may be noted that he does not say, 'I really ought to arise and go,' but 'I will arise and go.' The Greek words translated 'I have sinned against heaven' may mean either 'I have sinned heaven-high,' i.e. I have heaped transgression upon transgression till the sum of my sins is monstrous (cf. Ezra 9^6); or 'I have sinned against God,' heaven being the common Jewish periphrasis for God. (Cf. English 'Heaven forbid!' = 'God forbid!') The latter interpretation is preferable. 'In thy sight' is just a verbal variation for 'against thee.' (Cf. 1 Sam. 7^6, 20^1.) The confession to the father means simply 'I have sinned against God and against thee.' Strict justice would disown him as a son; but perhaps mercy will accept him as a servant.

20. The resolve is followed by action, and the action by a response from the father far beyond anything the son had dared to expect. The eyes of the father are towards the far country, and he sees the son while the son is still a long way off. He knows only one emotion, pity for his son in his wretched condition. He runs to meet him, embraces him and kisses him. (Cf. Gen. 33^4; Acts 20^{37}.) The Greek word used for 'kissed' signifies no mere formal salutation: he 'kissed him tenderly.'

21 ff. These demonstrations of love and compassion do not turn the son from the resolve which he had taken before he set out for home. If anything, they make him realise more keenly the wrong that he has done. So he begins his confession. But no sooner has he declared that he is unworthy of the name of son, than the father breaks in with orders to the servants which show plainly that he is still a son in his father's eyes. The father's love is stronger than the son's sense of un-

worthiness. ‘ In the rabbinical literature the paternal-filial relation between God and man is a common theme. R. Akiba . . . “ Beloved (of God) are the Israelites, in that they are called sons of God; still more beloved in that it is made known to them that they are called sons of God ” (Dt. 14^{1}). R. Judah (ben Ila‘i) thought that the name sons was given them only when they behaved themselves like sons; but R. Meir refuted him by quoting passages in which they were called foolish sons (Jer. 4^{22}), untrustworthy sons (Dt. 32^{20}), breed of evil-doers, vicious sons (Is. 1^{4})—but sons notwithstanding. Instead of its being said to them, Ye are not my people, they shall be called sons of the Living God (Hos. 1^{10}). The relation is not annulled by sin ’ (Moore, *Judaism*, ii. 203). The criticism that might be made of scribes and Pharisees was that, in their dealings with the publicans and sinners, they failed to rise to the height of their own best thoughts about God.

The R.V. marginal addition to *v.* 21, ‘ make me as one of thy hired servants,’ although supported by some of the leading MSS., is almost certainly an interpolation from *v.* 19.

22–24. The returned prodigal instead of being treated as a servant, which was all he dared hope for, is received as a guest of honour. The ‘ best robe ’ is literally the ‘ first robe,’ i.e. first in quality and value. ‘ Put a ring,’ literally ‘ give a ring.’ The Greek reflects the Semitic idiom whereby the verb ‘ to give ’ is used in the sense of ‘ to place.’ The same usage appears in Lk. 12^{51}, above, p. 411. The articles ordered by the father are more than mere necessities; the prodigal is to have the best of everything. He is not put on a plain wholesome diet suitable to his situation, but made chief guest at a banquet in honour of his return. Joy that he has come back outweighs all else. The father may have thought of his son as lost or dead; but he has never ceased to think of him as his son. Cf. the note on *vv.* 21 ff., above. The son may have forgotten the father, but the father has never disowned the son.

25. With this verse the elder son comes into the centre of the stage. As depicted for us, he stands in sharp contrast both to his brother and his father. His sympathies are as narrow as his ideals are high. He is incapable alike of the reckless selfishness of his brother and the reckless unselfishness of his father. It is perhaps a hint as to his nature that the mere fact that there is any gaiety in the house is a phenomenon calling for an explanation. The Greek word translated ‘ music ’ may mean the sound of a number of instruments playing together or voices singing together; or it may be, as in Dan 3^{5}, the name of one musical instrument somewhat like the bagpipes.

26 f., 28, 29 f. In reply to the enquiry of the elder son a servant explains the reason for the merrymaking. His answer contains no criticism of the younger son. It gives the true answer; but leaves the elder brother to find out the full details for himself. But it conveys enough information to rouse the anger of the elder brother, who refuses to join in the rejoicings. What is the use of trying to do one’s duty if wastrels and scapegraces are to receive more consideration than upright and conscientious folk? So the father comes out and begs him to come in. It is to be noted that the father has to go out to both sons. The Greek tenses are significant: the father came out and was entreating him to come in, when he broke in on the entreaties with his accusations of unjust treatment. His years of faithful and

conscientious service have received no reward, while his brother's career of dissipation and debauchery has been celebrated with a great feast. The impression remains, however, that the chief reason why he never got so much as a kid to make merry with his friends was that he would not have known how to make merry if he had got it. His real annoyance is not for what he has not had, but for what his brother has got. Further, it would seem that any deprivation which the elder brother suffered merely meant that the capital which he must ultimately inherit grew so much the larger. It is the veal that sticks in his gullet, not the goat's-flesh. His references to his brother are in harsh and brutal terms. He disowns him as a brother and refers to him as 'this son of yours'—an expression of contempt, which is met in *v.* 32 by the rebuke, 'this brother of *yours*.' He paints the life of the prodigal in the worst possible colours. He says 'thy living' although the father had actually made over the money in question to the son. He is the only authority for the harlots, and he does not say whence he had this piece of information. We feel that he is not trying to be just, much less generous, to the repentant sinner.

31 f. The father's reply is the last word; and it is a word that expresses his love for both his sons. 'Son' is almost too stiff a rendering of the Greek. 'My dear boy' would be nearer to the spirit of the word. The assurance 'all that is mine is thine' is no doubt meant to tell the elder brother that the return of the prodigal does not affect his rights in any degree. He will inherit his whole share of the estate when the time comes. But no rights of the elder brother can prevent the father from rejoicing that the prodigal has returned; and the elder brother *ought* to share in the joy of his father. It would cost him nothing but a little kindness.

So the upshot of the matter is that the way of the father with the prodigal is God's way with sinful men and Jesus' way with publicans and sinners; and the last word of Jesus to the scribes and Pharisees who criticised Him is: 'It ought to be your way too.'

20. *THE CLEVER RASCAL* (174)

LK. 16^{1-9}

16 1 And he said also unto the disciples,
There was a certain rich man, which had
a steward; and the same was accused unto
2 him that he was wasting his goods. And
he called him, and said unto him, What is
this that I hear of thee? render the account
of thy stewardship; for thou canst be no
3 longer steward. And the steward said
within himself, What shall I do, seeing
that my lord taketh away the stewardship
4 from me? I have not strength to dig; to
beg I am ashamed. I am resolved what
to do, that, when I am put out of the
stewardship, they may receive me into
5 their houses. And calling to him each
one of his lord's debtors, he said to the
first, How much owest thou unto my lord?
6 And he said, A hundred [1] measures of oil.
And he said unto him, Take thy [2] bond,
and sit down quickly and write fifty.
7 Then he said to another, And how much
owest thou? And he said, A hundred
[3] measures of wheat. He saith unto him,
8 Take thy [2] bond, and write fourscore. And
his lord commended [4] the unrighteous
steward because he had done wisely: for
the sons of this [5] world are for their own
generation wiser than the sons of the light.
9 And I say unto you, Make to yourselves
friends [6] by means of the mammon of
unrighteousness; that, when it shall fail,
they may receive you into the eternal
tabernacles.

[1] Gr. *baths*, the bath being a Hebrew measure. See Ezek. xlv. 10, 11, 14.
[2] Gr. *writings*.
[3] Gr. *cors*, the cor being a Hebrew measure. See Ezek. xlv. 14.
[4] Gr. *the steward of unrighteousness*.
[5] Or, *age*.
[6] Gr. *out of*.

This parable has always presented difficulties for the interpreter: and like most of such difficulties they arise from trying to press the details of the story instead of seeking for the main point. The parable becomes comparatively simple as soon as we realise that it is part of the L collection of material which we have called the Gospel of the Outcast. We are, in fact, still concerned with the great questions: what is God's way with sinners? and what ought to be the way of religious men with sinners? It is the latter question that is uppermost in this story, so that it may almost be regarded as an appendix to the parable of the Prodigal Son. In that parable the criticism of the elder brother is that he fails to show the gracious and pitiful spirit of his father: or, in other words, that the religious Jews fail to rise to the height of their own faith in God in their dealings with the immoral and the irreligious. Here the criticism of the scribes and Pharisees is that their attitude to the publicans and sinners is not even good policy, much less good religion. If they would show kindness and friendship to the outcasts, it would turn out for the good of themselves as well as of the publicans and sinners.

1. This interpretation is not affected by the fact that Lk. represents the parable as addressed to the disciples; for it is no article of the Christian faith that members of the Church are immune from the worst kind of Pharisaism, or that Christians are never in danger of becoming censorious, intolerant, and self-righteous. And, in any case, the Pharisees are thought of as still present. Cf. *v.* 14.

We have to resist the temptation to make exegetical equations. The rich man does not represent God, nor does the steward represent a disciple or a Pharisee. The point of the parable lies in *v.* 8; and it does not depend on anything but the story itself. The Greek word translated 'steward' is used in the New Testament in three different senses: (*a*) of an overseer or head-servant responsible for the welfare and discipline of the rest of the household staff, as in Lk. 12^{42}, above, p. 409; (*b*) of a bailiff or estate-manager, as here; (*c*) of a civic official like our city-treasurer, as in Rom. 16^{23}. In the present case it is reported to the master that the steward is squandering the property entrusted to him. We are not told whether or not the charge is true; but in view of the subsequent behaviour of the steward we may well think that it was not unfounded. 'Wasting his goods,' cf. Lk. 15^{13}.

2 f., 4, 5 ff. The master takes immediate action. He orders the steward to hand over his accounts, and dismisses him from his post. The steward is evidently an employee and not a slave. If he were a slave his future would not be in doubt: he would be reduced to some menial post, not discharged. As it is, he is left wondering how he is to make a living. He is too soft for manual labour and too proud to beg. He must therefore live by his wits; and his plan is to show such kindness to his master's debtors that, when he is out of his present position, they will be under an obligation to entertain him. The fact that he will be robbing his master in carrying out the plan does not weigh with him. Having decided, he proceeds at once to action. Each debtor is interviewed; and we are given samples of the proceedings in two cases. Both debtors would seem to be persons who have purchased goods from the estate and have not yet paid for them. The steward holds their receipts for the goods, and now hands them back to be altered to the advantage of the debtors. In the first case the debt is in respect of 100 *baths* of oil. The *bath* is a Hebrew measure, and 100 *baths* may be computed to be = about

868 gallons. The bill is altered to 50 *baths*: that is, the debtor is presented with 434 gallons at the master's expense. The second debt is in respect of 100 *cors* of wheat = about 1,083 bushels. From the Mishnah (*Baba Metzia* 5^1, Danby, p. 355) it would appear that the price of wheat was 25 to 30 denars a *cor*; so that in reducing the debt from 100 to 80 *cors* the steward was making this debtor a present of 500 to 600 denars. In both cases the steward invites the debtor to do the falsifying of the accounts for himself.

8. 'His lord': the Greek text has simply 'the lord,' and it is still debated whether 'the lord' means the steward's master or Jesus Himself. Those who take the latter view point to a somewhat similar case in Lk. $18^{6\,ff.}$, where the commentator on the behaviour of the unjust judge is certainly Jesus Himself. In view of the beginning of *v.* 9, 'And I say unto you,' there can be little doubt that Lk. thought that 'the lord' in *v.* 8 meant the steward's master; and this probably means that that was the way in which the words were taken by the compiler of the source on which he is here dependent. And it may be urged that if we take 'the lord' as meaning Jesus the story ends rather abruptly. If we take 'the lord' to mean the master in the story, it is necessary to suppose that the steward's plan miscarried, and that somehow his master got to know what he was doing. If that were so, the master would be better able to pass judgement on the fraud considered merely from the point of view of its ingenuity, seeing that he had probably secured himself against pecuniary loss. On the other hand, if it is Jesus who is subject in *v.* 8, these suppositions are unnecessary: we do not need to know whether or not the scheme succeeded. We may, if we like, assume that it did. The difficulty, then, is that Jesus praised the dishonest steward; but this difficulty is largely imaginary. First the word 'praise' does not necessarily signify moral approval of the steward's plan. The ethical judgement on the plan is given in the description of its author as 'the unrighteous steward'; and the ground of the praise is given in the clause 'because he had done wisely.' It is the astuteness of the plan that is praised: and there is all the difference in the world between 'I applaud the dishonest steward because he acted cleverly' and 'I applaud the clever steward because he acted dishonestly.' Whether it is the employer or Jesus that speaks, we must take the purport of the speech to be: 'This is a fraud; but it is a most ingenious fraud. The steward is a rascal; but he is a wonderfully clever rascal.' The steward's cleverness is not an isolated phenomenon: it is part of the way of the world. The worldlings show far more *savoir faire* than the religious in dealing with their contemporaries. For even their roguery is often designed to procure them friends, while the pious only too often estrange those who might be friendly to them. The expressions 'sons of this world' (cf. 20^{34}) and 'sons of light' (John 12^{36}; 1 Thess. 5^5; Eph. 5^8) have no exact parallels in the Rabbinical literature; but the meaning of them is plain enough. With 'sons of light' we may compare 'every spirit of light' (*Enoch* 61^{12}), a phrase which, according to Charles, 'embraces good spirits, human and angelic'; also 'the spirits of the good who belong to the generation of light' (*Enoch* 108^{11}).

9. It may be doubted whether this verse belongs to the parable. The point of the parable is that if a bad man will take infinite trouble to get friends for his own selfish interests, the good man will surely take some trouble to make friends in a

better way and for better ends. The point of this saying is rather that by disposing of worldly wealth in the proper way, one will have treasure in heaven. The true parallel to this verse is in such sayings as Mt. $6^{19\,ff.}$; Mk. 10^{21}; Lk. $12^{33\,f.}$. The ' mammon of unrighteousness ' is an expression that has no exact parallel in the Old Testament or other Jewish literature. In the Targums we find the phrase ' mammon of falsehood ' and once (Targum on Hab. 2^{9}) ' mammon of wickedness.' Other passages which have a bearing on this verse are: *Enoch* 63^{10} where ' the mighty and the kings who possess the earth ' (63^{1}) say: ' Our souls are full of unrighteous gain, but it does not prevent us from descending from the midst thereof into the † burden † of Sheol '; *Ecclus.* 5^{8}: ' Trust not in unrighteous gains, for they shall profit (thee) nothing in the day of wrath.' The one idea that seems to cling to all these phrases, including perhaps ' the mammon of unrighteousness,' is that of ill-gotten gain, whether acquired by force or fraud. It is ' dirty money,' and doubtless all money gets dirty at some stage in its history, if we could trace it out. But there is another and more radical sense in which, for Jesus, mammon is unrighteous: it is a rival to God for the service and love of man. ' Ye cannot serve God and mammon.' The only effective way to deal with it is to force it into the service of God by converting it from selfish to unselfish uses. In this way it can be made to procure one ' friends.' It is probable that the word ' friends ' signifies God Himself. Use the mammon of unrighteousness in such a way that you gain the friendship of God. Then in the day when earthly possessions are no longer of any use ' they ' will receive you into the eternal tabernacles. ' They ' in this context most probably means God. In the Rabbinical writings it is a common way of avoiding the mention of the divine name to use the verb in the 3rd person plural, just as in this verse.

Thus what is counselled in this saying is something that will produce the opposite result to that indicated in *Enoch* 63^{10} or in the fate of Dives (Lk. 16^{19-31}); and we may leave the question open whether this verse would not stand more appropriately as the moral of the parable of Dives and Lazarus.

21. *SAYINGS ABOUT WEALTH* (174)

LK. 16^{10-12}

16 10 He that is faithful in a very little is
faithful also in much: and he that is
unrighteous in a very little is unrighteous
11 also in much. If therefore ye have not
been faithful in the unrighteous mammon, who will commit to your trust the
12 true *riches*? And if ye have not been
faithful in that which is another's, who
will give you that which is [1] your own?

[1] Some ancient authorities read *our own*.

10. This verse is unconnected with what precedes in *v.* 9 and with what follows in *vv.* 11 f. It could stand appropriately as a reflection on the promotion of the good servants in the parable of the Pounds (Lk. 19^{16-19}). In the Midrash, *Exodus Rabbah* (on Exod. 3^{1}), the principle is laid down that God ' does not give a big thing to a man until He has tested him in a small matter; and afterwards He promotes him to a great thing. This is illustrated by the cases of David and Moses. David was found satisfactory as a shepherd. ' The Holy One, blessed is He, said to him, " Thou hast been found faithful in the matter of the sheep: come

and be shepherd to my flock " (i.e. Israel).' Similarly, Moses was a good shepherd of his father-in-law's flock, and God took him to be shepherd of Israel. We may also compare the parable related by R. Simeon ben Eleazar (*Mekhilta* on Exod. 20[2]): A king appointed two overseers. One he put in charge of the store of straw, the other he put in charge of the treasury of silver and gold. He who was set over the straw turned out untrustworthy, and (at the same time) grumbled because he had not been set over the treasury of silver and gold. He who had been put in charge of the silver and gold said to him: ' Thou fool, thou hast been false in the matter of the straw; how much more in the matter of the silver and gold.' The point of this parable is that since the Gentile nations have failed to observe the simple moral rules (the so-called Noachide commandments: Moore, *Judaism*, i. 274 f.) given to them by God, it would be futile to give them the fuller code of the Jewish Law. In both Rabbinical parallels the contrast is between small and large opportunities of serving God: and it may be supposed that something of the same kind is intended in the saying of Jesus.

11. It may then be suggested that it is the same thought that is present in *v.* 11. The ' unrighteous mammon ' is just a way of speaking about worldly goods. These afford an opportunity for faithful service of God, if they are used in the right way. And all men are tested in this very way. If we cannot use the means and opportunities, which we now have, aright, what guarantee is there that we shall be any more satisfactory with larger opportunities and better means? It is perhaps worth considering whether this saying may not have at least an oblique reference to the kind of ambition among the disciples, of which we have record in Mk. 9[33-37], 10[35-45]; Lk. 22[24-27]. It would then be a hint that greatness in the Kingdom is measured by service in the world as it is. The question: ' Who will commit to your trust the true riches? ' is another way of saying: ' Will God commit to your trust the true riches? '

12. If this world's wealth is called ' the unrighteous mammon,' and if the true riches is the ' treasure in heaven,' then we may think of the former as foreign wealth considered from the point of view of a citizen of the Kingdom, and of the goods of the Kingdom as the true wealth of its citizens. If the citizens of the Kingdom are not faithful in their use of the foreign currency—this world's goods —can God give them their own currency—the treasure of heaven? The Greek words translated ' that which is another's ' can equally mean ' that which is foreign.' There are three different MS. readings in this verse. For ' that which is your own ' some MSS. have ' that which is our own,' and a few ' that which is mine.' The interpretation given of the saying is not affected by these variants. If we read ' our ' it means that Jesus includes Himself with those to whom He is speaking: He too belongs to the Kingdom and its wealth is His. The reading ' mine ' would imply that the disciples do not participate in the treasure of the Kingdom except as being admitted to share with Jesus in what is primarily His heritage. In any case the contrast between the treasure of the Kingdom and the ' foreign ' currency of the world remains.

On *v.* 13, which is assigned to Q, see above, p. 425.

22. *PRIDE CONDEMNED* (175)

LK. 16^{14-15}

16 14 And the Pharisees, who were lovers of money, heard all these things; and they
15 scoffed at him. And he said unto them, Ye are they that justify yourselves in the sight of men; but God knoweth your hearts: for that which is exalted among men is an abomination in the sight of God.

In these verses we have an isolated saying of Jesus condemning pride. As such it is suitably included in the collection of teachings which we have called the Gospel of the Outcast. The connexion with what goes before is, however, artificial. Lk. or the compiler of his special source has attempted to make a historical connexion where there is only a topical. The link between these verses and what precedes is provided by the words 'who were lovers of money.' This clause betrays itself as editorial by the fact that (1) what is condemned in the saying is not love of money but pride; and (2) the Pharisees were not in fact specially lovers of money. That charge would have fitted the Sadducees or the publicans very much better. The Pharisees certainly did not despise worldly possessions; but it was not they who held the great vested interests but the Sadducees; and it was not they who sold their country and their own souls for gain but the publicans.

Further, we may suspect that 'the Pharisees' is not original either. What precedes this saying in L is a series of sayings in which the contrast is drawn between worldly wealth and 'treasure in heaven.' The people who would be likely to scoff at such teaching were certainly not the Pharisees but the Sadducees who did not believe in any future life worthy of the name. To the Sadducees, and probably to them alone in Judaism, the words 'treasure in heaven' meant nothing at all. A further small point in favour of the view that this saying is addressed to the Sadducees is the fact that in that case we should have a play on their name in the saying itself. For the name Sadducee is connected with the root *sdk* = 'be righteous'; and this very root is used to translate 'justify yourselves' in the Palestinian Aramaic version of these verses. That some such play upon the name is intended is suggested by the curious phrasing of *v.* 15: 'Ye are they that justify yourselves,' which may mean: 'You are the people who, by taking the name "Sadducee," make public claim to be the party of righteousness.' But God looks deeper than party labels, and knows that the name does not correspond to any real righteousness within. It is rather the expression of an overweening pride, which is utterly detestable in God's sight. The last clause of *v.* 15 may be paraphrased: 'human pride is idolatry in God's sight.' In Jewish thought the word 'abomination' is practically a synonym for 'idol' and 'idolatry.' Cf. 1 Kings 11^{5}, 'Milcom the abomination of the Ammonites,' i.e. Milcom the national deity of the Ammonites; Dan. 11^{31}, 'They shall set up the abomination that maketh desolate,' with reference to the introduction of heathen worship into the Temple at Jerusalem.

There is an excellent parallel to this in the *Mekhilta* on Exod. 20^{18} (not Exod. 20^{21} as in Moore, *Judaism*, ii. 275, and elsewhere). 'All who are lofty of heart (i.e. proud) are called "abomination," as it is said (Prov. 16^{5}) "Every one who is lofty of heart is an abomination to the Lord"; idolatry is called "abomination," as it is said (Deut. 7^{26}) "and thou shalt not bring an abomination (i.e. an idol) into thine house." As idolatry pollutes the land and causes the Presence of God to withdraw from it, so also does pride.' Here in Rabbinical Judaism we have the clear recognition that human pride is as near being idolatry as makes no matter; and this passage confirms our interpretation of the saying of Jesus. Pride is idolatry in God's sight.

Now it is well known that the Sadducees were the aristocratic party in the Jewish commonwealth, holding the first place in riches and dignity. Josephus tells us that the Sadducean doctrines attracted none but the rich (*Antiq.*, XIII, x. 6) and those of the greatest dignity (*Antiq.*, XVII, i. 4). The insatiable love of wealth and the pride and insolence of the Sadducees are frequently alluded to in the *Psalms of Solomon* (see the Introduction to Ryle and James' edition, p. xlviii). So on all points we are justified in regarding this saying as probably directed against the Sadducees.

On *vv.* 16–18 (Q), see above, pp. 425–430.

23. *PARABLE OF DIVES AND LAZARUS* (177)

LK. 16^{19-31}

16 19 Now there was a certain rich man, and
he was clothed in purple and fine linen,
20 [1] faring sumptuously every day: and a
certain beggar named Lazarus was laid
21 at his gate, full of sores, and desiring to
be fed with the *crumbs* that fell from the
rich man's table; yea, even the dogs came
22 and licked his sores. And it came to
pass, that the beggar died, and that he
was carried away by the angels into
Abraham's bosom: and the rich man also
23 died, and was buried. And in Hades he
lifted up his eyes, being in torments, and
seeth Abraham afar off, and Lazarus in
24 his bosom. And he cried and said,
Father Abraham, have mercy on me, and
send Lazarus, that he may dip the tip of
his finger in water, and cool my tongue;
25 for I am in anguish in this flame. But
Abraham said, [2] Son, remember that
thou in thy lifetime receivedst thy good
things, and Lazarus in like manner evil
things: but now here he is comforted,
26 and thou art in anguish. And [3] beside
all this, between us and you there is a
great gulf fixed, that they which would
pass from hence to you may not be able,
and that none may cross over from thence
27 to us. And he said, I pray thee therefore,
father, that thou wouldest sent him to
28 my father's house; for I have five
brethren; that he may testify unto them,
lest they also come into this place of
29 torment. But Abraham saith, They have
Moses and the prophets; let them hear
30 them. And he said, Nay, father Abraham: but if one go to them from the dead,
31 they will repent. And he said unto him,
If they hear not Moses and the prophets,
neither will they be persuaded, if one
rise from the dead.

[1] Or, *living in mirth and splendour every day.*
[2] Gr. *Child.*
[3] Or, *in all these things.*

If the interpretation of *vv.* 14 f. given above is correct, we must ask whether this parable, which immediately follows it in L, may not also be intended as a warning to the same party. There are several considerations in favour of this view. (1) The description of the rich man in *v.* 19. He is wealthy; and the Sadducean party was the party of the wealthy. He wears purple, the colour associated with royal or quasi-royal dignity, and fine linen or lawn, the most luxurious fabric of the ancient world. The Sadducees were the aristocratic party in Judaism. He lived in luxury: so did the Sadducees. Anyone, in the days of Jesus, hearing this description would think at once of the priestly aristocrats of Jerusalem. (2) The dramatic contrast between the end of *v.* 22 and the continuation of the story in *v.* 23. The Sadducees did not believe in any real life after death. A man, in their view, achieved his full life in this world. If he lived on earth in felicity, died in peace, and was honourably buried, he had gained all that was to be gained: he had nothing further to hope for or to fear. This rich man obtains all that a Sadducee could expect; but the end of the Sadducean programme turns out not to be the end of the whole story. There is an unexpected continuation, which is described in *v.* 23. (3) The rich man, who has been sadly disillusioned by the turn of events, wishes (*vv.* 27–31) to warn his five brothers lest they come to the same unhappy end as himself. They are living as he lived in the belief that the grave is the end of all things. But if someone returned from the other side and told them the truth, they would realise that they must change their belief and their way of life. The reply of Abraham (*v.* 29) is significant. The brethren of the rich man are referred to the canonical Scriptures for proof of the life after death. *And those Scriptures were the only authority recognised by the Sadducees*, who rejected the additional doctrines of the Pharisees. And here it is to be noted that when Jesus undertakes to refute the Sadducean doctrine that there is no life beyond the grave, He appeals to the one authority which they recognised (Mk. $12^{26\text{f.}}$).

In view of these considerations it may be concluded that the original hearers of this parable would have recognised in the story the description of a typical Sadducee.

There are numerous parallels to the story of the rich man and the poor man, and their changed fortunes in the next world. The fullest collection is that of Gressmann in the *Abhandlungen* of the Prussian Academy (Phil.-hist. Kl., 1918, No. 7). The most interesting of these parallels is the Egyptian story of a rich man and a poor man, who are buried on the same day. In the under-world their conditions are reversed, and the change is explained as due to the fact that the poor man had been virtuous on earth, while the rich man had not. They now receive the appropriate rewards. The moral is that he who is good on earth receives good in the under-world, and he who is evil on earth receives evil in the under-world. The Jewish version of the tale occurs in several forms, of which the oldest appears to be that given in the Palestinian Talmud (*Hagigah*, II, 77*d*). It is as follows: ‘ Two godly men lived in Ashkelon. They ate together, drank together, and studied in the Law together. One of them died and kindness was not shown to him (i.e. nobody attended his funeral). The son of Ma‘yan, a tax-gatherer, died and the whole city stopped work to show him kindness. The (surviving) pious man began to complain; he said: “ Alas that no (evil) comes upon the haters of Israel ” (i.e. the wicked in Israel). In a dream he saw a vision; and one said to him: “ Do not despise the children of your Lord (i.e. the Israelites). The one (the pious) had committed one sin and departed (this life) in it (i.e. his mean funeral cancelled it); and the other (the wealthy publican) had performed one good deed and departed (this life) in it ” (i.e. his splendid funeral cancelled it). . . . After some days that godly man saw the godly one his (former) companion walking in gardens and parks beside springs of water (in Paradise). And he saw the son of Ma‘yan, the publican, stretching out his tongue on the edge of a river; he was seeking to reach the water, and he could not.’

In both the Egyptian version and the Jewish the point of the story is that in the next world men are rewarded or punished according to their behaviour in this. The similarities between these stories and the Lucan parable are sufficient to suggest the possibility that some such tale was current in Palestine in the days of Jesus, and was taken over by Him and adapted to His own purposes. Whether, as Gressmann thought, the story originated in Egypt and travelled thence to Palestine, there to be adapted by the Rabbis and also by Jesus, is another question. But, granting that Jesus has taken over and adapted a current tale to His own purposes, we still have to ask what is the purpose that He has in view. What is the point of the story as *He* tells it?

His version differs from the parallels in two respects. It has a prologue and an epilogue. The prologue gives the life-histories of the two men; and, very significantly, brings them into relation to one another. It is not that one was very rich and the other very poor, but that the rich man had the opportunity to help the poor man and would not take it. The epilogue (*vv.* 27–31) makes it clear why he would not help. He had believed all his life that he had only one life to live; and therefore he had spent it entirely in seeking his own satisfaction, and wasted no time on thought for others. The prologue and the epilogue are the parts of the parable that matter: and what they have to say is that the heartless conduct of the rich man is connected with his wrong beliefs. His selfish life goes with his bad religion. Translated into the terms of Jesus' own day: the Sadducees hold unworthy beliefs about God and man, and so their whole attitude to their fellow-men is wrong. The difference between the Pharisees and Sadducees in this matter is that whereas the Pharisee is in danger of despising and rejecting those who are ignorant and degraded, the Sadducee is entirely wrapped up in himself and shows a callous indifference to the lot of all who are unfortunate, good, bad, and indifferent alike.

19. The rich man has all the appurtenances of his station in life. His outer garment is dyed with the costly purple associated with royalty. His underclothing is of the finest linen, the most delicate and expensive fabric known to the ancient world, and regarded by the Rabbis as a mark of luxury. On 'fine linen' (*byssus*, Heb. *būṣ*), see *Encyc. Bib.*, col. 2800. The life of the rich man was one continual round of lavish entertainment. In some authorities for the text his name is given. The Sahidic version calls him Nineue. In Ps. Cyprian, *De Pascha Computus*, his name is Finæus, in Priscillian it is Phinees, and in a marginal note to the versified Bible of Peter of Riga it is Amonofis. It is unlikely that these names are anything but a later embellishment of the story.

20 f. The existence of Lazarus is in violent contrast to the life of the rich man. He was lying ill at the gates of the rich man's house. The verb translated 'was laid' is used of persons or animals prostrated by wounds or sickness. Cf. Mt. $8^{6, 14}$. There is no reason to suppose that Lazarus had been carried there to beg alms. His body was covered with ulcers, and he was in such poverty that he would gladly have eaten the bits that fell from the rich man's table. In this his lot was similar to that of the Prodigal in the far country (cf. 15^{16}). It is possible that the word translated 'beggar' represents the Aramaic *miskēnā*, which was used as a euphemism for 'leper.' Cf. Littmann in *Z.N.T.W.* xxxiv (1935), p. 31. He was so weak that he could not even drive away the vagrant dogs that nosed round him

and licked his sores, adding to his troubles, not relieving them. The name Lazarus is the Græcised form of the Hebrew name Eleāzār, shortened in Palestinian usage to Lazār, and meaning '(he whom) God helps.' He certainly had no help from man. The utter wretchedness of Lazarus is illustrated by the Rabbinical saying (*Beṣa* 32^b): 'There are three whose life is no life: he who depends on the table of another (for his food), he who is ruled by his wife, and he whose body is burdened with sufferings.'

22. The reversal of Lazarus' fortunes begins with his death. His soul is carried away to Paradise by the angels. In the Rabbinical literature the idea that the souls of the righteous are conducted by angels is first expressed by R. Meir (*c.* A.D. 150); but it is found at an earlier date in the *Testaments of the XII Patriarchs*, *Asher* 6^{4-6}: 'For the latter ends of men do show their righteousness (or unrighteousness), when they meet the angels of the Lord and of Satan. For when the soul departs troubled, it is tormented by the evil spirit which also it served in lusts and evil works. But if he is peaceful with joy he meeteth the angel of peace, and he leadeth him into eternal life.' The words 'into Abraham's bosom' can be paralleled from the Rabbinical literature. The two clear cases of the use given by Billerbeck (ii. 226) both refer to martyrs, who after their sufferings are in Abraham's bosom. The phrase may be interpreted in two ways. It may stand for the place next to Abraham in the heavenly banquet. (Cf. the similar expression in John 13^{23}.) Or it may be, more generally, a way of describing close and intimate fellowship. (Cf. John 1^{18} and the notes in Bernard's Commentary where similar expressions are adduced from Greek and Latin literature.) Both here and in the Rabbinical passages cited by Billerbeck the latter interpretation is the more suitable. It is to be noted that the destiny of Lazarus, as also of the rich man, is settled at death. There is no suggestion of an intermediate state pending a final judgement. Reward and punishment begin forthwith. There is, it seems, no ground in old Jewish belief for the notion either that 'Abraham's bosom' was a part of Hades set apart for the righteous, or that Paradise was located in Hades or Sheol (Billerbeck, ii. 226 f.).

The fate of the rich man is now described. He died and was buried. That, according to the belief of the Sadducees, should have been the end of the story. If a man lived prosperously and happily, died in peace, and was honourably buried, he had had all that a man could ever expect. Their creed is stated in a polemical passage in *Enoch* 103^{5-8} (transl. Charles):

'Woe to you sinners (i.e. Sadducees), when ye have died,
If ye die in the wealth of your sins,
And those who are like you say regarding you:
"Blessed are the sinners: they have seen all their days.
And now they have died in prosperity and in wealth,
And have not seen tribulation or murder in their life;
And they have died in honour,
And judgement has not been executed on them during their life."'

Here the statement of the Sadducean creed ends. It is followed by a contradiction from the Pharisaic point of view:

'Know ye that their souls will be made to descend into Sheol
And they will be wretched in their great tribulation.
And into darkness and chains and a burning flame where there is grievous judgement shall your spirits enter;
And the great judgement shall be for all the generations of the world. Woe to you, for ye shall have no peace.'

23. So it turns out that the belief of Dives was mistaken. There is something after death, and for the rich man it is punishment. It is important to observe just what the nature of the disillusionment is. The rich man, after his death, goes to the very place where, according to Sadducean belief, he would expect to go; but the place turns out to be quite different from the Sadducean picture of it. Hades is the regular equivalent in the LXX of the Hebrew Sheol; and in the earliest Israelite belief Sheol is the under-world, the shadowy abode of the dead, to which all men without distinction must come. There they remain as ghostly relics of their former selves. They still exist, but their existence is not worth calling life. There is nothing to hope for there and nothing to fear. It is just the dumping-ground for worn-out human beings. After the Exile this view of Sheol or Hades is modified. The belief in a resurrection begins to set limits to the period during which the dead remain in Sheol. The belief in retribution after death comes in at a later period and makes a distinction between the righteous and the wicked in Sheol. The belief in the immortality of the soul leads to the notion that the righteous go direct to Paradise after death. These factors work in various ways in modifying Jewish eschatology as held by the Pharisees; but they do not touch at all the beliefs of the Sadducees, who remain faithful to the old original idea of Sheol. What the rich man in the parable discovers with horror and amazement is that Hades is not what he believed it was, and what his brothers still believe it to be; but something more like the Pharisaic picture as given for example in *Enoch* 22. That is, Hades is something very like Gehenna.

24, 25 f. In his torments the rich man looks about for some help or relief, and perceives Abraham far away and Lazarus with him in Paradise. To them he appeals for mercy. He calls Abraham 'Father,' an indication that he himself is a Jew. The request for water recalls the Rabbinical parallel given above. There springs of water are part of the landscape of Paradise (cf. *Enoch* 22^{9}), and thirst that cannot be appeased is one of the torments of the damned (cf. 4 *Ezra* 8^{59}). The rich man recognises Lazarus and knows his name. It was not through ignorance that Lazarus lay untended at his gate. Abraham addresses the rich man as 'Child' (cf. 15^{31}). His reply is that the request ought not to be granted, and in any case cannot. The fates of the persons concerned are determined by God and it is not for Abraham or Lazarus to meddle in these matters. The same inscrutable decree that gave one abundance and the other misery on earth now reverses the lots. Had the rich man shown mercy in his lifetime he might have had mercy now. But in any case there is no way from the one state to the other; an impassable gulf lies between Paradise and Hades.

27 f. The rich man now thinks of his brothers, who are living as he had lived, believing what he had believed, and so dooming themselves to join him in torment.

He asks that Lazarus may be sent to them to testify to them. Of what? Of the only thing to which one returned from the dead could bear witness; the fact that there is a life beyond the grave, and the nature of it as retribution. The five brothers are in danger of punishment after death precisely because they do not believe in it. If an eye-witness were to go and tell them what had happened to Dives, they would be convinced, and amend their lives in order to avoid a like fate. The creed of the five brothers is the Sadducean creed.

29, 30. The reply of Abraham is that the Law and the prophetic books—the one authority recognised by the Sadducees—contain the belief which the brethren reject. (See above, p. 589.) Lazarus could not tell them the truth any more plainly than it is already told by Moses and the prophets. Dives persists that his brothers really would be impressed if someone returned from the dead to testify. But the last word is that those who reject God's revelation will not be convinced in this way.

The difficulty, felt by many, of believing that the description of the torments of the rich man in the parable can truly represent the mind of Jesus, is at least mitigated if we can suppose that the central portion of the parable is a popular tale which Jesus has adopted, and that the really characteristic and important matter is that which He has added to it by way of prologue and epilogue. We may then contend that the purpose of Jesus in this parable is not to give information about the next world. Rather the point is that there *is* a future life, and that the heartless selfishness of the Sadducees arises from the fact that they deny this truth. 'Let us eat and drink for to-morrow we die' means a low view of human life; and a low view of human life issues in callous indifference to the miseries of others. There is a striking parallel to this in the *Koran* (Surah 107^{1-3}):

> Seest thou not him who disbelieves in the Judgement;
> He it is who repels the orphan,
> And does not encourage the feeding of the poor.

If this interpretation of the purport of the parable is correct, we may reckon it also as a part of the 'Gospel of the Outcast,' teaching that God requires of man not only a merciful and understanding attitude towards the morally frail (as against the Pharisees), but also generous and gracious help for all the victims of poverty, sickness, or any other ill that may come upon man. The Sadducee could boast that he was not narrow-minded and strait-laced like his brethren the Pharisees. But he could not clear himself of the charge that he, who had the most abundant means and the best opportunities for showing a generous spirit, was remarkable only for hardness of heart.

24. *ON SERVING GOD* (181)

LK. 17^{7-10}

17 7 But who is there of you, having a
[1] servant plowing or keeping sheep, that
will say unto him, when he is come in
8 from the field, Come straightway and sit
down to meat; and will not rather say
unto him, Make ready wherewith I may
sup, and gird thyself, and serve me, till I
have eaten and drunken; and afterward
9 shalt thou eat and drink? Doth he
thank the [1] servant because he did the
10 things that were commanded? Even so
ye also, when ye shall have done all the
things that are commanded you, say, We
are unprofitable [2] servants; we have
done that which it was our duty to do.

[1] Gr. *bondservant*. [2] Gr. *bondservants*.

The opening verses of chapter 17 are derived from Q (see above, pp. 430–433). They are all clearly addressed to disciples; and this L passage, which is appended to them, may be taken to be spoken to the disciples also. The important question is whether it can be fairly included in the block of material which we have called the 'Gospel of the Outcast.' It can be argued that it would be in place in any context concerning the service of God, no matter what the nature of the service might happen to be. On the other hand we have clear indications in the teaching as to what Jesus conceived the service of God or the service of the Kingdom, in the special sense, to be. The business of a disciple as servant of God, in the full sense of the word, is to be the organ whereby the merciful love of God is manifested to men. The work *par excellence* of the disciple is to do what the Pharisee and the Sadducee fail to do. The Son of Man is come to seek and to save the lost; and the task of the disciple is that task. And there is no point at which he is entitled to say, 'I have done enough,' no point at which performance overtakes duty to God or the needs of men. The most devoted and tireless of the Apostles knew this; see 1 Cor. 9^{16ff}. See notes on Mt. 25^{14-30}, above, pp. 537–540.

7 f., 9. The endless claims of God's work are illustrated by the parable of the master and the slave. The slave has done a day's work, or what might fairly be deemed a day's work, on the farm. But on his return to the house he is not met with an invitation to sit down to a meal. Fresh tasks await him. He must prepare and serve food to his master; and when the master is satisfied, then he may attend to his own wants. Even when he has done all this he has not put his master under any obligation to him. He has not given anything that the master was not already entitled to demand.

10. The conclusion to be drawn from this example will then be something like this: if a mere man is entitled to make such far-reaching demands on the services of his servant, and that merely for his own profit and comfort, how much more is God entitled to require the utmost from His servants in the manifestation and extension of His Kingdom among men. So the conclusion might be drawn from God's side. Actually it is stated in terms of the disciple's obligation rather than of God's demands. So put it becomes: When you have done all that you can do, you have done no more than God is entitled to expect from you, and not enough to put God in your debt.

The difficulty in this verse lies in the word 'unprofitable.' The only other place in the New Testament where it occurs is Mt. 25^{30} in reference to a servant who had done nothing at all. That passage cannot help us here, where the servants have done all that they are commanded. The word is omitted by the better of the two MSS. of the Old Syriac version; and some scholars, on the strength of this omission, reject the word here and then take the sense to be, 'we are but servants; we have done only what we were bound to do.' It is urged that the emphasis is on the fact of being servants; not on a distinction between good and bad servants. But the point is that the servants *are* good, as good as they can be. And at their best they have not put God in their debt; they have only earned the right to be retained as servants; they have earned their keep. Or, in Pauline terms: 'If I preach the gospel, I have nothing to glory of; for necessity is laid upon me; for woe is unto me, if I preach not the gospel' (1 Cor. 9^{16}). The same thought is found in a saying of Rabban Johanan b. Zakkai (died *c.* A.D. 80): 'If thou hast wrought much in the Law claim not merit for thyself, for to this end wast thou created.' 'Unprofitable' here is much the same as 'having nothing to glory of,' or 'not claiming merit.'

25. *THE COMING OF THE KINGDOM* (183)

LK. 17^{20-21}

17 20 And being asked by the Pharisees, when the kingdom of God cometh, he answered them and said, The kingdom of God cometh not with observation:
21 neither shall they say, Lo, here! or, There! for lo, the kingdom of God is [1] within you.

[1] Or, *in the midst of you.*

This short passage presents serious difficulties. The first problem to be solved is that of deciding between 'within you' (R.V. text) and 'in the midst of you' (R.V. mg.). The difference of interpretation implied in the two renderings is of old standing, as may be seen from the following typical patristic quotations. For the sense 'within,' Origen on Joshua, *Hom.* xiii. 1. 'After the Lord Jesus has destroyed the king of sin from the city of our soul, our soul may become the city of God, and God may reign in it, and it may be said to us, "Behold the Kingdom of God is within you."' For 'in the midst of you,' Ephraim Syrus, *Commentary on the Diatessaron* (Moesinger 211): '"Behold the Kingdom is within your heart" which He (Jesus) said concerning Himself, who was standing in their midst.' This interpretation of Ephraim's is supported by the Old Syriac version and the Syriac Vulgate, both of which translate the Greek of Lk. in the same sense as R.V. mg. It must, however, be admitted that this rendering of the Greek word *entos* is not the obvious or natural one. Liddell and Scott do not recognise it. The natural way to translate *entos* is by 'within' or 'in': and this is confirmed by the fact that when Lk. means 'among' he writes *en mesō* (22^{27}).

But the matter does not end with this admission. For if the saying is authentic, *entos* is the translation of some Aramaic preposition; and both in Hebrew and Aramaic the corresponding prepositions are ambiguous in a way that *entos* is not. The ambiguity may be illustrated by a Rabbinical discussion which is recorded as having taken place in the middle of the second century A.D. on the meaning of the text in Exod. 17^7, 'Is the Lord among us (*bĕkirbēnū*) or not?' One Rabbi explains thus: The Israelites in asking this question meant to say, 'If He (God) provides us with food, like a king who dwells in a city (i.e. in the midst of his people), so that the city lacks for nothing, then we will serve Him; if not, we will rebel against Him.' The majority of the Rabbis, however, gave a different interpretation. The question meant: 'If we think our thoughts and He knows what we think (i.e. if He is literally within us and knows the secrets of each individual), then we will serve Him; if not, we will rebel against Him' (*Pesikta* 28^a). Here is exactly the same difference of interpretation as that between R.V. text and R.V. mg.; and here the difference of views is grounded in a real ambiguity in the meaning of the Hebrew word. The conclusion is that even if it be admitted that 'within' is the natural and proper translation of *entos*, *entos* itself is only one of the possible translations of the probable original Aramaic, which would equally well be translated by *en mesō*, 'among.' (Cf. Field's *Hexapla* on Exod. 34^{9}.)

We are thus driven back upon other considerations; and there are two which seem to be decisive in favour of the sense 'among' rather than 'within.' First it is the Pharisees who are addressed, and it is not likely that Jesus would say that the Kingdom of God was 'within' them. Such a statement would lay Him open to the obvious retort: 'Why then are you in open opposition to us?' Secondly, the Kingdom of God is not here under discussion as a state of mind or a disposition in men. It is thought of as something which is to come. It is a fact of history, not of psychology. Moreover, Jesus speaks elsewhere of men entering the Kingdom, not of the Kingdom entering men. The Kingdom is a state of affairs, not a state of mind. This state of affairs can come to pass in God's providence, and men may find their place in it. The whole weight of the teaching of Jesus elsewhere seems to be in favour of saying, 'Lo, the Kingdom of God is among you.'

There remains yet another problem: how are we to interpret 'Lo, the Kingdom of God is among you'? Is it (1) a description of the present state of affairs, or (2) a prophecy about the future? This question is still in debate.

The form of the Pharisees' question shows that they are thinking of the Kingdom as something still future. They believe that it will come; and they ask 'when?' That is, they ask the question which so many of the Apocalypses ask and attempt to answer. The answer of Jesus may mean that it is idle to ask *when* the Kingdom will come, since it is already present; or that the question cannot be answered, since the answer is known to God alone. For either reply we can quote supporting passages from the other teaching of Jesus. In favour of the first are such sayings as Mt. 12^{28}||Lk. 11^{20} (Q); Mt. $12^{41f.}$||Lk. $11^{31f.}$ (Q); Mt. $12^{5f.}$ (M); in favour of the latter Mt. 24^{37-41}||Lk. 17^{26-30} (Q); Mk. 13^{32-37}; Mt. $24^{43f.}$||Lk. $12^{39f.}$ (Q). On the whole the latter view seems preferable. We must then understand Jesus to say: The Kingdom does not come in such a way that one can make a programme of its coming. There are no premonitory signs and portents which may be observed so that one could say, 'Look at this and that; it cannot be far away now.' On the contrary it comes suddenly and unexpectedly. One moment the world is just its normal self: then Lo! the Kingdom of God is among you. This interpretation has two obvious claims to acceptance. It deals with the question asked; and the reply of Jesus agrees with His genuine teaching about the final consummation as given in the Q passage which follows immediately in Lk. (17^{23-30}, see above, pp. 433–436).

This interpretation of Lk. $17^{20f.}$ can be maintained without in any way minimising the importance of those other passages in which the Kingdom appears as a present reality at work in the world. The general view of the whole matter of the Kingdom as both present and future can best be realised in the parable of the Seed (Mk. 4^{26-29}). There the point of the story is not the contrast between small beginnings and large results; neither has it anything to do with the length or shortness of the time between sowing and harvest. It is that a man who sows seed sets in motion natural forces which go on inevitably until they reach their consummation in the harvest. So is the Kingdom of God. The ministry of

Jesus has set in motion supernatural forces which go on inevitably until they reach their consummation. The consummated Kingdom is now present in the world as really as the harvest is present in the sown field. How the growth takes place and when it will come to full fruition—these are questions which the sower cannot answer. They are God's affair. But that heavenly forces, as real as the mysterious forces of nature, are already at work in the world moving inevitably to the great consummation—of that Jesus has no doubt whatever. The Kingdom is a present reality working towards a future consummation.

26. *THE IMPORTUNATE WIDOW* (185)

Lk. 18^{1-8}

18 1 And he spake a parable unto them to
the end that they ought always to pray,
2 and not to faint; saying, There was in a
city a judge, which feared not God, and
3 regarded not man: and there was a widow
in that city; and she came oft unto him,
saying, [1] Avenge me of mine adversary.
4 And he would not for a while: but afterward he said within himself, Though I fear
5 not God, nor regard man; yet because this
widow troubleth me, I will avenge her,
lest she [2] wear me out by her continual
6 coming. And the Lord said, Hear what
7 [3] the unrighteous judge saith. And shall
not God avenge his elect, which cry to
him day and night, and he is longsuffering
8 over them? I say unto you, that he will
avenge them speedily. Howbeit when the
Son of man cometh, shall he find [4] faith
on the earth?

[1] Or, *Do me justice of*: and so in ver. 5, 7, 8.
[2] Gr. *bruise*.
[3] Gr. *the judge of unrighteousness*.
[4] Or, *the faith*.

The Evangelist's introductory note to this parable represents it as an exhortation to be instant in prayer to God. But an examination of the parable itself shows that the duty of praying is not the main point. The prayers of the righteous are taken for granted as much as the persistence of the widow in stating her claim. The true point is not that prayers should be made, but that God will answer the prayers of His servants. The object of the parable is not to encourage the habit of praying, but to induce that faith in God and His purposes of good, without which prayer cannot be anything but a formality. It is thus a word of hope and encouragement to the victims of oppression and injustice, and an integral part of the 'Gospel of the Outcast.' The message of the parable has close affinities with a striking passage in *Ecclesiasticus* (35 $^{12-20\ (14-26)}$; Charles, *Apoc. and Pseudepigr.*, i. 438 ff.), where the writer speaks of God's righteousness and His readiness to hear the cry of the oppressed:

Bribe not, for He will not receive;
And put not thy trust upon a sacrifice of extortion,
For He is a God of justice,
And with Him is no partiality.
He will not show partiality against the poor man,
And the supplications of the distressed He heareth.
He doth not ignore the cry of the fatherless,
Nor the widow, when she poureth out (her) plaint. . . .
The appeal of the lowly traverseth the skies,
And resteth not till it reach (its goal).
It shall not remove till God doth visit,

And till the righteous Judge executeth judgement.
Yea, the Lord will not tarry,
And the mighty One will not refrain Himself,
Till He smite the loins of the merciless,
And requite vengeance to the arrogant;
Till He dispossess the sceptre of pride,
And the staff of wickedness utterly cut down;
Till He render to man his due
And recompense people according to their devising;
Till He plead the cause of His people,
And rejoice them with His salvation.
[Beauteous is His favour in a time] of stress
As a rain-cloud in the season of drought.

1. The audience for this parable is, in the Lucan arrangement, the same as that of the preceding Q section (17^{22-37}), that is, the disciples (17^{22}). The Greek word (*enkakein*) translated 'faint' is very rare. In the Greek version of the Old Testament by Symmachus it occurs four times to translate a Hebrew verb meaning to loathe, abhor, dread. Something like this appears to be the meaning here: the disciples are not to 'get fed-up' with praying or 'be sick of praying.' Cf. 1 Thess. 5^{17}, 'Pray without ceasing.' Jewish teaching and practice did not favour incessant prayer. Three times in the day was the correct practice, based on Dan. 6^{10}. Cf. Moore, *Judaism*, ii. 221.

2 f. The character of the judge is not calculated to inspire any hope in the breast of a litigant who is not in a position to offer a bribe. Neither the laws of God nor public opinion can stir his conscience. The widow, on the other hand, is the very type of helplessness and defencelessness. Jerusalem devastated by the Babylonians is compared to a widow (Lam. 1^{1}). In the Old Testament great stress is laid on the duty of treating widows and orphans aright (Exod. $22^{22\,ff.}$) and on God's care for them (Ps. 68^{5}); and this duty is an essential part of true religion in the early Church (James 1^{27}).

4 f. The widow in the parable has no weapon but her own perseverance. She comes again and again before the judge, always with the same plea: 'Vindicate my rights against my opponent.' The situation would seem to be that the widow is the plaintiff in the case. Having failed to obtain satisfaction by other means, she appeals to the court to do her justice. The court, however, is not willing to act, and remains unwilling; so that the business becomes a war of attrition between the judge and the widow. The judge is represented as reflecting on this situation. He will not do justice out of respect for God's will nor out of regard for public opinion; but perhaps it will be best for his own convenience to grant the woman's request. The exact nature of the deciding consideration is not quite clear. The Greek of the latter part of *v.* 5 could be understood to mean that the judge fears a time when the widow, grown exasperated by the law's delays, will set about him and beat him black and blue. The verb translated 'wear me out' means properly to 'give a black eye.' It appears again in a more general sense in Paul's statement 'I buffet my body' (1 Cor. 9^{27}). Against the

notion of such a violent climax is the fact that the judge would know how to deal with such a burst of fury. Also the Greek tenses are against this interpretation. We should probably, therefore, prefer the translation given in R.V. text and understand that the judge dreads being continually pestered by the widow, and decides to put an end to it by doing her justice.

6–8^{a}. The comment of Jesus on the parable. If even an unjust judge can be induced to do justice, how much more will the righteous God, the judge of all the earth, do right. The ' elect ' of God : the Greek word translated ' elect ' is used in the Septuagint in several senses: (*a*) = choice, i.e. of the best quality. In this sense the word is used of animals and things; (*b*) = picked, especially of picked men—the idea that is expressed by *corps d'élite*; (*c*) the chosen of God, especially Israel as God's chosen people, or great men in Israel as God's chosen servants. This third use of ' elect ' seems to belong to the period of the Exile and after. Cf. Is. 42^{1}, 43^{20}, 65$^{9, 15, 23}$; Ps. 105$^{6, 43}$, 106^{5}; 1 Chron. 16^{13}; *Ecclus.* 46^{1}. David is God's chosen (Ps. 89$^{3, 19}$), as is Moses (Ps. 106^{23}); and God made the patriarchs His elect (2 *Macc.* 1^{25}). It is noteworthy that the idea of Israel as God's elect should appear not in the days of national greatness and prosperity, but in the period of humiliation and impotence. And it is probably significant that the term so often appears in parallelism to ' servant ' (Is. 65$^{9, 15}$; Ps. 105^{6}; 1 Chron. 16^{13}). The election is not in the first instance an election to privilege, but an appointment to service. It is in line with this that we find the ' elect ' of God in parallelism with His holy ones (*Wisdom* 4^{15}) or ' them that love Him ' (*Ecclus.* 47^{22}) or as another name for the righteous and in contrast to the impious (*Enoch* 1$^{1, 3, 8}$, 5^{7}). We might almost say that the mark of the elect is that they serve God by the sanctity of their lives. They are not the pampered darlings of Providence, but the *corps d'élite* in the army of the living God. Because they are what they are, they are foredoomed to suffering at the hands of the wicked; and in many cases the seal of election is martyrdom.

If this is the meaning of election it is easy to see why the elect cry to God day and night. We may compare the Greek text of *Enoch* 9$^{1-3}$: ' Then Michael, Uriel, Raphael, and Gabriel, looking down from heaven, saw much blood being shed on the earth. And they said one to another: " The voice of them that cry upon the earth; (and their cry comes up) as far as the gates of heaven. The souls of men make their suit saying: Bring our cause before the Most High." ' See also Rev. 6$^{9-11}$ and the passage from *Ecclus.* quoted above.

The words ' and he is longsuffering over them ' are difficult. It is possible to take the clause as meaning that God gives a patient hearing to the cries of the elect; but that is a very lame interpretation. The elect do not want a patient hearing: they want redress. They do not want God to go on patiently listening to their outcry: they want God to take action which will make their crying unnecessary. Yet, although this interpretation is unsatisfactory, there is no other that will fit the Greek text as it stands; and we are driven to suppose that the Greek itself is a misunderstanding of the Semitic original. In the Septuagint the Greek verb here translated ' is longsuffering ' corresponds to a Hebrew, which means ' postpones (his) wrath.' In Aramaic there is a similar idiom: ' removes his wrath to a distance.' There is a Rabbinical parable based on this idiomatic phrase (p. *Taanith*, II. 65^b). A king had two legions of troops. He wondered where he should keep them, and finally decided to have them at a distance from the capital on the ground that if the civilian population became troublesome, and he had to send for the troops, there would be time for the people to come to a more reasonable frame of mind before the troops arrived. So, it is argued, God keeps His wrath at a distance in order to give Israel time to repent.

So in this case it may be supposed that the original Aramaic meant 'and He postpones the wrath, which He has on their account,' i.e. He refrains from executing His wrath on those who persecute the elect, thus giving the persecutors time to repent and amend their ways. This would give an entirely satisfactory sense. What delays the vindication of the elect is the longsuffering of God towards their foes. In this connexion we may quote another Rabbinical saying from the same passage as the parable given above. It is attributed to R. Jonathan b. Eleazar (first half of the third century A.D.). Commenting on the phrase 'postponing anger' he remarks that in the Hebrew phrase the word for 'anger' is not in the singular number, but in the dual. This suggests that God postpones two angers, and so leads to the conclusion that God is longsuffering not only with the righteous but with the wicked as well.

8. In *v.* 8 the answer to the question of *v.* 7 is given. Although God is patient with the oppressors of His elect, yet the vindication will come, and come quickly. The connexion of the question in *v.* 8^b with the parable is not at all clear. By some commentators it is regarded as a later editorial comment on the parable, which is taken to end with the word 'speedily.' It may be noted that in the Palestinian Syriac Lectionary *v.* 8^a ends Lesson CXV, and *v.* 8^b begins Lesson CXVI. On the assumption that the saying is genuine and that it belongs to its present context, two ways of interpreting it seem possible. First, we may take 'the coming of the Son of Man' to mean the Parousia, as in Lk. 17^{22-30} (above, pp. 433–436). In that case the Parousia will be the vindication of the elect, and the question comes to mean: 'When the Son of Man comes, will anyone be looking hopefully for that consummation?' Alternatively 'Son of Man' may be taken, as in Lk. 7^{34} = Mt. 11^{19} (Q), above, p. 362, as a periphrasis for the first personal pronoun. In that case the parable may be taken to show what ought to be the attitude of men. They ought to have implicit faith that God will vindicate His elect. But when one looks for such faith and hope among men, does one find it? Cf. Lk. 7^9 = Mt. 8^{10} (Q), above, p. 355, and the parable of the Great Feast (Lk. 14^{16-24} (Q), above, pp. 420 ff.). In the latter parable we have the reply to the conventional piety that says, 'Blessed is he that shall eat bread in the Kingdom of God'; and the reply is in effect: 'You say that, but don't really mean it: you merely pretend to desire the Kingdom of God.' See *The Teaching of Jesus*, pp. 224 f. I still think the second line of explanation the better.

27 *THE PHARISEE AND THE PUBLICAN* (186)

LK. 18^{9-14}

18 9 And he spake also this parable unto
certain which trusted in themselves that
they were righteous, and set [1] all others
10 at nought: Two men went up into the
temple to pray; the one a Pharisee, and
11 the other a publican. The Pharisee

stood and prayed thus with himself, God,
I thank thee, that I am not as the rest of
men, extortioners, unjust, adulterers, or
12 even as this publican. I fast twice in
the week; I give tithes of all that I get.
13 But the publican, standing afar off,
would not lift up so much as his eyes
unto heaven, but smote his breast, saying,
14 God, [2] be merciful to me [3] a sinner. I
say unto you, This man went down to
his house justified rather than the other:
for every one that exalteth himself shall
be humbled; but he that humbleth
himself shall be exalted.

[1] Gr. *the rest*. [2] Or, *be propitiated*.
[3] Or, *the sinner*.

This parable obviously belongs to the 'Gospel of the Outcast.' It is addressed to all the friends of the elder brother in the parable of the Prodigal. According to R.V. this parable is spoken 'unto' the people in question; but the Greek preposition may also mean 'with reference to' or even 'against.' Lucan usage, however, is in favour of 'unto.' The parable is spoken to those 'who trusted in themselves that they were righteous, and set all others at nought.' The words 'trusted in themselves' are to be taken literally. They do not mean 'considered themselves to be righteous'; but 'believed in themselves' 'had faith in themselves' 'relied upon themselves.' The same construction appears in Lk. 11^{22}, where the strong man 'relied confidently on his armaments'; and, most instructively, in 2 Cor. 1^{9}, 'that we should not trust in ourselves, but in God.' The mark of the people attacked in the parable is their self-confidence and self-reliance in things religious. This consideration determines the meaning of the word 'that' in the following clause. The Greek word (*hoti*) may mean 'that' or 'because.' The latter translation is to be preferred here. The clause gives the ground of their self-confidence. It is not that they had a good opinion of themselves, to wit, that they were righteous; but that they really had the kind of faith in themselves and their own powers that weaker vessels are content to have in God, and that the ground of this confidence was their own achievements in piety and morality. They believed in themselves *because* they were able to live up to their own standard. And naturally they despised those who either did not acknowledge their standard or did not succeed in living up to it.

It is clear from the parable itself that the persons meant by this description are Pharisees. Josephus describes the Pharisees (*War*, i. 110) as 'a body of Jews with the reputation of excelling the rest of their nation in the observances of religion, and as exact exponents of the laws'; and the description of Josephus is confirmed by the confession of Paul (Phil. $3^{4\text{ff.}}$): 'If any other man thinketh to have confidence in the flesh (i.e. in man and things human, as opposed to God and God's grace), I yet more: circumcised the eighth day, of the stock of Israel, of the tribe of Benjamin, a Hebrew of the Hebrews; as touching the law, a Pharisee; as touching zeal, persecuting the church; as touching the righteousness which is in the law, found blameless.'

While it is clear that it is Pharisees that are meant by the description in *v.* 9, it is not certain that all Pharisees are covered by it. That spiritual pride was a real and ever-present danger in Pharisaism is sufficiently obvious. The danger was perceived by the great Hillel (*c.* 20 B.C.), who used to say (*Aboth* 2^{5}, Danby, p. 448): 'Keep not aloof from the congregation and trust not in thyself until the day of thy death, and judge not thy fellow until thou art come to his place.' If it be argued that such warning against a haughty, self-confident, and censorious attitude presupposes that there were some who had it (which is more than probable), it also means that there were others within the Pharisaic circle who perceived this subtle peril and strove to avoid it. We shall probably be near the truth if we think of the parable as directed not against the entire body of Pharisees, but against a certain section of them. See the discussion of the Speech against Pharisaism, above, pp. 386–397, 519–532.

10. The parable proper begins with *v.* 10. Two men, representing the two types of character, go up from the city to the temple-mount to pray. For the use of the Temple as a place of prayer see Lk. 1[10]; Acts 3[1]; Mishnah, *Tamid* 5[1] (Danby, pp. 586 f.). Besides such prayers as were incorporated in the regular daily ritual of the Temple, there were the private prayers and meditations of individuals who could use the Temple for this purpose not only at the times of the daily sacrifices, but also in the intervals between services. The two men who go up to the Temple for this purpose represent the two extremes in Judaism. The Pharisee is the type of complete devotion to the Law as the supreme standard of Jewish faith and morals. The publican represents the lowest stratum of Jewish life, those who fail miserably to live up to the religious and moral ideals of the nation.

11 f. Both men pray. Standing was the regular posture in prayer, though other attitudes were not rigidly excluded. There is great variation among the witnesses to the text at this point. The main alternatives are:

(*a*) The Pharisee stood and prayed thus with himself.
(*b*) The Pharisee stood and prayed thus.
(*c*) The Pharisee stood by himself and prayed thus.

In (*a*) ' prayed with himself ' must mean that he prayed silently. Does this fit the story? We are told that the custom was to utter the words of private prayer in an undertone (Moore, *Judaism*, ii. 222 f.). The second reading is colourless, and has nothing against it—or to recommend it. The third introduces a feature that is in keeping with the rest of the parable. The Pharisee stands aloof from the common herd of worshippers, thus doing one of the three things criticised by Hillel. Intrinsically, reading (*c*) is superior to the other two. It makes a real contribution to the story. Reading (*b*) contributes nothing, and (*a*) is mere conventional detail, which fills out the picture of the Pharisee but does nothing to make it live.

The content of the Pharisee's prayer is a catalogue of his own virtues. The first and larger part of the list mentions the vices from which he abstains; the second part draws the attention of God to certain evidences of his special piety. The catalogue is introduced by a thanksgiving to God, which we must regard as sincere. There is no ground for supposing that the Pharisee is a hypocritical humbug, or that his virtues are pretended. He is a respectable God-fearing man, and what he says about himself must be taken as true. He thanks God that he has been able to abstain from a number of things that are prohibited by God Himself in His Law. The unpleasant feature in the prayer is the self-satisfied comparison which the Pharisee makes between himself and those who do not belong to his party. It is, unhappily, very easy to slip from ' There, but for the grace of God, goes John Bradford ' to ' God, I thank thee, that I am not as the rest of men '; and it would be rash to contend that Pharisees were the only people who ever made this kind of slip. The difficulty of drawing the line between the two attitudes is illustrated by the prayer which R. Nechunya b. Ha Kana (*c.* A.D. 70) used to offer whenever he came out of the Rabbinical College (p. *Berakhoth*, II. 7[d]):

> I give thanks before thee O Lord my God, and God of my fathers, that thou hast appointed my portion with those who sit in the College and the Synagogue, and hast not appointed my lot in the theatres and circuses. For I labour and they labour. I am keen and they are keen. I labour to inherit Paradise and they labour to inherit the pit of destruction; as it is said (Ps. 16[10]) 'Thou wilt not leave my soul to Sheol; neither wilt thou suffer thy godly one to see the pit.'

'Extortioners': cf. Is. 10[1f.]. Possibly to be distinguished from the 'unjust,' as being those who wrong their fellows while managing to keep within the letter of the law; whereas the 'unjust' break the law in their greed of gain. 'Adulterers'; see on Lk. 16[18] (Q), above, pp. 428 ff. 'Or even as this publican': better, 'or, for that matter, like this publican.' The publican may not be guilty of any specially notorious crimes; but, take him all in all, he is a despicable creature.

In *v.* 12 the Pharisee names two matters in which he goes beyond the positive commands of the Law. A regular fast day twice in the week is not prescribed in the Law; and such evidence as we have on the practice tends to show that it was a self-imposed act of piety in strict Pharisaic circles. The motives lying behind the institution are obscure. The chosen days were Monday and Thursday, probably because they satisfied the double requirement of not interfering with the Sabbath celebrations, and of being well separated from one another. According to Billerbeck (ii. 244) there is no evidence that the Jews of this period, as a whole, had a regular weekly fast, either on one day or two. Nor is there any ground for thinking that the practice of fasting twice a week was regarded as obligatory by the whole body of Pharisees. The practice was essentially a voluntary observance undertaken by individuals.

Later the two fasts were explained as days of mourning for such national calamities as the destruction of the Temple: and this explanation found its way into Christian circles. Thus in a Greek MS. quoted by Juster (i. 308 n. 2) the Jews are said to fast on Mondays because it was on a Monday that the Temple was destroyed by Nebuchadnezzar, and on Thursdays because it was on a Thursday that the Temple was destroyed by Titus.

The Church took over the two fasts in the week, but altered the days. So in the *Didache* 8[1]: 'Let not your fasts be with the hypocrites, for they fast on Mondays and Thursdays, but do you fast on Wednesdays and Fridays.' In the *Apostolic Constitutions* (vii. 23[1]) it is explained that Wednesday is a fast because on that day the betrayal of Jesus was arranged between Judas and the Jewish authorities, and Friday because it was the day of the Crucifixion. Other passages to a like effect in Juster (i. 310 n. 5).

'I give tithes of all that I get.' Here again the Pharisee goes beyond the strict legal requirement, and probably beyond the interpretations of the scribes. See notes on Lk. 11[42] (Q), above, pp. 389 f.

13. The publican is overwhelmed by the sense of his own unworthiness, and rightly so. It is a great mistake to regard the publican as a decent sort of fellow, who knew his own limitations and did not pretend to be better than he was. It is one of the marks of our time that the Pharisee and the publican have changed places; and it is the modern equivalent of the publican who may be heard thanking God that he is not like those canting humbugs, hypocrites, and killjoys, whose chief offence is that they take their religion seriously. This publican was a rotter; and he knew it. He asked for God's mercy because mercy was the only thing he dared ask for.

14^{a}. The comment of Jesus on the story. Why does the publican go down justified rather than the Pharisee? The answer is that the decisive thing is not the past record, whether good or bad, but the present attitude towards God. Every moment before God is an opportunity to have life determined by the future rather than the past. The Pharisee asks nothing better than to go on in the way he is going. The one thing against him is that he is satisfied with life and with himself. God can do nothing for him because he lacks nothing. The publican has one point, and one only, in his favour: he is not satisfied. Where there is this heaven-born discontent, there is hope.

14^{b}. A floating saying (it appears in Mt. 18^{4}, 23^{12} and Lk. 14^{11} as well as here), which has attached itself to the parable in the course of tradition. It only serves to weaken the conclusion in *v.* 14^{a}.

The remainder of this chapter consists of material derived from Mk.; and the next piece of L material is the story of Zacchæus (19^{1-10}), a fitting pendant to the parable of the Pharisee and the Publican. In the parable Jesus pillories the Pharisaic attitude to these outcasts: in the case of Zacchæus He shows by His own example the more excellent way. With this narrative the section of L material, which we have called the 'Gospel of the Outcast,' comes to an end. These L passages from 15^{1}–19^{10} contain some of our Lord's deepest thought concerning the nature of God, some of His most searching criticism of the religion of His time, and at least one perfect example of His own way with sinners.

28. *THE PARABLE OF THE POUNDS* (195)

LK. 19^{11-27}

19 11 And as they heard these things, he
added and spake a parable, because he
was nigh to Jerusalem, and *because* they
supposed that the kingdom of God was
12 immediately to appear. He said therefore, A certain nobleman went into a far
country, to receive for himself a kingdom,
13 and to return. And he called ten [1] servants of his, and gave them ten [2] pounds,
and said unto them, Trade ye *herewith* till
14 I come. But his citizens hated him, and
sent an ambassage after him, saying, We
15 will not that this man reign over us. And
it came to pass, when he was come back
again, having received the kingdom, that
he commanded these [1] servants, unto
whom he had given the money, to be
called to him, that he might know what
16 they had gained by trading. And the
first came before him, saying, Lord, thy
pound hath made ten pounds more.
17 And he said unto him, Well done, thou
good [3] servant: because thou wast found
faithful in a very little, have thou
18 authority over ten cities. And the
second came, saying, Thy pound, Lord,
19 hath made five pounds. And he said
unto him also, Be thou also over five
20 cities. And [4] another came, saying,
Lord, behold, *here is* thy pound, which I
21 kept laid up in a napkin: for I feared
thee, because thou art an austere man:
thou takest up that thou layedst not
down, and reapest that thou didst not

22 sow. He saith unto him, Out of thine
own mouth will I judge thee, thou wicked
[3] servant. Thou knewest that I am an
austere man, taking up that I laid not
down, and reaping that I did not sow;
23 then wherefore gavest thou not my
money into the bank, and [5] I at my
coming should have required it with
24 interest? And he said unto them that
stood by, Take away from him the
pound, and give it unto him that hath
25 the ten pounds. And they said unto
26 him, Lord, he hath ten pounds. I say
unto you, that unto every one that hath
shall be given; but from him that hath
not, even that which he hath shall be
27 taken away from him. Howbeit these
mine enemies, which would not that I
should reign over them, bring hither,
and slay them before me.

[1] Gr. *bondservants*.
[2] *Mina*, here translated a pound, is equal to one hundred drachmas. See ch. xv. 8.
[3] Gr. *bondservant*.
[4] Gr. *the other*.
[5] Or, *I should have gone and required*.

This parable has a parallel in Mt.'s parable of the Talents (Mt. 25^{14-30}, above pp. 537–540). There are many differences in detail between the two narratives, so many that it is difficult to suppose that the two versions can be traced back to a common written source such as Q. Indeed, it has been doubted whether they can be the same parable. The most likely solution is that we have here two versions of an original parable, which have come down through different lines of tradition and suffered modifications in the process. The most striking difference between Mt. and Lk. is the additional narrative matter peculiar to Lk., contained in *vv.* 12, 14, and 27. The most recent commentator on Lk. (Hauck) regards these verses as forming a separate allegory, which has been incorporated with the parable of the Pounds, and has influenced the latter in places, e.g. *v.* 15 'having received the kingdom'; *v.* 17 'have thou authority over ten *cities*'; *v.* 19 five *cities*. Harnack, noting certain similarities between the additional matter in Lk. here and the additional matter in Mt.'s version of the parable of the Great Feast (Mt. 22^{1-14}, above, pp. 516–519), suggested that the additions in both cases were derived from a common source. But it must be confessed that the resemblances are far outweighed by the differences.

Much more impressive is the similarity between Lk.'s additional matter and the story told by Josephus (*War*, II, vi. §§ 80–100; parallel in *Antiquities*, XVII, viii.–xi.). There we are told how Herod the Great divided his kingdom by will among his family. The bequests required the confirmation of the Roman Emperor before they could become fully valid, and accordingly Archelaus set out for Rome to obtain confirmation of the bequest to him. He was followed by an embassy of the Jews sent to protest against his appointment; and, after hearing both parties, Augustus gave Archelaus half of Herod's kingdom, with the title of Ethnarch, promising, moreover, to make him king if he proved worthy of the title. The rest was divided into two tetrarchies, which Augustus presented to two other sons of Herod, Philip and Antipas.

In view of the parable of the Talents, it seems clear that the additional matter in Lk. is really addition. But it is not like Lk. to conflate in this way, and it may be suggested that the addition of this secondary matter had already taken place before Lk. got hold of the parable.

The effect of the additions is to make the parable, as it now stands, an allegory of the Christian life in the interim between the Ascension and the Parousia. The nobleman (Christ) has departed to a distant country (heaven) to receive a kingdom. Meanwhile he entrusts the management of his affairs to his servants (Christians). His citizens (the Jews) hate him and will not have him as king (the Jews deny the Messiahship of Jesus). But in the end he receives the kingdom and returns (the Parousia) to reward his servants according to their behaviour during his absence, and to execute judgement on the rebels (at the Last Judgement). With the removal of the additional matter, we get a parable whose main purport is the same as that of the Talents.

11. The opening verse effects a connexion between the immediately preceding story of Zacchæus of Jericho—'near Jerusalem'—and the parable. The motive ascribed to Jesus—'because they supposed that the Kingdom of God was immediately to appear'—is apt to the expanded parable, but not to the original form. This fact tends to confirm the suggestion that Lk. knew the parable only in its present state, in which the coming of the Kingdom in power during the lifetime of Jesus is clearly excluded; and we may suppose that *v.* 11 is Lk.'s own introduction to *vv.* 12–27, which were already before him as a single whole in his source.

'Near to Jerusalem': the distance from Jericho to Jerusalem is about 17 miles. See on Lk. 10^{30}, above, p. 554.

The expectation of the immediate appearance of the Kingdom is a feature also in the Marcan narrative. It underlies the request of the sons of Zebedee (Mk. 10^{35-45}) and the cries of the crowd at the entry into Jerusalem (Mk. $11^{9f.}$). It also appears in Acts $1^{6f.}$. This last passage indicates clearly enough what kind of kingdom was expected to appear. It is the restoration of sovereignty to the Jewish people, or, as the crowds express it in Mk. 11^{10}, the revival of the vanished glories of the 'Kingdom of our father David.' As against all this the expanded parable asserts (1) that the coming of the Kingdom will not take place forthwith, and (2) that when it does come it will not be a political upheaval culminating in the establishment of an Israelite Empire, but a Final Judgement in which loyalty and obedience will be rewarded and disloyalty and disobedience punished.

12, 14. The nobleman, who may originally have been Herod Archelaus, is here Jesus Himself. The departure to a distant country corresponds to the pilgrimage of Archelaus to Rome. Here it stands for the death and exaltation to heaven of Jesus. Note that in 22^{22} Lk. uses the same Greek verb (*poreuomai*—'go away') of the death of Jesus. In Palestinian Aramaic the verb *ăzal* is used in the same way both of going away and of 'departing this life.' Archelaus received his kingdom from Augustus: Jesus receives His from God. (Cf. Phil. $2^{8ff.}$.) 'And to return': the Kingship is conferred in heaven, but it is to be exercised on earth. The refusal of 'his citizens' applies to Archelaus, whose application to Augustus was actively opposed by his own subjects. It also fits the case of Jesus, who is rejected by the 'sons of the Kingdom.' Cf. John 1^{11}, 'He came unto his own, and they that were his own received him not.' The sending of the embassy is exactly paralleled in the case of Archelaus. Fifty deputies from Palestine appeared before Augustus to oppose his claims. How this feature in the story is applied to Christ is not clear. We may perhaps compare John $19^{15f.}$: 'Pilate saith unto them, Shall I crucify your King? The chief priests answered, We have no king but Cæsar,' and the words attributed by Josephus to the Jewish embassy before Augustus (*War*, ii. 90 f.): 'They implored the Romans to take pity on the relics of Judæa and not to fling what remained of it to those who were savagely rending it in pieces, but to unite their country to Syria and to entrust the administration to governors from among themselves (i.e. Roman governors). The Jews would then show that, calumniated though they now were as factious and always at war, they knew how to obey equitable rulers' (Thackeray's translation).

13. Archelaus before setting out for Rome had entrusted his castles and treasuries to his officers (Josephus, *War*, ii. 18 f.). With *v.* 13 the original parable may be taken to begin. The differences between Mt. and Lk. are striking. There are ten servants as against three in Mt. The distribution is equal: each servant receives one mina. In Mt. the amounts vary with the ability of the servants. The amounts entrusted are very much smaller in Lk. than in Mt.: about £4 each as against at least £1,000, £400, and £200.

Although ten servants are appointed (cf. the ten virgins, Mt. 25^{1}), only three of them appear in the account of the audit. On this point Lk. is in agreement with Mt. The number ten is significant in that it is ten and not twelve. The servants are not the Apostles. Further, G. Kittel has shown that in Palestine the number five was used constantly as a round number, much as we say, in a vague way, 'half a dozen.' Ten is then probably an extension of this usage, similar to our 'about a dozen.' Cf. the ten virgins (Mt. 25^{1}), five pairs of oxen (Lk. 14^{19}), ten sayings by which the world was created, ten generations from Adam to Noah and from Noah to Abraham, ten temptations of Abraham, ten miracles performed for Israel in Egypt and ten at the Red Sea, ten plagues of Egypt, ten temptations with which the Israelites tempted God, ten wonders wrought by God in the Temple, ten things created on the eve of the Sabbath (*Aboth* 5^{1-6}, Danby, pp. 455 f.). The number ten will then suggest that the story is of Palestinian tradition. Further, since only three of the servants appear at the reckoning, it may be supposed that the number ten belongs to the additional matter. In this connexion it may also be noted that the Greek verb here translated 'trade' also means 'to engage in State business.' These things may be indications that in *v.* 13 features from the original parable and the additional story have been conflated.

'Ten pounds,' lit. ten minas: the mina = 100 denars = rather less than £4. The whole sum entrusted to the servants is less than £40, not a large sum for a 'nobleman.' In Mt. the master hands over all his property. The smaller sums in Lk. suggest that the trust is really a test to discover which of the servants are fit for larger responsibilities.

15–19. We are not told how the servants employ themselves in the absence of the master (contrast Mt. 25^{16-18}). The narrative goes straight to the return of the nobleman, now confirmed in his rank as king. His first act is to examine the conduct of his servants during his absence. The results of the investigation are different from those in Mt. There the two good servants both succeed in doubling their capital. Here the first servant shows a profit of 1,000 per cent., the second 500 per cent. Only in the case of the third servant is there agreement between Mt. and Lk. The industrious servants are rewarded by being promoted to positions of high rank and responsibility in the kingdom of their master. Here we have doubtless to recognise the influence of the additional matter on the original parable, especially when we observe that in *v.* 24 the mina of the third servant is ordered to be handed over to the first. It is not clear that a matter of £4 can mean very much to one who is now governor of ten cities.

20 f. In the verses describing the reckoning between the third servant and the master Mt. and Lk. come nearest to one another. Yet there are considerable differences in detail. In Mt. the servant buries his talent: here he wraps the money in a 'napkin.' The Greek word here translated 'napkin' is a loan-word from the Latin *sudarium.* It is also naturalised in Aramaic. Besides this passage it occurs three times in the New Testament (John 11[44], 20[7]; Acts 19[12]). The word seems to signify some kind of scarf or neckcloth used in Palestine to protect the head and back of the neck from the heat of the sun. Billerbeck gives one Rabbinical passage from which it would appear that it was a custom to wrap up money in the folds of his garment.

'Thou art an austere man.' For 'austere' Mt. has 'hard.' 'Austere' is not a good rendering of the Greek word, which 'obviously means "strict, exacting," a man who expects to get blood out of a stone' (Moulton and Milligan, *Vocab.*, p. 93*a*).

'Thou takest up where thou layedst not down.' This clause is peculiar to Lk. Perhaps a current proverbial expression for a grasping person (Plummer). Parallels are quoted from Philo and Josephus.

22 f. The unprofitable servant is judged on the terms laid down by himself. On his own showing he is not only lazy, but a fool. If he did not wish to have his own industry exploited, he could have taken steps to show a profit without any expenditure of energy on his part.

24. Those 'that stood by,' i.e. the attendants on the king, his courtiers or his bodyguard. The introductory words are absent from Mt. The description of the first servant as having ten minas is not quite correct. He has eleven: one, his original capital, and ten, his profit.

25. This verse has no parallel in Mt. It is apparently meant to prepare the way for *v.* 26 by expressing surprise at the command of *v.* 24. The first servant has ten—really eleven—minas. What does he want with more? (The fact that the first servant is now governor of ten cities seems to be forgotten.) This objection is then answered in *v.* 26. But there are certain difficulties and awkwardnesses. Who are the speakers in *v.* 25? The most natural interpretation would be that they are the attendants who have just been mentioned. Plummer argued that *v.* 25 represented the remonstrance of the audience. They have been following the story and they object to the turn given to it by Jesus at this point. Why should the servant who already has most receive more? They think that He is spoiling the parable. In that case *v.* 26 is the reply of Jesus to His critics, and not the reply of the master in the parable. This explanation is certainly attractive. But there is a further difficulty. The whole of *v.* 25 is omitted by early and important authorities for the text of Lk.; and it is accordingly rejected as an interpolation by several scholars. In any case *v.* 26 begins very abruptly after *v.* 25, without any indication of who is speaking. We should have expected

some such words as 'But he said' or 'But he replied.' On the other hand, the omission of *v.* 25 by some of our authorities may merely be assimilation to the text of Mt.

26. The parable of the Pounds ends with *v.* 26, which has a close parallel in Mt. 25^{29}, see above, p. 540.

27. This verse belongs to the additional matter, which has been incorporated with the original parable. Unlike the other additional verses, this one has no parallel in the story of Archelaus as told by Josephus, though from what Josephus elsewhere tells us about that gentleman we might safely infer that he was quite capable of the kind of action described in this verse. For this savage treatment of defeated enemies there are numerous parallels in ancient history. The verse is doubtless meant to describe the fate that awaits the Jews who reject the Messiah. We may be horrified by the fierceness of the conclusion; but beneath the grim imagery is an equally grim fact, the fact that the coming of Jesus to the world puts every man to the test, compels every man to a decision. And that decision is no light matter. It is a matter of life and death. That is true of Christ which Wisdom says of herself (Prov. $8^{35 f.}$):

> Whoso findeth me findeth life,
> And shall obtain favour of the Lord.
> But he that sinneth against me wrongeth his own soul:
> All they that hate me love death.

29. *THE OFFENCE OF ENTHUSIASM* (196–197)

LK. 19^{37-40}

19 37 And as he was now drawing nigh, *even*
at the descent of the mount of Olives,
the whole multitude of the disciples
began to rejoice and praise God with a
loud voice for all the [1] mighty works
38 which they had seen: saying, Blessed *is*
the King that cometh in the name of the
Lord: peace in heaven, and glory in the
39 highest. And some of the Pharisees from
the multitude said unto him, [2] Master,
40 rebuke thy disciples. And he answered
and said, I tell you that, if these shall
hold their peace, the stones will cry out.

[1] Gr. *powers*.
[2] Or, *Teacher*.

Lk. 19^{37-44} would seem to be the L account of the entry into Jerusalem. Apart from a few verbal coincidences in *v.* 39, and those chiefly in a quotation from the Old Testament, the passage is quite independent of Mk. To *vv.* 39–40 we have a parallel in Mt. 21^{14-16} (M); see the discussion of this passage, above, pp. 512 f. Lk. differs from Mt. in several important particulars: time and place of the occurrence, the parties involved, and the wording of the reply of Jesus to the protesters. These differences are so great that some scholars maintain that we have in Mt. and Lk. the reports of two separate incidents. But it is more probable that we have two accounts of the same incident, which have come down through separate lines of tradition; and, on the whole, the Lucan version is freer from difficulties and probably more reliable.

37. The Lucan account locates the incident at the descent of the Mt. of Olives, i.e. at the point where the descent begins, the summit of the Hill. From

this point the pilgrims look across the Kidron valley to Jerusalem. 'Those who know the emotional potentialities of Orientals, who were here roused to great enthusiasm at beholding the longed-for holy city and by the consciousness of leading into it a Son of David who was, at the lowest estimation, a Man of God above all others, will not be astonished at the phrases used on that occasion. They suggested wishes the immediate fulfilment of which probably no one expected' (Dalman, *Sacred Sites and Ways*, p. 257).

The multitude of disciples praise God for the mighty works which they had seen. It is objected that there have been no miracles in the story, except that of the healing of Bartimæus, since Jesus healed the ten lepers on the frontiers of Samaria and Galilee (Lk. 17^{11}). This is so; but if we may lay some weight on the word 'disciples,' we may suppose that among them there would be those who knew of or had seen other mighty works at an earlier date. There is some manuscript authority for the alternative reading, 'for all the things which they saw happening'; and perhaps this ought to be preferred, not because it is easier than the other, but because it is more likely that the colourless 'happenings' would be altered to the more impressive 'mighty works' than that 'mighty works' should be reduced to 'happenings.'

38. With this verse cf. Mk. $11^{9f.}$. The Lucan form makes the cries very definitely the plaudits offered to the Messianic King. In so doing it probably makes explicit what is implicit in the Marcan version.

39. Certain Pharisees are shocked by the display. They appeal to Jesus to stop it. It is implied that only He can quiet the enthusiasm of His followers. The complaint is made in respectful terms. They address Jesus as 'Master,' or 'Teacher,' i.e. 'Rabbi'; and that is very respectful address among Pharisees. Why do the Pharisees object to the demonstration? The answer to this question is that in accordance with their principles they could do no other. If Jesus was hailed as king, that seemed to involve at once political rebellion against Rome; and it was a settled principle with the Pharisees that the only thing that justified revolt was interference with their religion. Their attitude to the Empire in practice was the same as that of St. Paul: 'Let every soul be in subjection to the higher powers: for there is no power but of God; and the powers that be are ordained of God. Therefore he that resisteth the power, withstandeth the ordinance of God: and they that withstand shall receive to themselves judgement. For rulers are not a terror to the good work but to the evil.' (Rom. 13^{1-3}, see the whole passage.) This may be paralleled by a saying of R. Hanina, the prefect of the priests, a younger contemporary of Paul: 'Pray for the peace of the ruling power, since but for fear of it men would have swallowed up each other alive' (*Aboth* 3^2, Danby, p. 450). On the whole question of the attitude of the Pharisees to the Roman Empire, see Moore, *Judaism*, ii. 112–118. It may, therefore, be supposed that the Pharisees, who objected on this occasion, believed that such outcry as the followers of Jesus were making was just asking for trouble.

40. In reply Jesus makes use of a proverbial expression. In Habakkuk (2^{11}) in reference to secret crimes it is said: 'The stone shall cry out of the wall, and the beam out of the timber shall answer it.' This is taken up in the Talmud (*Hagigah* 16*a*): 'Perhaps thou wilt say, Who witnesseth against me? The stones of a man's

house and the timbers of his house, these witness against him, as it is said, "For the stone shall cry, etc." (Hab. 2^{11}).' In these cases the inanimate objects cry out against the evil deeds of men. As Jesus employs the saying they proclaim the mighty acts of God. If men were dumb, the very stones would cry out that the Kingdom of God had drawn nigh. By the 'stones' we should probably understand the stones of the Holy City—particularly the Temple—to be meant. That inanimate objects might respond in some way to the great events of history was a common enough belief of the time. Thus at the death of Jesus the veil of the Temple is rent in twain. And Josephus (*War*, vi. 288–300) describes strange happenings in the Temple in the period preceding its destruction. The eastern gate of the inner court opened of its own accord at midnight. Voices were heard at night in the Temple; and so on. The very building seemed to be sensitive in some way to the coming disasters and to give warning of them. So also it might be argued the stones of Jerusalem would be in some way sensitive to the presence of that which is greater than the Temple and cry out, if men were insensitive and dumb.

30. *A LAMENTATION OVER JERUSALEM* (197)

LK. 19^{41-44}

19 41 And when he drew nigh, he saw the
42 city and wept over it, saying, [1] If thou
hadst known in this day, even thou, the
things which belong unto peace! but now
43 they are hid from thine eyes. For the
days shall come upon thee, when thine
enemies shall cast up a [2] bank about
thee, and compass thee round, and keep
44 thee in on every side, and shall dash thee
to the ground, and thy children within
thee; and they shall not leave in thee one
stone upon another; because thou
knewest not the time of thy visitation.

[1] Or, *O that thou hadst known.*
[2] Gr. *palisade.*

The lamentation over Jerusalem comes with tremendous dramatic effect in the midst of the jubilant enthusiasm of the crowd. The passage is a prophetic oracle, which reminds us of similar prophecies in the Old Testament. We may compare the utterance of Jeremiah (Jer. $8^{18\,ff.}$):

Incurable is my sorrow;
My heart within me is sick.
Hark! my people's cry of distress
  From the land far and near:
'Is Yahwe not in Zion?
  Is no King there?
Past is the harvest, ended the fruit-time,
  And we are not saved.'
For the ruin of my people I mourn,
  Horror hath seized me.
Is there no balsam in Gilead?
  No healer there?
Why then does no healing come
  For my people's hurt?

O that my head were waters,
And my eyes a fountain of tears!
That day and night I might weep
O'er my people's slain.
(Skinner's translation, *Prophecy and Religion*, pp. 125 f.)

In both cases we have the prophetic sense of the inevitability of the coming catastrophe and the genuine sorrow of a tender and sympathetic nature over the sufferings that must come upon the prophet's own people. There is a similar saying of Jesus, also peculiar to Lk., in Lk. 23^{28-31}, below, pp. 634 f. Burney (*The Poetry of our Lord*, p. 69) found evidence of poetic form in *vv.* 43–44 of the present passage; and it is possible that the whole saying, *vv.* 42–44, was originally in poetic form. To describe these verses as a Christian composition after the event is the kind of extravagance that brings sober criticism into disrepute.

42. The force of the unfinished sentence is ' If only thou hadst known, even now, at the eleventh hour, the things that would really make for thy peace, then the future would hold something better for thee than it now does. But thou art blind, and so walking blindly to disaster.' In ' the things which belong unto peace ' there is probably a play on the Aramaic word for ' peace ' (*shĕlāmā*) and the popular etymology of the name Jerusalem as meaning ' vision of peace ' or the like. (Cf. Heb. $7^{1f.}$.)

43 f. A prophetic description of the horrors of siege and destruction of the city. Compare Is. 29^{1-4}. The nature of the disasters sketched in these verses may perhaps give a clue to the nature of the failure which is their cause. Verses 43 f. depict the fate of a Jerusalem that has rebelled against Rome, a Jerusalem, that is, in which political ambition has been mistaken for zeal in the cause of God.

The first part of this passage describes the blockade of the city. The operation called ' casting up a bank ' actually took place at the siege of Jerusalem by Titus. From the account of Josephus (*War*, v. 262 ff.) it appears that the ' bank ' was an earthwork surmounted by a wooden palisade. At a later stage in the siege the place of this ' bank ' was taken by a stone wall encircling the city (*War*, v. 491 ff.), and preventing both the escape of the inhabitants and the bringing to them of supplies. When this encirclement is complete and effective the position of the defenders is truly desperate. However strong their own fortifications, however determined their resistance to the assaults of the besiegers, they must eventually succumb to famine. Then they fall an easy prey to the enemy. In *v.* 44 the sack and destruction of the city are described. The Greek verb translated ' dash thee to the ground ' means also—and originally—to ' lay level with the ground ' or ' raze to the ground.' It is probable that this original meaning is the meaning here. The city will be laid level with the ground. But this rendering obviously will not fit the following words, ' and thy children within thee.' This objection is easily met by taking the words in question as a circumstantial clause, a common Semitic idiom, describing the circumstances in which the main action takes place. What the verse says is that the city will be sacked and destroyed with its inhabitants in it. That is, they will not be allowed to evacuate the doomed city before destruction is let loose in it. The ' children ' of the city are, by another common idiom, its inhabitants, regardless of their age. It may be objected to this interpretation that if we translate our Greek verb by 'lay thee even with the ground,' it is tautologous to have to add, 'And shall not leave in thee one stone upon another.' But, as Burney pointed out (*loc. cit.*), if these verses are poetry, it is a case not of tautology but of parallelism; and the supposed tautology is really another argument for the correctness of the rendering.

'They shall not leave in thee one stone upon another': compare Mk. 13^{2} and parallels. In Hag. 2^{15} 'to lay one stone upon another' is used for 'to build.' The opposite phrase must signify 'to demolish.'

'Because thou knewest not the time of thy visitation.' The prime cause of the material disaster is a moral failure; and the moral failure is essentially a failure of religious insight. Inability to recognise the 'time of visitation' is the same thing as inability to 'interpret this time' (Lk. 12^{56} Q, above, p. 413). That is, it is the failure to recognise that 'the Kingdom of God is come nigh unto you' (Lk. $10^{9, 11}$ Q, above, p. 367; Lk. 11^{20}||Mt. 12^{28} Q, above, p. 378). The ministry of Jesus and His disciples is the 'visitation.'

The Greek word translated 'visitation' (*episkopē*) is commonly used to render the Hebrew word *pĕḳuddāh.* This Hebrew word stands chiefly for the visitation of God, in which He will execute judgement upon all that is opposed to His will. Thus in Jer. 6^{15}, after the arraignment of priests and prophets who deal falsely, it is said: 'Therefore they shall fall among them that fall: at the time that I visit them they shall be cast down, saith the Lord.' And in Jer. 10^{15}, of idols, 'They are vanity, a work of delusion: in the time of their visitation they shall perish. Cf. Is. 10^{3}, 24^{22}, 29^{6}. The force of the word comes out clearly in *Ecclus.* 18^{20}:

> Before judgement examine thyself,
> And in the hour of visitation thou shalt find forgiveness.

But the visitation, which is judgement on all unrighteousness, can also be an occasion of grace and mercy to those who are repentant, as this last quotation shows. This sense for 'visitation' appears also in *Wisdom* $3^{7 f.}$:

> 3^{1} But the souls of the righteous are in the hand of God,
> And there shall no torment touch them. . . .
> 7 And in the day of their visitation they shall shine forth,
> And as sparks in the stubble shall run to and fro.
> 8 They shall judge nations and have dominion over peoples;
> And their Lord shall be king for ever.

Similarly in *Wisdom* 4^{15}:

> Grace and mercy are with His (God's) chosen
> And His visitation with His holy ones.

It is this latter sense that is the sense in our passage. The 'visitation' has taken place in the mission of Jesus. The Kingdom of God has drawn near to

Israel in grace and mercy. But Israel is rejecting this proffered mercy and going determinedly on the road that leads to disaster. This is the tragedy over which Jesus weeps.

31. *A DETACHED SAYING* (204)

LK. 20^{18}

20 18 Every one that falleth on that stone shall be broken to pieces; but on whomsoever it shall fall, it will scatter him as dust.

This verse is given by the great majority of MSS. in Mt. 21^{44} as well as here. But it is most probably to be regarded as an interpolation in Mt., an example of the tendency to assimilate the text of the gospels. See above, p. 516. In Lk. it appears in the parable of the Wicked Husbandmen, a passage in which Lk. is following Mk. But the verse does not appear in Mk.; and the simplest explanation is that it is an insertion by Lk. It is not, however, likely that it is an attempt by Lk. to comment on what has gone before. More probably it is detached saying, which he incorporated here in what seemed to him a suitable place.

In Mk., which is here Lk.'s source, the parable is given in 12^{1-9}, ending with the declaration that the owner of the vineyard will come and destroy the wicked husbandmen, and give the vineyard to others. Then Mk. adds the quotation from Ps. $118^{22f.}$:

> The stone which the builders rejected,
> The same was made the head of the corner:
> This was from the Lord
> And it is marvellous in our eyes (Mk. $12^{10f.}$).

Lk. gives the parable substantially as in Mk. (Lk. 20^{9-16}). Then he adds the Psalm quotation; but gives only the first verse of it, 'The stone . . . corner' (20^{17}). Then follows the verse 20^{18}, which has no parallel in Mk. Finally, Lk. rejoins Mk. in describing the effect of all this teaching on the leaders of the Jewish community (Lk. 20^{19}||Mk. 12^{12}).

The verse added by Lk. is plainly an insertion. But it can hardly be comment on the stone which is made head of the corner. That stone is securely fixed in the building and is not likely to fall or be fallen upon. The stone in *v.* 18 is much more like the stone in Dan. $2^{34, 45}$, or that other in Is. $8^{14f.}$. A still closer parallel to our verse is in the Aramaic saying, possibly a proverb, preserved in the Midrash on Esther 3^{6}: 'If the stone falls on the (earthenware) pot, woe to the pot! If the pot falls on the stone, woe to the pot! In either case woe to the pot!'

Whether *v.* 18 is a genuine saying of Jesus, and if it is genuine, what He meant by it—these are questions which cannot now be answered with certainty, since we do not know the original context of the saying. All that can be said with confidence is that it probably came to Lk. as a genuine saying, and that he inserted it here in what seemed to him the most suitable context in his Gospel.

32. *THE APOCALYPTIC DISCOURSE*

This is the second apocalyptic discourse in Lk. The first, derived from Q, has already been discussed. See notes on Lk. 17$^{22\text{-}37}$, above, pp. 433–439. This second speech (Lk. 21$^{5\text{-}36}$) runs parallel to Mk. 13 and Mt. 24, and the relation of Lk. to Mk. presents one of the most complicated and difficult problems in the criticism of the Gospels. The essential issue is whether Lk.'s discourse is a free rewriting of Mk. or an independent account into which Lk. has incorporated a few passages from Mk. In other words, is the substance of Lk. 21$^{5\text{-}36}$ derived from Mk. or L? It may be that a final solution of the problem is not possible; but at least something can be done towards making the issues clear. We begin with an analysis of Lk. 21$^{5\text{-}36}$, dividing the material into three classes:

(*a*) Probably derived from Mk.: *vv.* 5–11*a*, 16–17, 21*a*, 23*a*, 26*b*, 27, 29–33

(*b*) Certainly not derived from Mk.: 11*b*, 18, 25*b*, 26*a*, 28, 34–36.

(*c*) Doubtful cases: *vv.* 12–15, 19, 20, 21*b*, 22, 23*b*, 24, 25*a*.

On the basis of this classification two theories are possible:

(1) The groundwork of the discourse is (*a*) + (*c*); and (*a*) + (*c*) is the Marcan apocalypse revised and in part rewritten by Lk. To this groundwork the Evangelist has added the fragments collected under the heading (*b*).

(2) The groundwork is (*b*) + (*c*), which may be regarded as the L version of the apocalyptic discourse. Into this discourse Lk has incorporated selected passages from Mk., namely those grouped under (*a*).

Both theories have the support of distinguished scholars. Those who uphold theory (1) have to maintain that Mk. has been severely edited and rewritten by Lk. in view of what happened at the siege and destruction of Jerusalem. Against this is the fact that in our study of the documents up to this point we have found little reason to think that Lk. was addicted to the practice of rewriting his sources. Further, there are observations in detail which tell against the hypothesis of Lucan rewriting.

(i) MK. 13^{11}	LK. 21$^{14\text{-}15}$
And when they lead you to judgement, and deliver you up, be not anxious beforehand what ye shall speak: but whatsoever shall be given you in that hour, that speak ye: for it is not ye that speak, but the Holy Ghost.	Settle it therefore in your hearts, not to meditate beforehand how to answer: for I will give you a mouth and wisdom, which all your adversaries shall not be able to withstand or to gainsay.

Cf. Lk. 12$^{11\text{-}12}$ Q (above, p. 402).

The word 'spirit' is a favourite word with Lk. It is not likely that he would have altered it in this case, especially in view of Lk. 12$^{11\text{f.}}$, where he gives the Q form of the saying without alteration.

(ii) The result of the supposed editorial rewriting of Mk. in Lk. 21$^{20\text{-}24}$ is to produce something that looks extremely like poetry (see notes on this passage). It is not usual for editorial revision to turn prose into verse.

The analysis of Lk. 21$^{5\text{-}36}$ must begin with *vv.* 5-7, a passage commonly regarded as derived from Mk. 13$^{1\text{-}4}$.

MK. 13^{1-4}

13 1 And as he went forth out of the temple, one of his disciples saith unto him, [1] Master, behold, what manner of stones
2 and what manner of buildings! And Jesus said unto him, Seest thou these great buildings? there shall not be left here one stone upon another, which shall not be thrown down.
3 And as he sat on the mount of Olives over against the temple, Peter and James and John and Andrew asked him privately,
4 Tell us, when shall these things be? and what *shall be* the sign when these things are all about to be accomplished?

[1] Or, *Teacher*.

LK. 21^{5-7} (Huck § 213)

21 5 And as some spake of the temple, how it was adorned with goodly stones and
6 offerings, he said, As for these things which ye behold, the days will come, in which there shall not be left here one stone upon another, that shall not be thrown down.
7 And they asked him, saying, [1] Master, when therefore shall these things be? and what *shall be* the sign when these things are about to come to pass?

[1] Or, *Teacher*.

There is no doubt that Mk. and Lk. here give the same thing—a prophecy by Jesus of the destruction of the Temple. But there is one striking difference. In Mk. the prophecy is given in reply to a remark by one of His disciples; and the whole of the following apocalyptic address is a private communication to Peter, James, John, and Andrew. In Lk. the persons who comment on the grandeur of the Temple, and so lead up to the prediction of its fall, are undefined. But in *v.* 7 it becomes clear that they are not disciples. For they go on to address Jesus as 'Teacher' (*didaskale*). Now in Lk. the disciples never address Jesus as *didaskale*. They use the more honorific terms 'Lord' (*kurie*) or 'Master' (*epistata*). It is only those outside the circle of the disciples who call Jesus 'Teacher.' (See Burkitt, *Gospel History and its Transmission*, p. 114.) We must therefore suppose that Lk. has altered a conversation between Jesus and His disciples into a public declaration.

But this supposition is more than difficult in view of what immediately follows in Lk. For, whatever we may think of *vv.* 8–11, there cannot be the least doubt that *vv.* 12–19 must have been spoken to disciples and not to the Jewish populace; and this fact must have been as obvious to Lk. as it is to us. On the hypothesis of Lucan editing of Mk. we are thus led to the position that Lk. made a quite pointless alteration in Mk., and one which immediately involved him in making a public speech out of what was obviously a private conversation. This seems unlikely.

Further, the Lucan passages *vv.* 8–11, 12–19 do not seem to deal with the question put in *v.* 7. For the question put concerns the destruction of the Temple and that only. The answer is not given till *vv.* 20–24. It is thus natural to suppose that originally Lk. 21^{5-7} was followed immediately by 21^{20-24}, and that the intervening passages have been inserted, probably at an earlier stage in the tradition than the composition of Lk. Now it is highly probable that Mk. 13 contains an early apocalyptic passage, which has been incorporated bodily into the chapter. It is to be noted that the question in Mk. 13^{4} appears to be a double one: when will the destruction of Jerusalem take place, and what will be the sign of the end of the existing world order? The Marcan form of the question prepares the way for a passage dealing with both topics in a way that the Lucan question does not. The passage thus introduced is the so-called 'Little Apocalypse,' which may be supposed to be represented by Mk. 13^{5-31}. (See my *Teaching of Jesus*, p. 262, n. 1.) If, as is likely, this little apocalypse was in circulation before Mk. was written, it may well have influenced the formation of the L material into its present shape. This would be the more likely if, as Hölscher maintains, the substance of Mk.'s little apocalypse (Mk. $13^{7f., 12, 14-20, 24-27}$) was composed in A.D. 40 under stress of the threatened profanation of the Temple by Caligula.

I am therefore inclined to think that Lk. 21^{5-36} is, in the main, a solid block of L material whose arrangement—and, to a considerable extent, its wording also—has been determined by the pre-Marcan 'little apocalypse.' No explanation is free from difficulties; and I am not confident that this hypothesis is a final solution of the problem. I only put it forward in default of a better.

MK. 13^{5-8}

13 5 And Jesus began to say unto them, Take heed that no man lead you astray.
6 Many shall come in my name, saying, I am *he*; and shall lead many astray.
7 And when ye shall hear of wars and rumours of wars, be not troubled: *these things* must needs come to pass; but the
8 end is not yet. For nation shall rise against nation, and kingdom against kingdom: there shall be earthquakes in divers places; there shall be famines: these things are the beginning of travail.

LK. 21^{8-11} (Huck § 214)

21 8 And he said, Take heed that ye be not led astray: for many shall come in my name, saying, I am *he*; and, The time is
9 at hand: go ye not after them. And when ye shall hear of wars and tumults, be not terrified: for these things must needs come to pass first; but the end is not immediately.
10 Then said he unto them, Nation shall rise against nation, and kingdom
11 against kingdom: and there shall be great earthquakes, and in divers places famines and pestilences; and there shall be terrors and great signs from heaven.

These verses, both in Mk. and Lk., I take to be derived from the 'little apocalypse.' It is difficult to suppose that the events enumerated here are indications that Jerusalem is about to be destroyed. They seem rather to be the premonitory signs of the final consummation. Mk. and Lk. run parallel for the most part. The order of events is: (*a*) appearance of false messiahs; (*b*) wars and disturbances—the break-up of the social order; (*c*) earthquakes, famines, pestilences, etc.—the break-up of the order of nature. According to Mk. these are the birth-pangs of the new age. But these premonitory signs do not lead up to anything immediately; for the next section in both Mk. and Lk. describes persecution of the disciples, and after that comes the account of the distresses in Judæa (Mk.) or the siege and destruction of Jerusalem (Lk.). Now in *v.* 11 Lk. has a sentence which has no parallel in Mk.: 'and there shall be terrors and great signs from heaven.' The natural continuation of this is in Lk. 21^{25}: 'And there shall be signs in sun and moon and stars.' We should therefore naturally suppose that Lk. $21^{8-11, 25-28}$ belong together, and that the whole passage has to do with the final consummation.

8. The Marcan parallel announces the rise of bogus messiahs. Lk. has a small addition. Besides the pretenders who say 'I am he,' there are others who announce that the time is at hand. These may be the false prophets who appear along with false Christs in Mk. 13^{22}. The injunction 'Go ye not after them' has no parallel in Mk. Cf. Lk. 17^{23} (Q), above, p. 434.

9–11. According to Mk. there will be wars and rumours of wars, or perhaps wars (at home) and news of wars (in other lands). Lk. has wars and tumults. The Greek word translated ' tumults ' stands for confusion and anarchy. It is war accompanied by a general break-down of civil order. This might well cause terror; but those who are forewarned will recognise in this upheaval a necessary stage in the passing of the old order. At the same time they will not be unduly elated, for there are still worse convulsions to come. There will be a period of world-wide war in which all nations and kingdoms will be involved. (The Lucan ' Then said he unto them,' which starts a new paragraph, is not an improvement on Mk. It is probably secondary.) This universal strife will be accompanied by convulsions of the natural order, earthquakes, famines, pestilences. The pestilences have no parallel in Mk., and look like an addition in Greek for the sake of the word-play on famines (*līmoi*) and pestilences (*loimoi*). The collocation of the two words is as old as Hesiod. The end of *v.* 11 is peculiar to Lk. Where Mk. has ' these things are the beginnings of travail,' Lk. has instead ' and there shall be terrors and great signs from heaven.' The ' terrors ' are, most likely, strange and unnatural events on earth, prodigies. Such things are described by Josephus (*War*, vi. 288 ff.). He relates, for example, how a cow brought for sacrifice gave birth to a lamb in the middle of the Temple court. By great signs from heaven are meant such things as Josephus mentions (§ 289): ' A star resembling a sword stood over the city, and a comet which continued for a year.' Cf. 4 *Ezra* 5^4 (Box's translation).

> Then shall the sun suddenly shine forth by night
> and the moon by day:
> And blood shall trickle forth from wood,
> and the stone utter its voice:
> The peoples shall be in commotion,
> the outgoings (?) (of the stars) shall change.

The description in Lk. 21^{8-11} seems to be leading up to the final consummation; but the story is interrupted by the introduction of a fresh topic.

(*a*) The Persecution of the Disciples (215)

MK. 13^{9-13}

13 9 But take ye heed to yourselves: for they
shall deliver you up to councils; and in
synagogues shall ye be beaten; and before
governors and kings shall ye stand for
10 my sake, for a testimony unto them. And
the gospel must first be preached unto all
11 the nations. And when they lead you *to*
judgement, and deliver you up, be not
anxious beforehand what ye shall speak:
but whatsoever shall be given you in that
hour, that speak ye: for it is not ye that
12 speak, but the Holy Ghost. And brother
shall deliver up brother to death, and the
father his child; and children shall rise
up against parents, and [1] cause them to

LK. 21^{12-19}

21 12 But before all these things, they shall
lay their hands on you, and shall persecute you, delivering you up to the
synagogues and prisons, [1] bringing you
before kings and governors for my name's
13 sake. It shall turn unto you for a testi-
14 mony. Settle it therefore in your hearts,
not to meditate beforehand how to
15 answer: for I will give you a mouth and
wisdom, which all your adversaries shall
not be able to withstand or to gainsay.
16 But ye shall be delivered up even by
parents, and brethren, and kinsfolk, and
friends; and *some* of you [2] shall they cause
17 to be put to death. And ye shall be

13 be put to death. And ye shall be hated of all men for my name's sake: but he that endureth to the end, the same shall be saved.

[1] Or, *put them to death.*

hated of all men for my name's sake.
18 And not a hair of your head shall perish.
19 In your patience ye shall win your [3] souls.

[1] Gr. you *being brought.*
[2] Or, *shall they put to death.*
[3] Or, *lives.*

The break in the narration is marked in Mk. by the words, 'But take ye heed to yourselves,' and in Lk., still more emphatically, by the words, 'But before all these things.' In what follows Mk. and Lk. are parallel in substance but very far apart in wording. And the differences in language are not easily explained as revision on the part of Lk. Reasons have already been given above (p. 615) for thinking that *v.* 14 of Lk. is not a rewriting of *v.* 11 of Mk. It is unlikely also that *v.* 12 of Lk. is a rewriting by Lk. of *v.* 9 of Mk. The Greek construction in Lk. *v.* 12 is, as Creed justly notes, very awkward: so awkward that it is scarcely credible that Lk., the stylist of the Synoptics, could have produced it out of the clear statement of Mk.

The impression left by a comparison of Mk. and Lk. in this passage is that of two independent versions of the same original; and the question arises whether the original may not be the 'Little Apocalypse' in its pre-Marcan state, and perhaps in Aramaic.

12. Lk. has additional matter at the beginning of the verse: 'they shall lay their hands on you and persecute you': and he omits the notice of the flogging, which appears in the corresponding verse in Mk. There does not seem to be any reason why he should have suppressed the beatings, since he himself records one in Acts 5^{40}.

13–15. The disciples will have to face the hostility both of Jew and Gentile authorities. They will be accused of heresy in the synagogues and of sedition before the civil rulers. (Cf. 2 Cor. $11^{24f.}$, where Paul states that he had received five synagogue floggings and three Roman scourgings with rods.) That which is heresy to orthodox Judaism and sedition to kings and governors is the preaching of Jesus as Lord and Christ (Acts 2^{36}). But all this persecution will provide opportunity for the disciples to bear witness to the truth: and that not merely what they think true, but a truth divinely revealed, whose very wording will be inspired. It is for this reason that the disciples are told not to prepare beforehand the speeches to be made. The speeches will be provided from above; and they will be unanswerable and irresistible. In *vv.* 14 f. the wording of Lk. is almost totally different from Mk.

The Greek word translated 'meditate' in *v.* 14 occurs only here in the Greek Bible. It occurs in Aristophanes of 'preparing' a speech, and again of 'rehearsing' a dance for a subsequent performance. The word evidently signifies more than 'meditation' about the matter of what is to be said. It is careful preparation of the actual words and even gestures.

16, 17. The hostility aroused against the disciples will cut across all human ties. This is the other side of the saying that he who does not 'hate' his relatives cannot be a disciple. It is more than likely that they will hate him. And in the case of some of the disciples this hatred will not be satisfied by anything short of their death. This hatred aroused by the name of Jesus will be universal.

In *vv.* 16 f. Lk. comes very close to Mk. in wording; indeed *v.* 17 agrees word for word with *v.* 13 of Mk. This close agreement in the middle of so much diversity is very striking; and even those who maintain the general independence of Lk. in this chapter admit that *vv.* 16 f. are probably inserted from Mk. There are two facts which seem to support this view. First, the whole passage, up to this point, suggests a successful defence by the disciples. They will be able to speak in such a way that their opponents will be overwhelmed. And this confident tone is as clearly present in *vv.* 18 f. Verses 16 f. seem somewhat foreign to this context. Secondly, the prophecy at the end of *v.* 16: ‘ Some of you they shall put to death ’ is not consistent with *v.* 18: ‘ Not a hair of your head shall perish.’ It is therefore quite possible that *vv.* 16 f. have been inserted from Mk. into their present context by Lk. It may be added that the omission of *vv.* 16 f. leaves a perfectly good connexion between *vv.* 15 and 18.

18. This verse has no parallel in Mk. There is, however, a similar saying in Q (Lk. 12^{7}||Mt. 10^{30}), see above, pp. 399 f. For the form of the expression cf. 1 Sam. 14^{45}; Acts 27^{34}. In both cases it is a way of saying emphatically that this human life will be preserved, not that the ultimate salvation of the persons concerned will be secured. The factual parallel in the Old Testament is such a story as that of the three faithful Jews in Dan. 3. They stand fast in their faith and suffer persecution for it; but even the fiery furnace cannot touch them. ‘ The fire had no power upon their bodies, nor was the hair of their head singed ’ (Dan. 3^{27}).

19. This verse says the same as *v.* 13^{b} in Mk., but in almost entirely different words. Endurance during the period of trial will have its reward. The time of persecution will pass and the day of vindication will come. And the faithful disciples will be there to see it.

If we omit *vv.* 16 f., the general impression made by the whole passage is that the disciples will meet with violent opposition and persecution; but that, by supernatural aid, they will be able to triumph over it and endure to the day of their vindication. They will be God’s representatives against an evil world; and God will look after His own, and bring them through to ultimate victory. The text of the whole discourse might well be the saying (Lk. 12^{32}): ‘ Fear not, little flock; for it is your Father’s good pleasure to give you the kingdom.’

After these digressions we return to the question raised at the beginning of the discourse in *v.* 7: when shall these things be and what will be the sign that they are coming to pass?—‘ these things ’ being the destruction of the Temple.

(*b*) The Fall of Jerusalem (216)

MK. 13^{14-20}

13 14 But when ye see the abomination of
desolation standing where he ought not
(let him that readeth understand), then
let them that are in Judæa flee unto the
15 mountains: and let him that is on the
housetop not go down, nor enter in, to
16 take anything out of his house: and let
him that is in the field not return back to
17 take his cloke. But woe unto them that
are with child and to them that give suck

LK. 21^{20-24}

21 20 But when ye see Jerusalem compassed
with armies, then know that her desola-
21 tion is at hand. Then let them that are
in Judæa flee unto the mountains; and
let them that are in the midst of her
depart out; and let not them that are in
22 the country enter therein. For these are
days of vengeance, that all things which
23 are written may be fulfilled. Woe unto
them that are with child and to them

18 in those days! And pray ye that it be
19 not in the winter. For those days shall
be tribulation, such as there hath not
been the like from the beginning of the
creation which God created until now,
20 and never shall be. And except the
Lord had shortened the days, no flesh
would have been saved: but for the
elect's sake, whom he chose, he shortened
the days.

that give suck in those days! for there
shall be great distress upon the [1] land,
24 and wrath unto this people. And they
shall fall by the edge of the sword, and
shall be led captive into all the nations:
and Jerusalem shall be trodden down
of the Gentiles, until the times of the
Gentiles be fulfilled.

[1] Or, *earth.*

This passage in Lk. raises the question of dependence on Mk. in an acute form. At two points there is word for word agreement with Mk.; in the first clause of *v.* 21, and in the first half of *v.* 23. The rest of the passage has hardly a word in common with Mk. A theory of dependence of Lk. on Mk. requires us to suppose that, with the exception of these two short pieces, Lk. has completely rewritten Mk., taking pains not to use any words already used by Mk. Not only so: we have also to suppose that Lk. has succeeded in throwing his rewriting into poetic form:

But when ye see Jerusalem compassed with armies
  Then know that her desolation is at hand.
Let them that are in the midst of her depart out;
  And let not them that are in the country enter therein.
For these are days of vengeance,
  That all things that are written may be fulfilled.
For there shall be great distress upon the land,
  And wrath unto this people.
And they shall fall by the edge of the sword,
  And shall be led captive into all the nations:
And Jerusalem shall be trodden down of the Gentiles,
  Until the times of the Gentiles be fulfilled.

It is much simpler to suppose that this poetical passage is independent of Mk., and that Lk. has incorporated into it the two short pieces from Mk. The general similarity in thought between Mk. and Lk. could then be explained by the hypothesis that we have in the two gospels two independent versions of the pre-Marcan 'Little Apocalypse.'

20. The difference between Mk. and Lk. is usually explained as due to the fact that Lk. has rewritten Mk. in the light of what happened in A.D. 70. But this is going a little too fast. It is more likely that Mk. 13[14] has been rewritten in the light of what happened in A.D. 40, when the Emperor Caligula decided to have his statue set up in the Temple at Jerusalem. Josephus tells us (*War*, ii. 184 f., Thackeray's translation):

'The insolence with which the emperor Gaius (Caligula) defied fortune surpassed all bounds: he wished to be considered a god and to be hailed as such, he cut off the flower of the nobility of his country, and his impiety extended even to Judæa. In fact, he sent Petronius with an army to Jerusalem to instal in the sanctuary statues of himself; in the event of the Jews refusing to admit them, his orders were to put the recalcitrants to death and to reduce the whole nation to slavery.'

The remarkable phrase used in Mk.—' the abomination of desolation '—is used in the book of Daniel (9^{27}, 11^{31}, 12^{11}) and in 1 *Macc.* (1^{54}, cf. 1^{59}, 6^{7}) to describe a similar profanation of the Temple, the erection therein of an altar (and statue?) to Olympian Zeus in 168 B.C. Any Jewish Christian reading Mk. 13^{14} would naturally interpret the ' abomination of desolation ' as meaning a new profanation of the Temple similar to that which had already occurred. And so, in fact, did early Christian interpreters. Thus Hippolytus says: ' The " abomination of desolation " is the image of the emperor which he set up in Jerusalem.' He also denies that the words refer to the events of A.D. 70. ' This was not fulfilled in the siege of Vespasian. There was in this nothing new; wars and sieges have often taken place.'

Further, the verses which follow in Mk. are very appropriate advice in case of an approaching siege. The best thing the inhabitants can do is to get out of the city before the investment is complete. But it is not specially relevant to a profanation of the Temple. The inhabitants do not mend matters nor improve their own case by fleeing from the city.

In view of these considerations I am inclined to think that the original form of this oracle predicted the destruction of Jerusalem in general terms, and that in Mk. and Lk. we have two independent versions of the prediction. The Marcan version has been modified to meet the crisis of A.D. 40, while the Lucan has escaped this editing, and gives the prediction in something like its original form. If Lk. 21^{20} is the answer to the question in Lk. 21^{7}, it may be thought to be a somewhat unsatisfactory reply. ' When will these things be and what will be the sign that they are about to happen? ' ' When you see Jerusalem surrounded by armies.' This is not very informative; but compare Lk. 17^{37} (Q): ' And they answering say unto him, Where, Lord? And he said unto them, Where the body is, thither will the eagles also be gathered together.'

21. The first clause of the verse is copied word for word from Mk. That it is an addition is clear from what follows. For ' Let them that are in the midst of her depart out; and let not them that are in the country enter therein ' must refer to Jerusalem. The reference to the inhabitants of Judæa thus breaks the sense. Except for this insertion the verse is entirely independent of Mk. It is to be noted that the two clauses peculiar to Lk. are in close parallelism. The motive for flight is obvious. It is the only way to escape the horrors of a siege.

22. And there need be no expectation that there will be a Divine intervention in favour of the city. The besieging armies are the instruments of Divine judgement. Jerusalem is doomed, and her fate is the fulfilment of what is written in Scriptures, of all the prophecies uttered against the rebellious nation. Cf. Hos. 9^{7}; Jer. 5^{29}, $26^{4ff.}$; Dan. 9^{26}.

23. The first half of this verse again agrees word for word with Mk. 13^{17}; and again it can be removed without detriment to the sense. It is to be noted that Lk. does not insert Mk. 13^{18}: ' And pray ye that it be not in the winter.' The omission may be an indication that Lk. is writing after A.D. 70; for, as a matter of fact, the siege took place in the summer (April to September). The latter half of *v.* 23 is again independent of Mk. in wording, though there are similarities of thought in Mk. 13^{19}. The Lucan form is in parallelism. The R.V. text

'land' is to be preferred to the mg. 'earth.' The reference is to the land and people of Israel, not to the earth and its inhabitants in general. The 'wrath' does not occur elsewhere in the teaching of Jesus in the Synoptics. It does, however, appear in the preaching of John the Baptist (Lk. 3^{7}||Mt. 3^{7} Q).

24. The 'wrath' will work itself out in three particulars: the slaughter of part of the population, the carrying away captive of the rest, and the total destruction of the city. For 'treading down' as a figure for desolation and destruction, see Dan. 8^{13}; 1 *Macc.* 3$^{45, 51}$, 4^{60}; Rev. 11^{2}. The period set for this desolation of Jerusalem is 'until the times of the Gentiles be fulfilled.' The meaning of the phrase is uncertain. It may mean merely the period during which the Gentiles are to be permitted to do their worst to Jerusalem (cf. Dan. 8$^{13\,f.}$, 12$^{5-13}$), or it may be the period allowed to the Gentiles in which they may themselves turn to God (cf. Mk. 13^{10}; Rom. 11^{25}). It is, in any case, a limited period; and it is not to be followed by the restoration of Jerusalem. As the text of Lk. now stands the expiration of this period is to be followed by—

(*c*) The Great Consummation (219

MK. 13$^{24-27}$

13 24 But in those days, after that tribulation, the sun shall be darkened, and the
25 moon shall not give her light, and the
stars shall be falling from heaven, and
the powers that are in the heavens shall
26 be shaken. And then shall they see the
Son of man coming in clouds with great
27 power and glory. And then shall he
send forth the angels, and shall gather
together his elect from the four winds,
from the uttermost part of the earth to
the uttermost part of heaven.

LK. 21$^{25-28}$

21 25 And there shall be signs in sun and moon
and stars; and upon the earth distress of
nations, in perplexity for the roaring of
26 the sea and the billows; men [1] fainting
for fear, and for expectation of the things
which are coming on [2] the world: for the
powers of the heavens shall be shaken.
27 And then shall they see the Son of man
coming in a cloud with power and great
28 glory. But when these things begin to
come to pass, look up, and lift up your
heads; because your redemption draweth
nigh.

[1] Or, *expiring*.
[2] Gr. *the inhabited earth*.

There is nothing here in Lk. corresponding to Mk. 13$^{21-23}$. Lk. 21^{25} seems to resume the discourse that was broken off at *v.* 11, which ends with the words, 'and there shall be terrors and great signs from heaven.' This might well be continued by 'in sun and moon and stars.' The words at the beginning of *v.* 25, 'And there shall be signs,' might then be regarded as a necessary addition in order to make a fresh start. The alternative is to regard Lk. 21^{25a} as an abbreviated version of Mk. 13$^{24, 25a}$. There is nothing in Mk. corresponding to *vv.* 25^{b} and 26^{a} of Lk.: 'and upon the earth . . . things which are coming on the world.' Lk. 21$^{26b\ 27}$, 'for the powers . . . great glory' is an insertion from Mk., which makes nonsense of the following verse (28) in Lk. For *v.* 28 is a message of hope. It says in effect: The darkest hour is the hour before the dawn. When the whole world seems to be falling to pieces about you, then you may be sure that a new world is coming to birth. But all this is out of place after *v.* 27. For with the coming of the Son of Man the redemption *has come.* Faith has given place to sight. The removal of the insertion from Mk. removes this difficulty, and gives a perfect sense. The whole world will be in a state of chaos, nations in perplexity, men terrified to death of what may happen next. When you see these things you—and you alone—will be able to hold up your heads, because you know that they are the signs that your vindication is at hand.

25 f. These verses describe tremendous convulsions in the order of nature. The whole natural world is affected. The signs in the heavenly bodies are mentioned by Lk. In Mk. they are more fully described. On the other hand, Lk. describes the upheaval of the sea which is not mentioned at all in Mk. For the imagery, cf. Ps. $65^{7f.}$. Behind the description may lie the Semitic horror of the sea, which comes to its sharpest expression in Rev. 21^{1}: 'And I saw a new heaven and a new earth: for the first heaven and the first earth are passed away; and the sea is no more.' But it is more probable that 'the roaring of the sea and the billows' describes the world reverting to primeval chaos. See the full collection of material in Dodd's *The Bible and the Greeks*, pp. 105 ff. The Greek word translated 'perplexity' has a fairly wide range of meanings. 'Perplexity' is hardly strong enough to describe the condition which is portrayed in this verse. It is more than mere puzzlement: it is the bewildered despair of men who find that there is nothing reliable or safe in the world any more. In *v.* 26 'fainting' is preferable to 'expiring.' The men are terrified to death but not dying of terror. They have no hope but only the expectation that there is still worse to come upon the world. It is the whole inhabited earth that is involved in these calamities, not as in *v.* 23 the land of Israel.

28. In the midst of this helpless terror the disciples will be calm and hopeful. They know the meaning of these disasters. It is the old order breaking up to make way for the new: and the more rapid the process of dissolution, the nearer the coming of their deliverance.

26^{b}, 27. The additional matter inserted from Mk. is a description, in terms borrowed from the book of Daniel 7^{13}, of the final consummation, which is also the 'redemption' of the faithful. The interpretation given in the book of Daniel itself (7^{27}) is that the 'Son of Man' is 'the people of the saints of the Most High.' If we apply the Danielic interpretation to the Danielic figure in its new context, the coming of the 'Son of Man' with power and great glory ought to mean the triumphant vindication of the faithful disciples. But this is not the usual interpretation. The coming of the Son of Man is held to be the return of the risen and glorified Christ at the Second Advent. That is, it is not itself the vindication of the saints but a preliminary thereto. For a discussion of the whole question of the interpretation of the phrase 'Son of Man' in the Synoptic Gospels see my *Teaching of Jesus*, pp. 211–234.

(*d*) THE PARABLE OF THE FIG TREE (220)

MK. 13^{28-29}

13 28 Now from the fig tree learn her parable: when her branch is now become tender, and putteth forth its leaves, ye
29 know that the summer is nigh; even so ye also, when ye see these things coming to pass, know ye that [1] he is nigh, *even* at the doors.

[1] Or, *it*.

LK. 21^{29-31}

21 29 And he spake to them a parable: Behold the fig tree, and all the trees:
30 when they now shoot forth, ye see it and know of your own selves that the summer
31 is now nigh. Even so ye also, when ye see these things coming to pass, know ye that the kingdom of God is nigh.

This parable is given in much the same terms by Mk. and Lk. It is reasonable to suppose that it has been taken over by Lk. from Mk. The parable is an excellent illustration of the piece of teaching just given concerning the end. As the shooting forth of the leaves is an indication of the approach of summer, so the terrible experiences, through which the disciples must pass, will be an indication that the consummated Kingdom of God is at hand.

29 f. Lk. has provided the parable with an introduction. He has also added the words, 'and all the trees.' The fig is not the only tree to advertise the approach of summer, even if it does so before most. The description of the bursting of the tree into leaf is fuller in Mk. Lk. adds the words 'of yourselves' to 'know.' Those who see these things happening do not need anyone to tell them that summer is now near. Their own common sense will tell them. Cf. Lk. 12^{57}, Q.

31. The application. When you see 'these things,' i.e. the calamities described in the previous section—not, however, the events described in *vv.* 26^{b}, 27—know that the Kingdom of God (Lk. supplies the subject of the clause) is near. Lk. omits the words of Mk, 'at the doors.'

In all that has hitherto been said the original question has not been precisely answered. The discourse gives indications from which the disciples may infer that the destruction of Jerusalem is about to take place or that the coming of the Kingdom in power is at hand; but the questioners have not been given any date at which they may be on the look-out for premonitory signs. The next section in Lk. contains two sayings taken from Mk.; and in one of these a terminus is fixed. The other saying is, in its present context, apparently meant as a strong confirmation of the preceding prophecies. Mk. has a third saying, which is not reproduced by Lk. (Mk. 13^{32}).

(*e*) Two Sayings (221)

MK. 13^{30-31}	LK. 21^{32-33}
13 30 Verily I say unto you, This generation shall not pass away, until all these things 31 be accomplished. Heaven and earth shall pass away: but my words shall not pass away.	**21** 32 Verily I say unto you, This generation shall not pass away, till all things be 33 accomplished. Heaven and earth shall pass away: but my words shall not pass away.

32. This saying gives a limit within which the prophecies are to be fulfilled. It is in substantial agreement with another saying (Mk. 9^{1}): 'Verily I say unto you, There be some here of them that stand by, which shall in no wise taste of death, till they see the kingdom of God come with power.' It is quite clear that in the primitive Church this was really believed, and that the accomplishment of all things and the coming of the Kingdom with power were related to the return of the risen and glorified Christ. The position of Mk. 13^{30} and Lk. 21^{32} makes it clear that the reference of 'all these things' or 'all things' is to the whole of the preceding complex of predictions, including persecution of the disciples, the destruction of Jerusalem, and the consummation of the Kingdom. But is this the original sense of the saying? When it is considered that the eschatological discourse is a complex of predictions, one might be tempted to argue that perhaps the saying did not originally apply to all, and to suggest that its reference is, let us say, only to the fall of Jerusalem. So far as Lk. is concerned, this view would be

supported by the fact that the original question in *v.* 7 appears to apply only to the fall of Jerusalem. On the other hand the saying in Mk. 9^{1} refers definitely to the coming of the Kingdom with power. It is, therefore, more likely that in the present case the saying (Mk. 13^{30}||Lk. 21^{32}) is meant to cover all the predictions in the discourse, and in particular that of the final redemption.

This view creates difficulty; for the final consummation did not come in the lifetime of the first generation of disciples. But it is to be noted that, in the nature of the case, it was a difficulty that would be felt more acutely in the first century, when the expectation was a living thing, than in the twentieth. And the Church of the first century survived the disappointment of its expectations. The case of St. Paul is instructive. From first to last he believes in the Parousia as the consummation of all things and the fulfilment of the Christian hope. But as time goes on he seems to become less interested in the question whether he will live to see it. And the reason is plain. In the earliest formulation of his eschatology the essence of the final consummation is given not in the creation of a new and better world but in the fact that we shall be for ever with the Lord (1 Thess. 4^{17}). That and nothing else is the complete fulfilment of the Christian hope. But by the time that Philippians comes to be written Paul is convinced that this same thing can be achieved in another way, by death—' to depart and be with Christ; for it is very far better ' (Phil. 1^{23}). Once this point is reached it ceases to be a matter of great personal moment whether or not the Parousia will occur in the lifetime of Paul or any other believer. If it does so, well and good: if not, that which is its crowning mercy will be found on the other side of the gate of death.

33. Here we have another saying whose connexion with the foregoing would seem to depend on verbal links more than on any continuity of thought. The saying is to be compared with that on the Law (Mt. 5^{18}; Lk. 16^{17}, above, pp. 427, 446). And it is probable that we should take this saying as having to do with the validity of the teaching of Jesus as a whole rather than with the smaller matter of the correctness of the predictions in the apocalyptic discourse. Doubtless the intention of the compiler was to give this word as a guarantee of the prophecies contained in the discourse; but we may doubt whether that is the original sense of the verse. More probably Jesus is claiming for His teaching as a whole an eternal validity. It is valid not only in the present age, but also for the age to come. The greatness of the claim is realised when we consider that it was a debated question among the Rabbis whether the sacred Law would continue in full force in the world to come. The saying in effect puts the teaching of Jesus on a higher level of authority than the Law. We have here the most striking example of that ' authority ' in Jesus which so amazed His hearers, an authority which rests on His assurance of knowing the Father and the Father's will.

(*f*) Closing Admonitions (223)

LK. 21^{34-36}

21 34 But take heed to yourselves, lest haply
your hearts be overcharged with surfeiting, and drunkenness, and cares of this
life, and that day come on you suddenly
35 as a snare: for *so* shall it come upon all
them that dwell on the face of all the
36 earth. But watch ye at every season,
making supplication, that ye may prevail
to escape all these things that shall come
to pass, and to stand before the Son of man.

This final exhortation is independent of Mk.; and, if we are right in regarding *vv.* 29–33 as inserted from Mk., it ought to be the continuation of *v.* 28. It may be noted that in that case we have a better connexion than the existing one. For *v.* 28 is a message of hope and encouragement. In the midst of disaster and despair the disciples are to be full of confidence. But this confidence is not to degenerate into carelessness. The elect dare not presume on their election. The worldly may say: ' Let us eat and drink, for tomorrow we die '; but woe to the disciples if they say: ' Let us eat and drink, for tomorrow comes the redemption.'

There are important parallels to this passage in 1 Thess. 5^{1-11} (cf. Rom. 13^{13}):

5 1 But concerning the times and the
seasons, brethren, ye have no need that
2 aught be written unto you. For yourselves
know perfectly that the day of the Lord so
3 cometh as a thief in the night. When
they are saying, Peace and safety, then
sudden destruction cometh upon them, as
travail upon a woman with child; and
4 they shall in no wise escape. But ye,
brethren, are not in darkness, that that
5 day should overtake you [1] as a thief: for
ye are all sons of light, and sons of the day:
6 we are not of the night, nor of darkness; so
then let us not sleep, as do the rest, but let
7 us watch and be sober. For they that
sleep sleep in the night; and they that be
8 drunken are drunken in the night. But
let us, since we are of the day, be sober,
putting on the breastplate of faith and
love; and for a helmet, the hope of salva-
9 tion. For God appointed us not unto
wrath, but unto the obtaining of salvation
10 through our Lord Jesus Christ, who died
for us, that, whether we [2] wake or sleep,
we should live together with him. Where-
11 fore [3] exhort one another, and build each
other up, even as also ye do.

vv. 1–3. Cf. Lk. $21^{34f.}$

v. 7. Cf. Lk. 21^{34a}.

vv. 8–10. Cf. Lk. 21^{36}.

[1] Some ancient authorities read *as thieves*.
[2] Or, *watch*.
[3] Or, *comfort*.

34. ' Lest haply your hearts be overcharged.' ' Heart ' is here, as in the Old Testament, the inner man, the soul as the seat of thought, will, and feeling. The soul becomes dull, heavy, insensitive, stupefied by self-indulgence and worldly cares. The Greek word rendered ' surfeiting ' (*kraipalē*) is most commonly used to describe the condition following on a drunken bout. It is ' the morning after the night before.' ' Drunkenness ' (*methē*) is ' the night before.' ' The cares of this life ' are, one may suppose, the ancient equivalent of ' a hard day at the office.' And between the ' hard day at the office ' and the ' lively evening at the night-club ' and the ' morning after,' the soul has little chance to be anything but dull and stupid, insensitive to great issues, and unprepared for crisis.

35. The crisis, when it comes, will be sudden, as sudden as the springing of a trap. For the figure cf. Is. $24^{17f.}$. And it will come upon all the inhabitants of the world without exception. The mere name of ' disciple ' will confer no immunity. Cf. Rom. 14^{10}; 2 Cor. 5^{10}.

36. It is therefore all the more necessary that disciples should be spiritually alert, fortifying themselves against the coming trials by prayer, or, in Paul's words, 'putting on the breastplate of faith and love; and for a helmet, the hope of salvation.' Only so will they be able to pass safely through the impending troubles and to face the judgement with confidence. To stand before the Son of Man could be the same as to 'stand in the judgement' (Ps. 1^5), i.e. to secure a favourable verdict in the judgement. Otherwise it may mean to stand in the presence of the Son of Man as acknowledged disciples and servants. Cf. Lk. 12^8.

In considering the discourse as a whole there are two important facts to be borne in mind. The first is that it presents a very different picture of the last days from that given in Q. In the Q statement (Lk. 17^{22-30}, above, pp. 433–436), the end of the existing order is a bolt from the blue. Here it is the climax of a long series of catastrophes. The second fact is that the discourse here is obviously a complex of predictions dealing with the fate of Jerusalem, the persecution of the disciples, and the termination of the whole existing world-order. These different prophecies have been woven into a single discourse. The natural conclusion to be drawn from these facts is that the simple straightforward account in Q is the original, and that the discourse in Mk. 13 and Lk. 21 is a later compilation.

What is the purpose of this compilation? One motive appears fairly clearly, and more clearly in Mk. than in Lk. 'The end is not yet' (13^7); 'these things are the *beginning* of travail' (13^8); the Gospel must first be preached unto all the nations' (13^{10}); 'he that endureth *to the end*, the same shall be saved' (13^{13}); 'in those days, *after* that tribulation' (13^{24}). There are also traces in Lk.: 'the end is not immediately' (21^9); 'Jerusalem shall be trodden down . . . until the times of the Gentiles be fulfilled' (21^{24}). The effect of all these little touches is to postpone the final consummation; and this is the effect also of the arrangement of the discourse. Persecutions, wars, the destruction of Jerusalem, natural catastrophes —these things are not so much stages leading up to the consummation as means of postponing it. The burden of the discourse is: 'Be ready for the coming of the Kingdom at any time; but don't expect it yet.'

Now we know that in the middle of the first century, some twenty years after the Crucifixion, the Church of Thessalonica was troubled about this question of the Parousia; and in 2 Thess. 2^{1-12} an explanation is offered why the great redemption must be delayed. The 'man of sin' must first be revealed, who will sit 'in the temple of God, setting himself forth as God' (cf. Mk. 13^{14}). The genuine Parousia must be preceded by a Satanic Parousia, the last great fling of the forces of evil. The end is not yet.

It is likely that if such questions arose in the young community at Thessalonica, they could still more easily arise in the Palestinian churches, where Christians had been awaiting the Parousia for a matter of twenty years. It is indeed possible that such questions arose in Palestine before they arose in the Gentile churches. If they were not raised within the community, they would almost certainly be raised by opponents outside. It is at least possible that what we call the 'Little Apocalypse' was put together in order to furnish an answer to these questionings. It is not necessary to suppose that the whole thing is an invention. Jesus undoubtedly taught that His disciples must undergo persecution. It is reasonably certain that

He prophesied the downfall of Jerusalem and the Temple. And He had something to say about the final consummation. That which is new in the apocalyptic discourse is not the matter, but the way in which it is put together, the way in which persecutions of disciples and tribulations in Judæa are used to push the final consummation into the future.

The discussion of Mk. 13^{14-20} and Lk. 21^{20-24} suggests that the form of the 'Little Apocalypse' incorporated in Mk. was already in existence about A.D. 40; and the general conclusion to which our consideration of the whole discourse leads is that Mk. and Lk. offer two versions of this Palestinian document.

33. *RANK IN THE KINGDOM OF GOD* (237b)

LK. 22^{24-30}

22 24 And there arose also a contention among them, which of them is accounted
25 to be [1] greatest. And he said unto them, The kings of the Gentiles have lordship over them; and they that have authority
26 over them are called Benefactors. But ye *shall* not *be* so: but he that is the greater among you, let him become as the younger; and he that is chief, as he
27 that doth serve. For whether is greater, he that [2] sitteth at meat, or he that serveth? is not he that [2] sitteth at meat? but I am in the midst of you as he that
28 serveth. But ye are they which have continued with me in my temptations;
29 and [3] I appoint unto you a kingdom, even
30 as my Father appointed unto me, that ye may eat and drink at my table in my kingdom; and ye shall sit on thrones judging the twelve tribes of Israel.

[1] Gr. *greater.*
[2] Gr. *reclineth.*
[3] Or, *I appoint unto you, even as my Father appointed unto me a kingdom, that ye may eat and drink, &c.*

This passage falls into three parts: (*a*) the dispute among the disciples and the comment of Jesus (*vv.* 24–26); (*b*) a further saying in parabolic form (*v.* 27); (*c*) a promise to the Twelve (*vv.* 28–30). To (*a*) there is a parallel in Mk. 10^{42-45}. The sons of Zebedee have tried to steal a march on the other disciples and secure for themselves the chief places in the coming Kingdom. The ten are naturally incensed at this; and Jesus rebukes the whole company in terms very similar to *vv.* 25–26 in this passage. Lk. in chapter 18, where he is following Mk., omits the story about the sons of Zebedee, although he has the incidents immediately preceding and following it. This suggests that Lk. already has another version of the dispute and the saying of Jesus, probably already connected with the Passion story, and that he drops the Marcan account in favour of his own, namely that which he gives here. Another incident which has some points of contact with the present passage is Mk. 9^{33-37}. To this there is a parallel in Lk. 9^{46-48}. There is no parallel to (*b*) in the Synoptics; but it is significant that in John 13 we have the story of how Jesus, at the Last Supper, did in fact perform the duty of a servant for the disciples, and afterwards set His act before them as an example to be followed. The third part (*c*) has a parallel in Mt. 19^{28} (M), see above, pp. 508 f. We should probably regard the whole passage *vv.* 24–30 as independent of Mk. and derived from Lk.'s special source.

The Lucan account differs from the Marcan in making the narrative framework of the sayings quite vague and general. In Mk. the dispute takes place on the road to Jerusalem; and the story as told by Mk. could hardly be fitted into the account of the Last Supper without violence. The Lucan framework is so vague that the incident could be fitted in almost anywhere. Why does Lk. put it here? It may be conjectured that the determining factor is the material which follows in (*b*) and (*c*). If there was a tradition that Jesus had washed the disciples' feet at the Last Supper, *v.* 28 would be very appropriate in its present context. And, in any case, the promise of places at the Messianic feast would be appropriate in an account of the Last Supper. In that case we might suppose that (*b*) and (*c*) are the elements which have determined the placing of the passage; and from that it would follow that the whole passage was already in existence as a single unit when Lk. put it into its present place in his narrative. There is great dramatic, even tragic, power in the way in which the dispute is brought into the story of the last meal of Jesus and the disciples. Nevertheless the narrative setting of Mk. seems inherently more probable.

24. For the introductory formula compare Lk. 9^{46}: 'And there arose a reasoning among them, which of them should be greatest.' This is Lk.'s abbreviated version of Mk. $9^{33\,f.}$. It is possible that Lk.'s introduction here is a similar condensation of a narrative that was originally more detailed. It was natural that there should be such disputes. The Gospel narratives make it plain that the Twelve were not equal in seniority. Some would seem to be of longer standing as disciples than others. And there certainly was an inner circle within the group: Peter, James, and John, with Andrew sometimes added. The fact that Jesus took this inner circle most fully into His confidence may well have given them a sense of their own importance. And it is to be noted that it is two of the inner circle who try to overreach the rest in the story told in Mk. 10.

25 f. The reply of Jesus is similar to that in Mk. $10^{42\,ff.}$. The way of the world is contrasted with the way of the Kingdom. In the heathen world ambition and pushfulness are natural, and he who is most domineering is treated with the greatest respect. Kings make themselves masters over their people, not merely in the sense that they keep order and good government in their territories, but also and primarily in the sense that the king is master and the rest of the people his servants. Those who show the greatest ability in bending the wills of others to serve their own purposes assume or are given the title of 'Benefactors.' The Greek word *Euergetēs* (Benefactor) was, in fact, assumed as a title by Ptolemy III of Egypt and by the Seleucid king Antiochus VII (Bevan, *The House of Seleucus*, ii. 237). The title was also occasionally conferred by the cities of the ancient world on outstanding men. The practice is somewhat similar to that of conferring the honorary freedom of a city in modern times. It was not necessary that the recipient of the honour should actually have bestowed any benefit on the city in question, so long as he was sufficiently great and powerful.

The way of the disciples is to be the opposite of this. The Lucan form of the saying is slightly different from that in Mk. Mk.'s version suggests that the way to greatness is the way of service. The only kind of primacy attainable in the community is that which comes of being most perfectly the servant of others. Lk.'s statement, on the other hand, seems to imply that there are in fact differences of rank. Some are by nature leaders. But they are not to give themselves airs on that account. Leadership is a form of service, not a kind of privilege.

27. A parable peculiar to Lk. It makes the same contrast as the previous

verses. The way of the world is to make a sharp distinction between those who wait and those who are waited upon. The logical issue of this is that he is greatest who sits while all others stand in attendance upon him. That is the way of the world. What is the way of the community of the followers of Jesus? There is no question who is chief in this circle. Jesus Himself is the acknowledged leader and head of the group. But He does not sit to be waited on. He stands among His followers as the servant of all. It is evident that such a saying as this would come with tremendous force, if it followed upon the washing of the disciples' feet (John 13).

28 ff. The concluding saying of the group has a parallel in Mt. 19^{28} (above, pp. 508 f.). The similarities in wording between the two forms are confined to the concluding words about sitting on thrones judging the twelve tribes of Israel. It should be noted that Mt. has ' twelve thrones,' whereas Lk. has only ' thrones.' Now there is a serious difficulty about the saying as Lk. gives it here. Is it conceivable that Jesus should have made this prediction concerning the Twelve at this point, when He knew that one of them was on the point of betraying Him? The fact that Lk. has omitted the ' twelve ' before ' thrones ' may be an indication that he was not unaware of this difficulty.

The saying is clearly a farewell-saying. It looks back over the period of the Ministry to praise the faithfulness of the Twelve in difficult and trying times. They have shared the trials of Jesus: they shall also share His future glory. Cf. Rom. 8^{17}. The construction of *v.* 29 is awkward, but the general sense seems to be clear enough. God has assigned the Kingdom to Jesus; and He assigns a share in it to His disciples. This share includes both the joy of the Kingdom—represented under the figure of feasting at the table of the Messiah—and its privileges and responsibilities—represented by the sitting upon thrones and judging. For a parallel to this way of thinking of the duties and rewards of the disciples compare Lk.'s parable of the Pounds (19^{11-27}, above, pp. 604–609).

34. *EXHORTATION TO PETER* (237c)

LK. 22^{31-33}

22 31 Simon, Simon, behold, Satan [1] asked
to have you, that he might sift you as
32 wheat: but I made supplication for thee,
that thy faith fail not: and do thou,
when once thou hast turned again,
33 stablish thy brethren. And he said unto
him, Lord, with thee I am ready to go
34 both to prison and to death. And he
said, I tell thee, Peter, the cock shall not
crow this day, until thou shalt thrice
deny that thou knowest me.

[1] Or, *obtained you by asking.*

The complete paragraph in Lk., as it now stands, contains *vv.* 31–34. But *v.* 34 is most probably derived from Mk., as are also the verses (59^{b}–62) which relate the fulfilment of the prediction in *v.* 34. It does not seem that the special source of Lk. contained the story of Peter's denial. Note that in *v.* 31 the apostle is addressed as Simon, whereas in *v.* 34 he is called Peter. Verses 31–33 are a self-contained unit, without *v.* 34; and the purport of them is not to foretell Peter's denial. What they do say is that all the disciples will be tried to the uttermost and that all will fail under the test; but that Peter will be the first to recover and restore the brethren. That Peter was, in fact, the first to see the

Risen Lord is attested by Paul (1 Cor. 15^{5}), and it is implied in Lk. 24^{34}: 'The Lord is risen indeed, and hath appeared to Simon'—note that the name Simon is used here. Elsewhere the first appearance is to Mary Magdalene either alone or along with another of the women followers of Jesus. The question then arises whether the saying is not a prophecy after the event, which puts into the mouth of Jesus a prediction of what actually happened. Against such a view is the fact that Peter was not the only person to have the vision of the Risen Christ. The Easter faith did not depend on his testimony alone. Further, it seems only natural that Jesus, knowing that His life on earth was nearing its end, and that the end would be of a kind that would be likely to shatter the faith of His followers, should look among them for one who would be most likely to come through the experience. And of the Twelve Peter seemed to Him the one of whom most could be expected.

31. The double vocative is characteristic of Lk. (Cf. 10^{41}, 13^{34}—proper names—and 8^{24}; also 7^{14}, where the true text repeats the vocative, 'Young man.') It is also a common Jewish usage. The picture of Satan desiring to put the disciples to the test is reminiscent of the Prologue to the book of Job. The similarity was noticed by Tertullian (*De Fuga* ii.). Both in Job and in Zech. $3^{1ff.}$ Satan appears as the accuser, whose purpose it is to bring the faults and weaknesses of men to the light of day. From that it is an easy step to incite men to sin in order to have something to expose. This idea appears in the *Testaments of the XII Patriarchs* (Benjamin 3^{3}): 'Fear ye the Lord, and love your neighbour; and even though the spirits of Beliar (= Satan) claim you to afflict you with every evil, yet shall they not have dominion over you.' The Greek word here rendered 'claim' is the same as that translated 'asked to have' in R.V. The sifting doubtless stands for severe trial of the faith and constancy of the disciples. And it is to be applied to all of them. Primarily it is the shameful death of their Master that is thought of; but the danger of hatred and persecution directed against the followers is also a reality.

32. While Satan appears as the adversary, Jesus is the advocate for His followers. His intercession is above all for Peter. If Peter can come through this trial, he will be the rallying-point for the rest. It is not expected that Peter will come through unscathed. His faith will be shaken; but Jesus believes that, in answer to His prayers, it will not completely fail. Peter may desert with the rest; but he will return; and when he returns he will strengthen the others.

33. But Peter has more confidence in himself. There is no need to speak of his turning back, for he will not fall away. He is ready to face imprisonment or death with Jesus.

If the analysis of the passage given above is correct, there is no reply to this bold claim. And there need not be. The event will show whether or not it can be fulfilled.

35. *THEN AND NOW* (237d)

LK. 22^{35-38}

22 35 And he said unto them, When I sent you forth without purse, and wallet, and shoes, lacked ye anything? And they
36 said, Nothing. And he said unto them, But now, he that hath a purse, let him take it, and likewise a wallet: [1] and he

that hath none, let him sell his cloke, and
37 buy a sword. For I say unto you, that
this which is written must be fulfilled in
me, And he was reckoned with transgressors: for that which concerneth me hath
38 [2] fulfilment. And they said, Lord, behold, here are two swords. And he said unto them, It is enough.

[1] Or, *and he that hath no sword, let him sell his cloke, and buy one.*
[2] Gr. *end.*

This short dialogue throws a brilliant light on the tragedy of the Ministry. It goes with the Q lamentation over Jerusalem (Lk. $13^{34\text{f.}}$||Mt. $23^{37\text{-}39}$); and, like that elegy, it is full of bitter disillusionment. The grim irony of *v.* 36 is the utterance of a broken heart. Jesus looks back on the earlier days when He sent the disciples out on the Mission journey. Then they could rely on the goodwill of the people. Now they cannot. Then they could expect hospitality and a friendly welcome. Now nobody will give them a crust or a copper, and he who kills them will think he does God a service. The 'friend of publicans and sinners' will be 'reckoned with transgressors,' and His life will end in defeat and ignominy. Jesus Himself has already accepted this necessity and found its meaning in the prophecies concerning the Servant of Jehovah. With His faith in God and conviction that His whole career has been ordered in accordance with God's will, there is only one way left of making sense of it all; and that is that the suffering and death of God's Servant will accomplish what His life of devoted service has failed to accomplish; that those who could not recognise the Anointed of God as He went about doing good will recognise Him on the Cross.

The disciples cannot see this. They are aware of the growing hostility of the people; but the irony of the saying about buying a sword is lost upon them. They see in it a token that the Master is at last going to rouse Himself to action. If He is for fighting, they are with Him. And they have two swords. They are ready to die like men. They are not ready to be led 'as a lamb that is led to the slaughter.'

They and He are at cross purposes; and Jesus breaks off the conversation. He must die alone.

35. The verse refers back to the Mission of the disciples (Lk. 10), and the list of things not carried by the disciples on that occasion tallies exactly with that given in 10^4 (see above, p. 366). Those were happy days. The missioners had returned with joy (10^{17}). Their work had been successful and the people had been friendly to them. They took no provision with them, yet they lacked nothing.

36. The comment of Jesus on all that is that it is no longer possible. If such a mission were undertaken now, the missioners would have to carry provisions and money, and a sword would be more useful than a cloak. The translation given in R.V. mg. is preferable to that in the text. It is exceedingly unlikely either that this verse is meant to prepare the way for the story of the armed resistance at the arrest of Jesus ($22^{49\text{f.}}$), or that Jesus is thinking of a situation in which He will perish but the disciples will succeed in cutting their way out. The verse has nothing to say directly on the question whether armed resistance to injustice and evil is ever justifiable. It is simply a vivid pictorial way of describing the complete change which has come about in the temper and attitude of the Jewish people since the days of the disciples' Mission. The disciples understood the saying literally and so missed the point; but that is no reason why we should follow their example.

37. In any case armed resistance would be of no use to Jesus; for His fate is already determined. He finds the true meaning of His own career in the poem of the Suffering Servant of Jehovah (Is. 53); and if that prophecy is to be the interpretation of His life, He must be 'reckoned with transgressors' (Is. 53^{12}). If, as is likely, the quotation is allusive, we ought to take into account the whole verse of Isaiah, especially: 'He poured out his soul unto death, and was numbered with the transgressors: yet he bare the sin of many, and made intercession for the transgressors.' This verse of Lk. is 'the sole unambiguous Synoptic reference to the Isaianic Servant passages; a most significant fact, considering the importance of these passages to the earliest Christian apologetic' (Easton).

The last clause of the verse is difficult. The Greek phrase translated 'that which concerneth me' (or, taking the variant reading, 'those things concerning me') is most easily understood, on the analogy of similar phrases in Lk. $24^{19, 27}$; Acts 1^{3}; Phil. 1^{27}, as meaning 'my story,' i.e. my career, my life. The marginal 'hath end' is better than 'hath fulfilment.' The whole clause thus seems to mean: 'For in truth my life is at an end.' That is, events are moving inevitably in one direction for Jesus. There can only be one end to His Ministry; and that is the end foreshadowed in the fifty-third chapter of Isaiah.

38. But the disciples are not prepared to accept defeat of this sort. There has been talk of swords, and that they can understand. It is not too late; and a decisive stroke might yet turn the tables in favour of the Master. They have devotion to Him. They are ready to hazard their lives in His defence. They hate the thought that He should be brought to shame and death (cf. Mk. $8^{32 f.}$ || Mt. $16^{22 f.}$). Jesus does not rebuke them. Nor does He try to explain further. He breaks off the conversation. The words 'It is enough' can scarcely refer to the swords. Two swords would not be enough. More probably we have here a Semitic idiom analogous to our 'That will do' to put a stop to a conversation. There is such an idiom in Biblical Hebrew, e.g. Dt. 3^{26}; and Rabbinical Hebrew has a similar idiom (Gen. R., ed. Theodor, p. 200 ll. 6 ff.). The effect of 'It is enough' is thus to put the closure on any further talk about armed resistance. Jesus must fulfil the rôle of the Servant. He has done it throughout the Ministry —it is significant that we naturally call it the Ministry—and He will play the part through to its tragic end. To fight against it is not just attempting to defy destiny. It is rejecting what for Jesus is the revealed will of God. With that the die is cast. Only God can now save Him from the Cross. In the light of this it is possible to understand a little better the prayer in Gethsemane (Mk. 14^{36}), and perhaps also the cry of dereliction (Mk. 15^{34}).

36. *THE FATE OF JERUSALEM* (248)

LK. 23^{27-31}

23 27 And there followed him a great multitude of the people, and of women who
28 bewailed and lamented him. But Jesus
turning unto them said, Daughters of
Jerusalem, weep not for me, but weep for
29 yourselves, and for your children. For
behold, the days are coming, in which
they shall say, Blessed are the barren, and
the wombs that never bare, and the
30 breasts that never gave suck. Then shall
they begin to say to the mountains, Fall
31 on us; and to the hills, Cover us. For
if they do these things in the green tree,
what shall be done in the dry?

27. This incident is placed by Lk. in the account of the procession from the court to the place of crucifixion. The usual crowd, drawn by curiosity, is in attendance. Among them are women, who moved to sympathy for the victim raise a lamentation over him, beating their breasts and wailing. Dalman (*Jesus—Jeshua*, p. 193) quotes a Rabbinical passage in illustration (*Sifre Dt.* § 308): 'When a man goes out to be crucified, his father weeps for him; his mother weeps for him and beats (her breast) for him; and the one says "Woe is me"; and the other says "Woe is me." But the real woe is to him who goes out to be crucified.' The Greek word translated 'bewailed' in R.V. is properly to beat oneself in token of grief.

28. The women lament the fate of Jesus. They raise the death-wail over Him in anticipation. He in His turn raises, as it were, the death-wail over Jerusalem in anticipation. The Holy City is doomed, and those who weep for Jesus might well weep for themselves if they knew what the future held in store for them. The address 'Daughters of Jerusalem' occurs in the Old Testament (Song of Songs 1^{5}; cf. Is. 3^{16}, 'Daughters of Zion'). 'Weep not for me' is not a prohibition except in grammatical form. The effect of the whole sentence is: If you only knew, you have better cause to weep for yourselves and your children than for me. For the form of the saying cf. Lk. 10^{20}.

29, 30. Verse 29 gives the reason why the women should weep for themselves rather than for Jesus. The phrase 'Behold, the days are coming' is a common introductory formula of prophetic oracles in the Old Testament. The future is such that what among Jewish women was a reproach and humiliation will be looked upon as a blessing. The childless woman will suffer; but she will not have the added torture of seeing her children suffer too. What the sufferings will be is not stated. But they will be so terrible that people will pray for some convulsion of nature to overwhelm them and put them out of their misery. The words are borrowed from the Old Testament (Hos. 10^{8}).

31. This verse is not a continuation of *v.* 30. It is most probably a proverbial saying with which Jesus ends what He has to say. Its purport appears to be: If crucifixion is the fate of one who has obeyed the will of God in all things, what will be the fate of those who flout the will of God at all points? We may compare the story related of Jose ben Joezer (2nd cent. B.C.). The Rabbi was being taken out to be crucified, and his nephew rode on horseback beside him mocking him. The nephew said to him: 'See my horse on which my master (the King) mounts me; and see your horse (the Cross) on which your master (God) mounts you!' The Rabbi replied: 'If such things (as you enjoy) come to those who offend Him (God), how much more will come to those who do His will.' The nephew said: 'And has any man done His will more than you?' (and yet you are crucified). He replied: 'If such things (as crucifixion) happen to those who do His will, how much more (and worse will happen) to those who offend Him.' A similar thought is expressed in 1 Pet. $4^{17f.}$: 'For the time is come for judgement to begin at the house of God: and if it begin first at us, what shall be the end of them that obey not the gospel of God? And if the righteous is scarcely saved, where shall the ungodly and sinner appear?'

EPILOGUE

It is scarcely possible to sum up the teaching in a few sentences; and any attempt to do so would inevitably produce a one-sided and distorted picture. For the teaching is not the Gospel, and Jesus is more than an inspired teacher of religion and morals. He was not called Saviour, Lord, and Christ by the early Church for being a great teacher or even an inspired prophet. The teaching is indissolubly bound up with the life and ministry of Jesus; and, as we have seen again and again, much of the teaching is only intelligible in its connexion with the ministry. The life and work of Jesus, His teaching, the mission of the disciples, the Cross and Resurrection, are all of a piece. For Jesus the teaching is an essential part of His life-work; but it is not the whole. The whole is the manifestation of the Kingdom of God as a present reality. Origen was right when he called Jesus *autobasileia*—the Kingdom itself.

This gives the fundamental explanation of our Lord's attitude to the Jewish Law, whether written or oral. He is not trying to effect a reformation of the theory and practice of Pharisaic Judaism, much less indulging in carping criticism of established institutions. He represents the Kingdom of God; and what He claims is that where the requirements of the Kingdom clash with the requirements of the Law, the former take precedence. That and nothing more; but it is an epoch-making claim.

It explains the paradoxes of the teaching and the life of Jesus.

His hearers were amazed by the authority with which He spoke. He dominated the crowds, and He was, without ever striving for mastery, easily the Master of His band of disciples. Yet He constantly insisted that He was the servant of all, and as constantly demonstrated the genuineness of that strange claim. The secret of His mastery and His service alike is that He was first and supremely the Servant of Jehovah. He sought first the Kingdom of God; and other things were added to Him.

The religious authorities were horrified by the freedom with which He criticised doctrines and practices hallowed by centuries of pious observance. Yet He was wont to go to the Synagogue on the Sabbath; and He enjoined the healed leper to do what Moses commanded in the matter of his healing. The explanation of this seeming inconsistency lies in the fact that the claims of the Kingdom of God take precedence of the requirements of the Law. But only the claims of the Kingdom: not private taste or fancy or convenience.

Respectable people were scandalised by the freedom and familiarity of His intercourse with the disreputable. He was nicknamed 'Friend of publicans and sinners.' Yet the quality of the friendship was determined by Him, not by the publicans and sinners. The friendship is a manifestation of the Kingdom of God: and one element in the conception of the Kingdom is that there is more joy in heaven over one sinner that repents than over ninety-nine righteous persons who do not need to repent. Not that God takes no pleasure in the righteous; but that the repentance of the sinner is the triumph of the Kingdom.

The rank and file of the Jewish nation were estranged in the end by His lack of patriotism. Yet He wept over the impending fate of Jerusalem; and He was executed as a political agitator along with two rebels against Rome. Again the explanation is in terms of the Kingdom of God, whose claims outweigh the claims of the Roman Empire *and* the claims of the ' Kingdom of our father David.'

If we ask what is this Kingdom of God that so dominates the life and words of Jesus and rides roughshod over established belief and practice, challenging all constituted authorities, the only answer is that it is the realisation of God's will in the world. It is God's will being done on earth as it is done in heaven. But what then is this will of God? For Pharisaic Judaism it was holiness and righteousness as revealed in the Law. For those Jews who nourished their souls on the Apocalyptic literature, there was added an intenser assurance of a Divine power that would destroy evil and vindicate righteousness, and that right early. For many the Kingdom of God meant the downfall of Rome and the exaltation of Israel to world-dominion. For Jesus the will of God is primarily the forgiving, reconciling, redeeming love of God. And being what it is, it must express itself in a Divine act for men rather than in a Divine demand upon men; though this demand follows inevitably upon the act.

The essence of the Gospel is that Jesus—His life and death and victory over death, His ministry, His teaching—Jesus is the divine act, the fulfilment of God's redemptive purpose, the incarnation of the Kingdom of God. The ministry of Jesus is no mere prelude to the coming of the Kingdom, nor even a preparation for it: it *is* the Kingdom at work in the world. His ethic is no mere ' interim ethic ' to bridge the gap between the present and the future: it is the will of God which, whenever and wherever the Kingdom comes, is done on earth as it is in heaven. God was in Christ reconciling the world unto Himself. It is probable that the key to the teaching and the ministry of Jesus, and indeed to the whole New Testament, lies in a single phrase, which expresses, as perfectly as words can, the supreme interest of our Lord, that for which He lived and died, for which He endured hardship, loneliness, and obloquy, that to which He gave His whole undivided devotion—not ' the Law and the Prophets,' not ' the Kingdom of our father David,' but ' the Kingdom of my Father.'

END OF BOOK II

SELECT BIBLIOGRAPHY FOR BOOK II

The following list does not give all the works consulted in the preparation of this commentary. Its purpose is rather to indicate the books which will be most useful to the student who wishes to go farther in the study of the subject.

The most convenient text is A. Huck's *Synopse der drei ersten Evangelien* (8th ed., 1931). This gives the Greek text of the Synoptic Gospels in parallel columns, with excellent cross-references. It has also an appendix containing the parallels from John. The text given is that of Tischendorf, and there is a useful *apparatus criticus*.

The standard Grammar of New Testament Greek, for English readers, is that begun by J. H. Moulton and now being completed by W. F. Howard.

For serious study of the text two works are indispensable: Moulton and Geden's *Concordance to the New Testament*, and Hatch and Redpath's *Concordance to the Septuagint*. Of dictionaries, the best combination in English is the *Greek-English Lexicon of the New Testament*, by Grimm and Thayer, supplemented by Moulton and Milligan's *Vocabulary of the Greek Testament*. If these are not available, there is the excellent *Manual Greek Lexicon of the New Testament* by Abbott-Smith. In German, W. Bauer's *Wörterbuch zum Neuen Testament* is altogether admirable. Another dictionary of the greatest importance is the *Theologisches Wörterbuch zum N.T.* edited by G. Kittel. It is being published in parts (Vols. I and II have already been published) and, when complete, will be a great encyclopædia of New Testament theology.

The most important documents illustrating the Jewish background of early Christianity are available in English translations. The extra-canonical Jewish books are collected in Charles's *Apocrypha and Pseudepigrapha of the Old Testament*. There is an excellent translation of the *Mishnah* by H. Danby. And the works of Philo and Josephus are in process of publication in the Loeb series. The history of the Jewish people during this period can be studied in E. R. Bevan's brilliant sketch, *Jerusalem under the High-Priests*. The fullest treatment is in Schürer's *Geschichte des Jüdischen Volkes im Zeitalter Jesu Christi* (4th ed.), and there is much important material in *Les Juifs dans l'Empire Romain*, by J. Juster. The finest account of the Jewish religion is G. F. Moore's *Judaism*.

For the study of the Synoptic Problem the reader is referred to Streeter's *The Four Gospels*, Stanton's *The Gospels as Historical Documents* (Pt. II), and—an indispensable tool—*Horae Synopticae*, by Sir J. C. Hawkins. Very important for the study of Q is Harnack's *Sprüche und Reden Jesu* (English translation, *The Sayings of Jesus*). A new solution of the Synoptic Problem is expounded in Bussmann's *Synoptische Studien*. Whether this theory is satisfactory remains to be seen; but there is much acute observation in Bussmann's three volumes.

In recent years there has been a determined attempt to get behind the documents embodied in the Gospels, and to study the material as it may have taken shape in oral tradition. A good introduction to this special line of research is furnished by V. Taylor's *The Formation of the Gospel Tradition*. The works of the leading representatives of the Form-critical school are accessible—in the main—only to those who read German; but what is perhaps the most important of them, the second edition of *Die Formgeschichte des Evangeliums*, by M. Dibelius, has recently been translated under the title *From Tradition to Gospel*. In this connexion mention may be made of Burney's demonstration, in *The Poetry of our Lord*, that much of the teaching of Jesus was delivered in poetic form.

Works devoted to the interpretation of the Gospels are legion. Here we can take account only of those which have a direct bearing on the teaching and of commentaries on the Gospels of Mt. and Lk.

The completest collection of material for the illustration of the teaching from the Jewish literature is Billerbeck's great *Kommentar zum N.T. aus Talmud und Midrasch*. Billerbeck gives a vast quantity of material from Jewish sources translated into German; and the task of the user of the commentary is to select from the store what is really relevant. In English we have the *Studies in Pharisaism and the Gospels*, by I. Abrahams, and C. G. Montefiore's two works: his Commentary on the Synoptic Gospels and his *Rabbinic Literature and Gospel Teachings*. Most important are Dalman's two books, both translated: *The*

Words of Jesus and *Jesus-Jeshua*. Schlatter's *Der Evangelist Matthäus* also contains much valuable Jewish material, especially from Josephus; and my *Teaching of Jesus* is an attempt to interpret the teaching on its Jewish background.

Of commentaries Wettstein's (1751) has yet to be superseded as a collection of illustrative material from Greek and Latin authors; and Bengel's *Gnomon* cannot be superseded. Of modern commentators in German Wellhausen is most stimulating and suggestive. J. Weiss (in Vol. I of *Die Schriften des Neuen Testaments*) did for German readers what the present work is designed to do for English readers. Among the most useful of German commentaries on the Synoptic Gospels are Klostermann's in Lietzmann's *Handbuch zum N.T.* (*Mt.* 2nd ed., 1927; *Lk.* 2nd ed., 1929). Zahn's big commentaries on Mt. and Lk. are learned and conservative. In English McNeile's commentary on Mt. and Plummer's on Lk. contain a great deal of useful information. A more recent commentary on Lk., which takes account of the newer research, is that of J. M. Creed.

In addition to the books mentioned there is much to be learned from the text-books of New Testament Theology and from the various '*Lives*' of Jesus. Two other books that must be mentioned are Otto's *Reich Gottes und Menschensohn*, a work which may well prove to be a turning-point in the study of the Gospels, and *The Parables of the Kingdom* by C. H. Dodd.

Finally, a few books of a supplementary nature: Dalman's exhaustive study of the topography of the Gospels is now available in English under the title, *Sacred Sites and Ways*. The student of the New Testament must also study the early Christian literature which was not included in the Canon. The collection known as *The Apostolic Fathers* is available with text and translation in the Loeb series (Kirsopp Lake); and the apocryphal Gospels, Acts, and Epistles have been brought together in translation by the foremost English authority on the subject in *The Apocryphal New Testament*, translated by M. R. James.

BOOK III. JESUS: THE REVELATION OF GOD

Introduction

GOOD TIDINGS

THE book which lies before us for comment and elucidation is called, like the three which precede it, a 'Gospel.' It is so called because it brings 'Good Tidings' to its readers. If, as the Christian Church in every age has declared, this title is justified, the chief task of the commentator is so to expound the book that this message of good tidings shall be heard.

These 'Good Tidings' have to do with a historical figure known to us as Jesus the Christ. He, as far as we know—like the Buddha and Socrates before him—wrote nothing. His message was conveyed by spoken word and living example. He wrote in lives, not in books. For our knowledge, therefore, of His own 'Gospel' we have only two sources: first, the books of those who either themselves saw Him live and heard Him speak or who derived their knowledge from eye-witnesses and hearers; second, the lives of those who were either directly or indirectly influenced by His example and His teaching. It is obvious that the two sources are inter-related, for the books about Jesus were written by those who were influenced by Him. Among these books is 'The Gospel according to St. John,' as it is commonly known.

It is obviously one of the greatest books of religion ever written—if not indeed the greatest. And it purports to be all about Jesus. He is its central theme. It is His own 'Gospel' it seeks to declare, His own life it seeks to portray. Had Jesus never lived and taught this book could never have been written.

Yet here lies the perplexing problem which it raises in the mind of every serious reader. The Jesus it portrays is in some respects different from the Jesus of the Synoptic Gospels—so called because they give us a common view of the Master. The nature of these differences we shall unfold in a later paragraph. We here refer to them because they constitute in large measure what we might call 'the problem' of the Fourth Gospel. And while a modern commentator's *first* task is to set in the clearest possible light the 'Good Tidings' conveyed by the book, he cannot do this without a frank confrontation of this 'problem,' and some satisfactory, and satisfying, solution of it.

THE NEED OF PERSPECTIVE: THE WHOLE AND THE PARTS

A modern commentator's chief difficulty, therefore, becomes one of perspective. This Gospel is both a Glory and a Problem; but in seeking conscientiously to solve the problem one may easily envelop the glory in a fog of detailed argumentation. On the other hand, if one avoids the manifold critical issues, no intellectually satisfying elucidation of the Good Tidings is possible. True appreciation of a book requires that it be understood; and true understanding requires that it be appreciated. The familiar illustration of 'the wood' and 'the trees' will clarify the point at issue. The 'wood' is constituted of heterogeneous trees: without the trees there is no wood. Yet the 'wood' is itself a unity, and has a beauty of symmetry and colour to which each tree contributes, but which is itself more, and other, than the mere sum of the individual beauties of the several trees. Thus, there are those who, as we say, cannot see the wood for the trees; and, likewise, those who cannot discern the trees for the wood. A true appreciation of the wood requires at one and the same time the vision of the whole and the knowledge of the parts. The knowledge of the parts gives content and meaning to the vision of the whole; while the vision of the whole gives the sense of overshadowing unity by which the detailed parts are seen in true perspective.

Ever and anon in writing the following pages of this ' commentary ' we have been conscious of this difficulty of perspective. In studying the parts it is not easy to avoid clouding the vision of the whole. Yet a ' commentary ' must by its very nature be detailed. We can only hope that, in examination of particulars, our eyes do not become dim to the sublimity of the work as a whole.

THE NEED OF PSYCHOLOGICAL EXEGESIS

It is our conviction that the supreme need of the modern commentator on the Fourth Gospel is what we may call 'psychological exegesis.' By this we mean that a book can never be to us the author's own book unless we learn, as it were, to see with his eyes. The question a modern reader has continually to ask himself is, *What did the author himself think when he wrote?* No one can understand an author's book without sympathetic understanding of his mind. It is for this reason that only he who loves a man, or, at least, has some kinship with his mind, should write his biography. We should as little expect a colour-blind man to expound the glory of the art of painting, or a deaf person to interpret the meaning of noble music, as to expect a materialist, whether of the left or of the right, to understand so spiritual an author as the writer of this Gospel. Whatever is the expression of mind can only be understood, therefore, by those who have some kinship with the type of mind expressed. That is why men are divided in their literary, artistic, philosophical, and theological loyalties.

So often in the past we have had *dogmatic* exegesis, or *ecclesiastical* exegesis, of the books which compose the New Testament, when what was chiefly needed was a true and just *psychological* and *historical* exegesis. We have looked for a theological system instead of for living men. We so easily forget that the New Testament was written not by one writer but by many writers. Each writer, while the heir of common traditions and the sharer in common experiences, had his own heart and his own mind. Paul was not Peter, nor was Peter John. If they use the same words, the experience they wish to express is not necessarily the same experience. Each writer gives expression to the truth as he has seen it. And when, for example, he speaks of Jesus, he cannot but reveal himself as well.

Dogmatic exegesis has been inspired by the desire to find, or to safeguard, a theological system. Psychological exegesis is inspired by the desire to understand the inner experiences of living men. Dogmas are the later solidifications of insight. The Church itself as an institution has had a long history, in which it has been shaped by the motives and endeavours of many living men, and by many external forces. To arrive at a just appreciation of theological or ecclesiastical creations it is necessary to trace their history. To the history of every system of thought and of every institution, *many* minds, speaking in divers tones and with divers accents, have made their contribution. Thus it is, that to arrive at a true understanding of any book in the New Testament it is necessary to take our stand, if we can, with the author himself, and to seek, as far as may be, to see things as he saw them. We must stand where he stood.

It is undeniable that the author of this Gospel, whoever he was, fervently believed in the mission and message of Jesus, about whom he was writing. Some critical discussions of this Gospel rest upon the hypothesis that the Evangelist is writing about a theological abstraction, with the slenderest possible relation to a historical figure. Such a hypothesis is, to the present writer, certainly wrong. And if, as we hold, he had some measure of true and deep understanding of Jesus, he must have had some likeness of mind and spirit to Jesus. 'Jesus is known in so far as He is loved'—as the old Latin word has it. And, as we might say conversely, Jesus is loved in so far as He is known. Thus, even as an evangelist, to understand Jesus, had to have some likeness to Him, so we must have some sympathetic insight into an evangelist's mind if we would understand what he writes. As far as the Fourth Evangelist is concerned, his Gospel will always be a riddle unless its exegesis is inspired by intuitive discernment. Origen in his Commentary said something like this in his own very beautiful way when he wrote: 'No one can apprehend the meaning of this Gospel except he have lain on Jesus's breast and received from Jesus Mary to be his Mother also. Such an one must he become who is to be another John, and to have shown to him, like John, by Jesus Himself, Jesus as He is. . . . What a mind, then, must we have to enable us to interpret in a worthy manner this work, though it be committed to the treasure-house of common speech, of writing which any passer-by can read, and which can be heard when read aloud by anyone who lends to it his bodily ears?' A modern critical historian of the Life of Jesus—Dr. Maurice Goguel of Paris—has sounded the same note, though, of course, from a critical standpoint far removed from that of Origen. 'It is on psychology that, in the last analysis, must rely every attempt to understand the life of Jesus.' [1] No one can understand Jesus without some likeness, however feeble, to Him. Likewise, no one can understand the Fourth Evangelist without some spiritual kinship with him, and some insight into the historical situation he was confronting.

A. THE PROBLEMS RAISED BY THIS GOSPEL

Before we seek to elucidate the purpose and meaning of the Gospel, let us look, first, at the problems it presents. These are of two main kinds. The first has to do with its precise historical character and value. The second has to do with its literary structure. Under the first type of problem comes the question of its relation to, and differences from, the Synoptic Gospels. Under the second type of problem comes the question of its literary unity. Though these two types of problem obviously to some extent involve one another, it will be well to look at them separately.

[1] *Vie de Jésus*, p. 196.

1. *RELATION TO THE SYNOPTIC GOSPELS*

Differences

The attentive reader of the four Gospels receives an immediate impression of certain differences between the Fourth Gospel and the other three. The latter—in spite of the characteristic peculiarities of Matthew, Mark, and Luke—have a certain family likeness; while the former has features putting it in a class by itself. These differences have to do with the scene and duration of the Ministry of Jesus, with the nature and form of His teaching, and with specific incidents. A few of these main differences may be tabulated as follows:

1. The Synoptic Gospels represent the Ministry of Jesus as chiefly in Galilee, the Fourth Gospel as mainly in Jerusalem.

2. The Synoptic Gospels record only one Passover visit of Jesus to Jerusalem, and that at the end of the public Ministry; they may, therefore, be read as confining this Ministry to one year. The Fourth Gospel records three Passover visits to Jerusalem—in 2^{13}, 6^{4}, and 13^{1}—and therefore indicates that the public Ministry covered, at least, a period of between two and three years.

3. According to the Synoptic Gospels, Jesus does not announce His Messiahship; they suggest that the views of Him entertained by the disciples developed during their intercourse with Him, perhaps also that His own consciousness and estimate of His Person and Mission came to gradual fruition. In the Fourth Gospel His Messianic vocation is avowed and acknowledged from the first.

4. In the Synoptic Gospels the style and general emphasis of the teaching of Jesus is not that of the Fourth Gospel. There is an unmistakable Johannine style in which the teaching of Jesus is recorded. Indeed, so distinctive is this style that in several places in the Gospel it is impossible to say confidently where the words of Jesus are meant to end and where the comment of the Evangelist is meant to begin. Jesus, that is, speaks in precisely the same style as the Evangelist himself uses in recording his ensuing reflections. Then, further, according to the Synoptic Gospels, as Mark says (4^{34}), 'without a parable spake He not unto them'; in the Fourth Gospel Jesus does not speak in 'parables,' but in allegories. Yet further, the main theme of the teaching of Jesus in the Synoptic Gospels is the Kingdom of God; in the Fourth Gospel it is Jesus Himself. Where in the Synoptic narrative we find pithy ethical and spiritual precepts, illustrated by parables told in an objective manner, in the Fourth Gospel we find long discourses by Jesus about His own status as the unique revealer of spiritual blessing, illustrated by allegories told in a subjective manner. This difference of emphasis and of theme is very strikingly seen in the numerous 'I am' passages in the Fourth Gospel. In these sayings Jesus declares in the first person singular that *He is* 'the bread of life,' 'the light of the world,' 'the door of the sheep,' 'the good shepherd,' 'the resurrection and the life,' 'the way, the truth, and the life,' 'the true vine.' Nowhere in the Synoptic Gospels do we find this type of utterance. What Jesus *was*, He does not there declare in formal, categorical statements, but, rather, implies by the ethical and spiritual sublimity of His utterance and by the 'authority' which pervades it.

5. Differences in specific incidents are many. In the body of the Com-

mentary we shall seek to elucidate the inner significance of the numerous Johannine omissions and additions; but, in the meantime, the following conspicuous differences should be noted by the reader who wishes to reach a just and true solution of the problem before us.

(*a*) The cleansing of the Temple which in the Synoptic record comes at the end of the Ministry, in the Fourth Gospel comes at the beginning (2^{14-16}).

(*b*) The story of ' the raising of Lazarus,' which in the Fourth Gospel seems to lead to the arrest of Jesus, is not found in the Synoptic Gospels. There are other noticeable differences in the ' miracles ' recorded which will be noted later, one of the most obvious being the absence from the Johannine narrative of the casting-out of demons and unclean spirits which holds a conspicuous place in the Synoptic story.

(*c*) In the Fourth Gospel there is no account of ' the institution ' of the Lord's Supper or Eucharist; though there are passages from which it is possible clearly to read the author's conception of ' the sacramental principle.'

(*d*) In the Synoptic Gospels the Crucifixion takes place on the 15th Nisan, in the Fourth Gospel on the 14th Nisan. In other words, according to the first three Gospels Jesus was crucified on the day of the Passover Feast; the Last Supper there synchronising with the Passover: according to the Fourth Gospel Jesus was crucified on the morning of the day when the Passover lambs were killed, prior to the Feast in the evening; the Last Supper, therefore, in this Gospel being on the night before the Passover.

Agreements and Resemblances

Side by side, however, with the recognition of differences between the Fourth Gospel and the other three, there grows in the mind of the attentive reader the conviction of certain likenesses and agreements. If there are family resemblances between the three Synoptic Gospels, there is also sufficient in common between the Johannine Gospel and them to show that it itself is not in a position of ' splendid isolation.' On the one hand, it was clearly meant to be read by those acquainted with the general Synoptic tradition. It presupposes, that is, some knowledge of those Gospels. We cannot, of course, say whether the earliest readers of the Fourth Gospel had all read the Synoptic Gospels: it is inherently likely, we think, that most of them had. But at least we may say that the Johannine author presupposes a general knowledge of them on the part of his readers. A few illustrations will make this clear. In $1^{32 ff.}$ the Fourth Evangelist implies a knowledge of certain circumstances associated with the Baptism of Jesus, an incident which he does not himself record. In 3^{24} he alludes in passing to the fact that ' John had not yet been cast into prison,' an event to which he does not elsewhere refer. He speaks of ' the twelve ' (6^{67}), and so implies an acquaintance with the fact, unrecorded by him, that Jesus had chosen twelve especially intimate companions.

On the other hand, a close examination of the Gospel reveals not only that the author presupposed a general familiarity with the Synoptic Gospels, but also that he made some specific use of them in writing his own Gospel. He reproduces various unusual phrases used by Mark in his Gospel—for example, ' two hundred penny worth of bread ' (6^{7}; cf. Mk. 6^{37}), ' ointment of spikenard ' (12^{3}; cf. Mk. 14^{3}), a somewhat ' vulgar ' Greek word for ' bed,' κράβαττος (5^{8-9}; cf. Mk. 2^{11-12}). Inasmuch as Jesus spoke in Aramaic, the identity of these phrases suggests that our author was so familiar with the language of Mark that at times it flowed spontaneously through his pen. Further, there are resemblances, both of words and of narrative details, between the Fourth Gospel and Luke's Gospel, which reveal some dependence of John upon Luke. Some illustrations of this will be noted in the body of the Commentary. Suffice it here to say that the consensus of opinion among competent students is that the Fourth Evangelist was sufficiently familiar with both Mark and Luke as to reproduce in places the very language they employed.

This does not mean that our author wrote his Gospel with Mk. and Lk. open before him. His knowledge of these Gospels had much more probably become fused in his own creative mind; so that it was not *of set purpose* that he reproduced what others had written. Anyone to-day writing or speaking about Samuel Johnson will probably reproduce words or phrases found in Boswell; but he is not necessarily either quoting Boswell from memory or writing with the famous biography open in front of him. Much in Boswell has entered into the Johnson tradition, and it is thus hardly possible for anyone to write or speak about Johnson without reproducing sayings and incidents from that tradition.

At least, however, the evidence is sufficient to show that the Fourth Evangelist was very familiar with the language of Mark and Luke. That he had also read Matthew is, we think, entirely probable; for it is difficult to imagine that an author as interested in Jesus as he undoubtedly was should not have read so important a book—the Christian world was not so big that Gospels circulating in different localities should not have been known outside those localities. From a close examination it would seem, however, that the Fourth Evangelist does not make the same use of the First Gospel as he does of the other two. The reason for this *may* have been that the Apocalyptic and Judæistic emphasis and outlook of the Gospel of Matthew were distasteful to him.

From all this, one conclusion at least stands out clearly. The Fourth Evangelist, while familiar with the tradition manifest in the Synoptic Gospels, wrote his own Gospel in striking independence of them. The marks of a very original and creative mind are indelibly imprinted on his Gospel. He is poles asunder from the authors whose books are reproductions of the thoughts and language of their predecessors. He wrote his own book, and in his own way. In places his Gospel *supplements* the others; in places, probably, it *corrects* the others—as for example in the date of the Crucifixion; in places it *adopts* phrases and details found in the others. But we shall look to his Gospel, neither to find a detailed supplementation, nor a detailed correction, nor a careful adoption of what the others have written. It has too striking features of the positive, constructive, and creative mind for us to conclude that these were his *primary* motives in writing. He had larger purposes in view, a more urgent personal insight and point of view to express.

Before, however, we seek to eludicate that purpose, and so to arrive at the *meaning* of the Gospel, let us look at the second type of problem—namely, the question of its literary structure.

2. *LITERARY STRUCTURE OF THE GOSPEL*

This Gospel leaves upon the mind the impression that it was the work of one author. It bears upon itself, as much as, say, the *Æneid* or the play of *Hamlet*, the stamp of a single mind, and that, the mind of a transcendent genius. There is no book in the New Testament which bears more clearly upon its face the marks of one personality.

Yet there has been much discussion, and dispute, on this question of the unity of the Gospel. 'Partition theories' have been maintained by some; 'revision theories' by others. On the hypothesis that there are certain 'inequalities' and 'incongruities' in the Gospel, the endeavour has been made to analyse the book into one or more pre-existing sources. Other students, unable to defend this 'partition' hypothesis, have maintained that the Gospel as we now have it has undergone a process of *editing*. For a careful discussion of this issue the reader may be referred to *The Gospels as Historical Documents*, by Dr. V. H. Stanton, Part III, pp. 32–73.

We cannot but feel that theories of 'partition' are interesting speculations which reveal a certain myopic ingenuity of mind. It has recently been amusingly said, by one discussing some of the more extreme of these theories: 'If the sources have undergone anything like the amount of amplification, excision, rearrangement and adaptation which the theory postulates, then the critic's pretence that he can unravel the process is grotesque. As well hope to start with a string of sausages and reconstruct the pig.' [1] Using a kindred illustration, we would say that the incredibility of these partition theories arises from the fact that it involves the creation of a very considerable pig by the process of adding a number of little pigs together. The Gospel, in other words, is not a string of heterogeneous parts: it is a unified and organic whole. The author had, no doubt, like every other author, many sources of information at his disposal; but a variety of sources does not make a book of genius. It takes a mind of genius to do that. Of this we may be quite certain—this Gospel did not come by uniting fragment to fragment. Nor, like some modern books, was it the work of a committee. The figure employed by Strauss about a hundred years ago is still in large measure appropriate to this Gospel: it is like the seamless robe of our Lord.

A careful and detailed examination of the Gospel confirms, we believe, this impression of unity derived from the reading of the whole. The book, like some great works of music, has a few recurring themes. It is more like a symphony of Beethoven than like a book of tunes—as, for example, Mendelssohn's 'Songs without Words.' It is, that is, a complete and harmonious work in which several themes are fused into one transcendent whole. The impression of the diversity of theme and melody is merged and lost in the impression of the underlying identity to which each makes its contribution. What Browning's musician claimed for his art we may claim for the Fourth Evangelist.

But here is the finger of God, a flash of the will that can,
Existent behind all laws, that made them and, lo, they are!
And I know not if, save in this, such gift be allowed to man,
That out of three sounds he frame, not a fourth sound, but a star.

[1] B. H. Streeter in *The Four Gospels*, p. 377.

Further, this unity is seen not only in the recurrence of a few main themes: it is manifest also in the plan and contents of the Gospel. The Gospel divides itself naturally into two clear parts. After the Prologue, in which the author enunciates his main theme, there comes the first section setting forth the essential Witness of Jesus and the Conflict it occasions. There follows the second section, devoted to the Witness of Jesus among His friends on the night of His Betrayal, and to the Final Issue of the Conflict in His Passion and Resurrection. The Gospel has clear marks of the architectonic mind: only, let us add, this has come not by careful elaboration or by close ratiocination, but by a certain intuitive insight and a certain artistic sense of fitness. The structural coherence of the Gospel has the organic unity of a fruit, not the artificial completeness of a manufactured article. A former commentator said of this Gospel: 'In the whole range of literature there is no composition that is a more perfect work of art, or which more rigidly excludes whatever does not subserve its main end.' [1] This is probably to put the point too strongly; but *in the main* it is a true judgement.

More can be said for a very early editorial revision of the Gospel. Yet, in the absence of external evidence, we may not speak confidently even here. Endeavours have been made to show that in various places the sequence of the thought is interrupted, or the character of the prevailing thought contradicted, by certain passages; and these are, thus, attributed to a somewhat clumsy editor. This hypothetical editor, it is held, freely embodied his own comments in the text of the Gospel, as, for example, in such a passage as 5^{28-29}, where an intrusion of Apocalyptic views at variance with the main teaching of the Gospel is held by some to be evident.

Whether the Gospel as we have it has undergone editorial revision we do not know, and probably shall never know. The looseness of structure that some see in the Gospel we confess we do not see. There is, however, one passage of which we may fairly confidently say that it did not form part of the original Gospel. This is the passage about the woman taken in adultery, in 8^{1-11}. It is possible also that the Gospel may have originally circulated without the twenty-first chapter. The issues involved in relation to these two passages are discussed in the body of the Commentary.

Another theory, which has received considerable approval, is that many passages in the Gospel have been displaced from their original order. This conclusion was suggested by a number of seeming breaks in the logical, or chronological, sequence of the narrative. Two outstanding illustrations of these suggested misplacements may be here given. (1) Chapter 5 describes the activity of Jesus in Jerusalem: to the surprise of the reader, chapter 6 begins, 'After these things Jesus went away to the other side of the sea of Galilee'; chapter 7, following this account of a Galilean ministry begins, 'And after these things Jesus walked in Galilee.' By the simple process of reversing chapters 6 and 5, it is suggested, we should have a coherent narrative. (2) The second illustration comes from the section of the Gospel containing the addresses of Jesus to His intimate disciples. In 14^{31} Jesus says, 'Arise, let us go hence,' and to the surprise of some readers there follow the long discourses in chapters 15, 16, 17.

[1] Marcus Dods in *The Gospel of St. John* (the Expositor's Bible), vol. i, p. ix.

Many suggestions have been made to arrive at what some interpreters have felt to be a more consistent order for these discourses—that which meets with much approval being that chapters 15 and 16 should be interposed between 13^{30a} and 13^{30b}.

This issue, from the very nature of the case, cannot be dogmatically decided. It is of course 'possible,' that, by some mischance or other, at a very early date the sheets of papyrus on which probably the Gospel was written may have become disarranged. If, however, some disarrangement took place, one might have expected that those who tried to rearrange the sheets would have perceived the 'difficulties' of order which have inspired the hypotheses of many modern investigators. It is a mistake to imagine that the first intelligent men were born in our times. This consideration suggests the possibility that the order of the Gospel, as it has come down to us, was indeed the original order; and that the early copyists did not alter this order—in spite of a lack of logical coherence, which they could hardly avoid noticing—for the simple reason that it was the order in which they believed the Gospel had left the hand of the Evangelist.

This raises the important question of the type of mind of the author, and his method of writing. On this we shall write later. But in the meantime it is well to consider the following question. May it not be that the 'difficulties' felt by many modern investigators arise from their desire to impose a logical or chronological scheme upon the Gospel which may have been foreign to the mind of the author himself? In trying to make a book conform to standards of our own, we may fail to understand the author's type of mind. Not only so, but by the multiplicity and diversity of our schemes of rearrangement we are in danger of making our conclusions a laughing-stock to those not yet bereft of a sense of humour.

To ourselves the issue is not an important one, inasmuch as we do not think the author himself sought to give anything in the nature of a precise chronological narrative. His mind did not work in any systematic manner. No doubt he wrote different passages at different times. As we suggest in various relevant places in the ensuing exposition, the Evangelist did not write without interruption. Like every intuitive, mystical and artistic mind, he wrote when he saw—and not till he saw. What he wrote sprang out of his meditations, and not out of a process of conscious rationalisation. He did not tie his ideas together with philosophical dexterity, nor bind his narratives together with scientific acumen. This is transparently obvious to those who sit down without prepossessions before the Gospel, seeking not to prove ingenious theories but to learn from it what it has to say and how the author sought to say it. The Evangelist will, for example, begin a narrative and omit to finish it: as in the story of Nicodemus, who, he tells us, came to Jesus by night, with what issue to the inquirer he leaves us to guess; or as in the story of the Greeks who came seeking to see Jesus—which is the only thing the Evangelist has to say about them. Or, again, the Evangelist will use the phrases 'after these things' and 'after this' with the very vaguest chronological reference. The use of such a phrase may quite possibly indicate a resumption of the pen by the author—in somewhat similar fashion to a modern writer's use of such a phrase as 'And now' with which he may begin a new point of a discourse or a new paragraph in a narrative. The phrase 'after these things,' or 'after this,' very probably marks a sequence in the author's own mental reconstruction, or construction; not a sequence in the narrated events themselves. The phrase is found in 2^{12}, 3^{22}, 5^{1}, 5^{14}, 6^{1}, 7^{1}, $11^{7,11}$, 13^{7}, $19^{28,38}$, and 21^{1}.

If the reader will ponder upon such facts as these, he will see that the Evangelist had no intention of writing a strictly coherent or historical narrative. The question of hypothetical disarrangements would only be important for the understanding of the Gospel on the theory that its purpose was historical. Being unable to acquiesce in such a hypothesis, we must leave the issue to be discussed by those of ingenious mind.

Our hesitation in accepting any rearranged order for the Gospel is strengthened when we note the variety of the rearrangements suggested. They are almost as numerous as their authors. In this Commentary the order of the Revised Version is followed, but the more important of the suggested transpositions are discussed, each in its own context.

B. THE AUTHOR—HIS MIND, AND HIS PURPOSE

Fénélon, in one of his *Dialogues of the Dead*, puts into the mouth of Socrates when he is conversing with Confucius, these words: 'A book is a dead thing which does not reply to the unforeseen and diverse difficulties of each reader; a book passes into the hand of men incapable of making good use of it; a book is susceptible of many meanings contrary to that of the author.' When he wrote this, Fénélon was giving a kind of psychological *apologia* for the fact that Socrates chose to speak, and not to write. At any rate, most of us know that it is easier to misunderstand an author's book than to misunderstand the author himself when he speaks to us in living tones. A book records, a voice speaks. Here, however, we have a book to interpret: and every commentator, and every reader, is called to the hard task of entering thereby the sanctuary of the author's mind.

Now, for our understanding of the Fourth Evangelist's mind our only source of knowledge, practically speaking, is the Gospel he wrote. We have no biography of him to which we can turn for the unlocking of the secret places of his consciousness. It follows, therefore, that the two questions: (1) the mind and purpose of the author, and (2) the nature and meaning of the Gospel, are inextricably intertwined. It is the Gospel which tells us what kind of mind the author had; and it is the nature of the mind of the author which is the clue to our comprehension of the Gospel he wrote. For that reason, it is difficult to decide whether we ought first to speak of the nature and meaning of the Gospel, or, first, of the mind and purpose of the author. We have decided on the latter order; and have done so, in consequence of the fact that his mind and purpose seem to us to shine clearly through what he has written. Having sought to understand his mind, we can then go on to seek to unfold the essential meaning of his Gospel, and to elucidate its central themes, as he himself understood them.

THE TRADITIONAL VIEW

But, first, something must be said about the traditional view of the authorship of this Gospel. For if that view is accepted it will materially affect our estimate of the book itself.

Until the nineteenth century the Gospel was almost universally accepted as the work of the Apostle John, the son of Zebedee. Not only was he regarded as the witness of the scenes narrated, and the hearer of the discourses spoken by Jesus; it was he also, it was held, who, late in life, wrote the record we have before us. On this view, a very great historical value will be placed upon the Gospel; and when, for example, we find divergences from the Synoptic tradition we shall be compelled, either to set about constructing a ' harmony ' of the four Gospels, or, to revise that tradition in the light of these reminiscences of one who was, on this traditional hypothesis, a personal witness of the whole Ministry of Jesus.

The *external* evidence for this traditional view, it must be noted, is exceedingly strong. Irenæus is a witness to the fact that at the end of the second century there was a widely received tradition which ascribed the Gospel to the Apostle John, the son of Zebedee. Eusebius, in his *Ecclesiastical History* (v. 20), has preserved for us a letter written by Irenæus to Florinus, a Roman presbyter who had embraced heretical views, in which he wrote: ' For I saw thee, when I was still a boy, in Lower Asia in company with Polycarp, when thou wast faring prosperously at court, and endeavouring to stand well with him. I distinctly remember the incidents of that time better than events of recent occurrence; for the lessons received in childhood, growing with the growth of the soul, become identified with it; so that I can describe the very place in which the blessed Polycarp used to sit when he discoursed, and his goings out and his comings in, and his manner of life and his personal appearance, and the discourses which he held before the people, and how he would describe his intercourse with John and with the rest who had seen the Lord, and how he would relate their works. And what were the accounts he had from them about the Lord and about His miracles, and about His teaching; how Polycarp, as having received them from eyewitnesses of the life of the Word, used to give an account harmonising on all points with the Scriptures. To these discourses I used to listen at the time, by God's mercy which was bestowed upon me, noting them down, not on paper, but in my heart; and by the grace of God I constantly ruminate upon them faithfully.' The same Irenæus, in his treatise *Against the Heresies* (III, I, i), says that ' John, the disciple of the Lord, who also had leaned upon His breast, did himself publish a Gospel during his residence at Ephesus in Asia.'

Further, a letter written by Polycrates, Bishop of Ephesus, towards the close of the second century, to Victor, Bishop of Rome, has come down to us, in which he said: ' Moreover John, martyr [or ' witness '] and teacher, who leaned on the Lord's bosom and became a priest wearing the sacerdotal plate [' petalon '] he also fell asleep in Ephesus ' (Eusebius, *Ecclesiastical History*, v. 24). A bishop of the Ephesian Church may be supposed to know something of the history of the Church of which he is bishop, especially of events dating only about a century before the time in which he was writing.

Further, a number of stories of early origin have come down to us telling of the life of the Apostle John in Ephesus. One of them describes his abhorrence of the views of a certain gnostic heretic, Cerinthus, whom he encountered by chance in a bath in Ephesus. Another relates that in his old age he used continually to remind the members of the Ephesian Church of the one thing needful. 'My little children, love one another.' There is obviously a very strong tradition that the John who had leaned on the Lord's bosom had been one of the 'great luminaries' of the Ephesian Church, and that he had died in old age in Ephesus.

Of late years some investigators have disputed the value of this tradition. There are a few fragments of late 'evidence,' suggesting that John the Apostle had suffered an early martyrdom in Jerusalem, like James his brother. The evidential value of these fragments has been widely discussed, and has inspired

great argument
About it and about.

To some—as, for example, to the late Dr. R. H. Charles—they afford conclusive testimony for the early martyrdom of the Apostle. To others—as for example to the late Dr. James Drummond—the evidential value of these fragments is nil. To the present writer, the tradition associating John the Apostle with the Church of Ephesus is so strong that much more, and better, evidence on the other side than we have got would be necessary for its rejection.

THIS TRADITIONAL VIEW INACCEPTABLE

But if it be granted that the Apostle lived and died in Ephesus, must we also accept the tradition that he was the actual author of the Gospel? To seek an answer to that question, we have to turn to the evidence of the Gospel itself.

(*a*) The Beloved Disciple

There are a number of references in the Gospel—in 13^{23-25}, $19^{26,35}$, $20^{2f.}$, and $21^{7,20}$—to 'the disciple whom Jesus loved.' The two questions arising are: Who was this disciple? and, Did he write the Gospel? The traditional view is that he was John the Apostle, and that he wrote the Gospel. Our own conclusion is that he was John the Apostle, but that he did not himself write the Gospel.

With regard to the first question—namely, the identity of this disciple—there has been much debate. Some writers regard him as 'a purely ideal figure.' Others say that he was a historical figure, but that we have no means of knowing who he was. Others maintain that he was John the Apostle. That he was the Apostle John seems to be clear to the present writer, on the following grounds.

In the first place, it accords with the general tradition of the Church, that John the Apostle had been among the most intimate of the disciples of Jesus. In the Synoptic Gospels Peter, James, and John stand in an especially close relation to the Master. The beloved disciple is anonymous in the Fourth Gospel. He is certainly not Peter, who is expressly mentioned in association with him. Almost as certainly he is not James.

In the second place, John, the son of Zebedee, if not the beloved disciple, is nowhere referred to in this Gospel. Westcott well stressed this point a generation ago: 'While it appears incredible that an apostle who stands in the Synoptists, in the Acts (3^1, 4^{13}, etc.), and in St. Paul (Gal. 2^9), as a central figure among the Twelve, should find no place in the narrative, the nameless disciple fulfils the part which would naturally be assigned to St. John.'

In the third place, it is significant to note that 'John the Baptist' is always in this Gospel referred to as 'John,' without any descriptive epithet. Since the beloved disciple stands in a category by himself to the author, it is natural that he should thus refer to the Baptist.

We conclude that the beloved disciple was John the Apostle.

(*b*) Was the Beloved Disciple the Author of the Gospel?

Verse 24 in the 21st chapter emphatically says that he was. 'This is the disciple which beareth witness of these things and wrote these things: and *we know* that his witness is true.' But from the form in which this attestation of authorship is written, we conclude that it does not come from the author himself. The verse was, no doubt, added by those who wished to claim that John the Apostle, the beloved disciple, had himself written the Gospel—perhaps, as Westcott and others suggested, by the Elders of the Ephesian Church. Are we compelled to acquiesce in the truth of this claim?

It has been pointed out that while there is MS. evidence for the omission of v. 25 in chapter 21, there is no MS. evidence for the omission of v. 24. That is, this attestation of authorship is found in every text of the Gospel which has come down to us.

Yet there are other considerations which lead us seriously to question the *precise* truth of this statement. Let us look at them.

In the first place, we find it very difficult, indeed psychologically incredible, to suppose that the author of the Gospel should refer to himself as 'the disciple whom Jesus loved.' The nearer the Apostle John was to the mind of Jesus, the less likely is it that he should himself claim a pre-eminence in the affection of the Master. A close disciple of a revered Apostle might naturally so describe him; but a humble and spiritually minded Apostle, in our view, would not so describe himself. Apart from this 24th verse of the 21st chapter there is nothing in the Gospel itself to suggest that the beloved disciple was the author. And if we were to-day to read this Gospel without this verse, we should naturally conclude that the author was speaking of someone other than himself when he spoke of 'the beloved disciple.'

In the second place, some of the considerations already referred to make it exceedingly doubtful that so intimate a disciple as John, the son of Zebedee, wrote the Gospel. Let the reader bear in mind the following facts. The Gospel, while presupposing a knowledge of the Transfiguration and Gethsemane, does not narrate these incidents. John, the son of Zebedee, according to the Synoptists, had been chosen by Jesus to be especially near to Him on these occasions. Silence regarding scenes that must, surely, have been unforgettable to those who witnessed them, is difficult to account for. Further, the author's reproduction, in places, of the very language of the Synoptic records is more naturally explained on the hypothesis that he was not himself one of the Twelve. Such dependence upon the writings of those who were not themselves of the inner band of disciples, by one who was, is psychologically improbable. It is as if we were asked to believe that one who had first-hand knowledge of the hero of his biography should be content to use the second- or third-hand knowledge of others. Yet further, the form in which the teaching of Jesus is given in this Gospel is more naturally explicable on the hypothesis that the writer had not himself been a very close and intimate disciple of Jesus. We should expect one of the Twelve to be less free with the presentation of the teaching of Jesus than this author obviously is. One who was of the inner band would be expected to control his dramatic faculty, in the interest of precise historical fidelity, more than this Evangelist certainly does. It is clear that Jesus spoke in parables: our author records none. It is clear, also, that Jesus only gradually disclosed 'the Messianic secret': of this gradual disclosure the author says nothing. Had he been one of the Twelve—to whom this consciousness of Messianic vocation was a 'mystery' almost to the last—he would hardly have felt free to place Jesus' fully developed consciousness of mission at the very beginning of the Ministry. Indeed, the whole dramatic and allegorical presentation of the inner mind of Jesus, which, as we hope to show, is the key to the Gospel's meaning, is more likely to come from a disciple of John the Apostle than from John the Apostle himself.

These considerations compel us to reject the precise truth of the statement in 21^{24}. Some modern readers may conclude from this that we hold guilty of a moral offence those who inserted this statement in the Gospel. Such a conclusion betokens a lack of the historical imagination. What we call 'literary morals' were not then what they are now. Books were ascribed to an author when he was only indirectly associated with their authorship. The concern for scientific exactitude belongs to modern historical writers. It is necessary at this point to remember that *exactness* of mind is not necessarily *insight* of mind: if we remember this, we shall not hastily speak either of the high 'literary morals' of our own time, or of the low 'literary morals' of past ages. Books of profound psychological insight were written in the days of old: and books laden with scrupulously sifted detail, but lacking such insight, are written in these days. Unless we bear these facts in mind, we shall not estimate aright the way in which the teaching of Jesus is presented in this Gospel: nor shall we have a sympathetic understanding of the minds of those who inserted this verse—which 'guarantees' the apostolic authorship of the Gospel. If, as we hold, the Apostle John was 'the beloved disciple,' and if the author was very dependent upon him, it is easy to perceive how this Gospel came to be regarded as 'according to St. John,' and easy to explain how this attesting verse was added.

(*c*) Who Precisely Was the Author?

Such evidence as we possess is insufficient to warrant a wholly confident reply. The entire question bristles with perplexing problems, as the reader will no doubt already feel. The issue is difficult enough in itself, and has become even more perplexing to the reader who seeks to weigh up the arguments and counter-arguments set forth in the voluminous literature covering this field. Statements are made and challenged: patristic references are scrutinised and confident conclusions drawn from them, only to meet with equally confident counter-conclusions. The issue has become a veritable jungle, and through the thicket of discussion it has become almost impossible to find any path upon which the average intelligent man may walk without challenge, or without meeting the barrier of some new critical growth. It may be, that the future will have to acquiesce in the conclusion that the author is some great anonymous personality whose mind is revealed in the Johannine writings.

The Elder John.—Nevertheless, before accepting such a conclusion, it is well to consider the suggestion that the author is 'the Elder John' who also lived at Ephesus towards the close of the first century. In a very famous passage recorded by Eusebius, the Church historian (*Ecclesiastical History*, iii. 39), Papias is quoted as expressing his preference for oral testimony in comparison with that of books. 'But if I met with anyone who had been a follower of the Elders, I made it a point to inquire what were the declarations of the Elders—what was said by Andrew, Peter, or Philip; what by Thomas, James, John, Matthew, or any other of the disciples of the Lord; what is said by Aristion, and the Elder John, disciples of the Lord; for I do not think that I derived so much benefit from books as from the living voice of those that are still surviving.' Eusebius himself goes on to make the following comment. 'It is here proper to observe that the name of John is twice mentioned: the former of which he mentions with Peter and James and Matthew, and the other Apostles, evidently meaning the evangelist. But in a separate point of his discourse, he ranks the other John with the rest not included in the number of Apostles, placing Aristion before him. He distinguishes him plainly by the name of Elder. So that it is here proved that the statement of those is true who assert that there were two of the same name in Asia, that there were also two tombs in Ephesus, and that both are called John to this day; which it is particularly necessary to observe.' Later in his *Ecclesiastical History* (vii. 25) Eusebius quotes Dionysius of Alexandria who, writing about the middle of the third century, mentions the two tombs of the two Johns at Ephesus. Again, in the *Apostolical Constitutions* (vii. 4) dating from the fourth century, we are told that as bishops of Ephesus there were 'Timotheus ordained by Paul, and John by John.' There is further evidence in the New Testament itself for the conclusion that there was an 'Elder John' in Ephesus. Three letters are there found attributed to John, and they are very closely allied in thought and style with the Fourth Gospel. They are anonymous, but for the fact that the writer of the second and third calls himself 'the elder.'

An additional piece of evidence in support of the view that there were two Johns, both well-known figures to the Church, may be referred to. Dr. Mingana discovered in a Syriac MS. of the New Testament before the Gospel of John the following statement: 'The holy Gospel of our Lord Jesus Christ [according to] the preaching of John *the younger*.' The MS. is relatively modern, but is, Dr. Mingana holds, a faithful copy of a much older original to be ascribed, probably, to about A.D. 750. According to the statement, there must have been to the writer two Johns, one older than the other. The older John, we may suggest, was the Apostle John: the younger John may well have been the John we call the 'Elder' or 'Presbyter'—the name 'Elder' or 'Presbyter' was not meant to indicate his age in relation to any other John. Here there is evidence of a tradition in the

Syrian Church that the Fourth Gospel was connected with a John who was not the Apostle. Needless to say, the statement does not deny that there was some connexion between the Gospel and John the Apostle; but what it does say is that it was according to the preaching or teaching of John the younger. Further, in the same MS., at the end of the Fourth Gospel, there is the following statement: 'Here ends the writing of the holy Gospel [according to] the preaching of John who spoke in Greek in Bithynia.' The fact that this John is here described as speaking in Greek does not, of itself, conflict with the view taken in this Commentary, that the author of the Gospel thought naturally in Aramaic. Yet further, at the end of the same Syriac MS. there is a treatise, attributed by the scribe to Eusebius of Cæsarea, in which it is stated that when the John who was banished to Patmos returned to Ephesus he was followed by three of his disciples. Among these three is another John, to whom, we are told, the first John granted priesthood and the episcopal see after him. The John who is the disciple of the first John is, we are told, 'the disciple who wrote the revelations, as he states that he heard all that he wrote from the mouth of John the evangelist.' In regard to this rather cryptic reference, two suggestions, according to Dr. Mingana, can be made. One is that the word 'evangelist' here after the name of John does not necessarily mean a declaration that he actually wrote the Gospel; it may only allude to the fact that he was the John under whose name the Fourth Gospel was, in popular belief, written. Another is that the word 'revelations' does not refer to the Book of the Revelations, which book was excluded from the canon of the Syrian Church; and that it may well refer in a general descriptive sense to the Gospel. We are well aware that these suggestions are not *imposed* upon us by the language; but they are, at least, *possible*, encountering no inherent unlikelihood. And taken in this sense they lend additional support—for what it is worth—to the view we have taken as to the authorship of the Gospel. (See *Bulletin of the Rylands Library*, vol. 14, pp. 333–39.)

Support of the view that the Gospel was written, not by the Apostle John but by a disciple of his, is found in the anti-Marcionite Prologue to the Fourth Gospel preserved in certain Spanish MSS. of the Vulgate. As long ago as 1901 the late Prof. F. C. Burkitt drew attention to this evidence, declaring that it 'gives the earliest form known to us of a very remarkable theory of the origin of the Fourth Gospel' (*Two Lectures on the Gospels*, p. 94). The theory referred to—the one supported in this Commentary—is that the author was a disciple of John the Apostle, and not the Apostle himself. In 1928 D. Donatien de Bruyne published a careful examination of these Latin Prologues to Mark, Luke, and John, in which he declared that he was 'convinced that they were Roman, anti-Marcionite, and of the second century' (article in *Revue Bénédictine*, 1928, entitled 'Les Plus Anciennes Prologues Latines des Évangiles,' p. 214). This view of these Prologues is now generally accepted by scholars.[1] If we could be certain as to the precise meaning of this Latin Prologue to the Fourth Gospel emanating from the second century, it would be a highly important witness to the precise authorship of the Gospel. Unfortunately the text is corrupt, and this, with the absence of definitive punctua-

[1] For a discussion of these Prologues see *The Expository Times*, Sept. 1936, article by Dr. W. F. Howard.

tion, leaves its exact significance uncertain. Nevertheless, it is sufficiently clear to warrant the conclusion that the Gospel was written by a disciple of John and at the suggestion or 'dictation' of John—the John referred to being, presumably, the Apostle. The following is a translation—the Latin text will be found at p. 491 of *Novum Testamentum Latine*, Wordsworth and White; also at p. viii of the English ed. of the Huck-Lietzmann *Synopsis of the First Three Gospels*: 'The Gospel of John was revealed and given to the churches by John while he was yet in the body, as one Papias by name, bishop of Hierapolis, disciple of John and dear to him, related in the *Exoterica* at the end of the five books, indeed he wrote the Gospel at John's dictation. But Marcion the heretic, when he was disapproved by him because of his wrong opinions, was cast out by John. Indeed this person had brought writings, or letters, to him from the brethren who were in Pontus.' Who is this 'dear disciple' of John? As the Latin stands, he is Papias. The whole text, however, is obscure. Prof. Burkitt suggested that some words had fallen out, and added: 'I should not wonder if in the original form of the statement "the disciple of John and dear to him" referred not to Papias but to the writer of the Gospel.' At least, however, it is clear that this second-century Latin Prologue connects the Gospel with John the Apostle, and attributes the writing of it to a disciple of his.

The presence of two Johns at Ephesus, one a disciple of the other, might very naturally give rise to some of the confusions that attend the tradition on this question of authorship. If we suppose that the author of the Gospel was also the author of the Epistles—a conclusion which commends itself to the linguistic expert as well as to the intelligent layman who is sensitive to literary atmosphere and style—then it may very reasonably be concluded that the writer of them all was John the Elder.

But if we refrain from a dogmatic decision as to the precise identity of the author, there are certain facts which we may confidently declare about him.

In the first place, we conclude that *he was a Jew*. The evidence for this statement is scattered through the Gospel and will be noted in the course of our elucidation. Suffice it here to say that his familiarity with Jewish customs of thought and life, his literary style, and his religious faith, all lead to this conclusion. Speaking of the style of this Gospel, so distinguished a linguistic expert as the late Dr. J. H. Moulton said: 'The Fourth [Gospel] . . . with the Johannine Epistles (which no one with the faintest instinct of style would detach from it) belongs to a writer correct enough in grammar, but simple to baldness, and with no sense of idiom: Greek was with him no mother tongue.' As far as the religious thought of the author is concerned, it is dominated by the conviction, which runs through the Old Testament—namely, that the purpose of the Eternal God is manifest in the events in time. If he is—as seems to us indisputable—in the succession of the 'mystics,' let it be clear that he is a *Hebraic* 'mystic.' Eternity was not sundered from history, but revealed in history. There is no more Jewish writer in the New Testament than the Johannine evangelist. The conclusion of Loisy that the author was 'one converted from paganism,' and 'a master of gnosis rather than an apostle of faith' can, to our own view, be unhesitatingly rejected.[1] One of whom we may confidently say, at least, that he *thought*

[1] See Loisy's *Le Quatrième Évangile* (2nd ed., 1921), p. 66.

in Aramaic—some maintain, indeed, that he *wrote* the original Gospel in Aramaic [1]—whose mind was dominated by that sense of the Divine Presence and Purpose so characteristic of the prophets of Israel, was—we feel convinced—no convert from paganism.

In the second place, *he was a Palestinian Jew.* Here again the evidence for this conclusion is scattered through the Gospel and will be noted at the relevant places in the ensuing exposition. The topographical knowledge, the references to the Temple and its ceremonies, the familiarity with Jewish ideas of the time in Palestine, the understanding of the Old Testament in the original Hebrew, all point to that conclusion.[2] 'The evidence,' said the late Dr. Sanday, 'is overwhelming that the author of the Gospel was a Jew and (as I think) also a Jew of Palestine. The best critics admit this, and it is hardly worth while to stay to prove it' (*Criticism of the Fourth Gospel*, p. 128).

Passing from these conclusions, which we may regard as certain, we come to a third conclusion, which, to the present writer, gives coherence to the whole purpose and thought of the author. This is, that *he may himself very probably have had some contact with Jesus.* We do not maintain, as the late Bishop Westcott so strongly contended a generation ago, that the author was an eye-witness of the whole public Ministry of Jesus. He was not, that is, one of the Twelve. Nevertheless, the statement in the Prologue, 'we beheld his glory,' etc., may very well be expressive of the *personal* experience of the author, as well as of the Apostle John. Now there is one place in the Gospel where he himself may be specifically referred to. In 18^{15}, where he is narrating the story of the ecclesiastical trials of Jesus, he tells us that He was led bound to Annas: he then goes on to write, 'And Simon Peter followed Jesus, and so did *another disciple.* Now that disciple was known unto the high priest and entered in with Jesus into the court of the high priest.' Many commentators have identified this disciple with 'the disciple whom Jesus loved,' for what reason it is difficult to discover. Behind this mysterious reference to 'another disciple,' there may well be a reference to the author himself. If this be so, it supports the suggestion we make, that behind the narrative of the closing scenes in Jerusalem there is the first-hand testimony of the author himself. There is one other place in the Gospel where the author may be directly referring to himself. In the 34th and 35th verses of the 19th chapter, the Revised Version reads: 'Howbeit one of the soldiers with a spear pierced his side, and straightway there came out blood and water. And he that hath seen hath borne witness, and his witness is true: and *he* knoweth that he saith true, that ye also may believe.' The question is: Who is this 'he' referred to in the *latter part* of this attestation? The Greek word used here is ἐκεῖνος, and it is at least possible—Dr. Torrey in his *New Translation of the Four Gospels* regards it as highly probable—that the author

[1] For example, Burney, in *The Aramaic Origin of the Fourth Gospel*; and Torrey, in *The Four Gospels, a New Translation.*

[2] Carpenter (*The Johannine Writings*, p. 257) says that the Evangelist's quotations from the O.T. 'point to a greater familiarity with the books of the Canon than it seems reasonable to ascribe to a Greek convert.' Torrey (*op. cit.*, p. 330) says: '*All* the quotations in this Gospel are from the Hebrew. . . . The quotations are all made from memory, and with the customary freedom of choice and arrangement.'

is here referring to himself. In that case the translation would run; ' And he who saw this testified to it, and his testimony is reliable—and *I myself* know that his word is true—that you also may believe.' Such a use of ἐκεῖνος (*that one*) would correspond to the use of ' one ' in English by some speakers when they speak of themselves—as, for example, ' one says,' or ' one did,' etc. Dr. Torrey's suggestion is that the Aramaic *hahu gabra* was translated by the Greek *ekeinos*: he says that this Aramaic phrase was ' a common Jewish substitute for the pronoun of the first person singular.'[1] The fact, further, that the author was only brought into touch with Jesus during His last days in Jerusalem would give an additional psychological explanation for the absence of any ' Messianic secret ' from the Gospel. One who only personally remembered Jesus when He made full claim to Messianic vocation might very well read the end into the beginning. The fact, further, that he was of priestly family would explain his seeming familiarity with what happened at meetings of the Sanhedrin (7^{45-52}, 11^{47-53}, 12^{1ff}., etc.).

The author was, thus, one belonging to a priestly family, nurtured in the cradle of Jewish sacerdotal influences, and in some way—we know not how—brought to ' the light ' in the fellowship of Jesus. It is tempting to think that woven into the allegorical story of Lazarus in chapter 12 there is a personal experience of the author himself, raised to new life by the Master. If this were so, it would partly explain the central and dramatic place which the author gives to this story. And further, the hypothesis that the author belonged to a priestly family in Jerusalem may help to explain the mysterious reference in the letter of Polycrates, already mentioned, to the John who wore the ' sacerdotal plate.' Polycrates was given to confusing people of the same name: he, for example, confuses Philip the Evangelist with Philip the Apostle. He may, therefore, in speaking of 'John who leaned on the Lord's breast '—have confused him with the John who, on our hypothesis, was of priestly family, settled in Ephesus, was a personal disciple of John the Apostle, and had a position of authority in the Church there. He, it is very conceivable, might have on solemn Christian occasions worn the gold plate which his priestly fathers had worn in the service of the Temple. We ourselves baptise our heirlooms to fresh occasions and to new duties. How much more, one who believed that Jesus fulfilled all that was best in the religious past of his fathers.

Our view as to the author, therefore, places the Gospel in the first century. Such dating, it may be here said, is in accord both with a proper understanding of the Gospel itself, and with the evidence from without. In the Rylands Library in Manchester may be seen what is regarded as ' the earliest known fragment of any part of the New Testament, and probably the earliest witness to the existence of the Gospel according to St. John.' It is a fragment of papyrus found in Egypt, and contains on one side part of verses 31–33 and on the other side part of verses 37–38, of chapter 18 of our Gospel. It belongs—we are assured—to the first half of the second century. If the Gospel was circulating in Egypt in the first half

[1] Even if the Evangelist did not *write* his Gospel in Aramaic, the fact that he *thought* in Aramaic renders the suggestion not impossible. How often have we heard one to whom English was not a native language give a literal translation into our speech of an idiom peculiar to his own language.

of the second century—and Egypt is a far cry from Ephesus—it is safe to say that this fragment supports a date in the first century for the Gospel. (See *An Unpublished Fragment of the Fourth Gospel*, ed. by C. H. Roberts.)

THE AUTHOR'S PURPOSE

We have not to indulge in dubious conjecture as to the author's purpose in writing. He himself tells us what it was. ' Many other signs therefore did Jesus in the presence of the disciples, which are not written in this book: but these are written, that ye may believe that Jesus is the Christ, the Son of God; and that believing ye may have life in His name.' These were probably the last words of the Gospel as the Evangelist, at least originally, intended that it should end. From this statement it is clear that the author was not writing just for his own edification. He was thinking of a specific body of readers; and these were no doubt members of the Christian community. He wished so to tell the story of Jesus that they would be confirmed in their faith in Him, as God's anointed one and God's unique ' son '; and that thus they would know the life which it was His mission to bring. The Evangelist wrote, therefore, under the impulsion of a completely disinterested desire to lead his fellow-Christians to what he believed to be the essential truth about the historic Jesus. He was, in the best sense, an apologist. He had a message to declare about Jesus, and he wished men to know the fullness of ' life in His name.' In other words, he had the mind of an evangelist. He believed that he had ' Good Tidings ' to declare: his work was to be a ' Gospel.' Every other motive of the author was subservient to this central purpose. He had, as we shall go on to maintain, certain very characteristic qualities of mind; but all these were pervaded and directed by his missionary zeal. He sat down to write no argumentative theological treatise, nor to set forth a dispassionate philosophical discussion. Those who have no sympathy with this dominating purpose of the author, cannot hope to understand his book. Community of heart and mind will alone open his book to us.

This deliberate design dictated what he chose to say, and, partly, how he chose to say it. He might have recorded, as he says, ' many other signs '; but such an addition was unnecessary to his purpose. His Gospel, both in substance and in plan, was inspired by his deliberate design. Convinced that Jesus had a unique knowledge of the Eternal Father and that He had a unique Divine vocation to fulfil, the Evangelist wrote as the prophet of the Master's own Message.

THE AUTHOR'S CHARACTERISTICS OF MIND

One may, however, be in sympathetic appreciation with an author's dominating purpose, but without understanding of his qualities of mind. It is therefore necessary to elucidate the mental and spiritual characteristics of the Fourth Evangelist, so far as they are revealed to us in his Gospel.

(*a*) A Mind of Genius

The most obvious fact about the author is that he is a man of transcendent genius. His intellect soars, like the eagle in its flight. He who wrote this Gospel wrote one of the great books of the world. Approached without any prepossessions, it is seen to have upon it the stamp of a profound and original mind. It opens up to the reader new and wide vistas. Like a great work of music, it chastens and cleanses the spirit. The only possible answer to any who protest that they cannot see or feel this greatness, is—*It's there.* The truth of what some will regard as the 'hard' saying of Pascal is inescapable: 'The more mind we have, the more do we observe men of original mind: it is your commonplace people that find no difference between one man and another.'

(*b*) A Unitive Mind

Now whatever else a work of genius is, or is not, it is a unity. No book is truly great which does not convey the impression of wholeness. In a play of Shakespeare, for example, the various parts, the heterogeneous characters, are all somehow blended by the mysterious alchemy of a transcendent mind to form a coherent unity. Artistic or philosophic genius creates the one out of the many. The Fourth Evangelist does this. His Gospel is pervaded by one atmosphere. Like Bach, the more he changes his subjects the more he is the same. At whatever page we open the Gospel, we cannot mistake the pervasive quality of the writer's mind. Here is a book which is at the farthest possible remove from a *catena* of extracts. Like Shakespeare, and other great writers, he no doubt depended upon others for much of his material: but materials do not make a book, just as canvas, palette, brush and paints do not make an artist, or a bat and ball a cricketer. A mind of creative and artistic genius is here.

(*c*) A Dramatic Mind

Further, his mind was dramatic. He saw things in sharp outline, and in very distinct colours. His opening words at once reveal this positive and dramatic quality of mind. 'In the beginning was the Word, and the Word was with God, and the Word was Divine.' This is not a philosophic setting forth of a thesis to be carefully examined, elaborated, and proved. It is the emphatic assertion of a conclusion which pervades the whole Gospel that is to follow. The author does not write to clarify his mind; he writes to tell what he has seen, and what he believes.

The nature of the antitheses reveals this same dramatic quality of mind. Light is throughout contending with Darkness, Truth with Falsehood. Sharp distinctions are everywhere. Historical figures like Judas, the ecclesiastical rulers, and Pilate, are so presented as almost to personify all those qualities of mind and character which set themselves to combat Jesus. We misunderstand the nature of the Evangelist's mind if we ask, 'Was Judas *wholly* treacherous, were the ecclesiastical leaders *all* bitter opponents of Jesus, was Pilate *only* a vacillator?' Perceiving the dramatic character of the author's mind and method, we shall draw the necessary deductions when we seek to estimate the precise historical value of his portraitures. We know that life does not present us with quite the sharpness of distinctions that we find in this Gospel: and the author was as much aware of this fact as we are. He is concerned with essential qualities of mind, and when he sees these revealed in those who are opposed to Jesus, he does not find it necessary to set forth any counterbalancing factors in the whole psychological situation. If we remember this characteristic of his mind, we shall be assisted to a true understanding of the many ' polemical ' references to ' the Jews ' which occasion so much difficulty to many readers, otherwise sympathetic with the Evangelist's mind.

When he speaks of ' the Jews,' he no more means *all* the Jews than did those who in the respective warring nations in 1914–1918, when they wrote of reprehensible deeds perpetrated by ' the Germans,' ' the British,' ' the French ' or ' the Italians '—as the case might be—mean *all* the Germans, or *all* the British, or *all* the French, or *all* the Italians. This is the first point to remember. The second point to remember is this dramatic quality of mind of the Evangelist, and his profound and intuitive sympathy with the mind of Jesus. He does not ' hate ' the Jews; but he ' hates ' their hate. To him, ' the Jews ' symbolised the Darkness which hated the Light, the ' sons of the devil ' who hated the Son of the Father. He hated the hatred which so many of the ecclesiastical and religious leaders manifested to Jesus. This ' hatred ' was an inversion of his ' love ' of the truth and the light, as they were revealed in Him who was the Truth and the Light. His was a love, quick in its insight, vehement in its intensity, throbbing with moral passion. His ' love ' and ' hate ' were of the kind of which Tennyson speaks:

Dowered with the hate of hate, the scorn of scorn,
The love of love.

The third point to remember is the Evangelist's insight into the intrinsic value of man—an insight derived from Jesus Himself. Thus his ' polemic ' is, as we have said elsewhere, ' a dramatising polemic begotten of an insight into the essential significance of man. The dramatic genius of the author has overleapt itself, and so can be read, by those unsympathetic with his mind, as indicating an exclusiveness in the gospel and spirit of Jesus. Such a reading of the Gospel, however, should be corrected by a reading of the Gospel in its entirety. The light shines upon all, but all do not see it. The very fierceness of these seemingly polemical passages springs from the overmastering insight that no man is saved in spite of himself, that the reception of truth has its human conditions. These conditions are fulfilled in those who realise their own utter need ; they never can be fulfilled in those who are self-seeking, in those who esteem cleverness above insight, in those who are ecclesiastics before they are truthful men. All this has come from Jesus Himself, but it shines upon us in this Gospel, through a medium which distorts it because of the very intensity of the author's sympathy with it—a distortion which, doubtless, was also partly occasioned by the bitter polemical situation through which the Church had passed.' [1]

This dramatic quality of mind is very vividly revealed in the *dialogues* of the Gospel. Let the reader consider, for example, the discourse with Nicodemus in chapter 3, or that with the Woman of Samaria in chapter 4, or that with the Jews at Capernaum in chapter 6. He will see a similarity of dramatic presentation which obviously owes a great deal to the author's own mind. There is in each case an appropriate setting, then a declaration by Jesus of some great spiritual truth, then a resultant misunderstanding or denial, and then, finally, a fuller elucidation by Jesus of His message. These dramatic dialogues remind

[1] *The Meaning and Message of the Fourth Gospel*, pp. 230–231.

us in some respects of that form of dramatic and dialogic presentation of which the Book of Job is the outstanding illustration in literature—a book issuing, let us remember, from the same race as the Fourth Gospel. For one of the best illustrations in the Gospel of this dramatic character of the author's mind, the reader may be referred to the closing verses of chapter 6. This passage, and kindred dramatic passages, we discuss in the body of the Commentary.

The more we study this Gospel the more we see that it has many of the characteristics of a great drama. The present commentator has been tempted to analyse it into Scenes and Acts; but that, perhaps, would be to create a false impression in the minds of many readers. Nevertheless, the Gospel reads like great drama. The sense of inevitability broods over the whole. Through recognitions and refusals, acceptances and oppositions, the Gospel reaches the predestined end. It is our purpose to maintain that this sense of inevitability is not just the creation of the dramatic and artistic mind of the author; it is his *transcription* of that brooding and trustful sense of Divine destiny which belonged to the inner consciousness of Jesus.

(*d*) An Intuitive and 'Mystical' Mind

Further, his mind was of what we may call the intuitive character. He was known in the early centuries as a 'theologos,' but it would be a mistake to regard him, at least without qualification, as a 'theologian.' There are theologians *and* theologians. Often to-day a 'theologian' is regarded, primarily, as one whose task is to think coherently about Christianity as a system of Doctrines which have come down through the centuries. As a result, the 'theological temper' of mind is conceived of as primarily intellectual, and, since the theologian has something vital to defend, as almost necessarily pugnacious. This quality of mind explains that byword of history, the 'odium theologicum.'

Augustine, in a very famous saying, declared, however, that 'it is the *heart* that makes the theologian.' He knew very well, of course, that the 'heart' cannot be sundered from the 'head,' without the death of both; but what he wished there to assert was, that without the religious quickening of the whole depth of a man's mind he will not make the true theologian.

Now in this sense the author of the Fourth Gospel can be justly called a 'theologian'—but only in this sense. We have called him a 'true apologist,' but his Gospel has few of the characteristics belonging to the extensive literature known as 'apologetics'—a literature of which it was truly said by R. H. Hutton that it was 'as a rule the most depressing and disheartening of all religious literature' (*Theological Essays*, p. 168). There is nothing in St. John to suggest as a sub-title to the book, 'Christianity defensively stated.' The author felt too deeply, and saw too vividly, to write in an argumentative manner. It is usually those who do not themselves see who argue pugnaciously. Contentious vehemence often cloaks a division in the mind. Those who 'protest too much' usually see too little. There is a quality of serene and positive directness in the writing of the seer; and this, as it is easy to understand, both irritates and tantalises the purely rationalistic mind, whether of the left or of the right.

A lack of understanding of this quality of mind has led to the dogmatic theologian's fundamental mistake with this Gospel. He has sought to find himself in it. That is, regarding certain dogmatic statements as essential to Christianity, he has read this same attitude of mind into the Evangelist. The Gospel thus became a *catena* of 'proof-texts.' The author came to be regarded as the father of metaphysical theology. Even those unsympathetic with this hard and rigid type of theology have acquiesced in such a misreading of the Evangelist. And, in their rebellion, they have declared him as largely responsible for the transmutation of the ethical and spiritual emphasis of Jesus into a speculative system of human thought, by assenting to which, it was held, salvation and eternal life are to be found.

The author's mind was positive, but not, in the theological or ecclesiastical sense, dogmatic. His Gospel, as it has been well said, 'betrays no intellectual interest in ideas or definition as such, apart from personal influences' (R. H. Hutton, in *Theological Essays*, p. 193). His language is more akin to poetry than to science, more expressive of direct insight than of elaborated reasoning. For this reason he creates: he does not systematise. 'St. John,' as it has been well said, 'has no liking for progress along an unending straight road; he loves a circling flight, like his symbol, the eagle. There is something hovering and brooding about his production; repetitions are in no wise abnormal with him.'[1] It is for this reason that his Gospel is misunderstood by those of 'systematic' mind. They cannot, or will not, understand that his thought comes by flashes of insight, not by the laboured process of orderly thought. The failure to understand how such a mind works has led, we believe, to many of the ingenious hypotheses of 'displacements' with which the labours of the last generation of critical students have made us so familiar. It is a mistake, for example, to look for an orderly advance in the thought of the Gospel in the 'discourses' recorded. These 'discourses' are really all concerned with the same few issues. The controversies of the Gospel are all, in a sense, but different aspects of the one controversy—the conflict of Light with Darkness, and Good with Evil. The opponents of Jesus are all, in a sense, the same opponents. It is imperative to remember this, when, for example, we seek to arrive at a just judgement on the order of chapters 5, 6, and 7. It does not follow that, because we can achieve a more orderly and systematic presentation of the teaching of Jesus by one of our suggested transpositions, therefore we have reached the Evangelist's own order of presentation. Let us beware of making the Evangelist as 'clever' as ourselves. (For a fuller elucidation of such considerations we refer the reader to page 765 of the Commentary.) This intuitive, and unsystematic, quality of mind confers a crystalline character upon the Evangelist's work. What he has felt and seen with confidence he tells; and, for this reason, he is able to quicken vision in receptive and sympathetic readers. What is 'poetic creation,' asked Carlyle in his book, *Heroes and Hero Worship*, 'but seeing the thing sufficiently?' In submitting such a creation as the Fourth Gospel to analytical scrutiny, we imperil its spirit. A poet, let us remember, is not understood by a pedestrian process of dissecting his verses.

[1] Deissmann, in *Light from the Ancient East*, p. 401.

This intuitive quality of mind enables the author to penetrate to the *significant*. He becomes sensitive to the essential. In a second-rate writer the significant and the insignificant keep jostling each other, till the reader's mind, like the author's, becomes confused. This Evangelist's mind was akin to that of the artist in Balzac's *Unknown Masterpiece*, who said: 'Perhaps one ought not to draw a single line; perhaps it would be better to attack the face from the centre, taking the highest prominences first, proceeding from them to the whole range of shadows to the heaviest of all.'

(*e*) An Allegorising Mind

Allied to these dramatic and intuitive qualities, there is what we may call a certain 'allegorising' strain in the author's mind. The precise extent of allegory in this Gospel is a highly debatable question; but its presence is indisputable. While it is necessary to repudiate the facile theory that his Gospel is allegory and nothing but allegory, it is also necessary to maintain that an unmistakable symbolical quality of mind throughout finds expression. It is here, perhaps, that the scientific Western mind finds it most difficult to reach a sympathetic understanding of the mind of the author. It is difficult in the West to believe that anyone could write in the language of fact and *himself* realise that he was writing in the language of metaphor or symbol. If authors in the West write allegories—such as *The Pilgrim's Progress* or *Gulliver's Travels*—they make it quite clear that they are not writing history. The reader is left in no doubt that the *whole* of what he is reading is allegory, and is not confronted with the perplexing task of distinguishing in the same book the historical from the allegorical. Here in this Gospel, however, we see revealed an obviously historical intention, with, at least in places, an obviously allegorical method. It is this intermingling of historical intention with dramatic and allegorical method which makes the author's mind so much of a riddle to Western minds. We find it difficult to understand a mind which can weave a symbolical weft into a historical warp. But this is precisely what the author does.

Illustrations of this 'allegorical weft,' as we venture to call it, are scattered through the Gospel: they are noted in the body of the Commentary. There is, for example, an unmistakable symbolism in the use of *numbers*. The 'five husbands' of the 'Woman of Samaria' is a clear instance of allegorism: so also is the 'thirty and eight years' of the infirmity of the man at the pool of Bethesda: so also is the 'one hundred and fifty and three' fishes referred to in the Epilogue. It is not by accident that the Evangelist includes *seven* 'signs' in his portraiture of Jesus. These allegorical 'signs' we discuss later in this Introduction, and also, in greater detail, in the body of the Commentary. From the very nature of the case, one cannot always be quite sure how far he merely *reads* allegory into historical traditions, how far he *alters* such traditions in the interests of symbolism, and how far he is, what we may call *creatively* allegorical. There are instances of all three attitudes in the Gospel. He will *use* a traditional setting, he will *adapt* it, and he will *create* a setting of his own—in each case seeking a suitable frame for the delineation of the spiritual truth incarnate in Jesus.

That Jesus Himself allegorised inner spiritual experiences is clear to every intelligent reader of the Synoptic Gospels. The most striking illustration of this is the story of the Temptation. The record as we have it must have been derived from Jesus Himself, inasmuch as none of the disciples was with Him at the time. And it is clear that in speaking to them of His inner conflict in the wilderness He gave vivid symbolical form to His rejection of the enticements suggested by the nationalistic and apocalyptic Messianic hopes of His day. This symbolical frame has, in all ages, been unimaginatively and literally regarded; with the result that readers have thought that Jesus felt He had the power to turn 'stones' into 'bread,' or that He really thought He might throw His body from the pinnacle of the Temple without physical injury. Or, again, when He spoke of 'casting' a 'mountain' into the sea, a little common sense, conjoined with a modicum of the historical and psychological imagination, will make clear the spiritual truth which Jesus was thus expressing. It may well be, further, that a good deal of the vivid apocalyptic language of the Gospels should be read in the light of this symbolical quality of the mind of Jesus.

In any case, it is clear that in respect of this allegorising quality of mind the Fourth Evangelist is in the line of Him whom he sought to portray. If Jesus Himself dramatised and allegorised the inner meaning of His experiences, why should it be thought a thing incredible that this author, who had drunk so deeply of His spirit, should have done the same?

Such a quality of mind was common in the Hebrew race to which Jesus and the Evangelist belonged. The Old Testament abounds in metaphor and symbol. 'Hebrew,' as it was said by an Old Testament interpreter of rare insight, the late Prof. R. H. Kennett, 'is essentially a language of poetry rather than of dogma.' [1] The first chapters of Genesis, for example, at once take us into the realm of symbolic narrative. The story of Creation is told with the vividness of an incident that might have happened before the writer's eyes. Instead of a metaphysical dissertation on a First Cause, we have a figurative story of God 'speaking' the universe into being. 'God said, Let there be light: and there was light.' The obtuseness of the Western mind is evidenced by the many irrelevant endeavours that have been made to interpret the 'days' of this Creation story as if they were meant by the writer to represent precise periods of time. The narrative of the 'Fall' is as obviously symbolical. The sacrificial rites of the Hebrews, likewise, reveal symbolism, the most notable, perhaps, being the rites of the Day of Atonement. Or, again, when a Hebrew says, 'the blood is the life,' he obviously means 'the blood *represents* the life.' The Prophets were always using metaphors and symbolism to set forth their moral and spiritual teaching. Isaiah, for example, begins his prophecies with the most varied use of metaphor and simile—vineyards, gardens of cucumbers, a besieged city, scarlet sins, burning tow. An extended elucidation of metaphor and allegory in the Old Testament is, of course, outside the scope of our work. But it is essential to those who would understand the mind of the Johannine author that they remember how naturally Hebrew writers expressed themselves in this wise.

[1] *The Church of Israel*, p. 193.

C. THE MEANING OF THE GOSPEL

What light have these characteristics of mind to throw upon the meaning of this Gospel—its meaning, that is, to the author himself? The body of the Commentary contains, of course, our detailed elucidation of this meaning. But here a more summary statement is called for, so that the reader, in approaching the Commentary, may know the main conclusions which have controlled the interpretation of details. Further, it is necessary to show how this 'meaning' meets what we have called 'the Problem' raised by this Gospel.

NOT PRECISE BIOGRAPHY

It will be clear at once that the Gospel is not a precise biography of Jesus. Indeed, in none of our Gospels have we anything corresponding to a modern biography. Like the authors of all ancient 'Lives,' the Evangelists were indifferent to the claims of scientific history. The Fourth Evangelist, with the qualities of mind we have noted, would be least of all the New Testament writers concerned with anything in the nature of an exact and complete biography of Jesus. A *unitive* mind makes the parts subservient to the whole. A *dramatic* mind heightens contrasts in order to set in vivid outline the portraiture of the central figure. An *intuitive* mind penetrates to the inner secret of his hero. A *symbolical* mind clothes eternal truth in the drapings of parabolic narrative.

We have already seen how the Evangelist did not himself think he was writing a historical or chronological narrative. Nor did he think that he was penning the precise words of Jesus in the 'discourses' of this Gospel. Here, again, it is necessary for the reader to exercise the historical imagination. He should remember, for example, that it was common to writers of antiquity to record the *substance of the thought* of historical characters in the form of what we call 'oratio recta.' Hebrew writers did not say that someone 'thought' a certain thing: instead, they express the *thought* of the person by placing upon his lips precise words which *mean* this thought. The Old Testament is full of illustrations of such a custom. The Hebrew way, for example, of saying that God created the universe was: '*God said*, Let there be light,' etc.: where no intelligent person will suppose that the author thought that God uttered these precise words. Again, in the story of Jacob's meeting with Esau in Gen. 32, the author records the unspoken thought of Jacob, when confronted with the inevitable meeting, thus: '*For he said*, I will appease him with the present that goeth before me, and afterward I will see his face; peradventure he will accept me' (Gen. 32^{20}). Again, in the narrative of the solitary Moses at the burning bush, the author expresses the *thought* of Moses thus: 'And Moses said, I will turn aside now, and see this great sight, why the bush is not burnt' (Exod. 3^{3}). Again, in the story of the departure of the Israelites from Egypt, the narrator writes: 'And it came to pass, when Pharaoh had let the people go, that God led them not by the way of the land of the Philistines, although that was near; *for God said*, Lest peradventure the people repent when they see war, and they return to Egypt' (Exod. 13^{17}). Again, we find the common expression in the Prophets, 'Thus saith the Lord,' with a record of precise words following: it is obvious that the prophet is thus giving expression to what he believes to be the *Mind* of God. It is needless to illustrate further what must be evident to all who are familiar with the Old Testament Scriptures.

A characteristic, in some respects similar, is found in classical literature. A familiar illustration is that of Plato's *Dialogues*. In them Socrates takes part in dialogues with various representative people, and expresses his thought with directness and precision. It is, however, clear that Plato did not think he was recording the very words of Socrates: at most he was conveying in dialogic form the central thoughts of the master.

Such illustrations will assist a modern reader to approach the ' discourses ' of Jesus in the Fourth Gospel with an understanding mind. He will be in a position to understand why it is that the Evangelist records the utterances of Jesus in the same style as his own reflections. He will see that while the author is seeking to unfold the inmost thought of Jesus, he is giving that thought a form, characteristic of his own mental qualities and aptitudes. At all times he seeks to be completely loyal to the mind of Jesus Himself; but his loyalty is that of the reflective disciple with a mind of his own, not the slavish loyalty of a Boswell recording the utterances of Samuel Johnson. It is this fact which makes it so difficult to decide what sayings of Jesus recorded in this Gospel were His exact words. In the body of the Commentary we shall note the numerous parallels in the Synoptic Gospels to the Johannine sayings of Jesus. This fact supports the authenticity of our Lord's teaching in John. We shall also note many sayings to which the Synoptists give us no precise parallel, but which are *en rapport* with the Synoptic teaching. This fact supports the view, expressed in 1901 by the late Prof. F. C. Burkitt, that ' the Fourth Gospel enshrines many true words of the Lord which would otherwise have been lost to us ' (*Two Lectures on the Gospels*, p. 71). Even so, however, the Evangelist's own mind is clearly manifest throughout in his presentation of the mind of Jesus. He does not hesitate, for example, to give to the ' sayings ' of Jesus a dramatic setting which may, like the platinum, act as a foil to the diamond: not does he hesitate to give dialogic form to the central issues which divided the mind of Jesus from the minds of His adversaries.

ESSENTIAL BIOGRAPHY

But though the Gospel is not a precise biography it is, what we may venture to call, essential biography. Here it is necessary to remember that a detailed, chronological record of everything a man said and did would by no means constitute a ' Life ' of him. A man's own *life* is a vital entity: therefore, what we call a ' Life ' must convey the impression of dynamic thought, emotion, and activity. A biography is most ' true ' when it enables us to discern the directing mind of its hero; in other words, when it assists us to enter the inner sanctuary of his whole consciousness. We know not any man if we know not something of that.

Plutarch began his ' Life ' of Alexander with a paragraph in which he set forth a kind of *apologia* for selective and intuitive biography. ' It being my purpose to write the lives of Alexander the king, and of Cæsar, by whom Pompey was destroyed, the multitude of their great actions affords so large a field that I were to blame if I should not by way of apology forewarn my reader that I have chosen rather to epitomize the most celebrated parts of their story, than to insist at large on every particular circumstance of it. It must be borne in mind that my design is not to write histories, but lives. . . . Therefore as portrait-painters are more exact in the lines and features of the face, in which the character is seen, than in the other parts of the body, so I must be allowed to give my more particular attention to the marks and indications of the souls of men.'

In seeking to analyse the mind of this author, as we have done, we have been seeking, in a measure, to read his consciousness. What we now seek to say, is that he himself when he wrote this Gospel was seeking to read and to portray the essential mind of Jesus. We have ventured elsewhere to describe this Evangelist as ' the historian of the consciousness of Jesus.'

That the author was in a position to be such a ' historian,' has already been maintained. He knew the Synoptic Gospels. He was, we believe, a disciple of John the Apostle in Ephesus—the favourite disciple, as we like to think, of the revered luminary of the Ephesian Church. He had himself, we have further suggested, known Jesus in Jerusalem in the closing weeks of His ministry there—perhaps owing his own moral and spiritual quickening to that encounter. His Gospel, therefore, is not to be regarded as, primarily, an ' ecclesiastical ' or ' theological ' document, controlled and dominated by the practical and speculative situation which existed when he wrote. It is primarily a very *personal* document, and is the expression of a penetrating insight into the mind of the historic Jesus. Into the mind of the Master he, by the very qualities of his own mind, saw more deeply than did the Synoptic writers. Whatever *more* the mind of Jesus was, it also was unitive, dramatic, intuitive, and symbolical. Jesus was often misunderstood, even by His intimate disciples: He was least misunderstood by the Johannine seer. To correct an imperfect appreciation on the part of the Synoptic writers of the interior, spiritual depth of the teaching of Jesus was, we cannot but think, one of his motives in writing. It was not that he saw what they did not: it was that he saw clearly what they saw fitfully. It was not that he sat down to write more correct ' history ' than they had done: it was that he wished to write a truer ' Life.' No more could we, or would we, dispense with the Synoptic Gospels, than the Fourth Evangelist would have dispensed—or did dispense—with them. The first three Gospels give the necessary background for a just appreciation of the Fourth Gospel. Without them we should be without many a realistic incident and many a searching ethical word, which are essential to the understanding of the mind of Jesus, in its entirety. But it is in the light of the conscious relation of Jesus to the Father—the burden of the Fourth Evangelist's message—that the inner meaning of the Synoptic narratives is discerned. The mission and message of Jesus then fall into place in the unity of His life: the motive-spring of all His words and acts stands revealed. The fount, whence flows the stream of all His ministries, gleams before our eyes, like the pool, clear and deep, on the summit of the hills.

Clement of Alexandria, in an oft-quoted passage preserved by Eusebius from the lost *Hypotyposes*, speaking of the writing of our Gospel says: ' John, last of all, perceiving that what had reference to the body in the Gospel of our Saviour was sufficiently detailed, and being urged by his familiar friends, urged also by the Spirit, wrote a *spiritual Gospel*.' If we may call this Gospel, in contrast to the Synoptic Gospels, a 'spiritual' Gospel, it is because the author has more deeply appreciated the spiritual source of the unexampled life. Here was One, our Evangelist knew, to whom God was *the* Reality. And it was because he saw this fact with such intuitive, direct penetration, that it is the beginning, middle, and end of his book.

This will not, of course, be taken to mean that the Gospel does not reflect the ecclesiastical and theological situation in the Evangelist's day. In respect of a number of issues, as we hope to show, it very clearly does reflect this situation. Certain tendencies of thought and practice in the Church he sought to correct: and to correct tendencies presupposes a knowledge of tendencies. Further, no mind that is really alive can write without reflecting the intellectual and institutional environment. But it is one thing to *reflect* an environment, it is another thing to be *dominated* by it. The prophet never allows himself to drift in the stream of prevailing thoughts and customs. It is his very function to see more deeply than his contemporaries, to emphasise and bring to light those eternal inner truths which are in danger of being obscured by dogmatic and institutional embodiments. Thus, the Johannine prophet sought to recall the Church of his day to the mind and message of Jesus.

The clue to what some have called the 'incompatibilities' between the Johannine portrait of Jesus and that of the Synoptists is to be mainly found in this fact. These differences are seen in their just proportions, when our author's central insight and concern are remembered.

The main difference is one more of *emphasis* than of content. On the one hand, the Fourth Evangelist states, as definitely as the Synoptists, that Jesus was subject to characteristic human experiences—see 4^{6}, 11^{35}, 13^{21}, 19^{28}. On the other hand, there is hardly anything said by him of the Divine consciousness of Jesus which cannot be paralleled in the other Gospels. But while the *total impression* left by the first three Gospels upon the reader's mind is that Jesus, whatever else He was, was truly a man, the *total impression* left by this Gospel on the mind is that Jesus had a unique Divine consciousness. The one does not deny what the others maintain, nor maintain what the others deny. The consciousness of the Father's Presence and the Father's Mission are, for example, as clearly revealed in the famous Q passage—Mt. 11^{25-27}; Lk. 10^{21-22}—as in the transcendent claims of Jesus in the Fourth Gospel, if these latter be rightly understood. The 'authority' with which Jesus speaks in the Synoptic discourses points to such a consciousness of God as the Fourth Evangelist emphasises throughout his Gospel.

Other differences between the Fourth Gospel and the others are to be rightly understood in the light of the Evangelist's own religious history and of his personal qualities of mind. A Jerusalemite disciple would be expected, for example, to say more about the witness of Jesus in Jerusalem than about the witness in Galilee. This is precisely what he does. He does not *deny* the considerable Galilean ministry of Jesus: indeed, his narrative presupposes it. As likewise the Synoptic Gospels in various places indicate a considerable ministry of Jesus in Jerusalem, which, however, they do not record. But the author knew the

Jerusalem situation *from the inside.* It was there, he knew, that the final issues were revealed. It was there that the tensions and antagonisms, involved in the Ministry of Jesus, were focused. He himself had, as we believe, felt those tensions in the depth of his own heart and mind. Not lightly would one who was of a priestly family place himself in opposition to the mind of his class. When as an old man he looked back on those early days of tension in Jerusalem, he saw more clearly, and felt more deeply, the nature of the issues at stake than he had then done. He knew that the real, the final, issue—seen from the standpoint of men and of time—which led to the Crucifixion, was the religious claim, involved in the religious consciousness, of Jesus. That was why he set this claim, and this consciousness, in the clearest possible light. That was why he was indifferent to the stages in the development of this claim, and this consciousness. And so he placed at the beginning of the Ministry, instead of at the end, the incident of the cleansing of the Temple: wishing at once to focus the thought of the reader on the unique, authoritative claim implied in the whole teaching of Jesus. From the standpoint of strict historical sequence, the Synoptists were, in both these issues, undoubtedly right. That Jesus came to fuller, and deeper, insight into the Divine Will for Him in the course of His advancing Ministry may be taken for certainty—even though the 'stages' in this 'development' must always be recognised as 'the secret' of Jesus Himself, and therefore only to be pondered with a measure of diffident reverence. Even the Synoptic Gospels give us no sufficient means for the tracing of this 'development': though they suggest that Cæsarea Philippi is a very important stage. The Fourth Evangelist, however, portrays the beginning in the light of what he knew to be the end. Jesus, he would say, *was* what He became. The tree is known by the fruit it bears.

It is along these lines that we can appreciate the 'I am' passages already referred to. They should, probably, be regarded as dramatic declarations of the Master's consciousness. What matters, the Evangelist saw, was *what Jesus knew Himself to be in the depth of His mind.* Jesus knew Himself to be a mediator of Light, of Truth, of Food, of Water, of Life to men. And so these 'I am' passages may be taken as the dramatisation of the author's insight into the inner sense of mission possessed by Jesus.

AN ELLIPSE WITH TWO FOCI

The Gospel therefore may be regarded as an ellipse with two foci. It is, that is, the curve described by a mind equally firmly held to two fixed points. One is the Historic Jesus: the other is the Eternal Father. The message of the Gospel is that the Historic Jesus is the unique revelation of God in time and place. The author has not himself invented this message. Nor is it just his own 'experience,' or even the 'experience' of the Church of his day. The main thing the author wished to say is that this message is involved in the whole mind and mission of Jesus. It is He Himself who is the truth uniting earth and heaven. It is He Himself who speaks the Father's Word, He Himself who does the Father's deed. The author is as much concerned to say that Jesus was the Father's own Act as to say that the Father was the Reality known to Jesus. The whole Gospel is instinct with Eternity. It is history viewed *sub specie æternitatis.* 'No one hath seen God at any time: the only begotten Son . . . he hath declared Him.'

THE HISTORICAL SITUATION CONFRONTING THE AUTHOR

We have left to the last part of this section on the 'Meaning of the Gospel' the question of the specific historical situation confronting the Evangelist. We have done this in the interests of perspective. For, as we have already maintained, the historical situation by no means dominated his thought—as, indeed, it never dominates any truly great and original mind. Those who write about this Gospel as if it is to be 'explained,' either by the literature of its day, or by the movements of its time, are singularly forgetful of one of the main facts which history unfolds to us. This is, that the man of genius preserves his identity of mind amid the battalions of competing interests, motives, books, and institutions which surround him. Such a fact should make the interpreter less ready to read the thoughts of others into the Gospel, and more ready to perceive how the author's own original mind controls the environing situation.

Some interpretations of this Gospel, based primarily upon an endeavour to understand the complexities of the life of the Church at the time, and not primarily upon an endeavour to understand the obvious transcendent genius of the author, see in it an attempted blending of various tendencies. The author, to this point of view, was continually trying to find a place within the system of his thought for opposing types of belief and practice. In one place in his Gospel, he is seen as a somewhat narrow ecclesiastic, holding that only those within the ecclesiastical institution can be partakers of salvation. In another place, he is seen as a spiritual prophet, who recognises that the mission of Jesus transcends all divisions of sect or race. In one place, again, he is seen as the father of all theological dogmatists, declaring that the only gateway to Life is by intellectual assent to some credal statement. In another place, he is seen as one who believes that moral fidelity and spiritual insight are the only gateway to the Kingdom. The author thus becomes a kind of psychological monstrosity: his mind the home of unreconciled and contending beliefs. Nothing, however, is clearer to a true psychological exegesis than that the Gospel is a coherent and unified presentation. However varied the tendencies in the Church, the author had reached his own profound and serene mental, moral, and spiritual position.

Yet there are features of the situation confronting the author in the Church of his time which *colour* his own presentation of the Gospel. The *main* issue which confronted him—apart from *subsidiary* issues such as Miracle, Apocalyptic, and Sacramental theory, on which we speak later—was the central issue with which in every age Christian thinkers have to deal. It was: How is Eternity related to time, and God to man? This issue comes to a head in Christianity, which claims that there has been a unique revelation, act, incarnation, of the Eternal God in the historic person of Jesus the Christ. The age-long endeavours of Christian thinkers has been to reach some statement which would make coherent such a declaration. The Church of the author's own day was coming to be acutely and forcibly confronted with this issue. And the Fourth Gospel is the Johannine seer's answer to it.

A full and detailed statement of the way in which the issue had been confronted, from the creation of the first Christian community in Jerusalem up to the closing decade of the first century, when the Evangelist wrote, would require a treatise. Here, however, let us try to see the situation in broad outline.

For a generation following the death of Jesus the tradition of His life and teaching had been somewhat precariously dependent upon oral testimony and upon some incidental written accounts of the Master's sayings and deeds. During this period the Apostle Paul, who was responsible for the founding of many of the scattered churches, had directed the main emphasis of his teaching to a message about the heavenly Christ. This emphasis of Paul is naturally explicable. In the first place, he had probably not himself seen Jesus in the flesh. In the second place, the outstanding fact of his *Christian* life was a spiritual experience on the Damascus road. The writing and dissemination of the Synoptic Gospels, with their emphasis on the Jesus of history, would tend to correct any danger that to some might be inherent in the teaching of an Apostle who had not himself known this Jesus. The main emphasis of Paul's Gospel was a *faith, centred on Christ as its objective basis*. The main emphasis of the Synoptic Gospels was *the faith of the historic Jesus Himself*. How were these two emphases to be related? That constituted a real problem in the last decade of the first century—as, indeed, it still does. One way of meeting the perplexity was the Gnostic way. There are evidences of rudimentary Gnosticism in the New Testament. Our Johannine author himself tells us of its existence. There were, he knew, those who were proclaiming that Jesus Christ had not come in the flesh—in other words, that the Eternal Mind of God had not been revealed in one who was truly bone of our bone and flesh of our flesh (see 1 Jn. 4^7; 2 Jn. *v.* 7). This Gnosticism, or Docetism, sought to deny the historical humanity of Jesus in the interests of a speculative mysticism.

Now the Johannine author, with the characteristics of mind we have noted, was uniquely in a position to meet this perplexity. He had, as we saw, a twofold emphasis. His thought was centred on the historic Jesus, but at the same time oriented to the Eternity of God. By his recognition and unswerving assertion of the Eternal *in* the consciousness of the historic Jesus, he lifted it above the realm of the mere flux of history. His Gospel was a Gospel *of God*—he knew that there was no 'Gospel' at all unless it was God's own Gospel: but it was a Gospel of God *incarnate in a real man*. Only through man's *consciousness* can the Eternal God be *known*. And what he maintains from the beginning of his work to the end, is that in one truly human consciousness God has been uniquely known: in one truly human life God Himself has uniquely lived: in the Mission that was fulfilled by One in time the Purpose of the Eternal Father was itself uniquely proclaimed. The Divine had declared itself in the human, the abiding in the transitory. The Eternal Word had become flesh in the person of Jesus. This was the message of the author's Prologue, as it was the declaration with which he began his first Epistle (1 Jn. 1^{1-3}). It is the central meaning of the whole Gospel.

D. SOME MAIN THEMES

In the body of the Commentary the main thoughts of the Evangelist are elucidated, in each case where the context demands it. It seems well, however, to state here in a more summary manner our interpretation of the Gospel on five main issues.

1. *CHRISTOLOGY*

What is called ' Christology ' means a reasoned statement of the relation of the Historic Jesus to the Eternal God: or, more positively, of how Jesus has for Christians ' the value and reality of God.' Strictly speaking, there is no reasoned or systematic Christology in this Gospel. It was written, as we have stated, not by a metaphysician but by a prophet. Christological discussion moves in the realm of abstract speculation; this Evangelist's thought moves in the realm of concrete, experienced reality. Every characteristic of his mind which we have noted fortifies the judgement that the Gospel is primarily a work, not of theology, but of religion.

It is at this point that the interpretation of the Fourth Gospel here offered differs most widely from some recent interpretations. Some interpreters maintain that the original ' moral and religious categories ' of Christianity have in this Gospel been replaced by ' metaphysical categories ' derived from a Hellenistic environment. The Gospel has been called, in a recent exposition, by one who devoted many years to erudite research, ' The Gospel of the Hellenists ' ; the fundamental presuppositions behind the whole interpretation of the late Dr. B. W. Bacon's book, so entitled, being that the Gospel is primarily a writing in terms of current Hellenistic thought, and meant to commend Christianity to a presumed theological and philosophical body of readers. The author, as Dr. Bacon says, ' sets out to interpret the Christian story and Christian experience to the new world of Hellenism by translating the Gospel into a form intelligible to Greek modes of thought.' (*Op. cit.*, p. 112.) One of the main buttresses for the abstract and speculative interpretation of the Gospel is the Logos Prologue. The question therefore arises: What did the author mean when he spoke of the *Logos*—translated in our versions ' Word ' ?

(*a*) The Logos

There is a considerable literature dealing with this question, in which the ancestry or derivation of the Logos concept is explored. It is, however, necessary at the outset to remember that the ' ancestry ' of an ' idea ' is not the idea itself. Every notion that we ourselves hold has its ancestry, going back into the whole region of the uncharted past of humanity. We have words to express these notions or ideas; but no one will suppose that the same words express precisely the same ideas in successive ages. With the intellectual and moral and spiritual progress of humanity the same words receive, and convey, a richer content of meaning. The word ' God ' does not mean the same to an enlightened Christian as it means to an Australian aboriginal who has learnt from missionaries a few of our religious terms. And even among highly cultured Christians, the term can be used in a variety of senses, corresponding to their intellectual, moral, and spiritual endowment and environment. Words are moulds into which living thought and experiences are poured; and the main task of the interpreter of any author in these high realms of the spirit is to understand the content of the mould employed. Words in this respect are like rites: they may endure unchanged through centuries of developing thought and experience. But to know what a rite means to any man, it is more important to know the man than to know the history of the rite. There are, as every student of the history of religious rites knows, pagan parallels to most of our Christian rites: but no intelligent man will suppose that the rites mean the same thing to the respective worshippers. Least of all will it be concluded that a profound and original mind means by the rites in which he participates, or by the words which he uses to express his thought, what either his predecessors or his contemporaries mean. 'It is misleading,' as Dr. W. N. Whitehead says, 'to study the history of ideas without constant remembrance of the struggle of novel thought with the obtuseness of language.' [1]

It is for this reason that we do not find it essential to our purpose to discuss the kindred Logos notions in the Mystery and Hermetic literature, in the writings of contemporary Stoics, or in Philo. In the philosophical literature of the period to which our author belonged, as it has often been pointed out, the Logos idea was as common as the idea of Evolution in our times. It meant different things to different men. To Philo, the Alexandrine Jew, for example, the Logos seems to have been regarded as some vague and indeterminate Divine Principle mediating between Transcendent Deity and the natural universe. Some interpreters have supposed that the Johannine author had borrowed the Logos idea from Philo, and so had sought to present Christianity in this semi-philosophical *milieu.* To our own view, this is in the highest degree improbable. Whether he had read Philo or not, we do not know, and never shall know. What we *do* know is that he was steeped in the Old Testament Scriptures. And if we wish to understand the historical ancestry of the Logos concept as he himself regarded it, we have to go back to these Scriptures.

The Prophets spoke of 'the *word* of the Lord' *coming* to them. The Hebrew 'dabar' (word) was translated in the Septuagint by the Greek 'logos.' The Prophets meant by such statements that they believed God had made known to them, in the depth of their own mind, His very thought and purpose. God's 'Word' was to them His *revealing activity.* When the creative activity of God in the universe as a whole was thought of, similar expressions were used by the Hebrew writer. 'God *said*, Let there be light; and there was light' (Gen. 1^{3}). The psalmist says: 'By *the word* of the Lord were the heavens made, and all their host by the breath of his mouth. . . . He *spake*, and it was done, He *commanded*, and it stood fast' (Ps. 33^{6-9}). In Ps. 46^{6-7} there is the same type of expression: 'The nations raged, the kingdoms were moved; *He uttered his voice*, the earth melted. The Lord of hosts is with us; the God of Jacob is our refuge.' To the psalmist, God's 'presence' is revealed when He 'utters his voice,' which 'melts the earth.' The same thought is found in Ps. 147^{18}, where the melting of ice is regarded as caused by the 'sending out of the word' of God. Or, again, in Ps. 148^{8}, all the elements of Nature are regarded as 'fulfilling God's word.' In the Wisdom

[1] *Adventures of Ideas*, p. 167.

literature of the Old Testament there is the same thought. 'Wisdom' is regarded as the revealing and creative activity of God. 'When God established the heavens, I was there. . . . When he marked out the foundations of the earth, I was by him, as a master-workman' (Prov. 8^{27-30}). Of 'wisdom' it is said in the *Wisdom of Solomon*, that 'she is a breath of the power of God, and a clear effluence of the glory of the Almighty' (Wis. 7^{25}). 'Against wisdom,' says the same writer, 'evil doth not prevail'—an expression which forcibly reminds us of the Evangelist's statement in his Prologue, that 'the light shineth in the darkness, and the darkness did not *overcome* it.'

When the Fourth Evangelist wished to express his faith that the Eternal God had never been inactive, never silent, he said: 'In the beginning was the Word, and the Word was with God, and the Word was Divine.' For ourselves, as for F. D. Maurice, we 'can conceive nothing more thoroughly Hebrew' than such a sentence. When the Evangelist wished to say that the Eternal God had uniquely revealed Himself to Jesus, had been uniquely operative in Jesus, and through Jesus, he said: 'The Word became flesh and dwelt among us.'

The view here taken of the Logos Prologue, therefore, is that in it the author sets forth in a concise dramatic statement the central ideas of his whole Gospel. The author, in speaking of God's 'Word,' is not borrowing a speculative conception from Hellenistic philosophical thought. He is expressing his fundamental faith in the revealing activity of God throughout all history. He goes on to express his central *Christian* conviction when he declares that a historical person, Jesus the Christ, is the incarnate expression of this revealing activity of the Eternal God. No one has ever seen God; but Jesus, who knew such intimate relation with Him, 'hath declared him.' The creative thought of God, operative through all the ages, is now uniquely manifest in Jesus: such is the key to this Gospel, and it is the message of the Prologue.

The same term 'logos' is frequently used in the later chapters of the Gospel in passages where the author's mind is clearly moving in the same orbit of thought. Let the reader take note of the following passages:

5^{24}: 'He that heareth my *word* and believeth him that sent me, hath eternal life."

5^{38}: 'Ye have not his *word* abiding in you; for whom he sent, him ye believe not.'

8^{31}: 'Jesus therefore said to those Jews which had believed in him, If ye abide in my *word*, then are ye truly my disciples.'

8^{37}: 'Ye seek to kill me, because my *word* hath not free course in you.'

8^{43}: 'Why do ye not understand my speech? Even because ye cannot hear my *word*.'

8^{51-52}: 'If a man hear my *word*, he shall never see death.'

8^{55}: 'I know him (the Father), and keep his *word*.'

10^{34-36}: 'Jesus answered them, Is it not written in your law, I said, Ye are gods? If he called them gods, unto whom the *word* of God came (and the scripture cannot be broken), say ye of him, whom the father sanctified and sent into the world, Thou blasphemest; because I said, I am the Son of God?'

12^{47-48}: 'And if any man hear my sayings (ῥημάτων) and keep them not, I judge him not: for I came not to judge the world but to save the world. He that rejecteth me, and receiveth not my sayings (ῥήματα), hath one that judgeth him: the *word* that I spake, the same shall judge him in the last day.'

14^{23-24}: 'If a man love me, he will keep my *word*: and my Father will love him and we will come unto him, and make our abode with him . . . and the *word* which ye hear is not mine, but the Father's who sent me.'

15^{3}: 'Already ye are clean because of the *word* which I have spoken unto you.'

17^{6}: 'I manifested thy name unto the men whom thou gavest me out of the world: thine they were, and thou gavest them to me; and they have kept thy *word*.'

17^{14}: 'I have given them thy *word*; and the world hated them, because they are not of the world, even as I am not of the world.'

17^{17}: 'Sanctify them in the truth: thy *word* is truth.'

17^{20-21}: 'Neither for these only do I pray, but for them also that believe on me through their *word*; that they may all be one.'

These passages make clear that when the 'word' of Jesus is spoken of, what is meant is, not what we mean by a *word*, but *the essential inner mind* which Jesus expresses. Those who have *this*, have eternal life. Men do not understand the *speech* of Jesus, because they are not in accord with His *mind*. As Jesus's 'word' is His mind, so God's Word is His 'Mind': and this 'Mind,' which in every age had found expression, in Jesus had found perfect incarnate expression. Thus the 'word' of Jesus is the Father's own 'word': as we have it in *vv.* 23–24 of the 14th chapter: 'Jesus answered and said unto him, If a man love me, he will keep my word: and my Father will love him, and we will come unto him, and make our abode with him. He that loveth me not keepeth not my words: and the word which ye hear is not mine, but the Father's who sent me.'

It is significant, further, to note that other New Testament writers spoke of Jesus as the 'logos' of God. The author of the Revelation uses this very phrase with reference to Jesus (Rev. 19^{13}). The author of the Epistle to the Hebrews says that 'the *logos* of God is living and active, and sharper than any two-edged sword, and piercing even to the dividing of soul and spirit, of both joints and marrow, and quick to discern the thoughts and intents of the heart. And there is no creature that is not manifest in his sight' (4^{12}). The same author in his opening verses tells us that God who had *spoken* to those of old 'by divers portions and in divers manners' has now *spoken* through 'a Son.' Luke in the introduction to his Gospel speaks of those who were 'eye-witnesses and ministers *of the logos*,' where it would seem that the genitive is connected with 'eye-witnesses' as well as with 'ministers'—the reference, therefore, would be to the Word incarnate in Jesus.

Again, in Acts 13^{48} we are told that as the Gentiles in Antioch of Pisidia heard the preaching of Paul and Barnabas 'they were glad and glorified the *logos* of God.' And in Acts 18^{5} we read that 'when Silas and Timothy came down from Macedonia, Paul was constrained by the *logos*, testifying to the Jews that Jesus was the Christ.' In each of these cases the natural interpretation is that by the 'word' of God is meant the 'Spirit' or revealed mind of God, and not any mere written word.

From all this, it is clear that the author does not begin his Gospel with *a theory* of the Person of Christ. He begins with a declaration of his religious faith in Jesus. It was only later, from the second half of the second century onwards, that leading thinkers of the Church, such as Clement and Origen, sought to fuse this Johannine teaching with speculative Logos conceptions derived from Greek metaphysics. The result of this fusion was such a doctrine as 'the eternal generation of the Son,' as taught by Origen. It requires, however, to be said that, however legitimate or rationally necessary this development, the Johannine author did not himself dwell in this speculative realm.

(*b*) The Filial Consciousness of Jesus

We have called our author 'the historian of the consciousness of Jesus.' The secret of that consciousness was the certitude of God possessed by Jesus. This certitude is expressed throughout the Gospel by the ascription to Jesus of the descriptive title, 'the Son.' This figure was used by Jesus Himself. When He thought and spoke of God, He called Him 'Father.' This was the least inadequate symbol by which He could describe God. Obviously, it sprang out of His uniquely intimate knowledge of God. Jesus called Himself 'Son': this is the symbol by which He sought to express the relation of intimate love and dependent trust which He enjoyed with God. It is clear that, both when Jesus called God 'Father' and when He spoke of Himself as 'Son,' He was giving verbal expression to that whole consciousness of God which was the very secret of His being. In each case we have a figure of speech to unfold the profound spiritual consciousness of Jesus. Neither, as far as Jesus Himself was concerned, was a *dogmatic inference*: both arose as the expression of the *immediate intuition* of Jesus. He taught men to think of God as 'Father' because He Himself had known Him as such. He called men to a life of 'sonship,' because He Himself lived such a life. A metaphysic of Reality has been *read into* this unique spiritual consciousness of Jesus. It should be recognised that this *in-reading* is really an *out-reading*. In other words, our Christological statements are endeavours to *explicate*, in terms consonant with our whole philosophy, what belongs to the inner consciousness of Jesus.

The Fourth Evangelist recognised clearly that this 'Filial consciousness' was the inmost truth about Jesus, and was the real clue to all His outward activities. That is why he says in *v.* 14 of the Prologue that 'the Word became flesh.' He is here only giving formal expression to the unique consciousness of God possessed by Jesus. That is why the Prologue is the key to the comprehension of the whole Gospel, and not, as Harnack and others have maintained, a kind of philosophical and dogmatic introduction with which the rest of the Gospel has nothing in common. Jesus is 'the incarnate Word' because He knew Himself to be the unique Son. Both are different ways of expressing the same reality of consciousness. Thus the author's declaration that 'the Word became flesh' is really the declaration of the whole mind of Jesus Himself.

This 'Filial consciousness' of Jesus has two sides. One is *Dependence*; the other is *Intimacy*. Both these facts of consciousness are expressed by the term 'Son.' A son knows himself to be subordinate to, and dependent upon, his father: he is also in unique fellowship with his father's mind. Throughout the Gospel both this Dependence and this Intimacy are continually expressed,

Jesus recognises Himself always as *subordinate* to God. 'My meat is to do the will of him that sent me,' says Jesus in 4^{34}. He says again, in 6^{38}: 'I came not to do mine own will but the will of him who sent me.' In the 5th chapter, the Jews seek to kill Jesus, we read, because 'He called God his own Father, making himself equal with God' (5^{18}). The reply of Jesus in the following verses reveals wherein our Lord's consciousness of Sonship *did* consist. As if to deny that He made Himself 'equal' with God, He begins by asserting His own subordination. 'Verily . . . the Son can do nothing of himself but what he seeth the Father doing.' Jesus then goes on to assert the *uniqueness* of His Sonship, a uniqueness involved in the nature of the Mission He is called to fulfil. Nevertheless, it is clear that the Jews misunderstood Jesus. When they accused Him of blasphemy they were really misunderstanding His teaching about God. His thought of God was not theirs. Jesus nowhere claimed 'Deification.' What He did claim was a spiritual knowledge of the One Father, on whom He knew Himself to be completely dependent, and whom in all things He sought to obey. In the closing discourses of the Gospel Jesus gives repeated expression to His subordination to the Father. 'The Father that dwelleth within me, he doeth the works' (14^{10}). 'The Father is greater than I' (14^{28}). 'I have kept my Father's commandments' (15^{10}).

Just as clearly, however, Jesus claims unique *intimacy* with God. This is so clearly set forth throughout the Gospel that it is hardly necessary to illustrate by quoting separate passages. Every claim made by Jesus to special Mission on behalf of God involves this intimacy. He is only God's agent because He knows God. He can only mediate eternal life because He is in unique fellowship with the Source of that Life. All that Jesus claims to do is the expression of what He claims to be.

When, therefore, the Evangelist speaks of Jesus in the Prologue as 'a unique—or only—son from the side of a father' (*v.* 14), he is only giving expression to the unique consciousness of the Father which was possessed by Jesus. This figure of 'sonship' came naturally to one who belonged to the Hebrew race. Thus Isaiah speaks of the day star as a 'son of the morning' (Is. 14^{12}); and the *Proverbs* speaks of 'the sons of affliction' (Prov. 31^{5}). To share or express the quality of a thing was to be a 'son' of that thing. 'A son of light,' for example, is one who is enlightened, and who is therefore in a position to enlighten others. 'A son of peace' is one who has the quality of peace in the depths of his mind, and who thus brings peace wherever he goes and in whatever he does. Such a circumlocution, as Dr. Deissmann pointed out, is no mere idle circumlocution, 'but is due to the more vivid imagination of the Oriental, who looked upon any very intimate relationship—whether of connexion, origin, or dependence—as a relation of sonship, even in the spiritual sphere.' [1] Jesus frequently uses such a phrase in the Gospels. He speaks of 'the sons of the bride-chamber' (Mk. 2^{19}, Mt. 9^{15}, Lk. 5^{34}): He called the sons of Zebedee 'Boanerges,' which means, 'sons of thunder' (Mk. 3^{17}); He used the phrase 'the sons of the kingdom' (Mt. 8^{12} and 13^{38}), and the phrase 'a son of Gehenna' (Mt. 23^{15}). Judas is called in the Fourth Gospel 'the son of perdition' (17^{12}). In Luke's Gospel Jesus speaks

[1] *Bible Studies*, p. 161.

of 'a son of peace' (Lk. 10^6), 'the sons of this age' (Lk. 16^8 and 20^{34}), 'the sons of light' (Lk. 16^8), and 'sons of the resurrection' (Lk. 20^{36}). In the Fourth Gospel Jesus says, 'While ye have the light, believe on the light, that ye may become sons of light' (12^{36}). Paul used similar phrases. In *1 Thessalonians* he says: "Ye are all sons of light and sons of the day' (1 Thess. 5^5). He uses also the phrase 'the sons of disobedience' (Col. 3^6; Eph. 2^2, 5^6).

'Sonship,' it is clear, meant to Jesus 'partaking of the nature of.' Since He enjoyed unique fellowship with the Father, it was inherently natural for Him to describe this in terms of sonship. Its primary significance is the significance it had for Jesus Himself. 'Sonship' to the Father expressed a reality to the consciousness of Jesus. When the Church afterwards came to speak of Jesus as 'Son of God,' it used a language which would be understood in different ways, according to the cultural heritage of those employing the designation. Such a title, for example, was frequently ascribed to the Roman Emperors. When, therefore, it was used by Jewish-Christian missionaries in the Græco-Roman world it would, at first, be understood in the light of its application to the Emperor. In our own days the designation 'Son of God' is understood in many ways, varying with the intellectual, moral, and spiritual enlightenment of those who hear, or use, the phrase. For this reason, therefore, it is ever necessary to remember that its primary and dominating meaning for the Christian must be its meaning for Jesus Himself. The whole depth of that meaning cannot, of course, be sounded by us. We should have to be Jesus to know the whole secret of Jesus. Nevertheless, it is clear from the Gospel records that what Jesus expressed by the term 'Son,' as applied to Himself, was the intimacy and dependence of His conscious relation to the Father. It was only because He knew God as Father that He thought of Himself as 'Son.' That 'knowledge' was no speculative inference: it was an immediate and direct intuition. In seeking to trace the long course of the Church's speculations in Christology, it is of paramount importance to go back to the New Testament records, that we may learn the meaning of the phrases Jesus Himself used. 'Sonship,' it is clear, did not mean to Him what we may call *physical derivation*. Nor did it mean to Him the speculative, metaphysical conclusion reached by the Church in the fourth and fifth centuries. It arose out of His direct knowledge of the Father, and His obedience to the Father's will.

In our own judgement, the Fourth Evangelist himself used the title in reference to Jesus in this profoundly spiritual sense. The title 'Son of God,' found so frequently in this Gospel, is not to the author—such is our belief—what we may call a 'theological' title. The title was used by him to convey what the Master's own 'Sonship' meant to Himself. It proclaimed, in other words, the unique consciousness which belonged to Jesus, the unique Divine quality of His whole mind and work. He places the title on the lips of Jesus: this is his way of giving dramatic expression to the inner consciousness of the Master. Just as he places on the lips of Jesus the specific claims, 'I am the way, the truth and the life,' 'I am the bread of life,' 'I am the door,' 'I am the light of the world,'—all this to give dramatic expression to the mind and mission of Jesus—so he places on His lips the title 'Son of God.' This, he would say, is what Jesus essentially was. The Evangelist's mind, in other words, was moving in the same moral and spiritual orbit as the mind of Jesus Himself had moved. He uses the same Hebrew idiom as Jesus Himself had used.

(*c*) The Son of Man

The same may be said of the title ' Son of man,' also found in this Gospel. We do not believe that it, either, is to the Evangelist a ' theological ' title. This title, which was used by Jesus Himself, was retained by the Fourth Evangelist: it is used by him, as we believe, to express the fact of the real, though exceptional, humanity of Jesus. It has not in the Fourth Gospel the apocalyptic associations which it has in the earlier Gospels. In the 14th verse of the Prologue the Evangelist wrote that ' the Word *became flesh* ': when he uses this title ' Son of man ' he wishes to say the same thing—namely, that Jesus was indeed truly man. He who was ' Son of God ' is also ' Son of man.' He who partook of the nature of the Father partook also of the nature of humanity. ' Sonship,' as we have maintained, meant to the author ' partaking of the nature of.' Jesus, who because of His unique knowledge of God was the unique Divine Son, was yet bone of our bone and flesh of our flesh. So the author retains the Messianic title which Jesus Himself had used, and by so doing maintains the thesis and emphasis of the Prologue. The Eternal Word has spoken—as the Evangelist would say—in one who was truly man; and not, as the Docetists were beginning to say, in one whose humanity was but an illusory garment.

There are twelve occasions in the Gospel where this title ' Son of man ' is found —in 1^{51}, $3^{13, 14}$, 5^{27}, $6^{27, 53, 62}$, 8^{28}, $12^{23, 34}$, 13^{31}. It is significant that in several of these passages the title is associated with some symbolical expression of the unique fellowship Jesus enjoyed with God. This association is the Evangelist's way of saying what he has said in the Prologue—namely, that there is real correspondence between heaven and earth, and that this correspondence was uniquely manifest in Jesus. Let us think, for example, of the first use of the title—in 1^{51}. ' Ye shall see the heaven opened, and the angels of God ascending and descending upon the Son of man.' This is a record, in pictorial and allegorical language, of the signal manifestations, to be witnessed by the disciples during the Ministry of Jesus, of the unique communion with God which He knew. The passage is expressive of that intercourse between heaven and earth which was manifest throughout the whole Ministry of Him who was truly man. The references in 3^{13} and 3^{14} express the same truth. ' And no one hath ascended into heaven but he that descended out of heaven, even the Son of man (omitting ' which is in heaven '). And as Moses lifted up the serpent in the wilderness, even so must the Son of man be lifted up: that whosoever believeth may in him have eternal life.' Here also the Evangelist is giving expression, in his dramatic and allegorical way, to the consciousness of Jesus. In the first chapter, the Evangelist used the figure of ' angels ' ascending and descending: here he uses the figure of Jesus, the Son of man, Himself ' ascending ' and ' descending.' The ' ascent ' of the Son of man to heaven is the Evangelist's way of speaking of the *direct knowledge* of God possessed, and won, by Jesus: the ' descent ' of the Son of man from heaven is his way of speaking of the *source or origin* of the experience and mission of Jesus. It is clear that Jesus is not here speaking of a memory of a pre-existent life in heaven, nor of a miraculous coming down out of heaven. What He is saying—or what His whole consciousness, so expressed by the Evangelist, is saying—is that He who was truly man partook of the heavenly nature of God.

We must leave to the Commentary itself an elucidation of the several narratives in which the title 'Son of man' is found. Before, however, leaving this discussion we wish to point out that on the single occasion in which the title is associated with 'judgement,' it is clear that it is no eschatological 'Son of man' who executes judgement. The reference is in 5^{27}. 'And he (God) gave him authority to execute judgement, because he is Son of man.' We discuss later the meaning of 'judgement' in this Gospel. It is sufficient here to say that the 'judging' mission belongs to 'the Son'—not to an apocalyptic 'Son of man.' If the passage is studied in the light of its context, this will be evident. What the Evangelist would say is that the sifting process of eternity was uniquely manifest when the human Jesus was here among men. Jesus Himself had this assurance that His life and ministry was one of such 'judgement.'

The use of the title 'Son of man' is, therefore, no more a 'theological' title to the Evangelist than is the title 'Son of God.' The use of both titles springs out of *experience*, and not out of speculation—whether the apocalyptic speculations of visionaries who took their visions literally, or the 'metaphysical' speculations of those who took their cerebrations on abstractions as identical with reality. Each title expresses what was a *fact* in the *experience* of Jesus: the title 'Son of God' expressing the experience Jesus had in the depths of His consciousness and through the whole range of His outward activities of the Father God; the title 'Son of man' expressing the fact that Jesus was truly man, and not the semblance of man.

(*d*) Pre-existence

One of the crucial issues for the Christology of this Gospel is what is sometimes called the claim to pre-existence supposed to be explicit in certain utterances of Jesus. 'Before Abraham was, I am,' Jesus is declared as saying in 8^{58}. In the high priestly prayer, Jesus speaking to the Father says: 'And now, O Father, glorify thou me with thine own self with the glory which I had with thee before the world was' (17^{5}). How have these utterances to be regarded?

We have sought to interpret these, and other kindred utterances of Jesus in this Gospel, in the body of the Commentary; and must therefore point the reader to these detailed elucidations. Here, however, a few words may be said, to indicate the general point of view from which such passages are envisaged.

What the words say is that Jesus had a life transcending the categories of time and of space: the words do not mean that Jesus claimed a *memory* of a life prior to His life in the flesh. Jesus is not speaking of a 'pre-existent' life—such a phrase is, indeed, a contradiction in terms. He is speaking of a *pre-temporal* life—if we may venture to use the expression. It will be noted that in the first passage referred to—in 8^{58}—Jesus does not say, 'Before Abraham was, *I was*': He says, 'Before Abraham was, *I am*.' This 'I am' corresponds to the other uses of the same phrase in this Gospel. It is a dramatic declaration of the essential quality of the life known and lived by Jesus. Just as the life of Jesus was 'truth,' 'bread,' 'water,' 'way,' 'door,' 'resurrection'—every figure expressing some spiritual quality in the life and ministry of Jesus—so His life, in its essential nature, was grounded in the eternal nature of God Himself. It partook of the very 'Being' of Him who was 'I am that I am' (Exod. 3^4). It was a life, not of time, but of eternity. To understand the passage as meaning that the author claimed for Jesus a *memory* of an existence in time prior to His appearance in this world, is to misunderstand completely both the author himself and the Gospel he wrote. It is as much to misunderstand his mind as to conclude that he thought Jesus claimed to be literal water, or literal bread. The whole emphasis of the Gospel is on life in its eternal and essential quality. Eternal life is not a life of never-ending *duration*; it is a life of perduring essence. It is this life which Jesus knew, and which He, no doubt on many occasions, claimed in the presence of His disciples to possess. In such a controversy with the Jews as we find in the eighth chapter, it is natural to suppose that Jesus would use the reference to Abraham in order to express to the materialistic minds of His hearers the reality of a life He knew, unbounded by the categories of time and of space. It is clear that the hearers of Jesus did not understand Him. What He said to them was that the life He knew was *qualitatively different* from all existence which is measured in years: He is not saying that He has *memory* of an existence *greater in duration* than the years which have elapsed since the days of Abraham.

The basis for these 'pre-existence' passages in the Gospel is the transcending sense of God possessed by Jesus, and the unique sense of Divine mission accompanying it. Such a life was qualitatively complete: and this is what these 'pre-existence' passages were meant to declare. It has often been noted that the Jesus of the Synoptic Gospels nowhere asserts His 'pre-existence': nor, indeed, is it possible to think that He ever did so. If the profound spirituality of the Johannine Gospel is understood, it will be seen that this Gospel is at one with the Synoptic Gospels on this very issue. What Jesus knew, and what He claimed, was a life of intimate fellowship with the Father. This is the whole significance of the famous 'Q' passage—Mt. 11^{25-27} and Lk. 10^{21-22}. This utterance has often been interpreted as if it were an importation into the Synoptic Gospels of ideas foreign to them. It is, we have been told, 'a bolt from the Johannine sky'; by which is meant that it is a theological or metaphysical interpretation read back—in a so-called Johannine *metaphysical* fashion—into the consciousness of Jesus. If, however, the Johannine Gospel be really understood, it will be seen to be, not a metaphysical, but a religious and spiritual document. It was written by an author who believed, not in the pre-existence of Jesus, but in the Eternity of the Word of which Jesus was the incarnate expression. This belief was not his own discovery, or—as some would say—his own invention. It was a belief expressive of the essential consciousness, and claim, of Jesus Himself. And what the Fourth Evangelist is seeking all the time to do in his Gospel, is to transcribe into dramatic and allegorical language the claim inherent in the whole life of Jesus. That life was the timeless life of eternity.

It is far from our purpose here to suggest that the later 'explications' and 'definitions' of the Church in this realm of Christological speculation were 'mistaken.' They were not 'mistaken'; but they were 'inadequate.' The human mind being what it is, we cannot avoid the task of thinking things together, as far as we may. And this is the inner meaning of the whole history of theological thought. The history of theology is just the history of the mental life of the Church. Nor can we avoid the task of ' defining ' our central beliefs. What we call ' definition ' is necessary to our own intellectual integrity—we must say as clearly as we can what we believe: it is, also, a *practical* necessity to the teaching office of the Church. Children in all ages—and *of* all ages—learn by ' definitions.' The Church's Trinitarian and Christological formulations must be approached from this point of view. They are provisional, and not final, statements.

The Johannine author was not concerned with statements or definitions of the Person of Christ. He was concerned with the unveiling of His inner life. He believed that the secret of Jesus was His consciousness of the Father. He had the simple and direct mind which belongs to religious genius. In the present confused state of Christian thought the Church needs this type of mind more than any other. We need to be recalled from the myopic engrossment with theological formulæ to the spiritual reality all such formulæ seek to express. We shall then—and not till then—see our statements and definitions in right perspective. We shall no longer regard them as sacrosanct. We shall not repudiate the task of achieving less inadequate statements and definitions. But in all such theological activity we shall be inspired by spiritual insight. Such insight will make for simplification. We cannot forbear here from quoting the words of one of the most eminent of our modern philosophers: ' Theology intervenes to satisfy the rational mind of man with reasoned justifications of what it has taken over from actual faith, and in doing so no doubt it renders a great service to thought, attempting as it does to illuminate religion by the current notions of philosophy. But at the same time it imposes upon religion a mass of learning and tradition which are apt to stifle the mind of man in its effort after simplicity in its religious statements. Religions come thus to be choked by their own overgrowth of plants which draw their life from the religion, but may surround its central feeling with a paling which may shut out direct vision . . . . Such a simplification will not come from theologians nor from philosophers, but, if at all, from some simple-minded but profound religious genius sensitive to future needs. Even it will have its mythology in order to be humanly accessible, but its mythology will be credible to the men of to-day.' [1]

The insight necessary for the Christological definitions of the future belonged, we believe, to the Johannine author. Jesus, he saw and he said, was the unveiling of the Father's mind. How did he know this ? we ask. There is only one answer which has any validity in it: that is, that this truth belonged to the whole consciousness of Jesus. In the last analysis all Christological statements take us back to the inner mind of Jesus Himself. And when the Johannine author said that Jesus was the unveiling of the Father he said what he believed to be true to the inmost thought of Jesus Himself. It was from this inner consciousness of the Father's presence that all the claims of Jesus arose. If that consciousness was but a self-deception, then the whole of Christology is one vast mistake. The Johannine evangelist believed profoundly that the consciousness of Jesus was the

[1] Professor Samuel Alexander in *Science and Religion*, pp. 140–1.

clue to the Mind and Purpose of God. The consciousness of Jesus, to him, was no self-deception of Jesus Himself: it was what Jesus Himself claimed it to be—the *Self-manifestation* of the Father Himself. This is what Jesus meant when He said, 'I and the Father are one.' The Father—who was always *other* than Jesus, 'greater' than Jesus—was Himself speaking through the mind of Jesus: this is what Jesus claimed. In making this claim Jesus never *equated* Himself with the Father. The Father, to Jesus, was always the Transcendent Other. The 'oneness' of Jesus with the Father sprang out of His 'dependence' upon the Father. 'Dependence' and 'oneness' are *one* experience—not *two*.

The function of all Christological statements is to conserve the belief that in the whole life of Jesus there is a unique unveiling of the Father in time and place. 'The real reason,' if we may be permitted to quote words we have written elsewhere, 'why the Christian belief in the "Historic Incarnation" has outlived many of the inadequate arguments and formulas by which it has been buttressed and defined is that its vitalising centre has been a Johannine insight into the unique manifestation of the Eternal and Divine in the person of Jesus.' [1] In the last analysis, every form of Christological statement leads back to, and must rest upon, the consciousness of Jesus Himself. Let us not make the mistake of imagining that a Christological statement is true because a majority of Christian thinkers say so. It is only true if the consciousness of Jesus says so.

2. *MIRACLES*

Into the whole question of *Miracle*—a question involving historical, scientific, psychological, and philosophical investigation and discussion—it is not possible here to enter.[2] What we are really concerned with is the mind of the Evangelist. We wish to know what was his intention when he related the 'miracles' found in his Gospel. This, like the symbolical quality of the author's mind, raises one of the most perplexing questions to the modern reader.

In the body of the Commentary we have sought to elucidate the Evangelist's intention in respect to these 'miracle' narratives, each in its own context. We have, therefore, no intention to repeat here what is there said; but merely to indicate briefly and summarily the point of view which has dictated these elucidations.

1. Firstly, it is important to note that the Evangelist gives *seven* such 'miracle' incidents—excluding, that is, the Resurrection of Jesus. They are:

(1) The turning of water into wine ($2^{1ff.}$).
(2) The healing of the nobleman's son ($4^{46ff.}$).
(3) The healing of the impotent man at Bethesda ($5^{1ff.}$).
(4) The feeding of the five thousand ($6^{5ff.}$).
(5) The walking on the water ($6^{15ff.}$).
(6) The restoration of sight to the blind man ($9^{1ff.}$).
(7) The raising of Lazarus ($11^{1ff.}$).

Clearly, the choice of *seven* such incidents is significant of the allegorical or symbolical characteristics of the author's mind.

[1] *The Meaning and Message of the Fourth Gospel*, p. 147; in which book the reader will find a fuller exposition of the 'Christological' point of view expressed above.

[2] I have discussed the relevant issues at some length in *Miracle in History and Modern Thought.*

2. Secondly, these incidents are called 'signs.' In the Marcan narrative—apart from the spurious ending—the word 'signs' is only used in a hostile sense: in this Gospel the word is used to designate these incidents narrated as having been wrought by Jesus. The Fourth Evangelist, on the other hand, never uses the term 'mighty works' to denote these 'signs': while such a term is commonly employed in the Synoptic Gospels. From this it is clear that the Evangelist is chiefly concerned with that which is 'signified' by the 'signs' narrated. In other words, the centre of gravity in his thought is not the narrated incident, but that which is *signified* by the narrative. His precise motive in these narratives is to unfold different aspects of the moral and spiritual ministry of Jesus. This is clear from the fact that the narrative of the 'sign' is frequently followed by discourses in which the spiritual truths signified are elucidated: no thoughtful reader will suppose that these discourses were regarded by the author himself as following the 'signs' narrated. These 'signs' are thus viewed by the Evangelist himself as symbolical of the inner truth and mission of Jesus. Their place in the narrative is determined by the Evangelist's concern to portray the spiritual ministries of Jesus. What he himself wished supremely to say was that Jesus could effect in the moral and spiritual realm the transforming, sustaining, enlightening, and life-giving ministries of which these narratives are the 'signs.' 'The centre of gravity,' as it has recently been said, 'is always, not in the historic facts but in the words to which they serve as a frame, and of which sometimes—the multiplication of loaves, the healing of the man born blind, the resurrection of Lazarus—they are the allegorical expression.' [1]

3. Thirdly, as to the precise basis in historic fact on which these stories rest, it is impossible to dogmatise. In the judgement of the present writer, the author was in most cases freely and dramatically allegorising some historical tradition. There must have been a good deal of such tradition from which the Evangelist could choose what would serve his purpose. But, whatever the historical tradition, the Evangelist does not hesitate to give it a setting and a form which will serve his main intention—which is to unfold the spiritual ministry of Jesus. From this fact, it is clear that the Evangelist is not really interested in the incident as such. If he had been, he would not have taken such liberties as he obviously has taken with the historical setting.

The healing of the nobleman's son in chapter 4, for example, is probably a free rendering of the Synoptic story of the healing of the centurion's servant (Mt. $8^{5ff.}$ and Lk. $7^{6ff.}$). In the Synoptic story the centurion meets Jesus when He is entering Capernaum: in the Fourth Gospel the nobleman meets Jesus in Cana—where the first sign is recorded as having taken place—twenty miles from Capernaum. The 'boy' in the first narrative becomes a 'son' in the Johannine narrative.

Again, the story of the impotent man at Bethesda bears certain resemblances to the story of the paralytic in Mk. 2^{1-12}; and it is possible, here also, that the Fourth Evangelist is adapting the Marcan incident to his own purpose. Whether this be so, or whether the Evangelist is using some other incident of healing which took place in Jerusalem, at least we can be certain that he does not hesitate to adapt the traditional incident so as to serve as a suitable frame for his allegorical

[1] Goguel in *Vie de Jésus*, p. 135.

portraiture of the spiritual ministry of Jesus. The ' thirty-eight years ' of the narrative is quite clearly not a historical statement to him. It is inserted into the narrative by the author from his recollection of the narrative of Dt. 2^{14}, where we are told that the Israelitish wanderings from Kadesh-barnea to the brook Zered covered a period of thirty and eight years. To the Evangelist, the number is symbolical of a period of spiritual impotency which was brought to an end by the life-giving ministry of Jesus.

Again, in the story of the feeding of the multitude in chapter 6—the one incident in the Ministry of Jesus prior to His last visit to Jerusalem which is recorded in all four Gospels—the Evangelist held himself free to alter the details of the narrative as he had read it in the Synoptic Gospels. We have discussed at some length in the Commentary itself what the story probably meant to the Evangelist. Here it is sufficient to say that to him, in all probability, the story was an allegory of the spiritual ministry of Jesus. He was, indeed, the bread of man's inner life. What the author here does is to treat a story, familiar to the Church, in an allegorical manner, and with an allegorical motif. The long discourse which follows is sufficient to reveal what is in his mind. Thus also is to be understood the Evangelist's record of the walking on the water. Here, again, he found a story familiar to the Church through the narratives in Mt. (14^{22-23}) and in Mk. (6^{45-52}). It was no nature-marvel to him; least of all was it to him—what these stories have often been to a certain type of apologist—a ' proof ' of the Divinity of Jesus. It was an allegory of the succour which Jesus brought to His disciples in their hours of deepest need, and of that haven of fulfilled desires and aspirations to which He brought them.

Again, the story of the blind man in chapter 9 is no doubt based upon some traditional incident where Jesus restored sight. The Evangelist knew of such a ministry of Jesus from the Synoptic Gospels: Mark, for example, records two such incidents—in 8^{23} and 10^{46}. In all probability the Fourth Evangelist's story is a free rendering of some incident which took place in Jerusalem; but it is clear that what he is really concerned to do is to unfold the mind of Jesus on spiritual blindness and spiritual sight.

It remains, lastly, to say a few words at this point on the first and the last of these seven ' signs '—the turning of the water into wine at Cana, and the raising of Lazarus. Both are to be regarded as allegories. We have discussed them in some detail in the body of the Commentary, and it is unnecessary to say here what is there said. In each case we may assume that the Evangelist used some traditional incident for his point of departure; but in each case we may also be perfectly certain that he is with complete freedom adapting and embellishing these traditions to subserve his main purpose—which is, to lay bare the transforming and quickening spiritual ministries of Jesus. No one will understand what the Evangelist himself was seeking to say in these narratives if he does not remember the type of mind he possessed. It is as clear as anything can be that he had not a scrupulously historical mind. The dramatic and allegorical nature of his mind stands out with unmistakable clearness on every page of his Gospel—to those who will take the trouble to read and study it carefully. Why, then, should it be supposed that the Evangelist is only scrupulously historical in these 'miracle' narratives? We recognise his dramatic symbolism in innumerable places in his Gospel. Why should we be forbidden to see it in these narratives? To our own view, the Evangelist no more thought he was narrating precise history when he recorded the turning of the water into wine than he did when he narrated the conversation of Jesus with the woman of Samaria.

We have no wish to dogmatise on the precise historical incidents behind these 'sign' narratives. We have not the requisite data to decide in each case beyond a peradventure. It seems clear that when the Evangelist wrote there was a considerable body of stories of the 'works' of Jesus floating about in vague and indeterminate form. The author chose such as commended themselves to his primary purpose. He felt himself completely free to alter them in order to bring into more striking relief the spiritual significance of Jesus and the nature of the Mission He accomplished. To our own view, it is in the highest degree psychologically improbable that the Evangelist believed he was in these narratives recording precise history.

4. Fourthly, throughout the Gospel Jesus is portrayed as seeking to bring men to a 'faith' in Him which transcends the mere belief that is based on works performed. The author, it is transparently obvious, believed that Jesus little valued the kind of faith which was based on 'signs and wonders.' It is just as clear that he himself shared this conviction of Jesus. Let us note, for example, his record of the meeting of Nicodemus with Jesus. Nicodemus is rebuked for the reason he gave for his approach to Jesus. 'No man,' says Nicodemus, 'can work the signs which thou doest except God be with him.' To this Jesus replies, 'Except a man be born from above he cannot see the activity of God.' The 'sign' of God, that is, can only be seen by the spiritually awakened mind; spiritual things are spiritually discerned. Again, in 4^{47-48} Jesus seeks sharply to recall the nobleman of Capernaum from a belief dependent upon 'miracles': 'Except ye see signs and wonders ye will not believe.' Again, in 6^{26} Jesus rebukes those who sought him because of loaves: 'Ye seek me, not because ye saw signs, but because ye ate of the loaves and were filled.' The 'sign' obviously was not, to the Evangelist, what is usually called 'the miracle of the feeding of the five thousand': the narrative was but to him the framework of the truth symbolised—the truth, namely, that Jesus was here to impart eternal food for the spirit of man.

The whole emphasis of this Gospel is that God's 'sign' is Jesus—one who incarnates perfect knowledge of, and obedience to, the Holy Will of the Father. Men in every age lust for 'signs' of another kind. They want 'proofs' to convince the spiritually blind that God is not on the side of the big battalions. They want to see the big battalions overthrown by bigger battalions. In this they forget, 'Not by might, nor by power, but my Spirit, saith the Lord of hosts.' This lust for signs is sometimes a relic of materialism of creed, sometimes a witness to the tension in men's minds between faith and doubt.

'No sign,' groaned he;
'No stirring of God's finger to denote
He wills that right should have supremacy
On earth, not wrong.'

Wherever the light of Truth, of Love, of Sacrificial Obedience shines, *there* is God's 'sign.' This is the light which flowed from Jesus. Here in Jesus, to the Johannine author, was the 'stirring of God's finger.' But many, as he continually tells us, saw no 'finger of God' in Jesus. The 'incarnate Word' was no coercive, or demonstrative, 'sign' of God. Throughout this Gospel the note is insistently sounded that there is no 'miracle' of God's activity such as will compel all men to see. In this, universal human experience accords with the Johannine author.

This being without any doubt the Evangelist's main message about Divine 'signs,' there is additional substantiation for the conclusion already reached—namely, that he did not think of physical marvels as 'evidencing' Divine activity. The 'marvels' which he narrated were all, to himself, parables. That being so, the 'inconsistency' which many commentators have seen in his attitude to 'signs' is not really there at all. This 'inconsistency,' which has been attributed to him, has been held to consist in the fact that while he insists on the evidential value of these physical marvels he also disparages the kind of faith which rests upon them. The 'inconsistency' is not, however, in the mind of the Evangelist. The fact that he disparages throughout the Gospel the kind of belief which requires these 'miracles' supports the conclusions already reached on the parabolic nature of these stories to himself.

3. *THE SACRAMENTAL PRINCIPLE*

In closest correspondence with the emphasis in this Gospel on the necessity of the insight of faith to the perception of Divine 'signs,' is its teaching on what may be called 'the Sacramental Principle.' The Fourth Evangelist—who neither records the Baptism of Jesus nor the 'institution' of the Lord's Supper or Eucharist—has been frequently regarded as the foremost teacher in the New Testament on the subject of Christian Sacraments. Such a statement is open to divers and diverse interpretations; and it is clear that it needs elucidation. It is truer to say that the Fourth Evangelist is the foremost teacher in the New Testament on 'the Sacramental Principle.'

What is this principle? It is, that the physical can be the vehicle of the spiritual, the visible of the invisible. So understood, this principle runs through the whole of the Fourth Gospel. 'The Word,' says the Evangelist 'became flesh, and dwelt among us (and we beheld his glory, glory as of the only begotten from the Father), full of grace and truth.' The eternal activity of God was revealed in the life of one who was bone of our bone and flesh of our flesh. The God whom no one has ever seen was manifest in Jesus. This is the central theme of the Gospel. The 'sacramental principle,' so adumbrated, pervades the whole narrative.

There is, however, nothing in this Gospel to suggest that the physical is a *necessary* medium of the spiritual: indeed, the whole Gospel is the most emphatic repudiation of such an idea. Side by side with the author's central affirmation that the Word of God was made flesh in Jesus, is his declaration that many did not hear this 'Word.' Many, having eyes to see, did not see: having ears to hear, did not hear. The Incarnate One could not compel men to see or to hear.

Spiritual things are spiritually discerned, is the recurring refrain of this Gospel. 'Except a man be born from above, he cannot see the kingdom of God'—this word, spoken to Nicodemus, is but a transcription into specific utterance of the continuous declaration made by the whole mind of Jesus.

Physical symbols, and physical contacts, may *occasion* spiritual experience; but they do not *necessarily convey* it. Else were the whole world spiritually minded; and Jesus had never been rejected. To Wordsworth 'the meanest flower that blows' could give

Thoughts that do often lie too deep for tears.

But such 'thoughts' are not given to those who cannot, or will not, think. 'A primrose by a river's brim' may be sacramental to some men: it was not so to Peter Bell. Likewise, the 'flower in the crannied wall,' of Tennyson: it may adumbrate to us 'what God and man is,' or it may be nothing more than a bit of matter. 'Earth's crammed with heaven, And every common bush aflame with God,' wrote Mrs. Browning. But she knew enough of the facts of life to add:

But only he who sees takes off his shoes,
The rest sit round it, and pluck blackberries,
And daub their natural faces unaware
More and more from the first similitude.

The crowd *thronged* Jesus, we read in Mark's Gospel, but one woman in that crowd *touched* Him with faith. The grace of God is never an *impartation*: it is always a *gift;* and a gift requires a *receiver*. Two men may see a cross: to one it is a mere 'gibbet'; to another it is the symbol of the way by which the world may be 'overcome,' and, indeed, was 'overcome' by Jesus. The window lets in the light, but not to the blind. It reveals the wide-stretching landscape, but not if we close our eyes. Nor is what we see dependent merely upon the window, and upon our physical eyesight: it is dependent on our whole mental and spiritual perceptiveness. The whole universe is sacramental, but only if we are spiritually awake. This is the higher sacramentalism of the teaching of Jesus: a teaching which no New Testament writer has more firmly grasped than the Fourth Evangelist. It is the sacramentalism of the Christian mystics of all the centuries. It found beautiful expression in the lines of George Herbert:

Teach me, my God and King,
In all things Thee to see,
And what I do in anything
To do it as for Thee.

A man that looks on glasse,
On it may stay his eye;
Or, if he pleaseth, through it passe,
And then the heav'n espie.

The fundamental difference between this 'sacramental principle' and what may be called—by, of course, an abuse of language—the 'magical principle' is here revealed. To the first, the physical is the vehicle of the spiritual, *to those who have eyes to see*: to the second, the physical, in and by itself, conveys the spiritual. To the first, the insight of faith is essential to every sacrament: to the second, the 'opus operatum' is the only essential. The outward world touches the inward world, but only through the spirit. What we call 'salvation' is not, and never can be, an external *operation*: it is an experience known within the whole personal life, and revealed through the whole range of its activities. There is no 'regeneration' which is not a *real* regeneration of the heart, mind, and will. 'Not everyone that saith, Lord, Lord' enters into the Kingdom of heaven. Not everyone who perceives the outward sign receives the spiritual truth signified. Not everyone who eats the bread receives the Bread of Life. Not everyone who is baptised with water is inwardly cleansed.

Jesus taught His disciples to regard the physical, the external, the form, the institution, as servants, and not masters, of the spirit of man. He Himself, 'as his custom was,' attended the synagogue. But when the outward form and symbol was put to wrong uses, when in and for itself it was esteemed, then He was, as He could not but be, the spiritual iconoclast. He was full of moral and spiritual indignation at the use to which His 'Father's house' was put. He occasioned the wrath of the Pharisees by His attitude to the Sabbath. 'The sabbath was made for man, and not man for the sabbath,' He said. All this is true to the Johannine portraiture of Jesus, to his delineation of His essential spirit. In this, Jesus was in the line of the prophets of Israel; as, indeed, His interpreter himself was. Those prophets, when they witnessed the abuses of the sacrificial system in their day, called upon the people with such ethical and spiritual fervour to put first things first, that, ever since, commentators have disputed furiously as to whether they were 'abolitionists,' or only 'reformers.'

It is only in the light of this essential emphasis of the Fourth Gospel that what are regarded as the specific references to the Christian Sacraments will be understood. It is one of the soundest principles of exegesis, that the part is understood in the light of the whole. A man's words have their meaning within the whole context of his ideas. The profounder a man's mind is, the more true is this principle; the more necessary is it to the understanding of his mind. Small minds are a jumble of unrelated and discordant ideas: big minds remain true to a few central and fundamental beliefs. These beliefs are expressed in different ways; conveying thus the impression of the complexity and manifoldness of life itself. But variety of expression does not bespeak discordance of ideas. An underlying unity is revealed in the fabric to whose making the many strands of diverse colours have gone.

In the body of the Commentary we have sought to elucidate the inner meaning of the specific sacramental references of this Gospel. The reader is referred to the comments on the following passages of the Gospel for our interpretation.

First, in $3^{5ff.}$: 'Except a man be born of water and the Spirit, he cannot enter into the kingdom of God,' etc., where it has often been thought that the reference to being born 'of water' indicates that to the Evangelist the rite of baptism is essential to spiritual regeneration. The meaning of the passage can only be understood in the light of the teaching of the whole paragraph.

The second main 'sacramental' passage is, of course, the discourse in the sixth chapter on the ' bread of life,' with the references to eating ' the flesh ' and drinking ' the blood ' of Jesus. Here again the inner meaning of the teaching can only be grasped in the light of the essential message of the Gospel in its entirety. No interpretation could be more opposed to the mind of Jesus, or to the mind of His evangelist, than that ' flesh ' means physical flesh, or ' blood ' physical blood; or that ' eating ' and ' drinking ' signify the physical acts which in literal speech they signify. The thought of the whole passage moves on the highest plane of morality and spirituality.

The third main ' sacramental ' passage is in 19^{34}, where we read that when one of the soldiers pierced the side of Jesus, as He hung on the Cross, ' straightway there came out blood and water.' It is clear that there is a symbolical reference here. But the real question is: What did the ' blood and water ' symbolise to the Evangelist? What he would say is, that there issues from the completely dedicated life of Jesus, spiritual cleansing and spiritual sustenance. This ' flows ' to the life of the nations.

There are other sacramental references in the Gospel, which we seek to elucidate later, each in its own context. The above, however, are the chief—with the exception of the most important of all, namely, that implied in the way the Evangelist tells the story of the Last Supper. There, instead of recording the words of Jesus, in which, as is often said, He ' institutes ' the Eucharist as a rite, he tells the story of the feet-washing. The main feature of that Supper to the Evangelist is the acted parable which unfolds its inner meaning. There have been endeavours innumerable to explain away the author's silence about the words of ' institution ': but to *explain away* is not to *explain*. We do not, for example, *explain* the omission by pointing out that silence does not bespeak ignorance. Assuredly, it does not. But it does bespeak something to the Evangelist. That the Fourth Evangelist—with his continual and pervasive emphasis on the true ' sacramental principle '—should be the only Evangelist to omit all reference to the solemn words of Jesus, ' This is my body,' raises indeed an issue of the highest importance for those who would understand his mind—and, let us add, the mind of Jesus. It is not enough to say that he does not feel it necessary to repeat what was already familiar to his readers. The only satisfactory explanation of the Evangelist's omission, and of his addition, is that he is seeking to recall the Church to the profoundly spiritual inner meaning of the words and acts of Jesus on that solemn occasion. To eat the ' flesh ' or the ' body ' of Jesus, to drink of His ' blood,' is to partake by faith of His spirit: it is to manifest the same spirit of humility and of selfless sacrifice which He so perfectly incarnated. All other eating and drinking is vain. It is of the highest significance for the message of the Evangelist—which is the very message of Jesus Himself—to note, that the only disciple who is recorded as having received the bread is Judas. To him, says our author, Jesus gave the ' sop '—the morsel of bread dipped in the wine. And of Judas we read that when he had received the sop ' Satan entered into him.' ' Understandest thou what thou readest ' might well be the question put to the modern reader when he peruses this Johannine narrative. ' It is the spirit that quickeneth; the flesh profiteth nothing.' The ' words ' of Jesus—that is, His essential mind and spirit—*they* are spirit and are life.

That the Church in the Evangelist's day required this elucidation of the mind of Jesus on ' the sacramental principle,' we may take for granted. *How much* it required this reminder, we do not know—but may surmise. The Mystery cults, with their magical emphasis, spoke an *easy* word to the needs of humanity. Thus, and thus, was ' salvation ' to be found—by this initiatory rite, by that rite which ensured communion with deity. No, would say the Johannine author; but only as the cleansing was an inward cleansing, only as the partaking was a real moral and spiritual act. The Church of Jesus, he would say, rightly preserves the outward and visible signs; but her essential task is to make these rites a reality in the lives of His followers.

4. *JUDGEMENT*

In the body of the Commentary, the teaching of the Gospel on Judgement is elucidated, whenever the passage demands it. It is not necessary, therefore, to repeat here what is there said. Yet it is desirable to state what we conceive to be the main clue to the teaching of the Gospel on this issue.

It is clear that in the early years of the Church Christians looked for a speedy end of ' the world.' They associated this end with a coming-again of the Messiah on the clouds of heaven, and believed that His coming would be a great Judgement Day. These Apocalyptic ideas find expression in the *earlier* Epistles of Paul: traces of their presence are plainly found, also, in the teaching of Jesus recorded in the Synoptic Gospels.

The striking fact is that the Fourth Evangelist has no place in his thought for these visionary ideas of an approaching cataclysmic Judgement Day. What is the explanation of this fact?

The whole question as to the place of Apocalyptic in the teaching of Jesus is too intricate to be entered upon here. Our own view, let it be briefly said, is that Jesus was not the deluded Apocalyptic visionary which the views of some modern students presuppose. It is exceedingly probable that symbolical Apocalyptic language employed by Jesus to express His thought was misunderstood. The explanation, therefore, of the fact that no visions of an Apocalyptic Judgement Day loom before the eyes of the Fourth Evangelist lies in the fact that he is returning to the essential moral and spiritual emphasis of Jesus Himself. In this Gospel the teaching of Jesus, we believe, is set forth in its original purity. The Evangelist is unfolding the essential meaning which that teaching had for the Master's own consciousness. Judgement is not future, but present. Rather, perhaps, we should say it is *Eternal*, not Temporal. It is a process of sifting of the true from the false, the good from the evil, which is ever in operation. This Judgement will, of course, reach its climax; but this climax is not conceived by the author as belonging to a specific point of future time. ' The resurrection of judgement ' of which the author speaks, is his symbolic way of expressing in the language of his day the quality of *finality* which is inherent in a spiritual blindness and moral disobedience when persisted in. In the inexorable logic of Eternity, evil and falsehood are brought to ' final ' judgement by the Spirit of Truth. The author, like Jesus, saw all things *sub specie æternitatis*. Judgement, like eternal life, is of quality, of essence, not of quantity or of time. The attitude which men adopted to Jesus was *decisive* for themselves: it revealed their essential nature. Such an attitude, if persisted in, involves a *final* judgement: and, in such, the winnowing-instrument is ever the same—the qualities of Grace and Truth which were uniquely manifested in the historic Jesus.

Judgement, therefore, is *intrinsic* to life. Life in its eternal and essential quality was incarnate in Jesus. Therefore it can be said that 'the Father hath committed judgement to the Son' ($5^{22ff.}$). This is not the language of the Apocalyptic imagination. For, as the passage continues, 'The hour . . . *now is* when the dead shall hear the voice of the Son of God.'

The Johannine author's phrases about Judgement can only be understood by those who have some insight into his mind. He uses traditional language to express his thought—or rather to express the thought of Jesus. But to understand the thought it is necessary to penetrate to the meaning of the language for his consciousness. Jesus Himself continually used current modes of speech, but it would be a profound mistake to imagine that the use of current modes of speech indicated His acceptance of current modes of thought. Every great and original thinker struggles with the language of his day to express ideas which transcend the ideas of his contemporaries. For this reason he is misunderstood by the majority. Conventional phrases which he uses lead these at first to suppose that he is seeking to convey the ideas with which they are familiar. But a little later he is found using language which does not conform to their current ideas. They then become mystified: they have lost their bearings—'we know not what he saith' is the language of their perplexity. They cannot make his teaching cohere. His thought escapes the meshes of their linguistic and ideational net. All this is true of the eschatological teaching of Jesus. His profoundly spiritual thought struggled with the inadequacies of symbolical language and customary figures of speech. Words and figures were not equal to the subtlety and rarity of His teaching. The Johannine author had a profounder insight into the mind of Jesus than any other New Testament writer, and a 'quicker' *rapport* with it. It is for this reason that his own language gives rise to conflicting interpretations. He can tell us in one place that 'the Father hath committed judgement to the Son,' and later attribute to Jesus the words, 'I judge no man' (8^{15}), and yet later, 'I came not to judge the world, but to save the world' (12^{47}). He can speak of this judgement as *present*, and later speak of a 'last day.' In one chapter he can ascribe to Jesus the words: 'Verily, verily, I say unto you, He that heareth my word, and believeth him that sent me, hath eternal life, and cometh not into judgement, but hath passed out of death into life' (5^{24}) ; in the next chapter he can attribute to Jesus these words, when He is speaking of him who believes on the Son, 'I will raise him up at the last day' (6^{40}). Modern readers ask: How *can* we make to cohere the idea that the true believer has *now* passed from death into life and does not come into judgement, with the idea that this same true believer will be raised up at the 'last day'? And many modern interpreters, feeling that there is an incoherence of thought, attribute the latter idea to someone who redacted the Gospel. On the contrary, we suggest that in such a phrase as 'the last day' the Evangelist is using the language of *time* to convey an idea which is not of time. When he speaks of 'Word' he does not mean a spoken word. So when he speaks of 'day' he does not mean a period of time; nor when he speaks of ' last ' does he mean a point of time. What he means when he speaks of ' the last day ' is the quality of finality. The life which belongs to the spiritually regenerate man has in it a quality of eternity; and that quality will be completely sifted from every trace of evil in a consummation which indwells the thought and purpose of God.

The Johannine author is not looking for a catastrophic coming of the Messiah to pass a *last* judgement upon men. He knows that alienation from that life which was incarnate in Jesus involves of itself spiritual death. And when he speaks of ' those in the tombs ' hearing His voice he is not thinking of those who are *physically* dead; nor when he speaks of them as *coming forth* is he thinking of a general physical resurrection at a ' Great Assize.' The crudities of mediæval fancies did not belong to the Evangelist. He *knew*, in other words, that he was using figurative and symbolical language. Judgement is not a temporal episode, but an eternal fact. And because it is *eternal* fact, it is *universal* fact. So we read, ' ALL that are in the tombs shall hear his voice, and shall come forth; they that have done good, unto the resurrection of life; and they that have done ill, unto the resurrection of judgement ' (5^{29}). Even though they are ' in the tombs ', they cannot but listen to this voice. But what is it to *listen*? Not, to *obey*. The voice of eternity is an *authoritative* voice: it *requires* either obedience or disobedience. To stop the ears to this voice is one way of listening; it is the way of disobedience. To hear with the inward moral and spiritual ear is the way of obedience.

In all the language of the Evangelist there is a conscious symbolism. The very word which is translated ' judgement ' means a ' separating,' a ' sifting.' The Latin word *cribrum*, a sieve, comes from the same Greek root as the word *krisis*. Symbolism indwells all the language of religion. The Evangelist was not of those who mistake the symbol for the reality. He pours the moral and spiritual thought of Jesus into the symbolical religious moulds of his day—in this he was only following the method of Jesus Himself. He hoped to speak to the mind of his readers through the symbols he employed. But, like every great spiritual thinker, his language was not wholly understood. Such misunderstanding, by those of literalist mind, is the almost inevitable penalty incurred by the spiritual seer who uses symbolical language. The history of religion is, in part, the story of the misunderstanding of the prophets by the majority.

In the Commentary itself we seek to elucidate the meaning of the language of ' judgement ' to the mind of the Evangelist: and therefore refer the reader to the comments on the following passages—3^{16-21}, $5^{19\ ff.}$, $6^{39-40,\ 54}$, 11^{24-26}, $12^{31,\ 47-48}$. All this language has its meaning in the context of the central thought of the Gospel, which is that of ' Life.' To the unfolding of that thought we now turn.

5. *ETERNAL LIFE*

Perhaps the most characteristic phrase in the Fourth Gospel—if we may say that any one phrase is more characteristic than others which are also distinctive —is the phrase ' eternal life.' He who knows what ' eternal life ' means to the Evangelist has the essence of his Gospel. He who knows not this, knows nothing.

The phrase is found in a few places in the Synoptic Gospels. It occurs in the narrative of the rich young man, who asks Jesus: ' what shall I do that I may inherit eternal life.?' (Mk. 10^{17}; Mt. 19^{16}; Lk. 18^{18}.) The same phrase is used by 'a certain lawyer' in Lk. 10^{25}, who, however, Luke says, only asked in order to 'tempt' Jesus. In the teaching given by Jesus, subsequent to the interview with the rich young man, the phrase itself is used by Him: whoever, says Jesus, leaves house, or brethren, or sisters, or mother, or father, or children, or lands, for His name's sake and for the Gospel's sake 'shall receive . . . in the age to come eternal life.' (Mk. 10^{30}; see Mt. 19^{29} and Lk. 18^{30}.) In this passage it seems clear that the Synoptic Evangelists understood Jesus to mean by 'eternal life' a life in some Messianic age which was yet to be. The phrase is also found in the parable of the Judgement, as recorded in Mt. 25: there we read that the righteous shall go 'into eternal life' (*v.* 46). These are the only places in the Synoptic Gospels where the phrase 'eternal life' is found. There are, however, a few places in these Gospels where the word 'life,' without the adjective 'eternal,' is used in a qualitative sense which brings it into the closest relation to the phrase as found in the Fourth Gospel. In Mt. 7^{14}, for example, Jesus says: 'For narrow is the gate, and straitened the way, that leadeth unto life, and few be they that find it': a teaching which reminds us of the passage in Ps. 16^{11}: 'Thou wilt shew me the path of life; In thy presence is fulness of joy; In thy right hand there are pleasures for evermore.' Again, in Mk. 9^{43-45}—with the parallel passage in Mt. 18^{8}—Jesus speaks of that quality of life which is reached along the road of discipline and sacrifice: 'And if thy hand cause thee to stumble, cut it off: it is good for thee to enter into life maimed, rather than having thy two hands to go into Gehenna, into the unquenchable fire. And if thy foot cause thee to stumble, cut it off: it is good for thee to enter into life halt, rather than having thy two feet to be cast into Gehenna.' Such a Synoptic passage reminds us at once of the teaching of Jesus in Jn. 15 where He says: 'Every branch in me that beareth not fruit, he taketh it away: and every branch that beareth fruit, he cleanseth—or pruneth—it, that it may bear more fruit' (15^{2}). Again, in Mk. 8^{35}—with the parallel passages in Mt. and Lk.—Jesus speaks of that true life which only comes through the sacrifice of material interests: 'For whosoever would save his life shall lose it; and whosoever shall lose his life for my sake and the gospel's shall save it.' And in Lk. 14^{26} Jesus says that if a man 'hate' not the interests of time, 'and his own life also,' he cannot be His disciple. This life of discipleship, however, is the true life, for which the world were well lost. (See Mt. 16^{24-26}.) Once again, in Lk. 12^{15}, Jesus uses the word 'life' in the same transcendent and spiritual sense, where He says: 'a man's life consisteth not in the abundance of the things which he possesseth.'

It is, however, to the Fourth Gospel that we must go to find the consummation of all religion expressed in terms of 'eternal life.' The phrase itself is used repeatedly—in $3^{15, 16, 36}$, $4^{14, 36}$, $5^{24, 39}$, $6^{27, 40, 47, 54, 68}$, 10^{28}, $12^{25, 50}$, $17^{2, 3}$. In many other places in the Gospel, however, the same thought is present where the word 'life,' without the adjective 'eternal,' is used. These are so numerous that they need not here be enumerated.

What is this 'eternal life' of which Jesus speaks in the Fourth Gospel, this 'life' which it was His mission to bring to men?

It is clear that the thought expressed is that of a quality of life inherent in

Himself. The whole conception is on the loftiest plane of spiritual communion and ethical endeavour. It is a life of transcendent quality and of timeless reality. This life is not a mere 'existence,' and is not to be measured in terms of mere duration. It is the 'life' of which Paul speaks, when he says in his first Corinthian Epistle—'All things are yours, whether . . . *life*.' Clearly, Paul was not there thinking of physical existence—which is no exclusive possession of the true Christian: he was thinking of *life* as men ought to know it and live it. And it should be a *present* possession. This is true to the whole emphasis of the teaching of Jesus in the Fourth Gospel. Eternal life is not some speculative existence at some point of time in the distant future. It is the reality of life as known here and now. 'Eternity,' wrote Boetius in his *De Consolatione Philosophiae*, 'is the complete possession of unlimited life all at once.' 'Whosoever believeth in him *hath* eternal life' (3^{16}). 'Verily, verily, I say unto you, He that believeth *hath* eternal life' (6^{47}). 'Verily, verily, I say unto you, Except ye eat the flesh of the Son of man and drink his blood, ye have not life in yourselves. He that eateth my flesh and drinketh my blood *hath* eternal life' (6^{53-54}). 'And this is life eternal, that they should know thee the only true God, and him whom thou didst send, even Jesus Christ' (17^{3}). 'These are written, that ye may believe that Jesus is the Christ, the Son of God; and that believing ye may have life in his name' (20^{31}).

This life is the life which Jesus Himself knew, and the life of which He was the incarnate manifestation. In the Prologue we read of the eternal Logos, that 'in him was life, and the life was the light of men': and later, in the great incarnational affirmation, the Evangelist says that 'the Word became flesh and dwelt among us, and we beheld his glory, glory as of the only begotten from the Father, full of grace and truth.' That is, the transcendent quality of life which is inherent in God Himself was uniquely revealed in the historic life of Jesus. The same truth is stated in the fifth chapter: 'For as the Father hath life in himself, even so gave he to the Son also to have life in himself' (5^{26}). That is, to Jesus who lived in perfect harmony with God belonged that transcendent quality of life which had its source in the Father. It was because Jesus knew such life, that He called God, and always thought of God as, Father. He thought of Himself as 'Son' because He was in perfect fellowship with the Father. He was, therefore, a sharer in the Father's own life. What is fellowship but *sharing*? The Source of this life was God; the Giver of this life was God. Jesus always regarded Himself as the *transmitter* of this life, and not as its originating Source. He was a transmitter in virtue of that which He had *received* from the Father. Thus, Jesus says in the sixth chapter: 'my Father giveth you the true bread out of heaven. For the bread of God is that which cometh down out of heaven, and giveth life to the world'; Jesus then goes on to say, 'I am the bread of life: he that cometh to me shall not hunger, and he that believeth on me shall never thirst' (6^{33-35}). In this passage Jesus clearly states that the sustenance of man's true life is in God—it comes down out of heaven. He also goes on to say that He knew Himself to be the transmitter of this Divine sustenance to men. He is the bread of life, in virtue of the fact that He has received this sustaining life from the Father. In the same chapter Jesus says: 'It is the spirit that quickeneth; the flesh profiteth nothing: the words (ῥήματα) that I have spoken unto you are spirit, and are life'

(6^{63}). What Jesus here says is that His own essential mind is the medium of life to men: and the words of Jesus—not His verbal speech—are the expression of the *incarnate Word*. The *word* of Jesus is therefore not His, but the Father's who sent Him (14^{24}). The sustenance of this life in Jesus was in doing the Father's will: 'My meat,' He said, 'is to do the will of him that sent me and to accomplish his work' (4^{34}). This life belonged to Jesus in so far as He did the Father's will: God's will, that is, was the very life of Jesus. It was because He Himself had eaten that He could give to men to eat. But it is no magical impartation to men: they, and they alone, eat the bread which He has to give who partake of His own spirit, and do the will of God which He Himself does. So He says: 'Work not for the meat which perisheth, but for the meat which abideth unto eternal life' (6^{27}). In all these passages—to which more might be added, and will be noted in the course of the ensuing elucidation in the Commentary—there is the clear declaration that this 'eternal life,' of which Jesus knew Himself to be the mediator, has its Source in God. Eternal life, therefore, is that quality of life which is inherent in God Himself.

The appropriation of this life is through that act of the whole personality which is called in the Fourth Gospel 'believing' on Jesus. It has often been noted that the noun for 'faith' never once occurs in the Fourth Gospel—and only once in the Johannine Epistles, namely, in 1 Jn. 5^{4}. Instead of the noun 'faith,' however, the verb 'to believe' (πιστεύειν) is repeatedly found. The absence of the noun, and the continual presence of the verb, is highly significant. The Evangelist does not dwell in the realm of dogmatic abstractions, but in the realm of concrete activities of the personality. He knows that 'belief,' to be of any worth, must be the expression of the whole life of a man. A 'belief' is *a man's belief*: it is not an abstract statement achieved by the speculative faculty of other people, however intellectually competent such people may be. The gateway to eternal life is not acquiescent assent to the dogmatic formulas which a majority of the Church's ablest speculative thinkers have been able to achieve. It is the enlightened and obedient acceptance of the spiritual truth revealed in Jesus. It is not obedience to what we are told, an obedience imposed by the infallibility claims of those who call upon us to make the surrender. It is insight into the truth itself: and the obedience, in this case, is intrinsic to the insight itself. Truth is never *imposed*; it always *imposes itself*. It springs out of reality; because it is the expression of reality. In this sense Jesus Himself is *the truth*—His life, that is, reveals what God is like, and what God wishes men to be and to do.

There are numerous passages in the Fourth Gospel where it is clear that 'believing' is regarded as much more than mere acquiescence in statements made by Jesus. In the Prologue, for example, it is used as a synonym for 'receiving': 'as many as *received* him, to them gave he the right to become children of God, even to them that *believe* on his name' (1^{12}). The Johannine author certainly does not mean by *receiving* the Divine Logos, or by *believing on his name*, a mere intellectual assent to His Being. Those who *receive* Him are those who are 'born . . . of God.' Thus *believing* is the act of the spiritually awakened nature; it involves *fellowship* with God. To become a 'son' of God means the same in the Fourth Gospel as entering into life, or as having eternal life. Such 'believing' is also called 'knowing'; and it is clear that to the Evangelist 'knowledge' is not 'of things we see.' 'This is life eternal, that they should *know* thee the only true God, and him whom thou didst send, even Jesus Christ.' To 'know' God is the same as to 'receive' the Divine Spirit; which, again, is the same as to 'believe on his name.' In the sixth chapter, Jesus says; 'this is the will of my Father, that every one that beholdeth the Son, and believeth on him, should have eternal life' (6^{40}). Thus to the Evangelist, *knowing* Jesus, and *believing on* Him, mean the self-same thing: it is through this fellowship of thought and purpose with Jesus that eternal life is found. Again in the seventh chapter, the Evangelist says that he who *believes* on Jesus will become as a life-giving stream of water; he will be a channel of the Divine Spirit. 'He that believeth on me, as the scripture said, out of his belly shall flow rivers of living water. But this he spake of the Spirit, which they that believed on him were to receive' (7^{38-39}). Jesus Himself was the *water of life*, in virtue of His perfect fellowship with the Father: His disciples themselves will become channels of that cleansing and thirst-quenching stream, in virtue of their fellowship with Him. Again in the twelfth chapter Jesus says: 'While ye have the light, believe on the light, that ye may become sons of light' (12^{36}). Those, that is, who *believe on* the light become partakers of the nature of light—they are 'sons of light.' *Light* is one of the names for an essential quality of the Divine nature in this Gospel; and it is one of the names for Jesus Himself, who partook, in the depths of His consciousness and through the whole range of His life of obedient service, of the Divine nature. To be a 'son' of God is to share in all the moral and spiritual qualities of the Divine Being; and among all these qualities is that of illumination, or revelation. Yet once again, the last word of the Gospel—as originally penned—states the author's purpose in writing: 'these are written that ye may believe that Jesus is the Christ, the Son of God; and that believing ye may have life in his name' (20^{31}). No understanding reader of this Gospel can peruse what the author has written without seeing that to him *believing in the name of Jesus* is much more than a theoretical assent to His Messiahship, or to His Sonship. It is nothing less than that fellowship with the mind of Jesus, that practical identification with His Mission, which issues in eternal life, the life that is life indeed.

In many ways the first Epistle is an elaboration, and unfolding, of the ideas which are germane to the Gospel—it was written, as we believe, by the Evangelist. 'Knowledge' of Jesus, we there read, is only found where 'the love of God' is found; and such 'knowledge' belongs only to those who 'walk even as he walked.' 'Hereby know we that we know him, if we keep his commandments. He that saith, I know him, and keepeth not his commandments, is a liar, and the truth is not in him: but whoso keepeth his word, in him verily hath the love of God been perfected. Hereby know we that we are in him: he that saith he abideth in him ought himself also to walk even as he walked' (1 Jn. 2^{3-6}). Later in the same epistle he writes: 'Beloved, let us love one another: for love is of God; and everyone that loveth is begotten of God, and knoweth God. He that loveth not knoweth not God; for God is love' (1 Jn. 4^{7-8}). Eternal life is the life of perfect love: this life has its Source in God, for 'God is love.' The Evangelist says again in his first Epistle what he said in his Gospel—that ' no man hath beheld God at any time ' (1 Jn. 4^{12}). But he goes on to say that Him, whom we shall never behold with the eye of flesh, we may *know* in ethical and spiritual communion: ' if we love one another, God abideth in us, and his love is perfected in us: hereby know we that we abide in him, and he in us, because he hath given us of his Spirit ' (1 Jn. 4^{12-13}). Thus, *knowledge* of Jesus is the same as *abiding in* Jesus—the figure of which Jesus makes so much use in the Fourth Gospel. To *love*, to *abide*, to *know*, and to *believe* are all but different ways of describing the reality which is called *eternal life*. ' And this is his commandment, that we should believe in the name of his Son Jesus Christ, and love one another, even as he gave us commandment. And he that keepeth his commandments abideth in him, and he in him. And hereby we know that he abideth in us, by the Spirit which he gave us ' (1 Jn. 3^{23-24}).

All this the Fourth Evangelist learned, whether directly or indirectly, from Jesus. It is the insight of Jesus Himself which he expresses. Nothing was farther from the mind of Jesus than that eternal life was a reward of correct beliefs—as we may see from the Synoptic Gospels as well as from this Gospel. It is a man's ' spirit ' which, in the eyes of Jesus, is the criterion of his religion. ' Not everyone that saith unto me, Lord, Lord, shall enter into the kingdom of heaven, but he that doeth the will of my Father which is in heaven.' Many of the ' righteous ' shall in the Day, according to the parable in Mt. 25, find themselves approved, when they do not remember to have acknowledged or recognised Him in speech or formal belief. ' Inasmuch as ye did it unto one of these my brethren, even these least, ye did it unto me.' And, on the other hand, those who did not remember ever to have passed Him by, find themselves among the ' goats.' ' Inasmuch as ye did it not unto one of these least, ye did it not unto me.' In none of the Gospels is the test of real religion submission to an external authority, or conformity to ceremonial or precept. ' By their fruits ye shall know them.' Nothing entering into a man defiles him. It is ' out of the heart ' that proceed both everything that can be called good and everything that can be called evil. Thus it is only the ' pure in heart ' who can see God, or discern His perfect purity. The main concern of our Lord in His teaching was not to add to the stock of men's information; it was to kindle the insight of their own souls and to elicit a personal obedience to the principles that guided His own life. For that reason, we are told, He taught in parables, so that people should see with their own eyes, or not at all. He did not enunciate dogmatic formulas or rules of behaviour. There was a pearl of great price, but it had to be sought for diligently and sacrificially before it could be found. He Himself was not concerned to write down anything for the facile and fallacious solution of the later problems of His disciples. His aim was not to add to the number of ' authorities ' to which the future could turn, as to a codified past. In this He differed from ' the Scribes ' of all the ages and all the races. The people who heard and saw Him recognised the difference, when they said of Him, *not* that He taught *from authorities*, but that He taught *with authority*. They recognised, that is, that here was one whose life was *intrinsically* authoritative, whose teaching had upon it the *self-evidencing* stamp of truth.

It is the Fourth Evangelist's fidelity to this ' mind ' of Jesus which has attracted to it the saints, the seers, the mystics, of all the centuries. This Gospel gives no support to materialistic conceptions of a magical impartation of 'immortality.' In spite of certain assertions which are confidently made by exegetes, we maintain that it was at the farthest possible remove from the Evangelist's mind to declare that a physical immersion in water, or a physical partaking of material food, was necessary to the reception of eternal life. The phrases he uses can only be understood in the light of his mind, in the context of his own ideas. Eternal life, he says, comes by the regeneration of the whole nature. The 'believing' attitude of which he speaks is not the acquiescence in certain dogmas. It is, as it has recently been expressed, 'the active consent of personal adherence.'[1] It is, in other words, real discipleship, and not fictitious discipleship. It is fully compatible with the 'doubt' of which Browning speaks in *Rabbi Ben Ezra:*

Rather I prize the doubt
Low kinds exist without,
Finished and finite clods, untroubled by a spark.

It is the 'Faith' of which Robert Hugh Benson speaks in *Christian Evidences*:

Now God forbid that Faith be blind assent,
Grasping what others know; else Faith were nought
But learning, as of some far continent
Which others sought,
And carried thence, better the tale to teach,
Pebbles and shells, poor fragments of the beach.

Now God forbid that Faith be built on dates,
Cursive or uncial letters, scribe or gloss,
What one conjectures, proves, or demonstrates :
This were the loss
Of all to which God bids that man aspire,
This were the death of life, quenching of fire.

Nay, but with Faith I see. Not even Hope,
Her glorious sister, stands so high as she.
For this but stands expectant on the slope
That leads where He
Her source and consummation sets His seat,
Where Faith dwells always to caress His feet.

Nay then, if proof and tortured argument
Content thee—teach thee that the Lord is there,
Or risen again; I pray thee be content,
But leave me here
With eye unsealed by any proof of thine,
With eye unsealed to know the Lord is mine.

Nor does this Gospel contain any doctrines of 'heaven' and 'hell' such as have commended themselves to cosmic geographers. The whole conception of 'eternal life' is on the loftiest plane of spiritual communion and ethical endeavour.

[1] Bacon, *The Gospel of the Hellenists*, p. 347.

It does not decay with the disappearance of apocalyptic hopes and fantasies. It is not rendered obsolete with the progress of spiritual enlightenment. As the notion of ' heaven,' as a place of *reward* for conformity, whether in belief or in cult, becomes obsolescent, the conception of eternal life advances and grows. Eternal life is not the *reward* of virtue; it is the life of virtue itself. He who knows this life is like the ' Gnostic ' of whom Clement of Alexandria speaks: ' By reason of his surpassing holiness the Gnostic would rather pray without receiving than receive without praying. For his whole life is prayer and converse with God, and if he be free from sin he shall surely receive what he desires.' This is the ' Gnosticism ' of Jesus, as He is portrayed in the Fourth Gospel. This is the ' knowledge ' which itself is eternal life. It is the ' abundant life ' which in the tenth chapter Jesus declares it His purpose to minister. ' I came that they might have life, and might have it abundantly.' It is the wholly disinterested love of God, the wholly selfless obedience to Him, the wholly satisfying fellowship with Him.

But while it is ' known ' here, it is not *fully* known. A wholly disinterested love of God is hard to find among men. Obedience is at best but partial. Communion is clouded. The goal seems to fade for ever as we move towards it. Will it ever be reached? And, even if we may hope that it may be reached, who can now say what that goal will be like? Who could describe it but him who has seen it? It is not *described* for us in the Johannine Gospel. But there is implicit in the creed which underlies the whole teaching of Jesus in this Gospel the certainty that nothing that belongs to true life will ever pass away. The qualities which belong to this ' life ' are the qualities which belong to the very life of God Himself —Light and Love. These qualities in men are always the ' gift ' of God: God is other than His ' gifts,' and other than His ' sons ' who *receive* the gifts. Jesus Himself, the Unique Son, was the Father's own gift: and in all things the Son acknowledged that the Source of His life was the Father. As He, the Son, went forth to the Garden, with the Cross looming before Him, He knew that He was but returning to the Father. And He said to His disciples: ' Let not your hearts be troubled: believe in God, believe also in me. In my Father's house are many mansions; if it were not so, I would have told you; for I go to prepare a place for you.' There are many ' abodes,' corresponding to the character of the work done, and the work still to do. For those who seek to accomplish the Father's work it can be said, in complete fidelity to the message of Jesus in the Johannine Gospel:

No work begun shall ever pause for death.

' I meditate,' wrote Wordsworth to Sir George Beaumont, ' upon the Scriptures, especially the Gospel of St. John, and my Creed rises up of itself, with the ease of an exhalation, yet a fabric of adamant.'

' In the beginning was the Word, and the Word was with God, and the Word was God.'

' And the Word became flesh, and dwelt among us.'

' This is life eternal, that they should know thee, the only true God, and him whom thou didst send, even Jesus Christ.'

' And the world passeth away, and the lust thereof: but he that doeth the will of God abideth for ever.'

TEXT AND COMMENTARY

The Gospel According to St. John

THE PROLOGUE: THE INCARNATION OF THE WORD

JN. 1$^{1-18}$

1 1 In the beginning was the Word, and
the Word was with God, and the Word
2 was God. The same was in the beginning
3 with God. All things were made by him;
and without him was not anything made
4 that hath been made. In him was life;
5 and the life was the light of men. And
the light shineth in the darkness; and the
6 darkness apprehended it not. There came
a man, sent from God, whose name was
7 John. The same came for witness, that
he might bear witness of the light, that all
8 might believe through him. He was not
the light, but *came* that he might bear
9 witness of the light. There was the true
light, *even the light* which lighteth every
10 man, coming into the world. He was in
the world, and the world was made by
11 him, and the world knew him not. He
came unto his own, and they that were his
12 own received him not. But as many as
received him, to them gave he the right to
become children of God, *even* to them that
13 believe on his name: which were born,
not of blood, nor of the will of the flesh,
14 nor of the will of man, but of God. And
the Word became flesh, and dwelt among
us (and we beheld his glory, glory as of the
only begotten from the Father), full of
15 grace and truth. John beareth witness of
him, and crieth, saying, This was he of
whom I said, He that cometh after me is
become before me: for he was before me.
16 For of his fulness we all received, and
17 grace for grace. For the law was given by
Moses; grace and truth came by Jesus
18 Christ. No man hath seen God at any
time; the only begotten Son, which is in
the bosom of the Father, he hath declared
him.

In these verses, which form the Prologue or Preface to the Gospel, the Evangelist declares his central theme. He is going to write about the Incarnation of the Eternal Word.

Whether the author wrote these verses first, or wrote them last, it is interesting, though not important, to conjecture. Many a modern author writes his Preface after he has concluded his book: this Preface thus contains the distilled essence of his whole thought. For the labour of composition serves to clarify the mind, and to give sharp and vivid outline to what the writer wished to say. 'The last thing that we discover in writing a book is to know what to put at the beginning,' as Pascal had the insight to declare. When the Evangelist wrote, however, his thought was already mature. From out of a profound and brooding mind he sat down to express what already he vividly saw and deeply felt. An atmosphere of mature serenity pervades the whole Gospel. The Preface may probably, therefore, have been the first words the Evangelist penned. It must not be regarded as a detached 'doctrinal proem,' or as a kind of philosophical jumping-off board: it is integral to the whole Gospel. Some have sought to recognise in it 'a poem in three strophes,' with prose additions in, for example, *vv.* 6–8 and 12*b*–13. While, however, the thought of the Evangelist is expressed in poetical form, there is no reason for supposing that he did not write the whole Preface himself.

Milton began his epic, *Paradise Lost*, with a similar introduction, in which he declared his theme. He was going to write, it will be remembered, 'Of man's first disobedience,' and how 'One greater man' restored us. Even so, the Johannine author is going to write of how the Eternal Word of God became incarnate in the historic Jesus.

The Gospel will thus be 'an ellipse with two foci.' The Evangelist's thought, that is, will revolve round two fixed points. One is Eternity: the other is History. One is the Unseen God: the other is the Jesus whose glory, he says, 'we beheld.' Mrs. Hamilton-King expressed the author's central theme when she wrote:

For this world, the Word of God is Christ.

1–2. The opening sentence comes with the abruptness of settled conviction and unhesitating insight. The Gospel begins, not with a philosopher's careful discussion, but with a seer's dramatic statement. It is interesting to compare it with the opening of the Jewish philosopher Spinoza's *Ethics*. Spinoza begins with a series of definitions—he tells us what he means by 'Cause of Itself,' 'Substance,' 'Attribute,' 'Mode,' 'God,' etc. The Evangelist begins with his conclusions. The one begins by defining his terms, the other by asserting his message. The Evangelist, for example, leaves the reader to define the central term he employs in this prologue. That term is *Logos*, translated in our English versions *Word*. Goethe, it will be remembered, suggested in *Faust* four different translations. 'In the beginning was the *Word* (Wort) . . . the *Thought* (Sinn) . . . the *Power* (Kraft) . . . the *Deed* (That)'—deciding upon the last. Such a translation would be not inappropriate to the Evangelist's thought. For what he wishes to say is that the *Creative Thought* of God has been *operative* from all eternity.

'In the beginning . . .' These are the words of a Jew steeped in the thought and language of the Hebrew Scriptures. 'It is Moses, not Plato, who is revived in the Ephesian teacher,' as F. D. Maurice said, more than two generations ago. 'In the beginning God created the heaven and the earth,' are the opening words of the Old Testament Scriptures: and they lived in the mind of this Christian Jew, belonging to the race of Abraham, of Moses, and of the Prophets—the race of Jesus Himself. The undertone of the Johannine author's thought is God, the Reality of all realities, from whose Creative mind all existence has sprung. His mind can find no ground save in God. When in these modern days we grope our way, by the light of our theories of Evolution, back to the beginning of things, we find—what? Is it—'Back—back to nothingness!'? But who that has not lost all sanity will tell us that out of 'nothingness' has proceeded man's thought, and prayer, and sacrifice, and love? If, then, we are unable, as sane men, to take so desperate a leap of sheer unbelief, what else can we say but what the Johannine prophet said? 'In the beginning was the Eternal Divine Word.'

God is not for the Evangelist, as He is for the merely rationalist mind, just a necessary hypothesis to account for the universe. The assurance of God is for him—as for the late Baron von Hügel—'not anything built up by mere human reasoning, no clever or subtle hypothesis, nothing particularly French or German or English.' This assurance for our author had been mediated through all the experiences of life, and had been given unmistakably in the depths of his moral and spiritual consciousness.

God for the Evangelist has never been the silent, the distant, the inactive God. So he begins, not with the thought of an Absolute, existing in or for Itself: but with the thought of an Eternal, Ever-present, Ever-creative Mind. When he speaks of *the Word* that was *with God*, and was *Divine*, he is not thinking of a Being in any way separate from God, or of some *Hypostasis*. The later dogmatic Trinitarian distinctions should not be read *into* his mind—however legitimately, in the light of a philosophy that was not his, they may be read *out of* his mind. It may be possible to maintain with the late Bishop Westcott—indeed the general consensus of Christian opinion holds that it is not only *possible* but *rationally necessary*—that 'the absolute, eternal, immanent relations of the Persons of the Godhead furnish the basis for revelation.' But, to our view, such a judgement is not so much exegesis of the passage as interpretation of it in the light of the dogmatic history of the three centuries subsequent to the Evangelist's writing. The Evangelist is seeking to say that God Himself, in His ineffable being, is the source of all Creation and of all Revelation. An author's language in this transcendent realm will confuse us, unless we have some *rapport* with his mind and some understanding of his cultural heritage. So here the Evangelist takes a well-known term (Logos), does not define it, but unfolds what he himself means by it. In the Introduction we have sought to show that the idea belonged to the Old Testament, and is involved in the whole religious belief and experience of the Hebrew Scriptures. It is a most fitting term to express his message. For a man's 'word' is the expression of his 'mind'; and his 'mind' is his essential personality. Every mind must express itself, for activity is of the very nature of mind. 'A mind quite vacant,' or quite inactive, is not a 'mind.' Thus the author speaks of the 'Word' that was *with* God, and was *Divine*, to express his conviction that God has ever been Active and Revealing Mind. God, by His very nature, cannot sit in His heaven and do nothing. When later in the Gospel Jesus says, 'My Father worketh hitherto' He is saying what the Evangelist himself says in this first verse of the Prologue.

3. 'All things were made by him; and without him was not anything made that hath been made.' In the Introduction, when speaking of the *Logos*, we have set forth parallels in the Old Testament Scriptures to the central thought of this verse. In the *Epistle to the Hebrews*—whose teaching is 'like that of St. John, characteristically Palestinian'[1]—we have a strikingly similar utterance: 'By faith we understand that the worlds have been framed by the word of God, so that what is seen hath not been made out of things which do appear' (Heb. 11^3). Here is the same thought of the creative activity of God—though ῥῆμα is used here, expressing, no doubt, a single act of the Divine mind. The Evangelist may probably here have been thinking, further, of a belief, held by some in his day, and widely current in the second century—the Gnostic belief, namely, that matter itself is Eternal. It was part of his intention to rebut such a belief. No, he would say, the whole universe came into being by the purposive act of God. It was neither self-made, nor was it made by a Great External Artificer. It is the expression of the living mind of the living God.

4. Life is the highest manifestation of the activity of the Divine Word, and this Divinely originated life has been for the illumination of men. 'In him was life, and the life was the light of men.' The author is here thinking of the rational, moral, and spiritual illumination which has flowed to humanity from Him who

[1] Westcott, *Epistle to Hebrews*, p. lxi.

is the Divine Source of all good. All the light that has come to man in his searching for truth, in his obedience to the claims of duty, in his awareness of spiritual reality, has had its source in the Mind of God; and, if faithfully accepted and followed, will lead man back to Himself.

Thus at the outset the author expresses his lofty view of the spiritual nature of man. It was said of old: ' the mind of man is the throne of the Godhead.' Clement of Alexandria said: ' the soul of the righteous man is " God's own resemblance, effigy divine." ' Augustine said: ' if you dig deep enough in every man you find divinity.' Man's spiritual nature is eternal because it partakes of the nature of its Source.

The heroes and the saints
Thy messengers became;
And all the lamps that guide the world
Were kindled at Thy flame.

The words of the Psalmist may have been in the Evangelist's mind at this point: ' With Thee is the fountain of life, and in Thy light shall we see light.' (Ps. 36^9.) ' God,' says our author in his First Epistle, ' is light, and in him is no darkness at all.' (1 Jn. 1^5.)

An interesting, and attractive, translation of verses 3 and 4—which does not materially alter the exegesis—is that of the late Prof. B. W. Bacon [1]:

All things came into being through him;
Without him nothing received existence.
Through him the creation was suffused with life,
And the life was the guiding-light of men.

5. Amid the darkness of man's disobedience and ignorance, the Divine Light has always shone, and never been overcome. ' And the light shineth in the darkness; and the darkness overcame it not.' Here it will be noted that the Evangelist never seeks to *explain* ' the origin of evil.' He does not, that is, ask, Why darkness? and, Whence darkness? He leaves such speculative questions unasked and unanswered. He tells us in his First Epistle that there is no darkness in God: ' God is light and in him is no darkness at all.' (1 Jn. 1^5.) He accepts the fact of moral and spiritual darkness, attributing it to the disobedient will of man. Yet this darkness, as he adds, has never mastered the light.

The Greek word translated ' apprehended ' in the R.V. very probably means, as we have suggested, ' overcame,' or ' mastered.' The meaning of ' apprehending ' and of ' mastering ' almost merge into one another in our common speech. We may, for example, speak either of ' apprehending ' an author's thought, or of ' mastering ' it; and when we have mastered it, we may be said to have ' subdued ' it to our own purposes. To-day we might express the author's thought by saying that in every age God has witnessed to Himself in all that is true and good and beautiful; and that in no age has this witness been quenched. It was in the light

[1] *The Gospel of the Hellenists*, p. 243.

of this thought that Tertullian spoke of 'the witness of the soul by nature Christian.' It was the same thought which inspired the true and beautiful catholicity of the old poem:

Many man for Cristes love
Was martired in Romayne,
Er any Christendom was knowe there,
Or any cros honoured.

6–9. At this point the author's thought leaves these transcendent regions and turns to a man in history, John the Baptist. This abrupt transition may at first sight seem strange to a modern reader. But if he remembers the historical situation confronting the author, he will find here another clue to his mind and purpose. On the one hand, it is fitting that, before he comes to the great proclamation of the 14th verse, he should make reference to the forerunner. On the other hand, it is essential to his purpose that he should at the earliest opportunity assert the Baptist's complete subordination, as a teacher and prophet, to Jesus, the incarnate Word. When we place alongside this passage *vv.* 15, 20–23 and 26–27, it will be seen that the Evangelist wishes at the very outset of his Gospel to declare the subordination of John to Jesus. In the later verses of the chapter he singles out that part of the Baptist's teaching in which he himself affirmed his subordination to the Master, the latchet of whose shoe he was not worthy to unloose. Why should the Evangelist wish so emphatically to do this? Probably the reason is here. In his day there was a strain of teaching in the Church at Ephesus which was more akin to that of the Baptist than to that of Jesus. It may even be that there were those who were giving a position to the Baptist superior to that given to Jesus (see, e.g., Acts 18^{25}, 19^{1-7}). We learn from the *Clementine Recognitions*—a third-century document—that some of the disciples of John the Baptist had separated themselves from the followers of Jesus, declaring that their own master was the Christ.[1] Thus in the light of this consideration these references to John are seen, not to be a digression, but to be in full harmony with the Evangelist's whole intention. He wishes to give the supreme place to Jesus only among men. There have been many witnesses, and one historical forerunner, to the Truth and Grace of God: but there has been One only who has incarnated that Truth and Grace. So while the Evangelist would gladly recognise the truths which 'in manhood darkly join,' he would, with Tennyson—

Yield all blessing to the name
Of Him that made them current coin.

John was not the Light but came to bear witness to the Light. The real, the genuine light, which enlightens every man—the Baptist included—was then about to come into the world.

10–13. In *v.* 10 the Evangelist strikes another note, repeatedly heard throughout the Gospel. It is the tragic note of the world's opposition in every age to the good

[1] *Clementine Recognitions*, i. 54.

and to the true. Before the Incarnate One had appeared, the Divine life and truth, through which all created things had come, had been disowned by a world that should have been God's own. Yet not by all men. The rejection had never been universal. In every age the world has been saved by the few: always there have been those who would not disown their heavenly origin and destiny—else, indeed, the light had been overcome by the darkness. These were very 'sons' of God, 'sons' not by virtue of race or human ancestry—nor, as we should add to-day, by any credal or ecclesiastical ancestry—but by the allegiance of the whole being, itself the Divine gift, to God. 'Believing in God's name,' to the author, does not mean mere intellectual assent to the Divine existence: it means the trustful assent and obedient adventure of the whole personality to what God essentially is, and wills. This, again, is another of the author's favourite notes, and will be sounded again and again in his Gospel. He never speaks of 'faith,' the noun; but is always speaking of 'believing,' the verb. The use of the verb instead of the noun suggests the orientation of his whole mind. He is concerned, not with an abstraction about which men may argue, but about a *concrete activity* of the human personality. He is more concerned with 'believing' than with a 'creed.' Creeds are only of value in so far as they are the expression of the personal act of mind and heart and will. When they become as mere ramparts behind which the timid shelter, or as static formulas about which men dispute for disputing's sake, they are dead, and deadening. Thus the author, we are convinced, would have sympathised with what Tennyson *meant* when he said—though in his own 'creedless' days he could not have expressed it in Tennyson's way:

> *There lives more faith in honest doubt,*
> *Believe me, than in half the creeds.*

Indeed, he said pretty much the same thing in his First Epistle: 'He that saith that he is in the light, and hateth his brother, is in the darkness until now.' (1 Jn. 2^9.)

14–18. In *v.* 14 the Evangelist announces the text of his whole Gospel, and the central affirmation of Christianity. 'The Word became flesh.' When he so speaks he does not, of course, mean that the Eternal Word *became* a piece of flesh: what he means is that the Eternal Word *was manifest* in one who was flesh of our flesh and bone of our bone. The verb 'became' here must not be taken in a literalist, or unimaginative way. A dramatic poet is speaking, not a dogmatic theologian, or a speculative philosopher, or a careful scientist. He does not say that the Eternal Word *coincides*, in a spatial manner, with the Jesus of history. He would, therefore, have been merely bewildered by the kind of question which those who have completely misunderstood his mind have raised: such a question, for example, as, How are we to conceive that the cosmic functions of the Word were attended to during the life of the historic Jesus? The Evangelist, to repeat, does not say that the activity of God was *exhausted* by His self-manifestation in Jesus. With Paul he would say that 'Christ is God's' (1 Cor. 3^{23}): he would not say that 'God is Christ's.' The *presence* of God in Jesus does not, to the Evangelist, involve His *absence* from the rest of the universe. The Grace of God which *filled* Jesus was not, as a consequence, *used up*. 'From not a place, not a moment, not a creature, did the divine tide ebb to make the flood that rose within the soul of Christ.'

The Eternal Word 'dwelt' among us, he adds. The verb might be translated 'tabernacled': it reminds his readers of the Old Testament narrative of the 'tabernacle' of God placed in the centre of the tents of Israel. (See Exod. $40^{34f.}$.) Jesus was the 'tabernacle of God among men.' This tabernacle of flesh was no Gnostic or Docetic illusion—such as some in the Evangelist's day who were calling themselves Christian were beginning to say. God has been made known *in a Man*, not in the illusion of a man.

There is no more important question for a right understanding of the Evangelist's mind, and for a true interpretation of his Gospel, than this issue. It is the same issue as we have discussed in the Introduction—namely, What did the author's language mean *to himself*? The literalist mind often imagines that the verbs 'to be' and 'to become' have a precise, and invariable, connotation. A scrutiny of the literature of mankind would at once reveal the falsity of such a conclusion. Such verbs are commonly used to express, not *the identity of coincidence*, but *the similarity of nature*. In other words, they are used in a metaphorical sense. When, for example, it is said in this Gospel that Jesus *is* Water, or Bread, or Shepherd, or Way, or Door, or Vine, it should hardly be necessary to point out that the Evangelist does not think that Jesus is *identical* with whatever is connoted by such terms. So when he said that 'the Word became flesh' it should be hardly necessary to point out that he did not mean that the Eternal Word became *identical* with the Jesus of history—any more than did the Rabbis, when they spoke of the Torah as 'bread,' as 'light,' as 'water,' mean that it was identical with these physical entities. He did not think that the Thought and Activity of God was a 'quantity' which could be *exhausted* in One unique Life, leaving all other lives bereft, or empty. He did not think in terms of that distinction between 'degree' and 'kind' which is so often used by those who imagine that thereby they conserve the uniqueness of Jesus. It is a distinction which has been borrowed from the sphere of physical reality, and even there is losing its precision. In the moral and spiritual sphere, clearly, it is used in a symbolical sense, and has meaning only in such a sense.

So when the Evangelist says, 'The Word became flesh and dwelt among us,' he is using the language of metaphor to convey his central Christian faith in Jesus—the faith, namely, that the Eternal Word had uniquely spoken in Him. His language, we repeat, is not the language of philosophical definition. To the author, the uniqueness of Jesus *consisted in what He was*, not in what *definitions came to declare Him to be*. Our human statements and definitions are always 'abstractive.' The Evangelist has a 'concrete' and 'pictorial' mind. The failure to understand the Evangelist at this point has led many to the conclusion that he is 'the father of metaphysical Christology,' and, therefore, responsible for the later ecclesiastical obscuration of the ethical and spiritual emphasis of Jesus. This is a mistaken conclusion: but it will endure until it is perceived that the Evangelist did not think in terms of the category of 'substance'—a category which was so congenial to the Greek mind.

'We beheld his glory,' says the Evangelist. The 'glory' is the manifestation of the essential being. 'The heavens declare the glory of God,' wrote the Psalmist. Whatever awakens us to the reality of the presence of God is a manifestation of the Divine glory. *Tintern Abbey* was this to Wordsworth. *The Thames* was this to Francis Thompson. The '*flower in the crannied wall*' was this to Tennyson. To the Johannine author, the Divine glory was uniquely seen in Jesus. And—as we might paraphrase his words—if we would describe this glory, so full as it was of grace and of reality, how more fittingly than to say that it was the glory of one who knew himself to be as the only son of his father. So uniquely did the Divine Presence dwell within Jesus, so intimate, so trustful, so obedient was this fellowship—like that, again, between a father and his only son—that though no one has ever seen God, yet as we read His life and pondered His secret we said, Surely God is here in very presence.

This is the Evangelist's message in the 18th verse. God in the Infinite Splendour of His being no one ever has seen. Not indeed that He would hide Himself from men's eyes—' 'Tis only the splendour of light hideth Thee.' But Transcendent Deity, thus hidden by excess of light, is revealed in Him who is that light for this world.

In *v.* 15, for the second time in the Prologue, the Evangelist emphasises the subordination of the Baptist to Jesus. He does so by placing words on the lips of John in which he speaks of Jesus as 'he that cometh after me,' the same expression as in *v.* 27. The Coming One has already superseded His forerunner. This is what the Baptist again says in 3^{30}: 'He must increase, but I must decrease.' This supersession by Jesus arises, not from the fact of His coming *later in time* than the Baptist, but from the fact of His *inherent worth*—as the Baptist says here, 'for he *was* before me.' Jesus *must* increase, because He is *inherently* greater—an 'increase' which came to its final fruit on the Cross, on which the world thought He had been finally superseded! When the Evangelist puts the words, 'he *was before* me,' on the Baptist's lips he is expressing, not temporal priority, but eternal, or intrinsic, 'priority.' The phrase does not refer to the relative ages of Jesus and the Baptist—as a matter of fact, John was born about six months before Jesus: nor does it refer to what is usually called by exegetes and theologians the 'pre-existence' of Jesus. The language of *time* is used to express the notion of *quality*, as in the utterance found at 8^{58}, 'Before Abraham was, I am.' The *precedence* ascribed to Jesus has nothing to do with the notion of 'precedence' as it is found in the world. There, 'precedence' has to do with the forms and shows of things, not with inherent value. The hollowness of such 'precedence' was always being revealed by Jesus to those who had eyes to see and ears to hear, and will be repeatedly manifest in the ensuing chapters of the Gospel. Among men there may well be a fitness in giving 'precedence' to age; but age, in itself, confers no real *precedence* upon a man. In the world the good does not always 'supersede' the bad, nor the better the good, nor the best the better. But in the eternal world of spiritual reality the good *of necessity* supersedes the bad, the better the good, the best the better. It is in this sense that Jesus supersedes the forerunner: and not in the sense that He is older in time. It is difficult for those who are accustomed to think of 'precedence' and 'supersession' in terms of the values of the world to understand the Evangelist's thought at this point. If the reader will but remember the following fact he will be in a position to penetrate to the meaning here: those who believe in a 'personal Devil' do not thereby indicate their belief in his real precedence over the saints and seers who were born less than seventy years ago.

In this expression of the supremacy and uniqueness of Jesus Christ—an expression which continues to the end of the 18th verse—the Evangelist is not only giving utterance to the mind of the Baptist, and not only giving utterance to his own mind: he is giving utterance to the essential mind of Jesus Himself. For He had claimed—as we know from the Synoptic Gospels—to 'supersede,' or 'fulfil,' the Law given by those of old. Thus in the 17th verse—'For the law was given by Moses; grace and truth came by Jesus the Messiah'—the Evangelist reveals his fidelity to the consciousness of the historic Jesus. He who knew Himself to be the *Anointed* of God sought to reveal to men the Divine *grace* and *truth.* Clearly, He could only reveal what He Himself *knew,* or what had been revealed to Himself. The 'grace' of God is the self-giving love of God to sinful men: this 'grace' Jesus was always teaching to men by saying and by parable, and of this 'grace' He knew Himself to be the incarnate vehicle. (See, e.g., 3^{16} and our suggested interpretation.) So also Jesus was always declaring to men, both by lip and by life, the 'truth' about God and human life; and of this 'truth' He was convinced in the depths of His consciousness that He was the incarnate expression. Thus later in this Gospel—14^{6}—Jesus declares, 'I am the truth.'

It will be seen that to the two ideas, 'grace' and 'truth,' which are found in *v.* 14, there is added in this 17th verse the *Messianic* idea—for 'Jesus Christ' were better translated 'Jesus the Messiah'; the word 'Christ' was not to the Evangelist a proper name as it has become to ourselves. Thus in one brief verse is summed up a great part of the message of the whole Johannine Gospel.

This 'grace' manifest in Jesus, the incarnate word, the Evangelist has just declared—in the 16th verse—to have been experienced in the lives of 'all'—that is, all the members of the Christian fellowship of whom he is especially thinking as he writes. 'Of his fulness we *all* have received, even grace succeeding to grace.' This 'grace' is not—as has sometimes been suggested—the 'grace' of the Gospel *instead of,* or *in exchange for,* the 'grace' of the Law: for the Evangelist goes on in the 17th verse to contrast the grace mediated by Jesus the Messiah with the Law mediated by Moses. It is, rather, 'grace *upon* grace'—as when a man may say that blessing *upon* blessing has come to him. Out of the *plenitude,* or *perfection,* of being manifest in Jesus the Christ—either of these words is a better translation than 'fulness'—grace upon grace has flowed to His disciples, like the continuous stream of rays which descend to mankind from the sun.

Thus it is that in these verses we are meant to find, not just the Evangelist's own testimony to the truth and grace in Jesus, and not just the Baptist's testimony, but the testimony of Jesus Himself. Grace and truth could only be known to flow *from* Jesus the Christ in so far as grace and truth dwelt *within* Him. If we are in doubt as to whose testimony we are hearing in *vv.* 16–18, whether the Evangelist's or the Baptist's—for the verses can suitably be included in the direct speech of the Baptist recorded in *v.* 15—let us remember that the *whole* Gospel is the testimony of the inner mind of Jesus. It matters not whether the direct speech of the Baptist was meant by the Evangelist to conclude at *v.* 15, or to embrace the whole passage up to the 18th verse. What matters is that the Evangelist is transcribing the inmost mind, claim, and mission of Jesus Himself.

It should be noted that the correct reading of *v.* 18 is disputable. But whether we should read 'The only begotten Son,' or as in the R.V. margin, 'God only begotten,' the meaning differs little. In each case there is a reference to the unique Sonship of Jesus. The Evangelist is not here indulging in metaphysical speculations. He is expressing the *fact* of the unique Divine consciousness and life of Jesus; and he does so by vivid figures of speech which come naturally to his mind. As a Hebrew writer, he uses metaphors without introducing such explanatory phrases as 'as it were'—phrases by which we to-day when writing make it clear to the reader that we speak in figures. In Ps. 2[7] there is an example of this. 'The Lord said unto me, Thou art my son; This day have I begotten thee.' What the Psalmist here meant was that an assurance of the Divine Presence had been given to him, so that he awoke to the reality of a life completely dependent upon God. This assurance was so vivid that he felt as if he were that day 'begotten' of God. Further, the Evangelist knew that Jesus Himself had been accustomed to speak of His knowledge of the Father in this figurative way. So, he says here that Jesus was 'only begotten'—unique in His sense of the Father's presence, unique in the filial obedience He rendered to the Father: He was 'in the bosom of the Father'—that is, in the relation of closest and tenderest intimacy and affection with the Father. The Evangelist's metaphors rise directly out of the *fact* of the unique life of Jesus. They are a poet's way of describing the fact: they are not a metaphysician's way of *explaining* it—or, as often happens, of *explaining it away*. If we regard his metaphors and allegories as dogmatic definitions we are not expounding the mind of the Evangelist; but only seeking to construct an apologetic to meet *our own* intellectual necessities. His is the language not of dogma, but of insight.

When God undertook to write a Creed for humanity, He gave not a 'law' (*v.* 17), not words inscribed whether on stone or on vellum which might change their meaning through the course of the centuries, but a Perfect Man. People may argue about words, but no one who is truthful can dispute the reality of a life of perfect goodness. Religion itself is a life and must be lived.

And so the Word had breath, and wrought
With human hands the creed of creeds
In loveliness of perfect deeds,
More strong than all poetic thought.

And, we may add, in complete fidelity to the Evangelist's thought, more strong than all *dogmatic* thought. This is the Christian message of the Incarnation: it is not the dogma *about* the Incarnation. Christianity is the mind of God expressed in the Perfect Historic Life.

But, someone may say, it is only a man who speaks, and not God. To which we must reply: How else can God speak to man except through man? In Goethe's *Iphigenia in Tauris*, Thoas says:

''Tis not a god, 'tis thine own heart that speaks.'

To which Iphigenia replies:

''Tis only through our hearts the gods can speak to us.'

Only the moral can reveal the Moral: only the spiritual the Spiritual. If God is Pure Spirit, Perfect Goodness, then, whatever else He be, when He would show to man—in so far as man is able to receive it—what He is like, it must be through a Man who displays these attributes. Thomas Traherne expressed the truth thus:

To see the fountain is a blessed thing,
It is to see the King
Of Glory face to face: but yet the end,
The glorious, wondrous end is more;
And yet the fountain there we comprehend,
The spring we there adore:
For in the end the fountain best is shown,
As by effects the cause is known.

PART I (I. 19–XII.)

The Witness of Jesus and the Conflict it Occasions

A. EARLIER WITNESS OF JESUS, AND THE RESPONSE

JN. I^{19}–IV

THE WITNESS OF THE BAPTIST

JN. I$^{19-34}$

1 19 And this is the witness of John, when the
Jews sent unto him from Jerusalem priests
and Levites to ask him, Who art thou?
20 And he confessed, and denied not; and
21 he confessed, I am not the Christ. And
they asked him, What then? Art thou
Elijah? And he saith, I am not. Art thou
the prophet? And he answered, No.
22 They said therefore unto him, Who art
thou? that we may give an answer to
them that sent us. What sayest thou of
23 thyself? He said, I am the voice of one
crying in the wilderness, Make straight the
way of the Lord, as said Isaiah the pro-
24 phet. And they had been sent from the
25 Pharisees. And they asked him, and said
unto him, Why then baptizest thou, if thou
art not the Christ, neither Elijah, neither
26 the prophet? John answered them, saying, I baptize with water: in the midst of
27 you standeth one whom ye know not, *even*
he that cometh after me, the latchet of
whose shoe I am not worthy to unloose.
28 These things were done in Bethany beyond
Jordan, where John was baptizing.
29 On the morrow he seeth Jesus coming
unto him, and saith, Behold, the Lamb of
God, which taketh away the sin of the
30 world! This is he of whom I said, After
me cometh a man which is become before
31 me: for he was before me. And I knew
him not; but that he should be made
manifest to Israel, for this cause came I
32 baptizing with water. And John bare
witness, saying, I have beheld the Spirit
descending as a dove out of heaven; and
33 it abode upon him. And I knew him not:
but he that sent me to baptize with water,
he said unto me, Upon whomsoever thou
shalt see the Spirit descending, and abiding
upon him, the same is he that baptizeth
34 with the Holy Spirit. And I have seen,
and have borne witness that this is the
Son of God.

The author, having proclaimed his central theme in the Prologue, now launches upon the main field of his work. His intention is to show how the Incarnate Word manifested Himself among men.

He does this *in his own way.* That way is the way of dramatic and allegorical presentation. It is not the way of strict history. We are not, therefore, to look at the narratives which follow with the eye of the scientific historian. We are to look at them *through the Evangelist's own mind.* The nature of that mind, we have sought to elucidate in the Introduction.

He begins with the witness of the Forerunner to Jesus. And he *chooses* that part of this witness which subserves his purpose. He makes no reference to the perfervid apocalyptic utterances found in Mt. 3^{1-12}. The Church of his day had gone astray through this emphasis. What the Evangelist is concerned to say is that John knew, and declared, himself to be subordinate to Jesus. The forerunner had pointed his hearers not to himself, but to the Master; and any in the Church who gave superior honour to John are therein denying the witness of John himself. The Baptist's followers are corrected from their leader's own testimony. Later, in 3^{22-30}, we find an even more striking assertion by the Baptist of the supremacy of Jesus.

This witness of John is given a setting of impressively dramatic fitness. A deputation, consisting both of the Sadducean party and of the Pharisaic party, comes from Jerusalem, asking of John who he is. In this narrative of a commission of inquiry the Evangelist dramatises the nationalism, the conservatism, the intolerance of those sections of his own race which had rejected Jesus; confronting them, at the beginning of his Gospel, with the Baptist's witness to the uniqueness of Jesus. Here for the first time he speaks of 'the Jews' in his own characteristic way (see Introduction, p. 664). This setting may have some historical tradition behind it: but the way in which it is staged—Sadducees and Pharisees curiously combined, the manner in which their questions are put, reflecting the popular Messianic expectations of the day—and the emphatic threefold denial by John that he is the Messiah (*v.* 20), clearly reveal the dramatising mind of the author. If not Messiah, is he then Elijah, who was by some expected to come to make ready the world for Messiah (see Mt. 17^{9-13})? No. If not Elijah, then '*the* prophet' of Dt. 18^{15}? No. Who then is John? A 'voice.' He is a voice, as of the herald referred to by the prophet of the exile, calling to men to prepare 'a highway' through the trackless desert for the coming of the kingly servant. (Is. 40^{3}.) The burden of the chapter from Isaiah quoted by the Baptist is 'Behold your God.' Men and nations have thought of God in false and unworthy ways. God now comes to speak through Perfect Man to the conscience of all men. The 'voice' heralds the 'Word.' As Ephraim in his *Epiphany Hymns* put it: John was the voice, but not the Word. Theophylact in his comment said: 'When the voice has been uttered, it dies into the air, and is no more.'

But if John makes no other claim for himself but this, why should he audaciously practise such a rite as that of baptism? The answer of the Baptist in *v.* 26 takes us to the heart of the message and mission of Jesus Himself. While the Baptist was concerned with the outward symbol of a purificatory rite, the Master who followed was concerned with the inward grace of moral and spiritual renewal. 'I baptize with water,' but 'He . . . baptizeth with the Holy Spirit' (*v.* 33). It is as if the Evangelist would say to the readers of his day, The water is a symbol, a symbol hallowed by long custom, but only a symbol; true cleansing comes by the impartation of the Spirit which indwelt Jesus, and which it was His mission to bestow. The water is a sign, and not the thing signified. The sensible vehicle must not be confounded with the spiritual reality. 'All the perfumes of Arabia will not sweeten this little hand,' said Lady Macbeth. Nothing external can cleanse the mind: nothing material can purify the spirit. The mind is healed and saved by mind, the spirit by spirit.

It was said by the Rabbis: 'Every office which a servant would do for his master, a scholar should perform for his teacher, except loosing his sandal-thong.' John says of his Master: The latchet of His shoe I am not worthy to unloose.

The 'Bethany beyond Jordan' referred to in *v.* 28 is unknown, and seems to have caused many speculative surmises in the early centuries. Origen and others substituted Bethabara for it. Some modern students suggest its identification with Beth-Nimrah, north-east of Jericho, on the east side of Jordan: this may be the place referred to in Josh. 13^{27}.

29. There follows a striking witness of the Baptist, hallowed in the devotional literature of the Church: 'Behold, the Lamb of God which taketh away the sin

of the world.' The precision of the dating—' on the morrow '—is probably the precision of the dramatist and not of the scientific historian. The utterance itself, and its setting, are to be regarded likewise.

The narrative does not record the baptism of Jesus by John, but presupposes it. The Baptist says that he had beheld ' the Spirit descending as a dove out of heaven, and it abode upon him.' We do not think that the Evangelist is here ascribing to the Baptist an objective vision of a dove, or what appeared to the physical sight as a dove. He was familiar with the records of Mark and Matthew, who spoke of this vision of the dove as belonging to Jesus only, and with the record of Luke, who described it as a vision given to all present. What he himself is saying is that the descent of the Spirit upon Jesus was as the descent of the peaceful, gentle dove; and he has in his mind the contrast of the warlike coming which many had associated with the Messiah's advent. Isaac Watts was true to the thought of the Evangelist when he wrote his beautiful hymn:

Come, Holy Spirit, heavenly Dove.

Jesus was Messiah because of the ' heavenly Dove ' which rested upon Him: He was not Messiah because of the sign of an earthly dove.

Further, the two striking sayings recorded by the Evangelist can only be properly understood in the light of his own mind, and of his purpose in writing. The first is: ' Behold, the Lamb of God, who is to take away the sin of the world.' May Jesus have had some intimate conversation with the Baptist, in which He unfolded His conception of vocation as the Suffering Servant, referred to in Is. 53^{4}, who was ' a lamb led to the slaughter '? But if this had been so, the later doubt and disappointment of the Baptist, as referred to in Mt. $11^{2ff.}$, is difficult to account for. Further, nowhere in the Synoptic Gospels does John speak like this of Jesus. There, the Messiah is to come to cut down and to destroy (Mt. 3^{10-12}). Here, he comes to suffer for the sins of ' the world.' We suggest that it is only on a mistaken view of the Evangelist's mind that we need try to harmonise these accounts. He is here giving expression at the beginning of the public ministry to Jesus' own mature conception of His mission, and to the experience of liberation from sin which His disciples have found in His fellowship. Towards the close of the Ministry, as we learn from the Synoptists, Jesus came to regard His mission in the light of the Suffering Servant whom the prophet of the exile likened to a ' lamb that was led to the slaughter.' The Evangelist was aware of this; and he here gives dramatic expression to the mind of the Master, who knew both that His mission was for the *world* and that it was for the deliverance of men from sin.

The title ' the lamb of God ' also recalls the Paschal Lamb in the *Exodus* story of the Passover. The slaying of the lamb delivered the Israelites from the fear of death, and gave them strength for the journey from the Egypt of bondage to the Promised Land of liberty. So may have thought the Evangelist—Jesus, by His obedient following of the Divine Will, sought to deliver the world from the bondage of its fears and of its sins.

In this passage, and throughout the Johannine writings, ' sin ' is not regarded as an abstract entity whose ' penalty ' Jesus bears; but as a concrete reality in the lives of men, which, in life and death, He sought to remove. The world's sins are ' taken away ' when the world ceases to sin. To take away sins in this sense was precisely what Jesus sought to do: and this is what many of His disciples, among them the Evangelist himself, had found that Jesus *did* for them. Later in this Gospel these clues to the mind of Jesus will be followed by the author. He will seek to show, on the one hand, that the thought of the Master transcended all bounds of race or nationality, and, on the other hand, that He ever sought the deliverance of men from sin.

The second utterance is: ' And I have seen and have borne witness that this is the Son of God.' Here also the Evangelist has interpreted the mind of Jesus Himself, and at the very beginning of his Gospel has once more put in the clearest light the central fact about that mind—the unique filial consciousness of God.

In the Synoptic Gospels we are told that at the Baptism there came to Jesus an assurance of ' sonship.' ' Thou art my beloved son '—this was the word heard inwardly by Jesus (Mk. 1^{11}). To know himself as ' Son ' of God, was to know God intimately and dependently in the depths of His consciousness. The Evangelist thus places upon the lips of the Baptist a declaration which expresses the assurance that inspired and guided all the acts and words of Jesus. He is not making John the mouthpiece of a speculative dogma about the ' Sonship ' of Jesus: he is making him the herald of the unique religious consciousness of Jesus.

THE CALL AND WITNESS OF THE FIRST DISCIPLES

JN. 1^{35-51}

1 35 Again on the morrow John was stand-
36 ing, and two of his disciples; and he looked
upon Jesus as he walked, and saith, Be-
37 hold, the Lamb of God! And the two
disciples heard him speak, and they fol-
38 lowed Jesus. And Jesus turned, and beheld them following, and saith unto them,
What seek ye? And they said unto him,
Rabbi (which is to say, being interpreted,
39 Master), where abidest thou? He saith
unto them, Come, and ye shall see.
They came therefore and saw where he
abode; and they abode with him that day:
40 it was about the tenth hour. One of the
two that heard John *speak*, and followed
him, was Andrew, Simon Peter's brother.
41 He findeth first his own brother Simon,
and saith unto him, We have found the
Messiah (which is, being interpreted,
42 Christ). He brought him unto Jesus.
Jesus looked upon him, and said, Thou art
Simon the son of John: thou shalt be
called Cephas (which is by interpretation,
Peter).
43 On the morrow he was minded to go
forth into Galilee, and he findeth Philip:
and Jesus saith unto him, Follow me.
44 Now Philip was from Bethsaida, of the city
45 of Andrew and Peter. Philip findeth
Nathanael, and saith unto him, We have
found him, of whom Moses in the law, and
the prophets, did write, Jesus of Nazareth,
46 the son of Joseph. And Nathanael said
unto him, Can any good thing come out
of Nazareth? Philip saith unto him,
47 Come and see. Jesus saw Nathanael coming to him, and saith of him, Behold, an
Israelite indeed, in whom is no guile!
48 Nathanael saith unto him, Whence
knowest thou me? Jesus answered and
said unto him, Before Philip called thee,
when thou wast under the fig tree, I saw
49 thee. Nathanael answered him, Rabbi,
thou art the Son of God; thou art King of
50 Israel. Jesus answered and said unto
him, Because I said unto thee, I saw thee
underneath the fig tree, believest thou?
thou shalt see greater things than these.
51 And he saith unto him, Verily, verily, I
say unto you, Ye shall see the heaven
opened, and the angels of God ascending
and descending upon the Son of man.

It is the Evangelist's purpose in these opening chapters to give an impressive series of witnesses to the truth as it was in Jesus. He has given the witness of the Forerunner. There follows the witness of the disciples. After that comes the witness of a Pharisee—Nicodemus (chap. 3). And then follow the two witnesses, of the woman of Samaria and of the nobleman of Capernaum (chap. 4). There is nothing haphazard in this choice or in this arrangement. It is the story of enlarging witness to the truth as it was in Jesus. The Evangelist is marshalling his witnesses to the truth of his statement in the Prologue, namely, that the Word was made flesh. The circles widen, until at last they include the Gentile world. From the Forerunner to the intimate disciples, from the intimate disciples to the Jerusalem Pharisee, from the Jerusalem Pharisee to a Samaritan woman, from a Samaritan woman to a Gentile nobleman—such is the Evangelist's intention in these narratives. What he would say is that the claim of Jesus to unique knowledge of the Father, and of a mission transcending the limits of geography and race, was witnessed to in the experience of the divers classes who came into spiritual contact with Him.

The first call of Jesus is to two disciples of the Baptist: to Andrew and to an unnamed disciple who is usually regarded as John the son of Zebedee, the Apostle John (see *vv.* 35 and 40). If this supposition is correct—and we see no reason to reject it—it will explain the reference to time in *v.* 39, 'it was about the tenth hour,' that is, ten hours after sunrise, or about 4 p.m. While, as already indicated, we do not look for chronological accuracy in this Gospel, yet here and there are indications of time which *may* be historical. On the hypothesis that the Apostle John's teaching and reminiscences were a main source for the Evangelist, this otherwise insignificant reference to the time of day is naturally explained. Andrew (see 6^{8} and 12^{22}), who plays a minor part in New Testament history, brings his much more prominent brother Simon Peter. Philip, often called 'practical' Philip (see 6^{5}, 12^{21}, 14^{8}), finds Nathaniel, usually identified with Bartholomew, the customary companion of Philip in the Synoptic narratives, and brings him to Jesus. Brother brings brother, and friend brings friend—thus the circle widens from a family relationship to one that is independent of the ties of blood.

The main feature of the narrative—if we are to understand, that is, the Evangelist's intention—is found in the definite confession of the Messiahship of Jesus by Andrew in *v.* 41, by Philip in *v.* 45, and by Nathanael in *v.* 49. We have here three emphatic declarations of the Messiahship of Jesus, corresponding to the three emphatic declarations by the Baptist that he himself is *not* the Messiah. In the Synoptic Gospel the Messiahship of Jesus is not confessed by the disciple till Cæsarea Philippi (Mk. 8^{29}; Mt. 16^{16}). What the Fourth Evangelist is concerned to do is to set in clearest relief the consciousness of Messianic vocation possessed by Jesus. And so a 'secret,' which was only later unfolded by Jesus to the disciples with a true teacher's eliciting reserve, is openly and emphatically declared at the very beginning of the Ministry. It is as if the author would say, Whatever else Jesus was, or felt Himself to be, He knew Himself to be the anointed of the Lord. From the Baptism and the Temptation this sense of mission dominated the mind of Jesus. The disciples only slowly came to realise this. The Johannine author, however—himself not one of the intimate disciples—reads the beginning from the end. The whole life of Jesus, he believed, was controlled by His sense of vocation. If we may use an illustration from a very different realm of consciousness, the early followers of Napoleon did not know, and would not guess, when he first set out for Paris, the high ambition that was surging in the depth of his mind. The later historian, reading the whole story in the light of its *dénouement*, sees the end in the beginning, and the beginning in the end. It is a man's consciousness which explains the man. Even so, the Johannine author had learned—in the fellowship, we believe, of John, ' the beloved disciple ' —that the sense of Divine vocation had been directing the steps of Jesus from the earliest days of His ministry.

42. Another illustration of the Evangelist's freedom with chronological sequence is found in *v.* 42. The rugged character of Simon had gained for him the Aramaic name of *Kephas*, which became *Petros* in Greek, in English *Peter*, the ' rock-man ' (cf. *Pierre*, in French). This name had in all probability been given by Jesus to Simon much later (see Mt. 16^{16}). Paul frequently refers to Peter as *Kephas*, but the Aramaic name appears in no other Gospel but the Fourth—another fact suggesting that the author was a Jew familiar with Aramaic.

51. The chapter ends with the symbolic statement: ' Ye shall see the heaven opened, and the angels of God ascending and descending upon the Son of man.' The Old Testament is full of such symbolism; and it is only the prosaic and unimaginative mind which fails to penetrate the symbolical husk to the spiritual kernel enclosed. Unfortunately, the ' civilised ' Western mind tends to become less and less imaginative, less and less poetic. Macaulay says sweepingly in one of his essays that ' as civilisation advances poetry almost necessarily declines.' It is, at least, certainly true that the allegorical and symbolical method of thinking and writing in Eastern countries has often been misunderstood in the West. ' Understandeth thou what thou readest ? ' is a question which continually forces itself upon a modern Western reader when he ponders the symbolic language of the Old and New Testaments. We must not mistake poetic symbolism for pedestrian prose. We must not forget that language is the *mirror* of thought: it is not itself thought.

What, therefore, this symbolical utterance declares is that the disciples of Jesus will see in His life and ministry signal manifestations of the Divine presence and power. It is a record in pictorially fitting language of the ' traffic ' between the soul of Jesus and the eternal realm. Such language was no doubt used by Jesus Himself. The figure of the heavens opening is found in the Synoptic Gospels in the narrative of the Baptism of Jesus (Mt. 3^{16}; Lk. 3^{21}; Mk. 1^{10}). The ascent and descent of angels was a metaphor employed in the familiar Old Testament story of Jacob's dream recorded in Gen. 28. ' And he dreamed, and behold a ladder set up on the earth, and the top of it reached to heaven: and behold the angels of God ascending and descending on it.' (Gen. 28^{12}.) In the infancy of humanity ' heaven ' is always thought of as ' up there '—' up above the bright blue sky,' of the children's hymn. The symbol of *a place above* has remained, with the advance in mental, moral, and spiritual enlightenment—only, now, the symbol is seen to be *but* a symbol. Such a symbol, therefore, of a *ladder* was peculiarly appropriate to express the belief that there was relationship between earth and heaven, between history and eternity, between man and God.

It is for this reason that such a story as that of 'Jacob's ladder' has appealed so much to the religious mind. That ladder is a symbol of the experience and conviction of spiritual men of all ages—that God speaks to humanity, that communion is possible between heaven and earth—and not just in *this* place or in *that* place, in *this* rite or in *that* rite. This 'ladder' is *everywhere* where men awake to the reality of the world of the spirit: 'angels of God' are *ever* 'ascending' and 'descending' upon it. It is a 'ladder,' 'pitched,' as Francis Thompson saw, 'betwixt Heaven and Charing Cross.'

But (when so sad thou canst not sadder)
Cry;—and upon thy so sore loss
Shall shine the traffic of Jacob's ladder
Pitched betwixt Heaven and Charing Cross.

And the 'angels,' as the same mystical poet so well knew, who 'ascended' and 'descended' that 'ladder' were not confined to place, season, or event.

The angels keep their ancient places;—
Turn but a stone, and start a wing!
'Tis ye, 'tis your estrangèd faces,
That miss the many-splendoured thing.

When the Fourth Evangelist, therefore, wrote these words in the 51st verse—using a figure which, no doubt, Jesus Himself had employed—he would think of the familiar story of Jacob. It is possible, also, that he may have been familiar with some of the allegorical speculations of the Rabbinical teachers on this narrative in Genesis.[1] The primary thought, however, in what he himself writes in his Gospel is that during the coming Ministry of Jesus, which he is about to narrate, there will be signal manifestations of the intercourse between heaven and earth. Jesus Himself is the 'ladder' connecting earth with heaven. Within His soul there was a continuous celestial traffic: and the disciples would come to know this, as they companied with Him, beholding 'his glory.'

The title 'Son of Man' is here first used in this Gospel. The Evangelist retains the primitive title, but it has in his thought, as we believe, no apocalyptic associations. He here uses it to express the true, though exceptional, humanity of Jesus; and the profound sense of Messianic vocation which belonged to His deepest consciousness. 'The title Son of Man, used in immediate proximity with King of Israel (*v.* 49), still carries with it a Messianic meaning, but takes it out of Jewish associations into the sphere of universal humanity. Jesus is the type or centre of mankind on earth, quickened by heavenly powers to do the Father's will.'[2]

Before closing the chapter it should be clearly noted that here at the beginning of the Gospel the author has declared four main themes in his symphony of Good Tidings. He has spoken of:

[1] Odeberg gives many illustrations of such allegorical interpretations in *The Fourth Gospel*, etc., pp. 33 ff.
[2] J. E. Carpenter, *The Johannine Writings*, p. 366.

1. Eternity ever in traffic with History;
2. A unique incarnation of the Eternal Word in the historic Jesus,
3. Whose Filial Consciousness is the key to His Person, and to
4. The unique Divine Mission He sought to fulfil.

THE FIRST 'SIGN' AT CANA OF GALILEE

JN. 2^{1-12}

2 1 And the third day there was a marriage
in Cana of Galilee; and the mother of
2 Jesus was there: and Jesus also was
bidden, and his disciples, to the marriage.
3 And when the wine failed, the mother of
Jesus saith unto him, They have no wine.
4 And Jesus saith unto her, Woman, what
have I to do with thee? mine hour is not
5 yet come. His mother saith unto the
servants, Whatsoever he saith unto you,
6 do it. Now there were six waterpots of
stone set there after the Jews' manner of
purifying, containing two or three firkins
7 apiece. Jesus saith unto them, Fill the
waterpots with water. And they filled
8 them up to the brim. And he saith unto
them, Draw out now, and bear unto the
ruler of the feast. And they bare it.
9 And when the ruler of the feast tasted the
water now become wine, and knew not
whence it was (but the servants which had
drawn the water knew), the ruler of the
10 feast calleth the bridegroom, and saith
unto him, Every man setteth on first the
good wine; and when *men* have drunk
freely, *then* that which is worse: thou hast
11 kept the good wine until now. This
beginning of his signs did Jesus in Cana
of Galilee, and manifested his glory; and
his disciples believed on him.
12 After this he went down to Capernaum,
he, and his mother, and *his* brethren, and
his disciples: and there they abode not
many days.

The Evangelist in the first chapter has in his own way made two great assertions about the historic Jesus. The first is that He was the unique 'Son,' a hallowed title which he uses to give expression to that filial sense of the Father's presence which was the mainspring of His whole life. The second is that out of this filial consciousness of God there arose His sense of Messianic vocation. This consciousness of mission reached its peak, when, towards the close of His life, He regarded it in the light of the Servant of Isaiah, suffering vicariously for the deliverance of humanity from sin. In dramatic narrative the author sets forth the witness of the Baptist and the early disciples to these two controlling facts of the consciousness of Jesus.

He now relates a story, found in no other Gospel, which in every age has been a source of mingled perplexity and edification. The familiar words of the Marriage Service are at once recalled to the memory. Christ, it is there said, sanctioned and adorned this holy estate 'with His presence and first miracle that He wrought in Cana of Galilee.' One of the holiest experiences of life has been made doubly sacred, for multitudes in every age, by the reading of words which record a wedding where at the beginning of His Ministry Jesus was one of the guests. On the other hand, many have listened to such words with a certain misgiving, a certain hesitation, even a certain rebellion. How, they have said, can we believe that anyone, however holy in life, however unique his consciousness of God, either could or would turn the great quantity of wine referred to—some scores of gallons—into wine? No one else has ever turned water into wine in a moment of time. What then, they ask, are we to make of a narrative which seems plainly to mean that the author believed that Jesus had done so unparallelled a deed, and for, seemingly, so trivial a reason?

We have discussed in the Introduction the question of the intention of the author in these ' miracle ' narratives (p. 687.). Here we have to ask, What was his precise intention in this narrative of the turning of the water into wine? Did he *intend* to narrate a historical incident when 120 gallons of water were changed into wine by Jesus? *Or*, did he intend to write an allegory? And, if the latter, what did the allegory *mean* to him?

This, we suggest, is the only proper approach to the question. So often in the past the reader has felt that the right approach to the story was by raising the question *of historic fact*. In other words, he has said, The water was either turned into wine, or it was *not* turned into wine. The prior question—so seldom asked—is, What did the author himself seek to say?

Many readers, in reply to that question, will say that it is transparently obvious that the author was narrating what *he himself* believed to be historical fact. They will point out that the narrative is full of ' statements of fact '—' on the third day,' ' in Cana of Galilee,' ' the Mother of Jesus was there,' ' Jesus also was bidden and his disciples, to the wedding,' ' the wine failed,' etc.

When, however, the average intelligent reader looks again at the story, certain hesitations *as to the author's own meaning* will creep into the mind. First, he will ponder on the enormous quantity of wine—six waterpots, each containing two or three firkins apiece, in all 120 gallons. There is, the meditating reader will say to himself, no greater marvel in changing a million gallons of water into wine than in changing a single gallon: but he will not be able to withhold the question as to whether such a quantity does not seem wholly disproportionate, especially at the end of the feast, to the requirements of the guests; which will lead to the further question as to whether an author, such as the present Evangelist obviously is, *could* have meant this as *sober fact*. The reader will contrast the obviously moral and spiritual emphasis of the whole Gospel with a stupendous display of power merely to help a host embarrassed by the thirst of his guests. Surely there is some other explanation of the author's own motive in the writing of this narrative?

This hesitation will be increased when the reader notes the way in which the supposed narrative of transmutation is unfolded. After the waterpots have been filled to the brim with water, the words of Jesus are: ' Draw near, and bear to the ruler of the feast.' The narrative continues: ' and they bare it. And when the ruler of the feast tasted the water (now) become wine (and he knew not whence it was, but the servants who had drawn the water knew),' etc. There is here no explicit statement that *Jesus changed the water into wine*. There is, instead, the statement that *this water was now become wine*. This latter statement, some will say, *implies* the former statement. Nevertheless, the reader who really tries to see with the author's own eyes will note *his way* of narrating the story. Further, the reader will at this point begin to meditate upon the indisputably allegorical nature of the author's mind. No candid reader will deny, whatever his view of these ' miracle stories,' that there is a good deal of allegory in the Gospel. When, for example, the author says, ' The Word *became* flesh,' he did *not* mean that the ' Word ' had been changed into a piece of flesh. Yet it is the same verb in each case. We therefore suggest that when we read of water *becoming* wine, the author means that the word ' becoming ' should be interpreted in some such fashion as ' being the vehicle of '—a meaning which corresponds to the symbolical language in *v.* 14 of the Prologue. Our suggestion, that is, is that the author himself had no more intention of narrating a literal metamorphosis of water into wine than he had of narrating a literal metamorphosis of the ' Word ' into flesh.

If the reader still hesitates, in view of the crowd of seemingly narrative details, to accept this interpretation let him turn to another book written by a Hebrew author—the Book of Jonah. It is now almost universally acknowledged that the famous story of Jonah in the belly of the great fish is an allegory. Yet there are just as many narrative ' details ' in the one story as in the other. Then *why* should an allegorical interpretation be enforced in one case, and inadmissible in the other?

Let us now present our own positive interpretation of the author's meaning. He was seeking to express the transformations which the life of Jesus had achieved in His disciples and friends. This was his *main* intention. We are well aware of the precariousness of seeking to unfold in any exact outline the precise relation, in the author's own mind, of historical event to allegorical teaching: but we venture to make the following suggestions. First, that the author had heard testimony from John the Apostle of a certain wedding which Jesus had attended, in which He shared, and added to, the joys and festivities of the occasion. Second, on the basis of this historical tradition, the Evangelist pondered some of the sayings of Jesus with which he was familiar—' keeping the good wine until the end,' the ' new wine in old bottles ' (Mk. 2^{22}), the ' sons of the bride chamber,' in contrast to the disciples of the Baptist (Mk. 2^{19}), and the words at the Last Supper when Jesus told the disciples that he would drink no more wine with them till the Kingdom of God should come. The Evangelist, doubtless, had himself often pondered upon the ' old wine ' of Judaism, which had served his fathers well. He remembered, further, that Jesus had never sought to destroy, but to fulfil. Thus, from out of his meditations, there comes this story where thought is clothed in vivid narrative form, the whole overmastering desire being to express the significance of the unseen spiritual and moral reality manifest in Jesus.

Let the reader, further, note the points in the story which obviously accord with allegorical narration. First, the ' wedding ' itself. In the Synoptic Gospels it is a symbol for the reign of God. Second, the ' six ' waterpots may well have symbolised to the author ' the value of Judaism during the six days of the world-week.' Third, the words of Jesus, in *v.* 4, in His reply to the appeal of His mother, suggest that the Evangelist is, as he usually does, attributing to Jesus at the beginning of His Ministry the mature consciousness of vocation which, as we gather from the Synoptic narrative, was only His as He neared the end. ' Lady (there is no rebuke in the word used in addressing His mother), what have I to do with thee? mine hour is not yet come.' What is this ' hour '? It is His death, which will mean His glorification. Fourth, the word ' sign ' is used by the Evangelist, and this fact, as we stressed in the Introduction, is significant of his intention.

Here, therefore, some incident and some words of Jesus are fused in the creative imagination, and by the spiritual insight, of the author, into a kind of parable. The incident and the words are treated by the Evangelist with the utmost freedom. If he had been asked the question as to what he believed was scientific fact in his narrative, he would probably have answered that he did not know. Traditional incidents on which he had for many years meditated had taken in his mind an incisive and dramatic form suitable to become the vehicle of his central purpose. The historical incident to him was of little or no importance. It has but served the Evangelist as a rough frame in which to place a portrayal of the vivifying and transforming spiritual Ministry of Jesus. The 'glory' of Jesus is being manifested: the spiritual and moral excellence that were in Him were being displayed. The whole narrative is essentially a parabolic and imaginative symbol of the 'glory' of Jesus. It is this 'glory' which is 'signified' by the 'sign.' 'We beheld His glory,' wrote the author in the Prologue, 'full of grace and truth.' These spiritual qualities of 'grace and truth' are here displayed.

We ourselves are the inheritors of the symbolism of the Johannine author when we speak of 'the new wine of the Gospel.' To the Rabbis the Torah was likened to wine. One Rabbinic statement is: 'As wine rejoices the heart in a temporal manner, so the Torah rejoices the heart after a spiritual manner.' Paul had the same symbolism in his thought when he wrote in his Ephesian epistle: 'Be not drunken with wine, wherein is riot, but be filled with the Spirit, speaking one to another in psalms and hymns and spiritual songs, singing and making melody with your heart to the Lord.' (Eph. 5^{18-19}.) So the Fourth Evangelist thinks in this narrative of the person and message of Jesus which transformed the 'water' of Jewish purificatory rites into the 'wine' of a moral and spiritual Gospel.

Before leaving this narrative, the reader may be reminded of another suggestion that has sometimes been made. This is, that the Evangelist has here borrowed a pagan fable and baptised it into Christ. There was a widespread Greek legend that on certain annual occasions Dionysus, the renewer of life, produced wine in a miraculous manner. Further, it has been pointed out that the date of such Dionysian festivals was the night of January 5–6. Now, the Christian festival of the Epiphany (or Manifestation) was in the second half of the second century celebrated in honour of the Baptism of Jesus on January 6, being regarded as the day of His spiritual birth. 'It seems, therefore, in a high degree probable that the Christian festival of the Epiphany was designed by those who first observed it, to take the place of a Dionysian commemoration, just as the later date for the festival for the human Birth of Christ was attached to the Mithraic festival of the birthday of the unconquered Sun on December 25.'[1] The theory has been maintained that the Fourth Evangelist had begun this process by transforming 'the miracles of Dionysus into an imaginative symbol of the glory of Christ.' The theory is interesting, but, to the present writer, it is fanciful to suppose that the Evangelist was here influenced by such legends. The symbolism of wine was widespread, and it is much more likely that the Hebrew Christian who wrote this Gospel was using a familiar metaphor used by Jesus, and some incident in His Ministry, and that from these two sources he had written the parable before us.

[1] J. E. Carpenter, *op. cit.*, p. 380.

THE WITNESS IN THE TEMPLE

JN. 2^{13-25}

2 13 And the passover of the Jews was at
hand, and Jesus went up to Jerusalem.
14 And he found in the temple those that sold
oxen and sheep and doves, and the
15 changers of money sitting: and he made a
scourge of cords, and cast all out of the
temple, both the sheep and the oxen; and
he poured out the changers' money, and
16 overthrew their tables; and to them that
sold the doves he said, Take these things
hence; make not my Father's house a
17 house of merchandise. His disciples remembered that it was written, The zeal of
18 thine house shall eat me up. The Jews
therefore answered and said unto him,
What sign shewest thou unto us, seeing
19 that thou doest these things? Jesus
answered and said unto them, Destroy this
temple, and in three days I will raise it up.
20 The Jews therefore said, Forty and six
years was this temple in building, and wilt
21 thou raise it up in three days? But he
22 spake of the temple of his body. When
therefore he was raised from the dead, his
disciples remembered that he spake this;
and they believed the scripture, and the
word which Jesus had said.
23 Now when he was in Jerusalem at the
passover, during the feast, many believed
on his name, beholding his signs which he
24 did. But Jesus did not trust himself unto
25 them, for that he knew all men, and
because he needed not that any one
should bear witness concerning man; for
he himself knew what was in man.

Every attentive reader of the Gospels must have noted that the incident usually known as 'the Cleansing of the Temple " is placed by our Evangelist at the beginning of the Ministry, and by the Synoptists at the close of the Ministry (see Mt. 21^{12-13}; Mk. 11^{15-17}; Lk. 19^{45-46}; see also Mal. 3^{1-3}). What are we to make of this seeming historical discrepancy? The three possible answers are: (1) that there were two such incidents, and so both accounts are chronologically accurate; (2) that there was only one such incident, and the Synoptists place it in its correct historical order; (3) that the Fourth Evangelist gives it its right setting. We do not propose to immerse ourselves in a discussion on this issue. The view here taken is that the Evangelist places at the opening of the Ministry an incident which came at the end. The undoubted fact that his mind is untroubled about chronological accuracy alone suggests this. Further, it is natural for him to place such an incident at the beginning, inasmuch as it focuses at a very vivid point the ethical and spiritual consciousness of Jesus, when confronted by the exclusive claims and unspiritual emphases represented by the Temple religion. The Evangelist has already shown himself unconcerned with any *development* in the Messianic consciousness of Jesus. Here also he reveals this unconcern. The incident follows fittingly on the first 'sign' of the grace and truth incarnated in Jesus. The Evangelist will now set forth another 'sign' of Jesus. That unique Life, which in its ethical and spiritual sublimity has transformed for His followers the water of Judaism into the wine of the Gospel, will now be revealed in its prophetic and authoritative character. The hollowness of religion when divorced from spiritual and ethical purpose will be unveiled. The life-giver is also the destroyer. The Mission of Jesus is negative as well as positive. That which corrupts the life of spiritual worship will be destroyed. The bringer of peace comes to make war on all mummeries, hypocricies, and shams. He will come 'suddenly to his temple.' And 'who shall stand when he appeareth? For he is like a refiner's fire and like fullers' soap' (see Mal. 3^{1-3}).

The author was very familiar with the incident, having read of it in the other Gospels, and having probably heard it from the Apostle John. Having, therefore, written about the first 'sign,' his mind travels at once to another. 'What sign shewest thou?' say the Jews in *v.* 18. Every reader must have noted how a word will often quicken into life a whole train of thoughts slumbering in the deep places of the mind. Is it too hazardous to suggest that the author, having written of one 'sign' of Jesus, at once feels the appropriateness of recording another incident which signifies a truth amplifying and complementing the first?

The incident and its significance for Jesus can only be understood if we imaginatively reconstruct the scene. The temple market for the sale of sacrificial animals was in the outer court of the Gentiles. Between it and the inner court, into which the Gentiles must not enter, were barriers and posted notices—similar in intention to the notices we have seen nailed to trees in the grounds of a monastery in France forbidding any woman further access. These notices were in this case carved on stone tablets. The outer court, therefore, where the scene took place was the only place where the Gentiles might gather for prayer or instruction. The existence of a market here could well be defended by the authorities, on the plea that it was in the interests of the pilgrims that they should have victims certified as fit for sacrifice. This, however, inevitably lent itself to abuse. A 'house of prayer' tended to become little better than a house of merchandise. How was it possible to pray amid the squabble and unseemly excitement of buying and selling, of the bleating of sheep, and the shouting of money-changers? A place that should have stood as a symbol for the freedom of access of all nations in prayer to God, had become a place associated with sordid pecuniary interests. The modern traveller to some Continental pilgrimage centres of healing will be able to *feel* the situation.

This explains the prophetic zeal of Jesus. It was here, probably, that as a boy of twelve He had discussed the Scriptures with the Rabbis. The scene before Him now would make any such discussion, meditation, or prayer impossible. 'Take these things hence,' He says, 'make not my Father's house a house of merchandise.' He who is full of 'grace' cannot be indifferent to what is ungracious. He who is full of 'truth' cannot but seek to extirpate the false. There is a tolerance which is intolerable to the truth-loving; and there is an acquiescence in parades and formalities in which the spiritually minded cannot acquiesce. We are told that there are some in our days who find 'difficulty' in this prophetic and spiritual zeal of Jesus here. Rather should we find difficulty if from His life had come no such protest. The author recalls the impression made upon the disciples by this zeal: doubtless he knew what John the Apostle had felt and thought, and how a familiar passage from the Psalms (69^9) had occurred to his memory. 'His disciples remembered that it was written, The zeal of thine house shall eat me up.' There was in Jesus not only the gentleness of patient understanding, but a virility of moral indignation, in the presence of all bigotries and prides, such as does not always belong to the 'humble saint.' He who would be, to use Wesley's words, 'the friend of all and the enemy of none,' must seek to destroy whatever is the enemy of the best interests of mankind. He who would not 'quench the smoking flax,' could not but seek to stifle the smoking gunpowder. He who would not 'break the bruised reed,' could not but condemn those who would cause his little ones to stumble.

Jesus here calls the Temple '*my* Father's house.' Here we have once more expressed the unique filial consciousness of Jesus.

18. The question follows in *v.* 18: 'What sign shewest thou unto us, seeing that thou doest these things?' Here once again the author's mind is seen working in accord with the psychological law of the association of ideas. With the freedom of the dramatic historian he at this point inserts a symbolic and enigmatic word of Jesus which was, it is significant to note, used against Him at His trial (Mk. 14^{58}, 15^{29}; Mt. 26^{61}, 27^{40}). 'Destroy this temple, and in three days I will raise it up.' The saying was misunderstood. How could a temple that had taken forty-six years to build be rebuilt, if destroyed, in a day or two? The temple of Zerubbabel had taken forty-six years to build—begun in 559, the first year of Cyrus, and completed in 513, the ninth year of Darius. Or perhaps the suggestion refers to the alterations of Herod, which at the time of the incident may have been forty-six years in process—these alterations, begun in 20 B.C., were not completed till A.D. 63.

The symbolism of Jesus was misunderstood in His day, as in every age it has been misunderstood. What He meant was that if they succeeded in destroying the true worship of Him whom he knew to be the Father, in this place, he would raise another 'temple' in the lives of His followers. This would be the true 'temple of his body.' God's temple is where He is known and worshipped. A temple ceases to be such when it is a centre of nationalist purposes or mercenary interests. These necessarily 'destroy' it. Jesus does not say that He destroys the 'temple': it is the tendencies revealed before Him which will destroy it. It is then that it becomes unto them 'desolate.' (Mt. 23^{38}.) But Jesus, Himself the very Shekinah (Tabernacle) of God, knew that He was called to reveal to men wherein true worship of the Father consisted. If, then, this 'temple' be destroyed, as it was being destroyed, another 'temple' was being raised by Him in the hearts and minds of men. This is a temple 'not made with hands.'

That this interpretation of the words of Jesus is the true interpretation is, to our mind, evidenced by the form of the question in Mk. 14^{58}, where the accusation against Him is that of saying, 'I will destroy this temple that is made with hands, and in three days I will build another *made without hands*.' It is further evidenced by the form of the charge against Stephen in Acts 6^{14}: 'We have heard him say that this Jesus of Nazareth shall destroy this place, and *shall change the customs which Moses delivered unto us*.' Stephen had understood the saying of Jesus, that is, in reference to the transformation of the 'customs' of Mosaic ritual and worship. Jesus was going to build a new temple, in so far as He was going to inspire the old with new spiritual meaning. And Stephen, in his reply (Acts 7^{48-50}), reminds them that 'the Most High dwelleth not in houses made with hands; as saith the prophet, The heaven is my throne, and the earth the footstool of my feet: What, manner of house will he build me? saith the Lord: Or what is the place of my rest? Did not my hand make all these things?' Jesus, thus, in this saying, was regarded by Stephen as in the succession of the prophets whose concern was with the inward realisation of the Divine presence, the worship of Him in spirit and in truth.

Afterwards this utterance was regarded by the disciples as a prophecy of the crucifixion and the resurrection of Jesus. We can well understand how the disciples came to read this prophecy of the resurrection into the words of Jesus. For it was His Resurrection which had confirmed their wavering allegiance to the spiritual Kingdom for which He died. So as they looked back they said: *That* was the event which inaugurated the new Kingdom, the new Church.

The second chapter closes with some pregnant words which reveal the mind of Jesus towards that kind of belief which rested upon physical marvels. 'He knew what was in man' by intuitive penetration, and could distinguish a spurious form of faith which rests upon evidential 'proofs,' from that true faith which is the whole attitude of heart, mind, and will. In this conflict there is here presented another of the recurring themes of the Gospel. Jesus, whose whole life was 'the life of faith,' penetrated to the depths of truth and falsity in men's souls. He would not therefore *trust* Himself, or His cause, to those who claimed 'belief,' but had no 'faith.' 'Not with such allies' would He seek to commend the truth. The inherent incompatibilities were manifest to Him. In every age these have been so speciously disguised as 'rational necessities' that they have deceived all but the elect. 'Not everyone that saith unto me, Lord, Lord, shall enter into the Kingdom of Heaven, but he that doeth the will of my Father which is in heaven.' And, we might add, in essential fidelity to the Great Master's teaching and spirit: Not every one that saith, I believe because of these 'evidential' signs, shall enter the Kingdom of Heaven; but he who loves truth so much that he will follow whithersoever it leads. This is true faith, whose twin constituents are *trust* and *obedience.*

The traditional interpretation of the 'knowledge' here ascribed by the Evangelist to Jesus is that it is a 'supernatural' knowledge, or—to put the matter less ambiguously—that it is 'omniscience.' It has been said that, according to the Fourth Evangelist, 'the perspectives of the future are all open to his vision.' If this is what the Evangelist *meant*, then his portraiture of Jesus would seriously conflict with the portrait of a Jesus who 'grew in knowledge.' There are a number of places in this Gospel where the same kind of 'knowledge' is ascribed to Jesus—in 1^{48}, 4^{19}, 5^{42}, $6^{61, 64}$, 13^{11}. To our own view, the Evangelist meant in such passages to claim for Jesus what Matthew had claimed for Him in 9^{4} of his Gospel. Jesus, said Matthew, knew *the thoughts* of men. In other words, he wishes to say that Jesus had insight into men's motives. Such insight belongs to men in varying degrees. It is an *intuitive* knowledge, and not a scientific knowledge. It does not open to its possessors the pages of future history: but it does, in varying measures, open the pages of men's hearts and minds. That Jesus had such knowledge in a pre-eminent degree we may be certain. Those who have this intuitive insight into the characters of men are seldom surprised by their deeds. It gives to them a feeling as if they were looking on at a drama unfolding before them to a predestined end. Beginning, middle, and end become fused in a consciousness of unity and inevitability. The Fourth Evangelist—himself a man of intuitive genius—had also this quality of mind: he was therefore able to feel it with dramatic intensity in the person of Jesus, whose inner mind he seeks to delineate. Here and there we may feel that he gives too forcible expression to the sense of mastery over His circumstances possessed by Jesus; but if we make due allowance for the dramatic intensity of the Evangelist's mind, we shall be able to understand what he is wishing to say. He knew that Jesus had prophetic insight to a pre-eminent degree. This insight was not the kind of ' knowledge ' of which the ' dogmatists ' speak, and in which alone they can believe. It is the knowledge which sees into the life of men and of things.

THE WITNESS TO NICODEMUS

JN. 3^{1-21}

3 1 Now there was a man of the Pharisees,
named Nicodemus, a ruler of the Jews:
2 the same came unto him by night, and
said to him, Rabbi, we know that thou art
a teacher come from God: for no man can
do these signs that thou doest, except God
3 be with him. Jesus answered and said
unto him, Verily, verily, I say unto thee,
Except a man be born anew, he cannot see
the kingdom of God. Nicodemus saith
4 unto him, How can a man be born when
he is old? can he enter a second time into
5 his mother's womb, and be born? Jesus
answered, Verily, verily, I say unto thee,
Except a man be born of water and the
Spirit, he cannot enter into the kingdom
6 of God. That which is born of the flesh is
flesh; and that which is born of the Spirit
7 is spirit. Marvel not that I said unto thee,
8 Ye must be born anew. The wind
bloweth where it listeth, and thou hearest
the voice thereof, but knowest not whence
it cometh, and whither it goeth: so is every
9 one that is born of the Spirit. Nicodemus
answered and said unto him, How can
10 these things be? Jesus answered and said
unto him, Art thou the teacher of Israel,
and understandest not these things?
11 Verily, verily, I say unto thee, We speak
that we do know, and bear witness of that
we have seen; and ye receive not our wit-
12 ness. If I told you earthly things, and ye
believe not, how shall ye believe, if I tell
13 you heavenly things? And no man hath
ascended into heaven, but he that descended out of heaven, *even* the Son of man,
14 which is in heaven. And as Moses lifted
up the serpent in the wilderness, even so
15 must the Son of man be lifted up: that
whosoever believeth may in him have
eternal life.
16 For God so loved the world, that he
gave his only begotten Son, that whosoever
believeth on him should not perish, but
17 have eternal life. For God sent not the
Son into the world to judge the world; but
that the world should be saved through
18 him. He that believeth on him is not
judged: he that believeth not hath been
judged already, because he hath not believed on the name of the only begotten
19 Son of God. And this is the judgement,
that the light is come into the world, and
men loved the darkness rather than the
20 light; for their works were evil. For
every one that doeth ill hateth the light,
and cometh not to the light, lest his works
21 should be reproved. But he that doeth
the truth cometh to the light, that his
works may be made manifest, that they
have been wrought in God.

The third chapter is obviously connected in the Evangelist's mind with the closing verses of the second chapter. The meeting of Jesus, and His discourse, with Nicodemus illustrate and elucidate the central thought of those verses. The necessity of a spiritual birth is the positive message of this incident, as the insufficiency of a belief grounded on external signs was the negative message of the verses preceding. It is as if the Evangelist would say: Jesus would not trust His cause to those whose religious life rested on belief in external marvels, but only on those who have spiritual insight into the truths of the Kingdom. That this is the sequence of his thought is seen from the opening words of Nicodemus to Jesus: ' Rabbi, we know that thou art a teacher come from God: for no man can do these signs that thou doest, except God be with him.' The answer of Jesus at once directs Nicodemus away from the external to the internal, away from the 'sign' to the thing signified, away from the material to the spiritual. 'Verily, verily, I say unto thee, Except a man be born from above (or, anew),[1] he cannot see the kingdom of God.'

The way in which this incident is narrated shows once more the complete freedom with which the Evangelist deals with historical incident. Nicodemus is introduced as a Pharisee and 'a ruler of the Jews,' that is, a member of the Sanhedrin. The two later references to him in the Gospel—in 7^{50} and 19^{39}—suggest that to the author he is a real historical figure. A cautious and perplexed, but loyal, disciple of Jesus—he came 'by night.' Later in this *private* interview Jesus is made to speak as though to a larger audience: '*Ye* must be born anew' (*v.* 7); '*Ye* receive not our witness' (*v.* 11). From this it is clear that the author is not giving a verbatim report of a private conversation—which, indeed, could only be known to Jesus and to Nicodemus. He is unfolding the essential mind of Jesus; and though Nicodemus was no doubt a real historical figure, and though there is probably some historical basis for the interview, yet the author treats the incident as but a vehicle for expressing what he knew to be a central theme in the teaching of the Master. In the Synoptic Gospels that theme is expressed in a somewhat different form: 'Except ye turn and become as little children ye shall in no wise enter into the kingdom of heaven' (Mt. 18^{3}). The main thought, however, is the same. The religious life has its springs in the depths of a man's inner life. It is a birth 'from above.' It is a knowledge of the eternal, and its source is the Eternal Word. Its true 'sign' is an inward moral and spiritual perception, a quickening or renewal of the mind, whereby old things are passed away, and all things have become new. Our sophistications have to be stripped from us, and we are to become 'as little children.' Jesus was working with the very inadequate medium of human language, and in our blindness we wish to press His figures of speech to what is felt to be their logical issue, forgetting that 'the letter killeth, but the spirit giveth life.' It is necessary to see that the various metaphors used by Jesus are all different ways of expressing the same few eternal truths. When, for example, he speaks of the *Kingdom of God*—a phrase used in this Gospel very rarely but frequently found in the Synoptic Gospels—what he means is the *reign* of God in the lives of men. By connecting the *Kingdom of God* with the necessity of a *birth from above* in this third verse, the truth of each is revealed. The Kingdom is the Kingdom of those morally and spiritually quickened: the new birth is evidenced by a life of complete obedience to the King. So the Kingdom consists of the 'sons of God,' who, as we were told in the Prologue, 'were born not of flesh, nor of blood, nor of the will of man, but of God.' These are they who welcome 'the light,' and walk by it. The Kingdom cometh not by observation, nor can it be reached by the short-cuts of external artifice. It is never *imposed*: it is *seen*. 'Except a man be born from above he cannot *see* the Kingdom of God.' The Kingdom will only come in human society as men are born anew: or, as it used to be said, the soul of all regeneration is the regeneration of the soul.

4. Nicodemus, the religious ruler, is perplexed. 'How can a man be born

[1] Either translation is possible; but whether the metaphor is one of *space* or of *time*, the meaning of Jesus is not affected.

when he is old?' Those outside organised religion have no monopoly of spiritual blindness. It is found in ecclesiastical courts, as well as in Cæsar's house. Another of the recurring themes of this Gospel is the perplexity which the teaching of Jesus occasions, the misunderstanding which it both encounters and evokes. His answer sought to make dark things luminous. He speaks of the necessity of being born 'of water and the spirit.' The reference to 'water' recalls the rite of baptism and probably symbolises the cleansing act of surrender. It is clear that to the Evangelist the word 'water' here is used in a symbolical sense. The variety of the figures he uses in his Gospel—the variety indeed of the figures Jesus Himself employed—is sufficient to show that these were but symbolical of some moral and spiritual truth. The emphasis is never upon the thing itself but upon the thing signified—whether the thing be Word, Water, Bread, Door, Way, Vine. The Evangelist makes frequent use of 'water' as a symbol in his Gospel—in the 'sign' at Cana in the second chapter, in the story of the woman of Samaria in the fourth chapter, in 7^{34}, and in 19^{34}. It was a symbol with a variety of meanings, as is clear from the Old Testament. This variety obviously arises from the many uses of water—it cleanses, it quenches thirst, it is an agent in germination, etc. Mystical writers have delighted in such a symbol, with so varied and so extensive a suggestiveness. In the Rabbinical literature widespread use was made of 'water' as a symbol, not the least noteworthy being its use as a procreative symbol.[1] It is probable, however, that when the Evangelist used it here, he was thinking of it as a symbol of cleansing or purification—the meaning of the symbol in the baptismal rites of civilised humanity. Ezekiel used it in this sense: 'And I will sprinkle clean water upon you, and ye shall be clean: from all your filthiness, and from all your idols, will I cleanse you' (Ezek. 36^{25}). It is significant for the thought of the Evangelist here, that in this same passage of Ezekiel the prophet goes on to speak of 'a new heart' and 'a new spirit' which the Lord will put within His people: that is, the *cleansing water* and the *new spirit* are conjoined in his thought. It is the same combination in the thought of the Evangelist in this fifth verse, where Jesus speaks of being 'born of water and the spirit.'

From all this it is clear that while the Evangelist is probably thinking of the symbolic rite of baptism, his thought is at the farthest possible remove from any magical sacramentalism. In other words, he does not mean that the physical act of immersion in water is indispensable to spiritual quickening. Those who so interpret this reference isolate it from the whole context of the mind of Jesus as expressed in this Gospel. The passage does not say that the Spirit necessarily comes to those who are immersed in water. Against such a misinterpretation the succeeding verses should sufficiently warn us: 'That which is born of flesh is flesh: and that which is born of spirit is spirit.' Jesus further elucidates His meaning by referring to the incalculable and unfettered action of the Divine Spirit. In our English translation of *v.* 8, the figure of the *wind* is used by Jesus to illustrate that action. The word, however, translated 'wind' is also the word

[1] Hugo Odeberg has gathered many illustrations of this usage in his book, *The Fourth Gospel, Interpreted in its Relation to Contemporaneous Religious Currents in Palestine and the Hellenistic-Oriental World*, pp. 48 ff.

translated 'spirit.' This double meaning is suggestive. The passage, however, might probably be more truly rendered: 'The Spirit breatheth where he wills and thou hearest the voice thereof, and knowest not whence he comes or whither he goes: thus it is that every one is born of the Spirit.' In any case, what Jesus here says is that material conditions do not limit, or prescribe, the action of the Spirit of God. The Divine Spirit is always speaking, always acting: not just *here* in this act, or *there* in that place. A Jewish verse from a Mediæval Doxology, 'Praise to the living God,' expresses the same thought.

His Spirit floweth free,
High surging where it will:
In prophet's word He spake of old,
He speaketh still.

Francis Thompson, our own poet, gave expression to the thought in his lines:

The drift of pinions, would we hearken,
Beats at our own clay-shuttered doors.

9. In answer to the further bewilderment of the religious ruler—'How can these things be?'—Jesus expresses His own surprise that one called to teach in the nation of the prophets should be blind to these things. In the further answer of Jesus in *v.* 11, the words of the followers of Jesus are heard: 'We speak that we do know, and bear witness of that we have seen.' This might be said to be the voice of the true Church of Christ transmitted through the testimony of the inner mind of Jesus Himself. To Him the spiritual was the real, and the invisible the visible. The Evangelist, that is, is expressing both the mind of Jesus and the mind of His followers in His fellowship. Jesus is speaking of 'heavenly things'; and it is he, the Son of Man, whose converse is with 'heaven,' who bears the good tidings of the heavenly.

In *v.* 13 is found the same figure of 'ascent' and 'descent,' already found in 1^{51}. He that 'ascended' is he that 'descended,' even the Son of Man. Jesus to the author is he that 'cometh from above,' and 'he that cometh from heaven' (3^{31}; see also $6^{38, 42, 62}$). He alone 'ascended to heaven': that is, He is in unique fellowship with the Father. He 'descended from heaven': that is, He is the expression in time and place of Eternity—the Father's very 'Word.' The figure of 'ascending' and 'descending' is used in the Old Testament for 'a knowledge of the Holy One.' In Prov. 30^{4} we read: 'I have not learned wisdom, neither have I the knowledge of the Holy One. Who hath ascended up unto heaven, and descended?' Such a figure came naturally to the Jewish author of this Gospel. Indeed, it might well have come naturally to Jesus Himself. Many of the figures which the Evangelist uses, Jesus had used before him—wine, shepherd, light, bread, etc.—as we know from the Synoptic Gospels. It is exceedingly probable, therefore, that in this 13th verse the Evangelist, in speaking of the Son of Man *ascending* and *descending*, is but putting in his own way a metaphor which Jesus Himself had employed. He, it is clear, had claimed a unique *knowledge* of the Father: He had also avowed that His knowledge of the Father was *the Father's own gift.* The intimacy of communion which Jesus claimed to have with God is always conjoined with a sense of complete dependence upon God. These are the two thoughts expressed in this 13th verse. He who hath *ascended* is He who hath *descended*: that is, the *knowledge* which Jesus had of God is the *revealing act* of God Himself. The *knowledge* of God is expressed in terms of an *ascent to heaven*: the *revealing act* of the Father is expressed in terms of a *descent from heaven.* The Evangelist, that is, is not making a dogmatic or a speculative statement here: he is giving expression to the mind of Jesus Himself. The *exclusiveness* of the utterance—' no man hath ascended into heaven, but he that descended out of heaven, even the Son of man '—is the Evangelist's way of expressing what Jesus Himself had said in the famous Q passage. ' All things have been delivered unto me of my Father: and no one knoweth the Son, save the Father, neither doth any know the Father, save the Son, and he to whomsoever the Son willeth to reveal him (Mt. 11^{27}; Lk. 10^{22}). Jesus there claimed a knowledge of *all things pertaining to the Kingdom*; but it had been *delivered* to Him from the Father—that is, it was a *descent,* to use the Fourth Evangelist's figure. The revealing mission of the Son has its *origin* in God. That *reciprocal* knowledge —Son knowing Father, and Father knowing Son—has yet its *originating Source* in God Himself. The uniqueness of spiritual knowledge which Jesus Himself enjoyed, and claimed, is here expressed by the Fourth Evangelist, when he puts upon the lips of Jesus the words: ' No man hath ascended into heaven, but he that descended out of heaven, even the Son of man.' He who incarnates the Eternal Word is *very man.*

That this exclusiveness is not a *literal* exclusiveness is clear from the whole context of the passage. All men who are spiritually regenerate may be said to *ascend* and *descend.* Yet, says the Evangelist, there is One on whom the Divine Spirit has descended in such measure that He is the mediator of Life to men.

The closing words of *v.* 13—' which is in heaven '—are to be regarded as an ' interpretative gloss,' added by a later hand to express a more developed, or more speculative, Christology than is found in this Gospel.

14. The paragraph ends with the striking words of *vv.* 14 and 15. Jesus here uses the familiar story of the lifting up of the brazen serpent which brought healing to those who had been bitten by the serpents in the wilderness (see Num. 21^{9} and *Wis.* 16^{5-7}), to symbolise His own ministry of life-giving to men. Our Lord Himself may well have used such a story, and the Evangelist here gives it a dramatic form to express the conviction which Jesus held towards the close of His Ministry, namely, that His death on the Cross would bring healing and life to the nations. What the Evangelist here does is to dramatise the later consciousness of Jesus when He was confronted with death. The meaning of His life was focused in the spirit in which He went to the Cross: His ministry of life, eternal life, was there fulfilled in that consummating act of obedient acceptance.

Many commentators have read a *double* meaning into the verb ' be lifted up ' in this 14th verse: suggesting, that is, that there is the thought of the *Exaltation* of Jesus as well as of His Crucifixion. Westcott, for example, maintained this view; declaring that the passage of Jesus ' through the elevation on the cross to the elevation on the right hand of God was a necessity (*must*) arising out of the laws of the divine nature.' It is probable, however—to our own view—that the Evangelist was thinking specifically of the crucifixion of Jesus when he wrote these words. In 8^{28} and in 12^{32} the same verb is employed, and in each case it is the Crucifixion that is referred to. In the first of these two passages Jesus says to the unbelieving Jews: 'When ye have *lifted up* the Son of man, then ye shall know that I am he.' This 'uplifting' is clearly a reference to the Crucifixion, and not to the Exaltation—for unbelieving Jews would not be said by the Evangelist to 'exalt' Jesus to the Father. In the second passage Jesus says: 'And I, if I be *lifted up* from the earth, will draw all men unto myself.' This 'uplifting' is also clearly a reference to the Crucifixion; for the Evangelist at once adds the interpretative comment, 'but this he said, signifying by what manner of death he should die.'

When the Evangelist places upon the lips of Jesus so early in his Gospel the words that He '*must be* lifted up' on the Cross, he is only translating the overwhelming sense of Divine mission which possessed the soul of Jesus. In other words, he is giving dramatic expression to that faith in the Father which guided all the steps of the Master—which guided Him even to the Cross. In the faith that it was the Father's will for Him, Jesus suffered unto death: in the faith that His death would be the means of life to men, He was uplifted on the Cross.

In the R.V. a new paragraph begins at *v.* 16 and continues to *v.* 21. This might suggest that the words of Jesus end at *v.* 15, and that now the Evangelist himself continues in comment, exposition, and interpretation. Such a division, however, is misleading if it suggests to the reader that such clear lines of division between the words of Jesus and the words of the Evangelist are discernible. In the former verses, the mind of Jesus is expressed through the mind of this spiritual interpreter: in the later verses, the mind of the interpreter is the vehicle for the expression of the mind of Jesus. In both, the thought is that of Jesus, the mode of presentation that of the author.

The key words of this paragraph are Love, Life, and Judgement—and in that order. The nature of God is Love. The purpose of His Love is that men may have Life. But His purpose does not operate by compulsion: it involves a Judgement—a judgement which is intrinsic to the Fatherly relation of God to His children. The universe is no magical universe. God compels no man to receive His gifts. *Reception* of the Divine Grace always involves a free and willing co-operation on the part of man. So, while the Divine nature is without partiality, it is also without arbitrariness. His gifts are for all, but their reception depends upon moral and spiritual conditions.

16. In the 16th verse the Evangelist gives expression, in one of the greatest passages of Scripture, to the mind of Jesus Himself and to the conviction that flowed from Him to His followers. Jesus knew the Father with the intimacy of an only son's knowledge of his father. This knowledge was one of perfect harmony of mind, heart, and purpose. In this knowledge Jesus knew Himself to be 'given' by the Father. His knowledge of the Father, His obedience to the Father, His mission for the Father, is all of the Father's *grace*. These are *gifts*: they are not earned. They are the Father's gifts of Love, for He Himself is Love.

Love always gives, and He who knows the Source of Love always Himself *gives.* The life of Jesus was *given.* He knew Himself to be the medium of the Father's Love for the 'world.' The Divine Love, Jesus knew, embraced the *world,* not just a few elect believers (1^{29}, 6^{51}, etc.). The *end* of the mission was to bring 'eternal life' to men. The conviction that this was His mission dominates the consciousness of Jesus throughout this Gospel. He was here to *give* it, not just to *promise* it for a life beyond the grave. He gives what He *knows* He has. This 16th verse is therefore the expression in summary form by the reflecting mind of the Evangelist of the inner consciousness of Jesus.

But 'eternal life' has conditions for its reception. If its source is in the quickening grace of the Divine Spirit, as Jesus has said to Nicodemus, how comes it that some see and some do not see, that some 'perish' and some find 'eternal life'? The answer of the mind of Jesus to this perennial problem of humanity's speculation is also found in these verses. Life comes to those who 'believe on him,' or 'believe in his name.' Now, there could be no profounder misreading of such passages than the suggestion that the *way* is by formal assent to a dogma. Eternal Life is not a 'reward' of correct beliefs. 'Believing' is the act, and orientation, of the whole personality. It belongs to those who with trustful insight have accepted the Father's Word and Deed. These love the light, and walk in it. They *do* the *truth*—a remarkable Johannine phrase found elsewhere in the New Testament only in 1 Jn. 1^{6}—they do not just *assent* to a *statement* of truth. There are, however, those who 'do not believe,' that is, who hate the light and do evil. This is the *Judgement.* It is not an external, or imposed, judgement: it is an internal and intrinsic judgement. This Gospel does not speak of a future Apocalyptic judgement: it speaks of a present judgement which is inherent in life itself as God has ordered it. 'This is the judgement, that the light is come into the world, and men love the darkness rather than the light, for their works were evil.' The Son does not come to judge but to save; as the light does not come to make shadows but to enlighten. Nevertheless, when the light comes it makes shadows. Light reveals the true and the false. Truth itself is the great divider of life. Love would embrace the 'world,' but there are many who reject it. The impure flee the pure. The lovers of darkness hide from the light—scurrying away like cockroaches into their holes. There is no *arbitrariness* in this Divine universe. Judgement is rooted in the equity of God.

The mind is its own place, and in itself
Can make a hell of heaven, a heaven of hell.

The lovers of the light—the doers of the truth—come to the light when it shines. They welcome it, they do not flee from it. It is then made manifest that the very springs of their life are 'in God.' God's will is seen to be their law. All the 'works' they do have their source in a life of dedication to the Divine Will, of fellowship with the Divine nature. 'He that doeth the truth comes to the light, so that it becomes manifest that his works are wrought in complete harmony with the mind of God.'

THE SECOND, AND LAST, WITNESS OF THE BAPTIST

JN. 3^{22-36}

3 22 After these things came Jesus and his
disciples into the land of Judæa; and there
23 he tarried with them, and baptized. And
John also was baptizing in Ænon near to
Salim, because there was much water
there: and they came, and were baptized.
24 For John was not yet cast into prison.
25 There arose therefore a questioning on the
part of John's disciples with a Jew about
26 purifying. And they came unto John, and
said to him, Rabbi, he that was with thee
beyond Jordan, to whom thou hast borne
witness, behold, the same baptizeth, and
27 all men come to him. John answered and
said, A man can receive nothing, except it
28 have been given him from heaven. Ye
yourselves bear me witness, that I said, I
am not the Christ, but, that I am sent
29 before him. He that hath the bride is the
bridegroom: but the friend of the bridegroom, which standeth and heareth him,
rejoiceth greatly because of the bridegroom's voice: this my joy therefore is
30 fulfilled. He must increase, but I must
decrease.
31 He that cometh from above is above all:
he that is of the earth is of the earth, and
of the earth he speaketh: he that cometh
32 from heaven is above all. What he hath
seen and heard, of that he beareth witness;
33 and no man receiveth his witness. He
that hath received his witness hath set his
34 seal to *this*, that God is true. For he whom
God hath sent speaketh the words of God:
for he giveth not the Spirit by measure.
35 The Father loveth the Son, and hath given
36 all things into his hand. He that believeth
on the Son hath eternal life; but he that
obeyeth not the Son shall not see life, but
the wrath of God abideth on him.

Verses 22–30 are felt by many to follow somewhat awkwardly the earlier verses of the chapter. The interview with Nicodemus takes place, the Evangelist says, in Jerusalem, which is, of course, in Judæa. But here we read: 'After these things came Jesus and His disciples into the land of Judæa.' How, it is asked, could they 'come' where they already were? In consequence of this awkwardness of sequence, the passage is usually transposed—by some to follow the Galilean incident, 2^{1-12}, by others to follow 3^{31-36}. There is, however, no MS. evidence for such transpositions. And it may well be that they are dictated by a mistaken estimate—or rather by a lack of sympathetic understanding—of the Evangelist's mind and mode of writing. Engrossed as his mind has been in presenting, in *vv.* 16–21, the thought of Jesus on God, on eternal life, and on judgement—where in a few pregnant sentences he gives us the distilled essence of many of the sayings of Jesus—he returns, probably after a lapse of time, to the composition of his Gospel. We suggest that the phrase, 'after these things,' may indicate that the author is taking up his pen again after an interval. It is clear, from an examination of the phrases, 'After this' and 'After these things,' that the author himself has no chronological intention. If the reader will consider carefully the passages in the Gospel where these two phrases occur—2^{12}, 3^{22}, $5^{1,14}$, 6^{1}, 7^{1}, $11^{7,11}$, 13^{7}, $19^{28,38}$, 21^{1}—he will see that the idea of temporal sequence is not in the Evangelist's mind. 'After this' or 'After these things' are phrases which roughly correspond to the 'And now,' with which a modern author will begin a new paragraph. It indicates a sequence in the author's mind, not in the narratives themselves.

Another way of explaining the sequence in our text is as follows: 'the land of Judæa' may to the author be in contrast to the city of Jerusalem; just as a modern writer may speak of the 'counties' or 'shires' of England in contrast to London, the Metropolis.

What the Evangelist is now intent on saying is, once again, that John's baptismal ministry is but preparatory to the Ministry of Jesus. He has already stressed this in the first chapter. He will say it again before the Baptist disappears from the narrative. It is significant that each time the Baptist is introduced into the narrative it is to bear witness, not to himself or his own work, but to the life and work of Jesus. The Evangelist answers the exorbitant claims of the Baptist's followers at the time he was writing by unfolding the mind of the Baptist himself. This intention of the Evangelist is seen in the emphatic statement in *v.* 24, where it is declared that the public ministry of Jesus *preceded* the imprisonment of John. The Synoptic narrative (Mk. 1^{14}; Mt. $4^{12, 17}$) may have suggested that Jesus' work did not begin till John's was finished, and might therefore have lent colour to the idea that Jesus was only *completing* the work of his predecessor.

The Evangelist tells us here, in *vv.* 22 and 26, that Jesus Himself baptised, a statement which in 4^2 is seemingly withdrawn. This contradiction can be dealt with in two ways. *Either* the parenthetical note in 4^2 was inserted by a later editor; *or* what the author meant to say in chapter 3 was that, not Jesus but His disciples baptised. In the light of *v.* 26, the former is by far the more reasonable supposition. It is probable that Jesus himself baptised, having Himself submitted to the rite. Such a baptismal ministry of Jesus in the early days of his public work should serve to put the whole question of the sacramental rite in its proper historical perspective. It could not at this time *signify* to Jesus what Christian baptism afterwards came to signify in the Church. Christian sacramental rites, like Christian dogmas, have a history; and they can only be understood in the light of that history. The author, by reminding his readers that Jesus Himself baptised in the early stages of His Ministry, is recalling them to the Master's own mind on the place of these rites in the religious life. To that mind, there was *no necessary connexion* between an age-long rite and the 'grace' which it signified. The 'value' of any rite is the *real value it has for the worshippers*. Jesus Himself used an old rite—He was a fulfiller, not a destroyer. But the value of the rite to Him was in that which it signified to Himself, and not either in the rite itself or in that which it signified to predecessors. It is, therefore, a profound misreading of the author's mind to regard this passage as a later ecclesiastical justification of the centrality of Christian baptism.

25. The jealousy of some of the Baptist's disciples for his prestige is answered by the forerunner himself. What, they wanted to know, could be the relation of the purificatory baptisms of Jesus and of John? Were both 'valid,' to use our modern word? Or, What did these baptisms *mean*? What were their respective 'values'? The reply of the Baptist points his questioners to the truth which Jesus Himself had expressed in the interview with Nicodemus: 'A man can receive nothing except it have been given him from heaven.' Inward purification and renewal are from above. Disputations about the relative 'value' of baptismal rites leads to forgetfulness of the Divine source of the grace signified. That grace has come down to men through Christ; for He is the Word 'from above.' He is 'the bridegroom'; John is but a friend who 'standeth and heareth him,' and 'rejoiceth greatly because of the bridegroom's voice.' In these words the author is, with the freedom manifest throughout his Gospel, placing upon the lips of

John some of the ideas central to the mind of Jesus Himself. The Master had used this figure of the bridegroom to indicate His close relation to His followers (Mk. 2^{19-20}). The metaphor was familiar to readers of the Old Testament. The relation of Jehovah and His people was imaged in the relation of the Bridegroom and Bride (Exod. 34^{15}; Dt. 31^{16}; Hos. 2^{19}; Ezek. 16; Mal. 2^{11}: Ps. 73^{27}). The relation of Christ to the Church was similarly described in the books of the New Testament with which our author was familiar (2 Cor. 11^{2}; Eph. 5^{32}; Rev. 19^{7}, 21^{2}, etc.). The figure expresses the *unique* relation of Christ to His followers. It is intimate and possessive.

This testimony of the Baptist is to be regarded as an expression of the mind of Jesus Himself, and of His followers in His intimate and abiding fellowship. The author does not make the Baptist say all that the Church came to mean when it spoke of the relation of Christ to the Church. The ecclesiastical and theological form given to the figure of the bridegroom and bride belonged neither to the mind of Jesus nor to the mind of the Evangelist. In other words, neither Jesus nor the Evangelist thought of *an Institution* as the 'Bride of Christ.' Jesus, and His evangelist, thought of a real intimacy, a real harmony, in the depth of the whole personal nature; and not of a formal or institutional bond. There could be those who said, 'Lord, Lord,' who were not His; and those who belong to the Institution, who were no friends of the bridegroom, least of all, to be accounted His 'bride.' The Baptist was, indeed, the friend of the bridegroom. His joy was fulfilled in hearing the bridegroom's voice; for the bridegroom's friends, his voice is as 'the sound of many waters' (Rev. 19^{6}). He who was a 'voice' is silent before that of the voice of the bridegroom. The voice of the Baptist is hushed before that of the Word. 'He must increase, but I must decrease.' There is no bitterness or sadness in this. The herald had done his work. His witness is no longer necessary, for the Word is here.

31. In the paragraph, *vv.* 31–36, the Evangelist ceases to use the Baptist for the transmission of his own insight and reflection. Having given voice to the mind of the forerunner for the last time, his own meditation takes wing, and soars above any narrative limitation. Following on the thought of Him who is to increase while all His followers decrease, the Evangelist, in a passage of profound insight, expresses some of the central truths of Jesus Himself. He who knew Himself to be 'from above,' is *above all His followers* (not, *above all things*). In the Synoptic Gospels, Jesus had frequently made magisterial claims for Himself (cf. Mt. 11^{25-27}, and many other passages). There was something unique in our Lord's knowledge of the Father: and out of this unique knowledge sprang naturally His claims to the obedience of His followers. The Fourth Evangelist is here giving expression to this uniqueness and this supremacy of Jesus. In all others, he says, the 'earthly' is mixed with the 'heavenly.' The contrast between 'earthly things' and 'heavenly things' was a familiar one to the Evangelist. It had been used by the Jewish writer of the *Wisdom of Solomon*: 'And hardly do we divine the things that are on earth, And the things that are close at hand we find with labour; But the things that are in the heavens, who ever yet traced out?' The Evangelist himself had just narrated the story of Nicodemus, and the teaching of Jesus about the life 'from above.' He had recalled

his readers to the difficulty men had in receiving the teaching of Jesus with regard to ' heavenly things ' (*v.* 12).

In Jesus, and through Jesus, the pure unsullied light of eternity shines. The ' witness ' He bore was the knowledge He had of the Father. It was a ' witness,' says the Evangelist, of what Jesus had ' seen and heard ' (*v.* 32). All knowledge of the eternal can only be expressed by such figures as those of ' seeing ' and ' hearing.' How else could they be described? Those who ask for the extirpation of metaphor from the language of religion know not what they say.

' And no man receiveth his witness.' In view of what the Evangelist has said in *v.* 26 about ' all men coming ' to Jesus, how are we to understand these words? We have two keys to the author's thought. Firstly, many may come but few may receive. It is only they who have ears to hear, who can hear: ' the natural man receiveth not the things of God '; ' spiritual things are spiritually discerned.' Secondly, the author's conviction of the radical nature of this division, and of this necessity, is expressed with dramatic intensity. ' No man,' he says, ' receiveth his witness.' Yet he himself had received this witness; and all who had ' done the truth ' had ' come to the light.' What the author, therefore, means to say is that no one, unless illumined by the Light from above, receives the witness of God. It is but another way of saying what Jesus has already said in this chapter—that only those who are born from above can see the Kingdom of God in Jesus. He who is the Word of God, speaks the words of God; for God has given to Him of His spirit in no niggardly measure (*v.* 34). In Him were revealed the truth and grace of God without bounds. All our human thoughts of God are bounded by the limitations of our faculties. We cannot comprehend Him to perfection. Often in our blindness we deny the reality of the Light in its splendour. But the Light is there for those who have eyes to see. Who can deny the reality of Goodness? Or the splendour of Beauty? Or the peremptoriness of Truth? These are God's ' witnesses ' in human life, and were incarnate in the Son. The followers of Christ have found that these ' witnesses ' to God in our human life satisfy the deepest needs and aspirations of men's hearts and minds. ' He that hath received his witness hath set his seal to this, that God is true ' (*v.* 33).

It is the Son who has fullness of spiritual endowment. ' The Father loveth the Son and hath given all things into His hand.' Because Jesus knew Himself to be Son, ' all things ' pertaining to the Kingdom are at His disposal. The passage ends with the same message of ' eternal life ' and ' judgement,' given earlier in the chapter. He that ' *believeth* on the Son ' is contrasted with him who ' *disobeyeth* the Son.' This contrast shows once again that ' belief ' to the author does not mean mere intellectual assent. It is a belief that obeys. Such ' belief ' means the possession of eternal life in the midst of time: ' he *hath* eternal life.' But he who disobeys is a stranger to this life. Instead of being in spiritual union with God, he is alienated from Him. This separation the Evangelist calls ' the wrath of God.'

THE WITNESS TO THE WOMAN OF SAMARIA

JN. 4^{1-42}

4 1 When therefore the Lord knew how that
the Pharisees had heard that Jesus was making and baptizing more disciples than John
2 (although Jesus himself baptized not, but
3 his disciples), he left Judæa, and departed
4 again into Galilee. And he must needs
5 pass through Samaria. So he cometh to
a city of Samaria, called Sychar, near to
the parcel of ground that Jacob gave to
6 his son Joseph: and Jacob's well was there.
Jesus therefore, being wearied with his
journey, sat thus by the well. It was
7 about the sixth hour. There cometh a
woman of Samaria to draw water: Jesus
8 saith unto her, Give me to drink. For his
disciples were gone away into the city to
9 buy food. The Samaritan woman therefore saith unto him, How is it that thou,
being a Jew, askest drink of me, which am
a Samaritan woman? (For Jews have no
10 dealings with Samaritans.) Jesus answered and said unto her, If thou knewest
the gift of God, and who it is that saith to
thee, Give me to drink; thou wouldest have
asked of him, and he would have given
11 thee living water. The woman saith unto
him, Sir, thou hast nothing to draw with,
and the well is deep: from whence then
12 hast thou that living water? Art thou
greater than our father Jacob, which gave
us the well, and drank thereof himself, and
13 his sons, and his cattle? Jesus answered
and said unto her, Every one that drinketh
14 of this water shall thirst again: but whosoever drinketh of the water that I shall give
him shall never thirst; but the water that I
shall give him shall become in him a well
of water springing up unto eternal life.
15 The woman saith unto him, Sir, give me
this water, that I thirst not, neither come
16 all the way hither to draw. Jesus saith
unto her, Go, call thy husband, and come
17 hither. The woman answered and said
unto him, I have no husband. Jesus saith
unto her, Thou saidst well, I have no hus-
18 band: for thou hast had five husbands;
and he whom thou now hast is not thy
19 husband: this hast thou said truly. The
woman saith unto him, Sir, I perceive that
20 thou art a prophet. Our fathers worshipped in this mountain; and ye say, that
in Jerusalem is the place where men ought
21 to worship. Jesus saith unto her, Woman,
believe me, the hour cometh, when
neither in this mountain, nor in Jerusalem,
22 shall ye worship the Father. Ye worship
that which ye know not: we worship that
which we know: for salvation is from the
23 Jews. But the hour cometh, and now is,
when the true worshippers shall worship
the Father in spirit and truth: for such
doth the Father seek to be his worshippers.
24 God is a Spirit: and they that worship him
25 must worship in spirit and truth. The
woman saith unto him, I know that Messiah cometh (which is called Christ): when
he is come, he will declare unto us all
26 things. Jesus saith unto her, I that speak
unto thee am *he*.

27 And upon this came his disciples; and
they marvelled that he was speaking with
a woman; yet no man said, What seekest
thou? or, Why speakest thou with her?
28 So the woman left her waterpot, and went
away into the city, and saith to the men,
29 Come, see a man, which told me all things
that *ever* I did: can this be the Christ?
30 They went out of the city, and were com-
31 ing to him. In the mean while the dis-
32 ciples prayed him, saying, Rabbi, eat. But
he said unto them, I have meat to eat that
33 ye know not. The disciples therefore said
one to another, Hath any man brought
34 him *aught* to eat? Jesus saith unto them,
My meat is to do the will of him that sent
35 me, and to accomplish his work. Say not
ye, There are yet four months, and *then*
cometh the harvest? behold, I say unto
you, Lift up your eyes, and look on the
fields, that they are white already unto
36 harvest. He that reapeth receiveth wages,
and gathereth fruit unto life eternal; that he
that soweth and he that reapeth may rejoice
37 together. For herein is the saying true,
38 One soweth, and another reapeth. I sent
you to reap that whereon ye have not
laboured: others have laboured, and ye
are entered into their labour.

39 And from that city many of the Samaritans believed on him because of the word
of the woman, who testified, He told me
40 all things that *ever* I did. So when the
Samaritans came unto him, they besought
him to abide with them: and he abode
41 there two days. And many more believed
42 because of his word; and they said to the
woman, Now we believe, not because of
thy speaking: for we have heard for ourselves, and know that this is indeed the
Saviour of the world.

This whole passage may be subdivided into three paragraphs, as in the R.V. There is, however, a manifest sequence of thought, evidencing an interior unity in the complete section. We therefore propose to interpret it in the integrated completeness which it had to the Johannine author.

The characteristics of the Evangelist's mind are once more evidenced in this truly sublime chapter. The incident has been regarded in two ways. It has been taken, firstly, as a precise record of historical fact. It has been taken, secondly, as 'creative allegory.' We suggest, as a third way of interpreting the narrative, that a real historical incident in which Jesus met and conversed with a woman of Samaria is allegorised and dramatised by the Evangelist in order to make it the vehicle of the essential mind of the Master. We shall therefore be prepared for a measure of allegorical creation; but it is probably creation *within* historical incident, the whole being designed by the author to give expression to the essential teaching of Jesus. There are, as we believe, four factors to be remembered by those who would reach a true estimate of the narrative. Firstly, there is some historical fact; secondly, there is the 'literary realism' of the dramatic artist; thirdly, there is his allegorising motif; and finally, there is, as the *main clue* to the whole, the dominating desire on the part of the author to unfold to the Christians of his day what the Master Himself had taught. It can be hardly doubted that the dialogue between Jesus and the woman is largely of a symbolical character: it was designed by the Evangelist to give expression to the profound and spiritual universalism implicit in the teaching of Jesus.

It is possible that when the Evangelist wrote this chapter, he also had in mind the extension of the Gospel of Jesus beyond the confines of Judaism. He was doubtless familiar with the passage in the first chapter of the *Acts*, where the disciples are called to be the 'witnesses' of Jesus 'both in Jerusalem, and in all Judæa and Samaria, and unto the uttermost part of the earth' (Acts 1^8). Samaria was the part of the outside world nearest to the Jew. So when the Evangelist narrated this, largely symbolical, incident, he had in mind, not only the immediate situation which confronted Jesus Himself, but the mission which confronted His disciples after the Crucifixion and Resurrection. With such a thought in his mind, he would recall the Church of his own day to the essential mind of Jesus Himself. That mind, he would say, transcended the bounds of nationality and race. The Mission which Jesus came to fulfil was circumscribed by the frontiers neither of sect nor of creed. He, indeed—so the Evangelist meant to declare—fulfilled the religion of Samaria as well as of Judæa. He revealed the true meaning, indeed, of every traditional faith of men.

It is necessary to remember all these factors in the Evangelist's intention if we would understand the narrative.

1–6. The chapter follows fittingly upon the closing verses of the third chapter. Having spoken about baptismal rites, the author proceeds to expound the inmost thought of Jesus. The theme of the chapter is suggested by the reference to water—a clear case of 'association of ideas' in the mind of the Evangelist. He will say what 'water' really signified to Jesus. Water purifies: but *from what* does it purify? What kind of defilements does it remove? Water assuages thirst; but what kind of thirst does it assuage? The narrative which follows is the answer of the mind of Jesus to these questions.

The Pharisees had heard that Jesus is baptising more disciples than John.

Jesus departs from Judæa for Galilee. 'He *must needs* pass through Samaria,' for Samaria was in the direct line between Judæa and Galilee. A possible alternative, though longer, route was through Peræa; but to meet this woman of Samaria Jesus 'must needs,' the Evangelist says, 'pass through Samaria.' It is probable that the phrase 'he *must needs* pass through Samaria' has a double meaning to the Evangelist. It expresses, that it is not merely a necessity arising out of geographical convenience, but a necessity arising out of the sense of an imperious mission possessed by Jesus (see also 3^{14}). He halts in the heat of midday—'it was about the sixth hour'—by a well, famous in Israel's history, outside the small town of Sychar, to-day identified with 'Askar, lying to the east of Mt. Ebal. This was Jacob's well (Gen. 33^{19} and 48^{22}), recalling the days prior to the sectarian and tribal divisions that had sundered the race sprung from his loins. No more fitting or suggestive place for teaching which transcended the divisions of race and sect!

7. To Jesus, seated alone by a well that must have inspired many historical reflections, there comes a woman of Samaria. He asks that she may give Him to drink. The divisions and misunderstandings of the different branches of the one race are reflected in the woman's question of surprise. 'How is it, that thou, being a Jew, askest drink of me, which am a Samaritan woman?' The explanatory note found in *v.* 9—'For Jews have no dealings with Samaritans'—is omitted by some ancient authorities, and *may* have been inserted in the narrative by a later writer. Otherwise, the words may be taken as a kind of aside, in which the Evangelist himself explains to readers unfamiliar with the historical situation the inner significance of the woman's question. It is a question meant by the author to give dramatic expression to an age-long feud between two branches of the same race, a feud going back probably to the colonisation by Assyria, referred to in 2 Kings 17^{24}. There was acute dissension between Samaritans and Jews at the time of the Return from the Exile (Ezra 4 and Neh. 6); and this led the Samaritans to build a temple on Mt. Gerizim, rivalling the Jewish temple in Jerusalem. They claimed to be descendents of the ten tribes, and to be in possession of the true religion of Moses. They accepted the Pentateuch, and transmitted it in a Hebrew text which has only slight variations from that of the Jews. They rejected the Jewish temple and priesthood as schismatic, and declared that the true sanctuary chosen by God was not Zion but this Mt. Gerizim, over against Shechem. The sanctity of this site they sought to prove from the Pentateuch, reading Gerizim in Dt. 27^{4}.

10. The answer of Jesus continues the unfolding of a dramatic and allegorical situation. In 3^{16} the Evangelist had said that Jesus is *God's gift* to the race, and that this gift is the medium of eternal life to all who truly believe. Here, in Jesus's answer in *v.* 10, the same truth is expressed in another setting. 'If thou knewest the gift of God, and who it is that saith to thee, Give me to drink: thou wouldest have asked of him and he would have given thee living water.' By this answer—strikingly dramatic in its setting—the positions of seeker and giver are reversed by the Evangelist. The seeker becomes the giver and the giver the seeker. All this is true to the *real situation* which confronted Jesus, no doubt a thousand times, in His Ministry. Men and women who had material food and drink to

offer the wayfaring Son of Man awoke in His presence to deeper needs which He could satisfy. But it is not necessary to look to the details of the narrative for precise historicity. It continues with strikingly realistic touches, recalling us to the vivid pages of Bunyan's allegories. 'Sir, thou hast nothing to draw with and the well is deep: from whence then hast thou that living water? Art thou greater than our father Jacob which gave us the well, and drank thereof himself, and his sons, and his cattle?' The misunderstandings of the mind of Jesus, in the days of His flesh, as in every successive age, are once more expressed by the Evangelist. This Divine teacher is very patient with His spiritually dull hearers—'the bruised reed he does not break.' So in *vv.* 14 and 15 He leads the woman gently, by a statement that quickens her dawning sense of spiritual reality, into the deep waters. 'Every one that drinketh of this water shall thirst again: but whosoever drinketh of the water that I shall give him shall never thirst; but the water that I shall give him shall become in him a well of water springing up unto eternal life.'

This is the cardinal truth which the passage proclaims. The recurring theme of the whole Gospel is eternal life, of which the Word is the vehicle. It is here likened to 'living water'—water, that is, which flows perennial and fresh from the spring. In the Hebrew language the water of a spring was called 'living' water (Gen. 26^{19}). And in Hebrew religious thought such 'living water' represented the living energy proceeding from God. Jeremiah, for example, speaks of God as 'the fountain of the living waters' (Jer. 2^{13} and 17^{13}). Isaiah speaks of waters 'breaking out' in the wilderness, and streams in the desert (Is. 35^{6}). The prophet of the Exile called to the people: 'Ho, every one that thirsteth, come ye to the waters' (Is. 55^{1}). Ezekiel writes a parable about the waters which go forth from the temple (Ezek. 47). These passages—to which many might be added—show that to the Old Testament writers flowing water was a symbol for the knowledge of God which brought life to men. The Rabbis regarded water as a symbol for the *Torah*, the Law of the Lord, which was held by them to convey all true knowledge of Divine things.[1] In the *Odes of Solomon* the same figure repeatedly occurs. 'Fill ye waters for yourselves from the living fountain of the Lord, for it is opened to you: and come ye all ye thirsty, and take the draught; and rest by the fountain of the Lord. For fair it is and pure and gives rest to the soul. Much more pleasant are its waters than honey; and the honeycomb of bees is not to be compared with it. For it flows forth from the lips of the Lord and from the heart of the Lord is its name.'[2]

The figure of water, as we have already seen, is used frequently by the Fourth Evangelist. It was doubtless also frequently used by Jesus Himself. Among the beatitudes Mt. records one in which Jesus declared the blessedness belonging to those who 'hunger and thirst after righteousness' (Mt. 5^{6}). These shall be filled. Human need, that is, will be met by God's bounty. This is the message of the Fourth Gospel. God's bounty is Jesus Himself. The spiritual thirst which God implanted within man is quenched by the gift of spiritual life of which Jesus knew Himself to be the channel. He was conscious in the depths of His

[1] See, for example, the illustrations cited by Odeberg, *op. cit.*, pp. 158 ff.
[2] *The Odes and Psalms of Solomon*, J. Rendel Harris, p. 130.

being of a source of life which had its fount in God; and believed Himself to be the mediator of the vital energies of God to men. Thus, only the waters of which He was the channel could quench the thirst of humanity. All other waters—of the earth and of the flesh—but mock men's thirst; they do not quench it. For, as the Evangelist says in his first Epistle, they but pander to 'the lust of the flesh and the lust of the eyes, and the vain glory of life'; and these are not of the Father, but of the world (1 Jn. 2^{16}). Even the *Torah*—preserved by Samaritan and by Jew—could not give abiding satisfaction to this thirst. What men need is a *fountain*, and not a stagnant pool: not a static law, but a living spirit.

And this 'living water' is *in* man—'it becomes *in him* a well of water.' It is not, that is, a magical impartation. It is an inward and spiritual reception. Man can only be enduringly satisfied by that which becomes *his own* in the unplumbed depths of his own rational, moral, and spiritual nature. Then, to use the language of Is. 58^{11}, he becomes 'like a spring of water, whose waters fail not.' The source of life has not to be pursued through the things of space or time. The height and the depth, say, It is not in me. Things present and things to come respond, It is not in me. It is nigh thee, in thy heart and in thy mind. The Kingdom of heaven, said Jesus, is within you. Like happiness, it is not to be found in the external and evanescent. Restless pursuit of shadows engenders inevitable *ennui*. We find it *within*, or nowhere.

16. The narrative now takes a striking turn, in which, as we cannot but think, the allegorising mind of the author is seen creatively at work. The reference to the 'five husbands' of the woman indicates, to some former commentators, precise historical fact, revealing a 'supernatural' knowledge on the part of Jesus of some unhappy details in the past life of the woman. We suggest that this is to misunderstand both the mind of Jesus and the mind of the Evangelist. For, in the first place, though our Lord's knowledge was unique in the moral and spiritual realm, it was, as far as historical and scientific matters of fact were concerned, conditioned as ours is conditioned. And, in the second place, nowhere in the Gospel is the allegorising motif of the Evangelist more clearly seen than here. From the days of Origen, commentators have seen allegorical significance in the reference to 'five husbands'—though, it is necessary to add, this interpretation has been usually accompanied by the acceptance of the strict historicity of the narrative. Those who point to the 'vividness' of the narrative, in proof of its 'actuality,' forget that this dramatic vividness pervades the Gospel: it is evidence of the character of the author's mind, and not of the precise historicity of his narrative.

Josephus, in his *Antiquities* (ix. and xiv. 3), speaks of 'five gods' of Samaria; and in the passage from 2 Kings 17, which we have already cited, there is the canonical account of how the King of Assyria brought men to colonise Samaria from Babylon, from Cuth, from Hamath, from Avva, and from Sepharvaim, and of how these five bodies of colonists established the worship of their deities in Samaria (2 Kings 17^{30-31}). What, therefore, the Evangelist wishes to say here, is to remind his readers of the 'religious adultery' of Samaria's past, personified in this 'woman of Samaria,' and of the 'irregular' union of Samaria in the time of our Lord to the service and worship of Jehovah. 'He whom thou now hast is not thy husband': this signifies the ignorant worship of the Jehovah of Israel referred to in *v.* 22. This interpretation is supported by the fact that in the Old Testament 'adultery' was often referred to in a moral and spiritual sense. Jeremiah, for example, said that 'backsliding Israel committed adultery' (3^{8}); and Ezekiel said that 'with their idols they have committed adultery' (23^{37}). The Johannine author, who belonged to the same Hebrew race, used with complete naturalness similar language. Such language is the certain clue to his meaning here.

From the thought of this wanton, impure worship of God, the Evangelist now goes on to expound that true worship as taught by Jesus. It is a passage which transcends all the limitations of race and of cultural heritage. When, in the ages to come, humanity in its unity and completeness is able to erect some temple symbolical of the One Religion, over its portico may well be inscribed the words of Jesus in *v.* 24: 'God is Spirit: and they that worship him must worship in spirit and in truth.' The Evangelist, however, has his own dramatic approach to that culminating word. Here is Mt. Gerizim hard by Jacob's well, with its temple enshrining the worship of Samaria. 'Our fathers worshipped in this mountain': so speaks the woman. In distant Jerusalem is the temple of the Jews: 'And ye say that in Jerusalem is the place where men ought to worship.' Which, if either, is right? The answer of Jesus directs the mind, not to the *place*, which is subsidiary, but to the Being and Nature of God, which is essential. 'Woman, believe me, the hour cometh when neither in this mountain, nor in Jerusalem, shall ye worship *the Father*.' Jews and Samaritans dispute about a *place*. Jesus lifts the whole question to the highest realm, when He says that the true worship of the future will be inspired by right thoughts of God—even the thought of God which flowed out of the depth of His own personal knowledge, God as Divine Father. When men know God as the Divine Father they do not separate, and fight, on a question of the *place* where He ought to be worshipped.

22. The 22nd verse seems, at first sight, to be a startling expression of narrow nationalism, following as it does upon so striking a universalism as is found in the 21st verse. It is not really so, when understood in its setting, and in the light of the mind and intention of the author. When he puts into the mouth of Jesus the words, 'Ye worship that which ye know not,' He is but giving expression to what Paul said, in another context, to the Athenians on Mars Hill, 'Him therefore that ye ignorantly worship, him declare we unto you.' The 22nd verse follows naturally the emphasis on the *nature* of God in *v.* 21. The true worship of the future will involve a worship of God whose nature the Samaritans have not truly known: this God will be *the Father* whom Jesus has made known. Their ignorance was partly due to the fact that their Bible contained only the five books of the Law; the Prophets had no place in their Scriptures. In the second part of this 22nd verse—'we worship that which we know: for salvation is of the Jews'—the Evangelist is giving expression to the superior religious tradition enshrined in the Jewish Scriptures. 'Salvation is of the Jews'—in the sense that the unfolding of the Divine Mind had reached a higher point in a religious tradition which contained Prophets and Writings as well as the Law, and therefore was a truer and worthier preparation for Christ, who, though in the line of the prophets, was

'more than a prophet.' There is no exclusive nationalism, therefore, in the passage, but merely a recognition of the whole religious tradition of Israel which Jesus was come to fulfil.

23–24. That this is the true significance of the passage is seen, further, in the light of the sublime and spiritual universalism of the these following verses. The three particularisms, to which all religion in the world is prone, are each transcended—the particularism of *place*, the particularism of *race*, and the particularism of *book*. God is 'Father,' and God is 'Spirit.' The Father *seeks* the worship of His sons: it is not that the subject abjectly offers his gifts to the Despot. Those who know that God is 'the seeking Father' know that He is worshipped in *any* place where the human spirit is found of Him. They who worship the Father belong to no one race or clime. The only test of worship is the sincerity and reality of the worshipper—never in the colour of his skin or the order of his caste. The perverse loyalty to the letter of a specific sacred book is transcended by a larger loyalty to God who is Spirit, from whom all Truth has proceeded.

25–26. All this, we suggest, springs directly from these revolutionary words. They come, we are convinced, from the mind of the incarnate Word. It is little wonder that after such words, the Evangelist, again with complete chronological indifference, unfolds in another dramatic statement the unique Messianic consciousness and claim of Jesus. 'The woman saith unto him, I know that Messiah cometh. . . . Jesus saith unto her, I that speak unto thee am he.' Such teaching comes from one whose Messiahship transcended every exclusive, and materialistic, conception held by the sons of men.

27–38. At this point, descriptive narrative begins again. The disciples return with the food they have procured, to find to their surprise that Jesus is in conversation with the woman. Whether this statement of their surprise is another touch of 'literary realism,' or a reminiscence derived by the author from the Apostle John, we do not, and never shall, know. It is possible that this is part of the framework of historical incident which the Evangelist has used. Such surprise was natural to those familiar with Rabbinical custom and precept, and, indeed, with the prevailing Eastern view of womankind. 'Let no one talk with a woman in the street, no, not with his own wife,' was a precept of the Rabbis. 'Better that the words of the law should be burned than delivered to women,' it was said. Yet the disciples' surprise, the Evangelist tells us, was not expressed to Jesus: 'yet no man said, What seekest thou? or, Why speakest thou with her?' Such a record seems to spring from some transmitted personal recollection of the impression of the inscrutable which the disciples had in the presence of Jesus. Their momentary surprise was merged and lost in their conviction that His mind transcended their own. Though, however, they did not understand Him, they knew Him sufficiently to know that they did not. To know that we do not know, is the first step to knowledge.

In the absence of the woman—who, the Evangelist says, has returned to the town—Jesus reminds them that he has had meat to eat that they know not of. The record of the disciples' thoughts, when Jesus said this, is of the highest interest, for it throws a whole flood of light—and incidentally and unintentionally, which makes it more significant—upon their inmost thought in regard to what is usually called the ' miraculous power ' of Jesus. ' Hath any man brought him aught to eat? ' they ask each other. *It never entered their minds that He would or could work a ' miracle ' in order to feed Himself; as, for example, that he could or would turn stones into bread.* The reply of Jesus reminds them of the real food which has been His spiritual nourishment. Every servant of his fellows knows the deep satisfaction and refreshment of spirit which comes out of an act of self-forgetful ministry. This satisfaction and refreshment of spirit was no rare experience to Jesus: it was His daily meat. And the sustaining quality of it arose out of the sense of mission, the feeling of dependence, which was His. His meat was to do, not His own will, but the will of Him that sent Him, and to finish His work. Self-dependence is no sustaining food: it is a narcotic that saps the vital energies. The filial dependence and obedience which were perfectly exemplified in Jesus sustained Him to the Cross itself.

It is important for the student of the *thought* of the Johannine author to note the language employed in the 34th verse: it will serve to make many rough places plain in this Gospel. The translation of our version says exactly what the author himself meant; though it is not an exact translation of the Greek. What the Evangelist understands the mind of Jesus to say is that His meat consisted in *the doing* of His Father's will—His sustenance was derived from what He did. The Greek, on the other hand—if literally translated—means that His meat was *in order that* He might do the Divine will (ἵνα ποιῶ). This is an illustration of the fact that the author was thinking in Aramaic when he wrote. For, as it has been well said, ' men who thought in and spoke Aramaic would, on learning Greek, be disposed to use whatever phrase they might adopt as the translation of some expression in their own vernacular with the same extended and ambiguous meaning as in the Aramaic original. Thus, for example, they would probably not distinguish accurately between ἵνα ποιῶ (" that I may do ") and ποιεῖν (" to do "), and if they adopted the former as the translation of their infinitive in the one sense, they would be apt to use it in the other also. But whatever the influences may be which have moulded Biblical Greek, whether the language of the New Testament represents the actual living tongue of Greek-speaking Orientals, as seems probable, or not, a study of the Greek Testament by itself is sufficient to show that ἵνα (" that ") with the subjunctive does not necessarily possess a final sense, but corresponds rather to the Hebrew and Aramaic infinitive with the preposition " to." '[1] A similar use of ἵνα with the subjunctive is found in several places in this Gospel—in, for example, 8^{56}, 9^{2}, 15^{8}—and in each case the thought is one *of fact*, and not one *of purpose*. In other words, the mind of the Evangelist moves in the realm of *experience*, not in the realm of *speculation*.

Nor was it what is usually called ' success ' which sustained the spirit of Jesus. His harvest of success was not a present or visible harvest. Inasmuch as a few seeds have taken root in a Samaritan woman's heart He knew the joy of the first-fruits of a spiritual harvest. When in the springtime the farmer looks on his fields and sees the first shoots appearing green above the soil, he anticipates the harvest which lies four months or so ahead. Such is a parable of all service in the Kingdom of God. The task of Jesus was to sow the seed—and he who has seed to

[1] R. H. Kennett, in *The Church of Israel*, p. 150.

sow is greater than he who has a harvest to gather. Where shall seed be found except from Him who is at the source of life itself? Yet the work of the two, sower and reaper, though distinct, issues in a common joy. The disciples have been sent to reap a harvest not of their own sowing; in accord with the familiar proverb, ' One soweth and another reapeth.' But this proverb, which *might* be understood to express the inequalities of life, is taken by Jesus to express the higher equalities of Eternity, where the co-operative service of sower and reaper issues in the common joy of ' fruit unto eternal life.'

39–42. The whole section ends with the witness of the Samaritans to Jesus, resultant upon their experience of Him. The Evangelist narrates the stages of this experience, stages which belong to the growth of most of the convictions which guide men's lives. There is *first* the testimony of other people. ' And from that city many of the Samaritans believed on him because of the word of the woman.' No one comes into the world with ready-made convictions: they have to be *won* in the whole experience which life brings, in the response to its whole environment. But first there is the testimony of those who have gone before. That has to be sifted and weighed. The *second* stage is when the acceptance of the testimony of others is transmuted by personal experience into the convictions by which we live and die. ' So the Samaritans besought him to abide with them.' Many more, we are told, believed, not because of another's testimony, but because of what they had heard of His ' word ': ' for we have heard for ourselves, and know that this is indeed the Saviour of the world.' It is significant that this faith of which the Evangelist speaks rests upon no ' wonders,' except the ' wonder ' of personal intercourse with Jesus. Out of personal fellowship rises the assurance of His ' Saviourhood.' The Evangelist, though he elsewhere speaks of the *saving* work of Jesus (3^{17}, 12^{47}), only here in his Gospel speaks of Jesus as ' Saviour of the world.' The only other use of the title in the New Testament is by the same author in 1 Jn. 4^{14}. The title comes naturally to the pen of one who knew both what Jesus sought to do, and what He had succeeded in doing. To deliver men from every form of sin was the mission of Jesus: this mission had been accomplished in the life of the Evangelist himself. It was, he says, a *universal* mission. Jesus thought in terms of ' the world.' He was indeed ' Saviour of the world.'

The dramatic nature of the Evangelist's mind is clearly revealed by the setting he gives to the narrative just unfolded. The welcome received by Jesus in Samaria, among those with whom the Jews had ' no dealings,' stands in striking contrast to the reception He had received in Jerusalem. It also serves as a dramatic foil to the reception about to be accorded to Jesus in Galilee, in the narrative which follows.

THE SECOND ' SIGN ' AT CANA OF GALILEE

JN. 4^{43-54}

4 43 And after the two days he went forth
44 from thence into Galilee. For Jesus himself testified, that a prophet hath no
45 honour in his own country. So when he
came into Galilee, the Galilæans received
him, having seen all the things that he did
in Jerusalem at the feast: for they also
went unto the feast.

46 He came therefore again unto Cana of
Galilee, where he made the water wine.
And there was a certain nobleman, whose
47 son was sick at Capernaum. When he
heard that Jesus was come out of Judæa
into Galilee, he went unto him, and besought *him* that he would come down, and
heal his son; for he was at the point of
48 death. Jesus therefore said unto him,
Except ye see signs and wonders, ye will in
49 no wise believe. The nobleman saith unto
him, Sir, come down ere my child die.
50 Jesus saith unto him, Go thy way; thy son
liveth. The man believed the word that
Jesus spake unto him, and he went his
51 way. And as he was now going down,
his servants met him, saying, that his son
52 lived. So he inquired of them the hour
when he began to amend. They said
therefore unto him, Yesterday at the
53 seventh hour the fever left him. So the
father knew that *it was* at that hour in
which Jesus said unto him, Thy son
liveth: and himself believed, and his whole
54 house. This is again the second sign that
Jesus did, having come out of Judæa into
Galilee.

The narrative, as it stands in our English translation, goes on to tell us the *reason* for the return of Jesus to Galilee: 'for Jesus himself testified that a prophet hath no honour in his own country.' This, to most minds, would seem a good reason for His not going there; and it has therefore been suggested that what the Evangelist meant was that Judæa, not Galilee, was 'his own country.' This, however, is a very forced explanation; it is much better to take the reference as indicating the country of His upbringing. The same saying is found in Mt. 13^{57}, and Lk. 4^{24}, where it certainly refers to His own country round Nazareth. It may be that the 'for' in *v.* 44 is not meant by the Evangelist to indicate a motive, or reason, in the mind of Jesus for going to Galilee. Prepositions can be loosely and curiously employed; and in this case the 'for' may be used by the Evangelist to express a *connexion in his own mind*, as interpreting the mind of Jesus. What he wishes to say is that Jesus did not think it well to stay where He was receiving much honour, but that He was inwardly impelled to go to His own neighbours, even though not much honour could be expected from them. The history of every people and every age testifies to the fact that a prophet is seldom understood by his immediate associates. It was not in accord with the mind of Jesus, says the Evangelist, to stay where the welcome was greatest, or the difficulties least.

The incident of the healing of the nobleman's son, associated with Cana of Galilee, is in some respects similar to the healing of the centurion's servant recorded in Mt. $8^{5\,ff.}$ and Lk. $7^{6\,ff.}$. In each case, there is *healing at a distance*, and in each case *persistence of entreaty* is rewarded. There are, however, marked differences in the two narratives. The centurion of the Synoptic account is here an officer of Herod, Tetrarch of Galilee. In the first narrative he meets Jesus as He is entering Capernaum, in the second he goes twenty miles away to Cana. Further, the sick 'boy' of the Synoptists is here a 'son.' With these facts before us, all we can say is that the narrative of the Fourth Evangelist *may be* a free rendering of the Synoptic incident, designed to set forth the mind of Jesus on the relative values of different kinds of faith. The Evangelist does not hesitate to alter, or to accentuate, narrative detail in order to give a more dramatic setting to the inner thought of the Master.

This is a case of what we should to-day call 'telepathic' healing. Such a phrase, however—it is necessary to remember—merely hides our ignorance. For, while 'telepathy' may be regarded, with many competent students of psychical research, as established scientific fact, what it is that operates, and how it is that it operates, we do not know. In regard to the whole question of the healing ministry of Jesus, the reader must be referred to fuller discussions elsewhere.[1] Certain things, however, may here be said. *First*, that Jesus did cure people by other than ordinary medical methods. *Second*, that kindred healings have been related in many ages and among many peoples. *Third*, that such healings, obviously, do not 'evidence' the truth of the heterogeneous beliefs held by those who performed them. *Fourth*, that the explanation is to be sought in the realm of the unexplored potencies of the spirit, and of its action on the body. In the case of Jesus, that potency, operating in accord with psychical laws which are to us as yet obscure, was very remarkable. Thus, *fifthly*, these healings must not be regarded as 'miracles' in the old sense of that much used, and much abused, word; that is, they are not, of necessity, events which by their very nature are incapable of subsumption under law. We are not living in a magical universe. No event is, as we believe, without its antecedent causative factors. It is the business of science to discover these factors, and to employ the knowledge so gained in the interest of maimed and sick humanity.

Such issues, however, did not concern our author. His main concern here is not with the cure but with the teaching of Jesus on faith. The faith of the Samaritans, who believed because of their fellowship with Jesus, stands in contrast to the faith based on 'signs and wonders.' Jesus said to this nobleman: 'Except ye see signs and wonders ye will not believe.' The words are expressive of the mind of Jesus at all times and in all places, not just in this place and at this time. It will be noted that they are here spoken not to an individual—the plural 'ye' is used. It is clear that the judgement of Jesus on 'faith' differs from that of those who in different ages have said: 'Except we have miracles we cannot believe in God.' A good deal of religious apologetic, which declared that faith without miracles lacked one of its necessary supports, comes under the implied condemnation of Jesus. The faith which Jesus approved is faith in the reality of the living God, whose glory was manifest in the grace and truth uttered by the whole personality of Jesus. No one has seen God at any time, nor 'proved' Him from 'miracles.' If we do not find the 'super-natural' in the mind of Jesus we shall never find it in physical 'wonders.' As a former commentator on this Gospel said: 'There is a faith which responds to the glory of Christ's personality, which rests on what He is, which builds itself on the truth He utters, and recognises that all spiritual life centres in Him; it is this faith He approves.'[2] Yet Jesus did not let the inadequate faith of needy people prevent Him from giving what healing power He felt able in the circumstances to give. To the cry of real human need, however superstitious its faith, the Master was not deaf. 'Sir,' said the nobleman, 'come down ere my child die.' 'Go thy way; thy son liveth.'

Some have guessed that this 'nobleman' was Chuza, 'Herod's steward' (Lk. 8^3); some that he was Manæn, Herod's foster-brother (Acts 13^1).

The Evangelist closes this narrative with the statement that this was 'the

[1] We ourselves have discussed the issues at considerable length in *Miracle in History and in Modern Thought*.

[2] Marcus Dods.

second sign that Jesus did.' It will be noted that *both* are associated with Cana of Galilee. The nature of the mind and ministry of Jesus, and the nature of the response elicited, are being unfolded. That Ministry sought to lead men to the real belief which rises out of spiritual fellowship with Him who was the 'Word made flesh.' This fellowship is 'eternal life.'

B. LATER WITNESS OF JESUS, AND THE GATHERING CONFLICT

JN. $5–12^{36}$

The Evangelist now enters upon what may be conveniently regarded as the second subdivision of the First Part of the Gospel. These divisions are not arbitrarily read into the Gospel by the reader: they are latent in its dramatic structure and content. In the first subdivision of Part One the Evangelist has been portraying the self-revelation of Jesus to selected and significant individuals—the Baptist, the disciples, Nicodemus, the woman of Samaria, the nobleman of Galilee. In the second subdivision of Part One, which begins with chapter 5, he is going to depict the gathering conflict which the more public ministry of Jesus occasions. This conflict will attain its climax in the events narrated in Part Two.

The key-note of this subdivision is Conflict. The presence of the incarnate Word divides men. The witness of Jesus leads to acute controversy. There broods over the section the clouds of impending storm.

THE SIGN AT THE POOL OF BETHESDA (OR, probably, BETHZATHA)

JN. 5^{1-9}

5 1 After these things there was a feast of the
Jews; and Jesus went up to Jerusalem.
2 Now there is in Jerusalem by the sheep
gate a pool, which is called in Hebrew
3 Bethesda, having five porches. In these
lay a multitude of them that were sick,
5 blind, halt, withered. And a certain man
was there, which had been thirty and eight
6 years in his infirmity. When Jesus saw him
lying, and knew that he had been now a
long time *in that case*, he saith unto him,
7 Wouldest thou be made whole? The sick
man answered him, Sir, I have no man,
when the water is troubled, to put me into
the pool: but while I am coming, another
8 steppeth down before me. Jesus saith unto
him, Arise, take up thy bed, and walk.
9 And straightway the man was made whole,
and took up his bed and walked.

In this narrative the Evangelist's aim is to give a dramatic setting for the controversy with 'the Jews' which follows. The main issues round which the controversy gathers are set forth in realistic light. They are, chiefly, two: first, the attitude of Jesus to the Sabbath; second, His conscious relation to the Father. Should the Gospel be treated as a drama, the second act would begin here.

By some commentators chapter 6 is transposed so as to follow chapter 4. This transposition, for which, as Westcott a generation ago pointed out, there is no MS. authority, has been felt by various interpreters—from the fourteenth century onwards—to allow a better chronological scheme for the respective incidents narrated in chapters 5 and 6. For example, the feast referred to in 5^1 could then be identified with 'the Passover' which 'was at hand' in 6^4; and the reference to going away 'to the other side of the sea of Galilee' in 6^1 would follow naturally upon the incident in 4^{46-54} at Cana of Galilee: and the reference in 7^{21} to the 'one work' wrought in Jerusalem which had caused the multitude to marvel would be brought nearer to the Bethesda incident, to which it obviously refers.

The conjecture is interesting; but it may well be dictated by a desire to confer a chronological accuracy and concern to the Evangelist of which there are few signs in his Gospel. The phrases, 'after these things' and 'after this,' were vague and indeterminate phrases to the author, as we have already indicated. To imagine that by the phrases he meant '*soon after* these things' is to misunderstand his mind. The Hebrew writer of the *Book of Chronicles* used the phrase 'after this' in a similar somewhat indefinite sense. For example, in 1 Chron. 20^{3-4} we read: 'And it came to pass *after this* that there arose war at Gezer with the Philistines.' If the reader will compare the parallel narratives in 2 Samuel he will see that the phrase 'after this' covers about nine chapters of Samuel. In the absence, therefore, of external evidence for the transposition, it must be regarded as 'not proven.' We shall here take the Gospel as it has come down to us.

The Evangelist speaks of 'a feast' in 5^1, but what feast he has in mind—whether Tabernacles, Purim, or Pentecost—or whether, indeed, he has any specific feast in mind, we do not know. What the Evangelist *does* wish to say is that Jesus visited Jerusalem during the feasts, when the capital would be thronged by pilgrims. The statement in the Synoptic Gospels that Jesus had *often* appealed to Jerusalem accords well with the frequency of such visits. (See Mt. 23^{37} and Lk. 13^{34}.)

The incident which follows bears a few resemblances to the story of the healing of the paralytic in Mk. 2^{1-12}. For example, there is the same command: 'Arise, take up thy bed and walk.' Here it is significant to note that our Evangelist uses the same 'vulgar' word *krabatton*, 'bed,' which neither Mt. nor Lk. uses. (This word, as we noted in the Introduction, is used by Mk.) Further, each healing takes place on the Sabbath, and occasions religious controversy. It is impossible to say with confidence whether the author is adapting the Marcan incident to his purpose, or whether some other incident in Jerusalem forms the framework for his obvious purpose. This purpose, clearly, is the unveiling of the mind of Jesus and the controversy which His teaching occasioned. At least we may say with confidence that, here again, there is free adaptation of some traditional incident. For example, it is difficult to think that the 'thirty-eight years' referred to in *v.* 5 has not some allegorical or symbolical significance to the author. In Dt. 2^{14} we are told that the time taken by the Israelitish wanderings in the wilderness from Kadesh-barnea to the brook Zered was 'thirty and eight years.' Is it not that the author inserts this period of time because it symbolises to him a period of spiritual impotency prior to the full enrichment of life which Jesus is now bringing to those who have faith in Him: a period of 'homelessness' prior to the unveiling of the Father's heart which constitutes the

Mission of Jesus? The 'promised land' was close at hand. If the reference to 'thirty-eight years' is not to be taken historically, it is difficult to imagine that our author inserted it haphazardly: this being so, we have to look for a symbolical interpretation. And if there is symbolism in the number thirty-eight, there may well be, to the author, symbolism in other details of the record. The impotent man himself may symbolise the Jewish nation, seeking vainly for spiritual healing from its own appointed ordinances, and now about to receive such blessing from One who is able to bestow it.

The 'pool of Bethesda' referred to seems to have been filled by a natural spring; but where it was, or what its precise name, we do not know. Probably Bethzatha (R.V. mar.) was the name used by the author. 'Bethesda' means 'house of mercy': 'Bethzatha' means 'house of the sheep.' The name of this pool is not found in any other writer, though Josephus tells us that *Bezetha* was the name of the northern part of the city. If the author was, as we have suggested, a Jerusalemite Jew, the statement in *v.* 2, 'Now there is in Jerusalem by the sheep gate a pool, which is called in Hebrew Bethesda, having five porches,' is expressive of his personal recollection of a place, which at the time he was writing may well have been destroyed, in the destruction of the city by the Romans. The passage in brackets—part of *v.* 3 and the whole of *v.* 4—is not found in the best MSS., and was no doubt added by some later scribe who wished to embody some traditional legend which would explain the presence of the sick by the pool. The passage may have embodied the superstitious belief of the sufferers who resorted thither. Legends of angels giving healing virtue to water are not uncommon. In our own country, as in most other countries, there are disused and almost forgotten wells which at one time enshrined kindred beliefs. The present popularity of such pilgrimage shrines as that of Lourdes in the Pyrenees bears testimony to the tenacity with which men hold to belief in the miraculous efficacy of water. Spring-water is symbolic of life itself; and in every age, and among all peoples—from the Hindus who frequent Benares to bathe in the flowing waters of the Ganges, to the multitudes who flock from European countries to the Pyrenees to bathe in the waters of the sacred grotto in Lourdes—all kinds of 'super-natural' healing properties have been attributed to it. Perhaps it is sufficient to say here that the persistence of such beliefs is partly explained by a modicum of cures effected by the 'faith' of the sick—by the 'faith' in itself, not by the intellectually conceived object towards which the 'faith' is directed. When the reader next visits some deserted holy well in some lonely country place, let him remember the days when the waters before him inspired in many the hope of physical healing. The well is now forgotten, he will remember, save by the antiquarian; and its desertion bears testimony to the fact that it was not the water which cured, but the expectation with which it was associated. Thus the reader will be reminded that, if it is not angels who trouble the water, there are obscure moral and intellectual energies which can speak to, and revive, the spirit of man in ways we cannot yet trace, but to whose potency the modern study of psycho-therapeutics bears abundant testimony. The mistaken beliefs associated with the holy wells and rivers of all ages and countries serve as a reminder of something other than superstition: they bear testimony to an inter-relation of body and spirit in man which we have not yet traced, and to potencies which the study of physical medicine may well obscure.

That in some way Jesus was able to bring healing to the sick will not, therefore, in these psychological days, be denied. The Evangelist's narrative of this healing—which, as we have suggested, is doubtless embellished in the interest of allegory—is not, however, his main concern. It is but a text on which he hangs a dramatic unfolding of the mind of Jesus and the conflict which that mind occasioned.

Arthur Hugh Clough in his poem 'Bethesda' has some suggestive thoughts inspired by this narrative:

I saw again the spirits on a day,
Where on the earth in mournful case they lay;
Five porches were there, and a pool and round,
Huddling in blankets, strewn upon the ground,
Tied-up and bandaged, weary, sore, and spent,
The maimed and halt, diseased and impotent.

. . . . .

But what the waters of that pool might be,
Of Lethe were they, or Philosophy;
And whether he, long waiting, did attain
Deliverance from the burden of his pain
There with the rest; or whether, yet before
Some more diviner stranger passed the door
With his small company into that sad place,
And breathing hope into the sick man's face,
Bade him take up his bed, and rise and go.

The Resulting Controversy

JN. 5^{10-18}

5 Now it was the sabbath on that day.
10 So the Jews said unto him that was cured,
It is the sabbath, and it is not lawful for
11 thee to take up thy bed. But he answered
them, He that made me whole, the same
said unto me, Take up thy bed, and walk.
12 They asked him, Who is the man that said
unto thee, Take up *thy bed*, and walk?
13 But he that was healed wist not who it
was: for Jesus had conveyed himself
away, a multitude being in the place.
14 Afterward Jesus findeth him in the
temple, and said unto him, Behold, thou
art made whole: sin no more, lest a worse
15 thing befall thee. The man went away,
and told the Jews that it was Jesus which
16 had made him whole. And for this cause
did the Jews persecute Jesus, because he
17 did these things on the sabbath. But
Jesus answered them, My Father worketh
18 even until now, and I work. For this
cause therefore the Jews sought the more
to kill him, because he not only brake the
sabbath, but also called God his own
Father, making himself equal with God.

The cure takes place on the Sabbath. It is significant that the only other cure narrated by the Evangelist as performed by Jesus in Jerusalem—that of the blind man at the Pool of Siloam in chapter 9—also takes place on the Sabbath. Each occasions and inspires the hostility of the religious leaders in Jerusalem. The author, it is clear, wishes to direct the attention of the reader to the main motives of the conspiracy against Jesus. They are two: first, because He did these things on the Sabbath; second, because His whole attitude seemed to them to involve a claim to be 'equal with God' (*v.* 18).

In brief and pregnant scenes the story is dramatically told. In the first scene, the man is confronted with 'the Jews,' the name given by the author to the enemies of Jesus. In these passages the author's mind is frequently misunderstood. He does not of course mean that all Jews were enemies of Jesus. The bitter polemical situation through which the Church had passed, and was passing, when he wrote, in part no doubt occasioned his use of the phrase. During the war years, it was customary for people in the respective warring nations to refer in general terms to 'the Germans,' 'the British, 'the French,' etc., as those responsible for reprehensible deeds. Yet no one who said, for example, that 'the Germans' or 'the British' or 'the French' had killed with their bombs hundreds of helpless civilians, dreamt that he would be understood to say that *all* Germans or Britons or French did these things. It is necessary to exercise historical imagination and to have psychological insight when we read this Gospel: it will make many rough places plain. The dialogue, then, in this first scene between the man and 'the Jews,' narrated in *vv.* 10–13, unfolds the first motif of the conflict. The sick man has no right to be carrying his mat on the Sabbath. Such an action 'is not lawful.' The Jews might have quoted the words of Jeremiah in 17^{21-22} to enforce the point: 'Take heed to yourselves and bear no burden on the sabbath day, nor bring it in by the gates of Jerusalem: neither carry forth a burden out of your houses on the sabbath day.' The scene ends with the man's statement that he does not know who it is who has healed him and told him to take up his bed.

The second is a very brief scene in which Jesus, the real 'breaker of the law,' meets the man in the temple. His words in *v.* 14 point away from physical healing to the moral and spiritual restoration which it was His real mission to bestow. 'Sin no more lest a worse thing befall thee.' A man's suffering *may* be caused by his own sin; but it is not the teaching of Jesus that all physical suffering is the result of sin. Perhaps the man whom the author has in mind is suffering for personal sin. More probably, however, the words of Jesus are meant to direct the thought of the reader to the moral and spiritual issues which were involved in the ensuing controversy.

The next scene is merely suggested by *vv.* 15 and 16. The man meets the Jews again, and tells them that it was Jesus who was responsible for his healing. Their reason for persecuting Jesus is now directly expressed—it was 'because he did these things on the sabbath.' The religion of formal enactment is confronted by the religion of spiritual freedom. The religion of the spirit challenges the religion of the letter. The universalism of the mind of Jesus is opposed by the particularism of those who stood by a specific code. The Synoptists narrate that to Jesus sacred seasons and places were meant to be ministers to bless men, not chains to fetter men. All institutions are but means, not ends. 'The sabbath was made for man, not man for the sabbath.' (Mk. 2^{27}.)

17. The last scene in this section—*vv.* 17 and 18—gives expression to the essential mind of Jesus on this and kindred issues. 'My Father worketh hitherto and I work.' In this profound and striking utterance the two reasons for the

antagonism to Jesus are met and answered. What does the saying mean? First of all, it expresses that unique filial consciousness of Jesus, which the author has seen to be the secret of His mind. In whatever He does He is doing the will of His Father. Secondly, the saying expresses the continuous, unresting activity of God. *He* had never, on any ' day of rest,' ceased to work. His creative and revealing activity had never been suspended. The Divine Providence does not stand still. To think of God as resting in inactivity from His universe is to conceive of Him as apart from it, instead of as operative within it. If God is the Ground, as well as the Creator, of the universe, then it is His sustaining and directing mind which keeps all things in being. In the *Letter of Aristeas* (210) King Ptolemy asked one of the seventy translators of the Hebrew Scriptures into Greek: ' What is the mark of true piety? ' The answer given is: ' To perceive that God constantly works in the universe, and knows all things.' Our author begins his Gospel by asserting the eternity of the ' Word,' that is, of the Divine Thought and Activity; and goes on in the 14th verse to say that this Divine Word has been incarnated in Jesus. This same thought is, in the third place, proclaimed here: ' and I work.' The Evangelist's affirmation in *v.* 14 of the Prologue is here affirmed as the self-proclamation of Jesus Himself. The Prologue, as we have maintained, does not stand by itself as a kind of detached philosophic prelude to the Gospel. It gathers up the main ideas of the Gospel. That Jesus knew Himself to be the medium of the Divine Mind and Purpose is the key to the whole meaning of this Gospel.

18. We do not, therefore, regard the 17th verse as expressive of later developed formal theology. It is expressive of the religious consciousness of Jesus. He also, like the Father, works continuously; for it is the Father who works in Him and through Him. The saying does not stand alone. To elucidate it we have to put it alongside many other passages which say the same thing in other ways. Jesus does what He sees the Father doing (5^{19}). He does nothing of Himself. ' He that sent me is *true*,' that is, steadfast, unchanging, trustworthy (8^{26}). In the light of such and kindred passages in the Gospel, the saying recorded in the 17th verse means that Jesus knew Himself to be in uniquely close fellowship with the ever-working, ever-revealing God of the universe. It is this latter claim which focuses the hostility of the religious rulers. In calling God His own Father, He seemed to them to be making Himself ' equal with God ' (see also 10^{33}, 19^{7}). Jesus Himself never used such a phrase, or made such a claim. ' The Father,' He declared, ' is greater than I.' Nowhere more clearly than in this Gospel is the complete dependence of Jesus on the Father more emphatically and continuously expressed. (See Introduction, iv, 1.)

The Resulting Discourse of Jesus

Jn. 5^{19-47}

5 19 Jesus therefore answered and said unto
them,
Verily, verily, I say unto you, The Son
can do nothing of himself, but what he
seeth the Father doing: for what things
soever he doeth, these the Son also doeth
20 in like manner. For the Father loveth the
Son, and sheweth him all things that himself doeth: and greater works than these
will he shew him, that ye may marvel.
21 For as the Father raiseth the dead and
quickeneth them, even so the Son also

22 quickeneth whom he will. For neither
doth the Father judge any man, but he
hath given all judgement unto the Son;
23 that all may honour the Son, even as they
honour the Father. He that honoureth
not the Son honoureth not the Father
24 which sent him. Verily, verily, I say unto
you, He that heareth my word, and
believeth him that sent me, hath eternal
life, and cometh not into judgement, but
25 hath passed out of death into life. Verily,
verily, I say unto you, The hour cometh,
and now is, when the dead shall hear the
voice of the Son of God; and they that
26 hear shall live. For as the Father hath
life in himself, even so gave he to the Son
27 also to have life in himself: and he gave
him authority to execute judgement, be-
28 cause he is the Son of man. Marvel not
at this: for the hour cometh, in which all
that are in the tombs shall hear his voice,
29 and shall come forth; they that have done
good, unto the resurrection of life; and
they that have done ill, unto the resurrection of judgement.
30 I can of myself do nothing: as I hear, I
judge: and my judgement is righteous;
because I seek not mine own will, but the
31 will of him that sent me. If I bear witness of myself, my witness is not true.
32 It is another that beareth witness of me;
and I know that the witness which he
33 witnesseth of me is true. Ye have sent
unto John, and he hath borne witness unto
34 the truth. But the witness which I receive
is not from man: howbeit I say these
35 things, that ye may be saved. He was the
lamp that burneth and shineth: and ye
were willing to rejoice for a season in his
36 light. But the witness which I have is
greater than *that of* John: for the works
which the Father hath given me to accomplish, the very works that I do, bear
witness of me, that the Father hath sent
37 me. And the Father which sent me, he
hath borne witness of me. Ye have
neither heard his voice at any time, nor
38 seen his form. And ye have not his word
abiding in you: for whom he sent, him ye
39 believe not. Ye search the scriptures,
because ye think that in them ye have
eternal life; and these are they which bear
40 witness of me; and ye will not come to me,
41 that ye may have life. I receive not glory
42 from men. But I know you, that ye have
43 not the love of God in yourselves. I am
come in my Father's name, and ye receive
me not: if another shall come in his own
44 name, him ye will receive. How can ye
believe, which receive glory one of
another, and the glory that *cometh* from
45 the only God ye seek not? Think not that
I will accuse you to the Father: there is
one that accuseth you, *even* Moses, on
46 whom ye have set your hope. For if ye
believed Moses, ye would believe me; for
47 he wrote of me. But if ye believe not his
writings, how shall ye believe my words?

The author's method of presenting the mind of Jesus is nowhere more clearly seen than in this chapter. First, there is a narrative setting for the presentation. Second, there is the statement of the resulting misunderstanding. Third, there is the fuller unfolding of the teaching of Jesus in answer to this misconception. The chapter contains a kind of Thesis, Antithesis, and Synthesis. The paragraph before us sets forth the Synthesis. It is divided conveniently by the R.V. into two sections at *v.* 29; though there is little in the paragraph itself to suggest a very clear division. In the first section, the Sonship of Jesus is elucidated. In the second section, appeal is made to various witnesses in support of this Sonship.

19–29. There are three main ideas in this unfolding of the Sonship of Jesus. First, the *dependence* of the Son on the Father (*v.* 19). Second, the *life-giving* mission of the Son (*v.* 21, etc.). Third, the *judging* mission of the Son (*v.* 22, etc.). The Sonship of Jesus is the dominating refrain. In nearly every verse there is reference to 'the Son.' This repetition is strikingly dramatic, as the reader will discover if he will read the verses aloud. The whole should be regarded, not as the precise words of Jesus, but as a faithful transcript of His essential mind.

(*a*) The *filial dependence* of Jesus. If, as Schleiermacher maintained, religion in essence is a sense of conscious dependence, then Jesus had that sense in a unique degree. His whole life was controlled by the felt conviction that He was but an instrument in the hands of the Father. There is nothing more certain about the mind of Jesus than this. This sense of dependence sprang out of His unique filial consciousness. This is the meaning of *vv.* 19 and 20. As an only son knows the love of his father, so did Jesus feel assured of the Father's love; and out of this reciprocated love there issued the 'works' He had already done, and the 'greater works'—of moral and spiritual quickening—He had yet to do.

(*b*) The *life-giving mission* of Jesus. This profound thought runs through the Gospel. It is here expressed in *vv.* 21, 24, 25, 26, 28, 29. There is a vivid symbolism here which may easily delude the unimaginative Western reader. The reference to 'the dead hearing the voice of the Son' (*v.* 25), and to those 'in the tombs' hearing His voice (*v.* 29), is to those who are *spiritually* dead, not to those *physically* dead. Many interpreters have supposed that the Evangelist is thinking in *v.* 29 of a general physical resurrection at the Great Assize. Others—for example, Wendt—feeling that this is the meaning of the verse and recognising that it is a thought alien to this Gospel, regard the verse as an interpolation of someone redacting the Johannine source. Not so do we understand the author's meaning. Heaven for him is *life*, not environment. The author is using traditional language, but his thought has to be understood in the light of the whole Gospel. What he is saying is that it is the mission of Jesus to bring the eternal life of the spirit to man, a mission which he has seen fulfilled in his own experience and in that of multitudes of the friends of Jesus. The language, to the author himself, is clearly symbolical. He would—to say the least—have been *surprised* if a literalist reader had asked him how 'the dead' could 'hear.' He uses the same symbolism in the story of Lazarus in chapter 11: the 'Lazarus, come forth' is clearly, to our own view, dramatic allegorisation, akin to the *coming forth* of those who are *in the tombs* in this passage.

It should be manifest to every reader, not wholly devoid of the historical imagination, that by the 'dead' the Evangelist neither means those who are physically dead nor the completely annihilated. The 'dead' are sufficiently alive to be able to 'hear.' They hear 'the voice of the Son of God': that is, the spiritually dead will be awakened when they hear the voice of the incarnate Word. Those who 'hear' this voice are those who obey it. They are not merely hearers of the word, but doers. The Evangelist—true to his Hebrew mentality—is giving expression to *the fact* of the life-giving mission of Jesus; he is not indulging in *speculations* about a problematical future. So also, when he speaks of 'all that are in the tombs' hearing the voice of Him who knew Himself to be the Divine Son. The Evangelist uses a vivid and realistic figure of speech—like Ezekiel before him. Ezekiel, it will be remembered, had used a similar metaphor in chapter 37 of his prophetic book. In that famous allegory the 'dry bones' had *heard* 'the word of the Lord' (Ezek. 37^4). What were these 'dry bones' to Ezekiel? He tells us in *v.* 11: 'These dry bones are the whole house of Israel: behold, they say, Our bones are dried up, and our hope is lost; we are clean cut off.' It is, therefore, clear that to the prophet the 'dry bones' represent the *living* Jews—probably the exiles in Babylon. It is possible that the familiar passage in the Book of Daniel should be similarly understood: 'And many of them that sleep in the dust of the earth shall awake, some to everlasting life, and some to shame and everlasting contempt. And they that be wise shall shine as the brightness of the firmament; and they that turn many to righteousness as the stars for ever and ever " (Dan. 12^{2-3}). What this writer in the Maccabean period is probably saying is that living Jews scattered among heathen communities will be restored to Judæa.[1]

What we wish to say, therefore, is that the Fourth Evangelist was not alone in using such realistic metaphors as those he employs in *vv.* 25 and 29 of this chapter. Those who are ' in the tombs ' are those who are in need of spiritual quickening. Similar metaphors are used in our modern day. All the language of spiritual quickening, or of spiritual emancipation, is the language of metaphor. Jesus himself had used the metaphor of ' death.' In the parable of the prodigal Son, the father says: ' This my son was dead and is alive again.' (Lk. $15^{24, 32}$).

(*c*) The *judging mission* of Jesus. This thought is inwoven with that of the life-giving mission of Jesus, and runs through the same verses. Judgement, to the mind of the author, is the inevitable *sifting* effected by truth and grace. It is the cleavage which goodness always causes. It is the light and the shadow which the shining of the sun always brings. The Latin word *cribrum*, a sieve, it is significant to note, comes from the same root as the Greek word for judgement. Judgement to the author is therefore *intrinsic* to life itself: it is not extrinsic or imposed from without. Life itself judges us. Retribution is an ' eternal ' fact, not a temporal occurrence. Every choice of evil is a ' judgement.' It separates us from eternal life. If our minds *have* to think in pictures or symbols, let us ever seek to penetrate to the reality symbolised. Our human ' law-courts ' are but a figure of speech. Our thought of a distant ' day ' which we call the ' Last Assize ' is only pictorial language suited to the frailty of our finite minds. The reality behind the language is that the world is a moral world because it is the world of the Holy Father. Every time men are confronted by Beauty, or by Truth, or by Goodness they are judged. These three are everywhere. But some love Ugliness, tamper with Truth, combat Goodness. Who, then, or what judges us? The Christian answer is: It is the Word, the Eternal Thought and Purpose of God in life, which judges. This Word was incarnate in Jesus. To say that He is the Judge is to say that intrinsic to life itself, as God created it, is the ever-present Spirit of His truth and grace. He who was grace and truth incarnate divided those to whom he preached and among whom He witnessed. Those who received Him were entering into eternal life; those who rejected Him were excluding themselves from that life—they were already judged (see $3^{18f.}$, $5^{22, 27}$, 9^{39}, 12^{48}). The attitude adopted to Jesus was decisive for themselves: it revealed their essential nature. This judgement runs through all life: it is not merely *temporal episode*, but *eternal fact*.

One of the main convictions which have inspired this Commentary is that *the Johannine author seeks to give dramatic expression to the meaning which the apocalyptic ideas have for the consciousness of Jesus*. This is what Jesus *meant* by His apocalyptic imagery. The Evangelist, in other words, is not spiritualising and ethicising the ideas of Jesus; he is expressing the essential spiritual and ethical content which they had for Jesus. In this we find ourselves in agreement with a former interpreter, who said that here there is ' an interpretation and explanation of the inner

[1] This interpretation was maintained by the late Prof. R. H. Kennett. See his *The Church of Israel*, pp. 181 ff.

meaning which these ideas had for the consciousness of Jesus himself' (Wendt, *Teaching of Jesus*, ii, p. 307). The attitude of men to Jesus was a historical illustration of that which was 'eternal.' This judgement, therefore, is universal; and it is effected by the eternal Word. The author expresses this in vivid and dramatic language in *v.* 29; and, like all the figures for heaven and hell, it has been taken as literal statement of historic fact. The author is thinking throughout, however, not in terms of time, but in terms of eternity. Like Jesus, he sees all things *sub specie æternitatis.* Judgement, like eternal life, is not future but present. Rather, *it is.* And inasmuch as it is eternal fact, it is universal fact. It is a judgement that applies to the *dead*, as well as to the *quick.* '*All* that are in the tombs shall hear his voice, and shall come forth; they that have done good, unto the resurrection of life; and they that have done ill, unto the resurrection of judgement.' Those 'who are in the tombs' cannot but listen to this voice. To stop the ears is *one* way of listening: it is to pass a sentence of judgement upon oneself.

Still, as of old,
Man by himself is priced.
For thirty pieces Judas sold
Himself, not Christ.

30–47. *Witnesses to the Sonship of Jesus.*—This paragraph expounds the ideas already expressed, and does so by setting forth the several witnesses to the Sonship and Mission of Jesus. The key-note of the paragraph is witness. These verses are put in the form of a kind of apologetic substantiation of the lofty claims of Jesus. The judgement which He is exercising is no arbitrary, or self-seeking, judgement: it arises from *what He is.* The *justice* of this judgement arises from the fact that Jesus's life consists in its complete dependence upon, and harmony with, the will of the Father who had sent Him. It is only this fact which makes the judgement *valid.* Judgement, in other words, springs out of the very nature and will of God. It is the Son who judges, because Sonship consists in obedient fulfilling of the Father's will.

32. Hence, the first witness appealed to is that of *God Himself.* 'It is Another' that beareth witness within the whole mind of Jesus. That Other is God. It is significant for the whole interpretation of the Gospel that in this passage, where appeal is made to the witnesses for the Mission and Claim of Jesus, the primary witness is found *within the consciousness* of Jesus.

33–35. The second witness is that of the Baptist. Here the verses in the Prologue are recalled, in which the Baptist is spoken of as bearing witness to the Light, while not himself the Light. This is another indication of the oneness of the Prologue with the rest of the Gospel. The Baptist is here spoken of as 'a burning and shining lamp.' He is, that is, not the originating source of light. The lamp burns, and burns away: the light abides. The lamp shines, illuminating the darkness and bringing joy 'for a season': the Light is self-luminous, and eternal.

36. Thus, the third witness is found in the *works* of Jesus. When the Evangelist speaks of 'the works' (τὰ ἔργα) of Jesus he means the whole outward expression of His mind in act and word. This was a manifestation of a unique filial communion, issuing in filial obedience.

37–38. So the fourth witness is the same as the first—namely, that of the Father Himself, known within the unique consciousness of Jesus. This witness of the Father has not to be regarded as a physically audible voice, nor as a physically visible epiphany: for, as the author says in the Prologue, ' no one hath seen God at any time.' It was a witness within the consciousness of Jesus. The Father cannot be discovered *without*, in nature and in history, till He is known *within*. The Jews had not believed in Jesus the Word of God, because this ' word ' was not abiding in them. They might say that they had found God in their own history, in their own Scriptures: but inasmuch as they were blind to the Light shining before them, deaf to the Word spoken in their presence, they were but deceiving themselves. They searched the Scriptures because they imagined that in their pages they would find eternal life. But how can we *find*, without the enlightened mind? There is an idolatry of the letter of the Bible which blinds to its intrinsic and eternal worth. To regard the Scriptures as a source for ' proof-texts ' of our favourite doctrines is the kind of superstitious use of the Bible which Jesus here condemns. It is akin to that implied in the Rabbinical saying: ' he who has acquired the words of the Law has acquired eternal life.' Jesus was no doubt often confronted with the blindness of much of the Rabbinical investigation of the Scriptures. It could be as minute and ingenious as some modern interpretations of the Fourth Gospel. Its search for *hidden* meanings often closed the mind to the spiritual truth which lay open on the surface. So also Jesus must have been often confronted with a rigid conformity to the letter of the Law, conjoined with a denial of its inner spirit and meaning. There were those who had ' made void the word of God ' because of their tradition (Mk. 7^{13}; Mt. 15^{6}). There were those who had taken away ' the key of knowledge ' of the Scriptures: ' they entered not in themselves, and those who were entering in they hindered.' (Lk. 11^{52}.)

39–40. But, rightly regarded, the *Scriptures* bear witness to the Word. This is the fifth witness of the passage. The Scriptures bear witness to the continuous revealing activity of God, that is, to His Word. They bear witness to Jesus, in the sense that that Word has been incarnate in His life of filial communion and obedience. It is for this reason that for the Christian to-day, as for Luther in the sixteenth century, ' Christ is Lord and King of Scripture ': He is, that is, both the crown and the criterion of revelation. If ' the Jews ' had but ' come ' to Jesus—that is, if they had but listened to the witness of His unique person—they would have found in Him the life that is eternal. In every age the letter killeth, but the spirit giveth life.

41–47. In these closing verses of the chapter the unbelief of ' the Jews ' is assigned its *moral* cause. Lack of faith, in this Gospel, is not caused by intellectual difficulty. Faith itself is as much a moral as an intellectual quality. It is the right orientation of the whole personality. So it is their moral and spiritual standards that are wrong, when they reject Him who comes revealing the very character of the Father. The ' love of God ' is not in them; for that love, of its very nature, is self-giving, self-forgetful, never seeking material or selfish interests. If they have the ' love of God '—the phrase is only used here in this Gospel, and only in Lk. 11^{42} in the Synoptic Gospels—they would receive Him who manifested that love in thought and deed. Instead, they have the love of men. It is men's approval they really value (see also 12^{43}). To love flattery is not to love truth. How, then, could they receive one who showed what *self-denial* really was? By their very nature they were only ready to receive one of kindred spirit to their own. In this Moses himself condemns them in the Scriptures which they blindly search. Moses, on whom they have set their hope, is their accuser. For his prophetic spirit sought to deliver from all false gods, and himself had looked forward to a coming prophet (Num. 21^{9}; Dt. 18^{15}). They worship the letter of Moses, while they have killed the spirit of Moses. His insights had become entombed in structures created for their perpetuity. This happens in every age to the prophets. If, then, they cannot perceive and accept the written words of Moses, how can they believe the words of Jesus?

THE 'SIGN' OF THE LOAVES AND FISHES

JN. 6^{1-14}

6 1 After these things Jesus went away to
the other side of the sea of Galilee, which
2 is *the sea* of Tiberias. And a great multitude followed him, because they beheld
the signs which he did on them that were
3 sick. And Jesus went up into the mountain, and there he sat with his disciples.
4 Now the passover, the feast of the Jews,
5 was at hand. Jesus therefore lifting up his
eyes, and seeing that a great multitude
cometh unto him, saith unto Philip,
Whence are we to buy bread, that these
6 may eat? And this he said to prove him:
for he himself knew what he would do.
7 Philip answered him, Two hundred
pennyworth of bread is not sufficient for
them, that every one may take a little.
8 One of his disciples, Andrew, Simon
9 Peter's brother, saith unto him, There is a
lad here, which hath five barley loaves,
and two fishes: but what are these among
10 so many? Jesus said, Make the people sit
down. Now there was much grass in the
place. So the men sat down, in number
11 about five thousand. Jesus therefore took
the loaves; and having given thanks, he
distributed to them that were set down;
likewise also of the fishes as much as they
12 would. And when they were filled, he
saith unto his disciples, Gather up the
broken pieces which remain over, that
13 nothing be lost. So they gathered them
up, and filled twelve baskets with broken
pieces from the five barley loaves, which
remained over unto them that had eaten.
14 When therefore the people saw the sign
which he did, they said, This is of a truth
the prophet that cometh into the world.

We have already discussed the question as to whether this chapter should be transposed so as to follow chapter 4. Another suggested transposition must here be noted. *Vv.* 15–24 of chapter 7 would seem to follow naturally upon chapter 5. There seem, at least at first sight, good grounds for the theory that there has been at this point some dislocation of the text. The following are the main reasons for such a conclusion. (1) Chapter 5 ends with a reference to the two 'writings' of Moses: the question in 7^{15} seems, therefore, to arise naturally—'How does this man know *writings* (or *letters*: it is the same Greek word, γράμματα). (2) Further, 7^{25}, in which the dwellers in Jerusalem express their surprise that Jesus should be the object of mortal hatred to the rulers, seems a more natural sequel to 7^{14}. (3) Chapter 5 began with a discussion of the Sabbath controversy, and the themes which arise and are dealt with in the rest of the chapter are the same as in 7^{15-25}. (4) In 7^{18} Jesus speaks of those who seek their own glory, in similar language to that used in 5^{41-43}. (5) In 7^{22} Jesus answers their rigid views of the Sabbath by appealing to their own law-giver Moses, just as He had done in 5^{46}. (6) In 7^{23} there seems to be a definite reference to the cure at Bethesda of chapter 5. Such a reference seems to presuppose that it is in the mind of the questioners of Jesus: and how, it will be asked, could this be if there is the considerable interval of time which the present order of the text requires?

For this suggested rearrangement of the text, however, there is no MS. evidence. If there *is* dislocation, it will have to be attributed to some very early copyist. Let us, however, bear in mind that our difficulties with the text of the Gospel may be of our own creation. Chronological accuracy meant little to this author. The Gospel was not written at one sitting. It had taken probably many months, or even years, to write. Thoughts he wished to express burned themselves deeply into his mind through long brooding. Situations may have become fused in such a mind, so that details which seem to us to require another setting were not felt *by him* to require it. The controversies of this Gospel are really all the same controversy; the issues are all the same issues; the opponents of Jesus are all the same opponents. In this Commentary the order of the Gospel, even at this point, is followed as it has come down to us.

The opening verses of the chapter contain the narrative of the loaves and the fishes. This is the one incident in the Ministry of Jesus prior to His last visit to Jerusalem which is recorded in all four Gospels. It is found in Mt. 14^{13-21}, in Mk. 6^{30-34}, and in Lk. 9^{10-17}. The account of the Fourth Evangelist is most akin to that of Mk.; but there are details peculiar to his own narrative—as, for example, the place taken in the story by Philip, Andrew, and the boy, the reference to the Passover in *v.* 4, and the enthusiasm of the crowd, with its attendant dangers, in *v.* 15. The Evangelist, in some of these instances, may be preserving traditional details derived from the Apostle John. His concern, however, is not so much with the 'sign' as such, as with that which it signified. Once again he gives us a narrative which affords a fitting setting for the unveiling of the mind of Jesus. The profound discourses on the bread of life, with the misunderstandings and disputations which arise, form the substance of the chapter. Before, however, elucidating this teaching, it is necessary to confront the question as to what the author was really seeking to say in this narrative of the feeding of the five thousand.

The first thing to be said is that the author was familiar with the story recorded in the other three Gospels, and that he found it of great significance. So much is indisputable. The second thing to be said is that the Evangelist felt himself completely free to alter some of the details of the traditional narrative. Let us look at some of these alterations, to see if they cast any light on the precise meaning which the story had for him.

1. We note, first, the abruptness of the transition in 6^{1}, an abruptness which is characteristic of his manner of writing (see 3^{22}, 10^{22}, 12^{1}). There is, that is, no endeavour on his part to give an exactly historical setting to the story, such as is found in the Synoptists.

2. If we compare the story in Jn. with the story of Elisha in 2 Kings $4^{42f.}$ we shall note certain striking resemblances *which are absent from the Synoptic accounts.* In John's account alone we read about a παιδάριον (R.V., *lad*; Moffatt, *servant*) who has loaves and fishes; and in the narrative in 2 Kings 4 this very word is used in the LXX of Elisha's *servant* who exclaims, prior to the 'multiplication'

of the loaves, at the impossibility of feeding the hundred men with the barley loaves in his sack. Further, John alone tells us that the loaves were *barley* loaves, and these are the type of loaves referred to in 2 Kings 4^{42}. From this it seems permissible to suppose that the Evangelist had pondered and brooded over the traditional story recorded by the Synoptists in association with the story of Elisha's feeding of the hundred men; and that he inserted these details in his desire to declare that a prophet greater than Elisha was here, 'the prophet that cometh into the world.' (*v.* 14.)

These two points make it clear that the author did not regard the story as he had read it, or as he had heard it, as sacrosanct record. The main question remains: What precisely did the narrative mean for him? The question presents itself to a modern man in this way: Did he believe that these few loaves and fishes were miraculously increased so as to satisfy the physical hunger of a vast concourse of people? It is more difficult to answer such a question than a first reading of his narrative would lead us to suppose. Most readers conclude at once, on the perusal of the story, that, whatever may really have happened, the author at least believed in a miraculous multiplication of the loaves and fishes. In a similar manner, most readers *used* to conclude that the author of the book of Jonah believed in a three days' residence of Jonah in 'the belly of the great fish.' Why should it be thought incredible that one author allegorised and not another? The Evangelist may surely have taken a familiar story and, *without himself assenting to a traditional miraculous interpretation*, may have employed it in order to convey what was to him of primary importance, namely, the moral and spiritual significance of Jesus. It is not possible to dogmatise as to what the author himself believed precisely happened. In point of fact, we do not know what happened. We *do* know that scientific accuracy is not to be found in any of the Gospels. Nevertheless, we have the *whole emphasis* of this Gospel to guide us when we seek to read the mind of its author. It is his obvious intention to show from the teaching of Jesus that a faith resting upon 'signs and wonders' is a very inadequate faith. When he gives a narrative of a 'sign,' he does so only in order to say that real faith exists only where the spiritual truths signified are perceived and followed. The suggestion we therefore make is that, like many a spiritual and truthful Christian thinker since his day, he set no store on traditional nature-marvels: but that he used the two narrated in this chapter as a setting for the essential spiritual message of the Master. If, as we have suggested, the Cana story is the creative allegorising of some historical fact, the story of the loaves and fishes may be regarded as, *to the author himself*, the allegorising of an already existing narrative. As to what he thought happened on that memorable day when Jesus was with the crowd, we may not speak without a peradventure. But, at least, we know that a man's emphasis is the man. And the *whole emphasis* of the chapter is that Jesus is the bread of man's spiritual life. In our own judgement, the story to the Evangelist was a parable.

A few further points in the narrative should be noted. The author is the only New Testament writer who calls the Lake of Galilee 'the Sea of Tiberias' (6^{1}; see also 21^{1}). This name was used by classical writers, being derived from the name of Herod the Tetrarch's capital, built by the lake. The reference to a Jerusalem feast in *v.* 4 reminds us once again of the mentality of the author. In all that he narrates he has as a kind of mental background Jerusalem and all that it represents. In *v.* 6 the author expresses his conviction that the actions of Jesus were determined by His own insight into situations, and were not dependent upon the counsel of His disciples.

THE WALKING ON THE SEA

JN. 6^{15-25}

6 15 Jesus therefore perceiving that they
were about to come and take him by
force, to make him king, withdrew again
into the mountain himself alone.
16 And when evening came, his disciples
17 went down unto the sea; and they entered
into a boat, and were going over the sea
unto Capernaum. And it was now dark,
and Jesus had not yet come to them.
18 And the sea was rising by reason of a great
19 wind that blew. When therefore they had
rowed about five and twenty or thirty
furlongs, they behold Jesus walking on the
sea, and drawing nigh unto the boat: and
20 they were afraid. But he saith unto them,
21 It is I; be not afraid. They were willing
therefore to receive him into the boat:
and straightway the boat was at the land
whither they were going.
22 On the morrow the multitude which
stood on the other side of the sea saw that
there was none other boat there, save one,
and that Jesus entered not with his disciples into the boat, but *that* his dis-
23 ciples went away alone (howbeit there
came boats from Tiberias nigh unto the
place where they ate the bread after the
24 Lord had given thanks): when the multitude therefore saw that Jesus was not
there, neither his disciples, they themselves got into the boats, and came to
25 Capernaum, seeking Jesus. And when
they found him on the other side of the
sea, they said unto him, Rabbi, when
camest thou hither?

This familiar story, recorded also by Matthew (14^{22-23}) and Mark (6^{45-52}), is introduced by our Evangelist—and by him only—with a statement about the misdirected and misguided enthusiasm of the crowd. They misunderstand the nature of the Kingdom. They wish to make Jesus to be other than Himself. The enthusiasm of the crowd is as blind as was the antagonism of the rulers in Jerusalem. Here, once again, the Johannine author reveals his penetrating insight into the spiritual nature of the claims and Mission of Jesus. The rulers misunderstood the claims of one who knew the Father in unique filial trust and obedience. The crowd misunderstood the nature of His Mission. His spiritual consciousness antagonised the traditional orthodoxy of the first: His spiritual Mission was hidden to the materialistic aims of the second.

When we ask, What did the author himself believe to be the precise historical fact behind his narrative? the same issues arise as were discussed in the previous section. It has often been pointed out that the Greek preposition ἐπί in *v.* 19 can mean 'by' as well as 'upon.' The same phrase, when used in 21^1, certainly means 'on the sea-shore.' It has therefore been suggested that the author is here narrating that Jesus was here walking *by the edge* of the sea. But the statement of the disciples' *fear* in *v.* 19 suggests that there was something very unusual to the author in this appearance of Jesus. We make the same suggestion in this case as in the story of the loaves and fishes: namely, that the author is using a story familiar to the Church as a vehicle for a spiritual message. In this case, as in the former, the nature-marvel suggested by the traditional story meant little or nothing to him. It was a story known to the Church, and he used it, not to assert that a Jesus who could walk on water must be Divine, but as an allegory of the succour the Master had brought to His friends in their hours of spiritual and moral need, and of the true haven of men's deepest desires to which His presence brings. The Evangelist may well have had in his mind when—and he alone—narrated that 'straightway the boat was at the land whither they were going' (*v.* 20), the passage from Ps. 107^{30}: 'He bringeth them into the haven where they would be.' Jesus, the Light and Truth of God in the flesh, was doing what their fathers in the Old Testament had found the Divine Presence to accomplish. Francis Thompson had insight into the author's essential meaning when he wrote:

Yea, in the night, my Soul, my daughter
Cry—clinging Heaven by the hems
And lo, Christ walking on the water
Not of Genesareth but Thames!

The presence of Jesus had brought succour to His friends in the days of His flesh. And to the author, the unseen presence of the Divine Spirit of Jesus had often been the harbinger of peace to His storm-tossed followers of the Church. This was a presence not localised, but transcending the limitations of space: known, not by physical contact, but in spiritual fellowship. If, as we have suggested, in the discourse that follows, the author is seeking to express the real mind of Jesus as to wherein true eucharistic feeding consists, it is exceedingly suggestive that he prefaces it with a narrative pregnant with the allegorical thought that Jesus is to be found when least expected. 'Lo here, Lo there,' men say, the presence of the Saviour is to be found—'in this rite,' 'in this bread consecrated according to ecclesiastical rules.' Not so, saith the mind of Jesus through this author; but wherever and whenever men deeply need the succour of His presence, He is near.

THE DISCOURSE ON THE BREAD OF LIFE

JN. 6^{26-40}

6 26 Jesus answered them and said, Verily,
verily, I say unto you, Ye seek me, not
because ye saw signs, but because ye ate of
27 the loaves, and were filled. Work not for
the meat which perisheth, but for the
meat which abideth unto eternal life,
which the Son of man shall give unto
you: for him the Father, *even* God, hath
28 sealed. They said therefore unto him,
What must we do, that we may work the
29 works of God? Jesus answered and said
unto them, This is the work of God, that
ye believe on him whom he hath sent.
30 They said therefore unto him, What then
doest thou for a sign, that we may see, and
31 believe thee? what workest thou? Our
fathers ate the manna in the wilderness;
as it is written, He gave them bread out of
32 heaven to eat. Jesus therefore said unto
them, Verily, verily, I say unto you, It was
not Moses that gave you the bread out of
heaven; but my Father giveth you the
33 true bread out of heaven. For the bread
of God is that which cometh down out of
heaven, and giveth life unto the world.
34 They said therefore unto him, Lord, ever-
35 more give us this bread. Jesus said unto
them, I am the bread of life: he that
cometh to me shall not hunger, and he
that believeth on me shall never thirst.
36 But I said unto you, that ye have seen me,
37 and yet believe not. All that which the
Father giveth me shall come unto me; and
him that cometh to me I will in no wise
38 cast out. For I am come down from
heaven, not to do mine own will, but the
39 will of him that sent me. And this is the
will of him that sent me, that of all that
which he hath given me I should lose
nothing, but should raise it up at the last
40 day. For this is the will of my Father,
that every one that beholdeth the Son,
and believeth on him, should have eternal
life; and I will raise him up at the last day.

The long discourse that follows to the end of the chapter is obviously a series of discourses bound into a unity by one dominating and pervasive theme. Once again the characteristics of the author's mind are clearly revealed. He is quite indifferent to precise historical record, or to exact chronological order. The section of the discourse now to be considered is narrated as addressed to ' the multitude ' in the open air by the sea of Galilee. A controversy follows with ' the Jews,' and the resulting teaching of Jesus is given in ' the synagogue at Capernaum ' (*v.* 59). The remainder of the chapter is devoted to teaching given to ' many of his disciples,' and, finally, to ' the Twelve.' The circles grow progressively smaller as the chapter proceeds. The audience, in the dramatic mind of the author, is reduced from ' the multitude ' to ' the Jews,' from ' the Jews ' to ' many of his disciples,' from ' many of his disciples ' to ' the Twelve ': and, for one vivid moment, in the closing two verses of the chapter, the light is thrown upon one dark, enigmatic figure who seems to haunt the background of the author's thought.

As in the previous chapters, the theme is given a setting in a narrative that is in part historical and in part allegorical creation. Loaves and fishes mean *food*: the Evangelist will, therefore, unfold the mind of Jesus on the food that is eternal. As His teaching transforms men (chap. 2), as His spirit quickens men (chap. 3), as His Mission is to assuage man's deepest thirst (chap. 4), as His life of service led to a true knowledge of the ever-living, ever-revealing Father (chap. 5), so He is God's sacramental food for the souls of men (chap. 6).

26. The discourse is introduced by a sentence which throws a revealing light upon the mind of Jesus as to nature-marvels. ' Ye seek me not because ye saw signs, but because ye did eat of the loaves and were filled.' By ' signs ' here the Evangelist obviously is thinking of *the things signified*. This is his way of telling his readers that to Jesus those who sought Him because of the material help He could give them, instead of because of what *He really was*, were much in need of teaching. This verse conclusively shows, at least, that eating of loaves was not the ' sign.' The author's *signs* are really the *things signified*. Here there is once more an implied criticism of that spurious faith which is assent based upon ' wonders,' and ' proofs ' or ' evidences.' The author wished to deliver the Church from a false emphasis upon a few debatable nature-marvels. That he did not succeed in this endeavour is manifest from the apologetic literature of nineteen hundred years.

27. In contrast with that inadequate faith which is mere assent based upon a physical wonder the author gives expression, in the succeeding verses, to the twin centralities of the Master's Message. The first is that the *real gift* He is here to bestow is something not material but spiritual, not temporal but eternal. The second is that the belief required for the acceptance of this gift is not assent to a physical wonder which men cannot understand, but a moral and spiritual response of the whole nature of man to the truth as it is in Jesus. These two are never divorced in the Johannine Gospel. All is of the Divine Grace: but the reception of the Divine Grace is conditioned by true faith. Hence, he begins in *v.* 27 with an emphasis on man's *working*. The words recall the passage in Is. 55^2— ' Wherefore do ye spend your labour for that which satisfieth not ? ' This is a food which the Son—who is also Son of Man, knowing man's heart, for He had a man's

heart—is here to *give*: and He who is the giver of this eternal life has been *sealed* by God; that is, He has the accrediting witness both in His own consciousness and in the work He is doing, that this is *God's* gift.

28–33. But—the question comes, betokening a complete misunderstanding of the mind of Jesus—what must they do for God in order to *earn* His gift? What religious duties must they perform which they do not already perform? The answer of Jesus is that the work demanded never *earns* God's gift: the work required is that they *believe on* Him who comes with this ' sealed ' mission from the Father. This ' believing on ' Jesus is not mere assent to any wonder He may have worked: it is, as everywhere in the Gospel, the assent of the whole personality, in trust and in obedience, to Jesus. What then—the misunderstanding of falsely based faith is again expressed—is the evidential sign which Jesus gives to them? Their fathers had, they believed, received miraculous manna from God in the wilderness. Such a rejoinder, put into their mouth by the author, obviously does not suggest that to him the story of the loaves and fishes was akin in wonder to the manna story, and throws further significant light on what he himself thought about the incident. The reply of Jesus in *vv.* 32–33 is to direct their thought to Him who is the Source of every good, the God who is known to Jesus as Father. The Father's true bread for His children is ' the bread of life ': it is the gift ' from above.'

34–40. In the succeeding verses the climax of this discourse is reached and expounded. It is once more significant that this culminating message is a dramatic declaration of the essential mind of Jesus in relation to the Father. The passage is introduced by an appeal parallel to that of the Samaritan woman in 4^{15}, but in deeper and more poignant tones. ' Sir, evermore give us this bread '—the cry of humanity's deepest need in every age. It is the cry that finds expression in Thomas Aquinas's *O esca viatorum*:

O bread to pilgrims given,
O food that angels eat,
O manna sent from heaven,
For heaven-born natures meet,
Give us, for Thee long pining,
To eat till richly filled ;
Till, earth's delights resigning,
Our every wish is stilled.

The reply is the declaration that He who is the incarnate Word is that bread. What they are asking for is already before them, if they are but willing to receive. Jesus Himself is the bread of life. In the story of the Temptation as recorded in Mt. 4 Jesus reminds the tempter in the words of Dt. 8^3, 'Man shall not live by bread alone, but by every word that proceedeth out of the mouth of God.' This is the very thought of Jesus here. As their fathers knew that the soul's sustenance was the life-giving, revealing ' word ' of God, so He, the incarnate Word, was Himself that true bread. If they will only *come* to Him—come, not as they have now come, in physical presence, but *come* with the whole needy personality—their hunger will be satisfied. If they will but believe on Him—believe with the whole aspiring and consenting mind—their thirst will be assuaged. Augustine expressed the truth thus: 'We do not come to Christ by running or walking, but by believing, not by the motion of the body, but the will of the mind.' Their present coming has not been a true coming, their present seeing has not been a true seeing (*v.* 36). Seeing of their kind is not true seeing, as believing because of outward or physical marvels is not true believing. True belief in Jesus is not by the compulsion of demonstrative sign or of conclusive logic. It is only those whom the Father gives to Jesus who come to Him (*v.* 37). Such a statement must not be understood as if either Jesus thought, or the author meant to say that He thought, that God gives to a few privileged men a special faculty denied to others. What it means is that the author was deeply aware that many did *not* come to Jesus, did *not* see any Divine truth in Him, or hear any Divine word from Him. Yet, he adds—as if to correct a possible misunderstanding to which His words might give rise—that any who truly come to Jesus will never be rejected, or go empty away. Some came, and some did not come, to Jesus—that was historic fact. The author, revealing again a characteristic of the Hebrew mind, assigns this to God as ultimate Cause—but without meaning either to suggest that God has favourites or that man is not a free agent. The Evangelist, that is, does not seek to give, or to imply that Jesus gives, any speculative solution of the problems presented by theological determinism on the one hand and moral responsibility on the other. In the first part of the sentence He expresses the great truth enshrined by the word *Grace*—whoever comes is drawn by the Father: He expresses the great correlative truth of man's *freedom and moral responsibility* in the second part of the sentence—' coming ' is a voluntary act. The author, however, was not concerned with the later theological controversies on these issues. Chrysostom said of this passage: ' Our Lord's words do not destroy our free agency, but only show that we need Divine assistance.'

In the concluding verses of this section (*vv.* 38–40) we are again led to the inmost mind of Jesus. He Himself is here, not to do His own will, but the Father's. And He knows that the Divine will for Him is that He may ' lose nothing ' of all the Father has given Him; but that He should ' raise it up at the last day.' This is a profound, and, at first sight, perplexing verse. What does it mean? It is important to note that the ' all ' referred to is in the neuter. The thought of Jesus seems to outrun the boundary of human personalities, as we regard them, and to encompass a larger entity of which they form part in the integrated frame of nature itself. It is also important to note that the phrase ' the last day ' is found only in St. John—in $6^{39, 40, 44, 54}$, 11^{24}, 12^{48}. (In 1 Jn. 2^{18} the author speaks of ' the last hour '; and the plural occurs in Acts 2^{17}, James 5^{3}, and 2 Tim. 3^{1}.)

Does this language, *to the author*, mean that he accepts current eschatology, and that he attributes it to the mind of Jesus? Most commentators so regard it. Our own view is that the author uses language expressive of *time*, to convey ideas which are not of time. When, for example, he speaks of *eternal* life, he does not mean, primarily, a never-ending existence: he thinks in terms of *quality*, not of quantity, of real value, not of temporal duration. The ' last ' day is, therefore, the *decisive* day, the *culminating* day, the day when the sifting is complete. The 'day' is not of time; nor is the 'last' of time. They are both of eternity. In similar manner we should interpret the verb 'raise' used by the Evangelist. It would be as profound a misinterpretation of his meaning to hold that he is thinking in terms of *space* here as that he is thinking in terms of *time* when he speaks of 'the last day.' Through the inadequacy of language and the limitations of our minds, we are compelled to use words such as these when we seek to express, whether to ourselves or to others, the reality of a life unbounded by space and time. Jesus Himself—as well as the author of this Gospel—suffered from such limitations: and for this reason they were misunderstood—and always will be misunderstood by those who do not share, at least in some small degree, the nature and quality of their experiences. It will be noticed by every attentive reader that the language of space pervades this Gospel. We read of the Spirit 'descending' (1^{34}), of angels 'ascending and descending upon the Son of man' (1^{51}), of being 'born from above' (3^{3}), of *ascending* into heaven and *descending* out of heaven (3^{13}), of the dead *coming forth* and going unto the resurrection of life or unto the resurrection of judgement (5^{29}), of 'the bread which came down out of heaven' ($6^{51, 58}$), and many kindred phrases. All such language is symbolical —'when I was a child I thought as a child.' So, when the Fourth Evangelist puts into the mouth of Jesus the saying, 'I will raise him up' he is thinking of the *resurrecting spiritual Ministry* of Jesus: this life of which Jesus was the incarnate vehicle is the means to the complete entrance to Eternal life.

The facile mistake of many commentators is to treat a phrase apart from the mind of its user. How often to-day do we use the same words and mean quite different things. For that reason words are often the darkeners of counsel. We have to find out, not what a man says, but what a man means. *Words* are static things, but *meanings* are not. *Meaning* is integral to consciousness; and, because of this, the man of narrow consciousness interprets the man of rich and wide consciousness as meaning by the words he uses just what he himself is able to mean. It is not perceived that each mind has its own *constellation of ideas*. Just as most philosophic and mystical writers to-day use the word 'final' as connoting something qualitatively or essentially final, so the writer of this Gospel used the word translated 'last.' What, therefore, he says here is this. That Jesus is the expression of the mind and will of the Father in time and place, that all who come to Him in obedience and faith will, in this fellowship of the life eternal, come to attain a completely glorified, transfigured life. When the sifting is complete the new life will be complete. In the 40th verse the neuter is changed, and the thought of Jesus is that of the eternal hope for 'everyone' who sees and believes in the Son. The *completeness* of the restoration, that is, will *not* mean the merging of personal beings in an impersonal Absolute, the absorption of the many rivers of personal life in the one ocean of impersonal being.

The Resulting Controversy, and Fuller Elucidation of the Truth

JN. 6^{41-51a}

6 41 The Jews therefore murmured concerning him, because he said, I am the bread
42 which came down out of heaven. And
they said, Is not this Jesus, the son of
Joseph, whose father and mother we know?
how doth he now say, I am come down
43 out of heaven? Jesus answered and said
unto them, Murmur not among yourselves.
44 No man can come to me, except the
Father which sent me draw him: and I
45 will raise him up in the last day. It is
written in the prophets, And they shall all
be taught of God. Every one that hath
heard from the Father, and hath learned,
46 cometh unto me. Not that any man hath
seen the Father, save he which is from
47 God, he hath seen the Father. Verily,
verily, I say unto you, He that believeth
48 hath eternal life. I am the bread of life.
49 Your fathers did eat the manna in the
50 wilderness, and they died. This is the
bread which cometh down out of heaven,
that a man may eat thereof, and not die.
51 I am the living bread which came down
out of heaven: if any man eat of this
bread, he shall live for ever.

41–42. Here once again the thesis is followed by the antithesis, the presentation of the mind of Jesus by the misunderstanding it provoked. The challenge of *vv.* 41 and 42 is put into the mouth of ' the Jews '—once again the author's phrase which personifies the encompassing darkness which sought to ' master ' the light. The ground of this challenge is the lowly origin of Jesus, and reminds us forcibly of the same objection found in the Synoptic Gospels (Mk. 6^{3}; cf. Lk. 4^{22}). Is this reference to ' the son of Joseph, whose father and mother we know,' an indication of a view, generally accepted, that Joseph was the earthly father of Jesus? It may well be so. The Fourth Evangelist—at least this can be said—nowhere makes reference to a ' virgin birth ' of Jesus. The Patristic commentators, who, let us remember, accepted these words as the very words spoken by the opponents of Jesus, regarded this verse as showing that these Jews *did not know* of the virgin birth. To-day we cannot regard the words as *the very words* spoken by any specific individuals. They are the dramatic representation of the whole situation created by Jesus: and, so taken, they at least indicate the view generally held in the days of His flesh that the ' father ' and ' mother ' of Jesus were Joseph and Mary.

43–51. The answer of Jesus, which embraces the rest of this section, is a further elucidation of the thoughts of the previous section. Again, the whole truth has its ground in the nature of Him whom Jesus knew as Father. ' God ' is not a metaphysical formula to be assented to, but a Father to be trusted and obeyed. It is ' the Father ' who sends the Son, ' the Father ' who draws those who come to the Son; the Son Himself in whom is incarnate the Word which finally and completely raises men. This latter part of the 44th verse need not be regarded, as is now often suggested, as inserted by another hand into the narrative: it harmonises with the whole structure of the Gospel. In the first part of the verse there is the same assertion of Grace as in *v.* 37: in the latter part of the verse there is the same assertion of the completeness of restoration in Christ as in *vv.* 39 and 40. Nor was there anything revolutionary, or subversive of true prophetic teaching, in this message of Jesus (*v.* 45). He had come not to destroy, but to fulfil. Nothing is truer to the mind of Jesus as portrayed by the Synoptists than this 45th verse. In Is. 54^{13} it had been said, ' Ye shall all be taught of God.' A God who teaches all His children is both Father and Eternal Word. He speaks *directly* to heart and mind within, not merely indirectly by transmitted letter and law. Thus it is that those who have heard the Father's voice come to the Father's incarnate Word. To accept a code would lead them to expect another code: to hear a voice would lead them to expect a living presence. Yet this *direct* speaking of God to men is not seeing God in His fullness and glory—' no one hath seen God at any time ' (1^{18}). The Evangelist, it is very obvious, uses the verb ' to see ' in various senses, as indeed we all do. He can tell us that ' no one ' has ever *seen* God; he can also say, as here, that He who is of God, the unique Son, has *seen* the Father; he can also say, as in 14^{9}, that He who hath *seen* Jesus hath *seen* the Father. It is obvious, however, that what the Evangelist is expressing throughout are the self-same truths—that spiritual things are spiritually discerned, and that the unique discerner of spiritual truth is the incarnate Son, who thus reveals to God's other sons what they had not seen so fully and completely as He Himself has.

47–51. In the verses which conclude this section there are the same contrasts as in the previous section. There is physical bread and there is spiritual bread: there is physical existence and there is eternal life. In the 51st verse we find the first reference to the ' flesh ' of Jesus, which He gives ' for the life of the world.' Inasmuch as the thought expressed by this word ' flesh ' forms the key to what follows, it will be well to take the second part of this 51st verse with the following section.

The Flesh that is Given

JN. $6^{51b\text{-}71}$

6 51^{b} yea and the bread which I will give is
my flesh, for the life of the world.
52 The Jews therefore strove one with
another, saying, How can this man give
53 us his flesh to eat? Jesus therefore said
unto them, Verily, verily, I say unto you,
Except ye eat the flesh of the Son of man
and drink his blood, ye have not life in
54 yourselves. He that eateth my flesh and
drinketh my blood hath eternal life; and I
55 will raise him up at the last day. For my
flesh is meat indeed, and my blood is
56 drink indeed. He that eateth my flesh
and drinketh my blood abideth in me, and
57 I in him. As the living Father sent me,
and I live because of the Father; so he that
eateth me, he also shall live because of me.
58 This is the bread which came down out of
heaven: not as the fathers did eat, and
died: he that eateth this bread shall live
59 for ever. These things said he in the
synagogue, as he taught in Capernaum.
60 Many therefore of his disciples, when
they heard *this*, said, This is a hard saying;
61 who can hear it? But Jesus knowing in
himself that his disciples murmured at
this, said unto them, Doth this cause you
62 to stumble? *What* then if ye should behold the Son of man ascending where he
63 was before? It is the spirit that quickeneth; the flesh profiteth nothing: the
words that I have spoken unto you are
64 spirit, and are life. But there are some of
you that believe not. For Jesus knew
from the beginning who they were that
believed not, and who it was that should
65 betray him. And he said, For this cause
have I said unto you, that no man can
come unto me, except it be given unto him
of the Father.
66 Upon this many of his disciples went
back, and walked no more with him.
67 Jesus said therefore unto the twelve,
68 Would ye also go away? Simon Peter
answered him, Lord, to whom shall we
go? thou hast the words of eternal life.
69 And we have believed and know that thou
70 art the Holy One of God. Jesus answered
them, Did not I choose you the twelve,
71 and one of you is a devil? Now he spake
of Judas *the son* of Simon Iscariot, for he it
was that should betray him, *being* one of
the twelve.

This section of the discourse is, as already noted, in three paragraphs: the first, spoken to ' the Jews,' the second (from *v.* 60), to ' many of the disciples,' the third (from *v.* 66), to ' the twelve.' The whole passage, however, is a unity: to break it up would be like putting one movement of a great symphony on three gramophone records.

Various subsidiary points, like, for example, ' the Son of man ascending where he was before ' (*v.* 62), have been elucidated in previous contexts. The statement in *v.* 64 that Jesus knew from the beginning who they were that believed not, is to be interpreted in similar manner to 6^6. The insight of Jesus, says the Evangelist, into every situation was unique and *original*; it was not *derived* from external events, but given in intuitive conviction. The author is here giving dramatic expression to this unique intuitive faculty of Jesus, whereby He took the initiative in every situation—a faculty which made Him solitary in every company.

The interpretation of these verses depends upon our whole estimate of the author's mind and purpose in writing. If we regard this Gospel as an ecclesiastical and theological document, written in the interest of the institution as such, or of its formal theology as such, or of its sacramental rites as such, we shall conclude that there is here an endeavour to justify the eucharistic rite as it was coming to be celebrated in the Church at the close of the first century. If, on the other hand, we regard the Gospel as a presentation, in dramatic and allegorical form, of the ethical and spiritual teaching of Jesus, we shall interpret the language here used in the light of this dominant purpose, and of the type of mind manifested. What we have suggested is that the Evangelist is seeking to ethicise and spiritualise the sacramental rites of the Church, in the light of his insight into the essential mind of Jesus Himself. Such an interpretation is accordant with the Gospel in its entirety and in its manifest unity. His words here, as elsewhere, have to be interpreted in the light of his own mind, not in the light of other people's minds. The greater and deeper the mind of an author, the more certain we may be that isolated utterances have their meaning in relation to the whole context of his ideas and of his central purpose. So transparent a genius as the author of this Gospel is not guilty of setting before his readers a heterogeneous mass of discordant ideas. There is an obvious unity of transcendent spiritual purpose pervading his Gospel; and it is, to the present writer, impossible to conceive that the author is intuitive seer in one chapter, a narrow ecclesiastic in the next, a rigid sacerdotalist in the next—and so on. A great book is governed by a few great and simple ideas; and one of the greatest religious books of all time is no exception to this rule.

The *sacramental principle*, in the truest sense of that much-abused phrase, pervades this whole Gospel. To the author, the visible is ever the medium of the invisible—*for those who have eyes to see*. No one has seen God at any time, but Jesus, the Word has declared Him—*to those who have ears to hear*. Everywhere in the Gospel there is this emphasis; and all human experience corroborates it. The physical is sacramental of the spiritual, *but on spiritual conditions*. The external will touch the spirit, *but only through the spirit*. The material will reach the centre of man's spiritual being, *but never of itself*. Always and everywhere there is the condition—of faith, of insight, of obedience. Without one's five senses physical contacts mean nothing, and convey nothing. To a blind man a sunset is not sacramental. To a deaf man, a symphony is not sacramental—unless, like Beethoven, he has written it himself. Incense means nothing, conveys nothing, to one who has no sense of sight or of smell. The mind is reached through the body, but it is only in so far as the physical that is *without* can in some way speak to the consciousness that is *within*, that the outward can be sacramental. Nothing, in other words, is sacramental *in and by itself*. *Grace* is a spiritual gift, and requires spiritual conditions for its reception. If it were otherwise, both the Giver and the Gift were degraded—as also the receiver.

The sacramental principle, so understood, dominates this passage. What is this 'flesh' of Jesus which is 'given' to man to eat? What this 'blood' of Jesus, without which His hearers have no light in themselves? There is, without doubt, a eucharistic reference. But what does the reference mean? For ourselves, we agree with the late F. D. Maurice who said, speaking of this passage: 'If you ask me, then, whether he is speaking of the Eucharist here, I should say, "No." If you ask me where I can learn the meaning of the eucharist, I should say, "Nowhere so well as here."'

Some interpreters feel that the references to eating flesh and drinking blood indicate that they are 'explanatory additions' to the original Gospel; inasmuch as they are on a 'lower plane' than the rest of the Gospel.[1] Such a conclusion, for which there is no MS. evidence, is, we suggest, based upon a misunderstanding of the words employed, and of the ideas meant by the author to be conveyed.

What the Evangelist is seeking to do here is to express, in the vivid, realistic language that was becoming hallowed in the Church, the truth that the historic Jesus is the mediator—and supremely in His death—of that Divine sustenance required by the spirit of man if he is to know eternal life. When the author says 'flesh' and 'blood,' he no more means the physical realities which these denote than when he says that Jesus is 'light,' or 'door,' or 'vine,' or 'bread' or 'water.' The 'flesh' and 'blood' represent in vivid, realistic manner Jesus Himself in His essential, and human, spirit of unique faith and of perfect obedience—which faith and obedience were supremely manifest in the Cross. There He gave His 'flesh' and 'blood'; that is, there He dedicated His whole unique human self to God and to His fellows. To eat His flesh and to drink His blood is, therefore, to partake of His essential spirit: it is to 'abide in him,' and to have Him abiding in us (*v.* 56). This figure of 'abiding' in Him, and He in us, and He Himself in God, is found frequently in the later chapters of the Gospel, where it means what it here means. It signifies identification in moral and spiritual purpose. It is not something physical, or temporal, or local; it is something spiritual and eternal. Ignatius had understood this language when he wrote: 'Do ye therefore arm yourselves with gentleness and be renewed in *faith*, which is the *flesh* of the Lord, and in *love*, which is the *blood* of Jesus Christ.' Elsewhere the same Ignatius said that the *Gospel* is 'the flesh of Jesus.' Augustine in his moments of insight had seen this—as when he said, in words which might have been spoken by the author of this Gospel: 'Crede et manducasti,' 'believe, and thou hast eaten.'

[1] So, e.g., J. Estlin Carpenter in *The Johannine Writings*, p. 428.

Later in the chapter, at *v.* 63, the author—as if to show that any materialistic view of eucharistic practice and belief was far removed from his mind—goes on to answer the objections to this 'hard saying' of Jesus. For the mind of Jesus was 'hard' to most in the days of His flesh, and was becoming 'harder' still in the author's day. 'It is the spirit that quickeneth, the flesh profiteth nothing: the words that I speak unto you, they are spirit and they are life'—not the sayings in and by themselves, but the truth and the grace of which the mind of Jesus was the vehicle. Surely any honest exegesis of *the eating the flesh of Jesus*, and *the drinking of His blood*, must relate them to these words in the succeeding 63rd verse. The meaning of the words, 'Except ye eat the flesh of the Son of man, and drink his blood, ye have not life in you,' is revealed and elucidated in the words which follow. The passage is a harmonious unity, not a disconnected mass of discordant ideas.

One further thought is inherent in the terms 'flesh' and 'blood' as here employed. It has already been suggested that, as distinguished from 'bread,' 'flesh' and 'blood' indicate the thought of the death of Christ on the Cross. They also suggest the teaching of Jesus at the Last Supper. In the Introduction it was noted that there is no account of the institution of the Lord's Supper in this Gospel. But the *inner meaning* of the teaching of Jesus on that solemn occasion is here given—with the author's usual disregard for chronological exactness, when the dramatic and pedagogic framework of his Gospel demands it. The author has in mind that occasion, and its teaching, in this passage. The reader will note, in support of this suggestion, that this chapter ends with the announcement of Judas's treachery: later, in $13^{21ff.}$, he narrates this treason in its proper historical setting. When, therefore, the author is here expounding the essential teaching of Jesus given at that supper in the upper room, his mind leaps to the tragic figure of Iscariot who, then, went out into 'the night.' Perhaps, further, the Evangelist may have had an especial reason in this case for taking out of its historic setting this teaching of Jesus about eating and drinking the emblems of His body and blood. He knows the superstitious views which are in his day being associated with the Eucharist: and so, *of set purpose*, he takes it out of a setting which, in every age, has been quoted in support of materialistic views. He knows the spiritual teaching, of which the Supper was but the occasion, the vehicle: and he gives that teaching in a setting which will free it from the possibility of misunderstanding. Partaking of Christ's flesh and blood had no *causal* association with the eating of material bread or the drinking of material wine. The whole partaking is faith's appropriation of the essential mind and spirit of Christ, of which the bread and wine are symbols and vehicles.

That this interpretation of the references to eating the 'flesh' and drinking the 'blood' of Jesus is the true interpretation of what the author sought to say, and of what Jesus Himself said in the days of His flesh, is, we think, confirmed when we remember that such language was by no means peculiar to him: it was common in the religious literature of the world. Here, as elsewhere, we have to be on our guard against the facile fallacy of concerning ourselves with an author's *words* instead of with his *ideas*. We speak of *taste*, when we mean æsthetic appreciation. We speak of *tact*, when we mean sympathetic perception of how we ought to act towards other people. Such language was common in the Hebrew literature familiar to the Evangelist. There are few more complete misunderstandings of the Evangelist's mind than that which regards him as indebted for his *ideas* to the Mystery cults with their magical eating and drinking. The parallels in language have obsessed many myopic students of words, who have concluded that the use of the same words means the acceptance of the same ideas. There is little doubt but that in the second century the Church had come to imbibe some of the *ideas* of the Mysteries; but to suppose that the Johannine author had done so, is only possible by first closing the mind to what he has written.

The Old Testament speaks frequently of the *face* of God, of the *hand* of God, of the *heart* of God—and kindred expressions—when not even the dullest or most prosaic reader to-day finds it necessary to believe that the writer was using these terms literally. In Genesis we read of the *body* of the day ($17^{23, 36}$), and in Exodus (24^{10}) of the *body* of heaven. In Proverbs (9^5) Wisdom speaks and says: 'Come eat of my bread, and drink of the wine I have mingled.' The prophet of the Exile (Is. 55^1), in his exhortation says: 'Ho, every one that thirsteth, come ye to the waters, and he that hath no money; come ye, buy and eat.' In *Ecclesiasticus* (24^{21}) Wisdom says: 'They that *eat* me shall hunger for more; And they that *drink* me shall thirst for more.' In the collect for the second Sunday in Advent we pray that we may 'read, mark, learn, and *inwardly digest*' the Scriptures, when no one supposes that a *physical* act is implied. Even the vivid and realistic verb in *vv.* 56–58 of this chapter in Jn. (τρώγω—to chew, to gnaw, in classical Greek) does not mean that the author was thinking of any physical act. In our own enlightened days we talk of 'chewing the cud' of an author's thoughts, when we mean that we are meditating upon them. Perhaps some unimaginative scholar in the centuries to come will conclude that we meant a physical act, when we used so realistic an expression! That this is the author's *meaning* when he uses this realistic verb is supported by the further fact that when in 13^{18} he translates Ps. 41^9, he uses the same verb τρώγω, where the Septuagint employs the usual verb.

Such metaphors were used by Jesus Himself. He speaks of *hungering* and *thirsting* after righteousness, and of being *filled* (Mt. 5^5). He speaks of *eating* the *leaven* of the Pharisees, when He means partaking of their spirit (Mk. 8^{15}, Mt. 16^6, Lk. 12^1). He speaks of *drinking* the cup, when He means spiritual acceptance of the Father's will (Mk. 10^{38}, etc.). At the Last Supper the words: 'Take eat, this is my body,' 'this is my blood,' are recorded as having been spoken by Him. The disciples at the time did not misunderstand this language, nor did the author of this Gospel. The Church later on *did* misunderstand; and to correct such misunderstanding was one of the author's purposes in writing. That he was aware of such misunderstandings is clear from the dramatic expression given to them throughout the Gospel. 'How can these things be?' 'How can this man give us his flesh to eat?' In every thesis we have such an antithetical refrain. Nicodemus had raised the same kind of materialistic objection which 'the Jews' here raise: 'How can a man be born again when he is old?' (3^4). It is supremely significant that in the two discourses which have been interpreted to establish the materialistic sacramentarian views of the author—chapters 3 and 6—there is embedded in the narrative the expression of the materialistic misunderstandings which the discourses themselves meet and correct.

There are few more urgent necessities for the modern Christian than for him to penetrate beneath the venerable forms and phrases of the past to the moral and spiritual realities to which they give expression. It is for that reason that this Gospel is the most modern document in the New Testament.

It should be noted, before leaving this sacramental passage, that there is some textual evidence for an early preference for 'body' over 'flesh' in *vv.* 51 and 54. This seems to show *either* that the author's language to some seemed too materialistic, *or* that his original language was altered in a materialistic direction. Our own view is that the language, 'flesh' and 'blood,' is the author's own language, used by him to express moral and spiritual realities.

68–69. The closing verses of this section bring two of the Twelve into dramatic relief—Peter and Judas. The confession of Peter in *vv.* 68 and 69 is the Fourth Evangelist's account of the confession of the Apostle at Cæsarea Philippi, recorded by the Synoptists (Mk. $8^{27f.}$; Mt. $16^{31f.}$; Lk. $9^{18f.}$). We see again the chronological indifference of our author. Here, he feels, is a dramatic setting too good to be missed, too allegorically appropriate to be lost. So he takes the confession of Peter out of its historical setting and places it against the denial that is growing within the soul of Judas. The confession of Peter here is to the *inward* character of a holiness derived from, or belonging to, God, which was possessed by Jesus. He was 'the holy one of God.' The confession is not that Jesus is a worker of nature-marvels, but that He is 'holy.' Holiness is the true 'sign' of God in human life. This confession is of the highest significance for an understanding of the Fourth Evangelist's mind. He had penetrated to the *values* of Jesus.

On the other hand, Judas stands before us as representing a fundamental 'unbelief' in the essential mind and mission of Jesus. It is significant that Judas is called here 'the son of Simon Iscariot'; for Iscariot indicates the name of a place, or town—probably Kerioth, a town of Judah (cf. Josh. 15^{25}). Judas, therefore, was a strict Judæan, the only member of the chosen Twelve who was not a Galilean. Thus, the 'unbelief' of 'the Jews' has its representative even within the chosen Twelve. 'One of you is a devil,' are the words which the Evangelist uses to give expression to the mind of Jesus about Judas. What do the words mean? As used by the Evangelist they mean, first, that the character and tendencies of Judas were not hidden from the unique insight of Jesus. The Evangelist is *not* thinking that Jesus chose Judas *in order that* he should betray Him. In other words, the Evangelist is not concerned, as so many patristic exegetes were concerned, with the speculative problem of Judas's 'election' in order to accomplish man's salvation. It will perhaps be sufficient to give but one such interpretation—it will serve to reveal the width of the gulf separating our modern intellectual world from the patristic and mediæval world. Bede—according to Aquinas—commenting on this passage, says: 'Or we must say, that He elected the eleven for one purpose, the twelfth for another: the eleven to fill the place of Apostles, and persevere in it unto the end; the twelfth to the service of betraying Him, which was the means of saving the human race.' The

Evangelist, we would say, does not dwell in this speculative realm. What he means to say is that in this man who had become one of the Twelve there had very soon been manifest a lack of sympathy with the mind and mission of Jesus; and that this moral and spiritual alienation did not take Jesus by surprise. Acts which seem to us to be sudden and spontaneous have a long history. When the betrayer in 13³⁰ goes out into 'the night,' the Evangelist does not wish the reader to think that this 'night' has come suddenly. By such a passage as 6⁷⁰⁻⁷¹ he would say that the shadows had already been gathering in the mind of Judas. Second, the word 'devil' used here comes from a verb which means 'to accuse' (διαβάλλω): a 'devil' here means one who has the characteristics of a slanderer, or a perverter of the truth. When in 8⁴ Jesus says to 'the Jews': 'Ye are of your father the devil,' the meaning is that they partake of that spirit which perverts good into evil, and evil into good. Judas was seemingly following Jesus, but he was not really in fellowship of spirit with Jesus (see, e.g., 12⁴ and 13²). He was following his own purpose and hopes, not those of Jesus. His values were not those of Him who has just been confessed to be 'the holy one of God.' He desires to find, not holiness, but *power* in the Messiah; not the light of truth which is self-luminous, but the thunderbolt of authority which compels men to acquiesce. All the 'temptations' of Jesus have their source in the spirit of him whom the Evangelist says here is 'a devil.'

Nowhere is the dramatic nature of the Evangelist's mind more clearly seen than in these closing verses of the chapter. After unfolding the conflict between insight and sight, between belief and unbelief, he here presents us at the close with two sharply-contrasted figures within the chosen band, by whom the conflict is symbolised.

THE WITNESS AT THE FEAST OF TABERNACLES AND THE ENSUING CONTROVERSY

The Feast of Tabernacles

JN. 7^{1-13}

7 1 And after these things Jesus walked in
Galilee: for he would not walk in Judæa,
because the Jews sought to kill him.
2 Now the feast of the Jews, the feast of
3 tabernacles, was at hand. His brethren
therefore said unto him, Depart hence,
and go into Judæa, that thy disciples also
may behold thy works which thou doest.
4 For no man doeth anything in secret, and
himself seeketh to be known openly. If
thou doest these things, manifest thyself to
5 the world. For even his brethren did not
6 believe on him. Jesus therefore saith unto
them, My time is not yet come; but your
7 time is alway ready. The world cannot
hate you; but me it hateth, because I
8 testify of it, that its works are evil. Go ye
up unto the feast: I go not up yet unto
this feast; because my time is not yet ful-
9 filled. And having said these things unto
them, he abode *still* in Galilee.
10 But when his brethren were gone up
unto the feast, then went he also up, not
11 publicly, but as it were in secret. The
Jews therefore sought him at the feast, and
12 said, Where is he? And there was much
murmuring among the multitudes concerning him: some said, He is a good man;
others said, Not so, but he leadeth the
13 multitude astray. Howbeit no man spake
openly of him for fear of the Jews.

This is the third visit of Jesus to Jerusalem narrated by the Evangelist. The first visit gave a dramatic setting to the prophetic authority of Jesus—the incident of the cleansing of the Temple in 2[13-25]—and to the teaching to Nicodemus on the new life in chapter 3. The second visit gave a dramatic setting to the claim of Jesus to teach the subservience of institutions like the Sabbath to the well-being of man, this claim being based upon the unique knowledge of the Father possessed by Jesus (chap. 5). This third visit, associated with the Feast of Tabernacles, gives a peculiarly fitting setting to the increasing controversy which gathers round the claims of Jesus to be the 'tabernacle of God with men,' and to be the source of the 'living waters' flowing from His disciples (*v.* 38). What we have to note is that the Evangelist's setting of the teaching and of the ensuing controversy is neither precisely historical, nor is it just accidental. The setting is chosen for the controversy, and the controversy for the setting. The essential mind of Jesus is once again presented; the misunderstanding and hostility it encountered and provoked are once again delineated. But they are presented and delineated against a background which itself symbolises the moral and spiritual truth declared, and the falsehood opposed. Yet once again, the Evangelist exercises the freedom of the dramatic artist and of the intuitive seer. We misunderstand his mind and purpose if we seek for a precise chronological scheme for his Gospel, or if we treat these controversies as verbatim records of specific incidents and of precise words spoken thereat. There is a unity of presentation here which belongs to artistic and imaginative genius of the highest order. And this is fused and suffused with the heat, and glow, of a spiritual insight into the truth as it was in Jesus, which belongs to the greatest saints and seers of Christianity.

It has already been pointed out that a great deal of the teaching of Jesus in this Gospel is presented against a background of these Jewish feasts in Jerusalem. While it is here suggested that *for the most part* the dramatic inter-relation of the setting and of the form of the teaching belongs to the Evangelist's own mind, we must also allow for the exceeding probability that Jesus Himself had utilised these festival occasions for the presentation of His teaching. His own words would, without doubt, have reference to the state of mind of the people in Jerusalem at the time. Every true teacher uses his 'occasions' for the presentation of his message. A teacher or preacher who is alive to the historical and intellectual environment will always adapt the *form* of his message to the whole situation. On great national, and international, occasions, or on the great festivals of the Church, a real preacher will be alert to make these subservient to his ethical and spiritual purpose. It is, therefore, impossible to conceive that so uniquely vital a mind as that of Jesus would let such occasions in Israel's history go by without seeking to relate them to His Gospel, or to translate their temporal language into the language of eternity. For this reason, then, we must be ready to acknowledge that *the Evangelist was probably in many cases only dramatising an already dramatic situation.* Nevertheless, the *form* of presentation in this Gospel owes *more* to the Evangelist's own mind than to the historical situation. The chapter before us, therefore, has to be regarded, neither as a precise transcript from life, nor as a complete imaginative creation on the part of the author. Rather, it is the transmutation and transfiguration of the historical reality of the essential mind and teaching of Jesus into a variety of imagined dramatic encounters. And this transmutation and transfiguration was effected in a mind where there was no heat without light, nor light without heat.

This Feast of Tabernacles, which took place at the time of the ingathering at the end of summer, and which lasted, at first, seven days (Dt. 16^{13}), recalled to the Jews the days when their fathers had dwelt in tabernacles in the wilderness, and when the tabernacle of God had preceded them in their wilderness journey. Later in Israel's history, according to Num. 29^{35}, an eighth day was added to the feast, a day of ' solemn assembly '; and we know from Nehemiah 8^{18} and 2 *Mac.* 10^{6}, that this day was observed after the Exile. Josephus in his *Antiquities* (III, x. 4) refers to this eighth day, and no doubt this is ' the last day, the great day of the feast,' mentioned in *v.* 37 of this chapter.

The whole festival commemorated the march through the desert. Two features of the journey were especially prominent. The first was ' the pillar of fire ' which guided them by night. The second was the rock whence had issued waters to assuage their thirst. We may, therefore, take the three key ideas of this Feast as symbolised by the three words—*Tabernacle*, *Light*, and *Water*. It is not mistaken ingenuity on our part to see the fittingness of these symbolical words to the messages conveyed in this and the succeeding chapters. We cannot be certain as to how far, *to the author's own mind*, the Feast of Tabernacles extends in his narrative. Probably at least to the end of chapter 8, and possibly through chapter 9. That being so, we shall note that in the former part of the seventh chapter there is a *twofold* emphasis which harmonises with the ' tabernacle ' idea. The first is that of the unique indwelling of God within Jesus; the Eternal Word had ' tabernacled ' in Him (1^{14}). The second is that of the *transitory*, and transitional, nature of the present tabernacle of God in Jesus (*vv.* 14–36). This *transitory* idea is suggested by two facts in the history of the wilderness pilgrimage: first, the tents or ' booths ' used by their fathers—' I made the children of Israel to dwell in booths when I brought them out of the land of Egypt ' (Lev. 23^{43}); and second, the tabernacle in which God was thought to dwell had long since perished, or been lost. Both these ideas are fused and allegorised in the verses which speak of Jesus as being but ' a little time ' with them (*vv.* 34 and 36). We shall note, further, that in the latter part of the chapter there is the teaching on ' *the rivers of living waters* ' which are for those who truly thirst (*vv.* 37–44). And, finally, we shall note that 8^{12} begins the *author's own* 8th chapter, with the declaration that Jesus is the ' *light* of the world.'

The chapter has a striking character of animation, and of what we might call ' dramatic confusion.' We get the impression from the narrative of a Jerusalem full of people of diverse motives and natures. There is a pervasive atmosphere of confusion, suggested by the play and interplay of conflicting attitudes to Jesus. The situation is working up to its inevitable climax. There is the strife of contending voices. There is the bewilderment arising from a state of increasing tension. The river is running no longer quietly and serenely, but with turgid and uneven flow. It is like a day at the beginning of autumn when ominous calm is followed by distant rumblings, and when sudden alternations of temperature presage some violent change in the weather. The variety of figures referred to in the narrative, and of the feelings which govern them, is the author's way of creating this impression. We read of 'the Jews,' of 'his brethren,' of 'the multitudes,' of 'the people of Jerusalem,' of 'the Pharisees,' of 'the chief priests and the Pharisees,' and, once more, of 'Nicodemus.' We read of vague and anxious questionings, of heated and confused debate. Almost the whole gamut of the emotions is struck—fear and hope, hate and love, hesitation and certitude, wondering belief and misgiving unbelief.

1–5. The chapter is introduced by a statement to explain the absence of Jesus from Jerusalem during the period of six months from 'the Passover' referred in 6^4 to the Feast of Tabernacles. The growing hostility of 'the Jews' is known to Jesus, says the Evangelist. Jesus therefore 'walks' in Galilee. This hostility of 'the Jews,' however, has its counterpart in the blindness of his brethren (*vv.* 3, 5). Theirs was a different kind of 'unbelief'—not reasoned or settled, but partial and arising out of a misunderstanding of the mind of Jesus. Among them, light alternated with darkness; while among 'the Jews' darkness held full sway. It is the difference between the unbelief of an earnest, but bewildered and spiritually untutored, mind, and the unbelief of rigid, unbending traditionalism or ecclesiasticism. The first will often be perplexed by a prophet's words and actions, but the truth that is in his heart will always in the end win their loyalty, even if it is a bewildered loyalty. The second will stifle the misgivings that the prophet's sincerity and truth evoke in their antagonised minds, and these stifled misgivings will thus add fuel to the fire of their passionate opposition. Thus, in every age we find zealous men gnashing upon the prophet and seer with their teeth; stoning, burning, and crucifying him with their words, if not always with their hands.

These 'brethren' of Jesus shared the mistaken faith of those who lusted after signs and wonders. They wanted Jesus to go up to Jerusalem to convince 'the disciples' there by striking 'works.' A goodness which dwells 'in secret' did not seem to them to be essential goodness. They thought the criterion of goodness was its publicity. They did not know that whenever goodness seeks to parade itself it ceases to be goodness: it then reveals its essential quality of propagandist sham. Light is not here to draw attention to itself, but to shine in its own right, and to dissipate by its intrinsic quality the surrounding darkness. Wherever it is, it does this, whether in secret or in public, whether in 'the dark unfathomed caves of ocean,' or in the hurly-burly of Vanity Fair. 'Show thyself to the world' is the specious temptation to which the worldly mind always listens, but to which the unworldly mind is always deaf. Jesus had already met that temptation at the beginning of His ministry and overcome it. It recurs, but its sting had been drawn in that first encounter. When it appears in the mind of a Judas (called 'a devil'), or in the mind of an unregenerate Simon (called 'Satan,' Mt. 16^{23}), it is 'mastered,' as the true light has always in the end mastered the darkness.

6–9. Thus, the words of Jesus in reply express the knowledge He has of these inner antagonisms, and of the spontaneous certitude which guided Him in all He said and did. *His* time was not yet come: *their* time was always ready. He stands solitary among His disciples, conscious of a mission which could not be theirs, aware of an antagonism to this mission which, therefore, could not be *known* to them. The world never hates its own, but only its Divine enemy. The world loves those who pander to the self-delusions of its proud pomps and fond fantasies. It hates those who strip its nakedness and pretensions bare. The sons of the darkness know their friends. So Jesus goes 'not yet': nor indeed until the command comes *from within*.

The 'time' to which Jesus refers in this passage is the time of opportunity, or the occasion whose fitness He Himself must decide. The Greek word used (καιρός) is only found in St. John in this passage, and is not to be confused with the 'hour' of Jesus, to which the Evangelist frequently refers. When the author speaks of the 'hour' of Jesus—or places the word on the lips of Jesus—he would seem to be thinking of the end of the Ministry of Jesus on the Cross. When he places upon the lips of Jesus the phrase 'my time,' he means that the occasion did not seem as yet opportune to Jesus to *manifest Himself to the world* (*v.* 4). As far as the disciples were concerned, there was nothing to interfere with the fitness of the occasion for them. *Their* appearance in Jerusalem had not within it the decisive issues involved in *His* appearance.

10–13. The disciples go up openly to the feast. Jesus follows at a time and in a manner decided by His own insight. The Evangelist is always reminding us that the actions of Jesus were never dictated by external pressure, but arose from the initiative of His own luminous and directing spirit. The contrast between this visit to Jerusalem of the solitary pilgrim, unnoticed among the crowd, and the 'triumphal entry' of $12^{12\text{f.}}$ is striking; and suggests, once again, the dramatic contrasts which appealed to the Evangelist's mind. Bede read a somewhat forced 'mystical' meaning into this stay in Galilee and visit 'in secret' to Jerusalem. 'The mystical meaning is, that to all those carnal persons who seek human glory, the Lord remains in Galilee; the meaning of which name is, "passing over"; applying to those His members who pass from vice to virtue, and make progress in the latter. And our Lord Himself delayed to go up; signifying that Christ's members seek not temporal but eternal glory. And He went up secretly, because all glory is from within; that is, *from a pure heart and good conscience and faith unfeigned*' (1 Tim. 1^5). Augustine had carried farther this 'mystical' interpretation. He wrote: 'Our Lord went up in secret, to represent the figurative system. He concealed Himself at the feast itself, because the feast itself signified that the members of Christ were in a strange country. For he dwells in tents who regards himself as a stranger in the world.'

Though, however, He came 'in secret,' His presence is suspected, and 'the Jews' seek for Him. Evil is restive at the proximity of the unknown presence of good. 'The multitudes' are, however, divided in their views of Him. To some He is 'a good man.' To others He has too much influence with 'the multitude'—for had not some wanted to make Him a king? Yet such divisions, says the Evangelist, are as yet secret—'for fear of the Jews.' Authority has not yet spoken, so let us beware of committing ourselves. Thus, in every age 'safety first' has been erected into a moral principle.

The Discussion with 'the Jews' in the Temple at the Midst of the Feast

Jn. 7^{14-24}

7 14 But when it was now the midst of the
feast Jesus went up into the temple, and
15 taught. The Jews therefore marvelled,
saying, How knoweth this man letters,
16 having never learned? Jesus therefore
answered them, and said, My teaching is
17 not mine, but his that sent me. If any
man willeth to do his will, he shall know
of the teaching, whether it be of God, or
18 *whether* I speak from myself. He that
speaketh from himself seeketh his own
glory: but he that seeketh the glory of him
that sent him, the same is true, and no
19 unrighteousness is in him. Did not
Moses give you the law, and *yet* none of
you doeth the law? Why seek ye to kill
20 me? The multitude answered, Thou hast
21 a devil: who seeketh to kill thee? Jesus
answered and said unto them, I did one
22 work, and ye all marvel. For this cause
hath Moses given you circumcision (not
that it is of Moses, but of the fathers); and
23 on the sabbath ye circumcise a man. If a
man receiveth circumcision on the sabbath, that the law of Moses may not be
broken; are ye wroth with me, because I
made a man every whit whole on the
24 sabbath? Judge not according to appearance, but judge righteous judgement.

The suggested transposition of these verses has already been discussed (pp. 764 f.), and the decision reached was to leave them where all our MSS. place them—namely, here.

14. The central theme here is the same as that of chapter 5; but it has its fitness in the dramatic context of this chapter as much as in that of chapter 5. It is a mistaken understanding of the Evangelist's mind that demands the transposition of this theme. For it is one of the recurring themes of the Gospel. The theme is the *unique authority of Jesus derived from His unique knowledge of the Father's will.*

The visit to the Temple 'in the midst of the feast' is made openly. Within the precincts of 'his Father's house' there is no need, nor any possibility, for Him to be 'in secret.' The things of the Spirit have to be openly proclaimed. The antagonism of the Jews is now represented as that of the 'academic' mind—the mind that knows what everyone else has said but knows not what itself has to say. This 15th verse is to be interpreted in its context. It is not, therefore, an expression of real surprise at the profound teaching of one who is unlettered—such as we find in Mk. 1^{22} (see also Lk. 2^{47}). It is an expression of the exclusive pretensions of 'the schools.' How can one who is not of 'the schools' dare to speak thus? They forget there is only *one* real school, the School of Life and of Reality; and that our organised 'schools' frequently exist for the perpetuation of the subsidised 'infallibilities' of the past. Wherever there is 'an institution,' there are to be found the bones of some unlettered seer at its doors. The answer of Jesus in *v.* 16 points to the one source of truth in God Himself, by whom He knows Himself commissioned to teach. It is God's will He seeks to accomplish; and if anyone really *wills*, with the whole integrated personality, to do that will, he will recognise the authentic note of Divine teaching in the words of Jesus. This famous 17th verse, which has rightly afforded so much comfort to strong ethical souls, must not be isolated from its context. It does not mean that if a man really centres his whole personality on doing the Divine will as it is known to him, he will arrive at a perfectly articulated doctrinal position, or at dogmatic statements which will answer every perplexity of the logical intellect. It means that the truthful spirit comes to those truths of eternity by which Jesus lived and died. In other words, it is the truthful who recognise Him who is Truth; but to recognise Jesus as Truth does not mean that assent is necessarily given to what a majority of Christian thinkers have said *about* Him. For the Truth *in* Jesus is bigger and deeper than all the 'truths' which have been codified *about* Jesus. Self-will and the desire for self-glorification are the marks of the False: the disinterested and dedicated desire to glorify God is the mark of the True. The Son is recognised by the other sons: the Elder Brother by His brethren.

19. Those who belonged to the school of the Law of Moses had missed the spirit of their teacher, and the essence of his teaching, through their idolatry of the letter. The Law was in their books, but not in their hearts. And so they would kill Him who fulfilled the Law of Moses, out of their idolatrous love. Murder has frequently thus justified itself, as the records of the martyrs of all ages and of all faiths abundantly show. The Cross of Calvary itself is a vivid reminder of all the deaths that have been regarded as 'necessary' to the preservation of letter and of institution. In this utterance of Jesus—'Why seek ye to kill me?'—we have the Evangelist's way of expressing the growing hostility of which Jesus Himself was conscious. The seed of their hatred was already blossoming: it would soon bear its fatal fruit. But though this blossoming was hidden in the depth of a few hearts and minds, it was known, suggests our author, to the unique intuition of Jesus. The reply of 'the multitude' in *v.* 20 is the author's way of expressing the hidden and secretive character of this mortal hatred. Such an intuition on the part of Jesus is, to the crowd, disordered fancy—'Thou hast a demon,' they say. Penetrating insight into motives that are base, and that frequently deceive their owners themselves, is often regarded as subjective hallucination.

21–24. The reply of Jesus recalls the situation of chapter 5: the 'one work' in the Evangelist's mind is the healing there narrated. The meaning of this passage—at first sight so peculiar—is as follows. Jesus, in an answer which breathes the serenity both of assured insight and of logical decisiveness, reminds them that He has performed *one* act of labour *on the Sabbath*, and that this technical breach of the Law has astonished them. But let them look to their own acts. Let them consider that the law of circumcision, prior to Moses in origin (Gen. 17^{10}, 21^{4}), demanded that in this instance at least the Sabbath law should be overridden. For if the eighth day after birth occurred on the Sabbath, circumcision must nevertheless be performed. If, then, this rite, indicative of a *partial* restoration of man's nature, be permitted, why should they be working themselves into anger when the *whole* man is cured on the Sabbath? Let them, then, not judge by the external act, but by the inward motive and meaning. A true and just judgement is based upon insight into the purpose for which law exists, upon the good it seeks to conserve, upon the motives which inspired its fulfilment.

Some of the early teachers of the Church have interesting comments to make on this passage. Augustine, for example said: 'He who cast out devils, was told that He had a devil. Our Lord, however, in no way disturbed, but retaining all the serenity of truth, returned not evil for evil, or railing for railing.' Bede said of the same passage: 'Wherein He left us an example to take it patiently, whenever wrong censures are passed upon us, and not answer them by asserting the truth, though able to do so, but rather by some wholesome advice to the persons.' Alcuin commented on the answer of Jesus thus: 'Circumcision was given for three reasons; first, as a sign of Abraham's great faith; secondly, to distinguish the Jews from other nations; thirdly, that the receiving of it on the organ of virility might admonish us to observe chastity both of body and mind.' Augustine said: 'What is circumcision but a robbing of the flesh, to signify the robbing of the heart of its carnal lusts.'

The Controversy Intensified

JN. 7[25-36]

7 25 Some therefore of them of Jerusalem
said, Is not this he whom they seek to kill?
26 And lo, he speaketh openly, and they say
nothing unto him. Can it be that the
rulers indeed know that this is the Christ?
27 Howbeit we know this man whence he is:
but when the Christ cometh, no one
28 knoweth whence he is. Jesus therefore
cried in the temple, teaching and saying,
Ye both know me, and know whence I
am; and I am not come of myself, but he
29 that sent me is true, whom ye know not. I
know him; because I am from him, and he
30 sent me. They sought therefore to take
him: and no man laid his hand on him,
31 because his hour was not yet come. But
of the multitude many believed on him;
and they said, When the Christ shall come,
will he do more signs than those which
32 this man hath done? The Pharisees
heard the multitude murmuring these
things concerning him; and the chief
priests and the Pharisees sent officers to
33 take him. Jesus therefore said, Yet a little
while am I with you, and I go unto him
34 that sent me. Ye shall seek me, and shall
not find me: and where I am, ye cannot
35 come. The Jews therefore said among
themselves, Whither will this man go that
we shall not find him? will he go unto the
Dispersion among the Greeks, and teach
36 the Greeks? What is this word that he
said, Ye shall seek me, and shall not find
me: and where I am ye cannot come?

The next scene in the Act at the Feast of Tabernacles intensifies the confusion of motives and the conflict of desires. It represents a situation in which some know their mind about Jesus and some do not; a struggle in which it is not very easy to distinguish friend and foe. Such a situation is true to experience when any society feels itself to be moving irresistibly to a conflict where the issues are not clearly envisaged. It has been manifest in many an ecclesiastical Council, engaged in civil war for the Faith. Socrates, the Church historian, speaking of the later phases of the Arian controversy in the fourth century, says: 'What took place resembled a fight in the dark, when no man knew whether he struck at friend or foe.' The Fourth Evangelist has the dramatist's and the seer's power of conveying this impression of inchoate and confused strife.

The scene is represented as also taking place 'in the temple' (*v.* 28). The narrative enables us to see knots of people in the open court furtively discussing the issue. Here are a few of the inhabitants of Jerusalem, not pilgrims from afar. *Their* discussion is the author's way of giving expression to the *popular* objection to the Messianic claims of Jesus. Their minds are, however, swayed by different arguments. Some point out the mortal hostility of the rulers. Others give the reminder that, nevertheless, Jesus is being left alone. Then why, if the rulers want to kill Him, do they leave Him alone? Is it that among the rulers themselves there are divided counsels, some thinking He is Messiah and some that He is not? The conclusion, however, reached by this knot of the natives of Jerusalem is: He cannot be Messiah, for we know His family history, and the place of His origin. There is here again an echo of the 'Can any good thing come out of Nazareth?' of 1[46]. As for the origin of Messiah, His coming will be mysterious, an emergence of the unknown from the unknown A rabbinical saying confirms the Evangelist's accurate knowledge of the popular Jewish expectation: 'Three things are wholly unexpected, Messiah, a god-send, and a scorpion.'

28–30. In the answer of Jesus we have the author's way of presenting the Master's mind in relation to this popular Messianic view. To counter the false notion of mystery, the Evangelist tells us that 'Jesus *cried in the temple.*' The mysterious secrecy of the popular view is presented against the open unreserve of Jesus and of His teaching. It is not for all who have ears to hear and eyes to see. There is no magical mystery about His coming or about His methods. They know Him, indeed, as far as His family history is concerned—so far their statement is true. But true Messiahship has nothing to do with family or geographical origin. It consists in the unique sense of mission given to the Son by the real Father whose nature they know not. The God whom they remembered at this Feast as having 'tabernacled' with their fathers in the wilderness was with them in real presence in Jesus. This was mystery, not of the mere conundrum or of magic, but of spiritual reality.

31. This assertion of the moral and spiritual quality of Messiahship meets with a hostility which is yet held in check by a factor which to the opponents of Jesus was inscrutable. While they wanted to take Jesus, yet no one laid hands on Him, for His hour was not yet come. In this sentence the Evangelist gives to his narrative the sense of the inscrutable Providence of which Jesus knew Himself to be the vehicle. An hour is yet to come, and Jesus sees it looming dimly ahead; but it is 'not yet.'

31–33. In the 31st verse the Evangelist introduces us to yet another of the conflicting and confused attitudes taken with respect to Jesus. It is a belief in Him that is inadequately based. Those who represent this attitude are pointing to visible signs, rather than to invisible reality. Their faith is based upon an argumentative calculation that no Messiah of popular expectation could do more than 'this man' has done. Chrysostom, commenting on this passage, said: 'Minds of the grosser sort are influenced not by doctrine, but by miracles.' Significantly enough, it is this growing popular but mistaken assent to Jesus's claims which unites the two chief enemies of Jesus—'the Pharisees' and 'the chief priests.' This is the first reference in the Fourth Gospel to the latter. They represent the hierarchy in Jerusalem: together with the Pharisees they indicate the Sanhedrin, the supreme council of the Jews in Jerusalem at the time of the Roman occupation. The Pharisees, representing austere traditionalism in religion centred in synagogue worship, learn of the growing popular feeling; report it to the hierarchy, who represent the sacerdotalism of temple worship; and together they send their 'police' to arrest Jesus. The significant point to note in this passage is the nature of the cause which unites the 'chief priests' and 'the Pharisees' in their common action. Life brings strange bed-fellows together. Minds that have a common irritant sympathise with each other.

Often a common enmity for a third party will unite *for a time* divergent and opposed interests. The common enmity in this case has its basis in the popular, but mistaken, support Jesus is receiving. This at least must be summarily stopped; and to achieve this end two parties, representing incompatible interests, come together.

33–34. These verses can only be understood in the light of the dramatic purpose and spiritual insight of the author's mind. We are not to think that the author means Jesus to say these precise words to the officers who are come to arrest Him. The words have an application transcending any specific historical context. By them the author gives expression to Jesus's consciousness of an impending end to His temporal ministry. When that end comes He will go to the Father. This 'going to the Father,' however, is not to be conceived as a *spatial* departure; for Jesus says, 'Where *I am* ye cannot come.' He is 'with them' in bodily presence (*v.* 33); but only those who are of His spiritual lineage can be where He, in His essential being, is. Some see in these words a reading backwards of the *Ascension* into the mind of Jesus at this time. The Ascension may have been in the Evangelist's mind, but it is the Ascension understood in its spiritual reality and significance. The words also suggest, as we have earlier indicated, the thought of the *temporary tabernacles* represented in the Tabernacle festival. The tabernacle of Jesus's physical body was but a temporal dwelling-place of the Divine Spirit. There was 'the house not made with hands, eternal in the heavens.'

35–36. The bewilderment occasioned by the mind and teaching of Jesus is once again expressed. All that 'the Jews' can make of this 'departure' of Jesus is a physical departure to those Greek-speaking Jews of the Dispersion, and to the Greeks themselves. The saying is characteristic of the Evangelist's mind. He reads the *fact* of the preaching by the Church to Hellenist and to Hellene, back into an ironical anticipation of 'the Jews.' It is as if he would say: the Jesus who in the days of His flesh transcended the divisions of Judæa, Samaria, and Galilee, accomplished in spiritual presence with His Church an even wider liberation, an even more signal breaking down of racial barriers. What seemed so absurd to 'the Jews' was accomplished when Jesus returned to the Father.

The Last Day of the Feast

JN. 7^{37-52}

7 37 Now on the last day, the great *day* of the
feast, Jesus stood and cried, saying, If any
man thirst, let him come unto me, and
38 drink. He that believeth on me, as the
scripture hath said, out of his belly shall
39 flow rivers of living water. But this spake
he of the Spirit, which they that believed
on him were to receive: for the Spirit was
not yet *given*; because Jesus was not yet
40 glorified. *Some* of the multitude therefore,
when they heard these words, said, This is
41 of a truth the prophet. Others said, This
is the Christ. But some said, What, doth
42 the Christ come out of Galilee? Hath not
the scripture said that the Christ cometh
of the seed of David, and from Bethlehem,
43 the village where David was? So there
arose a division in the multitude because
44 of him. And some of them would have
taken him; but no man laid hands on him.
45 The officers therefore came to the chief
priests and Pharisees; and they said unto
46 them, Why did ye not bring him? The
officers answered, Never man so spake.
47 The Pharisees therefore answered them,
48 Are ye also led astray? Hath any of the
rulers believed on him, or of the Pharisees?
49 But this multitude which knoweth not the

50 law are accursed. Nicodemus saith unto
them (he that came to him before, being
51 one of them), Doth our law judge a man,
except it first hear from himself and know
52 what he doeth? They answered, and said
unto him, Art thou also of Galilee?
Search, and see that out of Galilee ariseth
no prophet.

37–38. The 'last day' of the feast was in all probability the eighth day to which reference has already been made (cf. Lev. 23^{36}). It was the 'great day,' because the closing day; perhaps also because the ritual on this day focused the whole meaning of the feast. On each day libations of water were brought from the pool of Siloam, symbolising the water given their fathers in the wilderness (Exod. 17^{6}), symbolising, also, their prayer for abundant water in the next harvest season. 'Bring the libation of water at the Feast of Tabernacles, that the showers may be blessed to thee,' it was said by one of the Rabbis. When the water was offered by the priest, the words of Is. 12^{3} were chanted: 'With joy shall ye draw water out of the wells of salvation.' This symbolism explains the teaching given in *vv.* 37 and 38. The punctuation of these verses is uncertain; but in all probability the full stop should come, not after 'and drink' at the close of *v.* 37, but after 'believeth on me' in *v.* 38. The translation then would read: 'If any man thirst, let him come unto me, and he that believeth on me let him drink. As the scripture hath said, "Out of the midst of *him* (i.e. Christ)—or out of the midst of Her (i.e. Jerusalem)—shall flow rivers of living water".' Chrysostom suggested yet another punctuation. 'We should read, "He that believeth in Me, as saith the scripture," putting the stop here; and then, "out of his belly shall flow rivers of living water": the meaning being that that was a right kind of belief, which was formed on the evidence of scripture, not of miracles.'

We cannot be quite certain as to the precise scripture the Evangelist had in mind in this reference. Probably he had many passages from the Old Testament in his thought; for example, Exod. 17^{6}, where there is the account of the water flowing from the rock; perhaps also, Is. 12^{3}, 44^{3-5}, 55^{1}, 58^{11}; perhaps also, Ezek. 47^{1}, where we read of waters issuing from the threshold of the house and coming down 'on the south of the altar'; perhaps also, Ps. $46^{4f.}$, where we read of 'a river, the streams whereof make glad the city of God, the holy place of the tabernacle of the Most High'; perhaps also, Zech. 14^{8}, where we read that 'in that day living waters shall go out from Jerusalem.' The symbolism of flowing water was very familiar to the Hebrew mind, as we saw when discussing the story of the woman of Samaria in chapter 4. There is a spiritual thirst which the Divine Spirit in Jesus can assuage. 'So then if we thirst,' as Augustine said, 'let us go not on our feet, but on our affections, not by change of place, but of love.'

If we take the R.V. translation of *v.* 38, the meaning is, that from the true believers on Jesus will issue spiritual blessings to bring refreshment to others. This is a similar thought to that expressed in 4^{14}; except that here the emphasis is on the communication to others of blessing already received. It is he who receives who can, and who must, give. We are reminded of Bunyan's lines:

There was a man, the world did think him mad,
The more he gave away, the more he had.

The living waters that flow for the healing of others do not dry up, for their source is in the Divine Life—in that 'Spiritual Rock' which is Christ, to which Paul refers in 1 Cor. 10⁴. Augustine has a beautiful comment on this passage, taking it in this sense: 'The belly of the inner man is the heart's conscience. Let him drink from that water, and his conscience is quickened and purified; he drinks in the whole fountain, nay, becomes the very fountain itself. But what is that fountain, and what is that river, which flows from the belly of the inner man? The love of his neighbour. If anyone, who drinks of the water, thinks that it is meant to satisfy himself alone, out of his belly there doth not flow living water. But if he does good to his neighbour, the stream is not dried up but flows.'

If we put a full stop after 'believeth on me,' we may *either* take the meaning to be that *Jesus Himself* is the fountain of these living waters (translating 'out of *His* belly,' that is, out of the midst of Him), *or* we may take the phrase 'out of *Her* belly,' etc., to refer metaphorically, as suggested in the above translation, to Jerusalem. The vivid word 'belly' here used means merely the *centre* or *midst*. Jersualem, for example, to the Jews was regarded as 'the navel' of the universe. In Prov. 20^{27} the word 'belly' means the seat of man's inner life: 'The spirit of man is the lamp of the Lord, Searching all the innermost parts of the belly.' The author no more meant 'belly' to be taken literally than he meant 'flesh' and 'blood' to be taken literally in chapter 6. It is his vivid way of saying: 'Out of the very centre of His being.' We have here another illustration of the Hebrew type of mind of the author, for such a mind was accustomed to make kindred references to parts of the body.[1]

39. The further comment of the Evangelist found in the 39th verse continues the same symbolism. Living water is emblematic of the Spirit. The author is looking back to the teaching of Jesus in the light of Pentecost and the growth of the Church. He knew that it was after the Passion and Resurrection that a signal outpouring of spiritual blessing had come to the followers of Jesus. The Cross and Resurrection of Jesus are His 'glorification.' The Fourth Evangelist does not, like Paul, distinguish the 'humiliation' of Christ from His 'exaltation.' To him the death and resurrection are inseparably one 'manifestation.' They are the supreme example of that principle which finds expression in 12^{23-26}. Life comes through death: so the Cross itself is Victory (12^{32-33}). The 'glorification' of Jesus is not a 'reward' given to Him for His life of suffering obedience. Such obedience is *intrinsically one* with the glorification. The Spirit comes in the path of suffering. Spiritual life flows from Him who incarnated eternal life. The gift of the Spirit comes to men, not as a magical outpouring or as a reward for correct belief or institutional obedience, but as intrinsic to the life of faith and obedience of which we are partakers in Christ. The Spirit was given to those who 'believe on him'; and, once again, it is necessary to remember that, to the Evangelist, 'belief' is not formal intellectual assent, but the whole dedication of the personality in trust and obedience to the Father whose grace and truth are incarnate in Jesus.

Jesus Himself, according to the Evangelist, had looked beyond His death to

[1] κοιλία. Burney suggests that the Greek κοιλία was due to a misunderstanding of the Aramaic, a confusion of מְעִין 'belly' (cf. Dan. 2^{32}) with מַעְיַן 'fountain.' So the translation would be: 'As the scripture hath said, Rivers shall flow forth from the *fountain* of living waters' (an allusion to Ezek. 47^{1}). Torrey also appeals to the Aramaic, rendering 'As the scripture says, *Out of the midst* of Her (i.e. Jerusalem) shall flow, etc.' (See Torrey, *op. cit.*, p. 201 and p. 323.)

an outpouring of His spirit upon His disciples (see chapters 14–17). Thus the author here expounds the later thought of Jesus when he says that 'the Spirit was not yet, for Jesus was not yet glorified.' Some early copyists thought that the phrase 'the Spirit was not yet' might be misunderstood—seeming to suggest that as yet *there did not exist* the Spirit—and so added 'given.' What, however, the author says is that the Spirit was not yet abundantly *present* or *operative*; and no intelligent reader of the Gospel in its entirety could misunderstand his meaning. In the first chapter, for example (1^{33}), we have the Baptist's words about 'the Spirit descending and abiding upon' Jesus; and the frequent references to the Spirit presuppose His existence, both in Jesus and in all the followers of the Light. The author, however, looking back through the experience of Pentecost and the later triumph of the Church, finds the supreme fulfilment of this promise of life-giving streams of water to have come later, after the 'glorification' of Jesus in death and resurrection. This was historic fact; but it is not necessary to suppose that the Evangelist attributes to Jesus a precise foreknowledge of what was to happen. Verse 39 is the author's comment and interpretation, in the light of the history of the Church as known to him; but it also expresses, in dramatic and epigrammatic form, a principle which runs through the whole teaching of Jesus.

40–44. These verses once again express the confusion and division among the hearers of Jesus. Like all the other passages in the chapter, they are to be taken as the Evangelist's pointed and dramatic way of expressing the disordered reactions of the people in Jerusalem to His whole teaching and person, and not just to a teaching given on a specific occasion. 'Some of the multitude' think Jesus to be 'the prophet' spoken of by Moses (see 1^{21} and 6^{14}); others, that He is the Messiah himself (see *v.* 26). Yet others give expression to the ironical type of rejoinder which Nathanael uses in the first chapter. How could one whose home was in Nazareth of Galilee fulfil the conditions necessarily involved in the Messiah's family and birthplace—namely, that he be 'of the seed of David' (see Ps. 89^{3-4}), and be from Bethlehem, the village of David (see Mic. 5^2 and 1 Sam. 16^1)? Once again, the Evangelist, as in *v.* 30, suggests that 'the hour' of Jesus was not yet come for His arrest. These do not *seek* to take Jesus, as in *v.* 30, but are so confused in their views that they are only *inclined* to take Him.

45–52. The closing verses give a fittingly dramatic end to the chapter. As we read these verses we seem to be in that company of priests and doctors, watching the expressions of surprise, of suspicion mingled with fear, of incredulous anger, and of vehement scorn which sweep over their Semitic faces as they confront their 'officers' and Nicodemus. A writer who can in a few lines suggest such a picture is one of the geniuses of literature. With a few sure strokes of the brush the impressionistic picture is unforgettably drawn.

The temple police referred to earlier in the chapter present their report to 'the chief priests and Pharisees.' They have not arrested Jesus, they say, because, like the Galileans of whom Mt. tells us in 7^{28-29}, they have been impressed by the authoritative nature of His teaching. The Evangelist suggests, in the reply given by the Pharisees in *vv.* 47 and 48, that it was the *officers themselves* who were impressed by the words of Jesus, and not just that they were debarred from arresting Him by the influence His message and personality were having on the people. Verse 49 suggests that the latter consideration was an additional factor; it expresses the contempt of the Rabbis for the crowd, unlearned in the Law. One of their sayings was: ‘ No rude man fears sin, and no vulgar person is pious.’ The intervention of Nicodemus has a significant fitness to the artistic and dramatic unity of the Gospel. One who belongs to the Sanhedrin itself raises his protest, but with the cautious ‘ wisdom ’ we should expect from the man portrayed in the third chapter, and referred to later in the Gospel (19^{39}). He does not plead openly for Jesus; he raises a principle of law, and suggests the illegality of their procedure. The Law itself requires that they may be impartial judges (Dt. 1^{16}), and that every report should be judicially investigated in the light of the motive which may be behind it (Exod. 23^{1}). His intervention is brushed aside with the contempt and haste which characterise those whose minds are made up before the evidence is presented. Even to suggest that the Messiah may be from Galilee is to brand the suggester with the same name of the true Jew's contempt—a ‘ Galilean.’ Messiahship to them was a matter to be decided by genealogy and by geography. The central Messianic conception of the Gospel—grounded as it is in the moral sublimity and spiritual insight of Jesus—stands confronted with the crude formalities of proof-texts, and lineage, and earthly habitation. The real evidence for Jesus's Messianic vocation, they could not, and would not, see. They could not believe that a prophet's truth rests in what he says and what he is, not in any kind of ‘ succession ’ to which he can lay claim. In their unbridled haste to give Nicodemus his *coup de grace* they suggest that no *prophet* has arisen from Galilee, forgetting such names as Jonah, Nahum, and others. The psychological insight of the Evangelist is once again evidenced.

THE WOMAN TAKEN IN ADULTERY

JN. 7^{53}–8^{1-11}

7 53 [And they went every man unto his
8 1 own house: but Jesus went unto the
2 mount of Olives. And early in the morning he came again into the temple, and all
the people came unto him; and he sat
3 down, and taught them. And the scribes
and the Pharisees bring a woman taken in
adultery; and having set her in the midst,
4 they say unto him, Master, this woman
hath been taken in adultery, in the very
5 act. Now in the law Moses commanded
us to stone such: what then sayest thou of
6 her? And this they said, tempting him,
that they might have *whereof* to accuse him.
But Jesus stooped down, and with his
7 finger wrote on the ground. But when
they continued asking him, he lifted up
himself, and said unto them, He that is
without sin among you, let him first cast a
8 stone at her. And again he stooped down,
and with his finger wrote on the ground.
9 And they, when they heard it, went out
one by one, beginning from the eldest,
even unto the last: and Jesus was left alone,
and the woman, where she was, in the
10 midst. And Jesus lifted up himself, and
said unto her, Woman, where are they?
11 did no man condemn thee? And she said,
No man, Lord. And Jesus said, Neither
do I condemn thee: go thy way; from
henceforth sin no more.]

This striking and most significant story did not form part of the original Gospel. It is not found in our oldest Greek MSS., with a single exception (Codex D). Indeed, as the late Bishop Westcott said, ‘ It is omitted by the oldest representatives of every kind of evidence ’—that is, the evidence of the versions, and of the early Fathers, as well as of the MSS. Further, both the style and the vocabulary indicate that it does not belong to this Gospel. The reader must be referred to linguistic and critical discussions for the substantiation of this statement.[1] Even the reader of the R.V. translation will, however, note differences in style and in general ' tone ' between this passage and the rest of the Gospel.

Then where, we ask, did it come from, and why was it inserted here in this Gospel? In the first place, the story was current in the third century, and in the fourth century and onwards it was inserted in different places in the Gospel, and also by some MSS. in St. Luke after chapter 21. Further, while its origin and history cannot now be traced, it was in all probability known to Papias, for Eusebius, the Church historian, speaking of Papias, says that ' he gives another story of a woman who was accused of many sins before the Lord, which is also contained in the Gospel according to the Hebrews ' (*H.E.*, iii. 39). Papias may have used this story, familiar to him and to his readers, to illustrate the passage in Jn. 8^{15}, where Jesus says: ' Ye judge after the flesh, I judge no man.' It might then have come to be regarded as belonging to this section of Jn. From being a kind of footnote, it came to be incorporated in the text of the Gospel itself. In any case, it is a very fitting comment on Jn. 8^{15}, and bears upon the face of it marks of authentic history. Many of the Fathers did not seem to like its moral very much; as it might be taken to make light of the sin of fornication. That may partly account for their refusal to regard it as genuine. Perhaps the best comment here is that of F. D. Maurice: ' I wish I were as sure that their conclusion was wrong, as that their reason for wishing the story away was unsound.'

The incident arises out of the desire of the ' Scribes and Pharisees ' to ' tempt ' Jesus. The ' Scribes and Pharisees ' are frequently referred to in the Synoptic Gospels: nowhere else in this Gospel are ' the Scribes ' referred to. Further, there are several places in the Synoptic Gospels where we read of such endeavours to put Jesus in a difficulty. Here, as in Mt. 22^{18}, they seek to impale Him upon one of the horns of a dilemma. Is the penalty of stoning, imposed for such an offence in the Law, to be meted out or not? (Cf. Dt. $22^{23f.}$.) They were not concerned with the maintenance of high moral standards when they brought the woman to Jesus: they were concerned with placing Him in what to themselves would have been a difficult position. They were very clever. Such cleverness is always discomfited by the directness of simple truthfulness. Their fine-spun webs are brushed aside. Their unworthy motives are laid bare by a simple act and by a single word. The simple act—that of stooping down and writing on the ground, as if Jesus was oblivious of the dilemma in which their cleverness was placing Him—is that of one who is *thinking* before them. There is a silence which speaks, and a quiet act which shouts aloud. The simple word is devastating in its effect—' He that is without sin among you, let him cast the first stone.'

The word is devastating because it speaks to the depth of their own natures. Sin, they know in their hearts, does not consist in the outward act, but in the inward motive and in the secret thought. Jesus had said this in Mt. 5^{28}—' I say unto you, that everyone that looketh on a woman to lust after her hath com-

[1] See especially Westcott, vol. 2, pp. 379–81; Bernard, vol. 2, pp. 715 ff.

mitted adultery with her already in his heart.' And there is that in the depth of every man which recognises its truth.

Jesus does not condemn or judge them, but makes them judge themselves. The truth itself is the judge. Jesus does not make light of sin. He treats it infinitely more seriously than they were doing—*and they know it.* So they go out, one by one.

Nor, when Jesus is confronted by the woman, does He condemn, or judge, her. Who can justly judge but God Himself, who knows every hidden motive, every conspiring circumstance, every millstone that has been hung about the necks of men and women and little children by environment and heredity? Burns had this question in his mind when he wrote:

What's done we partly may compute,
But know not what's resisted.

Browning, also, was thinking in terms of a just, ominiscient judgement, as against that of the ' vulgar mass,' when he wrote—thinking here not of the ' things done,' but the ' things undone ':

Not on the vulgar mass
Called ' work,' must sentence pass,
Things done, that took the eye and had the price;
O'er which, from level stand,
The low world laid its hand,
Found straightway to its mind, could value in a trice :

But all, the world's coarse thumb
And finger failed to plumb,
So passed in making up the main account ;
All instincts immature,
All purposes unsure,
That weighed not as his work, yet swelled the man's amount.

Thoughts hardly to be packed
Into a narrow act,
Fancies that broke through language and escaped;
All I could never be,
All, men ignored in me,
This, I was worth to God, whose wheel the pitcher shaped.

So, in refusing to condemn her, Jesus does not make light of sin. There is a judgement which springs, not from what He might have said, but from what He was. The truth in Him rebuked the lie in the Scribes and Pharisees. The purity in Him condemned the lust in her. Whittier had penetrated to the essential truth of the story when he wrote :

Thou judgest us : Thy purity
Doth all our lusts condemn ;
The love that draws us nearer Thee
Is hot with wrath to them.

'Go thy way; from henceforth sin no more.'

JESUS THE LIGHT OF THE WORLD : THE CONTROVERSY IN THE TREASURY

JN. 8^{12-20}

8 12 Again therefore Jesus spake unto them,
saying, I am the light of the world: he that
followeth me shall not walk in the dark-
13 ness, but shall have the light of life. The
Pharisees therefore said unto him, Thou
bearest witness of thyself; thy witness is
14 not true. Jesus answered and said unto
them, Even if I bear witness of myself, my
witness is true; for I know whence I came,
and whither I go; but ye know not whence
15 I come, or whither I go. Ye judge after
16 the flesh; I judge no man. Yea and if I
judge, my judgement is true; for I am not
alone, but I and the Father that sent me.
17 Yea and in your law it is written, that the
18 witness of two men is true. I am he that
beareth witness of myself, and the Father
19 that sent me beareth witness of me. They
said therefore unto him, Where is thy
Father? Jesus answered, Ye know neither
me, nor my Father: if ye knew me, ye
20 would know my Father also. These
words spake he in the treasury, as he
taught in the temple: and no man took
him; because his hour was not yet come.

This 8th chapter continues the controversies raised at the Feast of Tabernacles in the 7th chapter. The two chapters are integrally one in the thought and purpose of the Evangelist. The teaching of Jesus here, and the controversies which ensue, have *in the author's mind* as their background that same Feast. Light, like flowing water, was one of the central thoughts symbolised by the festival. The pillar of fire had, so tradition said, guided the people by night in the wilderness. This tradition was commemorated and symbolised by the lighting of four great candelabra in the Court of the Women where the Treasury was situated (*v.* 20). And it is again significant of the dramatic character of the author's mind that he gives the Treasury as the setting of this discourse: for around the court in which it stood were these large candlesticks illumining the gloom of the temple precincts at night-time. Further, the Court of the Women was the most public part of the temple. It was here, in the most frequented court, where men and women could mix, that the teaching about Jesus, the *Light* of *the World*, is given. The lights of the court suggests the figure of speech used; its publicity, the universalism of the illuminating mission of Jesus. In the Synoptic narrative (Mk. $12^{41f.}$ and Lk. 21^{1}) the sight of a poor widow placing her two mites in the treasury box had inspired one of the most penetrating messages of Jesus. It is not a mere adventitious guess to suggest that the least-fenced court of the temple indicated the unfenced nature of the message of which Jesus knew Himself to be the vehicle.

We cannot dogmatise on the question as to whether these words—'I am the light of the world'—are the precise words uttered by Jesus. On the one hand, nowhere in the Synoptic Gospels have we any record of Jesus using the familiar

'I am' of the Fourth Gospel; though His person, as there portrayed, *is* what in St. John He declares Himself to be. It is in accord with the presentation and interpretation, here suggested, of this Gospel to suppose that in these 'I am' passages the author is dramatising his insight into the religious consciousness of Jesus and His religious significance for mankind: he thus puts upon the lips of Jesus words which directly claim all this.

What matters, however, is not whether Jesus used these precise words, but whether *He was*, in the depth of His moral and spiritual consciousness, 'the light of the world'; and whether, what in His conscious relation to the Father He knew Himself to be called to be, He *really was* in the experience of men. Both these conditions were historically fulfilled.

The figure of 'the light' is one of the recurring metaphors of the Gospel. In the Prologue the eternal Word is 'the light of men,' and 'the true light which lighteth every man coming into the world' (1^4 and ^{9}); and in successive chapters the ideas associated with light are repeated. It was a metaphor familiar to Hebrew writers. 'The Lord is my light,' said the Psalmist (Ps. 27^1). 'In thy light shall we see light' (Ps. 36^9). The prophet of the Exile declared that the Servant of Jehovah would be 'a light of the Gentiles' (Is. 42^6, 49^6). The writer of *Proverbs* said: 'the path of the righteous is as the shining light, that shineth more and more unto the perfect day' (Prov. 4^{18}). And Malachi had proclaimed that 'unto you that fear my name the sun of righteousness shall arise with healing in his wings.' The figure expresses the spiritual illumination and quickening which have their source in God. Light comes to 'dissipate the clouds beneath,' to 'scatter all the night of nature,' to 'pour eyesight on our eyes.' The thoughts conveyed by the metaphor of light have inspired some of the noblest hymns of Christendom, and have been the vehicle of all true and deep religious experience.

No figure is more suitable than Light to express certain aspects of the transcendent reality of God. It does not, of course, say everything a Christian would wish to say. The word 'Father' expresses much that the word 'Light' does not say. Yet when we ponder on what light is to man, how suggestive and true to the spiritual universe is this figure. The beautiful words of Thomas Traherne in his *Centuries of Meditations* express better than any words we can find what we would wish to say. 'Place yourself therefore in the midst of the world as if you were alone, and meditate upon all the services which it doth unto you. Suppose the Sun were absent, and conceive the world to be a dungeon of darkness and death about you; you will then find his beams more delightful than the approach of Angels; and loath the abomination of that sinful blindness whereby you see not the glory of so great and bright a creature, because the air is filled with its beams. Then you will think that all its light shineth for you, and confess that God hath manifested Himself indeed, in the preparation of so divine a creature. You will abhor the madness of those who esteem a purse of gold more than it. Alas, what could a man do with a purse of gold in an everlasting dungeon?—It raiseth corn to supply you with food, it melteth waters to quench your thirst, it infuseth sense into all your members, it illuminates the world to entertain you with prospects, it surroundeth you with the beauty of hills and valleys. It moveth and laboureth night and day for your comfort and service; it sprinkleth flowers upon the ground for your pleasure; and in all these things showeth you the goodness and wisdom of a God that can make one thing so beautiful, delightful and serviceable, having ordained the same to innumerable ends.'

What this twelfth verse says, therefore—as also 9^5—is that Jesus, who is Himself dependent upon the Father for all He is and does, is the vehicle of the Father's illuminating and quickening will for the world. The Light which no one can see, has 'declared Itself' in Jesus, so that we can now see. God, who is absolute Light (1 Jn. 1^5), has so quickened and illumined the mortal Jesus that He has become the medium for Its transmission to all men. There are rays which, like the infra-red rays, and the X-rays, no human eye can detect, but which may, by suitable instruments, be made the means of photographing invisible objects. Even so, while no one can see God as He is, the Perfect Man has made Him visible.

We are reminded of the lines of Robert Southwell, the sixteenth-century English poet:

In heavenly sunne lye hidd eternall lightes,
Lightes cleere and neere, yet them no eye can see.

We are also reminded of the lines, and the profound insight revealed therein, of Cosmo Monkhouse:

How many colours do we see set,
Like rings upon God's finger? Some say three,
Some four, some six, some seven. All agree
To left of red, to right of violet,
Waits darkness deep as night and black as jet.
And so we know what Noah saw we see,
Nor less, nor more—of God's emblazonry
A shred—a sign of glory known not yet.
If red can glide to yellow, green to blue,
What joys may yet await our wider eyes
When we rewake upon a wider shore!
What deep pulsations exquisite and new!
What keener, swifter ruptures may surprise
Men born to see the rainbow and no more!

What man sees is not the criterion of *existence*, but it is the criterion of his *knowledge*. Man is not, as Protagoras said, the measure of things: he is the measure of things *as known to him*. Our knowledge of things is not the measure of Reality, for It is greater than our limited senses and faculties reveal. It is the Light which enables us to see; but what we see does not *exhaust* Reality. Nor does our capacity for seeing *create* Reality. It is Reality which has created our capacity for seeing. There would have been no eye to see unless there had first been the Creative Light which summoned it into the tension and task of evolutionary existence. All the light which flows upon our world is derived from a source beyond itself. We do not create the light, it creates us. All our systems, and creeds, and arts, and sciences, are, to use Tennyson's words,

but broken lights of Thee,
And Thou, O Lord, art more than they.

But Jesus is the truest ' image of the invisible God ' man has seen. The beautiful vesper hymn of the Eastern Church is perhaps the least inadequate comment on a verse of such transcendent suggestiveness.

Hail, gladdening Light, of His pure glory poured,
Who is the Immortal Father, Heavenly, Blest,
Holiest of Holies, Jesus Christ, our Lord.

13. The objection of the Pharisees to this claim—that it was but Jesus's own witness to Himself and, therefore, could not be depended upon—is the root objection made in every age to the claim which the moral and religious nature of man always makes. Religion, to some, is but illusion; it is that experience by which man deludes himself to the intrinsic meaninglessness of life. It is interesting to find this same fundamental objection put upon the lips of the Pharisees by the Evangelist. In this he was not only true to the historical situation, but true to the situation in every age. For there are types of so-called religious apologetic, which, distrusting the intrinsic claims of religion itself, seek to put in its place ' external evidences ' and ' institutional safeguards.' How can light convince us that it *is* light except by what it does for us? We do not demonstrate that light is light by treatises, or by analyses of its constituent rays. It is only *light* to us when it illumines and quickens us. Just as *water* is only thirst-quenching to us when we drink it, and not when we analyse it into hydrogen and oxygen; so light is only illumining when we *see* by means of it, and not when we argue about it. Anyone can, *to his own satisfaction*, confute the claim which Beauty makes, by saying, I do not see it; or the claim inherent in Goodness, by saying, I do not hear it; or the self-evidencing nature of Truth, by saying, I do not know it. But man does not *create* Goodness, or Truth, or Beauty; and to say that he cannot *see* them is to condemn himself, not them. If a blind man says he does not see the light of the sun, that is to deny, not the existence of the sun, but the fact of his own visual capacity. As the sun's rays fall upon the faces of those who see and those who do not see, so does the Light of God's presence, like the rain, fall upon all; but some affirm, and some deny. What, however, they should deny, is not that God reveals Himself, but that they do not, or will not, see.

14. Thus, the answer of Jesus, while it remains an affirmation of His own personal consciousness, points—if we may use the language of philosophy—to the objective reality whence it is derived, and to which it witnesses. This is the same affirmation as we found in 5^{31-32}. The evidence Jesus gives is His own essential nature—not quotations from the Old Testament, not demonstrative marvels. He *knows* the Father, the Source and the Goal of His life. Jesus is directing their thought, not to Himself, but to the Objective Fount of Light which has welled

up in Himself. Chrysostom interpreted this verse as indicating that Jesus implicitly claims Godhead. After quoting the words, 'even if I bear witness to myself, my witness is true,' he goes on to say: 'Surely God is a competent witness to Himself.' This interpretation is a reading of later theological ideas into the passage; it is not what the passage itself says. In the verse itself Jesus does not, as indeed He never did, equate Himself with God; but says that it is His knowledge of the Father which gives Him His certitude, and that this knowledge is itself derived from the Father.

15–18. In the following verses—very difficult for a modern reader to understand—Jesus distinguishes His way of judging from that of the Pharisees. He did not come judging by appearances, or from the letters of a book. The Pharisees searched the Scriptures to find out how and when the Messiah was to come (7^{52}). Jesus judged no man in that way; nor was He here in order to condemn. Judgement and condemnation are intrinsic to eternal life itself as the Father has revealed and quickened it in Jesus Himself. So while Jesus was not here to judge *in their way*, yet the sifting which His presence achieves among men is *just*, because it has its origin in the Father whom He knows. If, however, they *will* appeal to their Law, let them remember the legal maxim of Dt. 19^{15} (see also Dt. 17^{6} and Num. 35^{30}), to the effect that the testimony of *two* is required to establish a valid judgement. So the testimony of Jesus, while it is the testimony of His own experience, is yet also the testimony of the Father who speaks in Him and through Him. These 17th and 18th verses should be regarded as a kind of *argumentum ad hominem*. They suggest the distinction that runs through the Gospel, between God and Jesus Himself—God the Originating Father, and Jesus the receiver and medium of the Father's revelation and activity.

19–20. The 19th verse expresses the misunderstanding which, to the Johannine author, usually follows some profoundly spiritual utterance of Jesus. The Pharisees want to know *where* is His Father. Let Him define His meaning; let Him say *where* His Father dwells. The answer of Jesus sounds the depth of their crude, traditionalist and materialist notions. The Father was everywhere speaking and working; and here before them in the life and work of Jesus Himself. If they knew the Perfect Man they would know the Father; and if they knew the Father they would know Him who lived in the trust and obedience of the unique Son. This, again, to their blind minds is blasphemy. But, once again, they do not take Him, for His hour was not yet come.

The Warning of Spiritual Death

JN. 8^{21-30}

8 21 He said therefore again unto them, I go
away, and ye shall seek me, and shall die
in your sin: whither I go, ye cannot come.
22 The Jews therefore said, Will he kill himself, that he saith, Whither I go, ye cannot
23 come? And he said unto them, Ye are
from beneath; I am from above: ye are of
24 this world; I am not of this world. I said
therefore unto you, that ye shall die in
your sins: for except ye believe that I am
25 *he*, ye shall die in your sins. They said
therefore unto him, Who art thou? Jesus
said unto them, Even that which I have
also spoken unto you from the beginning.
26 I have many things to speak and to judge
concerning you: howbeit he that sent me
is true; and the things which I heard from
27 him, these speak I unto the world. They
perceived not that he spake to them of the
28 Father. Jesus therefore said, When ye

have lifted up the Son of man, then shall ye know that I am *he*, and *that* I do nothing of myself, but as the Father taught me, I
29 speak these things. And he that sent me is with me; he hath not left me alone; for I do always the things that are pleasing to
30 him. As he spake these things, many believed on him.

These profound verses develop and unfold the key thought of Jesus in this Gospel, and cannot, therefore, be understood apart from the Gospel as a whole. If anyone would understand *any* passage in this Gospel he must first grasp with the hands of his mind, or see with the eyes of his spirit, its main ideas. Apart from this appropriation, and insight, the word will be as if it had not been spoken, the light will be as if it had never shone.

The teaching here is, once again, put in dramatic dialogue form. Jesus asserts a spiritual truth (*v.* 21): 'the Jews' misunderstand (*v.* 22). Jesus further expounds His thought (*vv.* 23, 24): they remain incredulous (*v.* 25). Jesus again seeks to reveal His inmost mind (*vv.* 25–26): they still do not understand (*v.* 27). It is the conflict in every age between the things visible and the things invisible, the things physical and the things spiritual, the things temporal and the things eternal. The 'natural man' misunderstands the spiritual; the misunderstanding, when centred in the will, becomes *irritation* at the insistent assertion of spiritual reality; the irritation issues in unbridled *exasperation*; unbridled exasperation ends in determined and final *hostility*. And, finally, Jesus in a few vivid sentences sums up the whole meaning of His mission and of His person (*vv.* 25–29). Once again, we have not verbatim or chronological record, but insight into, and dramatic portraiture of, the essential mind of Jesus when confronted with those who believed not. It will be best to expound these verses in the light of their central ideas.

In the first place, there pervades the whole paragraph the thought of an impending consummation of the earthly ministry of Jesus. When He says, 'I go away' (*v.* 21), and 'when ye have lifted up the Son of man' (*v.* 28), the Evangelist is giving expression to the conviction which came to Jesus in the closing weeks of His earthly ministry that the cup of suffering and sacrifice had to be drunk by Him to the dregs; but that this earthly end would be no *final* end; it would be the accomplishment of the Father's purpose. It would indeed be a 'glorification'; a Victory, not a defeat; the Father's Goal, not the world's goal. 'The Jews' would 'lift Him up,' but this would only reveal His essential nature. The thought here is similar to that expressed in 3^{14}.

In the second place, there throbs through the passage the thought of impending 'doom' for those who are alienated from the Father, and who exemplify this separation from God by their rejection of His incarnate Word. When Jesus says: 'Ye shall seek me and die in your sin' (*v.* 21), and 'except ye believe that I am he, ye shall die in your sins' (*v.* 24), the Evangelist is giving expression to the conviction of Jesus that *sin* is alienation from God; it is blindness to truth: it is, therefore, exemplified in that attitude of bitter and blind hostility to Jesus, who knew Himself to be the vehicle of the Father's mind and will. The phrase to 'die in sin,' or 'in sins,' is twice used in this passage. There is a slight difference in the two passages, which can be brought out in English by translating the first, 'in your sin ye shall die,' and the second, 'ye shall die in your sins.'

Is the thought expressed that of physical death, or that of spiritual death? In other words, is the meaning that they will come to the end of their mortal life in a state of sin; *or* that their sin will *itself* be so deep-seated as to involve spiritual death? Perhaps both thoughts are suggested, but the *main* thought is that sin is *itself* the loss of eternal life, and issues, therefore, in spiritual death. Such an idea is expressed in the Old Testament. Ezekiel, for example, says: 'The soul that sinneth, it shall die' (Ezek. 18^4; see also Ezek. 3^{18} and 33^8). The LXX reading of Prov. 24^9 is, 'the foolish shall die in sins.' The thought of Jesus is that the issue confronting 'the Jews' is a momentous one. His sojourn among them is brief: unless, then, they will respond to the truth incarnate in Him (*v.* 24), inevitable spiritual death is the issue. Their persistent blindness to the truth expresses itself, now in bitter mockery—'will he kill himself?' (*v.* 22), that is, 'will he descend to those depths of Gehenna reserved for those who murder others and murder themselves? then indeed we cannot follow him'—now in a mere dull and determined closing of the mind (*v.* 27). In a moral universe the persistence of such an attitude of sheer negation issues in a state of final negation—the complete separation from eternal life. The barriers to life are of their own raising, and they may rise so high as to shut out every ray of the Light of Life.

In the third place, there dominates every other note in the passage the unique conscious relation of Jesus to the Father. This is expressed in the familiar language of the Gospel. Jesus is 'from above': He is 'not of this world' (*v.* 23). He is 'sent' by the Father, and He only speaks what He has 'heard' from Him (*vv.* 26–27). He does nothing of Himself; the Father who teaches Him is 'with Him,' never leaving Him alone; so all He does springs out of His desire to please the Father, never to please self (*vv.* 28–29). The earthly life of Jesus is in time; but His real life is in eternity. The fleeting life will end, but is the prelude to a 'return' to the Divine source of that eternal life which was His in the midst of time. The Cross itself is the complete manifestation of this fellowship with the Father which He knows, of this complete dependence upon Him, of this perfect fidelity to His will (*v.* 28). It will reveal, says Jesus, 'that *I am*' (not, 'that I am he'); that is, 'that my true being' is *in God.* This is the mind of Jesus about His Cross. Here, there is no doctrine of a Son placating the anger of His Father; no dogma of a separation in existence between Him who offers, and Him to whom the offering is made. The meaning of the Cross is that it is the obedient self-offering of Him who knows Himself to be in full harmony with the Father's will. It is, therefore, even more the Father's Cross than the Cross of Jesus. In other words, it is an Eternal Cross, and not just a Cross in time and place.

25. A few words must be added upon a verse which has occasioned much perplexity. The answer of Jesus in *v.* 25 to the question, 'Who art thou?' is given in the R.V. as follows: 'Even that which I have also spoken unto you from the beginning.' The Greek is difficult to translate. The R.V. margin suggests as an alternative translation: 'How is it that I even speak to you at all?' The R.V. rendering is almost certainly wrong. There is, however, an alternative to the R.V. marginal translation. The words may be rendered: 'Essentially (I am) what I am saying to you.' If we accept the R.V. marginal translation,

the meaning is that no verbal speech of Jesus will answer a question, the answer to which is given by His essential person. As in 10^{24}, they want a plain answer to a plain question. The answer of Jesus is: 'What good is it for me to speak to you in the plain way you say you desire? It would make no difference to you, for language says nothing to those who will not hear.' If we accept the other suggested rendering—namely, 'essentially (I am) what I am saying to you'—the meaning is: 'My essential person is the answer to your question.' It will thus be seen, that whatever translation be adopted, the kernel of the truth expressed is the same. It is, that spiritual reality is spiritually discerned.

Freedom Only by the Truth: the Father of Truth and the Father of Lies

JN. 8$^{31-59}$

8 31 Jesus therefore said to those Jews which
had believed him, If ye abide in my word,
32 *then* are ye truly my disciples; and ye shall
know the truth, and the truth shall make
33 you free. They answered unto him, We
be Abraham's seed, and have never yet
been in bondage to any man: how sayest
34 thou, Ye shall be made free? Jesus
answered them, Verily, verily, I say unto
you, Every one that committeth sin is the
35 bondservant of sin. And the bondservant
abideth not in the house for ever: the son
36 abideth for ever. If therefore the Son
shall make you free, ye shall be free in-
37 deed. I know that ye are Abraham's
seed; yet ye seek to kill me, because my
38 word hath not free course in you. I speak
the things which I have seen with *my*
Father: and ye also do the things which
39 ye heard from *your* father. They answered
and said unto him, Our father is Abraham.
Jesus saith unto them, If ye were Abraham's children, ye would do the works of
40 Abraham. But now ye seek to kill me, a
man that hath told you the truth, which
I heard from God: this did not Abraham.
41 Ye do the works of your father. They
said unto him, We were not born of fornication; we have one Father, *even* God.
42 Jesus said unto them, If God were your
Father, ye would love me: for I came
forth and am come from God; for neither
have I come of myself, but he sent me.
43 Why do ye not understand my speech?
Even because ye cannot hear my word.
44 Ye are of *your* father the devil, and the
lusts of your father it is your will to do.
He was a murderer from the beginning,
and stood not in the truth, because there
is no truth in him. When he speaketh a
lie, he speaketh of his own: for he is a liar,
45 and the father thereof. But because I say
46 the truth, ye believe me not. Which of
you convicteth me of sin? If I say truth,
47 why do ye not believe me? He that is of
God heareth the words of God: for this
cause ye hear *them* not, because ye are not
48 of God. The Jews answered and said
unto him, Say we not well that thou art a
49 Samaritan, and hast a devil? Jesus
answered, I have not a devil; but I honour
50 my Father, and ye dishonour me. But I
seek not mine own glory: there is one that
51 seeketh and judgeth. Verily, verily, I say
unto you, If a man keep my word, he
52 shall never see death. The Jews said unto
him, Now we know that thou hast a devil.
Abraham is dead, and the prophets; and
thou sayest, If a man keep my word, he
53 shall never taste of death. Art thou
greater than our father Abraham, which
is dead? and the prophets are dead:
54 whom makest thou thyself? Jesus answered, If I glorify myself, my glory is
nothing: it is my Father that glorifieth
me; of whom ye say, that he is your God;
55 and ye have not known him: but I know
him; and if I should say, I know him not,
I shall be like unto you, a liar: but I
56 know him, and keep his word. Your
father Abraham rejoiced to see my day;
57 and he saw it, and was glad. The Jews
therefore said unto him, Thou art not yet
fifty years old, and hast thou seen Abra-
58 ham? Jesus said unto them, Verily,
verily, I say unto you, Before Abraham
59 was, I am. They took up stones therefore
to cast at him: but Jesus hid himself, and
went out of the temple.

This long paragraph, which cannot, without breaking up the homogeneity of the thought, be split into sections, illustrates once more the author's method of presenting the mind of Jesus. He takes two central conceptions—Truth and Freedom—and unfolds the teaching of Jesus about them. In doing this, the misunderstandings of the Master's own age, of the Evangelist's age, and of every subsequent age, are expressed and answered. The answers of Jesus deepen the perplexity, for that is grounded, not in serious and anxious inquiry, but in the blind determination of the whole nature. The perplexity hardens into exasperated hostility, and then, at the end of the chapter, into open violence (*v.* 59).

The tones of Jesus seem to become severer as the chapter proceeds. Some modern Christians find difficulty here. The difficulty arises largely from a lack of historical imagination, and of psychological insight. Let us put ourselves into the mind of the author, and endeavour to feel as he feels. He is himself living in the dramatic presentation of a scene which depicts the pure, serene, assured spiritual and moral insight of Jesus confronted by an incredulity and antagonism based upon false Messianic expectations and alienation from the loving Father of men's spirits. Living himself in this presentation, He gives sharp and realistic force both to objection and to answer. The moral and spiritual issues presented are historically true: the psychological situation portrayed is no imaginative creation on the part of the author. But the whole mode of presentation is coloured by the very intensity of the author's penetration into the situation, and by his quick sympathy with the truths expressed by the lip and by the life of Jesus.

31–32. The controversy is between Jesus and ' those Jews which had believed him.' If the whole section be taken as expressive of such a controversy, it must be taken as unfolding in succinct and dramatic narrative the teaching of Jesus, by which He sought to bring such Jews to a more spiritual faith in Him. The seeming severity of the words of Jesus is not necessarily out of accord with the nature of such an audience. For, the *good* is always the enemy of the *best*; and to lead a partial, but satisfied, insight up to a complete insight is often more difficult, and requires a sharper emphasis, than to inspire faith in those dissatisfied with their unbelief.

In all ages, however, there have been commentators who have felt that the nature of the Jewish controversialists changes in the course of the paragraph. Augustine, for example, suggested that at *v.* 33 ' it was not those who believed but the unbelieving multitude that made this answer.' The reference of Jesus, again, in *v.* 37, to His questioners, as those who seek to kill Him, would seem to corroborate this suggestion. Probably we have here a case where the dramatic imagination of the author outruns his narrative. He begins this section by envisaging Jesus confronted by Jews who were partially sympathetic. They ' believed him ' (with Dative)—such a faith is not the complete acceptance expressed when the Evangelist speaks of those who ' believe *in* him ' (with εἰς and Accusative). But as the situation develops in the Evangelist's mind, the antitheses become sharper between their faith and that of Jesus—until the author envisages, not partially sympathetic, but wholly unsympathetic Jews. Doubtless also, the intensity of the Evangelist's feeling here is partly explicable by the bitter controversies between Jew and Christian which he himself had witnessed.

Jesus begins by reminding them that true discipleship consists in *abiding in*

His word: that is, not just in giving assent to occasional sayings when they can be made to accord with their own preconceived ideas, but in a continuous and harmonious assent of the whole personality to the mind of Jesus. Those who *abide in His word* have *His word abiding in them* (cf. 5^{38}). The verb ' to abide,' as used by the Evangelist, expresses continuous fellowship, as opposed to sporadic assent. Such *abiding* will lead to a knowledge of the truth which will make them free. *Truth*, to the Evangelist, is not merely intellectual: it is moral and spiritual. To know the truth is to be in harmony with God who is absolute truth, and with Jesus who is the incarnate expression of God. The phrase to a modern reader seems very abstract, and suggests just the assent of the intellect to a series of propositions which are *true*. To the author, Truth is incarnate in Jesus. In Him is revealed both the nature of God and His *will* for men. Later in the Gospel Jesus says, ' I am the truth ' (14^6). Thus, to know the truth is ' to believe in ' Jesus—to have insight into life as He reveals it, and to obey the will of God as He unfolds that will. So *Freedom* is the inseparable companion of Truth—freedom, which consists not in self-centred licence but in obedient and self-forgetful service. Self-love imprisons the soul. The love of God liberates it. His service is perfect freedom.

Truth can only prevail by suasion, never by constraint. It rules by right, not by might. It reigns; it does not tyrannise. It is as a monarch in a democratic state; never as a dictator in a totalitarian state.

33. Once again, the moral and spiritual nature of Christ's teaching is misunderstood. In this case it is political, racial, and religious pride which begets their perverse misunderstanding. Are they not of the seed of Abraham? Their chosen and privileged race, they say, has never been in bondage. Such an assertion on their part, at first sight, at least, seems a statement contrary to historical fact; for the fathers were in bondage to the Egyptians, to the Babylonians, to the Persians under Antiochus Epiphanes, and, in the time of our Lord, to the Romans. What, however, they mean is that they have always as a people preserved inviolate their proud national and religious consciousness. If they have had to acknowledge the rule of conquerors, they have never accepted such dominion *in their hearts*. Thus, they resent the suggestion that there is any freedom which they have still to win. Their protest is that of those who, by protesting too much, reveal a subconscious awareness that their boasted freedom of race was delusive. Those who ' protest to much ' have not serenity of inward and assured conviction.

34–38. The answer of Jesus points to the essential character of freedom. Rousseau began his epoch-making book, *The Social Contract*, with the words: ' Man was born free, and everywhere he is in chains.' The whole question is: What is the nature of these bonds? The answer of Jesus is that the loss of freedom is evidenced, not by political fetters, but by moral fetters. To commit sin is to become ' the bond-servant ' of sin. The connexion in thought between the 34th, the 35th, and the 36th verses is not easy at first to perceive: it has the elusiveness that often characterises a deeply spiritual narrative. The connexion seems to be here. To sin is to become a slave of sin—where ' sin ' is almost personified as a despotic master. The author's thought, however, is not bound to this figure. He at once goes on to think of this state of servitude, not in reference to that which *causes it*, but in reference to the privileges of which it deprives us. So he thinks of slavery to sin as slavery in a household where we are meant to have the freedom of sons. 'The bond-servant abideth not in the house for ever; the Son abideth for ever.' Our suggestion here is that 'the son' in *v.* 35 has the same meaning as in *v.* 36; and not, as in the R.V., where it is taken to refer in the first case to *any* son, but in the second case to Jesus Himself. The natural interpretation is to take 'the Son' in each case as referring to Jesus. The meaning, therefore, is as follows. Jesus, whose life is one of perfect fellowship with the Father, has complete security in the Father's house—in contrast to the slave whose place is for ever insecure. Jesus, who is Himself 'the truth,' is the mediator of that moral and spiritual truth which will make the slave to be as a son. The unique Son would have His brethren to be also sons in the household of God.

Jesus goes on to acknowledge their racial descent from Abraham. But 'sonship,' in His sense, is constituted, not by physical ancestry, but by kinship of mind and heart with the unique Son. Him they are seeking to kill, thereby revealing that His word makes no progress in them. This shows that the 'father' of their household is not the Father whom Jesus knows. (We take the R.V. translation here, and not that of the R.V. margin.)

38–42. From the 38th verse onwards the narrative develops the contrast of 'the two fathers.' The Jews maintain, again with a perverse misunderstanding, their physical descent from Abraham. Jesus replies that inasmuch as they have not the mind and will of Abraham they are not his spiritual children. Abraham, the father of the faithful, was a lover of God. How could they be *his* children when they wanted to kill Jesus, *a man* who had unique fellowship with the Father? It will be noted that *v.* 40 is the only place in the New Testament where Jesus is described, baldly, as 'a man.' This frank confession of the humanity of Jesus comes more naturally from our first-century Evangelist than from a second-century writer.

Their deeds, says Jesus, show who their real 'father' is. They cannot attribute the paternity of evil purposes to one like Abraham. At this point, they claim that God is their Father (*v.* 41). They are still perversely thinking in terms of racial heritage, not of spiritual kinship. God, they say, is their Father because they 'were not born of fornication.' The thought here may possibly be that of literal bastardom, and it is conceivable that the words, in that case, contain a satirical allusion to slanderous stories about the birth of Jesus. Origen suggested that their reply shows that they were 'bitterly insinuating that our Saviour was the offspring of adultery.' Probably, however, the main thought is metaphorical: that is, their allegiance to Jehovah was unsullied by idolatrous practices, like, for example, that of the Samaritans (see 4^{18}, also 8^{48}). In any case, they do not understand that to Jesus 'Sonship' consists in spiritual likeness to God, not in having racial prerogatives. Jesus does not condemn their assumption of the name Father; indeed, it was His mission to reveal the Father. What He *does* condemn is their wrong notion of what constitutes sonship. Sonship is ethical and spiritual harmony with God. As Augustine put it, commenting on this passage: 'When does God become anyone's Father except when he keeps His commandments?' No one is a son of God because he can claim saints and seers for his 'fathers.' There is only one test of spiritual succession, and that is spiritual likeness. So Jesus goes on to say that if they were the children of God they would love the unique Son, who knows Himself sent to do the Father's will.

43–44*a*. They hear the speech of Jesus, but they do not understand it, because they cannot hear His 'word.' It is one thing to hear a man's utterance: it is another thing to appropriate his thought. Jesus was the expressed thought of God, and so is called God's Word. His own expressed thought is also called here His 'word,' as distinct from His verbal speech. The paternity of their murderous thoughts can only be 'the devil,' for he has been a murderer 'from the beginning.' A real effort of mind is called for, on the part of the reader, if he would not misunderstand this 44th verse. What Jesus is saying is *not* that there has been a kind of second God *from the beginning*, a Manichæan Evil Power always existing side by side with the Good Power. That this is not what Jesus means—or what the Evangelist means Him to say—is obvious from the words which follow—'he stood not in the truth.' Truth existed prior to the Liar. Life existed prior to the Murderer. Here Jesus teaches, therefore, no fundamental dualism. What He says is that in human history there has been from the beginnings of our human story a self-seeking, murderous, lying will in man. The symbolical story of the Fall in Genesis, and of Cain and Abel (see 1 Jn. 3^{12}), may have been in the Evangelist's thought when these words were written. Lies belong to the same family as the lie that deceived Eve in the Garden. Murderous thoughts are of the lineage of the dark deed of Cain when he killed Abel. But we can only *lie* when there is a truth to deny; and we can only *murder* when there is a life to kill. All truth and life are from God—not from the Devil. The difference between the good and the bad is not a difference in their creative origin. It is a difference in their personal will. If we may use a figure used by Origen in commenting on this passage, a *bad eye* is not different *in kind* from a *good eye*: the difference is that one sees rightly and one sees wrongly. Augustine put the truth this way: 'the Jews were children of the devil by imitation, not by birth.'

This passage is of the very highest significance for the understanding both of the mind of Jesus and of the mind of the author. The teaching is not concerned with the speculative problem of metaphysical origin. It is concrete, not abstract. It is expressed in terms of psychological and historical fact. *They* are 'of their father the devil' who have murderous, lying thoughts. The very preposition used—'*out of* the devil'—is also used of true sonship to the Father. Jesus is the true Son, '*out of* the above' (8^{23}), because He does the Father's will, and has the Father's mind. We too shall be 'sons,' 'out of' the Father, when we have His mind and do His will (8^{47}). To be 'of the devil' is to manifest a spirit of evil; to be 'of the world' is to manifest the spirit that finds satisfaction in the temporal and physical. To be 'of the Father' is to manifest the Divine 'glory,' the grace and truth which have their source in God. The contrast is not, to the author, one of 'metaphysical origin'; it is one of 'nature.' And a man's 'nature' was what he *revealed* in his life. These differences of 'nature' lead back, of course, to metaphysical questions of origin and source; but in these passages the author's thought is centred upon *experienced fact.*

44*b*–47. The second part of *v.* 44 can be translated in two ways—either as in the R.V., or as in the R.V. margin. The reference, that is, may be either to 'the devil' or to 'a man.' In the first case, the meaning is: 'When the *devil* speaketh a lie he speaketh what belongs to his own nature; for he is a liar and the father of the lie.' In the second case, the meaning is: 'When *a man* speaketh a lie he speaketh out of his own nature, for his father also is a liar.' The former is more harmonious with the context. As for Jesus Himself, He speaks the truth; that is why they do not believe Him. Truth is congenial to the truthful. As for themselves, not one of them has accused Him of sin. Then why, if He speaks the truth, do they not believe Him? The only possible answer is that they are not 'of God.'

48–50. To this 'the Jews' reply that Jesus was but proving what they had been thinking about Him—namely, that He was 'a Samaritan,' and mad. The Samaritan was regarded by the Jew as a despised foe. When, therefore, they called Jesus 'a Samaritan' they meant a bitter taunt. He had been called mad—possessed by a demon—before (7^{20}), and was called so again (10^{20}). The point of inconvenient home-truths is often turned aside by irony and taunt—as here. In His reply Jesus ignores their taunt; but with complete serenity reminds them that to honour God is not a sign of madness. He it is who has the right to pronounce judgement.

51–55. The words 'verily, verily' in this Gospel either introduce a new thought, or summarise the previous thought. The verses beginning at *v.* 51 clinch the teaching of Jesus in the whole paragraph. To keep His 'word' is to participate in the life that is eternal; for to keep His 'word' is to have His mind, and to do as He does. 'Heaven and earth shall pass away,' said Jesus, in one of His sayings recorded in the Synoptic Gospels, 'but my *words* (λόγοι) shall not pass away' (Mt. 24^{35}; Mk. 13^{31}; Lk. 21^{33}). The 'words' of Jesus are the Truth of which He is the incarnate expression. They, therefore, endure when all things visible, like the unsubstantial pageant, vanish, and leave not a wrack behind. So here, in this Johannine saying, whoever has the 'word' of Jesus partakes of His own eternity: 'he shall never see death.' Such a life is itself eternal, and is exempted from the frustration and termination for which 'death' stands. Such a concept of eternity meets with derisive misunderstanding. 'The Jews' can understand the life that is lived *in years*, but not the life that is lived *in deeds*: the life that is measured by the beats of a clock, but not that valued in terms of heart-beats. Was not Abraham himself dead? and the Prophets also? To talk of a life transcending death was another sign of madness to them. Again Jesus, as in the 49th verse, leads their thought, in His reply, to the Eternal Father whom He knows, and whom they know not. This passage reminds us of the Synoptic saying of Jesus, that 'God is not the God of the dead, but of the living' (Mt. 22^{32}; Mk. 12^{27}; Lk. 20^{38}). To know the Father is to partake of this Eternal Life.

56–57. In the 56th verse Jesus goes back to the thought of Abraham whom they have called their father, and with whose 'greatness' they wish Him to compare His own. Abraham had *longed* to see His day, and he saw it and was glad. The Greek verb in the text, which means 'rejoiced' or 'exulted,' is found in an unusual construction; and it has been suggested that a wrong meaning was given in the Greek to the Aramaic word employed, and that the latter means 'longed' or 'prayed.'[1] The meaning is that Abraham had longed for the assurance of a day when in his seed all the families of the earth should be blessed; and that with the vision of faith he had *seen* that day with gladness of heart (Gen. 12^{3}). The same thought is expressed in Heb. 11^{17}, where we read that Abraham 'had gladly received the promises.' Jesus here says that the day of fulfilment of that hope of blessing to *all* the families of the earth is 'His day': that is, He is here with spiritual blessing which transcends all divisions of race and time.

Again 'the Jews' perversely misunderstand. How can one not yet fifty years old say he has been 'seen' by Abraham?[2] The reference to 'fifty years old' is a reminder that Jesus had not yet reached the climax of His complete manhood (see Num. 4^{3}). It may also have been the source of an early tradition in the Church to the effect that Jesus was between forty and fifty at the Passion, a tradition which was said to have had its origin in St. John. Chrysostom had read 'forty' instead of 'fifty'; but this, no doubt, represented an endeavour on his part to reconcile the text with the tradition that Jesus was about thirty years of age when He entered upon His public ministry (Lk. 3^{23}).

58–59. The answer of Jesus, summing up in one dramatic sentence a consciousness and a sense of mission transcending the limitations of time and place, is introduced by the significant words, 'Verily, verily.' The words do not mean that Jesus claimed a *memory* of an existence *prior* to Abraham. He was truly man, and did not come into the world with a memory of a pre-temporal life. So to think, would make a riddle of Jesus, and, instead of enhancing His Glory, would detract from it. It would also destroy the whole truth of *the Incarnation.* For that doctrine does not say that Jesus was God, but that He was 'God manifest in the flesh.' The Apollinarian heresy denied that Jesus had a human spirit, maintaining that this was replaced in Him by the Divine Logos. Such a view of the person of Jesus is not only based upon a misreading and misunderstanding of the Gospel records, but presents us with no *real* Incarnation. Instead of being able to see God revealed in perfect humanity, we should be seeing 'the union of a maimed or mutilated humanity with the divine'; and the result would be, as the late John Caird pointed out, that in Jesus we should have 'a divine nature in union with the nature of an animal.'[3] What the words of Jesus mean is that He had a life transcending the categories of space and time. He knew the Father in a fellowship of unique intimacy: He obeyed the Father with the filial devotion as of any only son. This was true life, eternal life. Jesus does not say, 'Before Abraham was, *I was*,' but, '*I am*.' The whole emphasis is on life in its essential, eternal quality. This is a life, not of greater duration than the years

[1] Burney, *op cit.*, p. iii. Torrey translates 'prayed.'
[2] Codex Siniaticus, the uncorrected text of Codex Vaticanus, and the Sinai Palimpsest read: 'hath Abraham seen thee?' This is probably the correct text.
[3] *Fundamental Ideas of Christianity*, vol. 2, pp. 155–6.

which have elapsed since Abraham, but a life qualitatively different from all existence which is measured in years. This is a life that partakes of the essential life of God Himself. For He, Jehovah, is 'I am that I am' (Exod. 3^{14}). Jesus, His incarnate Word, manifested that eternal life in the midst of time. The Grace and Truth incarnated in Jesus is not a creation in time. It belongs to eternity. It is older than the foundations of the earth, and newer than the green shoot now pushing its way through the soil. It was both Original and original. It is at the origin of the universe, in God. It gives its originality to every new splendour of beauty, truth, and goodness in each successive age. In Jesus this life was perfectly manifest. His originality consisted in His unique incarnation of the Original Word. This is the message of the Historic Incarnation

To these Jews this claim is blasphemy. It is not, as so many commentators maintain, that they had now understood Him: it is that they *have now finally misunderstood Him.* In this they have not been alone.

They would stone Him, but He eludes their unbridled fury and passes out of the temple. As Gregory beautifully points the moral: 'The truth flies the company of an unhumbled soul.'

THE 'SIGN' OF THE MAN BORN BLIND: AND THE RESULTING CONTROVERSY

The Healing

JN. 9^{1-12}

9 1 And as he passed by, he saw a man
2 blind from his birth. And his disciples
asked him, saying, Rabbi, who did sin,
this man, or his parents, that he should be
3 born blind? Jesus answered, Neither did
this man sin, nor his parents: but that the
works of God should be made manifest in
4 him. We must work the works of him
that sent me, while it is day: the night
5 cometh, when no man can work. When
I am in the world, I am the light of the
6 world. When he had thus spoken, he
spat on the ground, and made clay of the
spittle, and anointed his eyes with the
7 clay, and said unto him, Go, wash in the
pool of Siloam (which is by interpretation,
Sent). He went away therefore, and
8 washed, and came seeing. The neighbours therefore, and they which saw him
aforetime, that he was a beggar, said, Is
9 not this he that sat and begged? Others
said, It is he: others said, No, but he is like
10 him. He said, I am *he*. They said
therefore unto him, How then were thine
11 eyes opened? He answered, The man
that is called Jesus made clay, and
anointed mine eyes, and said unto me, Go
to Siloam, and wash: so I went away and
12 washed, and I received sight. And they
said unto him, Where is he? He saith, I
know not.

Those who accept the general standpoint from which this commentary is written will feel it unnecessary to fit this narrative, with the teaching and controversy arising, into a chronological scheme. The Evangelist does not tell us, for example, whether he wishes the reader to regard this incident in association with the Feast of Tabernacles—which seems to cover chapters 7 and 8—or whether he wishes us to regard it in association with the Feast of the Dedication referred to in 10^{22}. Endeavours, based upon no MS. evidence, have been made to rearrange sections of chapters 9 and 10, in order to present a more harmonious continuity in the narrative. Here we take the chapters as we find them.

We are not, of course, to suppose that this incident is meant by the Evangelist to follow immediately upon the violent ending of the 8th chapter. His mind moves from that atmosphere of storm to one of calm. Yet this story of the healing of the man born blind is—when we remember the nature of the Evangelist's mind —in natural and fitting sequence to the discourse of Jesus which began with the announcement, 'I am the light of the world': a discourse, further, which ended in an expression of violent hostility on the part of 'the Jews.' This chapter focuses that teaching in a graphically told incident; the incident itself giving rise to another of those controversies on the mind and mission of Jesus which pervade this whole section of the Gospel.

The incident is found only in this Gospel, but it is permissible to believe that the author is using some historical tradition, as a narrative framework, for the fuller presentation of the mind of Jesus. He is not, that is, inventing a story. With the freedom of the dramatic artist, he is using, and adapting, an authentic tradition in order to set forth in vivid light the issues involved between Jesus and the authorities in Jerusalem—issues which reach their climax in the story of the Crucifixion. We may not dogmatise on the question as to what in the story is precise history, and what is parabolic representation. But, once again, the *main* interest of the Evangelist is to portray the mind of Jesus. The two features of this story which afford him the background for this portrayal are: first, the fact that the healing was *on the sabbath*, and, secondly, the fact that it was concerned with *sight*. The first raises once more the issue as to the person of one who could break the Sabbath law. The second leads to a further unfolding of the mind of Jesus on spiritual blindness and spiritual sight.

1–2. The incident is introduced by a question on the part of the disciples which shows that the great philosophical questions of the schools arise out of the questions which every thinking man cannot but ask. The metaphysician's task is really only to try to answer the questions of simple, thoughtful men. Here, then, is a man born blind. *Why* should this be? That is the question. It is the same question as the writer of the Book of Job sought to confront in his dramatic poem; the same question which writers of all ages and races and creeds have asked. The *form* of the question, as the disciples put it here, is interesting and suggestive. Is it the man's own sin, or his parents' sin, which has caused his blindness? To them, that is, there seemed only one kind of answer to the problem of pain and suffering—namely, that *sin* is responsible. They left the question open as to *whose* sin was responsible, but not the question as to the causality of *sin itself*. The suggestion implicit in their question—that the sin of the man himself may have been the cause—seems to involve that they thought he could have sinned prior to birth. Thus, the alternative would be: *either* that the sin was committed in his mother's womb, *or* in a previous state of existence. It is doubtful, however, whether either of these ideas was really harboured by the disciples of Jesus; though it has been pointed out that some of the Rabbis had discussed the first possibility, and that, at least in later Judaism (see *Wis.* 8^{20}), the belief in the pre-existence of souls had been held. Origen, the Christian theologian, had firmly maintained, it will be remembered, this latter belief; and the Eastern doctrine of Karma and Transmigration has been felt by a very large section of the human race to give an answer to the riddle of human suffering.

Some in our own times have felt that the doctrine of *eternal life* requires some kind of doctrine of a pre-incarnate individual life. Wordsworth expressed some such belief.

Our birth is but a sleep and a forgetting:
The Soul that rises with us, our life's Star,
Hath had elsewhere its setting,
And cometh from afar:
Not in entire forgetfulness,
And not in utter nakedness,
But trailing clouds of glory do we come
From God who is our home.

Probably, however, the disciples when they asked the question did not envisage very clearly the alternatives involved. That suffering was *retributive*, they believed, like the friends of Job; and that the iniquity of the fathers is visited upon the children, they also believed (see Exod. 20^{5}).

3–5. Jesus does not answer this speculative problem, though we know from the Synoptic record that He firmly repudiated the idea that all human suffering and natural calamity was directly retributive—as witness Lk. 13^{2-4}. He here directs the thoughts of the disciples away from a metaphysical question to the man before them, and to the light *for the present guidance of life* which will flow from the cure to be performed. Jesus confronted life as He found it, believing at all times in the Father without whom no sparrow falls to the ground; believing, also, in the Father whose 'glory' He was here to reveal. His was the faith which both *accepted* and *combated*. He accepted with patient endurance His own sufferings, believing that they were the Father's will for Him, and that they would be fruitful for the blessing of the race. He *accepted*, also, the fall of the sparrow, and such natural calamities as the fall of the tower of Siloam. But He also was ever active in combating evils. So, after saying that this blindness is to be an *occasion* for the manifestation of the Divine purpose, He goes on to say in the 4th verse that He Himself is the vehicle of this Divine activity. While Jesus saw all things *in the light of eternity*, He knew that He was *in time* to reveal the purpose of eternity. He did not, that is, acquiesce in inevitable destiny, or in a universe statically preordained. He Himself *worked* to reveal the purpose of eternity.

He *must* work the works of the Father: the sense of mission and of dependence throbbing through these words is true to the whole consciousness of Jesus as revealed in the Fourth Gospel. This sense of mission is conjoined here with a sense of urgency and of impending consummation. It is still day, but the night is fast approaching in which no man can work. 'Man goeth forth to his work until the evening,' said the Psalmist (Ps. 104^{23}). While He is still in the world the day endures, for He Himself is here as its illuminant. The 'day-time' is whatever time wherein we work the works of the Father. The Evangelist is thus here giving us another glimpse into the inmost mind of our Lord as He began to confront His coming sufferings.

6–7. The use of spittle in the cure reminds us of an ancient, widespread belief in its healing potency. Fasting saliva was held to be especially efficacious in cases of eye-trouble. Both Suetonius (*Vespas.* 7) and Tacitus (*Hist.* iv. 8) tell us how Vespasian used it in restoring sight to a blind man. On a marble tablet at the temple of Asclepius on the island in the Tiber at Rome there is the following second-century inscription: 'To Valerius Aper, a blind soldier, the god revealed that he should go and take blood of a white cock, together with honey, and rub them into an eye-salve and anoint his eyes three days. And he received his sight, and came and gave thanks publicly to his god.' Mark records an instance of the use of spittle by Jesus in the case of another blind man (8^{23}); and also of its use in the case of a man suffering from deafness and an impediment of speech (7^{33}). The question which a modern man asks here is this: Did Jesus Himself regard the spittle as a means to the cure, or did He merely employ a familiar agency in order to awaken the faith of the blind man? The answer is, We do not know. It is perhaps significant that physical means were employed. We are only beginning to explore the inter-relation of the physical and the spiritual, and only beginning to confront a *Uni*verse, where Faith and Science are not opposed, but where Faith has its scientific means, and Science has its foundation in Faith.

The pool of Siloam has often been interpreted in an allegorical sense. The name is derived from a Hebrew verb (שׁלח) meaning *to send.* The pool was so named because its waters were 'conducted' thither by an aqueduct from the Fountain of the Virgin. Isaiah refers to 'the waters of Siloam which go softly' (8^{6}) as a symbol of the Divine guidance and nourishment of Israel, in contrast to the waters of Euphrates, which symbolise the earthly power of Assyria. It is indisputable that there is allegory in this Gospel; but it is a difficult question to decide in each specific case what precisely is allegory and what precisely is historical event. It has been suggested by commentators, from Chrysostom downwards, that the name symbolises Christ Himself, who was 'sent' of God (6^{29}). Others, who regard this Gospel as an 'ecclesiastical' document, written in the interest of a *high*—or *low*, according to the point of view—sacramental practice and belief, see here an analogy to Christian baptism. They suggest that Jesus's insistence upon 'washing' is the Evangelist's way of saying that the rite of baptism is necessary for the perfecting of the healing and illuminating work of Christ. It is, so the suggestion runs, by the sacramental washing that man's spiritual blindness is taken away and that he enters upon the new life of faith. This interpretation of the incident we regard as fanciful, and as based upon a fundamental misconception of the author's mind and purpose. The idea that outward washing is indispensable to spiritual illumination is an importation of ideas into a Gospel which is essentially at variance with them.

It is interesting to remember that such a 'sacramental' interpretation of this 'washing' has been frequent from Augustine downwards. He, for example, writing of this incident, said: 'The man did not see immediately he was anointed; that is, was, as it were, only made a catechumen. But he was sent to the pool which is called Siloam, that is, he was baptised in Christ, and then he was enlightened.'

It is better to take this narrative as enshrining a historical incident. The pool of Siloam was a well-known pool in Jerusalem, south of the temple area, lying at the mouth of the Tyropœon Valley (see Neh. 3^{15}); and it is possible that the Evangelist, having written ' Siloam,' remembered both its etymological meaning and its use by Isaiah in 8^{6}. *He himself*, if he wrote his Gospel in Greek, may have added for his Greek-speaking readers the explanatory note, ' which is by interpretation Sent.' If, however, the Gospel was originally written in Aramaic, this note would be added by the translator.

The remainder of the incident is graphically told, and hardly requires comment. They are the words of a dramatic artist, not of a systematic metaphysician. The Evangelist, it is clear, knows how to tell a story.

The Controversy between the Healed Man and the Pharisees

JN. 9^{13-34}

9 13 They bring to the Pharisees him that
14 aforetime was blind. Now it was the
sabbath on the day when Jesus made the
15 clay, and opened his eyes. Again therefore the Pharisees also asked him how he
received his sight. And he said unto
them, He put clay upon mine eyes, and I
16 washed, and do see. Some therefore of
the Pharisees said, This man is not from
God, because he keepeth not the sabbath.
But others said, How can a man that is a
sinner do such signs? And there was a
17 division among them. They say therefore
unto the blind man again, What sayest
thou of him, in that he opened thine eyes?
18 And he said, He is a prophet. The Jews
therefore did not believe concerning him,
that he had been blind, and had received
his sight, until they called the parents of
19 him that had received his sight, and asked
them, saying, Is this your son, who ye say
was born blind? how then doth he now
20 see? His parents answered and said, We
know that this is our son, and that he was
21 born blind: but how he now seeth, we
know not; or who opened his eyes, we
know not: ask him; he is of age; he shall
22 speak for himself. These things said his
parents, because they feared the Jews: for
the Jews had agreed already, that if any
man should confess him *to be* Christ, he
should be put out of the synagogue.
23 Therefore said his parents, He is of age;
24 ask him. So they called a second time
the man that was blind, and said unto
him, Give glory to God: we know that this
25 man is a sinner. He therefore answered,
Whether he be a sinner, I know not: one
thing I know, that, whereas I was blind,
26 now I see. They said therefore unto him,
What did he to thee? how opened he
27 thine eyes? He answered them, I told
you even now, and ye did not hear:
wherefore would ye hear it again? would
28 ye also become his disciples? And they
reviled him, and said, Thou art his dis-
29 ciple; but we are disciples of Moses. We
know that God hath spoken unto Moses:
but as for this man, we know not whence
30 he is. The man answered and said unto
them, Why, herein is the marvel, that ye
know not whence he is, and *yet* he opened
31 mine eyes. We know that God heareth
not sinners: but if any man be a worshipper of God, and do his will, him he
32 heareth. Since the world began it was
never heard that any one opened the eyes
33 of a man born blind. If this man were
34 not from God, he could do nothing. They
answered and said unto him, Thou wast
altogether born in sins, and dost thou
teach us? And they cast him out.

This healing, like that of Bethesda recorded in chapter 5, takes place on the Sabbath. It is for this reason that the author records it. He does not let us forget the two main issues which divided Jesus and the religious authorities—the attitude to the Law, and the claim to unique and eternal knowledge of God. The author knew what he wanted to say: it is for that reason that his Gospel is an artistic and dramatic unity. These pages were not ' random recollections.' The Evangelist selects his incidents, and presents them in his own free and dramatic fashion. Likewise, he chooses the main features of the teaching of Jesus, presenting them against the background of beliefs and opinions to which it is opposed.

As in the case of the Bethesda healing, therefore, this incident is the basis for a controversy; and the controversy leads up to a claim to unique Sonship by Jesus. The actors in this dramatic scene are: first, the healed man and 'the Pharisees'; later, 'the Jews' and the parents of the man. The controversy is *about* Jesus, but He Himself is not present—another illustration of the dramatic power of the author. Jesus is the invisible mind which dominates the situation.

The play and interplay of the divergent motives of different minds give striking realism to the scene. On the one hand, 'the Pharisees' are portrayed as blindly preoccupied with a point of law; but 'others' find it difficult to evade the facts. These latter reveal that rare type of mind which is willing to examine traditional beliefs in the light of present experience (*v.* 16). Thus, the Pharisees themselves are divided.

'The Jews' are introduced in *v.* 18, and the term, as usual in the Gospel, indicates the whole hostile section of the people. They begin by denying the fact; but when this attitude becomes impossible, through the testimony of 'the parents' and of the man himself, they achieve a psychological *tour de force*: 'give glory to God,' they say to the man; 'we know that this man is a sinner' (*v.* 24). In the interests of their presupposition, the fact is denied until it is shown to be undeniable: it is then *verbally* accepted, but without being permitted to assail the same presupposition. Their self-complacency is preserved at the expense of their intellectual integrity. But when the man himself, in his direct simplicity, presses home the fact of his cure upon their presupposition, they lose their self-control and *cast him out* from the place of their meeting (*v.* 34). They do not 'excommunicate' the man, for only the Sanhedrin could do that. The man's parents had been afraid of such an issue for their son, for they had heard that anyone confessing Jesus to be Messiah should be 'excommunicate.' The Greek word (ἀποσυνάγωγος), so translated, is only found in the New Testament in this Gospel—here at 9^{22}, at 12^{42}, and at 16^{2}.

The attitude of the healed man is presented with sure psychological insight. His first word about Jesus to the Pharisees is that He is 'a prophet' (*v.* 17), a confession similar to that of the Samaritan woman in 4^{19}. When confronted with the traditional beliefs of 'the Jews,' he stands firmly on the ground of personal experience. Let them *explain* the fact as best they can; he *knows* it. But when they become irritated at his obstinacy, he becomes more persistent and confident. He gains in clearness and conviction as they lose in assurance. As falsehood makes them weak, so truth makes him strong. He indulges in irony at their expense. Their weakness disguises itself in a cloak of scornful disdain. Finally, their disdain is exasperated to the point of fury. There is only one thing left for them to do: they use force—thereby revealing their final weakness. This has been a common way of dealing with minorities which had truth on their side. It was the way by which they afterwards dealt with Jesus. Those who cannot be answered must at least be silenced. Light, however, does not cease to shine because men deny it; nor does the tide cease to flow at their command.

The Result and Meaning of the Sign: Faith in the Son of Man

JN. 9^{35-41}

9 35 Jesus heard that they had cast him out;
and finding him, he said, Dost thou
36 believe on the Son of God? He answered
and said, And who is he, Lord, that I may
37 believe on him? Jesus said unto him,
Thou hast both seen him, and he it is that
38 speaketh with thee. And he said, Lord, I
39 believe. And he worshipped him. And
Jesus said, For judgement came I into this
world, that they which see not may see;
and that they which see may become
40 blind. Those of the Pharisees which were
with him heard these things, and said
41 unto him, Are we also blind? Jesus said
unto them, If ye were blind, ye would
have no sin: but now ye say, We see:
your sin remaineth.

35–38. In this final paragraph the Evangelist seeks to show how a true faith in Jesus is reached by this man; and contrasts it with the blindness of some of the Pharisees. These verses contain the underlying motif of the story. What the author is concerned to say is that Jesus is the bringer of spiritual life to those who have eyes to see.

On the one hand is a sincere, but somewhat perplexed, man. He had called Jesus 'a prophet' (*v.* 17). Personal experience had given him assurance and courage to confront traditional orthodoxy. It remains for the Evangelist to portray the final stage in his progress to discipleship. Jesus, hearing that he has been cast out, finds him. It is worth being cast out by falsehood to be found by the truth. The question asked by Jesus is, 'Dost thou believe in the *Son of Man*'?—for this title, and not 'Son of God,' is found in the best MSS. The man seems to be puzzled by the title, as were the people referred to later in 12^{34}. Jesus in His answer claims the title for Himself. The man confesses, both in word and act, that he believes in Jesus. This is not the 'faith' of those who say 'Lord, Lord,' with the lip, or with the speculative intellect, and deny that Lordship in the life. It is a 'faith' which *worships*: that is, it is the devotion and dedication of the whole being to the grace and truth incarnate in Jesus. The eyes of his spiritual nature are now open.

39–41. On the other hand are the Pharisees whose spiritual blindness remains. When Jesus is here presented as saying, 'For judgement came I into this world,' the question naturally arises: How can this be reconciled with such utterances of Jesus in this Gospel to the effect that He Himself does not judge, or condemn (8^{15}, etc.)? In the story of the woman taken in adultery Jesus does not judge in words, but His pure presence is itself the inexorable judge. This is the meaning of this 39th verse. Jesus is not before them with any *motive* of judging them: yet He knows that His very presence among men divided them. The Greek word (κρίμα) used here means the *result* of the *act of judging* (which latter is κρίσις). The presence of Him who is incarnate Truth separates the true from the false. Those who love the truth, even if they are in darkness, come to it and are made to see. They are 'the babes' of whom Jesus speaks in Lk. 10^{21} and Mt. 11^{25}. Those who pride themselves on their traditional wisdom, shun the light when it shines upon them in their own day. They know so much that they have nothing more to know. The last word of God, they think, has been said, and His last deed done. They cannot see, when they *will* not to see: they cannot hear, when they *will* not to hear.

The petulant remonstrance of ' some of the Pharisees who were with him ' is that they certainly are not among the blind. Jesus takes them at their word, and presses home the lesson of the responsibility which privilege confers. Here He neither asserts nor denies their blindness. Their condemnation comes from their own claim. They are witnesses against themselves. If they had not the capacity to see the light, their blindness would not be sin. But inasmuch as they claim the ability to see, and yet deny the light before them, their sin *abides.* Their blindness is a *moral* blindness, for which they are themselves responsible. Such sin is intrinsic to the nature. Unlike the sins of ignorance, or of circumstance, it has an *enduring* quality. It was of such sin that Jesus spoke His solemn words on the ' eternal sin ' against the Holy Spirit which hath never forgiveness (Mk. $3^{28, 29}$).

THE ALLEGORY OF THE GOOD SHEPHERD: AND THE CONTROVERSY AT THE FEAST OF DEDICATION

The Good Shepherd and the False Shepherds

JN. 10^{1-21}

10 1 Verily, verily, I say unto you, He that
entereth not by the door into the fold of
the sheep, but climbeth up some other
way, the same is a thief and a robber.
2 But he that entereth in by the door is the
3 shepherd of the sheep. To him the
porter openeth; and the sheep hear his
voice: and he calleth his own sheep by
4 name, and leadeth them out. When he
hath put forth all his own, he goeth
before them, and the sheep follow him:
5 for they know his voice. And a stranger
will they not follow, but will flee from
him: for they know not the voice of
6 strangers. This parable spake Jesus
unto them: but they understood not what
things they were which he spake unto
them.
7 Jesus therefore said unto them again,
Verily, verily, I say unto you, I am the
8 door of the sheep. All that came before
me are thieves and robbers: but the sheep
9 did not hear them. I am the door: by
me if any man enter in, he shall be
saved, and shall go in and go out, and
10 shall find pasture. The thief cometh
not, but that he may steal, and kill, and
destroy: I came that they may have life,
11 and may have *it* abundantly. I am the
good shepherd: the good shepherd layeth
12 down his life for the sheep. He that is a
hireling, and not a shepherd, whose own
the sheep are not, beholdeth the wolf
coming, and leaveth the sheep, and
fleeth, and the wolf snatcheth them, and
13 scattereth *them*: *he fleeth* because he is a
hireling, and careth not for the sheep.
14 I am the good shepherd; and I know
15 mine own, and mine own know me, even
as the Father knoweth me, and I know
the Father; and I lay down my life for
16 the sheep. And other sheep I have,
which are not of this fold: them also I
must bring, and they shall hear my
voice; and they shall become one flock,
17 one shepherd. Therefore doth the
Father love me, because I lay down my
18 life, that I may take it again. No one
taketh it away from me, but I lay it
down of myself. I have power to lay it
down, and I have power to take it again.
This commandment received I from my
Father.
19 There arose a division again among
20 the Jews because of these words. And
many of them said, He hath a devil, and
21 is mad; why hear ye him? Others said,
These are not the sayings of one possessed
with a devil. Can a devil open the eyes
of the blind?

The chapter-division here may mislead the reader into thinking that the Evangelist is giving an entirely new address of Jesus. These verses, on the contrary, are regarded by him as continuing the words spoken to the Pharisees at the close of chapter 9. They are connected with it, and arise directly out of it. The suggestion has been made that *vv.* 19–29 of the 10th chapter should be transposed, in the interest of sequence, so as to follow immediately upon 9^{41}. Such a transposition, however, is unnecessary, for there is a very fitting sequence in the order of the Gospel as we have it: nor is there any MS. evidence for the change.

At the close of the 9th chapter Jesus has been speaking to the leaders of the religious life of Israel, the Pharisees. Their mission, as they themselves would claim, was to be the guide of the thought and practice of the people. Those who claim to guide others must themselves be able to see clearly. This, as Jesus had said, was what they could not do. They were ' blind guides.'

It is out of this thought that this teaching of Him who is the true Shepherd of the sheep takes its natural and fitting rise. Once again, we are not to think of these words as the verbatim report of one address of Jesus, nor that the ideas which it contains were expressed in one precise form or on one specific occasion. What the author is doing is to set forth, in his own way, some essential elements in the teaching and conscious mission of Jesus, against the background of the opposed and opposing teaching of some of the Pharisaic guides.

The teaching is in the form of allegory. The word translated ' parable ' in *v.* 6 (παροιμία) is not the word so translated in the Synoptic Gospels, and should not be used here. A parable is a story. This is not a story, but rather an extended and amplified metaphor. There are no ' parables ' in the Fourth Gospel. Instead, we find in this Gospel allegories of the Good Shepherd and the Door, of the Bread, of the Light, and of the Vine. The same metaphor of the shepherd is found in the Synoptic Gospels, but there it is found in parabolic context. In Mt. 18^{12-13} and Lk. 15^{4-6} there is the parable of the shepherd who leaves the ninety-nine sheep within the fold to go out and find the one lost sheep. And in Mt. 15^{24} Jesus had said that He was not sent but unto the lost sheep of the house of Israel. When Jesus looked on the multitudes He had compassion on them, for they were to Him as sheep without a shepherd (Mk. 6^{34}; Mt. 9^{36}). These passages from the Synoptic Gospels show that such a metaphor had been often employed by Jesus. Even so, it is to the Fourth Evangelist that we owe its *extended* use in this allegorical form.

The main difference between the Synoptic and the Johannine presentation of the teaching on the Shepherd is that, in the former, the emphasis is on the poor, blind *sheep* who need such a shepherd as Jesus knows Himself to be: and, in the latter, the emphasis is on the blind hireling *shepherds* whose concern is not really for the sheep—the sheep that need such a shepherd as He knows Himself to be. Some interpreters have magnified the differences between the emphasis in the Synoptic Gospels and the emphasis in St. John—holding, for example, that the teaching in the latter lacks the comprehensive charity of that in the former. The difference in presentation is, however, naturally explicable if we remember that the same metaphor can be used by the same teacher in different contexts, and with different audiences in mind. When Jesus is confronting the needs of the weary and wandering sons of men, He thinks of His own mission to lead them to a safe fold. When He is confronting the blind, and interested, self-sufficiency of traditional teachers of religion, He thinks of the qualities which belong to the true, disinterested shepherd who, if needs be, will give his life for the sheep. The contrast, that is, requires no laboured and fanciful exegesis; but arises as naturally as it is psychologically and historically explicable. To see in the Johannine use of the metaphor a narrow polemic dating from the second century, and constructed in the interests of an exclusive ecclesiastical fold, or of a theologically elect, is a perverse misunderstanding of a passage which carries on the face of it its own essential meaning.

The metaphor is one that was congenial to the Hebrew religious mind. How more naturally would a pastoral people express religious thought? Abraham, Moses, and David were shepherds. When men speak of God, they use the language of their own interests and occupations. How else can they speak of Him but in such figures. The symbols used by the Prophets are borrowed from the conditions and circumstances of their lives, coloured and controlled by their moral and spiritual insight. To the Hebrews God is the rock that shelters and defends, the light that illumines, the voice that speaks His word, the wisdom that maketh wise, the shepherd who leads and tends his sheep. 'The Lord is my shepherd,' said the Psalmist (23^1). God is 'the shepherd of Israel' (Ps. 80^1). When the prophet of the Exile wished to speak of the Divine care of the nation, he used some of the most beautiful words ever written: 'He shall feed his flock like a shepherd: he shall gather his lambs in his arms, and carry them in his bosom; and shall gently lead those that are with young'—words which received from Handel a musical setting as beautiful as themselves.

The Old Testament, also, has many references to false shepherds, who have not the real interests of the sheep at heart. Ezekiel, for example, said: 'Thus saith the Lord God; Woe unto the shepherds of Israel that do feed themselves! Should not the shepherds feed the sheep? Ye eat the fat, and ye clothe you with the wool, ye kill the fatlings; but ye feed not the sheep' (34^{2-3}). Zechariah said: 'Woe to the worthless shepherd that leaveth the flock! The sword shall be upon his arm, and upon his right eye; his arm shall be clean dried up, and his right eye shall be utterly darkened' (11^{17}). Here it is significant to note that a characteristic of the 'worthless shepherd' is his blindness—the very combination of figures attributed in this Johannine passage to these Pharisees.

The figure, then, would come naturally to the mind of Jesus: and the Old Testament itself reveals the same variety of usage as is found in the Synoptic and Johannine Gospels. He had often, no doubt, in His journeyings through Galilee, Samaria, and Judæa, witnessed such scenes as are here so graphically allegorised—the sheepfold with its doorkeeper who opens the door for the shepherd; the sheep that are known individually, and by name, to the shepherd whose voice alone they will obey; the robber who climbs into the fold when he cannot gain entrance by the door. All this is a realistic transcript from pastoral life.

The metaphor is here used with complete freedom. In some of the verses Jesus is the shepherd; in others He is the door that leads into the sheepfold. As *the shepherd*, He is contrasted with the hirelings: as *the door*, He is contrasted with the 'other ways' by which the robbers seek entrance to the fold. Some interpreters suggest that the two figures were used on separate occasions by Jesus, and that they are here woven into one discourse by the Evangelist. Probably, however, the figures were *often* used by Jesus in such a context as this; it is not, therefore, necessary to suppose that *two* addresses are woven into one, but rather that a whole body of the Master's teaching and emphasis is concentrated into this passage.

1–6. The 9th chapter had closed with the solemn words of Jesus to the religious leaders of the Jews, who were 'blind.' The words, 'Verily, verily,' which open this chapter, are the grave prelude to a discourse which sets forth the issue in unmistakable outlines. This is characteristic of the author's way of presenting the mind of Jesus. The issue involved is amplified here by the use of allegory. Here is a sheepfold, with its open courtyard, into which entrance is gained by a door: behind it is the building where the sheep are kept at night. The shepherd will always enter by the door, which will be opened for him by the doorkeeper: the robber will climb over the encircling wall. The sheep recognise the voice of their own shepherd, and each flock will follow him alone whose voice is known. The shepherd knows his sheep one by one, and each knows him.

This allegory, says the Evangelist in *v.* 6, is not understood. Such misunderstanding is the mark of the type of mind represented by these hearers. They are familiar with the figure as employed in sacred texts; but they never see the meaning of the texts they quote. Such worship a dead word and deny the living voice. The implications and applications of sacred Scriptures are not inquired into. Is it not enough that here is an infallible word? Theirs was the subtlest and surest of all forms of atheism: they do not dream that He who once spoke can speak to-day.

7–18. The meaning of the allegory is now expounded. In the first part of the passage Jesus says that He is 'the door of the sheep.' The function of a door is to permit entrance and exit. It is the way to security and to rest: it is also the way to the freedom of 'fresh woods and pastures new.' Both these thoughts are emphasised in the 9th verse. The first thought is familiar to the reader of the Synoptic Gospels. Jesus had used beautiful words of invitation: 'Come unto me all ye that are heavy laden and I will give you rest' (Mt. 11^{28}); and later in this Gospel He tells His disciples that His own peace He gives to them (14^{27}). He also says: 'I am the way' (14^{6}). What, therefore, in the first place, the figure of the door means is that Jesus knew Himself to be a minister of spiritual strength and security to men. He had said, in 7^{37}, 'If any man thirst, let him *come unto me*, and drink.' He would be familiar with the beautiful figure in Isaiah 32^{2}: 'A man shall be as a hiding place from the wind, and a covert from the tempest.' The Psalmist had regarded God as his 'hiding place' (32^{7} and 119^{114}). Hosea had spoken of 'a door of hope' (2^{15}). It is not necessary, therefore, with so many commentators, to regard this figure as an importation into this Gospel of later rigid ecclesiastical views. The figure is coherent with the mind of Jesus as it is known to us: esoteric ecclesiastical ideas were absent, we are convinced, from His mind, and from that of the Fourth Evangelist. Jesus knew Himself to be the minister of eternal life to man—as man.

The second thought suggested by the figure of the door is that of *the way to liberty.* The 'sheep go in *and go out*' to find pasture. Again, it is true to the mind and mission of Jesus to say that He regarded Himself as the way that *leads to life.* In the Synoptic Gospels (Mt. 7^{13}; Lk. 13^{24}) there is a saying of Jesus in which He speaks of the 'narrow door' which leads to the full life of the Kingdom. The life of 'the Kingdom' in the Synoptic Gospels is the 'eternal life' of the Fourth Gospel. Jesus is the *way* to that life. If the 'door' is 'narrow,' the 'life' to which it leads is not. The few who find that door enter thereby to the life that is life indeed. Such a life, of which Jesus is the mediator, is not a life of acquiescence and repose: it is a life of freedom and adventure. His followers have to walk as well as to rest; but in their journey they will have 'the light of life' to guide them. A fold is good for security, but too much security is worse than too little. A fold that is never opened will become a cemetery; as a mind that never adventures into the wide universe which environs us will speedily decay and die. The truly 'dark' ages of humanity are the ages when men timidly acquiesce in what the past has to tell them. The ages of light are the ages when men accept the light of the past to guide their steps into the unknown future. Too much we think of the Church of Christ as a door to safety; and too little as a gateway to adventurous life. Too much we teach men to depend upon others; and too little do we see that the mission of Jesus was to lead men to that true independence of spirit where obedience springs out of personal vision. It is not surprising that Jesus came into collision with the ecclesiastical authorities, and institutions, of His day.

8. In the 8th verse Jesus is contrasted with those teachers and leaders of the people whose chief concern was to get, and not to give. These are 'thieves and robbers,' because they have not come in the name and in the spirit of which He was the incarnate expression. He was come to minister life: all who sought to serve themselves were as those who came to steal. These had come 'before' Jesus, in the sense that they *obscured* the spirit which was in Him. We must not read this 8th verse apart from the whole context of the thought. Jesus does not say that He is the *only* teacher. What He *does* say is that a teaching which is not inspired by the spirit of which He is the incarnate manifestation is not an imparting, but a robbing. In the Prologue we read that the Word had lightened every many coming into the world. The passage before us has to be interpreted as meaning, therefore, that all who have not been illumined by the spirit which He incarnated were as those who would serve themselves and not the sheep. They do not enter by the door of service or of truth, but climb over by the way of self-interest or of traditional privilege. Theirs is the method of compulsion, not of invitation. Their entrance is by stealth, not by open approach.

The voice of these, Jesus adds, the sheep do not hear. This is a difficult saying. For in every age the sheep seem to be beguiled by the wolf in sheep's clothing. Yet while this is so, such a thief has his day. The minds of men can be exploited for a time by those who wish to *use* them, and not to *serve* them. But there is a deep instinct in humanity which recognises the voice of the true shepherd. A dog may be allured, and betrayed, by the thief's offer of poisoned food; yet, it knows that the voice is not that of its master. The ways, then, of craft or of violence are in the long run self-defeating. This is the message of the Cross.

10. The contrast between Jesus and the false teachers is continued in the following verses. The false teachers are represented under the figure of 'thieves,' or 'hirelings'; but Jesus is now regarded as 'the good shepherd' who comes to give the abundant life. The one figure merges naturally and inevitably into the other. Jesus is both door and shepherd. It has been pointed out that in the Sahidic version 'shepherd' was substituted for 'door' in *v.* 7; and Dr. Torrey has noted that 'in the Aramaic language the two words resemble each other so closely that they might easily be confused in a connext permitting either, and in which both have already been used.' The same Aramaic student makes the suggestion that 'this error caused the insertion of *v.* 9, without which the designation of Jesus as the *door* would remain without illustration or other support.'[1] The suggestion is ingenious—probably too ingenious. In view of the absence of external evidence for the suggestion that *v.* 9 is a later addition to the text, it is much better to leave the passage as it has come down to us. And it is psychologically quite natural to have the two figures side by side. 'It cannot be too strongly insisted upon,' said the late Dr. R. H. Kennett, in *The Church of Israel* (p. 155), 'that a Hebrew attached no importance to consistency of metaphor, and as a matter of fact, so as to yield perfect sense, could blend together figures in a way which to our more prosaic minds is almost grotesque.'

There is no suggestion in *v.* 10 of an elect few on whom it was the mission of Jesus to bestow this abundant life. He is here to give to all who will receive. Nothing would be farther from the thought of Jesus, whether in these verses or anywhere else in the four Gospels, than the idea that outside an institution there is no salvation. The test of one's Christianity is the life manifested. This life is no narrow, or negative, way of living. It is life to the full, where every faculty is properly employed in the rich comprehensiveness of developed personality. The contrast is not between one institution and another, but between the true teacher and the false teacher. The true teacher wishes to *elicit* the full individual life of his pupils: the false teacher to *impose* his own opinions. The latter is a 'thief' of personality, for his chief concern is for the aggrandisement of personal or institutional prestige.

11–13. In these verses the contrast between the 'shepherd' and the 'hirelings' is seen in the spirit which they manifest. The hireling cares chiefly for his pay. His motive is narrow self-interest. He will do for the sheep what he *must* do in order to earn his pay; but that is all. Such, however, is not real work, but, as Carlyle would say, a mere quackery. It fails at the test of danger. There are hirelings in all walks of life. In the realm of Art they prostitute the creative impulse to profit and popular applause. In the realm of Religion they stifle the heavenly voice at the call of expediency or of fear. No true service is ever rewarded from without: its real reward is intrinsic to itself. The servant finds joy in service, not in the applause of others. All true work is its own gain. Such a worker, believing that he exists to serve a higher purpose than his own, forgets himself and the dangers which encompass him. The hireling, believing that the sheep exist for him, and not he for the sheep, seeks to save his own skin when his flock is in peril. The good shepherd's sole concern is for the flock: he will

[1] *The Four Gospels: A New Translation*, pp. 207 and 324.

surrender his own life in their interest. He 'fears' God—and no one, and nothing, else.

14–15. Here, again, the thought is expressed that the Shepherd knows the sheep, and the sheep know the Shepherd. It is not necessary to read into these verses a claim on the part of Jesus to a 'supernatural' knowledge of those who are 'elect.' Jesus knows 'His own,' as every lover of truth *knows* the lovers of truth. Truth penetrates all disguises. Those who serve the interest of time rather than the interests of eternity, sooner or later expose themselves. They may deceive themselves, but not Him who is incarnate love and truth. Further, fellowship always involves *mutual* recognition. *His own,* also, *know Him*: that is, within the depths of a true man's nature there is response to the truth. This mutual knowledge, which existed between Jesus and His true friends—such a one as the perplexed man who had been made to see—is akin to the fellowship which Jesus has with the Father. It is as if He would say to us, that every fellowship of the lovers of truth, of goodness, and of beauty, has its reality and ground in the very nature of God. The perfect lover of men knows the perfect love of the Father. 'We know,' says our author in his first Epistle, 'that we have passed from death unto life because we love the brethren' (3^{14}). The unique Son had this knowledge in a unique degree. This mutual knowledge of the Son and the Father is expressed in the Synoptic Gospels in the famous Q passage in Mt. 11^{25-27} and Lk. 10^{21-22}: and is to be interpreted as a real moral and spiritual fellowship uniting Jesus to the Father. The speculative, or metaphysical, interpretation of this came later. This complete dedication of Jesus to the will of the Father led Him in the end to the Cross itself. Thus, He laid down His life for the sheep. In treading the road which ended on Calvary, He who knew Himself as a unique Son was completely at one with the Father's own nature and will. In giving His life for the sheep, He was but manifesting in time the self-giving of God from all eternity. The 'at-onement' which Jesus Himself knew, He wanted all His brethren to know: and when they *know* it, there is a real 'at-onement'—but not before.

From the earliest times Christian art has represented the Good Shepherd in association with a sacrificing death. In the catacombs of Rome during the second and third centuries, rude drawings of the Shepherd who gave His life for the sheep were made. Matthew Arnold's sonnet gives fitting expression to the inwardness of the situation:

The infant Church! of love she felt the tide
Stream on her from her Lord's yet recent grave.
And then she smiled; and in the Catacombs,
With eye suffused but heart inspired true,
On those walls subterranean, where she hid
Her head 'mid ignominy, death, and tombs,
She her Good Shepherd's hasty image drew—
And on His shoulders, not a lamb, a kid.

16–19. The thought of Jesus here, once more transcends the particularity of any specific 'fold.' There are in the world many 'folds,' but the 'one flock' will come from many different 'folds.' There was a Jewish fold, and many of the Jewish leaders of the time regarded it as a very exclusive fold. To belong to it, one had to belong to a chosen race, or else to conform to specific rites. In the Apostolic age—as we know from the *Acts of the Apostles* and the Epistles of St. Paul—there was a very great danger that the Christian flock should be required to belong first of all to this Jewish fold. Through the insight, and courage, of St. Paul this danger was averted. The danger, however, was not overcome—as the history of the Church abundantly shows. Greater concern has often been manifested for the 'one fold,' of which Jesus never speaks, than for the 'one flock,' of which He does speak. Unity has been thought of in terms of privilege, of order, of succession, of creed, instead of in terms of insight and fellowship and obedience to the Shepherd—instead of, that is, in terms of *life*. Man builds a fold; but God makes a flock. The ideal of Christian unity to be striven after is that of the flock, and not that of the fold. It is of the utmost importance, if we would understand the mind of Jesus, and the mind of this spiritual Evangelist, to note the difference between the 'flock' and the 'fold.' The distinction is clear in the Greek; and is accurately reproduced in such a version as the Sinaitic Syriac MS.[1] George Matheson had drunk deeply of the teaching of Jesus here when he wrote:

Gather us in: we worship only Thee:
In varied names we stretch a common hand;
In diverse forms a common soul we see;
In many ships we seek one spirit-land:
Gather us in.

Thine is the mystic light great India craves,
Thine is the Persian's sin-destroying beam,
Thine is the Buddhist's rest from tossing waves,
Thine is the empire of vast China's dream;
Gather us in.

Some seek a Father in the heavens above,
Some ask a human image to adore,
Some crave a spirit vast as life and love:
Within Thy mansions we have all and more;
Gather us in.

The Shepherd of such a flock is He who gives His life for them. That is why the Father was completely satisfied with the Son (*v.* 17). He was perfectly satisfied because the Son was doing what was always in the Father's own heart and mind. In this passage there is no thought of the Son placating the Father's 'wrath.' The Father 'loves' Jesus, because He is doing what it is of the Father's own essential nature to be always doing. It is a *voluntary* act, but it is a voluntary act of *obedience* to the Father. The only act that has within it *eternal* freedom is that

[1] See *Light on the Four Gospels from the Sinai Palimpsest.* Smith and Lewis, p. 158.

which is inspired by obedience to a Purpose and a Will transcending our own. All else partakes of the licence of mistaken self-interest.

19–21. This section of the chapter ends with the customary statement of the conflicting views occasioned by the teaching of Jesus; and reminds us of 7^{43} and 9^{16}.

The Controversy at the Feast of Dedication

JN. 10^{22-42}

10 22 And it was the feast of the dedication
23 at Jerusalem: it was winter; and Jesus
was walking in the temple in Solomon's
24 porch. The Jews therefore came round
about him, and said unto him, How long
dost thou hold us in suspense? If thou
25 art the Christ, tell us plainly. Jesus
answered them, I told you, and ye
believe not: the works that I do in my
Father's name, these bear witness of me.
26 But ye believe not, because ye are not of
27 my sheep. My sheep hear my voice, and
28 I know them, and they follow me: and I
give unto them eternal life; and they
shall never perish, and no one shall
29 snatch them out of my hand. My
Father, which hath given *them* unto me,
is greater than all; and no one is able to
30 snatch *them* out of the Father's hand. I
31 and the Father are one. The Jews took
32 up stones again to stone him. Jesus
answered them, Many good works have
I shewed you from the Father; for which
33 of those works do ye stone me? The
Jews answered him, For a good work we
stone thee not, but for blasphemy; and
because that thou, being a man, makest
34 thyself God. Jesus answered them, Is it
not written in your law, I said, Ye are
35 gods? If he called them gods, unto
whom the word of God came (and the
36 scripture cannot be broken), say ye of
him, whom the Father sanctified and
sent into the world, Thou blasphemest;
37 because I said, I am *the* Son of God? If
I do not the works of my Father, believe
38 me not. But if I do them, though ye
believe not me, believe the works: that
ye may know and understand that the
Father is in me, and I in the Father.
39 They sought again to take him: and he
went forth out of their hand.
40 And he went away again beyond
Jordan into the place where John was at
the first baptizing; and there he abode.
41 And many came unto him; and they said,
John indeed did no sign: but all things
whatsoever John spake of this man were
42 true. And many believed on him there.

Every careful reader of the Gospel will feel that in this passage one of the dramatic climaxes of the Gospel is reached. Discourse after discourse of Jesus has been given, all with a view to presenting His inmost thought, His essential claims, His imperious sense of mission. In each case misunderstanding and hostility have resulted. Here a final statement is given; and a last appeal made to the Jews. Thereafter the drama moves to its inevitable end. The misunderstandings are complete: the hostility is final. Nothing remains but the final withdrawal from Jerusalem, and the final return.

22–23. The Evangelist begins the passage: 'Now (δέ) it was the Feast of Dedication in Jerusalem.' The R.V. marginal translation, 'At that time' (τότε), suggests a close connexion with the preceding passage. Probably, the translation suggested in the text is truer to what the Evangelist wrote and thought. Some of the MSS. support one translation, some the other. It has been clear throughout that the Evangelist is not concerned with precise chronology. What he wishes now to do is to associate this final appeal of Jesus to the Jews with another of the Jewish feasts; and, this time, with a feast which took place in the depth of winter. It was the *winter* of the misunderstanding and hostility which Jesus encountered. This was the last feast prior to the Passover Feast in the spring which was to see His death; and it is exceedingly probable that Jesus had on this occasion taught in Jerusalem, and that the final issues between Himself and the religious rulers had then been revealed in sharp and unmistakable outline. Nevertheless, there is symbolism as well as history in the narrative. This is seen in the reference to 'winter.' The author, that is, does not merely refer to the season of the year. His readers—at least many of them—would know without being told, that the feast of Dedication took place in the winter: just as a European would know without being told that Christmas falls in winter. A suggestive interpreter of this Gospel—the late Dr. E. A. Abbott—says, speaking of this passage: 'The language may be, as it were, sympathetic with the subject. The Gospel has recently introduced (Jn. 8[12]) the subject of the revelation of Christ as the Light of the world, and the Evangelist may wish to suggest to his readers that the Light is fast sinking towards the horizon, at least for those unbelieving Jews who regard Him as a blasphemer.'[1] Gregory the Great put it thus: 'The season of cold was in keeping with the cold malicious hearts of the Jews.'

The feast of the Dedication commemorated the Maccabean restoration of the services of the Temple in 165 B.C. after its three years' profanation by Antiochus Epiphanes. The history of the festival is found in the *First Book of the Maccabees* in the 4th chapter, and in the *Antiquities* of Josephus (XII, vii. 7). Beginning on the 25th of December, the Feast lasted for eight days. It was called 'the Feast of Lights,' perhaps because of the light and liberty that followed the Persian domination. Lamps were lit at this festival, as at that of the Tabernacles: they would symbolise the rejoicing associated with the rededication it commemorated.

The Evangelist here associates it with a final rejection of Him who was come to bring light and liberty to the people. The teaching of Jesus is given under the shelter of Solomon's porch (see Acts 3[11] and 5[12]). The Evangelist himself had probably known this porch, and had himself, as we suggest, companied with Jesus during these last months in Jerusalem. Looking back over the long vista of the years, he remembers that the Temple which was now a ruin was then the scene of an encounter between His Lord and the religious rulers of the Jews—an encounter which decided the final action that was to follow a few months later.

24–25. 'The Jews' ask what is, seemingly, a straightforward question, to which a plain answer is demanded. Does Jesus claim to be Messiah? Let Him answer Yes, or No. He has been saying all kinds of things to them about His mission—that He was Water, Light, Bread, Shepherd, Son of Man. All these statements have, seemingly, said nothing to them. He had been living before them: this also has, seemingly, said nothing to them. Will their mental 'suspense,' then, be ended if they receive the 'plain' answer they want? 'Plain' questions of this nature are never 'plain.' Every teacher knows that before he answers a question he must first know what the question means. No one can answer a man's *question* till he understands a man's *meaning*. The same question may mean a thousand different things on the lips of a thousand different questioners. If a man says he believes in God, we are not told much unless he goes on to say what kind of a God he believes in. Terse and definite answers are possible—and indeed desirable—to certain kinds of questions; in, for example,

[1] *The Fourfold Gospel*, p. 131.

the realm of the outward facts of life. But in the realm of unseen, spiritual realities it is often not possible to be concise without being blind and narrow. The more completely honest a teacher is, the more he will refuse to take refuge in misleading affirmations or negations. F. D. Maurice found it almost impossible to give a direct answer to a question. 'Shall we know each other hereafter?' asked an eager lady of him. 'How little do we know each other now,' was the reply. Direct answers to direct questions can be honestly given, where no ambiguity is possible. But there are times when the direct answer would make confusion worse confounded. This is evidenced in certain theological definitions, which not only imprison spiritual experience in dogmatic statements, but, under their capacious canopy, shelter heterogeneous and contradictory conceptions.

The question that really matters about Jesus is not whether or no, or at what precise time in His ministry, He claimed to be Messiah. The important question is the nature of His consciousness, and the character of His mission as He Himself conceived it? This involves the question as to the motive and manner by which He sought to achieve that mission. To such questions this whole Gospel is the Evangelist's answer. He is seeking throughout to give as 'plain' an answer as he can to the question here put into the mouth of 'the Jews.' But he does not deceive himself into thinking that his presentation of the mind of Jesus will *coerce* the belief of those who will read what he writes. Certitude will not come to his readers by assenting even to his own insight; but only as the truth, known and experienced by himself, quickens into personal insight their own fully integrated minds.

Everything Jesus had been saying to these blind and hostile hearers has shown that His view of God was not theirs: and that His conception of life and of religion was poles asunder from that which they held. What, therefore, they had *in their mind* had been as completely answered as it could be answered. Know a man's values and you know the man. Discover the springs of his inward and outward life, and he is revealed more completely than in a thousand autobiographical statements, carefully prepared with future readers in mind.

Thus the answer of Jesus is neither Yes, nor No. This refusal is in accord with all we know of His mind. He did not seek to 'define' truth: He lived it. He never harboured the thought that assent to concise definition was the way to life. So, instead, He points them to what He has already been telling them, by lip and by life. The secret of His life was the knowledge of the Father. So harmonious is His mind with that of the Father that His own works are never His own; they are the Father's works (*v.* 37).

26–27. Jesus cannot *compel* them to see this—as no one can be *compelled* to see the spiritual sublimity of this Gospel. A dogmatic declaration would not make it 'evident' to them. They cannot see by proxy. Certitude in spiritual matters is not gained by resting upon what anyone else says: it is only gained by personal spiritual discernment. The one possible conclusion, therefore, to be derived from their failure to see is that they lack spiritual vision. To use the figure which Jesus has been employing, they 'are not of his sheep.' A sheep that does not recognise the voice of a shepherd makes it plain that it does not belong to his flock. If men say they do not perceive the beauty of a sunrise, they are not condemning the sunrise: they are condemning themselves. This 26th verse strikes one of the recurring notes of this Gospel. It was struck resoundingly in the Nicodemus narrative, and can be heard in every chapter that follows—by those who have ears to hear. It is mere blindness to the meaning of this Gospel to say that this verse teaches a doctrine of a privileged elect. Augustine gave the lead to this type of interpretation of the Gospel: this can be said, while remembering the profound spiritual insight which at other times, and in other places, he revealed. This was, for example, his comment on this 26th verse: 'He saw that they were persons predestinated to eternal death, and not those for whom He had bought eternal life, at the price of His blood.' On the contrary, this Gospel *does* teach on every page the necessity of spiritual discernment. The central message of this Gospel is that Eternity is revealed in time, God in man. But a 'revelation' presupposes not only a Revealer, not only a medium through which the Revelation is given; but also, one who can *see* what is revealed. This vision is not a magical, or esoteric, impartation to an elect few; it is the prerogative of all who will respond to, and follow, the truth as it is revealed to them. Such are 'his sheep,' made known to Jesus in their attitude to Him. They demonstrate the fact that they are His sheep by following Him.

This whole emphasis is in completest accord with the teaching of Jesus in the Synoptic Gospels. Jesus came not to call the righteous, but sinners to repentance (Mt. 9^{13}; Mk. 2^{17}: Lk. 5^{32}). The 'righteous' Pharisee is contrasted with the 'unrighteous' Publican. *The first*, in the estimation of 'the world,' are *the last* in eternity. It is a *narrow gate* that leads to life, and few there be that find it: but the gate is narrow, and the entrants are few, not because of an inscrutable Divine decree, but because it is a *moral and spiritual way* that leads to this life.

28–29. Those who follow Him become partakers of that eternal life which is perfectly manifest in Himself. This is a life, not subject to physical dissolution; and not at the mercy of the violent hands of robbers. His sheep are compassed about by enemies; but the Good Shepherd brings to them a life which is stronger than death and circumstance. This 28th verse has often in the past given rise to theological discussions on the question of 'the final perseverance of the saints.' Such interpretations move on a speculative plane of thought which is not that of this Gospel. What Jesus here says is that He knows it to be His mission to bring eternal life to men. No one shall *forcibly* take from them this life. He does not say that 'no one *can* snatch,' but that 'no one *shall* snatch' them from His hand. As far as *His* care is concerned, it will not be found wanting. He is a Shepherd who neither slumbers nor sleeps. But this is not to say that a sheep may not wander, or may not one day listen to the defrauding and enticing voice of the robber. It is here that the figure of 'the sheep' breaks down—as every figure of speech breaks down if pressed into realms of thought for which it was not intended. Man is more than a sheep. He is a rational and moral being. There is no compulsion even in the solicitude of the Good Shepherd.

The 29th verse can be translated and understood in different ways, according to which of the textual variants is accepted. The best MSS. should be thus translated: 'that which my Father hath given me is greater than all.' The meaning, in this case, will be that the life of eternity, which is the Father's gift to Jesus, is 'greater' than every potency of earth: no one can snatch this away, for it is 'in the hand of the Father'—it is, indeed, of His own very Being. Such an interpretation of this translation is in accord with the whole thought of the Gospel, and is preferable to another which has often been offered—namely, that it is 'the Church' which is here referred to. Bishop Westcott interpreted the passage in this latter sense: 'the faithful regarded in their unity, as a complete body are stronger than every opposing body'—so he paraphrased the clause; but this does not harmonise with the rest of the passage, nor, indeed, with the rest of the Gospel. The translation of the R.V. is based upon other Greek MSS.; and the meaning, in such case, would be that the *Father Himself* is greater than all things. Inasmuch as the Father's gift is *of His own essential nature*, such a translation is, at least, in full harmony with the whole thought of Jesus. It matters little whether we read that the Father Himself is greater than all, or that that essential life of the Father which belongs to His children is greater than all. The Johannine author expresses the same thought in his first Epistle: 'Ye are of God, my little children, and have overcome them: because greater is he that is in you than he that is in the world' (4^4).

30. The climax of the passage is reached in this striking utterance, where Jesus claims to be 'one' with the Father. From the early centuries it has been perhaps more often quoted in Christological discussions than any other passage in the New Testament. Into these controversies it is not possible here to enter. The comment of Augustine will be a sufficient reminder to the modern reader of the nature of such controversies. He said: 'Mark both these words, *one* and *are*, and thou wilt be delivered from Scylla and Charybdis. In that He says *one*, the Arian, in *we are* the Sabellian, is answered.' Here, however, the *main* issue must be noted. The first, and most important, canon for the interpretation of *any* passage is that it should be interpreted in the light of the whole context. Now, throughout this Gospel Jesus is portrayed as One who had a unique sense of the Father's presence, and a unique consciousness of dependence upon Him. To read the 'numerical oneness' of Jesus with the Father into this passage, therefore, is to do the utmost violence to the mind of Jesus, and to the intention of the Evangelist. Later in the Gospel, Jesus declares: 'The Father is greater than I' (14^{28}). Further, precisely the same phrase expressive of 'oneness' is used in the 17th chapter, where Jesus speaks of the true unity of His followers. It is therefore obvious that the 'oneness' here spoken of is not a claim by Jesus —or a claim by the author for Jesus—to *identity* with the Father. It is the *same* claim that has been made throughout the Gospel—a claim to unique fellowship in mind and will with the Father. The only difference is that here it is expressed in terse, dramatic form. The theologians of the later centuries read back into this profoundly spiritual utterance of Jesus a claim on His part to identity of 'οὐσία' (essence) with the Father. What, however, they were seeking to do, was not to understand what Jesus said, but to fit His utterance into a metaphysical framework which they regarded as necessary. In doing this they came perilously near to enveloping the Jesus of the Gospels in a cloud of abstract speculation. This can be said, while at the same time we recognise the inevitability of philosophic or metaphysical statement. What, however, we have to see is that 'oneness'

and ' dependence ' explain each other—they do not contradict each other. Only he is ' one ' with God who lives in complete *dependence* upon Him: he seeks only to do One Will. Only *he* is completely dependent upon God who is in perfect fellowship with God: his knowledge of the Father is the fount of his very being. If the consciousness of Jesus is, as we must maintain, *one* consciousness, we are not at liberty to play ' oneness ' against ' dependence ' in a feat of spurious metaphysical dialectic. The two experiences are one; and the closer man lives to God the more clearly he sees that this is so. Neither did Jesus Himself claim, nor did the Fourth Evangelist claim for Him, a ' metaphysical ' identity with the Father. The oneness which Jesus had with the Father was the same kind of oneness which existed between Himself, the Shepherd, and His sheep; and the same kind of oneness as should exist between all the members of the true flock of God. Indeed, the only sure ground for such a fellowship in humanity, such as the teaching of Jesus envisaged, is that there is something eternal in humanity, something derived not from the fleeting shows of earthly things, nor from institutional or racial convenience or profit. And that something is eternal, because it is of God's own nature. The message of Christianity is that in Jesus was seen such perfect, such eternal, fellowship, here within the confines of mortality. This is the ground of hope for the fulfilment of that day when men will be one, even as Jesus was one with the Father. The islands are now separate, often isolated and solitary in the ocean. But beneath the sea they are one. And men will be one, because their potential oneness exists in the very being of God, and received its prophetic manifestation in Jesus, the first-born among many brethren. In Him was revealed both God's nature, and *God's will for humanity*. It was the mission of Jesus to mediate to men that life of God which is the only true and unifying centre for the whole human race. Without this life of God in man, the several Churches will never be brought to the Shepherd's own Unity. Without this eternal reality in humanity, all who work for national and international understanding would be but ploughing the sands. Their labour and prayer—to change the figure—would but go up in the smoke of a racial civil war. The broken arcs, however, will become the perfect round. The inescapable divinity in humanity will never let him rest till the goal is reached.

THE DEFENCE OF JESUS AGAINST THE ACCUSATION OF BLASPHEMY (10^{31-39})

31–33. This profoundly spiritual claim of Jesus was blasphemy to the Jews. They thought that He, a man, was making himself God. They were both right and wrong. They were right in seeing that Jesus was claiming to speak with the authority of truth, and that this authority was grounded in a unique knowledge of God. They were wrong in thinking that He claimed a unique relation to *their kind of God*. People often think that they have said something truly Christian when they say that Christ was ' very God of very God.' This indeed is a very hallowed phrase, symbolising an imperishable truth. But it is the expression of Christian truth, *only* if the latter phrase, ' of very God,' is understood in the light of the whole truth about God revealed in Jesus. If we say that He was ' very

God *of very God*,' and mean by the latter part of the phrase, an absentee God of the Deists, or an Impersonal absolute of the Pantheists, or the sectarian deity of so many 'plain' people—then, indeed, it is *not* a Christian utterance at all. Let not so-called Christians condemn these Jews, for an orthodoxy may be precisely as blameworthy. The only difference is here: that the Jews regarded as 'blasphemy' what many so-called Christians claim as 'orthodox' truth. The division between Jesus and these Jews was not a difference between *blasphemy* and *reverential humility*. It was Jesus who was truly humble, and truly reverent: it was the Jews who were really proud, and really blasphemous. The final blasphemy is to sin against the light. The division between Jesus and these Jews, in other words, arose from *two different conceptions of God*. To Jesus God was Father: to them, He was the arbitrary Potentate of a few favourites in a favourite race. This is a difference which has come down through the centuries. And the first task of a truly Christian thinker is to *Christianise* the conception of God.

34–38. That all this is true to the mind of Jesus is seen in the striking words He quotes from Ps. 82^6, in reply to the charge of blasphemy. This 34th verse has been often on the lips of those who have been regarded as 'heretics.' They were often in the thought, and on the lips, for example, of Abelard. Let us see what they mean. The Jews are charging Jesus with blasphemy because He speaks in this intimate way of God. But how do their own Scriptures speak? These say that God Himself, the supreme Judge, called earthly judges 'gods' (see Exod. 21^6). How then can there be blasphemy in His own filial claim? It is obvious that the verse is a kind of *argumentum ad hominem*. The Jews are 'hoist with their own petard.' It is not that Jesus admits He is claiming to be 'one' with their kind of God. He is showing that, *on their own reasonings*, the Scriptures are as much guilty of their charge as He Himself. But Jesus does this only to lead them at once to the true knowledge of the Father, whose will He does and whom He knows in perfect filial fellowship.

Once again, the Evangelist narrates that the claim and mission of Jesus leads His enemies to conspire His arrest. His claim at the Feast of Dedication to 'oneness' with the Father issues in the same manifestation of open hostility as His claim at the Feast of Tabernacles to a life transcending time (8^{58-59}). It is clear that the two claims interpret each other. 'Before Abraham was I am,' points to the non-temporal nature of the life He knew: 'I and the Father are one' points to the source of that life in the Father Himself. In each case 'the Jews' seek to take Jesus and to stone Him; in each case He escapes out of their hand.

Retiral of Jesus Beyond the Jordan (10^{40-42})

40–42. This passage forms a brief interlude between the teaching of Jesus in Jerusalem, in which He asserted His spiritual oneness with the Father, and the events which lead to His final return thither to be crucified—save for the brief period of suspense referred to in 11^{54-57}. A period of calm follows a period of controversy. It is, however, but the calm before the final storm.

Jesus withdraws to Peræa on the eastern side of the Jordan where His ministry began. There is a psychological fitness in such a retiral. Knowing that the hostility of rulers and Pharisees was reaching its zenith, He retires to the scenes of His first public work, there to await the inward call to return. This visit to Peræa is recorded in the Synoptic Gospels, and is doubtless historical. (Mk. 10^1; Mt. 19^1.) It is tempting to try to imagine the thoughts and emotions both of Jesus and His disciples, when, after the storm and stress of the past years, they find themselves where they had first linked their lives in one school, with Jesus as master and the disciples as pupils. The return to a scene which had meant so much to both, must have revivified the splendour, and the poignancy, of the succeeding experiences. It is perhaps significant that the last reference to the Baptist in the Gospel is an emphasis on the subordination of his mission to that of Jesus. It is as if the Evangelist wished to stress, here for the last time, to those in His day who thought too much of the Baptist and too little of Jesus, that the earliest followers of the forerunner were among those who in the days of Jerusalem's hostility remained loyal to the transcending mission of Him who had been called ' the lamb of God.' The welcome given to Jesus in Peræa serves as a foil to the hostility of Jerusalem. ' Many believed on him there.'

THE ' SIGN ' OF THE RAISING OF LAZARUS AND CAIAPHAS'S COUNSEL OF DEATH

The ' sign ' of ' the raising of Lazarus,' like the Cana ' sign ' in chapter 2, presents one of the crucial issues for the understanding and interpretation of the Fourth Gospel. Every reader of the Gospels has noted that there is nothing corresponding to this story in the Synoptic narratives. In the first three Gospels there are, it is true, two stories of ' raisings from the dead '—that of Jairus's daughter (Mk. $5^{22\,\mathrm{ff.}}$ and parallel passages), and that of the son of the widow of Nain (Lk. $7^{11\,\mathrm{ff.}}$). But neither of these stories has the significant and controlling place in the narrative which the Lazarus story has in St. John. Not only is it that Lazarus had been ' dead four days ' (*v.* 39), but it is this ' sign ' which finally decides the rulers to achieve the death of Jesus (*vv.* 47 ff.). It is difficult to imagine that if this story is historical, it could have been omitted by the Synoptists. Even those commentators who regard the narrative as, *in its main features*, historical acknowledge that they can give no satisfactory explanation of this silence. Thus, the narrative focuses at a vivid and burning point most of the contentious questions to which this Gospel gives rise.

The same issues arise here as have been discussed in the passages dealing with the other Johannine ' signs.' This, the reader will note, is the *seventh* of these: and—if we take the Resurrection as belonging to a category all its own, and the twenty-first chapter as not forming part of the first draft of the Gospel—the last. The number of the ' signs ' is itself significant for the author's purpose and meaning, seven being the perfect number to Semitic peoples. The ' works ' the Evangelist has chosen to write about have been carefully chosen—and in most cases symbolically and dramatically embellished—from a large mass of stories circulating in the Christian communities. Neither their nature nor their number has been chosen in haphazard fashion. In this Gospel everything is narrated to subserve a dominant purpose.

This commentary is written from the standpoint that no one can understand this Gospel who does not seek to penetrate into the mind and dominant motif of the Evangelist. In every perplexing question which arises, the main issue for any *psychological* interpreter is: What did the *author himself mean*?

Before embarking, therefore, upon detailed comment on this chapter, we must seek to answer this question. The issues arising will be clearly seen if we ask such questions as these. Did the Evangelist himself believe that he was narrating precise historical fact? *Or*, is he presenting the mind and mission of Jesus in the framework of a strikingly realistic allegorical narrative? It is sheer blindness to psychological motivations to say—as has been said by both religious and anti-religious polemical writers—that the scene was either an *imposture* or *fiction*. The mistake behind such a conclusion lay in forgetfulness of the author's own mind and purpose. No one, surely, would dream of calling an allegorical narrative an ' imposture.' A work is only an ' imposture ' if the author sought to *deceive* his readers: it is not an ' imposture ' if some of his readers have deceived themselves as to what the purport of his narrative really is. To call it a ' fiction ' is likewise inappropriate. The book of Jonah, for example, is neither a ' fraud ' nor is it just ' fiction.' All these judgements are dictated by preconceived opinions; not by a frank and painstaking desire to enter imaginatively and understandingly into the mind of the author himself.

The reader is referred to the discussion preliminary to the Cana story—as also to the Introduction—for the general standpoint which we regard as essential for the understanding of the author's meaning in these ' sign ' narratives. They are not by him regarded as scientific history. On the basis of some incident circulating in the Church, his meditating mind has erected vivid and realistic narrative, designed to be the vehicle for expressing the main themes of the mind and mission of Jesus. Or, to use a more appropriate figure, such traditional incidents were woven into the striking fabrics found in this Gospel, by the shuttle of a remarkable dramatising and allegorising mind. There is warp of historical narrative, and there is woof of the author's own mentality; but what is precisely warp and what precisely woof it is not possible now to say. Of this, however, we may be certain. The author was not one to allow any traditional story to pass through his mind without being modified, or elaborated, in the process. His mind was not just the transmitter of tradition. Reminiscence and tradition were shaped, both consciously and unconsciously, to his high spiritual purpose.

The realistic details which so much impress every reader of this Lazarus story must not, therefore, be regarded as evidence of scientific accuracy of narrative. What Bishop Westcott here called ' dramatic vividness ' belongs not only to precise history, but also—and indeed more frequently—to imaginative and allegorical creation. Shakespeare is more vivid than Hallam, Victor Hugo than Mignet. Carlyle's *French Revolution* is more dramatically graphic than volume 8 of the *Cambridge Modern History*. Such books as *Job*, *Jonah*, *Pilgrim's Progress*, *Robinson Crusoe*, and *Gulliver's Travels*—to give but a few examples almost at random—lack nothing in vivid portraiture and coherent unity of theme. Given a mind of dramatic and artistic genius, details conveying the impression of living structure are as inevitable as are the bare facts of history which reveal the work of the prosaic and unimaginative plodder. If a narrative is so vivid and living that we feel that we are looking on at a scene taking place before our eyes, we may be perfectly certain that the writer has more than scientific precision of mind. It is a psychological fact that scientific exactitude seldom goes with dramatic and artistic insight. If realistic and detailed narrative and portraiture are to be the criterion of exact scientific history, many of the works that are obviously not such will have to be reckoned as such; and many of the works that are usually claimed to be such will have to relinquish their claim.

We have already noticed the *freedom* with which the Fourth Evangelist deals with incidents and discourses in the life of Jesus. We have found it difficult, for example—indeed impossible—to decide when Jesus ceases to speak and the author begins to expound. We have also noted that the incidents are not placed in any exact chronological order: they are placed, and handled, by the Evangelist to subserve his essential purpose. Who will mourn at this, save those who ask for what has not been given? Who will cry that it is ' fantastic ' to find allegory in this narrative, save those who are engaged in an unhappy and discordant inner mental strife with traditional conceptions, which they *wish* to keep, but cannot? Many a commentator has gone down to his grave tortured with divided loyalties: feeling, on the one hand, that Christianity stood or fell with miracles, and, on the other hand, knowing that in the interests of *truth* he *must* make concessions which undermined his position.

It has already been noted that the account of the cleansing of the Temple, which in all probability belonged to the closing week of the ministry of Jesus, is placed by this Evangelist at the beginning of his record. An event, that is, which to the Synoptists had an important place in the psychological motivations which led to the tragedy of the Cross, is thus replaced in St. John by this narrative of Lazarus, which is portrayed as having a similar effect. Many lines of evidence, therefore, verge on the position which is here maintained—namely, that the Evangelist is freely recreating and embellishing some historical incident, in the interests both of his allegorical portraiture of the mind and mission of Jesus, and of the dramatic fitness and coherence of his Gospel. The story, then, is to be regarded as a parable of the spiritual mission of Jesus : this was to bring eternal life to men. It is also a parable of that faith in Him which had, in Christian experience, been the gateway to such life. In the previous chapters, Jesus has been portrayed as ' the living water,' ' the bread of life,' ' the light of the world,' ' the good shepherd,' ' the door.' These are metaphors which he who runs may read. In this chapter He is ' the resurrection and the life ': here he who runs will not read so easily. Yet the narrative is clearly designed to set forth the truth that Jesus is the resurrection and the life. The key to the meaning of the whole narrative is found in the 25th verse, where Jesus says to Martha: ' I am the resurrection and the life; he that believeth on me, even if he die, yet shall he live, and whosoever liveth and believeth on me shall never die.' Jesus has within Himself that commanding authority whereby He can raise the dead from a state of moral and spiritual corruption: He can free them from the fatal bonds of Pharisaic teaching. This authority springs out of His filial consciousness and of His sense of Messianic mission. This is expressed in the reply of Martha in the 27th verse: 'I have believed that thou art the Christ, the Son of God, even he that cometh into the world.' The author's purpose is thus to declare that Jesus enjoyed such intimate fellowship with God that He knew Himself called to be the medium to men of that life transcending the dissolution of the earthly tabernacle. It is the Evangelist's conviction that Jesus was both Son and Messiah; and it is this conviction which controls and shapes the whole narrative.

There is no reference in the Synoptic Gospels to this Lazarus, the brother of the two sisters: but in Lk. $16^{19\,ff.}$ there is the familiar parable of the rich man and 'a certain beggar named Lazarus.' It is tempting to surmise that the Evangelist has woven the allegory out of an admixture of the Lucan parable and some incident in the life of one who was a brother of Mary and Martha. While this is, and must be, conjecture, yet it is conjecture which harmonises with what we know of the Evangelist's mind, and, also, with certain details in the parable itself. As far as the Lucan parable is concerned, it is significant to note that its theme is the life after death. The rich man in Hades wishes Father Abraham to send Lazarus back to earth to warn his brethren of the place of torment awaiting the unrighteous. And Abraham's answer is: 'If they hear not Moses and the prophets, neither will they be persuaded, if one rise from the dead.'

With all diffidence, therefore, we make the following suggestions as to the source and origin of this allegorical narrative. *First*, the author had personal knowledge of this 'Lazarus of Bethany,' who through the ministry of Jesus had been saved from the corruption of moral and spiritual death. The figure of *being brought back to life* had been used by Jesus Himself of a *moral and spiritual restoration*. In the parable of the prodigal son, the father says to the elder brother: 'This thy brother was dead and is alive again' (Lk. 16^{31}). The Evangelist, therefore, is only dramatising a metaphor used by Jesus Himself. *Second*, the author was familiar with the Lucan parable about the life after death: a parable which no doubt in the early Church, as in the later centuries, had given rise to a great deal of perplexity. In this parable the villain of the piece was a rich man; who appeals from Hades across the gulf to 'Father Abraham'—thus suggesting that he was of those who had in the flesh, like the Pharisees of the Fourth Gospel, falsely claimed to be of the spiritual lineage of Abraham. *Thirdly*, out of these two strands the author weaves the fabric of this parabolical narrative; which thus, at one and the same time, portrays Christ as the bringer of eternal life, and reveals the dire consequences of a life centred on narrow temporal and selfish hopes. Lazarus, to the Evangelist, symbolises the life transformed by the power of Jesus: the hostile Jews symbolise those who will not be persuaded of the truth 'even if one rise from the dead.'

THE PRELUDE TO THE SIGN

JN. 11^{1-16}

11 1 Now a certain man was sick, Lazarus
of Bethany, of the village of Mary and
2 her sister Martha. And it was that
Mary which anointed the Lord with
ointment, and wiped his feet with her
hair, whose brother Lazarus was sick.

3 The sisters therefore sent unto him, saying, Lord, behold, he whom thou lovest
4 is sick. But when Jesus heard it, he said,
This sickness is not unto death, but for
the glory of God, that the Son of God
5 may be glorified thereby. Now Jesus
loved Martha, and her sister, and
6 Lazarus. When therefore he heard that
he was sick, he abode at that time two
7 days in the place where he was. Then
after this he saith to the disciples, Let us
8 go into Judæa again. The disciples say
unto him, Rabbi, the Jews were but now
seeking to stone thee: and goest thou
9 thither again? Jesus answered, Are
there not twelve hours in the day? If a
man walk in the day, he stumbleth not,
because he seeth the light of this world.
10 But if a man walk in the night, he
stumbleth, because the light is not in him.
11 These things spake he: and after this he
saith unto them, Our friend Lazarus is
fallen asleep; but I go, that I may awake
12 him out of sleep. The disciples therefore
said unto him, Lord, if he is fallen asleep,
13 he will recover. Now Jesus had spoken
of his death: but they thought that he
14 spake of taking rest in sleep. Then
Jesus therefore said unto them plainly,
15 Lazarus is dead. And I am glad for
your sakes that I was not there, to the
intent ye may believe; nevertheless let us
16 go unto him. Thomas therefore, who is
called Didymus, said unto his fellow-
disciples, Let us also go, that we may
die with him.

The Evangelist is now entering upon the closing section of the first main part of his Gospel. The whole work is divided into two parts almost equal in size. The first is the record of the public ministry of Jesus: the second covers the few hours prior to the Passion, the Cross itself, and the Resurrection. He has been portraying with the insight and power of dramatic genius the nature of the challenge which Jesus made to the traditional religious views of the Jerusalem of His day. A sense of the impending and inevitable end has been haunting the reader. In the 11th and 12th chapters, which close this first section, the misunderstanding and hostility of 'the Jews' are given a setting which conveys to the reader, more clearly than a long and laboured discussion could do, the sense that all has been done and said by Jesus that could be done and said. The hour is now at hand.

1–3. A message is brought to Jesus in Peræa from a home in Bethany outside Jerusalem, in which He had, doubtless, often stayed while He ministered in the capital. This Bethany the author clearly distinguishes from 'the Bethany (Bethabarah?) beyond Jordan' of 1^{28}. Luke in 10^{38} speaks of 'the village of Mary and Martha,' but does not tell us where it was. In the 2nd verse the Evangelist tells us that this Mary, whose brother Lazarus was, is she who anointed Jesus and wiped His feet with her hair. The story itself he narrates in the succeeding chapter. Many commentators have suggested that this verse is a note inserted later by some redactor: there is, however, no MS. evidence for this. Luke in $7^{37ff.}$ records a similar incident of 'a woman who was a sinner': and Mark in $14^{3ff.}$ (the parallel passage is Mt. $26^{6ff.}$) tells us that in the last week of the life of Jesus 'in the house of Simon the leper . . . there came a woman having an alabaster cruse of ointment of spikenard very costly, and she brake the cruse and poured it over *his head*.' Whether there were two such incidents—one earlier in the Ministry and one during the last days—we do not know. But, in any case, it would seem that the Johannine author identifies this Mary of Bethany with Mary Magdalene. This is the Mary of whom it is recorded in Mk. 14^{9}: 'Wheresoever the gospel shall be preached throughout the whole world, that also which this woman hath done shall be spoken of for a memorial of her.' It is perhaps significant that the author finds it necessary to refer to this Mary in order to identify 'Lazarus.' Was 'Lazarus' the real name of a real person? Or a *nom de plume* of a real person? Or a fictitious name given to an imaginary person? At least, the words, 'whose brother Lazarus was sick,' suggest that there is little which is precisely historical behind the narrative: for it is difficult to suppose that a historical person who had been raised to life, after being dead for four days, would need to be identified in this way. Would not his name, in such a case, be so familiarly known that it would need no such laboured identification?

4. The reply of Jesus in *v.* 4 recalls the words about the blind man in 9^{3}. There it was stated that his blindness was 'that the works of God should be made manifest in him.' Here it is said that the sickness of Lazarus is 'for the glory of God, that the Son of God may be glorified thereby.' What the author would say is that the Divine presence is once again manifested in the regenerating activity of Him who knew Himself to be as a Son. God's 'glory' was seen in Jesus, who was both Light and Life. He made blind men to see, and dead men to live. It should be noted that only here and in 5^{25} and 10^{36} does the Evangelist put the title 'Son of God' on the lips of Jesus.

5. In the 5th verse, which speaks of Jesus *loving* the members of this household, the author would remind his readers that the historical Jesus was no impassible being, nor that His 'love' for men lacked the individual and affinitive qualities which it has in ourselves. The 'reformer,' who claims to *love humanity*, often, thereby, merely disguises his supreme interest in, and love for, himself. He *loves himself*, as the purveyor of what he thinks is for the good of the mass. Jesus was a man of natural and deep sympathies, and He both inspired, and responded to, the love of individuals. In this, He showed Himself a true 'Son' of the Father: for the Father loves, not abstractions, but *men*. To Him, as Jesus teaches in the Synoptic Gospels, the hairs of each man's head are all numbered.

6–10. The delay of Jesus, and His decision to return to Judæa, is so narrated by the author as to represent Jesus as the master of His circumstances, and not their slave. Previous passages—like 2^{4} and 7^{6-8}—convey this same impression. The action of Jesus is never hurried: He moves when He Himself *sees* what He must do. The disciples remind Him of the net of hostility which lies in wait for Him in Judæa. In His reply Jesus, as in 9^{4}, expresses His intuitive conviction that 'the day' of His public ministry has not yet reached its end. There are twelve hours in the day, and the twelfth hour has not yet struck. The apprehensions of the disciples are contrasted with the serenity of Jesus. The sun is still shining, for He has the inward assurance of a duty to fulfil. The way to His death is in a path of light. In the Synoptic Gospels we read that Jesus, when He envisaged His coming death in Jerusalem, regarded the way that led thereto as illumined for Him by the Father's will. Peter had acknowledged Him as the anointed of God because, as Jesus said, he had had it revealed to him, not by flesh and blood, but by the Father in heaven. But when the same Peter sought to dissuade Him from going to Jerusalem, Jesus regarded this as a voice of Satan, savouring not of the things of God but the things of men (Mt. 16^{23}).

Jesus says, also, that what is true of Himself is true of others. *Anyone* who acts in obedience to the constraining voice of duty walks without stumbling by a light that never was on land or sea: his is a light within to guide. But anyone who acts in obedience to self-seeking interests walks uncertainly, for he is without the inner light to guide him. Opposition will deflect him; the lure of competing self-interests will cause him to waver. He has no steady celestial Gleam to follow; but only many delusive will o' the wisps. The time-server always walks uncertainly in the darkness. He is the *benighted* man.

Augustine's somewhat fanciful interpretation of the passage, ' Are there not twelve hours of the day,' is worth recalling. To what, he asks, do these words refer? ' Just that to point Himself out as the day, He made choice of twelve disciples. If I am the day, He says, and you the hours, is it for the hours to give counsel to the day? The day is followed by the hours, not the hours by the day. . . . It was not, then, without a purpose that the Lord made choice of twelve disciples, but to indicate that He Himself is the spiritual Day. Let the hours then attend upon the Day, let them preach the Day, and by the preaching of the hours may the world believe in the Day. And so in a summary way it was just this that He said; Follow me, if ye would not stumble.' Such an interpretation contains beautiful spiritual truth which is harmonious with the rest of the Gospel. And it is clear that ' the light ' referred to in *vv.* 9 and 10 is, to the author, both the *inner light* and the *light manifest in Jesus*. It is in accord with the whole context of ideas in this Gospel that the spiritual illumination which has its seat within each man is also regarded as fully expressed in Jesus, the light of the world. But it is difficult to suppose, with Augustine, that the ' twelve hours ' symbolise the ' twelve disciples,' either to Jesus Himself or to the Evangelist. And, in any case, it is well to remember that Augustine and the other Fathers who allegorised these passages maintained at the same time their precise historicity. To them there were *two meanings* in all such narratives—the literal and the spiritual.[1]

11. The narrative continues with the symbolical reference of Jesus to the ' sleep ' of Lazarus, ' our friend,' from which He goes to arouse him. It would seem here that to the mind of the Evangelist ' Lazarus ' represents all the ' friends ' whom Jesus had awakened to newness of life. Death, whether physical or spiritual, is in all literature thought of under the figure of sleep. To primitive man sleep and physical death seemed very much alike: and in all probability the first words coined by humanity to express these two facts would be very similar. Death was ' the long sleep ' from which one did not wake up in this life. Sleep and trance were regarded as the temporary, death as the permanent, absence of the spirit from the body. In accord with this idea, many savage peoples regard it as highly dangerous to arouse a sleeper suddenly; for his spirit may not have had time to return. Even more dangerous is it to move a sleeper; for the spirit on returning might not be able to find its body. It is an egregious mistake, therefore, to suppose that Christianity has been the only religion to speak of death as a sleep; though it is true to say that Christianity has given deeper and fuller significance to the metaphor. The New Testament frequently speaks of

[1] Dr. Torrey has suggested, on the basis of his hypothesis of an Aramaic original of this Gospel, that the latter part of the 10th verse should be translated, ' because the light is not *in it* ': for he says, that in the Aramaic there would be no difference between ' in it ' and ' in him ' (the difference in Greek is between *αὐτῷ* and *αὐτῇ*: it is interesting to note that D has *ἀυτῇ* here).

what we call physical death as a sleep—thirteen times in all.[1] The use of the figure is as old as reflecting man. It is interesting to remember that our word 'cemetery' is from the root Greek verb meaning *to sleep*.

To the student of Greek it is also interesting to note that the word used by Jesus in the 11th verse translated 'awake out of sleep' is not elsewhere used in the New Testament. It is a Hellenistic word, and is used in the LXX both of waking up from normal sleep, and of waking up from the sleep of death. In the former sense it is used in 1 Kings 3^{15} of Solomon waking up from a dream; in the latter sense it is used in Job 14^{12}, where Job says that 'till the heavens be no more' men who have died 'shall not be roused out of their sleep.' It is clear that the word lends itself well to the allegorical purpose of the Evangelist.

12–14. The Evangelist expands these allegorical thoughts about 'death' and 'sleep' in *vv.* 12–14. The disciples take the reference to sleep literally. Jesus answers that Lazarus is 'dead.' Such an expression does not in any way preclude the view here taken that to the author the whole narrative is allegorical. Both 'sleep' and 'death' are words used in all languages in a metaphorical manner. We say, for example, that a man's conscience, or his mind, is *asleep*; or that his moral and spiritual nature is *dead*. Indeed, most of our language about unseen realities is derived from language which was originally expressive of physical realities. Such words as 'impression,' 'emotion, 'contact,' 'conscience,' 'spirit,' illustrate this fact. There is no reason, therefore, to suppose that the Evangelist could not expand a common metaphor. Indeed, from what we know of his type of mind we may confidently say that such imaginative expansion was natural to him.

15. The expression of gladness in *v.* 15 has created much difficulty to those who have regarded the narrative as historical. These have felt that it is inconceivable that Jesus—possessing, as He did, so deeply sympathetic a spirit—should have spoken of *being glad* when, on their hypothesis, He knew of the physical death of Lazarus, a cause of so great sorrow to the sisters. Even though this death was to be the occasion of His working a miracle, these commentators have felt that the words cannot be from Jesus, for they represent what seems a 'Stoic pose': such an attitude being inconsistent with the manifestation of deep human feeling in *vv.* 33, 35, and 38. This difficulty, we suggest, is created by the hypothesis of historicity. Once it is seen that the narrative is mainly allegorical drama, we need not be uneasily employed in seeking to reconcile what seem to be contradictory expressions of the emotions of Jesus. If the author makes Jesus express joy at what later causes Him deep grief, it is but a case of his dramatising faculty overleaping itself, and so tending to stultify the psychological coherence of his allegory. Dramatic genius in an author is always a peril: it may, as here, very easily distort the message by a psychologically false accentuation. In a few places in this Gospel the Evangelist did not avoid this peril—for example, in 6^6, 8^{24}, 11^{42}, 17^9. What, however, he wishes to express here is the joy which filled the mind of Jesus on every occasion when His disciples were brought to deeper and fuller faith in Him. For the moment, He has forgotten the psychological situation he is creating in the grief of the sisters and of Jesus Himself. He is

[1] The Greek verb κοιμᾶσθαι meant both 'to sleep,' and 'to sleep the sleep of death,'

intent upon declaring the joy of Jesus when men are brought to the light and liberty of truth. He conceives of the disciples as brought to fuller faith by the 'sign' which he is about to narrate. It has never been in the Evangelist's mind to express any joy on the part of Jesus at an inadequate belief based on wonders. We have already seen how one of his main purposes throughout the Gospel is to show the unsatisfactory nature of such a belief to the mind of the incarnate One. Jesus, says the Evangelist, was not present when Lazarus died: that is his way of saying that when the mind incarnate in Jesus is truly present with any man, he cannot see spiritual death. 'Let us go *unto him*'—that is, not to a dead body, but to one who needs spiritual restoration.

This 15th verse also expresses the whole scale of values possessed by Jesus. His mission to regenerate men was not repudiated when personal risks barred the way. No personal danger deterred Him. Indeed, the only real 'danger' to Him was in seeking to disobey His mission. Those who seek, in the interests of selfish convenience, to avoid the perils of circumstance or of opposition, find themselves engulfed in the final peril: they have lost their souls (see Mt. 16^{26} and similar passages). What boots it to prolong existence and lose eternal life? Life is only dangerous because of its greatness. When it loses its danger it loses its eternal worth.

16. Thomas, usually thought of as 'the doubter,' but more truly regarded as the independent 'prover,' is portrayed as one who did not quite know what it was all about, except that he envisaged the peril of Jesus. So he calls his fellow disciples to face the mortal danger into which the Master proposes to run. Such an attitude is true to what the Evangelist says of Thomas in 14^{5} and 20^{25}. It has more of true 'faith' in it than the empty protestations of those who say, 'Lord, Lord,' and do not do the will of the Divine Father. It is significant that it is Thomas who says this. It would seem that this is the Evangelist's way of commending a faith manifest in works. He understood and sympathised with the kind of disciple whom Thomas represented. The Synoptists record no incident of him. It was the Fourth Evangelist who recognised the abiding importance in Christianity of his type of mind. One way to understand the message of Jesus is to follow Him. This is what Jesus Himself said when, in the Synoptic Gospels, He told the disciples that it is they who take up the Cross and follow Him who are His true disciples.

Thomas is a Hebrew name which means 'twin.' It is found in the Old Testament in Gen. 25^{24} and 38^{27}, in *Song of Songs* 4^{5} and in 7^{3}: where it is translated in the LXX by *Diduma*. Three times in this Gospel, when Thomas is mentioned, there is the explanatory addition, 'who is called Didymus'—here, at 20^{24} and 21^{22}: this addition is made in no other passage in the New Testament. In all probability the insertion was for the sake of Greek-speaking people in the Evangelist's day. These may probably have come to refer to Thomas by the name used in the Greek Old Testament Scriptures to translate 'Thomas'; just as *Cephas* came to be generally referred to as *Peter*—each name signifying 'rock' (cf. 1^{42}). It may also be that the name was felt appropriate to his character. Perplexity in him is mixed with faith, despondency with courage. He will not say more than he thinks, but what he does think will determine his action. He was not one of the many whose creed outruns their actions. His action revealed, and created, his creed. Later traditions, of doubtful value, tell us that he was a missionary to Parthia and to India, that he was martyred, and that his supposed grave was pointed out in Edessa in the fourth century. The apocryphal *Acts of Thomas* date from the second century, and cannot be attributed to him.

The Scene at Bethany

JN. 11^{17-32}

11 17 So when Jesus came, he found that he
had been in the tomb four days already.
18 Now Bethany was nigh unto Jerusalem,
19 about fifteen furlongs off; and many of
the Jews had come to Martha and Mary,
to console them concerning their brother.
20 Martha therefore, when she heard that
Jesus was coming, went and met him:
21 but Mary still sat in the house. Martha
therefore said unto Jesus, Lord, if thou
hadst been here, my brother had not
22 died. And even now I know that, whatsoever thou shalt ask of God, God will
23 give thee. Jesus saith unto her, Thy
24 brother shall rise again. Martha saith
unto him, I know that he shall rise again
in the resurrection at the last day.
25 Jesus said unto her, I am the resurrection,
and the life: he that believeth on me,
26 though he die, yet shall he live: and
whosoever liveth and believeth on me
shall never die. Believest thou this?
27 She saith unto him, Yea, Lord: I have
believed that thou art the Christ, the
Son of God, *even* he that cometh into the
28 world. And when she had said this, she
went away, and called Mary her sister
secretly, saying, The Master is here, and
29 calleth thee. And she, when she heard
it, arose quickly, and went unto him.
30 (Now Jesus was not yet come into the
village, but was still in the place where
31 Martha met him.) The Jews then
which were with her in the house, and
were comforting her, when they saw
Mary, that she rose up quickly and went
out, followed her, supposing that she was
32 going unto the tomb to weep there. Mary
therefore, when she came where Jesus
was, and saw him, fell down at his feet,
saying unto him, Lord, if thou hadst
been here, my brother had not died.

17–19. The Evangelist now introduces us, in the second scene of his dramatic allegory, to the situation at Bethany on the arrival of Jesus. Lazarus 'had been in the tomb four days already.' This reference to 'four days' has intrigued many commentators from the earliest days. In the 39th verse we are told that he had been 'dead' four days; though the reader will note that the word 'dead' here is printed in italics in the R.V., to indicate that it is not in the original. Burial soon after death, we are thus reminded, is the custom in eastern countries. Those who maintain the historicity of the narrative take the reference to 'four days' as a proof of the magnitude of the miraculous power of Jesus: it shows that corruption would now be held to have set in, and that Jesus had either held it in abeyance, or had reversed a natural process in a moment of time. Those who, on the other hand—like the present interpreter—regard the narrative as, to the author himself, allegorical can take the 'four days' as his way of expressing the 'exceeding deadness' of Lazarus. This is his way of saying that here Jesus was confronted with a spiritual mortification which was seemingly past hope of regeneration. The early commentators made the most of both these positions, maintaining on the one hand that the 'four days' was a statement of history, and on the other hand that it contained a somewhat esoteric symbolism. Augustine, for example, in his remarkable commentary on the Gospel, after telling us that the whole narrative is precise history, goes on, in page after page, to point out its suggestive symbolism. But the question of a modern reader never seemed to arise in his mind: namely, did the *author himself* mean *both* these positions. It is obvious that few, if any, of the Fathers had the truly *historical* spirit. The symbolism which Augustine reads into the 'four days' of this passage, we may confidently say, was in his own mind, and not in that of the Evangelist. There are, he says, *four stages* of spiritual death. The *first* is that into which man is born, owing to original sin. The *second* is that which follows the violation of the moral law planted in his nature. The *third* is that which is the penalty of the breach of the written law of Moses. The *fourth* is that which finally ensues upon the transgression of the gospel. 'Now deservedly he stinketh'—as Augustine vividly adds. Such a mode of interpretation has affinities with heterogeneous and mutually contradictory modern interpretations of this Gospel. His maintenance of historicity pleases conservatives: his theological allegorising pleases those who deny any historicity to the Gospel, or who see in it an unmistakable *theological* document. We ourselves see allegory in this passage, but it is spiritual allegory, not theological allegory. The Evangelist himself, we are convinced, would have been exceedingly surprised at the theology of 'four deaths' imported into his narrative by Augustine.

20 ff. The portrayal of Martha and Mary by the Evangelist is true to what from the Lukan story in Lk. $10^{38 f.}$ we should expect. The first is the busy mistress of the house, eager in homely service, quick to express in speech what she thinks. It is she who goes to meet Jesus, and expresses to Him with precipitation her thoughts. The second is meditative and self-distrustful; of deep feeling not easily expressed in speech. She stays at home to await the coming of Jesus. Nor was it until the Master sent to call her that she 'rose quickly and went unto Him,' without telling her purpose to those with her (*vv.* 29 and 31). The first gives expression both to words of reproach and words of confidence in the presence of Jesus (*vv.* 21–22). The second, by act more than by word, gives utterance merely to humble devotion and resigned trust in His presence (*v.* 32). Her grief is expressed in wailing and tears (*v.* 33). It is the first who makes the practical remonstrance in *v.* 39. The second is in the background, standing silently by. The Evangelist contrasts the two sisters in these two vivid strokes; and the fact that this contrast is, as we may conclude, mainly true to historical fact, is not out of accord with the allegorical nature of the narrative. It is, indeed, psychologically most natural to suppose that the author will weave his allegory out of the strands of history.

25. The key, however, to the author's meaning is found, as we have already indicated, in the words of Jesus spoken in the discussion with Martha in the absence of Mary. He tells her first, in *v.* 23, that her brother shall rise again; then in *v.* 25 that He Himself is the resurrection and the life, that the dead shall rise through faith in Him, and that those who live through faith in Him shall never die. The Evangelist is setting forth the striking contrast between the traditional views of the day on the resurrection and the teaching of Jesus. The resurrection of which Martha speaks is to come on some distant day in the future. It was a vague and uncertain hope, affording little or no strength for the present. The 'Last Day' is too far off to mean anything to those immersed in the struggles, tensions, and sorrows of the present day. They can neither envisage it, nor can

they picture how the disintegrated bodies of men will be raised. It is all so distant —and so impossible. These words of Martha in *v.* 24 express the general belief of the Jews of the time—with the exception of the Sadducees. It would seem that such a doctrine of the resurrection of dead bodies on the Judgement Day had its origin among the Jewish apocalyptic writers. According to the usual interpretation, it is expressed in Dan. 12^2: ' And many of them that sleep in the dust of the earth shall wake, some to everlasting life, and some to shame and everlasting contempt.' [1] On the other hand, the resurrection of which Jesus speaks is not a vague and distant hope: it is a present reality. It is a reality of which He knows Himself called to be the mediator. The words, ' I am the resurrection and the life,' concentrate in one dramatic sentence the claim inherent in the whole consciousness of Jesus. Nothing is here said which has not already been said in this Gospel (see 5^{21} and 6^{39}). But it is now said in one of those striking ' I am ' utterances so characteristic of the Fourth Gospel. We have already noticed how the eternal reality of which Jesus, in virtue of His unique consciousness of the Father, knew Himself to be the channel to men, is claimed in this Gospel by the phrase ' I am.' He is the Water, Bread, Light, Shepherd, Door, Way, Truth, Vine, Resurrection, and Life. Everything that men need most He was here to give. He was the Water to quench the thirst of men, the Bread to feed them, the Light to illumine them, the Door through which entrance was found to life, the Way to the Father, and the Truth about everything that matters most. Here every quality is summed up in this striking saying, ' I am the resurrection and the life.' *Life* includes all its qualities. He who has *life* has all. He who gives *life* gives all. Jesus is the *resurrection* because He is the *life*. Only the living can call the dead to life. Jesus is the *resurrection* in that He incarnated the truth and grace of God which awake men from the death of falsehood and evil. Such life, which belongs to those who believe with the whole being in Jesus, is not subject to the dissolution which is the inevitable fate of the body. Jesus is ' the life,' in that this life had its fullest expression in Him. No one can give what he has not got. Jesus gives this life to men because He has it. And those who have it ' shall never die.' Just as the Gospel has been saying repeatedly that men are ' judged ' *now*, so this passage says that the ' resurrection ' is *now*. It is *now*, or *never*: and because it is *now*, it is *ever*. All the figures which Jesus uses of Himself are figures to express, not a temporal or future reality, but an *eternal* reality. He is ' water,' and water quenches man's thirst *now*: He is bread, and bread feeds *now*. Stagnant water is not the water of life. Bread that is left unused is not the bread of life. Thus Jesus is ' resurrection and life,' *now*. Men speculate about a future day which they have called the day of the ' general resurrection.' What Jesus says is that the coming to life should be *here* and *now*, and that the life which thus comes transcends the dissolution of what we call *matter*, and the passage of what we call *time*.

It is in the highest degree significant that the Fourth Evangelist never speaks of a ' general resurrection.' Resurrection is regarded as the result of ' believing on Jesus ' ($6.^{40}$): that is, it is itself part and parcel of that ' belief.' This shows conclusively, surely, that to this Evangelist the resurrection of man is a *spiritual*

[1] See, however, pp. 760–1, for another interpretation of the Daniel passage.

fact, just as 'judgement' is. The resurrection life is of eternity, not of time. It is not concerned with the reintegration of physical particles on some future day. It is the reintegration, here and now, of the whole Divine personal life. Sin disintegrates: the incarnate Word reintegrates. The Evangelist knows nothing of those crude materialistic notions of 'the general resurrection' which, like an outworn garment, religious humanity is now casting aside. In this he is fundamentally true to the teaching of Jesus. Eternal life is the life of God in the human soul. As Jesus shows in Mk. 12^{26-27}, it is because God is the living God of men's spirits that the life of fellowship with Him which they know will be deathless. As dust returns to dust, so soul returns to soul. The truth for which the phrase 'the general resurrection' stands is one of the same order as that for which the phrase 'the last day' stands. It is a 'resurrection' which is not partial but complete, not particular but general; not a restitution of individuals, but a restitution of all things when the purposes of the One Father of all are accomplished. The glory of God will be finally seen when the particularities of individuals, of races, of sects, of religions, will find their home in God.

The Sign

JN. 11^{33-44}

11 33 When Jesus therefore saw her weeping,
and the Jews *also* weeping which came
with her, he groaned in the spirit, and
34 was troubled, and said, Where have ye
laid him? They say unto him, Lord,
35 36 come and see. Jesus wept. The Jews
therefore said, Behold how he loved him!
37 But some of them said, Could not this
man, which opened the eyes of him that
was blind, have caused that this man also
38 should not die? Jesus therefore again
groaning in himself cometh to the tomb.
Now it was a cave, and a stone lay against
39 it. Jesus saith, Take ye away the stone.
Martha, the sister of him that was dead,
saith unto him, Lord, by this time he
stinketh: for he hath been *dead* four days.
40 Jesus saith unto her, Said I not unto thee,
that, if thou believedst, thou shouldest
41 see the glory of God? So they took
away the stone. And Jesus lifted up his
eyes, and said, Father, I thank thee that
42 thou heardest me. And I knew that
thou hearest me always: but because of
the multitude which standeth around I
said it, that they may believe that thou
43 didst send me. And when he had thus
spoken, he cried with a loud voice,
44 Lazarus, come forth. He that was dead
came forth, bound hand and foot with
graveclothes; and his face was bound
about with a napkin. Jesus saith unto
them, Loose him, and let him go.

33. The narrative of the sign is prefaced with a moving description of the distress and grief of Jesus. Those who take the whole record as historical have given many fanciful suggestions to explain precisely what this 'groaning in spirit' was, what had occasioned it, and how such grief could be reconciled with the divinity of Jesus. Was this 'groaning in spirit,' they have asked, 'indignation,' whether at the hypocritical Jewish mourners, or at their unbelief, or at the momentary triumph of death? Or, was it not 'indignation' at all, but an inward 'chafing' of spirit? [1] Did Jesus weep because of the grief of the sisters? And if so, why should He do so when He is going to remove the cause of their grief? Or did He weep because this grief confronted Him with the whole poignant situation? Or because the life to which He was going to recall Lazarus from the tomb was to be a life of great sorrow and suffering? These and kindred

[1] The Greek verb used here is only found in Mk. 1^{43}, 14^{5}; Mt. 9^{30}; Jn. 11^{33}, ^{38}.

questions have been asked—with varying degrees of profit. For ourselves, taking the main features of the narrative as allegorical, we can understand how the author wishes his readers here to understand that the Jesus of whose life-giving mission he speaks was not an impassive 'Divine' being, but one who in all points felt as we felt, knew life's poignant perplexities as we know them. Speculations on the precise significance of the emotion designated by these words are unprofitable. What the author *does* mean to say is that Jesus was truly and perfectly man. The tranquillity of a soul that could not be broken by opposition was shaken by the sorrow and suffering of His fellows. The fountain of His tears was unstopped, never by self-pity, but by compassionate sympathy for others. Only twice in the four Gospels are we told that Jesus *wept*—once when He wept tears of compassion over Jerusalem (Lk. 19^{42}), and here where He weeps with His friends.

36–37. The Evangelist, as has been his custom, records the diverse reactions of 'the Jews' to the words of Jesus. Once again they are divided. Some are sympathetic; others are full of scorn.

When they are come to the tomb, the Evangelist reminds us—through the statement of Martha in *v.* 39—of the 'four days' which have elapsed since the death of Lazarus. This reference has been discussed earlier. Here it should be noted that there was a Jewish tradition to the effect that the mourning did not reach its height till the third day; for it was held, during the first three days the spirit wandered about the sepulchre hoping to be able to return to the body; but that on the fourth day, when the face changed in aspect, it hovered near no longer but took its departure. Such traditional beliefs were by no means confined to the Jews.[1] It was after three days, it was held, that the countenance was changed. Jonah, as we read in the Old Testament allegory, was 'three days and three nights' in the belly of the great fish (Jon. 1^{17}). Without doubt, this reference by the Evangelist is his way of speaking, in the traditional idiom of his time, of a spiritual death which was complete.

38–40. The opening of the tomb, says the Evangelist, was closed by a stone. Some early commentators, in their eager quest to find an allegorical meaning in every verse of the Gospel, found one here. Augustine, for example, said that the stone represented the Law. 'Dead under the stone, guilty under the law. For you know that the law which was given to the Jews, was inscribed on stone. . . . What meant, then, the words, "Take ye away the stone"? . . . Take away the weight of the law; preach grace.' To attribute such a thought to the Evangelist, however, is to make him the kind of theologian which he certainly was not. His allegories, as we have said, were not *theological* allegories, but *spiritual* allegories. We look, therefore, for no symbolism here. To take the main motive of the Evangelist in this narrative as allegorical, it is not necessary to look for it in every realistic detail.

41–42. In these verses the Evangelist tells us once again that Jesus in all things recognised His dependence upon the Father. To Him, Jesus prayed: from Him, Jesus received the life which was the source of spiritual quickening to men. All

[1] See, for example, the illustrations given by Westcott in his Commentary on the Gk. text of the Gospel, vol. 2, p. 100.

that He did was of God, not of Himself. The harmony of will between Jesus and God was such that the Father heard Him ' always ': for He always sought the Father's will. The sentence—' because of the multitude which standeth round I said it '—has often caused difficulty: it is the author's way of saying that Jesus always wished people to know that the secret of all His spiritual and moral power was the Father. The Evangelist does not say that *Jesus's prayer* was made for the sake of the multitude; but that *His thanksgiving* was for their sakes. Jesus, in other words, would always have people know that He did nothing of Himself. When men were recalled to spiritual life, it was not done by a personal and privileged power peculiar to Himself. Such men as ' Lazarus ' issued from the death of sin to the eternal life of which He was the incarnate manifestation. His life was a life of prayer. *We* have *occasional* moments of dependence upon the Father when we seek not our own will but His will—not our selfish requests, but His glory. Such moments were not occasional to Jesus.

43-44. The cry, ' Lazarus come forth,' is dramatic allegorisation. The incarnate Word has spoken, and life has been awakened. We are recalled to the words of 5^{28-29}—' The hour is coming in which all that are in the graves shall hear his voice, and shall come forth.' The Word is the life-giver. In 1 Thess. 4^{16} Paul says that the Lord descends ' with a shout,' and the dead in Christ are raised. When the voice of the Word is truly heard, the spirit of man awakes to the life that is eternal. Man's ' last enemy ' is not *physical* death, which were better called by the Christian—in the words of St. Francis—' most kind and gentle death.' That ' enemy ' is *spiritual death*. And the voice that spoke in Jesus promises the ultimate victory over *that* enemy. The statement in the 44th verse is also dramatic allegorisation: ' He that was dead came forth, bound hand and foot with grave-clothes; and his face was bound about with a napkin.' Those who regard the whole narrative as historical seek to maintain that these ' grave-bands ' do not preclude the possibility of movement. Surely, however, the Evangelist has here given to us another clue to his allegorical motif. Who can conceive of movement when the limbs are closely bound, and the whole face covered? What the author would say is this: Those whom Jesus raised to spiritual life were often, as this ' Lazarus,' so bound by evil fetters, so blinded by their sins, that emergence to the new life and the new light would seem impossible. Yet, in spite of their fetters and their blindness, they *did* emerge from death, and, having emerged, they were loosed from their bands and made free. Such a verse as this from the hymn of Charles Wesley expresses what the Evangelist would say:

Long my imprisoned spirit lay
Fast bound in sin and nature's night;
Thine eye diffused a quickening ray—
I woke, the dungeon flamed with light;
My chains fell off, my heart was free,
I rose, went forth, and followed Thee.

Those who maintain that the author is writing history—or that he thinks that he is writing history—are perplexed by the fact that the story ends here. There is not a word about the emotions of Mary and Martha, not a word about their meeting with Lazarus, not a word about the overwhelming astonishment which must have come, on the historical hypothesis, upon the bystanders. This perplexity of such interpreters arises out of their hypothesis of historicity. It disappears, however, on the hypothesis here maintained. The Evangelist has said what he wanted to say—namely, that the incarnate Word had regenerative power. His allegory is complete with the restoration of 'Lazarus.' He is no longer interested in depicting motives. He was only concerned in giving a dramatic setting to the main truth He wished to declare. That having been said, the story ends. He has said all he wanted to say.

The speculations of those who maintain the historicity of the narrative have been further devoted to the after-life of Lazarus. These have had to remind themselves that of this after-life nothing is known. There are a few legends of no value, dating centuries after the Gospel. One of them is the somewhat grim story that he was never afterwards known to smile. To those who think that the death from which Lazarus was raised was a physical death, Tennyson's lines in *In Memoriam* will seem a happier issue:

Where wert thou, brother, those four days?
There lives no record of reply,
Which telling what it is to die
Had surely added praise to praise.

Browning, it will be remembered, devoted his *Epistle of Karshish* to an imaginative reconstruction of the after-experiences of Lazarus—the whole being based on the supposition that the Fourth Evangelist was seeking to write literal history. To Browning, Lazarus was as a 'grown man' who 'eyes the world now like a child': who

will wait patient to the last
For that same death which must restore his being
To equilibrium, body loosening soul
Divorced even now by premature full growth.

Had the Fourth Evangelist read this poem of Browning he would probably have read it as he read his own narrative—that is, he would have taken it as dramatic allegory. His own thought, however, was not concerned with Lazarus; but only with Jesus, 'the resurrection and the life.' And so, having told us that, in obedience to the voice of Jesus, Lazarus 'came forth' from the tomb of sin, he says no more. What more is there to say? Has not the 'sign' been told? That 'sign' was the manifestation of the resurrecting ministry of Jesus.

Caiaphas's Counsel of Death to the Sanhedrin

JN. 11^{45-53}

11 45 Many therefore of the Jews, which
came to Mary and beheld that which he
46 did, believed on him. But some of them
went away to the Pharisees, and told
them the things which Jesus had done.
47 The chief priests therefore and the

Pharisees gathered a council, and said,
What do we? for this man doeth many
48 signs. If we let him thus alone, all men
will believe on him: and the Romans will
come and take away both our place and
49 our nation. But a certain one of them,
Caiaphas, being high priest that year,
said unto them, Ye know nothing at all,
50 nor do ye take account that it is expedient
for you that one man should die for the
people, and that the whole nation perish
51 not. Now this he said not of himself:
but being high priest that year, he prophesied that Jesus should die for the
52 nation; and not for the nation only, but
that he might also gather together into
one the children of God that are scattered
53 abroad. So from that day forth they
took counsel that they might put him to
death.

The regenerating mission of Jesus is the link which leads to the final decision of the Sanhedrin to compass His death. The chain is now complete. The Word has spoken. The Light has shone. The Life has quickened. Some have heard, and some have not. Some have seen, and some have not. Some have been quickened, and some have not. The deaf, the blind, the dead, will now seek to prove that it is they who hear, who see, who live. They will silence the blasphemous Voice. They will master the deceitful Light. They will kill the false Life. Theirs, they imagine, will be the last word. Marvel of marvels!

They are gathered together in council, chief priests and Pharisees. They disagree in many things; but are agreed in one thing—Jesus must die. They are probably not agreed in their reasons as to *why* He must die, nor as to *the way* in which He must die. The Pharisees were chiefly concerned with His 'blasphemy': the chief priests, being Sadducees, were chiefly concerned with the appeal He was making to the people. The first regarded themselves as standing for the faith 'once for all delivered to the saints'; the second, for the prestige of the institution, and their own pre-eminent place therein. The first belonged to that line in humanity which has transmitted the 'odium theologicum' through the ages; the second to that line which, in the interests of the settled order, has scorned all 'enthusiasms.' To the first, Jesus was a blasphemer because He did not believe in their kind of God: to the second, He was a fanatic because He did not acquiesce in the finality of orders and of institution. The first were chiefly afraid of a disturbance in the people's religious beliefs, the second, of a disturbance of their customs. It was their common fear of *disturbance* which brought them together to decide how Jesus must die. For these disturbances were bound to end in civil troubles, especially with the Passover Feast just at hand. There might even be some new Messianic movement. This would mean action by Rome, involving the loss of whatever privileges they still possessed.

How, then, must He die? Probably they were, as we have suggested, in acute disagreement on this issue also. A death by stoning would have pleased the Pharisees—though probably it was their irresoluteness on this point which called for a decisive utterance. Such a death, some of them would feel, would have been their own affair, and Rome need not be called in. It had already, however, been abortively tried (see $10^{31\,f.}$ and 11^{8}); and, as the Sadducees would be quick to point out, might well intensify both the civil disturbances they feared and the interference of Rome they wished to avoid.

The word of worldly-wisdom was spoken by the ecclesiastical statesman of the company. When an assembly is perplexed as to what to do, the time has arrived for the astute mind. The Pharisees are too direct in their methods—at least they had the merit of forthrightness. A Sadducean way was better. Let Him die at the hands of Rome. The end they all have in view will be reached without tumult, and without the loss of their own prestige. Rome can do nothing, if Rome herself decides His death. Order will be kept and popular feeling will speedily abate. *They* will emerge with their privileges intact, and the author of all their troubles in His grave. *It is expedient* for them all *that one man should die for the people*. If He be handed over to the Roman power as an upstart king, the nation and its privileges are secure—perhaps the Sadducean way of saying that their own position was secure.

The speaker, writes the Evangelist, was Caiaphas, 'being high priest that year.' It was not, of course, that he was thinking—as a good shepherd should have thought—of the people, his flock. 'It is expedient *for you*,' he says. It is the word of a hireling shepherd 'who careth not for the sheep.' This Caiaphas is represented by the Evangelist as the conspiring mind which acts in the supposed interests of 'the nation' (see $18^{13-14, 24,}$ and ^{28}). Luke speaks of him in his Gospel (3^{2}), and Matthew in the chapter in which he narrates the story of the Crucifixion (Mt. 26^{3} and ^{57}). He is also referred to in Acts 4^{6}. He was the high priest in that fateful year. Josephus calls him *Joseph Caiaphas*, and tells us that he followed Annas his father-in-law in the high priesthood, holding the position during the procuratorship of Pontius Pilate.

51. The Evangelist reminds us in *v.* 51 that, as high priest and representing the theocratic rule, he spoke as one who was believed to have the prophetic mind. From various passages in the Old Testament we see that the high priest was expected to speak words of prophecy (see Exod. 28^{30}; Lev. 8^{8}; Num. 27^{21}). We cannot be certain whether these words of Caiaphas were historical or no. It may possibly be that the author is reporting a traditional utterance which may have come down through the medium of such a one as Nicodemus. Being himself, as we have suggested, at this time a young man of priestly family, he would learn at once of such an utterance. Or, it may be that here again we have an utterance of dramatic fitness, attributed by him to one who represented the divine headship of the people. The Evangelist, looking back over the years to the destruction of Jerusalem, when 'the nation' in a very real sense may be said to have perished, may well have attributed to Caiaphas an utterance of which—in the sense primarily suggested—history had proved the falsity. Caiaphas had wanted to serve their Temple and their nationality. Rome was becoming tired of the troubles in this obscure Judæan province, and may well have been contemplating its destruction. Caiaphas, seeking to avoid this, would make of Jesus a kind of scapegoat. But—thought the Evangelist—he only deferred for thirty or forty years the destruction that was feared. The sword was stayed for a season, but later it fell with ruthless severity. And yet—so the Evangelist may have meditated—while this Temple and all for which it stood was destroyed, the death of Jesus was to be fruitful in a way none of the priests in His day ever dreamed. So he makes Caiaphas say more than he knows; and, by the irony of history, to prophesy an end diametrically opposed to the one he had in view. His words are pregnant with a meaning which was true, both to the conscious mission of Jesus and to the experience of His disciples. That mission was for the

spiritual well-being, not of one nation only, but of all nations. The Cross, which consummated that mission, would be a message to all the scattered families of men; and would gather them 'into one'—so that, to recall the words of 10^{16}, there should be 'one flock having one shepherd.' The unifying power of humanity will be the Cross, and all for which it stands. This is what the Evangelist sees in these words attributed to Caiaphas. It is obvious that from now onwards, his Gospel is dominated by the thought of the Crucifixion, its meaning and its mission.

A Brief Period of Suspense

JN. 11^{54-57}

11 54 Jesus therefore walked no more openly
among the Jews, but departed thence
into the country near to the wilderness,
into a city called Ephraim; and there he
55 tarried with the disciples. Now the
passover of the Jews was at hand: and
many went up to Jerusalem out of the
country before the passover, to purify
56 themselves. They sought therefore for
Jesus, and spake one with another, as
they stood in the temple, What think ye?
57 That he will not come to the feast? Now
the chief priests and the Pharisees had
given commandment, that, if any man
knew where he was, he should shew it,
that they might take him.

The final Passover is at hand. The roads and villages on the way to Jerusalem are thronged by pilgrims who wish to reach the city some days before the festival began. Thus they would have time for the necessary rites of purification. 'Every man,' it was said, 'is bound to purify himself for the Feast' (see Lev. 7^{21}; Num. 9^{10}; 2 Chron. $30^{17ff.}$). The Evangelist calls this feast, as in 2^{13}, 'the passover *of the Jews*'—no doubt distinguishing it from 'the Christian passover,' which Paul had in mind in 1 Cor. 5^{7-8}.

Jesus, says the Evangelist, withdraws to the country near to the desert, to a village called Ephraim, some thirteen miles north-east of Jerusalem. There is no other mention of this Ephraim in the New Testament, but it is mentioned by Josephus in connexion with Bethel. In 2 Chron. 13^{19} the two places are also named together. They were probably near to one another.

The twelve hours of the day are nearing their end. The night approaches; but Jesus seeks, in a quiet retreat, some moments for preparation. His disciples are with Him. It is, however, busy noon-day for 'the chief priests and Pharisees.' They have their preparations to make, as well as Jesus. Their commandment is issued, that whoever knows where Jesus is must declare it to them. They are ready 'to take him.'

The Evangelist conveys in these few verses the impression of contrast. On the one hand, the repose and serenity of Jesus—on the other hand, the haste and confusion in Jerusalem. While He prepares to go to the Feast, the people excitedly ask themselves, Will He come or will He not come? Or again, there is the contrast between the self-preparation of Jesus, and the plottings of the rulers. Jesus, the people, the rulers! The first and the last making ready in their respective ways; the second, the tools of confused emotions and conflicting purposes.

THE FINAL RETURN TO JERUSALEM: AND THE FINAL PUBLIC WITNESS

We reach in this chapter the close of the first main section of the Gospel. The public witness of Jesus now ends. It ends as it began, in conflict and division. The Evangelist has shown, in each presentation of the teaching of Jesus, how some have believed and some have opposed; and, in each case, the forces of unbelief have seemed to be more powerful than the forces of belief. As the narrative advances the unbelief hardens into hostility, and at last into a decision to compass the death of Jesus. In this chapter, the author narrates three scenes, each of which closes with the same assertion of hostility. The first is the anointing at Bethany. Here is portrayed a unique manifestation of devotion to Jesus in the intimacy of a family circle; but the incident ends in *v.* 10 with a declaration of death on the part of the rulers. The second is the triumphal entry into Jerusalem. Here the enthusiasm of the people becomes as fuel to the fire of the hatred of the Pharisees (*v.* 19). The third is the request of the Greeks. In this case the desire of Gentiles to see Jesus stands in contrast to a misunderstanding and a hostility from which Jesus 'hides himself' (*v.* 36). Once again, therefore, the nature of the author's mind and of his method is clearly in evidence.

The Anointing at Bethany

JN. 12^{1-11}

12 1 Jesus therefore six days before the passover came to Bethany, where Lazarus
was, whom Jesus raised from the dead.
2 So they made him a supper there: and
Martha served; but Lazarus was one of
3 them that sat at meat with him. Mary
therefore took a pound of ointment of
spikenard, very precious, and anointed
the feet of Jesus, and wiped his feet with
her hair: and the house was filled with
4 the odour of the ointment. But Judas
Iscariot, one of his disciples, which should
5 betray him, saith, Why was not this ointment sold for three hundred pence, and
6 given to the poor? Now this he said,
not because he cared for the poor; but
because he was a thief, and having the
bag took away what was put therein.
7 Jesus therefore said, Suffer her to keep it
8 against the day of my burying. For the
poor ye have always with you; but me
ye have not always.
9 The common people therefore of the
Jews learned that he was there: and they
came, not for Jesus' sake only, but that
they might see Lazarus also, whom he
10 had raised from the dead. But the chief
priests took counsel that they might put
11 Lazarus also to death; because that by
reason of him many of the Jews went
away, and believed on Jesus.

In commenting on the 2nd verse of the 11th chapter reference was made to the three traditions in the Gospels on an anointing of Jesus by a woman. The reader should compare these three carefully, as narrated in Mk. $14^{3ff.}$ (parallel passage, Mt. $26^{6ff.}$), Lk. $7^{36ff.}$, and Jn. 12^{1-8}. This comparison will clearly reveal to the reader the nature of the mind of the Johannine author. It is obvious, in the first place, that he is familiar both with Luke's story of the earlier anointing, and with Mark's story of the later anointing. For in his narrative there are features borrowed from each. His story agrees with Lk. in that it is an anointing of the *feet*, not of the *head* as in Mk., and that the woman wipes the feet of Jesus with her hair. His story agrees with Mk. in that the incident takes place in the closing week of the Ministry, and in Bethany outside Jerusalem; also, in the fact that 'ointment of spikenard'[1] is used, and that the anointing is regarded as in some way related to the forthcoming burial of Jesus. Further, his narrative agrees with Mk. in that in both there is a statement about the waste of the ointment, and in both there is the rebuke of Jesus—'the poor ye have always with you, but me ye have not always.'

There are, however, features in the Fourth Evangelist's story which are not in either of the other two narratives. It is he alone who suggests that the anointing takes place in the house of Martha and Mary: in Lk. it takes place in the house of Simon the Pharisee, and in Mk. in the house of Simon the leper. Further, the Fourth Evangelist tells us that the woman who anointed was Mary the sister of Martha: in the other two narratives she is unnamed, though Lk. tells us that she was 'a sinner.' Yet further, our Evangelist says nothing about the woman's tears, which, in Luke's account, fall upon the feet of Jesus—but inserts a strange statement that she wiped *the ointment* from the feet of Jesus. Still further, the Fourth Evangelist tells us that it was *Judas* who complained about the waste of the precious ointment; while Mk. tells us generally that it was made by 'some of them.'

The commentators and theologians of all the centuries have discussed these three narratives. Some, like Clement of Alexandria and Tertullian, have regarded them as three versions of the one incident; with the resultant identification of Mary of Bethany, Mary Magdalene, and the 'sinful woman' of Lk. 7. Mary Magdalene—that is, Mary of Magdala, a village near to Capernaum—is referred to by Luke in 8^2 just after his story of the anointing, as she 'from whom seven devils had gone out.' In the spurious appendix to Mark's Gospel the author says that there the risen Jesus 'appeared first to Mary Magdalene, from whom he had cast out seven devils' (Mk. 16^9). Now this Mary Magdalene is referred to in all four Gospels as one of the women who went to the tomb of Jesus to anoint His body. The Fourth Evangelist was, therefore, no doubt thinking of this Mary Magdalene and of Mary of Bethany as one and the same woman, when he wrote the words in 12^7, 'Suffer her to keep it against the day of my burying.'

The question, however, of especial interest to the interpreter of this Gospel is here: What light does the narrative throw upon the Evangelist's mind? This, conclusively: that he freely chose features from both Mark's and Luke's narratives, and did not hesitate to embellish them in the interests of his own presentation of the situation. Whether he thought that Luke and Mark narrated two distinct incidents, we do not know. Some have supposed that the same Mary had anointed Jesus twice—once when she was reclaimed from a life of sin, and later, when having returned to her family in Bethany, she re-enacted the incident of her reclamation. This is the view which has been generally held in the Latin Church. What, however, we may safely say is that the Fourth Evangelist did not seek to write precise history; and we cannot use his account to show, either that the incidents recorded by Mk. and Lk. were the same incident, or separate incidents.

[1] The adjective here is *pistikos,* and is found elsewhere in the N.T. only at Mk. 14^3. Its meaning is uncertain. It may mean 'real' or 'genuine,' being taken as derived from *pistis,* faith: that which is *faithful* is that which is genuine, as opposed to that which is spurious—the ointment was 'genuine nard.' Or, the adjective may indicate that the ointment was prepared from the oil of the *pistachio nut* which, we are told, is used to this day for similar purposes in Syria.

With Mark's and Luke's narratives before him, he created his own story in the interests of his own dramatic and allegorical purpose. Details from each are fused in his own creative mind.

His dominant purpose, we suggest, was in the first place to set the unstudied devotion of this Mary over against the mind of the betrayer. Dramatic contrast runs through this Gospel. The Evangelist has never hesitated to create and heighten such contrasts out of the materials he has before him. He has shown how belief strives with unbelief, light with darkness, from the first day of the public ministry of Jesus. He has already, in one vivid sentence—6^{71}—indicated that this strife had even penetrated to the inner sanctuary of the chosen Twelve. He recreates, therefore, this incident of the anointing in order to set in contrast the uncalculating devotion of a woman who had been a sinner, and the critical and covetous scrupulousness of one who belonged to the inner band. Mary's act is as open as the sun. Judas's words as as obscure as the night. The motives of the one are as clear and spontaneous as those of a child. The motives of the other are as hidden and indirect as those of the hireling. The one can give no rational 'reason' for her act. The other can give many quite satisfactory 'reasons' for his words. But the one whose heart has reasons which the reason knoweth not, is *true*: the other whose head can give reasons which the heart knoweth not, is *false*. The act of the one is self-*less*: the words of the other are self-*ish*. Mary leaves the feast more devoted than before: Judas leaves it with the seed of treachery growing apace in his mind. In the one case understanding blossoms into devotion: in the other misunderstanding matures into hatred.

No other evangelist, it should be noted, has said anything about Judas being a 'thief.' Matthew, Mark, and Luke—except for the bare statement, 'who also betrayed him' (Mt. 10^{4}; Mk 3^{19}; Lk. 6^{16})—do not prepare us by the record *by any act* of Judas for his treachery. The Fourth Evangelist *does* prepare his readers: so that in his Gospel the treachery of Judas comes to them with no surprise. In this, the author reveals the artistic and dramatic quality of his mind. Whether the author had some independent knowledge of Judas, we do not, and shall never, know. What we *do* know is that he uses the characteristics he attributes to him as a foil to the devotion of Mary. If we should conclude that the covetousness he assigns to Judas is the Evangelist's own creation, we shall not conclude that it indicates any 'hatred' for a specific individual, or a wish to vilify him. Judas, like 'the Jews,' is to the author an embodiment of 'darkness.'

In the second place, his purpose was to stress the symbolical fitness of the anointing in view of the approaching crucifixion. The words of Jesus in *v.* 7 clearly reveal this purpose. It is difficult to know how we should translate these words. Some would suggest—for example, Dr. Torrey—that the words of Jesus are a question. 'Let her alone: should she keep it for the day of my burial?' This translation implies that she has *already* by this act anointed Him with *all* the ointment, and that there was no reason why she should have kept it till He was dead. Such a translation harmonises with the statement of Mk. that the flask of the ointment *was broken*, and all its contents used (Mk. 14^{3}). Others translate: 'Suffer her to keep it—that is, what has not been used—against the day of my burial'; or 'Let her alone: it was that she might keep it against the day of my burying.' This translation suggests that the present anointing is only preparatory to that other anointing when He was dead. But, as against this latter translation, it should be remembered that the later anointing was done, according to the Evangelist, by Joseph of Arimathæa and Nicodemus (19^{38-40}), and that when Mary went to anoint the body on the first day of the week, the body was no longer there (Jn. 20^1; Mk. 16^1). The difficulties are obvious. It is better, on the whole, to take the first translation, as indicative of what the Evangelist really had in his mind. He is, that is, regarding this anointing as a symbolical anointing of Jesus *prior to* His crucifixion. This is precisely what Mark says in 14^8: 'She hath anointed my body aforehand for the burying.'

The Evangelist declares his message by symbols. In this, he was true to the teaching method of Jesus Himself. For He had regarded, according to Mark, the anointing in Bethany as a symbolical anointing of His body that was soon to suffer death. Some have suggested that the Evangelist even wished to symbolise a spiritual message by his statement that 'the house was filled with the odour of the ointment.' It has been pointed out that the Fourth Evangelist omits the prediction, found in Mk. 14^9, that 'wheresoever the gospel shall be preached throughout the whole world, that also which this woman hath done shall be spoken of for a memorial of her.' This prophetic promise would, then, be replaced by the diffusion of the perfume through the house. The late Bishop Westcott quoted a Rabbinic saying where the same symbol is used. 'Good oil spreads its fragrance from the inner chamber to the hall; a good name reaches from one end of the world to the other.' Augustine in his commentary on this verse said: 'The world is filled with the fame of a good character; for a good character is as a pleasant odour.' Perhaps, however, such an interpretation is to attribute a *too minute* allegorical purpose to the Evangelist's mind. It would, however, harmonise with the view that to the author 'Mary' is but a symbol for the Church.

Before leaving this narrative, which we have endeavoured to expound in its essential features, one other point should be noticed. The Evangelist dates this anointing 'six days before the passover.' Mark, in 14^1, dates it 'two days' before the Feast—that is, on the Wednesday. Which dating is correct, we do not know. The chronological indifference of our author would suggest that his date should not be regarded as historical; though if, as we have suggested, he was a Jerusalemite Jew who had been in touch with Jesus during the closing weeks of His Ministry, it *may be* that here he is definitely correcting the Synoptic dating. On the other hand, it is possible that he is concerned merely with symbolical fitness in his reference to 'six days before the passover.' This day would probably be Nisan 10—though there are differences of opinion on the point, some maintaining that the day was Saturday, Nisan 9—and this was the day, according to Exod. 12^3, on which the lamb was set apart for the Feast. In the first chapter of the Gospel John the Baptist had said: 'Behold the lamb of God that taketh away the sin of the world.' The same thought of the sacrificial lamb may well have been in the mind of the Evangelist in this narrative.

The reference to Lazarus in *vv.* 9 and 10—as also in *vv.* 1 and 2—of this chapter will seem to some to forbid the allegorical interpretation of the incident which we have accepted. It will be said: How can we imagine that the author himself sought to write allegorically when these verses so definitely presuppose historical fact? The objection is specious, but arises, we suggest, from a failure to understand the mind of the Evangelist. If, as we have maintained, he was allegorising some historical incident, there is no reason why his mind should not continue to think of 'Lazarus' as he has portrayed him in his dramatic allegory. The reference to 'Lazarus' no more presupposes the precise historicity of the 'raising' to the Evangelist, than does the reference to the 'water made wine' in 4^{46} presuppose the precise historicity, in the mind of the Evangelist, of the incident at Cana of Galilee in chapter 2. In each case, the dramatic allegorist recalls an incident, recreated under an allegorising motif, in his previous narrative.

The Triumphal Entry into Jerusalem

JN. 12^{12-19}

12 12 On the morrow a great multitude that
had come to the feast, when they heard
13 that Jesus was coming to Jerusalem, took
the branches of the palm trees, and went
forth to meet him, and cried out,
Hosanna: Blessed *is* he that cometh in
the name of the Lord, even the King of
14 Israel. And Jesus, having found a
young ass, sat thereon; as it is written,
15 Fear not, daughter of Zion: behold, thy
King cometh, sitting on an ass's colt.
16 These things understood not his disciples
at the first: but when Jesus was glorified,
then remembered they that these things
were written of him, and that they had
17 done these things unto him. The multitude therefore that was with him when
he called Lazarus out of the tomb, and
raised him from the dead, bare witness.
18 For this cause also the multitude went
and met him, for that they heard that he
19 had done this sign. The Pharisees therefore said among themselves, Behold how
ye prevail nothing: lo, the world is gone
after him.

The *second* scene portrayed by the author in this closing chapter of the first main section of his Gospel is that of the 'triumphal' entry into Jerusalem. It is narrated here as *following* the anointing by Mary; in Mk. it is recorded as *preceding* that anointing (Mk. $11^{1ff.}$). The custom of the Church in commemorating the entry on 'Palm Sunday' is based on the Fourth Gospel: though it is based on the view that the anointing took place on Saturday, Nisan 9, the entry, therefore, falling on Sunday, Nisan 10.

Probably we have here another illustration of the Evangelist's chronological indifference. He omits details which the other evangelists give, and inserts points which they omit. Nevertheless, the essential features of the incident as narrated by Mark are retained. The Evangelist tells that Jesus rode on an ass, but does not say anything about how, or where, the ass was found. He relates that the people took 'branches of the *palm* trees' with them when they went to meet Jesus; while Mark and the other Synoptic writers merely say they took 'branches which they had cut from the fields.' Further, like Mark, he quotes the passage from Ps. 118^{26}: 'Hosanna! Blessed is he that cometh in the name of the Lord'; but, where Mark says that it is the *Kingdom* that comes, our Evangelist says it is 'the King of Israel' who comes. Luke also (19^{38}) narrates the saying, to the effect that it is the 'King' who comes. Yet further, the Fourth Evangelist quotes—as Matthew alone, apart from him, had done (Mt. 21^{4})—the words of Zechariah's prophecy, 'Behold, thy King cometh, sitting on an ass's colt' (Zech. 9^{9});

but he adds a statement peculiar to his own Gospel—' these things understood not his disciples at the first: but when Jesus was glorified, then remembered they that these things were written of him, and that they had done these things unto him ' (*v.* 16).

These facts clearly reveal the author's intention in this narrative. Probably he had the three Synoptic narratives of the incident before him when he wrote—Mk. 11^{7-10}; Mt. 21^{4-5}; Lk. 19^{35-38}—but his narrative is freely created in the interests of his own purpose. He wishes to portray this entry of Jesus into Jerusalem as the entry of one who was a kingly victor, but not a king in the common meaning of that term. Jesus is twice called ' king,' but the passage from Zechariah which he quotes shows what kind of king He was. And the reference to ' *palm* branches ' is a symbolic representation of the *victory* He was come to achieve. The details which the Fourth Evangelist inserts are such, therefore, as to heighten the allegorical and dramatic symbolism of the entry. No other evangelist has said that *palm* branches were used by the people: and no other evangelist has the *two* distinct references to the *kingship* of Jesus.

13. First, then, the reference to the *palm branches*. Palm branches, according to Lev. 23^{40}, were to be carried by the people during the rejoicings of the Feast of Tabernacles. When Simon Maccabeus entered Jerusalem in triumph, ' he entered with thanksgiving and branches of palm trees and with harps and cymbals and with viols and hymns and songs; because there was destroyed a great enemy out of Israel ' (1 *Macc.* 13^{51}). And when his brother, Judas Maccabeus, delivered Jerusalem from the Syrians, the people ' bare branches and fair boughs, and palms also, and sang psalms' (2 *Macc.* 10^{7}). In the Book of the Revelation (7^{9}) the great multitude who stand before the throne and before the lamb are ' clothed with white robes, and palms in their hands.' The palm was widely regarded as the emblem of victory in the world of the Evangelist's day. He did not insert this reference fortuitously. It is part of the symbolism which conveyed the meaning of the incident as he saw it. Jesus—as victor, not as vanquished—was entering the Jerusalem which had rejected Him. The Cross would not be His defeat, but His glorification. We have already seen how, to the Evangelist, the ' glorification ' of Jesus was as much the *Cross* as the Resurrection. The palm branches symbolise, then, the *triumph* of the Passion. That it was so to the *mind of Jesus Himself*, we have already maintained. The author has here, once again, symbolised the essential consciousness of Jesus. He has given dramatic narrative form to an essentially spiritual claim on the part of Jesus.

Secondly, the words from Ps. 118^{26} with which the people greeted Jesus. This was a refrain customarily sung at the Feast of Tabernacles, when palm branches also were carried by the worshippers. The word *Hosanna* is a Hebrew invocation which means, by etymology, ' Save, we beseech thee.' The branches borne by the people at the Feast of Tabernacles were also called *Hosannas*. The word is left untranslated in our English version, being merely transliterated—like the words *Amen*, *Hallelujah*, and *Sabbath*. When the people shouted ' Hosanna,' that does not mean that *they themselves* meant that they were hailing Jesus as Saviour. Like the words *Good-bye* and *Adieu*, it was used by those who did not trouble about its original, or etymological, meaning. Yet it is congruous with the mind of the Evangelist, as it is revealed to us in his Gospel, to suppose that to him the word was a symbolic representation of the saving mission and claim of Jesus. If, therefore, we are to do justice to what the *Evangelist himself* meant to convey, we should render the word ' Hosanna ' by some such phrase as, ' Save, we beseech thee.' Our Lord was entering Jerusalem, as He believed, for the last time; and in obedience to what He felt to be the Father's will for Him. That will was a *saving* will. He was come to deliver men from all that withheld them from eternal life. The Evangelist, in combining ' palm branches ' with the ' Hosanna,' is saying: Jesus came to Jerusalem as the *Victorious Saviour*.

Further, the words, ' even the king of Israel,' express the Messianic claim and consciousness of Jesus. We do not know how far, or in what sense, these people regarded Jesus as Messiah. At least, we are sure that they did not understand what Jesus's own mission was, nor what His claim to Messiahship meant to Himself. The later events of the Passion week in Jerusalem make that clear. Nathanael, it will be remembered, had confessed, in the opening chapter of the Gospel; ' Thou art the King of Israel ' (1^{49}). The Evangelist, then, narrates the incident so as to mean: Jesus came to Jerusalem as the Victorious Saviour *who is King*.

14–15. Further, Jesus rides on *an ass*. Mark and Luke had recorded that Jesus rode on *a colt*: Matthew had used both words, ' colt ' and ' ass.' The Fourth Evangelist, thus, like Matthew, sees in this entry of Jesus, riding on an ass, the symbolism of the vision of Zechariah. What was this symbolism? The earliest commentators have regarded the riding on a young ass as symbolising the *humility* of Jesus. Chrysostom very beautifully said that Jesus entered Jerusalem ' not driving chariots like the rest of the kings, not demanding tributes, not thrusting men off, and leading about guards, but displaying His great meekness hereby.' It is a mistake, however, to think that the ass necessarily symbolised humility. In the West it is regarded as a very humble beast of burden: in the East as a very valuable beast of burden, where also it is used for riding. Ahithophel (2 Sam. 17^{23}) and Mephibosheth (2 Sam. 19^{26}) rode upon asses. The riding upon the ass by Jesus symbolised, both to Himself and to the Johannine author, the *nature of His mission*. It was a mission of *Peace*. The horse and the chariot to the Hebrews were symbolical of warlike forces. Men fear those whose mission is war: they do not fear those whose mission is peace. Hence, the author preludes the prophecy from Zechariah which he quotes, with the words, ' Fear not '—words which are not themselves used by Zechariah in this place. The Evangelist is thinking of Zechariah's prophetic vision, but he is not thinking of his precise words. The choice of an ass, instead of a horse, by Jesus is, the Evangelist feels, of the highest significance. It revealed both what Jesus sought to do, and what the Church of later years had found in His fellowship.

Jesus comes, therefore, as one who would *appeal* to men, not as one who would *coerce* men. The demand He makes is a high and exacting one; but it is a peaceful one. He calls men to *see*, and to *live*—not to *fight* and to *die*. The enemy from whom He would deliver them is no external enemy. The freedom He would give is no mere liberty of circumstance. He comes as the Prince of Peace.

16. The Evangelist tells us that it was only later that the disciples understood

the significance of the act. Jesus had been familiar with the vision of Zechariah. He remembered the vision of the king riding upon an ass who would destroy chariot and horse and battle-bow. 'Rejoice greatly, O daughter of Zion; shout, O daughter of Jerusalem: behold, thy king cometh unto thee: he is just, and having salvation; lowly, and riding upon an ass, even upon a colt the foal of an ass. And I will cut off the chariot from Ephraim, and the horse from Jerusalem, and the battle-bow shall be cut off; and he shall speak peace unto the nations: and his dominion shall be from sea to sea, and from the River to the ends of the earth.' The act of Jesus, in entering Jerusalem upon an ass, had not been fortuitous. He was expressing in symbolic and dramatic manner what He was seeking to do and how He was seeking to do it. He was appealing in a striking and public manner to the people thronging the road to Jerusalem. But it was no popular appeal He was making. He claims to be God's Anointed One; but He is more concerned to show the nature of the mission for which He was anointed. Many of the people recognise that He claimed to be Messiah; but they did not recognise what true Messiahship meant to Jesus. Brooding over this whole narrative is the thought of the Passion which is to follow in a few days. To the people, the thought of a criminal's cross on which Jesus would hang would have quenched every rejoicing and silenced every Hosanna. How could a king be crucified? A victor slain? In this popular demonstration there may have been some who saw truly, but they were few. To most the mark of the victor was Death—but the death *of others*, not His own. To Jesus, the mark of the victor was the Cross. His kingdom was to be a kingdom not of this world.

It was the meaning of the symbolic act to the mind of Jesus that the Evangelist says the disciples did not see till afterwards. Even their conception of Messiahship was not *His*. It was only later that they came to understand what was in the Master's mind. The Fourth Evangelist's insight into that mind was clear and deep—clearer and deeper than that of any other writer in the New Testament.

Thus the key to the meaning of the whole incident is in three words: Victory, Kingship, Peace. In the war that lies ahead the King of Peace will get Himself the Victory; but not a victory on which men's hearts were set, or over a foe they deemed to be great.

Henry Vaughan, our seventeenth-century mystical poet, expressed the inner significance of the incident in his verses:

Come, drop your branches, strew the way,
Plants of the day!
Whom sufferings make most green and gay.
The King of grief, the man of sorrow
Weeping still, like the wet morrow,
Your shades and freshness comes to borrow.

Put on, put on your best array;
Let the joyed road make holiday,
And flowers, that into fields do stray,
Or secret groves, keep the highway.

Trees, flowers, and herbs ; birds, beasts, and stones,
That since man fell, except with groans
To see the Lamb, come, all at once,
Lift up your heads and leave your moans !
For here comes He
Whose death will be
Man's life, and your full liberty.

19. The scene ends with the assertion of the same hostility which broods over every manifestation of the mind of Jesus. 'The world is gone after him,' so the Pharisees think. It is the desperate cry of those who over-rate the significance of numbers.

The Inquiry of the Greeks

JN. $12^{20\text{-}36a}$

12 20 Now there were certain Greeks among
those that went up to worship at the
21 feast: these therefore came to Philip,
which was of Bethsaida of Galilee, and
asked him, saying, Sir, we would see
22 Jesus. Philip cometh and telleth Andrew: Andrew cometh, and Philip, and
23 they tell Jesus. And Jesus answereth
them, saying, The hour is come, that the
24 Son of man should be glorified. Verily,
verily, I say unto you, Except a grain of
wheat fall into the earth and die, it
abideth by itself alone; but if it die, it
25 beareth much fruit. He that loveth his
life loseth it; and he that hateth his life
in this world shall keep it unto life
26 eternal. If any man serve me, let him
follow me; and where I am, there shall
also my servant be: if any man serve
27 me, him will the Father honour. Now is
my soul troubled; and what shall I say?
Father, save me from this hour. But for
28 this cause came I unto this hour. Father,
glorify thy name. There came therefore
a voice out of heaven, *saying*, I have both
glorified it, and will glorify it again.
29 The multitude therefore, that stood by,
and heard it, said that it had thundered:
others said, An angel hath spoken to him.
30 Jesus answered and said, This voice hath
not come for my sake, but for your sakes.
31 Now is the judgement of this world: now
shall the prince of this world be cast out.
32 And I, if I be lifted up from the earth,
33 will draw all men unto myself. But this
he said, signifying by what manner of
34 death he should die. The multitude
therefore answered him, We have heard
out of the law that the Christ abideth for
ever: and how sayest thou, The Son of
man must be lifted up? who is this Son
35 of man? Jesus therefore said unto them,
Yet a little while is the light among you.
Walk while ye have the light, that darkness overtake you not: and he that
walketh in the darkness knoweth not
36 whither he goeth. While ye have the
light, believe on the light, that ye may
become sons of light.

The third scene in this chapter is one in which the meaning of the death of Jesus to Himself is unfolded. The setting is a request from some 'Greeks' to see Him. It is the one incident recorded by the Evangelist between the public entry into Jerusalem and the Last Supper. The scene has a peculiar dramatic fitness in the whole setting of the Gospel ; and this forbids our building too much on its historicity. Though some such incident may well have happened in the closing days of the Ministry in Jerusalem, yet the Evangelist's chief concern is the unfolding of the consciousness of Jesus in this dark hour. The Evangelist uses the incident as a frame for the discourse of Jesus which follows. Having narrated the request of the Greeks, he says nothing more about them. He does not tell us, for example, whether they were admitted to the presence of Jesus. They are shadowy figures introduced, not in their own interest, but in the interest of the presentation of the mind of Jesus. What the author wishes to say is this: Jesus regarded His death as necessary to the Father's will for Him, and for the consummation of His work.

The whole paragraph can be divided into three parts. There is, first, the inquiry (20–22). There is, second, the answer of Jesus, with the accompanying voice from heaven (23–33). There is, third, a final warning by Jesus (34–36).

20–22. These were not *Hellenists*, or Greek-speaking Jews, but 'proselytes of the gate.' They were such 'devout Greeks' as consorted with Paul and Silas at Thessalonica (Acts 17[4]). Those who take the narrative as precisely historical, point to the fact that it is to Philip they make their request. He, like Andrew, has a Greek name; and it has been thought that he may have been of Greek lineage, and, therefore, completely at home with their language. He was from 'Bethsaida of Galilee,' in the north-east corner of the province of Galilee, where doubtless many Greek families were found. The request is expressive of the religious needs and aspirations of the best men in the Gentile world. 'We would see Jesus.' The Evangelist himself had such a cry in his mind when he wrote his Gospel. He is seeking to show to men what Jesus was really like. The scenes and discourses of his Gospel are all penned under the dominating desire to show Jesus to men—what He really was in the depth of His unique mind, and what He really sought to do in the complete dedication of His life to the Father's will.

23–32. The reply of Jesus is so profound—and yet so simple—that the commentator feels that the words might well be left to speak their own message. Careful analytical scrutiny of such words may so easily hide from us their essential 'word.' It is impossible not to believe that this is the teaching of the historic Jesus. If some of the details of the narrative-setting belong to the Evangelist, the teaching itself belongs to Jesus. They are a transcript of the Master's essential mind.

No one can tell us all that Jesus thought and pondered during the closing days of His earthly pilgrimage. It is His own words that tell us best His secret. And the words before us have a fitness for these last days which bespeak their essential truth. He sees His earthly end approaching in Jerusalem. It comes to one in the full vigour of life. Did not the thought arise within Him: so little done, so much to do? So many wide fields of the Gentiles in which to sow the seed, so small the Palestinian field in which the seed has been sown! Was it too late to seek these wider fields and to accomplish a more extensive mission? But no. The thought of the wider fields, waiting for the sowing, recalls the lesson of Nature's own seed. The glorification by the Cross is the Father's way to the harvest. *Eternal* harvests are garnered by ways that are *eternal*. Popular applause seems good; but it is a delusive good. In compassing sea and land men may feel that they are doing much work; but lasting good is a work of eternity, where values, and not numbers or miles, are the standard of success. Does not Nature herself say this? The corn of wheat has to fall into the ground and die, if there is to be a resulting harvest. Jesus, like all the other, and lesser, seers of humanity, had lived close to Nature, and had pondered Nature's lessons. As we know from the Synoptic Gospels, He had spoken of His work as a sowing of seed in different kinds of ground. Here He speaks of the law of sacrifice which the destiny and function of the seed itself discloses. Some corn is eaten; and some is sown. What is eaten is of immediate profit; what is sown is of lasting profit. For the latter by dying in the ground, brings forth the grain which—ever by the same process—will be fruitful for all the ages to come. Seed that is immediately consumed is *dead*. Seed that is sown dies but to live in an abundant harvest. Death in one case, is a *final* issue; in the other, it is an issue in which are stored the living potencies of the future.

So is it with His own life—and with every other life. For Himself, the way of the Cross was the way of life. For all others the same law holds. He who would live for the immediate present will lose eternal good. His values are of time, not of eternity; of sense, not of spirit; of self, not of the Father. Such a life disintegrates with the inevitability of 'dust to dust, ashes to ashes.' It has no future—or, rather, no eternity. It partakes of the transitoriness of the materialistic shows of a delusive world. Its end is death. But he who would renounce the vanities of immediate profit and of selfish ends will gain eternal good. Wrapped up in the sanctuary of his life is a seed which, being sown in the ground of sacrificial service, has the potencies of eternity within it. For the life which is *given* partakes of the very life of God, whose nature it is to give. Not only is it fruitful to others: it is fruitful in and by itself. Eternity is hid in its heart. Such a life seems to the world to be imprisoned: but its prison is a womb. Its end is life.

27–30. Jesus therefore would not be saved from His hour, no matter how 'troubled' His human soul was by the tension of His experiences. The Evangelist does not record the Agony in Gethsemane, but it is that agony, and that triumph of faith, which is expressed in these verses. The 'voice out of heaven' is the assurance to the mind of Jesus in His last days that this way of the Cross was indeed the Father's way for Him. It is, says the Evangelist, a voice 'out of heaven'—that is, it is the Voice of the Father, heard and witnessed within. The people—so the author continues—thought they heard an *outward* witness, but there was only *one* witness for Jesus—the inward witness. Whether a *physical* phenomenon ever accompanied the spiritual experiences of Jesus, we do not know. Spiritistic interpreters do not regard such as impossible, or, indeed, as unlikely. The Evangelist is no doubt familiar with the tradition in the Church about the physically audible words reported to have been heard at the Baptism and at the Transfiguration—though he narrates neither. What happened on those occasions happened on this occasion. On three unforgettable moments in the life of Jesus His disciples had gained, perhaps from the radiance from His face, an irrefutable testimony of what was happening in the depths of His consciousness. Each was a moment of action; and each was a moment of renunciation. Each was a call to service—but to service through suffering and humiliation.

The Evangelist would not say here that any physically audible sound was heard. It was a 'voice from heaven.' It was not for *His* sake but *for their sakes*. These verses—28–30—are a narrative transcript of the certitude of Jesus, at the critical moments of His ministry, of the Father's mission for Him. This is their primary import. But they convey at the same time the tradition of a physically audible sound. In recording the latter the Evangelist makes it perfectly clear that what matters is the inward witness, not any outward witness. Verse 30—a difficult verse—should be taken as the Evangelist's dramatic—and distortingly dramatic—way of saying this.

31. So assured is Jesus that it is the Father's mission He is fulfilling, that *already* victory is seen in His death. 'Now' is the world judged: 'Now' is its Prince overthrown. The power of evil in the world has found nothing in Him. His victory is the sure presage of the final victory. He has overcome the world; and, as the Johannine author elsewhere interprets the mind of Jesus, it is the same kind of faith as that which Jesus perfectly incarnated which gives men the victory as well. 'This is the victory that hath overcome the world, even our faith' (1 Jn. 5^4).

32. And, further, this victory, consummated on the Cross, will be the bond which will draw men to Himself in a *universal* fellowship. 'I will draw *all men*.' Once again, the universalistic note peals forth in this Gospel. The word of Jesus in *v.* 32 does not say *when* or *how* His Cross will consummate the Kingdom He seeks to establish. What it does say is that this final manifestation of the Divine Word incarnate in Him will be a universal bond. There is that, deep-planted in all men—however different in race, culture, or credal opinion—which will respond to this drawing. It is the faith of Jesus that sacrificial love is the key to the Father's heart and mind; and the key to the future. The Cross is the emblem of the purpose, and the final victory, of God. If it is difficult at times to believe this, let us remember that it was the last conviction on which Jesus built His life. The love which is *of God* will prevail. The truest word which Eternity has ever spoken in time was spoken by a Cross on Golgotha.

34–36. The final passage in this section of the chapter is the warning answer of Jesus to the credulity of 'the multitude.' It was the 'multitude' which had shouted 'Hosanna'; it was the 'multitude' which misunderstood His mind. 'Who is this Son of man?' they asked. Such hopes as they had could not be reconciled with a suffering Messiah. The belief that the Christ would abide for ever seemed taught in the Old Testament Scriptures—in such passages as Is. 9^7, Ps. 89^4, 110^4, and Ezek. 37^{25}. Nor could their narrow desires be fulfilled in a kingdom of *men*: their king was to be, not Son of man, but Son of David.

The answer of Jesus to difficulties, which were begotten of traditional and sectional views of the Messianic kingdom, is that it is for them to walk by the light which is shining before them in Himself. They had been walking by the broken lights of the long distant past. They want as King one who 'abides for ever.' If they will follow the Light which shines before them through Him, they will not be overtaken by darkness—whatever the future has in store. They will become veritable 'sons of light,' bearing within them the light that is eternal. Jesus had used the phrase 'sons of light,' as we know from Lk. 16^8. He means by it those who are spiritually enlightened. The 'sons of light' are the 'sons of the Father,' for the Father is the Source of Light. The genitive, 'of light,' indicates the *essential quality* of a man. Thus a 'son of light' is an *enlightened man.*

The Evangelist's Judgement on the Final Rejection of Jesus by the Jews

JN. 12^{36b-43}

12 36b These things spake Jesus, and he departed and hid himself from them.
37 But though he had done so many signs before them, yet they believed not on
38 him: that the word of Isaiah the prophet might be fulfilled, which he spake,

Lord, who hath believed our report?
And to whom hath the arm of the Lord been revealed?

39 For this cause they could not believe, for that Isaiah said again,

40 He hath blinded their eyes, and he hardened their heart;
Lest they should see with their eyes, and perceive with their heart,
And should turn,
And I should heal them.

41 These things said Isaiah, because he saw
42 his glory; and he spake of him. Nevertheless even of the rulers many believed on him; but because of the Pharisees they did not confess *it*, lest they should be put
43 out of the synagogue: for they loved the glory of men more than the glory of God.

The Evangelist gives in these verses his own summing up of the rejection of Jesus. As a Jew, he naturally turns to the Old Testament for some illuminating word on so strange, so perplexing, an issue. Paul, before him, had sought in Rom. 9–11 to see a way through so dark an enigma of history. It is difficult for us to-day to appreciate how great a perplexity this rejection must have seemed to the Jewish Christians of the first century. Why should their nation, with so rich a heritage of religious insight, have rejected Jesus? The answer of the Evangelist is found in the Book of Isaiah. Like Paul in Rom. 10^{16}, he remembers the great passage on the Suffering Servant in Is. 53, and quotes its first verse, where the prophet speaks of the unbelief in his day. Unbelief in Israel, he sees, was not confined to the day when Jesus taught and lived. God's 'words' in the prophet's 'report' had not been believed: the 'work' of God's 'arm' had not been seen. The Evangelist then quotes from Is. 6^{10}—as Jesus Himself had done (Mk. 4^{12}), and also Paul (Acts 28^{26}). This passage attributed the unbelief of Israel to blindness. Our author does not immerse himself—like some of the later 'theologians' of the Church—in issues which the human mind can never resolve. He did not, that is, undertake the task of Milton's angels, who—

reasoned high
Of providence, foreknowledge, will and fate,
Fixed fate, free will, foreknowledge absolute;
And found no end in wandering mazes lost.

As in the rest of the Gospel, the only answer given is that spiritual blindness is the cause of the rejection of the spiritual. Those who refuse to see, lose the power to see. Those who will not obey, lose the power to obey. It was, thought the Evangelist, because Isaiah was illumined by the glory afterwards incarnate in Jesus that he saw what he saw and spoke as he spoke. Yet the rejection of Jesus was not complete; for 'even of the rulers many believed on him.' Their belief, however, was not less blameworthy than the unbelief of the majority; for it found no expression in open avowal. Self-interest or worldly wisdom robbed them of the moral courage without which faith is dead. 'They loved,' says the Evangelist, in a word which sums up the whole moral and spiritual issue, 'the praise of men more than the praise of God.' The honour which comes from men was prized far above the honour which comes from God.

The Summing Up of Jesus Himself

JN. 12^{44-50}

12 44 And Jesus cried and said, He that
believeth on me, believeth not on me, but
45 on him that sent me. And he that beholdeth me beholdeth him that sent me.
46 I am come a light into the world, that
whosoever believeth on me may not abide
47 in the darkness. And if any man hear
my sayings, and keep them not, I judge
him not: for I came not to judge the world,
48 but to save the world. He that rejecteth
me, and receiveth not my sayings, hath
one that judgeth him: the word that I
spake, the same shall judge him in the
49 last day. For I spake not from myself;
but the Father which sent me, he hath
given me a commandment, what I should
50 say, and what I should speak. And I
know that his commandment is life
eternal: the things therefore which I
speak, even as the Father hath said unto
me, so I speak.

Some students of the Gospel transpose—without any MS. authority—these verses, so as to follow the first part of *v.* 36. So taken, the verses would thus precede the paragraph we have just sought to interpret. Such students feel that this final warning of Jesus naturally follows the warning in *v.* 36; and naturally precedes the summing up of the Evangelist. For ourselves, however, there seems a fine appropriateness in the place the verses have in all our MSS. The Evangelist's last word in this first main section of his Gospel will be, not his own, but that of Jesus. His dramatic method, and chronological unconcern, are again clearly evidenced. We leave the verses, therefore, where we find them. Let us not try to impose upon him a method, and a concern, which were not his.

The verses themselves need no detailed interpretation, for they but reiterate the main notes in the teaching of Jesus already given. The Evangelist places upon the lips of Jesus here, in one final passage, what he knew to be central to the Master's mind. The dominating note is the unique filial certitude of the Father possessed by Jesus. The other notes in the whole chord sounded in these verses are: first, that it is belief in Jesus which dispels darkness; second, that the function of Jesus is to save and not to judge; third, that rejection of Jesus is itself a judgement; fourth, that the Father's will as expressed in Jesus is eternal life. These are the truths which the incarnate Word speaks. 'So I speak,' says Jesus. These are, indeed, the truths which Jesus did teach. They are the essential aspects of His message. 'He that hath ears to hear, let him hear.'

PART II (XIII–XX)

The Witness of Jesus among His Friends on the Night of the Betrayal, and the Final Issue of the Conflict in His Passion and Resurrection

The Evangelist now enters upon the second main section of his Gospel. This is devoted to the witness of Jesus to His intimate disciples on the night of the Betrayal, and to the final issue of the whole conflict between Light and Darkness, between Belief and Unbelief, in the Passion and Resurrection. No one who has studied the Gospel carefully can fail to see that this division belongs to the author's own mind. It is not imported into the Gospel by the reader: it was consciously before the mind of the Evangelist. He was aware of the contrast, and accentuates it. He has closed the 12th chapter with a summing up of the teaching of Jesus. He begins the 13th chapter with the dramatic word—*The hour is now come.* The hour which, as he has kept reminding us throughout the first section was yet to come—in 2^{4}, $7^{8,\ 30,\ 39}$, 8^{20}—is here.

This section itself is divided into two main subsections. There is, first, the witness of Jesus before His intimate disciples. This covers chapters 13–17. There is, second, the story of the Passion and the Resurrection. This covers chapters 18–20.

A. THE WITNESS OF JESUS AMONG HIS FRIENDS ON THE NIGHT OF THE BETRAYAL (13–17)

AT THE LAST SUPPER: THE FOOT-WASHING

JN. 13^{1-20}

13 1 Now before the feast of the passover,
Jesus knowing that his hour was come
that he should depart out of this world
unto the Father, having loved his own
which were in the world, he loved them
2 unto the end. And during supper, the
devil having already put into the heart
of Judas Iscariot, Simon's *son*, to betray
3 him, *Jesus*, knowing that the Father had
given all things into his hands, and that
he came forth from God, and goeth unto
4 God, riseth from supper, and layeth aside
his garments; and he took a towel, and
5 girded himself. Then he poureth water
into the bason, and began to wash the
disciples' feet, and to wipe them with the
6 towel wherewith he was girded. So he
cometh to Simon Peter. He saith unto
him, Lord, dost thou wash my feet?
7 Jesus answered and said unto him, What
I do thou knowest not now; but thou shalt
8 understand hereafter. Peter saith unto
him, Thou shalt never wash my feet.
Jesus answered him, If I wash thee not,
9 thou hast no part with me. Simon
Peter saith unto him, Lord, not my feet
only, but also my hands and my head.
10 Jesus saith to him, He that is bathed
needeth not save to wash his feet, but is
clean every whit: and ye are clean, but
11 not all. For he knew him that should
betray him; therefore said he, Ye are not
all clean.
12 So when he had washed their feet, and
taken his garments, and sat down again,
he said unto them, Know ye what I have
13 done to you? Ye call me, Master, and,
14 Lord: and ye say well; for so I am. If
I then, the Lord and the Master, have
washed your feet, ye also ought to wash
15 one another's feet. For I have given you
an example, that ye also should do as I
16 have done to you. Verily, verily, I say
unto you, A servant is not greater than
his lord; neither one that is sent greater
17 that he that sent him. If you know these
things, blessed are ye if ye do them. I
18 speak not of you all: I know whom I have
chosen: but that the scripture may be
fulfilled, He that eateth my bread lifted

19 up his heel against me. From henceforth
I tell you before it come to pass, that,
when it is come to pass, ye may believe
20 that I am *he*. Verily, verily, I say unto
you, He that receiveth whomsoever I
send receiveth me; and he that receiveth
me receiveth him that sent me.

1–3. The Evangelist begins with his account of the Last Supper. His introduction in the first three verses is characteristic of his mind and of his method. He here interprets the consciousness of Jesus. Firstly, he tells us that Jesus was aware that 'his hour was come.' Secondly, he tells us that the love of Jesus which inspired all His service was now to be seen in an act of uttermost devotion; 'having loved his own which were in the world he loved them *to the uttermost*.' The love, here referred to, is love for 'his own.' The seeming *exclusiveness* does not, of course, contradict anything which the author has already said about the *universality* of the loving mission of Jesus. It is the author's way of directing the thought of his readers to the *intimacy* of the scene and of the words now to be narrated, and to the *boundlessness* of the love of Jesus now to be manifested. Thirdly, he tells us that while the treachery in the mind of Judas was known to Jesus, yet the Lord's actions were the *free* expression of His unique and authoritative knowledge of God. The treachery did not *dictate* the action of one who did what He *knew* in the depths of His consciousness He must do.

The incident before us throws a vivid light, not only upon the mind of Jesus, but upon the mind of the Evangelist. In order to do justice to both, it is necessary —before commenting on the foot-washing—to consider two important questions. First, the date of the Supper to the Evangelist, and second, the absence from his narrative of the 'institution' of the Lord's Supper.

(1) According to St. Mark, the Last Supper took place on the evening of 'the first day of unleavened bread, when they sacrificed the passover' (Mk. 14^{12}). He therefore holds that the Last Supper was the passover meal, or at any rate that it took place at the time of that meal. This is also the view of Matthew ($26^{2, 17, 19, 20}$) and Luke ($22^{1, 7, 13, 14}$). The Fourth Evangelist, on the other hand, dates the Last Supper on the day before the passover feast, as is clear from *vv.* 1 and 29 of this chapter and from *v.* 28 of the 18th chapter. In the latter passage we are told that the passover was not eaten till the evening of the day on which Jesus was crucified.

Which day is correct? There are good grounds for concluding that on this issue the Fourth Evangelist's date should be accepted. The first ground is that of *intrinsic probability*. Mark himself tells us (14^{2})—see also Mt. 26^{5}—that the Sanhedrin wish to avoid the arrest and death of Jesus on the day of the Feast. It is difficult to believe that the Procurator would have permitted such a trial and death on an important festival. There is a second ground, which may be regarded as an important piece of *external evidence*. The Eastern Church has always used *leavened* bread for the Eucharist: this implies the tradition of the Fourth Gospel.

If the Fourth Evangelist's date be accepted, the Crucifixion took place at the time when the passover lambs and kids were being sacrificed. We have seen that such symbolism appealed greatly to the author; and we can believe that he would not have hesitated—if necessary—to alter a date to suit his symbolical purpose. The probability, however, in this case, is that the appropriateness of the symbolism was already to hand in the day on which the Crucifixion took place. Further, since Jesus treated this Last Supper as a Paschal meal, it is easy to understand why the Synoptic evangelists came to read it as such.

(2) In the second place, there is the Evangelist's omission of any reference to the 'institution' of what is variously called by Christians the Lord's Supper, Holy Communion, and the Eucharist. What can be said of this?

It cannot be said, in the first place, that his omission indicates that he was not acquainted with it. The dramatic and symbolic action of Jesus, when He took the bread, broke it, and gave to the disciples, saying, 'This is my body,' was obviously familiar to him—he had read the Synoptic accounts and that of Paul. That he should not have narrated this acted parable of Jesus raises a very interesting question: for, from the obvious nature of his mind, this is just the kind of incident we should expect him to record. His omission of what are often called 'the actual words of institution'—namely, 'this do in remembrance of me'—raises another interesting question, giving rise to issues more debatable than the former omission. It seems clear, from a study of the four relevant New Testament passages—Mt. 26^{26-29}; Mk. 14^{22-25}; Lk. 22^{15-22}; 1 Cor. 11^{23-25}—that Paul is our only authority for these words of 'institution'; though it has to be remembered that he tells us definitely that this was part of what he had 'received' from the tradition of the Church of his day.

What we have to do is to *explain* this silence, and not just to *explain it away*. Silence does not bespeak ignorance; but it does bespeak *something*. An author's *silences* give as valid a clue to his mind and purpose as his *insertions*. They throw light on his *emphasis*; and, let us not forget, a man's emphasis is the man. 'What you shout, I whisper: what you whisper, I shout.' We merely *explain away*, therefore, this silence when we say—as is frequently said—that 'if the Eucharist as it was developing in the practice and doctrine of the Church at the end of the first century, was an unwarrantable deduction from what passed at the Last Supper, the Johannine author was bound to have revealed the fact.' Such a statement does not *explain* his silence. The Evangelist had his reasons for what he left unsaid, as well as for what he said.

He does not record the story of the 'institution' of the Lord's Supper, not because he was unaware of that solemn breaking of the bread in the Upper Room and of the words of Jesus on that occasion; but because he had something which to him, *in the circumstances of his day*, was more important to emphasise. It is clear, from the whole Gospel, that the Evangelist's central intention was to elucidate the Master's deeply spiritual teaching. It was his view—to use the words of a recent interpreter of this Gospel—'that the Synoptists had imperfectly appreciated the higher and more spiritual side of the Master's teaching.'[1] It was also, we believe, his view that an imperfect appreciation of the mind of Jesus was responsible for certain false emphases in the Church of his day on Institution and on Eucharistic rite. Much that the Church was 'shouting,' Jesus had but 'whispered': much that the Church but 'whispered,' Jesus had 'shouted.' The Evangelist, therefore, will shout aloud the essential message of Jesus. It is not that to him the Institution was unnecessary; nor did he wish that the remem-

[1] Dr. Percy Gardner, in *The Ephesian Gospel*, pp. 54–55.

brance of the solemn breaking of the bread on the night before Calvary should be allowed to disappear from the Church's ordinances. It was that to him the *inner significance* of what happened in that upper room was in danger of being overlaid by materialistic beliefs; that the husk was in danger of being prized to the neglect of the kernel; that the spirit was in danger of being killed by the form which was created for its continuance. We know of no other satisfactory *explanation* of his silence about the symbolical breaking of the bread. This explanation of his silence arises naturally from the whole meaning of the Fourth Gospel as we have sought to interpret it. The very centrality of the Eucharistic rite in the Church at the close of the first century, instead of explaining that silence, makes it inexplicable on any other understanding of the author's mind. Once grant that, to the author himself, the rite *in and by itself* was essential to Christianity, and we have the psychologically impossible task of explaining why he alone of the four Evangelists has nothing to say about the solemn breaking of the bread which was the centre and basis of the rite. What the Evangelist would say is that the Last Supper was in essence a real love-feast, in which Jesus showed His disciples that those who truly partake of His spirit are those who are cleansed from all pride, and manifest always the spirit of humility and brotherly love.

(3) This leads to a third issue—the presence in his narrative of the incident of the foot-washing; for this incident elucidates the inner spiritual meaning of the breaking of the bread. In the previous chapter the Evangelist narrates the anointing of the feet of Jesus by Mary; here he narrates the washing of the disciples' feet by Jesus. The dramatic parallelism and contrast of the two incidents was, no doubt, in the author's mind.

No other evangelist has recorded this story. To him it takes the place of the breaking of the bread, because it unfolds the inner meaning of the act of Jesus. The Evangelist, both in the incident itself and in the discourses which follow, would lead us to the essence of the Master's religion. How often is a rite performed when its meaning and principle are forgotten. The Evangelist, yet once again, is concerned less with the 'sign' than with the thing signified. He would correct a false sacramentalism by revealing the true sacramentalism of Jesus as revealed in His act and in His discourse. He would recall the Church, not to what Jesus *said* at the solemn breaking of the bread, but to what He *meant*. What He *meant* was revealed in an incident the other Evangelists had missed. Was it that they did not know of it? Or was it not that they did not see its importance? It is a psychological law that we remember to record what seems to us significant. By nothing do men more clearly unveil the secrets of their inner life than by the subjects they discourse of in conversation, or the events they record in their writings.

It is so much easier to worship a word than to understand, and to follow, a deed. We enshrine the word, 'This is my body,' in our eucharistic services, but forget that to partake of Christ's body is to partake of His spirit. The *test* of our partaking is not the kind of bread we eat, or the circumstances under which we eat it: it is the spirit we manifest in our lives. So, the foot-washing becomes an empty image, and the 'This is my body' a magical word. The humbling lesson is forgotten; and the word about the body is so interpreted as to give prestige and power to those without whom a saving rite cannot be observed. All such tendencies the Johannine author would correct. And he would correct them by recalling to his readers the mind of Jesus. Implicit in his narrative is a protest against abuses to which ecclesiastical officials were becoming prone. By recalling the solemn occasion when Jesus washed His disciples' feet, he would show that the Last Supper, so far from being the foundation of a rite where privileged officials can do what no other godly Christian can do, was itself the most signal manifestation of the spirit of humility and brotherhood. The only privilege conferred by Jesus on His followers was that of humble service. Paul had the same message to give to the elders and overseers at Miletus when he spoke of his own example in 'serving the Lord with all lowliness of mind'; and when he reminded them of 'the words of the Lord Jesus, how that he himself said, It is more blessed to give than to receive' (Acts 20^{18-35}). It is the same message to the elders as in 1 Pet. 5^{5}—'gird yourselves with humility, to serve one another.'

We are here taking this incident of the feet-washing as historical. It is, of course, possible that this narrative is the Evangelist's own creative allegorical representation of the inner significance of the Last Supper. Such is the view of some recent interpreters of the Gospel. For example, Dr. Goguel in his recent *Vie de Jésus* says: 'The episode of the feet-washing is a representation or an allegory of the Supper. It is an artificial narrative which is but the translation into act of the word that Luke attributes to Jesus during the course of the last evening: "I am in the midst of you as one who serveth."' It may be that this is so. But, on the other hand, it is not at all improbable that *Jesus Himself* had indicated by this symbolical act the meaning of the Supper.

We cannot say at what precise time during the Supper Jesus washed His disciples' feet. It was, the Evangelist says, 'when they were at supper': not, as the Authorised Version renders the phrase in *v.* 2, 'supper being ended.' Probably we should regard the incident as taking place, not as they entered the room from their journey, but at some time during the meal itself. It was an 'acted parable.' Luke tells us ($22^{24ff.}$) that there had arisen a contention among them as to which should be the greatest. Could anything that Jesus had to say to them be understood with this darkness in their mind? So His *act* speaks to them. The willingness to perform the humblest acts of service is the mark of true greatness. He Himself was in the midst of them as He that serveth (Lk. 22^{27}). He does what to the ancient world was the act allotted to the slave. Bishop Westcott in his commentary referred to a Rabbinic comment on Ezek. 16^{9}: 'Among men the slave washes his master; but with God it is not so.' Jesus tried to teach the world this truth, both by precept and by life. Without humility there can be no true greatness. Its opposite is pride, always impatient and easily offended—the mark of the hireling, and of the despot, of him who loves self most. 'Humility,' said St. Theresa, 'is Queen and Empress of, and Sovereign over, all virtues. In fine, one act of true humility in the sight of God is of more worth than all the knowledge, sacred and profane, in the whole world.'

Thus, the acted parable speaks also a lesson about *cleansing*. It symbolises, at one and the same time, the *humility* which must belong to the followers of Jesus, and their need of *cleansing*. Foul things had lodging among them: dark stains on the heart and on the mind. Judas was present, and though he was not the only one who needed to be cleansed, his sin was the darkest. It is He who knows, and manifests, the Father's heart who can cleanse from pride, from covetousness, from all that stains the mind. Jesus later—in 15^2—says that His teaching has cleansing power. Here was such teaching in act. The washing of the feet is symbolical of the inner cleansing of which they all have need, and of which Jesus knew Himself, through His communion with the Father, to be the agent. In his First Epistle the Evangelist—perhaps thinking of this symbolical act on the night before the Crucifixion—sees the death of Jesus as that which consummated His cleansing mission: 'If we walk in the light as he is in the light, we have fellowship one with another, and the blood of Jesus his son cleanseth us from all sin' (1 Jn. 1^7).

6–11. The symbolical nature of the act is made manifest in the reply of Jesus to the self-confident shrinking expressed by Peter. There is a combination, in Peter's first refusal to allow Jesus to wash His feet, of genuine recognition of the Mastership of Jesus and of impatient self-will. This is true to the character of Peter as we know it from the Synoptic Gospels (see Mt. 16^{22}). The hardest lesson for the self-confident man to learn is that he has much still to learn. So when Jesus meets his remonstrance by telling him that the symbolical act will one day be made plain to him, he only the more determinedly demurs. His sudden change of mood as seen in *v.* 9 is again characteristic of his mind. If without washing of the feet he cannot have part with Jesus—that is, cannot be a sharer in His work—then let his whole body be cleansed. Jesus replies—using perhaps a familiar proverb—that he who is already bathed needs only that the dust of travel be washed from his feet. He that is bathed needeth not save to wash his feet.

There have been many interpretations of this 10th verse, some of them curious and far-fetched. Augustine, for example, saw in it a reference to the rite of Christian baptism, thus interpreting it in the light of later ecclesiastical practices and beliefs. These are his words: 'The Truth declares that even he who hath been washed has still need to wash his feet. What, my brethren, think you of it? save that in holy baptism a man has all of him washed, not all save his feet, but every whit; and yet, while thereafter living in this state, he cannot fail to tread on the ground with his feet. And thus our human feelings themselves, which are inseparable from our mortal life on earth, are like feet wherewith we are brought into sensible contact with human affairs; and are so in such a way, that if we say we have no sin, we deceive ourselves, and the truth is not in us. And every day, therefore, is He who intercedeth for us washing our feet: and that we, too, have daily need to be washing our feet, that is, ordering aright the path of our spiritual footsteps, we acknowledge even in the Lord's prayer, when we say, " Forgive us our debts, as we also forgive our debtors." For if " we confess our sins," as it is written, then verily is He, who washed His disciples' feet, " faithful and just to forgive us our sins, and to cleanse us from all unrighteousness," that is, even to our feet wherewith we walk on the earth.'

What Jesus wishes to show to the disciples is that His act in washing their feet is merely symbolical of the inner cleansing of the proud spirit needed for the service that lay before them. It is one thing to submit to a symbolical act—as we should put it, one thing to be baptised with water, one thing to partake of eucharistic elements—and another to be inwardly clean. 'Ye are not all clean,' said Jesus. Judas had his part in the symbolical rite, but he remained in need of cleansing. The symbol has cleansing efficacy only to those who appropriate its spiritual significance. Submission to the rite did not chasten his pride or wash away his hostile resolve. It is 'from within, out of the heart of man' that all defiling evils proceed (Mk. $7^{20\,ff.}$).

12–17. These verses unfold the meaning of the act. It is well to call Jesus Teacher and Master; but the test of discipleship is in following the example He has shown. Longfellow had understood the mind of Jesus on discipleship when he wrote:

Not he that repeateth the name,
But he that doeth the will.

In his First Epistle Peter had remembered not only the whole emphasis of the teaching of Jesus but these specific incidents of the night of the Betrayal, when he wrote: 'Christ also suffered for you, leaving you an example that ye should follow his steps' (1 Pet. $3^{21\,ff.}$). The Fourth Evangelist records here another of the 'beatitudes' of Jesus—'if ye know these things, blessed are ye if ye do them.' To the New Testament writers, the 'example' of Jesus is always an example of some form of humble, sacrificial service.

To follow the example of Jesus in foot-washing does not mean a theatrical re-enacting of the incident. Not but that there may be profit in the reminders which the custom, familiar at different times and in different places in Christendom, has conveyed. The practice of ceremonial foot-washing on Maundy Thursday goes back to the early centuries, and came to be recognised as a necessary rite, to be performed by the Pope, all Christian kings, prelates, priests, and nobles. In England the king washed the feet of as many poor men as his own years since birth. At Peterborough Abbey Wolsey, in 1530, made 'his maund in Our Lady's Chapel, having fifty-nine poor men whose feet he washed and kissed.' James II was the last English sovereign to perform the rite, William III delegating the washing to his almoner. The rite is still observed in the Latin and the Greek Churches. But while the custom can be an effective reminder of the humble service to which the followers of Jesus are called, it would be idle to say that this is to 'follow his example.' Arrogance of spirit can co-exist with an act of theatrical humility, violent methods which *deny* Jesus with symbolical acts which *copy* Him. It is difficult for the worldling not to sneer when he sees travesties of humility, meekness, and self-sacrifice cloaking acts of pride and of persecution. Let his satirical laugh be the sword that pierces our spirit, awaking us once more to the mind that was in Christ.

18–20. The 18th verse recalls us to the strange and sinister figure of Judas. He is *with* them, but not *of* them. He sits at the feast, a stranger. Outward submission to the rite is not inward submission to the mind of Jesus. The psalmist, in Ps. 41^{9}, had spoken of the treachery of an intimate friend: such a treachery was about to be manifested towards Jesus by one whom He had chosen. The 19th verse may be taken in two ways. On the one hand, it may be interpreted as following on the thought of *v.* 17, *v.* 18 being regarded as parenthetical. In this case, the meaning of *vv.* 19 and 20 will be: 'If you follow my example and do as I do, you will discover hereafter the Divine source of such a way of life (" that *I am*," not " that *I am he* "). Men who receive you will be receiving me, and, receiving me, will be receiving him that sent me.' On the other hand, *v.* 19 may be taken as following directly upon *v.* 18, and as the Evangelist's way of expressing a warning given to the disciples by Jesus of the coming treachery of Judas. When the betrayal takes place, instead of perplexing them, it will confirm their faith in Him. With F. D. Maurice we prefer the former interpretation.

AT THE LAST SUPPER: THE RETIRAL OF JUDAS INTO THE NIGHT

JN. 13^{21-30}

13 21 When Jesus had thus said, he was
troubled in the spirit, and testified, and
said, Verily, verily, I say unto you, that
22 one of you shall betray me. The disciples looked one on another, doubting
23 of whom he spake. There was at the
table reclining in Jesus' bosom one of his
24 disciples, whom Jesus loved. Simon
Peter therefore beckoneth to him, and
saith unto him, Tell *us* who it is of whom
25 he speaketh. He leaning back, as he
was, on Jesus' breast saith unto him,
26 Lord, who is it? Jesus therefore answereth, He it is, for whom I shall dip the
sop, and give it him. So when he had
dipped the sop, he taketh and giveth it to
27 Judas, *the son* of Simon Iscariot. And
after the sop, then entered Satan into
him. Jesus therefore saith unto him,
28 That thou doest, do quickly. Now no
man at the table knew for what intent he
29 spake this unto him. For some thought,
because Judas had the bag, that Jesus
said unto him, Buy what things we have
need of for the feast; or, that he should
30 give something to the poor. He then
having received the sop went out
straightway: and it was night.

This strikingly realistic scene, in which Jesus unmasks the traitor who then retires into the night, raises once again the issue which has already been discussed—how far, namely, the narrative is based upon personal recollection, and how far it is free dramatisation of a scene recorded in the other Gospels. If the ' disciple whom Jesus loved '—here first referred to in this way in the Gospel—is John the son of Zebedee, and if, as is here suggested, his teaching forms one of the main sources for the presentation for the Evangelist, it is very probable that such personal reminiscence is at the basis of this narrative. On the other hand, there is a dramatic quality in the passage which suggests that the Evangelist was dealing with his source or sources with the freedom of the artist bent on emphasising the allegorical significance of the scene.

The reader should himself compare the three Synoptic narratives—in Mk. 14^{18-21}; Mt. 26^{21-25}; Lk. 22^{21-23}—with that of the Fourth Evangelist. From this comparison he will note that all four Gospels tell us that Jesus indicated to the disciples at the Supper that His betrayer was one of them. The Fourth Evangelist alone, however, records that Jesus, by means of the ' sop ' definitely indicated to the ' disciple whom Jesus loved ' who the traitor was: and he, we may presume, communicated his knowledge to Peter. Yet the narrative goes on to record that when Jesus, after having given Judas the sop, said to him, 'That thou doest, do quickly,' ' no man at the table knew for what intent he spake this to him.' One would have supposed that at least ' the disciple whom Jesus loved ' would have surmised the meaning of the cryptic utterance of Jesus recorded; and if he, along with Peter, knew for what purpose Judas was leaving them, they would surely have sought to prevent his departure. We know some of the characteristics of John the son of Zebedee and of Peter—the one a 'son of thunder,' the other the impetuous defender of Jesus with the sword. We should naturally conclude that some such action, or attempted action, on their part would be psychologically inevitable.

The conclusion to which we are driven is that this narrative is as 'cryptic' as its ending in *v.* 30. The Evangelist is concerned, not so much with psychological coherence, as with dramatic allegorical contrast. There are four chief actors in the scene—Jesus, Peter, John, and Judas. It is a conflict of light and darkness, ending with the withdrawal of Judas into the night: the night, not only of physical gloom but of spiritual alienation from the Father revealed in Him who was the Light. The decisive moment for Judas, says the Evangelist, was when he received the sop: it was then that 'Satan entered into him.' Luke, it will be remembered, in 22^{3}, says that it was *before* the Last Supper that 'Satan entered Judas.'

It seems obvious that there is dramatic symbolism to the author in the 'entry of Satan into Judas' immediately after his reception of the sop. Mark merely tells us that the betrayer would be he who dipped with Jesus in the dish—Mk. 14^{20}; also Mt. 26^{23}. The Fourth Evangelist heightens the contrast between the fellowship which Jesus would share with Judas and the closing of the latter's heart to such fellowship; and he does so by saying that Jesus offers a love-token, or token of honour, to Judas—for the giving of a morsel to the honoured guest was an Eastern custom. The reception of the love-token, to the Fourth Evangelist, brings to a head the hostile intention of Judas: in Luke, and probably in historical reality, the decisive step had already been taken by Judas.

What, therefore, the Evangelist would say is that the more Jesus dealt affectionately and entreatingly with Judas, the more Judas hardened his heart against Him. Jesus did not abate to the end His effort to scatter with the light of His love the darkness which was creeping over the heart of Judas. Is it not the author's way of recording the patient love of Jesus with those who refused Him—such, for example, as is recorded in the words: 'O Jerusalem, Jerusalem, which killeth the prophets, and stoneth them that are sent unto her! How often would I have gathered thy children together, even as a hen gathereth her chickens under her wings, and ye would not' (Mt. 23^{37}; Lk. 13^{34}).

The question often debated—whether Judas ate of the broken bread at the Last Supper—is here answered by the Fourth Evangelist. Yes! he would say, he did indeed eat it, for to him it was especially offered. Jesus gave to Judas the piece of bread dipped in the wine. The two symbols of the outpoured love were received by him.

The offering of the morsel to Judas was the Evangelist's symbolical way of speaking of the offering of the love of Jesus to Judas which he spurned. As the broken bread symbolised the life given on the Cross, so the sop offered to Judas is symbolical of that same self-giving in love. The Evangelist does not narrate 'the breaking of the bread'; but in relating the offering of the morsel dipped in wine to Judas he says all that the former had said—*and more.* And the *one thing more* which this latter act said, was that the self-giving of Jesus was not only for such disciples as had responded to His love, but was also for Judas—and such as

Judas—who bitterly spurned that love. This is why the Evangelist says in *v.* 21, at the beginning of this narrative, that Jesus 'was troubled in the spirit.' He has already told us twice that Jesus was 'troubled'—in 11^{33} and in 12^{27}. But this third is the deepest 'trouble' of Jesus, because it is caused by the treachery of a familiar friend. In such a treachery 'does he not wish us to try to imagine, however faintly, how profound and piercing must have been that stab of sin which penetrated that infinite calm of the Lord's inmost being?' [1]

In fine, the whole narrative of the 'sop' given to Judas takes the place in the Fourth Gospel of the broken bread which was given to all the disciples. It is the same symbolism; only intensified and made more strikingly dramatic. For the receiver is he who betrayed Jesus. And his reception of the bread and wine, so far from making him a partaker of the essential mind of Jesus, brings to a head his diabolical intention.

As to the *motives* which inspired Judas to his act of treachery, it is impossible, with the slight evidence we have in our Gospels, to speak dogmatically. Volumes might be written on the theme—but they would for the most part be the work of the psychological imagination. But certain things may be said with confidence. The fact that he had chosen to follow Jesus shows that he was no betrayer from the beginning. Nor is it probable that his motive was the desire for pecuniary gain. In all probability his alienation from Jesus grew with his growing recognition that Jesus refused the rôle of a political Messiah.

And to be wroth with one we love
Doth work like madness in the brain.

B. THE LAST DISCOURSES OF JESUS (13^{31}–17)

These discourses, and the place they occupy in the Fourth Gospel, raise some of the most important issues for the understanding and interpretation, both of the mind of the historic Jesus and of the mind of the Evangelist. It is necessary, therefore, that these issues should be frankly considered before any endeavour is made to expound the discourses in detail.

The two questions on which these issues hinge are: firstly, in what precise order are we to suppose that the discourses stood in the Gospel as it left the hand of the Evangelist? And, secondly, are we to regard them as the precise words of Jesus? Or as the reflections of the Evangelist? Or as a combination of the words of Jesus and the reflections of the Evangelist? These two issues involve one another to some extent; though, it is obvious, the second issue is by far the more important of the two.

Firstly, *the order of the discourses.* Many readers of the Gospel have felt that the order of these discourses as we have them does not present a natural sequence of thought. The most 'awkward' sequence, it is felt, is that presented by the closing verse of the 14th chapter. Jesus there says, 'Arise, let us go hence'; and, to the surprise of many readers, the long and intimate discourses of chapters 15, 16, and 17 immediately follow. Many rearrangements have been suggested which would give, it is thought, a more fitting sequence to the chapters in question.

[1] E. A. Abbott, *The Fourfold Gospel*, p. 162.

One is that chapters 15 and 16 should be placed in the middle of *v.* 31 of the 13th chapter. In such a case, we should have the following sequence: 13^{31a}, 15, 16, 13^{31b-38}, 14, 17.

Another suggested rearrangement is that chapter 14^{25-31} should be transposed to the end of chapter 16, and so give, it is felt, a fitting close to the discourse covered by 14^{1-24}, 15, and 16.

Another suggestion is that chapters 15 and 16 should be interpolated between 13^{20} and 13^{21}.

Yet a fourth suggestion is that chapters 15 and 16 should be placed between 13^{35} and 13^{36}.

In this Commentary we follow the order of the Gospel as it has come down to us. In doing so, we do not say that any one of these conflicting suggestions is necessarily incorrect. What we do say is that with the complete absence of any MS. authority for any one of them, it is much more likely that our present order is the original order. It is, of course, ' possible ' that ' pages ' of the original MS. were accidentally transposed—no modern author who has any considerable knowlege of the fallibilities of printers and proof readers would say that in the days before printing, when there was necessarily much less oversight and control in respect to MSS., such was ' impossible.' It is, of course, also ' possible ' that some later editor himself made transpositions of the original ' logical ' and ' harmonious ' text. If he did, at least he has to his credit that he has been the means of providing scope for the ingenuity of us moderns. These are only two ' possibilities ': many more, without any undue feat of the imagination, might be suggested.

The only real objection to the present order is that it is felt to involve an illogical or unchronological sequence. Such an objection, in our own judgement, is in large measure dictated by the demand that the Evangelist *ought* to have conformed to more modern standards of writing. Our study of the Gospel up to this point has already made it abundantly clear that the author had a mind of his own, and a way of writing which is not that of us moderns. Is it not possible that he would have been, shall we say, mildly surprised and perhaps a little amused, at our modern endeavours to achieve a logical harmony for his writings? A little of the grace of humour would have saved many critics from their dogmatic pronouncements on the *original* order of the discourses. For ourselves, we can conceive of very many transpositions, in addition to those already mentioned, which would give a ' harmonious ' and ' logical ' order. But the ' satisfactory ' nature of these mutually divergent hypotheses permits us to smile at our own cleverness.

Perhaps a simple question might now be asked. *Why* should not chapters 15 and 16 have been written by the author after ' Arise let us go hence '? He is not writing precise history. If a modern writer were to make his hero give expression to such an utterance, he would no doubt go on to tell us, first, that they went hence, second, the time at which they went, and, third, the place to which they went. As a matter of fact, to make chapter 17 follow this verse does not lessen the ' difficulty '—if it be a difficulty; for a long soliloquy or prayer of Jesus follows the statement. And, further—if we must argue about *order*—it might be maintained that there is a fitness in regarding 13[34] as *preceding* 15[12]: for, in the *first* reference to this 'commandment' to love one another, we should expect it to be called 'new.' According to our present order, this expectation would *not* be disappointed; according to many suggested transpositions, such expectation *would* be disappointed.

Or, again, *why* should not chapters 15 and 16 follow the statement in 14[30], 'I will no longer talk much with you'? This sequence is only a 'difficulty' on the supposition that the author is either narrating, or thinks he is narrating, the precise words of Jesus. And even on one or other of these hypotheses of transposition, it is only a 'difficulty' on the additional hypothesis that such words can only mean that the discourse is like the 'finally' of a preacher's sermon. (As a matter of fact, we have heard many sermons where the preacher *very early* in his discourse says he is only going to say 'a few words,' and then goes on to say a few thousand.)

Yet, again, *why* should not 16[5]—'None of you asketh me, Whither goest thou?'—follow 13[36], where Peter, it has been noted, asks that very question? Even if the reader takes the discourses as the precise words of Jesus, or as meant to be so taken, why should it be regarded as impossible for a question which was asked at the beginning, to be now no longer asked?

If the reader is looking for 'inconsistencies' of this nature, he will find them on nearly every page of the Gospel; and to remove them all would require a rearrangement of almost the whole Gospel. Most of the suggested transpositions of this Gospel leave in our own mind the thought that their authors are either 'too clever' or not 'clever' enough.

Secondly, *the nature of the discourses.* In all the previous discourses of this Gospel, the Evangelist has been seeking to lay bare the essential mind of Jesus. It is impossible in any single instance to say what are, and what are not, the precise words of Jesus, and what the precise words of the Evangelist. Without doubt, authentic sayings of the Master were known to the author; and he has sought to be completely loyal to such words as those he knew. But it is also clear that, as far as their *form* and *occasion* are concerned, they have been stamped by the impress of his own profound meditation, and coloured by the clarity of his own insight. In no part of the Gospel is it more difficult to distinguish with any kind of dogmatism between the precise words of Jesus and the meditative and dramatic colouring of the Evangelist than in these chapters. On the one hand, every reader must feel that here he is in touch with the mind of our Lord. Here One is speaking, greater than the Evangelist. If these be the words of the Evangelist, he cannot be less than another Jesus. But he himself has told us that it is the mind of Jesus he is seeking to lay bare. No great writer has made smaller claim to originality than the Fourth Evangelist. The most 'original' of the evangelists acknowledges on every page that his work is a transcript of the thought and teaching of Jesus. He acknowledges himself to be but a scribe of One greater than all the other sons of men. On every ground, therefore, we are constrained to believe that the essential content of these discourses is primarily due to Jesus Himself. On the other hand, we cannot be certain that all these discourses were spoken on a single evening; nor can we deny that in different places their form, and perhaps their substance, owes something to the Evangelist himself. All we can say is that the transcendent sublimity of the words of Jesus has lifted the mind of the Evangelist into a realm where they take an almost perfect harmony of form and setting.

The view, therefore, taken here about the nature of these chapters is thus roughly as follows. Valedictory teaching was given by Jesus to His disciples on the night of the Betrayal. This teaching ended with a prayer in which Jesus poured forth His mind in the presence of the Father, the disciples standing by reverently and with solemn awe. The Evangelist had learned in the school of John the Apostle the substance of these utterances. He had meditated upon them with the quickened insight of one who had lived for long in the spirit of Jesus. When he came to write them down, they had become welded in his mind with the whole substance of the message and person of Jesus, and with his own application of their truth to the need and situation of the Church in his own day.

One other thing remains to be said. This ' welding ' of the historical speech of Jesus with the reflective interpretation and insight of the Evangelist himself is a ' psychological ' explanation of the discourses as we have them. ' Psychology,' however, says nothing about the ultimate question of ' inspiration.' Those of us who believe that all the highest work of man's spiritual faculty are the result of an illumination which comes ' from above,' will not hesitate to declare our conviction that here the Divine Helper, spoken of by Jesus Himself in these discourses, was quickening and enabling an author of fully consecrated mind to apprehend and to state things beyond our temporal and sensory ken.

1. *ON THE DEPARTURE OF JESUS AND THE COMING HELPER* (13^{31}–14)

The Hour is Now Come

JN. 13^{31-38}

13 31 When therefore he was gone out, Jesus
saith, Now is the Son of man glorified,
32 and God is glorified in him; and God
shall glorify him in himself, and straight-
33 way shall he glorify him. Little children, yet a little while I am with you.
Ye shall seek me: and as I said unto the
Jews, Whither I go, ye cannot come; so
34 now I say unto you. A new commandment I give unto you, that ye love one
another; even as I have loved you, that
35 ye also love one another. By this shall
all men know that ye are my disciples,
if ye have love one to another.
36 Simon Peter saith unto him, Lord,
whither goest thou? Jesus answered,
Whither I go, thou canst not follow me
now; but thou shalt follow afterwards.
37 Peter saith unto him, Lord, why cannot
I follow thee even now? I will lay down
38 my life for thee. Jesus answereth, Wilt
thou lay down thy life for me? Verily,
verily, I say unto thee, The cock shall not
crow, till thou hast denied me thrice.

31–32. The dramatic nature of the words of Jesus in *v.* 31, following upon the statement that when Judas went out ' it was night,' is so striking that the least imaginative reader should be able to feel their import. The loyal friends are left alone with Jesus. He who was a traitor to His mind and spirit has gone to do his part in the work that must end in the Cross. It is ' Now ' that the Son of man is glorified. The glorification of Jesus is now begun. His mind is now wholly devoted to His act of complete self-sacrifice. And in this, God Himself is glorified: for the Eternal embraces the Historic; the conquest of Jesus in time and place is the expression of the conquest of evil by God. Once again, the darkness has been overcome. An eternal fact has here its historic expression. The 32nd verse expresses the same truth; but declares that it is God Himself who is the agent in the glorification of Jesus. The whole of this Fourth Gospel is written round the theme—the Word *of God*. What Jesus does, God does. It is the eternal which is operative in time. Some interpreters would see in this 32nd verse the profound idea expressed in the Athanasian Creed—that the Incarnation is consummated 'by taking of the manhood into God.' Probably, however, the metaphysics of this statement were not in the author's mind when he wrote the words—nor, indeed, in the mind of Jesus. It is obvious, however, that here the 'glorification' of Jesus is envisaged, not just in the historic fact of the Cross, but in the whole future to which the Cross was but the prelude. For we read: 'God *shall* glorify him in himself.' And it is no distant event: '*straightway* shall he glorify him.'

33–35. This reference to the future leads at once to the thought of the impending separation. 'Little children,' says Jesus—it is an affectionate and intimate mode of address, corresponding to the untranslatable '*mes enfants*' with which a French general will address his soldiers—and goes on to warn them that the time of their sojourning together in the flesh is short. The 'new commandment' comes with added meaning to them after the incidents of the Supper. The humility of the Master, and the treachery of one of the disciples, have both been witnessed. 'Love one another, even as I have loved you.' This is the one thing needful. But how difficult it is: as the history of humanity shows, even the history of the Christian Church itself. Those who have called themselves the disciples of Jesus have not always been 'known' to men by this sign, and this bond. The sign has not always been witnessed: the bond has often been snapped. The tests of membership in Christ's Church have included belief in dogmatic statement and obedience to the laws of the institution; but have not always included *love to one another*. Yet, in the light of these words of Jesus, this is the *Open Sesame* to the Kingdom. Surely from this we may conclude that it is impossible to equate the true Church of God with any one institution—least of all with any which claims the *exclusive* right to that name. The true Church includes all who love as Jesus taught men to love. 'We know,' says our author in 1 Jn. 3^{14}, 'that we have passed from death unto life, because we love the brethren.' Of John the Apostle Jerome records the story that in his old age he used continually to repeat these very words to the brethren of the Church—'Little children, love one another.' When they, tired of the reiterated word, asked why he kept saying this, he replied: 'Because it is the Lord's commandment: if this be fulfilled it is enough.'

36–38. The new commandment of selfless love is followed by Peter's self-confident assertion of fidelity. Again we feel the dramatic contrast. The Evangelist places the story in his own setting, as will be seen by comparing his account with those of Mk. ($14^{27\,\mathrm{f.}}$), of Mt. ($26^{31\,\mathrm{f.}}$), and of Lk. ($22^{31\,\mathrm{f.}}$). Matthew follows Mark in saying that the warning to Peter was given on the road to Gethsemane. The Fourth Evangelist agrees with Luke in regarding the Upper Room as the scene of the warning. But he alone associates it with the announcement of the 'going away' of Jesus. This 'going away' is conceived, both as a severance from the bonds of mortality, and as the complete victory of the eternal Spirit in an act of uttermost sacrifice. Peter cannot 'now' follow Jesus: for, on the one hand, not yet is the hour for his severance from the bonds of mortality; and, on the other hand, not yet is the hour—referred to again in 21^{19}—when he must suffer martyrdom. (This tradition seems to be read back by the author into these words in *v.* 36.) Further, it is the Johannine Evangelist who alone places the warning to Peter after the 'new commandment' of Jesus. In so doing He wishes to show that Peter, and all such as Peter, have a long way to travel before they reach the goal of humble and selfless love. 'Love,' said Paul, 'vaunteth not itself, is not puffed up.' Peter, with all his splendid qualities, has yet an ingredient in his virtues which robs them of the one thing needful. One day his delusion that *his* is a fidelity which can with complete self-assurance confront every peril, will vanish. He will then be a sadder, a wiser, and a more loving man. The washing of the feet had not taught him the lesson that without humility there can be no Christian love. If we say we have all courage, complete devotion, entirety of love, the truth is not in us. To protest our devotion over-much is not the sign of the serenity of humble and selfless love. It is both the sign, and the father, of weakness. Even before the crowing of the cock betokens the coming of another day, Peter will have thrice denied Jesus.

The Goal and Purpose of the Departure of Jesus

JN. 14^{1-4}

14 1 Let not your heart be troubled: ye
2 believe in God, believe also in me. In
my Father's house are many mansions; if
it were not so, I would have told you; for
3 I go to prepare a place for you. And if I
go and prepare a place for you, I come
again, and will receive you unto myself;
that where I am, *there* ye may be also.
4 And whither I go, ye know the way.

These words, among the most familiar and the most sustaining words of Jesus, speak their own undying message. The commentator feels that they might well be left as they are, without detailed exposition or analytical discussion. All our comments wither and die; but the words of Jesus grow not old nor perish with the years. The literature of Christendom tells us of the central place this chapter has had in the hearts and minds of her seers and of her soldiers. When the words were read by Lockhart to Sir Walter Scott, during his last illness, he said: 'Well, this is a great comfort: I have followed you distinctly and I feel as if I were yet to be myself again.' Florence Nightingale wrote: 'For myself, the mystical and spiritual religion of St. John's Gospel, however imperfectly I have lived up to it, was and is enough.'

It is a message to bring reassurance and peace to perplexed and disquieted men. If we are to look for sequence of thought, we find that this message follows appropriately upon the two thoughts of the preceding paragraph. Jesus is going away; and the devotion of the most heroic among the disciples is to be found wanting. These two notes, struck one after the other, awake disquiet and dismay in their minds. No one likes his best friend to go whither he cannot be followed: least of all, when that going away is associated with the thought of a failure of one's own devoton to his mind and cause. Separation itself is bad enough; but the separation which, every time it is remembered, speaks of

Deeds undone that wrankle and snarl, and hunger of their due
Till there seems nought so despicable as you
In all the grin of the sun,

—that were bitterness indeed.

To this universal trouble of mankind Jesus speaks in these words to His disciples. We take both verbs in this first verse as in the imperative. 'Believe in God—and believe in me.' What is the essential meaning of the Fourth Gospel but this—that we are called to a belief in God as He is revealed in Jesus? It is no bare or abstract Theism which the Gospel proclaims. It is a *Christian* Theism: that is, it is a belief in 'the God and Father of our Lord Jesus Christ.' Right from the Prologue this is the Gospel's essential message. The Eternal has been declared in Jesus. To believe in God is good; but in what kind of God do we believe? The Christian message to a world of perplexed, disquieted, and doubting men is: Believe in the kind of God made known to us by Jesus, the kind of God He Himself knew and obeyed. It is the inseparability of these two beliefs which the Church has, despite every false emphasis, sought to maintain in her dogmatic Trinitarian and Christological statements.

To Jesus death was not a cessation of life in the grave: it was a going from one 'abode' to another 'abode' in the one 'house' of the one Father. Our English word 'mansion' has become hallowed by usage in this passage. It is well to remember, however, that it is the same word that is found in *v.* 23, where it is translated 'abode.' There is only one 'house,' but there are many 'rooms.' The language is figurative, as all language dealing with spiritual existence must be. Jesus is 'going away'; but when He says this we shall not think of *motion in space.* He is going to the *Father's house*; but we shall not think of heaven as located. 'Heaven' is that state of life where God *indwells* man—when, as the 23rd verse says, God makes His 'abode' in man. It is the life of eternity: it is the life where the Father dwells and rules. This 'house,' says Jesus to the disciples, was *theirs* as well as *His.* They, too, would have 'abodes' there. He goes to get theirs ready. As we make ready our rooms for our expected guests, so, says Jesus, 'I go to prepare a place for you.' Their coming will be expected, and will be prepared for in the house not made with hands eternal in the heavens.

If this had not been so, He would have told them. Throughout the Gospel Jesus has been speaking of the 'Father's house,' using different figures and expressing different aspects of the life that was life indeed. He has taken it for granted that they will see the implications of His message. To Him *eternal separation* is a contradiction in terms. True life is eternal, and involves fellowship. Where there is life that is life indeed, there is no death that is death indeed. Therefore, He does not say, 'Because it is so, I tell you'; but, 'If it were not so I would have told you.' Nor will the disciples be left to their own unaided strength in the journey to that 'abode.' He will 'come again.' Again, we have the truth of spirit expressed in the language of time and space. Jesus does not mean what we mean by ' coming ' or ' going.' What He says is that the Divine Spirit which constitutes His own essential life will be their guide and stay. The spiritual thought of Jesus struggles with the medium of poor human words to express the reality of a life of abiding fellowship.

The Difficulties of Thomas and Philip

JN. 14^{5-11}

14 5 Thomas saith unto him, Lord, we know
not whither thou goest; how know we the
6 way? Jesus saith unto him, I am the
way, and the truth, and the life: no one
7 cometh unto the Father, but by me. If
ye had known me, ye would have known
my Father also: from henceforth ye
8 know him, and have seen him. Philip
saith unto him, Lord, shew us the Father,
9 and it sufficeth us. Jesus saith unto him,
Have I been so long time with you, and
dost thou not know me, Philip? he that
hath seen me hath seen the Father; how
sayest thou, Shew us the Father?
10 Believest thou not that I am in the
Father, and the Father in me? the words
that I say unto you I speak not from
myself: but the Father abiding in me
11 doeth his works. Believe me that I am
in the Father, and the Father in me: or
else believe me for the very works' sake.

5–7. Thomas and Philip are the spokesmen of two difficulties. The difficulty of the first is that both the *goal* and the *way* thereto are unknown. The knowledge of the Father, which had been the centre of the teaching of Jesus, is the goal: Jesus knew Himself to be the mediator of that knowledge. This is what Jesus had meant when He said: ' Whither I go ye know, and the way ye know.' They had not, however, understood. So Jesus answers that He Himself is ' the way, the truth, and the life.' There is here gathered into one pregnant utterance the whole mind and mission of Jesus. A *way* unites two places: its function is to heal divisions, to bridge gulfs of separation, to lead men home. Jesus is the way, uniting two worlds, bridging the gulf of separation between time and eternity, between man and God. *Truth* is correspondence with reality. God is Reality, and Jesus is Truth because He knows God. In Him there was perfect correspondence with God. It is not just that Jesus *speaks* the truth: He *is* truth. All the *real* questions of men are answered, not by what Jesus says in speech, but by what He was in His essential being. He did not answer all our speculative questions. But His *life* itself is the answer to all the final questions. He is the truth about God, and about human life itself: He is the truth by which men live and die. It was no doubt such a thought which inspired Browning's familiar lines in *A Death in the Desert*:

I say the acknowledgement of God in Christ,
Accepted by thy reason, solves for thee
All questions in the earth and out of it.

It is the incarnate Word who gives meaning to life and to the universe. It is within the context of the incarnational belief that the questions involved in life itself receive the only really satisfactory, and satisfying, answer. So, also, Jesus is the *life*—life in its essence, not life as physical or durational existence. He is the way to life, and the truth about life, because He is life itself. To know Jesus is to know the Father: for it is He who leads to the Father, is the truth about the Father, and incarnates the Father's very life. The three ideas—Way, Truth, Life—are incorporated into one saying in the 3rd verse of the 17th chapter: ' This is life eternal, that they should know thee the only true God, and him whom thou didst send, even Jesus Christ.'

8–11. The difficulty of Philip is expressed in words which voice the deepest need of humanity. He who had brought Nathanael and the Greeks to Jesus (1^{46}, 12^{20}) had not really ' known ' Him to whom he had brought them. He had ' seen ' without ' seeing.' Physical sight is not spiritual sight. Unable to comprehend this distinction, he asks for a ' theophany,' such as he believed had been given (Exod. $33^{17ff.}$), and promised of old (Is. 40^{5}). If he can only have a physically visible manifestation of the Father, he thinks, his mind will be satisfied. Blind and deluding thought! As if the spirit in man can ever be satisfied with physical appearance! A God who could be seen in this way would be no God: as a God who could be defined would no longer be God—' Le dieu défini, c'est le dieu fini.' In every age men delude themselves with the notion that if they could have an indisputable ' sign ' of God to their physical senses, or an irrefragable ' proof ' of God to their intellects, they would be satisfied. They do not know that religion is *life*, and is its own ' sign ' and its own ' proof.' There is a *sign* and a *proof* that spring out of religion itself; and, in comparison with these, the other ' signs ' and ' proofs ' for which men crave are like the sea-water—they mock man's thirst, they do not quench it. Jesus has been revealing the Father to Philip and the rest since first they began to company with Him. The knowledge of the Father has been the secret of His whole mind: to convey such a knowledge to them has been one of the main purposes of His mission. His essential being lay there. All His ' words ' and ' works ' were expressive of their source in the Father. If, then, Philip cannot with the directness of spiritual vision see the Father in Jesus—if, that is, his mind, like that of many, must work backward from the ' words ' to the Speaker, from the ' works ' to the Worker—then let him believe ' for the very works' sake.' What a man does reveals what he is. A good deed reveals a good nature. It is the ultimate conviction of Jesus that God is ' Father ': every ' work,' therefore, expressive of the highest conception of fatherhood which man can attain, reveals the Father.

The Promise of the Helper

Jn. 14^{12-24}

14 12 Verily, verily, I say unto you, He that
believeth on me, the works that I do
shall he do also; and greater *works* than
these shall he do; because I go unto the
13 Father. And whatsoever ye shall ask in
my name, that will I do, that the Father
14 may be glorified in the Son. If ye shall
ask me anything in my name, that will I
15 do. If ye love me, ye will keep my com-
16 mandments. And I will pray the
Father, and he shall give you another
Comforter, that he may be with you for
17 ever, *even* the Spirit of truth: whom the
world cannot receive; for it beholdeth
him not, neither knoweth him: ye know
him; for he abideth with you, and shall be
18 in you. I will not leave you desolate: I
19 come unto you. Yet a little while, and
the world beholdeth me no more; but ye
behold me: because I live, ye shall live
20 also. In that day ye shall know that I
am in my Father, and ye in me, and I in
21 you. He that hath my commandments,
and keepeth them, he it is that loveth

me: and he that loveth me shall be loved
of my Father, and I will love him, and
22 will manifest myself unto him. Judas
(not Iscariot) saith unto him, Lord, what
is come to pass that thou wilt manifest
thyself unto us, and not unto the world?
23 Jesus answered and said unto him, If a
man love me, he will keep my word: and
my Father will love him, and we will
come unto him, and make our abode
24 with him. He that loveth me not
keepeth not my words: and the word
which ye hear is not mine, but the
Father's who sent me.

The words 'verily, verily,' as is customary in this Gospel, form a prelude either to a passage which sums up the significance of what has gone before, or a passage which gives expression to a consummating truth.

12–15. In the first part of the passage, Jesus speaks of the work His disciples are called to continue when He is gone. If they but 'believe on' Him—that is, if their whole mind is grounded in Him, and seeks to be loyal to *His* mind—then the kind of spiritual works He has done they also will do: and, indeed, their work will be farther-reaching in its effects. These 'greater works' are not, to the Evangelist—nor to Jesus—greater physical marvels. The 'works' of which Jesus is speaking are the works which reveal the Father. Jesus Himself in His essential person was the Father's true 'sign.' They also, in so far as they were in harmony of spirit with Jesus, will do the same works of the Spirit which He did. And their 'works' will be greater, inasmuch as His departure from earth to the Father's immediate presence will release new Divine powers, and so lead to a fulfilment of the mission He Himself had begun.

The releasing of these new energies is associated in *vv.* 13 and 14 with prayer 'in the name of' Jesus. This great promise occurs several times in these great discourses—in chapter 15 at *v.* 16, and in chapter 16 at *vv.* 23, 24, and 26. What makes such prayer efficacious? *Not* that the name of Jesus is formally introduced into it. This Gospel knows nothing of the magical efficacy of mere words or mere acts in and by themselves. True, and efficacious, prayer had been offered in every age by the sons of light, by those who had been enlightened by the pre-incarnate Word. The 'name' signifies the reality adumbrated by the person who bears the name. So, to pray 'in the name of Jesus' is to pray as He prayed, with complete trust and obedience. Such prayer cannot be selfish, cannot be centred on material blessings for narrow temporal ends. It is Jesus who has taught the world, as no one else has done, what true prayer is. His was a fellowship with the Father, full of humility, full of trust, full of forgiveness, full of passionate longing and consecrated zeal for the eternal well-being of men. Anything asked in *His* name receives its answer. But if we would understand these words, let us remember the Cross to which the consecrated prayer of Jesus took Him. Such faith is also 'love,' as the 15th verse, immediately following, shows. To pray in the name of Jesus is to *love* Him; and to love Him is to follow Him in thought, word, and deed.

16–21. In these verses is found the first of the series of promises given by Jesus in these discourses of the 'Comforter.' The Greek word is 'Paraclete,' and is only found five times in the New Testament—in Jn. $14^{16, 26}$, 15^{26}, 16^{7}; 1 Jn. 2^{1}. Its exact equivalent in English is difficult to decide. The word comes from a verb, παρακαλέω, meaning 'to call to one.' The English word 'advocate' (Latin 'advocatus') corresponds to the Greek word, and is used to translate it in the revised version of 1 Jn. 2[1]. The preferable translation is 'Helper,' or—if we are to use the word hallowed by Wyclif, by Tyndale, and by the Authorised Version—'Comforter.' The disadvantage of using the word 'Comforter' here is that not every reader will remember that it is formed from the verb 'to comfort,' that is, to strengthen. The word means much more than one who consoles. The 'Comforter' is the sustainer and counsellor of the spirit of man; and while this sustenance and counsel will include consolation, it will include much more. The promise of Jesus is that His disciples can be assured that if they pray 'in His name,' and follow Him with the whole heart and mind, they will have Divine guidance and Divine sustenance.

The main question for him who would understand the mind of Jesus and the mind of the Evangelist at this point, is: Did Jesus Himself speak of 'another Comforter'? Or, is this the Evangelist's theological interpretation—or misinterpretation—of His mind? And if Jesus did speak in this way of 'another Comforter,' what precisely did He mean?

The view here maintained is that if we can approach these passages on the Spirit, without the prepossessions derived from later dogmatic history, we shall see that the essential teaching is harmonious with the whole mind of Jesus as it is known to us. If, on the other hand, we find—and mistakenly find—in these passages the trinitarian distinctions, long afterwards reached by the Church in her endeavours to achieve a coherent doctrinal statement of the revelation of God in Jesus and of the quickened life which after His death and resurrection came to the Church, we shall be led to regard the passages as theological after-interpretations. It will therefore be seen that the fundamental question as to the nature and purpose of this Gospel is involved in the issue before us. In the Introduction we have set forth the general point of view from which this question, and kindred questions, are here approached.

It is of the highest importance to note how the subject is here introduced. Jesus has spoken of the greater spiritual works to be done by His disciples. These 'works' will be done, in so far as they pray 'in His name,' and in so far as they are wholly devoted to His mind and purpose. The washing of their feet has shown one aspect of His mind: His death on the morrow will show forth His mind completely. It must have seemed an impossible task and mission He was giving to His disciples. 'No,' he says, 'it is not impossible. As it is not impossible to me, so neither need it be to you. Of myself, I also can do nothing; but the Father's Spirit indwelling has guided me in my uncertainty and strengthened me in my weakness. This same Spirit will be your Guide and Helper, in so far as you are bound together in a fellowship of humble loving service and of wholly consecrated endeavour. This Helper will be *ever* with you. His presence will not be governed by physical contacts, as my presence with you has been governed. His presence among you will be wholly spiritual, and, therefore, not subject to the limitations of bodily and temporal conditions. The world of fleshly interests and materialistic concerns will not 'know' this Helper; but *you* will know Him, for He will indwell you. You will not, therefore, be left as weak and bewildered orphans. The bond of intimate family unity will not be broken on my departure. The Spirit who has sustained me will come to you. The world will see me no more; but you will have the inward vision of, and contact with, the Spirit who has guided me. This knowledge will be to you as it is to me, life—eternal life, the life that is life indeed. And in such spiritual communion you will know the reality of the life which binds me to the Father, which binds you to me, and me to you. Your fellowship will reveal the true nature of all spiritual union—your union with me, and my union with the Father. This whole spiritual quickening has, as its central condition, the complete devotion of heart and mind and will to my spirit and purpose. And such devotion is wholly reciprocal: those who are thus devoted are loved by the Father Himself, and by me who have tasted so completely of that love.'

We have sought to paraphrase these verses, 16–21, in order to make clear what we believe the Evangelist was seeking to convey. He is conveying the parting message of Jesus to the disciples. His method of conveying it will be understood if we have *rapport* with his mind, as he, we believe, had *rapport* with the mind of Jesus. The difficulty which many modern readers feel, when they note that the Helper is sometimes regarded as Jesus Himself, and sometimes as 'another,' will disappear with a little psychological insight. For in this *seeming* contradiction we have substantial psychological fact. Jesus could, at one and the same time, convey the idea to His disciples that it was the Divine Spirit indwelling Himself who would come to them, *and* that this Spirit was other than Himself. The Spirit was *in* Himself; but it was also *from* the Father. Just as He knew Himself to be completely dependent on the Father for word and work, so He would say to His disciples that the Spirit who was to come would be One other than Himself—none other than the Spirit proceeding eternally from the One Source of all good, of every Word, of all Light—even from God Himself.

22–24. This spiritual revelation thus promised by Jesus to His true disciples raises a perplexity in the mind of Judas Thaddeus, the Judas less conspicuous than his namesake the betrayer (see Lk. 6^{16}; Mk. 3^{18}; Mt. 10^{3}). Why, he wants to know, should this revelation be confined to the disciples of Jesus? The perplexity probably arose out of a still-mistaken view of the nature of the manifestation to be given. The question of Judas evidences the false Messianic conceptions which lingered in the minds of the disciples long after the death of Jesus. Such Messianic hopes as they held, and continued to hold, demanded public demonstrations, not private revelation. So he wants to know why Jesus should reveal Himself to them and not to the world. The answer of Jesus points the disciples, yet once more, to the *conditions* and the *nature* of this revelation. It belongs by its very nature only to those who love the things Jesus loved and do the things He did. It is then that they experience that spiritual fellowship which He calls an 'abode' or 'dwelling' of God in the soul—it is the same word as is translated 'mansion' in *v.* 2. As for those who are not His friends, they will not seek to keep His word or to be fashioned by His spirit. And inasmuch as His words spring out of His fellowship with the Father, in spurning them they will be shutting themselves out from such fellowship.

The Gift of Peace

JN. 14^{25-31}

14 25 These things have I spoken unto you,
26 while *yet* abiding with you. But the
Comforter, *even* the Holy Spirit, whom
the Father will send in my name, he shall
teach you all things, and bring to your
remembrance all that I said unto you.
27 Peace I leave with you; my peace I give
unto you: not as the world giveth, give I
unto you. Let not your heart be
28 troubled, neither let it be fearful. Ye
heard how I said to you, I go away, and
I come unto you. If ye loved me, ye
would have rejoiced, because I go unto
the Father: for the Father is greater than
29 I. And now I have told you before it
come to pass, that, when it is come to
30 pass, ye may believe. I will no more
speak much with you, for the prince of
the world cometh: and he hath nothing
31 in me; but that the world may know that
I love the Father, and as the Father gave
me commandment, even so I do. Arise,
let us go hence.

25–27. These verses bring to a fitting close the first of these last discourses—or, if it is preferred, the first part of this last discourse. Jesus is leaving them. While still with them in visible and audible presence He is speaking these things to them. But much of what He has said they did not understand—as witness the interjections of Peter, of Thomas, of Philip, and of Judas Thaddeus. When, however, He was no longer with them in bodily presence His Helper, even that Spirit of holiness which comes from the Father, will be their teacher. He will make the meaning of His words clear to them, and reveal to them all the things pertaining to the life of the Spirit of which they were to be ministers. Their minds will be quickened to see all the things that matter, and to remember all that is worth remembering.

27–28. Such spiritual insight and discernment brings peace with it, the very peace which He Himself knows. It is thus His legacy to them. But it is a legacy given and received not according to the ways of the world. For it is not a material possession which may be stolen or squandered. It is a spiritual possession which the world can neither give nor take away. This peace is not the delusive sense of security which comes to those who belong to a large institution; it is not a possession such as is claimed by those who build barriers to keep their treasure to themselves. It is an inward possession: it may belong to him who is in a minority of one, or to him who would spend all his treasure on others. It comes not with striving without, or with crying within. The world slays its foes, and calls the result Peace. The Church has often done the same. 'Not as the world giveth, give I unto you,' said Jesus. Jesus, and the Evangelist, would be very familiar with the words of the prophet of the Exile: 'There is no peace . . . to the wicked' (Is. 48^{22} and 57^{21}). His peace can only come His way.

Thus, there is no need for them to be troubled or fearful. His going away is but the prelude to a richer coming. For His departure is to the immediate presence of the Father. This should be a cause of joy, not of fear, to them. For how can we but rejoice when those we love reach the haven of their desire? So He whom they would love is returning to the Father's own home, to the dwelling of Him from whose unsearchable greatness His own strength is derived.

29–31. Thus He has told them of His approaching departure to the Father, and of the Father's gifts which they may expect. Their belief will then be fortified and deepened. But before that day of fulfilment dawns, there are hours of darkness to be passed through. The prince of darkness is already marshalling the enemies of the light. Righteousness will *seem* to be overthrown; but it will be but a *seeming* overthrow. For this prince *had nothing in Jesus*. There was nothing in Jesus, that is, to which unrighteousness could lay claim. Like claims like. The prince of darkness claims control over all things dark; but is abashed and discomfited by the prince of light. As it has ever been, the darkness will not master the light. And so His Cross, instead of being the victory of darkness, will reveal to the world itself the love of Jesus for the Father, a love that gave Him strength to follow unfalteringly up the *via dolorosa* to Calvary.

The last words of the chapter—' Arise, let us go hence '—indicate that to the author there is a break in the discourse. These words have already been referred to in the light of the suggested transposition of chapters 15 and 16: and the conclusion was reached that, if we perceive the author's method of writing, there is no difficulty in accepting the order of the discourses as we have them. It is only on the view that the author is giving a historical record of the course of events, or an exact account of the discourses of Jesus, that these closing words of the fourteenth chapter are a difficulty at this point. That he is not so doing has been abundantly obvious. We do not find it necessary, therefore, to speculate on the place where chapters 15 and 16 were spoken. Former interpreters of the Gospel have suggested *either* that these chapters were spoken by Jesus to the disciples as they still lingered in the room prior to the departure for Gethsemane, *or* that, having left the room, the little company had halted on the way to Gethsemane (see 18^{1}), and that, perhaps in the Temple precincts, these discourses were given. There is nothing more inherently unlikely in such suggestions than in the various transpositions of the text suggested to-day. It is impossible, however, to dogmatise on such issues. All that is here stressed is that the author inserts these words in his Gospel at this point to indicate a break in the speech of Jesus. It may very well be that the author, having written chapter 14, put down his pen; and that he did not return to his work until the impulse to write returned to him—perhaps after many days.

The same two Greek verbs, it should be noted, are found in Mk. 14^{42} and Mt. 26^{46}: ' Arise, let us be going.' In these Synoptic passages the words are spoken by Jesus at Gethsemane just before His arrest.

An interesting, though highly speculative, suggestion has been made—by Dr. Torrey—that the original Aramaic words may have been: ' I will arise and go hence.' In this case the ' going hence ' would be to the Father's immediate presence: and thus the thought would entirely harmonise with the central theme of the chapter.[1] Socrates, it is pointed out, used a similar euphemistic phrase of his approaching death in the *Phaedo* (66).

2. *THE ALLEGORY OF THE VINE: THE MISSION OF THE HELPER* (15, 16)

We are taking chapters 15 and 16 together, as giving the second of the group of discourses associated by the Evangelist with the night of the Betrayal.

[1] See *Harvard Theol. Review*, pp. 341 f.: also *The Four Gospels: a New Translation*, p. 326.

The Spiritual Union

JN. 15^{1-10}

15 1 I am the true vine, and my Father is
2 the husbandman. Every branch in me
that beareth not fruit, he taketh it away:
and every *branch* that beareth fruit, he
cleanseth it, that it may bear more fruit.
3 Already ye are clean because of the word
4 which I have spoken unto you. Abide
in me, and I in you. As the branch
cannot bear fruit of itself, except it abide
in the vine; so neither can ye, except ye
5 abide in me. I am the vine, ye are the
branches: He that abideth in me, and I
in him, the same beareth much fruit: for
6 apart from me ye can do nothing. If a
man abide not in me, he is cast forth as a
branch, and is withered; and they gather
them, and cast them into the fire, and
7 they are burned. If ye abide in me, and
my words abide in you, ask whatsoever
ye will, and it shall be done unto you.
8 Herein is my Father glorified, that ye
bear much fruit; and *so* shall ye be my
9 disciples. Even as the Father hath
loved me, I also have loved you: abide
10 ye in my love. If ye keep my commandments, ye shall abide in my love; even as
I have kept my Father's commandments,
and abide in his love.

The figure of the vine may well have been suggested to Jesus by the supper of which they had partaken. They had drunk a cup from the vine, emblem of the outpouring of His life in sacrificial love. Often, as they had walked to the Mount of Olives, they had seen the vines growing on the hillsides. Every time they had entered the Temple they had seen the vine carved upon its gates, symbol of the true Israel. The vine indeed was a very familiar metaphor as applied to Israel. The word of the Lord had spoken through Jeremiah to Israel: 'Yet I had planted thee a noble vine, wholly a right seed: how then art thou turned into the degenerate plant of a strange vine unto me?' (Jer. 2^{21}). Again, to Ezekiel the word of the Lord had come saying: 'Son of man, what is the vine tree more than any tree, the vine branch which is among the trees of the forest?' (Ezek. $15^{1ff.}$). The same prophet wrote: 'Thy mother was like a vine, in thy blood, planted by the waters: she was fruitful and full of branches by reason of many waters' (Ezek. 19^{10}). In Ps. 80 at *v.* 8 we read: 'Thou broughtest a vine out of Egypt: Thou didst drive out the nations, and plantedst it.' It is clear that the vine had been to the prophets—what trees, running brooks, and stones had been to the Duke in *As You Like It*—a book from which they had read Divine lessons, a sermon which had proclaimed to them the ways and will of God. The vine had appeared on the Maccabean coins as the emblem of the nation. The metaphor, therefore, was one very familiar both to Jesus and the disciples: and it is unimportant, even if interesting, to speculate on what suggested it here. The important question is not what suggested it, but what it suggests.

The metaphor of the vine might suggest many things and be used in a multitude of ways. It was doubtless used frequently by Jesus in His teaching (see Mk. $12^{1ff.}$, Mt. 21^{28} and $21^{33ff.}$; Lk. $20^{9ff.}$). There is, however, a peculiar appropriateness in the message it conveys to the disciples during the last hours they had with Him in the flesh. It is a declaration of the condition, and the need, of fruitfulness. If the key to the 14th chapter is Peace, the key to the 15th chapter is Fruitfulness.

1–2. Jesus Himself is the true, the genuine vine. He is, that is, the source of the life of the true Israel. The nation which was to have been the Lord's vine had become a degenerate plant, bringing forth but wild grapes (see Is. 5^{1}).

Yet there is a genuine vine of which the Father Himself has been the Husbandman. The life of this vine, which had ever proceeded from the Father, was the very life incarnate in Jesus. The Father who was its source had always tended it, cutting completely away the fruitless branches, pruning the fruitful branches in order that they might become more fruitful.

The *main* thought behind the metaphor is that of the *one Source of spiritual life* among men. Humanity should be as a *vine*, of which the life incarnate in Jesus is the vitalising unity. Men are not isolated sticks, but branches deriving their true life from the one vine out of which they spring. The metaphor is one expressive of the true unity purposed by God for the race in that life incarnate in the Son. Paul used the figure of the ' body ' to express this unity. Jesus Himself used the figure of the vine and its branches. A limb cut off the body no longer lives: a branch severed from the vine immediately dies. The fellowship in the life eternal has an organic unity derived from the one Divine life which is its source and the condition of its continuance.

3–6. This is a truth of the most far-reaching application. Jesus, however, applies it at once to the little fellowship He has created. These His disciples have been ' cleansed ' or ' pruned ' through His ' word '—through, that is, the whole manifestation of the Eternal of which He was the medium. In the 10th verse of the 13th chapter He had said, 'Ye are clean, but not all,' excepting the betrayer from the success of the cleansing mission of His spirit among them. Let them remain implanted in Him, so that He may remain the life of their fellowship. The two clauses, ' Abide in me ' and ' I in you,' constitute at once the condition and the source of their fruitfulness. It is only as the branch is united to the stem that the life flowing through the stem can vitalise it to fruitfulness. ' Abide in me ' is a moral command, addressed to those who are more than branches of a vine: the metaphor is therefore here transcended into that of a *personal* relationship. If, however, they *will* to remain in Him, to do as He does, in the spirit of humble sacrificial service, the life of which He is the incarnate medium will make them as a fruit-bearing vine. Separate from this life, they must be fruitless, for fruit is the expression of life. From machines men get manufactured articles; but only from the living tree is it possible to get sustaining fruit. The message is one our mechanised age needs to ponder. Fruit, in any society, is the expression of that spirit of service running through all its members and pervading all its activities. Without that spirit there can be no real fruit; but only artificial products which mock and deceive man's need. They are dead things, to be cast into the fire and burned. In the organic unity of a truly Christian society, ' the fruits of the spirit,' as Paul calls them in Galatians, will be found in abundance.

7–8. Such an organic fellowship in Christ results in prayer ' in his name.' (See 14^{13}.) This is always answered, for it seeks always the Father's will. Such fellowship, also, results in the fruits of obedience and of love: and just as the Father is glorified in the Son, so He becomes glorified in the disciples, for by these fruits they reveal that they are the Son's disciples. John Smith, the Cambridge Platonist, beautifully expressed the thought of this 8th verse, in *The Excellency and Nobleness of True Religion*: ' Our Saviour hath best taught what it is to live to God's glory, or to glorify God, viz. to be fruitful in all holiness, and to live so as that our lives may shine with His grace spreading itself through our whole man.'

9–10. This whole fellowship is grounded in the eternal love of the Father which Jesus knew. Of this originating love, He has been the channel to them. Let them, then, abide therein. The spirit of obedience to Him will secure this permanent union; as His own obedience to the Father has secured it for Himself. Love and obedience are, therefore, correlatives. While the eternal love of the Father is the ground of all true fellowship, our human obedience is the condition of its continuance. Such obedience is both the way to eternal life and one of its essential constituents. 'I persuade myself,' said Ralph Cudworth, the Cambridge Platonist, 'that no man shall ever be kept out of heaven for not comprehending mysteries that were beyond the reach of his shallow understanding, if he had but an honest and good heart that was ready to comply with Christ's commandments.'

A Union of Friends

JN. 15$^{11-16}$

15 11 These things have I spoken unto you,
that my joy may be in you, and *that* your
12 joy may be fulfilled. This is my commandment,
that ye love one another,
13 even as I have loved you. Greater love
hath no man than this, that a man lay
14 down his life for his friends. Ye are my
friends, if ye do the things which I com-
15 mand you. No longer do I call you servants; for the servant knoweth not what
his lord doeth: but I have called you
friends; for all things that I heard from
my Father I have made known unto you.
16 Ye did not choose me, but I chose you,
and appointed you, that ye should go and
bear fruit, and *that* your fruit should
abide: that whatsoever ye shall ask of the
Father in my name, he may give it you.

In these verses this union is shown to result in perfect friendship between Christ and His disciples. In the first place, His own joy would be theirs. This joy did not consist in the absence of pain or perplexity: for He had been 'troubled in spirit' over the betrayer, and would know very soon the anguish of Gethsemane and the feeling of complete isolation on the Cross. It is the joy of complete obedience to the Father. If they obey Him they will know His joy. Obedience to Him means that they love one another as He loves them. His is the love which impels a man to sacrifice his life for his friends: than this no love is greater. They are his friends in so far as they live in obedience to His spirit. This 13th verse, it is interesting and significant to remember, was one of the favourite texts of Abelard, and constituted the bed-rock of his view of the reconciling love of God in Christ.

15–16. He calls them no longer servants but friends. The difference between the friend and the servant is the difference between the willing obedience that springs from knowledge of, and loyalty to, the Master's own purposes, and the reluctant obedience that springs from ignorance of those purposes. The friend gladly does what he is doing, for he knows *why* he is doing it. The slave does his work perfunctorily, for he does not see the end which is in His master's view. Both the friend and the slave obey; but the service of the first is perfect freedom, and of the second degrading servitude. Obedience is ennobling if it issues from love for the Master's person, and loyalty to His mind and purpose—for it is then the obedience of a *man*, a being with a rational, moral, and spiritual nature. But obedience is degrading if it is blind unthinking work, as of a horse in a tread-mill. The disciples of Jesus are His friends because He has made known to them the Father's purpose which He, with them, seeks to fulfil.

To be a 'friend' of Jesus, then, was to be a sharer in His inmost thoughts and purposes. Throughout His Ministry, Jesus had been seeking to unfold to His disciples His knowledge of the Father, and the nature of the mission the Father had given Him to accomplish. He had formed them into a 'school' for this very purpose. To them He had declared more freely than to others 'the mystery of the kingdom of God' (Mk. 4^{11}). Luke also records that Jesus had called His disciples 'friends,' and, significantly enough, at a time when He was speaking of the persecutions they would have to face. 'And I say unto you, *my friends*, Be not afraid of them which kill the body, and after that have no more that they can do' (Lk. 12^{4}). The disciples of Jesus are indeed His *friends* when they can confront their persecutions in the spirit and faith with which He confronted His.

This conception of a 'friend,' as one that 'knoweth what his lord doeth,' was one familiar to Hebrew writers. Abraham was called 'the friend of God'—2 Chron. 20^{7}, Is. 41^{8}, and Jas. 2^{23}. He was so called because He was believed to be a sharer in the thought and purpose of God: as it is said in Gen. 18^{17}, 'Shall I hide from Abraham that which I do?' The Jerusalem Targum here has, 'from Abraham *my friend*.' Philo says, giving expression to the same thought: 'For wisdom is God's *friend* rather than *bond-servant*: wherefore also (the sacred writer) says clearly about Abraham, "Shall I hide it from Abraham *my friend*?"'[1] Such 'friendship' was of the same nature as 'prophecy': for the 'prophet' had knowledge of the Divine will. So Amos said: 'Surely the Lord God will do nothing, but he revealeth his secret unto his servants the prophets' (Amos 3^{7}). As the 'prophets' of God had had revealed to them the mind of God, so the 'friends' of Jesus are they who have become partakers of the Word what was incarnate in Jesus.

In this fellowship of service, let them remember that while their obedience to the Master arises out of their own moral choice, yet their Master has first chosen them. There is no really stable religious life which does not arise out of the conviction of the prevenient grace and call of God. This is not to teach a narrow and exclusive doctrine of election. But it is to emphasise that the 'friends' of Christ are, yet, not self-appointed masters of their work or destiny. They have their appointed place in a Vine which creates and sustains them. Such an assurance of 'call' takes away all self-sufficient pride: for the life that flows into the branches from the stem of the vine is the sap of humility.

The Ensuing Hatred of the World

JN. 15^{17-27}

15 17 These things I command you, that ye
18 may love one another. If the world
hateth you, ye know that it hath hated
19 me before *it hated* you. If ye were of the
world, the world would love its own: but
because ye are not of the world, but I

[1] See Abbott, *Johannine Vocabulary*, p. 293.

chose you out of the world, therefore the
20 world hateth you. Remember the word
that I said unto you, A servant is not
greater than his lord. If they persecuted
me they will also persecute you; if they
kept my word, they will keep yours also.
21 But all these things will they do unto you
for my name's sake, because they know
22 not him that sent me. If I had not come
and spoken unto them, they had not had
sin: but now they have no excuse for
23 their sin. He that hateth me hateth my
24 Father also. If I had not done among
them the works which none other did,
they had not had sin: but now have they
both seen and hated both me and my
25 Father. But *this cometh to pass*, that the
word may be fulfilled that is written in
their law, They hated me without a
26 cause. But when the Comforter is
come, whom I will send unto you from
the Father, *even* the Spirit of truth, which
proceedeth from the Father, he shall bear
27 witness of me: and ye also bear witness,
because ye have been with me from the
beginning.

17–20. This spiritual union of friends encounters, and must encounter, the hatred of the world: such is the theme of the closing section of the chapter.

The command to love one another is first repeated, as if to contrast the union so created with the hatred it will occasion in the world. This is one of the recurring themes of this profoundly moral and spiritual Gospel. As Jesus Himself was not exempt from opposition and hate, so neither will His true disciples be. Such opposition is an implicit testimony to the disciples' identity with their Master. He has called them 'friends'; but they are still His servants, and as such will follow Him in the road that occasions persecution from the world.

21–25. This hostility on the part of the world is *occasioned* by the disciples' fidelity to 'his name'; but it is *grounded* in blindness to the Father of love from whom He has come. Goodness does not *cause* hatred, but gives it occasion for its manifestation. This is a terrible and searching word, and reveals the intensity and dramatic quality of the Evangelist's perception of the opposition between Light and Darkness. Men hated Jesus primarily because of what they themselves were. The goodness in Him roused to fury the evil that was in them. Their hate for Him revealed their hate for the Father. Thus, their hatred for Him was *gratuitous*, like that to which the Psalmist refers in Ps. 35^{19} and Ps. 69^{4}. It was the pure hatred which drew its very sustenance from contact with goodness. This is the real hell.

26–27. The chapter, however, does not close on this terrible note. The Helper is coming, and with Him at their side the hatred of the world will be powerless, both over themselves and over the truth which is their cause. For the Helper is the Spirit of truth, proceeding from the Father, who is the Fount of truth, and bearing witness to Jesus who is the incarnate expression of truth. The disciples themselves, in virtue of their fellowship with Him since the beginning of His public ministry, will bear the same witness. The words of *v.* 26, 'which proceedeth from the Father,' were the centre of the Church's discussion in the later centuries on the 'procession' of the Holy Spirit. It is necessary, however, here to say that the speculative distinctions drawn between the 'eternal generation' of the Son from the Father, and the 'eternal procession' of the Spirit from the 'Father *and the Son*' (the phrase used by the Latin Church), or from the 'Father *through the Son*' (the phrase used by the Greek Church), do not belong to the mind of the Fourth Evangelist—or to the mind of Jesus. These distinctions must not be *read into* the mind of Jesus, even if they be *read out of* it.

The World and the Helper

JN. 16^{1-11}

16 1 These things have I spoken unto you,
that ye should not be made to stumble.
2 They shall put you out of the synagogues: yea, the hour cometh, that whosoever killeth you shall think that he
3 offereth service unto God. And these
things will they do, because they have
4 not known the Father, nor me. But
these things have I spoken unto you, that
when their hour is come, ye may remember them, how that I told you. And
these things I said not unto you from the
5 beginning, because I was with you. But
now I go unto him that sent me; and
none of you asketh me, Whither goest
6 thou? But because I have spoken these
things unto you, sorrow hath filled your
7 heart. Nevertheless I tell you the
truth; It is expedient for you that I go
away: for if I go not away, the Comforter
will not come unto you; but if I go, I will
8 send him unto you. And he, when he is
come, will convict the world in respect of
sin, and of righteousness, and of judge-
9 ment: of sin, because they believe not on
10 me; of righteousness, because I go to the
11 Father, and ye behold me no more; of
judgement, because the prince of this
world hath been judged.

The sequence of thought follows on unbroken from the 15th chapter to the 16th. The whole chapter is dominated by the thought of the coming Helper and His testimony, which is the theme of the closing verses of chapter 15. The thoughts of the previous chapters recur, like the themes in the several movements of a symphony. The thought of Jesus has been coloured as it has passed through the medium of the author's mind: the message has been transmuted through the Evangelist's reflections on the subsequent conflict of the world with the true Church of Christ. Yet the mind of Jesus speaks its essential message through the whole chapter, to those who have ears to hear.

1–4*a*. The world, while full of falsehood, will yet be full of zeal. In every age there have been adherents of religion who have manifested their earnestness by excommunicating, or unchurching, those who sought a wider fellowship and revealed a deeper charity than that known to themselves. These persecutions have in every case been justified as ' necessary to the preservation ' of dogma or of institution—just as the crucifixion of Jesus was justified by the Church of Israel in His day. Let not the disciples find in this experience, when it comes to them, a cause of stumbling. They will be expelled from the Synagogue, excluded from the very fellowship which sought to perpetuate the spirit of the prophets. They would even be killed by zealous defenders of the faith once for all committed unto the saints. All this would be offered as an act of devoted zeal in the service of God. Such zeal is, however, the zeal that is not according to knowledge—or to love. It springs from blindness to the Father who is the source of truth and love, and from blindness to the Son who is the incarnate expression of these Divine qualities. When these experiences come to the disciples, they will remember how this opposition of Darkness to Light, of Falsehood to Truth, was the burden of His closing message to them.

46–47. All this, says Jesus, had not been told them at first. Future trials for His disciples, it will be remembered, had been referred to earlier in the Ministry by Jesus, according to the Synoptists (Mt. $5^{10\,f.}$; Lk. 6^{22}). But while He was with them, the brunt of the attack would fall on Him. Not till He was gone from them would they know ' these things '—that is, the full nature of the enemy, and their relation to the Helper. His mission on earth is now nearing completion. Yet the disciples, absorbed in their own grief at impending loss, too little think of the issue in store for Him, and the issue in store for themselves. 'Whither goest thou?' is not the burden of their thoughts; but, 'What sorrow fills our own hearts.' (We would say, in parenthesis, that it is mere clever stupidity which regards *v.* 5 as inconsistent with the questions of Peter and Thomas in 13^{36} and 14^{5}.) For Jesus, the issue is a return to the immediate presence of the Father. For them, the issue is the coming of the Helper. 'It is therefore expedient' for them that He should go away. The loss of His physical presence will have abundant compensation in the presence of the Helper whom He will send. The psychological appropriateness of the two forms of speech found in these discourses —" *I* will come to you,' and 'I will send *him* unto you'—has been already discussed. Into this distinction must not be here read an endeavour on the part either of Jesus or the Evangelist to elucidate *the doctrine* of the Holy Spirit. These attempted elucidations came later, in response to another kind of mission than that which Jesus Himself, or His Evangelist, knew. From this passage, in bygone days, it was sought to show that the return of Manhood to the Godhead was a necessary preliminary to the Mission of the Spirit. What, however, Jesus is here expressing is His certitude that His going will not be a loss to them, but a gain. The Spirit of the Father who has been His own helper, will be at their side in a plenitude of power unknown to them before.

8–11. This mission of the Helper will be directed to convicting the world in respect of sin, of righteousness, and of judgement. The Spirit, that is, will be *their* helper, by helping the cause to which Jesus has called them—not by conferring personal blessings upon them. No passage in the New Testament more clearly shows that the sustaining joy of a Christian man is to be found, not in blessings for himself, but in the extension of the kingdom of Christ. The 'expediency' is envisaged solely in reference to the mission of the Spirit, a mission transcending all selfish or individual interests. That mission is one of convicting and convincing advocacy. The metaphor of these verses is that of the law-court. The Helper is their advocate in the coming Trial in the world, where the issues to be dealt with are three. The whole passage would seem to be coloured by the contentions of the early Church with the Jews, and the charges and counter-charges made in the tension of that controversy.

The first issue is *Sin*. The Jews had regarded Jesus as a sinner—9^{24}, 18^{30}— and had thus justified His death at their hands. The disciples would be able to answer that it was 'the righteous one' they had slain (see Acts 2^{23} and 7^{52}). The Helper would be the disciples' advocate in this trial, and would show convincingly that the Jews, in killing Jesus, had been blind to the Divine truth and love manifest in Him. *They* were the sinners, not He. The history of human thought during the last nineteen hundred years shows that this convicting mission has been fulfilled. There is no man of truth left to-day in the world who seeks to justify the crime of the Crucifixion. This is not to say, however, that there is not the spirit which re-enacts such a crime. The Helper's mission is needed, therefore, as much to-day as in any past day: and the *sin* of which we need to be convicted is of the same nature as that of those who crucified Jesus. We ourselves have not been convicted of sin by the Advocate until we are willing and ready to confess *their* sins as our own.

The second issue is *Righteousness*, inseparable from the first issue of Sin. The Jews had regarded themselves as the custodians of righteousness (see Lk. 18^{9}): and had tried to persuade themselves that in effecting the death of Jesus they were doing service to the God of all righteousness. The disciples would be able to answer that it was 'the prince of life' whom they had crucified (Acts 3^{15}). The Helper would be the disciples' Advocate also, for when Jesus went to the Father, the Helper would vindicate the cause of righteousness in the tribunal of men's minds. Let not therefore the disciples think that the cause of righteousness was defeated in the seeming defeat of the Cross. That Cross would one day be seen to exemplify, as no other event in history, the Father's own way. As Lowell wrote:

Though the cause of evil prosper,
Yet 'tis truth alone is strong;
Though her portion be the scaffold,
And upon the throne be wrong—
Yet that scaffold sways the future,
And, behind the dim unknown,
Standeth God within the shadow,
Keeping watch above His own.

The third issue is *Judgement*, inseparable from the other two issues. 'Judgement' is one of the major themes of this Gospel. The Jews would bring Jesus to their own paltry judgement, and would hold Him worthy of death. This judgement they would seek to vindicate in the days to come. Futile vindication! The Helper will carry on the work of sifting which has been manifest in all that Jesus has said and done. As 'the prince of this world' had been 'judged' by the truth that was in Him, so the Spirit of Truth, when He was gone, would be ever bringing home to the hearts and minds of men the whole judgement inherent in the life He had lived, and in the death He had died. Let not therefore the disciples be intimidated, or deceived, by that spirit of unrighteousness which sought dominion over men. The prince of evil had found nothing in Jesus. His dominion therefore is illusory. He has been already judged. The sifting of eternity has been manifest once and for all in the life of Jesus.

The Disciples and the Helper

JN. 16^{12-15}

16 12 I have yet many things to say unto you,
13 but ye cannot bear them now. Howbeit
when he, the Spirit of truth, is come, he
shall guide you into all the truth: for he
shall not speak from himself; but what
things soever he shall hear, *these* shall he
speak: and he shall declare unto you the
14 things that are to come. He shall glorify
me: for he shall take of mine, and shall
15 declare *it* unto you. All things whatsoever the Father hath are mine: therefore
said I, that he taketh of mine, and shall
declare *it* unto you.

The mission of the Helper is not only to convict the world: it is to guide the disciples themselves into all needful truth. The first mission is, in a sense, negative, or, as we might say, preparatory. The second mission is positive. The disciples are called to be teachers; but they themselves must first be taught. Jesus has been their teacher; but much that He has said they have not understood, and much more has been left unsaid owing to this same inability to understand. 'Ye cannot bear them now'—this is the principle behind the progressive self-revelation of God throughout history. The teacher can only reveal his mind progressively to his pupils, the father only gradually to his children. The more they know, the more they are able to know. The measure of their future knowledge is determined by the insight already gained.

The Helper is none other than the Spirit of Truth, and He will be their continual guide in the days to come. This is one of the great liberating thoughts of all men of insight. It belonged to Jesus Himself. He sought to deliver men from the worship of their final dogmas. He incarnated the Spirit of the Father whose way was to lead men progressively and increasingly into the truth. To the truth-loving the Spirit of Truth comes to guide into deeper truth. 'There is,' said Henry More, the Cambridge Platonist, 'a kind of sanctity of soul and body that is of more efficacy for the receiving and retaining of divine truths than the greatest pretences to discursive demonstration.' When Lessing said that if he had to choose between two proffered gifts of God—one, truth, the other, search for truth—he would unhesitatingly choose the latter, he was saying nothing contrary to the mind of Jesus. For the search for truth is the condition, both of the reception of truth and of the guidance from above. It was the teaching of the mediæval mystic and prophet Joachim of Floris, in *The Eternal Gospel*, that: the age of the Father was past; the age of the Son was passing; the age of the Spirit was yet to be.

This religion of the Spirit, however, will not invalidate the religion incarnate in Jesus. For the Helper 'shall take of the things' of Jesus and declare them to His disciples. The guiding Spirit does not guide men away from Christ, but only guides to a deeper understanding of what He was and did. He will help men to tread that 'way' to the Father which Jesus in His essential person was; to know that 'truth' of the Father incarnate in Him; to find that 'life' of eternity which He revealed. Pfleiderer spoke of 'the fatal ban of historicism, which seeks God's revelation only in the records of a dead past, and thus loses the power of finding it in the living present.' [1] But, let us remember, there is a *fruitful* historicism, which recognises in the facts of Christian history the source and the inspiration of the capacity to discover God's revelation in the living present. And the most fruitful fact of history for the Christian philosopher is in the fact of Jesus Himself. 'He shall glorify me: for he shall take of mine, and shall declare it unto you.' This is the watchword of those who would remain faithful to the twin centralities of Christianity—'Jesus, Word of God incarnate,' and 'Holy Spirit, Giver of Life and Light.'

[1] *Early Christian Conception of Christ*, p. 170.

Joy After Sorrow

JN. 16^{16-24}

16 16 A little while, and ye behold me no more;
and again a little while, and ye shall see
17 me. *Some* of his disciples therefore said
one to another, What is this that he saith
unto us, A little while, and ye behold me
not; and again a little while, and ye shall
see me: and, Because I go to the Father?
18 They said therefore, What is this that he
saith, A little while? We know not what
19 he saith. Jesus perceived that they were
desirous to ask him, and he said unto
them, Do ye inquire among yourselves
concerning this, that I said, A little while,
and ye behold me not, and again a little
20 while, and ye shall see me? Verily,
verily, I say unto you, that ye shall weep
and lament, but the world shall rejoice:
ye shall be sorrowful, but your sorrow
21 shall be turned into joy. A woman when
she is in travail hath sorrow, because her
hour is come: but when she is delivered
of the child, she remembereth no more
the anguish, for the joy that a man is born
22 into the world. And ye therefore now
have sorrow: but I will see you again,
and your heart shall rejoice, and your joy
23 no one taketh away from you. And in
that day ye shall ask me nothing.
Verily, verily, I say unto you, If ye shall
ask anything of the Father, he will give
24 it you in my name. Hitherto have ye
asked nothing in my name: ask, and ye
shall receive, that your joy may be
fulfilled.

In these verses the thought of Jesus reverts to the sorrow filling the disciples' mind at His approaching departure. This sorrow, He says, will be turned into joy.

16–23. After a little while they will no longer behold Him in the flesh: and again after a little while they will see the abiding reality of His spiritual being with the eye of intuition and of faith. The two verbs in *v.* 16, translated ' behold ' and ' see,' are different: we have sought in our paraphrase to express the meaning of that difference. The ' seeing ' Him after a little while, while probably, to the Evangelist, including the Resurrection visions, embraces the whole spiritual insight into His person and work which it was the Helper's mission to give to them. The thought, therefore, is in the directest relation to the preceding verses. It is the Helper who is to declare His reality to them: it is the Helper who after a little while will quicken their inward vision so as to ' see ' Him. The disciples are perplexed. ' We know not what he saith.' Their confusion, said the Evangelist, is perceived by Jesus. Every teacher of insight and sympathy knows when his students do not follow him. He may seek to remove their confusion either by a fuller exposition of his thought, or—if he perceives that such will not avail in the present stage of their mental and spiritual development—by an emphatic declaration of his own moral and spiritual conviction. If they cannot understand his explanations, at least let them know the convictions on which his life is grounded. This is the way of Jesus here. He does not seek to answer their perplexities: they will have to come their own way to the truth. But what He *does* do is to seek to convey His own faith and hope to them. What causes their weeping will cause the world's rejoicing. Let not that trouble them. Their sorrow will be turned into joy. Their pains are but the pains of travail. When the child is born, the pain of the mother is forgotten in her joy. So will it be with them. At present they have sorrow because they are no longer to see Him in the flesh. There is still a selfishness at the basis of their sorrow. The joy that is to come to them will be grounded in the fact that new spiritual quickening has come to men. Theirs will then be the joy, not of the receiver of life, but of the transmitter of life. And *He* will see them again. Not only is it that they will *see* Him again; but in the eternal realm of the spirit they will be the object of His interest and regard. He will 'see' them. This will bring a joy not to be taken from them by any man. For this joy will rest, not on the evidence of their own senses, but on the conviction that the Christ to whom their faith is directed has the interests of the Kingdom of Truth, of Faith, and of Love for ever in His view. The ground of their joy will be nothing less than the Father revealed in Himself. The joy of the Lord will be their strength.

23–24. When that conviction becomes the ground of their joy, they will ask Him no such questions as are now troubling their minds. It is not that they will cease to ask the questions such as man in his finiteness cannot help but ask. It is that the way of asking the questions will be different. In that day it will be with them—as it was afterwards to be with Newman: a thousand difficulties will not constitute a single real doubt. The questions they ask will arise out of a faith that all life's real questions will have their answer in the truth about God and life revealed in Himself. They will then ask the Father *in His name* for spiritual truth and moral fidelity, not for answers to questions which arise out of fundamental doubt as to whether there is a Father and whether He Himself is His incarnate expression. What they ask will in that day be asked in complete fidelity to the vision of the Father as He Himself has declared Him: such requests are always answered. Hitherto they have been asking questions arising out of their lack of insight into Truth itself: they have not been asking 'in his name.' But every right asking will, instead of increasing their perplexity, merely increase their deep-seated joy.

His Victory, the Foundation of their Peace and Joy

JN. 16[25-33]

16 25 These things have I spoken unto you
in proverbs: the hour cometh, when I
shall no more speak unto you in proverbs,
but shall tell you plainly of the Father.
26 In that day ye shall ask in my name: and
I say not unto you, that I will pray the
27 Father for you; for the Father himself
loveth you, because ye have loved me,
and have believed that I came forth from
28 the Father. I came out from the Father,
and am come into the world: again, I
leave the world, and go unto the Father.
29 His disciples say, Lo, now speakest thou
30 plainly, and speakest no proverb. Now
know we that thou knowest all things,
and needest not that any man should ask
thee: by this we believe that thou camest
31 forth from God. Jesus answered them,
32 Do ye now believe? Behold, the hour
cometh, yea, is come, that ye shall be
scattered, every man to his own, and
shall leave me alone: and *yet* I am not
alone, because the Father is with me.
33 These things have I spoken unto you,
that in me ye may have peace. In the
world ye have tribulation: but be of good
cheer; I have overcome the world.

These verses close this second address, or series of addresses, associated with the night of the Betrayal. They state in a few summary words the nature of the mission of which Jesus knew Himself to be the medium, and state it in order to meet the need of His disciples. What more He has to say will not be said *to them*, but to the Father Himself. This passage, therefore, is the climax of His discourse *to them*.

25–28. So far He was speaking to them in symbols, or proverbs. The vine and the branches, His going away, the coming of the Helper, the woman in travail—all this was symbolical speech, confusing to the literalist or materialist mind, but a window to those who knew how to look and what to look for. But when He is gone from their physical sight and the Helper has quickened their inward hearing, they will hear the unmistakable message of the Father. The tongue of their souls will be unloosed, and they will ask the Father in His name. They must not think that He will have to plead with a reluctant Father to give them what they need. The Father's love is assured them, both because of what He eternally is, and because of the response they have already been making to that love in receiving His incarnate word. As for the incarnate One, by His death He returns to the immediate presence of the Father.

29–30. This seems 'plain' speech to the disciples. They have not had to wait, they think, till they find 'plainness' in spiritual reality itself. They have even now, they imagine, something definite on which they can rest. No 'mystical' symbols, or allegorical fancies, here. The time has *even now* come when they need ask Him no more questions. How clearly the Evangelist's own mind is revealed in the way by which He expresses the confident, and over-confident, faith of the disciples at this point. They are still resting upon the fact that a word has been said to them, not upon their insight into the nature of that word itself. In other words, it is still a faith in 'signs and wonders,' or, as we might say, a faith based upon an 'external authority.' They are more confident, but confidence is not of necessity faith.

31–32. The answer of Jesus is to ask them to question their own faith. Can the confidence they have that He is the incarnate expression of the Father's heart and mind endure the shock of His coming death, and of their own desertion of Him? Is not their confidence still that of sight, not that of insight? Will not such fail them in the hour of trial? As for Himself, desertion by friends cannot disturb His faith. His fellowship with the Father will be His strength. If from out the tension of that hour on the Cross He has to cry that He *seems* to be forsaken, yet the Father is still with Him. The Father's will is His peace.

33. All that He has said has been meant to lead them to such a peace. Tribulation awaits them in the world—trouble, confusion, hatred, and strife. Let the courage begotten of assured faith in Him abide. He Himself has overcome this world of trouble, confusion, hatred, and strife. Spirit has been triumphant over circumstances. Death is swallowed up in victory.

'This,' wrote the Evangelist in his First Epistle (5^{4-5}), 'is the victory that overcometh the world, even our faith. And who is he that overcometh the world but he that believeth that Jesus is the Son of God.' 'Thanks be unto God who giveth us the victory through our Lord Jesus Christ,' wrote Paul in his first Corinthian Epistle. Such faith, expressed by two New Testament writers—so different, yet so alike—was derived from the incarnate Word, whose whole life upon earth calls forth to His disciples in every age, 'Courage, I have overcome the world.'

3. *JESUS'S PRAYER TO THE FATHER FOR THE DISCIPLES* (17)

This chapter contains what has often been called the High-Priestly Prayer of Jesus—sometimes the Prayer of Consecration, sometimes the Intercessory Prayer. It is difficult to find a phrase that suitably describes it. That it is a ' prayer ' is clear from the opening verse, where Jesus, ' lifting up his eyes to heaven,' addresses the Father. He has been speaking to the disciples: He now speaks directly to God. Yet it is a ' Prayer ' to which we have no precise parallel in the Gospels. It is more an outpouring of the soul of Jesus as in the presence of the Father, of whom He is immediately conscious, than a series of petitions addressed—like so many of *our* prayers—to a Being dwelling in remote and transcendent splendour.

The voice of Christendom has said that this is a ' Holy of Holies '; and no commentator can approach it without the diffidence belonging to a sense of reverential awe. The place whereon we stand is holy ground. ' To peep and botanise ' on this ground were indeed sacrilege—*unless* our scrutiny and interpretation are governed by that reverence for truth itself which is the basis and substance of all other reverence. To such a reverence nothing can be really irreverent: the tasks of the true critic or interpreter, whatever his field, partakes of the spirit of Him who said, ' Thy word is *truth* ' (*v.* 17).

Critical scrutiny, therefore, being compatible with reverence, it will be seen that this ' Prayer ' is not an exact report of *one* prayer of Jesus. The language throughout is Johannine. Further, here and there we find in the chapter definite indications of the Evangelist's reflection and interpretation. In *v.* 3, for example, we cannot imagine that Jesus, speaking intimately to the Father, would think or speak of Himself in the third person as ' Jesus Christ.' Nor is it possible to think that Jesus, in such converse with God, would acquaint Him with a fulfilment of prophecy such as is recorded in *v.* 12.

Yet, on the other hand, it is not possible to believe that the whole prayer is an original composition of the Evangelist himself. The certitude of the Father's presence and of the Father's will which throbs through the whole prayer is the certitude of Jesus Himself. The consciousness of His own mission revealed in the prayer is that which pervades the whole Gospel. The sense of the task awaiting His disciples in the world is wholly akin to the mind of Jesus as already manifested. All this, we cannot but feel, is a transcript from the consciousness of the historic Jesus. And that there had come down to the Evangelist—probably through the Apostle John—a tradition incorporating the substance of this prayer on the night of the Betrayal, is, in our judgement, the only theory which does justice to the ' Prayer ' as we have it. As already suggested, this is not to say that the Evangelist has not embodied into the ' Prayer ' phrases, and perhaps sentences, which may have belonged to other occasions; nor is it meant to claim precise historicity for every phrase and sentence embodied. What we do wish to maintain is that *in substance* the prayer is a true transcript of the mind of Jesus when confronted with His approaching death on the Cross.

From what we know of the inmost mind of Jesus, we may say that this is the kind of prayer we should *expect* Him to make. Few of our Lord's personal prayers were overheard by others. That prayer was as the 'vital breath' of Jesus we know from the Synoptic Gospels. 'In the morning, rising up a great while before day, he went out, and departed into a solitary place, and there prayed,' wrote Mark at the beginning of his Gospel (Mk. 1^{35}). 'And it came to pass in those days, that he went out into a mountain to pray, and continued all night in prayer to God,' wrote Luke (6^{12}). Such references to the prayer-life of Jesus are frequent in the Gospels: though, from the very nature of the case, such prayers were neither heard nor recorded. Yet the few of which we *have* a record are consonant both with this prayer and with the mind therein revealed. For example, we should expect that His prayers would begin with 'Father'—for this is how Jesus always thought of God. And that this was so is seen from such Synoptic passages as Mt. 11^{25}—the closest parallel to this prayer—Lk. 22^{42}, $23^{34, 46}$ (see also Jn. 11^{41} and 12^{27}). Or again, many of the 'notes' of what is usually called The Lord's Prayer are heard in this chapter—notably the sense of the Divine Father, whose 'name' was to be 'hallowed,' whose 'will' was to be done, whose children were to be guarded in the hour of temptation and kept from evil. That these were the burden of our Lord's thought in His intercessory fellowship with the Father is clear. And that they are the leading themes of this prayer is also clear to anyone who will meditate upon it. In other words, the revelation of the deepest consciousness of Jesus in this chapter is consonant with what we already know of that consciousness.

The Evangelist does not say where the prayer he records was uttered. This silence has led to many guesses—the Upper Room, the Temple Courts, the road to Gethsemane. On the ground of fitness, the late Bishop Westcott suggested the Temple Courts. 'One spot alone, as it seems, combines all that is required to satisfy the import of these last words, the Temple Courts. . . . Nowhere, as it seems, could the outlines of the future spiritual Church be more fitly drawn than in the sanctuary of the old Church. Nowhere, it is clear, could our High Priest more fitly offer His work and Himself and believers to the Father, than in the one place in which God had chosen to set His name.' It *may be* so: but we do not know, and never shall know.

The whole prayer naturally divides into three parts. In the first—*vv.* 1–8—Jesus prays for Himself; in the second, for His intimate disciples—*vv.* 9–19; in the third, for the disciples of the unborn ages—*vv.* 20–26. The prayer in its entirety focuses and recapitulates the central thoughts of the Gospel.

The Son's Prayer for Himself to the Father

Jn. 17^{1-8}

17 1 These things spake Jesus; and lifting up
his eyes to heaven, he said, Father, the
hour is come; glorify thy Son, that the Son
2 may glorify thee: even as thou gavest him
authority over all flesh, that whatsoever
thou hast given him, to them he should
3 give eternal life. And this is life eternal,
that they should know thee the only true
God, and him whom thou didst send, *even*
4 Jesus Christ. I glorified thee on the
earth, having accomplished the work
5 which thou hast given me to do. And
now, O Father, glorify thou me with thine
own self with the glory which I had with
6 thee before the world was. I manifested
thy name unto the men whom thou gavest
me out of the world: thine they were, and
thou gavest them to me; and they have

7 kept thy word. Now they know that all
things whatsoever thou hast given me are
8 from thee: for the words which thou gavest
me I have given unto them; and they received *them*, and knew of a truth that I came forth from thee, and they believed that thou didst send me.

1. The prayer begins with our Lord's customary mode of address to God—'Father.' All the teaching of Jesus was controlled by the sense of the Father's presence, and the mission given Him to fulfil. That mission was now on the verge of consummation. The hour was come. This sense of impending consummation has dominated the mind of Jesus throughout these last chapters. It is an hour of 'glorification.' So intimate and sure is the certitude of the Father's presence possessed by Jesus that, in spite of the evil agency of men, He regards that glorification of Himself in sacrificial death as the fulfilment of the Father's own purpose and the means of the Father's own glorification. When the Father glorifies the Son, the Son glorifies the Father. When the Son offers Himself, the Father is seen for what He essentially is. The Cross, in revealing a perfect filial relationship, reveals also the Father's own nature. It is a prayer of acknowledgement, and of acceptance. Jesus acknowledges the Divine will for Him, and accepts it. This is the essence of all true prayer. To God alone the glory. 'Thy will, not mine, be done.'

2–3. Conscious that His mission has the inherent power of Divine authority, and that it is for all men, Jesus prays that all of which He was the vehicle should be imparted to His disciples.[1] This 'eternal life' consists in the 'knowledge' of the one true God, and in Jesus the Anointed One whose mission it was to reveal Him. Such 'knowledge' is the apprehension of God, in faith and obedience, by the whole nature of man. This third verse is the double command of the first verse of the 14th chapter in another setting. 'And this is life eternal, that they should know thee the only true God, and him whom thou didst send, even Jesus Christ.' It is clear that the Evangelist is here giving his own expression to the consciousness of Jesus, and to the experience of the disciples in His fellowship.

4–5. The mission of Jesus is now at its completion. Throughout, He has sought to reveal the Father: His earthly end perfects that work. The 5th verse leads to some of the profoundest questions raised by the Gospel, and can only be understood in the light of such other 'pre-existence' passages as 8^{58}, on which we have already commented. The passage gives expression to that unique sense of the presence of the Father possessed by Jesus, by which He transcended the categories of time and space. His consciousness—we speak with reverent diffidence—should not be regarded as a *memory* of a pre-temporal existence: it was—we will venture to say—a present assurance of the Eternal Father. The language of time expresses a consciousness of eternity. The idea of a qualitative completeness of life is conveyed by the idea of priority. The Church has sought to conserve this reality of the consciousness of Jesus in her dogmatic formulas. All such formulas are an inadequate expression of the reality—though they may well have been the least inadequate that could be found at the time.

[1] It has been suggested by Dr. Torrey in *The Four Gospels: a New Translation* (p. 322), that the Greek here may be a mistaken rendering of an original Aramaic, and that the translation should probably be: 'According as thou hast given him authority over all flesh, to give eternal life to all those whom thou hast given him.' The Greek πᾶν (neuter) and αὐτοῖς (masculine plural) are certainly awkward.

6–8. In these verses Jesus speaks to the Father of the mission He has accomplished in the lives of His disciples. These have been ' given ' Him by the Father—it is not Himself who has *won* them. How true this sense of ' givenness ' is to all who live in the Father's eye. Nothing is ' earned ': all is ' given.' And it is the Father's own ' word ' the disciples have kept. The whole end of His teaching had been to lead them from Himself to the Father who was the source of His own words. He has sought all the time to wean them from an inadequate clinging to wonder and sign, and from a false emphasis upon the visible and the terrestrial. He could only be their ' Master,' as they acknowledged the Father, greater than Himself, whose mission He had to fulfil. Now they are coming to see that the visible is not itself the invisible, but only the way to it. Real spiritual belief has begun to take root within them. The greatest joy that can come to any spiritual teacher is when he is able to lead his pupils away from himself to the One Source of Truth whence he himself has derived and derives his own sustenance. Until that day comes they are as children who have still to be carried, and have not yet learned to walk. It is a false Christology which suggests that this joy could not belong to Jesus.

Jesus's Prayer for His Intimate Disciples

JN. 17^{9-19}

17 9 I pray for them: I pray not for the
world, but for those whom thou hast
10 given me; for they are thine: and all
things that are mine are thine, and thine
are mine: and I am glorified in them.
11 And I am no more in the world, and
these are in the world, and I come to
thee. Holy Father, keep them in thy
name which thou hast given me, that they
12 may be one, even as we *are*. While I was
with them, I kept them in thy name
which thou hast given me: and I guarded
them, and not one of them perished, but
the son of perdition; that the scripture
13 might be fulfilled. But now I come to
thee; and these things I speak in the
world, that they may have my joy fulfilled
14 in themselves. I have given them thy
word; and the world hated them, because
they are not of the world, even as I am
15 not of the world. I pray not that thou
shouldest take them from the world, but
that thou shouldest keep them from the
16 evil *one*. They are not of the world, even
17 as I am not of the world. Sanctify them
18 in the truth: thy word is truth. As thou
didst send me into the world, even so sent
19 I them into the world. And for their
sakes I sanctify myself, that they themselves also may be sanctified in truth.

9. The prayer is now directed to these His intimate disciples in whom true belief has begun to find root. He is making requests for these who have been ' given ' Him by the Father. It is concerning them that He now prays, not concerning the world. Only a blind and unsympathetic reader can interpret these words as indicating indifference on the part of Jesus to the world. The mode of expression here—accentuating the exclusion of the world from the prayer—is no doubt that of the Evangelist. What he wishes to convey is that in this prayer of Jesus on the night of the Betrayal He prayed first for Himself, and then specifically for His intimate disciples.

10–12. These disciples, inasmuch as they have received the Divine truth incarnate in Jesus, are of God the Father. ' They are thine,' says Jesus. And such is the fellowship in mind and will which Jesus has with the Father, that what is Jesus's is the Father's, and what is the Father's is Jesus's. This passage is in the closest correspondence of thought with the passage in Mt. 11^{25-27}, where it is stated that there is perfect reciprocal knowledge between the Father and Jesus. Jesus is ' glorified ' in these disciples, inasmuch as their spiritual insight and moral fidelity are a memorial of His own essential person. Whatever manifests the nature of Jesus ' glorifies ' Him—whether it be the Cross on which He hung, or the disciples whom He left behind to follow in His steps. They are to continue in the world, while He goes to the Father. May the Father of all holiness—this is the burden of the prayer—keep in His own sanctity these His disciples; that their unity in mind and endeavour may be the spiritual unity already existing between Himself and the Father. Their ' oneness ' is no spurious, or spectacular, union, such as men delude themselves into thinking they have when they obliterate diversities in the interests of mechanical uniformity. It is a unity of mind and purpose—the same kind of unity as is referred to in 10^{16}, where Jesus speaks of the ' one flock.' The real difficulty from which Jesus wished His disciples to be delivered was the undesirable diversity caused by the sectarian spirit, not the desirable diversity caused by the manifoldness of the gifts of God to His children. ' If thy heart be as my heart, give me thy hand,' said John Wesley.

All except one have so far been kept true to this fellowship: the exception being Judas ' the son of perdition,' the son, that is, of ' loss.' There is a play upon words in the Greek, which might be conveyed in English by such a translation as, ' None was lost but the son of loss '; or, ' None perished but the son of perishing.' The reference by the Evangelist is to Ps. 109^{8}.

13–17. Jesus now prays that the eleven who are left may come to a full knowledge of His own joy. Such a joy consists in having the ' word ' of Jesus, that is, in having His essential mind and spirit. No one can know the joy of service but one who serves, nor the joy of humility but one who is humble, nor the joy of sacrifice but one who offers himself. If we sought more to manifest the mind of Jesus, we should not find it necessary to seek restlessly for His joy. Joy is a product of the spirit. It can belong to the disciples amid the opposition of the world. Indeed, that opposition is not something to be fled from. All that needs to be fled from is evil. While *in* the world, His disciples are not *of* the world; even as Jesus Himself is in the world and not of it. So He prays that the Divine Father will consecrate, or sanctify, them in that whole life of truth incarnate in Himself, the Father's ' word.' To be ' consecrated in the truth ' is to live in that realm of the spirit where Jesus had His home. There is only truth where there is sanctity, and only sanctity where there is truth. The spiritual universe is one, not two: hence he who is a stranger to either sanctity or truth is a stranger to both. The Father's ' word ' is truth, says Jesus. This is another way of saying what the Gospel has said from the Prologue onwards—that Jesus is the Father's incarnate ' Word.'

18–19. Thus the disciples will fulfil His mission in the world, as He Himself has fulfilled the Father's mission. It is to the end that they should be truly consecrated in the whole service which lies before them that He devotes Himself in sacrificial death.

Jesus's Prayer for the Disciples-to-be

JN. 17[20-26]

17 20 Neither for these only do I pray, but for
them also that believe on me through
21 their word; that they may all be one;
even as thou, Father, *art* in me, and I in
thee, that they also may be in us: that
the world may believe that thou didst
22 send me. And the glory which thou hast
given me I have given unto them; that
23 they may be one, even as we *are* one; I in
them, and thou in me, that they may be
perfected into one; that the world may
know that thou didst send me, and lovedst
24 them, even as thou lovedst me. Father,
that which thou hast given me, I will
that, where I am, they also may be with
me; that they may behold my glory,
which thou hast given me: for thou
lovedst me before the foundation of the
25 world. O righteous Father, the world
knew thee not, but I knew thee; and
26 these knew that thou didst send me; and
I made known unto them thy name, and
will make it known; that the love wherewith
thou lovedst me may be in them,
and I in them.

20–21. The prayer now embraces the disciples to be—those who are to believe in the incarnate Word through the 'word' of His intimate disciples. Did Jesus here pray, as has often been said, for 'the whole estate of Christ's Church militant here upon earth'? If the question means to suggest that Jesus envisaged such a future for His followers as is to-day seen in the organised communities now calling themselves the several branches of that Church, the answer must be in the negative. But if it means that Jesus thought of His mission as one that was to be carried on after His death by His disciples; if it means that He believes that His own death would inaugurate an extension of that mission outside the field of Palestine—the answer must be in the affirmative. His prayer is, that these disciples-to-be may know the same unity as that for which He has already prayed on behalf of His present disciples. This is a real unity of spirit, not a formal union of organisation. The first may exist without the second; and the second without the first. This is a fact of experience, not a theory on which to argue. All the phrases used in this Gospel of the unity of the Church emphasise its spiritual character. It is such a unity of spiritual and ethical fellowship as existed between Jesus and the Father. The *end* of this unity is that the world may, with the whole mind, believe in the Father's gift of the incarnate Word. The 'world' will never believe this through a regimented union of churches; but only where Christians put first things first, and dwell together in perfect charity, without the pride, vain-glory, and worldly wisdom which it itself knows so well. Jesus does not pray that the world should believe *in itself*, in, that is, the qualities it itself manifests. He prays that it may accept the whole truth of the Father incarnate in Him. This can only come when His followers incarnate the same truth, manifest the same spirit.

22–24. The 'glory' which Jesus has received from the Father He has given to the disciples. That is, even as the Father has manifested Himself in Jesus, so Jesus has been the channel of the Divine self-manifestation to others. This 'glory' constitutes the unity of the children of light. The Splendour of the Father revealed in the Son makes all the other sons to become one family of light. When they live as sons they will know the Love the Father bestows upon His sons. They will thus be *with Him* who has incarnated the Father's nature, beholding thus that Eternal Glory which is Eternal Love. 'God,' says the Evangelist in his First Epistle, 'is love.' This 24th verse expresses the same truth in language of unfathomable depth. God has *always* manifested Himself; and that self-manifestation has ever been as the giving and receiving of Love. 'For thou lovedst me before the foundation of the world.'

25–26. In the closing words of the prayer Jesus says that the world has not known the *Righteous* Father—has not known, that is, the righteousness and love which are of the essence of the Divine nature. Jesus Himself, in virtue of His filial fellowship, has so known God, has so revealed Him, and will continue so to declare Him by the Spirit. The final petition of Jesus is that the Divine Love may indwell the disciples, so that they may come to the knowledge of that spiritual union adumbrated in the allegory of the vine: 'that the love wherewith thou lovedst me may be in them, and I in them.'

C. THE PASSION AND RESURRECTION OF JESUS (18–20)

The third main section of the second part of the Gospel is now reached. We have thought it well to include the Betrayal, the Arrest, the twofold Trial, the Crucifixion, and the Resurrection in one main subdivision. For they constitute a unity within the larger unity of the second main part of the Gospel: which part is embraced within the still larger unity of the Gospel as a whole. These divisions, and subdivisions, should help a modern reader to see the whole Gospel as it was begotten in the mind of the Evangelist. The entire work was written to convey the essential mind of Jesus. The first part is devoted to the public witness of Jesus: the second part to the private witness of Jesus. The whole self-revelation of Jesus both encounters and occasions hostility. This hostility now reaches its climax in scenes which at the same time reveal in a culminating manner the mind of Jesus and the mind of His opponents. It is the final battle between Light and Darkness. Both are here seen for what they essentially are. The Darkness which deems itself to have conquered is seen in the Resurrection to have been itself overcome. That is why the whole work is rightly called a 'Gospel'—that is, Good Tidings. That is why the Passion and the Resurrection have always been, and always must be, the centre of the Gospel. Everything that Jesus has said about Himself is focused in the way He went to His death. Everything He has said about the Father is revealed on a Cross, whereon the Son incarnates the Father's own mind and purpose. The Cross, we sometimes say, is the victory of Jesus over the world's last circumstance. It is, however—this is the message of Jesus Himself—more than the triumph of one human spirit in time. It is the triumph of Eternity itself. The Prologue is essentially and inseparably one with the Passion and Resurrection. These are events in time and place ; but they are the deeds of the Eternal Word. The Cross and Resurrection have their ultimate meaning in that whole context of the Gospel which shows that the 'Word' has never been silent, but has now become incarnate in Jesus. The four books we call 'Gospels' are so called because they spring out of the conviction—a conviction which had its fountain in the mind of Jesus Himself—that Eternity is here revealed in time, that God has spoken in man, that the Father's mind is incarnate in Him who knew Himself to be the Son.

The differences and agreements here between this Gospel and the other three raise questions of the highest interest for the historian of the closing hours of the life of Jesus. And inasmuch as any interpretation of the mind of Jesus must be based on the historic facts, these issues are of the highest importance for the Christian philosopher and teacher. Some of these will be noted in the course of the exposition. It seems well at this point, however, to point out: first, the *main* omissions of the Fourth Gospel, and, second the *main* addition of this Gospel, in relation to the Synoptic Gospels.

1. *The main omissions.*—The chief is *the agony in the Garden of Gethsemane*, recorded by all three Synoptists. The Fourth Evangelist, further, omits *the examination at night before the Sanhedrin in the house of Caiaphas*, recorded by Mark and Matthew; as also *the meeting of the Council at daybreak*, recorded by all three Synoptists.

2. *The main incident peculiar to the Fourth Gospel.*—This is *the examination before Annas*, father-in-law of Caiaphas.

There are, of course, many other differences between the Fourth Gospel and the other three, in respect of the incidents and utterances covered by these chapters. The careful student of the Gospels will place the relevant four narratives side by side in separate columns—Mk. 14^32 ff.; Mt. 26^36 ff.; Lk. 22^40 ff.; Jn. 18^1 ff.—and will thus be able to see at a glance the extent and nature of these lesser divergences. From such an examination he will discover the problematical nature of all the 'harmonies' which have sought to make a complete and consistent chronological and topographical narrative of the Betrayal, the Arrest, and the Trials. It is clear that there were different streams of tradition in regard to the events of the Passion in the early Church; and no effort was ever made by a scientifically minded historian in the first century to write a complete and consistent narrative.

There is, however, *one* impressive point of agreement between the Fourth Gospel and the others. *There are two trials*—one ecclesiastical and one civil. It is exceedingly difficult to decide on the precise measure of responsibility for the death of Jesus belonging to the Jewish and Roman authorities respectively: further, on the questions of jurisprudence raised by the twofold trial there are differences of opinion. Both in regard to the ecclesiastical trial and in regard to the civil trial the question of legality arises. Yet that the Jewish and Roman authorities were both involved in the trial of Jesus is the unanimous view of the four evangelists. Before the religious tribunal the charge against Jesus was one of blasphemy. Before the tribunal of Pilate the charge was that Jesus had set Himself up as a King. To the Jewish authorities the crime of Jesus therefore was a *religious* one. To the Roman authorities it was a *political* one. The final word of condemnation came from the Roman tribunal; and the manner of death—crucifixion—was that imposed by Rome upon civil and political criminals. Does this mean that Jesus was found guilty of a political crime? Or does it mean that Pilate betrayed the impartial integrity of the Roman law in deference to utilitarian motives? The latter is the conclusion to which we are driven by our narratives. Death by crucifixion was only legally justifiable on the ground that Jesus was guilty of a political or civil crime. That He was not regarded by Pilate as guilty of such a crime is evidenced by all four Gospels. According to the Marcan tradition, while Pilate does not pronounce Jesus to be innocent, it is yet clear that he so regarded Him. According to the Fourth Evangelist—and to Luke—Pilate definitely declared Jesus to be innocent (Jn. 18^{38}, $19^{4, 6}$; Lk. $23^{4, 14, 22}$). We are therefore left with the necessity of explaining the motives of Pilate in handing over to a Roman death one whom he himself regarded as guiltless of any crime which would have merited it. Whatever may have been the motives of Pilate—and it is well to remember that only if we had access to his inmost mind and to the whole historical and psychological situation should we be in a position to speak with assured conviction—at least it is clear that he acted against his better judgement, and in deference to ignoble considerations. There may be some doubt as to whether he was swayed by motives of personal advantage, or whether, caught in a network of considerations of civil prudence, he refused to take the strong and just line of cutting the network and letting Jesus go free.

Our main concern in the exposition that follows is, by an understanding of the mind of the Evangelist, to penetrate as far as we may into the mind of Jesus.

THE ARREST AND TRIAL BEFORE THE HIGH PRIEST AND PILATE (18–19^{16})

The Arrest

JN. 18^{1-11}

18 1 When Jesus had spoken these words,
he went forth with his disciples over the
brook Kidron, where was a garden, into
the which he entered, himself and his
2 disciples. Now Judas also, which betrayed him, knew the place: for Jesus oft-
times resorted thither with his disciples.
3 Judas then, having received the band *of*
soldiers, and officers from the chief priests
and the Pharisees, cometh thither with
4 lanterns and torches and weapons. Jesus
therefore, knowing all the things that
were coming upon him, went forth, and
5 saith unto them, Whom seek ye? They
answered him, Jesus of Nazareth. Jesus
saith unto them, I am *he*. And Judas
also, which betrayed him, was standing
6 with them. When therefore he said unto
them, I am *he*, they went backward, and
7 fell to the ground. Again therefore he
asked them, Whom seek ye? And they
8 said, Jesus of Nazareth. Jesus answered,
I told you that I am *he*: if therefore ye
9 seek me, let these go their way: that the
word might be fulfilled which he spake,
Of those whom thou hast given me I lost
10 not one. Simon Peter therefore having a
sword drew it, and struck the high priest's
servant, and cut off his right ear. Now
11 the servant's name was Malchus. Jesus
therefore said unto Peter, Put up the
sword into the sheath: the cup which the
Father hath given me, shall I not drink it?

It has already been noted that the Evangelist does not narrate the agony in Gethsemane (Mk. 14^{32-42} and parallel passages). But that he was familiar with the story as recorded in the Synoptic Gospels is clear from the 11th verse of this chapter, where Jesus, speaking to Pilate, uses the words: 'The cup which the Father hath given me, shall I not drink it?' These are the words of one who has emerged in triumphant serenity of purpose from the tension of that inner conflict narrated by the Synoptists. 'Remove this cup from me,' so Mark records his words in 14^{36}: 'howbeit not what I will, but what thou wilt.'

Why, then, a modern reader asks, did he not record the whole scene in Gethsemane? All we can say in answer to such a question is that he did not find it necessary to his purpose to do so. One *might* have assumed that an author with the dramatic type of mind obviously belonging to the Fourth Evangelist would have been eager to record an incident which so vividly revealed the tension of spirit of Jesus at this time. Before adopting that assumption, however, it is necessary to remember that the Evangelist throughout has been indifferent to the chronological stages in the development of the mind of Jesus. He is concerned less with the inward struggle in the consciousness of Jesus than with the triumphant issue. Thus from the first chapter Jesus is assured of His full Messianic vocation, and does not hesitate to proclaim it. So here, the Evangelist is not so much concerned with the conflict within the spirit of Jesus, as with the fact that in that conflict His consciousness of filial mission emerged triumphant. That the Evangelist was not ignorant of this conflict is clear, not only from the 11th verse of this chapter already referred to, but from such a passage as 12^{27}, where he records Jesus as saying: 'Now is my soul troubled: and what shall I say? Father, save me from this hour? But for this cause came I unto this hour.' The conclusion has sometimes been drawn from the omission of any narrative of the Agony in Gethsemane, that the Evangelist did not find it consistent with his Christology, and so of set purpose omitted it. Such a conclusion is mistaken, and is begotten of two fundamental errors of interpretation—as we, at least, regard them. The first error is a misinterpretation of his Christology: the second error is a misinterpretation of the nature of His mind. These two errors are in reality one. As far as his Christology is concerned, the Evangelist has never hesitated to portray the human emotions and limitations of Jesus. As far as his mind is concerned, what he wanted to do was, not to deny how Jesus *came to be* what He was, but *to proclaim what He essentially was and did become.* His omission, in other words, is not dictated by theological preoccupations but by His overmastering insight into the victorious spirit of Jesus. It is not that he has any apologetic interest in obscuring the tension in the spirit of Jesus. It is that he has so penetrative an insight into the victorious faith and obedience of Jesus, that he omits the record of details of the inner conflict, in which and by which the victory was achieved.

1–3. He tells us in *v.* 1 of 'the garden'—not naming it, as Mark (14^{32}) and Matthew (26^{36}) do—which was 'over the brook Kidron.' This was a winter stream dividing the Temple-mount from the Mount of Olives, and is frequently referred to in the Old Testament (see 2 Sam. 15^{23}; 1 Kings 2^{37}, 15^{13}; 2 Kings 23^{46}; 2 Chron. 29^{16}; Jer. 31^{40}). The Fourth Evangelist alone gives this reference to Kidron, and it seems a clear indication of his knowledge of the locality. The name 'Kidron' is a transliteration of the Hebrew adjective for 'dark' or 'black,' but it became confused in the LXX and in some of the Greek MSS. with the Greek word for 'of the cedars' (Kedron). The fact that cedars grew on the slopes of the Mount of Olives helps to explain the confusion. The Hebrew name was known no doubt to our Hebrew author, and used by him; and originally meant the stream that was dark owing to mud, or—a less likely supposition—that it was dark owing to the shadows cast by the trees. The Evangelist tells us that to this garden Jesus was wont to repair with His disciples. As Jesus was not now seeking to evade arrest, we may surmise that, through the betrayal act of Judas, spies had followed the party to Gethsemane. It was thither, probably towards midnight, that Judas led the 'cohort' of Roman soldiers—no doubt a detachment of a 'cohort,' for a 'cohort' consisted of six hundred men—and the Temple police to arrest Jesus. The reference to the 'cohort'—only found in the Fourth Gospel—is significant; and indicates that, to the Evangelist, steps had already been taken by the Jewish authorities to associate the civil power with themselves in the charges to be preferred against Jesus. Such an association is inherently likely, and affords some substantiation for the view that the author himself had been with Jesus during the closing days in Jerusalem.

Some interpreters hold that there is no historical foundation for this reference to the Roman soldiers at the arrest, concluding that the author inserted it for symbolical reasons. The whole historical situation, however, makes it much more probable that the Evangelist here is stating historic fact—which, of course, would have its own dramatic and symbolical significance for his mind.

4–7. The Evangelist, desiring perhaps once more to emphasise that Jesus was not taken aback by circumstances, but rather that He was treading a path which He felt intuitively to be the Divine will for Him, omits the story of the kiss of Judas. In his account, Jesus at once takes the initiative and avows Himself to be the Jesus of Nazareth whom they were seeking. According to our MSS. this open avowal by Jesus disconcerted the arresters, who, we are told, retreated in hesitation, some falling to the ground. That the author is not narrating any 'miraculous' falling to the ground will be obvious to the reader. If we accept the words in the Revised Version as the words employed by the Evangelist himself, we shall conclude that what he wished to say was that some of them stumbled and fell. An exceedingly interesting suggestion, however, has here been made by Dr. Torrey in his new translation of the four Gospels. By the change of a single letter in the two Greek verbs translated 'went backwards' and 'fell'—a copyist's mistake which was not uncommon—the translation would run as follows: 'And Judas also, which betrayed him, was standing with them. When therefore he said unto them, I am he, he went backwards and fell to the ground.' It is, thus, Judas 'who was so overwhelmed by the sense of what he had done, as he saw the eyes of his master fixed on him, that every vestige of strength left him and he collapsed.' [1] Such a translation explains the express reference to Judas at this point and is psychologically natural and coherent with the whole incident.

8–9. Jesus submits Himself to His arresters, telling them to allow His eleven to go free. The Evangelist recalls the words, expressive of the solicitude of Jesus, he has only recently written—in 17^{12}—and finds in this request of Jesus a speedy manifestation of that solicitude, and thus, a partial fulfilment of the words.

10–11. The incident of the smiting of the servant of the high priest follows immediately upon this manifestation of Jesus's care and thought for His disciples. It would seem that to the author the strong contrast presented itself of the true shepherd's solicitude for His disciples, and the spurious militaristic concern of Peter for His Master. While the incident is narrated in all four Gospels, the Fourth Evangelist alone gives us the names of the assailant and the assailed—Peter and Malchus respectively. It is clear that there was a tradition in the Church

[1] Torrey, *op. cit.*, p. 327.

of such an incident, and the names supplied by the Fourth Evangelist are probably correct. On the other hand, it has been pointed out that the name 'Malchus' was derived from the root of the Hebrew word for 'king.' With this in mind, some interpreters would suggest that there is creative dramatic symbolism in this narrative. '"These Jewish High Priests," John seems to say, "were wicked in the worst sense, far worse than Pilate. They were given over by God to pronounce a verdict in accordance with their ingrained injustice—externally High Priests of the Lord but internally ministers of Satan, the ruler of this world. Most appropriately therefore was their servant and representative called Malchus, or king. And, when this servant of theirs went forth to lay hands on Jesus, most appropriately was his *right* ear cut off by the sword so that he lost that symbol of *righteous hearing* which was bestowed by the Law of anointing on Aaron and his successors."'[1]

Augustine—who, it must always be remembered, accepted the precise historicity of the whole narrative—read his own symbolism into the passage; and this merits our recollection. 'The interpretation of Malchus is, one who is destined to reign. What, then, is signified by the ear that was cut off in the Lord's behalf, and healed by the Lord, but the renewed hearing that has been pruned of its oldness, that it may henceforth be in the newness of the spirit, and not in the oldness of the letter? Who can doubt that he, who had such a thing done for him by Christ, was yet destined to reign with Christ? And his being found as a servant, perhaps also to that oldness that gendereth to bondage, which is Agar (Gal. 4^{24}). But when healing came, liberty also was shadowed forth.'

At least, we know that there was a tradition in the Church of such an incident: and it is not improbable that the Fourth Evangelist has given the correct names. The silence of the other evangelists as to the names of assailant and assailed is naturally explicable when we remember that both were probably alive for thirty or forty years after the incident. As to the question of the exact historicity of the incident, it is probable that the author was more concerned with its dramatic fitness than with the precise event that happened. He agrees with Luke—22^{51}—in saying that it was the 'right' ear, but, unlike Luke, he does not record that Jesus restored the ear to the servant. What he wishes to emphasise is the attitude of Jesus during the arrest. The Master would not have His disciples take the sword on His behalf. Matthew in his narrative tells us that Jesus said to the assailant: 'Put up again thy sword into its place: for all they that take the sword shall perish with the sword' (Mt. $26^{52\text{f.}}$).

There was a 'cup' which He must drink: it was the Father's will for Him, and He receives it with His whole heart and mind and will. This figure of the 'cup' is one that is used frequently in the Old Testament—as, for example, in Ps. 11^{6}, 75^{8}; Ezek. $23^{31\text{ff.}}$; Is. 51^{17}, etc.—and came naturally to Jesus, deeply versed as He was in these Scriptures. The 'cup,' which was seemingly being 'given' by the hatred of men, was accepted by Jesus without embitterment and without having recourse to false allies. It was *accepted*, because He knew it to be the Father's own cup. Such a sublime *acceptance* is difficult, both to our intellectual dealing with the problem of evil, and to our own practical attitude in life. But, *in the last*

[1] E. A. Abbott, *The Fourfold Gospel*, pp. 62–63.

resort, the insight of faith involves, to him who treads the path of moral duty, the *acceptance* of whatever is meted out by the world to such obedience. We know of only One Man—the perfect Son of man—who so harmoniously combined the spirit which *combated* evil in all its forms, and the spirit which so perfectly *accepted* it, without the rancour, the bitterness, and the doubt that it occasions in ourselves. Thanks be to God for this unspeakable gift!

The Preliminary Jewish Trial, and Peter's Denials

JN. 18^{12-27}

18 12 So the band and the chief captain, and
the officers of the Jews, seized Jesus and
13 bound him, and led him to Annas first;
for he was father in law to Caiaphas,
14 which was high priest that year. Now
Caiaphas was he which gave counsel to
the Jews, that it was expedient that one
man should die for the people.
15 And Simon Peter followed Jesus, and
so did another disciple. Now that disciple was known unto the high priest, and
entered in with Jesus into the court of the
16 high priest; but Peter was standing at the
door without. So the other disciple,
which was known unto the high priest,
went out and spake unto her that kept
17 the door, and brought in Peter. The
maid therefore that kept the door saith
unto Peter, Art thou also *one* of this man's
18 disciples? He saith, I am not. Now
the servants and the officers were standing *there*, having made a fire of coals; for
it was cold; and they were warming
themselves: and Peter also was with
them, standing and warming himself.
19 The high priest therefore asked Jesus of
20 his disciples, and of his teaching. Jesus
answered him, I have spoken openly to
the world; I ever taught in synagogues,
and in the temple, where all the Jews
come together; and in secret spake I
21 nothing. Why askest thou me? ask them
that have heard *me*, what I spake unto
them: behold, these know the things
22 which I said. And when he had said
this, one of the officers standing by struck
Jesus with his hand, saying, Answerest
23 thou the high priest so? Jesus answered
him, If I have spoken evil, bear witness
of the evil: but if well, why smitest thou
24 me? Annas therefore sent him bound
unto Caiaphas the high priest.
25 Now Simon Peter was standing and
warming himself. They said therefore
unto him, Art thou also *one* of his disciples? He denied, and said, I am not.
26 One of the servants of the high priest,
being a kinsman of him whose ear Peter
cut off, saith, Did not I see thee in the
27 garden with him? Peter therefore denied again: and straightway the cock
crew.

The account of the preliminary Jewish trial and of Peter's denial, which we take as one narrative for comment, is divided into four brief paragraphs in the Revised Version. Commentators have always found it difficult to make a coherent narrative out of these verses as they stand. The difficulty arises partly through a desire to harmonise this narrative of a preliminary examination of Jesus before Annas with the Synoptic narratives where Annas is not mentioned; and partly through a desire to deliver the Evangelist from making what has been called 'a most astounding contradiction.' It is necessary to look somewhat closely at these two issues: for though they may seem to involve us in tortuous argumentation upon unessentials, yet they have importance for the understanding of the Evangelist's mind and the nature of his Gospel.

The first point is the silence of the Synoptists in regard to the preliminary trial before Annas. In these Gospels the trial of Jesus is a kind of official Jewish trial before Caiaphas—a trial by the Sanhedrin—which took place in the morning. The Fourth Evangelist is obviously acquainted with this trial before Caiaphas, for he definitely tells us in *vv.* 24 and 28 of this chapter that Jesus was taken from

Annas to him; but he does not say anything about what happened when Jesus was confronted with Caiaphas and the Sanhedrin. From very early times transpositions of these verses have been made and suggested, in order to meet what were felt to be difficulties in the way of a 'harmony.' The Sinaitic Syriac Palimpsest, for example, gives the verses in the following order—12, 13, 24, 14, 15, 19, 20, 21, 22, 23, 16, 17, 18, 25, 26, 27, 28, 29, 30, 31. If the reader will take the narrative in such order, he will note that the trial thus recorded is before Caiaphas, not before Annas—this being consistent with the Synoptic account. The reader will also note that the story of Peter's denial is thus given in a continuous, instead of in a divided, narrative.[1]

The second issue—the 'astounding contradiction' supposed to be inherent in the narrative as we have it in our best MSS., and, of course, in our Revised Version—is in the fact that Annas, who is, so the author tells us, the father-in-law of Caiaphas the high priest, is himself, presumably, regarded as 'the high priest' in *v.* 19; and yet the author goes on to say that Annas sent Jesus bound to 'Caiaphas the high priest' (*v.* 24). Surely, it is held, the author would not perpetrate such incoherences in his narrative. In other words, he could not say —so it is held—these three things: first, that Annas was 'father-in-law to Caiaphas who was high priest that year' (*v.* 13); second, that the examination of Jesus was before Annas 'the high priest'; and, third, that he it was who sent Jesus 'bound to Caiaphas the high priest' (*v.* 24). There must, it is thought, be some confusion in a text which calls both Annas and Caiaphas 'high priest.' The transposition of the order given in the Sinaitic Syriac Palimpsest, beside harmonising the Johannine narrative with that of the Synoptists, delivers the author, it will be noted, from such a 'self-stultification,' as it has been regarded. The same deliverance of the author is achieved by a much simpler transposition, namely, by placing *v.* 24 between *vv.* 13 and 14. The Authorised Version, it will be noted, sought to evade the difficulties inherent in this narrative by an even simpler alteration. The 1611 version translated the aorist 'sent,' in *v.* 24, as a pluperfect 'had sent.' If the Evangelist wrote that 'Annas *had* sent' Jesus bound to Caiaphas, the 'trial' which precedes would be naturally understood as a trial before Caiaphas. The Authorised Version translation, however, is inadmissible, and is but an endeavour to evade the difficulty.

The reader will now wish our reasons for following the narrative as we have it in the Revised Version.

In the first place, it is the narrative as found in our most dependable MSS.

In the second place, it is easier to understand why this narrative was altered—as in the Sinaitic Syriac—than to understand why, if it did not give the original order, it should have persisted. Those who alter are conscious of difficulty—their 'difficulty,' however, may be the result of a mistaken understanding of the Evangelist.

This leads to the third, and really important, point. Annas *had been* high priest, and a very famous high priest, maintaining a position of great influence throughout his life. Josephus tells us that among those who succeeded him in the office were not only his son-in-law Caiaphas, but also his five sons. It is

[1] See *Light on the Four Gospels from the Sinai Palimpsest*, by Smith Lewis, p. 171.

therefore not at all a psychological absurdity for the author to refer to him as 'high priest.' In the Acts of the Apostles (4^6) Annas is also called 'the high priest,' on an occasion when he was not the *ruling* high priest (see also Lk. 3^2). If, for example, we could imagine a very famous 'Archbishop of Canterbury' being alive when his successor is enthroned in Canterbury, we should not be surprised if an author were to call each of them by the same title 'Archbishop.' Further, in *v.* 13 the Evangelist clearly says that Caiaphas was the high priest 'that year'—*that fateful year*, that is—thus distinguishing him from Annas who would be in a general way regarded as 'high priest' (see also Jn. 11^{49}). What, therefore, has been regarded as an 'astonishing contradiction' and 'self-stultification' on the part of the Evangelist, will not appear so to those who exercise the historical imagination.

It is well, however, to say that a precise harmony of all the evangelical narratives of the trials of Jesus is not possible. The view here taken is that the Fourth Evangelist is narrating in his own way a preliminary and informal examination of Jesus in the house of Annas. This *may* have been the same examination as is recorded in Mk. $14^{53\,\text{ff.}}$, where, however, Annas is not mentioned by name. The author's account here may well—we suggest—be based on his own recollection.

We have already suggested that the Evangelist—then a very young man—may have been with Jesus during these last days in Jerusalem. Was he the *other disciple* referred to in *vv.* 15 and 16 of this chapter? Some have supposed him to be 'the beloved disciple'; which raises again the question as to who 'the beloved disciple' was. To our view the beloved disciple was John the Apostle, and this other disciple was not he. If the author meant here to refer to him whom he has called 'the disciple whom Jesus loved,' we should expect him so to refer to him at this point. What he does is to refer somewhat vaguely and mysteriously to 'another' disciple. We conclude that the author is here referring to a disciple other than the beloved disciple. Further, it is not probable that John the Apostle, a fisherman of Galilee, would be 'known to the high priest.' Suggestions—more ingenious than wise—have been made to account for such an acquaintanceship: as, for example, that the apostle's family may have provided the high priest's household with fish, or that the high priest may have met the apostle and his family while holidaying in Galilee. With a little imagination one could make hundreds of kindred bizarre and fantastic suggestions. Let us smile at them and pass on. One who was 'known to the high priest' was, no doubt, a young man belonging to a priestly family. That the author was this young priestly disciple is a suggestion coherent with the characteristics of the Gospel as we have it. It may help also to explain the perplexing reference, discussed in the Introduction, of Polycrates, Bishop of Ephesus at the end of the second century, to the John who wore the 'sacerdotal plate.' [1]

The scene, then, which the Evangelist has in mind is roughly this. Jesus is

[1] E. A. Abbott made the somewhat far-fetched suggestion that this disciple 'known to the high priest' was Judas Iscariot, and that the Evangelist intends us to distinguish this friend of the high priest from 'the disciple whom Jesus loved.' On this supposition, we have another illustration of *dramatic antithesis*. One was the 'bosom friend' of Caiaphas, the murderer of Jesus, the other the bosom friend of Jesus Himself (*Miss. Evan.*, i, pp. 18 ff.).

brought in bonds by the mixed body of Roman and Jewish arresters to Annas. Peter and the Evangelist himself follow. The latter gains admission at once into the court, and uses his influence to secure the admission of Peter, who would otherwise have been left in the street. Such is the scene. The Evangelist's chief interest, however, in his narrative is to set forth the dramatic contrast between the serene faith and fidelity of Jesus in this hour of His trial and the uncertainty and infidelity of Peter. There is a psychological fitness in the position of *vv.* 19–24; for they come between two stages in the denial of Peter. The diamond of the Lord's unwavering fidelity to His mission is flanked on either side with the dull foil of Peter's infidelity. Such dramatic contrasts were seen and vividly felt by the Evangelist, as he watched the scene in sombre and questioning perplexity—which through the days that followed grew to deep and utter abhorrence of every base purpose and motive on the part of the enemies of Jesus. He conveys the contrast as it presented itself to his mind by the order and setting of his narrative.

First, then, the denial of Peter.—' It was,' says the Evangelist ' cold.' Nights in Jerusalem, nearly 3,000 feet above sea-level, can be cold even at Easter time. Beside the historical fact, however, the Evangelist may have been thinking of the ardour in the soul of Peter, so recently revealed in the garden, which has now spent itself. The fire has died down; the cold ashes remain. A fire burns in the courtyard. Thrice Peter denies that he is a disciple of the arrested Jesus. The mistaken zeal has given place to cold denial. Twice the Evangelist tells us that Peter was warming himself—in *vv.* 18 and 25. His spirit as well as his body needed heat. When the morning came, heralded by the crowing of the cock, he has denied his Master thrice.

Is there anything in the Evangelist's narrative to throw light upon the mind of Peter during this trial hour? For it is *his* trial—and the trial of everyone present—as well as the trial of Jesus. To adjudicate on the motives of any man is a difficult and delicate task, from which anyone who knows the intricacies and uncertainties of his own mind will shrink. Is it cowardice? But Peter was not, at least in the ordinary sense, a coward. For at least he has followed Jesus to the house of His enemies. And had he not struck his blow in the garden? This, indeed, showed zeal. But was it zeal enkindled at the flame of insight into the mind of Jesus? *Or*, was it not zeal begotten of his own over-weening self-confidence? The latter kind of zeal may not quail before soldiers and rulers, for in meeting these it is showing how strong it itself is. But let it be confronted with the inconspicuous questioning of a servant, and it will be caught off its guard; for there is here no self-esteem to be defended, no self-confident zeal to be manifested. A little more self-distrust, a little more real humility, and his courage would have had the steadfastness of the ' rock ' symbolised by his name.

The way the Evangelist tells the story of Peter's threefold denial may help our insight a little into the mystery of his mind on that fateful night. His first denial is, seemingly, in order to escape unwanted notice on his entry into the courtyard. His second and third denials are narrated immediately following the record of the examination of Jesus and His dismissal to Caiaphas. During that examination might he not have confirmed from his own experience the spiritual nature of the teaching of Jesus? The words of Jesus at this preliminary investigation are: ' Why askest thou me? Ask them that have heard me, what I spake unto them: behold these know the things which I said ' (*v.* 21). There was in the courtyard one who might have come forward to meet such a questioning—*but he did not come.* (The ' other ' disciple—probably the Evangelist himself—who was also present was yet too young and inexperienced to understand the whole significance of what was happening.) Was it that Peter still wanted Jesus to think and to act as he now knew He would not think and act? Was it, that is, that he did not find himself in that essential sympathy with the non-political, non-violent purposes of Jesus, which would have made him a self-forgetful defender of His cause? At least, he did not intervene in such a way as Jesus would, we think, have approved. Thus the second denial follows naturally as Jesus is led away, and when the servants, taking their eyes from the accused, have time to look around. The question which follows this second denial, coming we are told from a kinsman of him whom Peter had struck in the garden, is one fraught with serious danger. The third denial follows.

Thomas Hardy in his poem, *In the Servants' Quarters*—too long to be quoted here—has given rein to his imagination in describing the denials of Jesus.

Secondly, the examination of Jesus.—The Master's strong serenity of purpose stands contrasted with His disciple's weak and troubled indecision. At this preliminary and informal investigation, the inquiry, we are told, is first about *the disciples of Jesus*—probably their type and number; and secondly, about *His teaching.* The two issues involve one another. The character of a man's teaching determines the character of his followers. In His answer—found only in the Fourth Gospel—Jesus therefore says nothing in reply to the first query; and to the second merely refers them to the frankness and publicity of His speech. The question is answered with a question. What can He say that He has not already said openly? They had employed secret and treacherous means to arrest Him, when His ways have been clear and open. Implicit in the reply of Jesus is His insight into the subtle and veiled insincerity of the inquiry. Such a reply is as an arrow of truth which goes home to its target. The startled discomfiture which it causes manifests itself in a burst of self-deceptive fury, and Jesus is violently struck by an officer standing by. If a self-revealing truth is not *received*, it will goad to unbridled violence against him who declares it. The darkness of falsehood once again hates the light of truth. This one blow, in the Fourth Gospel, takes the place of many violent insults referred to in the Synoptic Gospels, there associated with the trial before Caiaphas. (See Mk. 14^{65}; Mt. $26^{67\,f.}$; Lk. $22^{63\,ff.}$.) The words of the attendant are, ' Answerest thou the high priest so? ' Behind this reply there is the implication that truth must be silent in the presence of men's delusive ' authorities.' 'Twas ever so. The precept of Jesus in Mt. 5^{39}—' resist not him that is evil '—refers not to the intrinsically resisting quality of truth and truthfulness, but to the manner and motive of the resistance. Truth will always resist falsehood, but it will resist by its own pure and truthful ways. It will resist by being itself. Even ' high priests ' have to be answered if they love not the truth; but the answer should be given—as here by Jesus—with the quiet candour of serenity, and without argumentative or pugnacious heat.

THE CIVIL TRIAL BEFORE PILATE (18^{28}–19^{16})

JN. 18^{28-40}

18 28 They lead Jesus therefore from Caiaphas into the palace: and it was early;
and they themselves entered not into the
palace, that they might not be defiled,
29 but might eat the passover. Pilate
therefore went out unto them, and saith,
What accusation bring ye against this
30 man? They answered and said unto
him, If this man were not an evil-doer,
we should not have delivered him up
31 unto thee. Pilate therefore said unto
them, Take him yourselves, and judge
him according to your law. The Jews
said unto him, It is not lawful for us to
32 put any man to death: that the word of
Jesus might be fulfilled, which he spake,
signifying by what manner of death he
should die.
33 Pilate therefore entered again into the
palace, and called Jesus, and said unto
him, Art thou the King of the Jews?
34 Jesus answered, Sayest thou this of thyself, or did others tell it thee concerning
35 me? Pilate answered, Am I a Jew?
Thine own nation and the chief priests
delivered thee unto me: what hast thou
36 done? Jesus answered, My kingdom is
not of this world: if my kingdom were of
this world, then would my servants fight,
that I should not be delivered to the
Jews: but now is my kingdom not from
37 hence. Pilate therefore said unto him,
Art thou a king then? Jesus answered,
Thou sayest that I am a king. To this
end have I been born, and to this end am
I come into the world, that I should bear
witness unto the truth. Every one that
38 is of the truth heareth my voice. Pilate
saith unto him, What is truth?
And when he had said this, he went
out again unto the Jews, and saith unto
39 them, I find no crime in him. But ye
have a custom, that I should release unto
you one at the passover: will ye therefore
that I release unto you the King of the
40 Jews? They cried out therefore again,
saying, Not this man, but Barabbas.
Now Barabbas was a robber.

The proceedings before Caiaphas, narrated by Mark and Matthew, are briefly referred to, but are not described. Nor is the formal decision of the Sanhedrin recorded. That sentence passed upon Jesus required the concurrence of the Roman authorities, before it could be executed. The civil trial therefore follows the ecclesiastical trial. Jesus is led to the Prætorium, the official residence of Pilate, the Roman governor. The traditional view is that this was in Antonia, to the north-west of the Temple precincts; but the reference may be to the palace built by Herod the Great on the western hill of the city.

'It was,' says the Evangelist, 'early.' What had been done by the Jewish religious authorities had been done in the darkness. We are told that formal meetings of the Sanhedrin could not be held earlier than 6 a.m. If the term that is used here by the Evangelist for 'early' means, as it usually means, the fourth watch (see Mk. 13^{35})—that is, from 3 a.m. to 6 a.m.—then the trial of Jesus before the Sanhedrin was illegal. Furtiveness and haste, at least, seem to have been the marks of the ecclesiastical trial. The Passover day began in the evening at 6 p.m.—accepting, that is, the date of the Crucifixion as given by the Fourth Evangelist. The Jewish authorities, therefore, would wish the sentence executed without delay. They have 'religious' scruples about the date of the execution, but not about their own motives. They deluded themselves that sacredness belongs to seasons instead of to purposes and values. They have further scruples about entering the Prætorium, for if they had entered a house from which all leaven had not been removed they could not partake of the Passover that evening (see Exod. 12^{15}). The Fourth Evangelist alone tells us of this scruple. It is another clue to the nature of his mind, and to that whole conception of religion which he has learned from Jesus. With unthinking and unimaginative approval, the words have been read in every age, by those whose spiritual insight the letter has killed. Let us ponder well the words—' they entered not into the palace, that they might not be defiled.' If the words say nothing to us, we are dead while we live.

29–32. Pilate is now for the first time mentioned by the Evangelist. He rejects the scruples of the religious authorities, with the ' wisdom ' of the sceptical statesman to whom all religions are *useful*. What, he wishes to know, is the charge against Jesus? Their answer is evasive. Jesus had been condemned by the Sanhedrin for blasphemy; but this is a *religious* crime, outside the jurisdiction of Pilate. They wish the Procurator, therefore, to sentence Jesus on the mere ground that *they* consider Him worthy of death. In other words, they ask for a confirmation of their decision, not for an examination of their judgement. Pilate, however, is here represented as seeking to conform to the ideals of Roman justice, and at the same time to save Jesus from death. ' If you will not specify his crimes, then judge him yourselves,' he says—knowing full well the answer they would make to such a proposal. To inflict the death penalty was outside their legal competence. Their reply to this effect is regarded by the Evangelist as bearing out the conviction which had been maturing in the mind of Jesus—namely, that His death would be at the hands of Rome (see 12^{32-33}). The Jewish authorities wanted His death, but they wanted the Romans to effect it. They might have tried to *stone Him*, and if they had done so their illegal act would perhaps have been overlooked by Pilate. But, besides their uncertainty about the attitude of Pilate, there was their uncertainty about the attitude of the people. Jesus must have penetrated their thoughts, and doubtless it was His insight into the working of their minds which first led Him to speak of His death by crucifixion.

33–38. Their charge, therefore, becomes one of *treason*. The examinations of Jesus by Pilate are private. These two dialogues—recorded in *vv.* 33–38 of this chapter, and *vv.* 8–11 of the 19th chapter—are only recorded by the Fourth Evangelist. They have a striking dramatic fitness. It seems clear that the Evangelist is himself dramatising this situation when Pilate is confronted with Jesus—for, as he himself tells us, it was a private examination. Ideas central to the whole mind of Jesus are given dramatic expression.

The charge before Pilate is that Jesus had claimed to be King; this was a charge to which the representative of the Roman Emperor *must* listen. A charge of blasphemy meant nothing to him: it was outside his jurisdiction as Procurator, and outside his concern as a sceptical Roman. The way in which the Jewish enemies of Jesus shift their ground, from a religious to a political charge, is in keeping with the subtle malignity they personify in this Gospel.

So the theme of this first dialogue is Kingship; and we have presented in contrast the spiritual mission of Jesus and the sceptical materialism of Pilate. Jesus neither declares plainly that He is a King, nor denies that He is a King. Instead, He seeks to unfold to the mind of the sceptical Procurator wherein true kingship consisted. The kingship inherent in Jesus's consciousness of the Father, and of His own mission, is not the idea of kingship held by Pilate. To the governor kingship involved an earthly kingdom, to be maintained by military might. To Jesus kingship involved a spiritual kingdom, to be established and maintained by spiritual means. Jesus is King of a kingdom of truth. Out of His unique fellowship in the life eternal there has come to Him unique insight into the truth of eternity. It is for this reason that He *must* bear witness to the truth. He who knows truth is king in the kingdom of truth-seekers. To him those who are of the truth naturally gravitate. The kingdom of truth has no frontiers of race. It is a kingdom, not just for the Jews, whom Pilate so heartily despises, but for all the lovers of truth. To this claim of Jesus there comes the half-sceptical, half-scornful, perhaps half-jesting, reply of Pilate—made familiar to English readers by Bacon's famous essay. 'What is truth? said jesting Pilate, and would not stay for an answer.'

The idea of truth is inseparable from the idea of God. If the second is uncertain, so is the first. He who denies one denies both. Truth incarnate stands before Pilate, but he will not listen to its word. No one can hear the voice of truth who does not follow it. Pilate is sceptical about a spiritual kingdom. How could he be otherwise when he was refusing to obey the spiritual and moral truth which was speaking to him in Jesus? Some doubts reveal a central love of truth; just as some so-called beliefs reveal a central hatred of it. But Pilate's doubts were, probably, not of that kind. A man's attitude to truth is shown, not by his elaborated utterances but by his instinctive attitudes, by his unthinking and spontaneous reactions. Pilate reacts to the speech of Jesus with a sceptical or jesting rejoinder. He could not do otherwise; for in the depths of his mind and conscience he was already stifling, or seeking to stifle, the voice which bade him liberate one who was innocent. So his spoken scepticism is but the outward form of that fundamental scepticism seated in the central sanctuary of his mind. No one really believes in truth who refuses to follow it. And no one *can* believe in truth who does not acknowledge its imperious right to be followed. Right and truth are to the Fourth Evangelist one idea, not two. Like the Psalmist, he believed that God desired truth in the inward parts. He who is not an obedient servant in the kingdom of right and truth is the final atheist. The truth is not in him; and can, therefore, never come out of him. Duty is imperative and he who follows it is on the road of truth. 'Unto the upright there ariseth light in the darkness.'

39–40. To Pilate there is no political danger in one with such visionary claims. So he wishes to release Jesus. The Evangelist, omitting the Lucan story of the attempted transference of the trial to Herod (Lk. $23^{7 ff.}$), tells us that Pilate sought to take advantage of a Passover custom of releasing a Jewish prisoner. 'But ye have a custom, that I should release unto you one at the passover: will ye therefore that I release unto you the King of the Jews?' This custom is not directly referred to, as far as we know, except in our Gospels (see Mt. 27^{15} and Mk. 15^{6}). It is a custom, however, which harmonises well with what is known of the Roman method of provincial administration. Such methods were on the whole tolerant, and mindful of the religious scruples of Rome's numerous subject peoples. The Evangelist, no doubt, inserts this reference to this 'custom,' in order to unveil the hesitations in the mind of Pilate. He wishes—so the Evangelist would say—to annul the sentence of the Sanhedrin, and at the same time to reveal a pretended scrupulous regard for the sacredness of their Festival seasons. The custom of granting ‘ amnesties ’ is one with which colonial administrators have been familiar in all ages. Further, by so releasing Jesus, Pilate would be at one and the same time acquiescing in the guilt of Jesus —and thus, not putting himself into open opposition to the *decision* of the Sanhedrin—and refusing to acquiesce in their *sentence.* He would thus, at the same time, be absolving Jesus from a punishment which he knew to be unjust. It would therefore seem that Pilate wished to avoid an open conflict with the Sanhedrin, and at the same time to save his conscience from the burden of what he knew would be a crime. Pilate's proposal is that of the weak man who wishes to make the best of two worlds.

In Mark's Gospel (15^{8}) it is the people who first make the demand for such an act of grace: whereas here it is Pilate himself who suggests it. Further, in Mt. (27^{17}) Pilate himself offers the Jews the alternative—Barabbas or Jesus; whereas here the suggestion that Barabbas should be released comes spontaneously from the people. In both (Mk. 15^{11}) and (Mt. 27^{20}) the suggestion that Barabbas should be chosen comes from the priests.

It will thus be clear that the Johannine account has the succinctness of vivid drama. ‘ They yelled again, Not this man but Barabbas. Now Barabbas was a robber.’ The Evangelist has not told us of any previous yelling of the crowd; but he now says that they do it ‘ again.’ The suggestion has been made that the ‘ again ’ is the ‘ inadvertent addition ’ of a scribe who remembered Mk. 15^{13} —‘ and they cried out *again*, Crucify him.’ Perhaps, however, the Evangelist himself wrote, ‘ They cried out therefore again,’ his pen inadequately expressing the rapidity and vividness of his thoughts. It is a dramatic contrast surging up in his mind, between the King Jesus and the robber Barabbas, which inspires this condensed and striking brevity.

Mark, in 15^{7}, says that Barabbas was one of a band of rebels and murderers: the Fourth Evangelist merely says he is a robber. This gives the Evangelist the opportunity for the dramatic symbolism so congenial to his mind. The 13th chapter closed with the words, ‘ And it was night.’ This chapter closes with a symbol, just as vivid—‘ Now Barabbas was a robber.’ Jesus, the Son of the Divine Father, is the good shepherd who gives His life for the sheep. Bar-abbas —the name, as has been noted since Origen's time, means ‘ son of the father ’— represents the hireling who comes as a thief and a robber (see chap. 10). He is the son of another father (see Jn. 8^{44}, etc.), and it is he whose release is shouted for by those who are the sons of the same father of evil. Thus, the Evangelist sees a dramatic fulfilment of the word of Jesus just recorded. Those who are of the truth hear *His* voice: the sons of falsity shout for *Bar-abbas.*

THE CIVIL TRIAL—*continued*

JN. 19^{1-16}

19 1 Then Pilate therefore took Jesus, and
2 scourged him. And the soldiers plaited
a crown of thorns, and put it on his head,
and arrayed him in a purple garment;
3 and they came unto him, and said, Hail,
King of the Jews! and they struck him
4 with their hands. And Pilate went out
again, and saith unto them, Behold, I
bring him out to you, that ye may know
5 that I find no crime in him. Jesus
therefore came out, wearing the crown of
thorns and the purple garment. And

Pilate saith unto them, Behold, the man!
6 When therefore the chief priests and the
officers saw him, they cried out, saying,
Crucify *him*, crucify *him*. Pilate saith
unto them, Take him yourselves, and
crucify him: for I find no crime in him.
7 The Jews answered him, We have a law,
and by that law he ought to die, because
8 he made himself the Son of God. When
Pilate therefore heard this saying, he was
9 the more afraid; and he entered into the
palace again, and saith unto Jesus,
Whence art thou? But Jesus gave him
10 no answer. Pilate therefore saith unto
him, Speakest thou not unto me? knowest
thou not that I have power to release
thee, and have power to crucify thee?
11 Jesus answered him, Thou wouldest have
no power against me, except it were
given thee from above: therefore he that
delivered me unto thee hath greater sin.
12 Upon this Pilate sought to release him:
but the Jews cried out, saying, If thou
release this man, thou art not Cæsar's
friend: every one that maketh himself a
13 king speaketh against Cæsar. When
Pilate therefore heard these words, he
brought Jesus out, and sat down on the
judgement-seat at a place called The
Pavement, but in Hebrew, Gabbatha.
14 Now it was the Preparation of the passover: it was about the sixth hour. And
he saith unto the Jews, Behold, your
15 King! They therefore cried out, Away
with *him*, away with *him*, crucify him.
Pilate saith unto them, Shall I crucify
your King? The chief priests answered,
16 We have no king but Cæsar. Then
therefore he delivered him unto them to
be crucified.

1. Pilate, still wishing to save Jesus from death, seeks another way of achieving this end, while at the same time placating the hostile desires of 'the Jews.' He is caught in the net, woven as much by his own weakness, as by the machinations of the Sanhedrin. He will neither acquit Jesus nor condemn Him. Thus, he inflicts the Roman punishment of scourging upon Him; hoping, perhaps, that this might satisfy the Jewish accusers and judges. That this was his motive is substantiated by the Lucan Gospel, where Pilate says: 'I will therefore chastise him and let him go' (Lk. 23^{22}). In Mark and Matthew, however, the scourging follows the sentence of crucifixion; and this would be the strictly legal order of proceedings. Yet the strict legality of the proceedings is highly dubious; and we are therefore justified in reading the motives of Pilate in the light of the Fourth Evangelist's narrative.

2. After the scourging comes the mockery. Let the mock-king, or the mock-victor, be arrayed as one. Thus, in Mk., Mt., and Jn., Jesus is made to wear a crown of thorns and the purple robe. In both Mk. ($15^{15\,ff.}$) and Mt. ($27^{26\,ff.}$) this dramatic mockery follows the sentence of crucifixion: in the Fourth Gospel, it precedes it. Our author's narrative is again psychologically coherent; for it portrays Pilate as treating Jesus with a lack of seriousness which well accords with a desire to save His life. Surely this helpless visionary, so arrayed, cannot be worthy of the death they wish inflicted upon Him!

3–5. After the mockery and the reviling by the soldiers—'Hail, King of the Jews' breathes contempt both for Jesus and for the Jewish nation—comes the second declaration by Pilate of the innocence of Jesus. There follows his dramatic and enigmatic word—'Behold the man.' Much has been written on these words. *Ecce homo*—they are familiar as the title of picture and of book. The words are only in the Fourth Gospel, and have the characteristic dramatic quality which we have discovered throughout. To Pilate himself the words were probably an expression, half of pity, half of contempt. 'Here is the man who claims to be a king! Would you have so helpless a dreamer crucified?' The comment of Augustine reveals penetrating psychological insight. 'Jesus goes forth wearing the crown of thorns and the purple robe, not resplendent in kingly power, but laden with reproach; and the words are addressed to them, Behold the man! If you hate your king, spare him now when you see him sunk so low; he has been scourged, crowned with thorns, clothed with the garments of derision, jeered at with the bitterest insults, struck with the open hand; his ignominy is at the boiling-point, let your ill-will sink to zero. But there is no such cooling on the part of the latter, but rather a further increase of heat and vehemence.'

To the author, however, the words of Pilate, 'Behold the man,' declare that here was *the* Man—the Man in whom the Word had tabernacled, the Perfect Man, whose Glory was even now being manifested in the humiliation of His Passion.

6*a*. To which the cry of the priests and their officers responds: 'Crucify him, crucify him.' The light, indeed, shineth in the darkness, and the darkness apprehendeth it not. They will crucify the Perfect Man. They will place Truth once more on the scaffold, once more place Wrong on the throne; and what they will do will be done in the name of religion itself. 'When therefore the *chief priests* and officers saw him, they cried out, saying, Crucify him, crucify him.' So speaks the Evangelist—and yet we are told by blind expositors that the Fourth Evangelist was a narrow and rigid ecclesiastic—surely one of the greatest psychological perversions and critical aberrations ever achieved in the history of literary interpretation.

6*b*–7. To which Pilate in impotent exasperation replies by inviting them to take the responsibility for the crucifixion they desire. 'Take him yourselves and crucify him; for I find no crime in him.' He knows, and they know, that if Jesus is to be crucified, he, and not they, must take full responsibility both for the sentence and for its execution. Pilate's reply reveals a spirit exacerbated by its own impotent rebellion against the inhuman 'theological hate' of which Jesus is the innocent victim. For the third time he affirms the innocence of Jesus, just as the Lucan evangelist had done before him—Lk. 23[4, 14, 22]. In their reply, the *real* charge they have against Jesus finds expression. 'We have a law, and by that law he ought to die, because he made himself the Son of God.' Pilate's emphatic 'I'—'for myself, I find no fault in him'—is countered by their equally emphatic 'we'—'for ourselves WE have a law.' The vacillating Roman Procurator is confronted by the determined ecclesiastics. The clever administrator meets those who are cleverer than himself. He has some moral scruples which would deter him from the deed: they have religious scruples which would drive them to it. Was it not written in Lev. (24[16]) 'And he that blasphemeth the name of the Lord, he shall surely be put to death'? What is a moral law written in the heart in comparison with such a law imprinted on a Book! The Letter indeed would kill, and did kill—both themselves, and Jesus. They worship a different God from Jesus—a lesser God even than the God of the sceptical Pilate. He at least has some awareness of a law of justice and of humanity: they have a law before which the claims of the moral law 'primordially insculpted in men's hearts' are as if they had not been.

Thus, the exasperation of Pilate has caused the religious rulers to reveal what is in the depth of their mind. 'It is *blasphemy* we accuse him of. He has made himself the Son of God.' The charge of *treason* had been on their lips, while the charge of *blasphemy* had been in their hearts. How familiar is the fact that it is in the heat of exasperated debate that inmost motives are revealed.

8–9. Pilate, at this, becomes 'the more afraid.' Something in the personality of Jesus has been rapping, and knocking, and seeking to find entrance in his soul. It was not, as with Browning's Bishop Blougram, 'a sunset touch,' or 'a fancy from a flower bell,' or 'a chorus-ending from Euripides,' which was calling him to awake out of his torpor. It was the voice of eternity speaking through the incarnate Word. Unheard, it would not be silenced: disobeyed, it would not be denied. An increasing *awe* gathers in his mind—such an awe as comes to men when they regard themselves as 'safe' within their sceptical solutions which are no solutions, within their negations which cannot stifle the great Perhaps. Thus his question, when once more face to face with Jesus in the privacy of the Prætorium: 'Whence art thou?' With troubled misgiving he asks the question to which the whole Johannine Gospel is the answer. 'In the beginning was the Word and the Word was with God and the Word was Divine. . . . And the Word became flesh and dwelt among us.'

To his question, however, Jesus gives no verbal answer. What can mere *words* say to those who will not listen to the Word? The Eternal Logos has already been speaking to him: in the depths of a mind which had reached the conviction of the innocence of Jesus the answer had already been given. Why does he not obey *that* word? Can any further light come to a man who *will not* obey when Duty whispers low to him, 'Thou must'?

10–11. The silence of Jesus irritates the man who sought every escape, but the one possible escape. When we will not do what we *know* to be right, we take delusive refuge in the externalities of office. 'Speakest thou not unto me? Knowest thou not that I have power to release thee, and power to crucify thee?' The whole emphasis of this reply of Pilate is on his own personal power—'*unto me* speakest thou not?'—not on the inner authority of impartial justice. By this, he shows that he is no longer the representative of truth. It is not he who is judging truth: it is truth that is judging him.

In the reply of Jesus, the Evangelist gives utterance to that serenity of the Master's spirit which arose out of the knowledge that it was the Father's will, not the will of man, that was being accomplished. As far as Pilate's power is concerned, while he exercises it in virtue of human authority, yet he ought to recognise that the authority of human justice rests on the authority of Divine justice: his own power, therefore, ought to be regarded as delegated. In using his power in the interests of what he knows to be injustice, he will be guilty of sin. Yet the sin of the Jewish authorities who have delivered Jesus to him is greater than his; for they are taking their stand on religion itself, and in the name of God whom they *say* they recognise they are denying religion itself. The greatest of all sins, therefore, are those done in the name of religion. They are the sins of sins. 'If therefore the light that is in thee be darkness, how great is that darkness.'

It has often been noted that the Fourth Evangelist continually emphasises that the Jewish guilt was greater than the Roman guilt. He does this, not because he is in the grip of a 'philo-Roman tendency'—as has been sometimes suggested—and therefore wished to relieve the Roman authorities of all responsibility for the death of Jesus. As a matter of fact, no one can read this narrative without perceiving that he diagnosed the Roman part in that guilt just as clearly, and justly, as he did the Jewish part. 'Thou ailest here—and here,' he would say to the civil administration as represented by Pilate. But what he saw with penetrating clarity, and felt in the very depths of his being, was that the *real* guilt belonged to the religious authorities. 'He that delivered me unto thee,' Jesus says to Pilate, 'hath greater sin.' Might we not say the same when we read of the handing over of Joan of Arc by the religious authorities to the military authorities? Her *burning* was the act of English military authorities, and they cannot be absolved—any more than could Pilate—from a measure of responsibility. But if the Fourth Evangelist had been narrating that burning, would he not have said to them: 'They that delivered Joan unto you have the greater sin'? He does not absolve Pilate; he reveals Pilate as he was in the depth of his mind. He does not wish to discharge the Roman authorities from responsibility, in the interests of an 'apologetic' endeavour, as has been maintained by some interpreters of this Gospel. We have been told, for example, that he wished to remove the difficulties in the way of the Roman world embracing Christianity; and that, to effect this, he wishes to remove the impression that Jesus had been a *rebel* in the eyes of Rome. For how could Roman citizens accept a Gospel which had been preached, and incarnated, in one who had been an insurgent against the imperial power? [1] Such is the argument which seeks to find in the Johannine narrative a motive of an 'apologetic' order. The Evangelist has a motive, but it is not this motive. He was concerned with an 'apologetic,' but it was not this type of apologetic. His motive is to portray the inwardness of the situation. His 'apologetic' is concerned with leading Jew, and Greek, and Roman to that Gospel of Truth incarnated in Jesus.

12. The light has not yet been quenched in Pilate's mind, and he seeks a way of releasing Jesus. No way, however, can he find that will not demand a resoluteness of purpose which he does not possess. The Evangelist so narrates these scenes as to convey the sense of the inevitability of the end to be reached. This is the work of the highest dramatic genius. 'The stars in their courses' are in league against his vacillating endeavours to release Jesus. It is not to be; for Pilate is what he is, and not as we would wish him to be.

Not in our Stars,
But in ourselves, dear Brutus, that we are underlings.

'The Jews' returned to their political charge: 'If thou release this man, thou art not Cæsar's friend; every one that maketh himself a king speaketh against Cæsar.' Pilate seems to be presented with a conflict of loyalties. He had already assured himself that the kingship inherent in the claims of Jesus was of a different order than the kingship of Cæsar. Yet a danger to his own position as Procurator might well arise from crafty insinuations in the ears of the suspicious Emperor, Tiberius, that he was indifferent to rebellion. It is significant that the final, and decisive, attempt of the Jewish authorities to make Pilate the tool of

[1] See, for example, Goguel's *Vie de Jésus*, pp. 450 ff.

their purposes is by exploiting his own fears. These fears may not have been groundless; for his conduct as Procurator of Judæa may well have exposed him to a Jewish attack before the Emperor. Most of our knowledge of Pilate's rule is derived from Josephus. The Jewish historian tells us of various incidents in his administration which reveal both want of tact and weakness of character. One such illustration had to do with his policy in regard to the Jewish prejudice against images. Rome had sought so far to conciliate this prejudice as to remove from her military standards the figures of the Emperor. Pilate, at the beginning of his period of administration, had caused the standards, bearing the figure of the Emperor, to be carried into Jerusalem. When the Jews had sought for their removal he refused any conciliation. A riot resulted, and Pilate was compelled to yield. Another illustration of the same lack of tact was revealed when he utilised money from the Temple treasury for the building of an aqueduct.[1] Philo records—in *Legatio ad Gaium*, 38—an incident in his administration when, through similar lack of consideration for the religious scruples of the Jews, he is threatened with an appeal on their part to the Emperor. 'This threat exasperated Pilate to the greatest degree,' so Philo records Agrippa as saying, 'as he feared they might go on an embassy to the Emperor, and might impeach him with respect to other particulars of his government—his corruptions, his acts of insolence, his rapine, and his habit of insulting people, his cruelty, and his continual murders of people untried and uncondemned, and his never-ending gratuitous and most grievous inhumanity.' This reads like an exaggerated and biased account of the delinquencies of Pilate; nevertheless, it reflects the feelings of the Jews of the time. He was obviously open to attack, and feared it.

13–15. Pilate's decision is now taken. He takes his seat upon the tribunal that he may pronounce the sentence of death. Some interpreters have supposed that the meaning of this passage is that Pilate seated *Jesus* on the tribunal, in order, presumably, to deride both Jesus and the Jews—'Behold your King!' The time for jesting, however, is over. It is Pilate himself who takes his seat on the tribunal. The name of the site of this tribunal is given by the Evangelist in both its Greek and Aramaic name. The Greek name means *the Mosaic Pavement*: the Aramaic name is of uncertain derivation, and may mean either 'an elevated place' or 'a mosaic.' The judgement-seat stood on a dais of mosaic pavement outside the Prætorium, and here, in public, the sentence is pronounced. The day was the Preparation of the Passover, that is, the Friday of the Passover week: the time was about noon. Mark tells us that the Crucifixion took place at 'the third hour' (15^{25}), and various unsuccessful endeavours have been made to harmonise these divergent statements. The Church has followed the Johannine chronology here, the solemn service of Good Friday being from twelve noon till 3 p.m. Noon was a more likely hour for the Crucifixion than 9 a.m. With bitter irony the words of Pilate are spoken, 'Behold your King.' This exasperates to fury the accusers of Jesus. 'Away with him,' they cry. To which Pilate makes the ironical rejoinder, 'Shall I crucify your King?' Whereupon—the crowning apostasy of Judaism, as it has been regarded—the official leaders of the Jews reply, 'We have no King but Cæsar.'

[1] *Antiquities*, XVIII, iii, 1 and 2.

It is clear that the Evangelist is dramatising history. The situation itself had all the elements of the greatest drama; and it is penned by an author who felt in the very depths of his mind its tragic contrasts and issues. It will be noted that it is the 'chief priests'—not just 'the Jews,' not just even 'the chief priests and the officers'—who cry, 'We have no King but Cæsar.' It is as if the Evangelist would say—it was the *official* representatives of Judaism who repudiated Him who came in the line of the prophets to fulfil the noblest Messianic hopes. It is difficult to suppose that the Jewish religious leaders *intentionally* disavowed their theocratic faith, in declaring their allegiance to Cæsar. What they *did* do was to disavow Jesus. He at least was no king of theirs. Rather Cæsar than Jesus! It is too much, therefore, to say that by their words they made 'a solemn recantation of the faith which had kept alive the national existence from age to age.' Yet the Evangelist may well have felt that this was indeed what they were doing.

16. The chief priests have said the last word. No further word is recorded by the Evangelist as having been spoken by Pilate. The final responsibility is theirs. Matthew tells us (27^{24-25}) that he 'took water, and washed his hands before the multitude, saying, I am innocent of the blood of this righteous man: see ye to it. And all the people answered and said, His blood be on us and on our children.' The Fourth Evangelist dramatically *suggests* this repudiation of responsibility by Pilate. He speaks no further word. 'Then therefore he delivered him to them to be crucified.'

THE CRUCIFIXION (19^{17-42})

The Evangelist narrates the end in his own way. His record has its own emphasis, and details peculiar to itself. It is he who tells us that the Jews challenged the inscription of Pilate (*vv.* 20–22): it is he alone who records the last bequest of Jesus (*vv.* 25–27): it is he alone who preserves the four words from the Cross, 'Woman, behold thy son,' 'Behold thy mother,' 'I thirst,' and 'It is finished' (*vv.* 26–30): it is he alone who speaks of the piercing of the side, from which issued blood and water (*vv.* 31–37): it is he alone who narrates the ministry of Nicodemus (*v.* 39). Further, it is he who tells us that Jesus bore His own Cross, thus correcting, or at least supplementing, the story told in all Synoptic Gospels, that it was Simon of Cyrene who bore the Cross of Jesus.

It Is Finished

JN. 19^{17-30}

19 17 They took Jesus therefore: and he
went out, bearing the cross for himself,
unto the place called The place of a skull,
which is called in Hebrew Golgotha:
18 where they crucified him, and with him
two others, on either side one, and Jesus
19 in the midst. And Pilate wrote a title
also, and put it on the cross. And there
was written, JESUS OF NAZARETH, THE
20 KING OF THE JEWS. This title therefore
read many of the Jews: for the place
where Jesus was crucified was nigh to the
city: and it was written in Hebrew, *and*
21 in Latin, *and* in Greek. The chief priests
of the Jews therefore said to Pilate, Write
not, The King of the Jews; but, that he
22 said, I am King of the Jews. Pilate
answered, What I have written I have
written.
23 The soldiers therefore, when they had
crucified Jesus, took his garments, and
made four parts, to every soldier a part;
and also the coat: now the coat was
without seam, woven from the top

24 throughout. They said therefore one to
another, Let us not rend it, but cast lots
for it, whose it shall be: that the scripture
might be fulfilled, which saith,

They parted my garments among them,
And upon my vesture did they cast lots.

These things therefore the soldiers did.
25 But there were standing by the cross of
Jesus his mother, and his mother's sister,
Mary the *wife* of Clopas, and Mary Mag-
26 dalene. When Jesus therefore saw his
mother, and the disciple standing by,
whom he loved, he saith unto his mother,
27 Woman, behold, thy son! Then saith he
to the disciple, Behold, thy mother!
And from that hour the disciple took her
unto his own *home*.
28 After this Jesus, knowing that all
things are now finished, that the scripture
might be accomplished, saith, I thirst.
29 There was set there a vessel full of
vinegar: so they put a sponge full of the
vinegar upon hyssop, and brought it to
30 his mouth. When Jesus therefore had
received the vinegar, he said, It is
finished: and he bowed his head, and
gave up his spirit.

17. The execution took place 'without a city wall,' as the familiar hymn of Cecil Frances Alexander has it; or 'without the gate,' as the Epistle to the Hebrews has it (Heb. 13^{12}). Jesus sets out carrying His own Cross. 'Every criminal,' says Plutarch, 'carries his own cross.' The Evangelist would have us know that Jesus was not immune from the treatment accorded to other malefactors: though, perhaps, he saw in the fact that Jesus went out carrying His own Cross a symbol of the completeness and voluntariness of the self-offering of Jesus. Many of the Fathers regarded Isaac bearing the wood for the burnt offering as a type of Jesus bearing the Cross. The tradition of the Church has reconciled the Synoptic story of Simon with the Johannine narrative, by the natural explanation that it was when Jesus sank beneath the Cross that the Cyrenian was pressed into service.

The name of the site of the Crucifixion is given by the Evangelist—as also by Mark (15^{22}) and by Matthew (27^{33})—in Greek and Aramaic. *Golgotha*, or 'the place of a skull,' corresponds to the Latin *Calvaria*—from the noun *Calva*, the bald-scalp: whence we have our term Calvary. It may have been so called from the bare, skull-like shape of the hill where, it is suggested, the Crucifixion took place. The exact site cannot be decided with complete certainty. Tradition has it that the Church of the Holy Sepulchre stands upon the spot where the Cross of Jesus stood, a tradition going back at least to the time of Constantine in the fourth century. But it is uncertain whether this site was within or without the city wall in the time of Jesus. Many modern investigators hold that the Crucifixion took place upon the skull-shaped knoll above 'Jeremiah's grotto,' outside the present north wall of the city: this knoll is the place of public execution, according to Jewish tradition. Perhaps it was here that the Cross of Jesus stood, between 'two others,' as the Evangelist declares simply. Mark (in 15^{27}) and Matthew (in 27^{38}) tell us that these two were 'robbers': Luke (in 23^{33}) that they were 'malefactors.'

19–22. All the evangelists tell of the title on the Cross; but the Fourth Evangelist alone says that it was written 'in Hebrew, and in Latin, and in Greek'—as he alone relates that it was Pilate who wrote and placed it there. The first language was the national speech, the second the official language, the third the language for inter-provincial communication. In every age the readers of the Gospel have felt that to the author the three languages of the inscription symbolised the universality of the spiritual kingship of Jesus. It is He who fulfils the religious, the social, and the intellectual heritage of humanity. George Matheson may have been thinking of this inscription when he wrote:

Thine is the Roman's strength without his pride,
Thine is the Greek's glad world without its graves,
Thine is Judæa's law with love beside,
The truth that censures and the grace that saves;
Gather us in.

The title, however, to Pilate himself was placed there with a certain bitter irony: nor would he alter it to meet the wishes of the priests. What he has written, he has written. To the Evangelist this terse utterance of an obstinate man symbolises, no doubt, the *finality* of the truth that Jesus is the universal king.

23–24. Like the other three evangelists, our author narrates the parting of the garments among the soldiers; but he alone tells that they were divided into four parts—probably for the quaternion of soldiers; and he alone relates that the under-coat, or tunic, was 'without seam.' These two details have each their significance for the Evangelist. The first—suggestive of the group of four soldiers—is in dramatic contrast to the narrative which immediately follows, of another group of four by the Cross. While the first group callously appropriates His garments, the second group—of the four faithful women—in sorrow of heart has become partaker of His afflictions. The second detail peculiar to the Evangelist—the seamless tunic—*may* have symbolised for him the universal and spiritual high-priesthood of Jesus; for Josephus—in his *Antiquities*, iii. 7, 4—tells us that the coat of the High Priest was of one piece. (Exod. 28^{32}.) At least, the Evangelist sees in this distribution a fulfilment of Ps. 22^{18}. From Cyprian onwards, 'the seamless robe' has been used as a symbol of the Unity of the Church; but such an interpretation and use of the passage would only be made when the problem of preserving the unity of the Church became acute.

25–27. In contrast to the callously-minded soldiers are the four sorrowing women. Some interpreters have supposed that the Evangelist refers only to *three* women here—taking 'Mary the wife of Clopas' as explanatory of 'his mother's sister'; but it is highly improbable that sisters would have had the same name Mary. This 'Mary the wife of Clopas' is no doubt identical with 'Mary the mother of James the less and of Joses,' referred to in Mk. 15^{40}; and 'his mother's sister' is no doubt identical with Salome, the mother of the sons of Zebedee, referred to in the same Marcan passage. Our identification of 'the beloved disciple' with John the Apostle, the son of Zebedee, harmonises well with this incident; for there is a natural fitness in the words of Jesus which follow, whereby He commends His own mother to the care of His own maternal cousin—and her own nephew.

Some recent interpreters have taken this commendation of the 'mother' of Jesus to 'the beloved disciple' as being the author's way of allegorising the committing of the Jewish Church—the 'Mother' from which Christianity sprang—to the care of the true Christian community. The Evangelist is supposed to mean by his narrative here that the valuable elements in Judaism are now committed to Christianity. '"The mother of Jesus" would seem to represent the ancient faith—the " mother " that had given birth to Christianity—and Jesus commends her, as He dies, to the care of His beloved disciple. . . . What was valuable and permanent in Judaism has now passed over to Christianity: the " mother of Jesus " dwells in the house of His disciple.' [1]

While, however, the Evangelist's mind—as we have repeatedly seen—delights in symbolic meanings, it is a somewhat strained interpretation, as we cannot but feel, which suggests that he is not here thinking of real historical persons. The ' mother of Jesus ' means to him, as to the Synoptists, Mary the mother of Jesus; and ' the beloved disciple ' means to himself—what the phrase has meant throughout his Gospel—a specific individual, and, as we believe, John, the son of Zebedee and of Salome.

28–29. The Fourth Evangelist relates neither the three Lukan words from the Cross—Lk. $23^{34, 43, 46}$—nor the ' cry of desolation ' found in Mk. 15^{34} and Mt. 27^{46}. He also omits the interval of darkness, lasting for three hours, recorded by all three Synoptists. ' After this,' he says—a lapse of time which may cover this incident—and goes on to narrate two words from the Cross peculiar to his Gospel.

The first is, ' I thirst '—a saying which the author perhaps thinks of as a fulfilment of Ps. 22^{15}. This saying leads to the offer of the sour wine of the country; which, again, seems to him a fulfilment of Ps. 69^{21}. It is not to be supposed that in either this ' fulfilment ' of Scripture, or in the one which precedes—or in the one which follows this word of Jesus, recorded in *v.* 37—the Fourth Evangelist meant that these things were said *in order that* the Old Testament Scriptures might be fulfilled. What he means is that when he looked back to these incidents of the Crucifixion, and pondered upon them in the light of the whole revelation of God, he found words in those Scriptures in which he had been nurtured as a boy and which were still to him of imperishable value, to which he could point perplexed readers—words which spoke of similar experiences as having befallen those of old. Thus—as he would feel, and say—in these three Crucifixion scenes, what happened of old has been ' fulfilled ' in the death of Jesus.

Jesus was truly man, and knew all the experiences which the physical organism imposes upon the spirit. In recording, therefore, this word—' I thirst '—the Fourth Evangelist may probably have been thinking of that Docetic doctrine which denied the real humanity of Jesus. He may also have seen in this utterance, expressive of the *physical* thirst of Jesus, a symbolical expression of that spiritual thirst which the Father alone had satisfied during the years of His ministry, and would now completely satisfy as His spirit returned to Him whence it had come. Mk. 15^{36} —and (Mt. 27^{48})—tells us that the sponge full of vinegar was placed upon a ' reed,' and so given to Jesus. The Fourth Evangelist says that it was put ' upon hyssop,' which may either mean ' upon a stalk of hyssop,' or—by a slight alteration of the Greek word of the text—' upon a javelin.' The stick to which the sponge was fastened may have been a javelin belonging to one of the soldiers; and this is perhaps what the Evangelist said. *Hysso* (upon a javelin) might easily be mistaken by a scribe for *hyssopo* (upon hyssop).[2]

[1] E. F. Scott, *The Fourth Gospel*, pp. 74–75.

[2] Bernard has pointed out, in his *Critical Commentary*—vol. 2, p. 640—that this conjectural emendation is the actual reading of the eleventh-century Cursive, No. 476.

The esoteric symbolism which Augustine saw in this passage is worthy of our recollection, expressive though it is of a far-fetched ingenuity of interpretation foreign both to the thought of the Evangelist and to our own modern minds. 'He said, "I thirst"; as if it were, One thing still you have failed to do, to give me what you are. For the Jews themselves were the vinegar, degenerated as they were from the wine of the patriarchs and prophets; and filled, like a full vessel, with the wickedness of this world, with hearts like a sponge, deceitful in the formation of its cavernous and tortuous recesses. But the hyssop, whereon they placed the sponge filled with vinegar, being a lowly herb, and purging the heart, we fitly take for the humility of Christ Himself; which they thus enclosed, and imagined they had completely ensnared. Hence we have it said in the Psalm, "Thou shalt purge me with hyssop, and I shall be cleansed."'

30. The final word spoken by Jesus on the Cross, as narrated by our Evangelist, is, 'It is finished.' The task of Jesus is accomplished. The Father's own will for Him, He has now achieved. The victory of the spirit is complete. 'Fought the fight, the battle won.' All this, and more, the Evangelist understands the words to mean. To know with completeness what these words meant to Jesus, we should have to be Jesus Himself. But this Evangelist—who has so deeply penetrated His spirit, so truly portrayed His consciousness of a work to be done and a self-offering to be made—knows that whatever else the words say, they speak of a trust in the Father, and a fidelity to His will, without parallel among the sons of men. His work is accomplished. So also is the work of Pilate, and of the Jewish religious rulers. Yet nothing was finished. The work accomplished was just begun. The seed sown in the hearts of men would take root and bring forth fruit unto eternity. Enshrining the gloom of the Cross on Golgotha is the glory of the eternal world, and behind its seeming defeat the victory of Love and of Truth.

The Piercing of the Side

Jn. 19^{31-37}

19 31 The Jews therefore, because it was the
Preparation, that the bodies should not
remain on the cross upon the sabbath (for
the day of that sabbath was a high *day*),
asked of Pilate that their legs might be
broken, and *that* they might be taken
32 away. The soldiers therefore came, and
brake the legs of the first, and of the other
33 which was crucified with him: but when
they came to Jesus, and saw that he was
dead already, they brake not his legs:
34 howbeit one of the soldiers with a spear
pierced his side, and straightway there
35 came out blood and water. And he that
hath seen hath borne witness, and his
witness is true: and he knoweth that he
saith true, that ye also may believe.
36 For these things came to pass, that the
scripture might be fulfilled, A bone of
37 him shall not be broken. And again
another scripture saith, They shall look
on him whom they pierced.

It was the eve of the Sabbath, and a Sabbath in this case which coincided with Nisan 15, the first day of the Feast of unleavened bread. This Sabbath was therefore a 'high day.' The Fourth Evangelist alone records the request of the Jewish leaders that the bodies on the three crosses should be removed. The request was natural. Their law forbade that the bodies of criminals should be left on the gibbet after sunset (see Dt. 21^{22-23}); and Josephus states that in his time the bodies of criminals were buried before sunset of the day on which they were crucified. The fact that the Passover feast was about to begin made their request the more urgent, for the city was crowded with pilgrims. Let therefore every sign of a crime which might arouse slumbering passions be removed as speedily as possible. Such a removal would suit the Roman authorities as well as the Jewish. For it would save the first from criticism of their methods of political control, and the second from criticism of their methods of religious control.

The legs of the two malefactors are first broken, in order to hasten their death. When the soldiers came to Jesus they find, however, that He is already dead. So instead of breaking His legs they pierce His side with a spear, perhaps to ensure that what they take for death is not a swoon.

34. From the wound there immediately issued, says the Evangelist, ' blood and water.' Voluminous comment in every age has been made on this statement. It is clear, *in the first place*, that the Evangelist is narrating some historical reminiscence. Verse 35 states this as emphatically as it could be stated: ' he that hath seen hath borne witness, and his testimony is reliable; and he—ἐκεῖνος—knows that he saith what is true.'

The Evangelist, that is, is recording *ocular* testimony. This ocular testimony must not be taken as exact *medical* testimony. It was a resemblance to ' blood and water ' that was seen. A modern physician would not have called this appearance ' blood and water '; for he knows that real ' water ' does not issue from a wound. We must leave the medical authorities to discuss the question as to what physiological conditions would precede such an outflow of blood and water-like serum from a wound.[1] The point to be stressed is that the Evangelist is narrating some historical reminiscence; and one of his reasons for so definitely emphasising this memory was, doubtless, because he had in mind Docetic denials of the true humanity of Jesus. To those who were beginning to say that the body of Jesus was a mere phantom he would say: Out of His pierced side when He hung on the Cross issued the blood which is common to mortal humanity. In other words, it is the same message as he gives in the Prologue: ' The word *became flesh*.'

In the second place, however, the allegorical nature of the Evangelist's mind suggests that to him this appearance of ' blood and water ' symbolised the *life-giving* and the *cleansing* significance of the death of Jesus. He delights to find parabolic meaning in historical fact. That is why he speaks of Jesus as the ' Word ' that ' became flesh.' In his First Epistle the same author says that ' the *blood* of Jesus Christ his Son *cleanseth* us from all sin.' Thus, one may say that he is here showing the *inner spiritual meaning* of the sacramental rites of the Church. Many of the Fathers interpreted this issue of ' blood and water ' as typical of the two sacraments of the Church. Chrysostom, for example, says: ' Not without a purpose or by chance did those springs come forth, but because the Church consisteth of these two together. And those who are initiated know it, being regenerate by water and nourished by the Blood and Flesh. Hence the Sacraments take their beginning; in order that when thou drawest near to the awful cup thou

[1] The question was discussed nearly a hundred years ago by Dr. W. Stroud in *The Physical Cause of the Death of Christ* (1847).

mayest so approach, as drinking from the very side.' Augustine, speaking of the *opened* (aperuit) side of Jesus, says that it was ' thereby that, in a sense, the gate of life might be thrown open, from whence have flowed the sacraments of the Church, without which there is no entrance to the life which is the true life. That blood was shed for the remisson of sins; that water it is that makes up the health-giving cup, and supplies at once the laver and the cup.'

It is natural to suppose that the Evangelist thought of the two sacraments when he recorded this reminiscence. But we may be perfectly certain that he had not in his mind the theological views which the patristic interpreters found in the passage. As to what he himself thought, and felt, about the sacramental practices of the Church—on that issue we have already indicated our views, both in the Introduction and in relevant passages of the Commentary. He certainly did not inculcate any magical theory of these rites. What he wishes to do is to set forth the life-giving and cleansing mission of Jesus, to which these rites testify. The blood signifies the life: the water signifies cleansing. Cleansing of the spirit comes to those who by faith appropriate the life incarnate in Him who gave His life on the Cross in complete trust and obedience. Out of the complete self-dedication of Jesus there comes spiritual sustenance and cleansing to mankind. It is this symbolism which inspired the familiar verse of Toplady's hymn, ' Rock of Ages ':

Let the water and the blood,
From Thy riven side which flowed,
Be of sin the double cure,
Cleanse me from its guilt and power.

35. One final question arises from this passage. Who was this witness? The answer to this question involves the perplexing question as to the precise translation of this 35th verse. Is the person referred to in the phrase, ' *he* (ἐκεῖνος) knoweth ' the same as the witness referred to in ' he that hath seen hath borne witness '? The Revised Version suggests that he is the same, but the Greek by no means necessitates this identity. The ἐκεῖνος may be—as is maintained by Dr. Torrey in his *New Translation of the Four Gospels*—an idiomatic circumlocution for ' I '—somewhat corresponding to the ' one thinks ' used by some speakers when they refer to themselves. In this case the translation would run: ' he that hath seen hath borne witness, and his testimony is reliable: and *I myself know* that he saith what is true.' If such translation be accepted, the ocular witness will probably be that of John the Apostle, and the solemn asseveration of its truth that of the Evangelist, the friend of the high priest of $18^{15, 16}$, and the disciple of the Apostle in Ephesus. Other translators and interpreters have held that the ἐκεῖνος may refer to Jesus Himself, in accord with the usage of the First Epistle of John (1 Jn. 2^{6}, $3^{3, 5, 7, 16}$). In this case the Evangelist appeals solemnly to ' that master,' Christ Himself. The phrase would then be a formula of emphatic assertion, something like our ' God knows '—as Dr. Sanday suggested in *The Criticism of The Fourth Gospel* (p. 78). The translation in such case would run: ' He that hath seen hath borne witness, and his testimony is reliable: *the Master*

knows that he saith what is true.' If such translation be accepted, the ocular witness referred to may be either the Apostle John or the Evangelist himself. It should be noted that in the Epilogue to the Gospel—in 21^{24}—we find a similar asseveration.

36–7. Looking back on this event in the light of his meditations on the Old Testament Scriptures, the Evangelist sees a 'fulfilment' of two passages to which he now refers—Exod. 12^{46} and Zech. 12^{10}. The first passage speaks of the Passover Lamb, which had to be offered to God unmutilated. As Jesus hung on the Cross the Passover lambs were being slain. Yes, thought the Evangelist, and when Jesus offered Himself He also, as the True Passover Lamb, was offered perfect and entire. Paul used the same symbolism when he wrote in 1 Cor. 5^{7}: 'Christ our Passover is sacrificed for us.' The Evangelist may also have been thinking of the passage in Ps. 34^{20}, where of the righteous man it is said: 'He keepeth all his bones: not one of them is broken.' The second passage—from Zech. 12^{10}—speaks of the inhabitants of Jerusalem who penitently look upon some prophet whom they have pierced and slain. 'And I will pour upon the house of David, and upon the inhabitants of Jerusalem, the spirit of grace and supplication; and they shall look unto me (or *him*) whom they have pierced: and they shall mourn for him, as one mourneth for his only son, and shall be in bitterness for him, as one that is in bitterness for his first born.' Even so, thought the Evangelist, and thus their descendants gazed upon *The* Prophet whose side they, indirectly, had pierced. As the unbroken bones recalled to the Evangelist the Paschal Lamb, so the pierced side recalled the contrition expressed by Zechariah for an act of his people's hate. Could it be that even to the inhabitants of Jerusalem would come the penitence prefigured by the old prophet?

The Burial

JN. 19^{38-42}

19 38 And after these things Joseph of
Arimathæa, being a disciple of Jesus, but
secretly for fear of the Jews, asked of
Pilate that he might take away the body
of Jesus: and Pilate gave *him* leave. He
came therefore, and took away his body.
39 And there came also Nicodemus, he who
at the first came to him by night, bringing
a mixture of myrrh and aloes, about a
40 hundred pound *weight*. So they took the
body of Jesus, and bound it in linen cloths
with the spices, as the custom of the Jews
41 is to bury. Now in the place where he
was crucified there was a garden; and in
the garden a new tomb wherein was
42 never man yet laid. There then because
of the Jews' Preparation (for the tomb
was nigh at hand) they laid Jesus.

The Evangelist's narrative of the Crucifixion ends with the burial. Like the Synoptists, he records the request of Joseph of Arimathæa, and the burial of the body of Jesus in a tomb belonging to him. If he had not intervened, the body of Jesus, when removed from the Cross (*v.* 31), would have been thrown into a common pit. This Joseph was a wealthy member of the Sanhedrin—Mk. 15^{43} and Mt. 27^{57}—and a 'secret disciple' of Jesus, or, as Mk 15^{43} and Lk. 23^{51} say, one 'looking for the kingdom of God.'

The Fourth Evangelist alone tells us that Nicodemus was associated with Joseph in these last rites. He also was a 'secret disciple,' of whom the Evangelist has twice previously spoken—in 3^{1} and 7^{50}. To the Evangelist the words which he has recorded as spoken in the ears of Nicodemus, in $3^{15, 16}$, would seem already to be receiving a partial fulfilment. The Son of Man *has* been lifted up, and the secret disciples *have* looked upon him, and lost the timidity which is a barrier to the life which is life indeed. Nicodemus brings with him spices, kingly in kind and in quantity. When King Asa was buried—2 Chron. 16^{14}—they 'laid him in a bed which was filled with sweet odours and divers kinds of spices prepared by the apothecaries' art.' A hundred pounds weight of spices—about seventy pounds to our scale—is indeed a kingly gift, and could only come from one who was wealthy. It would be used for embalming the body, 'according'—as the Jewish evangelist reminds his Hellenistic readers, who were more familiar with rites of cremation—'to the Jewish burial custom.'

The Passover day began at six o'clock in the evening, now just at hand. So, as time was short, the body of Jesus was laid to rest in a garden hard by, in a tomb wherein never man had yet been laid. Matthew (27^{60}) says that this was Joseph's 'own new tomb.' So he who had not opened his whole heart to Jesus in life, opened to Him, when dead, the resting-place prepared for himself.

THE RESURRECTION (20)

The climax of the Gospel is now reached. The voice of the incarnate Word has been stilled in Death, but only for a time. The Light which from the beginning shone in the darkness without being overcome, has shone in the word, work, and death of Him who in time wore 'the eternal splendour.' Hid for a time, it appears again in incorruptible glory. Victory has remained with Life.

The Evangelist tells the story of the Resurrection in his own way, with an emphasis peculiar to his own mind. Some of the differences between his account and those of the Synoptists will be noted in the course of our elucidation and comment. Here it is sufficient to state that he makes no attempt to describe *the act* of the Resurrection, or to record a complete history of the Resurrection *appearances*, or to harmonise the Synoptic records he knew. Endeavours have been frequently made to force the four records into a 'harmony': they inspire no sense of certitude. It seems clear that there were two traditions in the Church as to the appearances of the Risen Jesus; one associating them with Jerusalem, the other with Galilee. The Fourth Evangelist—we are leaving the Epilogue on one side for the moment—follows the Jerusalem tradition. The events narrated in this chapter all take place in the Holy City.

The Evangelist's main concern is to show how faith in the Risen Lord was begotten in the minds of different types of His disciples. He chooses four scenes and incidents in which dull uncertainty, poignant sorrow, troubled fear, and anxious doubt are transcended through faith in the Risen and Triumphant Jesus. From the Easter Fact springs the Easter Faith. Uncertainty is transmuted into certainty, grief into joy, fear into peace, doubt into faith. The four main scenes of the chapter, which reveal these transformations, speak their culminating message in what Bishop Westcott called the 'last and greatest of the Beatitudes of the Church'—'Blessed are they that have not seen, and yet have believed' (*v.* 29).

The Empty Tomb

JN. 20^{1-10}

20 1 Now on the first *day* of the week
cometh Mary Magdalene early, while it
was yet dark, unto the tomb, and seeth
the stone taken away from the tomb.
2 She runneth therefore, and cometh to
Simon Peter, and to the other disciple,
whom Jesus loved, and saith unto them,
They have taken away the Lord out of
the tomb, and we know not where they
3 have laid him. Peter therefore went
forth, and the other disciple, and they
4 went toward the tomb. And they ran
both together: and the other disciple
outran Peter, and came first to the
5 tomb; and stooping and looking in, he
seeth the linen cloths lying; yet entered
6 he not in. Simon Peter therefore also
cometh, following him, and entered into
the tomb; and he beholdeth the linen
7 cloths lying, and the napkin, that was
upon his head, not lying with the linen
cloths, but rolled up in a place by itself.
8 Then entered in therefore the other disciple also, which came first to the tomb,
9 and he saw, and believed. For as yet
they knew not the scripture, that he must
10 rise again from the dead. So the disciples went away again unto their own
home.

1. 'While it was yet dark'—a mental as well as a physical darkness—Mary Magdalene comes to the tomb. The Evangelist is concerned with the awakening of the Resurrection joy in the mind of this Mary: he does not find it necessary to say, with Mark (16^{2}), that she was accompanied by two other women—though, that he was aware of this fact, seems clear from the second verse, where Mary says, '*we* know not where they have laid him.' It is this same concern which leads him to alter 'when the sun was risen' in Mark's account, to 'while it was yet dark.' The early dawn is neither a period of light nor of darkness: to the Evangelist it is a time which symbolises the darkness of sorrowing minds. 'It was yet dark'—the Light, that is, had not yet come to dissipate the gloom from their hearts.

Finding the stone removed from the tomb, she concludes that it has been violated and the body of Jesus taken away. Here there is no record of 'a young man arrayed in a white robe' (Mk. 16^{9}) or an 'angel' (Mt.28^{5}) who announces the Resurrection.

2–5. She runs to tell Peter and John the 'beloved disciple.' The story which follows has the vividness and realistic detail of historical reminiscence. The Evangelist doubtless knew these details from the beloved disciple, who must often have told the story of that unforgettable morning when he outran Peter to the sepulchre, how he hesitated to enter though not to look, how the disciple he had outrun entered before him, and how he himself entered and saw and believed.

6–7. With minute detail, found in no other Gospel, he tells us what the beloved disciple saw—'the linen cloths lying and the napkin that was upon his head not lying with the linen cloths, but rolled up—perhaps turban-like, as it had been wound round the head—in a place by itself.' What the beloved disciple saw caused him to believe. To believe what? we ask. This is the answer: 'For as yet they knew not the Scripture, that he would rise again from the dead.'

Into the question as to the precise *mode* of the Resurrection the Evangelist does not enter. 'Who rolled away the stone?'—a question debated much in patristic, mediæval, and modern times—he does not answer. At least, however, he says that the empty tomb begot the first belief in Peter and John. And from this it is clear that to him the Resurrection of Jesus involved what we may call the 'dematerialisation' of the physical body. The language he uses about the linen cloths and the napkin obviously implied his belief that the body had not been removed either by friends or by enemies. It had seemingly, to him, itself 'dematerialised,' and—though it is not possible here to dogmatise as to what was his own specific theory on the point—had probably, in his view, risen through the undisturbed grave-clothes and napkin.[1]

9. Nevertheless, the real emphasis of the Evangelist, in answer to our question as to *what* he believed, is found in this enigmatic 9th verse. What was this Scripture, we ask, which later spoke to them of the Resurrection? Commentators have in all ages pointed to Ps. 16^{10} as the specific Scripture referred to: 'Thou wilt not leave my soul to Sheol: Neither wilt thou suffer thine holy one to see corruption.' Does the author mean, then, that it was only later that this passage from the 16th Psalm occurred to their minds, and that in the light of it they came to feel there was a foretold necessity for the Resurrection of Jesus? Peter, according to the Acts ($2^{24\,ff.}$), had seen a reference to the Resurrection of Christ in this same passage, as also Paul (Acts 14^{10}). If this is what the Evangelist meant, at least it showed that, to him, the belief in the fact preceded the recollection of this specific Scripture; and not that the recollection of this Scripture created the belief in the fact. Is it not possible, however, that the Evangelist's thought is profounder than such an interpretation suggests? Need it be a *specific* Scripture to which he alludes? May he not here mean that they had not yet understood the central message of Scripture as he himself in this Gospel is now proclaiming it? To him that message was that of the Divine Logos, ever acting; the Light, never mastered; the Word, never silenced, which now had become incarnate in the Jesus they knew. How, then, could this Logos be silenced by physical death, this Light be quenched by the darkness of the tomb? So, he says, later the true disciples of Jesus came to read Scripture in the light of this revealing clue to its innermost meaning, and, thus, to see that the Divine Word that spoke *must* continue to speak, the Divine Light that shone *must* continue to shine. If they had had such insight on the morn of that first Easter Day, they would not have been surprised at what they found, and did not find, in the empty tomb.

The Appearance to Mary Magdalene

JN. 20^{11-18}

20 11 But Mary was standing without at the
tomb weeping: so, as she wept, she
12 stooped and looked into the tomb; and
she beholdeth two angels in white sitting,
one at the head, and one at the feet,
13 where the body of Jesus had lain. And
they say unto her, Woman, why weepest
thou? She saith unto them, Because
they have taken away my Lord, and I
know not where they have laid him.
14 When she had thus said, she turned herself back, and beholdeth Jesus standing,
15 and knew not that it was Jesus. Jesus
saith unto her, Woman, why weepest
thou? whom seekest thou? She, supposing him to be the gardener, saith unto
him, Sir, if thou hast borne him hence,
tell me where thou hast laid him, and

[1] I have discussed at length the many issues relative to the Resurrection in *Miracle in History and in Modern Thought*, chapter 7.

16 I will take him away. Jesus saith unto
her, Mary. She turneth herself, and
saith unto him in Hebrew, Rabboni;
17 which is to say, Master. Jesus saith to
her, Touch me not; for I am not yet
ascended unto the Father: but go unto
my brethren, and say to them, I ascend
unto my Father and your Father, and
18 my God and your God. Mary Magdalene cometh and telleth the disciples, I
have seen the Lord; and *how that* he had
said these things unto her.

There follows one of the most beautiful stories in all literature, found only in this Fourth Gospel. It is the story of the first appearance of the Risen Jesus, and given to her out of whom the seven devils had been cast. Mary having returned to the tomb remains there weeping after Peter and John have left. What, we ask, is historical fact in the scene which follows? 'Angels,' we are reminded, do not appear to us to-day. Did they appear to Mary, or did the author believe that they did? Those who have no dogmatic answers to these questions are not, therefore, sceptical of spiritual communications. Indeed, in many cases, it is because they believe so firmly in the reality of a spiritual universe that they hesitate to believe that we to-day are precluded from direct spiritual vision such as belonged to those of old. Those who believe in angelic visitations in the past, but unknown in our times, are not expressing a deeper conviction of spiritual communication than those who refuse to believe that spiritual communication has not the same channels in every age: what they are doing is to state a historical judgement in respect to a specific record. Twice previously in the Gospel the author has written of angels: once in 1^{52}, where the words 'ye shall see the heavens opened and the angels of God ascending and descending upon the Son of man,' attributed to Jesus, express to the Evangelist the reality of spiritual communion enjoyed by Jesus; and once in 12^{29}, where some of the people say that 'an angel' had spoken to Jesus. In the passage before us, however, we have the only passage in the Gospel where the author speaks of 'angels' *in his own narrative.* Now it is clear that the Evangelist, with the Synoptic Gospels before him, was familiar with the traditions of angelical visitations in connexion with the Resurrection. The passages in Mk. 16^{5}, Mt. 28^{2-7}, and Lk. 24^{4-7} were familiar to him. Such a tradition the Johannine author incorporates in the story of Mary he is recording. It is very possible, and perhaps probable, that the value of this tradition to him was wholly symbolical. The place where Jesus had lain was as holy a place as the mercy-seat was to his fathers, on either side of which they placed the golden cherubim (Exod. 25^{18-21}); or as the Holy of Holies in the temple of Solomon, which contained two colossal cherubim made of olive wood and overlaid with gold. The symbolism of the cherubim was retained by the prophets of Israel, even though it was a survival of a mythology they had discarded; and was used by them to express the way by which God's glory was revealed to men. The Johannine Evangelist, who is certainly in the succession of the Hebrew prophets, may therefore have himself inserted this tradition of angels because it symbolised for him the glory now to be revealed to Mary.

14–16. When Mary turns from the tomb, preoccupied with her grief, she fails to recognise the Risen Master before her. 'She turned about, and saw Jesus standing there, but knew not that it was he.' It is significant for any theory of the resurrection-body of Jesus at which we may arrive, that, in the first place,

Jesus never appeared to any but to His friends; and, in the second place, that some kind of spiritual insight or *rapport* was necessary on the part of the observer before Jesus was recognised (see Lk. 24^{16}; Jn. 21^{4}). Her first and natural thought is that the stranger, about at this early hour, must be the gardener; and she asks him whither the body of Jesus has been removed. 'Mary,' says Jesus. There is a way of pronouncing a name which unlocks the door of the hearer's understanding. The tones, the inflection, of the voice reveal what cannot be written down. The soul speaks through the voice, but not always through the written words. Mary starts, and cries in her own Aramaic speech, 'Rabboni,' meaning, as the Evangelist says, Master. The voice of the incarnate Word revealed to her what the outward form had failed to do. The apocalyptic writer of the New Testament had said that 'his voice was as the sound of many waters' (Rev. 1^{15}).

18. 'Cling not to me,' says Jesus—for the words translated in the Revised Version, 'Touch me not,' suggest, what is interpolated in some MSS., that Mary would have *clung* to Him as if to lose Him no more. And, according to our Greek text, he adds as a reason: '*For* I am not yet ascended unto the Father.' Does the Evangelist wish to say that when Jesus ascended, and no more appeared visibly to His disciples, a union would be possible transcending every condition of time and space, such a union as the Master Himself had spoken of in His farewell discourses? All earthly clinging will but blind the vision to the heavenly reality. Spiritual union is not of body but of spirit; and all that ties us to the senses may loosen our grasp of the unseen and eternal. The Eternal Word speaks its harmony to us,

But while this muddy vesture of decay
Doth grossly close it in, we cannot hear it.

Mary and the other disciples would have clung to a Jesus they could touch and see. No! is the message which the Johannine Evangelist transmits as the message of the Risen Master: such touching and seeing is but for a space, and is but a prelude to a fellowship with Him transcending all limitations of sense. Let them not cling to Resurrection appearances, but recognise that they must, like children, be weaned from the dependence upon the physical touch and sight, in order that they may enjoy the richer fellowship of the spirit in perfect freedom. Even so, we are told that physical blindness may make mental communion more certain and more rapid, by preventing the attention from being dispersed on outward things. 'The private and exclusive communion,' as F. D. Maurice put it, 'into which they had entered so imperfectly, must be merged in one in which all should share who would take up their lot as brethren of each other and of Him.'

On the basis of his theory of an Aramaic original, of which the Greek is a translation, Dr. Torrey suggests that the Greek here is a mistranslation of the Aramaic; which, being correctly translated, ran as follows: 'Touch me not: but before I ascend to my Father, go to my brethren and say to them, I am about to go up to my Father and your Father, to my God and your God.' With such a translation, the elucidation of 'Touch me not' we have sought to give, need not be changed.

17. The unique sense of the Father's presence possessed by Jesus is expressed in this 17th verse by the distinguishing 'my' and 'your.' There is only one Divine Father; but the Evangelist knew, and here says, that *to One* He was Father in a unique conscious communion. 'I ascend to *my* Father and *your* Father, and *my* God and *your* God.' This is the message to be carried to the still perplexed and materialistic minds of the disciples.

The Appearance to the Disciples

JN. 20^{19-23}

20 19 When therefore it was evening, on that
day, the first *day* of the week, and when
the doors were shut where the disciples
were, for fear of the Jews, Jesus came and
stood in the midst, and saith unto them,
20 Peace *be* unto you. And when he had
said this, he shewed unto them his hands
and his side. The disciples therefore
were glad, when they saw the Lord.
21 Jesus therefore said to them again, Peace
be unto you: as the Father hath sent me,
22 even so send I you. And when he had
said this, he breathed on them, and saith
unto them, Receive ye the Holy Ghost:
23 whose soever sins ye forgive, they are
forgiven unto them; whose soever *sins* ye
retain, they are retained.

The appearance to the disciples, assembled behind closed doors 'for fear of the Jews,' follows in the evening of that first Christian Sunday. The incident is referred to in Mk. 16^{14} and Lk. $24^{36ff.}$, but the Fourth Evangelist alone speaks of the closed doors, the fear of the Jews, and the absence of Thomas. He does not say where they were meeting; though he *may* have had in mind the room where the Last Supper was eaten. 'The doors were shut,' he says, when 'Jesus came and stood in the midst. He does not say *how* He came, but he leaves us to suppose that walls and doors did not, and could not, shut out the Risen Jesus. Yet he does not add what may be called 'the materialistic details' of Lk. 24^{42-43}—where it is said that Jesus ate material food in the presence of the disciples.

The story as told by the Evangelist reads like a fulfilment of promises given by Jesus in His Farewell Discourses. 'I will not leave you orphans: I come unto you,' He had said (14^{18}). He now comes. 'Peace I leave with you,' He had said (14^{27}). Peace is here the gift He imparts, before He is taken from their eyes. 'These things have I spoken unto you that *my joy* may be in you, and that *your joy* may be fulfilled' (15^{11}). Now, indeed, 'the disciples were glad when they saw the Lord.' He had prayed: 'As thou didst send me into the world even so sent I them into the world' (17^{18}). Once again He says before He leaves them: 'As the Father hath sent me even so send I you.' He had told them that the Helper who was to come to them, would convict the world of sin, and of righteousness, and of judgement (16^{7-8}). His departure from them synchronises with their reception of this gift, by which gift they will fulfil the Helper's ministry. 'Receive ye the Holy Spirit.'

22–23. These 22nd and 23rd verses have been the source of much controversy —as also the passage in Mt. 16^{19}, with which they are customarily associated. The question has been disputed whether this commission was given only to the ten or to a larger company of disciples: whether the power imparted belonged peculiarly to a visible society, and whether an 'apostolical succession' is necessary to the existence of this society, and so, to the perpetuation of the exercise of this privileged power. Such questions are all subsidiary to the main question, which is: What exactly do these words mean to the Evangelist himself? If we can find an answer to that question, the other questions will answer themselves.

It is clear that the Evangelist is here giving dramatic expression to the task the disciples of Jesus knew themselves called to fulfil in the world. He does not, for example, record the incident on the day of Pentecost with which he was no doubt familiar; but is, with his customary chronological indifference, reading back such signal experiences of spiritual power into the evening of that first Easter Day. The words, ' He breathed on them and saith unto them, Receive ye the Holy Spirit,' recall the day of Pentecost, with the rushing mighty wind symbolising the coming of spiritual power and insight. The figure employed—He *breathed* on them—came naturally to the mind of one in whose literature it was said that God *breathed* into man's nostrils so that he became a living soul. The Evangelist had already likened the coming of the Spirit to the ' wind which bloweth where it listeth ' (3^8). Further, the word translated ' receive ' is not a word, as used by the Evangelist, which means, an impartation to a passive recipient. The same word is used in 12^{48} of him who *receiveth not* the sayings of Jesus. The Spirit comes, therefore, not by magical impartation, but by moral and spiritual reception.

These words are not therefore to be regarded as the precise words spoken by Jesus; but as the statement of the Evangelist, in which he dramatises what he knew to be the Lord's mind with respect to the task committed to the disciples.

This task is one of ' remitting,' or ' forgiving,' *sin*. It is *not* the remitting, or excusing, of *punishment*. The debasing of the idea of sin to the idea of punishment is not derived from this Gospel, nor from the teaching of Jesus. It is therefore wholly foreign to the thought of the Evangelist—and to the thought of Jesus—to suggest that a power is given to certain individuals—privileged by birth, or race, or country, or specific creed, or institutional allegiance—to remit punishment which otherwise would fall upon the sinners whom they ' absolve.' It is *sin* that is to be ' remitted,' not punishment. And *sin* is only remitted when it is *sent away*—for this is the meaning of the term. In other words, it is *remitted*—when it *ceases*. Now *sin* is no abstraction. There is only *sin*, where there are *sinners*. To say, therefore, that sins are remitted means *no less* than that sinners *cease to sin*. This is the ' power ' given to the true disciples of Jesus. It is an *inherent* power, not an official power—which is no real ' power.' In virtue of the liberty from sin which the disciples of Jesus have found in His fellowship, they become the channels of that same liberating power. Consequent on their moral reception of the Spirit of Truth, they become the destroyers of Falsehood. Having received the Spirit of power, they become the extirpators of weakness. Having been enlightened by the spirit of light, they become the annihilators of darkness. No one can give what he has not got. The disciples of Jesus cannot impart what they have not received. They cannot be channels of a grace which has not first cleansed their own lives. They can only loose from the cords of sin in so far as they have themselves been loosed. It is a *real* ' remission of sins ' which they are called to exercise, not a fictitious verbal proclamation of an ' absolution ' which may give momentary emotional satisfaction to the hearer.

No man's sins are remitted by hearing a voice saying that the act of remission is accomplished. Our sins are remitted when we cease to sin—and not till then. Our lies are extirpated when we receive the Truth—and not till then. Our darkness is annihilated when we have the Light—and not till then.

This, then, is the task of the disciples of Jesus. It is only their task in virtue of their discipleship—in virtue, that is, of what they *are* in the depths of their whole personal being. By being 'the sons of light,' they banish the darkness. But the darkness may refuse the light. The slaves may be unwilling to repudiate their chains. In that case, they remain 'bound.' Their sins are 'retained'—not their *punishment*, but their *sins*. Jesus Himself was the supreme 'remitter' of sin. But many refused their liberation; and in refusing to be freed they bound their sin more firmly to themselves. This fact is certified in the experience of humanity. Those who remit sin become the unwilling agents in 'retaining' sin. They become the 'sifters' and 'judges' of humanity. They bind and loose. They remit and retain sins. Their 'authority' is intrinsic to their experience, and rests upon no other basis.

This being so, it is clear that there is no limitation here to any specific body of disciples—whether ten, or more. *All* who have the light are remitters of the darkness of sin. Liberating power is not confined to any class or order of men. It is wide as virtue itself. Its only confines are vice and evil, falsehood and superstition. This is the only doctrine of the power of remission and absolution which is taught by the Fourth Gospel—or by Jesus Himself; and it is the only doctrine substantiated by the history and experience of humanity. Those who have 'remitted' the sins of humanity are those who have 'hated' the sins of humanity. To belong to a privileged sect does not make us remitters of sin. But to belong to Christ does—that is, to be in such fellowship with His spirit that we share His hatred of it, and His separation from it.

Origen, commenting on the kindred passage in Mt. 16^{19} said: 'He who is gifted with self-control enters the gate of heaven by the key of self-control. He who is just enters the gate of heaven by the key of justice. The Saviour gives to those who are not overcome by the gates of hell as many keys as there are virtues. . . . If any who is not Peter, and has not the qualities here mentioned, believes that he can bind on earth like Peter, so that what he binds is bound in heaven, such an one is puffed up, not knowing the meaning of the Scriptures.'

The Appearance to Thomas

Jn. 20^{24-29}

20 24 But Thomas, one of the twelve, called
Didymus, was not with them when Jesus
25 came. The other disciples therefore said
unto him, We have seen the Lord. But
he said unto them, Except I shall see in
his hands the print of the nails, and put
my finger into the print of the nails, and
put my hand into his side, I will not
believe.
26 And after eight days again his disciples
were within, and Thomas with them.
Jesus cometh, the doors being shut, and
stood in the midst, and said, Peace *be* unto
27 you. Then saith he to Thomas, Reach
hither thy finger, and see my hands; and
reach *hither* thy hand, and put it into my
side: and be not faithless, but believing.
28 Thomas answered and said unto him,
29 My Lord and my God. Jesus saith unto
him, Because thou hast seen me, thou
hast believed: blessed *are* they that have
not seen, and *yet* have believed.

The doubt of the disciples finds typical expression in Thomas, the 'twin.' The incident is peculiar to the Fourth Gospel, and may be the Evangelist's way of dramatising the persisting perplexity and scepticism of the disciples. It is clear from the Synoptic Gospels that doubt did persist for a time among them; this will be seen by a perusal of Mt. 28^{17}, Mk. 16^{11-18}, and Lk. $24^{11 ff.}$. Yet the attitude of Thomas here is in accord with what the Evangelist had said of him in 11^{16} and 14^{5}; and it may well be that the narrative has its historical basis in some specific experience given to Thomas by the Risen Christ.

It is clear that the Evangelist is leading up to the crowning beatitude of Jesus, and to the original ending of his Gospel. He wishes to close his Gospel with what he knew to be the essential emphasis of Jesus Himself. Throughout his work he has been seeking to show the superiority of the 'faith' which is integral to spiritual insight, to that lower variety which rests upon external 'proofs' and 'evidences' of the senses. Apart from the Epilogue—which was undoubtedly added later—this is the final word of Jesus in this Gospel. 'Blessed are they that have not seen, and yet have believed.'

As in the previous appearance, the Evangelist emphasises that the *doors were shut* when Jesus appeared in the midst of the disciples. The Risen Jesus could be manifest to sense, but was not confined by physical barriers. Thomas says that he will not believe that the other disciples saw 'the Lord' unless he himself can see Him with the evidences of the Passion and Crucifixion upon Him. The print of the nails and the riven side will be evidences to him that it is indeed Jesus the Lord.

The words of Jesus in *v.* 27 meet the need which Thomas had expressed to the other disciples. Jesus stands before him with the marks of the Passion upon Him. The Evangelist does not tell us that Thomas *touched* Jesus. Some interpreters have concluded that the Evangelist wished to say that such sensuous contact *was* given to him; and among modern spiritistic exegetes the view has been held that such contact has to be interpreted in the light of the phenomena adduced in the literature of psychical research. It is possible, however, that what the Evangelist did wish to say was that it was not the physical touch which elicited the utterance of faith from Thomas, but the insight of Christ into the perplexed needs of his mind. For it was after the Risen Jesus had *spoken* to the perplexity of Thomas that he 'answered and said unto him, 'My Lord and my God.'

In this confession of Thomas the message of the Prologue receives its emphatic vindication and corroboration. 'My Lord,' he says: that is, It is indeed He whom I have followed and called my Lord. 'My God,' he says: that is, He whom I now recognise as my Lord is to me as God; He is 'God for me.' The Word had indeed become flesh for him: Jesus was indeed Divine. Thomas had beheld His glory, the glory as of the only begotten from the Father, full of grace and truth.

Pascal expressed the same truth as Thomas when he said: 'Christ is the God of men.' It was a genius of a different stamp—'Europe's sagest head,' Goethe—who said: 'There is in the four Gospels . . . the reflection of a greatness which emanated from the Person of Jesus, and which was of as divine a kind as ever was seen upon earth. If I am asked whether it is in my nature to pay Him devout reverence, I say—certainly! I bow before Him as the divine manifestation of the highest principle of morality.' Yet another, who learned much from Goethe but more from the race from which Jesus and the Johannine author came—Carlyle—said of Him whom Thomas called 'My Lord and my God': 'Our divinest symbol. Higher has the human thought not yet reached. A Symbol of quiet perennial, infinite character; whose significance will ever demand to be anew inquired into, and anew made manifest.'

29. Most of those who in the Evangelist's day could say with Thomas, 'My Lord and my God,' had not had such appearances vouchsafed to them. There were few, if any, left who had companied with Jesus in the days of His flesh: few who had witnessed the Crucifixion or had been partakers of the first visions of the Risen Jesus. What, then, of *their* faith? Was it insecurely grounded? The crowning word of 'the spiritual Gospel' is the word in which Jesus speaks of the blessedness belonging to essential spiritual faith. Faith itself is its own evidence. It is not sight, but insight: not logically verifiable evidence, or sensory impression. It is in the highest and best sense 'knowledge'—though not 'knowledge' of the things we see. What Tennyson called 'the forms of faith' are the inadequate expressions men have given to their 'Faith'; but 'the forms of faith' are not Faith itself. Some delude themselves with the idea that there is a 'knowledge' which belongs to the 'forms of faith' which does not belong to 'Faith' in itself. They forget that the only source of all knowledge, in any spiritual sense, is 'Faith'; and if there is any validity in 'the forms of faith' it is only because there is valid 'knowledge' in that activity of the deepest self which we call 'Faith.'

Max Planck [1] has recently said that every serious scientific worker realises that over the entrance to the temple of science are written the words: *Ye must have faith.* In other words, Science is concerned, not merely with the *description* of subjective sensory impressions, but with a real objective world existing independently of ourselves; and the assurance or 'knowledge' of such an objective world is given us by faith. The objective world of science can no more be 'proved' than can the Objective Spiritual Realm of religion.

Thou canst not prove the Nameless, O my son,
Nor canst thou prove the world thou movest in,
Thou canst not prove that thou art body alone,
Nor canst thou prove that thou art spirit alone,
Nor canst thou prove that thou art both in one:
Thou canst not prove thou art immortal, no,
Nor yet that thou art mortal—nay, my son,
Thou canst not prove that I, who speak with thee,
Am not thyself in converse with thyself,
For nothing worthy proving can be proven,
Nor yet disproven.

'Faith,' therefore, is necessary to our knowledge of all reality. In the 'knowledge' which spiritual faith gives there is a 'blessedness' without compare.

[1] In *Where is Science Going?*

It is blessedness, not happiness—least of all, pleasure. Blessedness belongs, says Jesus, to those who know the Truth, and have found the life that is life indeed.

Conclusion

JN. 20^{30-31}

20 30 Many other signs therefore did Jesus in the presence of the disciples, which are
31 not written in this book: but these are written, that ye may believe that Jesus is the Christ, the Son of God; and that believing ye may have life in his name.

The Evangelist has written what he wants to write, and concluded as he wanted to conclude. He adds these two verses to state in summary form the purpose he has had before him in writing. This purpose has dictated the method he has followed. In the interests of that purpose he has left many of the signs of Jesus untold. It is no meticulous biography he has sought to write. What he has written has been inspired by the desire that his readers may continue in believing that Jesus was indeed the Anointed of God, and the unique Divine Son. This has been the theme of his whole Gospel. In every chapter he has been unfolding the sense of Messianic vocation possessed by Jesus, and that Filial consciousness out of which the sense of vocation arose.

In such belief consists the 'life in his name.' It is a 'belief' which embraces the whole unified personality—the belief that is evidenced in the whole depth of a man's rational, moral, and spiritual nature. Not everyone that saith, Lord, Lord, has the belief that leads to this life.

Not he that repeateth the Name,
But he that doeth the will.

EPILOGUE (21)

The Gospel has reached a fitting, consistent, and unifying close. When the reader reaches the closing verses of the 20th chapter he feels he has reached the end, and would now quietly close the book to meditate upon the transcendent themes which, like strains of celestial music, have been haunting him throughout. Were the author to say more, the reader feels, it would be like building on an additional and projecting exit to a symmetrical structure: it would be like adding a portico to the completed Parthenon; or an additional movement to the Fifth Symphony of Beethoven. However perfect in itself the addition, it must, so one thinks, mar the integrated symmetry of the work.

Yet the 21st chapter follows. And as far as is known no copy of the Gospel was issued without this additional chapter.

A nice problem in scientific criticism and in psychological interpretation therefore presents itself to the careful student. This problem has inspired numerous long and intricate discussions, in which critics have engrossed themselves in answering, or seeking to answer, every point adduced by those who reached a different conclusion from themselves. Many of these discussions leave the reader with the impression that their authors have been more anxious to combat opponents than to arrive at truth. The two questions which arise are: first, was this chapter written by the author of the Gospel? Second, when and for what reason was it written? The two questions, however, involve each other, and are intrinsically inseparable.

Inasmuch as there is no external evidence for a text of the Gospel without this chapter, we have to reach a conclusion on these two issues, first, from the vocabulary and style of the chapter; and, second, from its coherence and harmony with the rest of the Gospel—entirely, that is, from internal evidence.

1. In regard to the first point—the vocabulary and style of the chapter—this is an issue on which linguistic experts reach diverse conclusions. The late Dr. Sanday reached this conclusion: 'The complete identity of thought and style, and the way in which this last chapter is dovetailed into the preceding . . . seem to prove that the last chapter is by the same hand as the rest of the Gospel' (in *The Criticism of the Fourth Gospel*, p. 81). This was also the view of Lightfoot, who wrote—in *Biblical Essays* (p. 195): 'Though an after-thought, this chapter was certainly written by the author of the Gospel.' This view was also maintained by Renan, Pfleiderer, Westcott, Drummond, Harnack, and many others—by interpreters, it should be noted, who had reached very divergent conclusions as to the precise historicity of the Gospel, as to its author, and as to the situation which called it forth. On the other hand, almost as imposing a body of linguistic students reach precisely the opposite conclusion, and do not hesitate to express their judgement with the assurance of critical conviction. After a careful examination of the points at issue, for example, Dr. Moffatt says: 'Even within the brief space of the appendix, idiosyncrasies of language and style appear which are practically sufficient to indicate another hand' (*Introduction to the Literature of the New Testament*, p. 572).

For ourselves, we are unable to dogmatise on this question. It seems clear that the Evangelist, at least originally, intended that his Gospel should close with the 20th chapter. But whether he himself added this chapter, or whether it was added by another hand, is a question we are unable to answer. On the one hand, there is—as we cannot but feel—an obvious resemblance in general feeling and spirit between this chapter and the rest of the Gospel. On the other hand, there are a number of words in the Appendix which are peculiar to this chapter of the Gospel. Those who maintain that the Evangelist himself wrote this chapter will explain these slight differences of language as without any psychological improbability: the same author will use new words after a lapse of time, and even after no lapse of time. On the theory that differences of language indicate a difference of authorship, most of the books that have ever been written would lose some of their chapters—those of the critics who maintain this view included. A completely stereotyped language or style is seldom found —except the language and style of a mind that is dead. Those, on the other hand, who maintain that the Evangelist himself did not write this chapter will explain the obvious resemblance in feeling and spirit which it has to the rest of the Gospel, as the result of the natural desire of the new writer to approximate the addition to what has gone before. And so we might go on, arguing *ad infinitum* on an issue which, on the evidence before us, can never be satisfactorily settled.

Without any desire to dogmatise on the issue, we propose to take this 21st chapter as added by the Evangelist himself. If he had been an artist, and only an artist, we might conclude with some kind of conviction that he would not himself have either made, or countenanced, this addition. But he himself was primarily an evangelist, and only secondarily an artist. If the claims of literary art and of his nobly apologetic purpose conflict, then the former will have to submit. Something more, he seems to feel, has to be said. He sees—let us suggest—the growing edifice of the Church of Jesus; he envisages the interior perils to which it will become increasingly subject. What is the *mission* of the disciples of Jesus, he asks, and what is the *essential condition* of successful discipleship? There leaps before his kindling mind—' Stung by the splendour of a sudden thought '—a vision which answers both these questions. He therefore becomes wholely willing to mar the symmetrical proportions of his work in the interests of his transcendent theme and his concern for the children of the Church.

AN ALLEGORY OF THE MISSION AND REQUISITE OF THE DISCIPLES OF JESUS

I. *THE MISSION*

THE APPEARANCE AT THE SEA OF TIBERIAS

JN. 21^{1-14}

21 1 After these things Jesus manifested
himself again to the disciples at the sea
of Tiberias; and he manifested *himself* on
2 this wise. There were together Simon
Peter, and Thomas called Didymus, and
Nathanael of Cana in Galilee, and the
sons of Zebedee, and two other of his dis-
3 ciples. Simon Peter saith unto them, I
go a fishing. They say unto him, We
also come with thee. They went forth,
and entered into the boat; and that night
4 they took nothing. But when day was
now breaking, Jesus stood on the beach:
howbeit the disciples knew not that it was
5 Jesus. Jesus therefore saith unto them,
Children, have ye aught to eat? They
6 answered him, No. And he said unto
them, Cast the net on the right side of
the boat, and ye shall find. They cast
therefore, and now they were not able to
7 draw it for the multitude of fishes. That
disciple therefore whom Jesus loved saith
unto Peter, It is the Lord. So when
Simon Peter heard that it was the Lord,
he girt his coat about him (for he was
naked), and cast himself into the sea.
8 But the other disciples came in the little
boat (for they were not far from the land,
but about two hundred cubits off),
9 dragging the net *full* of fishes. So when
they got out upon the land, they see a fire
of coals there, and fish laid thereon, and
10 bread. Jesus saith unto them, Bring of
the fish which ye have now taken.
11 Simon Peter therefore went up, and drew
the net to land, full of great fishes, a
hundred and fifty and three: and for all
there were so many, the net was not rent.
12 Jesus saith unto them, Come *and* break
your fast. And none of the disciples
durst inquire of him, Who art thou?
13 knowing that it was the Lord. Jesus
cometh, and taketh the bread, and
14 giveth them, and the fish likewise. This
is now the third time that Jesus was
manifested to the disciples, after that he
was risen from the dead.

There are undoubted marks of allegory in this beautiful story, but it is a perplexing question as to what is the precise historical basis on which the author has constructed his allegory. The reader will note that there are close resemblances between this narrative and that in Lk. 5^{1-11}. The Lucan story tells of a remarkable catch of fish by Peter, James, and John—the latter two being the sons of Zebedee—at the opening of the ministry of Jesus; the story ends with the statement of Jesus, 'Fear not, from henceforth thou shalt catch men.' This Lucan narrative of what has been usually called 'the miraculous draft of fishes' is not found in Mk. or in Mt.—though the same call is doubtless expressed in Mk. 1^{16-20} and in Mt. 4^{18-22}, where Jesus says to Peter and Andrew, 'Come ye after me, and I will make you to become fishers of men' (Mk. 1^{17}). The two striking similarities between the Lucan story and the Johannine story, are the catch of fish and the call to Peter to become a fisher—or, to use the figure employed in this 21st chapter, a shepherd—of men. The Johannine story also recalls the narrative in Mt. 14^{28-31} where Peter attempts to walk on the water to Jesus.

It seems clear that there was a tradition in the Church of a remarkable catch of fish by some of the disciples on the Lake of Galilee, associated with the presence of Jesus on the shore. While Luke uses this tradition as the framework for the original call of the disciples, the Fourth Evangelist embodies with it another tradition current in the Church, of an appearance of the Risen Jesus in Galilee. The existence of this other tradition is evidenced from Mk. 16^{7}—and Mt. 28^{7}—where the disciples are told that they will see the Risen Jesus in Galilee: it also survives in the apocryphal Gospel of Peter—dating from about the middle of the second century—which gives 'the earliest uncanonical account of the Passion that exists.' The fragment of this Gospel of Peter which has come down ends thus: 'Now it was the last day of unleavened bread, and many were coming out of the city and returning unto their own homes because the feast was at an end. But we, the twelve disciples of the Lord, were weeping and were in sorrow, and each being grieved for that which had befallen departed unto his own house. But I, Simon Peter, and Andrew my brother took our nets and went unto the sea: and there was with us Levi the son of Alphaeus, whom the Lord . . .' The lost ending of Mk.'s Gospel might conceivably throw light on this traditional appearance of the Risen Jesus—but, again, it might not.[1]

Our conjecture, therefore, is as follows. On the basis of these two traditions—the draft of fishes and the appearance of the Risen Jesus in Galilee—the Evangelist constructs an allegory of the mission of the disciples of Jesus. Just as, on the basis of some wedding incident, the Evangelist constructed the allegory of the water made wine in chapter 2, or on the basis of some raising akin to that of Jairus's daughter, he composed the allegory of the 'raising of Lazarus.' The mission of the disciples had early been conceived under this figure of fishing. Jesus had called them to be 'fishers of men'—Mk. 1^{17}, Mt. 4^{19}, and Lk. 5^{10}. He likened the Kingdom to the net cast into the sea which gathered every kind of fish—Mt. 13^{47}. Further, the fish very soon became the emblem of the Christian.

The allegory is in two parts, and each part is necessary to the other. In the first part, using the story of the draft of fishes, the Evangelist seeks to unfold the world-wide mission of the disciples of Jesus. In the second part, using probably some traditional story, which exemplified that Peter having learnt his lesson

[1] Harnack, for example, held that the lost ending of Mark contained this tradition (*Luke the Physician*, p. 227). Streeter, in *The Four Gospels* (pp. 355–356), sets forth five considerations in support of the view 'that Jn. 21 represents either the lost end of Mark or an oral tradition more or less its equivalent.'

became a humbler and a wiser man, the Evangelist seeks to emphasise the one essential to adequate discipleship—namely, love to Christ. The whole allegory, therefore, might be given as its title, as we have suggested: '*The Mission and Requisite of the disciples of Jesus.*'

1. The scene is 'the sea of Tiberias,' as the author, alone among the New Testament writers, calls the Sea of Galilee. There are *seven* disciples gathered by the Lake, among them 'the sons of Zebedee'—here first referred to in the Gospel—and 'two other of his disciples.' It is difficult not to conclude that the number *seven* was deliberately chosen by the Evangelist in pursuance of his allegorical motif. Simon Peter—spokesman and leader among the disciples—proposes that they go fishing. Their fishing *that night* is vain—as in the Lucan story the fishing had been vain during the night hours (Lk. 5^{5}). Perhaps the Evangelist is here again thinking allegorically: for to him 'night' speaks of spiritual darkness, and 'the breaking of the day' is associated with the presence of Him who is the light of the world, on the shore. In the dim light of early dawn Jesus is not recognised—as He had not been recognised by Mary. Even when He addresses them with an intimate 'children'—or 'boys' (παιδία); it is not the same word as in 13^{33}, where the Greek is τεκνία—they fail to respond: this time, unlike Mary, whose mind the *voice* of Jesus awoke to recognition. They have, they say, nothing to eat. Jesus bids them cast their net on the *right* side of the boat—a reference not found in the Lucan story, and which probably, once again, illustrates the symbolism of the Fourth Evangelist's narrative. The *right* side was the auspicious side, or the side of value—as it is in both the Old and New Testaments. For example, Ezekiel lies on his *right* side for Judah, while on his *left* side for Israel. (Ezek. 4^{4-6}.) Zechariah in 11^{17} speaks a Divine word of woe to the worthless shepherd that leaveth the flock, adding that 'the sword shall be upon his *right* eye,' which eye 'shall be utterly darkened'—the *right* eye being symbolical of the eye of spiritual vision. In Mt. 5^{29-30} Jesus says that the *right* hand, if necessary, should be cut off, and the *right* eye be plucked out. And it is at the *right* hand that the sheep are placed in the Judgement Day in Mt. 25^{33}. (To ourselves to-day the *right* hand is still the place of honour.)

There results such a catch that they are unable to draw the net into the boat for the multitude of fishes. Nevertheless, the net remains unbroken, the catch being taken in its entirety: whereas in the Lucan story, as it will be remembered, the nets were breaking. The perception of 'the disciple whom Jesus loved' is awakened, and he says to Peter, 'It is the Lord.' Success in spiritual work quickens spiritual insight and recognition. The beloved disciple is the first to recognise Jesus—'Jesus is known in so far as he is loved.' Simon Peter, however, while not the first to see, is the first to act. The disciple who is quickest in thought and profoundest in penetration, first detects the beloved Presence; while the impulsive Simon, accustomed to act first and think afterwards, will be the first to greet the Lord. He is 'naked,' but clothes his nakedness with a fisherman's garment before he jumps into the water to come to Jesus. Has not the Evangelist some symbolism in his mind here? He clothes himself in the garment of repentance. The figure is employed, it will be remembered, by Toplady in his hymn, "Rock of Ages," where he writes, *Naked, come to Thee for dress.*

The boat was about *two hundred cubits* from the shore: a statement which may be either the author's way of saying that Peter was not in danger of being drowned —cf. Lk. 5^7—or which may contain an additional symbolical suggestion. 'In the numerical symbolism of Philo it was resolved into two hundred, the first intimating purification from unrighteousness, the second representing the plenitude of perfect virtue.' [1] The late Dr. E. A. Abbott also maintained that the number two hundred represented repentance, and found a similar symbolical reference in the 'two hundred pennyworth of bread' referred to in Jn. 6^7—'two hundred pennyworth of bread' instancing, as he said, 'how John may (as often elsewhere) have retained an old tradition that adapted itself to spiritual interpretation, as if to say, "Not all the repentance in the world could suffice to *buy* bread to feed the Church; it must be received as the free gift of God."' [2]

The other disciples bring the boat to the shore, dragging with it the net full of fish. Though they were unable to haul the net into the boat, they were able to drag it to the land. Jesus has already prepared a meal of fish and bread for them: yet He bids them bring of the fish which they have now caught. It is Peter now, who, presumably, returns to the boat and himself drags the net to land—the net that was beyond the strength of the seven to pull into the boat. Obviously a symbolical, and not a historical, motif is responsible for these seeming inconsistencies.

The number of the fish caught is one hundred and fifty-three. Here there is unmistakable symbolism, as has been felt from the days of the first commentators on this Gospel. The interpretations of the symbolism have been as numerous as they have been quaint and far-fetched. Origen pointed out that the number could be taken as representing the Trinity: $3 \times 50 + 3$. Another suggestion was that 100 stands for the Gentiles, 50 for the Jews, and 3 for the Trinity. Yet another Trinitarian interpretation was that the number was reached by adding 144 to 9, the first being the square of the number of the disciples, the second the square of the symbol of the Trinity. Augustine sponsored yet another quaint and fanciful suggestion: that 153 was the 'potentiality' of 17—that is, the sum of the successive digits—1, 2, 3, 4, 5, . . . 17; the number 17 being itself the sum of 10—representing the ten commandments—and 7—representing the sevenfold gifts of the Spirit. The Christian 'net' therefore, consists of those who keep the Decalogue and are filled with the Spirit. Such are a few of the fantastic theological interpretations of the number. The most likely of all the suggestions made to interpret the symbolism of the number 153, however, is that referred to by Jerome. He says, commenting on Ezek. 47^{10}, that Latin and Greek natural historians declare that there were a hundred and fifty-three known species of fish. It has been pointed out that Oppianus, whom alone Jerome refers to by name, was too late in date to be known by the author of this narrative. Yet it is probable that the view had been expressed long before Oppianus: for he, it may be taken for granted, had not himself counted the number of species of fish in the sea. The number therefore to the Evangelist had no dogmatic Trinitarian significance, but rather an *experiential* significance. What he wished to say was

[1] J. E. Carpenter, *The Johannine Writings*, p. 246.
[2] *Ency. Bib.*, vol. 2, p. 1797.

that the disciples of Jesus, if they were true to His spirit, would proclaim an inclusive and universal Gospel. 'All ranks and conditions of men' must be won to discipleship. The command found in Mt. 28^{19}—to 'make disciples of all the nations'—is here expressed in the form of an allegory.

12–13. Jesus bids them to come and break their fast. They all now know that it is the Lord. Jesus takes the bread and the fish, and gives to them. It is a meal in miniature, corresponding to the meal with the multitude recorded in chapter 6, without, however, the eucharistic word.[1] The meal symbolises to the Evangelist that spiritual feeding upon Christ whose inner significance he is now about to unfold. Such feeding is the first essential in all true discipleship.

14. This is now, says the author, the *third* time that Jesus was manifested to the disciples, a statement which harmonises the narrative with the two previous appearances recorded in $20^{19\,ff.}$ and $20^{26\,ff.}$

2. *THE ESSENTIAL CONDITION OF DISCIPLESHIP*

THE RESTORATION OF PETER

JN. 21^{15-19}

21 15 So when they had broken their fast,
Jesus saith to Simon Peter, Simon, *son* of
John, lovest thou me more than these?
He saith unto him, Yea, Lord; thou
knowest that I love thee. He saith unto
16 him, Feed my lambs. He saith to him
again a second time, Simon, *son* of John,
lovest thou me? He saith unto him,
Yea, Lord; thou knowest that I love thee.
17 He saith unto him, Tend my sheep. He
saith unto him the third time, Simon, *son*
of John, lovest thou me? Peter was
grieved because he said unto him the
third time, Lovest thou me? And he
said unto him, Lord, thou knowest all
things; thou knowest that I love thee.
Jesus saith unto him, Feed my sheep.
18 Verily, verily, I say unto thee, When
thou wast young, thou girdedst thyself,
and walkedst whither thou wouldest: but
when thou shalt be old, thou shalt stretch
forth thy hands, and another shall gird
thee, and carry thee whither thou
19 wouldest not. Now this he spake,
signifying by what manner of death he
should glorify God. And when he had
spoken this, he saith unto him, Follow me.

The second part of the allegory follows naturally upon the first part. The figure of fishing is replaced by the figure of shepherding. It has been characteristic of the Evangelist's way of writing to base a spiritual discourse upon some traditional incident. The incident is shaped and embellished in order to supply a frame for the teaching of Jesus. So it is here. The incident of the fishing—itself treated in a symbolical manner—leads up to the teaching of Jesus that without love to Himself and His cause no disciple can accomplish the work to which He calls them. The teaching itself, however, is here given a narrative setting; which suggests that the Evangelist is using some traditional story of the restoration of Peter after the Crucifixion and Resurrection. The inner meaning of the meal they have just received from Jesus is now unfolded. They who eat truly the bread which Jesus gives are they who are devoted to Himself and His cause. Judas had eaten the bread dipped in the wine, which Jesus had given him, but had not partaken of Him in his heart by faith with thanksgiving. The inner meaning of the Last Supper had been unfolded in the incident of the feet-washing,

[1] It is interesting to note that both the Sinaitic Syriac palimpsest and Codex Bezæ insert the eucharistic word in the passage: 'Jesus took the bread and the fish, and *blessed* them and gave to them.'

as if to show that only *they* have truly eaten who manifest the spirit of Jesus in humble acts of service. The seven have eaten of the bread and fish; and now, as if to show that they have truly eaten, Peter—who after the last meal in the Upper Room had shown that he had not truly eaten, in that he had just a few hours later denied Jesus—now thrice protests a devotion which, as the Evangelist and the Church knew, found its consummation in a martyr's death. He, at least, has now partaken of Christ in his heart by faith with thanksgiving.

That Jesus had required of His disciples a completely devoted zeal is seen from the Q passage variously recorded in Mt. $10^{37\text{f.}}$ and Lk. $14^{26\text{f.}}$. A love to be sundered by no family ties, a love which will lead wherever Jesus Himself goes—even to the Cross—is the love requisite to the true disciple. This same teaching is in the Fourth Gospel made the indispensable requisite of the shepherding and teaching mission of the disciples; and at the same time its exemplification in Peter, who *did* follow to the end, is the Gospel's final sacramental emphasis.

As Peter had thrice denied, so here he thrice affirms his love—that, as Augustine put it, ' his tongue may not yield a feebler service to love than to fear, and imminent death may not appear to have elicited more from his lips than present life.' As is pointed out in the marginal notes in the Revised Version, two verbs—ἀγαπᾶν and φιλεῖν—are used in the story for ' love.' To a modern reader it would seem that whatever be the precise connotation of the two verbs, the author means to express some significant truth by the distinction. The first of the two verbs is used by Jesus in His first two questions, in each case Peter answering with the second of the two verbs. In His third question Jesus changes the verb to that which Peter has used in his replies. When, however, we come to examine carefully the Evangelist's use of the two verbs in the rest of the Gospel, we discover that they are used by him interchangeably. Both verbs are used for God's love for man, for the Father's love for the Son, for Jesus's love for men, for men's love for Jesus, and for men's love for other men.[1] With the linguistic evidence of the rest of the Gospel before us, therefore, any interpretation based upon differentiation of connotation of the two verbs must be precarious and problematical. Many commentators have suggested that the first verb—ἀγαπᾶν—' has more of judgement and deliberate choice ' in it; and that the second verb—φιλεῖν—' has more of attachment and peculiar personal affection.' On the basis of this suggested difference in connotation, an interesting interpretation of the three questions and answers might be drawn out: showing, for example, on the one hand, a gradual declension in the demands made by Jesus—the comparison ' more than these ' (probably, other *disciples*) being omitted in the second question, and Peter's own word being used in the third question; and, on the other hand, showing a growth in the humility of Peter, when in his third reply he is both ' grieved ' that Jesus has had to descend to his word, and is ready to throw himself and his protestation upon the absolute insight of Jesus.

If a difference was read by the Evangelist into the two words, it probably corresponds to the temperament and character of Peter himself. He was a man of warm emotional nature. Such men act first and think afterwards. Their

[1] Bernard in his *Critical Commentary*, vol. 2, pp. 702 ff., gives a complete list of the relevant passages in the Gospel.

actions are governed not so much by settled, deliberately-embraced principles as by personal attachments. This gives their service an emotional zest which makes for popular leadership; but also may lead them to vacillate uncertainly when principles are at stake—as, for example, Peter showed in his controversy with Paul in Gal. $2^{11 ff.}$. The quality of Peter's discipleship and leadership—arising from the essential quality of his mind—is therefore revealed in the verb expressive of warm personal attachment to Jesus. The ' love ' of which, on the other hand, Jesus speaks is that on which Paul writes in his Hymn to Christian Love in 1 Cor. 13. *Agape* is that devotion characteristic of him whose mind is governed by unswerving insight and deliberately-embraced principle. It suffers long, is always humble, does not mistake outward shows for inward reality, has within it reliability and steadfastness. Has not the Evangelist—so we might tentatively suggest—read into these two verbs such differences in the quality of the discipleship and leadership which must have been exemplified within the circle of the Apostles themselves?

At least, the questions of Jesus and the answers of Peter reveal that the Evangelist's purpose was to unfold the growing humility of Peter's mind. He had claimed a devotion to Jesus surpassing that of the other disciples—Mk. 14^{29}; Jn. 13^{37}. He will not now say that he loves Jesus more than the others do—for that surely is the meaning of the phrase ' more than these,' and not, as has been suggested, ' more than these things,' that is, the secular life of fishing to which he had returned. And in his third reply Peter omits the confident ' Yea, Lord,' as if to show that he leaves what is in his heart to the Master's own insight.

The commands of Jesus follow the protestation of Peter's love. There are, here also, slight differences in the commissions given by Jesus which probably had some significance for the mind of the Evangelist. We must not read into these commissions the later distinctions between ' laity ' and ' clergy '—a distinction which, by the fallacy of anachronism, was held to be involved in the difference between ' lambs ' and ' sheep.' Such a distinction was at the farthest possible remove from the mind of the Johannine author: as also was the conception of the ' primacy ' of the Roman pontiffs. The only primacy Jesus, or the Fourth Evangelist, recognised was the ' primacy ' conferred by spiritual insight, by selfless humility, and by complete obedience. All other ' primacy ' savours of the world and its perishing lusts. All the disciples of Jesus are ' pastors,' as all are ' fishers.' He who loves the Good Shepherd will love His flock. He will see men as Jesus saw them, ' sheep not having a shepherd '; and his service of thankful love will be to nourish and guide them. The heart of a shepherd beats in every disciple's breast.

Nevertheless, there are differences in the commissions.

First, ' Feed my lambs ': that is, nourish those who are as children in the Gospel. ' I fed you with milk, and not with meat,' said Paul to the Corinthian Christians in 1 Cor. 3^2. The lambs that cannot yet seek their own food have to be carefully nourished. ' Whosoever,' said Jesus, ' shall cause one of these little ones that believe on me to stumble, it were better for him that a great millstone were hanged about his neck, and he were sunk into the sea ' (Mk. 9^{42} and parallel passages).

Second, ' Tend my sheep '—προβάτια, the *young* sheep, is probably the correct reading: that is, be as a shepherd to my young sheep.[1] The true pastor will lead his sheep into the green pastures, and, if necessary, go out to find the lost.

Third, ' feed my sheep '—πρόβατα, the flock including young and old: that is, nourish the whole flock of God.

18–19. When the Evangelist wrote these words Peter was already dead. These verses give the first expression to the tradition that he died a martyr's death; and Tertullian, writing about the beginning of the third century, accepts this tradition and says that Peter died by crucifixion at Rome. Origen says that Peter, in accord with his own wish, was crucified head downwards. The Evangelist interprets the words of *v.* 18 as having had their fulfilment in this death by martyrdom suffered by Peter. It seems clear that he has adapted some words spoken by Jesus to Peter to harmonise both with his narrative here and with the traditional nature of his death. It may be that those words originally only expressed the increasing *dependence*—the increasing destruction of self-will—that would come to Peter as age advanced. In the years to come he who has girded himself so confidently for the tasks of life will know his own mind to be girded. The unfettered confidence of youth will become transmuted to a wholly dependent devotion. Self-will will be finally broken in Peter, as he comes, after much storm and stress, to a complete submission to the will of the Father. In such surrender of his own will, he will, indeed, be following Jesus Himself. But when the Evangelist records, ' when thou wast young, thou girdest thyself,' he is obviously thinking of what he has just written in *v.* 7—' he girt his coat about him.' And, further, when he writes, ' thou shalt stretch forth thy hands, and another shall gird thee,' he is obviously thinking of the stretching out of the hands on a cross. By such a death Peter would ' glorify God.'

The final word to Peter is ' Follow Me.' Such a call had come to him at the beginning of the ministry of Jesus. It may well have come again after the Crucifixion. How much more we see, as life moves on, in the old cause to which we once surrendered! How much deeper seem the words of every great teacher on each successive reading! We see what we have the capacity to see. The moral and spiritual life is what in our blindness or insight we make it to be. To follow Jesus meant now to Peter the complete surrender of his self-will to the higher purposes of the Father. This had led Jesus to the Cross. And in writing the words the Evangelist read into them the fact that Peter had indeed followed Jesus there.

A Misunderstood Saying about the Beloved Disciple

JN. 21[20-23]

21 20 Peter, turning about, seeth the disciple
whom Jesus loved following; which also
leaned back on his breast at the supper,
and said, Lord, who is he that betrayeth
21 thee? Peter therefore seeing him saith
to Jesus, Lord, and what shall this man
22 do? Jesus saith unto him, If I will that
he tarry till I come, what *is that* to thee?
23 follow thou me. This saying therefore
went forth among the brethren, that that
disciple should not die: yet Jesus said not
unto him, that he should not die; but, If
I will that he tarry till I come, what *is*
that to thee?

[1] The Vulgate here has *agnos*, as in the first commission, and *oves* in the third: though it does not distinguish ' feed ' from ' tend,' in each case translating by *pasce*.

In these concluding verses, the Evangelist answers a difficulty that had presented itself to many in the Church of his day. We cannot be certain what is the historical basis for this dialogue between Peter and Jesus. Some would take the *vv.* 20–22 as a record of an actual conversation in which Jesus rebuked the curiosity of Peter—a curiosity which is also instanced in 13^{24}, where Peter wants to know who is the traitor. Others go farther and hold that in such a dialogue Jesus had expressed His will that the beloved disciple should remain alive until 'His coming.' In all probability, however, we should take this dialogue as the free creation of the Evangelist; in which he seeks to answer a difficulty to many minds created by the death of John the Apostle. He, the beloved disciple and the last surviver of the Apostolic company, had, we have presumed, recently died. The saying of Jesus in Mk. 9^1—'there be some of them that stand here which shall in no wise taste of death till they see the kingdom of God come with power'—had been mistakenly interpreted by the Church to mean that some of the inner band of the disciples would not die before a catastrophic 'coming.' The last had now died, and there had been no such 'coming.' The Evangelist, who has throughout his Gospel sought to correct the false eschatological views of the Church, now tells his readers that the inner mind of Jesus might be thus expressed: 'If I will that he tarry till I come, what is that to thee?' In other words, the mind of Jesus was not concerned with specific times and seasons. The passage expresses in Johannine language the uncertainty and ignorance expressed by Jesus in the saying recorded in Mk. 13^{32} and Mt. 24^{36}: 'Of that day knoweth no one, not even the angels of heaven, neither the Son, but the Father.' Jesus, as the Evangelist reminds his readers, had never said that the beloved disciple would survive till any special day. What He *had* stressed was that times and seasons were in the hands of the Divine Father, and that for each disciple the path of the Divine Will must be faithfully followed without concern for such issues. 'Follow thou me,' says Jesus. The task of the Church in each successive age is to follow in the path in which Jesus led the way: it is not for her to 'stand gazing up into heaven.'

The form of words in which the mind of Jesus on this issue is here expressed has, it will be noted, a certain enigmatic ambiguity, corresponding to the uncertainty of the minds of the followers of Jesus in the Church. The Evangelist neither at this point gives support to those who believe in an apocalyptic 'day,' nor to those who believe that in every great crisis in human affairs there is 'a coming of the Lord.' Without doubt, the second conception would have been more in accord with his mind. What he *does* emphasise is the paramount need for the mind untroubled with questioning about times and seasons, and for the fidelity which follows Jesus to the end.

An Appended Postscript

JN. 21^{24-25}

21 24 This is the disciple which beareth witness of these things, and wrote these things: and we know that his witness is true.
25 And there are also many other things which Jesus did, the which if they should be written every one, I suppose that even the world itself would not contain the books that should be written.

These verses form a kind of appendix to the Appendix. They raise another nice point in criticism. Were they written by the Evangelist? Or were they attached to the Gospel prior to publication?

Those who maintain that John the son of Zebedee was the author of the Gospel as we have it, *necessarily* come to the conclusion that another hand has written at least this 24th verse: for the Apostle himself could not have written '*we* know that *his* witness is true.' These, therefore, will conclude that the 24th verse was appended to the Gospel before its circulation, and probably by the elders in the Church in Ephesus. Such was the view of Westcott and others.

Yet, it is difficult to imagine that the Gospel could ever have been regarded as concluded at the 23rd verse. If the Evangelist himself added this 21st chapter it is inherently of the highest improbability that he could have concluded with such a statement as we find in this 23rd verse. And even if the 21st chapter was added by another hand, it is difficult to imagine that this other writer, whoever he was, could have regarded *v.* 23 as a fitting conclusion to so integrated a work. This difficulty can be met by supposing that *v.* 25 was the ending of the Gospel, as it left the hand of the Evangelist, and that *v.* 24 was inserted as a kind of attestation.

Many hypotheses are possible, and it is not difficult to make out some kind of a case for them all. Our own view is as follows. Probably this 24th verse was inserted by the elders in the Church of Ephesus. They tell us that it is 'the beloved disciple' who 'beareth witness of these things, and wrote these things'; and that *they* know that his witness is true. The beloved disciple, we have concluded, is the Apostle John, the son of Zebedee. He is the witness behind the whole Gospel. When the elders at Ephesus say that he *wrote* these things, they did not necessarily mean that he wrote the Gospel as we have it—any more than the Evangelist himself meant that Pilate had *himself* written the inscription and had *himself* put it on the Cross, in the statement in 19^{19}: 'Pilate wrote a title and put it on the Cross.' What they wish the readers of the Gospel to know is that *it rests upon the authority of the Apostle*. Probably he himself wrote a good deal of what he taught in his 'Asram' in Ephesus; just as a Christian teacher to-day in a theological college writes out much of what he says to his students. This 24th verse, therefore, does not contradict the conclusion as to authorship reached in this commentary. The Evangelist transmitted the essential thought of the Apostle John, and no doubt in some places his very words. It would be natural for the Ephesian Church to issue this Gospel with a statement of this nature, attesting that behind it, is the authority of the great Apostle whose spirit, as well as whose bones, rested among them. In so doing they are not to be regarded as guilty of what, to modern standards, might be condemned as literary dishonesty. It indicates a signal act of the historical imagination to speak of such an attestation as 'forgery' or 'fraud.' As a matter of fact, there are books in both the Old and the New Testaments whose authors we do not, and shall never, know, which yet have from the earliest times been attributed to authors who, to the best of our critical knowledge, could not have written them. The Evangelist himself, the intimate disciple of the Apostle, would be not unwilling for his Gospel to appear with such a clause attesting the apostolic source of its main witness. He who has so often written in his Gospel that Jesus ' said ' this and that, when he himself knew that he was giving, not the precise words uttered by Jesus, but an interpretation and elucidation of his essential thought, would not have the scruples of a modern scientific historian when he read this attestation. Knowing his indebtedness to ' the beloved disciple,' his own revered teacher, he would rejoice to know that his work went forth to the Church with a statement which would at all times indicate its dependence upon so beloved an apostolic witness. No monetary desires—as in modern instances—would dissuade him from acquiescing in such an attestation. He wrote neither for money nor for personal glorification. He wrote for the Christians of his day. He was willing to efface himself in the interests, first of the message about Jesus he had to convey, and, second, of the apostle at whose feet he had learned so much of that message.

25. Thus the last word of his Gospel is to remind his readers of the fragmentary nature of his Gospel, and of its inadequacy to its inexhaustible theme. For this is what he would say in the striking hyperbole with which he closes: ' I suppose that even the world itself would not contain the books that should be written.' Pedantic and myopic critics of such hyperbole may be reminded that the Evangelist had sufficient intelligence to know that books which were written *in* the world could be contained *by* the world. They fail to understand the author. He began with the Word, through which the world was made. He has written throughout his Gospel of Him who was the incarnate Word, revealing to those who had eyes to see, the God whom no man had ever seen. Now as he closes he asks himself: What *is* his own book? What indeed are *all* the books that might be written on so transcendent a theme? A world of books cannot suffice to utter the Word made flesh. ' Christianity,' he might be saying to us, ' is not *my* book, nor a whole universe of books. It is the Eternal Grace and Truth of the Divine Father incarnate in Jesus.'

So with an overmastering insight into the inexhaustible truth as it was in Jesus, he closes by saying that an adequate record of that life will never be written. All our Gospels are glimpses:

They are but broken lights of Thee,
And Thou, O Lord, art more than they.

END OF BOOK III

SELECT BIBLIOGRAPHY FOR BOOK III

The following bibliography is not meant to be exhaustive. It is designed to point the reader to some of the more important books in English—whether historically or intrinsically important—that have appeared during the last few generations. For the descriptive epithets and characterisations applied to some of the books, the present author must take full responsibility: they are the expression of his own judgement.

Abbott, E. A.: *From Letter to Spirit.* 1903. A suggestive study in the application to passages in the Gospels of what Abbott called 'Targumistic phenomena.' Its characteristic dedication was: 'To the unknown author of the Fourth Gospel, the noblest attempt at indirect biography where direct biography was impossible.'

—— *Johannine Vocabulary.* 1905.
—— *Johannine Grammar.* 1906.
—— *The Fourfold Gospel.* 5 vols. 1913–17.
Like the above, these three works are full of interesting, and sometimes brilliant, sometimes fanciful, suggestions.

Appasamy, A. J.: *The Johannine Doctrine of Life: A Study of Christian and Indian Thought.* 1934. Has insight and suggestiveness.

Bacon, B. W.: *The Fourth Gospel in Research and Debate.* 1910. An important critical study.

—— *The Gospel of the Hellenists.* 1933. A posthumous work, giving the mature conclusions of Dr. Bacon. A stimulating and important book, but full of fanciful conjecture.

Bernard, J. H.: 'St. John,' in the *International Critical Commentary* series. 2 vols. 1928. A learned and comprehensive commentary, but excessively conservative.

Burney, C. F.: *The Aramaic Origin of the Fourth Gospel.* 1922. An important linguistic study designed to maintain the thesis of the title.

Carpenter, J. Estlin.: *The Johannine Writings.* 1927. A mature and suggestive study of the thought of the Apocalypse and of the Fourth Gospel. Valuable.

Charnwood, Lord: *According to St. John.* 1925. Interesting and, in places, acute. An assault upon some critical positions from the standpoint of 'common-sense.'

Dods, Marcus: 'The Gospel of St. John,' in *The Expositor's Bible.* 2 vols. 1891. A commentary of religious value; based, however, on a view of the Gospel no longer possible of acceptance.

—— 'St. John,' in *The Expositor's Greek Testament.* 1897.

Drummond, J.: *An Inquiry into the Character and Authorship of the Fourth Gospel.* 1903. Maintains the Apostolic authorship, but rejects the traditional view of the character of the Gospel.

Gardner, P.: *The Ephesian Gospel.* 1915. A suggestive study of the presumed historical background and of the thought of the Gospel.

Garvie, A. E.: *The Beloved Disciple.* 1922. An interesting series of studies, based upon the view that 'the witness,' 'the evangelist,' and 'the redactor' have each contributed to the Gospel as it now is.

Holland, H. S.: *The Fourth Gospel.* 1923. A republication of two essays on the character, purpose, and authorship of the Gospel, written from a conservative standpoint.

Howard, W. F.: *The Fourth Gospel in recent Criticism and Interpretation.* 1931. A valuable recent survey. Learned and fair-minded.

Hügel, F. von.: Article, 'John, Gospel of St.,' in *Encyclopædia Britannica.* Eleventh edition An important study.

Hutton, R. H.: *Theological Essays.* Second edition, revised. 1876. Essay 7, on 'The Historical Problems of the Fourth Gospel.' Historically interesting.

Jackson, H. L.: *The Problem of the Fourth Gospel.* 1918.

Lewis, F. W.: *The Disarrangements of the Fourth Gospel.* 1910. One of the first studies in English of the thesis suggested by the title.

Lofthouse, W. F.: *The Father and the Son.* 1934. A suggestive study of Johannine thought in its application to a Christian theological statement.

MacGregor, G. H. C.: 'John,' in *The Moffatt New Testament Commentary.* 1928. A recent, and suggestive, commentary.

Maurice, F. D.: *The Gospel of St. John: a Series of Discourses.* 1857. A commentary in the form of discourses by a theologian of insight and depth.

Nolloth, C. F.: *The Fourth Evangelist.* 1925. A conservative study of the place of the Fourth Gospel in the development of Christian thought.

Odeberg, H.: *The Fourth Gospel: interpreted in relation to contemporaneous religious currents in Palestine and the Hellenistic-Oriental world.* 1929. An important study of the Rabbinical and Gnostic parallels in thought and language to the Fourth Gospel.

Sanday, W.: *The Criticism of the Fourth Gospel.* 1905. Lectures on the character of the Gospel, written from a conservative standpoint which Dr. Sanday afterwards relinquished.

Schmiedel, P. W.: *The Johannine Writings.* Eng. tr. 1908.

Scott, E. F.: *The Fourth Gospel: its Purpose and Theology.* 1906. A strong book, important both historically and intrinsically. Lacking in appreciation of the 'mystical' element in the Evangelist's mind.

Strachan, R. H.: *The Fourth Gospel: its significance and environment.* 1917. A suggestive exposition of the Gospel.

—— *The Fourth Evangelist: dramatist or historian?* 1925. Suggestive.

Streeter, B. H.: *The Four Gospels: a Study of Origins.* 1924. Part III of this important study deals with the Fourth Gospel.

Tayler, J. J.: *The Fourth Gospel.* 1867. One of the first attempts in English to confront the problems, historical and theological, raised by the Fourth Gospel.

Torrey, C. C.: *The Four Gospels: a New Translation.* Revolutionary. Dr. Torrey's translation is based upon the conviction 'that the four who gave to the world our Greek Gospels, all learned men and masters of the language which they were using, did not produce their curious jargon by "thinking in Semitic," but, as their predecessors did, by translating.' To him, the Fourth Gospel was written in Aramaic prior to the year 70, and 'was carried out of Palestine by one of the Christian fugitives, to be translated and put in circulation at a later day.' In addition to the translation, the book contains a discussion on 'The Origin of the Gospels' and a body of 'Notes on the new readings.'

Dr. Torrey's views demand, and are receiving, careful examination; it is recognised that they raise real issues, but New Testament experts are, in the main, critical.

Wendt, H. H.: *The Gospel according to St. John: an Inquiry into its Genesis and Historical Character.* Eng. tr. 1902.

Westcott, B. F.: 'The Gospel according to St. John,' in *The Speaker's Commentary.* 1880.

—— *The Gospel according to St. John: the Greek text with Introduction and Notes.* 2 vols. 1908.

The above two Commentaries are of abiding value, though based on a conservative estimate of the nature of the Gospel now no longer possible of acceptance.

Wright, C. J.: *The Meaning and Message of the Fourth Gospel.* 1933.

Index of Scriptural References

MARK

Book I, pp. 1–297. Book II, pp. 299–639. Book III, pp. 641–958.

MATTHEW

Book I, pp. 1–297. Book II, pp. 299–639. Book III, pp. 641–958.

LUKE

JOHN

Book I, pp. 1–297. Book II, pp. 299–639. Book III, pp. 641–958.
Italic figures in the Johannine references indicate passages in Book I.

Book I, pp. 1–297. Book II, pp. 299–639. Book III, pp. 641–958.

Italic figures in the Johannine references indicate passages in Book I.